Psychological Perspectives on Human Sexuality

Lenore T. Szuchman

and

Frank Muscarella

John Wiley & Sons, Inc.

New York • Chichester • Weinheim • Brisbane • Singapore • Toronto

To the members of the Department of Psychology at Barry University

Library of Congress Cataloging-in-Publication Data:

Psychological perspectives of human sexuality / edited by Lenore T.
    Szuchman and Frank Muscarella.
        p.   cm.
    Includes index.
    ISBN 0-471-24405-8 (cl. : alk. paper)
    1. Sex.   2. Sex (Psychology)   I. Szuchman, Lenore T., 1948–
II. Muscarella, Frank, 1958–   .
HQ21.P77   1999
306.7—dc21   99-30531

Printed in the United States of America.

10 9 8 7 6 5 4 3 2 1

Preface

This book is a collection of critical reviews of the scientific literature on topics in human sexuality that are of research interest to a broad audience of social scientists. In addition, each review provides some practical guidance to mental health professionals. The intent of the book is to be consistent with the scientist-practitioner tradition in which application is based on theory and empirical evidence. The scientist-practitioner emphasis has not often been applied to the field of sexology, perhaps because sexology is the product of influence and collaboration from many disciplines. Thus, disparate and sometimes conflicting approaches have defined the field. In this book, we use a predominantly psychologically based empirical perspective. Nonetheless, the varied tones of the chapters reflect the differences in training and perspectives of the contributors.

We have three audiences in mind. First, we would like to fill a gap in the training of graduate students in applied mental health programs. In the area of human sexuality, it seems that we often fail to educate the scientist half of the scientist-practitioner. Students often get a smattering of sexuality research in some of their content areas, and they may have been exposed to an undergraduate course in human sexuality. However, sometimes they are not well educated in human sexuality as an area of scientific inquiry.

The second audience is a professional group of clinicians and researchers potentially in need of a research-based state-of-the-art review. These would include, for example, people who are in general clinical practice who cannot keep up with this specialized literature but recognize the need to do so, especially in the face of the abundant and compelling pop psychology treatments in the field.

Finally, we would like to provide a means to introduce advanced undergraduates to this field as potential investigators themselves. The typical undergraduate human sexuality textbook addresses them very personally, differently from the way theories of personality or cognitive psychology texts do. Unfortunately, sensationalized and unreliable material from popular psychology may fill the gap for students. Advanced undergraduate students may become excited enough to devote their careers to this research if they come under the direct influence of a scholarly book written by leaders in the field.

A unique feature of this book is the selection and organization of the topics. In identifying topics for study, in addition to the expected chapters, we have included chapters on subjects that have only recently come to the attention of the scientific and mental health communities, such as genital surgery on children and Internet sex. Furthermore, some of the traditional areas of study have been regrouped to emphasize their impact on society and on definitions of normalcy. For example, chapters on sexual orientation and gender/transgender issues are not presented here as minority sexual behaviors. Rather, they are presented along with love and fantasy to indicate that, just as love and fantasy are common elements of "normal" sexuality, healthy, functional people all have a sexual orientation and also fit somewhere on a gender continuum.

We gratefully acknowledge the effort and cooperation of all of the contributors to this volume. We would like to thank our editor at Wiley, Jennifer Simon, for her patience and encouragement. Linda Bacheller, our graduate assistant, was a great help, and we are very grateful to her. Finally, we would like to thank Lenore's husband, Mark Szuchman, and Frank's partner, Doug Garber, for encouraging us to do this book and for making their own sacrifices so that we could.

LENORE T. SZUCHMAN, PHD
FRANK MUSCARELLA, PHD

Contributors

Paul R. Abramson, PhD
Professor of Psychology
University of California–Los Angeles

Sylvain Boies, PhD
Counselling Services
University of Victoria
Victoria, British Columbia

Stephanie Both, MA
Department of Clinical Psychology
University of Amsterdam

Donn Byrne, PhD
Distinguished Professor and Head
Social-Personality Program
Department of Psychology
State University of New York at Albany

Karen S. Calhoun, PhD
Professor
Department of Psychology
University of Georgia

Cheryl Chase
Executive Director
Intersex Society of North America
  (ISNA)
San Francisco, California

Sandra S. Cole, PhD
Professor and Director
The University of Michigan Health
  System
Comprehensive Gender Services
  Program
Ypsilanti, Michigan

Al Cooper, PhD
Clinical Director, San Jose Marital
  and Sexuality Centre
Santa Clara, California
Training Coordinator
Counseling and Psychological
  Services, Cowell Student Health
  Services
Stanford University

Christine A. Courtois, PhD
Psychologist, Private Practice and
  Clinical Director
The CENTER: Post-traumatic
  Disorders Program
The Psychiatric Institute of
  Washington
Washington, DC

Dallas Denny, MA
Consultant
The University of Michigan Health
  System
Comprehensive Gender Services
  Program
Ypsilanti, Michigan

Alan L. Ellis, PhD
Research Associate
Center for Research and Education in
  Sexuality (CERES)
San Francisco State University

Walter Everaerd, PhD
Professor
Department of Clinical Psychology
University of Amsterdam

A. Evan Eyler, MD
Director of Primary Care Services
The University of Michigan Health
    System
Comprehensive Gender Services
    Program
Ypsilanti, Michigan

Jay R. Feierman, MD
Clinical Professor
Department of Psychiatry
University of New Mexico School of
    Medicine

Lisa A. Feierman, MD
Resident Physician in Psychiatry
Department of Psychiatry
University of New Mexico School of
    Medicine

P. Sándor Gardos, PhD
Oxygen Media
San Francisco, California

Ronald Goldman, PhD
Executive Director
Circumcision Resource Center
Boston, Massachusetts

David Greenfield, PhD
Psychological Health Associates
West Hartford, Connecticut

Tim Hammond
Executive Director
National Organization to Halt the
    Abuse and Routine Mutilation of
    Males (NOHARMM)
San Francisco, California

**John M. Kellett, MB, BChir & MA
Cantab**
Department of Geriatric Medicine
Saint George's Hospital Medical
    School
University of London
London

Ellen T.M. Laan, PhD
Senior Researcher
Outpatient Clinic for Psychosomatic
    Gynecology and Sexology
University Hospital of Leiden
Assistant Professor
Department of Clinical Psychology
University of Amsterdam

Hanny Lightfoot-Klein, MA, FAACS
Independent Researcher
Tucson, Arizona

Marlene Maheu, PhD
Clinical & Consulting Psychologist
Pioneer Development Resources
San Diego, California

Anthony McCormick, MA
Project Director
Department of Psychiatry
Psychiatric Institute
University of Illinois at Chicago

Robert W. Mitchell, PhD
Associate Professor of Psychology
Eastern Kentucky University

Linda R. Mona, PhD
Research Associate
World Institute on Disability
Oakland, California

Lena Nilsson Schönnesson, PhD
Associate Professor of Social Work
Department of Social Work
Göteborg University
Göteborg, Sweden
Licensed Psychologist
Psychosocial Center for Gay and
Bisexual Men
Stockholm City Council
Stockholm, Sweden

Julie A. Osland, BA
Graduate Assistant
Social-Personality Program
Department of Psychology
State University of New York at
Albany

Roberta L. Paikoff, PhD
Associate Professor of Psychology in
Psychiatry
Psychiatric Institute
University of Illinois at Chicago

Steven D. Pinkerton, PhD
Assistant Professor
Center for AIDS Intervention
Research
Department of Psychiatry and
Behavioral Medicine
Medical College of Wisconsin

Kenneth S. Pope, PhD
Independent Practice
Norwalk, Connecticut

Pamela C. Regan, PhD
Director
Social Relations Laboratory
Department of Psychology
California State University,
Los Angeles

Michael W. Ross, PhD
Professor
WHO Center for Health Promotion
Research and Development
School of Public Health
University of Texas

Lynda M. Sagrestano, PhD
Assistant Professor
Department of Psychology
Southern Illinois University

Sandra L. Samons, DCSW
Private Practice and Affiliate
The University of Michigan Health
System
Comprehensive Gender Services
Program
Ypsilanti, Michigan

Mark Spiering, MA
Department of Clinical Psychology
University of Amsterdam

Janneke van der Velde
Department of Clinical Psychology
University of Amsterdam

David A. Wagstaff, PhD
The Methodology Center
College of Health and Human
Development
Pennsylvania State University

Amy E. Wilson, MA
Department of Psychology
University of Georgia

Contents

Introduction

Three forces contribute to the direction of contemporary scientific inquiry into human sexuality: the conceptualization of normalcy, the nature of the cultural climate, and concern for sexual victimization. We have been guided by these themes in the selection of topics for this book.

NORMALCY

Groups of individuals who have been regarded as socially marginal and thus "abnormal" are challenging the status quo and demanding that society broaden its tolerance for diversity in expressions of human sexuality. Consequently, behaviors and expressions of human sexuality that were once considered out of the range of normalcy are beginning to be seen as acceptable variation within scientific paradigms. The phenomenon of sociopolitical themes influencing scientific paradigms in general, and paradigms in sexology in particular, is common in the history of science and sexology.

Sexual orientation is a good example of a change in the conceptualization of normalcy that is well underway for both the scientific community and a significant sector of the general public. Few readers would be surprised to find our chapter "Sexual Orientation" (not *homosexuality*) located in the section of core issues rather than relegated to a section whose topic is "sexual minorities." This may be a significant paradigm shift for many sectors of the scientific community. However, at a broader sociocultural level, the shift is less consistent. This reconceptualization began primarily as a political movement by those adversely affected by the personal consequences of the old paradigm. Their activity ultimately influenced scientific thinking, as evidenced by the depathologization of homosexuality in the *DSM*. If such a profound shift occurs in society, future scientists emerging from this society may well be inclined to further change scientific paradigms regarding this topic.

The next major movement from abnormal to normal may be precipitated by the transgender community and social scientists working with this community. This community, along with its advocates in the mental health professions, is currently exerting pressure on both the mental health and general communities. They are presenting a gender continuum rather than accepting the traditional male-female dichotomization that necessarily pathologizes transgender. Although this may sound dubious to the scientific community and shocking to the general public, scientific beliefs change. We are reminded of the fact that 100 years ago, women who actively pursued orgasms were considered abnormal, given the diagnosis of nymphomania, and, in some cases, "treated" with clitorectomies. The paradigm shift concerning gender is still very much in the future, and we are only at the beginning stages of the process. In fact, this may be the first text for mental health professionals that reflects this reconceptualization.

Another compelling example of a politically active group urging the scientific mainstream to rethink definitions of normalcy is the intersexual community. In this case, they are advocating for the acceptance of greater diversity in anatomical structure. Standard medical practice calls for reshaping the genitalia of some infants and children to meet current conceptions of "normal" size and shape for a given sex. Intersex advocates argue that such procedures are motivated by misguided concern for aesthetic conformity rather than by appropriate concern for psychosexual adjustment. Similarly, members of the disabled community argue that many of their psychosexual difficulties arise from societal constraints on the conceptualization of appropriate sexual partners.

CULTURAL CLIMATE

The 1960s gave American society a legacy of sexual openness, freedom, and permission to seek sexual fulfillment. In fact, we are continually made aware that pleasure from sex is an essential right. Thus, for example, the emphasis on the female orgasm in the popular press has gone from sensational and pervasive to matter-of-fact. However, there are exceptions, and this legacy has not been left to all groups.

Society is uneasy about the sexual expression of some groups, for example, the elderly and the disabled. Many prefer to think of both of these groups as asexual. But of course, a fair number of older adults have always been sexually active and satisfied. Now, the arrival of hormone replacement therapy, the enthusiastic public endorsement of Viagra, and the aging of the 1960s generation have brought the sexuality of older adults into public awareness and sharp focus. Likewise, the Americans with Disabilities Act of 1990 has made the general population more aware of the disability community and their needs. However, the acknowledgment of the sexuality of disabled persons has not attained the same level of public awareness.

Sexual pleasure is limited physically by genital mutilation. In our culture, there is general agreement that the genital cutting performed on girls in some African cultures constitutes a gross violation of the individual's right to sexual fulfillment. Some have argued that a similar violation and consequent abrogation of the individual's right to sexual fulfillment occurs routinely in the United States in the "corrective" genital surgery performed on intersexuals and in the circumcision of male infants. The medical establishment in our own culture might not agree with the parallel; nevertheless, it is beginning to discuss changes in standard practice.

There are cultural constraints on sexuality that are considered acceptable by scientists and the general public and, therefore, less controversial. For example, adolescents and people with HIV/AIDS, whose urges we consider to be legitimate, are nevertheless encouraged to exercise certain restraints. Additionally, there are groups such as rapists and pedophiles who victimize others, thus impelling society to attempt to constrain their behavior. Psychologists have been asked to develop interventions for all of these groups.

A new cultural force, the Internet, is causing society some discomfort in terms of its impact on sexual experience and expression. We are only now beginning to ask the questions that will help us understand the problems brought about by the Internet and their solutions. At the broadest sociopolitical level, raising questions about controlling the Internet conflicts fundamentally with cultural beliefs about constitutionally protected rights. Nevertheless, questions have already arisen for which we have few clear answers, and research must proceed for society to properly weigh the risks in the contexts of those rights. What are the real dangers that are lurking for children? How extensive is the risk posed by sexual predators? What are the implications of sexually graphic Internet conversations? It is commonly accepted that sexual fantasy is a healthy and integral component of sexual expression. The Internet is a new venue for fantasy, and its implications for sexual expression are unclear. For example, is a "cyber-affair" an enhanced fantasy or adultery? Is a person who spends an hour in an S & M chat room going to be better or worse off than the person who spends an hour with an explicit S & M magazine? What are the implications for mental health professionals who will be confronted with questions about sexual behavior and the Internet when they lack the traditional, empirically based norms and guideposts for making clinical judgments?

VICTIMIZATION

Inescapably, some forms of sexual expression lead to the victimization of their targets due to a variety of factors, such as the targets' youth, psychological vulnerability, and physical vulnerability. The identification of effective treatment guidelines for victims of incest and rape has become a priority. Also, there has been a significant controversy concerning the therapist's role in the recollection of purported abuse. Although some controversy remains and some cases of victimization may be dubious, one outcome for the mental health field is that people who have such trauma in their history have felt more comfortable in coming forth and seeking help. Also, perhaps as a result of the increased awareness of sexual victimization in general, mental health professionals themselves are more aware of and concerned about sexual misconduct in their own ranks.

This theme also touches on the topic of paraphilias. Currently, it would seem that society is more concerned with paraphilic behavior that involves victims, such as pedophilia, than with victimless fetishistic behavior. Consequently, research and intervention agendas reflect this impetus and direction.

THE FUTURE

The chapters in this book represent what we consider to be the most important topics in human sexuality in the year 2000. Some of these topics have a long history, such as female and male sexuality and paraphilias. Others have become important only within the past few decades, for example, sexual misconduct and HIV/AIDS. Still others seem to be at the cusp of their importance at the beginning of the twenty-first century. We will soon know whether or not those predictions are accurate.

PART I

BACKGROUND

CHAPTER 1

Research in Human Sexuality

DAVID A. WAGSTAFF, PAUL R. ABRAMSON, and STEVEN D. PINKERTON

I N THIS INTRODUCTORY chapter, we provide an overview of many of the important elements that define contemporary research on human sexuality. We hope that our material facilitates the reader's enjoyment and appreciation of the interesting and informative chapters that follow. Given the limits of time and space, we had to be selective and undoubtedly excluded a number of important research areas and developments. However, we have tried to provide a broad sampling of the many flavors that constitute contemporary sex research. In this chapter, we touch on such fundamental questions as What (and who) do sex researchers study? What kinds of issues do sex researchers examine? What methods do they use?

The chapter is loosely organized in four sections. In the first, we consider definitions and, specifically, the meanings that individuals and researchers associate with the words "sex" and "research." In the second section, we discuss some of the theories that guide sex research programs and currently provide the theoretical basis for interventions that are designed to prevent sex-related social problems (such as sexually transmitted infections and unwanted pregnancies). In the third section, we consider some of the methods used to collect data on human sexuality. We close, in the last section, with a discussion of clinical applications and our perspective on the future of sex research.

Preparation of this chapter was supported, in part, by NIDA center grant P50-DA10075 awarded to the Center for the Study of Prevention through Innovative Methodology, Pennsylvania State University, and by NIMH center grant P30-MH52776 awarded to the Center for AIDS Intervention Research, Medical College of Wisconsin.

WHAT IS SEX?

Sex, like love, is a many splendored thing. It also has many definitions, which have given rise to an equal number of misconceptions. One of the most fundamental confusions concerns the difference between "sex" and "gender." Sex, of course, has a dual meaning, referring both to a physical activity and to a physical characteristic. The latter is often confused with gender (roughly, one's sense of femaleness or maleness), which is perceived internally and negotiated (i.e., socially constructed and affirmed through interaction with other individuals). The distinction is subtle. Although most sexual characteristics form a continuum from "male" to "female," the genome of most males has both an X and a Y chromosome, and most men exhibit typically male secondary sexual characteristics, such as penile development. The male *sex* is thus defined by physical characteristics. In contrast, the male *gender* is defined by a confluence of psychological and social considerations. At the psychological level, we can define a person's *gender identity* as his or her subjective self-perception of maleness or femaleness. On this basis, gender identification is inherently psychological: a physiologically male individual can perceive himself as female, and vice versa. However, cultural influences are also evident in gender identification. Culture defines what it means to be male or female to the extent that the individual's culture determines the appropriate *gender roles* for men and women. Indeed, the term "gender" is often used to denote the cultural, social, and psychological *experience* of belonging to a particular sex or fitting into a particular gender role. For example, one might ask, What is it like to be a woman in contemporary America?

Sex researchers concern themselves with all the various meanings of "sex" and "gender," as well as a number of related and not-so-related issues. The long list of topics they study includes (but is not limited to) the physiology and anatomy of the reproductive tract; potential physical determinants of maleness and femaleness, including genetics, hormones, and neurophysiology; the intricacies of human sexual responses, including mechanisms of arousal, orgasm, and resolution; sexual attraction, whether heterosexual, homosexual, bisexual, asexual, or some mix; individualistic expression of sexuality and what it means to adopt, or identify with, a particular sexual orientation; the role of fantasy in healthy and "deviant" sexuality; the etiology, prevalence, and expression of various paraphilias (nonnormative sexual attractions and practices), such as necrophilia, bestiality, sadomasochism, and various fetishes; what it means to be male or female in a particular culture, and the determinants of gender identity; the social and individual ramifications of sexual behavior, including unwanted pregnancies and sexually transmitted infections (STIs) such as human immunodeficiency virus (HIV); the commercialization of sex, especially pornography and prostitution; and the psychological determinants and consequences of sexual behavior and ideation. Some sex researchers specialize in tracking the history of sexual mores; in how societies regulate sexuality; in how human sexual behaviors compare with those of closely related primates; or in cross-cultural comparisons of sexual expression. Given the importance of sex to the continuation of the human species, it is perhaps not surprising that the study of human sexual behavior should encompass such an extensive and varied range of topics. (Like the rest of this volume, however, the remainder of this chapter will focus primarily on psychological aspects of human sexuality.)

As the preceding discussion suggests, the vocabulary of sex research contains some ill-defined terms. However, the use of some inexact language in science is not uncommon. As Peter Medawar observed, biology would not exist if its technical terms had to be defined precisely (Medawar & Medawar, 1983). For different reasons, the same may be true for research in human sexuality. This ambiguity in the meanings assigned to and the uses of sexual terminology arise from two inextricably linked sources: intrapsychic variability and cultural differences. The former refers to the idiosyncratic ways that people define sex and sexuality for themselves; the latter refers to the ways that different cultures define these concepts.

INTRAPSYCHIC DIFFERENCES

There are many interesting anecdotes that illustrate the ways that different individuals think about sex. Our favorite is the following. A psychology professor was studying contraceptive neglect among pregnant teenagers attending a support group for unwed mothers. Prior to assessing their contraceptive experiences, the professor asked a number of standard sex questions, including, "Are you now or have you ever been sexually active?" One teen answered no. Puzzled by this enigmatic response, the professor asked the pregnant teen how she could claim she was never sexually active. Her telling reply was, "I just kind of lie there." To this teen, the phrase "sexually active" referred to the amount of energy that one put into sex! The professor and every other study participant understood the phrase differently. To them, it meant engaging in sexual intercourse—the *active* participation of all parties was not required.

The phrase "sex differences" also means different things to different people. When some individuals use the phrase, they are often referring to gender, gender roles, and/or gender differences. The latter are critical to sexuality itself, both on the psychological level and the genetic level (Margolis & Sagan, 1986). Recently, the concept of two genders has been challenged with the view that there are (or can be) more than just male and female (L. Cohen, 1995; Herdt, 1994). The Hijra of India provide a fascinating example (L. Cohen, 1995). The Hijra are castrated genetic males, who perceive themselves as neither male nor female, and whose social and sexual roles do not fit into either category. Thus, they are a "third gender," a group of individuals who do not fit neatly within the traditional strictures of sexual dimorphism. These examples are meant to emphasize the fact that researchers need to choose their words carefully. They also suggest that the way individuals think about sex is curiously personal—and the way individuals *think* about sex often influences or reflects how they *act*. For example, individuals who believe that masturbation is sinful express and experience the act differently from those who believe that it is essential to sexual health (Abramson & Mosher, 1975, 1979; D. Mosher & Abramson, 1977; Pinkerton & Abramson, 1999).

Accommodating these kinds of individual differences, particularly in a country as culturally diverse as the United States, is a difficult task. In large national surveys of sexual behavior, a standard terminology is clearly needed; therefore, clinical language is typically used (Binson & Catania, 1998). However, not all research participants understand the clinically correct terms for the sexual anatomy and for common (and uncommon) sexual behaviors. Indeed, as many as 25% of Americans with fewer than 12 years of schooling may have difficulty understanding terms such as "vaginal intercourse" and "anal intercourse," which frequently appear in the instruments that researchers use to obtain data on sexual behaviors that confer risk for HIV transmission (Binson & Catania, 1998). In addition, the evidence suggests that men are more likely than women, and minority respondents are more likely than White respondents, to have trouble understanding these terms. These findings suggest that, whenever possible, survey respondents should be provided with definitions of the relevant terms (e.g., "vaginal intercourse") before being asked questions about their own behavior. Additionally, these findings suggest that researchers should ensure that the questionnaires and interview forms used to obtain sexual behavior data are tailored to the population of interest and are both culturally and developmentally appropriate. In some cases, researchers will have more success if they use slang or "street" language to describe sexual behaviors and show greater sensitivity when asking questions (Mays & Cochran, 1990).

Ultimately, sex researchers need to be clear about the definitions they use and acknowledge the fact that other individuals—especially research participants, but also other researchers—may use different definitions. Unfortunately, there is no "one size fits all" solution to this difficulty. Although some individuals may feel more comfortable discussing their sexual behavior using clinical terms such as "vaginal intercourse" or "cunnilingus," others may not understand these terms, or may instead prefer to use slang or vernacular equivalents. The challenge for sex researchers is to correctly gauge which terms would be most acceptable and appropriate given the particular research population and the aims of the study. Conducting focus groups or otherwise eliciting input from the study population prior to finalizing survey or interview instruments can be extremely helpful in this regard.

Cultural Differences

In the past, people believed that the cultural world followed the same laws as the natural world. In particular, the cultural world was viewed as an adaptation designed to best serve the needs of men and women. As such, they believed in an objective cultural reality that could be reliably ascertained: those who studied the cultural world merely needed to observe it and deduce the functions it served. This was as true for sex as for any other phenomenon worthy of investigation.

This view changed in large part as a result of the work of postmodern writers such as Foucault (1978) and Sedgwick (1990). These writers "deconstructed" sex, demonstrating that the concept of "natural" sex was highly capricious and often politically or religiously motivated. In their view, although heterosexuality might be prized by most societies, there is no inherent validity for this valuation. Instead, the greater value placed on heterosexuality arose from pervasive religious emphases on procreation and the (heterosexual) relationships that promote this end. Thus, if heterosexuality were considered more "natural" than homosexuality, it was only because society deemed it so.

Thoughts on the nature of female orgasm provide another example of the social construction of sex. In the sixteenth century, particularly in midwifery manuals, female orgasm was presumed routine and necessary for conception (Laqueur, 1990). (Some formulations of this belief held that women, like men, released "sperm" when they had an orgasm, and that it was the mixing of the male and female sperm that formed a fetus.) However, by the nineteenth century, many doctors had rejected this popular theory and began to doubt the reality of female orgasm (i.e., they doubted that women were *capable* of orgasm). The two views reflect radically different conceptualizations; if holding one of them made it easier or more difficult for a woman to achieve orgasm, we should not be surprised. Psychologists have long known that "expectancy is a self-fulfilling prophecy."

Both cultural variability and the cultural construction of sex are evident in historical and contemporary conceptualizations of homosexuality. Japan has a long and celebrated history of male homosexuality, particularly among the samurai and certain sects of Buddhist monks (Leupp, 1995; Pinkerton & Abramson, 1997). There are no legal proscriptions on homosexuality or laws concerning the practice of sodomy in Japan. This historical experience contrasts sharply with that of other countries, particularly the United States, where homosexuality has been vigorously penalized and pathologized. Indeed, the Western concept of homosexuality—in which homosexual behavior is considered deviant and the practice thereof defines someone as a different sort of person (i.e., a "homosexual")—is basically a nineteenth-century invention. It differs significantly from the way other cultures organize erotic desire for persons of the same sex. In the Sambia culture of Papua, New Guinea, for example, all teenage boys are expected to undergo a period of ritual homosexual behavior prior to establishing a lifelong, heterosexual marital relationship. The Sambia do not consider the boys who engage in oral sex with one another to be "homosexual," but instead believe that the ingestion of semen plays a critical role in masculinizing the receptive partner, helping him to achieve the strength and courage required of men in this fierce warrior society. In contrast, in the traditional Mexican culture of male "machismo," the "passive" or receptive partner of a male-male sexual dyad is considered to be homosexual, whereas the "active" or insertive partner can still claim a heterosexual identity (Carrier, 1995). Finally, in the United States, Kinsey's claim that approximately 10% of the male population had engaged in at least one same-sex encounter has been widely misinterpreted to mean that 10% of the male population *is* homosexual. Thus, when viewed cross-culturally or historically, it is clear that there is no standard set of behaviors or feelings that constitute the construct of homosexuality (Greenberg, 1988; Herdt, 1997). Similar comments apply to many other fundamental conceptual constructs.

Such examples have clear implications for research on human sexuality. First, they suggest that many sex-related constructs—the bread and butter of the psychological study of human sexuality—are socially constructed, rather than fixed aspects of the natural world. They also demonstrate the immense variability of these constructs when viewed historically or cross-culturally. Third, they remind us that the meaning given to a construct by a culture is often politically or religiously motivated. Thus, exceptional care should be taken in how such constructs are defined and investigated. Finally, as noted in the preceding section, the instruments (e.g., questionnaires and interview forms) used to measure individual sexual behavior should be culturally appropriate for the target population.

A PHILOSOPHY OF SCIENCE

To conduct research, it is essential to understand the purpose and methods of research, as well as the philosophical foundations of the scientific enterprise. In this section, we briefly summarize the contributions of three important philosophers of science: Francis Bacon, Thomas Kuhn, and Sir Karl Popper.

MODELS OF THE SCIENTIFIC ENTERPRISE

In the prescientific era, people believed they could determine if a statement was true by consulting religious texts or previous work by respected authorities (preferably Greek). Francis Bacon (1620/1956) changed this when he proposed that researchers use observation and experimentation to determine the validity of scientific conjectures. In particular, he proposed that researchers observe and make records of the phenomenon in which they are interested, and then develop a theory on the basis of what they observe, a process known as *scientific induction*. Theory was important because it facilitated interpretation of the available data and yielded predictions that the researcher could test through further experimentation. If the findings agreed with the researchers' predictions, the theory survived; if they did not, the theory was revised to take into account the new observations. Thus, research was conceived as an iterative, self-correcting process, in which theory and observation are partnered with an experimental method.

According to the Baconian model, "normal science" operates via a three-stage process of hypothesis formation, testing, and revision. Scientific knowledge grows as more elaborate and extensive theories are proposed and tested according to the above model. Thomas Kuhn (1962) challenged this view of normal science and offered an alternative explanation for the growth of scientific knowledge and the origin of scientific revolutions. Scientific revolutions are reflected in conceptual changes of a fundamental kind and radical alterations in the standard or accepted explanations for natural phenomena (J. Cohen, 1985). The emergence and acceptance of Darwin's theory of natural selection is an obvious example. Kuhn added to our understanding of scientific revolutions by highlighting the manner in which such revolutions evolve. Contrary to prevailing wisdom, Kuhn argued, scientific revolutions do not come about as the result of the practice of normal science, or the accumulation of evidence from successive experiments, in accordance with the Baconian method. Instead, Kuhn believed that scientific revolutions result from so-called paradigm shifts, precipitated by a crisis in the current state of science. That is, with the emergence of evidential patterns that cannot be explained by existing theories, a crisis occurs, followed by a revolution that produces a new paradigm. The theory of natural selection illustrates Kuhn's argument. This theory did not result from a series of prior experiments, but from Darwin's careful observations of nature. In time, natural selection was accepted because it provided a more robust theory than the prevailing religious and Lamarckian explanations of evolutionary change.

Sir Karl Popper's (1972, 1983) work has been highly influential and represents another radical departure from normal science. Popper (1983) contends that a theory should be accepted as a statement of empirical science (as opposed to a statement of belief, for example) if and only if it is possible for researchers to collect data that could potentially refute it. Like Bacon, Popper makes the clear distinction between a scientific theory that can be proven false and religious dogma that cannot. He believes that "scientific theories are distinguished from myths merely in being criticizable, and in being open to modification in light of criticism" (1983, p. 7). In fact, Popper concludes that the unifying characteristic of all "true" sciences is that their theories are subject to criticism and revision. Researchers must be able to conduct independent tests of each leading explanation of the phenomenon of interest; the more rigorous and frequent the test, the more satisfactory the explanation (Popper, 1957, 1972). Scientific progress, then, is marked by better and better explanations (Popper, 1972).

In summary, theory and experimentation form the basis of scientific research. In our view, the role of experimentation is multifaceted. It can be used to verify a hypothesis or to discredit it in accordance with Popper's doctrine of falsifiability, or it can be used to more thoroughly investigate a phenomenon and thereby assist with the formulation of new or better explanations.

PRINCIPLES OF STUDY DESIGN

Although the scientific method as outlined in this chapter provides a framework for the conduct of certain types of research, it is not often applied to the study of human sexuality, which relies instead on other modes of inquiry and validation. Residing primarily in the social sciences, the study of human sexuality has embraced methods characteristic of the early life (agricultural) and social sciences, particularly in the design of experiments and the analysis of data.

As W. Cochran (1976) suggests, the seeds of contemporary study design and data analysis were sown in English fields in the eighteenth and nineteenth centuries. The best of these comparative agricultural experiments used systematic layouts, careful measurement, replication, and concurrent controls. A major advance in statistical practice occurred in 1908 when William Gosset, writing under the pseudonym of Student, published a paper on the distribution of errors about the sample mean (Boland, 1984; G. Box, 1984; J. Box, 1981; Student, 1908). The statistic and distribution were subsequently named in Student's honor (i.e., Student's t-statistic). Gosset's paper was important because it showed that it was possible to study the exact distribution of a sample statistic. In addition, it showed how one could use data to draw conclusions when the sample size was small. Prior to the paper's publication, statistical theory was based primarily on what was known about the distribution of statistics in large samples (and, in fact, many years would pass before researchers used the small sample statistic that Gosset proposed in his paper).

Extensive use of probability theory in the design and analysis of agriculture experiments began in 1919 when R. A. Fisher joined the Rothamsted Experimental Station as its first statistician (G. Box, 1984; J. Box, 1980). Fisher was interested in determining how experiments might be designed so that they provide the clearest answer. In the first article that he published on the subject, R. Fisher (1926) introduced the principle of randomization and the use of factorial designs, which required the researcher to vary simultaneously two or more factors that were believed to affect the outcome. (In a text published in the preceding year, R. Fisher (1925) introduced a larger audience to the analysis of variance, tests of statistical significance, and the 5% significance level.) Unlike earlier researchers who were concerned with obtaining a precise estimate, Fisher was concerned with a study's validity and efficiency, recognizing that statistical rigor could not substitute for inadequate design. Fisher's proposed use of randomization (into treatment and control groups) was not accepted initially by his colleagues, who favored the use of systematic designs. However, his arguments eventually gained broad acceptance, and randomization became the distinguishing characteristic of the "true" experiment and the standard against which most social science research studies, including studies of human sexuality, are judged today. Of no less importance to the current study of human sexuality were the other principles that Fisher introduced or championed: factorial arrangements (and the idea that outcomes are determined by multiple causes), replication, the use of concurrent controls, and careful measurement (a principle that is reaffirmed when researchers assess the reliability and validity of their scales and instruments).

THEORY

In the physical sciences, theory development represents a search for the laws of nature. Such laws are presumed to exist; however, it has proven difficult to find laws that hold without exception, exactly, and throughout time (Kemeny, 1959). Where sex is concerned, the goal is often more humble. What many researchers want from a theory of human sexuality is a good explanation. Thus far, sex researchers have had to be satisfied with good explanations because research findings have yielded relatively few consistently verifiable facts. The latter are required to construct a scientific theory and, in particular, a fully mathematized theory capable of expressing universal laws of behavior (Abramson, 1990).

CONTRIBUTIONS FROM THE LIFE SCIENCES

Darwin's theory of evolution by natural selection represents one of the few exceptions. It is a "true" scientific theory that appears to be a law of nature. Evolutionary theory has also given rise to a fertile area of sexuality research known as evolutionary psychology by some, and as sociobiology by others. This research focuses on how the physical and social environments in which humankind evolved have shaped the way we think and act. The fundamental theoretical assumption that underlies this incipient program of research is that many (if not most) physical and behavioral traits evolved millions of years ago as solutions to problems of relevance to either survival or reproduction (these behavioral solutions are known as "adaptations"). Evolutionary psychology differs from other evolutionary theories, including sociobiology, in its explicit focus on the innate psychological mechanisms through which particular adaptations are expressed. (For more on evolutionary psychology, see Buss, 1994; Cosmides & Tooby, 1987; H. Fisher, 1982, 1992; Symons, 1979, 1992, 1995. For additional information on sociobiology, see Barkow, 1980; E. Wilson, 1975.)

According to evolutionary psychological theory, the physical features that people find attractive are precisely those that have been reliably correlated with reproductive success throughout human existence. Symons (1995) argues that the appearance of youth and healthfulness is universally associated with female sexual attractiveness because these qualities act as de facto markers for reproductive fitness. Consequently, he predicts that in all societies in which women attempt to alter their appearance—through cosmetics, diet, exercise, and dress—they will do so in a manner that accentuates the appearance of youth and health. Conversely, men are assumed to have inborn mechanisms for detecting these qualities in women (Symons, 1995). Notice that in this example, Symons begins with a broad theoretical framework (evolutionary psychology), which is then narrowed down to a specific, testable hypothesis (women can be expected to accentuate the appearance of youth and health).

There are several notable biologically based theories of human sexual behavior and sexual desire. Most biologically based theory and research owes a debt of gratitude to the pioneering work of John Money and his colleagues. Money argued for developmentally focused research on sexuality (including sexual orientation, gender differentiation, and gender identification). In this model, sexuality begins in the womb, under the combined influences of genetics and hormones (Money & Ehrhardt, 1972). Recently, Dean Hamer and his colleagues gained much notoriety for identifying a genetic site that appeared to be correlated with an increased incidence of familial male homosexuality (Hamer, Hu, Magnuson, Hu, & Pattatucci, 1993). Genetic influences are also apparent in studies of twins: even when raised separately, twins are more likely to have the same sexual orientation than are nontwin siblings (because twins share more genes than do nontwins, this suggests that sexual orientation may have a heritable component) (e.g., Bailey & Pillard, 1991; Bailey, Pillard, Neale, & Agyei, 1993). This does not, of course, explain *how* genetic differences influence sexual behavior and especially sexual orientation. One possibility, popularized by Simon LeVay (1991, 1993), is that genetic differences lead to neuroanatomical and/or neurophysiological differences between gay and straight individuals.

Contributions from the Humanities

The field of human sexuality is also deeply indebted to theories developed within the humanities, in particular, those founded on postmodernism, deconstructionism, and feminism. As mentioned previously, the works of Michel Foucault and Eve Kosofsky Sedgwick have been highly influential, as have the writings of Thomas Laqueur (1990) and Judith Butler (1990). Collectively, these authors have provided insights on the ephemeral nature of sexual constructs. Their theories have been elaborated upon and extended by many authors. To name a few: Marjorie Garber (1992) has considered cross-dressing; Lillian Faderman (1991), the history of lesbian life; Constance Penley (1997), sex in popular culture (notably, "slash fiction," in which fictional characters, such as *Star Trek's* Spock and Kirk, are cast into improbable sexual relationships); Martine Rothblatt (1995), the historical and legal stature of binary gender differentiation; Cindy Patton (1985), sex and its relation to disease; Camille Paglia (1990), art and decadence; Laura Kipnis (1996), pornography; Carol Vance (1984), pleasure and danger; and Jeffrey Weeks (J. Weeks & Holland, 1996), sexual civilizations.

Contributions from the Cognitive Sciences

In another area of active theorizing, several researchers have proposed models to explain how women and men behave in sexual situations. One of the best known of these is Simon and Gagnon's "script theory" (1984; Gagnon & Simon, 1973), which borrows from the more general notion of behavioral scripts that has been popularized by cognitive scientists (e.g., Schank & Abelson, 1977). As the name implies, a script is a stereotypical set of behavioral responses and expectations that are appropriate for a particular scenario. For example, a restaurant script might include expectations regarding the waiter's behavior ("He will bring me a menu"), the service that will be provided ("They will cook and serve me food"), and the need to pay for what is ordered, as well as particular behavioral responses that will be required (taking a seat, choosing from the menu, ordering, eating, tipping, paying, etc.). Because the interaction follows a well-defined script, the individual knows what to expect and how to act. According to sexual script theorists, people also have scripts for how to behave in sexual situations, including specific scenarios for dating, foreplay/sexual play, and intercourse. Recently, script theory has been applied to the question of how men and women choose when (and with whom) to practice safe or unsafe sex (Seal, Wagner, & Ehrhardt, 1999).

Contributions from Mathematics

Although a number of mathematical models of sexual behavior have recently been proposed or reexamined within the context of the ongoing HIV epidemic, this area remains one of the least well-developed areas of sexual theorizing. Most existing models focus on the relationship between sexual behavior and viral transmission, but tell us little about human sexual behavior per se (E. Kaplan, 1995). Among the most influential sexual transmission models are the population-level models of Anderson and May (1988; May & Anderson, 1987); the individual-level, Bernoulli-process model examined by Pinkerton and Abramson (1993, 1998); and the social network models of Morris (1994; Morris & Kretzschmar, 1995; Morris, Pramualratana, Podhisita, & Wawer, 1995; Morris, Zavisca, & Dean, 1995).

Contributions from Prevention Research

Health psychologists and prevention researchers have used a number of theories to design programs and behavior change/risk-reduction interventions that address adolescent pregnancy and the transmission of sexually transmitted infections (especially HIV). Four are described here: the Health Belief Model, the Theory of Reasoned Action, Social Learning/Self-Efficacy Theory, and the Theory of Transtheoretical Change.

The Health Belief Model has been the focus of numerous studies (Becker, 1974; Brown, DiClemente, & Reynolds, 1991; Condelli, 1986; Eisen, Zellman, &

McAlister, 1992; Hiltabiddle, 1996; Janz & Becker, 1984; Kirscht & Joseph, 1989; Maiman & Becker, 1974; Rosenstock, Strecher, & Becker, 1988, 1994). The model assumes that an individual's choices and subsequent behaviors reflect a rational decision-making process. Further, it assumes that an individual's decisions are based on her perception of how susceptible she is to the threat (e.g., unwanted teenage pregnancy), how severe the consequences are, and the relative costs and benefits of adopting the various risk-reduction behaviors (use an effective contraceptive, remain abstinent).

The Theory of Reasoned Action (Fishbein & Ajzen, 1975) and the Theory of Planned Behavior (Ajzen, 1991; Ajzen & Madden, 1986) are similar to the Health Belief Model: all three are cognitive models and, as such, do not give much weight to emotion or to individuals' motivations and drives. The Theory of Reasoned Action focuses on individuals' intentions to engage in the target behavior. For example, an individual's intentions to use condoms are assumed to be a function of his or her attitudes toward condom use, and the salience and valence of the condom use attitudes held by significant others (friends, sexual partners, parents). Despite the fact that it provides no direct role for emotion, the Theory of Reasoned Action has been applied extensively to the study of sexual behavior (Baker, Morrison, Carter, & Verdon, 1996; S. Cochran, Mays, Ciarletta, Caruso, & Mallon, 1992; Fishbein & Middlestadt, 1989; W. Fisher, Fisher, & Rye, 1995; Hecker & Ajzen, 1983; L. Jemmott & Jemmott, 1991; Morrison, Gillmore, & Baker, 1995; Terry, Gallois, & McCamish, 1993).

Bandura's Social Learning Theory (1977b) and his Self-Efficacy Theory (Bandura, 1977a, 1982; Strecher, DeVellis, Becker, & Rosenstock, 1986) are also widely used in behavior change and HIV prevention research. The former reminds researchers that sexual behaviors, like most behaviors, are learned. The latter serves to focus attention on the fact that individuals will adopt a recommended behavior (e.g., use condoms with a new partner) only if (a) they believe that they can enact the behavior (ask and, if necessary, insist that the new partner use condoms) and, (b) they believe that the behavior will achieve the desired outcome (prevent HIV infection and/or pregnancy). Because the related social cognitive theory is used frequently in clinical practice, Social Learning Theory and Self-Efficacy Theory have provided the rationale for many sexual risk-reduction interventions (Bandura, 1989; Basen-Engquist & Parcel, 1992; Heinrich, 1993; J. Jemmott, Jemmott, Spears, Hewitt, & Crus-Collins, 1992; Joffe & Radius, 1993; Kasen, Vaughan, & Walter, 1992; L. Lawrance, Levy, & Rubinson, 1990; Levinson, 1986; D. Rosenthal, Moore, & Flynn, 1991; Schinke, Holden, & Moncher, 1989; K. Weeks, Levy, Zhu, et al., 1995).

The fourth theory that we mention is the Theory of Transtheoretical Change (Prochaska & DiClemente, 1983). This theory differs from the three other theories of behavior change in that it views change as a process, specifically, a sequence of five stages: precontemplation, contemplation, preparation, action, and maintenance. Although it has its origins in studies of smoking cessation, it has been applied to sexual behavior change and in the design of STI/HIV prevention interventions (Centers for Disease Control and Prevention, 1993; Grimley, Prochaska, Velicer, & Prochaska, 1995; Grimley, Riley, Bellis, & Prochaska, 1993; Santelli, Kouzis, Hoover, Polacsek, Burnell, & Celentano, 1996).

INTEGRATIVE THEORIES OF HUMAN SEXUAL BEHAVIOR

There are surprisingly few overarching theoretical integrations of human sexual behavior. As a consequence, fundamental questions such as Why does sex feel good? and What determines erotic preferences? have largely been left unexplored. We note two exceptions to our generalization.

In a recent book, Abramson and Pinkerton (1995) examined the central role of pleasure in motivating and shaping human sexual experience. They argued that reproduction is a by-product of the human desire for sexual pleasure, rather than the other way around. The implications of this seemingly obvious but ultimately nontrivial shift in how individuals conceptualize sexuality extend from the debate over the legitimacy of homosexuality, to the prosecution of pornographers, to the practice of safer sex.

The work of Robert Stoller provides another example of a theoretically rich investigation of human sexuality, and especially "deviant" sexuality (e.g., see Stoller, 1985; Stoller & Herdt, 1985; Stoller & Levine, 1993). Stoller, a psychoanalytic psychiatrist by training, hoped to answer basic questions about human sexual desire by exploring the "fringes" of socially normative behavior. For instance, he offers the following psychoanalytic explanation for the development of male transvestism (Stoller, 1971). According to Stoller, as young boys, most transvestites suffer the humiliation of being dressed in girl's clothes by their (usually female) relatives—a symbolic act of castration. This leads to later cross-dressing because, for the adult transvestite, dressing as a woman reaffirms his masculinity by juxtaposing the threat of castration symbolized by his feminine attire with that supreme marker of maleness, his intact penis.

Although our task is to consider research on *human* sexuality, we recognize that there is much to be gained by examining theories of primate sexuality. Here, we recommend the works of Mary Pavelka (1995), Frans de Waal (1989, 1995), and Kim Wallen (1995).

METHODS

This section discusses several important methodological considerations for conducting human sexuality research. The first issue concerns how individuals are selected for participation in a study, or more precisely, how individuals are *sampled* from a population, with the hope that the results obtained from this sample can be generalized to the larger population. Next, we discuss some of the many methods that have been developed for obtaining information about people's sexual behavior, including surveys, interviews, focus groups, direct observation, and clinical and laboratory research.

SAMPLING

Sampling has come to play a critical role in both qualitative (descriptive) and quantitative research on human sexuality. Because researchers do not have the time, money, ability, or inclination to observe all members of the study population, they must observe and assess a select number of individuals from the population (the study sample). Sampling theory, methods, and practices ensure that an adequate number is selected and that the individuals selected are representative of the larger population. They also serve as a form of social control, ensuring that researchers have not purposefully selected individuals with characteristics that favor the researcher's hypothesis.

One example of a conventional sampling design is provided by the school-based surveys that assess sexual behaviors among high school students (Centers for Disease Control and Prevention, 1990). With a conventional design, selection of the classrooms and of individuals within each classroom does not depend on what has been observed in other classrooms or in the particular classroom. Once the sampling frame (roughly, a list of the schools, classrooms, and students to be considered for inclusion in the study) is determined, the probability that an individual will be selected as a member of the study sample can be calculated. Imagine that a researcher is interested in determining the proportion of sexually active high school students who drink beer or other alcoholic beverages shortly before intercourse. If the sampling design calls for the researcher to sample schools, then classrooms within schools, and then individuals within classrooms, each individual will have a known probability of being included in the study sample. The inclusion of John, who has sex with Jennifer and is a close friend of Joe, will not affect Jennifer's chances of being included (and vice versa). More important, if only a few students within the selected schools have had sexual intercourse, there may be an insufficient number to establish the prevalence and determinants of the behavior of interest (alcohol use before sex). When the researcher does not take into account the distribution of the characteristic in the population, a conventional sampling design will probably provide a poor estimate of the characteristic that the researcher wanted to assess (Thompson, 1997).

Compared to conventional sampling designs, ethnographic studies have a much greater potential to reach a larger number of individuals who possess the characteristic or engage in the behavior. Such studies use a variety of techniques such as *snowball sampling* or *chain referral sampling*. Snowball sampling may be the best known of the various techniques (Biernacki & Waldorf, 1981; Faugier & Sargeant, 1997; Van Meter, 1990). The term has been used to describe two types of network sampling procedures. For one type, a few identified members of the population are asked to identify other members who are asked to identify other members of the population (Kalton & Anderson, 1986). This procedure is useful for generating a sampling frame. For the second type of snowball sampling, members are asked to identify a fixed number of other members, who are asked to identify other members, for a fixed number of rounds (Goodman, 1961). This procedure is useful for identifying and estimating the number of mutual relationships or social circles in the population. Although these techniques provide a relatively inexpensive way of identifying individuals who are members of the intended study population, they may make it difficult to determine the extent to which the specific, sample-based study findings are representative of the larger population (Kalton, 1993; Thompson, 1997).

So-called adaptive sampling designs have been developed to sample populations that are "hidden" or difficult to reach and assess in a timely and resource-efficient manner or to estimate characteristics that are difficult to sample using conventional designs (e.g., the level of contamination in hazardous waste sites; the number and serostatus of men who have sex with men; the health status of commercial sex workers; condom use attitudes among undocumented migrant workers). With adaptive sampling, each step of the sampling process is determined by what the researcher has observed on the previous step (Thompson & Seber, 1996). Thus, in ascertaining the prevalence of a sexually transmitted infection in a particular area, public health officials might select and test individuals at random. (Some of the difficult ethical issues associated with STI research are considered in a later section of this chapter.) If one of these individuals tests positive, all of that person's friends and contacts are tested, and so on. As suggested by the research on social networks, adaptive cluster designs have particular appeal for studying drug use and sexually transmitted infections because the latter are not uniformly distributed within the population.

DATA COLLECTION

Data on the most accessible aspects of human sexuality—attitudes, beliefs, intentions, norms, behaviors, practices, and functioning—typically are obtained through face-to-face interviews, focus groups, self-administered questionnaires, computer-assisted personal interviews, and audio-enhanced computer interviews. With the exception of the recent computer-assisted methods, an extensive literature addresses the advantages and disadvantages of each of these tools (Clement, 1990; Coreil, 1995; Fetterman, 1998; Fowler, 1993; Gilbert, Fiske, & Lindzey, 1998; Jorgensen, 1989; Lavrakas, 1993; Locke & Gilbert, 1995; McCracken, 1988; Morgan, 1993; Ward, Bertrand, & Brown, 1991). Other sources of data on human sexuality include observational techniques, which have been used to study the sexual behavior of individuals, couples, and cultural groups; laboratory research, which has been used to test causal hypotheses; and clinical research, which has been used to study and assist individuals experiencing sexual problems.

Interview

Various interviewing methods have been used to study human sexuality (e.g., semistructured vs. structured; face-to-face vs. computer-assisted personal interview). The most famous example of an interview-based study may be the Kinsey reports on the sexual behavior of American males and females (Ellis, 1954; Kinsey, Pomeroy, & Martin, 1948; Kinsey, Pomeroy, Martin, & Gebhard, 1953). When data are obtained through face-to-face interview, the interviewer can respond quickly and appropriately upon hearing information that is inconsistent or incomplete. However, the use of interviews to obtain sexual behavior data, especially about sensitive behaviors such as extramarital relationships, has its disadvantages. In addition to being a time-intensive and relatively costly means of gathering data, a face-to-face interview may contribute to individuals reporting information that is biased or inaccurate. That is, individuals may respond in a socially desirable manner (Catania, Gibson, Chitwood, & Coates, 1990; Paulhus, 1991), and their responses may be affected by their perceptions of and reactions to the interviewer and/or the interview situation (Benney, Riesman, & Star, 1956; Catania, Binson, Canchola, et al., 1996; Colombotos, Elinson, & Loewenstein, 1968; J. Freeman & Butler, 1976; Grimes & Hansen, 1984; T. Johnson, Hougland, & Moore, 1991; Kadushin, 1972; McBee & Justice, 1977; Shuman & Converse, 1968).

Imagine that you are a graduate student conducting a study of individuals' reactions to pornography. As part of the study, you show a pornographic movie to a group of mature undergraduate students. Suppose that the students like you and can identify with you because you look like one of them, and that they find the film enjoyable, arousing, and humorous. The next day, your professor repeats the study (i.e., shows the movie) with a different group of undergraduates. The professor is a no-nonsense social scientist and the students have long been intimidated by her. Unlike the students who viewed the movie on the previous day, these students find the movie distasteful and the whole experience anxiety producing. The different experiences of the two groups of students indicate that experimenter characteristics (such as age, gender, race/ethnicity, clothing, and status) can affect individuals' reactions to sexually explicit movies (Abramson, Goldberg, Mosher, Abramson, & Gottesdiener, 1975; for related work on reactions to double entendres, see Abramson & Handschumacher, 1978).

A face-to-face interview constitutes a social interaction between two individuals and is therefore subject to the demands associated with most social situations. Unplanned social influences that are perceived and acted on by study participants are referred to as *demand characteristics:* participants encode cues that suggest something about the research hypothesis, infer the correct hypothesis or a hypothesis that results in the same behavior, and then act in a manner consistent with the inferred hypothesis (cf. Shrimp, Hyatt, & Synder, 1991). Demand characteristics are treated as an experimental artifact because they, and not the experimental manipulation, are responsible for the observed outcome. For example, in one study, women were either told or not told that the researchers were interested in studying the symptoms women experienced during the menstrual cycle (AuBuchon & Calhoun, 1985). After eight weeks of weekly assessment, the researchers found that "informed" women had reported more negative psychological and somatic symptoms at the premenstrual and menstrual phases of their cycle than did the remaining women. In this study, the two conditions associated with demand characteristics were met: the "informed" women thought they knew the purpose of the study, and they behaved accordingly. (Notice the similarity to the placebo effect that is often observed in medical trials.)

Interviewers and experimenters can also be influenced by their perceptions of both study participants and the study contexts. More important, experimenters' expectancies or beliefs about the likely reactions of study participants can bias the data they obtain (R. Rosenthal, 1978, 1980; R. Rosenthal & Rosnow, 1968; R. Rosenthal & Rubin, 1978). Although researchers cannot completely eliminate such influences, they should acknowledge them and try to reduce their impact by using a representative sample of experimenters (interviewers). (The rationale underlying the need for a representative group of study participants holds as well for a representative group of experimenters or interviewers.)

Focus Groups

A focus group consists of approximately 8 to 12 individuals who meet as often as necessary with a group facilitator (or moderator) to discuss a topic identified by the facilitator. (The purpose of the discussion is to generate information of principal use to the facilitator.) Focus groups provide researchers with an opportunity to study individuals' beliefs, attitudes, values, norms, and experiences within the context of a group interaction (Asbury, 1995; Carey & Smith, 1994; Knodel, 1995; Krueger, 1988; Morgan, 1988, 1993; Vaughn, Schumm, & Sinagub, 1996). In addition to the information generated during the group discussion, focus groups provide researchers with an opportunity to listen to and see how individuals talk to and interact with one another. As with other qualitative research methods, the data are transcribed, coded, and analyzed. Although many researchers have used focus groups in conjunction with in-depth interviews and questionnaires, researchers have also used focus groups to develop interviews and assist with the wording of questionnaire items.

The primary advantage of the focus group is its capacity to provide the researcher with insights into the psychological, social, economic, political, and cultural contexts that serve to define, promote, and constrain individuals' choices and behaviors. In particular, focus groups can provide researchers with several detailed and subtle perspectives in a relatively short period of time. As with any research tool, there are disadvantages associated with its use. First, the number of participants who are asked to speak for the study population is limited by necessity (and it is not too difficult to see how a selection bias could result in information that is not representative of the study population). Second, and more important, the group is subject to the same dynamics that can influence any other group. Discussion can be dominated by one or more individuals, especially if the moderator is not sufficiently experienced, and individuals may censor themselves or conform to the opinions expressed by other group members. Third, the use of multiple moderators at several sites may pose a strong challenge to the researcher's ability to achieve comparability within and across sites.

The use of focus groups as a research tool can be traced to work done in the 1930s. In recent years, the method has been used by researchers in different countries to study diverse topics in human sexuality, including the context of adolescent pregnancy in Nicaragua (Berglund, Liljestrand, Martin, Salgado, & Zelaya, 1997); women's knowledge and attitudes toward a proposed antenatal STI screening/treatment program in Haiti (Desormeaux et al., 1996); awareness and knowledge of sexually transmitted infections among married women living in rural Bangladesh (Khan, Rahman, Khanam, et al., 1997); child sexual abuse in Zimbabwe (Meursing, Vos, Coutinho, et al., 1995); sexual attitudes and views of male and female sexuality among married adults living in Bangkok (Knodel, Low, Saengtienchai, & Lucas, 1997); and sexual decision making among adolescent African American males (Gilmore, DeLamater, & Wagstaff, 1996).

Survey

To avoid the potential biases associated with face-to-face interviews, many researchers use self-administered questionnaires to collect sensitive information. By using a questionnaire, researchers seek to give respondents greater privacy when considering their responses to potentially embarrassing questions and greater flexibility in deciding when and where the information will be obtained. However, with this transfer of control to the respondent, the researcher may not be able to make appropriate adjustments when respondents report inconsistent data or decline to answer items. Moreover, with a self-administered questionnaire, some respondents may misunderstand the "skip patterns" designed to elicit information from specific individuals (e.g., "If 'No' go to Question 4a; if 'Yes' go to Question 4b"), and other respondents may not be able to read and comprehend some of the items.

To address concerns about the validity and reliability of information gathered through interview and self-administered questionnaire, a number of researchers have used telephone interviews (Bastani, Erickson, Marcus, et al., 1996; Catania, Coates, Stall, et al., 1992; Gibb, MacDonagh, Tookey, & Duong, 1997; Mishra & Serxner, 1994; Slutske et al., 1998) and computer-assisted data gathering (Bloom, 1998; Millstein & Irwin, 1983; Romer et al., 1997; Schneider, Taylor, Prater, & Wright, 1991). To varying degrees, these tools give respondents a greater sense of privacy and mitigate the social influence effects attributable to an interviewer's physical appearance or demeanor, although responses may still be influenced by the interviewer's vocal characteristics (Oksenberg, Coleman, & Cannell, 1986). Computer-assisted approaches are receiving increased attention because they permit individuals to respond privately while giving researchers the opportunity to (a) ask questions in a language spoken by the respondent; (b) ask the respondent additional questions if inconsistent or incomplete information is offered; (c) automate skip patterns and thereby ensure that the respondent is asked the appropriate questions; and (d) ensure that comparable information is gathered from respondents with various levels of reading skills.

Although the Kinsey Reports (Kinsey et al., 1948, 1953) were and still are recognized for their comprehensive look at the sexual behavior of U.S. males and females, most researchers appreciate the fact that the data were not representative of any larger population (W. Cochran, Mosteller, & Tukey, 1954; Turner, Danella, & Rogers, 1995). Indeed, until recently, much of what was known about sexual behavior was obtained from volunteers, clinical studies, and small samples. This situation has changed dramatically in the past thirty years, during which time a number of surveys of nationally representative populations (e.g., adolescents, young men and women, households) have been conducted. Typically, in these surveys a trained interviewer conducts face-to-face interviews with respondents in a private setting and a self-administered questionnaire is used to obtain the most sensitive data. Examples of surveys using this format include the 1971, 1976, and 1979 National Survey of Young Women (Zelnik & Kim, 1982); the 1979 National Survey of Young Men (Zelnik & Kanter, 1980); the 1988 and 1990 National Survey of Adolescent Males (Sonenstein, Pleck, & Ku, 1989); the 1991 National Survey of Men (Tanfer, 1993); and the 1992 National Health and Social Life Survey (Laumann, Gagnon, Michael, & Michaels, 1994). The National Health and Social Life Survey may be the most comprehensive survey of the sexual behavior of the general population that has been conducted to date (Laumann et al., 1994).

Examples of telephone survey include the population-based National AIDS Behavioral Surveys that were initiated in 1990 (Catania et al., 1992). The surveys obtained sexual behavior and HIV-risk data on a random sample of individuals residing in 23 U.S. metropolitan areas that accounted for a significant proportion of AIDS cases (e.g., Binson, Dolcini, Pollack, & Catania, 1993). In a recent example of the potential of computer-assisted surveys, researchers used laptops outfitted with an audio-enhanced, self-interviewing software program to obtain data from participants in the 1995 National Survey of Adolescent Males. Their findings suggested that estimates of sensitive and/or illegal behaviors (e.g., male-male sexual contact, injection drug use, engaging in sex while drunk or high, engaging in sex with someone who injected drugs) obtained with a self-administered questionnaire may underestimate true prevalence of the behavior (Turner, Ku, Rogers, Lindberg, & Pleck, 1998).

Additional data on sexual behavior in the United States is provided through the General Social Survey, which has been conducted each year since 1972 (e.g., J. Davis & Smith, 1994; T. Smith, 1991); the recurring National Survey of Family Growth, which provides detailed information on the sexual and contraceptive behavior of women aged 15 to 44 (W. Mosher & Bachrach, 1995); the National Health Interview Survey, which has been fielded continuously since 1957 and provides information on the health of the civilian, noninstitutionalized U.S. population (National Center for Health Statistics, 1958, 1989); the National Longitudinal Survey of Youth, an annual study of individuals who were between the ages of 14 and 21 in 1979 (Center for Human Resource Research, 1995); and the biennial Youth Risk Behavior Survey of nineth- to twelfth-grade students conducted by the Centers for Disease Control and Prevention (Kolbe, 1990).

Direct Observation

There is, of course, a much more direct means than surveys or interviews for learning about people's sexual behaviors—namely, observing them in the act. Observational studies, which sometimes include physiological measurements in addition to direct observation, are especially useful for obtaining information about the physical aspects of human sexuality. The most famous study to use this methodology is Masters and Johnson's (1966) investigation of the physiology of human sexual response. In their laboratory studies, they watched individuals and couples engaging in masturbation and intercourse, making detailed notes of observed physical changes (such as "sexual flush") and measuring physiological changes (such as penile circumference or vaginal lubrication). On the basis of these observations, they postulated that both men and women proceed through four distinct phases in their "sexual response cycles": excitement, plateau, orgasm, and resolution (Masters & Johnson, 1966). Although their theoretical integration of the physical data has been challenged (e.g., Robinson, 1976), Masters and Johnson are widely acknowledged for their pioneering use of observational and physiological measurement techniques.

Directly observed, laboratory investigations of human sexuality such as Masters and Johnson's are relatively rare. A more common observational technique is the ethnographic study, in which the researcher observes the population of interest (e.g., a society such as the Sambia or a social group such as injection drug users) in the natural environment. Ethnographic methods have historically been associated with the fields of anthropology and sociology, but are now employed by behavioral researchers of many stripes who wish to study sensitive human behaviors—especially sex and illicit drug use—in their naturally occurring contexts. This method is typically used to gather detailed descriptive data regarding the behaviors of the population of interest, rather than as a means of directly testing a specific hypothesis.

One of the keys to a successful ethnographic study is to minimize reactivity among the study participants. That is, their behavior should not be influenced in any way by the presence of the ethnographer. One approach requires that the ethnographer try to "blend into" the environment, so that the subjects of the study become accustomed to his or her presence and begin to react to it much as they would to any other feature of the natural environment. This is a passive, detached, and highly noninteractive ideal, and one that, like *Star Trek's* Prime Directive, is next to impossible to achieve. Instead, many ethnographers become *participant-observers* in the cultures they study. As participant-observer, the researcher becomes an acknowledged part of the culture, sometimes participating in the rituals or other activities of the group he or she is studying.

Usually, in ethnographies of sexual behavior, the emphasis is on observation rather than participation. Participation in general, and especially in studies of sexual behavior, raises questions of (a) reactivity among study subjects (i.e., is their behavior affected by the ethnographer's participation?); (b) the objectivity and validity of the ethnographer's account (can he or she objectively describe his or her own behavior, and is his or her experience typical of the culture or unique to his or her role as an outsider?); and (c) the ethics of engaging in or condoning potentially dangerous, illegal, or socially proscribed activities (such as illicit drug use, unsafe sex, or sex in public). These issues are highlighted in Humphries's (1970) famous ethnography of men who seek anonymous sex in public restrooms, *Tearoom Trade*. Conducting an observational study of men engaged in an illegal activity in a very small, confined space (public park restrooms, or "tearooms" in the argot of the men who frequent them) presented Humphries with a number of methodological difficulties to overcome. Initially, Humphries assumed the role of a "straight" (i.e., a man who enters the restroom solely to use the toilet) while attempting to observe the sexual activities in the tearooms, but as a straight, Humphries could remain in the tearoom for a short time only, during which his interest in the sexual goings became highly conspicuous. Worse, most sexual activity would cease as he approached the restroom. He soon realized that he needed to find a way to integrate himself into the tearoom trade subculture ("trade" refers to men who engage in homosexual activities but who do not self-identify as gay). For ethical reasons, Humphries rejected adopting an active sexual role and instead assumed the role of voyeur/lookout, or "watchqueen." In this role, Humphries was an accepted part of the tearoom sex scene (thus limiting the reactivity of the study population) and could freely observe the sexual behaviors of others, provided that he also performed his watchqueen duties by warning participants of the approach of straights, "chickens" (teenagers), and police officers (Humphries, 1970).

More generally, the anthropological literature makes clear that it is difficult to obtain accurate records of human sexual behavior (Abramson, 1992b; Abramson & Herdt, 1990; Herdt, 1981; Herdt & Stoller, 1989; Mead, 1961). Margaret Mead (1961), who is most famous for her investigations into adolescent sexuality in Samoa (Mead, 1928/1961), describes many of the difficulties. She notes as a starting point that human sexual behavior is intimately linked with privacy. As a result, there is an inherent tension between the individual's desire to be protected from unsolicited intrusion and the researcher's desire to make a public record that can be examined by others (Abramson, 1990; Abramson & Pinkerton, 1995; Mead, 1961). Similarly, Mead notes that sexuality is characterized in almost every society by gaps in awareness (e.g., accurate descriptions of genitalia) and specific taboos (e.g., homosexuality) that contribute to an inability or unwillingness to talk about one's sexual behavior. Finally, Mead asserts that there is no cultural rationale for describing honestly one's sexual behavior and that there are discrepancies between institutionalized statements of what is appropriate sexual behavior and actual sexual behavior and practices.

In the past thirty years, more methodological concerns have been raised regarding cultural prohibitions and unconscious processes that make the assessment of sexual behavior an extraordinarily difficult objective. For example, Abramson and Herdt (1990) describe two levels of bias in the cross-cultural assessment of sexual practices. The first level is related to the language used to identify culturally sensitive categories. Is there a generic category for "prostitute," or is the category gendered? (Compare "hustler" for male to "hooker" for female.) How may these labels be used, in what contexts, and by whom? More important, to what extent do situation-specific meanings and behaviors bias individuals' responses to questions about sexual behavior?

The second level of bias is related to the manner in which sexuality-related ethnographic information is collected, and in particular, with interviewing protocols. When one considers the linguistic context and the need for culturally sensitive procedures, the question of where individuals should be interviewed arises immediately. Should the interview be conducted in public or in private? Should the individuals conducting the interviews be of the same culture, gender, social class, and sexual orientation as the interviewee? An ethnographer usually works alone and establishes a close, personal relationship with the social group members participating in the study. The ethnographer will learn their language and customs, participate in the group's activities, and perhaps live with them. Although these practices undoubtedly enhance trust and facilitate understanding, the literature on interviewer/experimenter effects and the fierce debates about the impact of specific anthropologists (e.g., Margaret Mead; see D. Freeman, 1983) argue forcefully for the use, when possible, of multiple investigators with different sociodemographic characteristics.

STUDY OF SOCIAL NETWORKS

One area that has seen an explosive growth in the use of ethnographic methods is the study of social networks. A social network analysis focuses on the relationships among social entities or actors and the patterns and implications of those relationships (Wasserman & Faust, 1994). More important, it focuses on the interactions among the actors, as opposed to the attitudes, beliefs, intentions, and behaviors of an individual actor. This perspective has grown in popularity because many important aspects of social life are conducted by individuals organized into social networks (Galaskiewicz & Wasserman, 1994). It has become increasingly important to ethnographers studying urban life because an understanding of the social network is necessary to obtain information on less public events and establish relationships with key informants (J. Johnson, 1994). The social network perspective has also grown in importance because it is well suited to studying the injection drug use and sexual networks that transmit HIV and other sexually transmitted infections (Anderson & May, 1991; Morris, 1994; Neaigus, Friedman, Curtis, et al., 1994; Rhodes, Stimson, & Quirk, 1996; Rothenberg, Potterat, & Woodhouse, 1996). In particular, a social network perspective recognizes the fact that, like many material goods, drugs and infections are exchangeable and, as such, travel routes that connect interdependent social networks (e.g., from individual transactions in shooting galleries to mass distribution by drug cartels). In addition, and unlike many epidemiological models, a social network perspective recognizes the fact that individuals do not select their drug and/or sexual partners at random: sociodemographic characteristics strongly influence interaction opportunities and define the appropriate groups from which one can select one's friends, neighbors, associates, and partners.

Ethnographers have made a number of important contributions to the study of human sexuality and sexual behavior. Their work continues to show that public proclamations (surface-level material) can often be unreliable; that subtle methods can yield detailed information about the social experiences of individuals and their social networks; and that rapport and intimate understanding are critical (Abramson, 1992a).

CLINICAL RESEARCH

Clinical research, naturally enough, is research that is conducted in a clinical setting (e.g., a hospital, clinic, or physician's or therapist's office); with a clinical population (e.g., men with erectile dysfunction or postoperative transsexuals); or that concerns clinical issues related to sexuality (e.g., physical aspects of sexual satisfaction). The most frequently studied clinical issues concern the diagnosis and treatment of difficulties with specific aspects of sexual attraction, arousal, and performance.

Clinical research often adopts a case study approach, in which one or more persons with the condition of interest are described in detail. For example, Coleman and Bockting (1988) describe a 36-year-old female-to-male transsexual who was "heterosexual" prior to sex reassignment surgery and "homosexual" after it—that is, who was attracted to men both before and after surgery. This case study illustrates the separability of the concepts of gender identity and sexual orientation, in that the patient sought surgery to bring her (female) anatomical sex into alignment with her (male) psychological gender, even though the surgery also transformed her from a "straight" woman into a "gay" man. Importantly, it also demonstrates a critical scientific function of case studies: if properly documented, they can serve as disconfirmatory counter-examples to prevailing theories (e.g., that gender identity and sexual orientation are inexorably connected). Moreover, case studies can offer deep insight into the causes and correlates of the study condition and thereby can help researchers generate testable hypotheses (Abramson, 1992a). Although the generalizability of case study findings is limited, the case study approach makes up in specificity what it lacks in generality.

Large-scale clinical studies are often undertaken to evaluate the efficacy of new treatments for various forms of sexual dysfunction, or to assess the relationship between sex and other health-related issues. As an example of the latter category, a recent study published in the prestigious *British Medical Journal* suggests that maintaining an active sex life can have beneficial effects on life expectancy; specifically, the authors found evidence of a dose-response relationship, such that men with greater orgasmic frequency exhibited a significantly lower risk of death from coronary heart disease (Davey Smith, Frankel, & Yarnell, 1997).

Erectile dysfunction is also commonly associated with other medical conditions, such as hypertension, diabetes, and depression, as well as with psychogenic factors. In 1998, the Food and Drug Administration (FDA) approved a new drug for the treatment of erectile dysfunction on the basis of 21 randomized, double-blind, placebo-controlled trials (Lamberg, 1998). According to the FDA, the new drug, Viagra (oral sildenafil), led to at least some improvement in 7 of 10 men with erectile dysfunction, compared to 2 of 10 men who reported improved functioning when given a placebo. Surprisingly, perhaps, the clinical efficacy trials relied on a self-report measure, the International Index of Erectile Dysfunction, rather than on direct physiological measurement of erectile function, such as nocturnal erections (Lamberg, 1998).

More generally, the fourth edition of the venerable *Diagnostic and Statistical Manual of Mental Disorders* (*DSM-IV*) (American Psychiatric Association [APA], 1994) defines sexual dysfunction as a problem characterized by a disturbance in both sexual desire and the psychophysiological changes that precipitate sexual arousal or orgasm. Such problems are often accompanied by distress and relationship difficulties. They are also surprisingly common: in one study of "happily married couples," 40% of the men reported erectile or ejaculatory dysfunction and 63% of the women reported arousal or orgasmic dysfunction (Frank, Anderson, & Rubinstein, 1978). From a diagnostic perspective, research tends to focus on precipitating factors (e.g., relationship conflict, medical cofactors) and delineating specific syndromes (e.g., sexual desire disorders) (H. Kaplan, 1979; Stuart, Hammond, & Pett, 1988; Zilbergeld & Kilmann, 1984). Therapy research tends to focus more on developing specific treatment formats (e.g., masturbation training for female orgasmic dysfunction) that are drawn from different treatment modalities (e.g., behavioral, cognitive, marital, psychodynamic) (Masters & Johnson, 1970; Rosen & Leiblum, 1992; Schover & LoPiccolo, 1982; Zilbergeld, 1992).

Another main area of clinical research concerns the diagnosis and treatment of sexual attraction disorders. For many years, homosexuality was conceptualized as a psychiatric problem because it represents a deviation from the statistical norm in terms of sexual attraction (i.e., unlike most of the population, homosexuals are sexually attracted to members of their own sex). Homosexuality was thus considered deviant. The larger question, however, is whether this "deviation" encompasses identifiably pathological psychological processes, or whether sexual attraction is simply a form of diversity, like skin or eye color, or a preference for brunettes over blondes.

Although political and religious issues did (and continue to) play a significant role in this debate, the scientific question of whether homosexual attraction is pathological was largely settled in the 1950s and 1960s by researchers such as Evelyn Hooker. Hooker (1957) administered a series of psychological tests to nonclinical samples of homosexual and heterosexual populations and demonstrated that there were no significant differences between the two populations. Subsequent research supported this finding, which precipitated a major change in how homosexuality was viewed. In the 1970s, the American Psychiatric Association passed a resolution that stated, "homosexuality per se implies no impairment in judgment, stability, reliability or general social or vocational capabilities" and removed homosexuality from its list of mental disorders (Allgeier & Allgeier, 1995).

At present, most sexual attraction disorders are characterized as *paraphilias*, which are defined as intense and recurring sexual feelings or behaviors involving nonhuman objects, suffering or humiliation, or nonconsensual activities (e.g., exhibitionism or acts involving children). The treatment of these disorders is also a focus of clinical research. Behavioral and cognitive therapies are the preferred technique (e.g., Marshall, Eccles, & Barbaree, 1991), although there is considerable debate about the effectiveness of treating sexual offenders, given the high recidivism rates that are often observed. Hormonal and other pharmacological therapies have shown some promise in this regard (Bradford, 1998; Gijs & Gooren, 1996; Rösler & Witztum, 1998). Related areas of treatment research also include improving techniques for counseling survivors of sexual assault and designing therapies for the nonoffending partner or parent in cases of incest (Finkelhor & Berliner, 1995). There is also an ongoing debate over the status and possible treatment of "sexual compulsivity" or "sexual addiction" (Abramson & Pinkerton, 1995; Coleman, 1991; Levine & Troiden, 1988; Quadland, 1985).

LABORATORY RESEARCH

Researchers conduct laboratory studies of human sexuality to test hypotheses about causal relationships. For example, Kelley, Byrne, Greendlinger, and Murnen (1997) used the context, sex of the viewer, and seven dispositional variables to predict heterosexual college students' affective and evaluative responses to three types of sexually explicit film; Murnen, Perot, and Byrne

(1989) studied situational determinants of and individual differences associated with female college students' coping reactions to unwanted sexual advances; and Przybyla and Byrne (1984) examined male and female college students' recall of and their affective and sexual/physiological reactions to erotic stimuli in the presence of auditory and visual distractions.

Researchers use laboratory settings because such settings give them greater control over conditions that could account for the hypothesized relationship. In particular, laboratory settings give researchers the ability to control the number, magnitude, and type of influences, as well as to constrain the manner in which these influences exert their effects on the causal relationship of primary interest. In turn, this control enhances the researcher's ability to conclude, when supported by the data, that the assumed cause and effect covary, and that this covariation cannot be attributed to alternative causes. Because the assumed cause precedes the effect in time, covaries with the effect, and is the most plausible explanation of that covariation, the researcher concludes that the hypothesized causal relationship holds. This is the logic behind studies conducted in laboratory settings.

On occasion, the nature of the research is such that the laboratory is the only place where it can be conducted. Studies of sexual response to stimuli spring to mind immediately. For example, Janssen, Vissenberg, Visser, and Everaerd (1997) conducted a study to compare two types of penile strain gauge (devices used to measure male sexual arousal). Laan, Everaerd, and Evers (1995) studied female sexual arousal to visual stimuli that were sexual, anxiety-inducing, sexually threatening, or neutral. The researchers measured vaginal pulse amplitude and blood volume, skin conductance, and heart rate—measurements best taken in the laboratory setting. However, even when instruments are not required to obtain data, researchers may want to take advantage of the privacy, quiet, and safety the laboratory provides.

When conducting a laboratory study, a researcher's primary concern has often been with the study's internal validity—the judgment that the observed statistical relationship was a true causal relationship (Cook & Campbell, 1976). Internal validity is a "diagnosis by exclusion." Confidence in the judgment that the study has high internal validity is achieved by eliminating (preferably by design and not by subsequent argument) the plausible challenges to the putative causal relationship. However, with an increased involvement in the body politic (e.g., social action research, applied social research, evaluation research, policy research) and with growing pressure to provide relevant answers to social problems (race relations, economic disadvantage, adolescent pregnancy, welfare dependency, violence and crime, HIV infection), researchers have given more attention to designing and analyzing studies that have more external validity. A finding from a study with high external validity is one that holds across populations and settings (Cook & Campbell, 1976).

Although laboratory studies have enhanced our understanding of human sexuality, questions have been raised about the generalizability of the findings obtained thereby. These questions reflect concerns about the nature of the set-ting and the task experienced by the study participants (i.e., concerns about the study's *ecological validity*). The questions also reflect concerns about the use of volunteers. Evidence suggests that the individuals who choose to participate in studies of human sexuality differ from those who do not choose to do so (Barker & Perlman, 1975; Bogaert, 1996; Kaats & Davis, 1971; Morokoff, 1986; Strassberg & Lowe, 1995; Wolchik, Braver, & Jensen, 1985; Wolchik, Spencer, & Lisi, 1983). Strassberg and Lowe found that undergraduate sex research volun-teers reported more positive attitudes toward sexuality, less sexual guilt, and more sexual experiences than nonvolunteers. Bogaert found that undergradu-ate male volunteers were more sexually experienced, more interested in sexual variety, and more erotophilic. In addition, volunteers were higher in sensation seeking and lower in social conformity than nonvolunteers. Morokoff found that unmarried female undergraduate volunteers had more noncoital sexual experience, more masturbatory experience, and less sexual inhibition than nonvolunteers. These and similar findings pose a serious threat to the external validity of study findings that are based on volunteers. Future research on human sexuality should make an effort to include more diverse populations and should take greater care to control for possible selection bias.

FIELD STUDIES

Field studies are defined by their location: they are research studies conducted *in the field* (as opposed to a research laboratory). Examples of field studies in-clude the HIV prevention intervention developed for mentally ill homeless men by Ezra Susser and his colleagues (Susser et al., 1998; Susser, Valencia, Miller, et al., 1995; Susser, Valencia, Sohler, et al., 1996; Susser, Valencia, & Torres, 1994). The intervention consisted of 15 sessions, which is more sessions than many other prevention interventions. Contributing to the risk of infection were cocaine and injection drug use, and unprotected sex. The intervention combined social cognitive theory skills training (i.e., role play, modeling, social reinforcement, and feedback) with various clinical approaches and activities. The latter were centered on the kinds of conversations, games, and activities that were routine to shelter life. Other researchers have offered similar cognitive-behavioral interventions to prevent sexually transmitted HIV infec-tion among adolescents (Jemmott, Jemmott, & Fong, 1992, 1998; St. Lawrence, Brasfield, Jefferson, Alleyne, & O'Bannon, 1995); gay men (Kegeles, Hays, & Coates, 1996; Kelly, St. Lawrence, Betts, Brasfield, & Hood, 1990; Kelly, St. Lawrence, Diaz, et al., 1991; Kelly, St. Lawrence, Stevenson, et al., 1992); and economically disadvantaged women (Kelly, Murphy, Washington, et al., 1994).

Field studies, prevention interventions, and planned program evaluations share many of the strengths and weaknesses of laboratory-based studies. In-deed, many graduate students in education and the social sciences receive training in the logic of experimental design, if they are not actually trained to conduct lab-based experiments. Thus, it should come as no surprise that field studies and prevention interventions rely on convenience samples. However, the evidence for volunteer bias in lab-based studies (e.g., Bogaert, 1992, 1996; Griffith & Walker, 1976; Morokoff, 1986; Nirenberg, Wincze, Bansal, et al., 1991; Strassberg & Lowe, 1995; Wolchik et al., 1983, 1985) suggests that the individuals who choose to participate in a prevention program differ from those who do not choose to do so. Prevention interventions may have high internal validity; however, the failure to address concerns about their external validity will result in their having less value to programmers and policymakers, and less support from the larger community.

MEASURES

It is often said that the fundamental activity that distinguishes science from other human pursuits is the taking of measurements. Indeed, it has been argued that without the successive refinement in measurement, scientific progress would cease and science would grind to a halt (Kemeny, 1959). With this emphasis on measurement, scientists have an obligation to demonstrate that their measures are valid and reliable. Taken once, the measure should provide an accurate value; taken repeatedly, it should provide consistent values.

SEXUAL BEHAVIOR AND SELF-REPORTS

Researchers who study human sexuality need to be particularly concerned about the validity and reliability of their measures because they often rely on individuals' reports of their sexual experiences. These self-reports reflect the experiences that individuals can recall and choose to share. Thus, when researchers study aspects of human sexuality that are socially mediated, they need to take into account the capacities and limits of human memory and the conscious and unconscious motivations that shape self-reports. In all fairness, all researchers who rely on self-report should proceed cautiously (even when the studied phenomenon is as public as weight gain; see Bowman & DeLucia, 1992).

Numerous studies and reviews have considered the validity and reliability of self-reports of sexual behavior. Many of the early studies reflect research on the sexual behavior of adolescents and young adults. The finding that adolescent, young adult, and adult males in the United States, Britain, France, New Zealand, and Norway report many more sex partners than their female counterparts has been one of the most consistent and troubling research findings (Wiederman, 1997). The suggested explanations for the discrepancy include some form of sampling bias (e.g., males have greater sexual contact with individuals such as young females or prostitutes who are not included in the study sample), response bias (e.g., differences in the way males and females define "sex" and "sex partner"), and/or outlier influence (i.e., men who report large numbers of partners may inflate the mean) (Morris, 1993; Wiederman, 1997).

More recent studies of the validity and reliability of self-report data reflect research on risk behaviors for sexually transmitted infections, specifically HIV infection (Abramson, 1988; Abramson & Herdt, 1990; Alexander, Somerfield, Ensminger, et al., 1993; Catania, Gibson, Chitwood, et al., 1990; Catania, Gibson, Marin, Coates, & Greenblatt, 1990; Coates, Calzavara, Soskolne, et al., 1988; Coates, Soskolne, Calzavara, et al., 1986; D. Cohen & Dent, 1992; Jaccard & Wan, 1995; James, Bignell, & Gilles, 1991; Kauth, St. Lawrence, & Kelly, 1991; McLaws, Oldenburg, Ross, & Cooper, 1990; Padian, Aral, Vranizan, & Bolan, 1995; Saltzman, Stoddard, McCusker, Moon, & Mayer, 1987; Turner & Miller, 1997; Upchurch, Weisman, Shepherd, Brookmeyer, et al., 1991; Zenilman, Weisman, Rompalo, et al., 1995). Concerns about the reliability of the data collected by HIV researchers are heightened because the behaviors that result in HIV transmission are illegal (injection drug use), stigmatized (anal intercourse), or difficult to enact (getting a reluctant partner to use condoms). On the whole, researchers have concluded that self-reports of sexual behaviors are reliable, particularly when the recall period is short and individuals are asked to recall salient behaviors. However, an uncritical treatment of individuals' reports of sexual behavior may be unwarranted.

In a recent experiment (Berk, Abramson, & Okami, 1995), half of the participants were asked to keep a daily diary for two weeks; the remaining participants were not. Within each group, participants were assigned to a memory enhancement, placebo enhancement, or no instruction condition. The purpose of the study was to provide an estimate of the error in the recall of (recent) sexual behavior, examine factors that might facilitate recall on a survey of sexual behavior, and provide further insight into how people experience and encode human sexual behavior. Although the study was weighted toward remembering recent sexual experiences (in that the recall period was the past two weeks and participants were explicitly encouraged to remember events as accurately as possible), the most striking finding was how little participants could remember about their sexual experiences. This was true even for the participants who kept a daily diary and wrote about their experiences. Furthermore, the nondiary participants reported more sexual behavior than did the diary participants, suggesting that individuals tended to inflate their sexual experiences without the help of a diary.

Why? Do the findings reflect error or chance, or do they suggest something about the processes associated with the encoding and recall of sexual experiences? The authors of the study believe the latter and have called for further study of the recall of sexual experiences as an adjunct to the assessment of sexual practices (Berk et al., 1995).

PHYSIOLOGICAL MEASURES

As we have discussed throughout this chapter, there are many obstacles to collecting valid and reliable data on human sexual behavior, including reliance on retrospective recall, social desirability effects, and experimenter effects. Conversely, there are several characteristics that facilitate the measurement of human sexuality. Unlike many psychological variables (e.g., guilt, depression), sex is often an overtly expressed behavior, which can be counted (e.g., "How often do you masturbate per month?") or measured physiologically (e.g., erectile tumescence). The latter is particularly significant because physiological assessment can provide several advantages in theory, measurement, and objectivity.

One of the most interesting physiological measurement techniques makes use of heat to indicate changes in sexual status. All objects—including humans—emit infrared energy as a function of temperature. This infrared energy (or "heat") can be measured through a process known as *thermography*. Thermography is a noninvasive means of detecting and photographing individual heat-generation patterns to indicate physiological condition and functional changes within (M. Bacon, 1976). Thermography is also a very useful physiological measure for studying sexual arousal in humans. Because pelvic vasocongestion and myotonia (increased blood flow and muscular spasms, respectively), both of which are associated with increased temperature, are the principal peripheral physiological responses that accompany sexual arousal, thermography is an excellent way of documenting the blood flow rate and transfer of heat that underlie the experience of being sexually aroused (Abramson, Perry, Rothblatt, Seeley, & Seeley, 1981; Abramson, Perry, Seeley, Seeley, & Rothblatt, 1981; Seeley, Abramson, Perry, Rothblatt, & Seeley, 1980). Thermography has also been useful in documenting an asymmetrical vasocongestive pattern in the pectoral region that accompanies the sexual response cycle (Abramson & Pearsall, 1983). Thus, unlike many paper-and-pencil social science measures, thermography represents a good match among object (sexual arousal), theory (heat distribution), and measurement scale (temperature).

A number of other physiological measures are useful for studying human sexual arousal. Probably the best-known examples are the penile strain gauge and the vaginal photoplethysmograph. The former can measure minute changes in penis size (including each pulse of blood in the penis), and the latter measures increased vaginal blood volume. These measures have been used, for example, to study men's and women's physiological reactions to sexually explicit films or pictures (Rosen & Beck, 1988). Of course, researchers need to be particularly sensitive when their experiments involve direct genital measurement (Abramson, Perry, Rothblatt, et. al., 1981). Using same-gendered experimenters, providing privacy to participants, and allowing self-placement and monitoring of genital devices should be employed when possible.

Besides genital blood flow, new technologies, such as magnetic resonance imaging (MRI), offer the possibility of examining other bodily responses that are instrumental to sexual arousal, including the role of the brain. Additionally, endocrinological studies of the hormonal changes that accompany or influence sexual behavior are very important and active areas of research (Meyer-Bahlburg, 1995; J. Wilson, 1995).

Personality Measures

There are several measures of specific personality traits that are germane to the topic of sex research; these be discussed momentarily. First, however, we discuss the relationship of sexual behavior to the comprehensive personality model of Hans Eysenck. (In this exposition, personality is viewed as an essentially stable component of the psyche that determines fundamental patterns of interaction between self and environment.)

Like many other contemporary personality theorists, Eysenck (1947; Eysenck & Eysenck, 1969) posited that personality could be factored into a small number of nearly orthogonal dimensions, or traits. The three dimensions proposed by Eysenck were (1) *extroversion,* a nonspecific mixture of sociability and impulsivity; extroverts are sociable, lively, active, assertive, and highly sensation seeking; (2) *neuroticism,* largely a measure of emotional instability; persons who are high in this trait tend to be anxious, depressed, tense, and to suffer from feelings of guilt and low self-esteem; and (3) *psychoticism,* which reflects asocial and atypical attitudes and tendencies, including cruelty, indifference to the feelings of others, and paranoia; highly psychotic individuals are characteristically aggressive, cold, egocentric, impersonal, and impulsive. Relative standing on these three dimensions (E-P-N) is assessed using the Eysenck Personality Questionnaire, together with a "lie scale" that is used to detect dissimulation and social conformity (Eysenck & Eysenck, 1975). (The labeling of Eysenck's three factors as extroversion, neuroticism, and psychoticism is misleading. For example, a high score on the psychoticism scale does not indicate psychosis in the clinical sense; nor does a high neuroticism score necessarily reflect neurosis in the Woody Allen sense.)

In his book, *Sex and Personality,* Eysenck (1976) made a number of concrete predictions regarding the relationships of E-P-N factors to sexual behavior, especially focusing on the expected correlation between extroversion and enhanced sexuality (Barnes, Malamuth, & Check, 1984). Empirical tests of these predictions suggest the following (see Abramson, 1973; Barnes et al., 1984; Eysenck, 1976; Giese & Schmidt, 1968). First, compared to introverted people, extroverted individuals are more likely to be sexually promiscuous and hedonistic; desire greater sexual variety; are more likely to have multiple partners; and experience greater enjoyment and satisfaction from engaging in conventional sexual activities. Those who are higher on the psychoticism scale are more likely to exhibit high libidos and to hold favorable attitudes toward unconventional sexual activities, including impersonal sex, premarital and extramarital sexuality, and coercion. High neuroticism scores are generally associated with increased guilt, decreased sexual enjoyment, and intolerance of premarital sex. The relationships of these and other personality variables (such as sensation seeking) to HIV risk taking is examined in Pinkerton and Abramson (1995).

One of the main drawbacks to the use of a comprehensive personality inventory such as Eysenck's is that it is *too general* and *too comprehensive.* What is needed in most research situations is a specific measure of the relevant sexuality construct. For example, a study of masturbation guilt requires an instrument that is devoted to assessing masturbation guilt. Fortunately, a number of specific measures exist, including ones for masturbation attitudes and guilt (Abramson & Mosher, 1975); sexual guilt and repression (D. Mosher, 1966, 1973); and erotophobia-erotophilia (Byrne, 1983; Byrne & Schulte, 1990), which measures attitudes toward sex-related materials and activities. A wealth of research utilizing these measures has established their utility (see, e.g., Abramson & Handschumacher, 1978; W. Fisher, 1980; Galbraith & Mosher, 1968; D. Mosher & Abramson, 1977; Schill & Chapin, 1972; Schwartz, 1973).

The best-known instruments for assessing sexual orientation and gender identity are the Kinsey scale and the Bem Sex Role Inventory, respectively. Kinsey measured sexual orientation along a 7-point continuum ranging from strictly heterosexual (0) to strictly homosexual (6), with various mixes of opposite-sex and same-sex sexual behaviors falling between these extremes (e.g., the midpoint of Kinsey's scale describes someone who engages in equal amounts of heterosexual and homosexual activity). However, sexual behavior is not necessarily congruent with sexual attraction or with sexual identity. For this reason, contemporary research often uses multiscale instruments that separately measure these different aspects of sexual orientation.

Rather than juxtaposing masculinity and femininity along a bipolar continuum, as earlier instruments had, the Bem Sex Role Inventory (BMSI) assesses them separately (Bem, 1974). The original form of the BMSI asks the respondent to rate himself or herself on 20 stereotypically masculine personality traits (e.g., assertive, dominant), 20 stereotypically feminine traits (e.g., compassionate, affectionate), and 20 filler items. (Later, a short form was devised that consists of half the number of items on the original.) Because the BMSI measures femininity and masculinity separately, a person can appear both highly masculine and highly feminine; such a person is considered *androgynous* (at the other extreme, someone who is neither masculine or feminine is labeled *undifferentiated*) (see, e.g., Ballard-Reisch & Elton, 1992; Hyde, Krajnik, & Skuldt-Niederberger, 1991; Taylor & Hall, 1982).

PSYCHOSOCIAL MEASURES

Although some researchers develop psychosocial scales and instruments for each new study they conduct, a number of these tools have been collected in book form and are available off the shelf for use by other investigators. For example, C. Davis, Yarber, Bauserman, Scheer, and Davis (1998) discuss more than 200 measures of sex-related states, traits, behaviors, and outcomes that have been used in research and clinical settings. In most instances, the instrument is provided along with information on its purpose, timing, scoring, interpretation, and psychometric properties (reliability, validity). The measures address over 50 areas, representing research on abortion, abuse, aging, arousal, attitudes, coitus, contraception, dysfunction, esteem, fantasy, gender identity, gender roles, harassment, homophobia, homosexuality, intimacy, molestation, orgasm, rape, relationships, sexual history, sexual risk, sexually transmitted infections, stereotypes, transsexualism, and vasectomy.

Numerous general social psychological measures can be found in Robinson, Shaver, and Wrightsman (1991). With one notable exception, the topics and measures are not specific to research on human sexuality. However, several of the theories underlying current behavior change and prevention interventions require that researchers use measures that are similar to the measures found in this reference.

ETHICAL ISSUES

Two issues arise immediately when considering the ethics of research on human sexuality. The first issue reflects the varied opinions regarding what is ethical, the nature of the information on human sexuality that individuals need, and the manner in which this information is to be obtained and shared with them. There are many opinions on these matters and much of what is offered is important. However, few research studies have addressed the underlying questions explicitly. That is the second issue. Although many sex researchers have to address ethical problems when they plan and conduct their studies, they seldom consider ethical problems per se to be an important focus for research.

Consider the question of who should participate in human sexuality studies. Presumably, we want participants of all races/ethnicities, both genders, all sexual orientations, and different age groups. However, should all participants be 18 or older, or can they be younger? Many of the critical questions about human sexuality have to do with its development. For example, some researchers are interested in determining when individuals become aware that they have sexual feelings for others. Although we have retrospective data and parental observations on this process, we rarely get firsthand information from children. Should we settle for retrospective data, or should we develop ethical methods that allow us to obtain data from children? Even when there is agreement on the question of who should participate, we may have concerns about the appropriateness of assigning treatments to individuals at random. The issues are particularly difficult when individuals in need are to receive a placebo, a "treatment" that is known to have no effect. A placebo is often used in a randomized trial when the researcher wants to determine if an active treatment impacts some outcome. For present purposes, the active treatment could be a new drug, a pregnancy prevention program, or an HIV prevention intervention. In the absence of any preexisting differences between treatment and control groups, data from a control group provide information on the outcomes that would have been observed among treated individuals in the absence of any treatment effect. Randomization bolsters the study's internal validity: it ensures that any differences observed prior to treatment are due to chance and not due, for example, to a selection bias exercised by the study participant, referring physician or therapist, social worker, or researcher. The use of placebo receives less challenge when there is no broadly accepted standard treatment that can serve as a control and the consequences of receiving an inert treatment are mild. Its use is challenged more when prior studies indicate that something may work for some individuals under some conditions and it is clear that the consequences of receiving an inert treatment are serious.

Different members of society also hold different opinions on the kinds of sex-related information and materials that should be available and how they should be disseminated. School-based sex education and condom distribution programs illustrate some of the current challenges. Although these programs are designed to reduce the risk of adolescent pregnancy and sexually transmitted infections, some critics argue that they violate religious principles or usurp a parental role and responsibility; others argue that they encourage children to be sexually active (the available evidence suggests that they do not; see Grunseit, Kippax, Aggleton, Baldo, & Slitkin, 1997; Kirby, 1984, 1985; Kirby, Short, Collins, et al., 1994; Kirby, Waszak, & Ziegler, 1991; Stout & Kirby, 1993). Because data can only address some of the concerns (e.g., whether education and condom distribution programs encourage youth to be sexually active, or whether parent-child relationships are damaged if trained teachers provide instruction on human sexuality), researchers, practitioners, and teachers must learn to communicate more effectively with parents and other community members.

Communicating with individuals about the purpose and nature of the study, as well as the risks and benefits of participation, is a necessary requirement for obtaining individuals' *informed consent*. Additionally, when researchers provide individuals with the information needed to make an informed decision, the latter are less likely to question researchers' motives and/or behavior. Clearly, individuals and the communities asked to host and support sex research are more likely to question a researcher's motives and behavior when they learn that they have been deceived. The infamous Tuskegee syphilis study, in which medical treatment was intentionally withheld from some southern African American men in order to study the course of untreated syphilis, may be the most well-known example of scientific misconduct involving multiple levels of deception, long-term efforts to see that participants did not receive treatment, and a legacy of mistrust and suspicion (Brandt, 1978; Silver, 1988; Thomas & Quinn, 1991). Although institutional review boards now operate to safeguard the rights of research participants and ensure that they receive adequate protection, researchers retain primary responsibility. Researchers should be as clear as possible about the nature and purpose of the study. Most important, they should make sure that individuals understand all of the information contained in the informed consent form before signing, and they should provide participants with a detailed debriefing (Perry & Abramson, 1980). When provided with such, the evidence indicates that individuals often find participating in sex research to be an interesting and enriching experience (Abramson, 1977).

Proper graduate training should be designed to equip sex researchers with sensitivity to others as well as the knowledge needed to conduct ethical research. However, another way to ensure that participants are treated ethically in sex research is to enhance their sexual literacy. The better informed participants are about sex, the more likely they are to participate in a knowledgeable and conscientious manner. In *Cultural Literacy: What Every American Needs to Know*, Hirsch (1987) argued that Americans were no longer culturally literate, and ignited an enduring controversy about the province and effectiveness of American education, formal and otherwise. We believe the same is true for "sexual literacy" (Abramson & Pinkerton, 1999). Being informed about sexual matters serves to ensure that sexual liabilities do not exceed potential benefits. As we have argued elsewhere (Abramson & Pinkerton, 1999), improving the sexual literacy of Americans is an important and laudable goal. To do this would require, at a minimum, that society begin to better support the structures that create sexual literacy, that is, sexual research and scholarship and the teaching of sexuality in schools, from elementary school through the university.

CLINICAL APPLICATIONS

Research on human sexual behavior has numerous clinical applications. The most obvious is the study of sexual dysfunctions (e.g., the inability to become aroused, achieve orgasm, or maintain an erection). Assessment of the type of dysfunction is one clinical application; treatment is another. Sex therapy is the primary method used to treat many sexual dysfunctions. However, the extraordinary attention recently given to the anti-impotence drug Viagra suggests that the present focus will shift increasingly to various forms of drug therapy. Indeed, a number of companies are investing a considerable amount of research effort and enormous amounts of money to develop drugs that enhance sexual performance and eradicate sexual dysfunction in men and women.

The study of sexual satisfaction in relationships is another clinical application of research on human sexuality. Marriage is an obvious focus for these studies (Perlman & Abramson, 1982). However, sexual satisfaction is equally important to elderly individuals (Kellett, 1991; Leiblum, 1990; Schiavi, 1990; Schlesinger, 1996; Segraves & Segraves, 1995); gay men, bisexuals, and lesbians (Dennen, Gijs, & van Naerssen, 1994; Rose, 1994; Rosenzweig & Lebow, 1992; Rosser, Metz, Bockting, & Buroker, 1997); disabled individuals (Cole & Cole, 1993; Mona, Gardos, & Brown, 1994; Pitzele, 1995; Sipski & Alexander, 1997); and individuals who are or are not married (Byers, Demmons, & Lawrance, 1998; K.-A. Lawrance & Byers, 1995; MacNeil & Byers, 1997). In fact, as a basic clinical issue, sexual satisfaction has enormous significance in terms of self-esteem and psychological health for most people, from adolescence onward.

Clinical applications also come in other forms. Because we tend to be sexually attracted to people whom we find physically attractive, studies of physical attractiveness can yield findings that have important implications for clinical practice (Byrne, 1997; E. Smith, Byrne, & Fielding, 1995). To examine the question of physical attractiveness in the context of psychotherapy, Murray and Abramson (1983) created a fictitious college student medical history form using gender-neutral writing and a set of psychological problems (e.g., lack of assertiveness, uncertainty about career choices). Four forms were created: two were purportedly written by males, and two were purportedly written by females. The researchers attached a photograph to each form that was previously rated for attractiveness (attractive, unattractive). In addition, they created a cover letter stating that UCLA was attempting to streamline its student mental health intake procedures, and needed therapists to help by evaluating a case for symptom severity and the potential for therapeutic success. Packets consisting of the cover letter and one of the four cases were sent to a randomly selected, nationwide sample of psychiatrists, psychologists, and social workers. Murray and Abramson found that the "attractive" cases were judged to have less severe symptoms, and that the therapists more willing to work with these cases and more confident of their ability to be successful with them.

Obviously, there are many more ways to apply the study of human sexuality to clinical issues. Recently, one important focus has been on risky sex and psychotherapy for HIV-infected individuals (e.g., Farber & Schwartz, 1997; Fontaine, 1995; Gunther, Crandels, Williams, & Swain, 1998; Henry, 1996; Kelly, 1998; Markowitz et al., 1998; Markowitz, Rabkin, & Perry, 1994; Millan & Caban, 1996; Sarwer & Crawford, 1994).

PROFESSIONAL DEVELOPMENT

Before we conclude our overview of research on human sexuality, we would like to mention some of the professional societies and journals that support and publish the kind of sex research that we have discussed. The principal focus of our survey is sex research, broadly defined, and on clinical applications such as sex education and therapy. Given our focus, we do not cover several sex-related disciplines (e.g., public health, HIV/AIDS, genitourinary medicine), each of which has professional organizations and publications that interest sex researchers.

Founded in 1957, the Society for the Scientific Study of Sexuality (SSSS) is the oldest organization in the United States that is devoted to the professional study of human sexuality. With over 1,100 members, the Society is also one of the largest sex research organizations in the world. According to the Society's literature, "SSSS brings together an international group of professionals who believe in the importance of both the production of quality research and the clinical, educational, and social applications of research related to all aspects of sexuality." Each year, the Society holds a national conference and three smaller regional conferences.

The Society's official publication, *The Journal of Sex Research (JSR)*, is arguably the nation's premier sex research journal. Published quarterly, *JSR* is "designed to stimulate research and to promote an interdisciplinary understanding of the diverse topic in contemporary sexual science." In addition to original reports of empirical research, the journal publishes theoretical essays, literature reviews, methodological notes, historical articles, clinical reports, teaching papers, book reviews, and letters to the editor. The Society also publishes the *Annual Review of Sex Research.*

Sex education and related topics are the focus of the Sexuality Information and Education Council of the United States (SIECUS). SIECUS is a national, nonprofit organization that was founded in 1964 to develop, collect, and disseminate information about human sexuality; to promote comprehensive sexuality education; and to advocate the right of individuals to make responsible sexual choices. SIECUS maintains a comprehensive sexuality library and publishes numerous pamphlets, booklets, and bibliographies for professionals and the general public alike. Their bimonthly journal, *SIECUS Report*, offers "ground-breaking articles written by prominent leaders . . . updates on relevant advocacy and legislative issues, timely reviews of newly released books and videos, and announcements for conferences and meetings." SIECUS's sister organization in Canada is called the Sex Information & Education Council of Canada (SIECCAN). SIECCAN publishes the quarterly journal *The Canadian Journal of Human Sexuality*, which covers a range of topics of interest to sexuality researchers.

The American Association of Sex Educators, Counselors, and Therapists (AASECT) was founded in 1967. AASECT is devoted to "promoting understanding of human sexuality and healthy sexual behavior." The association "certifies qualified health and mental health practitioners in dealing expertly and ethically with the sexuality concerns of individuals and couples" and offers a broad range of education and training activities. In addition, AASECT publishes *The Journal of Sex Education and Therapy.*

The International Academy of Sex Research has some 200 members. The Academy's official publication is the *Archives of Sexual Behavior.* This British journal is published bimonthly and "reports the latest research trends in the science of human sexual behavior, bringing together high-quality submissions from such diverse fields as psychology, psychiatry, biology, ethology, endocrinology, and sociology."

In addition to the aforementioned journals, individuals and researchers interested in human sexuality have access to journals that address different areas. For example, the quarterly *Journal of the History of Sexuality* "illuminate[s] the history of sexuality in all its expressions, recognizing various differences of class, culture, gender, race, and sexual orientation." Another quarterly, *Sexualities: Studies in Culture and Society*, publishes "articles, reviews and scholarly comment on the shifting nature of human sexualities." The similarly titled *Sexuality & Culture* provides a forum for "the discussion and analysis of ethical, cultural, psychological, social, and political issues related to sexual relationships and sexual behavior." The 1997 and 1998 volumes focused, respectively, on sexual harassment/sexual consent and sex work. Another quarterly, the *Journal of Psychology & Human Sexuality*, covers a broad range of sex-related topics from a variety of perspectives, including clinical, counseling, educational, social, experimental, psychoendocrinological, and psychoneurological research.

There are several special-interest journals related to sexuality. Gender, sex roles, and sexual orientation are the subject of *GLQ: A Journal of Lesbian and Gay Studies; Journal of Gay, Lesbian, and Bisexual Identity; Journal of Homosexuality;* and *Sex Roles: A Journal of Research*. Clinical and therapeutic issues are discussed in the *Journal of Gay and Lesbian Psychotherapy; Journal of Sex and Marital Therapy; Journal of Sex Education and Therapy; Journal of Social Work and Human Sexuality; International Journal of Impotence Research; Medical Aspects of Human Sexuality; Sexual Abuse: A Journal of Research and Treatment* (formerly, *Annals of Sex Research*); *Sexual Addiction & Compulsivity;* and *Sexuality and Disability*.

Having a number of professional organizations, each with its own unique focus, and having access to multiple avenues for communicating with other professionals are indeed blessings. However, to ensure that future researchers experience the same bounty, those of us who are currently active will need to become more involved in shaping and supporting the formal sex education that children, adolescents, and young adults receive at home, in school, and from health care and social service providers. Some of these individuals will participate directly in studies of human sexuality; almost all will be asked to support the funding of such studies. As we stated earlier, sexual literacy is an important societal goal that benefits the individual, the researcher, and society.

CONCLUSION

Sex and sexuality are important concerns of laypersons and sex researchers—and rightly so. The behaviors, the practices and patterns, and the thoughts and feelings reflected in the phrase "sex and sexuality" are fundamentally important to our individual and collective health and well-being, to our sense of who we are and our place in the world. Thus, whereas many Americans have been able to abandon social distinctions (and the inherent privileges that accompany such distinctions) based on social class, country of origin, and race, a good number are reluctant to abandon social distinctions based on gender and gender roles.

Research on human sexuality can play an important role in the ongoing transition. In particular, sex researchers can obtain accurate and timely information on the determinants of and mechanisms regulating all manner of sexual attraction and expression; on what it means to be male or female (straight, gay, lesbian, bisexual, or transsexual) in a particular culture; and on the individual and social consequences of sexual behavior. Because sex researchers continue to pay close attention to issues such as design (and, specifically, the design of the study, the items and instruments, and the sample) and data collection, their methods are often more persuasive to the lay public than other modes of inquiry and validation.

In this chapter, we have endeavored to show that sex research has benefited greatly from numerous insights and contributions from the life sciences (e.g., evolutionary psychology and biologically based theories of human sexual behavior), the humanities (e.g., the theories founded on postmodernism, deconstruction, and feminism), the cognitive sciences (e.g., script theory), mathematics (e.g., epidemiological modeling), and prevention research (with its theories and models of behavior change). We firmly believe that future contributions from these disciplines will continue to provide some of the impetus for the important work done by clinicians and other service providers.

However, we encourage sex researchers to consider more integrative theories of human sexual behavior. To date, the use of specific models of sexual behavior, rigorous methodologies, and sophisticated statistical techniques have not yielded satisfactory answers to important questions such as Why does sex feel good? or Why are we sexually attracted to given individuals (or objects of desire, as the case may be)? Clearly, more informative, comprehensive theories will be of greater use to clinicians working with individuals who are struggling with issues of sexual identity, as well as prevention researchers who often ask participants to enact behaviors that individuals find difficult to initiate and maintain (e.g., use condoms to avoid sexually transmitted infections).

REFERENCES

Abramson, P.R. (1973). The relationship of the frequency of masturbation to several aspects of personality and behavior. *Journal of Sex Research, 9,* 132–142.

Abramson, P.R. (1977). Ethical requirements for research on human sexual behavior. *Journal of Social Issues, 33,* 184–192.

Abramson, P.R. (1988). Sexual assessment and the epidemiology of AIDS. *Journal of Sex Research, 25,* 323–346.

Abramson, P.R. (1990). Sexual science: Emerging discipline or oxymoron? *Journal of Sex Research, 27,* 147–166.

Abramson, P.R. (1992a). *A case for case studies: An immigrant's journal.* Newbury Park, CA: Sage.

Abramson, P.R. (1992b). Sex, lies and ethnography. In G. Herdt & S. Lindenbaum (Eds.), *The time of AIDS: Theory, method and practice* (pp. 101–123). Newbury Park, CA: Sage.

Abramson, P.R., Goldberg, P.A., Mosher, D.L., Abramson, L.M., & Gottesdiener, M. (1975). Experimenter effects on responses to erotic stimuli. *Journal of Research in Personality, 9,* 136–146.

Abramson, P.R., & Handschumacher, I. (1978). Experimenter effects on responses to double-entendre words: Some additional implications for sex research. *Journal of Personality Assessment, 42,* 592–596.

Abramson, P.R., & Herdt, G. (1990). The assessment of sexual practices relevant to the transmission of AIDS: A global perspective. *Journal of Sex Research, 27,* 215–232.

Abramson, P.R., & Mosher, D.L. (1975). The development of a measure of negative attitudes towards masturbation. *Journal of Consulting and Clinical Psychology, 43,* 485–490.

Abramson, P.R., & Mosher, D.L. (1979). An empirical investigation of experimentally-induced masturbatory fantasies. *Archives of Sexual Behavior, 8,* 27–39.

Abramson, P.R., & Pearsall, E.H. (1983). Pectoral changes during the sexual response cycle: A thermographic analysis. *Archives of Sexual Behavior, 12,* 357–368.

Abramson, P.R., Perry, L.B., Rothblatt, A., Seeley, T.T., & Seeley, D.M. (1981). Negative attitudes toward masturbation and pelvic vasocongestion: A thermographic analysis. *Journal of Research in Personality, 15,* 497–509.

Abramson, P.R., Perry, L.B., Seeley, T.T., Seeley, D.M., & Rothblatt, A.B. (1981). Thermographic measurement of sexual arousal. *Archives of Sexual Behavior, 10,* 171–176.

Abramson, P.R., & Pinkerton, S.D. (1995). *With pleasure: Thoughts on the nature of human sexuality.* New York: Oxford University Press.

Abramson, P.R., & Pinkerton, S.D. (1999). Sexual literacy. In P.R. Abramson & S.D. Pinkerton (Eds.), *Made to be broken: Reflections upon sex and the law.* Manuscript under review.

Ajzen, I. (1991). The theory of planned behavior: Theories of cognitive self-regulation (Special issue). *Organizational Behavior & Human Decision Processes, 50,* 179–211.

Ajzen, I., & Madden, T.J. (1986). Prediction of goal-directed behavior: Attitudes, intentions, and perceived behavioral control. *Journal of Experimental Social Psychology, 22,* 453–474.

Alexander, C.S., Somerfield, M.R., Ensminger, M.E., Johnson, K.E., & Kim, Y.J. (1993). Consistency of adolescents' self-report of sexual behavior in a longitudinal study. *Journal of Youth and Adolescence, 22,* 455–471.

Allgeier, A.R., & Allgeier, E.R. (1995). *Sexual interactions.* Lexington, MA: D.C. Heath.

American Psychiatric Association (1994). *Diagnostic and statistical manual of mental disorders* (4th ed.). Washington, DC: Authors.

Anderson, R.M., & May, R.M. (1988). Epidemiological parameters of HIV transmission. *Nature, 333,* 514–519.

Anderson, R.M., & May, R.M. (1991). *Infectious diseases of humans: Dynamics and control.* New York: Oxford University Press.

Asbury, J.-E. (1995). Overview of focus group research: Issues and applications of focus groups (Special issue). *Qualitative Health Research, 5,* 414–420.

AuBuchon, P.G., & Calhoun, K.S. (1985). Menstrual cycle symptomatology: The role of social expectancy and experimental demand characteristics. *Psychosomatic Medicine, 47,* 35–45.

Bacon, F. (1956). *Selected writings: The great instauration.* New York: Modern Library. (Original work published 1620)

Bacon, M. (1976). Thermography—explanation and description. *Thermograph Quarterly, 1,* 8.

Baker, S., Morrison, D., Carter, W., & Verdon, M. (1996). Using the theory of reasoned action (TRA) to understand the decision to use condoms in a heterosexual STD clinic population. *Health Education Quarterly, 23,* 528–542.

Bailey, J.M., & Pillard, R.C. (1991). A genetic study of male sexual orientation. *Archives of General Psychiatry, 48,* 1089–1096.

Bailey, J.M., Pillard, R.C., Neale, M.C., & Agyei, Y. (1993). Heritible factors influence sexual orientation in women. *Archives of General Psychiatry, 50,* 217–223.

Ballard-Reisch, D., & Elton, M. (1992). Gender orientation and the Bem Sex Role Inventory: A psychological construct revisited. *Sex Roles, 27,* 291–306.

Bandura, A. (1977a). Self-efficacy: Toward a unifying theory of behavioral change. *Psychological Review, 84,* 191–215.

Bandura, A. (1977b). *Social learning theory.* Englewood Cliffs, NJ: Prentice Hall.

Bandura, A. (1982). Self-efficacy mechanism in human agency. *American Psychologist, 37,* 122–147.

Bandura, A. (1989). Perceived self-efficacy in the exercise of control over AIDS infection. In V.M. Mays, G.W. Albee, & S.F. Schneider (Eds.), *Primary prevention of psychopathology. Primary prevention of AIDS: Psychological approaches* (Vol. 13, pp. 128–141). Newbury Park, CA: Sage.

Barker, W.J., & Perlman, D. (1975). Volunteer bias and personality traits in sexual standards research. *Archives of Sexual Behavior, 4,* 161–171.

Barkow, J.H. (1980). Sociobiology: Is this the new theory of human nature? In A. Montagu (Ed.), *Sociobiology examined* (pp. 171–197). New York: Oxford University Press.

Barnes, G.E., Malamuth, N.M., & Check, J.V.P. (1984). Personality and sexuality. *Personality and Individual Differences, 5,* 159–172.

Basen-Engquist, K., & Parcel, G.S. (1992). Attitudes, norms, and self-efficacy: A model of adolescents' HIV-related sexual risk taking. *Health Education Quarterly, 19,* 263–277.

Bastani, R., Erickson, P.A., Marcus, A.C., Maxwell, A.E., Capell, F.J., Freeman, H., & Yan, K.X. (1996). AIDS-related attitudes and risk behaviors: A survey of a random sample of California heterosexuals. *Preventive Medicine, 25,* 105–117.

Becker, M.H. (1974). The health belief model and personal health behavior. *Health Education Monographs, 2,* 220–243.

Bem, S.J. (1974). The measurement of psychological androgyny. *Journal of Consulting and Clinical Psychology, 42,* 155–162.

Benney, M., Riesman, D., & Star, S.A. (1956). Age and sex in the interview. *American Journal of Sociology, 62,* 143–152.

Berglund, S., Liljestrand, J., Martin, F., Salgado, N., & Zelaya, E. (1997). The background of adolescent pregnancy in Nicaragua: A qualitative approach. *Social Science & Medicine, 44,* 1–12.

Berk, R., Abramson, P.R., & Okami, P. (1995). Sexual activities as told in surveys. In P.R. Abramson & S.D. Pinkerton (Eds.), *Sexual nature/sexual culture* (pp. 371–386). Chicago: University of Chicago Press.

Biernacki, P., & Waldorf, D. (1981). Snowball sampling: Problems and techniques of chain referral sampling. *Sociological Methods and Research, 10,* 141–163.

Binson, D., & Catania, J.A. (1998). Respondents' understanding of the words used in sexual behavior questions. *Public Opinion Quarterly, 62,* 190–208.

Binson, D., Dolcini, M., Pollack, L., & Catania, J. (1993). Multiple sexual partners among young adults in high-risk cities: The National AIDS Behavioral Surveys. *Family Planning Perspectives, 25,* 268–272.

Bloom, D. (1998). Technology, experimentation, and the quality of survey data. *Science, 380,* 847–848.

Bogaert, A.F. (1992). Volunteer bias in sex research: An exploratory study of self-reported autoerotic experiences. *Canadian Journal of Human Sexuality, 1,* 207–211.

Bogaert, A.F. (1996). Volunteer bias in human sexuality research: Evidence for both sexuality and personality differences in males. *Archives of Sexual Behavior, 25,* 125–140.

Boland, P.J. (1984). A biographical glimpse of William Sealy Gosset. *The American Statistician, 38,* 179–183.

Bowman, R.L., & DeLucia, J.L. (1992). Accuracy of self-reported weight: A meta-analysis. *Behavior Therapy, 23,* 637–655.

Box, G.E.P. (1984). The importance of practice in the development of statistics. *Technometrics, 26,* 1–8.

Box, J.F. (1980). R.A. Fisher and the design of experiments, 1922–1926. *The American Statistician, 34,* 1–7.

Box, J.F. (1981). Gosset, Fisher, and the *t* distribution. *The American Statistician, 35,* 61–66.

Bradford, J.M.W. (1998). Treatment of men with paraphilia. *New England Journal of Medicine, 338,* 464–465.

Brandt, A.M. (1978). Racism and research: The case of the Tuskegee Syphilis Study. *Hastings Center Report, 8,* 21–29.

Brown, L.K., DiClemente, R.J., & Reynolds, L.A. (1991). HIV prevention for adolescents: Utility of the health belief model. *AIDS Education & Prevention, 3,* 50–59.

Buss, D.M. (1994). *The evolution of desire.* New York: Basic Books.

Butler, J. (1990). *Gender trouble: Feminism and the subversion of identity.* New York: Routledge & Kegan Paul.

Byers, E.S., Demmons, S., & Lawrance, K.-A. (1998). Sexual satisfaction within dating relationships: A test of the interpersonal exchange model of sexual satisfaction. *Journal of Social & Personal Relationships, 15,* 257–267.

Byrne, D. (1983). The antecedents, correlates, and consequences of erotophobia-erotophilia. In C.M. Davis (Ed.), *Challenges in sexual science* (pp. 53–75). Lake Mills, IA: Society for the Scientific Study of Sex.

Byrne, D. (1997). An overview (and underview) of research and theory within the attraction paradigm. *Journal of Social and Personal Relationships, 14,* 417–431.

Byrne, D., & Schulte, L. (1990). Personality dispositions as mediators of sexual responses. *Annual Review of Sex Research, 1,* 93–117.

Carey, M.A., & Smith, M.W. (1994). Capturing the group effect in focus groups: A special concern in analysis. *Qualitative Health Research, 4,* 123–127.

Carrier, J. (1995). *De los otros: Intimacy and homosexuality among Mexican men.* New York: Columbia University Press.

Catania, J.A., Binson, D., Canchola, J., Pollack, L., Hauck, W., & Coates, T. (1996). Effects of interviewer gender, interviewer choice, and item wording on responses to questions concerning sexual behavior. *Public Opinion Quarterly, 60,* 345–375.

Catania, J.A., Coates, T.J., Stall, R., Turner, H., Peterson, J., Hearst, N., Dolcini, M.M., Hudes, E., Gagnon, J., Wiley, J., & Groves, R. (1992). Prevalence of AIDS-related risk factors and condom use in the United States. *Science, 258,* 1101–1106.

Catania, J.A., Gibson, D.R., Chitwood, D.D., & Coates, T.J. (1990). Methodological problems in AIDS behavioral research: Influences in measurement error and participation bias in studies of sexual behavior. *Psychological Bulletin, 108,* 339–362.

Catania, J.A., Gibson, D.R., Marin, B., Coates, T.J., & Greenblatt, R.M. (1990). Response bias in sexual behaviors relevant to HIV transmission. *Evaluation and Program Planning, 13,* 19–29.

Centers for Disease Control and Prevention. (1990). Sexual behavior among high school students—United States, 1990. *Morbidity and Mortality Weekly Report, 40,* 885–888.

Centers for Disease Control and Prevention. (1993). Distribution of STD clinic patients among a stages-of-behavior-change continuum—selected sites, 1993. *Morbidity and Mortality Weekly Report, 42,* 880–883.

Center for Human Resource Research. (1995). *NLS Handbook 1995.* Columbus, OH: Center for Human Resource Research, Ohio State University.

Clement, U. (1990). Surveys of heterosexual behavior. *Annual Review of Sex Research, 1,* 45–74.

Coates, R.A., Calzavara, L.M., Soskolne, C.L., Read, S.E., Fanning, M.M., Shepherd, F.A., Klein, M.H., & Johnson, J.K. (1988). Validity of sexual histories in a prospective study of male sexual contacts of men with AIDS or an AIDS-related condition. *American Journal of Epidemiology, 128,* 719–728.

Coates, R.A., Soskolne, C.L., Calzavara, L.M., Read, S.E., Fanning, M.M., Shepherd, F.A., Klein, M.H., & Johnson, J.K. (1986). The reliability of sexual histories in AIDS-related research: Evaluation of an inter-administered questionnaire. *Canadian Journal of Public Health, 77,* 343–348.

Cochran, S.D., Mays, V.M., Ciarletta, J., Caruso, C., & Mallon, D. (1992). Efficacy of the theory of reasoned action in predicting AIDS-related sexual risk-reduction among gay men. *Journal of Applied Social Psychology, 22,* 1481–1501.

Cochran, W.G. (1976). Early development of techniques in comparative experimentation. In D.B. Owen (Ed.), *On the history of statistics and probability* (pp. 3–25). New York: Marcel Dekker.

Cochran, W.G., Mosteller, F., & Tukey, J.W. (1954). *Statistical problems of the Kinsey Report on sexual behavior in the human male.* Washington, DC: American Statistical Association.

Cohen, D.A., & Dent, C. (1992). The validity of self-reported condom use. *American Journal of Public Health, 82,* 1563–1564.

Cohen, J.B. (1985). *Revolution in science.* Cambridge, MA: Harvard University Press.

Cohen, L. (1995). The pleasures of castration: The postoperative status of hijras, jankhas, and academics. In P.R. Abramson & S.D. Pinkerton (Eds.), *Sexual nature/sexual culture* (pp. 276–304). Chicago: University of Chicago Press.

Cole, S.S., & Cole, T.M. (1993). Sexuality, disability, and reproductive issues through the lifespan. *Sexuality & Disability, 11,* 189–205.

Coleman, E. (1991). Compulsive sexual behavior: New concepts and treatments. *Journal of Psychology & Human Sexuality, 42,* 37–52.

Coleman, E., & Bockting, W.O. (1988). "Heterosexual" prior to sex reassignment—"homosexual" afterwards: A case study of a female-to-male transsexual. *Journal of Psychology & Human Sexuality, 1,* 69–82.

Colombotos, J., Elinson, J., & Loewenstein, R. (1968). Effect of interviewer's sex on interview responses. *Public Health Reports, 83,* 685–690.

Condelli, L. (1986). Social and attitudinal determinants of contraceptive choice: Using the health belief model. *Journal of Sex Research, 22,* 478–491.

Cook, T.D., & Campbell, D.T. (1976). The design and conduct of quasi-experiments and true experiments in field settings. In M.D. Dunnette (Ed.), *Handbook of industrial and organizational psychology* (pp. 223–326). New York: Rand McNally.

Coreil, J. (1995). Group interview methods in community health research. *Medical Anthropology, 16,* 193–210.

Cosmides, L., & Tooby, J. (1987). From evolution to behavior: Evolutionary psychology as the missing link. In J. Dupre (Ed.), *The latest on the best: Essays on evolution and optimality* (pp. 277–306). Cambridge, MA: MIT Press.

Davey Smith, G., Frankel, S., & Yarnell, J. (1997). Sex and death: Are they related? Findings from the Caerphilly cohort study. *British Medical Journal, 315,* 1641–1645.

Davis, C.M., Yarber, W.L., Bauserman, R., Scheer, G., & Davis, S.L. (Eds.). (1998). *Handbook of sexuality-related measures* (2nd ed.). Thousand Oaks, CA: Sage.

Davis, J.A., & Smith, T.W. (1994). *General social surveys, 1972–1994: Cumulative codebook.* Chicago: National Opinion Research Center.

Dennen, A.A., Gijs, L., & van Naerssen, A.X. (1994). Intimacy and sexuality in gay male couples. *Archives of Sexual Behavior, 23,* 421–431.

Desormeaux, J., Behets, F., Adrien, M., Coicou, G., Dallabetta, G., Cohen, M., & Boulos, R. (1996). Introduction of partner referral and treatment for control of sexually transmitted diseases in a poor Haitian community. *International Journal of STD & AIDS, 7,* 502–506.

de Waal, F.B.M. (1989). *Peacemaking among primates.* Cambridge, MA: Harvard University Press.

de Waal, F.B.M. (1995). Sex as an alternative to aggression in the bonobo. In P.R. Abramson & S.D. Pinkerton (Eds.), *Sexual nature/sexual culture* (pp. 37–56). Chicago: University of Chicago Press.

Eisen, M., Zellman, G.L., & McAlister, A.L. (1992). A health belief model–social learning theory approach to adolescents' fertility control: Findings from a controlled trial. *Health Education Quarterly, 19,* 249–262.

Ellis, A. (Ed.). (1954). *Sex life of the American woman and the Kinsey Report.* New York: Greenberg.

Eysenck, H.J. (1947). *Dimensions of personality.* New York: Praeger.

Eysenck, H.J. (1976). *Sex and personality.* London: Open Books.

Eysenck, H.J., & Eysenck, S.B.G. (1969). *Personality structure and measurement.* San Diego, CA: Knapp.

Eysenck, H.J., & Eysenck, S.B.G. (1975). *Manual of the Eysenck personality questionnaire.* London: Hodder & Stoughton.

Faderman, L. (1991). *Odd girls and twilight lovers.* New York: Penguin.

Farber, E.W., & Schwartz, J.A.J. (1997). Changing conceptions of self and world through the spectrum of HIV disease: Implications for psychotherapy. *Journal of Psychotherapy Practice & Research, 6,* 36–44.

Faugier, J., & Sargeant, M. (1997). Sampling hard to reach populations. *Journal of Advanced Nursing, 26,* 790–797.

Fetterman, D.M. (1998). *Ethnography step by step: Sage applied social research methods* (Vol. 17, 2nd ed.). Thousand Oaks, CA: Sage.

Finkelhor, D., & Berliner, L. (1995). Research on the treatment of sexually abused children: A review and recommendations. *Journal of American Academy of Child and Adolescent Psychiatry, 34,* 1408–1423.

Fishbein, M., & Ajzen, I. (1975). *Belief, attitude, intention, and behavior: An introduction to theory and research.* Reading, MA: Addison-Wesley.

Fishbein, M., & Middlestadt, S.E. (1989). Using the theory of reasoned action as a framework for understanding and changing AIDS-related behaviors. In V.M. Mays, G.W. Albee, & S.F. Schneider (Eds.), *Primary prevention of psychopathology. Primary prevention of AIDS: Psychological approaches* (Vol. 13, pp. 93–110). Newbury Park, CA: Sage.

Fisher, H.E. (1982). *The sex contract: The evolution of human behavior.* New York: Quill Press.

Fisher, H.E. (1992). *Anatomy of love: The natural history of monogamy, adultery, and divorce.* New York: Norton.

Fisher, R.A. (1925). *Statistical methods for research workers.* Edinburgh, England: Oliver and Boyd.

Fisher, R.A. (1926). The arrangement of field experiments. *Journal of the Ministry of Agriculture, 33,* 503–513.

Fisher, W.A. (1980). *Erotophobia-erotophilia and performance in a human sexuality course.* Unpublished manuscript, University of Western Ontario.

Fisher, W.A., Fisher, J.D., & Rye, B. (1995). Understanding and promoting AIDS-preventive behavior: Insights from the theory of reasoned action. *Health Psychology, 14,* 255–264.

Fontaine, M.M. (1995). Issues of isolation and intimacy for the HIV infected, sexually addicted gay male in group psychotherapy. *Journal of Psychology & Human Sexuality, 7,* 181–191.

Foucault, M. (1978). *The history of sexuality.* New York: Pantheon Books.

Fowler, F.J., Jr. (1993). *Survey research methods: Sage applied social research methods* (Vol. 1). Newbury Park, CA: Sage.

Frank, E., Anderson, C., & Rubinstein, D. (1978). Frequency of sexual dysfunction in "normal" couples. *New England Journal of Medicine, 299,* 111–115.

Freeman, D. (1983). *Margaret Mead and Samoa.* Cambridge, MA: Harvard University Press.

Freeman, J., & Butler, E.W. (1976). Some sources of interviewer variance in surveys. *Public Opinion Quarterly, 40,* 79–91.

Gagnon, J.H., & Simon, W. (1973). *Sexual conduct.* New York: Aldine.

Galaskiewicz, J., & Wasserman, S. (1994). Introduction: Advances in the social and behavioral sciences from social network analysis. In S. Wasserman & J. Galaskiewicz (Eds.), *Advances in social network analysis: Research in the social and behavioral sciences* (pp. xi–xvii). Thousand Oaks, CA: Sage.

Galbraith, G.G., & Mosher, D.L. (1968). Associative sexual responses in relation to sexual arousal, guilt and external approval contingencies. *Journal of Personality and Social Psychology, 10,* 142–147.

Garber, M. (1992). *Vested interests.* New York: HarperCollins.

Gibb, D.M., MacDonagh, S.E., Tookey, P.A., & Duong, T. (1997). Uptake of interventions to reduce mother-to-child transmission of HIV in the United Kingdom and Ireland. *AIDS, 11,* F53–F58.

Giese, H., & Schmidt, A. (1968). *Studenten sexualitat.* Hamburg: Rowohlt.

Gijs, L., & Gooren, L. (1996). Hormonal and psychopharmacological interventions in the treatment of paraphilias: An update. *Journal of Sex Research, 33,* 273–290.

Gilbert, D., Fiske, S.T., & Lindzey, G. (1998). *The handbook of social psychology* (4th ed.). New York: McGraw-Hill.

Gilmore, S., DeLamater, J., & Wagstaff, D. (1996). Sexual decision making by inner city Black adolescent males: A focus group study. *Journal of Sex Research, 33,* 363–371.

Goodman, L.A. (1961). Snowball sampling. *Annals of Mathematical Statistics, 32,* 148–170.

Greenberg, D. (1988). *The construction of homosexuality.* Chicago: University of Chicago Press.

Griffith, M., & Walker, C.E. (1976). Characteristics associated with expressed willingness to participate in psychological research. *Journal of Social Psychology, 100,* 157–158.

Grimes, M.D., & Hansen, G.L. (1984). Response bias in sex-role attitude measurement. *Sex Roles, 10,* 67–72.

Grimley, D.M., Prochaska, J.O., Velicer, W.F., & Prochaska, G.E. (1995). Contraceptive and condom use adoption and maintenance: A stage paradigm approach. *Health Education Quarterly, 22,* 20–35.

Grimley, D.M., Riley, G.E., Bellis, J.M., & Prochaska, J.O. (1993). Assessing the stages of change and decision-making for contraceptive use for the prevention of pregnancy, sexually transmitted diseases, and acquired immunodeficiency syndrome. *Health Education Quarterly, 20,* 455–470.

Grunseit, A., Kippax, S., Aggleton, P., Baldo, M., & Slitkin, G. (1997). People's sexual behavior: A review of studies. *Journal of Adolescent Research, 12,* 421–453.

Gunther, M., Crandles, S., Williams, G., & Swain, M. (1998). A place called HOPE: Group psychotherapy for adolescents of parents with HIV/AIDS. *Child Welfare, 77,* 251–271.

Hamer, D.H., Hu, S., Magnuson, V.L., Hu, N., & Pattatucci, A.M.L. (1993). A linkage between DNA markers on the X chromosome and male sexual orientation. *Science, 261,* 321–327.

Hecker, B.I., & Ajzen, I. (1983). Improving the prediction of health behavior: An approach based on the theory of reasoned action. *Academy of Psychology Bulletin, 5,* 11–19.

Heinrich, L.B. (1993). Contraceptive self-efficacy in college women. *Journal of Adolescent Health, 14,* 269–276.

Henry, R.M. (1996). Psychodynamic group therapy with adolescents: Exploration of HIV-related risk taking. *International Journal of Group Psychotherapy, 46,* 229–253.

Herdt, G. (1981). *Guardians of the flute.* New York: McGraw-Hill.

Herdt, G. (Ed.). (1994). *Third sex/third gender.* New York: Zone.

Herdt, G. (1997). *Same sex/different cultures.* Boulder, CO: Westview Press.

Herdt, G., & Stoller, R.J. (1989). *Intimate communications: Erotics and the study of culture.* New York: Columbia University Press.

Hiltabiddle, S.J. (1996). Adolescent condom use, the Health belief model, and the prevention of sexually transmitted disease. *Journal of Obstetric, Gynecologic, & Neonatal Nursing, 25,* 61–66.

Hirsch, E.D., Jr. (1987). *Cultural literacy: What every American needs to know.* Boston: Houghton Mifflin.

Hooker, E. (1957). The adjustment of the male overt homosexual. *Journal of Projective Techniques, 21,* 18–31.

Humphries, L. (1970). *Tearoom trade: Impersonal sex in public places.* New York: Aldine.

Hyde, J.S., Krajnik, M., & Skuldt-Niederberger, K. (1991). Androgyny across the lifespan: A replication and longitudinal follow-up. *Developmental Psychology, 27,* 516–519.

Jaccard, J., & Wan, C.-K. (1995). A paradigm for studying the accuracy of self-reports of risk behavior relevant to AIDS: Empirical perspectives on stability, recall bias, and transitory influences. *Journal of Applied Social Psychology, 25,* 1831–1858.

James, N.J., Bignell, C.J., & Gilles, P.A. (1991). The reliability of self-reported sexual behavior. *AIDS, 5,* 333–336.

Janssen, E., Vissenberg, M., Visser, S., & Everaerd, W. (1997). An in vivo comparison of two circumferential penile strain gauges: The introduction of a new calibration method. *Psychophysiology, 34,* 717–720.

Janz, N.K., & Becker, M.H. (1984). The health belief model: A decade later. *Health Education Quarterly, 11,* 1–47.

Jemmott, J.B., III, Jemmott, L.S., & Fong, G.T. (1992). Reductions in HIV risk-associated sexual behaviors among Black male adolescents: Effects of an AIDS prevention intervention. *American Journal of Public Health, 82,* 372–377.

Jemmott, J.B., III, Jemmott, L.S., & Fong, G.T. (1998). Abstinence and safer sex HIV risk-reduction interventions for African American adolescents: A randomized controlled trial. *Journal of the American Medical Association, 279,* 1529–1536.

Jemmott, J.B., III, Jemmott, L.S., Spears, H., Hewitt, N., & Crus-Collins, M. (1992). Self-efficacy, hedonistic expectancies, and condom use intentions among inner-city Black adolescent women: A social cognitive approach to AIDS risk behavior. *Journal of Adolescent Health, 13,* 512–519.

Jemmott, L.S., & Jemmott, J.B., III. (1991). Applying the theory of reasoned action to AIDS risk behavior: Condom use among Black women. *Nursing Research, 40,* 228–234.

Joffe, A., & Radius, S.M. (1993). Self-efficacy and intent to use condoms among entering college freshman. *Journal of Adolescent Health, 14,* 262–268.

Johnson, J.C. (1994). Anthropological contributions to the study of social networks: A review. In S. Wasserman & J. Galaskiewicz (Eds.), *Advances in social network analysis: Research in the social and behavioral sciences* (pp. 113–151). Thousand Oaks, CA: Sage.

Johnson, T.P., Hougland, J.G., & Moore, R.W. (1991). Sex differences in reporting sensitive behavior: A comparison of interview methods. *Sex Roles, 24,* 669–680.

Jorgensen, D.L. (1989). *Participant observation: A methodology for human studies, Sage applied social research methods* (Vol. 15). Beverly Hills, CA: Sage.

Kaats, G., & Davis, K. (1971). Effects of volunteer bias in studies of sexual behavior and attitudes. *Journal of Sex Research, 7,* 26–34.

Kadushin, A. (1972). The racial factor in the interview. *Social Work, 17,* 88–98.

Kalton, G. (1993). Sampling considerations in research on HIV risk and illness. In D.G. Ostrow & R.C. Kessler (Eds.), *Methodological issues in AIDS behavioral research* (pp. 53–74). New York: Plenum Press.

Kalton, G., & Anderson, D.W. (1986). Sampling rare populations. *Journal of the Royal Statistical Society, Series A, 149,* 65–82.

Kaplan, E.H. (1995). Model-based representations of human sexual behavior. In P.R. Abramson & S.D. Pinkerton (Eds.), *Sexual nature/sexual culture* (pp. 353–370). Chicago: University of Chicago Press.

Kaplan, H.S. (1979). *Disorders of sexual desire.* New York: Brunner/Mazel.

Kasen, S., Vaughan, R.D., & Walter, H.J. (1992). Self-efficacy for AIDS preventive behaviors among tenth grade students. *Health Education Quarterly, 19,* 187–202.

Kauth, M.R., St. Lawrence, J.S., & Kelly, J.A. (1991). Reliability of retrospective assessments of sexual HIV risk behavior: A comparison of biweekly, three-month, and twelve-month self-reports. *AIDS Education and Prevention, 3,* 207–214.

Kegeles, S.M., Hays, R.B., & Coates, T.J. (1996). The Mpowerment Project: A community-level HIV prevention intervention for young gay men. *American Journal of Public Health, 86,* 1129–1136.

Kellett, J.M. (1991). Sexuality of the elderly. *Sexual & Marital Therapy, 6,* 147–155.

Kelley, K., Byrne, D., Greendlinger, V., & Murnen, S.K. (1997). Content, sex of viewer, and dispositional variables as predictors of affective and evaluative responses to sexually explicit films. *Journal of Psychology & Human Sexuality, 9,* 53–71.

Kelly, J.A. (1998). Group psychotherapy for persons with HIV and AIDS-related illnesses. *International Journal of Group Psychotherapy, 48,* 143–162.

Kelly, J.A., Murphy, D.A., Washington, C.D., Wilson, T.S., Koob, J.J., Davis, D.R., Ledezma, G., & Davantes, B. (1994). The effects of HIV/AIDS intervention groups for high-risk women in urban clinics. *American Journal of Public Health, 84,* 1918–1922.

Kelly, J.A., St. Lawrence, J.S., Betts, R., Brasfield, T.L., & Hood, H.V. (1990). A skills-training group intervention model to assist persons in reducing risk behaviors for HIV infection. *AIDS Education and Prevention, 2,* 24–35.

Kelly, J.A., St. Lawrence, J.S., Diaz, Y.E., Stevenson, Y., Hauth, A.C., Brasfield, T.L., Kalichman, S.C., Smith, J.E., & Andrew, M.E. (1991). HIV risk behavior reduction following intervention with key opinion leaders of a population: An experimental community-level analysis. *American Journal of Public Health, 81,* 168–171.

Kelly, J.A., St. Lawrence, J.S., Stevenson, Y., Hauth, A.C., Kalichman, S.C., Diaz, Y.E., Brasfield, T.L., Koob, J.J., & Morgan, M.G. (1992). Community AIDS/HIV risk reduction: The effects of endorsements by popular people in three cities. *American Journal of Public Health, 82,* 1483–1489.

Kemeny, J.G. (1959). *A philosopher looks at science.* New York: D.Van Nostrand.

Khan, M.A., Rahman, M., Khanam, P.A., Barkat-e-Khuda, Kane, T.T., & Ashraf, A. (1997). Awareness of sexually transmitted disease among women and service providers in rural Bangladesh. *International Journal of STD & AIDS, 8,* 688–696.

Kinsey, A.C., Pomeroy, W.B., & Martin, C.E. (1948). *Sexual behavior in the human male.* Philadelphia: Saunders.

Kinsey, A.C., Pomeroy, W.B., Martin, C.E., & Gebhard, P.H. (1953). *Sexual behavior in the human female.* Philadelphia: Saunders.

Kipnis, L. (1996). *Bound and gagged.* New York: Grove Press.

Kirby, D. (1984). *Sexuality education: An evaluation of programs and their effects.* Santa Cruz, CA: Network.

Kirby, D. (1985). The effects of selected sexuality education programs: Toward a more realistic view. *Journal of Sex Education & Therapy, 11,* 28–37.

Kirby, D., Short, L., Collins, J., Rugg, D., Kolbe, L., Howard, M., Miller, B., Sonenstein, F., & Zabin, L. (1994). School-based programs to reduce sexual risk behaviors: A review of effectiveness. *Public Health Reports, 109,* 339–360.

Kirby, D., Waszak, C., & Ziegler, J. (1991). Six school-based clinics: Their reproductive health services and impact on sexual behavior. *Family Planning Perspectives, 23,* 6–16.

Kirscht, J.P., & Joseph, J.G. (1989). The health belief model: Some implications for behavior change with reference to homosexual males. In V.M. Mays, G.W. Albee, & S.F. Schneider (Eds.), *Primary prevention of psychopathology. Primary prevention of AIDS: Psychological approaches* (Vol. 13, pp. 111–127). Newbury Park, CA: Sage.

Knodel, J. (1995). Focus groups as a qualitative method for cross-cultural research in social gerontology: Focus group research on the living arrangements of elderly in Asia (Special issue). *Journal of Cross-Cultural Gerontology, 10,* 7–20.

Knodel, J., Low, B., Saengtienchai, C., & Lucas, R. (1997). An evolutionary perspective on Thai sexual attitudes and behavior. *Journal of Sex Research, 34,* 292–303.

Kolbe, L.J. (1990). An epidemiological surveillance system to monitor the prevalence of youth behaviors that most affect health. *Health Education, 21,* 44–48.

Krueger, R.A. (1988). *Focus groups: A practical guide for applied research.* Newbury Park, CA: Sage.

Kuhn, T.S. (1962). *The structure of scientific revolutions.* Chicago: University of Chicago Press.

Laan, E., Everaerd, W., & Evers, A. (1995). Assessment of female sexual arousal: Response specificity and construct validity. *Psychophysiology, 32,* 476–485.

Lamberg, L. (1998). New drug for erectile dysfunction boon for many, "Viagravation" for some. *Journal of the American Medical Association, 280,* 867–869.

Laqueur, T. (1990). *Making sex: Body and gender from the Greeks to Freud.* Cambridge, MA: Harvard University Press.

Laumann, E.O., Gagnon, J.H., Michael, R.T., & Michaels, S. (1994). *The social organization of sexuality: Sexual practices in the United States.* Chicago: University of Chicago Press.

Lavrakas, P.J. (1993). *Telephone survey methods: Sampling, selection, and supervision, Sage applied social research methods* (Vol. 7). Newbury Park, CA: Sage.

Lawrance, K.-A., & Byers, E.S. (1995). Sexual satisfaction in long-term heterosexual relationships: The interpersonal exchange model of sexual satisfaction. *Personal Relationships, 2,* 267–285.

Lawrance, L., Levy, S.R., & Rubinson, L. (1990). Self-efficacy and AIDS prevention for pregnant teens. *Journal of School Health, 60,* 19–24.

Leiblum, S.T. (1990). Sexuality and the midlife woman: Women at midlife and beyond (Special issue). *Psychology of Women Quarterly, 14,* 495–508.

Leupp, C.P. (1995). *Male colors: The construction of homosexuality in Tokugawa Japan.* Berkeley: University of California Press.

LeVay, S. (1991). A difference in hypothalamic structure between heterosexual and homosexual men. *Science, 253,* 1034–1037.

LeVay, S. (1993). *The sexual brain.* Cambridge, MA: MIT Press.

Levine, M.P., & Troiden, R.R. (1988). The myth of sexual compulsivity. *Journal of Sex Research, 25,* 347–363.

Levinson, R.A. (1986). Contraceptive self-efficacy: A perspective on teenage girls' contraceptive behavior. *Journal of Sex Research, 22,* 347–369.

Locke, S.D., & Gilbert, B.O. (1995). Method of psychological assessment, self-disclosure, and experimental differences: A study of computer, questionnaire, and interview assessment. *Journal of Social Behavior & Personality, 10,* 255–263.

MacNeil, S., & Byers, E.S. (1997). The relationships between sexual problems, communication, and sexual satisfaction. *Canadian Journal of Human Sexuality, 6,* 277–283.

Maiman, L.A., & Becker, M.H. (1974). The health belief model: Origins and correlates in psychological theory. *Health Education Monographs, 2,* 336–353.

Margolis, L., & Sagan, D. (1986). *Origins of sex.* New Haven, CT: Yale University Press.

Markowitz, J.C., Kocsis, J.H., Fishman, B., Spielman, L.A., Jacobsberg, L.B., Fances, A.J., Klerman, G.L., & Perry, S.W. (1998). Treatment of depressive symptoms in human immunodeficiency virus–positive patients. *Archives of General Psychiatry, 55,* 452–457.

Markowitz, J.C., Rabkin, J.G., & Perry, S.W. (1994). Treating depression in HIV-positive patients. *AIDS, 8,* 403–412.

Marshall, W., Eccles, A., & Barbaree, S. (1991). The treatment of exhibitionists: A focus on sexual deviance versus cognitive and relationship features. *Behavior Research and Therapy, 29,* 129–135.

Masters, W.H., & Johnson, V.E. (1966). *Human sexual response.* Boston: Little, Brown.

Masters, W.H., & Johnson, V.E. (1970). *Human sexual inadequacy.* Boston: Little, Brown.

May, R.M., & Anderson, R.M. (1987). Transmission dynamics of HIV infection. *Nature, 326,* 137–142.

Mays, V.M., & Cochran, S.D. (1990). Methodological issues in the assessment and prediction of AIDS risk-related sexual behaviors among Black Americans. In B. Voeller, J.M. Reinisch, & M. Gottleib (Eds.), *AIDS and sex: An integrated and biobehavioral approach* (pp. 97–120). New York: Oxford University Press.

McBee, G.W., & Justice, B. (1977). The effect of interviewer bias on mental illness questionnaire responses. *Journal of Psychology, 95,* 67–75.

McCracken, G. (1988). *The long interview: Sage qualitative research methods* (Vol. 13). Newbury Park, CA: Sage.

McLaws, M.-L., Oldenburg, R., Ross, M.W., & Cooper, D.A. (1990). Sexual behavior in AIDS-related research: Reliability and validity of recall and diary measures. *Journal of Sex Research, 27,* 265–281.

Mead, M. (1961a). *Coming of age in Samoa.* New York: Morrow. (Original work published 1928)

Mead, M. (1961b). Cultural determinants of sexual behavior. In W.C. Young (Ed.), *Sex and internal secretions* (pp. 1433–1479). Baltimore: Williams & Wilkins.

Medawar, P.B., & Medawar, J.S. (1983). *Aristotle to Zoos: A philosophical dictionary.* Cambridge, MA: Harvard University Press.

Meursing, K., Vos, T., Coutinho, O., Moyo, M., Mpofu, S., Oneko, O., Mundy, V., Dube, S., Mahlangu, T., & Sibindi, F. (1995). Child sexual abuse in Matabeleland, Zimbabwe. *Social Science & Medicine, 41,* 1693–1704.

Meyer-Bahlburg, H.F.L. (1995). Psychoneuroendocrinology and sexual pleasure: The aspect of sexual orientation. In P.R. Abramson & S.D. Pinkerton (Eds.), *Sexual nature/sexual culture* (pp. 135–153). Chicago: University of Chicago Press.

Millan, F., & Caban, M. (1996). Issues in psychotherapy with HIV-infected Latinos in New York City. *Journal of Social Distress & the Homeless, 5,* 83–98.

Millstein, S., & Irwin, C. (1983). Acceptability of computer-acquired sexual histories in adolescent girls. *Journal of Pediatrics, 103,* 815–819.

Mishra, S.I., & Serxner, S.A. (1994). "It won't happen to me": Perceived risk and concern about contracting AIDS. *Health Values, 18,* 3–13.

Mona, L.R., Gardos, P.S., & Brown, R.C. (1994). Sexual self views of women with disabilities: The relationships among age of onset, nature of disability and sexual self-esteem. *Sexuality & Disability, 12,* 261–277.

Money, J., & Ehrhardt, A.A. (1972). *Man and woman, boy and girl: The differentiation and dimorphism of gender identity from conception to maturity.* Baltimore: Johns Hopkins University Press.

Morgan, D.L. (1988). *Focus groups as qualitative research: Sage qualitative research methods* (Vol. 16). Newbury Park, CA: Sage.

Morgan, D.L. (Ed.). (1993). *Successful focus groups: Advancing the state of the art.* Newbury Park, CA: Sage.

Morokoff, P.J. (1986). Volunteer bias in the psychophysiological study of female sexuality. *Journal of Sex Research, 22,* 35–51.

Morris, M. (1993). Telling tails explain the discrepancy in sexual partner reports. *Nature, 365,* 437–440.

Morris, M. (1994). Epidemiology and social networks: Modeling structured diffusion. In S. Wasserman & J. Galaskiewicz (Eds.), *Advances in social network analysis: Research in the social and behavioral sciences* (pp. 26–52). Thousand Oaks, CA: Sage.

Morris, M., & Kretzschmar, M. (1995). Concurrent partnerships and transmission dynamics in networks. *Social Networks, 17,* 299–318.

Morris, M., Pramualratana, A., Podhisita, C., & Wawer, M.J. (1995). The relational determinants of condom use with commercial sex partners in Thailand. *AIDS, 9,* 507–515.

Morris, M., Zavisca, J., & Dean, L. (1995). Social and sexual networks: Their role in spread of HIV/AIDS among young gay men. *AIDS Education and Prevention,* 7(Suppl.), 24–35.

Morrison, D.M., Gillmore, M.R., & Baker, S. (1995). Determinants of condom use among high-risk heterosexual adults: A test of the theory of reasoned action. *Journal of Applied Social Psychology, 25,* 651–676.

Mosher, D.L. (1966). The development and multitrait-multimethod matrix analysis of three aspects of guilt. *Journal of Consulting Psychology, 30,* 25–29.

Mosher, D.L. (1973). Sex differences, sex experience, sex guilt, and explicitly sexual films. *Journal of Social Issues, 29,* 95–112.

Mosher, D.L., & Abramson, P.R. (1977). Subjective sexual arousal to films of masturbation. *Journal of Consulting and Clinical Psychology, 45,* 796–807.

Mosher, W.D., & Bachrach, C.A. (1995). Understanding U.S. fertility: Continuity and change in the National Survey of Family Growth, 1988–1995. *Family Planning Perspectives, 28,* 4–12.

Murnen, S.K., Perot, A., & Byrne, D. (1989). Coping with unwanted sexual activity: Normative responses, situational determinants, and individual differences. *Journal of Sex Research, 26,* 85–196.

Murray, J., & Abramson, P.R. (1983). The effects of client gender and attractiveness on psychotherapists' judgements. In J. Murray & P.R. Abramson (Eds.), *Bias in psychotherapy* (pp. 129–167). New York: Praeger.

National Center for Health Statistics. (1958). The statistical design of the Health Household-Interview Survey. *Health Statistics* (DHHS PHS Pub. No. 584-A2). Washington, DC: U.S. Government Printing Office.

National Center for Health Statistics. (1989). Design and estimation for the National Health Interview Survey, 1984–94. *Vital and Health Statistics* (Series 2, No. 110. DHHS PHS Pub. No. 89-1384). Hyattsville, MD: U.S. Government Printing Office.

Neaigus, A., Friedman, S.R., Curtis, R., des Jarlais D.C., Furst, R.T., Jose, B., Mota, P., Stepherson, B., Sufian, M., Ward, T., & Wright, J.W. (1994). The relevance of drug injectors' social and risk networks for understanding and prevention of HIV infection. *Social Science and Medicine, 38,* 67–78.

Nirenberg, T.D., Wincze, J.P., Bansal, S., Liepman, M.R., Engle-Friedman, M., & Begin, A. (1991). Volunteer bias in a study of male alcoholics' sexual behavior. *Archives of Sexual Behavior, 20,* 371–379.

Oksenberg, L., Coleman, L., & Cannell, C.F. (1986). Interviewers' voices and refusal rates in telephone surveys. *Public Opinion Quarterly, 50,* 97–111.

Padian, N., Aral, S., Vranizan, K., & Bolan, G. (1995). Reliability of sexual histories in heterosexual couples. *Sexually Transmitted Diseases, 22,* 169–172.

Paglia, C. (1990). *Sexual personae.* New York: Vintage Books.

Patton, C. (1985). *Sex and germs.* Boston: South End Press.

Paulhus, D.L. (1991). Measurement and control of response bias. In J.P. Robinson, P.R. Shaver, & L.S. Wrightsman (Eds.), *Measures of personality and social psychological attitudes* (Vol. 1, pp. 17–59). San Diego, CA: Academic Press.

Pavelka, M.S.M. (1995). Sexual nature: What can we learn from a cross-species perspective? In P.R. Abramson & S.D. Pinkerton (Eds.), *Sexual nature/sexual culture* (pp. 17–36). Chicago: University of Chicago Press.

Penley, C. (1997). *NASA/Trek.* London: Verson.

Perlman, S.D., & Abramson, P.R. (1982). Sexual satisfaction in married and cohabiting individuals. *Journal of Consulting and Clinical Psychology, 50,* 458–460.

Perry, L.B., & Abramson, P.R. (1980). Debriefing: A gratuitous procedure? *American Psychologist, 35,* 298–299.

Pinkerton, S.D., & Abramson, P.R. (1993). Evaluating the risks: A Bernoulli process model of HIV infection and risk reduction. *Evaluation Review, 17,* 504–528.

Pinkerton, S.D., & Abramson, P.R. (1995). Decision making and personality factors in sexual risk-taking for HIV/AIDS: A theoretical integration. *Personality and Individual Differences, 19,* 713–723.

Pinkerton, S.D., & Abramson, P.R. (1997). Japan. In D.J. West & R. Green (Eds.), *Sociolegal control of homosexuality: A multi-nation comparison* (pp. 67–85). New York: Plenum Press.

Pinkerton, S.D., & Abramson, P.R. (1998). The Bernoulli-process model of HIV transmission: Applications and implications. In D.R. Holtgrave (Ed.), *Handbook of economic evaluation of HIV prevention programs* (pp. 13–33). New York: Plenum Press.

Pinkerton, S.D., & Abramson, P.R. (1999). *Masturbation: Sin and sensation.* Forthcoming.

Pitzele, S.K. (1995). Chronic illness, disability and sexuality in people over fifty. *Sexuality & Disability, 13,* 309–325.

Popper, K. (1957). *The poverty of historicism.* London: Ark.

Popper, K. (1972). *Objective knowledge.* London: Ark.

Popper, K. (1983). *Realism and the aim of science.* Totowa, NJ: Rowman & Littlefield.

Prochaska, J.O., & DiClemente, C.C. (1983). Stages and processes of self-change in smoking: Toward an integrative model of change. *Journal of Consulting and Clinical Psychology, 51,* 390–395.

Przybyla, D.P., & Byrne, D. (1984). The mediating role of cognitive processes in self-reported sexual arousal. *Journal of Research in Personality, 18,* 54–63.

Quadland, M.C. (1985). Compulsive sexual behavior: Definition of a problem and an approach to treatment. *Journal of Sex and Marital Therapy, 11,* 121–132.

Rhodes, T., Stimson, G.V., & Quirk, A. (1996). Sex, drugs, intervention, and research: From the individual to the social. *Substance Use & Misuse, 31,* 375–407.

Robinson, J.P., Shaver, P.R., & Wrightsman, L.S. (Eds.). (1991). *Measures of personality and social psychological attitudes. Measures of social psychological attitudes* (Vol. 1). San Diego, CA: Academic Press.

Robinson, P. (1976). *The modernization of sex: Havelock Ellis, Alfred Kinsey, William Masters, and Virginia Johnson.* New York: Harper.

Romer, D., Hornik, R., Stanton, B., Black, M., Li, X., Ricardo, I., & Feigelman, S. (1997). "Talking" computers: A reliable and private method to conduct interviews on sensitive topics with children. *Journal of Sex Research, 34,* 3–9.

Rose, S. (1994). Sexual pride and shame in lesbians. In B. Greene & G.M. Herek (Eds.), *Lesbian and gay psychology: Theory, research, and clinical applications. Psychological perspectives on lesbian and gay issues* (Vol. 1, pp. 71–83). Thousand Oaks, CA: Sage.

Rosen, R.C., & Beck, J. (1988). *Patterns of sexual arousal: Psychophysiological processes and clinical applications.* New York: Guilford Press.

Rosen, R.C., & Leiblum, S.R. (1992). *Erectile failure: Diagnosis and treatment.* New York: Guilford Press.

Rosenstock, I.M., Strecher, V.J., & Becker, M.H. (1988). Social learning theory and the health belief model. *Health Education Quarterly, 15,* 175–183.

Rosenstock, I.M., Strecher, V.J., & Becker, M.H. (1994). The health belief model and HIV risk behavior change. In R.J. DiClemente & J.L. Peterson (Eds.), *Preventing AIDS: Theories and methods of behavioral interventions* (pp. 5–24). New York: Plenum Press.

Rosenthal, D., Moore, S., & Flynn, I. (1991). Adolescent self-efficacy, self-esteem and sexual risk taking: Social dimension of AIDS (Special issue). *Journal of Community & Applied Social Psychology, 1,* 77–88.

Rosenthal, R. (1978). *Experimenter effects in behavioral research.* New York: Irvington.

Rosenthal, R. (1980). Replicability and experimenter influence: Experimenter effects in behavioral research. *Parapsychology Review, 11,* 5–11.

Rosenthal, R., & Rosnow, R.L. (Eds.). (1968). *Artifact in behavioral research.* New York: Academic Press.

Rosenthal, R., & Rubin, D.B. (1978). Interpersonal expectancy effects: The first 345 studies. *Behavioral and Brain Science, 1,* 377–415.

Rosenzweig, J.M., & Lebow, W.C. (1992). Femme on the streets, butch in the sheets? Lesbian sex-roles, dyadic adjustment, and sexual satisfaction. *Journal of Homosexuality, 23*, 1–20.

Rösler, A., & Witztum, E. (1998). Treatment of men with paraphilia with a long-acting analogue of gonadotropin-releasing hormone. *New England Journal of Medicine, 338*, 416–422.

Rosser, B.R.S., Metz, M.E., Bockting, W.O., & Buroker, T. (1997). Sexual difficulties, concerns, and satisfaction in homosexual men: An empirical study with implications for HIV prevention. *Journal of Sex & Marital Therapy, 23*(1), 61–73.

Rothblatt, M.A. (1995). *The apartheid of sex: A manifesto on the freedom of gender.* New York: Crown.

Rothenberg, R.B., Potterat, J.J., & Woodhouse, D.E. (1996). Personal risk taking and the spread of disease: Beyond core groups. *Journal of Infectious Diseases, 174*(Suppl. 2), S144–S149.

Saltzman, S.P., Stoddard, A.M., McCusker, J., Moon, M.W., & Mayer, K. (1987). Reliability of self-reported sexual behavior risk factors for HIV infection in homosexual men. *Public Health Reports, 107*, 692–697.

Santelli, J.S., Kouzis, A.C., Hoover, D.R., Polacsek, M., Burwell, L.G., & Celentano, D.D. (1996). Stage of behavior change for condom use: The influence of partner type, relationship, and pregnancy factors. *Family Planning Perspectives, 28*, 101–107.

Sarwer, D.B., & Crawford, I. (1994). Therapeutic considerations for work with persons with HIV disease. *Psychotherapy, 31*, 262–269.

Schank, R.C., & Abelson, R.P. (1977). *Scripts, plans, goals, and understanding: An inquiry into human knowledge structures.* Hillsdale, NJ: Erlbaum.

Schiavi, R.C. (1990). Sexuality and aging in men. *Annual Review of Sex Research, 1*, 227–249.

Schill, T.R., & Chapin, J. (1972). Sex guilt and males' preference for reading magazines. *Journal of Consulting and Clinical Psychology, 39*, 516.

Schinke, S.P., Holden, G.W., & Moncher, M.S. (1989). Preventing HIV infection among Black and Hispanic adolescents: Adolescent sexuality. New challenges for social work (Special issue). *Journal of Social Work and Human Sexuality, 8*, 63–73.

Schlesinger, B. (1996). The sexless years or sex rediscovered. *Journal of Gerontological Social Work, 26*, 117–131.

Schneider, D.J., Taylor, E.L., Prater, L.M., & Wright, M.P. (1991). Risk assessment for HIV infection: Validation study of computer-assisted preliminary screen. *AIDS Education & Prevention, 3*, 215–229.

Schover, L., & LoPiccolo, J. (1982). Treatment effectiveness for dysfunctions of sexual desire. *Journal of Sex and Marital Therapy, 8*, 179–197.

Schwartz, S. (1973). Effects of sex guilt and sexual arousal on the retention of birth control information. *Journal of Consulting and Clinical Psychology, 41*, 61–64.

Segraves, R.T., & Segraves, K.B. (1995). Human sexuality and aging. *Journal of Sex Education & Therapy, 21*, 88–102.

Seal, D.W., Wagner, L.I., & Ehrhardt, A.A. (1999). Sex, intimacy, and HIV: An ethnographic study of a Puerto Rican social group in New York City. *Journal of Psychology and Human Sexuality.*

Sedgwick, E.K. (1990). *Epistemology of the closet.* Berkeley: University of California Press.

Seeley, T.T., Abramson, P.R., Perry, L.B., Rothblatt, A.B., & Seeley, D.M. (1980). Thermographic measurement of sexual arousal: A methodological note. *Archives of Sexual Behavior, 9*, 77–85.

Shrimp, T.A., Hyatt, E.M., & Synder, D.J. (1991). A critical appraisal of demand artifacts in consumer research. *Journal of Consumer Research, 18*, 273–283.

Shuman, H., & Converse, J.M. (1968), The effects of Black and White interviewers on Black responses in 1968. *Public Opinion Quarterly, 35*, 44–68.

Silver, G. (1988). AIDS: The infamous Tuskegee study. *American Journal of Public Health, 78*, 1500.

Simon, W., & Gagnon, J.H. (1984). Sexual scripts. *Society, 22*, 53–60.

Sipski, M.L., & Alexander, C.J. (Eds.). (1997). *Sexual function in people with disability and chronic illness: A health professional's guide.* Gaithersburg, MD: Aspen.

Slutske, W.S., True, W.R., Scherrer, J.F., Goldberg, J., Bucholz, K.K., Heath, A.C., Henderson, W.G., Eisen, S.A., Lyons, M.I., & Tsuang, M.T. (1998). Long-term reliability and validity of alcoholism diagnoses and symptoms in a large national telephone interview survey. *Alcoholism, Clinical & Experimental Research, 22*, 553–558.

Smith, E.R., Byrne, D., & Fielding, P.J. (1995). Interpersonal attraction as a function of extreme gender role adherence. *Personal Relationships, 2*, 161–172.

Smith, T.W. (1991). Adult sexual behavior in 1989: Number of partners, frequency of intercourse and risk of AIDS. *Family Planning Perspectives, 23*, 102–107.

Sonenstein, F.L., Pleck, J.H., & Ku, L.C. (1989). Sexual activity, condom use and AIDS awareness among adolescent males. *Family Planning Perspectives, 21*, 152–158.

St. Lawrence, J.S., Brasfield, T.L., Jefferson, K.W., Alleyne, E., & O'Bannon, R.E., III. (1995). Cognitive-behavioral intervention to reduce African American adolescents' risk for HIV infection. *Journal of Consulting and Clinical Psychology, 63*, 221–237.

Stoller, R.J. (1971). The term "transvestism." *Archives of General Psychiatry, 24*, 230–237.

Stoller, R.J. (1985). *Observing the erotic imagination.* New Haven, CT: Yale University Press.

Stoller, R.J., & Herdt, G.H. (1985). Theories of origins of male homosexuality. *Archives of General Psychiatry, 42*, 399–404.

Stoller, R.J., & Levine, I.S. (1993). *Coming attractions: The making of an X-rated video.* New Haven, CT: Yale University Press.

Stout, J.W., & Kirby, D. (1993). The effects of sexuality education on adolescent sexual activity. *Pediatric Annuals, 22*, 120–126.

Strassberg, D.S., & Lowe, K. (1995). Volunteer bias in sexuality research. *Archives of Sexual Behavior, 24*, 369–382.

Strecher, V., DeVellis, B., Becker, M.H., & Rosenstock, I. (1986). The role of self-efficacy in achieving health behavior change. *Health Education Quarterly, 13*, 73–92.

Stuart, F., Hammond, C., & Pett, M. (1988). Inhibited sexual desire in women. *Archives of Sexual Behavior, 16*, 91–106.

Student. (1908). The probable error of a mean. *Biometrika, 6*, 1–24.

Susser, E., Valencia, E., Berkman, A., Sohler, N., Conover, S., Torres, J., Betne, P., Felix, A., & Miller, S. (1998). Human immunodeficiency virus sexual risk-reduction in homeless men with mental illness. *Archives of General Psychiatry, 55*, 266–272.

Susser, E., Valencia, E., Miller, M., Tsai, W.-Y., Meyer-Bahlburg, H., & Conover, S. (1995). Sexual behavior of homeless mentally ill men at risk for HIV. *American Journal of Psychiatry, 152*, 583–587.

Susser, E., Valencia, E., Sohler, N., Gheith, A., Conover, S., & Torres, J. (1996). Interventions for homeless men and women with mental illness: Reducing sexual risk behaviors for HIV. *International Journal of STD & AIDS, 7*(Suppl. 2), 66–70.

Susser, E., Valencia, E., & Torres, J. (1994). Sex, games, and videotapes: An HIV-prevention intervention for men who are homeless and mentally ill. *Psychosocial Rehabilitation Journal, 17,* 31–40.

Symons, D. (1979). *The evolution of human sexuality.* New York: Oxford University Press.

Symons, D. (1992). On the use and misuse of Darwinism in the study of human behavior. In J.H. Barkow, L. Cosmides, & J. Tooby (Eds.), *The adapted mind: Evolutionary psychology and the generation of culture* (pp. 137–159). New York: Oxford University Press.

Symons, D. (1995). Beauty is in the adaptation of the beholder: The evolutionary psychology of human female attractiveness. In P.R. Abramson & S.D. Pinkerton (Eds.), *Sexual nature/sexual culture* (pp. 80–118). Chicago: University of Chicago Press.

Tanfer, K. (1993). National survey of men: Design and execution. *Family Planning Perspectives, 25,* 83–86.

Taylor, M.C., & Hall, J.A. (1982). Psychological androgyny: Theories, methods, and conclusions. *Psychological Bulletin, 92,* 347–366.

Terry, D.J., Gallois, C., & McCamish, M. (Eds.). (1993). *The theory of reasoned action: Its application to AIDS preventive behavior.* Oxford, England: Pergmanon Press.

Thomas, S.B., & Quinn, S.C. (1991). The Tuskegee Syphilis Study, 1932–1972: Implications for HIV education and AIDS with education programs in the Black community. *American Journal of Public Health, 81,* 1498–1505.

Thompson, S.K. (1997). Adaptive sampling in behavioral surveys. *NIDA Research Monograph No. 167,* 296–319.

Thompson, S.K., & Seber, G.A.F. (1996). *Adaptive sampling.* New York: Wiley.

Turner, C.F., Danella, R.D., & Rogers, S.M. (1995). Sexual behavior in the United States, 1930–1990: Trends and methodological problems. *Sexually Transmitted Diseases, 22,* 173–190.

Turner, C.F., Ku, L., Rogers, S.M., Lindberg, L.D., & Pleck, J.H. (1998). Adolescent sexual behavior, drug use, and violence: Increased reporting with computer survey technology. *Science, 380,* 867–873.

Turner, C.F., & Miller, H.G. (1997). Zenilman's anomaly reconsidered: Fallible reports, ceteris paribus, and other hypotheses [comment]. *Sexually Transmitted Diseases, 24,* 522–527.

Upchurch, D.M., Weisman, C.S., Shepherd, M., Brookmeyer, R., Fox, R., Celetano, D.D., Colletta, L., & Hook, E.W., III. (1991). Interpartner reliability of reporting of recent sexual behavior. *American Journal of Epidemiology, 134,* 1159–1166.

Van Meter, K.M. (1990). Methodological and design issues: Techniques for assessing the representativeness of snowball samples. *NIDA Research Monograph No. 98,* 31–43.

Vance, C.S. (Ed.). (1984). *Pleasure and danger: Exploring female sexuality.* Boston: Routledge & Kegan Paul.

Vaughn, S., Schumm, J.S., & Sinagub, J.M. (1996). *Focus group interviews in education and psychology.* Thousand Oaks, CA: Sage.

Wallen, K. (1995). The evolution of female sexual desire. In P.R. Abramson & S.D. Pinkerton (Eds.), *Sexual nature/sexual culture* (pp. 57–79). Chicago: University of Chicago Press.

Ward, V.M., Bertrand, J.T., & Brown, L.F. (1991). The comparability of focus group and survey results: Three case studies. *Evaluation Review, 15,* 266–283.

Wasserman, S., & Faust, K. (1994). *Social network analysis: Methods and applications.* New York: Cambridge University Press.

Weeks, J., & Holland, J. (Eds.). (1996). *Sexual cultures: Communities, values, and intimacy.* New York: St. Martin's Press.

Weeks, K., Levy, S.R., Zhu, C., Perhats, C., Handler, A., & Flay, B. (1995). Impact of a school-based AIDS prevention program on young adolescents' self-efficacy skills. *Health Education Research, 10,* 329–344.

Wiederman, M.W. (1997). The truth must be in here somewhere: Examining the gender discrepancy in self-reported lifetime number of sex partners. *Journal of Sex Research, 34,* 375–386.

Wilson, E.O. (1975). *Sociobiology: The new synthesis.* Cambridge, MA: Harvard University Press.

Wilson, J.D. (1995). Sex hormones and sexual behavior. In P.R. Abramson & S.D. Pinkerton (Eds.), *Sexual nature/sexual culture* (pp. 121–153). Chicago: University of Chicago Press.

Wolchik, S.A., Braver, S.L., & Jensen, K. (1985). Volunteer bias in erotica research: Effects of intrusiveness of measure and sexual background. *Archives of Sexual Behavior, 14,* 93–107.

Wolchik, S.A., Spencer, S.L., & Lisi, I.S. (1983). Volunteer bias in research employing vaginal measures of sexual arousal: Demographics, sexual and personality characteristics. *Archives of Sexual Behavior, 12,* 399–408.

Zelnik, M., & Kanter, J.F. (1980). Sexual activity, contraceptive use and pregnancy planning among metropolitan area teenagers: 1971–1979. *Family Planning Perspectives, 12,* 230–231, 233–237.

Zelnik, M., & Kim, Y. (1982). Sex education and its association with teenage sexual activity, pregnancy, and contraceptive use. *Family Planning Perspectives, 16,* 117–126.

Zenilman, J.M., Weisman, C.S., Rompalo, A.M., Ellish, N., Upchurch, D.M., Hook, E.W., III, & Celentano, D. (1995). Condom use to prevent incident STDs: The validity of self-reported condom use. *Sexually Transmitted Diseases, 22,* 15–21.

Zilbergeld, B. (1992). *The new male sexuality.* New York: Bantam Books.

Zilbergeld, B., & Kilmann, P. (1984). The scope and effectiveness of sex therapy. *Psychotherapy, 21,* 319–326.

Zisook, S., Peterkin, J., Goggin, K.J., Sledge, P., Atkinson, J.H., & Grant, I. (1998). Treatment of major depression of HIV-seropositive men. *Journal of Clinical Psychiatry, 59,* 217–224.

CHAPTER 2

Male Sexuality

WALTER EVERAERD, ELLEN T. M. LAAN, and MARK SPIERING

Fish got to swim
and birds got to fly
I got to love one man till I die,
Can't help lovin' dat man of mine.

OSCAR HAMMERSTEIN, *Showboat*

I N THIS CHAPTER, we review male sexuality as it is described in current research. At least three perspectives are used in psychological approaches to
sexual issues: the body perspective, the emotional perspective, and the social and cultural perspective. In the discussion of different topics, we may
bring one particular perspective to the foreground; in our view, this often implies that the chosen perspective provides the best explanation for the topic.
Descriptions of sexual behavior and sexual experiences always connect with
normative and ethical points of view. We are aware of the variety of customs
and laws not only within the Western hemisphere, but across the world. However, our views are colored by the culture of The Netherlands. For example, we
do not always differentiate male-female from male-male relationships; thus,
many of our observations about male sexuality implicate both heterosexual
and homosexual men.

The review is divided in three sections: sexual pathways, sexual functioning, and sexual dysfunctions.

SEXUAL PATHWAYS

The Body in Context

Is there a sexual system? In the production of a sexual response, stimuli that are recognized as sexual by the brain are transformed into specific efferent messages. One way to understand this process is to think of the nervous system as a set of modules or nuclei that each contribute in a specific way to determine a sexual outcome. In this view, there are provisions in anatomically specified areas for the processing of sexual information. These areas recognize information as sexual and connect with other units which respond to the incoming information. If we were able to follow this neural processing, we would see the pathway for sexual information. Of course, there are many other processes that help to determine the expression of sexual response and that are not specifically sexual. Among these are emotional responses, muscular responses, and cognitions about a sexual response in an actual social situation.

The processing of sexual information can also be traced neurochemically. This view does not conflict with the modular view. Neuronal systems can be characterized both by their topography and by their neurochemical content, particularly amino acids, amines, peptides, and steroid receptors. Neurons can be classed into chemical categories according to genes they express that enable them to make or respond to a particular neurochemical (Herbert, 1996, p. 8). The role of a neuron, in this view, is not only determined by its specific anatomic location and connections but also by its use of transmitters.

The interaction of anatomical locations and neurochemical transmitters results in very complicated pathways that cannot be easily specified. The combined view provides a rich heuristic for the study of sexual functioning. However, a preliminary condition for the success of such studies is the specification of psychological processes and behavioral end points. Most of the work on anatomy and neurobiology of sexual response has been done with nonhuman animals. Sexual response, or sexual behavior, has been very narrowly defined as reproductive behavior. Transposition of the results of this work to human sexuality should be accompanied by an awareness of the social and cultural constructions in human sexual experience and behavior.

Is sex natural? Sexuality in humans and several animal species is typically prepared at birth. It needs growth, maturation, and learning. The advantage is considerable adaptability and, as a consequence, variability in what is sexual or sexy and which emotions and behaviors are implicated in sexual expression.

An answer to "Is there a sexual system?" will depend on one's point of view. Kolodny, Masters, and Johnson (1979) adhered to a sexual system view when they wrote:

> To define sex as natural means just as an individual cannot be taught to sweat or how to digest food, a man cannot be taught to have an erection, nor can a woman be taught to lubricate vaginally. Because the reflex pathways of sexual functioning

are inborn does not mean that they are immune from disruption due to impaired health, cultural conditioning, or interpersonal stress. . . . Although sexual responsivity is a natural psychophysiologic process, many learned behaviors or attitudes may be maladaptive from the viewpoint of sexual functioning—that is, they may interfere with rather than enhancing (or at least leaving undisturbed) the natural set of sexual reflexes. (p. 479)

Kolodny et al. (1979) did not specify what they meant by these sexual reflexes. In their text, reflexogenic erections are erections in response to tactile stimulation to the penis, as contrasted with psychogenic erections which come about through, for example, visual stimuli. These authors imply that there are natural, unlearned, or unconditional stimuli that, given appropriate conditions, will elicit the sexual reflexes. This may be so, but we do not know for certain whether there are such stimuli. For most functional men, "sex comes naturally," which means automatically, without purpose or without effort. From this subjectively and objectively observable state of affairs, the "naturalness" may impose itself as a probability. However, natural origin does not logically follow from these observations. Simplified, Kolodny et al.'s message is that sex comes naturally unless one (cognitively) interferes with it.

If one accepts the "natural psychophysiologic process," how can this process explain effects of voluntary fantasies, intentional seeking of sex, and cultural variations in sexuality? It predicts that in functional men, an adequate sexual stimulus, when it is attended, will produce a sexual response. Under all circumstances? Hopefully not: there are some social constraints to sexual expression.

Is there a hierarchical organization? "Natural" is not a helpful construct in understanding a sexual response, the subjective experience of sex, or sexual expression. Kolodny et al. (1979) consider the psychophysiological requirements that should be fulfilled to elicit a sexual response. However, most of these develop over time, after birth, in interaction with social and cultural factors. A more useful conceptualization may start from the notion that the various systems and mechanisms that "produce" sex are organized in a hierarchical manner. Various models of hierarchical organization have been proposed. Consider two examples. The idea of levels of integration in the central nervous system starts from the principle that higher parts of the brain coordinate and direct simpler components of action, which themselves are controlled by levels farther down in the nervous system (Mook, 1996). In such a model, at a lower level we may consider spinal reflexes; the higher brainstem provides the intermediate level for fixed movement patterns, and the hypothalamus integrates the patterns, thus producing directed movements and internal control. A second example is the stages approach in information processing. In its simplest form, this approach describes the processing of stimulus information from feature detection through elaboration and the generation of action plans into the execution of actions. More complex processing models add regulation modules (Frijda, 1986) or supervisory control modules (Jeannerod, 1997) to account for hierarchical and integrated processing. A hierarchical model may help us understand how sexual information survives the processing competition in the brain and eventually results in sexual action.

Whether a sexual response, for example, will be behaviorally expressed cannot be explained solely by the concept of sexual reflexes. For some men, the bodily feelings that arise as a consequence of sexual stimulation are enjoyable in themselves, even when it is not possible to act on these feelings. Some men will masturbate in such circumstances, and others will look for more sexual stimulation—visual, olfactory or tactile—or will look for a partner. Some men will not pay any attention at all to these feelings.

Before elaborating on hierarchical organization, we look a little more closely into sexual stimuli.

Sexual Response to What?

Remember your first sexual response? Did you know it was sexual, or did this interpretation appear after the experience? There may be no explicit memory of your first sexual response, and you may not remember that it was sexual. The most probable development is that sensations from tactile stimulation and later from visual, auditory, or olfactory stimulation were pleasurable and not sexual, like many other sensations for which labels and meanings have to be learned after the first experience. It is implied that stimuli are (cognitively) transformed into messages that eventually result in a sexual response and a subjective sexual experience in particular. Thus, a stimulus is not intrinsically sexual; it becomes sexual by its transformation. We have no certainty about the existence of so-called unlearned sexual stimuli. There is ample evidence that there are stimuli (e.g., tactile) that activate arousal in the physiological component of sexual response (Bancroft, 1989). However, this arousal alone is not sufficient to produce a subjective sexual experience. This experience ultimately depends on the individual's awareness and definition of the response as sexual (Everaerd, 1993).

Another important point is that a stimulus may convey several meanings depending on the circumstances or the individual's history. Different messages, in the same or in different individuals, may thus be accessed by the same stimulus. Sexual meaning and other meanings relevant for different emotions, such as anxiety, anger, or elation, may be present at the same time. The different meanings will be processed as different messages that, by further processing, may develop divergent physiological and behavioral responses and experiences.

A stimulus that (supposedly) triggers the sexual system is commonly called a sexual stimulus—a truly circular description. Tactile stimuli applied to the penis are often considered sexual because of the presumed direct spinal pathway that connects the afferent tactile information to the efferent vasomotor output. But afferent and efferent processes are connected by interneurons that allow modulation by higher-order processes (McKenna, 1998). Most men know that the experience of any gentle touch to the penis depends on the context wherein it is applied. The context may be sexually attractive or aversive. In the aversive context (e.g., a man touches a heterosexual man), the implied sexual meaning arouses aversion and shame, and generally not an erection.

There are three neural pathways to the genital area: the hypogastric nerve, the pelvic nerve, and the pudendal nerve. These pathways transmit signals for somatic (pudendal), sympathic (hypogastric), and parasympathic (pelvic) motor action (Stoeckart, Slob, & Moor-Mommers, 1995). The hypogastric nerve exits from the thoracolumbar part of the spinal cord, and the pelvic and pudendal nerve from the lumbosacral part of the spinal cord. It is hypothesized that the pelvic nerve mediates reflexive erections and that the hypogastric nerve mediates erections that originate from the brain, sometimes called psychogenic erections. Most of the evidence for the hypogastric pathway comes from studies with patients with spinal cord injuries. Men with lesions under T11-L2, where the hypogastric trunk exits, should retain psychogenic erections, whereas those with lesions higher than T11-L2 should not. Men with lesions higher than the lumbosacral area (S1-S3) should retain reflex-erections. In most cases, there will be no subjective experience from these erections if the afferent spinal pathway to the brain is disconnected through injury.

From available evidence, Sachs (1995) speculates that the hypogastric pathway contributes to erectile function through psychogenic mediation. It is likely that, via neural plasticity, psychogenic mediation is possible in men with spinal cord injuries. However, evidence in favor of this prevailing view is not compelling. It has been found that men with spinal cord injury, as compared to men with an intact spinal cord, could not accurately predict their erectile response to visual sexual stimulation (Kennedy & Over, 1990). According to Sachs, erections are normally mediated by the pelvic nerves. He adds an interesting note on ejaculation: "for those species in which the male ejaculates immediately upon insertion, e.g., canids and most ungulates, erection may be more directly controlled by the hypogastric nerve, which mediates ejaculation" (p. 217).

Sexual stimuli are of either sensory, fantasy, or memory origin. Some sensory information will arise from stimulation of tactile receptors in the penis. Most sensory and other information is mediated by the brain and will affect the penis and the genital area via complex neural pathways. Sensory information, whether auditory, olfactory, gustatory, tactile, or visual, may effectively arouse sexual response; men most easily and preferentially attend to information from the visual pathway. From an array of stimuli that range from verbal description of sexual scenes through slides to film with moving pictures, the moving pictures are the most efficient in terms of immediacy in intensity of sexual response (Bancroft, 1989; Dekker & Everaerd, 1989; Janssen & Everaerd, 1993). Sexual fantasy most often is based on, or at least connected with, retrieval of earlier experiences from memory (Leitenberg & Henning, 1995).

We do not know whether sexual preferences are determined at birth. What we do know is that we are born with a sensitivity for what we call sexual stimuli.

This sensitivity builds up in the course of development and becomes prominent around puberty and, although attenuated, remains active into old age.

We have already considered some of the anatomical prerequisites (e.g., genitalia and connections with the nervous system), and we mentioned chemical orchestration by (sex) hormones and neurotransmitters. During development and growth, there is interaction with the environment that builds up experience and potentiation of "sexual" stimuli. The social and cultural environment determines sexual expression and the meaning of sexual experience. And although all this sounds already quite complicated, sexual function is always connected with functioning of the person as a whole. Let us reiterate this with the musical metaphor used by Bermant (1995):

> Human sexuality emerges from the interdependencies of biology, personal awareness, and the facts and artifacts of public life. Ignoring for long any of these mutually dependent aspects of sexuality leads to a distorted understanding and inadequate accounting of the varieties of meaning sexuality has for individuals and cultures. A useful metaphor is that correct accountings of sexuality are not one-finger melodies—they are chords. But we cannot readily speak or write in chords, so we are limited in how accurate and comprehensive we can be in any single comment. (p. 343)

A Hierarchical Organization

We take at least two messages from Bermant's (1995) metaphoric chord. First, one cannot understand every aspect of sexuality from a one-finger melody, that is, the chemical processes in the cell or the social construction of sexual attractivity. Second, the chord is a parallel process; different but connected things happen at the same time, influencing each other, and for the listener, they may fuse into one melody.

We use an information processing approach to describe a hierarchical model. Our purpose is to understand how stimulus information is transformed into particular sorts of actions. Steven Pinker (1997) eloquently wrote: "the mind is not the brain but what the brain does, and not everything it does, such as metabolizing fat and giving off heat. . . . The brain's special status comes from a special thing the brain does, which makes us see, think, feel, choose and act. That special thing is information processing or computation" (p. 24).

Our model has to provide explanations for at least two phenomena. We have to explain how stimulus information is turned into specific sexual actions, for example, genital arousal, erection, and eventually orgasm and subjective experience of sexual excitement. In addition, to explain sexual expression, we have to elucidate how nonspecific, nonsexual behaviors are engaged and integrated into this process, for example, social interactions and access to sexual processing in potential partners.

There is an important distinction between what goes on in the domains of awareness and those processes that take place outside awareness. Guyton (1991), the famed physiology textbook author, reminds us that of all information processing going on in our bodies, we can become aware of only a tiny fraction; even most processing in the brain (and thus in the mind) is outside awareness. This is an important observation because people tend to use the awareness distinction to attribute causes of sexual response and behavior. So-called spontaneous sexual thoughts, spontaneous erections (Bancroft, 1989), are of unknown origin. In fact, people may not have been aware of their own processing. Spontaneity is also a problematic concept because it may be used as a romantic synonym for authenticity, which is a meaningful descriptor for emotional experience. The authentic quality may validate emotions connected with infatuation and infatuation itself.

When one looks up synonyms for spontaneous, for example in *Chambers Dictionary of Synonyms and Antonyms*, one finds free, impromptu, impulsive, instinctive, natural, unforced, unhesitating, unpremeditated, unprompted, untaught; then, unexpectedly, are the synonyms voluntary and willing. The first set of synonyms is relevant for male sexuality because these match male, perhaps macho, imagery of sexual motivation, and male vitality in general. "Voluntary" and "willing" apparently do not fit in this imagery; these words are linked with responsibility. And yet, there is an important trade-off between sexual vitality and responsibility. The more a man leans toward the vitality option for his causal attributions, the less responsibility he may claim. The stupendous consequence is that he cannot be held responsible either in good (functional) times or in bad times when he fails sexually (in dysfunction or offense).

The constructions of the mind—sometimes "dagger(s) of the mind, false creations," according to *Macbeth*—do not necessarily match the mechanics of the brain. Thinking in terms of a hierarchical model and being aware of its intricate complexity may help prevent the construction of a simplistic view of male sexuality.

PENILE ERECTIONS: PHYSIOLOGY AND PHARMACOLOGY

Erection and Ejaculation Mechanisms

In this section, we offer a noncomprehensive description of the mechanisms of erection and ejaculation. We do not elaborate in great detail on anatomy, psychophysiology, and neurotransmission. Our aim here is to provide a description that allows a basic understanding of mechanisms.

In the course of the previous sections, we have touched on a number of relevant topics. It should become clear that there exists a considerable imbalance in the knowledge about the molecular biology, anatomy, physiology, and pathology of peripheral mechanisms of erection, as compared with what is known about central mechanisms. The current focus on peripheral mechanisms stems from advances in knowledge about general smooth muscle physiology. The spectacular results of smooth muscle relaxant drugs draws attentional resources to that domain at the expense of the possibilities that reside in central nervous system control. Knowledge about central control of sexual processes is still very limited, although it is clear that central control is all-important (Guyton, 1991; McKenna, 1998; Rowland, 1995).

What we know about central control comes from animal research and some clinical studies about brain pathology and brain injuries. Regarding afferent pathways, for example, from the senses to the brain, it is not clear where transformation into sexual information takes place. Recently, a sketchy pathway has been described by McKenna, based mainly on animal data and, specifically, tracing studies in which anatomical projections are explored (McKenna, 1998; Nieuwenhuys, 1996). McKenna's views are summarized here. The medial preoptic area (MPOA) seems to be responsible for the recognition of sensory information as appropriate sexual targets. A high density of neurons that concentrate androgens is characteristic. In castrated animals, implantation of testosterone restores sexual behavior. The MPOA also integrates sexual information with sexual motivation and copulatory programs. The volume (larger in males than in females) of MPOA nuclei has been implicated in studies about homo/heterosexual preferences, without any certainty about the origin of this volume difference. The energizing or motivational component seems to reside in the medial amygdala. McKenna refers to the famous Klüver and Bucy reports about large temporal lobe lesions and the consequent hypersexual behavior in monkeys. This hypersexuality, that is, the removal of inhibitory control, seems not to reside in the amygdala but in an adjacent brain area (the piriform cortex), and is most likely related to executive functions of the forebrain. Discrete lesions of the amygdala did not induce hypersexuality in these monkeys. More often, it has been found that lesions of the amygdala disrupt sexual behavior.

From the MPOA, information is possibly passed to the periaquaductal gray (PAG) in the midbrain and from there to the spinal interneurons that connect with the hypogastric nerve, the pelvic nerve, and the pudendal nerve. The PAG projects to the nucleus paragigantocellularis (NPG), which in turn projects to the already mentioned spinal interneurons. The direct path from PAG to interneurons is excitatory, and the path from PAG through NPG is inhibitory. Serotonin is the transmitter responsible for inhibition in this pathway. This elucidates the clinical finding that SSRIs (selective serotonin reuptake inhibitors) may interfere with sexual function and premature ejaculation (Lane, 1997) and may be useful to retard ejaculation.

In 1989, Wagner, Gerstenberg, and Levin were able to show, using an electromyographic (EMG) measure, that upon viewing an erotic video, the tonic contraction of smooth muscles in the viewer's penile corpora cavernosa disappeared. This is the first observable sign of a beginning erection. Since 1989, there have been developments in the measuring method—needle as well as surface electrodes have been applied—but as yet there is no robust and subject-friendly procedure available (Sasso et al., 1997). Still, Wagner et al.'s landmark study opened the way to exploring functional neural pathways of early activation of sexual response in humans. In our lab, we attempted to create a psychological paradigm to measure the activational effects of visual sexual stimuli on sexual response. Because the cavernous EMG is not yet suitable for psychophysiological studies, we used reaction time in a classification task as a first approach (Janssen & Everaerd, 1993). Neutral (plant) and sexual primes below the awareness threshold were followed by consciously perceived sexual or plant targets that were to be classified as either "sexual" or "plant." Sexual primes showed shorter reaction times for sexual targets. In a separate study, no effect of primes on subjective sexual excitement ratings of the targets was found (Spiering, Everaerd, & Janssen, 1999). This paradigm will shortly be complemented by an EMG measure of the penile smooth muscle potential and will thus provide a useful window on information processing as it relates to neural erectile mechanisms.

Erection. The penis is made up of spongeous tissues, the ventral corpus spongiosum, and two dorsal corpora cavernosa, surrounded by a white membrane, the tunica albuginea. The cavernosal branches of the penile artery supply blood directly into the corpora. Blood is drained from the corpora via veins that pierce the tunica albiginea, to continue into the deep dorsal vein, or the cavernosal and crural veins. As mentioned earlier, penile blood vessels and smooth muscle in the corpora have motor sympathic and parasympathic innervation (hypogastric and pelvic nerves). The striated muscles outside the tunica albigunea are innervated by the pudendal nerve. Action of these innervations proceeds in a coordinated way. Interruption of these pathways, in particular the parasympathetic nerves, may preclude normal erections (Wagner & Saenz de Tejada, 1998).

For a description of the physiology of erection, we again follow Wagner and Saenz de Tejada's (1998) description. In the usual flaccid state, the smooth muscles of the corpora cavernosa are in tonic contraction. Relaxation of smooth muscles of the blood vessels and the spaces in the spongeous corpora causes inflow of blood. Through arterial pressure, the spaces expand and, in turn, this expands the tunica albuginea, with subsequent elongation and compression of the draining small veins. This occlusion of the small veins restricts outflow of blood. After ejaculation or cessation of sexual stimuli, the spaces in the corpora again contract.

Ejaculation. The neurophysiology of ejaculation is less well-known than the neurophysiology of erection. Following erection, the ejaculatory reflex normally is a second stage in sexual response. Repeated or sustained tactile stimulation and also intense visual stimulation may first result in erection; then, emission of semen in the urethra takes place through smooth muscle contraction of the internal sexual organs: the vas deferens, seminal vesicles, and smooth muscle of the prostate (the hypogastric nerve is also involved). At the start of inflow of semen in the urethra, the bladder neck closes to prevent semen from entering the bladder (as in retrograde ejaculation). Then ejaculation proper, the expulsion of semen, takes place through contractions of the pelvic musculature (the pudendal nerve is involved) (Segraves & Segraves, 1993).

Three components can be distinguished in the process of ejaculation: emission and bladder neck closure, ejaculation, and the experience of orgasm (Segraves & Segraves, 1993). Orgasm, the third component, is the subjective experience of the sensations that stem from contractions of emission and ejaculation. Orgasm is connected with perceptual mechanisms of attention and awareness. The quality of orgasm is connected with the intensity of sensations, attentional focus, and meaningfulness of the orgasmic event.

Sexual Pharmacology

What we call the chemical orchestration of the sensitivity of the sexual system is, in fact, a very complex and still fragmented field of knowledge. Recently, the effects on sexual function of a vast number of drugs (endogenous as well as exogenous chemical substances) have been reviewed and reported in *Sexual Pharmacology* (Crenshaw & Goldberg, 1996). The endogenous substances already constitute quite a list, which is here reproduced by way of illustration. Substances with sexual excitatory action are $alpha_1$ and $beta_2$ adrenergic activity, calcitonin-gene-related-peptide, cholinergic activity, dehydroepiandrosterone (DHEA/DHEAS), dopamine, endothelium-derived relaxin factor, estrogen (in women only), growth hormone, histamine, luteinizing hormone-releasing hormone (LHRH), nitric oxide (NO), oxytocin, prostaglandins, substance P, testosterone, vasoactive intestinal peptide (VIP), vasopressin, and zinc (replacement value only). Substances with sexual inhibitory action are $alpha_2$ adrenergic activity, angiotensin II, cortisol, estrogen (men only), melatonin, monoamine oxidase, neuropeptide Y, progesterone, prolactin, serotonin, and thyroid activity (Crenshaw & Goldberg, 1996). The list gives a coarse division of excitatory and inhibitory effects; in reality, effects are more subtle, as many substances exert both excitatory and inhibitory influences.

Androgens are the best-known sex hormones, although, like many other substances, their effects are not limited to sexual action; androgens also influence anxiety, aggression, feeding, learning, and memory. It has become clear that the brain is sensitive to androgens in relation to sexual function. Exactly how this influence takes place remains unanswered (McCarthy & Albrecht, 1996). In a number of studies, testosterone appeared to be necessary for cognitive sexual functioning (fantasy, sexual daydreaming, the experience of desire) and for erections during REM sleep periods. However, erections may be elicited by visual sexual stimulation with films or videos in men with very low levels of testosterone, for example, in hypogonadal men (Bancroft & Malone, 1995; Carani, Bancroft, Granata, Del-Rio, & Marrama, 1992; Schiavi, White, Mandeli, & Levine, 1997).

In hypogonadal men, a supplement of testosterone may induce spectacular changes in functioning and experience (Bancroft, 1989). In hypersexual sex offenders, drugs that inhibit androgen-receptor activity (Androcur,

Depo-Provera) decrease the frequency of sexual thoughts and fantasies and reduce sexual desire (Gijs & Gooren, 1996). There is no evidence that supplementing testosterone to eugonadal men improves aspects of sexual functioning. Men who use anabolic steroids to enlarge their muscular volume or for performance in sports are reported to be more sexually active. This may be due to nonsexual effects such as feeling healthy, disinhibited, and more aggressive (Bahrke, Yesalis, & Wright, 1996; Middleman & DuRant, 1996).

Monoamines such as dopamine, serotonin, and norepinephrine have various effects; a few will be described. Dopamine (apomorphine) increases the likelihood of erections in normal volunteers and in men with psychogenic erectile dysfunction. Serotonin has a reputation of inhibitory effect, but the many patients that use various SSRIs report mixed positive and negative effects on sexual functioning. In rats, it has been found that impairing serotonin transmission greatly enhances sexual functioning. Treated rats showed a dramatic change in ejaculation; whereas they usually ejaculated after 10 to 12 intromissions, they now needed only one or two (Pfaus & Everitt, 1995). Norepinephrine is released through the action of the alpha$_2$ receptor antagonist yohimbine, a long-standing aphrodisiac; it enhances erections, but only in younger men with erectile dysfunction (Crenshaw & Goldberg, 1996; Pfaus & Everitt, 1995; Rowland, Kallan, & Slob, 1997). Oxytocin, a peptide, is secreted during sexual activity in some animals (Hillegaart, Alster, UvnasMoberg, & Ahlenius, 1998); it also enhances ejaculation in men (Pfaus & Everitt, 1995).

Peripheral action of smooth muscle relaxing drugs has been extensively studied. When sildanafil (Viagra), which can be orally ingested to produce the desired effects, was made available, it caused spectacular media hype. Sildanafil is one of the phosphodiesterase-5 inhibitors that affects the breakdown of cyclic guanosine monophosphate (cGMP). With normal erotic stimulation, cGMP is the last step before smooth muscle relaxation. Sildanafil enhances the availability of cGMP by preventing its breakdown, hence its positive effect on erection (Goldstein, Lue, Padma-Nathan, Rosen, Steers, & Wicker, 1998).

The exploration of the chemical orchestration of sexual function has only begun to shed light on the many ways of influencing its processes. This research is part of a much larger transition in the way we look at biological processes in the body. Wells (1998) states:

> Tully and Yin have made flies with photographic memories, and with the backing of a major pharmaceutical company they hope to transfer some of that capability to humans. Whether or not they are the first to succeed, it seems almost inevitable that society will soon face the question of whether more—be it hair (Propecia), weight-loss (fen-phen), sex (Viagra), or now memories—is always better.

THE SOCIAL-DEVELOPMENT CONTEXT

In this section, we sketch a perspective that illustrates how male sexuality sensitivity is dependent on biological as well as contextual factors. Beginning with embryonic development, there is differentiation of the genitalia, which, after birth, develop a sensitivity for stimuli that we call sexual stimuli. In very young baby boys, touching the penis may (reflexively) result in erection; erections have even been observed in utero. There is a famous demonstration in a drawing by Rembrandt of an erection in a baby. Long-lasting erections (priapism) of various origin have been observed in newborns (Walker & Casale, 1997). From birth into old age, erections can be pharmacogically induced in males (Perovic, Djordjevic, & Djakovic, 1997). Touching and exploring genitals may induce erections and pleasurable feelings, supposedly without any sexual meaning attached to these experiences. In a German study, it was suggested that little girls have a more vague notion of their genitals and how they fit into the rest of their body than do little boys, as long as the boys are not hindered in the exploration of their genitals (Schuhrke, 1997). There are rare reports about prolonged self-stimulation to orgasm in boys less than 1 year old. There have been observations of rhythmical body movements, penile thrusting, sustained tension in muscles, and sudden relaxation with rhythmical contractions (Cohen-Kettenis, Wafelbakker, & Slob, 1995).

A pleasurable subjective experience suggests very early central (and not only spinal) mediation of the sexual response. In early childhood, curiosity about genitals and behavior involving genitals is usually discouraged. It is a first attempt at the social control of sexual functioning. There are differences in how this curiosity is met in boys and in girls. More important, during the child's discovery of the world, parents support the child with openly given cognitive and affective information, often excluding sex (Cohen-Kettenis et al., 1995). In spite of all this, children explore the "sexual" world by playing doctor and mimicking adult lovemaking. From early childhood till puberty, children elaborate on these experiences and develop sexual repertoires. There is wide variation among children, which is amplified by cultural and religious differences.

How the onset of puberty (pubarche, spermarche; arche = begin) takes place is not yet well understood, although there are speculations regarding the role of several substances, for example, serum leptin levels (Issad, Strobel, Camoin, Ozata, & Strosberg, 1998; Palmert, Radovick, & Boepple, 1998). The "pubertal motor" takes off when the hypothalamus begins to produce pulsatile GnRH (gonadotrophin-releasing hormone), which stimulates the pituitary to produce the gonadotrophin (stimulating the gonads) LH (luteinizing hormone). LH stimulates the gonads to produce "sex" (sex-specific, not sexual) hormones; in boys, testosterone is produced in the Leydig cells of the testes; in girls, estradiol is produced in the cells of the ovarian follicles. Some time before puberty, the adrenal cortex (adrenarche) has begun to produce androgens.

Testosterone is responsible for, among other things, further growth and adult sexual differentiation. The testes increase in size, the penis grows thicker and longer, pubic hair and body hair start to appear, and lowering of the voice begins (Martini, 1995). After some time, ejaculation will occur either in wet dreams or through masturbation (Cohen-Kettenis et al., 1995). Testosterone (and its related steroid metabolites; together they are called androgens) also sensitizes the brain to initiate and to sustain the sexual response. The effect of androgens on the sensitivity of the sexual system is strikingly demonstrated when patients with insufficient gonadal production are treated with androgens. The androgens very quickly increase sexual desire and sexual thoughts and fantasies. There is also an increase in nocturnal (REM sleep–related) erections and "spontaneous" erections, and mood is more positive and optimistic (Bancroft, 1989; Burris, Banks, Carter, Davidson, & Sherins, 1992).

It is clear that sexual sensitivity is a result of a very complicated interaction between the body and the (social) environment. This interaction may also be the framework for the development of sexual preference and sexual orientation. Bem's (1996) theory of how "the exotic becomes erotic" fits very well into this point of view: "It proposes that biological variables, such as genes, prenatal hormones, and brain neuroanatomy, do not code for sexual orientation per se but for childhood temperaments that influence a child's preference for sex-typical or sex-atypical activities and peers" (p. 320). In Bem's temporal sequence of development, "gender-conforming children will feel different from opposite-sex peers, perceiving them as dissimilar, unfamiliar, and exotic" (p. 321). Nonconforming children will have these feelings and perceptions about same-sex peers. Dissimilarity and unfamiliarity are sources of heightened autonomic arousal, which in later years will be transformed into erotic/romantic attraction. Bem's reasoning may also apply to the development of paraphilias. We will elaborate neither on orientation nor preference because these are the subjects of other chapters of this book.

From the onset of the "pubertal motor," a cascade of changes takes place, resulting in an increased expression of the sexual response. From the interactionist point of view, it is important to note that no discrete shift appears at any important biological step. The body develops in context, which means that the biological change, be it gonadarche, pubarche, or spermarche, is not a sufficient explanation of sexual development. Although mean age of gonadarche was found to be 12 years in girls and 14 years in boys, mean ages at first sexual attraction do not corroborate the hypotheses of discrete hormonal influence. For example, it has been found that in boys, the first same-sex attraction appears at age 9.6, the first same-sex fantasy at age 11.2, and the first same-sex activity at age 13.1. In girls, mean ages are 10.1, 11.9, and 15.2, respectively. There is no significant difference between heterosexual and homosexual development, nor between boys and girls (McClintock & Herdt, 1996).

What about growing older? Does sensitivity wane or even disappear? There are abundant data to show a decline with age in androgen levels (Vermeulen, 1996). Recently, there has been growing interest in an androgen steroid, dehydroepiandrosterone (DHEA), and its influence on the aging process in men. There is a very clear negative correlation between increasing age and sexual desire, sexual arousal, and sexual activity (Schiavi, 1996). But Schiavi could not establish a meaningful relationship between the decline in sexual function and hormone levels. In fact, studies involving androgen supplements did not show that they significantly improved sexual function, in particular erectile capacity. Despite hormone diminution, many men continue to have satisfactory sex lives, some men even into very old age.

SEXUAL FUNCTIONING

THE SEXUAL RESPONSE CYCLE

The section "Body in Context" above began with a very simple model: certain stimuli are recognized as sexual and produce a sexual response. Older models refer to the reproductive function of the sexual response to specify a sequence of physiological events. The sequence is best described by enumerating the classic diagnostic terms: *impotentia* (i) *concupiscentiae erectionis*, i. *ejaculationis*, i. *satisfactionis*, and i. *satisfaciendi*. Concupiscentiae (Cupido!) is the urge or desire to have sex. Not being able to experience satisfaction is i. satisfactionis, and not being able to give satisfaction to one's partner is i. satisfaciendi (Matussek, 1971).

Masters and Johnson presented their model of the sexual response cycle in 1964. There is a striking absence of the first phase (urge or desire) in the old model. Masters and Johnson proposed an excitement phase and, within that phase, a plateau phase, followed by the orgasm phase and a resolution phase. The plateau phase "describes a high degree of sexual arousal that occurs prior to reaching the threshold levels required to trigger orgasm" (Kolodny et al., 1979, p. 12). Time and again, Masters and Johnson have stressed that "it is important to recognize that the various phases of the response cycle are arbitrarily defined, are not always clearly demarcated from one another, and may differ considerably both in one person at different times and between different people" (p. 7). The well-known diagrams of the model "are only schematic conceptualizations of commonly observed physiologic patterns" (p. 9). Masters and Johnson very carefully describe how sexual response comes about: "Excitation occurs as a result of sexual stimulation, which may be either physical or psychic in origin. Stimulation arising in situations without direct physical contact is neither unusual nor unexpected, since many physiologic processes of the body occur as a result of thought or emotion" (p. 9). The purpose of the excitement/plateau/orgasm/resolution (EPOR) diagram is not to comprehensively reflect sexual response; rather, its use is restricted to illustration and to being a helpful guide in discussions about sexual response and some sexual dysfunctions.

In their physiological research, Masters and Johnson (1964) studied volunteers who were willing to accept and give various forms of sexual stimulation and who were also willing to uninhibitedly respond to that stimulation. Once they began to treat people with sexual dysfunctions, they used selection procedures to assure the same willingness in their patients to accept stimulation and to respond to it (Masters & Johnson, 1970). However, Masters and Johnson's original model was unable to accommodate desire disorders. Adoption of these treatment procedures in sex therapy quickly brought to light that the crucial prerequisite for success is willingness to engage in sexual interaction. Now, patients had to be both motivated for treatment and for sex. Thus, the old impotentia concupiscentiae reappeared under the name of "desire disorder" or "inhibited sexual desire." A desire (D) phase was added to the EPOR model, which then became the DEPOR model. Kaplan (1995) apparently wished to delete the plateau phase, which results in a DEOR model. Kaplan's work inspired the *DSM* construction of sexual function (American Psychiatric Association, 1994).

More Models and Psychology

There have been several attempts to study sexual function within an information processing framework (Everaerd, 1995). Several of these models of sexual function are discussed below.

Sexual function has been described as a sequence of physiological and psychological events. *DSM-IV* proposes a three-phase sequence consisting of desire, excitement, and orgasm (American Psychiatric Association, 1994) These phases are to some extent independent, although they also occur in a positive feedback fashion. Not only does the initial stimulus evoke a response, but also, under many conditions of sustained attention to that stimulus, the magnitude of the response is enhanced. Sexual desire is thought to increase to the extent that it cascades into, or triggers sexual excitement. To trigger orgasm, a higher level of excitement is necessary.

Both discrete and continuous processing have to be considered in a description of the sexual response cycle. Processing is discrete when desire has to occur before excitement can come about. It is continuous when desire and excitement co-occur or when one phase cascades into the other. A review of the literature makes clear that there is no satisfactory model to account for the response cycle as a whole; however, there are a number of attempts to explain the separate phases. In addition, attention to the different phases has not been well balanced. Most attention has been given to the excitement phase. Recently, there has been an increase in studies on sexual desire. Studies on orgasm are sparse. Further, more research effort has been devoted to male sexual function and dysfunction than to female sexual function and dysfunction.

Sexual Desire.   Until Moll's publication in 1897, the sexual impulse was seen as the expression of a "need of evacuation" (of male semen), or as a biologically driven impulse to reproduce. Moll proposed to distinguish between two component drives: first, the impulse of detumescence is aimed at the relief of tension in the sexual organs, and second, the impulse of contrectation is the instinct to approach, touch, and kiss another person, usually of the opposite sex (Ellis, 1933). The adequacy of such views has been challenged by evidence from several lines of investigation, including phyletic comparisons, effects of castration, and research on the periodicity of sexual desire (Hardy, 1964; Singer & Toates, 1987). As Beach (1956) concluded: "No genuine tissue or biological needs are generated by sexual abstinence. . . . What is commonly confused with a primary drive associated with sexual deprivation is in actuality sexual appetite, and this has little or no relation to biological or physiological needs" (p. 4).

Although there may not be an innate sexual impulse, conditions most likely exist that are innately pleasurable (e.g., local stimulation of the genitals and the experience of orgasm) (Hardy, 1964). According to Hardy, these conditions "form the constitutional base for the elaboration of sexual appetite" (p. 7). In his theory of sexual motivation, Hardy postulates that sexual motives are based on learned expectations; the learning is a result of actual experiences or imaginal processes. The pleasure that accompanies genital stimulation continues throughout life as an affective base for motivational development; many stimuli may become associated with it and may serve as cues leading to the elicitation of sexual desire (Hardy, 1964). On the other hand, habituation processes can occur in many sexual areas wherein the repetition of a given activity produces a diminished affective response (Beach, 1956). Sexual motives are not restricted to the learning of positive expectations (the "approach" type); motives may also be avoidant (as a result of negative expectations). However, most of the motivated behavior is ambivalent, based on a mixture of positive and negative expectations. Sources of negative affective expectations, for example, social sanctions and feelings of guilt, provoke inhibition or concealment of sexual expression.

Hardy's (1964) distinction between sexual motives fits well with Byrne's (1986) conception of erotophilia-erotophobia. Byrne also presumes the existence of an innate mechanism of sexual arousal (that is responsive to tactile stimulation) and claims that all human beings are probably born with erotophilic or positive emotional responses to sex. According to Byrne, the acquisition of positive (erotophilic) and negative (erotophobic) emotional responses to sex involves the pairing of sexual cues with emotion-producing reward or punishment.

The domain of sexual motivation also includes the study of sexual arousability, which has been defined as the individual's propensity for arousal given an adequate source of sexual stimulation. In Whalen's (1966) energetic view, sexual arousal (the current state of sexual excitement) and sexual arousability (the rate at which an individual approaches maximal arousal) together define sexual motivation. He distinguishes motivation from sexual activity (e.g., reported fantasy and desire) because sexual behavior can demonstrate motivation but is not part of motivation. Whalen is inspired by models that hypothesize the interaction of drive (arousal) and habit (behavior). According to Bancroft (1989), sexual arousability ("central arousability") is, together with cognition (e.g., internal imagery) and affect (mood states), one of the three dimensions of sexual appetite. In his view, sexual arousability points to a neurophysiological mechanism that determines the sensitivity to the sexual response system (its central and genital components) to internal and external stimuli. High arousability might imply a high sensitivity to external cues, revealing itself through an increased likelihood of central and genital responses. These responses could, in turn, lead to an increase in sexual thoughts and the experience of sexual appetite or desire.

Both Whalen (1966) and Bancroft (1989) view hormonal (i.e., androgen) factors as important determinants of sexual arousability. After reviewing the data available in 1966, Whalen concluded that androgens determine the responsiveness to erotic stimuli; they alter "the threshold for erotic stimulation." At present, however, the relationship between androgens and the sexual response appears to be much more complex. Recent empirical studies point to the possibility of two distinct sexual response systems: one that is androgen-dependent, and one that is not (Bancroft, 1989). As indicated in the section "Body in Context" above, erections during sleep and erections in response to erotic fantasy appear to be affected by androgen withdrawal and replacement. In contrast, mechanisms leading to erection in response to external erotic stimuli (e.g., erotic films) may remain intact despite androgen deficiency. Furthermore, the androgen-dependent system is believed to be linked with sexual desire; that is, levels of androgen seem to have an effect on sexual interest and sexual activity (Bancroft, 1989).

What are the implications of these findings for our understanding of the determinants of sexual arousability? According to Bancroft (1989), sleep erections give us "a 'window' into the central arousability system" (p. 77). This window allows the assessment of sexual arousability when it is "relatively independent of the effects of the environment or cognitive processes" (p. 72). Thus, the information obtained through this window relates primarily to the androgen-dependent response system itself, that is, to the responsivity of the sexual response system to internal stimuli (e.g., sexual imagery). The responsivity of the sexual response system to external stimuli depends, as is implied by Bancroft, on many other (i.e., cognitive and environmental) factors, the exact nature of this mechanism being less clear. In a discussion of changes in hormonal status in female to male transsexuality, it has been observed that two subjects with almost no androgen activity (due to androgen insensitivity) had the highest "libido" in the total study population (Gooren & Giltay, 1996). We may safely conclude at this point that this aspect of sexual arousability is less dependent on hormonal influences than was once believed.

Sexual motivation, to be a functional mechanism, has to respond both to the concerns of the organism (the energetic aspect) and to relevant environmental cues (the situational aspect). This interactive aspect has been highlighted in models of incentive-motivation (Singer & Toates, 1987). The energetic aspect *pushes* the individual toward the situation; the situation *pulls* the individual in its direction. The exploration of the mechanism of sexual motivation in humans has only recently begun. The push of motivation may increase through past experience, possibly in combination with various hormonal or other somatic factors. Motivation is dependent on the pull factors of the situation.

There is no motivation to be found in the organism; it is an emerging property that will come about when all conditions are fulfilled.

Sexual Arousal.   Sexual arousal may be produced by a multitude of external (e.g., visual and tactile) and internal (sexual imagery) stimuli. Furthermore, sexual arousal can be indexed with measures from three different response systems: verbal reports, physiological responses, and overt behavior (Lang, 1970). An adequate model or theory of sexual arousal should help explain how stimuli acquire sexual meaning, and how they lead to physiological (e.g., genital) responses, affective responses (e.g., conscious subjective experience of sexual arousal), and sexual behavior. Particular instances of discordance between response systems highlight the potential complexity of the mechanisms involved in the activation of sexual arousal.

Psychophysiological studies have shown that correlations between self-reported sexual arousal and genital responses are variable over situations, as well as between and within subjects (Janssen & Everaerd, 1993; Laan, Everaerd, van der Velde, & Geer, 1995b). Also, differential response patterns have been found between and within investigations. The phenomenon of discordance has led Bancroft (1989) to the conclusion that "we should not assume that, as the theoretical models of arousal have encouraged us to do in the past, central arousal and peripheral arousal are linked manifestations of the same process" (p. 73). Thus, a comprehensive theory of sexual arousal should not only explain how stimuli derive sexual meaning and bring about sexual responses, but it should also help explain the complex interrelationships between and among components of the sexual response.

Early models of sexual arousal postulate a preprogrammed sexual mechanism, which is activated by "adequate sexual stimulation" (Masters & Johnson, 1970). Such models have the appealing property of matching the experience that sexual arousal (in particular, the genital response) seems to occur in an "effortless" or "spontaneous" manner, as reported by many sexually functional men and women. These models, however, do not fully define the concept of "adequate sexual stimulation." Neither do they provide an explanation for the many regulatory processes related to voluntary control of the sexual response, nor can we understand the many variation in subjective experience and the complicated variation within and between subjects in relevant stimulus and response parameters.

Bancroft (1989) presented a theoretical schema for research on the sexual response, which he named the "psychosomatic circle of sex." Sexual appetite, central arousal, peripheral arousal, and genital response are considered to be the four principal elements in sexual arousal. In the model, a sequential order is introduced by postulating links between

(1) cognitive processes which influence (2) the limbic system and other parts of the brain, providing the neurophysiological substrate for our sexuality. This

system in turn influences the periphery via (3) the spinal cord and reflex centres within it, which, via peripheral somatic and autonomic nerves, control (4) genital responses as well as (5) other peripheral manifestations of sexual excitement. Perception, awareness and cognitive processing of these peripheral and genital changes complete the full circle. (p. 12)

The second component of sexual arousal, central arousal, refers to central nervous system (CNS) activation and attentional processes that underlie the cognitive processing of stimuli. Bancroft (1989) is not very specific, however, on the nature of the cognitive processes that activate the circle in response to sexual stimuli. For example, although tactile stimuli are considered an important source of sexual stimulation, he acknowledges, without further elaboration of the mechanisms involved, that "central processes can influence whether genital stimulation is perceived as erotic" (p. 66). Furthermore, although Bancroft recognizes the complexity of the interrelationships between and among the components of sexual arousal, he does not speculate about possible explanatory mechanisms. In general, psychological processes are considered important in this model, because cognitions mediate beliefs and expectations, and because of the role of awareness or perception of genital and somatic changes.

In 1977, Byrne introduced his Sexual Behavior Sequence model, which also defines arousal, affect, and cognition as the major determinants of sexual behavior. It suggests that the human sexual response may be contingent on both unlearned (e.g., tactile) and learned erotic cues. These cues may elicit physiological sexual arousal, affective (and evaluative) responses, and cognitive (i.e., informational, expectative, and imaginative) responses. Arousal affect and cognition guide and motivate instrumental acts. Such acts may have rewarding or punitive consequences that feed back into the system and influence subsequent behavior (Byrne, 1986). According to Byrne, the outcome of the sequence for an individual at a specific time depends on the relative magnitudes of the various internal and external forces that are operating with respect to this specific individual. Byrne's dimension of erotophobia-erotophilia, described earlier, is one of the central concepts in his sexual behavior sequence model. A large number of investigations have suggested the erotophobia-erotophilia dimension to be a useful one. For example, affective response has been shown to influence both individuals' willingness to experience erotic stimulation and the degree of subjective arousal and perception of genital sensation in response to erotic stimuli (Fisher, 1986). Byrne's model may be viewed as the most comprehensive attempt to date that delineates relevant interactive mechanisms of sexual arousal. However, as Rosen and Beck (1988) pointed out, given the complex network of feedback loops that it contains, the model has little predictive value.

Another recent model concerning interactive mechanisms in sexual arousal has been put forward by Barlow (1986). His working model of sexual dysfunction integrates much of what is known about the role of cognitive processes in sexuality and their consequences for emotional responses. Empirical evidence (reviewed by Barlow) has produced five factors that differentiate sexually functional from dysfunctional men:

> First, sexually dysfunctional subjects consistently evidence negative affect in the sexual context, whereas sexually functional subjects display more positive affect. Second, dysfunctional subjects consistently underreport their levels of sexual arousal and generally evidence diminished perceptions of control over their arousal. Third, dysfunctional men are not distracted by non-sexual-performance-related stimuli in that they evidence no decrease in erectile response, whereas sexually functional subjects are distracted and show decreases in sexual response. Fourth, dysfunctional men are distracted by performance-related sexual stimuli, whereas sexual arousal of sexually functional men is enhanced. Finally, anxiety inhibits sexual arousal in dysfunctional subjects but facilitates arousal in sexually functional subjects. (p. 146)

Together, these findings provided the basis for Barlow's model. The model is characterized by its emphasis on the interaction between autonomic activation and cognitive processes in the determination of functional and dysfunctional responding. The response patterns are conceptualized as forming either a positive or a negative feedback system. Both loops start with the perception of explicit or implicit demands for sexual performance. This perception results in either positive or negative affective evaluations, both triggering autonomic arousal. This increase in autonomic arousal enhances attention for those features (i.e., positive/erotic or negative/threatening) of the sexual situation that are most salient. Continued processing of erotic cues produces genital response and ultimately leads to sexual approach behavior. Continued processing of nonerotic issues (e.g., social consequences of not responding) produces a dysfunctional arousal pattern and ultimately leads to avoidance behavior.

A noticeable similarity between the models of Byrne (1986) and Barlow (1986) concerns the focus on affective and cognitive processes in the activation of functional and dysfunctional patterns of sexual arousal. Both models place special emphasis on the processing of erotic cues and the perception of physiological activation as mediators of the male sexual response. The perception of physiological activation (awareness of peripheral and genital changes) is also considered to be a prominent determinant of sexual arousal in Bancroft's (1989) model. Thus, in each of the models described, psychological (affective and cognitive) processes are perceived as an important window for our comprehension of the mechanism of sexual arousal.

Orgasm. It is generally agreed that we know very little about the neurophysiological mechanism of orgasm and the experience of orgasm. The latter seems to require input from spinal mechanisms to higher spinal and brain levels. Sensory information from the contracting muscles seems to contribute to the intensity of the experience. The existence of a separate central mechanism for orgasm is uncertain. In a few psychological studies, there has been some interest in orgasm as an altered state of consciousness and in the effects of focused and divided attention as determinants of the experience of orgasm (Dekker, 1993).

Motivation.   In our lab, we have been looking for metaphorical windows on activation and regulation of sexual motivation. From the onset, we looked for paradigms that would allow us to study action tendencies, stimulus intensity, and regulatory processes.

Action tendencies can be studied in:

Subjective reports about felt action tendencies or felt desire

The valence of sexual stimuli, which can be demonstrated with the startle paradigm, in which the defensive eye blink is modulated by positive or negative emotional stimuli (Lang, 1995)

Motor preparation, which can be demonstrated through the modulation of T-reflexes (Achilles tendon) by emotional stimuli. (We have opened the window of T-reflexes, as will be explained in a moment.)

Stimulus intensity has been a focus in a number of studies (e.g., Laan, Everaerd, & Evers, 1995a). It has become clear that sexual stimuli can be classified in a rank order that predicts intensity of physiological responses as well as that of subjective responses. Another approach to variation in stimulus intensity is the incentive motivation paradigm, which predicts that stimuli become more attractive through abstinence (Singer & Toates, 1987). Regulatory processes are numerous and, to a large extent, may be unconscious. However, our preliminary approach is to ask people about their tactical considerations when confronted with their own desires or the desires of other people.

Action Tendencies as Demonstrated in Motor Preparation.   From a functional perspective, sexual arousal is the first step in the unwinding energetics of sexual response. Autonomic nervous system (ANS) efferent activity has been the most widely used parameter for monitoring the presence and the intensity of the sexual response (Janssen & Everaerd, 1993; Laan & Everaerd, 1995b). As energetics develop, it is to be expected that early (somatic) motor preparation can be observed. To monitor early motor preparation, one may use modulation of reflexes by emotional arousal, including sexual arousal (Bonnet, Decety, Jeannerod, & Requin, 1997; Brunia & Boelhouwer, 1988). To this end, we were able to bring together the work on the T-reflex modulation of the Tilburg psychophysiology group and the Amsterdam sex and emotions research group's experience with studies of the sexual response. In a pilot study, we explored the modulation of T-reflexes by sexual arousal and anxiety.

Bonnet et al. (1997) studied the modulation of T-reflexes during the presentation of pictures from the International Affective Picture System (Lang, Öhman, & Vaitl, 1988). Pictures were designed to induce emotions varying in valence (positive to negative) and in intensity (low to high). Similar to what has been said about the sexual response, Bonnet et al. reasoned that emotional responses are preparations for actions. Thus, motor preparation and facilitation of motor responses can be monitored as an aspect of emotional processing. This motor facilitation is nonspecific relative to valence; no differences in the modulation of T-reflexes were found between negative and positive emotional states. As was expected, increasing emotional intensity resulted in increased reflex amplitudes.

Using, a somewhat different approach to induce emotional states, we used stimuli that had been explored in our earlier studies of sexual response (Laan et al., 1995a). The stimuli consisted of sexual, anxiety-inducing, sexually threatening, and neutral film clips. We expected the neutral film to have no modulating effects on the T-reflex. The other film clips were expected to facilitate T-reflexes, and we had no reason to expect a differential response.

In a study with a small sample of female students, we found that induced emotions indeed modulate T-reflex amplitude, whereas the neutral induction does not show this effect. As expected, there was no difference between anxiety and sexual film clips. In a second study, again with women, we induced sexual arousal with increasingly intense sexual stimuli. As expected, T-reflex amplitude increased with intensity of sexual stimulus.

An adequate sexual stimulus, a stimulus that matches an individual's sensitivity, will elicit several responses. These responses will get more intense depending on the significance of the stimulus (stimulus intensity) and on the allocation of attention (Mook, 1996; van der Molen, 1996). Both response facilitation and inhibition will determine the outcome. Once the individual is aware of his or her sexual arousal, he or she may indulge in a further attentional focus on sexual stimuli and look for more and other sexual stimuli or cognitively elaborate on sexual fantasies. The felt desire to act on the excitement will grow, and when a partner is available, sexual expression may continue in interaction with this partner. The gist of our model is exemplified when someone engages in the process of increasing excitement without conscious inhibitory regulation. Confronted with an unwilling partner, the individual may feel the strong imbalance between desire to sexually act and its social impossibility.

SEXUAL DYSFUNCTIONS

In this section, we review the *DSM-IV* dysfunctions and possible etiologies. First, we discuss some worries. After that, attempts at categorization of sexual problems are described. Next is a discussion of etiology and diagnostic procedures, followed by treatment of sexual dysfunctions.

WORRIES: TRY, TRY, TRY

Of course, there are very serious sexual problems with complicated etiologies and astounding pathophysiology or biographies. Still, those who have practiced sexology for some time know that patients worry about body parts, about performance, and about experience. Accepting the patient's worries and being able to give accurate information are prerequisites for helping people with sexual problems.

Frequency

Inhibited sexual desire is a common sexual problem. The (self) diagnosis rests on a conviction about "normal" desire and the "normal" frequency of making love. More important, desire predicts action. What is the reference for comparisons about frequency? In older works, it is always intercourse; one or two times per week is reported by 78% of respondents (Matussek, 1971). Jokingly, some therapists use the following rule: under 25, twice daily; between 25 and 35, try weekly; between 35 and 45, try weekly; between 45 and 55, try weekly; 55 and on, try, try, try. The joke is relevant because it points to the pressure to solve desire problems by prescribing how much desire there should be. But frequency follows desire, and not the other way around. Desire will vary with sexual sensitivity and availability of attractive partners, and will generally decrease in long-lasting relationships and with age (Everaerd & Laan, 1995).

Penis Too Short

We should always ask: Too little or too short in relation to what? Satisfying the partner? Visually or through coital stimulation? In terms of illusions about potency and penile volume or length? In terms of identity problems? There is more variation in length when the penis is flaccid than when it is erect. Length and circumference of the penis may contribute to the quality of the partner's experience, but this may depend on increased sensory stimulation as well as on idiosyncratic subjective appraisals. Most worries about length and volume are caused by "penile illusions." These may result from subjective constructions or from being uninformed about anatomy and the physiology of the sexual response.

Passion and Vigor

Older men, but also men who have had genital surgery, may become aware of changes in the vigor of their erections or the orgasmic contractions. In some cases, they refer to their earlier experience when they became "a little bit unconscious" through orgasm. The French refer to this phenomenon as *le petit mort*. Passion and vigor are part and parcel of very intense emotional experiences that will occur only under particular conditions such as infatuation, long periods of abstinence, and certain disinhibited states (e.g., being on holiday). Sometimes, passion and vigor refer only to vocal exclamations and muscular orgasmic spasms that people have witnessed in movies. People tend to compare such behavior to their partner's amount of desire and his or her expressions of passion.

DIAGNOSIS AND CATEGORIZATION

"If you refer to a dysfunction in something such as a relationship or someone's behavior, you mean that it is different from what is considered to be normal. . . . If someone has a physical dysfunction their body is not working properly" (Cobuild, 1995, p. 520). What is dysfunctional depends on function, and in this section, the relevant domain is functions of sex: attraction/bonding, lust/satisfaction, and reproduction. Recently, the norms shifted from a focus on reproduction to a focus on performance. We will distinguish dysfunctions of attraction/bonding and lust/satisfaction.

What is considered normal? If something is outside the normal range, is it then necessary to offer treatment? Often, there is no simple answer to these questions. Take as an example oral-genital contacts, an apparently normal kind of sexual interaction. Is it abnormal when a woman or a man does not like to perform oral stimulation of the penis? Many people do it, but how do they like it? Geer and Broussard (1990) demonstrated with Bentler's Gutmann scales of sexual interactions that men and women will rank items of sexual actions, varying from kissing, caressing over clothes, caressing under clothes, to intercourse, almost in the same order. So, to a large extent, they agree on what comes next in making love. The implicit supposition is that this rank order is also the rank order of lustfulness, pleasure, and excitement. Fair enough. However, Geer and Broussard doubted this and subsequently, using a paired comparison, asked their subjects to rank sexual acts in the order in which they found them sexually arousing. The results were surprising: there was a high correlation of both rank orders for men; for women, a low correlation was found. This was due to the ranking of actions that involved manual or oral manipulation of the genitals. These acts were turn offs for most women (Geer & Broussard, 1990). Why do women do things that are not in themselves sexually rewarding and may even be aversive? Is it to please the partner? Is it for his pleasure? Of course, it is also possible that there are other nonsexual rewards.

Description of Sexual Dysfunctions in DSM-IV

Since the introduction of *DSM-III*, the sexual response cycle (EPOR or DEOR) has been the frame of reference to distinguish sexual dysfunctions. In the current *DSM-IV* (American Psychiatric Association [APA], 1994), the description of the sexual response cycle includes subjective experience and "accompanying" physiological changes. In the defining criteria of some sexual dysfunctions, *DSM-IV* as compared to *DSM-III-R* no longer specifies subjective experience.

Hypoactive sexual desire disorder (302.71) is the "persistently or recurrently deficient (or absent) sexual fantasies and desire for sexual activity. The judgment of deficiency or absence is made by the clinician, taking into account factors that affect sexual functioning, such as age and the context of the person's life" (APA, 1994, p. 498). *DSM-IV* does not specify physiological changes that accompany fantasies or desire. Thinking about past sexual experiences, daydreaming about an attractive person, and sexual fantasies arouse the sexual system (Janssen & Everaerd, 1993; Laan et al., 1995; Leitenberg & Henning, 1995). Even without sustained attention for these cognitive activities, genital physiological changes might be observed. With sustained attention, genital response increases; when it reaches awareness, desire will ensue. There is no urge or desire without physiological sexual arousal in functional men. There may be desire for desire, but this condition is not meant in the definition of the diagnosis. The distinction in *DSM-IV* between desire disorders and arousal disorders is unclear, because arousal is a common denominator (Everaerd & Laan, 1995).

Sexual aversion disorder (302.79) is a desire disorder. The essential feature is the "persistent or recurrent extreme aversion to, and avoidance of, all (or almost all) genital sexual contact with a sexual partner" (APA, 1994, p. 500). Someone with this diagnosis typically reports anxiety, fear, or disgust when confronted with a sexual opportunity with a partner.

Male erectile disorder (302.72) is an arousal disorder. "The essential feature . . . is a persistent or recurrent inability to attain or to maintain until completion of the sexual activity, an adequate erection" (APA, 1994, p. 502). Subjective complaints were deleted as a diagnostic criterion to disallow a diagnosis based only on subjective experience. However, having an erection without the experience of subjective excitement is problematic. Men with sexual problems often underestimate their physiological arousal, that is, erections (Barlow, 1986).

Male orgasmic disorder (302.74) is the "persistent or recurrent delay in, or absence of, orgasm following a normal sexual excitement phase during sexual activity that the clinician, taking into account the person's age, judges to be adequate in focus, intensity, and duration" (APA, 1994, p. 509). Note that both absent and delayed orgasms may be accounted for in this diagnosis. When orgasm follows too quickly upon "normal" excitement, the next diagnosis has to be given.

Premature ejaculation (302.75) is the "persistent or recurrent ejaculation with minimal sexual stimulation before, on, or shortly after penetration and before the person wishes it. The clinician must take into account factors that affect duration of the excitement phase, such as age, novelty of the sexual partner or situation, and recent frequency of sexual activity" (APA, 1994, p. 511).

There is no diagnosis for the resolution phase, although some men may complain of headaches or a painful penis (Ferini-Strambi et al., 1996; Kaplan, 1993).

Dyspareunia (302.76) is one of the sexual pain disorders. It is "recurrent or persistent genital pain associated with sexual intercourse in either a male or female" (APA, 1994, p. 513).

The defensive spasm of the outer third of the vaginal musculature (vaginismus, 306.51) has a counterpart in anal sphincter contraction in some homosexual men (Everaerd & Dekker, 1982; Paff, 1985).

Etiology

We think that a close look at the *DSM-IV* description of the sexual response makes clear that the preferred point of view is a psychophysiological one. This is consistent with the view we described in the section on sexual pathways and sexual function. Moreover, it elucidates the futility of the psychogenic-biogenic controversy that for a long time dominated debates in sex research about etiology and pathophysiology. From the outset, we have proposed that there are different perspectives (body, emotion, culture), and to explain phenomena in the sexual domain, it may help to bring one perspective to the foreground. Men generally prefer explanations from the body perspective rather than from the emotion perspective. Recently, an enormous effort has been put forth in understanding the physiology of erection with no match in the striving for knowledge about vasocongestion and lubrication. Female disorders are preferentially explained within the emotional and social/cultural perspective. Why do we have this tendency to explain male problems with biological theory and female problems with psychological or social theory? Answers may range from the vulgar, unemancipated "men must perform and have to take initiative," or deplorable machine metaphors, to sophisticated explanations from evolutionary psychology. It is beyond the scope of this chapter to elaborate on this topic.

Pathway and Function Explanations of Etiology

We distinguished neuroanatomical and neurochemical contributions to sexual pathways and hence to sexual function. There are no adequate epidemiological data to estimate the prevalence and the causation of sexual dysfunction in the domain of neuroanatomy or neurochemistry, or in the genital tissues.

Laumann, Gagnon, Michael, and Michaels (1994) found in a random sample of 1,346 men that 3% reported pain during sex, 8.1% did not find sex pleasurable, 8.3% were unable to reach orgasm, 15.8% lacked interest in sex, 17% had anxieties about performance, 28.5% climax too early, and 10.4% are unable to sustain an erection. In the Massachusetts Male Aging Study of 1,209 40- to 70-year-old men, a different and higher prevalence was found for impotence (Feldman, Goldstein, Hatzichristou, Krane, & McKinlay, 1994). Complete impotence was found in 9.6% of the men, moderate impotence in 25.2%, and minimal impotence in 17.2%. The complete impotence group reported no sexual activity, no full erections, and no morning erections. There was a clear relation between age and probability of impotence. Having a disease clearly contributed to impotence probability. Compared with the 9.6% of men with complete impotence in the total sample, of the men with treated diabetes, 28% had complete impotence, those with treated heart disease 39%, and those with treated hypertension 15%. Percentages were reported for some untreated diseases: untreated ulcer 18%, untreated arthritis 15%, and untreated allergy 12%.

Clearly, there is considerable impact from disease. This may be due to a large number of factors, such as impaired neural signal conduction and processing, the interference of drugs (Crenshaw & Goldberg, 1996), decreased sexual sensitivity associated with endocrine diseases, and vascular and muscular defects. Some mental disorders also interfere seriously with sexual function (Glennon, 1990).

It is essential to consider the direct biological influence of disease on sexual pathways and function, but as important is the impact of the experience of illness. Disease may change body presentation and body esteem; ideal sexual scenarios may be disturbed by constraints that accompany illness. In many patients, sexual desire may decrease in connection with grief about the loss of normal health and uncertainty about illness outcome (Schover & Jensen, 1988). It is evident that there is a two-way interaction: bodily changes and diseases moderate cognitions, and cognition influences bodily function.

Sexual Function and Psychological Explanations

As in medical sex research, psychological researchers have put most of their effort into exploring erectile mechanisms, and much less into desire, orgasm, or resolution. Psychologists have chosen to study sexual function and the etiology of sexual dysfunction from different perspectives. It has been clear for a very long time that one's perception of sexual situations is primarily determined by personal experience, and to a lesser extent by the influence of culture (e.g., Freud, 1953).

Memory for Sexual Experiences. Autobiographical memory may uncover which meanings are attached to sexuality. These may be memories that are not easily and consciously retrieved because the crucial aspect is conditioned. Hans Eysenck (1972) used to recall the story of a patient who was unable to achieve orgasm in his bedroom, until he discovered that the wallpaper reminded him of his parents' bedroom. Changing the wallpaper solved his problem. These conditioned aspects of sexual stimuli and sexual situations in general have been called fetishistic when they have a positive valence and antifetishistic when they have a negative valence. Both may be bothersome when they inhibit sexual response toward a sincerely loved partner. People may not be aware of these turn-ons and turnoffs (Geer & Manguno-Mire, 1996).

There may be very negative experiences that are not recalled or not connected with the current sexual relationship. It is very disturbing to recognize that a current partner unwillingly evokes sad memories that may preclude sexual desire or excitement. These memories may also elicit very negative emotions of resentment without conscious recall of the source of these emotions (Janssen & Everaerd, 1993).

Relationship and Communication in Sexual Interactions. "If only we loved each other, sex would evolve spontaneously," some people conclude in desperation. Many therapists approach sexual problems in the same vein, and their diagnosis of the specific sexual problem is formulated in such terms as "bad and destructive relationship" or "immature partners." Of course, conflicting relationships easily disturb positive mood, which may be a precondition for sexual overtures. For most people, emotions connected with conflicts detract from erotic and sexual feelings (Heiman, Epps, & Ellis, 1995).

Masters and Johnson (1970) proposed that the couple rather than individual patient should be considered as the unit of analysis. In their introduction to the recent study about sexual behavior in the United States, Laumann et al. (1994) support this point of view:

> The objective of such [biological and psychological] research is to answer questions about why an individual exhibits certain sexual behaviors. But this line of inquiry can reveal only part of the story. . . . Sex involves negotiation and interplay, the expectation and experience of compromise. There is competition; there is co-operation. (p. 5)

Let us elaborate a bit on relationship factors and sexual desire. From a cognitive view on emotion and motivation mechanisms, it is not difficult to understand that different appraisals will eventually result in different emotional experiences. In the course of individual development and in the course of the development of relationships, numerous meanings may become associated with sexual situations and with the automatic and strategic aspects of the sexual response process. Thus, a sexual situation may function as a vehicle for many different positive and negative emotions and action tendencies connected with these different emotions. There may be as many motives related to sexual situations as there are attributable meanings. Levin (1994) provides a summary of motives that helps to illuminate this point:

> Coitus is undertaken not only for pleasure and procreation but also to degrade, control and dominate, to punish and hurt, to overcome loneliness or boredom, to rebel against authority, to establish one's sexuality, or one's achieving sexual competence (adulthood), or to show that sexual access was possible (to "score"), for duty, for adventure, to obtain favours such as a better position or role in life, or even for livelihood. Similarly, other sexual activities such as oral genital sex can be used to avoid coitus, as an act of degradation, or to give and receive pleasure, and not least, as an expression of love. (p. 125)

Several or all of these motives may fuel sexual motivation, but they may also kill it. To satisfy nonsexual motives, sexual desire is not strictly necessary.

One may wonder at the robustness of sexual response in confrontation with so many, apparently nonsexual motives. Motives may be unrelated, or they may mutually inhibit or facilitate each other. We think that in sexual situations, many nonsexual motives are associated with the rules for access to a partner. They may light the fire in one partner, but they may end whatever is left of sexual desire in the other.

Information Processing and Sexual Emotions. One would predict that a patient with a sexual disorder when confronted with a sexual situation will report meaning (cognitions) that predicts negative emotions, erectile failure, and avoidance of the sexual situation. An interesting point is that functional males, as compared with females, seem to be limited in the conscious emotional experience of sexual situations. Whereas women report many other positive and negative emotions concurrent with sexual excitement, reports of men are almost exclusively limited to sexual excitement (Dekker & Everaerd, 1989).

This selectivity in men's sexual experience may be attributed to the contribution of sensations in the genitalia. The peripheral feedback generated by vasocongestion may act as a specific indicator of the relevant meaning to be processed ("I feel that this is sexual"). The contrast between men and women would then be that in subjective experience, women process more situational cues and men more physiological cues. It is not easy to decide whether males are preoccupied with genital sensations, or whether peripheral feedback dominates the quality (content) and intensity of sexual experience. In both instances, men will be vulnerable to a weakening of sensations from the penis.

In emotion research, the contribution of peripheral feedback to emotions as they are subjectively experienced is still debated. For subjective sexual experience, this contribution is clear when considering more intense levels of subjective experience, and is most probable in the experience of orgasm. With less intense experience, the contribution of peripheral feedback to sexual experience is uncertain. There are some data to substantiate this. First, correlations between self-reported sexual excitement and penile engorgement are variable over situations as well as between and within subjects. Second, in a study using a habituation paradigm, O'Donohue and Geer (1985) found low correlations between physiological and subjective responses. Physiological response seems to habituate readily, whereas subjective response does not decrease at the same rate. Further, it has been observed that functional men tend to overestimate their genital arousal, whereas men with sexual dysfunction underestimate theirs (Barlow, 1986).

Conscious cognitive interference (e.g., worries, fear of failure) probably takes place in a late stage of the perceptual process. Further development of sexual responding is then inhibited, although there is some initial responding. Conceptually, this state of affairs is quite different from a very early association between a "sexual" stimulus and cues for nonsexual emotions (e.g., anxiety or depression). In the latter case, possibly as a result of conditioning, no initial sexual response will result.

Psychological theories on erectile dysfunction have emphasized the role of conscious cognitions. Theorizing started from the observations of Masters and Johnson (1970), which were still noted in the associated features section of *DSM-III-R*: "Almost invariably a fear of failure and the development of a 'spectator' attitude (self-monitoring), with extreme sensitivity to the reaction of the sexual partner, are present" (American Psychiatric Association, 1987, p. 292). Conscious cognitive interference has been explored both in experimental and treatment studies. These studies show that inhibition of subjective excitement and penile engorgement may be prevented by avoiding sexually irrelevant negative thoughts (Barlow, 1986). Later, these studies will be reviewed in some detail.

There is no evidence available on the role of conditioned inhibition in erectile disorders. However, there have been some attempts at conditioning penile tumescence. Generally, conditioning effects were weak (Geer, O'Donohue, & Schorman, 1986). Erectile disorders that are difficult to treat may benefit from a counterconditioning approach. However, counterconditioning may not be useful in instances of a more general inhibition sexual response that serves as a psychological defense. Anecdotal evidence shows that incidents of erectile failure may prevent confrontations with painful emotional experiences. This point is illustrated by a man who complained of erectile failure with his third sexual partner. His first and second partners both had died of genital cancer, but according to this patient, these dramatic events were unrelated to his erectile problem. In many attempts with his third partner, he experienced no response whatsoever. His response to masturbation, when alone, remained intact. "There is really no way to understand why I fail with her," he concluded.

Barlow's (1986) model of erectile dysfunction has already been mentioned in the section on sexual functioning. That which is felt or experienced in confrontations with "sexual" stimuli, according to Barlow, is specifically determined by peripheral physiological feedback. Thus, when confronted with sexual stimuli, expectations, or demands for sexual performance, the individual may feel threatened, hurt, and rejected. These negative emotions will be fed back into the system, eventually resulting in erectile failure in the short term and avoidance of such confrontations in the long term. In functional subjects, the dominant experience is sexual excitement and positive emotions. The co-occurrence of autonomic arousal feeds back on and facilitates the processing of sexual cognitions, and so further enhances sexual response. Thus, dysfunctional subjects seem to focus on or attend to task-irrelevant stimuli, at least when they wish to become sexually aroused. It is also possible, of course, that functional subjects discard or ward off threatening aspects of the situation. Eventually, they are "safe" from these threats by focusing on their sexual excitement, which obscures their emotional problems.

In the literature, there have appeared long lists of possible psychological factors contributing to the etiology or maintenance of male sexual disorders (Hawton, 1991). These proposed factors stem from different sources, such as restrictive upbringing, relationship discord, and reaction to illness. The common pathway to erectile disorder seems to be the processing of negative emotions.

Etiological Factors in Specific Dysfunctions

Most of the dysfunctions may be understood and explained on the basis of the etiological factors described above. However, there are some unique etiological factors associated with specific disorders.

Desire Disorders. The most radical view in cases of hypoactive desire is that there is nothing to desire for, or that earlier desire is lost. Many people are able to connect this state of affairs with their ongoing cognitions (fantasies and thoughts) about the object of desire, although this confrontation may be harsh and difficult to accept. Certainly, it may be easier to have the disease "hypoactive desire" than to admit that you do not like your partner (Everaerd & Laan, 1995).

There are two areas to evaluate in the case of desire problems. The first is the sensitivity of the sexual system. Both biological (e.g., hypogonadism) and biographical (e.g., sexual abuse) factors should be considered. The second is the "sexual" situation (e.g., no positive fantasies about partner) that gives rise to the complaints.

Arousal Disorders. Arousal disorders may be characterized as disorders of feeling and flow. Many men have problems attending to their feelings in sexual situations: "My penis should become hard when I want it to." This focus is on biological and behavioral performance, which is not a problem when the response is automatic and effortless. Once the response is disrupted, however, the only way to restore it is by attending to sexual feelings, without performance pressure.

Blood flow and vasocongestion in the penis and its neural control are important concerns in etiological evaluations. Numerous events may detract from attending to the sexual situation and sexual feelings. It is important to understand that attention to the stimulus is a sine qua non for response. For men with erectile problems, negative cognitions about sexual situations make sexual response improbable: "It should come when I want it"; "Will she blame me again for not loving her?" In most instances, these are not very sexy thoughts.

Orgasm Disorders. Too much (absent or delayed orgasm) or too little (premature ejaculation) control over the timing of orgasm typifies these disorders. Of course, when there is neural disease, sensory receptor thresholds may impair afferent signal conduction, and likewise, there may be disturbed efferent conduction (e.g., multiple sclerosis). In either case, patients tend to control their partners in ways that reinforce their problems. For example, men with delayed orgasm may try to stimulate their partners and thus shift the focus of their attention away from their own genitals, decreasing the likelihood of their own excitation. Men with premature ejaculation may direct their partners to minimize stimulation to help delay ejaculation without developing ejaculatory control.

However, the reasons for absent and delayed as well as premature ejaculation may be much more complicated. For example, prospect of pregnancy can be frightening for some men, resulting in very serious inhibitions. It is important to note that both disorders prevent men from intimately interacting with their partners.

Sexual Pain Disorders. When there is no disease, genital pain is often a consequence of mechanical friction when attempting penetration. In heterosexual coitus, this may be due to inadequate communication about the level of sexual excitement or the timing of coitus. In homosexual couples, it may be caused by improper lubrication of the anal meatus or because of anal sphincter contractions (similar to vaginismus in women). These contractions are a normal part of the defensive reflexes and should be taken as a sign of anxiety or fear of pain.

DIAGNOSTIC PROCEDURES

An ideal protocol for the assessment of erectile dysfunction should be constructed following theoretical and factual knowledge of the physiological, psychophysiological, and psychological mechanisms involved. The protocol then describes the most parsimonious route from presentation of complaints to effective therapy. It is relevant to consider not only financial costs, but also the nuisance to the patient caused by the suggested intervention. Strategic considerations in constructing protocols also depend on what is known about the rank order of most probable causes. This debate on strategies based on different presumed rank orders of causes underscores the need for theory and factual knowledge (Everaerd, 1993).

Clinical Interview

Assessment in a biopsychosocial context should start with a verification of the chief complaint. The aim of the initial clinical interview is to gather detailed information concerning current sexual functioning, onset of the sexual complaint, and the context in which the difficulty occurred. This information gathering may be aided by the use of a structured interview and paper-and-pencil measures regarding sexual history and functioning. An individual and conjoint partner interview, if possible, can provide additional relationship information and can corroborate data provided by the patient. The initial clinical interview should help the clinician in formulating the problem. It is important to seek the patient's agreement with the therapist's formulation of the problem. When such a formulation is agreed upon, the problem may guide further diagnostic procedures.

Many men with erectile dysfunction may be wary of psychological causes of their problem. Psychological causes seem to imply that the man himself is responsible for his problem. This may add to the threat to his male identity that he already experienced by not being able to function sexually. Considering the way a man may experience his problem, it can be expected that it will not be easy to explain to him the contribution of psychological factors. A clinician knowledgeable in biopsychosocial aspects of sexual functioning should be able to discuss the problem openly with the patient. Dysfunctional performance is meaningful performance in the sense that misinformation, emotional states, and obsessive concerns about performance inform the patient's "theory" of sexual functioning. When contrasting this information with what is known about variations in adequate sexual functioning, it is often clear that one cannot but predict that the patient must fail. For the clinician, a problem arises when, even with adequate stimulation and adequate processing of stimulus information according to the clinician's judgment, no response results, either at a physiological or a psychological level.

Psychophysiological Assessment

At this point, a number of assessment methods aimed at identifying different components or mechanisms of sexual functioning may be considered. In principle, two main strategies may be followed. First, although a psychological factor interfering with response cannot be inferred from the report of the patient, one can still suspect some psychological factor at work. Possibly, the patient is not aware of this factor; thus, he cannot report on it. Eliminating this psychological influence may result in adequate response. Second, perhaps, even with adequate (psychological) stimulation and processing, responding is prevented by physiological dysfunction. Physiological assessment may then aid in arriving at a diagnostic conclusion. The biopsychosocial approach predicts that it is inadequate to choose one of these strategies exclusively. The fact that sexual functioning is always psychophysiological functioning means that there may always be an unforeseen psychological or biological factor.

A psychophysiological protocol may incorporate any number of tasks that tap into the patient's information processing. In our lab, we have used tasks that originate from the work of Barlow (1986) in a protocol aimed at eliciting erections, which were monitored with circumference measures. Compared with clinical and other more invasive physical tests, the diagnostic accuracy—if problems are mainly caused by psychological factors—is about 80% (Janssen, Everaerd, van Lunsen, & Oerlemans, 1994).

Penile rigidity can be measured with a device that monitors radial rigidity by applying a predetermined force to a loop around the penis (Rigiscan by Urohealth Corporation). Changes in circumference reflect changes in radial diameter and rigidity (Rosen, 1998). Accuracy of waking erectile assessment (WEA) and Rigiscan measures in relation to diagnostic decisions is similar. A very simple and crude measure is the erectiometer. It consists of a felt collar that slides around the penis and is fastened to one end. The collar is calibrated in millimeters and will widen when force is applied by increasing circumference and pressure (Rosen, 1998). Rowland and colleagues reported a series of studies on tactile sensitivity of the penis (Rowland, 1998; Rowland, Geilman, Brouwer, & Slob, 1992). Men with premature ejaculation were found not to be hypersensitive to tactile stimulation. Details of psychophysiological measures for the sexual response system may be found in the *Handbook of Psychophysiology* (Geer & Janssen, in press).

TREATMENT OF SEXUAL DYSFUNCTIONS

The purpose of treatment is at least twofold: to improve the dysfunctional aspects of sexual response and to alleviate suffering and stress that accompany having a sexual disorder. Here we discuss treatments that are aimed at improving the dysfunction.

Medical Treatments of Male Sexual Dysfunctions

There is at this time no effective treatment to alleviate conditions associated with impaired neural conduction caused by disconnection (as in spinal cord injuries) or operations in the genital area (namely, prostate), and by peripheral or central neural disease (e.g., diabetes, multiple sclerosis, stroke). Recently, vascular (reconstructive) surgery to improve blood flow has been successful for a number of conditions. Mechanical devices to help attain erections (vacuum pump) or to provide continuous erections (penile implants) have been used.

Pharmacological treatment is on the increase. Testosterone may improve hypogonadal conditions. Hyperprolactinemia, caused by tumors of the pituitary, results in the production of high levels of prolactin, which inhibit the function of testosterone. Bromocryptine or similar drugs are used to alleviate these effects of prolactin. Corpora cavernosa smooth muscle relaxants are now widely used either in the form of injections, suppositories, or orally. As a treatment approach, injections have been relatively unsuccessful, resulting in fibrosis of the penis and eventual low compliance (Lottman, Hendriks, Vruggink, & Meuleman, 1998; Sundaram et al., 1997). Studies of oral and suppository administration are currently more in vogue (Goldstein et al., 1998; Wagner & Saenz de Tejada, 1998). It is as yet uncertain how these drugs will change clinical practice. For premature ejaculation, SSRIs have shown a salutory effect (Haensel, Klem, Hop, & Slob, 1998). What is to be expected in the next few years, in addition to the existing antiandrogen drugs, is the development of drugs that moderate central control of sexual response, in particular, drugs that modulate (hypoactive as well as hyperactive) sexual desire.

Psychological Treatments of Male Sexual Dysfunctions

There is a dearth of well-designed studies of the effects of medical treatments, and to our dismay, this is also true for psychological treatments, which are discussed below.

Approaches to Treatment.   The most important transformation of the treatment of sexual dysfunctions occurred after the publication of *Human Sexual Inadequacy* (Masters & Johnson, 1970). First of all, Masters and Johnson brought sex into the treatment of sexual problems. Before the publication of their seminal book, sexual problems were conceived as consequences of (nonsexual) psychological conflicts, immaturity, and relational conflicts. In most therapies for sexual problems, sex was not a topic of the therapeutic transactions. There were always things "underlying," "behind," and "besides" the sexual symptoms that deserved discussion. Masters and Johnson proposed to directly attempt to reverse the sexual dysfunction by a kind of graded practice and focus on sexual feelings. If sexual arousal depends directly on sexual stimulation, that very stimulation should be the topic of discussion. Here, the second important transformation occurred. A sexual dysfunction was no longer something pertaining to an individual; rather, it was regarded as a dysfunction of the couple. It was assumed they did not communicate in a way that allowed sexual arousal to occur when they intend to "produce" it. Masters and Johnson thus initially considered the couple as the "problem" unit. Treatment goals were associated with the couple concept: the treatment goal was for orgasm through coital stimulation. This connection between treatment format and goals was lost once Masters and Johnson's concept was used in common therapeutic practice. People came in for treatment as individuals. Male orgasm through coitus adequately fulfills reproductive goals, but it is not very satisfactory for many women because they do not easily reach orgasm through coitus.What has remained over the years since 1970 is a direct focus on dysfunctional sex and a focus on sexual sensations and feelings as a vehicle for reversal of the dysfunction.

What Masters and Johnson tried to achieve in their treatment model is a shift in their patients' focus of attention. We know now, from information-processing approaches to emotions, that attention to and evaluation of stimuli to a large extent determine processing and outcome (Frijda, 1986). In this chapter, we already touched on some examples of attentional focus and evaluation. Let us look at one of Masters and Johnson's interventions to elucidate this point. People with sexual dysfunctions tend to wait and look for the occurrence of feelings, instead of feeling what occurs. Hence, the spectator role. Their attention is directed toward something that is not there or does not exist, which is frustrating. In simplest form, Masters and Johnson proposed to redirect attention by using the following steps. First, they manipulate expectations by instructing the patient about what is allowed to occur and what is not. It is explained to the patient that nonsexual feelings are to be accepted as a way to accept sexual feelings later on, and therefore, sexual areas are excluded in the initial homework tasks. From a psychological point of view, this manipulation is ingenious; it directs attention away from sex—when you feel a caress on your arm, it may be pleasant, but (now) it is not sexual—however, at the same time, it defines sexual feelings as feelings in "sexual areas."

In this chapter, we cannot describe in any detail the large number of variations in approaches that build on Masters and Johnson's approach, nor the alternative approaches that have been developed. To attain a direct approach of sexual functioning, numerous variants of couple, communication, and group therapy have been used. Rational-Emotive Therapy has been used to change expectations and emotions. To remedy biographical memories connected with sexual dysfunction, psychoanalytic approaches have been used as well as cognitive behavior therapy approaches. There are specific interventions for some dysfunctions; for example, premature ejaculation has been treated with attempts at heightening the threshold for ejaculatory release (stop-start or squeeze techniques) (O'Donohue & Geer, 1993).

Validated Treatments for Male Sexual Dysfunctions.   Until recently, it was difficult to get an overview of treatments for sexual dysfunctions because any proposal about how to approach dysfunctions was valid. This has changed through the introduction of criteria for validated or evidence-based practice (American Psychological Association, 1995). From the timely review by O'Donohue, Swingen, and Dopke (in press) of psychotherapies for male sexual dysfunctions, it appears that the state of the art is far from satisfactory. Following the criteria of APA's Task Force, they found no controlled outcome studies for male orgasmic disorder, sexual aversion disorder, hypoactive sexual desire disorder, and dyspareunia in men. For premature ejaculation and for erectile disorder, there is evidence for the usefulness of psychological treatment. But effects are limited and often unstable over time.

Although we are firm supporters of the evidence-based practice movement, unqualified support would be disastrous for the practice of the treatment of sexual problems. The care for patients with sexual problems must be continued even without proof, according to the rules of "good clinical practice." The sensible clinician will learn to be very careful about any claims concerning either diagnostic procedures or treatments. Those engaged in research should understand that correct methodological doubts will not help a clinician to convince his or her patient of the usefulness of the treatment modality of choice.

CONCLUSION

Medical treatment, in particular, pharmacological treatment, is increasingly offering promising remedies for erectile disorder. However, these treatments are limited to smooth muscle relaxation and support for normal erectile processes. Of course, they do not change conflicted relationships. In addition, the contribution to the management of sexual problems remains to be established for medical treatment.

After a rise in interest in studies of psychological treatments in the 1970s and 1980s, there has been silence for about 10 years. Our interpretation is that this was caused by the unsatisfactory outcomes of these treatment-outcome studies. The trade-off between investment in these studies and outcome has not been very rewarding. Thus, the state of the art is unsatisfactory from the validated practice point of view.

REFERENCES

American Psychiatric Association. (1987). *Diagnostic and statistical manual of mental disorders* (3rd ed., rev.). Washington, DC: Author.

American Psychiatric Association. (1994). *Diagnostic and statistical manual of mental disorders* (4th ed.). Washington, DC: Author.

American Psychological Association. (1995). Training and dissemination of empirically-validated psychological treatments: Report and recommendations. *Clinical Psychologist, 48,* 3–24.

Bahrke, M.S., Yesalis, C.E., & Wright, J.E. (1996). Psychological and behavioural effects of endogenous testosterone and anabolic-androgenic steroids: An update. *Sports Medicine, 22,* 367–390.

Bancroft, J. (1989). *Human sexuality and its problems.* Edinburgh: Churchill Livingstone.

Bancroft, J., & Malone, N. (1995). The clinical assessment of erectile dysfunction: A comparison of nocturnal penile tumescence monitoring and intracavernosal injections. *International Journal of Impotence Research, 7,* 123–130.

Barlow, D.H. (1986). Causes of sexual dysfunction. *Journal of Consulting and Clinical Psychology, 54,* 140–148.

Beach, F.A. (1956). Characteristics of masculine sex drive. In M.R. Jones (Ed.), *Nebraska Symposium on Motivation* (pp. 1–31). Lincoln: University of Nebraska Press.

Bem, D.J. (1996). Exotic becomes erotic: A developmental theory of sexual orientation. *Psychological Review, 103,* 320–335.

Bermant, G. (1995). To speak in chords about sexuality. *Neuroscience and Biobehavioral Reviews, 19,* 343–348.

Bonnet, M., Decety, J., Jeannerod, M., & Requin, J. (1997). Mental simulation of an action modulates the excitability of spinal reflex pathways in man. *Cognitive Brain Research, 5,* 221–228.

Brunia, C.H.M., & Boelhouwer, A.J.W. (1988). Reflexes as a tool: A window in the central nervous system. *Advances in Psychophysiology, 3,* 1–67.

Burris, A.S., Banks, S.M., Carter, C.S., Davidson, J.M., & Sherins, R.J. (1992). A long-term, prospective study of the physiologic and behavioral effects of hormone replacement in untreated hypogonadal men. *Journal of Andrology, 13,* 297–304.

Byrne, D. (1977). Social psychology and the study of sexual behavior. *Personality and Social Psychology Bulletin, 3,* 3–30.

Byrne, D. (1986). Introduction. The study of sexual behavior as an interdisciplinary venture. In D. Byrne & K.K. Kelley (Eds.), *Alternative approaches to the study of sexual behavior.* London: Erlbaum.

Carani, C., Bancroft, J., Granata, A., Del-Rio, G., & Marrama, P. (1992). Testosterone and erectile function, nocturnal penile tumescence and rigidity, and erectile response to visual erotic stimuli in hypogonadal and eugonadal men. *Psychoneuroendocrinology, 17,* 647–654.

Cohen-Kettenis, P., Wafelbakker, F., & Slob, A.K. (1995). Seksuele onmtwikkeling en seksueel gedrag. In A.K. Slob, C.W. Vink, J.C.P. Moors, & W. Everaerd (Eds.), *Seksuologie voor de Arts* [Sexology for medical doctors]. Houten: Bohn, Stafleu, VanLoghum.

Crenshaw, T.L., & Goldberg, J.P. (1996). *Sexual pharmacology.* New York: Norton.

Dekker, J. (1993). Inhibited male orgasm. In W. O'Donohue & J.H. Geer (Eds.), *Handbook of sexual dysfunctions* (pp. 279–302). Boston: Allyn & Bacon.

Dekker, J., & Everaerd, W. (1989). Psychological determinants of sexual arousal: A review. *Behaviour Research and Therapy, 27,* 353–364.

Ellis, H. (1933). *Psychology of sex.* New York: New American Library.

Everaerd, W. (1993). Male erectile disorder. In W. O'Donohue & J.H. Geer (Eds.), *Handbook of sexual dysfunctions: Assessment and treatment* (pp. 201–224). Boston: Allyn & Bacon.

Everaerd, W. (1995). Information processing approach and the sexual response in human studies. In J. Bancroft (Ed.), *The psychopharmacology of sexual function and dysfunction* (pp. 175–184). Amsterdam, The Netherlands: Exerpta Medica.

Everaerd, W., & Dekker, J. (1982). Treatment of homosexual and heterosexual sexual dysfunction in male-only groups of mixed sexual orientation. *Archives of Sexual Behavior, 11,* 1–10.

Everaerd, W., & Laan, E. (1995). Desire for passion: Energetics of sexual response. *Journal of Sex and Marital Therapy, 21,* 255–263.

Eysenck, H.J. (1972). *Psychology is about people.* London: Penguin Press.

Feldman, H.A., Goldstein, I., Hatzichristou, D.G., Krane, R.J., & McKinlay, J.B. (1994). Impotence and its medical and psychosocial correlates: Results of the Massachusetts male aging study. *Journal of Urology, 151,* 54–61.

Ferini-Strambi, L., Oldani, A., Zucconi, M., Castronovo, V., Montorsi, F., Rigatti, P., & Smirne, S. (1996). Sleep-related painful erections: Clinical and polysomnographic features. *Journal of Sleep Research, 5,* 195–197.

Fisher, W.A. (1986). A psychological approach to human sexuality. In D. Byrne & K.K. Kelley (Eds.), *Alternative approaches to the study of sexual behavior* (pp. 313–371). London: Erlbaum.

Freud, S. (1953). *The standard edition of the complete psychological works of Sigmund Freud.* London: Hogarth Press.

Frijda, N.H. (1986). *The emotions.* Cambridge, England: Cambridge University Press.

Geer, J.H., & Broussard, D. (1990). Scaling sexual behavior and arousal: Consistency and sex differences. *Journal of Personality and Social Psychology, 58,* 664–671.

Geer, J.H., & Janssen, E. (in press). The sexual response system. In J. Cacioppo, L. Tassinari, & G. Bernston (Eds.), *Handbook of psychophysiology.* New York: Cambridge University Press.

Geer, J.H., & Manguno-Mire, G.M. (1996). Gender differences in cognitive processes in sexuality. *Annual Review of Sex Research, 7,* 90–124.

Geer, J.H., O'Donohue, W.T., & Schorman, R.H. (1986). Sexuality. In M.G.H. Coels, E. Donchin, & S.W. Porges (Eds.), *Psychophysiology: Systems, processes and applications.* New York: Guilford Press.

Gijs, L., & Gooren, L. (1996). Hormonal and psychopharmacological interventions in the treatment of paraphilias: An update. *Journal of Sex Research, 33,* 273–290.

Glennon, R.A. (1990). Serotonin receptors: Clinical implications. *Neuroscience and Biobehavioral Reviews, 14,* 35–47.

Goldstein, I., Lue, T.F., Padma-Nathan, H., Rosen, R.C., Steers, W.D., & Wicker, P.A. (1998). Oral sildanafil in the treatment of erectile dysfunction. *New England Journal of Medicine, 338,* 1397–1404.

Gooren, L.J.G., & Giltay, E.J. (1996). Risk associated with long-term androgen supplementation. In B.J. Oddens & A. Vermeulen (Eds.), *Androgens and the aging male* (pp. 205–222). New York: Parthenon.

Guyton, A.C. (1991). *Textbook of medical physiology.* Philadelphia: Saunders.

Haensel, S.M., Klem, T., Hop, W., & Slob, A.K. (1998). Fluoxetine and premature ejaculation: A double-blind, crossover, placebo-controlled study. *Journal of Clinical Psychopharmacology, 18,* 72–77.

Hardy, K.R. (1964). An appetitional theory of sexual motivation. *Psychological Review, 71,* 1–18.

Hawton, K. (1991). Sex therapy. *Behavioural Psychotherapy, 19,* 131–136.

Heiman, J.R., Epps, P.H., & Ellis, B. (1995). Treating sexual desire disorders in couples. In J.R. Jacobson & A.S. Gurman (Eds.), *Clinical handbook of couple therapy* (pp. 471–495). New York: Guilford Press.

Herbert, J. (1996). Sexuality, stress, and the chemical architecture of the brain. *Annual Review of Sex Research, 7,* 1–43.

Hillegaart, V., Alster, P., UvnasMoberg, K., & Ahlenius, S. (1998). Sexual motivation promotes oxytocin secretion in male rats. *Peptides, 19*, 39–45.

Issad, T., Strobel, A., Camoin, L., Ozata, M., & Strosberg, A.D. (1998, March 14). Does leptin signal for the onset of puberty in human? *Medicine Science*, 349–351.

Janssen, E., & Everaerd, W. (1993). Determinants of male sexual arousal. *Annual Review of Sex Research, 4*, 211–245.

Janssen, E., Everaerd, W., van Lunsen, R.H.W., & Oerlemans, S. (1994). Validation of a psychophysiological waking erectile assessment (WEA) for the diagnosis of male erectile disorder. *Urology, 43*, 686–696.

Jeannerod, M. (1997). *The cognitive neuroscience of action.* Oxford, England: Blackwell.

Kaplan, H.S. (1993). Post-ejaculatory pain syndrome. *Journal of Sex and Marital Therapy, 19*, 91–103.

Kaplan, H.S. (1995). *The sexual desire disorders: The dysfunctional regulation of sexual motivation.* New York: Brunner/Mazel.

Kennedy, S., & Over, R. (1990). Psychophysiological assessment of male sexual arousal following spinal cord injury. *Archives of Sexual Behavior, 19*, 15–27.

Kolodny, R.C., Masters, W.H., & Johnson, V.E. (1979). *Textbook of sexual medicine.* Boston: Little, Brown.

Laan, E., & Everaerd, W. (1995). Determinants of female sexual arousal: Psychophysiological theory and data. *Annual Review of Sex Research, 6*, 32–76.

Laan, E., Everaerd, W., & Evers, A. (1995). Assessment of female sexual arousal: Response specificity and construct validity. *Psychophysiology, 32*, 476–485.

Laan, E., Everaerd, W., van der Velde, J., & Geer, J.H. (1995). Determinants of subjective experience of sexual arousal in women: Feedback from genital arousal and erotic stimulus content. *Psychophysiology, 32*, 444–451.

Lane, R.M. (1997). A critical review of selective serotonin reuptake inhibitor–related sexual dysfunction: Incidence, possible aetiology and implications for management. *Journal of Psychopharmacology, 11*, 72–82.

Lang, P.J. (1970). Stimulus control, response control, and the desensitization of fear. In D.J. Levis (Ed.), *Learning approaches to therapeutic behavior change* (pp. 148–173). Chicago: Aldine.

Lang, P.J. (1995). The emotion probe: Studies of motivation and attention. *American Psychologist, 50*, 372–385.

Lang, P.J., Öhman, A., & Vaitl, D. (1988). *The international affective picture system.* Gainesville: University of Florida, Center for Psychophysiological Research.

Laumann, E.O., Gagnon, J.H., Michael, R.T., & Michaels, S. (1994). *The social organization of sexuality.* Chicago: University of Chicago Press.

Leitenberg, H., & Henning, K. (1995). Sexual fantasy. *Psychological Bulletin, 117*, 469–496.

Levin, R.J. (1994). Human male sexuality: Appetite and arousal, desire and drive. In C.R. Legg & D. Booth (Eds.), *Appetite: Neural and behavioral bases* (pp. 127–164). Oxford, England: Oxford University Press.

Lottman, P.E.M., Hendriks, J.C.M., Vruggink, P.A., & Meuleman, E.J.H. (1998). The impact of marital satisfaction and psychological counseling on the outcome of ICI-treatment in men with ED. *International Journal of Impotence Research, 10*, 83–87.

Martini, F. (1995). *Fundamentals of anatomy and physiology.* Englewood Cliffs, NJ: Prentice Hall.

Masters, W.H., & Johnson, V.E. (1964). *Human sexual response.* Boston: Little, Brown.

Masters, W.H., & Johnson, V.E. (1970). *Human sexual inadequacy.* Boston: Little, Brown.

Matussek, P. (1971). Funktionelle Sexualstörungen [Functional sexual disturbances]. In H. Giese (Ed.), *Die Sexualität des Menschen* [Sexuality of humans] (pp. 786–828). Stuttgart: Ferdinand Enke Verlag.

McCarthy, M.M., & Albrecht, E.D. (1996). Steroid regulation of sexual behavior. *Trends in Endocrinology and Metabolism, 7,* 324–327.

McClintock, M.K., & Herdt, G. (1996). Rethinking puberty: The development of sexual attraction. *Current Directions in Psychological Science, 5,* 178–183.

McKenna, K.E. (1998). Central control of penile erection. *International Journal of Impotence Research, 10,* S25–S34.

Middleman, A.B., & DuRant, R.H. (1996). Anabolic steroid use and associated health risk behaviours. *Sports Medicine, 21,* 251–255.

Moll, A. (1897/1898). *Untersuchungen über die libido sexualis* [Studies of sexual libido] (Vol. 1, parts 1 & 2). Berlin: Kronfeld.

Mook, D.G. (1996). *Motivation: The organization of action.* New York: Norton.

Nieuwenhuys, R. (1996). The greater limbic system, the emotional motor system and the brain. In G. Holstege, R. Bandler, & C.B. Saper (Eds.), *Progress in brain research* (Vol. 107, pp. 551–580). Amsterdam, The Netherlands: Elsevier.

O'Donohue, W.T., & Geer, J.H. (1985). The habituation of sexual arousal. *Archives of Sexual Behavior, 14,* 233–246.

O'Donohue, W.T., & Geer, J.H. (Eds.). (1993). *Handbook of sexual dysfunctions: Assessment and treatment.* Boston: Allyn & Bacon.

O'Donohue, W.T., Swingen, D.N., & Dopke, C.A. (in press). Psychotherapy for male sexual dysfunction: A review. *Clinical Psychology Review.*

Paff, B.A. (1985). Sexual dysfunction in gay men requesting treatment. *Journal of Sex and Marital Therapy, 11,* 3–18.

Palmert, M.R., Radovick, S., & Boepple, P.A. (1998, July). Leptin levels in children with central precocious puberty. *Journal of Clinical Endocrinology and Metabolism, 83,* 2260–2265.

Perovic, S., Djordjevic, M., & Djakovic, N. (1997). Natural erection induced by prostaglandin-E1 in the diagnosis and treatment of congenital penile anomalies. *British Journal of Urology, 79,* 43–46.

Pfaus, J.G., & Everitt, B.J. (1995). The psychopharmacology of sexual behavior. In F.J. Bloom & D.J. Kupfer (Eds.), *Psychopharmacology: The fourth generation of progress* (pp. 743–758). New York: Raven Press.

Pinker, S. (1997). *How the mind works.* London: Penguin Press.

Rosen, R.C. (1998). Sexual function assessment in the male: Physiological and self-report measures. *International Journal of Impotence Research, 10,* S59–S63.

Rosen, R.C., & Beck, J.G. (1988). *Patterns of sexual arousal.* New York: Guilford Press.

Rowland, D.L. (1995). The psychobiology of sexual function. In L. Diamant & R.D. McAnulty (Eds.), *The psychology of sexual orientation, behavior, and identity* (pp. 19–42). Westport, CT: Greenwood Press.

Rowland, D.L. (1998). A psychophysiological approach to assessing premature ejaculation. *International Journal of Impotence Research, 10,* S44–S48.

Rowland, D.L., Geilman, C., Brouwer, A.A., & Slob, A.K. (1992). New device for penile vibrotactile stimulation: Description and preliminary results. *Urological Research, 20,* 365–368.

Rowland, D.L., Kallan, K., & Slob, A.K. (1997). Yohimbine, erectile capacity, and sexual response in men. *Archives of Sexual Behavior, 26,* 49–62.

Sachs, B.D. (1995). Placing erection in context: The reflexogenic-psychogenic dichotomy reconsidered. *Neuroscience and Biobehavioral Reviews, 19,* 211–224.

Sasso, F., Stief, C.G., Gulino, G., Alcini, E., Jünemann, K.P., Gerstenberg, T., Merckx, L., & Wagner, G. (1997). Progress in corpus cavernosum electromyography (CC-EMG): Third international workshop on corpus cavernosum electromyography (CC-EMG). *International Journal of Impotence Research, 9,* 43–45.

Schiavi, R.C. (1996). Androgens and sexual function in men. In B.J. Oddens & A. Vermeulen (Eds.), *Androgens and the aging male* (pp. 111–128). New York: Parthenon.

Schiavi, R.C., White, D., Mandeli, J., & Levine, A.C. (1997). Effect of testosterone administration on sexual behavior and mood in men with erectile dysfunction. *Archives of Sexual Behavior, 26,* 231–241.

Schover, L., & Jensen, S.B. (1988). *Sexuality and chronic illness: A comprehensive approach.* New York: Guilford Press.

Schuhrke, B. (1997). Genitalentdecken im zweiten Lebensjahr [Discovering one's genitals during the second year of life]. *Zeitschrift fuer Sexualforschung, 10,* 106–126.

Segraves, R.T. (1998). Definitions and classification of male sexual dysfunction. *International Journal of Impotence Research, 10,* S54–S58.

Segraves, R.T., & Segraves, K.B. (1993). Medical aspects of orgasm disorders. In W. O'Donohue & J.H. Geer (Eds.), *Handbook of sexual dysfunctions* (pp. 225–252). Boston: Allyn & Bacon.

Sinclair, J., et al. (1995). *Cobuild English dictionary.* London: HarperCollins.

Singer, B., & Toates, F.M. (1987). Sexual motivation. *Journal of Sex Research, 23,* 481–501.

Spiering, M., Everaerd, W., & Janssen, E. (1999). *Priming the sexual system: Automatic versus non-automatic processing of sexual stimuli.* Manuscript in preparation.

Stoeckart, R., Slob, A.K., & Moor-Mommers, M.A.C.T. (1995). Fysiologie en anatomie van de seksuele respons. In A.K. Slob, C.W. Vink, J.C.P. Moors, & W. Everaerd (Eds.), *Seksuologie voor de arts* [Sexology for medical doctors] (pp. 45–91). Houten: Bohn, Stafleu, VanLoghum.

Sundaram, C.P., Thomas, W., Pryor, L.E., Sidi, A.A., Billups, K., & Pryor, J.L. (1997). Long-term follow-up of patients receiving injection therapy for erectile dysfunction. *Urology, 49,* 932–935.

van der Molen, M.W. (1996). Energetics and the reaction process: Running threads through experimental psychology. In O. Neumann & A.F. Sanders (Eds.), *Handbook of perception and action: Attention* (Vol. 3, pp. 229–276). London: Academic Press.

Vermeulen, A. (1996). Declining androgens with age. In B. Oddens & A. Vermeulen (Eds.), *Androgens and the aging male* (pp. 3–14). New York: Parthenon.

Wagner, G., Gerstenberg, T., & Levin, R.J. (1989). Electrical activity of corpus cavernosum during flaccidity and erection of the human penis: A new diagnostic method. *Journal of Urology, 142,* 723.

Wagner, G., & Saenz de Tejada, I. (1998). Update on male erectile dysfunction. *British Medical Journal, 316,* 678–682.

Walker, J.R., & Casale, A.J. (1997). Prolonged penile erection in the newborn. *Urology, 50,* 796–799.

Wells, W. (1998, July 24). Total recall. *HMS Beagle BioMedNet Magazine* http://hmsbeagle.com.

Whalen, R.E. (1966). Sexual motivation. *Psychological Review, 73,* 151–163.

CHAPTER 3

Female Sexuality

WALTER EVERAERD, ELLEN T.M. LAAN, STEPHANIE BOTH,
and JANNEKE VAN DER VELDE

That first Day, when you praised Me, Sweet,
And said that I was strong —
And could be mighty, if I liked —
That Day — the Days among —

EMILY DICKINSON (659)

I N THIS CHAPTER, we review women's sexuality. The focus is on research issues in women's sexual response and on sexual dysfunctions. In the history of sexological science, the study of women's sexuality has been neglected or has been obscured by comparisons with the sexuality of men. "Did women enjoy sex before 1900?" asked Shorter (1984) in his book on the history of women's bodies. Comparisons of the sexuality of women and men often aimed at increasing awareness of similarities in physiological and psychological mechanisms (Kolodny, Masters, & Johnson, 1979). Only recently have women been empowered to express their sexual concerns. Therefore, in current research about women's sexuality, the focus is on subjective meaning. This review is divided into two sections: psychological theories about women's sexuality and sexual dysfunctions.

THEORIES ABOUT WOMEN'S SEXUALITY

HISTORICAL PERSPECTIVES: THE DENIAL OF WOMEN'S SEXUALITY

One of the most important causes of the denial of women's sexuality is the virtual absence of women in science and the consequent dominance of male imagery about sexuality. Some serious authors literally describe sexual anatomy and physiology as a reflection of functional differences between women and men. Otto Weininger (1909), in his famous book *Gender and Character*, speculates about differences in sexual motivation between women and men. Two concepts determine sexual motivation; one is a drive to reduce the swelling of the genitals (detumescence), and the second is a drive for tactile interaction (contrectation). The first drive is caused by an accumulation of ripe sperm cells, the second by a need to be touched. Only men have the two drive components; detumescence does not occur in women. This becomes clear when considering the sexual act: the woman does not give something to a man, rather, the man delivers something to the woman. The woman then keeps both the man's and her own secretions. Anatomy provides another proof of this difference in sex drive: the male genitals are more prominent than the female genitals. Weininger was 23 years old when the book was published in 1903. Within 10 years, there were 25 editions in German and it was translated into most modern languages. The book's widespread impact helps explain the degree of depreciation of women and their sexuality.

The general idea in Western culture was that although women may have a disposition for sexual feelings, only a loving husband would arouse these feelings in decent and healthy women:

> In women . . . , especially in those who live a natural and healthy life, sexual excitement also tends to occur spontaneously, but by no means so frequently as in men. . . . In a very large number of women the sexual impulse remains latent until aroused by a lover's caresses. The youth spontaneously becomes a man; but the maiden—as it has been said—"must be kissed into a woman." (Ellis, 1903/1920, p. 241)

Stekel (1926/1967) believed that it was a man's task to awaken sexual feelings in a woman, a responsibility that should not be taken lightly:

> As a matter of fact it is the duty of every man whose wife is unfortunately anaesthetic to investigate for himself his marital partner's erogenous zones, adroitly, carefully until he discovers the areas or positions which are capable of rousing his wife's libido and of bringing on her orgasm during intercourse. (p. 133)

He disapprovingly remarked:

> There are men so brutally blunt and so selfish that they take no trouble to study their wives so as to become acquainted with their erogenous zones and learn to meet their particular desires. (p. 130)

Half a century before Weininger's work, a book entitled *The Functions and Disorders of the Reproductive Organs* by W. Acton (1857), a surgeon, passed through many editions and was popularly regarded as a standard authority on the subjects with which it dealt. The book was almost solely concerned with men; the author evidently regarded the function of reproduction as exclusively appertaining to men. He claimed that women, if "well brought up," are, and should be, absolutely ignorant of all matters concerning it. "I should say," this author remarks, "that the majority of women (happily for society) are not very much troubled with sexual feeling of any kind." The supposition that women do possess sexual feelings he considered "a vile aspersion" (Ellis, 1903/1920, p. 194).

It was not until the late nineteenth century, however, that Acton's view had become the dominant one. For thousands of years prior to this, scholars had assumed that conception could not take place without the woman having an orgasm (Laqueur, 1990, pp. 2–3). Thus, sexual pleasure for women was not only accepted, but considered essential. Yet, although sexual feelings in women were acknowledged, they were not always considered to be unproblematic. Shorter (1984) summarized the prevalent view of women's sexuality in the Middle Ages as follows: "Women are furnaces of carnality, who time and again will lead men to perdition, if given a chance. . . . Because the flame of female sexuality could snuff out a man's spirit, women had sexually to be broken and controlled" (pp. 12–13).

Ellis (1903/1920) had distinctive opinions about differences between women and men concerning the physiological mechanisms involved in sexuality. In men, the process of tumescence and detumescence was considered to be simple. In women,

> we have in the clitoris a corresponding apparatus on a small scale, but behind this has developed a much more extensive mechanism, which also demands satisfaction, and requires for that satisfaction the presence of various conditions that are almost antagonistic. . . . It is the difference, roughly speaking, between a lock and a key. . . . We have to imagine a lock that not only requires a key to fit it, but should only be entered at the right moment, and, under the best conditions, may only become adjusted to the key by considerable use. (p. 235)

It seems that phrases such as "an extensive mechanism behind the clitoris" served to conceal ignorance about physiological facts. Even today, scholars acknowledge that "it is glaringly obvious that we know so little about sexual arousal that we cannot answer some of the most elementary questions about the . . . human genital function" (Levin, 1992, p. 3).

In his excellent book on the role of the body in female sexuality, Laqueur (1990) demonstrated that conceptions about human sexuality were not the result of scientific progress. Instead, he argued, they were part of social and political changes, "explicable only within the context of battles over gender and power" (p. 11). Feminists have long criticized the notion that the behaviors and abilities of women are uniquely determined by their biology. This criticism led to an almost total rejection of the role of biology in the construction of gender (Birke & Vines, 1987). It also contributed, unfortunately, to an image of female sexuality devoid of the body. Masters and Johnson (1966) were the first to carefully study and describe the genital and extragenital changes that occurred in sexually aroused women. Recently, Tiefer (1991a) rightly critiqued their claim that the human sexual response cycle is a universal model for sexual response, not in the least because the concept of sexual desire was not included in the model, therewith eliminating "an element which is notoriously variable within populations" (p. 4). She argued that the human sexual response cycle, with its genital focus, neglects women's sexual priorities and experiences. Indeed, Masters and Johnson did not assess the subjective sexual experience of the 694 men and women who were studied. In addition, their emphasis on peripheral physiology, particularly the genital vasocongestive processes associated with sexual response, may reflect the influence of primarily male-dominated theorizing and research in sexology, with its inevitable emphasis on penile-vaginal sexual contact. Nevertheless, Masters and Johnson's studies led to the recently evolved field of sexual psychophysiology. This line of research, which clearly represents but a part of the broad concept of sexuality, seeks to study sexual arousal processes in both men and women, with a special emphasis on the interplay between subjective and physiological determinants of sexual arousal.

THE SEXUAL BODY

In the chapter on male sexuality, we have tried to formulate answers to whether there is a sexual system. The take-home message is that there is a provision in our bodies for specific sexual responses, but sexual expression in emotions and behavior depends largely on nonspecific sensory as well as motor capabilities. Our general theoretical approach was discussed in some detail in that chapter. In this section, we describe current knowledge about some key issues of women's sexual body.

Notes on Anatomy and Physiology

Recently, there has been a renewed discussion about the clitoris and connected erectile tissue. According to the *New Scientist*, a UK-based popular science journal, Helen O'Connell stated that she realized for the first time how little was known about women's sexual anatomy when she was studying for her urology surgical exams. "Even nowadays," she says, "textbooks routinely recycle decades-old, inaccurate illustrations of female sex organs, or omit diagrams altogether. The written accounts can also lack a certain something. One text describes female genitalia as the same as the guys' only turned inside out; another, as the 'poor homologue' of the male" (cited in Williamson & Nowak, 1998, p. 34). O'Connell points to a practical use of knowledge about nerves and blood vessels in women's genitalia. This information may help reduce the risks of nerve damage following operations. However, a more important message can be heard with priority. The title of the *New Scientist* article is "The Truth about Women." Women's sexual sensory capacities have been debated in Western scientific culture for more than 100 years.

Body sensations depend on the presence of sensory receptors; therefore, we like to know where receptors are for information that may eventually result in sexual feelings. Sensations may come about through all sensory modalities: visual, auditory, tactile, gustatory, and olfactory. Sensory thresholds may be influenced by varying levels of gonadal hormones over the menstrual cycle (Gandelman, 1983). Around ovulation, visual and olfactory thresholds appear to be lower. Prior to menstruation, lower pain sensitivity has been found (Parlee, 1983). For tactile thresholds, no cyclic changes have been found. The search for tactile "sexual" sensory receptors dominates sexological literature. It is important to observe that this search overlooks the point of view that the skin is our largest erotic organ (Musaph, 1977).

Clitoris and Surrounding Erectile Tissue

There is a considerable density of tactile receptors in the clitoris. The anterior (ventral is a synonym, meaning situated nearer the front part of the body) vaginal wall is also rich in tactile receptors. Freud (1953) entertained a developmental idea about excitability to explain how "a little girl turns into a woman" (p. 220). Remember that Freud's *Three Essays on Sexuality* first appeared in 1905, just two years after Weininger's *Gender and Character.* Freud explained that from the onset of puberty, libido increases in boys; at the same time, in girls, "a fresh wave of repression" occurs that affects precisely "clitoridal sexuality" (p. 220). The brake on the girl's sexuality will serve as a stimulus to the boy's libido. Then, in Volume 7 of the *Standard Edition* (1953) a crucial passage follows, about the "leading zones":

> When at last the sexual act is permitted and the clitoris itself becomes excited, it still retains a function: the task namely, of transmitting the excitation to the adjacent female sexual parts, just as—to use a simile—pine shavings can be kindled in order to set a log of harder wood on fire. Before this transference can be effected, a certain interval of time must often elapse, during which the young woman is anaesthetic. This anaesthesia may become permanent if the clitoridal zone refuses to abandon its excitability. (p. 221)

And then, in the next paragraph:

> When erotogenic susceptibility to stimulation has been successfully transferred by a woman from the clitoris to the vaginal orifice, it implies that she has adopted a new leading zone for the purposes of her later sexual activity. A man on the other hand, retains his leading zone unchanged from childhood. (p. 221)

Freud proves to be a child of his time when he formulates an explanation for women's anesthesia or frigidity. His suggestion that there are also tactile receptors in the anterior vaginal wall is correct. Currently, there is no evidence that the anterior wall becomes excitable at the expense of clitoral sensitivity. Contrary to Freud's belief, there is ample evidence, however, that women who learned to know their own sexuality through masturbation are able to transfer this knowledge (or is it skill?) to coital stimulation with a partner (Hite, 1976). For a long time, ideas similar to those of Freud have been used to suppress masturbation in girls and women. Even today, there are many women with a partner who feel guilty when masturbating.

The clitoris contains two stripes of erectile tissue (corpora cavernosum), which diverge into the crura (leglike structures) inside the labia majora. On the basis of recent anatomical studies, O'Connell, Hutson, Anderson, and Plenter (1998) proposed to rename these structures as bulbs of the clitoris. They also found that there is erectile tissue connected to the clitoris and extending backwards, surrounding the perineal part of the urethra. However, most anatomical facts have been known for a long time (cf. Grafenberg, 1950). There is a growing scientific and professional interest in these erectile structures. Smooth muscle relaxants, such as sildanafil (Viagra), may contribute to the swelling of the erectile tissues, similar to what occurs in penile erectile tissue. At the moment of this writing, it is uncertain how smooth muscle relaxants may contribute to women's sexual response. There may be some effects on lubrication and consequently on lowering pain at attempts of intromission of fingers or a penis. This may be relevant for women in the postmenopausal phase when lubrication subsides (S.A. Kaplan et al., 1999).

The Anterior Vaginal Wall: Other "Leading Zones"

When Masters and Johnson (1966) published their account of the physiology of the sexual response, they opposed Freud's theory of the transition of leading zones in women. According to these famous sexologists, the clitoris is richly endowed with nerve endings, which are extremely sparse in the vagina. Therefore, during coital stimulation, the clitoris is stimulated indirectly, possibly through the movement or friction of the labia. Masters and Johnson stressed the similarity of women and men; the homologous clitoris and penis thus became the leading zones. Again, Hite's (1976) data supported this point of view. Almost all women who reached orgasm through stimulation from coitus alone had a history of empowering masturbation experiences. Many women needed additional manual stimulation to orgasm during coitus, and an even larger number were unable to achieve orgasm during coitus (Hite, 1976).

Apparently, for women, coitus is not a very effective stimulus to orgasm. Coitus may give pleasurable emotional satisfaction, but for many women, it does not imply sexual satisfaction. One practical view arose from the observation that two people are involved in coitus. Both are attending to optimal conditions for intense arousal and orgasm for the man; the man may be more powerful, and the woman at the same time ignores her own concerns. In these cases, a shift in attentional focus will be helpful to reverse the conditions for orgasm (Everaerd & Dekker, 1981). One attempt to resolve issues of coital orgasm involves renewed attention to the leading role of the clitoris, the importance of masturbation, and relationship dynamics. Another route consists of a closer look at the anterior vaginal wall.

In 1950, Grafenberg published a landmark paper in which he provided an explanation for lack of orgasm or frigidity. Women's urethra, like men's, "is surrounded by erectile tissues like the corpora cavernosa. In the course of sexual stimulation, the female urethra begins to enlarge and can be felt easily. It swells out greatly at the end of orgasm. The most stimulating part is located at the posterior urethra, where it arises from the neck of the bladder" (p. 146). Grafenberg is convinced that arousal and orgasm may be induced in many ways: "there is no spot in the female body, from which the sexual desire could not be aroused" (Why did Grafenberg use a double negation?). However, "The intensity of orgasm is dependent on the area from which it is elicited" (p. 146). Cunnilingus is a practice resulting in great intensity, but then there is the spot in the anterior wall. The spot can be found easily: "Women tested this way [with a finger] always knew when the finger slipped from the urethra [as felt on the anterior wall] by the impairment of their sexual stimulation" (p. 146). Coitus in the so-called missionary position (ventral-ventral) prevents stimulation of the anterior wall. We have to understand our phylogenetic ancestry to find the adequate positions: "Contact is very close, when the intercourse is performed more bestiarum or à la vache i.e., a posteriori" (p. 148).

Sensitivity of the entire vaginal wall has been explored in several studies. In many cases, doctors, men as well as women, with their fingers touched different spots on the vaginal wall. At the same time, the women gave subjective reports about the experience of this tactile exploration (Alzate, 1985; Chua, 1997; Goldberg et al., 1983; Grafenberg, 1950). Weijmar Schultz, van de Wiel, Klatter, Sturm, and Nauta (1989) used an electrical stimulus for exploration under nonerotic conditions. All studies confirm sensitivity of the anterior vaginal wall, including the Grafenberg or G-spot, and sensitivity of the vaginal introitus at the 12 o'clock position.

Reports about G-spot sensitivity also, at least in some women, give accounts of more intense arousal and orgasm. This intense arousal and orgasm may elicit ejaculations, which may vary from expulsions of abundant lubrication fluid to spurts of fluid that may contain urine and paraurethra gland secretions. The spurts appear to originate from the urethra (Bèlzer, Whipple, & Moger, 1984; van der Velde, Klooster, Messelink, Gorgels, & Everaerd, 1999).

Menstrual Cycle, Hormones, and Sexual Sensitivity

In most mammals, estrogen (Greek *oistros*, mad desire) causes estrus around ovulation. Estrus is characterized by willingness to permit coitus, which is demonstrated behaviorally and by other signs. In nonhuman primates, the relationship is less strict between estrogen and willingness and actual frequency of sexual interactions (Dixon, 1998). In women, the relationship between cycle phase and sexual behavior is uncertain. Slob, Bax, Hop, Rowland, and van der Werff ten Bosch (1996) did find some effects on genital physiological arousal in a psychophysiological study. In both the follicular phase and the luteal phase, they induced arousal with films and tactile vibration in women who were between 18 and 45 years of age, had normal cycles, and were not using oral contraception. On subjective measures of sexual excitement, no cycle effects were found. A modest effect appeared for reported sexual desire in the follicular phase when subjects were for the first time exposed to the erotic film.

Androgens, particularly testosterone, seem to play an important role in women's sexuality. Androgens increase the sensitivity for sexual stimuli and have significant effects on women's sexual fantasies, sexual desire, and sexual arousal (Sherwin, Gelfand, & Brender, 1985). The use of androgens has so far been restricted to postmenopausal women, who may develop androgen deficiency (S.R. Davis, 1998; Fourcroy, 1998). Sarrel (1999), in a timely review of the role of androgens in menopause, concludes that the addition of androgens in hormone replacement therapy improves sexual symptoms. However, he is not very specific about when to apply this treatment.

Studies about the menstrual cycle and sexuality are complicated by many factors that may determine sexual response. Hormonal variations may be obscured by other, more potent factors, for example, relationship and aging.

In our discussion of women's sexual body, we have taken a sensory perspective; we described body areas rich in (tactile) receptors and reviewed the knowledge about sensitivity. In the section on sexual dysfunctions, we present data on anatomy and physiology in a discussion of sexuality and the pelvic floor. There we use a motor or output perspective.

ASSESSMENT OF FEMALE SEXUAL AROUSAL

Measuring Genital Vasocongestion

In 1975, Sintchak and Geer introduced a practical method for the measurement of genital arousal in women, using vaginal photoplethysmography. The vaginal photoplethysmograph was designed to monitor changes in vasocongestion of the vagina. According to Masters and Johnson (1966), vasocongestion is one of the earliest occurring and most reliable physiological correlates of female sexual arousal.

The most widely used type of vaginal photoplethysmograph is a tampon-sized device containing an infrared light-emitting diode as a light source and a phototransistor as a light detector. Changes in blood volume within the vagina produce changes in the amount of light scattered back to the light detector, as a result of the large difference in transparency between blood and bloodless tissue. Changes in blood volume within the tissue can therefore be easily recorded as changes in the output of the light detector. Two components of variation in vaginal blood volume can be recorded simultaneously. With AC coupling, a measure of vaginal pulse amplitude (VPA) is obtained, reflecting short-term changes in vaginal engorgement. Fluctuations in VPA reflect the phasic change in blood content or volume of the illuminated tissue at each heart beat, with larger amplitudes reflecting higher levels of vasoengorgement. When the signal is DC coupled, slowly developing changes in vaginal blood volume (VBV) are observed, which are thought to reflect pooling of blood in the vaginal tissue (Hatch, 1979).

There has been a great deal of controversy concerning the issue of which genital measure, VPA or VBV, is the most sensitive and reliable. Additionally, the issue of response specificity has been long overlooked. Weinman (1967) reasoned that the DC measure should be the more sensitive because blood volume changes produced by the heart (the AC measure) represent only a small fraction of total blood volume in a capillary bed. In studies that compared both signals, however, it was concluded that the AC measure is a more sensitive measure of sexual arousal (Geer, Morokoff, & Greenwood, 1974; Heiman, 1977; Osborn & Pollack, 1977; Weinman, 1967). Response specificity would also require the genital measures to be unresponsive to nonsexual emotional stimuli.

Recently, we compared specificity, sensitivity, and construct validity of VPA and VBV during sexual, neutral, and nonsexual emotional states (Laan, Everaerd, & Evers, 1995). We obtained responses from 49 healthy women to five-minute sexual, neutral, anxiety-inducing, and sexually threatening film excerpts. To determine the effectiveness of the experimental manipulations, subjective reports of sexual arousal and emotional experience and two autonomic measures (skin conductance and heart rate) were monitored along with the genital measures. Anxiety was chosen as the emotional state incorporated in the comparison, because the effect of mild anxiety on responses to sexual stimuli has been studied extensively (Hoon, Wincze, & Hoon, 1977; Palace & Gorzalka, 1990). Results of most studies showed an enhancing effect of anxiety to subsequent sexual arousal in functional subjects. These results will be supported if it can be established that anxiety in itself does not yield higher genital arousal levels, but only in interaction with a sexual stimulus. The sexually threatening film excerpt was included to assess sensitivity of the genital measures to more subtle sexual cues.

Results indicated that the stimulus conditions had the intended effects on subjective sexual arousal and emotional experience and skin conductance levels. Heart rate failed to discriminate among stimuli. The sex stimulus yielded highest levels of VPA and VBV relative to the other emotional stimuli and the neutral. In contrast to VPA, VBV was found to be insensitive to the sexual threat stimulus. The most striking difference between VPA and VBV was, however, that VBV was also responsive to the anxiety stimulus in that it showed a marked decrease after three minutes of stimulus presentation, coinciding with the most frightening part of the film excerpt. Some studies have found evidence of finger vasoconstriction under conditions of fear (Ekman, Levenson, & Friesen, 1983; Hoon et al., 1977; Palace & Gorzalka, 1990; Stemmler, 1989; Vanderhoff & Clancy, 1962). Similarly, VBV, in contrast to VPA, may have been affected by a process of vasoconstriction in the capillaries of the peripheral bed during the last three minutes of stimulus presentation.

We concluded that in terms of convergent and divergent validity, VPA is the superior measure. Convergent validity of VPA was substantiated in that this genital measure was highly reactive to the sex stimulus and moderately reactive to the sexual threat stimulus. In contrast, VBV was reactive to the sex stimulus only. Divergent validity of VPA was demonstrated by the absence of response to the nonsexual stimuli. VBV, however, was reactive to the nonsexual anxiety stimulus. Furthermore, the VBV measure suffered from base line drift over time, despite a 45-minute warm-up period prior to insertion. This measure has an additional complication in that it may show abrupt shifts in response levels due to movement (e.g., readjustment of one's position in the chair) that renders the obtained data useless.

An overview of the genital and extragenital changes in sexually aroused women will not be given here. Levin (1992) recently provided an excellent account of the physiology of human female sexual arousal. Several other textbooks (Bancroft, 1989; Rosen & Beck, 1988) describe in detail the physiological changes that occur during sexual arousal.

Measuring Subjective Sexual Arousal

Subjective sexual arousal is most often assessed by a single item, asking subjects to rate their feelings of subjective (sometimes called mental or cognitive) sexual arousal on a rating scale. The intermediate points of the scale may or may not have verbal descriptors. Some studies have assessed subjective sexual arousal by having subjects rate the degree to which they found the presented stimulus sexually arousing. C. Henson, Rubin, and Henson (1979; D.E. Henson, Rubin, & Henson, 1979) found ratings according to Griffitt's (1975) 7-point scale of genital reactions to be highly correlated with the physiological measurements used in their study (VPA in particular). Instead of the typical range, from not at all aroused to extremely aroused, Griffitt associated actual genital sensations with the seven points. On his scale, 1 corresponded to no genital sensations; 2 mild genital sensations; 3 moderate sensations; 4 slightly strong genital sensations; 5 strong genital sensation; 6 vaginal lubrication; and 7 orgasm.

Wincze, Hoon, and Hoon (1977) used an awareness of physiological changes scale to assess subjective sexual arousal. They were the first to use a continuous measure of subjective sexual arousal. A continuous measure allows for an evaluation of the relationship between subjective and genital measures throughout the entire stimulus interval. Wincze et al. constructed a lever that could swing through an approximately 90-degree arc, and which was mounted on a table enabling subjects to operate the lever effortlessly with one hand. By watching the position of the lever, subjects could see the degree of subjective sexual arousal they were indicating.

In our laboratory, subjective sexual arousal is assessed by four 7-point Likert scales, or visual analog scales. Following an erotic stimulus, subjects are asked to rate their subjective sexual arousal most of the time (overall sexual arousal), their strongest feeling of sexual arousal, their strongest genital sensations (using descriptors roughly similar to Griffitt, 1975), and their strongest extragenital sensations. Emotional experience is typically assessed by 7-point Likert scales.

In addition, in some studies, we used a continuous measure of subjective sexual arousal by means of a lever (Laan & Everaerd, 1995; Laan, Everaerd, Van Aanhold, & Rebel, 1993; Laan, Everaerd, van der Velde, & Geer, 1995). This lever is calibrated so that its placement determines how many of 10 lights are illuminated. The lever in the most rearward position illuminates one light, signaling no sexual arousal (or signaling no genital sensations, depending on the methodology of the particular study), and the lever in the most forward position illuminates all 10 lights, indicating maximum sexual arousal (or maximum vaginal lubrication). The lever is attached to either the right or left arm of a recliner chair, matching the subject's dominant hand. A corresponding bar with 10 red lightbulbs is placed underneath the TV monitor so that subjects need not look away from the screen to monitor their level of sexual arousal.

The Relationship between Subjective Sexual Arousal and Genital Arousal

A review of the literature on female sexual arousal revealed that there is little agreement between reported genital sensations and changes in genital vasocongestion. The majority of studies reported the degree of association between subjective sexual arousal and changes in genital vasocongestion. Across studies, correlations ran the gamut from nonsignificant to significantly negative to significantly positive. In contrast, correlations between genital and subjective sexual arousal in men are usually significantly positive, despite differences in methodology and procedures. Studies designed to compare female and male sexual arousal patterns in one experimental design, thus precluding methodological variation, consistently reported higher correlations in men than in women (Dekker & Everaerd, 1988; Heiman, 1977; Steinman, Wincze, Sakheim, Barlow, & Mavissakalian, 1981; Wincze, Venditti, Barlow, & Mavissakalian, 1980). Several explanations have been advanced for the low correlations between genital and subjective sexual arousal in women. First, the lack of a consistent pattern of correlations has been attributed to the various ways subjective sexual arousal was assessed (Geer et al., 1974). Nevertheless, whether discrete or continuous measures were employed, correlations between genital and subjective sexual arousal remained variable. Second, low correlations between measures have been thought to be the result of measurement error of the vaginal photoplethysmograph (Beck, Barlow, & Sakheim, 1983; Hatch, 1979). Third, Heiman (1977, 1980) suggested that at lower levels of arousal, women need external cues to help interpret the subjective experience. An underlying assumption, postulated earlier by sensory psychophysicists (Reed, Harver, & Katkin, 1990), is that at higher levels of arousal, agreement between measures would be higher. A related explanation is that women, if not instructed to do so, do not attend to the physiological cues of arousal (Korff & Geer, 1983). These latter two explanations will be discussed in more detail later.

Two obvious problems result from the findings regarding female sexual arousal. First, it seems that there are huge variations in the awareness of bodily sensations between subjects as well as within subjects over situations. Second, it is clear that bodily sensations, even when consciously processed, do not necessarily determine subjective sexual experience. Both facts suggest that there are other sources that determine subjective sexual experience. Nonetheless, a basic premise in models of sexual arousal (Bancroft, 1989; Barlow, 1986; Byrne, 1977, 1983; Korff & Geer, 1983) is that in the process of sexual excitation, subjective and genital arousal both increase and decrease simultaneously and proportionately.

The Relationship between Subjective Sexual Arousal and Sexual Behavior

To complicate matters further, not only does it seem that subjective sexual arousal and genital arousal correlate poorly in women but the relationship between subjective sexual arousal and sexual behavior is not straightforward either. For example, Geer and Broussard (1990) asked male and female subjects to complete two paired-comparison tasks using sentences describing sexual activities ranging from kissing to intercourse. They selected 14 items from Bentler's (1968a, 1968b) Heterosexual Behavior Scales that were thought to represent a typical sequence of heterosexual behaviors. Subjects were first asked to arrange each possible pair of behaviors in the order in which they would occur in a "typical heterosexual encounter." Then they were asked to order each pair of behaviors by their perceived arousal value. From these data, a sequence scale and an arousal scale were constructed. Although men and women agreed on the sequence of sexual activities, the degree to which they found the activities sexually arousing differed considerably. The male arousal scale closely approximated the male sequence scale. For women, however, there was a large discrepancy between the arousal scale and the sequence scale. A replication of this study in a Dutch sample yielded similar results (Janssen, Post, & Everaerd, 1993).

These findings suggest that, in contrast to men, women engage in sexual behaviors even when they do not regard them as sexually exciting. Similarly, Weijmar Schultz and van de Wiel (1991) found that women, one year after cervical cancer treatment or one year after hysterectomy for benign disease, reported more negative genital sensations during sexual arousal and coitus (pain, numbness, or tightness of the vagina) and less sexual arousal compared to an age-matched control group of gynecologically healthy women. Nevertheless, frequency of and motivation for sexual behavior with a partner for both patient groups was as high as in the control group. Weijmar Schultz and van de Wiel concluded that a woman's motivation for sexual interaction with her partner is not limited to the experience of sexual arousal. They suggested that women's "love ethos" makes them more inclined to adapt to the wishes of their sexual partner.

In sum, in women there appears to be not only a discrepancy between genital and subjective sexual arousal, but also a discrepancy between sexual behavior and subjective sexual arousal. This may suggest that for women, sexuality and sexual situations have more meanings than just sexual or lustful ones.

Sexual Arousal: The Cognitive Emotion Theory Perspective

In the field of sexual psychophysiology, the interrelationships between subjective and physiological phenomena of sexual arousal have only recently begun to be explored. In contrast, the interaction between physiological and cognitive processes in emotion research has been studied for a longer period of time. James's (1890/1950) body reaction theory has stimulated a debate in emotion research concerning the contribution of peripheral feedback to emotions as they are subjectively experienced, a debate that is still ongoing. Only a decade ago, Ekman et al. (1983) claimed that the experience of specific emotions is associated with distinct facial expressions and autonomic activity. This marked a return to James's position and a departure from the current view in emotion research that the physiological correlates of emotions are characterized simply by general and undifferentiated physiological arousal. Nevertheless, other emotion theorists judge the evidence for emotion-specific autonomic patterns to be inconsistent (Cacioppo, Berntson, & Klein, 1992; Stemmler, 1989). Frijda (1986) concluded that awareness of autonomic arousal may contribute to the intensity of emotional experience, but that such awareness is not indispensable for emotional experience per se.

The classic alternative to James's (1890/1950) position is the appraisal theory of emotion. Schachter and Singer's (1962) proposal of the cognitive arousal theory of emotions holds that the experience of emotion is based on the occurrence of both physiological arousal and a state of "emotional" cognition. They argue that internal bodily cues are secondary, and that, instead, situational cues play a primary role in the experience of emotion. For instance, it can be hypothesized that following the initial appraisal of a situation as sexual, erotic cues of the situation function both to arouse physiological reactions and the perceptions thereof, as well as to initiate simultaneously a cognitive labeling process. An important implication of the cognitive arousal theory is that a given situation will not be experienced as sexual, despite the presence of genital arousal, without the occurrence of the appropriate emotional attribution. Thus, a situation (a stimulus) is not intrinsically sexual; it becomes sexual by its transformation (Everaerd & Laan, 1994; Rosen & Beck, 1988).

Everaerd (1988) argued that sexual arousal fits the definition of an emotion as delineated by most cognitive emotion theorists. For instance, sexual arousal matches Ekman's (1984) definition of an emotion: it has evolved to deal with fundamental life tasks, and its antecedents and patterns of expression are emotion-specific. In addition, as with other emotions, sexual arousal has been described as having three components: neurophysiological-biochemical, behavioral expressive, and feeling experiential (Izard & Blumberg, 1985). Everaerd (1988) concluded that sexual arousal fits the characteristics of an emotion in many respects.

Lang (1984) thinks of the three response systems mentioned above as being "loosely integrated." He endorsed the concept of anxiety as a multisystem response (Lang, 1970):

> In human subjects, fear responses appear to be loosely integrated behavioral loops, in which somatic, verbal, and gross motor segments mutually influence each other, but are also controlled in part by separate, emotion-irrelevant events. To a considerable extent these response systems are bound to be idiosyncratic, emphasizing in their development and expression different output systems in different subjects. (p. 165)

For studies of sexual arousal, Lang's view implies that response systems differentially influence the expression of sexual arousal. Low correlations are to be expected between verbal reports and genital measures of sexual arousal.

Some attempts have been made to study sexual arousal from an emotion theory perspective. For example, Dekker and Everaerd (1988) applied Lang's bio-informational theory of emotions, which mainly concerns anxiety, to sexual arousal. In Lang's (1984) theory, it is postulated that information about emotional stimuli and responses is represented in memory as a propositional network. This network is activated when a person attends to information that matches the relevant stimulus or response propositions in the network. Lang hypothesized that the processing of emotional response results in the activation of response propositions, which in turn activate motor programs that produce the emotional response. Stimulus propositions activate an emotional response only when they are associated with response propositions. Dekker and Everaerd found, in support of Lang's theory, that subjects encouraged to focus on sexual stimuli as well as sexual responses showed stronger subjective and genital sexual arousal than subjects asked to focus on sexual stimuli only. This effect occurred in both men and women.

Our position is that sexual arousal is best construed as an integrated multi-modality processing system, consisting of subjective, physiological, and behavioral components. These components may be at least partially independent. We assume that this information-processing system includes parallel cognitive processing of both situational dimensions and bodily changes. As in cognitive emotion theories, this perspective provides us with the possibility of studying the interaction between cognitive processes and response systems.

Second, genital changes are necessary for subjective experience to attain a sexual quality. Although in emotion research, conflicting results concerning the importance of peripheral feedback for the experience of emotions are reported, one might argue that sexual arousal, unlike other emotions, involves quite specific bodily reactions. The role of peripheral feedback generated by vasocongestion may act as a specific indicator of the relevant meaning to be processed (e.g., "I feel that this is sexual"). Naturally, a basic premise of this specificity assumption is the accuracy assumption. That is, for the specific sexual bodily reactions to contribute to subjective experience of sexual arousal, people must be able to accurately detect these bodily reactions. The contribution of peripheral feedback from genital arousal seems relatively unambiguous when considering intense levels of genital arousal (e.g., orgasm), suggesting that genital arousal should be sufficiently intense to be consciously perceived. As noted earlier, there seem to be huge variations in the awareness of bodily sensations between subjects as well as within subjects over situations. These differences may be related to individual differences in genital responsiveness, individual differences in perception thresholds, individual differences in attentional focus, and the like. Nevertheless, it is predicted that the contribution of genital arousal to subjective sexual experience is a function of genital arousal intensity. No study to date has systematically investigated to what extent and in what way genital arousal intensity contributes to subjective report of sexual arousal in women.

Third, it is unlikely that genital arousal alone is sufficient to produce sexual experience. A stimulus may convey numerous meanings, depending on the circumstances or the individual's history. Sexual meaning and other meanings relevant to different emotions (e.g., anxiety, anger, and elation) may well be present at the same time. Different messages may thus be derived from the same stimulus, which, through further processing, may develop divergent subjective and physiological responses. It has been noted earlier that there is evidence that women may have more motives for sexual behavior than only lustful ones. Presumably, these motives vary from situation to situation. We hypothesize that women, to a large extent, use external (situational or stimulus) information to assess their subjective feelings of sexual arousal.

As Gagnon and Simon (1973) have argued, people have to learn to be sexual. This sexual learning includes linking cognitive and imagery processes to sexual feelings and behavior. Traditionally, society's double standard of sexuality has been less permissive to women than to men in the expression of sexual feelings, which may have resulted in a higher degree of uncertainty about sexual roles and sexual behavior in women than in men. As Stock and Geer (1982) put it: "Our culture has traditionally socialized women to believe that their sexual and romantic involvement should be central to their lives but, both cognitively and behaviorally, outside their locus of control" (p. 43). Negative sexual experiences, sexual harassment, or sexual abuse may add to this uncertainty. At the same time, these latter factors may cause women to attend to situational cues more vigilantly, because "Pleasure is one side of the sexual coin, but, for women, danger is the other" (Tiefer, 1991b, p. 3).

In other lines of research, outside the domain of sexuality, it has been argued that for women, external stimulus information is an important determinant for assessing internal state. In a recent review of gender differences in visceral perception, Pennebaker and Roberts (1992) stated that the strategy women use to perceive and define their emotions is more congruent with cognitive appraisal theories than James's (1890/1950) peripheralist view. They argued that in defining their internal states, women predominantly rely on stimulus information and men on bodily cues. In laboratory settings devoid of external cues, men are consistently more accurate than women at detecting physiological signals such as blood glucose levels, heart rate, and blood pressure levels. In natural settings replete with multiple situational cues, however, women and men are equally accurate in detecting their physiological states.

There is some evidence that women not only use stimulus information to a greater extent to estimate internal state, but they also attribute more meanings to a situation than do men. Dekker and Everaerd (1988) reported that subjective reports of sexual arousal of men were almost exclusively limited to sexual excitement, whereas women reported many other positive and negative emotions concurrent with sexual excitement. Preliminary findings of Fischer (1994) suggest that women attribute more meanings to and report more emotions in nonsexual situations (e.g., failing an exam, being cheated) than do men. In addition, there is supporting evidence for such a gender difference from research in nonverbal communication. Research in this field has consistently found that women pay more attention to and are better decoders of emotion-relevant facial and other nonverbal cues in other people than are men (DePaulo, Jordan, Irvine, & Laser, 1982; J.A. Hall, 1984).

Although we do assert that genital arousal in women contributes to subjective experience of sexual arousal, and that this contribution is a function of genital arousal intensity, genital cues in women may determine subjective experience to a lesser extent than external, situational cues. In contrast to erections in men, genital arousal in women is likely to produce fewer kinesthetic cues to facilitate conscious detection. Therefore, it is predicted that in women, appraisal of the situation will account for more of the variance in subjective experience of sexual arousal than feedback from genital sensations.

Response Agreement

To test the above-mentioned hypothesis, we conducted several experiments. Three studies were designed to manipulate conditions that were thought to have the potential of optimizing agreement between subjective and genital sexual arousal. One study investigated the influence of erotic film content on subjective and genital sexual arousal (Laan, Everaerd, van Bellen, & Hanewald, 1994). It was hypothesized that the discrepancy between both measures of sexual arousal that was observed in many earlier studies may have been the result of negative affect induced by the type of erotic film that was used. Until recently, male producers and directors, whose products focused on a male public, governed the erotic film industry. We investigated the extent to which an erotic film from a woman's perspective, highlighting the sexual pleasure of the female actor, was more capable of producing positive affect than the common, "man-made" film. We presumed that positive affect induced by the woman-made film would increase attentional focus on erotic cues, resulting in high correlations between subjective and genital sexual arousal.

Results showed higher subjective sexual arousal to the female-initiated, female-centered erotic film, but genital arousal to this film was no higher than arousal to the male-initiated, male-centered film. The fact that Heiman (1977) did find an effect of this sex-role dimension on genital arousal and Laan et al. (1994) did not was attributed to the weaker stimuli Heiman used in her study (i.e., erotic audiotapes).

In a study investigating the effects of performance demand on sexual arousal, it was found that this factor indeed proved to facilitate both subjective and genital sexual arousal in women (Laan et al., 1993). However, the effect of this experimental instruction was visible during erotic fantasy only, and not during the erotic film. Correlations between genital and subjective sexual arousal tended to be higher in the erotic film conditions. Similarly, in a study in which a positive sexual mood was induced before erotic stimuli were shown, not the mood manipulation but the erotic film conditions resulted in higher correlations (Laan, Everaerd, van Berlo, & Rijs, 1995). The erotic film yielded higher levels of genital and subjective sexual arousal than erotic fantasy. The positive sexual mood had no effect on subjective or genital sexual arousal, but only tended to attenuate negative emotional experience during the erotic film.

Thus, in all three studies, correlations between subjective and genital sexual arousal were overall low and statistically nonsignificant. Response agreement was not enhanced by positive affect, nor reduced by negative affect (Laan et al., 1993, 1994; Laan, Everaerd, van der Velde, et al., 1995). Rather, response agreement was enhanced by the erotic film.

Peripheral Feedback Hypothesis

These findings seem to support the notion that agreement between measures will be higher at higher levels of genital arousal (Heiman, 1977, 1980), because in all experiments, genital responses were highest in the erotic film conditions. It is difficult to investigate systematically whether higher levels of genital arousal would generate higher correlations between subjective and genital sexual arousal, because high levels of sexual arousal are rarely obtained in laboratory experiments. Hypothetically, one could measure female subjects' arousal during masturbation or other highly arousing sexual activity. In practice, however, such estimates may be unreliable due to movement artifacts interfering with responding. Similarly, vaginal muscle activity induced by orgasm seriously compromises the interpretation of vaginal photoplethysmographic records (Gillan & Brindly, 1979; Levin, 1992). Notwithstanding these practical difficulties, we attempted to study response agreement at varying levels of genital arousal by presenting subjects with 21 one-minute erotic film stimuli (Laan, Everaerd, van der Velde, et al., 1995). This design allowed us to compute individual correlations. We found that subjects with high correlations between genital and subjective sexual arousal did not have significantly higher levels of genital arousal than subjects with low correlations. Between subjects, genital and subjective sexual arousal were neither linearly nor curvilinearly related.

Clearly, as with other laboratory experiments, our results are valid for weak to moderate sexual arousal only. To test the assumption that response agreement increases with higher levels of genital arousal than are obtained by the

erotic film, we designed and are currently testing a device for vibrotactile stimulation to the clitoris. The vibrator itself is built in a 2 cm metallic cylinder (diameter 2 cm). The cylinder is placed in a tightly fitting natural rubber cup,
which at one end has the form of a rubber stopper. A property of natural rubber
is that it does not impair the vibratory motion that is generated by the vibrator.
This container is mounted on a flexible metal strap, lined with washable lycra
cloth, by pulling the rubber stopper through a hole in the cloth. The flexible
metal strap fits each subject's pelvis and can be individually adjusted such that
the rubber stopper touches the clitoris. A split in the cloth allows for the photoplethysmograph to be placed into the vagina so that photoplethysmographic
records can be taken during vibration. The advantage of this device is that vibrotactile stimulation can be applied without activity on the part of the subject.
Preliminary results suggest that this device produces high levels of genital
arousal. Furthermore, as long as subjects do not move the lower half of the body,
the photoplethysmographic records do not contain artifacts.

Perceiving Genital Sensations

Korff and Geer (1983) claimed that in our society, women, in contrast to men,
are not trained to attend to their genitals in sexual activity. They suggested,
therefore, that instructing women to attend to bodily responses during erotic
stimulation would enhance agreement between subjective and genital sexual
arousal. Indeed, they found significant individual correlations in 93% of the
subjects who had been instructed to attend to bodily activity, and in the condition in which subjects were instructed to attend to genital activity, all individual correlations were significant. These findings led Korff and Geer to
assert that the instruction to attend to bodily cues generated the high correlations between genital and subjective measures. They subsequently concluded
that their findings "begin to lay to rest the conclusion that the correlation between subjective and genital measures of sexual arousal for women is of necessity low" (p. 126). This conclusion may well be premature, for a number of
reasons.

First, Korff and Geer (1983) did not report whether the condition in which
women were instructed to attend to bodily activity yielded higher levels of
genital arousal than the other conditions, which may, in part, have caused the
high individual correlations. Second, even in the group that did not receive attentional instructions, 60% of subjects had significant correlations, and the
computed group correlation was high ($r > .70$). Most important, in all conditions, Korff and Geer employed a hierarchy of stimuli depicting a wide range
of sexual behaviors likely to produce varying degrees of sexual arousal. It
seems probable that usage of a hierarchy of stimuli itself contributed to high
response agreement. Indeed, both Wincze et al. (1977) and Steinman et al.
(1981) used a wide range of stimuli, ranging from kissing to intercourse, and
they found high individual correlations although subjects were not instructed
to attend to bodily cues. In contrast, Wincze et al. (1980) did not show their

subjects a wide range of different stimuli, and most individual correlations were nonsignificant.

We attempted to shed light on this issue by designing an experiment in which stimulus conditions were varied instead of attentional instructions (Laan, Everaerd, van Berlo, et al., 1995). Sixty-two female subjects were presented with 21 one-minute erotic film stimuli. In one condition, subjects were exposed to 21 uniform presentations of a one-minute film excerpt. In a second condition, subjects were shown 21 one-minute film excerpts that differed in content but were about equal in stimulus intensity. Subjects in the third condition were exposed to 21 one-minute film excerpts whose content gradually increased in stimulus intensity (ranging from kissing to intercourse). Concern about a possible response set in this third condition (the expectancy that a more arousing excerpt would be presented next, thereby influencing subjective report), which could explain possible higher within-subject correlations, prompted creation of a fourth condition in which subjects were shown the excerpts of the increasing condition in random, nonincreasing order.

All subjects were asked to move a lever to indicate to what extent they were experiencing genital sensations. Results showed that individual correlations were low in the first two stimulus conditions, which had resulted in a relatively stable pattern of genital arousal over trials. Only 24% of subjects had significant correlations in the first condition, and 14% in the second condition. In contrast, the third stimulus condition resulted in a linearly increasing pattern of genital arousal and was found to produce significant individual correlations between subjective and genital arousal in 74% of subjects. The pattern of subjective responses in the fourth condition, when rearranged into the order in which they were presented in the third condition, was equivalent to the one in the third condition. This gave us reason to assume that the high number of significant correlations in the third condition was not caused by a response set. Also, 71% of subjects in the fourth condition had significant individual correlations. Incidentally, mean subjective and genital arousal scores of the four conditions, obtained by averaging over the 21 trials, did not differ significantly. The same was true for mean individual variances in subjective and genital arousal scores.

To assess whether the high correlations in the third and fourth conditions were mediated by stimulus content, for each subject in these conditions partial correlations were calculated between subjective arousal and genital arousal with trial number (1 to 21) partialled out, and between subjective arousal and trial number with genital arousal partialled out. Trial numbers 1 to 3 represented kissing scenes; trials 4 to 6 were caressing, kissing, and mutual undressing scenes; and so on to trials 19 to 21, representing intercourse scenes. It was found that stimulus content and genital arousal explained equal amounts of the variance in subjective sexual arousal ($r = .30$ and $r = .36$, respectively, $p < .10$). Thus, even though in all conditions, subjects were alerted to use genital signs of sexual arousal to assess their subjective feeling state, reasonable response agreement was found only in the two conditions in which large differences in genital arousal and stimulus content occurred over trials.

These results are in agreement with Pennebaker's (1984) observation that we only encode changes in autonomic levels; if a stimulus remains constant, we will not perceive it. It seems, therefore, that the high correlations reported by Korff and Geer (1983) did not result merely from the instruction to attend to bodily or genital activity. Rather, their results seem to be a consequence of using a design in which subjects were shown a wide range of stimuli.

Sexual Arousal in Women and the Subjective Experience of Sex

It is time to speculate on why genital arousal is a less important factor in subjective sexual arousal for women than it appears to be for men. Women and men undergo quite different learning experiences in understanding their body's signals. Girls are generally discouraged from attending to their genitals. Steiner-Adair (1990), for instance, has argued that society's insistence on the shamefulness of menstrual events is a powerful socialization that encourages young women to turn away from and even mistrust their body's physiological cues. With regard to sexual arousal, women are more socialized to restrict knowledge of their genitalia (Gartrell & Mosbacher, 1984).

These observations may reflect cultural status differences between men and women. Individuals who exercise a lower degree of social power have been shown to be more attentive to and skilled at understanding social-emotional cues in their environment than are individuals higher in social status (Frieze & Ramsey, 1976; Snodgrass, 1985). Perhaps the observed gender differences are a by-product of their status-driven attention to such cues.

It is possible that, as a result of socialization pressures, women tend to downplay their subjective reports of sexual arousal. Alternatively, they may not have had the learning experiences that men had to become accurate perceivers of bodily signs of sexual arousal. For instance, in Western cultures, men have been consistently found to masturbate more than women (see Bancroft, 1989, for a summary of these gender differences; and Oliver & Hyde, 1993, for a meta-analysis of gender differences in sexuality in the United States). Perhaps masturbation is the learning experience par excellence in making an individual an accurate perceiver of bodily signs of sexual arousal. If learning experiences indeed are a key component in the discrepancy between genital and subjective sexual arousal in women, one would predict, in line with Korff and Geer's (1983) suggestions, that instructing women to attend to bodily cues may eliminate the observed gender differences. If women have learned not to pay attention to bodily signs in their childhood, they can be encouraged to learn at a later age. In fact, one of the underlying rationales in many sex therapy programs that favor masturbation exercises for women is this "monitoring hypothesis." We have argued extensively above, however, that the instruction to women to monitor their bodily changes did not necessarily cause them to do so. Instead, they may have judged increasing stimulus intensities.

It can be argued that, even if social learning is a contributing factor to the observed discrepancy between genital and subjective measures of sexual arousal, stimulus information may be a yet more important one. It makes sense first to screen the situation one finds oneself in before engaging in sexual behavior. The reasons for doing so are likely to be more compelling for women than for men, given the double standard and the higher incidence of sexual abuse in women. The fact that sexual behavior was not the focus in the present studies does not preclude this mechanism from operating in a laboratory setting as well. For instance, Dekker and Everaerd (1988) remarked that the women in their study tended to evaluate the erotic stimulus much more critically than did the men. We have observed that most women spontaneously report aspects of the stimulus they do not like. These critical evaluations may mirror a more general tendency of women to screen situational cues, in turn reflecting the many motives of women's sexuality.

A number of biological explanations of why women tend to use situational instead of bodily cues in assessing their subjective sexual arousal have been mentioned in the literature. One concerns the anatomical differences between men and women. Women have a less obvious physiological feedback system; their physiological cues may be more ambiguous than the clear erection cue for men. This anatomical difference extends beyond visual cues. High response agreement in men also occurs in laboratory research where the subject's lap is covered with a sheet. Tactile cues, generated, for instance, by an erection pressing against clothing or the sheet, may result in stronger agreement between subjective sexual arousal and genital arousal in men than in women. Research in the domain of brain lateralization showed that the degree to which individuals evidence strong hemispheric lateralization is linked to visceral detection styles. Men apparently show greater right-hemisphere lateralization along a number of domains compared with women (see McGee, 1979, for a review). Furthermore, it has been demonstrated that women are less lateralized in general than men, which may reflect women's relatively thicker corpus callosum (Oka et al., 1999; Springer & Deutsch, 1989). This finding in women may allow for greater integration of internal and external sources of information between the hemispheres (DeLaCoste-Utamsing & Holloway, 1982). Of course, if differences in lateralization do exist in men and women, the question whether such differences came about by evolution or maturation remains to be answered.

Is Genital Arousal an Involuntary Response?

A surprising finding of our studies was the ease with which healthy women become genitally aroused in response to erotic film stimuli. When watching an erotic film depicting explicit sexual activity, most women respond with increased vaginal vasocongestion. This increase occurs within seconds after the onset of the stimulus. This ease in genital responding suggests a highly automated response mechanism. Even when these explicit sexual stimuli are negatively evaluated, or induce no or only weak feelings of sexual arousal, genital responses are elicited (Laan et al., 1994). Similarly, women sustained considerable levels of genital arousal to a one-minute erotic film stimulus, even after 21 presentations of the same stimulus (Laan & Everaerd, 1995). This occurred despite the fact that positive affect decreased over trials. Surprisingly, we even observed this ease in responding in women with a testosterone deficiency.

In a study in which we compared responses of women with hypothalamic amenorrhea to those of normally menstruating women, we found significantly lower genital responses to erotic fantasy and a film excerpt depicting foreplay in the amenorrheic women. Genital responses to a strong film excerpt depicting cunnilingus and intercourse, however, were as high as in the women with testosterone levels within the normal range (Tuiten, Laan, Panhuysen, Everaerd, et al., 1996). These findings imply that there is a strong link between sexual stimuli and genital responses. This link may be automatic or highly prepared (Geer, Lapour, & Jackson, 1992).

According to Öhman (1986), automatic information-processing mechanisms can detect emotionally significant stimuli in a preattentive analysis, which primes physiological responses. Such a highly automated mechanism is adaptive from a strictly evolutionary perspective. If genital responding did not occur to sexual stimuli, our species would quickly disappear. For women, increase in vasocongestion produces vaginal lubrication, which obviously facilitates sexual interaction. One might be tempted to assume that, for adaptive reasons, the explicit sexual stimuli used in these studies represent a class of unlearned stimuli, to which we are born to respond. At this time, there are no data available to determine whether automatic processing should be attributed to unlearned, overlearned, or conditioned stimuli (Everaerd, 1993).

We hypothesize that genital arousal is induced by automatic processing of the sexual cues in the stimuli, and conscious cognitive elaboration of contextual cues may result in nonsexual subjective experience. It may be noted here that the most frequently found pattern of responding in our studies was that genital arousal occurred in response to sexual stimuli, whereas subjective sexual arousal was low or absent. Hardly ever was desynchrony between genital and subjective sexual arousal found to be the result of subjective sexual arousal without genital responding.

A prerequisite of automatic processing seems to be that sexual meaning resulting from visual sexual stimuli is easily accessible in memory. Sexuality may be represented in a semantic network such as proposed by Lang (1984). It would be of general and theoretical interest to explore representation of sexuality in memory and its role in activating and regulating genital response. From our studies, an obvious question is whether linguistic and pictorial representations in memory are fundamentally different, or whether differences in response appear only in the activating and first stages of sexual arousal. For instance, future research may find pictorial representations in memory to be linked to automatic and early stages of sexual responding, whereas linguistic representations may be connected with the regulation, elaboration, and conscious control of sexual responding.

What Is Sexual Arousal?

The findings we presented here raise the question of how we should define sexual arousal. It is clear that genital arousal is a poor predictor of subjective sexual experience, and vice versa, suggesting those genital signs alone are not sufficient to conclude that a woman is sexually aroused. We propose that both genital and subjective indices are necessary to reliably assess sexual arousal. In our perspective, sexual arousal cannot be defined adequately without subjective experience that determines the response to a given stimulus as sexual (Rosen & Beck, 1988). There are examples of genital responding in the context of nonsexual situations, such as increases in vasocongestion during rapid eye movement (REM) sleep. Such increases in blood flow during REM occur not only in men, but also in women (Fisher et al., 1983; Van-de-Castle & Kinder, 1968). In most instances, these physiological changes are not accompanied by erotic dream content nor by subjective experience of sexual arousal. In these cases, genital arousal should not be considered to be a sexual response.

The second rationale for our point of view is of a more philosophical nature. Obviously, subjective sexual experience is the proper reflection of an individual's concerns and self-determination. Furthermore, if genital responses are taken as the sole indication of sexual arousal, it would be possible to consider these responses during rape or other types of sexual abuse as proof that the woman consented to the abuse. We dismiss such alleged consent as nonsensical. After all, our studies showed that in women, genital responding may occur involuntarily, and that for subjective experience of sexual arousal, appraisal of the (stimulus) situation seems crucial.

SEXUAL DYSFUNCTIONS

DSM-IV AND THE CONSTRUCTION OF WOMEN'S SEXUALITY

In research and in clinical practice, the *Diagnostic and Statistic Manual of Mental Disorders*, 4th edition (*DSM-IV*) (American Psychiatric Association, 1994) is used to diagnose sexual dysfunctions. It is important to realize that the definitions of sexual dysfunctions are not value-free but are influenced by theories and professional beliefs about sexuality. Concepts such as frigidity and impotence were introduced at the beginning of this century. These concepts were derived from the then current beliefs about the etiology of sexual dysfunctions. Today, most clinicians and researchers do not use these concepts; rather, they speak about "low sexual desire" or "sexual aversion" and about "erectile dysfunction." A clear illustration of the influence of the so-called zeitgeist is seen in the history of the treatment of homosexuality in the *DSM*. *DSM-I* listed homosexuality as a specification of a sexual deviation in a sociopathic personality disturbance (American Psychiatric Association, 1952). In 1968, homosexuality was classified as a sexual deviation in *DSM-II* (American Psychiatric Association, 1968). In 1974 members of the American Psychiatric Association voted to drop homosexuality as a psychiatric disorder. *DSM-III* (American

Psychiatric Association, 1980) included ego-dystonic homosexuality as a disorder, but this was deleted in *DSM-III-R* (American Psychiatric Association, 1987) and *DSM-IV* (1994). Obviously, theories and beliefs about sexuality change over time.

The *DSM-IV* classification of sexual disorders has been derived from phases of the sexual response cycle presented by Masters and Johnson (1966). Their model describes the physiological changes that accompany the developing sexual reactions. Masters and Johnson paid little attention to the subjective experience of their subjects.

The laboratory findings of Masters and Johnson (1966) showed that men and women are equally capable of physiological responding. They stressed male-female similarity in the response cycle. This emphasized the capacity of women for sexual responding, dispelling popular myths concerning female sexuality. But the tendency to equate male and female sexual response may have unintentionally obscured sex differences. Genital arousal appears to be a less important factor in subjective sexual arousal for women than it appears to be for men (Laan & Everaerd, 1995). In the previous section, we reviewed evidence for the importance, especially in women, of other than genital arousal information in assessing their subjective sexual arousal.

According to Tiefer (1991b), the *DSM* draws the line between normal and abnormal sexual function exclusively on genital performances. In the *DSM*, genital performance during heterosexual intercourse is the essence of sexual function. Nongenital alternatives for sexual pleasure and expression have been ignored. Tiefer wonders why problems such as "too little tenderness" or "partner has no sense of romance" were excluded. These problems have been frequently reported by women (Hite, 1976). The response cycle model assumes men and women have and like the same kind of sexuality. Yet, various studies show that women care more about affection and intimacy, and men care more about sexual gratification in sexual relationships (Leiblum, 1998). There seems to be support for the cliché "Men give love to get sex, and women give sex to get love." Men and women are raised with different sets of sexual values. Tiefer concludes that focusing on the physical aspects of sexuality and ignoring other aspects of the sexual response cycle favors men's value training over women's.

Masters and Johnson's (1966) model incorporates an excitement phase, a plateau phase, the orgasm phase, and a resolution phase. H.S. Kaplan (1979) amended Masters and Johnson's four-phase cycle by adding as a first step the desire phase. In the *DSM-III* (1980), sexual desire disorder was included for the first time. In the more recent *DSM* versions, a distinction is made between low desire disorder and sexual aversion disorder. Problems with sexual desire are common in clinical practice. More women than men complain about low sexual desire (Laumann, Gagnon, Michael, & Michaels, 1994; Laumann, Paik, & Rosen, 1999).

By discussing two problems, we now elaborate on the definition of sexual desire disorder in *DSM-IV*: first, the validity of the sexual desire phase, and second, the values that are involved in the definition of low sexual desire. H.S. Kaplan's (1979) desire concept is comparable to the psychoanalytic concept of libido. It is the experience of specific sensations that motivates the individual to initiate or become responsive to sexual stimulation. The sensations are said to be produced by the activation of a specific neural system in the brain. H.S. Kaplan (1995) used the concept of homeostasis as it has been used to explain hunger and thirst. However, there is no good reason to compare sexual desire to states of deprivation, which are controlled by homeostasis (Robbins & Everitt, 1999). The desire phase is said to be generated by central mechanisms (limbic activation), and excitement and orgasm are associated with the stimulation of peripheral reflex pathways in the lower spinal cord. Rosen and Beck (1988) state that specifications for the different phases are lacking as are data in support of the differentiation of drive as a centrally mediated process versus excitement and orgasm as peripherally based processes. They conclude that the desire phase is lacking an operational definition and is linked inadequately to the other phases of sexual response, excitement, and orgasm. In the chapter on male sexuality, we proposed a model that specifies that desire is the subjective experience of action tendencies that depend on increases in sexual arousal.

Let us now turn to the problem of values involved in the definition of sexual dysfunctions. A definition of low sexual desire implies some standard; however, there is no standard for normal levels of sexual desire. This makes the diagnosis of low sexual desire very subjective. We have suggested that the sexual response cycle model favors men's sexual values over women's. We should be aware of the influence of a male bias in our standard of sexual desire, and its influence on decisions about deviations from that standard. There is controversy about gender differences in sexual desire: men seem to be more sexually desirous compared to women; men and women seem to desire different things in a sexual relationship. Using the male standard for sexual desire will undeservedly pathologize women's sexual desire

DSM-IV Diagnostic Classification of Women's Sexual Dysfunctions

In this section, we discuss women's sexual dysfunctions as they are described in the *DSM-IV*. We summarize the main features and characteristics of the female sexual dysfunctions. For each dysfunction, we discuss its prevalence, some theoretical points of view, and etiological factors.

Desire

Hypoactive sexual desire disorder (302.71) is the persistent or recurrent lack or absence of sexual fantasies and desire for sexual activity. The judgment of deficiency or absence is made by the clinician, taking into account factors that affect sexual functioning, such as age and the context of the person's life. The clinician can make his or her own judgment or use the patient's judgment as a criterion. The patient may complain about having less desire than she wants, or there may be a discrepancy in desire between the patient and her partner.

Desire may have changed over time, for example, an experience of less desire relative to the past.

Reliable information concerning the prevalence of low sexual desire in the general population is scarce (Laumann et al., 1994, 1999). In sexual problem clinics, low sexual desire is the most common sexual problem in women. Often, there is comorbidity of hypoactive sexual desire and one or more other sexual disorders, in most instances, sexual arousal disorder (Segraves & Segraves, 1991). According to H.S. Kaplan's (1979, 1995) psychodynamic model, the cause of low sexual desire is unconscious and consists of active suppression of sexual desire. Suppression occurs when severe anxiety is experienced during the desire phase of sexual activity. The intensity of the anxiety can vary, from mild anxiety such as performance anxiety, fear of success, and fear of pleasure, to deep sources of anxiety such as fear of castration or injury.

In contrast to the drive model, incentive motivation models stress the importance of an external stimulus to activate the sexual system. Singer and Toates (1987) state that sexual motivation develops from the interaction of a sexual stimulus and an internal state. The internal state is influenced by hormone levels and sexual deprivation. In this view, sexual motivation is not an innate trait but an emerging property that comes about when all conditions are fulfilled (Everaerd & Laan, 1995). There are three necessary conditions: (1) an intact sexual system, (2) a (sexual) stimulus matching with this system, and (3) opportunities and rules for access to sexual partners.

An incentive motivation model underlines the importance of the attractiveness of the stimulus. Attractiveness may be influenced by habituation. There is some evidence that sexual arousal habituates to repeated presentations of the same sexual stimulus in men (O'Donohue & Geer, 1985) and in women (Meuwissen & Over, 1990). Laan and Everaerd (1995) found habituation of subjective sexual arousal but no habituation of genital arousal in women. Habituation may be a mechanism in the etiology of sexual desire disorder.

Another possible mechanism is conditioning (Letourneau & O'Donohue, 1993). Extinction of sexual responding may occur when the partner's characteristics become less reinforcing, or when the stimulation by sexual interaction becomes less reinforcing. The association of unsavory stimuli with one's sexual partner, by classical conditioning, may lead to the experience of lower desire.

Other authors present a systemic model for explaining low desire. According to Verhulst and Heiman (1988), sexual desire problems are problems in synchronization between sexual partners. There can be "too little desire" but also "too much desire." Territorial or power issues in a relationship may result in a decrease of sexual desire. It is important to be aware of constraints of the model one employs because these impact diagnoses and the focus of treatment.

Recently, notable changes in social values and norms have influenced heterosexual relationships. As a consequence of women's emancipation, sex is no longer a man's "right" and a woman's "duty." Sexual contact presupposes mutual consent; negotiation about sexual desire has to take place. Profound differences in sexual desires are problematic in this situation. In our view, sexual desire, as a property of a sexual process, by definition changes over time. The automatic or spontaneous desire of beginning relationships will wane after some time. A couple may be unaware of the fact that, over time, their relationship has become flooded with nonsexual concerns. These nonsexual concerns fragment their involvement and decrease the attentional resources for sexual desire. We predict that abstinence and restricted access will increase desire only when the couple's internal state is already positive.

The difficult part for therapists, when confronted with these problems, is to set realistic goals for their patients. It may be possible to convert negative or hostile feelings into mild or even positive feelings. But even when therapy has been successful in this respect, it is still hard to eroticise these feelings. And when patients believe that such feelings should occur spontaneously, the task is virtually impossible. When mutual consent is guiding access, however, one must be prepared to actively and strategically mobilize sexual desire. Admittedly, this is not a very romantic view: negotiating will inevitably lead to the diminishing of the intensity of sexual feelings. Sex may become less dangerous but also less exciting (Everaerd & Laan, 1995).

Aversion

Sexual aversion disorder (302.79) is the persistent or recurrent extreme aversion to and avoidance of all (or almost all) genital contact with a sexual partner. First of all, we should note that in the definition, there is a strong emphasis on genital sexual contact. A person reporting no problems with intercourse but experiencing kissing and petting as aversive would not be diagnosed.

Sexual aversion can be general but also highly specific. In the latter case, the aversion may be specific to a sexual act, for example, oral sex, or to a particular aspect, such as sperm. The pattern of avoidance may vary from avoidance of genital contact to avoidance of all potential sexual situations. Often, in discussions on aversion disorder, "aversion" and "phobia" are used interchangeably. However, aversion implies disgust whereas phobia implicates fear and avoidance. There are two approaches to sexual aversion. Some authors have suggested that sexual desire disorder and sexual aversion disorder represent a behavioral continuum, with avoidance of sex as the unifying aspect. From this perspective, sexual aversion is a more extreme avoidance than low desire. In H.S. Kaplan's (1987) approach, desire and aversion are related but different. She reported that 25% of her clients who found sexual activity aversive also met the criteria for panic disorder, whereas only 2% of those with low desire had panic disorder. Women with sexual aversion can experience desire and enjoy sexual fantasies and masturbation; on the other hand, those with low desire can engage in sexual activity without anxiety. Two separate disorders assume different etiologies, yet, apart from the clinical evidence presented by Kaplan, there are no data supporting this (Gold & Gold, 1993).

The prevalence of sexual aversion disorder is unknown. Definitional and co-morbidity problems may obscure accurate rates for sexual aversion. In the case of a very specific aversion, a clinician can miss the diagnosis by failing to ask about a variety of sexual stimuli. Clinicians may find these questions too intrusive for the patient and choose to wait for the patient to bring up the topic. In clinical practice, this leads to a situation where a person is first diagnosed as having a desire disorder, then in the course of the treatment, when the response to different stimuli is discussed, the diagnosis has to be changed to aversion disorder.

All experiences in which sexual stimuli or sexual responses are associated with negative emotion may bring about aversion. Relationship problems, fear of pregnancy, or performance anxiety, but most of all sexual abuse are examples of aversive events. Negative experiences will be represented in memory as an emotion structure containing information about the event, response to the event, and its meaning. Many stimuli can activate this fear structure, resulting in emotional reactions and possibly flashbacks. The fear may generalize to all sexual encounters, eventually resulting in avoidance of sexual situations. Many clinicians point to women's experience of sexual trauma such as childhood sexual abuse or adult rape as a significant contributor to sexual aversion and desire problems.

Arousal

Female sexual arousal disorder (302.72) is the persistent or recurrent inability to attain or to maintain until completion of the sexual activity an adequate lubrication-swelling response of sexual excitement. The emphasis is on absence of physiological response to sexual stimulation; no reference is made to the subjective experience of sexual arousal. Moreover, what is meant by "completion of the sexual activity": masturbation to orgasm, sexual contact with a partner, or sexual contact including coitus? In the section on theories about women's sexuality, we discussed research evidence that, especially for women, physiological response may not coincide with subjective experience. Women's subjective experience of sexual arousal appears to be based more on their appraisal of the situation than on their bodily responses.

Thus, in the definition of female arousal disorder, probably the most important aspect of women's experience of sexual arousal is neglected. There is evidence that women with sexual dysfunction show less physiological response compared to sexually functional women (Palace & Gorzalka, 1992). Lack of or diminished experience of arousal can be the result of absent or weak genital response. The positive or negative effect of emotion on sexual arousal is another area needing more research. For instance, fear is often regarded as a cause of sexual arousal problems, but there is no experimental evidence for an inhibiting effect of fear on physiological arousal. On the contrary, genital arousal in response to an erotic film seems to be facilitated by preexposure to a threatening stimulus (Beggs, Calhoun, & Wolchik, 1987; Palace & Gorzalka, 1990).

In a National Health and Social Life Survey (Laumann et al., 1994), 19% of the participating women report lubrication problems. In a study among women attending a gynecology clinic, 13.6% reported this complaint (Rosen, Taylor, Leiblum, & Bachmann, 1993). There are many possible causes of sexual arousal disorder. First of all, there is the effect of different life stages on sexual arousal potential. This is due both to physiological changes that occur during the various stages and to accompanying life stresses. Knowledge about changes in genital and subjective arousal over the menstrual cycle is scarce. The same is true for arousal during and after pregnancy.

Sexual arousal has seldom been specifically assessed. Masters and Johnson (1966) examined physiological response patterns of six pregnant women and observed increased vasocongestion and lubrication. Self-reports of changes in sexuality during pregnancy generally show a decline in sexual enjoyment, with some indication that this decline is partially reversed in the second trimester. There may be a specific effect of pregnancy hormones. However, vasocongestion, physical symptoms such as morning sickness, and psychological factors such as changes in body image and fears concerning the baby's welfare should also be taken into account. During breast-feeding, prolactine levels are raised and estrogen levels are below normal. This hormonal environment may be expected to have a negative impact on sexual arousal. Besides hormonal influences, factors such as fatigue, stress associated with care of the newborn, episiotomy pain, and conflicts between partners can have their impact on sexual functioning (Gjerdingen, Froberg, Chaloner, & McGovern, 1993; Klein et al., 1994).

Masters and Johnson (1966) compared older and younger women and observed less labial vasocongestion and slower vaginal vasocongestion in older women. The rate and amount of vaginal lubrication were also observed to diminish with age. The effect of menopause on the vasocongestive component of arousal is not clear. In some studies a lower response to an erotic film for postmenopausal women was observed; in other studies, there were no differences between pre- and postmenopausal women (Laan & van Lunsen, 1997; Leiblum, Bachmann, Kemmann, Colburn, & Swartzman, 1983). Obviously, events that characterize a woman's life can have a strong influence on sexual arousal. In case of arousal problems, it is important to be aware of these influences in the diagnostic phase as well as in the treatment phase.

In classic psychoanalytic theories, the cause of sexual arousal disorders has been located in oedipal conflicts. Women may unconsciously inhibit feelings of sexual pleasure due to fear of the mother's jealous reactions to the child's success in winning the father. Another possibility is loyalty to mother through avoidance of sexual pleasure.

Many interpersonal factors within a relationship may affect a woman's sexual arousal. There may be a lack of adequate stimulation, or sexual interaction may be focused solely on the sexual wishes of the partner. Premature ejaculation of the partner may also preclude women's excitement. The partner may be unaware of the woman's preference for clitoral stimulation over vaginal stimulation. Often, women complain about a lack of intimacy during lovemaking. When conditions for becoming sexually aroused are not met, and coitus is taking place despite insufficient arousal and lubrication, this may result in pain. Eventually, this may turn into a vicious cycle of pain resulting in inhibited arousal, inhibited arousal resulting in pain, and so on. Another factor that may make it difficult to become aroused is anger toward the partner (Morokoff & Gillilland, 1993). Anger may lead the woman to focus on negative ideas about her partner that will inhibit sexual arousal. This hypothesis is in line with Barlow's (1986) model of sexual dysfunction suggesting that cognitive interference interacts with anxiety to produce inhibited excitement in both men and women. Barlow emphasizes that dysfunctional subjects focus on a task-irrelevant context. According to Morokoff and Gillilland (1993), traditional sex-role expectations will keep women from focusing on their sexual responses.

Orgasm

Female orgasmic disorder (302.73) is the persistent or recurrent delay in or absence of orgasm following a normal sexual excitement phase. The diagnosis of female orgasmic disorder should be based on the clinician's judgment that the woman's orgasmic capacity is less than would be reasonable for her age, sexual experience, and the adequacy of sexual stimulation she receives.

Many variations of inhibited female orgasm are possible. A woman may experience an inability to achieve orgasm through any means. A woman may be anorgasmic except through masturbation, or except for vibrator stimulation. She may be anorgasmic except for partner stimulation. A woman may never or seldom experience orgasm through coitus. Within the *DSM* diagnosis, numerous subtypes of inhibited female orgasm are all possible.

There is no single correct or "normal" way to achieve orgasm. Rooted in Freudian theory, there has been a long-standing debate regarding vaginal versus clitoral orgasm. We already discussed Freud's ideas in the section on theories. The Hite report (1976), for instance, revealed that only 30% of the women who were able to reach orgasm achieved this through coital stimulation. We now know that women can experience orgasm in different ways: by clitoral stimulation, by vaginal stimulation, by stimulation of the vaginal wall on sensitive areas (e.g., G-spot). Some women experience multiple orgasm and others do not, or only through a specific type of stimulation. There are indications that a considerable number of women do experience multiple or consecutive orgasms, about 40% in a large sample of professional nurses according to a recent study (Darling, Davidson, & Jennings, 1991).

Orgasmic problems can be primary (lifelong) or secondary (not lifelong), global (present across situations) or situational (Masters & Johnson, 1966). Approximately 10% of women have never experienced an orgasm (Hite, 1976; Laumann et al., 1994, 1999). The ability to achieve orgasm does not predict experience of orgasm during sexual activity with a partner. A significant number of women do not experience orgasm during sexual relations. In a study of the frequency of sexual dysfunction in 100 happy marriages, 48% of women reported difficulty getting sexually aroused, 33% reported difficulty maintaining sexual arousal, 46% reported problems achieving orgasm, and 15% never experienced orgasm during sexual activity with their partner (Frank, Anderson, & Rubinstein, 1978). These figures suggest that inhibited female orgasm is very common. The majority of women do not seek help: apparently, these women do not consider orgasm the most important sexual satisfaction. In her study, Hite asked women what gave the greatest pleasure in sex. The most frequently reported aspects were "emotional intimacy, tenderness, closeness, and sharing deep feelings with a loved one" (p. 630).

Due to the lack of knowledge of the neurophysiological basis of orgasm, there is very little to say about physical causes of inhibited female orgasm. Damage to the central nervous system, the spinal cord or peripheral nerves caused by trauma, or multiple sclerosis may lead to orgasmic difficulty. There is no evidence of orgasmic difficulty as a result of hormone deficiencies (Bancroft, 1989; Sipski, 1998).

For most women, orgasm is most easily achieved by masturbation. There are various reasons why women do not masturbate. Sometimes, they lack knowledge of how to do it, or they are held back by fears, feelings of guilt, or religious considerations. These women miss the best opportunity to learn how to achieve orgasm.

Pain

Dyspareunia (302.76) is recurrent and persistent genital pain associated with sexual intercourse. The genital pain can occur before, during, and/or after intercourse. The *DSM* states that the problem cannot be caused exclusively by a lack of lubrication; in that case, the disorder is classified as sexual arousal disorder.

Two forms of dyspareunic pain are distinguished: pain experienced at the vaginal introitus (or opening) and pain felt on deep penetration. The pain can vary from aching to burning, and may also vary in intensity and duration. In addition, we can distinguish pain during or after orgasm.

The complaint of dyspareunia is a common clinical presentation, but precise statistics regarding the incidence of dyspareunia are not available (Quevillon, 1993). In their U.S. survey, Laumann et al. (1999) found a prevalence of 7%. Pain associated with orgasm is a less frequently reported form of dyspareunia. The etiology of dyspareunia is often divided into organic and psychogenic causes. This distinction between two classes is not very helpful because in most of the cases, both organic and psychogenic factors are equal contributors to the dyspareunic pain. Organic factors commonly cited as causes of pain experienced at the vaginal outlet and vaginal opening are a rigid hymen, vulvar vestibulitis, episiotomy scars, inflammation of the Bartholin's glands or the clitoris, vaginal infections, or irritation due to the use of substances such as hygiene deodorants. Vulvar vestibulitis involves pain at small spots at the lower side of the vaginal opening. The pain appears in case of coitus, touch by a finger or tampon, or even by tight pants or cycling. In general, the small inflamed spots are visible. The cause of these inflammations is not clear; a possible cause may be hyperactive pelvic floor muscles. Vulvar vestibulitis can easily give rise to a vicious cycle of painful coitus, more muscle tension, more irritation of the spots, resulting in more pain, and so on. Pain felt on deep penetration can be caused by diseases, for example, pelvic inflammatory disease, endometriosis, and abnormality of the ovary.

Often, there is no clear organic cause for the pain reported by the woman. It is important to note that various factors can influence pain. Pain is not determined by tissue injury alone, but by a balance of influences competing at various levels of the nervous system. Pain is actually a summation of inhibitory and excitatory influences coming from the side of the injury and from higher modulating centers. Factors such as anxiety, fear, and motivation may amplify or dampen pain impulses (Bergeron, Binik, Khalife, & Pagidas, 1997; Meana, Binik, Khalife, & Cohen, 1997a, 1997b). An illustration of the fact that pain is not determined by physiological state alone is cases in which there is clearly visible irritation of the skin indicating vulvar vestibulitis but no subjective experience of pain. In other cases, there is a subjective experience of painful vulval skin but no visible irritated spots.

Discrepancy between the objective organic state and the subjective perception of this state is a well-known phenomenon. Pennebaker (1982) states, based on his symptom-perception research, that the correlation between self-report and a physiological measure is generally low (.30). Pennebaker defines a bodily symptom as a perception, feeling, or even idea of the state of the body. According to his symptom-perception theory, bodily sensations are based on information from physiological processes, information from the situation, and information stored in the memory of a person. The expectancies and hypotheses of a person regarding the meaning of physical symptoms will influence the perception and interpretation of bodily sensations. When there is a strong bodily sensation, such as intense pain due to severe tissue damage, the sensation will be interpreted as pain. But in the case of mild bodily sensations, these sensations can, depending on the situational context and the expectancy of a person, be interpreted as painful or pleasurable. A symptom-perception approach to sexual pain disorders may lead to more understanding of the complaints of women with dyspareunia without an obvious organic cause.

Psychological causes of dyspareunia often mentioned are negative feelings about sexuality, fear of sex, negative feelings toward the partner, and traumatic sexual experiences such as painful first intercourse, rape, or childhood sexual abuse. Fear of sex and traumatic experiences can lead to mild vaginismus. And negative feelings toward sex can have a strong influence on a woman's expectancies of a sexual situation and thereby on the interpretation of bodily sensations (Meana et al., 1997a).

Spasm of Vaginal Introitus

Vaginismus (306.51) is the recurrent or persistent involuntary spasm of the pelvic musculature surrounding the outer third of the vagina. The specificity of vaginismus varies. In some women, spastic contraction occurs only during attempts at penile insertion during sexual encounters. In other women, contraction occurs during any attempt at penetration, such as insertion of a tampon, finger, or speculum during a gynecological pelvic examination. The severity of the muscular spasm varies also. In some women, not only the musculature of the outer third of the vagina contracts, but also the adductor muscles of the thighs, the muscles in the upper legs, and sometimes the muscles in the back and neck. As in other sexual disorders, vaginismus can be distinguished as primary or secondary. If vaginismus has been present since the first coital attempt, the term primary is applied; when the woman has had an interval of successful penetration, the term secondary vaginismus is used (Reissing, Binik, & KhalifÈ, 1999).

There are no accurate estimates of the incidence of vaginismus (Beck, 1993). Estimates in clinical samples range from 8% to 55%. The differences in estimates are most likely due to variations in the definition of vaginismus. Beck states that it is possible that many women experience mild to moderate degrees of vaginismus but never seek help.

Women with vaginismus are, in general, capable of becoming sexually aroused, and they may experience orgasm. Most models of vaginismus emphasize the role of reflexive, involuntary spasm, which is accompanied by a fear of penetration. Often, a conditioning model of vaginismus is proposed, which relies on a combination of classical and operant learning processes to explain the conditioned fear response to penetration. Painful penetration could result from an organic cause, a painful pelvic examination, or sexual trauma. In some cases, such an experience can be determined, but in many cases, no clear initiating experience can be found. Very often, sexual assault is mentioned as the cause of vaginismus. It is important to note that sexual abuse may precipitate a variety of sexual dysfunctions in women and thus is not a specific cause of vaginismus.

THE PELVIC FLOOR AND WOMEN'S SEXUALITY

The pelvic floor covers the caudal opening of the bony pelvis. All the structures located between the pelvic peritoneum and the vulvar skin belong to the pelvic floor. Situated at the bottom of the abdominopelvic cavity, attached to the walls of the bony pelvis, the pelvic floor supports the abdominal and pelvic viscera. In addition, the urethra, vagina, and rectum pass through this layer. The pelvic floor has a function not only in micturition, defecation, parturition, and the evacuation of excretory products, but also in sex.

The function of the pelvic floor has two major aspects: first, it provides support to the organs in the abdominopelvic cavity; second, it functions as a doorway by opening and closing its orifices. This is essential for the filling and evacuation of bladder and rectum and for proper sexual function. Although the pelvic floor consists of different layers and muscles, it forms an integrated unit with all parts of the pelvic floor contributing to proper function.

Disturbance of pelvic floor function is often communicated as problems with (a combination of) micturition, sexuality, and defecation. These complaints can often be traced back to a hypoactive or hyperactive pelvic floor. Hypoactivity of the pelvic floor muscles may result in urinary and fecal incontinence, genital prolapse, and loss of sexual feeling. Hyperactivity of the pelvic floor may lead to hesitated micturition, bladder outlet obstruction, and eventually urinary retention. Other symptoms of hyperactivity of the pelvic floor are constipation, irritable bowel syndrome (IBS), and obstructed defecation. Sexual problems such as vaginismus, vulvar vestibulitis, dyspareunia, and erectile difficulties (Claes & Baert, 1993) may also be a consequence of a hyperactive pelvic floor. The hyperactivity of the pelvic floor also may explain pain in the genital and pelvic floor region.

Hypoactivity of the pelvic floor muscles in women is often attributed to nerve and muscle damage due to pregnancy and parturition. The mechanism underlying hyperactivity of the pelvic floor has not yet been elucidated. However, the relationship between complaints and pelvic floor hyperactivity has been described in the literature (Duncan, 1878; Segura, Opitz, & Greene, 1979).

Sexual Function

Vaginistic contractions interfere with coitus. They occur during attempts at penetration with, for example, a penis, finger, speculum, or menstrual tampon (American Psychiatric Association, 1994). The muscles involved in these contractions, the pelvic floor muscles, surround the urethra, vagina, and anus. These muscles are under voluntary control and play, among others, a role in holding urine and feces when there is an urge to void or defecate. However, the pelvic floor muscles can also contract involuntarily, as is shown during orgasm (Perry & Whipple, 1981; Segura et al., 1979). During vaginistic reactions, the pelvic floor muscles also contract involuntarily. These contractions are spastic as opposed to the rhythmic contractions during orgasm (Fertel, 1977).

Despite the growing interest in the pelvic floor muscles and their function, little is known about the characteristics of pelvic floor muscle activity in women with sexual dysfunctions. In the literature, lack of control over these muscles is often suggested as one of the explanatory factors of vaginismus (Fordney, 1978). For example, Barnes, Bowman, and Cullen (1984) suggested that patients with vaginismus have a faulty perception of vaginal muscle tone. According to the authors, these women fail to distinguish between a relaxed state and spasm and are unaware that tone can be voluntarily altered. Van der Velde and Everaerd (1999) investigated voluntary control over pelvic floor muscles in 67 women with vaginismus and 43 control subjects with no sexual or pelvic floor complaints. Pelvic floor muscle activity was measured using an intravaginal surface EMG device, developed by Perry (1987).

When investigating pelvic floor activity, both slow-twitch and fast-twitch muscle fiber activity are important. By performing short flick contractions as well as 10-second hold contractions, the activity of both types of muscle fibers is taken into account (Norton, 1996). Voluntary control over pelvic floor muscles was defined as the ability to contract and relax these muscles when instructed to do so.

The results indicated no difference between the women with and those without vaginistic reactions; there were no differences between groups in resting tone or ability to voluntarily control the pelvic floor muscles. However, the amount of control seems to be influenced by the severity of the pelvic floor complaints. Women with vaginismus and complaints related to micturition and/or defecation showed less activity during the short flick contractions of the pelvic floor muscles compared to the control women.

Since the early 1940s an increase in voluntary control over the pelvic floor muscles has been seen as one of the important components of treatment (S. Hall, 1952; Malleson, 1942; Norton, 1996). So-called Kegel exercises to contract and relax pelvic floor muscles are often advised (Barnes et al., 1984; Colgan & Beautrais, 1977; Fertel, 1977). Kegel (1952) was the first to employ a device to measure tension in pelvic floor muscles (Colgan & Beautrais, 1977; Perry, 1987):

> Pelvic muscles are often poorly developed, because demand for use has remained minimal since childhood. To meet these various problems an apparatus was designed, known as the Perineometer, which has proved fully satisfactory during the past five years. While women who possess awareness of function of the vaginal muscles are able to carry out active exercises once they have been carefully instructed, those who lack initial awareness of function require muscle education and progressive resistive exercise with the aid of the Perineometer. (Kegel, 1952; p. 523)

Glazer et al. (1995) reported treatment results of women with vulvar vestibulitis syndrome who were treated with biofeedback. Eighty percent of the women were able to resume intercourse after a treatment that focused on pelvic floor relaxation, coordination, and strength.

Diagnostic Methods

For clinical purposes, a thorough clinical interview is needed. The aim of the initial interview is to gather detailed information concerning current sexual functioning, onset of the complaint, and the context in which the problem occurs. Sexual history should be questioned. Regarding sexual history, the clinician should ask if the woman ever experienced sexual abuse. Some women do not feel safe enough during the initial interview to reveal such experiences; nevertheless, it is necessary to ask about sexual abuse to make clear to the patient that traumatic sexual experiences can be discussed. Besides sexual history, psychiatric and medical history should be addressed. If a stable sexual relationship exists, the nature of the general relationship should be questioned. After an individual interview, a conjoint partner interview is desirable to provide information concerning the relationship and possible (sexual) problems of the partner.

The initial interviews should help the clinician in formulating the problem and in deciding whether sex therapy is indicated. An important issue is the agreement between therapist and patient about the formulation of the problem and the nature of the treatment. To reach a decision to accept treatment, the patient needs to be properly informed about what the diagnosis and the treatment involve.

Tests

Self-report measures are available for female sexual dysfunction in general and for specific dysfunctions. These self-report measures can be used as a supplement to the clinical interview. For more information concerning these measures, we refer to the *Handbook of Sexual Dysfunction* (O'Donohue & Geer, 1993) and the compendium of sexuality-related measures of C.M. Davis, Yarber, and Davis (1997). As already stated in the chapter on male sexuality, self-report measures are not very useful for clinical purposes because they lack sensitivity and specificity with regard to causes of the individual patient's dysfunction. Depending on the nature of the complaint, the initial interviews may be followed by psychophysiological or medical assessments. Thus far, psychophysiological methods have not been in common use in clinical practice. The sections on assessment of female sexual arousal and on the pelvic floor give ample evidence of valuable diagnostic information that may be obtained.

The advent of pharmacological treatments that may support sexual response will necessitate the use of psychophysiological markers of sexual desire, of sexual arousal, and possibly of orgasm. The relevance of this approach has been demonstrated in a study by Laan and van Lunsen (1997). They compared VPA responses of premenopausal and postmenopausal women. Postmenopausal women displayed lower VPA before stimulation with an erotic film. However, during stimulation, both groups showed adequate vaginal response. This finding is relevant because lower pulse amplitude is commonly attributed to vaginal atrophy associated with menopause. The Laan and van Lunsen data indicate that complaints of vaginal dryness may be a reflection of problems with sexual arousal rather than vaginal atrophy.

Medical Assessment

There are several indications for medical assessment, for example, complaints of pain during sexual activity or complaints possibly related to menopausal age. Sometimes, a general physical examination including central nervous system or hormone levels is necessary, but in most cases, only genital examination is required. Carried out in a sensitive manner, a genital examination can have a diagnostic but also an educational effect. The clinician should be aware of the emotional impact of a physical examination and the importance of the timing. When a woman is very anxious about being examined, it may be appropriate to wait until she feels more secure. In cases of women who are not familiar with self-examination of their genitalia, it is preferable to advise self-examination at home before a doctor carries out an examination.

REVIEW OF TREATMENTS AND VALIDATED EVIDENCE

Treatment of Sexual Dysfunctions

In this section, we review treatments of women's sexual dysfunctions. In the chapter on male sexuality, we concluded that there is a large number of variations built on the sex therapy developed by Masters and Johnson (1970). Variants of couple, communication, and group therapy exist and approaches vary from cognitive-behavioral and psychoanalytic to rational-emotive therapy. It is impossible in this section to describe all variations in approaches. We briefly mention the most frequently used treatment approaches for women's sexual dysfunctions.

Low sexual desire is generally treated with the classical Masters and Johnson approach, using sensate focus exercises, interventions to minimize performance pressure, and communication training. In the treatment of sexual aversion, the focus is on decreasing anxiety, the common core of sexual aversions. Behavioral techniques, such as exposure, are most commonly used. Sometimes, when the phobic response is so strong that it interferes with the ability to respond to psychological treatment, medication is used during the first exposure steps (Everaerd & Laan, 1995; Shover & Leiblum, 1994).

Compared to the highly medicalized treatment of sexual arousal disorder in men, the treatment of female sexual arousal disorder is strongly focused on psychological aspects. There are some pharmacological treatments: in the case of estrogen deficiency, for example, hormone replacement is recommended (Sarrel, 1997, 1999). Studies on the effect of smooth muscle relaxants on sexual response in women have just started. Considering the discordance between physiological and subjective response in women, a very limited effect may be expected of this kind of pharmacological treatment on women's sexual satisfaction (Rosen, Phillips, Gendrano, & Ferguson, 1999). Psychological treatment of sexual arousal problems generally consists of sensate focus exercises and masturbation training, with the emphasis on becoming more self-focused and assertive.

For the treatment of primary anorgasmia, there exists a well-described treatment protocol (LoPiccolo & Lobitz, 1972). Basic elements of this program are education, self-exploration and body awareness, and directed masturbation. Because of the broad range of problems behind the diagnosis of secondary anorgasmia, there is no major treatment strategy for this sexual disorder. Depending on the problem, education, disinhibition strategies, and assertiveness training are used. It is important to identify unrealistic goals for treatment, such as achieving orgasm during intercourse without clitoral stimulation (Stock, 1993).

As noted before in the discussion of dyspareunia, there are multiple possible somatic and psychological causes of this disorder. Treatment should be tuned to the specific causes diagnosed and can vary from patient to patient. Behavioral interventions typically include prohibition of intercourse, and finger exploration of the vagina, first by the woman, then by her partner. Sensate focus exercises may be used to increase sexual arousal and sexual satisfaction. Kegel exercises and relaxation training can be recommended in cases of vaginismus or a high level of muscle tension in the pelvic floor.

Treatment of vaginismus commonly involves exposure to vaginal penetration by using dilators of increasing size or the woman's fingers. Kegel exercises may be used to provide training in discrimination of vaginal muscle contraction and relaxation, and to teach voluntary control over muscle spasm.

Validated Treatments for Women's Sexual Dysfunctions

Recently, several reviews of treatments for sexual dysfunctions following the criteria for validated or evidence-based practice have been published (Baucom, Shoham, Mueser, Daiuto, & Stickle, 1998; Heiman & Meston, 1997; O'Donohue, Dopke, & Swingen, 1997). Heiman and Meston concluded that treatments for primary anorgasmia fulfil the criteria of "well-established," and secondary anorgasmia studies fall into the "probably efficacious" group. They concluded with some reservations that vaginismus appears to be successfully treated if repeated practice with vaginal dilators is included in the treatment. Their reservations are due to a lack of controlled or treatment comparison studies of vaginismus. All authors concluded that adequate data on the treatment of sexual desire disorder, sexual arousal disorder, and dyspareunia are lacking.

In the chapter on male sexuality, we argued that, despite our support of the evidence-based practice movement, care for patients with sexual problems must continue even without proof, according to the rules of "good clinical practice."

NOTES

Some paragraphs about psychophysiological measures and cognitive emotion theory earlier have appeared in Laan and Everaerd (1995).

The information services of the Kinsey Institute provide extensive information on measurement and assessment at http://www.indiana.edu/~kinsey/bib-measures.html.

REFERENCES

Acton, W. (1875). *The functions and disorders of the reproductive organs in childhood, youth, adult age, and advanced life* (6th ed.). Philadelphia: Presley Blackstone. (Original work published 1875)

Alzate, H. (1985). Vaginal eroticism and female orgasm: A current appraisal. *Journal of Sex and Marital Therapy, 11,* 271–284.

American Psychiatric Association. (1952). *Diagnostic and statistical manual.* Washington, DC: Author.

American Psychiatric Association. (1968). *Diagnostic and statistical manual of mental disorders* (2nd ed.). Washington, DC: Author.

American Psychiatric Association. (1980). *Diagnostic and statistical manual of mental disorders* (3rd ed.). Washington, DC: Author.

American Psychiatric Association. (1987). *Diagnostic and statistical manual of mental disorders* (3rd ed., rev.). Washington, DC: Author.

American Psychiatric Association. (1994). *Diagnostic and statistical manual of mental disorders* (4th ed.). Washington, DC: Author.

Bancroft, J. (1989). *Human sexuality and its problems.* Edinburgh: Churchill Livingstone.

Barlow, D.H. (1986). Causes of sexual dysfunction. *Journal of Consulting and Clinical Psychology, 54,* 140–148.

Barnes, J., Bowman, E.P., & Cullen, J. (1984). Biofeedback as an adjunct to psychotherapy in the treatment of vaginismus. *Biofeedback and Self Regulation, 9,* 281–289.

Baucom, D.H., Shoham, V., Mueser, K.T., Daiuto, A.D., & Stickle, T.R. (1998). Empirically supported couple and family interventions for marital distress and adult mental health problems. *Journal of Consulting and Clinical Psychology, 66,* 53–88.

Beck, J.G. (1993). Vaginismus. In W. O'Donohue & J.H. Geer (Eds.), *Handbook of sexual dysfunctions: Assessment and treatment* (pp. 381–397). Boston: Allyn & Bacon.

Beck, J.G., Barlow, D.H., & Sakheim, D.K. (1983). The effects of attentional focus and partner arousal on sexual responding in functional and dysfunctional men. *Behaviour Research and Therapy, 21,* 1–8.

Beggs, V.E., Calhoun, K.S., & Wolchik, S.A. (1987). Sexual anxiety and female sexual arousal: A comparison of arousal during sexual anxiety stimuli and sexual pleasure stimuli. *Archives of Sexual Behavior, 16,* 311–9.

Belzer, E.G., Whipple, B., & Moger, W. (1984). On female ejaculation. *Journal of Sex Research, 20,* 403–406.

Bentler, P.M. (1968a). Heterosexual behavior assessment: I. Males. *Behaviour Research and Therapy, 6,* 21–25.

Bentler, P.M. (1968b). Heterosexual behavior assessment: II. Females. *Behaviour Research and Therapy, 6,* 27–30.

Bergeron, S., Binik, Y.M., KhalifÈ, S., & Pagidas, K. (1997). Vulvar vestibulitis syndrome: A critical review. *Clinical Journal of Pain, 13,* 27–42.

Birke, L.I.A., & Vines, G. (1987). Beyond nature versus nurture: Process and biology in the development of gender. *Women's Studies International Forum, 10,* 555–570.

Byrne, D. (1977). Social psychology and the study of sexual behavior. *Personality and Social Psychology Bulletin, 3,* 3–30.

Byrne, D. (1983). The antecedents, correlates and consequents of erotophobia-erotophilia. In M. Davis (Ed.), *Challenges in sexual science.* New York: Society for the Scientific Study of Sex.

Cacioppo, J.T., Berntson, G.G., & Klein, D.J. (1992). What is emotion? The role of somatovisceral afference, with special emphasis on somatovisceral "illusions." In M.S. Clark (Ed.), *Review of personality and social psychology: Emotion and social behavior* (Vol.14, pp. 63–98). Newbury Park. CA: Sage.

Chua, C.A. (1997). A proposal for a radical new sex therapy technique for the management of vasocongestive and orgasmic dysfunction in women: The AFE zone stimulation technique. *Sexual and Marital Therapy, 12,* 357–370.

Claes, H., & Baert, L. (1993). Pelvic floor exercise versus surgery in the treatment of impotence. *British Journal of Urology, 71*, 52–57.

Colgan, A.H., & Beautrais, P.G. (1977). Vaginal muscle control in vaginismus. *New Zealand Medical Journal, 86*, 300.

Darling, C.A., Davidson, J., Sr., & Jennings, D.A. (1991). The female sexual response revisited: Understanding the multiorgasmic experience in women. *Archives of Sexual Behavior, 20*, 527–540.

Davis, C.M., Yarber, W.L., & Davis, S.L. (1997). *Handbook of sexuality related measures.* Thousand Oaks, CA: Sage.

Davis, S.R. (1998, May). The role of androgens and the menopause in the female sexual response. *International Journal of Impotence Research, 10*, S82–S83.

Dekker, J., & Everaerd, W. (1988). Attentional effects on sexual arousal. *Psychophysiology, 25*, 45–54.

DeLaCoste-Utamsing, M.C., & Holloway, R.L. (1982). Sexual dimorphism in the human corpus callosum. *Science, 216*, 1431–1432.

DePaulo, B.M., Jordan, A., Irvine, A., & Laser, P.S. (1982). Age changes in detection of deception. *Child Development, 53*, 701–709.

Dixon, A. (1998). *Primate sexuality: Comparative studies of the prosimians, monkeys, apes, and human beings.* Oxford, England: Oxford University Press.

Duncan, J.M. (1878). Clinical lecture on vaginismus. *Medical Times and Gazette, 2*(1477), 453–455.

Ekman, P. (1984). Expression and the nature of emotion. In K.R. Scherer & P. Ekman (Eds.), *Approaches to emotion* (pp. 319–344). Hillsdale, NJ: Erlbaum.

Ekman, P., Levenson, R.W., & Friesen, W.V. (1983). Autonomic nervous system activity distinguishes among emotions. *Science, 221*, 1208–1210.

Ellis, A. (1920). *Studies in the psychology of sex.* Philadelphia: Davis. (Original work published 1903)

Everaerd, W. (1988). Commentary on sex research: Sex as an emotion. *Journal of Psychology and Human Sexuality, 1*, 3–15.

Everaerd, W. (1993). Male erectile disorder. In W. O'Donohue & J.H. Geer (Eds.), *Handbook of sexual dysfunctions: Assessment and treatment* (pp. 201–224). Boston: Allyn & Bacon.

Everaerd, W., & Dekker, J. (1981). A comparison of sex therapy and communication therapy: Couples complaining of orgasmic dysfunction. *Journal of Sex and Marital Therapy, 7*, 278–289.

Everaerd, W., & Laan, E. (1994). Cognitive aspects of sexual functioning and dysfunctioning. *Sexual and Marital Therapy, 9*, 225–230.

Everaerd, W., & Laan, E. (1995). Desire for passion: Energetics of sexual response. *Journal of Sex and Marital Therapy, 21*, 255–263.

Fertel, N.S. (1977). Vaginismus: A review. *Journal of Sex and Marital Therapy, 3*, 113–121.

Fischer, A. (1994). *The self-fulfilling prophecy of emotional woman: The case of powerless emotions.* Unpublished manuscript, University of Amsterdam.

Fisher, C., Cohen, H.D., Schiavi, R.C., Davis, D., Furman, B., Ward, K., Edwards, A., & Cunningham, J. (1983). Patterns of female sexual arousal during sleep and waking: Vaginal thermo-conductance studies. *Archives of Sexual Behavior, 12*, 97–122.

Fordney, D.S. (1978). Dyspareunia and vaginismus. *Clinical Obstetrics and Gynecology, 21*, 205–221.

Fourcroy, J.L. (1998, May). Issues and priorities in the development of drug treatments for female sexual dysfunction. *International Journal of Impotence Research, 10,* S121–S123.

Frank, E., Anderson, C., & Rubinstein, D.N. (1978). Frequency of sexual dysfunction in normal couples. *New England Journal of Medicine, 299,* 111–115.

Freud, S. (1953). *The standard edition of the complete psychological works of Sigmund Freud.* London: Hogarth Press.

Frieze, I.H., & Ramsey, S.J. (1976). Nonverbal maintenance of traditional sex roles. *Journal of Social Issues, 32,* 133–141.

Frijda, N.H. (1986). *The emotions.* Cambridge, England: Cambridge University Press.

Gagnon, J., & Simon, W. (1973). *Sexual conduct: The social sources of human sexuality.* Chicago: Aldine.

Gandelman, R. (1983). Gonadal hormones and sensory function. *Neuroscience and Biobehavioral Reviews, 7,* 1–17.

Gartrell, N., & Mosbacher, D. (1984). Sex differences in naming children's genitalia. *Sex Roles, 10,* 867–876.

Geer, J.H., & Broussard, D. (1990). Scaling sexual behavior and arousal: Consistency and sex differences. *Journal of Personality and Social Psychology, 58,* 664–671.

Geer, J.H., Lapour, K.J., & Jackson, S.R. (1992). The information processing approach to human sexuality. In N. Birbaumer & A. Öhman (Eds.), *The structure of emotion: Psychophysiological, cognitive, and clinical aspects* (pp. 138–155). Toronto: Hogrefe-Huber.

Geer, J.H., Morokoff, P., & Greenwood, P. (1974). Sexual arousal in women: The development of a measurement device for vaginal blood volume. *Archives of Sexual Behavior, 3,* 559–564.

Gillan, P., & Brindley, G.S. (1979). Vaginal and pelvic floor responses to sexual stimulation. *Psychophysiology, 16,* 471–481.

Gjerdingen, D.K., Froberg, D.G., Chaloner, K.M., & McGovern, P.M. (1993). Changes in women's physical health during the first postpartum year. *Archives of Family Medicine, 2,* 277–283.

Glazer, H.I., Rodke, G., Swenconius, C., Hertz, R., & Young, A.W. (1995). Treatment of vulvar vestibulitis syndrome with electromyographic biofeedback of pelvic floor musculature. *Journal of Reproductive Medicine, 40,* 283–290.

Gold, S.R., & Gold, R.G. (1993). Sexual aversion: A hidden disorder. In W. O'Donohue & J.H. Geer (Eds.), *Handbook of sexual dysfunctions: Assessment and treatment* (pp. 149–194). Boston: Allyn & Bacon.

Goldberg, D.C., Whipple, B., Fishkin, R.E., Waxman, H., Fink, P.J., & Weisberg, M. (1983). The Grafenberg spot and female ejaculation: A review of initial hypotheses. *Journal of Sex and Marital Therapy, 9,* 27–37.

Grafenberg, E. (1950). The role of the urethra in female orgasm. *International Journal of Sexology, 3,* 145–148.

Griffitt, W. (1975). Sexual experience and sexual responsiveness: Sex differences. *Archives of Sexual Behavior, 4,* 529–540.

Hall, J.A. (1984). *Nonverbal sex differences.* Baltimore: Johns Hopkins University Press.

Hall, S. (1952). Vaginismus as cause of dyspareunia: A report of cases and method of treatment. *Western Journal of Clinical and Experimental Hypnosis, 60,* 117–120.

Hatch, J.P. (1979). Vaginal photoplethysmography: Methodological considerations. *Archives of Sexual Behavior, 8,* 357–374.

Heiman, J.R. (1977). A psychophysiological exploration of sexual arousal patterns in females and males. *Psychophysiology, 14*, 266–274.

Heiman, J.R. (1980). Female sexual response patterns: Interactions of physiological, affective, and contextual cues. *Archives of General Psychiatry, 37*, 1311–1316.

Heiman, J.R., & Meston, C.M. (1997). Evaluating sexual dysfunction in women. *Clinical Obstetrics and Gynecology, 40*, 616–629.

Henson, C., Rubin, H.B., & Henson, D.E. (1979). Women's sexual arousal concurrently assessed by three genital measures. *Archives of Sexual Behavior, 8*, 459–469.

Henson, D.E., Rubin, H.B., & Henson, C. (1979). Analysis of the consistency of objective measures of sexual arousal in women. *Journal of Applied Behavior Analysis, 12*, 701–711.

Hite, S. (1976). *The Hite report.* New York: Dell.

Hoon, P.W., Wincze, J.P., & Hoon, E.F. (1977). A test of reciprocal inhibition: Are anxiety and sexual arousal in women mutually inhibitory? *Journal of Abnormal Psychology, 86*, 65–74.

Izard, C.E., & Blumberg, S.H. (1985). Emotion theory and the role of anxiety in children and adults. In A. Husain Tuma & J. Maser (Eds.), *Anxiety and anxiety disorders* (pp. 109–129). Hillsdale, NJ: Erlbaum.

James, W. (1950). *The principles of psychology.* New York: Dover. (Original work published 1890)

Janssen, E., Post, S., & Everaerd, W. (1993). *Sex differences in sexual behavior and arousal.* Unpublished manuscript.

Kaplan, H.S. (1979). *Disorders of sexual desire.* New York: Brunner/Mazel.

Kaplan, H.S. (1987). *Sexual aversion, sexual phobias and panic disorder.* New York: Brunner/Mazel.

Kaplan, H.S. (1995). *The sexual desire disorders. The dysfunctional regulation of sexual motivation.* New York: Brunner/Mazel.

Kaplan, S.A., Reis, R.B., Kohn, I.J., Ikeguchi, E.F., Laor, E., Te, A.E., & Martins, A.C. (1999). Safety and efficacy of sildanafil in postmenopausal women with sexual dysfunction. *Urology, 53*, 481–486.

Kegel, A.H. (1952). Sexual function of the pubococcygeus muscle. *Western Journal of Surgery, Obstetrics and Gynecology, 60*, 521–524.

Klein, M.C., Gauthier, R.J., Robbins, J.M., Kaczorowski, J., Jorgensen, S.H., Franco, E.D., Johnson, B., Waghorn, K., Gelfand, M.M., Guralnick, M.S., Luskey, G.W., & Joshi, A.K. (1994). Relationship of episiotomy to perineal trauma and morbidity, sexual dysfunction, and pelvic floor relaxation. *American Journal of Obstetrics and Gynecology, 171*, 591–598.

Kolodny, R.C., Masters, W.H., & Johnson, V.E. (1979). *Textbook of sexual medicine.* Boston: Little, Brown.

Korff, J., & Geer, J.H. (1983). The relationship between sexual arousal experience and genital response. *Psychophysiology, 20*, 121–127.

Laan, E., & Everaerd, W. (1995). Habituation of female sexual arousal to slides and film. *Archives of Sexual Behavior, 24*, 517–541.

Laan, E., Everaerd, W., & Evers, A. (1995). Assessment of female sexual arousal: Response specificity and construct validity. *Psychophysiology, 32*, 476–485.

Laan, E., Everaerd, W., Van Aanhold, M.T., & Rebel, M. (1993). Performance demand and sexual arousal in women. *Behaviour Research and Therapy, 31*, 25–35.

Laan, E., Everaerd, W., van Bellen, G., & Hanewald, G. (1994). Women's sexual and emotional responses to male- and female-produced erotica. *Archives of Sexual Behavior, 23,* 153–169.

Laan, E., Everaerd, W., van Berlo, R., & Rijs, L. (1995). Mood and sexual arousal in women. *Behaviour Research and Therapy, 33,* 441–443.

Laan, E., Everaerd, W., van der Velde, J., & Geer, J.H. (1995). Determinants of subjective experience of sexual arousal in women: Feedback from genital arousal and erotic stimulus content. *Psychophysiology, 32,* 444–451.

Laan, E., & van Lunsen, R. (1997). Hormones and sexuality in postmenopausal women: A psychophysiological study. *Journal of Psychosomatic Obstetrics and Gynecology, 18,* 126–133.

Lang, P.J. (1984). Cognition in emotion. Concept and action. In C.E. Izard, J. Kagan, & R.B. Zajonc (Eds.), *Emotions, cognition and behavior* (pp. 192–225). New York: Cambridge University Press.

Lang, P.J. (1970). Stimulus control, response control, and the desensitization of fear. In D.J. Levis (Ed.), *Learning approaches to therapeutic behavior change* (pp. 148–173). Chicago: Aldine.

Laqueur, T. (1990). *Making sex: Body and gender from the Greeks to Freud.* Cambridge, MA: Harvard University Press.

Laumann, E.O., Gagnon, J.H., Michael, R.T., & Michaels, S. (1994). *The social organization of sexuality.* Chicago: University of Chicago Press.

Laumann, E.O., Paik, A., & Rosen, R.C. (1999). Sexual dysfunction in the United States: Prevalence and predictors. *Journal of the American Medical Association, 281,* 537–544.

Leiblum, S.R. (1998, May). Definition and classification of female sexual disorders. *International Journal of Impotence Research, 10,* S104–S106.

Leiblum, S.R., Bachmann, G., Kemmann, E., Colburn, D., & Swartzman, L. (1983). Vaginal atrophy in the postmenopausal woman: The importance of sexual activity and hormones. *Journal of the American Medical Association, 249,* 2195–2198.

Letourneau, E., & O'Donohue, W. (1993). Sexual desire disorders. In W. O'Donohue & J.H. Geer (Eds.), *Handbook of sexual dysfunctions: Assessment and treatment* (pp. 53–82). Boston: Allyn & Bacon.

Levin, R.J. (1992). The mechanisms of female sexual arousal. *Annual Review of Sex Research, 3,* 1–48.

LoPiccolo, J., & Lobitz, W.C. (1972). The role of masturbation in the treatment of orgasmic dysfunction. *Archives of Sexual Behavior, 2,* 163–171.

Malleson, J. (1942). Vaginismus: Its management and psychogenesis. *British Medical Journal,* 216.

Masters, W.H., & Johnson, V.E. (1966). *Human sexual response.* Boston: Little, Brown.

Masters, W.H., & Johnson, V.E. (1970). *Human sexual inadequacy.* Boston: Little, Brown.

McGee, M.G. (1979). Human spatial abilities: Psychometric studies and environmental, genetic, hormonal, and neurological influences. *Psychological Bulletin, 86,* 889–918.

Meana, M., Binik, Y.M., Khalife, S., & Cohen, D.R. (1997a). Biopsychosocial profile of women with dyspareunia. *Obstetrics and Gynecology, 90,* 583–589.

Meana, M., Binik, Y.M., Khalifè, S., & Cohen, D.R. (1997b). Dyspareunia: Sexual dysfunction or pain syndrome? *Journal of Nervous and Mental Diseases, 185,* 561–569.

Meuwissen, I., & Over, R. (1990). Habituation and dishabituation of female sexual arousal. *Behaviour Research and Therapy, 28,* 217–226.

Morokoff, P.J., & Gillilland, R. (1993). Stress, sexual functioning, and marital satisfaction. *Journal of Sex Research, 30*, 43–53.

Musaph, H. (1977). Skin, touch, and sex. In J. Money & H. Musaph (Eds.), *Handbook of sexology* (pp. 1157–1164). Amsterdam, The Netherlands: Exerpta Medica.

Norton, P. (1996). Summary and paramount anatomy and physiology of the pelvic floor. In B. Schüssler, J. Laycock, P. Norton, & S. Stanton (Eds.), *Pelvic floor re-education and practice* (pp. 34–36). London: Springer-Verlag.

O'Connell, H.E., Hutson, J.M., Anderson, C.R., & Plenter, R.J. (1998). Anatomical relationship between urethra and clitoris. *Journal of Urology, 159*, 1892–1897.

O'Donohue, W.T., Dopke, C.A., & Swingen, D.N. (1997). Psychotherapy for female sexual dysfunction: A review. *Clinical Psychology Review, 17*, 537–566.

O'Donohue, W.T., & Geer, J.H. (1985). The habituation of sexual arousal. *Archives of Sexual Behavior, 14*, 233–246.

O'Donohue, W.T., & Geer, J.H. (1993). *Handbook of sexual dysfunctions: Assessment and treatment.* Boston: Allyn & Bacon.

Öhman, A. (1986). Face the beast and fear the face: Animal and social fears as prototypes for evolutionary analysis of emotion. *Psychophysiology, 23*, 123–145.

Oka, S., Miyamoto, O., Janjua, N.A., Honjo-Fujiwara, N., Ohkawa, M., Nagao, S., Kondo, H., Minami, T., Toyoshima, T., & Itano, T. (1999). Re-evaluation of sexual dimorphism in human corpus callosum. *Neuroreport, 10*, 937–940.

Oliver, M.B., & Hyde, J.S. (1993). Gender differences in sexuality: A meta-analysis. *Psychological Bulletin, 114*, 29–51.

Osborn, C.A., & Pollack, R.H. (1977). The effects of two types of erotic literature on physiological and verbal measures of female sexual arousal. *Journal of Sex Research, 13*.

Palace, E.M., & Gorzalka, B.B. (1990). The enhancing effects of anxiety on arousal in sexually dysfunctional and functional women. *Journal of Abnormal Psychology, 99*, 403–411.

Palace, E.M., & Gorzalka, B.B. (1992). Differential patterns of arousal in sexually functional and dysfunctional women: Physiological and subjective components of sexual response. *Archives of Sexual Behavior, 21*, 135–159.

Parlee, M.B. (1983). Menstrual rhythm in sensory processes: A review of fluctuations in vision, olfaction, audition, taste, and touch. *Psychological Bulletin, 93*, 539–548.

Pennebaker, J.W. (1982). *The psychology of physical symptoms.* New York: Springer-Verlag.

Pennebaker, J.W. (1984). Physical symptoms and sensations: Psychological causes and correlates. In J.T. Cacioppo & R.E. Petty (Eds.), *Social psychophysiology* (pp. 543–563). New York: Guilford Press.

Pennebaker, J.W., & Roberts, T.A. (1992). Towards a his and hers theory of emotion: Gender differences in visceral perception. *Journal of Social and Clinical Psychology, 11*, 199–212.

Perry, J.D. (1987). *Handbook of EMG perineometry.* Strafford: Perrymeter Systems.

Perry, J.D., & Whipple, B. (1981). Pelvic muscle strength of female ejaculators: Evidence in support of a new theory of orgasm. *Journal of Sex Research, 17*, 22–39.

Quevillon, R.P. (1993). Dyspareunia. In W. O'Donohue & J.H. Geer (Eds.), *Handbook of sexual dysfunctions: Assessment and treatment.* Boston: Allyn & Bacon.

Reed, S.D., Harver, A., & Katkin, E.S. (1990). Interoception. In J.T. Cacioppo & L.G. Tassinary (Eds.), *Principles of psychophysiology: Physical, social and inferential elements* (pp. 253–291). Cambridge, England: Cambridge University Press.

Reissing, E.D., Binik, Y.M., & KhalifÈ, S. (1999). Does vaginismus exist? A critical review of the literature. *Journal of Nervous and Mental Diseases, 187*(5), 261–274.

Robbins, T.W., & Everitt, B.J. (1999). Motivation and reward. In M.J. Zigmond, F.E. Bloom, S.C. Landis, J.L. Roberts, & L.R. Squire (Eds.), *Fundamental neuroscience* (pp. 1245–1260). San Diego: Academic Press.

Rosen, R.C., & Beck, J.G. (1988). *Patterns of sexual arousal.* New York: Guilford Press.

Rosen, R.C., Phillips, N.A., Gendrano, N.C., & Ferguson, D.M. (1999). Oral-phentolamine and female sexual arousal disorder: A pilot study. *Journal of Sex and Marital Therapy, 25*, 137–144.

Rosen, R.C., Taylor, J.F., Leiblum, S.R., & Bachmann, G.A. (1993). Prevalence of sexual dysfunction in women: Results of a survey study of 329 women in an outpatient gynecological clinic. *Journal of Sex and Marital Therapy, 19*, 171–188.

Sarrel, P.M. (1997). Hormone replacement therapy in the menopause. *International Journal of Fertility and Women's Medicine, 42*, 78–84.

Sarrel, P.M. (1999). Psychosexual effects of menopause: Role of androgens. *American Journal of Obstetrics and Gynecology, 180*, 319–324.

Schachter, S., & Singer, J. (1962). Cognitive, social, and physiological determinants of emotional state. *Psychological Review, 69*, 379–399.

Segraves, K.B., & Segraves, R.T. (1991). Hypoactive sexual desire disorder: Prevalence and comorbidity in 906 subjects. *Journal of Sex and Marital Therapy, 17*, 55–58.

Segura, J.W., Opitz, J.L., & Greene, L.F. (1979). Prostatosis, prostatitis or pelvic tension myalgia? *Journal of Urology, 122*(2), 168–169.

Sherwin, B.B., Gelfand, M.M., & Brender, W. (1985). Androgen enhances sexual motivation in females: A prospective, crossover study of sex steroid administration in the surgical menopause. *Psychosomatic Medicine, 47*, 339–351.

Shorter, E. (1984). *A history of women's bodies.* London: Penguin Books.

Shover, L.R., & Leiblum, S.R. (1994). Commentary: Stagnation of sex therapy. *Journal of Psychology and Human Sexuality, 6*, 5–30.

Singer, B., & Toates, F.M. (1987). Sexual motivation. *Journal of Sex Research, 23*, 481–501.

Sintchak, G., & Geer, J.H. (1975). A vaginal photoplethysmograph system. *Psychophysiology, 12*, 113–115.

Sipski, M.L. (1998, May). Sexual functioning in the spinal cord injured. *International Journal of Impotence Research, 10*, S128–S130.

Slob, A.K., Bax, C.M., Hop, W.C., Rowland, D.L., & van-der-Werff-ten-Bosch, J.J. (1996). Sexual arousability and the menstrual cycle. *Psychoneuroendocrinology, 21*, 545–558.

Snodgrass, S.E. (1985). Women's intuition: The effect of subordinate role on impersonal sensitivity. *Journal of Personality and Social Psychology, 49*, 146–155.

Springer, S.P., & Deutsch, G. (1989). *Left brain, right brain* (3rd ed.). New York: Freeman.

Steiner-Adair, C. (1990). The body politic: Normal female adolescent development and the development of eating disorders. In C. Gilligan, N.P. Lyons, & T.J. Hanmer (Eds.), *Making connections: The relational worlds of adolescent girls at Emma Willard School* (pp. 162–182). Cambridge, MA: Harvard University Press.

Steinman, D.L., Wincze, J.P., Sakheim, B.A., Barlow, D.H., & Mavissakalian, M. (1981). A comparison of male and female patterns of sexual arousal. *Archives of Sexual Behavior, 10*, 529–547.

Stekel, W. (1967). *Frigidity in women.* New York: Washington Square Press. (Original work published 1926)

Stemmler, G. (1989). The autonomic differentiation of emotions revisited. *Psychophysiology, 26*, 617–632.

Stock, W.E. (1993). Inhibited female orgasm. In W. O'Donohue & J.H. Geer (Eds.), *Handbook of sexual dysfunctions: Assessment and treatment* (pp. 253–278). Boston: Allyn & Bacon.

Stock, W.E., & Geer, J.H. (1982). A study of fantasy-based sexual arousal in women. *Archives of Sexual Behavior, 11*, 33–47.

Tiefer, L. (1991a). *Feminism matters in sexology.* Paper presented at the 10th World Congress of Sexology, Amsterdam, The Netherlands.

Tiefer, L. (1991b). Historical, scientific, clinical and feminist criticism of "the human sexual response cycle model." *Annual Review of Sex Research, 2*, 4–23.

Tuiten, A., Laan, E., Panhuysen, G., Everaerd, W., de Haan, E., Koppeschaar, H., & Vroon, P. (1996). Discrepancies between genital responses and subjective sexual function during testosterone substitution in women with hypothalamic amenorrhea. *Psychosomatic Medicine, 58*, 234–241.

Van-de-Castle, R.L., & Kinder, P. (1968). Dream content during pregnancy. *Psychophysiology, 4*, 375.

Vanderhoff, E., & Clancy, J. (1962). Peripheral blood flow as an indicator of emotional reaction. *Journal of Applied Physiology, 17*, 67–70.

van der Velde, J., & Everaerd, W. (1999). Voluntary control over pelvic muscles in women with and without vaginistic reactions. *International Urogynaecology Journal and Pelvic Floor Dysfunction, 10.*

van der Velde, J., Klooster, H., Messelink, E.J., Gorgels, J., & Everaerd, W. (1999). *Female ejaculation: An investigation of a controversy.* Manuscript in preparation.

Verhulst, J., & Heiman, J.R. (1988). A systems perspective on sexual desire. In S.R. Leiblum & R.C. Rosen (Eds.), *Sexual desire disorders.* New York: Guilford Press.

Weijmar Schultz, W.C.M., & van de Wiel, H.B.M. (1991). *Sexual functioning after gynaecological cancer treatment.* Unpublished doctoral dissertation. University of Groningen.

Weijmar Schultz, W.C.M., van de Wiel, H.B.M., Klatter, J.A., Sturm, B.E., & Nauta, J. (1989). Vaginal sensitivity to electric stimuli: Theoretical and practical implications. *Archives of Sexual Behavior, 18*, 87–95.

Weininger, O. (1909). *Geslecht un Charakter* [Sex and character]. Wien: Wilhelm Braumller.

Weinman, J. (1967). Photoplethysmography. In P.H. Venables & I. Martin (Eds.), *A manual of psychophysiological methods* (pp. 185–217). Amsterdam, The Netherlands: North-Holland.

Williamson, S., & Nowak, R. (1998). The truth about women. *New Scientist, 159*, 34–35.

Wincze, J.P., Hoon, P.W., & Hoon, E.F. (1977). Sexual arousal in women: A comparison of cognitive and physiological responses by continuous measurement. *Archives of Sexual Behavior, 6*, 121–133.

Wincze, J.P., Venditti, E., Barlow, D., & Mavissakalian, M. (1980). The effects of a subjective monitoring task in the physiological measure of genital response to erotic stimulation. *Archives of Sexual Behavior, 9*, 533–545.

PART II

CORE ISSUES

CHAPTER 4

Issues of Transgender

SANDRA S. COLE, DALLAS DENNY, A. EVAN EYLER,
and SANDRA L. SAMONS

TERMINOLOGY, GENDER DIVERSITY, AND THE PRIMACY OF GENDER

UNTIL THE MID-1990s, it was believed that transgendered individuals could be categorized as either transvestites or transsexuals. Male-to-female (MTF) transsexuals were considered to be of two types: primary and secondary (Person & Ovesey, 1974a, 1974b). Primary transsexuals were thought to be more "naturally" feminine (cf. Stoller, 1968b), to present for treatment at an earlier age, and to make better posttransition adjustments than secondary transsexuals, whose transsexualism gradually developed out of either heterosexual or homosexual crossdressing, although most MTF crossdressers were considered to be in an entirely separate category from transsexuals. Female-to-male (FTM) transsexuals were considered to be of only one type, masculine women who were sexually attracted to other women. Female crossdressers were believed not to exist. Some clinicians emphatically denied the existence of female crossdressers and FTM transsexuals who were sexually attracted to men, even when confronted by those whose existence they denied.

In the early 1990s, the dichotomous system of transgender labeling began to break down. Subsequent labels, which have grown primarily from self-description by transgendered persons, have included two-spirit (from Native American traditions), transgenderist, drag king, drag queen, genderblend, and androgyne, among many others. Even if the etiology of transsexuality could be definitely determined, it is difficult to envision a biologic or social etiologic

149

explanation that would adequately capture the diversity of gender behavior and self-perception evident within the transgender community.

As cultural norms have changed, gender expression has become more variable, both within the transgendered community and in the population at large. This diversity sometimes manifests itself in minor ways within traditional normative gender-role expression, and sometimes it does so in more overt ways. Sometimes, gender variability is a significant part of an individual's life and may be expressed openly to various degrees. For some, it means living all or nearly all the time in the gender role with which the person identifies most strongly. For a few, it results in a complete transition of gender role, accompanied by hormonal and anatomic transformation.

Given the diversity of personal expression and self-perception within the transgender community, historical terminology and categorization are currently being questioned. For the purposes of this chapter, the term "transgender" will be used to describe an individual who lives (full or part time) as a member of a gender that is incongruent with his or her anatomic sex, frequently with hormonal support. "Transsexual" will be reserved for persons who also seek sex reassignment surgery.

ETIOLOGY OF CROSSDRESSING AND TRANSSEXUALISM

Contextual Issues in Scientific Investigation

A great deal of effort has been devoted to attempts to explain transgender identity and behavior, with the net result that its cause or causes remain unknown. Aside from purely scientific motivations, there are strong political reasons behind the desire to explain the phenomena of both transgender behavior and homosexuality. Curiously, both those who condemn transgendered individuals and homosexuals and those who defend them seem equally anxious to obtain answers. One possible reason is the following: If homosexuality, transsexualism, or transvestism can be conclusively shown to be biological in nature, it can be argued that the individual cannot "help" the behavior. One could be said to be born transsexual or homosexual, and therefore could not be blamed or faulted. However, if it could be shown that there is not a biological etiology, it could be claimed that the individual "chooses" and, conversely, could choose not to be homosexual or transgendered. The individual is thus accountable and could be held to blame with impunity.

Such concern regarding possible etiology sidesteps a number of important issues. First, human behavior is exceedingly complex, the result of multiple causal mechanisms, and the nature of many of these mechanisms is thus far impossible to determine. Second, scientists have historically found it almost impossible to remain objective in such a politically charged atmosphere (see Gould, 1981, for an excellent example). Third, most people do not consider homosexuality a mental illness (indeed, the American Psychiatric Association [APA] removed homosexuality from their *Diagnostic and Statistical Manual of Mental Disorders* in 1980), and it is a matter of current debate as to whether the diagnosis gender identity disorder should remain in the next revision of the *DSM.* If homosexuality and transgender behavior are not illnesses, it becomes less important to determine their causes.

Furthermore, there is also the issue of personal freedom. Why should it matter if someone wishes to crossdress, change sex, or engage in same-sex sexual behavior? It is one's right to do so. Etiologic investigation (or speculation) has tended to obscure this central truth, so that the focus on human freedom of expression is lost.

Political concerns aside, what causes crossdressing and transsexualism? The short answer is, no one knows. The space limitations of this chapter do not permit an exhaustive review of the salient etiological theories, but several lines of research, in which initial results seemed to support either environmental or biological causes, are presented below. In some cases, preliminary conclusions did not survive further scrutiny; in others, definitive evidence is currently lacking.

ETIOLOGIC THEORIES

The likelihood of identifying a specific etiology of transsexualism appeared more promising prior to the recognition of behavioral diversity within the transgender community. By the 1970s, clinicians had identified several diagnostic categories to which transgendered persons could be assigned (cf. Person & Ovesey, 1974a, 1974b). At first, these categories seemed to be exhaustive. However, by the mid-1990s, transgendered persons were evidencing a great deal of diversity in their self-identities and gender expressions (Bolin, 1994), which had not been present (or at least had not been recognized) only a decade earlier (Bolin, 1988). As more members of the transgender community have come to question a system in which there are only two possible genders (male and female), the historical categories of crossdresser and transsexual have become but two of a number of other possible self-identities.

Freud was the first to elucidate a theory of gender as learned behavior. A number of psychiatrists have drawn on his developmental theory in attempts to show environmental causes for transsexualism and crossdressing. The late Robert Stoller (1967) believed that MTF transsexualism was caused by the child's failure to adequately separate from a bisexual "empty" mother who kept the child too close to her body during the first two to three years of life. Stoller believed that MTF transsexuals were "among the most feminine of males" (Stoller, 1968b), and he discounted as transvestites those males who identified as transsexual but did not look or sound like females. However, the family dynamics of many transsexuals did not support Stoller's theory, and a longitudinal study by Richard Green (1987) showed that extremely feminine boys like those studied by Stoller were more likely to grow up to be homosexual than transsexual. Perhaps most telling was Stoller's (1968a) revelation that the subject of an early case study had turned out to be "extremely feminine" as an adult only because she had been surreptitiously taking female hormones since puberty.

More recently, the "John/Joan" case has received a great deal of public attention. In the 1950s, John Money and his colleagues (Money, Hampson, & Hampson, 1957) concluded that gender identity was primarily learned rather than innate, was well formed by about age 3, and was thereafter quite resistant to change. Later, Money (1975) reported on the case of a 6-month-old boy whose penis had been accidentally ablated during circumcision. The parents were counseled by Money to raise the child as a girl and the intact twin brother as a boy. Follow-up reports (Money, 1984) indicated that "Joan," as the patient was called in the literature, was well-adjusted as a girl.

However, Diamond and Sigmundson (1997) discovered that at adolescence, Joan, who had been long unhappy as a female, began to live as "John," a male. John subsequently had surgery to construct a penis and married as a man (Colapinto, 1997). This case resulted in a great deal of media attention, as it suggested that biology plays more of a role in the formation of gender identity than does environment.

However, a second, similar case was recently followed up (Bradley, Oliver, Chernick, & Zucker, 1998). In this case, a male infant similarly reassigned as female after penile ablation chose to remain female-gendered in adulthood. It is possible that one day there will be a sufficient number of such cases identified to allow conclusions to be drawn about the relative roles of biology and environment in gender-identity formation.

Perhaps the most thorough review of the etiology of transsexualism was done by Hoenig (1985), who devoted several pages to a theory of causality that initially generated a great deal of enthusiasm. Hoenig notes that in 1979, the German gynecologist Wolf Eicher discovered that one of his MTF patients showed an absence of the histocompatibility (H-Y) antigen, which is typically present in males and absent in females. Eicher and his colleagues published several papers in which they presented their findings that MTF transsexuals tended to lack the H-Y antigen and FTM transsexuals tended to have the antigen (Hoenig, 1985, p. 54). A number of attempts were made to replicate Eicher et al.'s results, mostly without success (p. 60). Consequently, the H-Y antigen theory has fallen into disfavor. However, at one time, the prospect of an unambiguous genetic marker for transsexuality caused a great deal of excitement in the scientific community.

A similar burst of enthusiasm occurred in the research area of sexual orientation after the publication of two significant studies. LeVay (1991, 1996) reported that there was a difference in the hypothalamic structure of heterosexual and homosexual men. Zhou, Hofman, Gooren, and Swaab (1995) reported that the suprachiasmatic nucleus of the hypothalamus of MTF transsexuals tended to be smaller than the same area in females, whose suprachiasmatic nuclei were in turn smaller than those of nontranssexual males. Other teams are currently attempting to replicate LeVay's and Zhou et al.'s work; however, at present, their work is unreplicated and should be considered suggestive rather than definitive.

CONCLUSION

It is possible that, given sufficient time and further research, causal mechanisms for many human behaviors, perhaps even transsexualism, will be elucidated. Currently, however, it is clear that gender, like sexual orientation, is in many ways an individually based and self-perceived characteristic, the origins of which are not well understood. Gender (and transgender) may evolve in a variety of ways and should not be restricted by societal prejudice.

A BRIEF TRANSGENDER HISTORY

In recent years, a transgender history has begun to emerge. Compiled from ancient texts, turn-of-the-century works of cultural anthropologists, biographies and autobiographies, medieval legal documents, and even reconstructions from the scanty evidence of Paleolithic burials and campsites, it has gradually become clear that rather than being the aberrations that Western science has held them to be, same-sex relationships and cross-gender behavior have been present in all societies from the earliest times, and both the behaviors and those who exhibit them have been positively acknowledged by many cultures. It has become equally clear that throughout history, sexually and gender-variant people have filled well-defined social roles in a wide range of cultures, often as shamans, healers, entertainers, and storytellers (Feinberg, 1996, Chapter 3). Usually, these roles were filled by those who chose them, but sometimes individuals were deliberately selected (R. Green, 1998). Dragoin (1995) has speculated that the presence of members with a "two-spirit" nature may have provided a selective evolutionary advantage for tribal groups throughout human history. There is some evidence to support this point. Most notably, Whitam (1997) found that homosexual and transvestic males in many cultures tend to become entertainers of one type or another. R. Green and Money (1966), who studied extremely feminine boys in the United States, reported that they exhibited a variety of theatrical traits, including dressing up in women's clothing and "putting on shows" for their friends and families.

Because they did not emerge as distinct social identities until the twentieth century, accounts of what we today call homosexuality and transvestism have usually been conflated, so that they are not really distinguishable. Much of this history is scattered, and much has been systematically repressed and is lost to us. Still, a surprising amount of information has become available in recent years. This section reviews only a small amount of the accumulated evidence. (Those interested in further reading should consult sources such as

Ackroyd [1979], V. Bullough & Bullough [1993], Dekker & van de Pol [1989], Feinberg [1996], R. Green [1998], Herdt [1994], Ramet [1996], Taylor [1996], and Williams [1986].)

PREHISTORY

Our knowledge of human prehistory is limited; we know only what we can deduce from the fossil record. Unlike bones and stone tools, which tend to be preserved, the social behavior of our ancestors must be inferred from physical artifacts that can provide clues about such behavior. Understandably, making sense of complex social roles is a difficult task with such scanty evidence, and a variety of interpretations can be drawn using the same artifacts. Still, a transgender pattern has begun to emerge.

In his fascinating book, *The Prehistory of Sex*, Timothy Taylor (1996) points out paleontological evidence showing that early humans almost certainly engaged in a range of sexual behaviors as extensive as that displayed today. Citing evidence from ancient burials, cave paintings, pottery decorations, and carvings that display hermaphroditic figures, Taylor points out that from prehistoric times, some members of every society would likely have had androgynous physical traits, and a certain number—perhaps one individual per 1,000 to 2,000—would have been born with physical intersex conditions (pp. 63–65). Reaction to individuals with such characteristics could have included indifference, acceptance, rejection, and celebration. In many non-Western societies, Taylor notes, children are accepted as they are (p. 64). This is not universal, however; in some societies, intersex and gender-variant individuals may be treated badly, or even put to death (cf. Edgerton, 1964).

Individuals who crossdressed would have faced the same range of reactions, perhaps being ridiculed in some societies and in others being culturally constructed as members of the other sex or as members of a third sex (Taylor, 1996, pp. 210–212). Taylor describes carvings of androgynous figures who are full-breasted but potently phallic (pp. 130–131, 215–219) and burials containing sex-typed grave goods that differ from what would be expected from the physical characteristics of the skeleton (pp. 67, 212–214, Chapter 8). He notes that ambiguous physical measurements of some skeletons make them impossible to classify as either male or female (pp. 65–68), and suggests that the potent pharmacopeia of the time may have been used to deliberately produce estrogenic and androgenic effects: Paleolithic sex changes (pp. 212–214). Taylor's evidence comes from widely separated sites, suggesting that gender-variant behavior was widespread, not limited to a few small areas.

CROSS-CULTURAL ACCOUNTS

Before they came under the influence of Western missionaries, many modern hunter-gatherer groups had institutionalized social roles for gender-variant persons. These roles were part of the accumulated cultural wisdom of the tribes, having been passed down, like their language and other customs, from their ancestors. Institutionalized alternate gender (transgender) roles have been described in societies in all the continents except Antarctica, which until very recently has never sustained human habitation. Anthropologists have documented such roles in cultures including Polynesia (Besnier, 1994), Siberia (Czaplicka, 1914, cited in R. Green, 1998, p. 10), Eastern Europe (Dickemann, 1995), and Native North America (Kurti, 1996; Roscoe, 1988; Williams, 1986). Will Roscoe's *Living the Spirit* (1988, pp. 217–222) contains a six-page listing of North American Native tribes that had well-defined alternate gender roles.

Typically, individuals in alternate gender roles lived openly and without shame, wearing the clothing of and functioning socially as members of the "other" sex (see Herdt, 1994, for descriptions of such roles). Transgender roles were common in Western cultures before the rise of Christianity, when they began to be systematically eradicated (V. Bullough & Bullough, 1993, pp. 39–40, 45; Roscoe, 1994).

Although female social roles for those born male have been the more commonly documented across cultures than male social roles for those born female (cf. Roscoe, 1988, pp. 217–222), this may be at least partially due to a bias in reporting. Some societies had both roles. (For more information on cross-transgender roles in a variety of cultures, see Feinberg [1996], R. Green [1998], Herdt [1994], Ramet [1996], and Wheelright [1979].)

EARLY WRITTEN ACCOUNTS

Many societies, including Greek, Roman, East Indian, and Native American, have creation and other myths in which hermaphroditic or cross-gendered figures play prominent roles (see Bulliet, 1928, for an early review). These tales were passed down orally until the development of writing. Early manuscripts in Greek, Latin (R. Green, 1998), Sanskrit (Money, 1992), and Sumeric (Ochshorn, 1996) describe transgender behavior. Remarkably, the *Gospel of St. Thomas* talks positively about androgyny:

> When you make the two into one, when you make the inner like the outer and the outer like the inner, and when you make the male and the female into a single one so that the male will not be male and the female will not be female, then you will enter the kingdom of heaven. (Thomas, 22, in the *New Hammadi Library*, p. 121, cited in R. Green, 1998)

By all accounts, a number of the Roman emperors and several of the Egyptian pharaohs (both male and female) were transgendered (R. Green, 1998; Harrison, 1966; Margretts, 1951; Taylor, 1996). For instance, it is reported that the Roman Emperor Heliogabalus offered half his empire to any physician who could change his genitals from male to female (as cited in R. Green, 1998).

Transgender behavior was not only known but perhaps even common among the general populace of ancient cultures:

> Philo, the Jewish philosopher of Alexandria [Greece], wrote, "Expending every possible care on their outward adornment, they are not ashamed even to employ every device to change artificially their nature as men into women. . . . Some of them . . . craving a complete transformation into women, they have amputated their generative members." (as cited in R. Green, 1998)

The Roman poet Manilus wrote:

> These [persons] will ever be giving thought to their bedizement and becoming appearance; to curl the hair and lay it in waving ripples . . . to polish the shaggy limbs . . . Yeah! and to hate the very sight of (themselves as) a man, and long for arms without growth of hair. Woman's robes they wear . . . [their] steps broken to an effeminate gait. (as cited in R. Green, 1998)

Transgender roles were widespread in pre-Christian Europe and Eurasia as well (O'Hartigan, 1993; Roscoe, 1994). Early Christianity incorporated ritualized crossdressing (Torjesen, 1996), which survives in symbolic form in ecclesiastical robes even today, but transgender behavior and roles were systematically and often violently suppressed by Christian and Jewish cultures over a period of nearly 2,000 years (V. Bullough & Bullough, 1993, pp. 39–40, 45).

By the Middle Ages, fear of punishment, banishment, or even execution had driven transgender expression in the West underground, where it has largely remained. However, despite the danger of societal sanction, many individuals across the centuries have lived either openly or secretly in the clothing of and have sometimes passed as members of the other sex. Reports of men living as women and women living as men are common throughout the Middle Ages and into the modern era (V. Bullough & Bullough, 1993, Chapter 3; Dekker & van de Pol, 1989), including both commoners (Dekker & van de Pol, 1989) and royalty (Choisy, 1966; Gilbert, 1926; Kates, 1995). Dekker and van de Pol (1989) found records of hundreds of females who lived as men in the medieval Netherlands; no doubt, there were many more whose records did not survive, or whose records reflect unambiguous identities as men. There are also numerous accounts of "passing women" in other European countries and the early United States (cf. Wheelright, 1979). Historical accounts of women living as men are more common than accounts of men living as women. Perhaps women were more likely to take on cross-gender roles because they offered an escape from the strict social proscriptions placed on women (V. Bullough & Bullough, 1993, p. 51); perhaps it was easier for women to "pass" as men than it was for men to "pass" as women; perhaps punishment was less severe for passing women than for passing men; perhaps women were more likely to be discovered and revealed because their active sexual and social lives made them more public and thus more vulnerable to discovery; or perhaps there were simply more passing women than passing men. Passing women often took wives, and many volunteered for military service (Wheelright, 1979, Chapter 1). There are accounts of more than 150 female soldiers passing for male in the U.S. Civil War, and probably several times that number actually served (Lowry, 1994; E. Meyer, 1994).

A number of female and male saints transgressed gender roles, both in their behavior and in their manner of dress (V. Bullough & Bullough, 1993, Chapter 3; Torjesen, 1996). Most, in fact, became saints *because* of their crossdressing. The best-known saint is perhaps Joan of Arc of Orleans, who was put to death for, among other things, refusing to wear women's clothing (V. Bullough & Bullough, 1993, pp. 57–60). There is even a persistent rumor that Pope John VIII Anglicus was a woman who passed as a man until she gave birth to a baby during a Papal procession (V. Bullough & Bullough, 1993, pp. 55–57).

Twentieth-Century Accounts

Beginning about 1850, physicians began to take an interest in individuals who varied from the gender norms of the day (V. Bullough & Bullough, 1993, Chapter 9). The case studies of both Krafft-Ebing (1894) and Hirschfeld (1910, 1991) depict individuals who clearly conform to current-day definitions of crossdressers and transsexuals. Correspondence unearthed in a variety of Victorian newspapers (Farrer, 1987) shows that a significant number of English men were interested in crossdressing. Male crossdressing had been common in bawdy houses since at least the seventeenth century (Trumbach, 1989), and boy actors played female roles on the Elizabethan stage, and sometimes offstage (Howard, 1993).

The popularity of crossdressing continued with the establishment of gay nightclubs early in this century (Paulson, 1996), and thrives in the present day (cf. Aviance, 1996). Female and male impersonation was common in American vaudeville and British pantomimes (Slide, 1986) and in moving pictures almost from their inception (Bell-Metereau, 1993; Dickens, 1984). Some performers, such as Julian Eltinge, were careful to maintain a public façade of respectable heterosexuality (Moore, 1994, Chapter 8). Others were deliberately outrageous, but in general, crossdressing in public invited interference from the police, and much crossdressing took place behind closed doors (Paulson, 1996). Public crossdressing began to emerge only in the 1950s and 1960s, as female impersonators began to grow bolder (County, 1995) and when small groups of male crossdressers started to meet in secret in California and the Northeastern United States (V. Bullough & Bullough, 1993, Chapter 12).

THE TRANSGENDER COMMUNITY

The last several decades of the twentieth century have seen the rise of a *transgender community*, a broad-based alliance of transsexuals, transgenderists, crossdressers, other "nontraditionally gendered" persons and helping professionals who have formed support groups, information clearinghouses, and other organizations that serve the manifold needs of transgendered and transsexual persons. This community developed from a model of heterosexual crossdressing created by Dr. Virginia Prince and a medical-psychological model of transsexualism developed by Dr. Harry Benjamin.

THE HETEROSEXUAL CROSSDRESSING MODEL

Virginia Prince is the founder of the Hose and Heels Club, which was perhaps the first club in the United States for heterosexual crossdressers. Prince also founded the Foundation for Personality Expression (FPE), a national organization for heterosexual crossdressers, and was cofounder of Tri-Ess, The Society for the Second Self, which replaced FPE and which still exists. She was also editor of *Transvestia*, the first nationally circulated magazine for crossdressers (V. Bullough & Bullough, 1993).

In the pages of *Transvestia*, Prince developed a model of male heterosexual crossdressing, downplaying the importance of self-eroticism and homosexuality in crossdressing and emphasizing the evolution of a nonsexual "girl within," a social woman with male anatomy. At the time (the 1950s and 1960s), crossdressers were universally assumed to be homosexual. Prince demonstrated that this was not so by surveying her readers and publishing the results not only in *Transvestia*, but also in professional journals (Bentler & Prince, 1969a, 1969b; Prince, 1957). For more than 40 years, Prince has vigorously promoted her concept of the crossdresser as a heterosexual male. From a contemporary perspective, it is clear that although there are many thousands of heterosexual crossdressers, many gay and bisexual persons also crossdress.

THE MEDICAL-PSYCHOLOGICAL MODEL OF TRANSSEXUALISM

The 1950s also brought news of Christine Jorgensen and the notion that change of sex was possible (B. Bullough & Bullough, 1998; V. Bullough & Bullough, 1993; Denny, 1998a; Hamburger, Stürup, & Dahl-Iversen, 1953). Jorgensen was not the first transsexual, as male genitals had been surgically altered since ancient times (O'Hartigan, 1993) and sex reassignment using modern surgical techniques had been attempted as early as the 1930s (Abraham, 1931; Hoyer, 1933). However, the news of Jorgensen's sex change galvanized the press, introducing to the general public and scientists alike the notion that sex was not immutable, but open to change (Denny, 1998a).

Following the news of Jorgensen's sex reassignment, hundreds of men and women came forth to request sex reassignment (Hamburger, 1953). Harry Benjamin, a New York endocrinologist, began treating many of these individuals, and in 1966 published a text, *The Transsexual Phenomenon*, in which he defined the syndrome of transsexualism. Benjamin, an empathic soul who seemed to genuinely enjoy his transsexual patients, described them as profoundly miserable in their gender of original assignment, so much so that they were often unable to function and were at considerable risk of taking their own lives. Benjamin noted that medical science was unable to rid them of their compelling desire to change their sex or to give them peace of mind in their original bodies. Surely, he argued, the humane thing in select cases would be to give transsexuals relief from their suffering by altering their bodies with hormones and surgery and allowing them to live as members of the other sex. Benjamin pointed out the success of his own patients who had had sex reassignment. It should be noted that both the physicians and transsexuals of the time tended to follow the medical model, interpreting the transsexual experience in terms of misery and anguish. Transsexuals are no more likely to be suicidal or severely impaired than are other persons who present for mental health services.

Three years later, in 1969, Richard Green and John Money published an edited textbook that established a medical protocol for sex reassignment, based on their own experience at the new gender-identity clinic at Johns Hopkins University. Now there was not only a model for transsexualism, but a sex reassignment protocol from one of the most prestigious medical schools in the United States. Other universities started gender programs; within 10 years, there were more than 40 university-based gender clinics scattered across the United States. The universities disassociated themselves from their programs in 1979 and 1980, following the release of a report by Jon Meyer and Donna Reter (1979) that showed "no objective improvement" following sex reassignment. Meyer and Reter's report came under immediate attack (cf. Fleming, Steinman, & Bocknek, 1980) and eventually was found to be lacking in scientific validity (see Denny, 1992; Ogas, 1994). The clinics nonetheless closed, except two, which continued as private for-profit centers, and the program at the University of Minnesota, which came under the control of the Program for Human Sexuality after its original departmental sponsor disassociated itself (Walter Bockting, personal communication).

The closing of the university programs led to the eventual development of a market-driven sex-change industry (Denny, 1992) that made sex reassignment more widely available than ever before, frustrating those who had worked for the closing of the gender programs (McHugh, 1992). Today, professional services are available to practically anyone in the United States who desires to change his or her sex and has the financial means to do so.

Being a "Good" Transsexual

Despite the groundbreaking work of Dr. Benjamin and his associates, the Benjamin model ultimately resulted in a narrow definition of transsexualism. Those who varied from the prescribed characteristics were at risk of not getting treatment—in fact, of being declared nontranssexual by medical professionals and by their peers (cf. Newman & Stoller, 1974). To qualify for treatment, it was important that applicants report that their gender dysphoria manifested at an early age, preferably by age 3 or 4; that they had a history of playing with dolls as a child, if born male, or trucks and guns, if born female; that their sexual attraction was exclusively to the same biological sex; that they had a history of failure at endeavors undertaken while in the original gender role; and that they were able to pass successfully as a member of the desired sex (Denny, 1992).

The literature reported that transsexuals were manipulative and had high levels of psychopathology, had narrow and stereotyped notions of masculinity and femininity, and conformed to those stereotypes in their personal presentations; that they had a desire to disappear into the larger society after surgery, passing as nontranssexual; and that they viewed themselves as having been born into the wrong body because of some sort of birth defect or horrible joke of nature (Bolin, 1988). Most transsexuals do not, in fact, have such characteristics; the literature that suggests they do reflects the bias and sexism of the psychologists and physicians who wrote it (and perhaps of some of their clients, as well), often in keeping with the values of the dominant culture of the time (Denny, 1998b).

Benjamin's model postulated that there were but two sexes, and that the only alternative to remaining unhappily in the original gender role was to work hard to conform to the only available alternative. That is, one "changed sex," going from male to female or from female to male. The model did not question the society that created such restrictive gender roles or examine the possibility of living somewhere outside those binary roles. Those who were not interested in going from one polar extreme to the other were defined as nontranssexual and presumed to be crossdressers, even when they were profoundly gender dysphoric. Transsexualism itself was considered a liminal state, a transitory phase, to be negotiated as rapidly as possible on one's way to becoming a "normal" man or "normal" woman. The Benjamin model of transsexualism was held as the only valid model of transsexualism until the early 1990s, despite challenges from opponents to the concept of transsexualism per se (Kessler & McKenna, 1978; Raymond 1979; Socarides, 1969) and complaints from the clientele whom it was intended to serve.

THE TRANSGENDER MODEL

The 1990s saw the rise of a model that provided an alternative to both Benjamin's medical-psychological transsexual model and Prince's model of heterosexual crossdressing. Early in the decade, a transgender sensibility began to emerge, in which the notion of changing sex or remaining rigidly in one's original sex was replaced by the idea of multiple or even infinite sexes. Prince herself had advanced this notion in the 1970s, but it was overlooked until resurrected by Holly Boswell, Kate Bornstein, and others in the early 1990s (Bornstein, 1994; Boswell, 1991; Rothblatt, 1994). Perhaps even more profound (from the North American perspective) was the decoupling of sex, which is largely defined by anatomic phenotype, and gender (which is a psychological phenomenon, and which had previously been viewed as a function of anatomic sex). This process also furthered the dissolution of socially "correct" gender roles, both for transgendered persons and for other members of society. Those subscribing to the emerging transgender model tended to see themselves as both man and woman, or neither, or as something else entirely. Under this model, the in-between state somewhere between manhood and womanhood, unacknowledged under either Benjamin's or Prince's model, became a goal for which to strive, or at least a comfortable place at which to rest. As the decade draws to a close, the transgender model is pervasive throughout the transgender community and is beginning to have a significant impact in academia (cf. Wilson, 1998).

ISSUES OF SEXUALITY

Like everyone else, transgendered and transsexual persons experience sexual attraction to other human beings. Some are attracted to males, some to females, some to both, some are asexual, and some are attracted to other transgenders or members of other sexual or gender minorities. This mirrors the range of sexual attractions in the larger society. Labeling such attractions heterosexual or homosexual becomes a bit confusing (and perhaps irrelevant) in the case of transsexuals. Therefore, it is more informative to reference the gender or genders to which the transgendered individual is attracted. The authors of the most recent revision of the *DSM (DSM-IV)* recognized this and avoided the use of the terms homosexual and heterosexual in the section on gender identity disorders.

IDENTITY AND COMMUNITY

Before the mid–nineteenth century, the social identities of homosexual and heterosexual as we know them did not exist. Of course, men and women engaged in a wide variety of sexual behaviors; however, it was only when scientists began to take an interest in sexual behavior that the terms homosexuality and heterosexuality came into common usage.

Before the turn of the century, homosexual behavior and transgender behavior were commonly believed to be manifestations of the same underlying condition. Male homosexuality was believed to be due to a strong feminine element (cf. Ulrichs, 1994), and female homosexuals were considered "mannish" (Devor, 1995). Indeed, Radclyffe Hall's 1928 novel, *The Well of Loneliness*, which has long been considered to have a lesbian protagonist, features a crossdressing female protagonist who calls herself/himself Stephen and who almost certainly fits the diagnostic criteria for FTM transsexualism.

Transvestism was differentiated from homosexuality by Hirschfeld (1910), but Hirschfeld's work had little impact in the United States because it was not translated into English until the 1990s (Vern Bullough, personal communication).

Transsexualism was differentiated from transvestism by Benjamin (1966); before that, Christine Jorgensen and others who had sex reassignment were frequently called transvestites in the medical literature (cf. Hamburger, 1953).

The Stonewall Rebellion of 1969 saw the birth of the modern gay liberation movement (Duberman, 1993). In the immediate post-Stonewall period, a new homosexual culture emerged, in which stereotypes of feminine gay males and mannish lesbians were replaced by new social constructions of male and female homosexuality in which masculine dress and demeanor were embraced by most gay men, and most lesbians rejected "butch" identities. Almost immediately, the drag queens and kings who had instigated the fighting at Stonewall were marginalized by the movement because they were visually different from these emerging notions of straight-looking, straight-acting gay men and woman-identified lesbians (Brewster, 1970). Over the ensuing decades, bisexuals and then transgendered persons lobbied for and were (sometimes grudgingly) readmitted to the movement.

In 1985, when the International Foundation for Gender Education (IFGE) was formed in Boston through the efforts of Merissa Sheryl Lynn and others, transsexuals throughout the United States and Canada began to come into regular contact with one another. As soon as they established the necessary level of comfort, many began to admit to one another that they did not conform to Harry Benjamin's definitions of transsexuals or transvestites. As an open organization, IFGE welcomed both transsexuals and crossdressers, so for the first time, transsexuals and crossdressers came into regular communication. Within five years, this interaction resulted in the development of a worldwide transgender community and the development of the transgender model.

The transgender model minimized the differences between gay and straight crossdressers and transsexuals and helped the transgender community confront and begin working through its considerable homophobia. The transgender model was brought to the attention of the gay, lesbian, and bisexual community by an awakening transgender political movement and by the publication of transgender literature, such as Leslie Feinberg's (1993) novel, *Stone Butch Blues*, in which the protagonist rejected transsexualism in favor of an essential (FTM) transgender identity. Feinberg has also been an inspiration to many FTM transgendered people, who have long been in the shadow of MTFs, and who are now coming forth in large numbers (J. Green, 1998). Other emerging groups on the social and political landscape include FTM crossdressers, persons born intersexed, and persons who identify as genderblended or as members of other nontraditional gender identities.

The politicization of transgender identities has also been a common theme in the 1990s. Transgendered individuals have protested when their peers have been murdered, have lobbied for civil rights previously denied them, and have engaged in vigorous letter-writing campaigns and political demonstrations when they have been slandered by those in power. Civil rights protection for transgendered people has been achieved in Minnesota and more than a dozen cities throughout the United States. Transgendered voices have also begun to appear in the professional literature, from which they had previously been excluded (Denny, 1997), and transsexuals have begun to run for and be elected to public office and have begun to be out as prominent members in a variety of professions (cf. Wilson, 1998).

Transsexuals have also begun to criticize the medical literature, which has often treated them as mentally ill. At issue is the gender identity disorders section of the *DSM-IV*. The call for reform of the diagnostic category, gender identity disorder of childhood, has been of particular concern, as it is sometimes used to institutionalize gender-variant homosexual boys and girls and other gender-role nonconforming children and adolescents (see Burke, 1996; Scholinski, 1997). Also at issue are the Harry Benjamin Standards of Care, which place restrictions on access to body-altering medical treatment without empirical evidence that such restrictions are necessary or even advisable (Levine et al., 1998).

The rise of postmodern gender theory (cf. Butler, 1990; Foucault, 1979) has provided a new language for the discussion of transgender issues (Wilchins, 1997). The careful reader will notice that throughout this section, there has been no mention of gender identity disorder (except when naming the diagnostic categories in the *DSM*), or other language that would predispose the reader to view transgendered persons as mentally ill or otherwise deficient. When resorting to the traditional medical-psychological model, it is difficult to discuss transgendered people or their issues without using terms that imply or overtly state pathology. In view of the groundbreaking work Benjamin performed on behalf of his transsexual clients, it is ironic that the current Harry Benjamin International Gender Dysphoria Association Standards of Care (Levine et al., 1998) contain language that diminishes and demeans transsexuals. Further, it is lamentable that the new Standards of Care maintain and strengthen restrictions on access to treatment (in the absence of empirical evidence for the rationale) at the same time that the modern transgender model is gaining acceptance by an increasing number of professionals.

The transgender model, which offers an infinite number of gender identities and lifestyles, is much less restrictive than previous models, which emphasized and even required conformity. However, such a liberalization reflects the evolution of our cultural norms. As the twentieth century closes, one is struck by the degree to which gender roles and sartorial styles have changed in only one hundred years. From an era in which women wore nearly 20 pounds of clothing, were not allowed to vote, and were routinely arrested if they appeared on the streets wearing trousers ("Dressed in," 1911; "Girl dressed," 1911), we have arrived at a time in which the gender norms of 1900 or even 1950 are transgressed daily by practically every American citizen, including people who are opposed to those who are pushing the frontiers of acceptance today. Perhaps we will eventually arrive at a time in which people's clothing (and genitals) will cease to be a focus of public debate.

THE MEDICAL CARE OF TRANSGENDERED CLIENTS

A comprehensive discussion of the medical needs of transgendered persons is beyond the scope of this chapter. Nonetheless, it behooves the mental health practitioner who provides services to gender variant persons to acquire at least a basic knowledge regarding the effects of contragender hormone supplementation and the health maintenance needs of this population. A brief description of these facets of transgender health care has therefore been included below.

THE "SECOND PUBERTY"

Although natural pubertal development is completed by the later teen years, persons desiring the physical characteristics usually associated with the other gender can obtain some of them through the use of supplemental hormones at any stage of life. In essence, the transsexual or transgendered person who takes estrogens, progesterones, or androgens, at sufficient doses and for a sufficient duration, will experience a second puberty.

Pubertal Change and Irreversibility

The physical effects that the "second puberty" is able to achieve can be summarized with this caveat: *Hormones can stimulate change but cannot undo what has already occurred.* Once these biologically active compounds have acted on their target organs to produce specific physical effects, these become irreversible even after the hormones are withdrawn. Therefore, transsexuals and transgenders of any preexisting hormonal configuration will require a combination of hormonal and (perhaps) surgical therapies, depending on the previous development and the desired outcome.

FTM persons who utilize androgen supplementation (usually, injectable testosterone cipionate or a related compound) will experience effects such as deepening of the voice (through thickening of the vocal cords); increase in facial and body hair in a typical male pattern; and growth of the clitoris. Although reports of clitoral growth sufficient to permit intercourse exist, in most cases, surgical procedures will be required to achieve the size and morphology of a normal penis. Because the hair follicles of the scalp are also sensitive to the effects of testosterone, male pattern baldness may occur.

Development from the "first puberty" will not regress even after the hormonal pattern becomes that of a genetic male. Most FTM persons will require breast surgery with nipple relocation to create a male-appearing chest, and although menstruation will cease with sufficient testosterone supplementation, hysterectomy with removal of the ovaries is usually performed for cancer prevention. The changes of the "second puberty" are also permanent. If the FTM individual decides to return to life as a female, beard and body hair growth will not disappear as testosterone is withdrawn; electrolysis will be necessary. Clitoral growth and vocal changes will also remain unchanged.

The MTF person who undertakes hormonal transition faces the same caveat. Although she will develop breasts and experience a cessation of scalp hair loss (if male pattern baldness has already begun), estrogen supplementation will not raise the voice or greatly change the pattern of body hair growth. Most MTF individuals pursue speech therapy, and in some cases vocal cord surgery, to achieve a more feminine-sounding voice. Extensive electrolysis is often necessary to remove the beard and male pattern chest, neck, back, and abdominal hair. Most MTF persons also take antiandrogen agents, such as spironolactone, finasteride, or cyproterone acetate. However, although these medications can soften the skin so that electrolysis can be performed more easily and can potentiate breast development and testicular shrinkage, they cannot undo the development of the "first puberty" that has already occurred. Similarly, if estrogen is discontinued at a later time, the female breast morphology will persist unless surgery is performed.

Hormonal Safety during Transition

Although the "second puberty" can occur at any stage of life, adults who undertake hormonal transition face one disadvantage that adolescents do not: the loss of physiologic resilience that occurs with advancing age. Even during the months and years when sex hormone production is highest, adolescents do not normally develop complications such as elevated cholesterol and coronary artery disease (which can accompany testosterone use, especially at high levels) and deep vein thrombosis (which can result from elevation in serum estrogen levels). Unfortunately, middle-aged and older adults do experience these illnesses, especially if they smoke. The two most important contributions that the mental health practitioner can make to the physical well-being of transgendered clients who use hormones are to encourage them to seek care with a physician who is familiar with contragender hormonal therapy (and who will monitor the serum estrogen and testosterone levels on a routine basis to avoid inadvertent overuse) and to provide information about locally available smoking cessation groups and other resources.

HEALTH MAINTENANCE FOR TRANSGENDERED PERSONS

Transgendered and transsexual persons who are in the process of hormonal transition have the same needs for routine health maintenance as their age-matched, non-trans or non-transsexual/transgendered peers. These include such services as cervical cancer screening and mammography for women, prostate examinations for men, and colon cancer screening and coronary artery disease prevention for both (U.S. Preventive Services Task Force, 1996). Many transgendered clients receive these services from the same physicians who prescribe and monitor their hormonal therapies; others, especially those who by choice or of necessity are following a more "à la carte" approach to transition services, do not (and may be unaware of the need for these procedures). Other impediments to receiving appropriate health maintenance services include anatomic incongruity and a lack of preventive focus.

Anatomic incongruity refers to the apparent mismatch between an individual's appearance while clothed and while undressed, especially while undergoing medical procedures. Transgendered persons (even if they are posttransition) often demonstrate anatomic incongruity, which can be problematic if the examining clinician is unprepared for these findings. For example, a woman who is undergoing a rectal examination may be wrongly found to have a rectal mass, which is in fact her prostate. (She is a postoperative MTF transsexual; the prostate gland is not removed with sex reassignment surgery.) Or the clinician may note that a masculine-appearing gentleman has no hair on his back, chest, underarms, limbs, and pubic region, and wonder whether this indicates a disease state, a psychological disorder, or an unusual personal hygiene custom. This individual is simply a MTF crossdresser, although he may not wish to discuss his gender identity with the treating clinician unless previous rapport has been established.

Lack of preventive focus often results from the expenditure of time and financial resources that is characteristic of the transition process. An individual who is involved in regular therapy sessions, medical visits for hormonal monitoring and other associated care, plus family counseling or a support group, may have little enthusiasm for additional medical services such as mammography or colon cancer screening. In addition, for persons desiring sex reassignment surgery, attention to long-term health maintenance issues may be subsumed in the quest for this greatly anticipated short-term goal.

COOPERATION FROM THE MENTAL HEALTH PROFESSIONS

Therapists and other mental health practitioners who wish to assist their clients in maintaining physical health during and after the transition process can intervene in two ways. The first is to assist the client in achieving a long-term, preventive focus. The second is to communicate with regional medical providers and to develop referral lists of physicians who are knowledgeable regarding gender variance (or who are at least welcoming of sexual and gender diversity within their clientele).

When discussing the need for preventive medical care with a client who has been using a more "à la carte" or "hormones only" approach to health care services, it is often useful to point out that, although it is possible to have the experience of being both biologically male and female during the course of one's lifetime, each person still only experiences life in one body. If it is not properly cared for, life in the new gender will be compromised or shortened; that is, *your new self will come from your old self.* Even if the client does not care for his or her body because it is the wrong sex, the tissues from which it is formed represent the only source of materials for the "right sex" body, and in fact for life itself.

A further caveat for persons in transition, or in states of permanent anatomic incongruity, is that it is necessary to take care of a body part for as long as it is part of your body. MTF transgenders and transsexuals need prostate examinations throughout the adult lifetime. MTF persons who have developed female-morphology breasts should have mammograms, even if they have not yet come out in all arenas of life. And even fully masculinized FTM persons require cervical cancer screening if they have female internal anatomy. (One of the authors [AEE] has suggested the public health slogan, "Real men get Pap tests" for use in the FTM community.) Unfortunately, inattention to a body part does not keep it healthy or free of cancer.

If the client is aware of the need for preventive and routine medical services and has no financial limitation to obtaining them, it may be necessary to explore prior experiences in health care settings, especially episodes of abuse. If the client has a history of shaming, threatening, or inappropriate medical experiences, referral to a physician or other clinician who is known to the therapist and knowledgeable about transgender health (or willing to learn) can be lifesaving.

Clinicians who are particularly useful to transgendered clients include family physicians or gynecologists who are able to put preoperative and nonoperative FTM clients at ease during pelvic examinations, mammography technicians who are comfortable with masculine-appearing MTF patients, and urologists and gastroenterologists who are knowledgeable regarding gender variance and anatomic incongruity. It is often useful for therapists who provide services to transgender clients to develop a referral network of welcoming medical and mental health providers. Although there is currently no board certification available in transgender medicine, most physicians (and therapists) who devote a substantial proportion of their time to transgender practice are members of the Harry Benjamin International Gender Dysphoria Association and can be located through that organization.

The remainder of this chapter addresses clinical issues in the mental health care of transgendered persons and their families.

MENTAL HEALTH CARE OF TRANSGENDERED CLIENTS

Transgendered persons represent an emerging minority population in the world. Although mental health professionals currently in training will almost certainly be asked to provide services for clients with "nontraditional" gender identities in their future practices, few graduate programs currently include transgender mental health care in their curricula. This section provides a brief introduction to mental health practice with transgendered clients, including an overview of common clinical presentations, evaluation, diagnostic issues, therapy during the gender transition process, terminating therapy, multidisciplinary practice, and an introduction to the professional organizations and standards of care associated with transgender medical and mental health service provision.

PROFESSIONAL ORGANIZATIONS AND STANDARDS OF CARE

The Harry Benjamin International Gender Dysphoria Association Standards of Care

This association is best known for its Standards of Care, which are recognized throughout the world. However, they are also the source of a significant amount of controversy within both the transgender and professional communities. Among other things, the standards require mental health care and written endorsement from mental health providers as a condition for access to hormonal therapy and surgical sex reassignment, on the grounds that these procedures are permanent and profoundly life changing. The standards also require a period called the real-life experience, in which the individual is required to crosslive 24 hours a day for a full year, functioning as a member of the new gender, before genital surgery is undertaken.

The Harry Benjamin Standards place the mental health professional in the role of gatekeeper. Understandably, this can cause resentment in transsexual clients who desire hormones and surgery and must convince a therapist to authorize access. The Standards of Care do not have an empirical basis. Although there is a strong feeling among clinicians that adhering to the Standards results in better outcomes than providing treatment on demand, there are currently no data to either confirm or disprove that opinion.

In late 1998, the Association introduced revised standards that were considerably different from previous versions, not only in form, but in content. Although they are improved in some ways, they are controversial because they altered the long-unchanged procedures by which transsexuals qualify for hormonal therapy and sex reassignment surgery. Furthermore, the revised standards were not brought before the general membership of the Association for a vote. It remains to be seen whether the worldwide professional community will follow these standards in the same way it embraced earlier revisions.

The DSM

The *DSM-IV* (1994) provides a comprehensive listing of diagnostic criteria for hundreds of mental disorders. Insurance companies typically will not provide reimbursement for psychotherapy or other mental health treatments unless the claim includes a *DSM-IV* diagnostic code. Clients who do not meet the diagnostic criteria for a mental disorder do not receive coverage for therapy.

Gender identity disorder (GID) and transsexualism first appeared in the *DSM-III* in 1980, at the same time that homosexuality was removed. In the *DSM-IV*, the diagnosis of transsexualism was replaced by the more generic GID. Both transsexuals and transgenderists may be diagnosable with GID (see Table 4.1), provided they are experiencing substantial intrapsychic conflict, or if an important aspect of their social functioning is significantly impaired.

Table 4.1
DSM-IV Diagnostic Criteria for Gender Identity Disorder

A. A strong and persistent cross-gender identification (not merely a desire for any perceived cultural advantages of being the other sex).

In children, the disturbance is manifested by four (or more) of the following:

(1) repeatedly stated desire to be, or insistence that he or she is the other sex

(2) in boys, preference for cross-dressing or simulating female attire; in girls, insistence on wearing only stereotypical masculine clothing

(3) strong and persistent preferences for cross-sex roles in make-believe play or persistent fantasies of being the other sex

(4) intense desire to participate in the stereotypical games and pastimes of the other sex

(5) strong preference for playmates of the other sex

In adolescents and adults, the disturbance is manifested by symptoms such as a stated desire to be the other sex, frequent passing as the other sex, desire to live or be treated as the other sex, or the conviction that he or she has the typical feelings and reactions of the other sex.

B. Persistent discomfort with his or her sex or sense of inappropriateness in the gender role of that sex.

In children, the disturbance is manifested by any of the following: in boys, assertion that his penis or testes are disgusting or will disappear or assertion that it would be better not to have a penis. or aversion toward rough-and-tumble play and rejection of male stereotypical toys, games, and activities; in girls, rejection of urinating in a sitting position, assertion that she has or will grow a penis, or assertion that she does not want to grow breasts or menstruate, or marked aversion toward normative feminine clothing.

In adolescents and adults, the disturbance is manifested by symptoms such as preoccupation with getting rid of primary and secondary sex characteristics (e.g., request for hormones, surgery, or other procedures to physically alter sexual characteristics to simulate the other sex) or belief that he or she was born the wrong sex.

C. The disturbance is not concurrent with a physical intersex condition.

D. The disturbance causes clinically significant distress or impairment in social, occupational, or other important areas of functioning.

Code based on current age:

302.6   Gender Identity Disorder in Children

302.85   Gender Identity Disorder in Adolescents or Adults

Specify if (for sexually mature individuals):

Sexually Attracted to Males

Sexually Attracted to Females

Sexually Attracted to Both

Sexually Attracted to Neither

(continued)

Table 4.1   *(Continued)*

Gender Identity Disorder Not Otherwise Specified

This category is included for coding disorders in gender identity that are not classifiable as a specific Gender Identity Disorder. Examples include

1. Intersex conditions (e.g., androgen insensitivity syndrome or congenital adrenal hyperplasia) and accompanying gender dysphoria
2. Transient, stress-related cross-dressing behavior
3. Persistent preoccupation with castration or penectomy without a desire to acquire the sex characteristics of the other sex

---

Source: Diagnostic and Statistical Manual of Mental Disorders, 4th ed. (1994). Washington, DC: American Psychiatric Association.

The *DSM-IV* also contains the category transvestic fetishism, which is limited to heterosexual or bisexual males who obtain erotic gratification from crossdressing. Many MTF transsexuals do report a history of transvestic fetishism. However, this diagnosis is not appropriate for MTF transsexuals, just as a diagnosis of GID is not appropriate for transvestic fetishists (or other persons) who occasionally fantasize about being a woman.

Opinion is divided about whether GID should be removed from the forthcoming *DSM-IV-R*. Many transgendered and transsexual people, as well as many professionals, believe that a nonnormative expression of gender per se is not pathological. Further, because many insurance companies exclude coverage of all medical and psychological treatment associated with GID, this diagnosis may not, in fact, confer a financial advantage, and may serve only to stigmatize the individual. Others argue that inclusion of GID in the *DSM* holds out a promise of insurance reimbursement, without which many transsexual and transgendered people cannot hope to pay the considerable medical expenses related to transition to a new gender role. However, because of the stress associated with gender-variant living in an often hostile social environment, many otherwise healthy transgendered people are likely to meet the criteria for recognized *DSM-IV* disorders such as affective disorders, anxiety disorders, or adjustment disorders.

Differential Diagnosis.   GID should be reserved as a diagnosis only for those who are extremely conflicted about their gender identity. Only the most pervasive feelings and behavior are suitable for diagnosis of GID, and only when they cause significant distress or impairment in social functioning (see Table 4.1).

Most transsexual, transgendered, and crossdressing persons are mentally healthy. Others may bear the psychological marks of keeping their natures secret from the world for decades, or for having been institutionalized or physically or sexually abused because of gender-nonconforming behavior. Some transgendered clients have psychopathology that has come about because of the way they have been treated by an intolerant society (e.g., posttraumatic stress disorder). Of course, transgendered individuals may also have comorbid mental illnesses that are unrelated to the gender identity issue.

A number of psychiatric conditions can result in symptoms that can be mis-diagnosed as GID. These include schizophrenia, body image disorders, bipolar disorder (especially in its manic phase), obsessive-compulsive disorder, border-line personality disorder, ego-dystonic homosexuality, and (rarely) malinger-ing. Obsessive crossdressing has been reported as a result of brain damage, especially in the temporal lobe area. It is necessary to screen for these and other conditions when a potentially transgendered client presents for treatment.

If there is a long history of transgender feelings or behaviors predating the onset of other diagnoses, one can be fairly certain that the gender identity is-sues exist independent of them. Because the other diagnoses may be exacerbat-ing or masking the transgender issues, it is important to stabilize co-occurring conditions while continuing to evaluate the transgender concerns.

TREATMENT ISSUES

Transsexual, transgendered, and crossdressing persons present to mental health professionals with a variety of goals and needs. The transgender or transsexual client who consults a mental health professional may be asking for help in dealing with the frustration of living in the original role or the many stresses associated with a change of gender role; attempting to gain a better understanding of his or her transgender nature and life options; seeking au-thorization letters for hormonal therapy or sex reassignment surgery, as man-dated by the Harry Benjamin Standards of Care; asking for help with a life issue totally unrelated to his or her transgender nature; or presenting with a mixture of issues. Most often, however, the individual will be seeking help to deal effectively with his or her gender identity issue. Looking into this issue may or may not eventually lead to a decision to change gender roles on a full-time basis or to have surgery.

Several visits are often needed to complete a thorough assessment and clar-ify the expectations of both client and therapist and to form a mutually agree-able treatment alliance. This section discusses the initial assessment, the establishment of treatment goals and expectations, and the comprehensive evaluation.

Assessment

The clinician must carefully evaluate the client to determine how best to pro-ceed. Why has he or she presented at this particular time? What does he or she hope to gain from therapy? Is he or she in crisis? If so, then immediate action may be required to ensure the physical and psychological well-being of the client before a more comprehensive evaluation is undertaken. Most clients will, of course, not be in crisis and will readily provide an introductory de-scription of their reasons for seeking therapy.

It is important to evaluate the "whole client" and to avoid drawing premature conclusions, which can assign a diagnostic label that the client may find difficult to modify in the future. For example, a client may enter therapy as a self-identified transsexual, but discover that periodic crossdressing or nonsurgical crossliving is as far as he or she wants to go. If the therapist has already accepted the assumption of transsexuality, it may be hard for the client to retreat from it.

Transgendered and transsexual clients have often "grown up with a secret," that is, have of necessity hidden their gender-variant self-identity since childhood or adolescence. This can result in feelings of intense rage, shame, or guilt, which are often contained until the individual becomes overwhelmed and seeks therapy. Consequently, even in individuals who seem calm, initial assessment must address the degree of risk for suicide and other precipitous action. It is necessary to ask formal mental status questions, unless the preceding portion of the interview has clearly demonstrated that these are unnecessary. The client should be queried about his or her immediate concerns and asked, "Why did you decide to be seen *now,* instead of yesterday or next week?" The therapist should ask about the vegetative signs of depression and the common symptoms of anxiety, while concurrently attempting to create a reassuring milieu.

If the therapist anticipates a need for psychiatric consultation, he or she can routinize a request for psychiatric evaluation during a first appointment, or may require that the client see a psychiatrist as a condition for beginning treatment.

Establishing Treatment Goals, Expectations, and Limits

The therapist should review the expectations for treatment, provide information and reassurance regarding confidentiality, and discuss the therapeutic process, as a therapist would with any new client. If possible, the first appointment should be ended with a mutual understanding of the goals of the next two or three sessions. The first several sessions typically include exploring personal history and relationship patterns and constructing a geno/ecogram. The client should be asked his or her reason(s) for entering treatment and his or her initial expectations and goals for treatment.

Perhaps unfortunately, the therapist letters required by the Harry Benjamin Standards of Care can become the major focus of treatment. Sometimes, the client will demand a letter immediately. The therapist is then cast in the role of gatekeeper, withholding the letter until the client has complied with the waiting period and other requirements of the Standards of Care. This creates a dynamic that can be extremely damaging to the therapeutic relationship. Consequently, the letter must be negotiated. The letter should not be used as an incentive to force the client to conform to the therapist's wishes, but neither should it be given indiscriminately. During the first session, the therapist should bring up the issue of the letter, if appropriate, and negotiate with the client. Upon successfully concluding an agreement, a verbal or written contract can be devised and should be adhered to by both parties.

Comprehensive Evaluation

Once the initial assessment has been completed and the therapist and client have agreed to go forward with treatment, it is advisable to obtain a more extensive history. This may require another two or three sessions, but it is time well invested.

The *geno/ecogram* should include the extended family of both the individual and the spouse or partner(s), if the client is in a partnered relationship. It is often useful to ask for several adjectives to characterize each person and his or her relationship with the client. The therapist can ask about friends, neighbors, and coworkers, and end by inquiring whether there are other people who are or were important in the client's life.

A *mental health history* should be taken. Has the client seen a mental health professional before? Were there any psychiatric hospitalizations? Suicide attempts? Why was treatment sought, and what was its outcome? What is the mental health history of family members? The therapist will need to decide if there is sufficient reason to obtain records from previous treatment. If so, it will be necessary to obtain a signed release of information from the client.

It is important to determine the client's feelings about past interactions with mental health professionals. All too often, transsexuals and other gender-variant persons report that prior attempts to obtain help for their gender identity issues were disillusioning and that therapists were actually obstacles to treatment. If there is such a negative history, the therapist will need to work even harder to gain the confidence of the client.

An *individual and family health history* should be obtained. Is the client healthy? Has he or she had a recent physical examination? Have there been any hospitalizations or surgeries? Does he or she have any diseases or complicating medical conditions? If so, are they being treated? Does the client take any medications? Is there a need for HIV testing, and has the client been tested?

Health concerns such as diabetes, heart disease, or HIV may make it difficult or impossible for the client to obtain desired medical treatments such as hormonal therapy or surgery. The therapist should discuss this possibility with the client and help the client work through his or her feelings about the impact of the health concern on transition. It may also be important to obtain medical consultation early in the therapeutic process.

A *legal history* should include juvenile problems and adult legal involvements, including divorce and custody issues. Were there any arrests or incarcerations? Is there a police record or any open or pending case? Are there any indications of a substance abuse problem? Has the client been involved in any kind of illegal activity? If so, is it related to the client's transgender status (i.e., has the client faced discrimination that has made it impossible to maintain employment and forced him or her into sex work)? If a transgendered person has been taken into police custody for any reason while crossdressed, it is important to pursue a trauma history in as gentle and supportive a manner as possible.

The client's *religious beliefs and background* should be determined. Many transgendered clients experience tremendous internal conflict associated with religion, and often benefit from contact with a peer support group. In that setting, clients are likely to encounter other transgendered persons who share their religious struggle. The religious beliefs of family members and significant others may also have a powerful impact on the client.

Substance abuse is always a risk in individuals who are highly stressed. Consequently, a *substance use/abuse history* should be obtained. Has the client been previously or currently engaged in the misuse of alcohol or other drugs? Has he or she ever been arrested for use of illegal drugs, or entered a treatment program? Do other family members have histories of substance abuse?

What is the client's *education, employment, and military history?* How well does the client function in these areas of life? Does the client possess college degrees, professional licenses, or certifications? What type of discharge did the client receive from the military? How is the type of work that the client performs likely to affect the transition process? If the client is transsexual and pursuing full-time transgendered living, has he or she initiated the process of legal name change for needed documents? Is he or she eligible for Veterans' benefits?

What are the client's *hobbies and interests?* What sort of *social life* does he or she have? What sort of *support system* does he or she possess? How will the support system be impacted by gender transition? Will the client lose friends, family, or job? Will he or she be excluded from church, school, or social organizations? Does he or she have friends, a support group, or other sources of support in the new role?

It is also important to take a *sexual history.* Do other family members show atypical sex or gender indicators? Does the individual have a history of fetishistic arousal to crossdressing? Does this currently occur? How often does he or she masturbate, and with what fantasies? What is the client's history of sexual activity? Has he or she ever been in a sexual relationship? Has he or she ever been partnered or married? Have sex partners been male, or female, or both? How does the client feel about his or her sexual life? Does he or she currently have a sexual partner? If so, what is the perception of the partner's feelings about the client's gender issue? Finally, what is the client's sexual orientation? The therapist should keep in mind that a person unsure about his or her own gender identity may be unsure about what exactly *is* the "opposite" sex. It can be determined, however, if the client is attracted to males, females, both, or neither. Many transgendered people find themselves attracted to other transgendered people.

The therapist should help the client construct a *chronology of gender identity issues.* When did he or she first become aware of a sense of difference in regard to gender? How did awareness evolve? What were the client's fears, discoveries, reactions, consequences, beliefs, and feelings about the gender issue? How does the client perceive these issues currently? Has the client ever cross-dressed in private? In public? Has the client thought about or actually under-taken body alteration with hormones, electrolysis, or surgery? When did the client become aware of the transgender community? Has there been prior con-tact with support groups? Is he or she currently attending a support group?

One useful tool clients can employ to describe both current self-concept and its evolution over time is the Nine-Point Gender Continuum (Eyler & Wright, 1997). This schema is based on the premise that, like sexual orientation, gender identity is best understood as a continuum. As with the description of bisexu-ality on the Kinsey scale, individuals who consider themselves neither fully male nor fully female may describe themselves with a variety of distinct iden-tifications. Furthermore, when discussing gender, it is important to accommo-date both "nontraditional" (from a Western standpoint) gender identifications and the "gender agnostic"; that is, the individual who regards gender either as being a very fluid concept or as a notion that is irrelevant to the freely expres-sive person. The Nine-Point Gender Continuum can also be used by the "gen-der questioning" person to indicate self-concept at the beginning of therapy and can be revisited at later times in the therapeutic process. This gender schema is represented in Figure 4.1.

This may appear to be a daunting amount of material to gather, but a prac-ticed therapist can obtain a reasonably thorough history in two or three ses-sions. It will be helpful if the client understands that the therapist is gathering an overview to identify areas to return to later for further exploration, espe-cially if the therapist raises a sensitive issue during the history taking.

As the history is gathered, potential goals for therapy will evolve and be-come defined. At the conclusion of the comprehensive evaluation, the thera-pist and the client should be able to come to agreement about areas that warrant further exploration. Issues that are usually prominent during the middle stages of the therapeutic process include the transition itself and self-disclosure ("coming out").

The Therapeutic Process: Gender Transition and
Self-Disclosure ("Coming Out")

The Transition Process.   Transition is the term used to describe the process of moving physically, psychologically, and socially into the gender role with which the transgendered person most closely identifies. Many transgendered clients will find enough satisfaction in lesser measures of cross-gender expres-sion to make transition unnecessary. Some may defer transition until a time when their life better supports such a move, such as after children have been raised or employment advancement achieved. However, some clients will be prepared to live full time in the chosen gender role very soon, with or without surgery, and may well be prepared to make major sacrifices to do so.

The medical aspects of transition are discussed in a separate section of this chapter. However, even from the perspective of social interaction, transitioning

F	F/M	GB/F	O	U	B	GB/M	M/F	M
"Female-based" identities			"Nontraditional" identities			"Male-based" identities		

Female (F) I have always considered myself to be a woman (or girl).

Female with maleness (F/M) I currently consider myself to be a woman, but at times I have thought of myself as really more of a man (or boy).

Genderblended female predominating (GB/F) I consider myself (in some significant way) to be both a woman and a man, but somehow more of a woman.

Othergendered (O) I am neither a woman nor a man, but a member of another gender.

Ungendered (U) I am neither a woman, a man, nor a member of any other gender.

Bigendered (B) I consider myself bigendered because sometimes I feel (or act) more like a woman and other times more like a man, or sometimes like both a woman and a man.

Genderblended male predominating (GB/M) I consider myself genderblended because I consider myself (in some significant way) to be both a man and a woman, but somehow more of a man.

Male with femaleness (M/F) I currently consider myself to be a man, but at times I have thought of myself as really more of a woman (or girl).

Male (M) I have always considered myself to be a man (or boy).

- How do you perceive your gender currently? (Place a mark at the most appropriate place.)
- Have you understood your gender differently in the past?
- Do you think that this perception may change with time? If so, in which direction may it evolve?

Figure 4.1 The Nine-Point Gender Continuum.

from natal female to male (FTM) is quite different from transitioning from male to female (MTF). In addition, although there are probably about equal numbers of transgendered people of both natal sexes (Signorile, 1996), currently more MTF transsexuals, transgenders, and crossdressers have publicly self-identified in Western countries.

Gender-variant persons who are beginning therapy (and their therapists) should be made aware of the interaction among identified gender, personal valuation, and social acceptance. In a society with a paternalistic heritage (such as contemporary Western culture), maleness is more highly valued than femaleness in most contexts. FTMs often experience a rise in social status and income (without any change in credentials, only in sex), whereas MTFs are more likely to experience the reverse. Associates and family members may also find the decision of "a man to turn female" harder to understand than an FTM "freeing himself" of the female role. However, the majority of persons who undertake gender transition will experience some degree of censure. For example, an FTM who has previously identified "herself" as a lesbian and developed "her" social outlets in the lesbian community may find the experience of coming out as FTM to be a mixture of relief (at expressing his true self) and loss (of his lesbianism). One of the gifts of the transgender community to contemporary understanding of mental health and social context has been to increase social awareness regarding the spectrum of gender and to call into question cultural perceptions about sex and gender.

Social position and earning power also impact MTF and FTM transsexuals and transgenders at different times during the transition process. Despite recent progress and the achievement of partial equal rights legislation, women in general have less earning power than their male counterparts. For an MTF, this can result in a lower standard of living, which may come as a shock to the individual. If income changes occur, they may negatively affect the ability of the MTF person to pay for facial electrolysis (which is usually needed to negate one of the strongest male appearance cues) and perineal electrolysis, which is needed prior to MTF sex reassignment surgery. In most cases, electrolysis represents a time-consuming, painful, and expensive process that may require several years to complete. Conversely, although FTM persons may begin at a lower income level, and may therefore experience difficulty in paying for therapy and hormonal services. Improvement in income or insurance status will often be needed prior to sex reassignment surgery since this procedure is more expensive than male-to-female surgical procedures.

Consistent participation in therapy is necessary prior to the decision to begin hormonal therapy or to seek surgical procedures, as well as when other significant events such as coming out or beginning the first sexual relationship in the true gender are in progress. Although the transition process can often be completed within two or three years, both FTM and MTF individuals in transition will often experience times during which further progress will be delayed, either due to financial limitations or to practical considerations (such as the need for facial electrolysis prior to coming out, in the case of an MTF transgender or transsexual with extensive facial hair). This time can be well spent in discussing what it means to the person to be male or female (or some other identity), in identifying and addressing the obstacles that are likely to be encountered in the transition process, and in expanding the individual's experience and confidence in contragender expression. Other, concurrent life issues may also benefit from further attention during these times.

When sufficient medical and cosmetic alterations have been obtained, the process of coming out to the larger society, rather than to the client's closest friends and family, can begin. Coming out issues are discussed below.

Self-Disclosure (Coming Out).   The coming out process is the very essence of transition. It is truly a process rather than a single event. Early in the transition process, the therapist should inquire about the degree to which the client's transgender behavior is a secret: Who knows (or suspects)? Exactly what do they know? How long have they known? How did they learn about your identity (or behavior)? What is their attitude toward your transgender issues?

The therapist should also attempt to determine the risk for the transgendered person precipitously coming out to someone such as a supervisor or parent without carefully weighing the consequences. The therapist may wish to advise the client to defer this step until self-disclosure can be planned for in a way that will maximize the chances of a successful outcome. Concurrently, it is crucial that the therapist avoid giving the impression that transgender status should remain hidden as a shameful secret.

In most cases, it is optimal that the client's transgender status eventually be disclosed to select individuals; however, the therapist must allow the individual to make his or her own decision, after the ramifications of coming out have been thoroughly explored. The therapist may also assist the client in assessing the risks associated with going out in public in particular settings. For example, a client who goes to a restaurant or mall where he or she is well-known, or who ventures into a setting that poses a risk of physical attack or public ridicule may be exposing himself or herself to a higher degree of consequence than was anticipated.

The lack of childhood and adolescent gender-congruent socialization may pose additional, practical difficulties for persons who are just beginning the process of expressing their new gender role in public. Male-to-female "novice" crossdressers often lack skill with makeup and style of dress and may not have objective perceptions regarding how they appear to others. The client should be advised to proceed cautiously to reduce risk, while concurrently exploring ways of gaining skill and confidence through therapy, support groups, speech therapy, and so on. The client may be fearful about making contact with transgender social or support groups. If so, this fear can be used to increase self-awareness and to reinforce the realization that he or she may not be ready for other, even more public steps.

If there is imminent risk of discovery of gender-variant dressing or behavior by a specific individual, the advisability of "preemptive" self-disclosure should be explored. Otherwise, it is generally advisable to begin with the person who is most likely to be accepting and to respect the client's privacy. Friends and family are critical components in developing a support system. However, support is of limited value if that person cannot maintain confidentiality.

Often, the initial step is for the client to reveal his or her true gender to a parent or sibling. This revelation will raise its own questions: When will your mother allow you to show her a picture of you "the other way"? When will she meet you in person as a member of your true gender? When will your father be seen with you in public? How will he adjust to the new pronouns? Even in very supportive family relationships, parents usually experience their own grieving process at the loss of the adult child they "always thought they knew," at the loss of the name they chose at birth. This will be followed by their own struggle with coming out, as they tell friends and neighbors and acknowledge the transition with extended family members. Provision for offering therapeutic support to these family members is recommended.

During the coming out process, the client may need to be counseled not to announce intent to go further in transition unless it is certain that he or she will proceed. It may also be better not to make promises that may not be kept (or that will give away control of his or her life to another person). For example, a client who is pressured by his mother to promise not to reveal his transgender identity to his father, who is struggling with a chronic illness, may crave her acceptance sufficiently to promise. But it would be less problematic for the client to say, "I can only promise to take your feelings into consideration, but I will have to make my own decision based on my relationship with Dad." This will prevent the promise from becoming an additional obstacle in the coming out process.

In a majority of cases, coming out at work is a last step, after the client has taken hormones for an extended period of time, lived most of his or her life outside of work in the gender to which he or she is moving, and is ready for a legal name change, which would necessitate use of the new name for Social Security purposes. By then, the individual will have dealt with numerous other transition-related issues. If the person was married, he or she may (but is not required by law to) have gotten a divorce or redefined the marital relationship. When other issues have been cleared up first, the client is more free and better equipped to address work issues.

Clients may use the therapy setting as a source of both "reality testing" regarding gender-expression decisions and support during the sequential layers of the coming out process. One additional principle that should be emphasized to the client is that, if hormonal therapy is begun prior to coming out, it must be kept at a level at which the physical changes are not so noticeable that they will force premature disclosure.

The effects of hormonal therapy vary. Some people react very gradually; others blossom out in breasts or beard so quickly that it may force a more rapid outing of the transself. Therefore, the client should be close enough to this step that the physical changes will not precipitate a crisis. Some clients will benefit from low doses of hormones that do not produce rapid physical changes, but this varies considerably from one individual to the next. A physician who is experienced in transgender medicine should be able to offer a range of possible approaches to hormonal transition. Throughout the transition process, consultation among therapist, client, and physician is advisable.

After the desired physical changes have been obtained and the coming out process is reasonably complete, the transgendered or transsexual person will eventually desire termination of the therapy process. This is discussed in the following section.

Terminating Therapy

Readiness to terminate therapy will depend on the needs of the individual client and the treatment goals that have evolved during the therapy process. The extent and ease of the client's gender journey will also be major determinants in this regard. For clients who have undertaken full gender transition, practical considerations (e.g., whether and how to begin using the restroom of the other sex) may have been addressed along with intrapsychic and interpersonal issues earlier in treatment. Before the termination of therapy, socialization into the new gender role, including employment stability, should be reasonably complete. Further, if the client has chosen full transition with genital reconstructive surgery, issues that have been previously addressed may require further attention postoperatively, and additional material may be brought to the therapy sessions before termination is achieved.

The adjustment process for persons who undertake full gender transition is in some ways analogous to a period of adolescence (although fortunately, with the benefit of greater life experience and maturity prior to its onset). Varying the frequency of therapy sessions can be a useful technique as the client passes through different stages of the transition process, sometimes achieving a plateau and at other times contemplating new and perhaps major life change. Alternation between regular and less frequent sessions may be arranged several times before the therapy process is complete, and the continuing availability of the therapist for follow-up visits once or twice annually may be useful during the years immediately following the completion of transition. Nevertheless, the sense of closure is important. Client and therapist have shared a remarkable journey and can arrive together at the best plan for closure of this relationship.

The preceding portion of this chapter has described many of the issues involving individual transgender clients. It is also useful for mental health professionals to be familiar with the couple and family dynamics that often provide a context for the self-disclosure of transgender. These are discussed in the following section.

TRANSGENDER ISSUES FOR PARTNERS AND FAMILIES

One of the most important aspects of the transgender journey is coming out to family members, partners, and close friends. This step almost always precedes the decision to inform employers and coworkers, and may predate the real-life experience by months or years. Transsexual, transgendered, and crossdressing persons who are not in a partnered relationship and do not have children will nonetheless usually need to come out to their family of origin. For persons who are married, partnered, or parenting, this process may be even more complex. This section addresses issues frequently encountered in intimate partnerships, with or without children, in which one partner discloses to the other the fact of his or her transgender identity.

Disclosure

Couples and families will often present to a therapist in the wake of the disclosure or discovery of gender variance within the partnered relationship. Even if a prior therapeutic relationship exists with the transgendered partner, attention must be directed at this time to the partners and families whose own concerns may seem to be eclipsed by the presence of transgender in the relationship or family. The context of the discovery is also a crucial therapeutic consideration. *When, how, and from whom* the significant other or family learns that transgender is a part of their lives is fundamentally important. The partner may be dramatically influenced by these factors in his or her ability to grasp information, understand this change, then respond and integrate the presence and reality of transgender uniqueness into his or her own life and that of the family. For many, grappling with this new information can be stressful. Initial responses can resemble posttraumatic stress in those individuals who struggle with the discovery.

Female Partners and the Discovery of Transgender

Psychotherapeutic experience with the male partners of FTM or MTF transgenders is currently very limited. It is recognized that, to date, most partners of MTF and FTM individuals are female. One of the authors has conducted retreats and discussion groups for partners of transgendered persons for 16 years. Therefore, this section will report her experience with female partners of MTF and FTM individuals, with or without children.

The female partner of an MTF husband in a "traditional" marriage may feel challenged and conflicted in her multiple roles in the relationship and family as wife, lover, mother, and helpmate. She also may have her own career or employment responsibilities, and community and religious activities and responsibilities. It is generally observed that she will now also assume the larger responsibility of the necessity of "keeping the secret," as her confidence in her husband's judgment about discretion may be eroded, particularly if he is choosing public behaviors that risk his being identified or discovered. She will often recognize, and may live in fear of, the unforgiving attitude and punitive behavior of society toward people it considers variant or deviant (Goffman, 1963).

When the wife or lover learns of the partner's transgender identity is a crucial factor in the adjustment process. When transgender identity is known in the initial development of the relationship, whether heterosexual or lesbian, the couple can more satisfactorily integrate and develop their bond together. Discovery of transgender issues after the relationship has been established is considerably more complex (Talamini, 1982). Factored into the couple's therapeutic process must be an understanding of the length of the relationship, whether or not children are present in the family and their ages, the situation in which discovery took place, and how she emotionally experienced learning of the transgender aspect of her partner. Predictably, discovery of transgender after the dyad has had years of shared experiences can result in her experience of emotional trauma, specifically initial feelings of betrayal, revulsion, anxiety, paranoia, and intense competition.

How and from whom she learns will also influence her response. If he initiates the process of disclosure and reveals his transgenderism in an honest and truthful way, many couples will work toward resolution over time, often with strong indications that the couple will stay together in the long term (Brown, 1998). If the female partner discovers the clues or actual evidence herself, she may experience more intense feelings of betrayal, humiliation, shame, and revulsion. She may experience the desire to flee, may actually abandon the relationship, or, in her fear, rage, and betrayal, she may "out" her partner deliberately as retaliation. This reaction is potentially harmful to the entire family system, as once the "secret" is out, there is no recovery, and the couple and the family may be placed in a compromising and defensive social position, especially if the "outing" has occurred in particularly negative circumstances. More usually, the wife will fear exposure, social retaliation, and loss of her sense of privacy from the world outside her family and will therefore work to maintain the feared and deeply resented secret of transgender.

Coming Out (or Not) in Families with Children

The coming out process is often more complex in families with children, especially if transgender is still a secret from certain members of the family or others in the community (such as may be the case when the husband/father crossdresses but is not actively involved in pursuing public gender transition or sex reassignment surgery). Couples often seek professional assistance in grappling with these decisions. The choices about coming out must be made individually by each couple; considerations for the dyad (and therapist) include previous and current family construct, values, and styles of communication (Docter, 1988; Zuger, 1988, 1989). The ages of the children, communication patterns between parents and toward the children, prejudices, biases, social awareness, honesty, and truth-telling are other key assessment issues. In general, adolescents and pubescent youth are considered to be more vulnerable to negative emotional responses than either younger or older children, as they themselves are personally experiencing enormous physical, hormonal, and emotional changes and challenges to their bodies, feelings, gender identity, and sexual orientation.

Many families choose to wait until their children are older (e.g., late teens or twenties); some families decide to be open and to develop a sense of understanding and coping skills together; and some choose not to involve the children or other parts of the family at all, as long as they can manage such privacy.

Responses to Transgender: Emotional Evolution over Time

As indicated earlier, female partners of MTF or FTM persons may respond to the disclosure or discovery that their partner is transgendered with any of a variety of emotional responses and behaviors. These include feelings that may be described as a deep sense of betrayal, violation of trust, fear, competition with this "new" female (if the disclosing partner is MTF), shame, curiosity, anxiety, repulsion, embarrassment, isolation, challenge, sexual arousal, eroticism, desire to be supportive, sexual dysfunction, aversion, increased self-imposed responsibility to the family, cooperative determination, and feelings of abandonment. There is an enormous potential for a wide array of feelings and behavior that may vacillate over time, depending on the circumstances and life situation.

In addition, the female partner of a transgendered individual may experience further challenges to her own gender identity and sexual orientation. Most female partners of MTF persons identify themselves as heterosexual without a self-concept of being partnered with a woman. Indeed, most MTF individuals are attracted to women after transition as well, and some continue to refer to themselves as heterosexual, despite the fact that they are now women partnered with women. Similarly, the majority of partners of FTM are female with a lesbian self-identity and do not have a self-concept of being partnered with a male. Whereas the partner of an MTF may experience feelings of betrayal of the couple's commitment to each other or to a "traditional" marriage, the partner of an FTM may experience rejection from her lesbian community and may actively grieve over her perceived loss of lesbianism, which is her own true identity (Devor, 1998). In some cases, she may be pressured by her FTM partner to tell others that she is heterosexual, so that he can be regarded as a "real man."

Some female partners may be attracted to such challenges and explore the flexibility of their own gender identity, expanding their own self-concept of masculinity/femininity. Some bisexual women may enjoy the "mix" of developing gender characteristics within the same partner. However, many women respond to their partner's gender transition (or exploration) more negatively or with stoicism. (Having a transgendered partner is not, after all, the basis on which their relationship was initiated.) Most partners of transgendered individuals will express concern about how far the transgender journey will go: Will it include taking hormones and eventual surgery, including genital surgery? Will I be able to allow myself to stay in the relationship if these events occur? (It should be noted that, although some couples do not stay together during the gender transition process, the widespread belief that sex reassignment surgery will invalidate a legal marriage in the United States is false. Marriages end if the participants wish to terminate them, and cannot be ended by the state due to gender transition.)

Sexual Intimacy in Transgender Relationships

If the transgendered partner has been open with his or her female partner since the early stages of the relationship, then the gender journey may be experienced as a desired component of the sexual partnership, "freely chosen" and erotically embraced. However, when women enter romantic or committed relationships on the assumption that gender variance is not present, only to discover this reality at a later time, psychological stress and sexual dysfunction may occur.

Female partners of MTF transgendered individuals may experience a decrease in sexual desire, usually as a result of concerns and anxieties about the relationship. During the times of disclosure and transition, she may inadvertently neglect her own health, including sexual health. The most common informally self-reported sexual dysfunction of women after discovery of transgender in the partner is secondary anorgasmia. In the beginning, she may not be able to tolerate feminine expression by her male partner during intimacy, especially when the MTF partner refers to herself as a lesbian, experiences feminine feelings, and wants to be made love to as a woman. Other partners may be sexually aroused by the sexual opportunities presented by challenging traditional gender norms (Brown, 1998; Cole, 1998; Docter, 1988).

For the female partner of an FTM individual, the sexual issues may be quite different. She has been sexually active with her female partner in a lesbian relationship and may not be prepared to have familiar intimacy activities suddenly considered "off limits," such as sex play involving her FTM partner's breasts and female genitalia. It should also be noted that persons who are experiencing gender transition are not homogeneous in their own sexual responses. Some FTM and MTF individuals "divorce" their genitals, and consider them "off limits" for sexual pleasuring until after sex reassignment surgery. Others are accepting of or erotically enthusiastic about their genital "incongruence," especially if surgery is not desired or is far in the future.

In relationships in which the partner's transgender identity is unexpected or undesired, other more serious sexual and psychological sequelae may result. Women may become so distracted by the changes in their relationships that they neglect their own medical health (e.g., pap smears, breast exams, and general well-care). They may present symptoms of depression and posttraumatic stress disorder, especially when feeling enormous responsibility to "guard the secret" from family, friends, employers, church, and community. Serious consideration must also be given to the female partner's own previous sexual history and life experiences. These may influence her ability to accept and learn about her partner's true gender identity, particularly if she has previously experienced betrayal in childhood or adolescence through family alcoholism, divorce, incest, sexual exploitation, or rape (Cole, 1998). If she has experienced any of these issues in her youth, her reaction to the discovery that her partner is transgendered may resemble compounded posttraumatic stress syndrome.

Response from the Mental Health Professions

For all of these issues, partners and couples often benefit from counseling or psychotherapy with mental health providers who have training and experience with transgender issues and who are knowledgeable about the impact that nontraditional gender identities may have on partners, families, employment, and community (Cole, 1998). Therapists and physicians who are experienced in transgender health care are currently not available in many areas, although the Harry Benjamin International Gender Dysphoria Association and other organizations have provided increased professional cohesion in recent years. In the future, additional outreach efforts to network with other members of the professional community will promote continuity of medical and mental health well-care for transgendered individuals and their partners and families.

Partners frequently benefit from participation in partner/significant other support and social groups, which can offer empathy, advice, problem-solving opportunities, and personal sharing of feelings and concerns. The opportunity to discuss feelings about transgender in a nonjudgmental environment can be extremely important and is usually not available to the partner among her own personal confidants and friends (Weinberg & Bullough, 1988).

Other Issues in Transgender Therapy

North American families have usually been created around the dominant Western cultural paradigm in which gender is viewed as a dichotomy (women and men) that corresponds to the two sexes (female and male). When families learn that a transgendered person exists within their own family system, the response is often predictable and reflective of the social values of the culture in which they live (Rosenfeld & Emerson, 1998). Hence, the struggle to learn more about their transgendered family member may include elements of behaviors such as denial and grief.

Although families tend to move through recognizable stages as they learn to accommodate to these changes, the course of adaptation does not usually follow Kübler-Ross's (1969) theories of grief, death, and dying in a linear fashion. Progression through the stages of denial, anger, bargaining, depression, and acceptance is rarely direct and linear. Instead, the movement more closely resembles a kaleidoscopic journey in which individuals react and respond independent of one another and in different stages, depending on the circumstances. The emotional journeys of families are highly individual; individual members will have different experiences in each stage and will not necessarily experience these transitions at a similar pace.

When disclosure within the family is not managed in a constructive manner, threats and unrealistic boundaries may be imposed on the newly identified transgendered family member. Spouses and families may threaten rejection or force the transgendered person to leave. Partners may threaten to leave or may actually flee. Family mental health therapy made available to such partnerships or family systems may help manage feelings of loss and anger, prevent unnecessary family trauma, and mitigate long-term guilt, shame, and grief for all parties concerned. Family therapy can also help the family attain a level of stability that will allow all members of the family to function normally and can assist the family unit in learning needed problem-solving skills.

From a therapeutic standpoint, it is crucial for the partner and family to finally be able to abandon the desire to change the transgendered individual and accept the reality of the situation. This does not mean that approval always accompanies acceptance, but it does allow the family and partners to move on in their lives. Brown (1998) notes that, with regard to women with "closeted" transgender or crossdressing partners, "The overall trend observed was for greater acceptance over time, assuming that the woman obtained accurate information and access to other women living in similar circumstances" (p. 364).

Family therapists can positively influence the struggle and journey as the family attempts to integrate new information: possible disruption of the unit, new knowledge that is often uncomfortable and anxiety-producing, and an abiding concern about what others will think (Cole, 1998). In addition, many families report high satisfaction from association with peer support groups, which offer the opportunity to discuss, learn, and process with others who are also experiencing the journey of transgender.

Participation in support groups is particularly relevant for families of children and youth who exhibit nonconforming gender behaviors or who may be emerging as transgendered. Transgendered young people who are facing the pressures and confusion of gender-specific roles that may be contrary to their self-identity need love, support, and education. Family support is extremely important, but may be difficult for parents and siblings to provide as they themselves struggle with a complex and unfamiliar situation. Parents may experience isolation, disbelief, shock, anger, and shame. Groups such as Parents, Families, and Friends of Lesbians and Gays (PFLAG) often include transgendered members and provide support for families of transgendered youth. Networking with other parents may be highly effective in helping the family to gain comfort, understanding, confidence, and practice in effective coping strategies while striving to learn about, accept, accommodate, and embrace their transgendered youth (Xavier, Sharp, & Boenke, 1998). Therapists working with transgendered adolescents can facilitate the process of family acceptance and functional normalization through referral to supportive community groups. Participation in groups can also complement concurrent family therapy, the goal of which is to enhance family efforts to facilitate its own journey toward understanding and resolution, while supporting and respecting the transgendered child's unique personal journey.

Conclusion and Future Directions

An awareness of the variety of human gender expression and knowledge of the individual, dyadic, and family dynamics that accompany the transgender journey can provide the mental health professional with a foundation from which to assist transgendered persons and their loved ones. Due to the societal complexities that currently surround gender variance, it is essential to consult with colleagues who are experienced in this area of practice.

This chapter focuses on female partners only because clinical experience with male partners of MTF transgenders is very limited, and experience with husbands and male partners of FTM persons is nearly nonexistent. This should not be understood to imply that other transgender dyads do not exist, but only that they are less well studied. Nontransgendered partners reflect the entire continuum of gender identity themselves. Some partnerships consist of two transgendered persons (MTF and FTM, MTF and MTF, FTM and FTM), the previously described MTF and female, FTM and female, FTM and gay male, MTF and gay male, MTF and heterosexual male, and FTM and heterosexual male. In addition, many FTM persons have children from previous long-term heterosexual or lesbian relationships. Furthermore, although crossdressing was once defined as strictly an MTF phenomenon, it is clear from clinical experience that some women also crossdress to express gender variance or for erotic enjoyment. As the field of transgender studies matures, it will behoove mental health professionals to stay informed with respect to emerging issues for individuals, partners, and families.

MENTAL HEALTH CARE WITHIN A MULTIDISCIPLINARY TEAM

Many therapists who provide services to transsexual, transgendered, and crossdressing clients do so as solo practitioners, making referrals, as appropriate, to medical colleagues for hormonal or surgical therapies. An alternative approach, introduced by Richard Green and John Money in 1969, is practice within a multispecialty transgender health care team.

In the 1970s, there were approximately 40 university-based "gender programs" in the United States (Denny, 1992). Subsequently, transsexual medical care shifted largely to the private sector, with most providers offering either mental health or surgical services exclusively. Until recently, these programs neglected transgenderists, that is, people who crosslive full time without seeking sex reassignment surgery. Crossdressers have also experienced difficulties in obtaining needed medical services in a welcoming environment.

The pattern most commonly seen today is for independent practitioners to offer specific services such as counseling, electrolysis, hormonal therapy, sex reassignment surgery, and breast augmentation or reduction and to refer their transsexual and transgendered clients for other medical or mental health services. Transsexuals, transgenderists, and serious crossdressers have learned to shop "à la carte," selecting service providers based on price, reputation, services offered, and location.

The chief advantage to this à la carte approach is that the individual becomes his or her own case manager. He or she can choose from a menu of services and service providers, shopping for price or competence in much the same way that one might purchase a new car. This is also the chief disadvantage, for many transsexuals are not emotionally or intellectually prepared to undertake the difficult task of coordinating their transition. In addition, accurate medical knowledge regarding the safe use of contragender hormones has not been widely available, and many transgendered persons seeking a rapid transition have suffered medical complications from taking hormonal preparations inappropriately or from multiple simultaneous prescriptions.

Another disadvantage of the à la carte approach is that the various professionals who treat the client rarely have a chance to interact with one another. There is, therefore, insufficient opportunity to fully coordinate care, and care providers will, of necessity, make treatment decisions with less than full knowledge of the client's situation. Furthermore, significant health concerns may be overlooked or go unaddressed. Often, services are delivered far from the client's home, in another state or even out of the country, making follow-up difficult. This is of especial concern with regard to surgery, which can be followed by a variety of complications. If treatment-related health problems or complications develop, the treating physician may be unfamiliar with the client's history or the procedures used, and it may prove difficult to consult with a previous physician who practices in a distant time zone.

A third problem with the à la carte approach is that treatment of gender identity issues is a highly specialized field that requires particular competence. Some providers have only limited experience with gender identity issues. They may draw from personal experience, extrapolating about all transgendered people from contact with a very small number of individuals, or consulting textbooks containing obsolete or harmful information. Countertransference is common among health providers (Franzini & Casinelli, 1986; R. Green, 1969), and it is not uncommon for transgendered people to find themselves in the care of providers who try to "cure" them of their transgender feelings or who do not treat them with respect and recognition of their personal autonomy.

Also, as mentioned previously (under "Health Maintenance for Transgendered Persons"), under the à la carte approach, general health care is often overlooked both by transgendered people and by their care providers. The focus is often on crossliving, hormones, and surgery, to the exclusion of cancer prevention, cardiovascular risk reduction, and health maintenance services.

There are a number of advantages to the provision of services by an interdisciplinary team. The most important is that all services are provided at a single institution. The client can come to one location for preventive care, treatment of chronic illnesses, mental health services, speech (voice) therapy, electrolysis, facial plastic surgery, breast augmentation or reduction, sex reassignment surgery, and vocational counseling, all of which can be coordinated by a case manager or the primary care physician. Services are less likely to be duplicated, as they might be with the à la carte approach, and a wider range of health needs can be addressed in an integrated fashion.

Currently, such services are provided in the university sector by the University of Michigan Health Systems Comprehensive Gender Services Program in Ann Arbor. A number of other centers provide a variety of services but do not yet offer comprehensive health care to their transsexual and transgendered clients.

A historical disadvantage to gender programs has been compromise of the autonomy of the transsexual client. Actions into which transsexual persons have historically been coerced by gender programs as a condition for receiving services have included divorce, participation in research projects, conformance to stereotypic (e.g., "Barbie and Ken") gender presentations, heterosexual posttransition sexual orientation, commitments to alter their bodies with sex reassignment surgery, and departure from successful careers to take "gender-appropriate" jobs. Unfortunately, a recent survey (Petersen & Dickey, 1995) showed that throughout the world, transsexuals continue to be coerced into specific outcomes by gender programs. Petersen and Dickey's survey also revealed that some centers routinely exclude transsexuals they deem to be too old, too young, or too ugly, and those they feel will not "pass" well as members of the new gender. Unfortunately, some programs also still require their transsexual clients to crosslive full time as a condition for initiating hormone therapy. This practice is disruptive of the lives of transsexuals and places them at considerable danger for hate crimes, because without the masculinizing or feminizing effect of some period of time on hormones, they tend to be noticeably crossdressed in public. Since 1991, the American Educational Gender Information Service (AEGIS, 1997) has condemned the practice of enforced crossliving, and recently released a position paper stating that the practice of requiring crossliving as a condition for hormones is unethical.

Several centers in the United States have broken with the harmful and unethical traditions of their predecessors and, unfortunately, some of their contemporaries. The University of Michigan Comprehensive Gender Services Program and the Program in Human Sexuality at the University of Minnesota allow and encourage their clients to come to their own decisions regarding possible modification of their bodies. Furthermore, they take great pains to ensure that their clients are treated in a fair and ethical fashion. Other North American programs have modified their requirements and procedures over the years.

Mental health practitioners who care for transsexual, transgendered, and crossdressing persons should be alert for abuses of their clients' personal autonomy and should check to be sure all medical needs are met. Discussion of the client's previous experiences in the medical sphere should be routinely addressed in therapy, and the treating physician should communicate with previous physicians or the previous program case manager, when this is desired by the client.

Further Options

Therapists who do not engage in team practice will be best served by maintaining contact with other professionals who treat transgendered clients and their families. The American Association of Sex Educators, Counselors, and Therapists (AASECT) and the Harry Benjamin International Gender Dysphoria Association are two professional organizations through which such networking, support, and continuing education can occur.

REFERENCES

Abraham, F. (1931). Genitalumwandlung an zwei maennlichen transvestiten [Genital alteration in two male transvestites]. *Zeitschrift Sexualwissenschaft, 18,* 223–226.

Ackroyd, P. (1979). *Dressing up. Transvestism and drag: The history of an obsession.* New York: Simon & Schuster.

AEGIS. (1997). *Blanket requirement for real-life test before hormonal therapy: In our opinion, unethical.* American Educational Gender Information Service. Decatur, GA 30033-0724.

American Psychiatric Association. (1980). *Diagnostic and statistical manual of mental disorders* (3rd ed.) Washington, DC: Author.

American Psychiatric Association. (1994). *Diagnostic and statistical manual of mental disorders* (4th ed.) Washington, DC: Author.

Aviance, T. (1996, June). Dragathon: Drag past. Drag present. Drag future. Drag always. The 20th annual Miss Pittsburgh pageant celebrates community. *Planet Q, 3,* 30–31.

Bell-Metereau, R. (1993). *Hollywood androgyny* (2nd ed.). New York: Columbia University Press.

Benjamin, H. (1966). *The transsexual phenomenon: A scientific report on transsexualism and sex conversion in the human male and female.* New York: Julian Press.

Bentler, P.M., & Prince, C. (1969a). Personality characteristics of male transvestites: II. *Archives of General Psychiatry.*

Bentler, P.M., & Prince, C. (1969b). Personality characteristics of male transvestites: III. *Journal of Abnormal Psychology, 74*(2), 140–143.

Besnier, N. (1994). Polynesian gender liminality through time and space. In G. Herdt (Ed.), *Third sex, third gender: Essays from anthropology and social history* (pp. 285–328). New York: Zone Books.

Bolin, A.E. (1988). *In search of Eve: Transsexual rites of passage.* South Hadley, MA: Bergin & Garvey.

Bolin, A.E. (1994). Transcending and transgendering: Male-to-female transsexuals, dichotomy, and diversity. In G. Herdt (Ed.), *Third sex, third gender: Essays from anthropology and social history* (pp. 447–485). New York: Zone.

Bornstein, K. (1994). *Gender outlaw: On men, women, and the rest of us.* New York: Routledge & Kegan Paul.

Boswell, H. (1991). The transgender alternative. *Chrysalis Quarterly, 1*(2), 29–31.

Bradley, S.J., Oliver, G.D., Chernick, A.B., & Zucker, K.J. (1998). Experiment of nurture: Ablatio penis at 2 months, sex reassignment at 7 months, and a psychosexual follow-up in young adulthood [On-line]. *Pediatrics, 102*(1), E9. <.http://www.pediatrics.org/cgi/content/full/102/1/e9>.

Brewster, L. (1970). Editorial on Stonewall. *Drag, 1*(1), 4.

Brown, G.R. (1998). Women in the closet: Relationship with transgendered men. In D. Denny (Ed.), *Current concepts in transgender identity* (pp. 353–371). New York: Garland.

Bulliet, C.J. (1928). *Venus Castina: Famous female impersonators, celestial and human.* New York: Covici, Friede.

Bullough, B., & Bullough, V.L. (1998). Transsexualism: Historical perspectives, 1952 to present. In D. Denny (Ed.), *Current concepts in transgender identity* (pp. 15–34). New York: Garland.

Bullough, V.L., & Bullough, B. (1993). *Cross-dressing, sex, and gender.* Philadelphia: University of Pennsylvania Press.

Burke, P. (1996). *Gender shock: Exploding the myths of male and female.* New York: Doubleday.

Butler, J. (1990). *Gender trouble: Feminism and the subversion of identity.* New York: Routledge & Kegan Paul.

Choisy, Abbé de. (1966). *Adventures de l'Abbé de Choisy habillé en femme (1735)* [Memoirs of the Abbé de Choisy, dressed in women's clothing]. Mercure de France: Paris. (Original work published in 1870)

Colapinto, J. (1997, December 11). The true story of John/Joan. *Rolling Stone, 1*(775), 54–58, 60, 62, 64, 66, 68, 70, 72–73, 92, 94–97.

Cole, S.S. (1998). The female experience of femme: A transgender challenge. In D. Denny (Ed.), *Current concepts in transgender identity* (pp. 353–371). New York: Garland.

County, J. (with Smith, R.). (1995). *Man enough to be a woman.* London: Serpent's Tail.

Dekker, R.J., & van de Pol, L.C. (1989). *The tradition of female transvestism in early modern Europe.* New York: St. Martin's Press.

Denny, D. (1992). The politics of diagnosis and a diagnosis of politics: The university-affiliated gender clinics, and how they failed to meet the needs of transsexual people. *Chrysalis Quarterly, 1*(3), 9–20.

Denny, D. (1995). The paradigm shift is here! *AEGIS News,1*(4), 1.

Denny, D. (1996, May). Heteropocrisy: The myth of the heterosexual crossdresser. *Chrysalis: The Journal of Transgressive Gender Issues, 2*(3), 23–30.

Denny, D. (1997). Coming of age in the land of two genders. In B. Bullough, V. Bullough, M.A. Fithian, W.E. Hartman, & R.S. Klein (Eds.), *Personal stories of "How I got into sex": Leading researchers, sex therapists, educators, prostitutes, sex toy designers, sex surrogates, transsexuals, criminologists, clergy, and more* (pp. 75–86). Amherst, NY: Prometheus Press.

Denny, D. (1998a). Black telephones, white refrigerators: Rethinking Christine Jorgensen. In D. Denny (Ed.), *Current concepts in transgender identity* (pp. 35–44). New York: Garland.

Denny, D. (1998b). *Needed: A new literature for a new century.* Unpublished manuscript.

Devor, H. (1995, November). *More than mannish women: How female-to-male transsexuals reject lesbian identities.* Paper presented at the 1995 annual meeting of the Society for the Scientific Study of Sexuality, San Francisco, CA.

Devor, H. (1997, September). *A social context for gender dysphoria.* Symposium conducted at the XV Harry Benjamin International Gender Dysphoria Association, Vancouver, British Columbia, Canada.

Devor, H. (1998). *FTM: Female-to-male transsexuals in society.* Bloomington, IN: Indiana University Press.

Diamond, S., & Sigmundson, H.K. (1997). Sex reassignment at birth: A case report with long-term follow-up and clinical implications. *Archives of Pediatric and Adolescent Medicine, 150.*

Dickemann, M. (1995, February). *The Balkan sworn virgins: A European transgendered female role.* Paper presented at the First International Congress on Gender, Cross Dressing, and Sex Issues, Van Nuys, CA.

Dickens, H. (1984). *What a drag: Men as women and women as men in the movies.* New York: Quill.

Docter, R. (1988). *Transvestites and transsexuals: Toward a theory of cross-gender behavior.* New York: Plenum Press.

Dragoin, W. (1995, February). *The gynemimetic shaman: Evolutionary origins of male sexual inversion and associated talent?* Paper presented at the International Congress on Gender, Cross Dressing, and Sex Issues, Van Nuys, CA.

Dressed in men's clothes, chorus speeders arrested. (1911, February 26). *Atlanta Constitution*, p. C7.

Duberman, M.B. (1993). *Stonewall*. New York: Dutton.

Edgerton, R.B. (1964). Pokot intersexuality: An East African example of the resolution of sexual incongruity. *American Anthropologist, 66*, 1288–1299.

Eyler, A.E., & Wright, K. (1997). Gender identification and sexual orientation among genetic females with gender-blended self-perception in childhood and adolescence [On-line serial]. *The International Journal of Transgenderism, 1*(1). <http://www.symposion.com/ijtc0101.htm>.

Farrer, P. (Ed.). (1987). *Men in petticoats: A selection of letters from Victorian newspapers.* Liverpool: Karn.

Feinberg, L. (1993). *Stone butch blues.* New York: Firebrand Books.

Feinberg, L. (1996). *Transgender warriors: Making history from Joan of Arc to Ru Paul.* Boston: Beacon Press.

Fleming, M., Steinman, C., & Bocknek, G. (1980). Methodological problems in assessing sex-reassignment: A reply to Meyer and Reter. *Archives of Sexual Behavior, 9*(5), 451–456.

Foucault, M. (1979). *The history of sexuality.* London: Allen Lane.

Franzini, L.R., & Casinelli, D.L. (1986). Health professionals' factual knowledge and changing attitudes towards transsexuals. *Social Science and Medicine, 22*(5), 535–539.

Gilbert, O.P. (1926). *Men in women's guise* (R.B. Douglas, Trans.). New York: Bretano.

Girl dressed in male attire escorted to club for drink. (1911, February 20). *Atlanta Constitution*, p. 1.

Gould, S.J. (1981). *The mismeasure of man.* New York: Norton.

Goffman, E. (1963). *Stigma: Notes on the management of spoiled identity.* Englewood Cliffs, NJ: Prentice-Hall.

Green, J. (1998). FTM: An emerging voice. In D. Denny (Ed.), *Current concepts in transgender identity* (pp. 145–161). New York: Garland.

Green, R. (1969). Attitudes toward transsexualism and sex-reassignment surgery. In R. Green & J. Money (Eds.), *Transsexualism and sex reassignment* (pp. 13–22). Baltimore: Johns Hopkins University Press.

Green, R. (1987). *The "sissy boy" syndrome and the development of homosexuality.* New Haven, CT: Yale University Press.

Green, R. (1998). Transsexualism: Mythological, historical and cross-cultural aspects. In D. Denny (Ed.), *Current concepts in transgender identity* (pp. 3–14). New York: Garland Publishing, Inc. (Reprinted from *Transsexualism and sex reassignment* pp. 173–186 by R. Green & J. Money Eds., 1969, Baltimore: Johns Hopkins University Press)

Green, R., & Money, J. (1966). Stage-acting, role-taking, and effeminate impersonation during boyhood. *Archives of General Psychiatry, 15*, 535–538.

Green, R., & Money, J. (Eds.). (1969). *Transsexualism and sex reassignment.* Baltimore: Johns Hopkins University Press.

Hall, R. (1928). *The well of loneliness.* New York: Avon.

Hamburger, C. (1953). The desire for change of sex as shown by personal letters from 465 men and women. *Acta Endocrinologica, 14*, 361–375.

Hamburger, C., Stürup, G.K., & Dahl-Iversen, E. (1953). Transvestism: Hormonal, psychiatric, and surgical treatment. *Journal of the American Medical Association, 12*(6), 391–396.

Harrison, R.G. (1966). An anatomical examination of the pharaonic remains purported to be Akhenaten. *Journal of Egyptian Archaeology, 52*, 95–119.

Herdt, G. (Ed.). (1994). *Third sex, third gender: Essays from anthropology and social history.* New York: Zone Books.

Hirschfeld, M. (1910). *Die transvestiten: Eine untersuchung ber den erotischen verklei-dungstrieh.* Berlin: Medicinisher Verlag Alfred Pulvermacher.

Hirschfeld, M. (1991). *Transvestites: The erotic drive to cross dress* (M.A. Lombardi-Nash, Trans.). Buffalo, NY: Prometheus Books.

Hoenig, J. (1985). Etiology of transsexualism. In B.M. Steiner (Ed.), *Gender dysphoria: Development, research, management* (pp. 33–73). New York: Plenum Press.

Howard, J.E. (1993). Cross-dressing, the theater, and gender struggle in early modern England. In L. Ferris (Ed.), *Crossing the stage: Controversies on cross-dressing* (pp. 20–46). New York: Routledge.

Hoyer, N. (1933). *Man into woman: An authentic record of a change of sex. The true story of the miraculous transformation of the Danish painter, Einar Wegener (Andreas Sparrer).* New York: Dutton.

Kates, G. (1995). *Monsieur D'eon is a woman: A tale of political intrigue and sexual masquerade.* New York: Basic Books.

Kessler, S.J., & McKenna, W. (1978). *Gender: An ethnomethodological approach.* New York: Wiley.

Krafft-Ebing, R. von. (1894). *Psychopathia sexualis* (C.G. Chaddock, Trans.). Philadelphia: Davis.

Kubler-Ross, E. (1969). *On death and dying.* London: Macmillan.

Kurti, L. (1996). Eroticism, sexuality, and gender reversal in Hungarian culture. In S.P. Ramet (Ed.), *Gender reversals and gender cultures* (pp. 148–163). New York: Routledge & Kegan Paul.

LeVay, S. (1991). A difference in hypothalamic structure between heterosexual and homosexual men. *Science, 253*, 1034–1037.

LeVay, S. (1996). *Queer science: The use and abuse of research into homosexuality.* Cambridge: MIT Press.

Levine, S.B., Brown, G.B., Coleman, E., Hage, J.J., Cohen-Kettenis, P., Van Maasdam, J., Petersen, M., Pfafflin, F., & Schaefer, L. (1998, April–June). Harry Benjamin international gender dysphoria association's the standards of care for gender identity disorders [On-line]. *International Journal of Transgenderism, 2*, 2. Available: <http://www.symposion.com.ijt/ijtc0405.htm>.

Lowry, T.P. (1994). *The story the soldiers wouldn't tell: Sex in the Civil War.* New York: Stackpole Books.

Margretts, E.I. (1951). The masculine character of Harshepsut, Queen of Egypt. *Bulletin of the History of Medicine, 24*, 559.

McHugh, P.R. (1992). Psychiatric misadventures. *American Scholar, 61*(4), 497–510.

Meyer, E.L. (1994, January). The soldier left a portrait and her eyewitness account. *Smithsonian, 24*(10), 96–104.

Meyer, J.K., & Reter, D. (1979). Sex reassignment: Follow-up. *Archives of General Psychiatry, 36*(9), 1010–1015.

Money, J. (1975). Ablatio penis: Normal male infant sex-reassigned as a girl. *Archives of Sexual Behavior, 4*, 65–71.

Money, J. (1984). Part III: Matched-pair theory from two cases of micropenis syndrome concordant for diagnosis and discordant for sex of assignment, rearing, and puberty. *International Journal of Family Psychiatry, 5*, 375–381.

Money, J. (1992). Transsexualism and homosexuality in Sanskrit: 2.5 millennia of Ayurvedic sexology. *Gender Dysphoria, 1*(2), 32–34.

Money, J., Hampson, J.G., & Hampson, J.L. (1957). Imprinting and the establishment of gender roles. *AMA Archives of Neurology and Psychiatry, 77,* 333–336.

Moore, F.M. (1994). *Drag! Male and female impersonators on stage, screen and television.* Jefferson, NC: McFarland.

Newman, L.E., & Stoller, R.J. (1974). Nontranssexual men who seek sex reassignment. *American Journal of Psychiatry, 131*(4), 437–441.

Ochshorn, J. (1996). Sumer: Gender, gender roles, gender role reversals. In S.P. Ramet (Ed.), *Gender reversals and gender cultures* (pp. 52–65). New York: Routledge & Kegan Paul.

Ogas, O. (1994, March 9). Spare parts: New information reignites a controversy surrounding the Hopkins gender identity clinic. *City Paper, 18*(10), cover, 10–15.

O'Hartigan, M. (1993). The gallae of the Magna Mater. *Chrysalis Quarterly, 1*(6), 11–13.

Paulson, D. (with Simpson, R.). (1996). *An evening at the Garden of Allah: A gay cabaret in Seattle.* New York: Columbia University Press.

Person, E., & Ovesey, L. (1974a). The transsexual syndrome in males: I. Primary transsexualism. *American Journal of Psychotherapy, 28,* 4–20.

Person, E., & Ovesey, L. (1974b). The transsexual syndrome in males: II. Secondary transsexualism. *American Journal of Psychotherapy, 28,* 174–193.

Petersen, M.A., & Dickey, R. (1995). Surgical sex reassignment: A comparative survey of international centers. *Archives of Sexual Behavior, 24*(2), 135–156.

Prince, C.V. (1957). Homosexuality, transvestism and transsexualism: Reflections on their etiology and differentiation. *American Journal of Psychotherapy, 11,* 80–85.

Ramet, S.P. (Ed.). (1996). *Gender reversals and gender cultures.* London: Routledge & Kegan Paul.

Raymond, J. (1979). *The transsexual empire: The making of the she-male.* Boston: Beacon Press. (Reissued in 1994 with a new introduction by Teacher's College Press, New York)

Roscoe, W. (Ed.). (1988). *Living the spirit: A gay American Indian anthology.* New York: St. Martin's Press.

Roscoe, W. (1994, December). *Priests of the goddess: Gender transgression in the Ancient World.* Paper presented at the 109th Annual Meeting of the American Historical Association, San Francisco, CA.

Rosenfeld, C., & Emerson S. (1998). A process of supportive therapy for families of transgender individuals. In D. Denny (Ed.), *Current concepts in transgender identity* (pp. 353–371). New York: Garland.

Rothblatt, M. (1994). *The apartheid of sex: A manifesto on the freedom of gender.* New York: Crown.

Scholinski, D. (1997). *The last time I wore a dress.* New York: Riverhead Books.

Signorile, M. (1996, June). Last page: Transgender nation. *Out.*

Slide, A. (1986). *Great pretenders: A history of female and male impersonation in the performing arts.* Lombard, IL: Wallace-Homestead Book.

Socarides, C.W. (1969). The desire for sexual transformation: A psychiatric evaluation of transsexualism. *American Journal of Psychiatry, 125*(10), 1419–1425.

Stoller, R.J. (1967). Etiological factors in male transsexualism. *Transactions of the New York Academy of Sciences, 29*(4), 431–433.

Stoller, R.J. (1968a). A further contribution to the study of gender identity. *International Journal of Psycho-Analysis, 49,* 364–369.

Stoller, R.J. (1968b). Male childhood transsexualism. *Journal of the American Academy of Child Psychiatry, 7*(2), 193–209.

Talamini, J.T. (1982). *Boys will be girls: The hidden world of the heterosexual male transvestite.* Lanham, MD: University Press of America.

Taylor, T. (1996). *The prehistory of sex: Four million years of human sexual culture.* New York: Bantam Books.

Torjesen, K.J. (1996). Martyrs, ascetics, and gnostics: Cross-dressing in early Christianity. In S.P. Ramet (Ed.), *Gender reversals and gender cultures* (pp. 79–91). New York: Routledge & Kegan Paul.

Trumbach, R. (1989). The birth of the queen: Sodomy and the emergence of gender equality in modern culture 1660–1750. In M.B. Duberman, M. Vicinus, & G. Chauncey, Jr. (Eds.), *Hidden from history: Reclaiming the gay and lesbian past* (pp. 129–140). New York: New American Library.

Ulrichs, K.H. (1994). *The riddle of "man-manly" love: The pioneering work on male homosexuality* (M.A. Lombardi-Nash, Trans.) (Vols. 1 & 2). Buffalo, NY: Prometheus Press.

U.S. Preventive Services Task Force. (1996). *Guide to clinical preventive services* (2nd ed.). Baltimore: Williams & Wilkins.

Weinberg, T., & Bullough, V. (1988). Alienation, self-image and the importance of support groups for the wives of transvestites. *Journal of Sex Research, 24,* 262–268.

Wheelright, J. (1979). *Amazons and military maids: Women who dressed as men in pursuit of life, liberty, and happiness.* Unwin, England: Pandora Press.

Whitam, F. (1997). Culturally universal aspects of male homosexual transvestites and transsexuals. In B. Bullough, V. Bullough, & J. Elias (Eds.), *Gender blending* (pp. 189–203). Amherst, NY: Prometheus Press.

Wilchins, R.A. (1997). *Read my lips: Sexual subversion and the end of gender.* Ithaca, NY: Firebrand Books.

Williams, W.L. (1986). *The spirit and the flesh: Sexual diversity in American Indian culture.* Boston: Beacon Press.

Wilson, R. (1998, February 6). Transgendered scholars defy convention, seeking to be heard and seen in academe: A growing movement demands protection in anti-bias policies and attention for their ideas. *The Chronicle of Higher Education,* p. 68.

Xavier, J., Sharp, N., & Boenke, M. (1998). *Our trans children.* Transgender special outreach network of parents, families, and friends of lesbians and gays (PFLAG), 1101 14th St., NW, Washington, DC, 20055.

Zhou, J.-N., Hofman, M.A., Gooren, L.J.G., & Swaab, D.F. (1995, November). A sex difference in the human brain and its relation to transsexuality. *Nature, 378*(2), 68–70.

Zuger, B. (1988). Is early effeminate behavior in boys early homosexuality? *Comprehensive Psychiatry, 29*(5), 509–519.

Zuger, B. (1989). Homosexuality in families of boys with early effeminate behavior: An epidemiological study. *Archives of Sexual Behavior, 18*(2), 155–166.

CHAPTER 5

Sexual Orientation

ALAN L. ELLIS and ROBERT W. MITCHELL

ONE OF THE most controversial aspects of human sexuality is sexual orientation. In this chapter, we present an overview of the theoretical and research literature on sexual orientation. To do so, we have divided the chapter into five major sections: Defining Sexual Orientation, The History of Sexual Orientation and Mental Health, Research Issues, Theories of Sexual Orientation, and Therapy Issues.

From the outset, we should note that sexual desire for members of the opposite sex (heterosexuality) is the sexual orientation of the majority of individuals and is accepted as the norm in virtually all societies. As a result, controversy surrounding sexual orientation has focused primarily on those whose sexual orientation or desire is for members of the same sex (homosexuality), for members of both sexes (bisexuality), or for nonnormative sexual objects or activities (paraphilias). Throughout the twentieth century, the majority of the societal and academic discourse and research regarding sexual orientation has examined those whose sexual orientation is something other than heterosexual, particularly, homosexual sexual orientation. However, as early as 1905, Freud (1925/1962) wrote that heterosexuality is as much in need of explanation as homosexuality. Homoeroticism came to be the thing to be explained because, "contrary to Freudian counsel, heteroeroticism was assumed to be perfectly obvious and natural, so much the order of things as to be in no apparent need of explanation" (Murphy 1997, p. 19; see also Rosario, 1997a).

DEFINING SEXUAL ORIENTATION

The term "sexual orientation" has generally been used to refer to heterosexual, homosexual, or bisexual preference in choosing sexual partners (Bohan, 1996), or the range of preferences in choosing partners from completely homosexual to completely heterosexual (Kinsey, Pomeroy, & Martin, 1948; Kinsey, Pomeroy, Martin, & Gebhard, 1953). However, we use the term "sexual orientation" to refer to all sexual desires whether directed toward humans or not, whether acted on or only imagined, with the proviso that these be persistent desires. We include in sexual orientation not only desires for enactment of fantasies ("cognitive rehearsals," Saghir & Robins, 1973), but also desires in fantasy ("erotic ruminations," Binet, 1887) that may never coincide with a desire for enactment.

We are specifically interested in presenting theories that attempt to explain why a person is consistently sexually excited by a particular sort of object or activity. Possible sexually exciting "objects" are not only people of the same or opposite sex or both, but also things—clothespins, women's panties with their menstrual or orgasmic discharge, crystals, rubber clothing, a woman wearing velvet—and activities—having pies thrown in the face, wearing a diaper or dresses, touching an amputation or having one done to oneself, having snails and cockroaches crawl over one's body, or observing a woman squash a bug that was dropped on her shoulder (Berest, 1971; Bethell, 1974; Brand, 1970; Bulrich & McConaghy, 1979; Epstein, 1969; Gosselin & Wilson, 1980, 1984; Hirschfeld, 1948; Krafft-Ebing, 1886/1978; Mitchell, Falconer, & Hill, 1954; Money, 1986/1993, 1987/1993; Stekel, 1923/1952; Stolorow, 1975). Sexual orientations directed toward things or activities other than people are now called "paraphilias" (De Silva, 1995; Money, 1977; Stekel, 1923/1952), although a still common name for sexual orientations directed toward things is "fetishism" (Brand, 1970; Freud, 1925/1962; Stekel, 1923/1952). Many if not most people have particular preferences for types of people, such as red-haired men or skinny women wearing high heels, that might be considered a tendency toward fetishism (Gebhard, 1969; Grant, 1949). However, fetishes are usually looked on as "obligatory," in the sense that they are required for sexual excitement and orgasm (Greenacre, 1953, p. 79). Sexual orientations with a focus on particular body parts, such as breasts or foreskins (Khan, 1966), are also sometimes referred to as fetishism, although another term is "partialism" (Stekel, 1923/1952).

All of these terms refer to a person's relatively consistent and persistent directedness toward some thing or activity for sexual gratification. Thus, if a woman finds sex with a man to be something she is frequently interested in repeating in fantasy and/or reality, she would be characterized as having a heterosexual orientation. If she were also repeatedly sexually excited by fantasies of eating and becoming large and powerful (whether or not she had any desire to act on these fantasies), she would be characterized as having another sexual orientation toward eating and becoming large and powerful. Having once had a fantasy about having sex with a gorilla would not allow for classification as having a sexual orientation toward gorillas, but a repetitive fantasy of having sex with gorillas would. (Note that the sexual desire in sexual orientations is for something other than the self per se, such that a desire for masturbation or to have orgasm per se are not sexual orientations.)

An idea similar to our use of sexual orientation is "erotic orientation," which refers to "the most desired stimuli and responses leading to sexual climax or orgasm" (Langevin, 1985, p. 2). Langevin's (1983) focus is more on sexual fantasy than on sexual behavior: "Usually the most frequent behavior leading to orgasm reflects [someone's erotic] preference but not always. A married man can have intercourse thousands of times with his wife and yet prefer young boys with whom he may only have risked contact a dozen times" (p. 7). Langevin presumes that phallometric measures (indications of penile erection to particular stimuli) can "serve to establish an index of . . . erotic preferences" (p. 12) for men, yet it is hard to believe that a man who has had sex thousands of times with his wife would not find women (or at least his wife) sexually exciting, however much his fantasies were directed toward other sexual objects. One other problem is that a man may have a persistent fantasy (e.g., of having sex against his will) that he has no desire to actually experience (see Leitenberg & Henning, 1995).

Still, even if people never enacted—or had any desire to enact—some persistent fantasies, most people's persistent sexual fantasies seem likely to be related to their sexual behavior (especially when that sexual behavior is socially acceptable). The concept of the *lovemap* integrates fantasy and behavior into one concept. A lovemap is "a personalized, developmental representation or template in the mind and in the brain that depicts the idealized lover and the idealized program of sexuoerotic activity with that lover as projected in imagery and ideation, or actually engaged in with that lover" (Money, 1988, p. 126). Such a fusion of fantasy and behavior is problematic. Although people usually fantasize about things they have already experienced (Kinsey et al., 1948, pp. 510–511; Kinsey et al., 1953, pp. 164–165), both men and women can fantasize about things they've never experienced (and presumably can experience things they've never fantasized about).

Kinsey and his associates developed a scale of sexual preference, from 0 (exclusive heterosexuality) through 3 (bisexuality) to 6 (exclusive homosexuality) to characterize most people's sexual directedness toward other people (Kinsey et al., 1948, pp. 638–641). For Kinsey and his associates, fantasy and behavior were "two aspects of a single phenomenon" (Weinrich et al., 1993, p. 159), and both were integrated into the seven designations (from 0 to 6), which are useful for sociological and population-level analyses. Although they mentioned sexual fantasies or activities about animals, fetishism, and fantasies involving sadomasochism (Kinsey et al., 1948, pp. 510, 607; Kinsey et al., 1953, p. 164), these sexual orientations were apparently too infrequent to be objects of concern. Sexual fantasies during masturbation and in dreams were discussed, but little reference was made to fantasy during sexual interaction, except to say that it is more common among males than females (1953, pp. 668–669).

Building on Kinsey's concern with sexual preference is Storms's (1980) view of homoerotic and heteroerotic orientations as separable erotic orientations, with both present in individuals who have high sexual responsiveness to both males and females (bisexuals), or absent in individuals with low sexual responsiveness to both males and females (asexual). We further this splitting beyond the Kinsey continuum in our view of sexual orientation by positing that there may be multiple sexual orientations in individuals, some expressed in behavior, some expressed in fantasy, and some expressed in both.

Note that our view of sexual orientation is at times independent of people's self-designations (cf. Friedman, 1988). People may view themselves as gay, lesbian, bisexual, fetishistic, paraphilic, or heterosexual for many reasons (Bohan, 1996; De Cecco, 1981; Rust, 1993), and their behaviors and fantasies (and even their biological sex) may deviate markedly from these self-designations (Coleman, Bockting, & Gooren, 1993; Devor, 1993; Humphreys, 1970). Indeed, people can view sexual behavior, sexual desire, and sexual identity as independent (Adams, Wright, & Lohr, 1996; Laumann, Gagnon, Michael, & Michaels, 1994, pp. 298–301). Some people may find it more important to designate their sexual orientation than others do, some may be more attentive to fantasies than behaviors, and some may reverse this attention. For many individuals, sexual desires are to some degree fluid (De Cecco, 1981). Individuals who view themselves as homosexual or heterosexual may later develop sexual relationships that deviate from their self-label (Blumstein & Schwartz, 1977), and (judging from case studies) most people with paraphilias seem to develop sexual relationships with people.

THE HISTORY OF SEXUAL ORIENTATION AND MENTAL HEALTH

The study of sexual orientation and mental health for the greater part of the twentieth century has dealt with the treatment of homosexuality. That treatment has closely followed social mores and norms and, prior to 1973, homosexuality was considered a mental illness, a disease. In 1973, following several significant sociopolitical events in the history of gay rights (e.g., the Stonewall riots of 1969 that perhaps led to an increased awareness of and willingness to consider the research findings of the time), the American Psychiatric Association officially removed homosexuality from its list of mental disorders. The association issued the following position statement on homosexuality:

> Whereas homosexuality per se implies no impairment in judgment, stability, reliability, or general social or vocational capabilities, therefore, be it resolved that the American Psychiatric Association [APA] deplores all public and private discrimination against homosexuals in such areas as employment, housing, public accommodation, and licensing, and declares that no burden of proof of such judgment, capacity, or reliability shall be placed upon homosexuals greater than that imposed on other persons. Further, the [APA] supports and urges the enactment of civil rights legislation at the local, state, and federal level that would offer homosexual citizens the same protection now guaranteed to others on the basis of race, creed, color, etc. Further, the [APA] supports and urges the repeal of all discriminatory legislation singling out homosexual acts by consenting adults in private. (American Psychiatric Association, 1974)

A similar statement was also endorsed by the American Psychological Association's Council of Representatives in 1975 (p. 632).

The seminal work of Dr. Evelyn Hooker in 1957, in which she compared nonclinical samples of gay and nongay men and found no significant differences in psychological adjustment, helped lead to these changes in classification (Hooker, 1957; also see Bayer, 1987; Gonsiorek, 1991, for a review of the research and political actions that led to declassification of homosexuality as a mental illness).

THE SOCIOPOLITICAL ENVIRONMENT: HOMOPHOBIA AND ATTITUDES TOWARD LESBIANS AND GAY MEN

Although the mental health field has largely changed its view on the mental health issues of homosexuals, society at large continues to view homosexuals negatively. These negative views unfortunately result in acts of discrimination and violence against homosexuals. Previously, the term "homophobia" was commonly used to refer to prejudice and hostile behavior toward gay men and lesbians. However, there are few data to show that this behavior is associated with the physiological reactions that are characteristics of other phobias (Herek, 1996; Shields & Harriman, 1984). Indeed, heterosexual homophobic men show increased sexual arousal (as measured by penile tumescence) to images of male homosexual sex (Adams et al., 1996). Consequently, the term homophobia may be a misnomer. The term "heterosexism" is currently preferred over homophobia by most researchers as descriptive of antigay sentiment and behavior, especially as it is similar to other terms used to describe prejudice (e.g., sexism, racism, anti-Semitism; however, see Blumenfeld, 1992, for a discussion of why the use of the term homophobia is likely to persist). Heterosexism also lends itself more fully to descriptions of antigay sentiment and behavior at both the cultural and the individual level (Herek, 1996). Cultural heterosexism is similar to institutional racism and sexism, whereas individual or psychological heterosexism is the individual manifestation of cultural heterosexism.

The transition to the term heterosexism is fairly recent. As a result, the majority of the theory and research on attitudes toward gays and lesbians, as well as the popular press, uses the term homophobia. A key theoretical and research objective has been to better understand the underlying bases of homophobia. Homophobia appears to be based on four assumptions: (1) homosexuality is sinful/immoral; (2) it is "unnatural"; (3) it is a chosen form of behavior that can be changed; and (4) it can be taught to others (Marmor, 1998).

By better understanding the bases of homophobic or heterosexist tendencies, researchers, public policy analysts, and others hope to challenge the underlying assumptions and thereby reduce homophobic or heterosexist biases. In support of this approach, both anecdotal and empirical research demonstrate that heterosexuals who know someone who is gay are more likely to hold favorable attitudes and behave in a positive manner toward gay people (e.g., Ellis & Vasseur, 1993; Herek & Capitanio, 1996; Herek & Glunt, 1993; B. Powers & Ellis, 1996). The improvement in attitudes is thought to occur because direct contact with gay men and lesbians challenges erroneous stereotypes and beliefs, as well as assumptions such as those outlined by Marmor above.

Despite increasing contact with gay men, lesbians, and bisexuals, the majority of Americans remain uncomfortable with homosexuals and homosexual behavior, particularly as it relates to same-sex sexual desire between men. In a national telephone survey conducted by staff of the Survey Research Center at the University of California at Berkeley (in 1990 and 1991), 69.8% agreed with the statement that "sex between two men is just plain wrong," and 54.1% with "I think male homosexuals are disgusting" (Herek & Capitanio, 1996).

Still, increasing contact between gays and lesbians and heterosexuals has led to dramatic improvements in attitudes toward gays and lesbians over the past 30 years, and these attitudes continue to improve (Herek & Capitanio, 1996). Increasingly, heterosexuals are aware that they know a gay man or lesbian and, not surprisingly, the closer the contact with a gay person (male or female), the more favorable the attitudes toward gay people. The survey results also indicated that when heterosexuals were told directly by a gay person about his or her sexuality, the attitude was generally more favorable than if they knew about the person's sexuality secondhand. This finding supports the general belief that coming out to heterosexuals helps reduce prejudice toward gay people: "although coming out to loved ones exposes gay men and lesbians individually to the possibility of ostracism, discrimination, and even violence, it appears to be one of the most promising strategies for promoting the kind of societal change that will eventually end such stigma" (p. 422).

PREVALENCE OF GAY MEN AND LESBIANS

As more and more gay men and lesbians come out, the visibility of this group increases, and gay men and lesbians are no longer a hidden minority. However, because stigma and prejudice continue, it has been difficult to determine the exact numbers of gays and lesbians in the population. Efforts to do so have resulted in widely varying percentages, in part because of the difficulties inherent in differentiating between same-sex sexual behaviors and same-sex sexual identity (see next section).

With respect to occurrence of same-sex sexual behavior, Sell, Wells, and Wypij (1995) found that between 8.6% and 11.1% of females and 7.9% of males reported same-sex attraction after age 15. From these findings, they estimated that due to a likelihood of underreporting of such behavior, as many as 18% of females and 21% of males in the United States experience same-sex attraction or behavior after the age of 15. In another attempt to determine the numbers of gay men and lesbians, Laumann et al. (1994) used a probability sample and estimated that 7.5% of males and 7.7% of females experienced same-sex sexual attraction after puberty. Other studies have suggested that the percentages may be as low as 1% and as high as 20% (see Michaels, 1996).

One problem in assessing the prevalence of gay men and lesbians relates to how homosexuality is operationally defined as a construct: "Homosexuality is often treated as a unitary phenomenon that can be used to unambiguously differentiate persons into discrete categories. However, data from surveys of sexual behavior indicate that the distinction between the heterosexual person and the homosexual person is often imprecise" (Michaels, 1996, p. 61; see also Laumann et al., 1994). In fact, a great many people designated by researchers as homosexual in most research studies of the 1970s were actually bisexual in fantasy, behavior, and feelings (De Cecco, 1981). (Because of this overclassification of individuals as homosexual, it is not surprising that sex researcher Bell [1975] noted that there were so few bisexuals available for researchers at that time.) Such categorical looseness has been the norm. In some studies, heterosexuals might be defined as "any individual not known to the tester as a homosexual" (Thompson, Schwartz, McCandless, & Edwards, 1973, p. 121), or their heterosexuality might simply be "assumed" (Evans, 1969, p. 129). Lesbians might, on average, have had sex with more men than women, as in Loney's (1973, p. 345) study, and should be considered bisexual at least in their behavior. Even in people's self-categorizations, "homosexual behavior, desire, and identity are not completely overlapping" (Michaels, 1996, p. 61).

To the degree that homosexual behavior and same-sex sexual identities as constructs remain difficult to define and are stigmatized, and prejudice toward gay men and lesbians continues, consistent and relatively accurate estimates of the percentage of gay men and lesbians in the population are likely to remain elusive.

DEFINING SEXUAL ORIENTATION VERSUS SEXUAL IDENTITY

A key distinction for those interested in the study of sexual orientation is the difference between sexual orientation and sexual identity. Troiden (1988) notes that sexual conduct is primarily social in origin: "Existing sociocultural arrangements define what sexuality is, the purposes it serves, its manner of expression, and what it means to be sexual. This statement does not deny a biological substratum to human sexuality, but emphasizes the powerful role of social forces in shaping sexual conduct" (p. 123). Gagnon (1977) suggests the use of the term "human sexualities" as opposed to "human sexuality":

> There are many ways to become, to be, to act, to feel sexual. There is no one human sexuality, but rather a wide variety of sexualities. Had it been possible, I would have made the word "Human" plural as well. Just as there are many sexualities, there are many humanities, different ways of being sexual, different ways of being human. (p. i)

To the degree that sexual behavior itself is a social construct, the concept of sexual identity is dependent on the social and cultural beliefs of a given time and place. In the past 20 years, a number of researchers have studied the development of a gay or lesbian sexual identity. These theoretical developments are useful, but it is important to consider the historical and cultural limitations of such frameworks. For example, descriptions of "gay" culture at the turn of the century (the late nineteenth and early twentieth centuries) are inconsistent with current models of sexual orientation identity development. The current models are simply inadequate for explaining how people described their sexual identity based on their sexual behavior at that time (see Chauncey, 1994). Even so, for those working with gay men, lesbians, and bisexuals, the sociocultural factors that currently influence how these sexual identities are defined are relevant in helping them to integrate their sexuality with other aspects of themselves in this place and this time.

DEVELOPING A SEXUAL ORIENTATION IDENTITY

Again, because the academic research has focused on same-sex sexual issues, the concept of sexual orientation identity formation has centered on gay, lesbian, or bisexual identity development. Cass (1979, 1996) has developed the most widely cited and well-known model of lesbian and gay identity formation. Her model consists of six stages: (1) identity confusion, (2) identity comparison, (3) identity tolerance, (4) identity acceptance, (5) identity pride, and (6) identity synthesis.

The primary activity during identity confusion (Stage 1) is to address the confusion about who one is in light of one's behavior and/or sexual desire, and the cultural context in which one's desire is seen as negative and undesirable. This is one of the most challenging periods in sexual identity development as it brings up one of the key questions of existence, namely, Who am I? In identity comparison (Stage 2), the individual attempts to reconcile and cope with the feelings of alienation and difference resulting from identity confusion. The individual may look to others to understand whether or not holding a lesbian or gay identity may ultimately have more positive than negative consequences. During this stage, the individual is likely to say, I am probably gay or lesbian even if others think I am heterosexual.

During identity tolerance (Stage 3), the individual seeks to meet the social, sexual, and emotional needs that support his or her developing sexual identity.

Identity acceptance (Stage 4) involves a clearer perception of oneself as gay or lesbian although the inner sense of one's self as gay or lesbian is still tenuous. Cass (1996) notes, "given that individuals at this point are entrenched in the societal belief that heterosexuality is where power and acceptability lie, it is not surprising that little internalization of this experience of self has occurred" (p. 244).

During the stage of identity pride (Stage 5), the individual may pass through a period of devaluing heterosexuality in an effort to see his or her identity as legitimate and of value. A lesbian or gay self may be seen as "the preferred identity." As Cass (1996) notes, the combination of pride and anger (resulting from the perception of a strong cultural heterosexist bias) may lead the individual to abandon efforts to pass as heterosexual and to strongly announce his or her gay or lesbian identity.

In the final stage, identity synthesis, the individual begins to acknowledge and value supportive heterosexuals while perhaps further devaluing nonsupportive heterosexuals. To a large extent, however, the feelings of anger and alienation are resolved and the individual is able to develop a sense of "wholeness" that integrates his or her sexual identity. Cass (1996) suggests that this stage is "driven by notions of individuality, self-actualization, personal maturity, development, and other concepts" (p. 247).

Coleman's (1981/1982) similar five-stage model is also widely accepted. It consists of (1) pre–coming out (preconscious awareness), (2) coming out (acknowledgment), (3) exploration, (4) first relationships, and (5) integration. These five stages integrate most of the same conceptual issues and experiences as Cass's six stages, as do most other models of gay and lesbian sexual identity development.

As the sociocultural aspects of sexual identity continue to change, models of sexual orientation identity formation such as Cass's and Coleman's are likely to change. Indeed, it would probably be unwise to assume that all gay men and lesbians pass through the stages of identity development described in these models, particularly as these theories are largely based on case studies and there is limited empirical research to validate them. Even so, as examples of frameworks for understanding stages of sexual identity development, they have value as they offer a general awareness of the factors influencing sexual identity. To the degree that we see how these theories stand in need of revision, the sociocultural aspects of sexual identity will be further highlighted and understood.

MULTICULTURAL INFLUENCES ON ATTITUDES TOWARD HOMOSEXUALITY

In considering sexual identity, it is also important to acknowledge the challenges that face gay, lesbian, and bisexual individuals who must integrate ethnic, gender, and other identities with their sexual identity. People from African American, Latino, and Asian American backgrounds may fear loss of ethnic and cultural identity by being gay, lesbian, or bisexual, and also feel culturally and otherwise alienated from the predominantly White gay and lesbian community (Gonzalez & Espin, 1996; Jones & Hill, 1996; Nakajima, Chan, & Lee, 1996). Integrating multiple identities can present additional challenges to coming out for those whose identities are affected by sexism and racism in addition to heterosexism. Rosabal (1996) suggests that "it is impossible to grow up in a sexist, racist, and homophobic society without learning and internalizing messages [that devalue various aspects of identity]. However, it is possible to unlearn them" (p. 26). Equally, for a given culture or society, it is possible to learn new attitudes and beliefs regarding variations in sexual orientation.

In addition to identifying the challenges that ethnicity and other identities place on an individual, research in this area points out the sociocultural components of sexual identity. For example, Tafoya (1996) discusses the concept of "native two-spirit" people—the concept that one has both a male and a female spirit within—to illustrate how differing cultural backgrounds influence perceptions of sexual orientation. In many communities, two-spirit individuals are associated with power and spirituality and are thought to have a greater potential to exist on an integrated level. Tafoya quotes from W. Powers (1986, p. 188) the following description of the Winktes of the Lakota Indians: "the Winkte, variously translated as transvestite, hermaphrodite, homosexual, or more appropriately 'would be woman' . . . enjoyed a decided amount of prestige and high status. They were regarded as extremely sacred people who followed a particular lifestyle as a result of instructions received in visions." This description as well as other anthropological research indicate the degree to which perceptions of sexual orientation are culturally defined and constantly redefined. As Herdt (1996) states:

> We must be aware of the fundamental unpacking of the construct of homosexuality as a Western, typically culture-bound concept, in the sense that it implies a certain social role and identity that radiate largely from the 19th century, and these meanings as we now understand them are not present in other cultures and histories." (p. 66; see also Herdt, 1994)

Because of the historical and sociocultural influences on how sexual orientation is viewed, it is critical that research and theory remain current. The next section focuses on some of the issues that researchers wishing to study sexual orientation are likely to face.

RESEARCH ISSUES

The most fervent academic and research debate focuses on whether sexual orientation is the result of factors over which the individual has no control—essentialism—or is a choice made by the individual—social constructionism (see T. Stein, 1998). The debate over nature versus nurture is not unique to the study of sexual orientation and has been the source of debate regarding virtually every aspect of human behavior. Obviously, the middle road in this debate is a focus on genetic predispositions that are influenced by one's social environment.

With regard to sexual desire, there is a popular belief that research demonstrating a biogenetic explanation of sexual orientation offers a protection or "moral shield" for gay people. However, as Murphy (1997) notes, "there is no automatic correlation of social beneficence toward people with 'offensive' traits simply because those traits have an involuntary origin" (p. 76; see also Allen, 1997). One need only look at the prejudices associated with race and gender to validate this idea.

A key question is whether or not the etiology of homosexuality is really important. For example, Marmor (1998) argues,

> From an ethical perspective, the etiology of homosexuality, ideally speaking, should be of no importance whatever. Whether homosexuality is innate, acquired, consciously chosen, or any combination of these, the highest ethical imperative in a humanistic society mandates that gays and lesbians be treated no differently than any other religious, ethnic, or racial group, or indeed, than heterosexuals in general. The only reasonable ethical consideration is whether or not the overt behavior of any individual is harmful or destructive to others. (p. 20)

Others have noted that even asking the question regarding a biogenetic basis for homosexuality is problematic. As LeVay (1996), whose own work in this area is controversial, states, "it is hard not to think about the 'cause of homosexuality' without implying that heterosexuality is the 'normal' state that requires no explanation" (p. 5).

However, Marmor (1998) also argues that because therapists' views on etiology influence how they work with patients, an etiology that finds a biogenetic component for sexual orientation is likely to lead therapists to treat patients with same-sex sexual desire in a manner that facilitates acceptance and respect. In support of this view, Pillard (in E. Stein & Pillard, 1993, p. 98) notes that research supporting a genetic sexual orientation would be of benefit, as it will "get psychiatrists away from trying to convert sexual orientation."

Despite concerns regarding the ethics and motivation behind sexual orientation research, there is considerable evidence of the benefits that such research offers society and gay, lesbian, and bisexual individuals. For example, research has established that children raised by same-sex couples are as psychologically well-adjusted as those raised by heterosexual couples (Golombok & Tasker, 1996; Kirkpatrick, 1996; Patterson & Chan, 1996; Raymond, 1992). To the degree that the courts and society acknowledge such research findings, the experience of lesbians and gay men improves (e.g., lesbian mothers would not be denied custody of children solely because they are lesbians).

AVOIDING HETEROSEXIST BIAS IN RESEARCH

In addition to the work on biogenetic and social constructionist views of sexual orientation, there is a large body of research looking at the psychological factors associated with sexual orientation, including research on attitudes, the study of interpersonal relationships, and other social behaviors. A significant concern regarding this research is the degree to which *general* studies of human behavior may naïvely or deliberately exclude an awareness of those whose sexual orientation is not that of the majority. To the degree that a researcher ignores this population, he or she may be guilty of heterosexist bias, "conceptualizing human experience in strictly heterosexual terms and consequently ignoring, invalidating, or derogating homosexual behaviors and sexual orientation, and lesbian, gay male, and bisexual relationships and lifestyles" (Herek, Kimmel, Amaro, & Melton, 1991, p. 957). To avoid heterosexist bias, researchers should ask the following questions when formulating research questions (Herek et al., 1991):

Does the research question ignore or deny the existence of lesbians, gay men, and bisexual people?

Does the research question devalue or stigmatize gay and bisexual people?

Does the research question reflect cultural stereotypes of lesbians, gay men, and bisexual people?

Does the research question implicitly assume that observed characteristics are caused by the subject's sexual orientation?

If researchers fail to recognize that most samples include some lesbians, gay men, and bisexual participants, they are likely to weaken the overall research design, particularly in studies of interpersonal attraction, gender, and sexuality. As with any research design, the failure to account for additional variables that may influence the results threatens the internal validity of the study.

OTHER RESEARCH ISSUES

Another key research concern is the degree to which research studies protect participants, regardless of sexual orientation. Herek et al. (1991) suggest that researchers need to address the question of whether or not information that is obtained about sexual orientation and behavior for research purposes is truly confidential. Because of the stigma associated with homosexuality, research participants may fear negative consequences surrounding disclosure of their sexual orientation. It is the researcher's responsibility to ensure that any limits to confidentiality are understood and that these limits are clearly explained to participants.

The concern about confidentiality extends to a second research concern, namely, the potential difficulties associated with finding a representative sample given the cultural biases against disclosure of one's nonnormative sexual orientation (e.g., Herek & Glunt, 1993; Kite, 1991). To the degree that research findings are based on nonrepresentative samples, the validity of those findings is questionable, and the possibility of potentially harmful and inaccurate conclusions exists.

Ultimately, researchers must balance the need to better understand human behavior based on representative samples with the need to conduct ethical research that protects the rights and well-being of research participants. Reconciling these two demands will continue to be an important aspect of research on sexual orientation and will require ongoing scrutiny by researchers.

THEORIES OF SEXUAL ORIENTATION

Many theories about sexual orientation try to explain only one type of sexual orientation, such as male homosexual preference, or both homosexual and heterosexual preference, or fetishistic preference, with the implication that explanations for other sexual orientations are likely to be different. They very well may be, but this diversity of explanatory foci does not lend itself to grand theories of sexual orientation. To counter this parochialism, we present theories of homosexuality, theories of sexual preference, and theories of fetishism not only to see if they satisfy their objective but also as explanations of other sexual orientations. Many diverse explanations of homosexuality can be found in the reviews of Dynes (1987) and Weinberg and Bell (1972); explanations specific to other particular sexual orientations as well can be found in Langevin (1983) and Porter and Teich (1994).

One theory, though, that of Freud, is an important (though flawed) first attempt to provide a universal explanation for all sexual orientations and thus deserves elaboration. Freud's (1925/1962) theory has been exceedingly influential in later scientific explanations of sexual preference. Freud, himself a physician, relied on the research of other physicians, including Krafft-Ebing (1886/1978), Stekel (1923/1952), and Hirschfeld (1948), who described and classified sexual deviations (see Rosario, 1997b). We begin here with a brief summary of the general outline of Freud's theory, which is remarkably complex and which changed extensively over the course of his life.

FREUD

Freud's scientific analysis of sexual orientation marks the beginning of modern psychological theories, although certainly there were earlier theorists whose ideas he employed. Freud wished to provide a comprehensive theory to explain all human behavior and experience, of which sexuality was just one part. In his *Three Essays on the Theory of Sexuality* (1925/1962), he focused directly on sexuality. Freud began with the idea of a "sexual instinct" as a motivation to satisfy a biological need for sexual stimulation analogous to hunger. The sexual instinct is essentially sexual desire, something like lust or libido. Although Freud later (pp. 74–87) tried (unsuccessfully) to explain sexual desire as resulting from physical tensions combined with pleasure and unpleasure, he takes sexual desire largely as a given, something that itself does not require explanation.

Freud introduced two terms, sexual object and sexual aim, to discuss normative sexuality and its deviations. He initially defined the sexual object as the person desired, "the person from whom sexual attraction proceeds," but later included animals and things ("fetishes") as potential sexual objects; the sexual aim is "the act toward which the [sexual] instinct tends" and thus is integrally tied to sexual desire (1925/1962, pp. 1–2). Though not so clearly defined, what makes something "sexual" for Freud is apparently its relation to genital stimulation and orgasm.

Freud included homosexuality, pedophilia, and bestiality as deviations in the sexual object. The latter two he explained as resulting almost always from unavailability of more appropriate sexual objects, an exuberance of sexual impulses, or the availability of children and animals for people such as teachers and shepherds. Homosexuality ("inversion"), on the other hand, required more elaborate explanation, as neither innate nor experiential factors appear satisfactory. The innateness hypothesis required "the crude explanation that everyone is born with his sexual instinct attached to a particular sexual object" (1925/ 1962, pp. 6–7). The experience hypothesis suggested that "various accidental influences would be sufficient to explain the acquisition of inversion" (p. 7). Because the same experiential factors that were presumed to lead to homosexual desire for some people do not do so for others, Freud required a coordination between innate and experiential factors: experiences could not by themselves lead to homosexuality "without the co-operation of something in the subject himself" (p. 7).

In Freud's view, the sexual instinct (sexual desire) does not have a predetermined sexual object. Rather, the sexual instinct comprises components (rather than being unitary), and sexual desire directed toward a heterosexual object is not an inevitable consequence of ontogeny. Still, Freud's entire program assumed that a heterosexual object is fundamental: "One of the tasks implicit in object-choice is that it should find its way to the opposite sex," although there may be some "fumbling" along the way; object choices other than heterosexual ones indicate a sexual desire gone "astray" (1925/1962, p. 95).

Freud also considered deviations in sexual aim to be perversions because they "extend, in an anatomical sense, beyond the regions of the body that are designed for sexual union." Perverts "linger over the intermediate relations to the sexual object which should normally be traversed rapidly on the path towards the final sexual aim" (1925/1962, p. 16). Looking, kissing, cunnilingus, fellatio, and anal intercourse are sexual aims that appear to be, by definition, perversions. However, Freud viewed them as stopping points on the way to intercourse. He viewed deviant sexual aims and objects as resulting potentially from "fixations" on or "overvaluations" of aspects of another person or behaviors on the developmental path to heterosexual intercourse. In keeping with this idea, such sexual aims are now viewed as "courtship disorders" (e.g., Freund & Watson, 1993). In this view, voyeurism, exhibitionism, and sadomasochism are fixations on the steps leading to intercourse: looking, showing one's naked body, and male aggressiveness and female submissiveness, respectively. (However, someone interested only in both the penis and clitoris would not be viewed as "overvaluing" these parts of the body, as their conjugation is the presumed aim of sexual behavior.)

Although Freud's distinction between sexual object and sexual aim is useful in making clear that sexual desire is not likely to be inherently attached to an object (specifically, a heterosexual object), it is not always clear what is a sexual object and what is a sexual aim in any given instance. For example, if a woman desires cunnilingus with another woman, what is the sexual object: the other woman, the woman's genitals, the act of cunnilingus? Similarly, if a man finds that having his head shaved brings on orgasm, is this act a sexual aim or a sexual object? In essence, the thing sexually desired and the behaviors to be enacted for sexual satisfaction can be one and the same. Thus, it is not easy to distinguish between sexual object and sexual aim and, as Freud's analysis suggests, one's behavior (sexual aim) in relation to sexual satisfaction (usually operationally defined as orgasm) is related to the sexual object one desires.

Having set out the parameters of what needs to be explained in sexuality, Freud presented his models. He postulated that, in a boy, heterosexual desire results from the boy's initially undirected sexual desire taking his mother as his sexual object in unconscious fantasy, and from his competitive relation with his father in relation to his mother's affections. For several reasons (including the incest taboo, fear of castration derived from believing that girls' genitals are the result of castration, developing beyond parental authority), the fantasy images of the mother and father are diverted to those who resemble them, and the boy consequently desires women and feels competitive toward men (Freud, 1910/1959, 1922/1966). If the incestuous fantasies of the child are not diverted in this way, "fixation" of the sexual desire on nonheterosexual objects will ensue: "in view of the importance of a child's relations to his parents in determining his later choice of a sexual object, it can easily be understood that any disturbance of those relations will produce the gravest effects upon his adult sexual life" (Freud, 1925/1962, p. 94). Although Freud recognized fantasy as important in sexual development, it is an unconscious fantasy (for boys) of union with the mother. Dreams and daydreams were thought to reveal desires for or threats to union with the parent of the opposite sex (pp. 92–93).

According to Freud (1922/1959), homosexual desire is likely to result when the boy fixates on the mother (which makes desiring other women difficult), has excessive fears of castration and consequent overvaluation of the penis (which causes aversion to women and directedness to penises), and/or avoids rivalry with the father or with brothers by denying a desire for women because of the requirement that the love object have a penis. Freud (1925/1962, p. 96) also posited homosexual desire as likely when the boy is raised by a male figure, which causes the boy to desire men and be hostile to women. These are not his only models to explain male homosexuality, and many others can easily be derived using Freudian logic about the boy's relations with his mother and/or father (Tripp, 1975/1987, pp. 72–73).

Fetishes, a typically though not exclusively male preoccupation (Hirschfeld, 1948; Kinsey et al., 1953, pp. 678–681; Krafft-Ebing, 1886/1978; Stekel, 1923/1952), derive from mechanisms similar to those leading to homosexuality. Freud (1927/1959) felt that the fetish symbolizes for the boy the mother's castrated penis, and its presence allows the boy to avoid homosexuality "by endowing women with the attribute which makes them acceptable as sexual objects" (p. 200; see also Greenacre, 1953). He further suggested that "behind the first recollection of the fetish's appearance there lies a submerged and forgotten phase of sexual development" which the fetish "represents" (Freud, 1925/1962, pp. 20–21). Despite earlier writings to the contrary, Freud, at times, vacillated between thinking that "fetishism, as well as the choice of the fetish itself, are constitutionally determined" (pp. 20–21), and that the object that is a fetish is accidental (see also Binet, 1887). He maintained, however, that the potential for sexual perversions of various sorts is innate in everyone (Freud, 1925/1962, p. 37). The implications of fetishism for later Freudian theorists are myriad and unsystematic (Stoller, 1985, pp. 124–126).

Although Freud's intent was to apply his theory to all sexual orientations, it is a model based on males and required some revisions to apply to females (see, e.g., Freud, 1920/1959, 1925/1959, 1931/1959). For Freud, all people have a bisexual predisposition, but it is greater in women than in men. Freud (1931/1959) viewed women's sexuality as having three endpoints: asexuality, lesbianism, or heterosexuality. All women initially follow the same path. A girl is aware of the pleasure her clitoris ("with its masculine character," p. 255) brings, and views her mother as her sexual object. At some point, she "acknowledges the fact of her castration, the consequent superiority of the male and her own inferiority, but she also rebels against these thoughts" (p. 257). How a girl deals with these issues fixes her sexual desires as an adult. For example, according to Freud, she may turn away from sexuality because she recognizes that, as female, she is always inferior (asexuality); she may maintain her masculine character in hope of getting a penis and fantasize that she is a man (lesbianism); or she may turn away from her mother as sexual object (heterosexuality).

Freudian approaches generally pathologized nonheterosexual orientations until the 1970s and 1980s (Bayer, 1987; Lewes, 1988), and the assumption that sexual activity should develop toward and result in heterosexual intercourse came to be a mainstay of Freudian and some other models until this time. For example, one psychoanalyst who noted that homosexuals are like heterosexuals in the depth of their relationships, still felt that homosexuals engaged in extensive denial about the fact of their perversion and made emphatic claims about the superiority of homosexual love "in order to deny—what they all know—that, without normal intercourse, there is no real contentment" (Balint, 1956, p. 24). Another psychoanalyst simply stated that "heterosexuality is a more mature form of sexual behavior than homosexuality," and that nonheterosexual activities are "substitutes for intercourse" (Storr, 1964, p. 13). One other stated that "homoerotic object choice by preference is a confession of the inability to be competitively and reproductively heterosexual. Homosexuality is a relinquishment of the task imposed by puberty, and a return to genetically [i.e., developmentally] earlier, non-reproductive sexual gratifications" (Gadpaille, 1969, pp. 67–68). Contrary to these expectations, intercourse is not the preferred sexual activity of married or cohabiting heterosexual men (Blumstein & Schwartz, 1983).

Psychoanalytic and psychodynamic models derived from Freud's ideas presented sexual behavior and fantasy other than heterosexual as symbols of familial interactions, adolescent or childhood experiences, cross-gender desires, or sexual intercourse (Goldberg, 1975; Greenacre, 1953). Research commonly focused on familial relations (dominant mother, weak father, seduction), cross-gender identity (cross-dressing as child), or both (parental desire for opposite sex child) as predictors of homosexuality. However, the research often found extensive overlap between homosexual and heterosexual men, and between homosexual and heterosexual women even though there were statistically significant average differences (Evans, 1969; Loney, 1973; Shavelson, Biaggio, Cross, & Lehman, 1980; Thompson et al., 1973). Although all of these interpretations are still made by psychiatrists and psychoanalysts (Burch, 1993), most now favor biological explanations (for male homosexuality at least) (Vreeland, Gallagher, & McFalls, 1995).

BIOLOGICAL EXPLANATIONS

A wide variety of biological influences have been posited as leading to different sexual preferences or orientations, including differences in chromosomes, genes, hormone levels, or brain-hormone interactions in development causing masculinization or feminization, and sizes of particular brain areas, as well as natural and sexual selection. Where the evidence is clear, as in the research that has attempted to demonstrate chromosomal irregularities and differences in hormone levels, homosexuals and heterosexuals of the same gender show no differences. Unfortunately, the methods of gathering evidence and conceptual or theoretical bases for all the other such influences have been remarkably flawed, such that no unbiased view for or against many of these factors is possible. (For citations of original work and critiques, see Blanchard & Bogaert, 1997; Bohan, 1996; Byne & Parsons, 1993; De Cecco & Parker, 1995; Meyer-Bahlberg, 1977, 1979; Pillard, 1997.) We still have no good evidence of biological influences on sexual preference or sexual orientation. Strangely, many of the requirements to find evidence for a genetic (biological) theory of homosexuality described by Kinsey et al. (1948, pp. 662–663)—complete sexual history of individuals and their siblings, not assuming heterosexuality because people are married or homosexuality because other people say so—have been completely ignored in recent research. Biology is incorporated into other models for explaining sexual orientation. In the rest of this section, we consider some of these other models. Evidence supporting these theories is no better than for the biological models, but the theories themselves are worthy of greater explication.

ASSOCIATIVE LEARNING

One early model by Binet (1887) explained divergent sexual desires as deriving from an association of ideas: a chance experience that is sexually arousing will imprint the desire for a repetition of the experience, both in the subject's "erotic ruminations" and in action. Binet drew on Jean-Jacques Rousseau's (1782/1928) *Confessions,* in which Rousseau described his desires to be beaten by a woman for sexual pleasure as deriving from having been sexually aroused at age 8 when punished by his schoolmistress. Rousseau suggested that sexual arousal became attached to the beating and remained throughout his life. Freud (1925/1962) pointed out that Binet's theory could not account for the initial development of sexual orientation, as Rousseau had previously experienced heterosexual arousal when he incorporated the desire to be beaten into his sexual repertoire.

Research has shown that men's sexual interest in an object can be classically conditioned by temporarily pairing the object to already sexually stimulating images. For example, one study found that when men are shown pictures of boots just prior to pictures of "attractive, naked girls," they show penile responses to the boots (Rachman, 1966, p. 293; Rachman & Hodgson, 1968). However, other research indicates that heterosexual males' penile responses to a conditioned stimulus that has been paired with erotic movies are extremely weak compared to the responses to the unconditioned stimulus (images of sexually provocative females; Langevin, 1983, pp. 248–249). These findings call into question the idea that a fetish will develop any time something is paired with sexually arousing stimuli.

A more elaborate model suggests that fantasies repeatedly used while masturbating, many of which derive from real experiences, lead to nonnormative sexual interests (Abel & Blanchard, 1974; Marquis, 1970; McGuire, Carlisle, & Young, 1965). Given that males masturbate more than females, this model predicts higher rates of fetishism in males than in females. However, the theory is still problematic in that fetishes do not seem easily conditioned (Langevin, 1983; Leitenberg & Henning, 1995). In addition, boys who experience compulsory sexual activity with adult men in cultures where this is prescribed almost always eroticize the culturally appropriate female (Herdt, 1994; Stoller, 1985). It is possible that what becomes arousing is not a particular object, but a fantasy narrative surrounding the object, such that a script (an amalgam of multiple associations) is developed in relation to orgasm (Gagnon & Simon, 1973; Gosselin & Wilson, 1980). Sexual scripts (i.e., scripts related to genitally oriented interactions) appear to develop in heterosexual and homosexual males and females (Gagnon & Simon, 1973; Leitenberg & Henning, 1995), though fantasy used for sexual excitement is more common in middle-class than in lower-class males (Gagnon & Simon, 1973; Kinsey et al., 1948). Certainly, the content of most fantasies about sexual interaction is consistent with cultural sex roles as well as with gender differences in nonsexual fantasizing (Wagman, 1967). Men tend to have fantasies in which they are active and visually oriented, whereas females tend to have fantasies in which they are passive and focused on men's interest in them (Leitenberg & Henning, 1995).

TIMING OF SEXUAL MATURITY AND PEER GROUP

Some models suggest that sex-drive development is related to sexual preferences. Specifically, they posit that children who sexually mature early are
more likely to develop homosexual interests, and those who mature later are
more likely to develop heterosexual ones, an idea that goes back at least to
Freud (1925/1962, pp. 106–107). The belief is that boys who start puberty early
are more likely to be focused on maleness as they develop sexually than are
boys who mature later (Tripp, 1975/1987).

A similar but more complex model by Storms (1981) related sex-drive development and peer groups for both boys and girls as the most important factors
in the development of sexual fantasy, which itself leads to sexual orientation. In
Storms's view, those who experience early sex drive (measured as the onset of
masturbation) are more likely to have homosocial (same-sex) peer groups,
whereas those who experience sex drive later are more likely to have heterosocial peer groups. (A strong emotional bond with peers is presumed, and apparently accurately so; Maccoby, 1998.) Given that children are more likely to
eroticize what is available than what is not, children who develop sex drive
earlier will tend to eroticize same-sex people, and those who develop sex drive
later will tend to eroticize opposite-sex people. The fact that girls tend to show
sex drive later than boys (although girls mature sexually earlier) (see also
Leitenberg & Henning, 1995) suggests that homosexual desire should be less
common in women than in men, which is consistent with many estimates of the
prevalence of male and female homosexuality. Research indicating that
homosexual males have an earlier onset of puberty than heterosexual males
along with research finding that these males have more older brothers than heterosexual males (Blanchard & Bogaert, 1996a/1996b) support Storms's ideas.

Although Storms cites numerous studies whose findings are consistent with
his ideas, one recent large-scale study focusing on "exclusive" heterosexuals
(Kinsey ratings 0–1) versus "exclusive" homosexuals (Kinsey ratings 5–6)
found no relationship between onset of sex drive and sexual preference (Bell,
Weinberg, & Hammersmith, 1981a). Note, however, that Storms was interested
in explaining the "object" of erotic fantasy such that exclusive homosexual
preference need not be predicted by early sex drive. As a result, many of the
studies cited to support Storms's conclusions include bisexuals in the homosexual groups. Other evidence contradicts Storms's assertions. For example,
the average age of first heterosexual arousal for heterosexual males and of first
homosexual arousal for homosexual males was the same (11.6 years). In addition, the average age of first homosexual arousal for heterosexual males (12.9
years) and of first heterosexual arousal for homosexual males (13.1 years) was
later (Bell et al., 1981a, pp. 99, 106). (There were no differences in average ages
of first homosexual or heterosexual arousal for females in the latter study.)
Also, during childhood and adolescence, more "prehomosexual" than "preheterosexual" boys were likely to have had mostly girls as friends (directly

contrary to Storms's assumptions), but the great majority (81%–99%) of boys of both types had mostly boys as friends (pp. 84–85). Similarly, during childhood, more "prehomosexual" than "preheterosexual" girls were likely to have had mostly boys as friends (again, contrary to Storms's assertions). In addition, during adolescence, the frequency of having mostly boys as friends for both groups was very low (4%–13%), and overall, girls of both types were more likely to have had female rather than male friends (Bell, Weinberg, & Hammersmith, 1981b, pp. 77–81). In addition, "preheterosexual" boys and girls were usually more likely than "prehomosexual" children to have had a same-sex play group (pp. 78, 81).

PEER GROUPS ALONE

These data on the gender of children's peers indicate that sexually maturing adolescents tend to express sexual interest in those who have the opposite gender from the majority of their playmates. This "familiarity breeds contempt" hypothesis (Werner, 1979) suggests that the ordinary is not sexually interesting, and thus the unordinary is. More recently, the same explanatory mechanism has been labeled "exotic becomes erotic" (Bem, 1996). In this even more elaborated model, biological variables influence a child's temperament, which then influences his or her play interests. Children will tend to play with those who have similar interests, so more aggressive boys and girls generally play with boys, and less aggressive girls and boys generally play with girls. Gender-conforming children will feel different from other children that they perceive to be of the opposite sex, and gender-nonconforming children will feel different from children of the same sex. These experienced differences will increase arousal when the child is in the presence of those children of the type who feel different to him or her, which will be transformed into erotic/romantic attraction through a variety of possible mechanisms, including opponent processes or imprinting. Although this theory can account for most heterosexuals and those homosexuals who mostly had opposite-sex friends, most gay men had had same-sex friends (57%–59% of all Black or White gay males stated that more than half to all friends were boys in childhood, with 59%–60% in adolescence). In addition, a large percentage of lesbians had had same-sex friends (39%–43% of all Black or White lesbians stated that less than half to no friends were boys in childhood, with 57%–65% in adolescence; Bell et al., 1981b).

PEER GROUPS AND GENDER IDENTITY

A modern attempt (Friedman, 1988) to coordinate evidence with a Freudian analysis for male homosexuality suggests that it develops from feelings of either femininity ("effeminacy") or "unmasculinity" ("feeling of masculine inadequacy," p. 34) in childhood. According to Friedman, these feelings lead to self-representation in the form of gender-disturbed imagery and lack of intense friendships with masculine males. One's feeling of masculinity is affirmed by being accepted as masculine by other men or boys, such that unmasculinity or femininity arises from not being so affirmed. These feelings lead to "an intense longing for acceptable male companionship" (Friedman, 1988, p. 261; see, e.g., Green, 1987, p. 193). Friedman posits that "representation of the self during childhood as not masculine enough (according to some internal standard) appears to provide a psychological environment conducive to the genesis of homosexual fantasies" (p. 74). Once the homosexual fantasy becomes part of the core identity structure, it remains and is unchangeable. By implication, males who become heterosexual have feelings of masculine adequacy, which, for inexplicable reasons, is followed by heterosexual fantasies. Heterosexual males as boys engage extensively in aggressive rough-and-tumble play, which solidifies their sense of masculinity. Why any self-imagery in relation to gender standards leads to eroticized imagery is unknown (p. 253).

The relations among gender identity (designating oneself as male or female), gender role (behaving consistently with gender stereotypes), and sexual preference are complex (Harry & DeVall, 1978). The assumption that homosexual individuals are in some way deviant in relation to gender has a long history (Foucault, 1978; Kennedy, 1980), and even as recently as 30 years ago, "engaging in heterosexual relations" was posited as a component of accurate gender identity (Kramer, 1969, p. 56). The research does suggest that feminine boys and masculine girls (gender-nonconforming individuals) are more likely to become homosexually than heterosexually oriented (Green, 1987; Harry, 1983; Whitam, 1980). However, even though male adults who were feminine as children are more likely to enjoy receptive anal intercourse (Weinrich et al., 1992), and even though gender-conforming children are more likely to become heterosexually than homosexually oriented, this greater likelihood is not prescriptive (Bell et al., 1981a; Friedman, 1988; Green, 1987; Saghir & Robins, 1973). Why children are gender conforming or nonconforming is unclear, with hypotheses including genetic influences (Bell et al., 1981a), how gender-appropriately parents touch their children (Fleishman, 1983), and how masculine heterosexual fathers are (Green, 1987). When asked about their own adult gender characteristics, people's self-described feminine and masculine gender characteristics appeared unrelated to self-attributed sexual orientation as straight, bisexual, or gay, whereas erotic fantasies were more closely (and obviously) tied to such self-attributions (Storms, 1979). Many adult homosexuals do not show gender nonconformity, whereas "prehomosexual" children often do. This probably has to do with the desire to conform to gender stereotypes during adolescence (Harry, 1983; Whitam, 1980). Consequently, the belief that, as a class, adult gay men and lesbians have a crossed-sex gender identity and want to act like the opposite sex is in fact a cultural fiction with no empirical basis (Freund, Nagler, Langevin, Zajac, & Steiner, 1974, p. 259; Kinsey et al., 1948, p. 615; Storms, 1979).

Ultimately, our review of the various theories of sexual orientation indicates that they generally lack empirical support. They may provide a direction for research, but currently, they are suggestive at best, and inadequate at worst.

THERAPY ISSUES

For the greater part of the twentieth century, the study of mental health issues and homosexuality focused on changing a homosexual orientation to a heterosexual one. Efforts to change homosexual or bisexual orientations to a heterosexual orientation have focused on males, due to "a stronger and frequently more virulent reaction to homosexuality in men than to homosexuality in women in our society" (T. Stein, 1996, p. 525).

Efforts to change sexual orientation (referred to as conversion therapies) are the result of discomfort experienced either by the patient or by the therapist. Given the history of negative views regarding homosexuality, the desire by some (even many) individuals to change same-sex sexual orientation is not surprising. However, there is little evidence that such efforts are successful (Haldeman, 1994), and considerable anecdotal (e.g., Duberman, 1991; B. Powers & Ellis, 1996) and experimental (Drescher, 1998; T. Stein, 1996) evidence shows that they are potentially damaging to the patient. Patients who are exposed to sexual orientation conversion therapy are likely to experience an increase in the effects of existing internalized homophobia (or heterosexism) and interruption of the development of an integrated gay, lesbian, or bisexual identity. In general, the attempts at conversion are driven by an empirically unjustifiable belief that homosexuality is pathological (Gonsiorek, 1991). As T. Stein (1996) notes, the very titles of the books on "reparative therapy" (the latest form of conversion therapy) imply that "homosexuality represents something that is broken or sick" (e.g., Nicolosi's, 1993, *Healing Homosexuality*).

Those who espouse reparative therapy tend to do so on the basis of religious beliefs rather than scientific evidence (Drescher, 1998). In addition, the work of these therapists tends to be based on a number of misunderstandings of the theoretical work of Freud, Jung, and Adler. As Drescher pointedly asks, "What can be said of a therapist who believes that relationships among a whole class of people are flawed?" (p. 71). The degree to which a therapist's own beliefs should play a role in therapy has been an ongoing issue throughout this century. For example, in the psychoanalytic literature, the concept of absolute neutrality is discussed as the ideal for the therapist: "the feeling that is most dangerous to a psycho-analyst is the therapeutic ambition to achieve by this novel and much disputed method something that will produce a convincing effect upon other people. [This will] put him into a state of mind which is unfavorable for [the analyst's] work" (Freud, 1912, p. 115). Drescher (1998) writes that "absolute neutrality is an ideal that is rarely achieved" (p. 55). In addition, there are those who believe it is neither achievable nor desirable (Levenson,

1983; Spence, 1982). Drescher also notes that "in terms of sexual orientation, there is no such thing as a neutral analyst. Every analyst is homosexual, heterosexual or bisexual. This obliges a therapist, regardless of his sexual orientation, to monitor his own biases and to let patients know what those biases are" (p. 55).

SHOULD THE THERAPIST HAVE THE SAME
SEXUAL ORIENTATION AS THE PATIENT?

Although there are many situations in which a patient may feel more comfortable with a therapist who shares the same sexual orientation, an affirming therapist, regardless of sexual orientation, who works to integrate the patient's sexual orientation with other aspects of the "whole" person can be quite effective. Reflecting on his over 50 years of work as a heterosexual psychotherapist working with gay and lesbian clients, Marmor (1996) writes:

> Gay patients may also seek out nongay therapists for reasons pertaining to their idiosyncratic family dynamics. A nongay therapist can provide a corrective emotional experience as a warm and accepting father or mother surrogate for a patient whose parents were rejecting or lacking in understanding them. By the same token, gay or lesbian therapists serve equally effectively as healing parent surrogates to nongay patients in need of similar corrective emotional experiences. (p. 543)

WORKING WITH GAY MEN, LESBIANS, AND BISEXUALS

In addition to helping lesbians, gay men, and bisexuals to work toward integration of their sexual identity with other aspects of the self, a therapist may be called on to address areas of concern that are specific to this population. Scasta (1998) suggests that special consideration be paid to coming out to parents, coming out to children, bisexuality, and religious proscriptions. Additional issues that are likely to present themselves in therapy are differences in the dynamics of same-sex sexual relationships and issues surrounding coming out at work. Each of these areas will be discussed in greater detail below.

Coming Out to Parents

For most individuals whose sexual orientation differs from the majority, coming out to parents is often the most difficult step. Scasta (1998) suggests that the patient needs to be sure of his or her sexual orientation and have sufficient self-esteem to cope with possible rejection. Additionally, he recommends that statements such as "Mom, I need to let you know that I am gay" are preferable to such statements as "Mom, I think I'm gay" because of the denial that may arise by the parents or any attempts to "fix the problem" based on equivocation. The reactions of parents are varied, and the therapist may wish to prepare the patient for whatever reaction occurs by noting that, just as it most likely took the patient many years to come to terms with his or her sexual orientation, it may also take some time for parents to accept it. Again, the greater the patient's comfort with his or her sexual identity, the more he or she can patiently guide parents to a similar level of comfort.

Coming Out to Children

Only recently has this issue received attention, and there are no definitive answers about when or how a patient should come out to his or her children. Again, it is important that the individual feel comfortable with his or her sexual identity before sharing it with children. On a related issue, there is no evidence that being raised by a gay parent or parents increases the likelihood that a child will be homosexual (e.g., Kirkpatrick, 1996; Patterson & Chan, 1996). In addition, the research also shows that children raised by gay parents are as psychologically healthy as those raised by heterosexual parents (e.g., Gottman, 1990).

Bisexuality

The issue of bisexuality is controversial not only in society at large but also in the gay community. The controversy lies in the belief by some that bisexuality is a way of avoiding one's homosexuality. Because of the negative stereotypes and attitudes toward homosexuality, a claim to bisexuality may reflect avoidance, and many therapists report having clients who claimed initially to be bisexual and later acknowledged that they were gay or lesbian. Even so, it is inappropriate for a therapist to assume that all patients who claim to be bisexual are simply avoiding their own homosexuality. There are many individuals who, over the course of their lifetime, have significant sexual relationships with members of both sexes. As Scasta (1998) states, "the dilemma for the therapist is how to separate out true bisexuality, which may not need intervention, from homosexual denial" (p. 95). Scasta suggests that the solution is to avoid judgment as well as to have no preconceived agenda for the patient on this issue.

Religious Proscriptions

Therapists working with gay, lesbian, and bisexual clients are likely to find that many come from religious backgrounds that condemn homosexuality and bisexuality. Because therapists are taught to be neutral about religious beliefs, it can be particularly challenging to help a patient integrate his or her sexual identity with religious beliefs without encouraging the patient to consider other theological or spiritual perspectives. In any case, the therapist should not criticize a patient's religious beliefs even if those beliefs condemn the patient. However, the therapist should help the patient to work out his or her own approach to reconciling those conflicting beliefs.

Issues Specific to Same-Sex Sexual Relationships

Homophobia (or heterosexual bias) is psychologically harmful to lesbian and gay male couples (Klinger, 1996). Homophobia is expressed obviously as overt acts of discrimination and more subtly in the lack of societal legitimacy and legal protections that heterosexual couples receive. These overt and subtle acts of bias create issues in same-sex relationships that are somewhat specific to such relationships. For example, there is a greater burden placed on same-sex couples to protect themselves in the event of a serious illness or death. In addition, families may fail to recognize the couple as they do married members. Despite these additional challenges, studies of same-sex relationships indicate that they are often as committed and long term as heterosexual relationships (Berzon, 1988; Blumstein & Schwartz, 1983; Kurdek, 1995; McWhirter & Mattison, 1984, 1996; Peplau & Cochran, 1990; Silverstein, 1981).

Coming Out at Work

Therapists may also wish to better understand the issues that a gay or bisexual person faces regarding coming out at work. Coming out to parents may be the most difficult step in the coming out process, yet coming out at work presents a number of potential challenges to an individual, including fear that one may lose one's livelihood and experience other acts of discrimination (failure to receive promotions, raises, etc.). How a lesbian or gay identity is managed is a personal decision dependent on many factors, and some lesbian and gay individuals choose to pass as heterosexual to avoid potential problems (Elliott, 1993). Assisting lesbian and gay individuals in making decisions about self-presentation should be a key aspect of any counseling that focuses on career planning (Elliott, 1993). Although limited research has been done in this area (Ellis & Riggle, 1995), a number of books have been published that include anecdotal as well as theoretical discussions of this issue (Ellis & Riggle, 1996; Friskopp & Silverstein, 1995; McNaught, 1993; B. Powers & Ellis, 1995).

OTHER THERAPEUTIC ISSUES

In addition to the concerns that may be experienced by any gay man or lesbian, there are specific therapeutic issues for those in certain life stages. In particular, the challenges facing gay and lesbian youth require special consideration, as do those of older gay men and lesbians.

Working with Gay and Lesbian Youth

Hartstein (1996) notes that although a considerable amount of controversy exists regarding the relation between sexual orientation and suicide among youths, a report by the U.S. Department of Health and Human Services listed homosexuality as a risk factor for youth suicide. In that report, Gibson (1989) suggested that gay youth may make up 30% of completed U.S. suicides annually. Although this figure has been widely debated, it nevertheless indicates that gay youth appear to be up to three times as likely to commit suicide as their heterosexual peers.

Herdt (1989) identifies four factors that may affect the psychological well-being of lesbian, gay, and bisexual youth: (1) their invisibility, (2) the assumptions of peer and family that they are defective, (3) the stigmatization that follows the assumption of deviance, and (4) the assumptions by others that all lesbians and gay men are alike. The fact that these youth are often financially dependent on parents who may hold strong negative views of their sexual orientation further exacerbates these youths' vulnerability. In addition, these youth also suffer from a lack of positive role models (Plummer, 1989).

Not surprisingly, a number of studies have found that lesbian, gay, and bisexual youth are at high risk of suffering psychological difficulties because of the additional burdens associated with their sexual orientation and negative societal views (e.g., D'Augelli & Hershberger, 1993; Gonsiorek, 1988; Savin-Williams, 1990). For example, D'Augelli and Hershberger found that 63% of gay, lesbian, and bisexual youth reported feeling so worried or nervous in the preceding year that they could not function for a period of time; 38% said that they were severely depressed. As D'Augelli (1996) notes:

> Mental health professionals must take the lead in the development of affirmative services and the creation of supportive settings for lesbian, gay, and bisexual youth. We must not victimize these youth again by colluding with social and political forces that render them invisible. The need for interventions directed toward this population is intense and urgent. (p. 283)

Older Gay Men and Lesbians

As Berger and Kelly (1996) note, the research literature on aging often fails to consider older gay men and lesbians. The research that has addressed this group suggests that older gay men and lesbians may, in some ways, be better equipped to deal with certain aspects of aging than their heterosexual counterparts. For example, because older gay men and lesbians have developed strategies for dealing with stigma (as homosexuals), they are able to transfer those skills to dealing with the stigma society places on older persons. In addition, older gay men and lesbians, as a group, often have developed support systems that extend beyond the traditional family and/or relate to issues of being alone in older age in ways that differ (and may be more adaptive) than heterosexuals (Berger, 1995; Kimmel, 1989). However, older lesbians and gay men often face challenges of negotiating older age in a heterosexist society (Berger & Kelly, 1996). Many of the professionals working for agencies that offer social services and medical support to older individuals are either insensitive to the needs of older lesbians and gay men or openly hostile to this group. As a result, older lesbians and gay men may encounter additional difficulties in accessing the resources available to older persons. Helping these individuals meet their needs in a sometimes hostile environment is likely to be a key issue for therapists working with this population (see Beeler, Rawls,

Herdt, & Cohler, 1999; and Jacobs, Rasmussen, & Hohman, 1999, for recent work in this area).

SUMMARY

This chapter dealt with five major areas of the research and theory surrounding sexual orientation: defining of sexual orientation, sexual orientation and mental health, research, theories of sexual orientation, and therapy issues. The study of sexual orientation remains one of the most hotly debated and controversial areas of human sexuality. This presents members of society and the therapist community with a number of challenges, including further developing our understanding of how to reconcile negative stereotypes and beliefs with the positive life experiences of gay, lesbian, and bisexual individuals, and how to create an environment that supports the dignity and rights of those whose sexual orientation(s) differs from the mainstream majority. In addition, there are likely to be those who continue to be intrigued by the determinants of sexual orientation and who will conduct research and further develop theories on the origins of sexual orientation. Because of the social and political aspects of sexual orientation, those who conduct this research, as well as those who review and evaluate it, need to recognize how their own values and beliefs affect the research that is conducted and their reactions to it. This chapter was written based on a belief in the worth of all individuals, regardless of sexual orientation, and our interpretations are likely to have been affected by that belief. Nevertheless, we believe that the overwhelming majority of the research and theory on sexual orientation supports our interpretations.

REFERENCES

Abel, G.G., & Blanchard, E.B. (1974). The role of fantasy in the treatment of sexual deviation. *Archives of General Psychiatry, 30,* 467–475.

Adams, H.E., Wright, L.W., Jr., & Lohr, B.A. (1996). Is homophobia associated with homosexual arousal? *Journal of Abnormal Psychology, 105,* 440–445.

Allen, G.E. (1997). The double-edged sword of genetic determinism: Social and political agendas in genetic studies of homosexuality, 1940–1994. In V.A. Rosario (Ed.), *Science and homosexualities* (pp. 243–270). New York: Routledge & Kegan Paul.

American Psychiatric Association. (1974). Position statement on homosexuality and civil rights. *American Journal of Psychiatry, 131,* 497.

American Psychological Association. (1975). Minutes of the Council of Representatives. *American Psychologist, 30,* 620–651.

Balint, M. (1956). Perversions and genitality. In S. Lorand (Ed.), *Perversions: Psychodynamics and therapy* (pp. 16–27). New York: Gramercy.

Bayer, R. (1987). *Homosexuality and American psychiatry.* Princeton, NJ: Princeton University Press.

Beeler, J.A., Rawls, T.W., Herdt, G., & Cohler, B.J. (1999). The needs of older lesbians and gay men in Chicago. *Journal of Gay and Lesbian Social Services, 9*(1), 31–49.

Bell, A.P. (1975). Research in homosexuality: Back to the drawing board. *Archives of Sexual Behavior, 4,* 421–431.

Bell, A.P., Weinberg, M.S., & Hammersmith, S.K. (1981a). *Sexual preference: Its development in men and women.* Bloomington: Indiana University Press.

Bell, A.P., Weinberg, M.S., & Hammersmith, S.K. (1981b). *Sexual preference: Its development in men and women: Statistical appendix.* Bloomington: Indiana University Press.

Bem, D.J. (1996). Exotic becomes erotic: A developmental theory of sexual orientation. *Psychological Review, 103,* 320–335.

Berest, J.J. (1971). Fetishism: Three case histories. *Journal of Sex Research, 7,* 237–239.

Berger, R.M. (1995). *Gay and gray: The older homosexual man* (2nd ed.). Binghampton, NY: Haworth Press.

Berger, R.M., & Kelly, J.J. (1996). Gay men and lesbians grown older. In R.P. Cabaj & T.S. Stein (Eds.), *Textbook of homosexuality and mental health* (pp. 305–316). Washington, DC: American Psychiatric Press.

Berzon, B. (1988). *Permanent partners: Building gay and lesbian relationships that last.* New York: Dutton.

Bethell, M.F. (1974). A rare manifestation of fetishism. *Archives of Sexual Behavior, 3,* 301–302.

Binet, A. (1887). Du fétichisme dans l'amour [Fetishism in love]. *Revue Philosophique de la France et l'étranger, 12,* 143–167.

Blanchard, R., & Bogaert, A.F. (1996a). Biodemographic comparisons of homosexual and heterosexual men in the Kinsey interview data. *Archives of Sexual Behavior, 25,* 551–579.

Blanchard, R., & Bogaert, A.F. (1996b). Homosexuality in men and number of older brothers. *American Journal of Psychiatry, 153,* 27–31.

Blanchard, R., & Bogaert, A.F. (1997). The relation of closed birth intervals to the sex of the preceding child and the sexual orientation of the succeeding child. *Journal of Biosocial Science, 29,* 111–118.

Blumenfeld, W.J. (Ed.). (1992). *Homophobia: How we all pay the price.* Boston: Beacon Press.

Blumstein, P.W., & Schwartz, P. (1977). Bisexuality: Some social psychological issues. *Journal of Social Issues, 33,* 30–45.

Blumstein, P.W., & Schwartz, P. (1983). *American couples: Money, work, sex.* New York: Morrow.

Bohan, J.S. (1996). *Psychology and sexual orientation: Coming to terms.* New York: Routledge & Kegan Paul.

Brand, C. (1970). *Fetish: An account of unusual erotic desires.* New York: Senate, Random House.

Bulrich, N., & McConaghy, N. (1979). Three clinically discrete categories of fetishistic transvestism. *Archives of Sexual Behavior, 8,* 151–157.

Burch, B. (1993). Heterosexuality, bisexuality, and lesbianism: Rethinking psychoanalytic views of women's sexual object choice. *Psychoanalytic Review, 80,* 83–99.

Byne, W., & Parsons, B. (1993). Human sexual orientation: The biologic theories reappraised. *Archives of General Psychiatry, 50,* 228–239.

Cass, V. (1979). Homosexual identity formation: A theoretical model. *Journal of Homosexuality, 4,* 219–235.

Cass, V. (1996). Sexual orientation identity formation: A Western phenomenon. In R.P. Cabaj & T.S. Stein (Eds.), *Textbook of homosexuality and mental health* (pp. 227–251). Washington, DC: American Psychiatric Press.

Chauncey, G. (1994). *Gay New York: Gender, urban culture, and the making of the gay male world 1890–1940.* New York: Basic Books.

Coleman, E. (1981/1982). Development stages of the coming out process. *Journal of Homosexuality, 7,* 31–43.

Coleman, E., Bockting, W.O., & Gooren, L. (1993). Homosexual and bisexual identity in sex reassigned female to male transsexuals. *Archives of Sexual Behavior, 22,* 37–50.

D'Augelli, A.R. (1996). Lesbian, gay, and bisexual development during adolescence and young adulthood. In R.P. Cabaj & T.S. Stein (Eds.) *Textbook of homosexuality and mental health* (pp. 267–288). Washington, DC: American Psychiatric Press.

D'Augelli, A.R., & Hershberger, S.L. (1993). Lesbian, gay, and bisexual youth community settings: Personal challenges and mental health problems. *American Journal of Community Psychology, 21,* 421–448.

De Cecco, J.P. (1981). Definitions and meanings of sexual orientation. *Journal of Homosexuality, 6*(4), 51–67.

De Cecco, J.P., & Parker, D.A. (Eds.). (1995). *Sex, cells, and same-sex desire: The biology of sexual preference.* New York: Harrington Park Press.

De Silva, P. (1995). Paraphilias and sexual dysfunction. *International Review of Psychiatry, 7,* 225–229.

Devor, H. (1993). Sexual orientation identities, attractions, and practices of female-to-male transsexuals. *Journal of Sex Research, 30,* 303–315.

Drescher, J. (1998). Contemporary psychoanalytic psychotherapy with gay men: With a commentary on reparative therapy of homosexuality. *Journal of Gay and Lesbian Psychotherapy, 2*(4), 51–74.

Duberman, M.B. (1991). *Cures: A gay man's odyssey.* New York: Dutton.

Dynes, W.R. (1987). *Homosexuality: A research guide.* New York: Garland.

Elliott, J. (1993). Lesbian and gay concerns in career development. In L. Diamant (Ed.), *Homosexual issues in the workplace.* Washington, DC: Taylor & Francis.

Ellis, A.L., & Riggle, E.D.B. (1995). The relation of job satisfaction and degree of openness about one's sexual orientation for lesbians and gay men. *Journal of Homosexuality, 30,* 75–81.

Ellis, A.L., & Riggle, E.D.B. (1996). *Sexual identity on the job: Issues and services.* Binghampton, NY: Harrington Park Press.

Ellis, A.L., & Vasseur, R.B. (1993). Prior interpersonal contact with and attitudes toward gays and lesbians in an interviewing context. *Journal of Homosexuality, 25*(4), 31–46.

Epstein, A.W. (1969). Fetishism: A comprehensive view. In J.H. Masserman (Ed.), *Dynamics of deviant sexuality* (pp. 81–87). New York: Grune & Stratton.

Evans, R.B. (1969). Childhood parental relationships of homosexual men. *Journal of Clinical and Consulting Psychology, 33,* 129–135.

Fleishman, E.G. (1983). Sex-role acquisition, parental behavior, and sexual orientation: Some tentative hypotheses. *Sex Roles, 9,* 1051–1059.

Foucault, M. (1978). *The history of sexuality: An introduction* (Vol. 1). New York: Pantheon, Random House.

Freud, S. (1912). Recommendation to physicians practicing psycho-analysis. In J. Strachey (Ed.), *The standard edition of the complete works of Sigmund Freud* (Vol. 12, pp. 109–120). London: Hogarth Press.

Freud, S. (1959). Certain neurotic mechanisms in jealousy, paranoia and homosexuality. In *Collected papers* (Vol. 2, pp. 232–243). New York: Basic Books. (Original work published 1922)

Freud, S. (1959). Female sexuality. In *Collected papers* (Vol. 5, pp. 252–272). New York: Basic Books. (Original work published 1931)

Freud, S. (1959). Fetishism. In *Collected papers* (Vol. 5, pp. 198–204). New York: Basic Books. (Original work published 1927)

Freud, S. (1959). The passing of the Oedipus-complex. In *Collected papers* (Vol. 2, pp. 269–276). New York: Basic Books. (Original work published 1910)

Freud, S. (1959). The psychogenesis of a case of homosexuality in a woman. In *Collected papers* (Vol. 2, pp. 202–231). New York: Basic Books. (Original work published 1920)

Freud, S. (1959). The psychological consequences of the anatomical distinction between the sexes. In *Collected papers* (Vol. 5, pp. 186–197). New York: Basic Books. (Original work published 1925)

Freud, S. (1962). *Three essays on the theory of sexuality.* New York: Basic Books. (Original work published 1925)

Freud, S. (1966). *Introductory lectures on psychoanalysis.* New York: Liveright. (Original work published 1922)

Freund, K., Nagler, E., Langevin, R., Zajac, A., & Steiner, B. (1974). Measuring feminine gender identity in homosexual males. *Archives of Sexual Behavior, 3,* 249–260.

Freund, K., & Watson, R.J. (1993). Gender identity disorder and courtship disorder. *Archives of Sexual Behavior, 22,* 13–21.

Friedman, R.C. (1988). *Male homosexuality: A contemporary psychoanalytic perspective.* New Haven, CT: Yale University Press.

Friskopp, A., & Silverstein, S. (1995). *Straight jobs, gay lives: Gay and lesbian professionals, the Harvard Business School, and the American workplace.* New York: Scribner.

Gadpaille, W.J. (1969). Homosexual activity and homosexuality in adolescence. In J.H. Masserman (Ed.), *Dynamics of deviant sexuality* (pp. 60–70). New York: Grune & Stratton.

Gagnon, J.H. (1977). *Human sexualities.* Glenview, IL: Scott, Foresman.

Gagnon, J.H., & Simon, W. (1973). *Sexual conduct: The social sources of human sexuality.* New York: Aldine.

Gebhard, P.H. (1969). Fetishism and sadomasochism. In J.H. Masserman (Ed.), *Dynamics of deviant sexuality* (pp. 71–80). New York: Grune & Stratton.

Gibson, P. (1989). Gay male and lesbian youth suicide. In *Report of the Secretary's Task Force of youth suicide (Vol. 3): Prevention and interventions in youth suicide* (pp. 110–142). Washington, DC: U.S. Department of Health and Human Services.

Goldberg, A. (1975). A fresh look at perverse behaviour. *International Journal of Psycho-Analysis, 56,* 335–342.

Golombok, S., & Tasker, F. (1996). Do parents influence the sexual orientation of their children? Findings from a longitudinal study of lesbian families. *Developmental Psychology, 32,* 3–11.

Gonzalez, F.J., & Espin, O.M. (1996). Latino men, Latina women and homosexuality. In R.P. Cabaj & T.S. Stein (Eds.), *Textbook of homosexuality and mental health* (pp. 583–601). Washington, DC: American Psychiatric Press.

Gonsiorek, J.C. (1988). Mental health issues of gay and lesbian adolescents. *Journal of Adolescent Health Care, 9,* 114–122.

Gonsiorek, J.C. (1991). The empirical basis for the demise of the illness model of homosexuality. In J.C. Gonsiorek & J.D. Weinrich (Eds.), *Homosexuality research implications for public policy* (pp. 115–136). Newbury Park, CA: Sage.

Gosselin, C., & Wilson, G. (1980). *Sexual variations: Fetishism, sadomasochism and transvestism.* New York: Simon & Schuster.

Gosselin, C., & Wilson, G. (1984). Fetishism, sadomasochism and related behaviours. In K. Howells (Ed.), *The psychology of sexual diversity* (pp. 89–110). Oxford, England: Basil Blackwell.

Gottman, J.S. (1990). Children of gay and lesbian parents. In F. Bozett & M.B. Sussman (Eds.), *Homosexuality and family relations* (pp. 177–196). Binghampton, NY: Harrington Park Press.

Grant, V.W. (1949). A fetishistic theory of amorous fixation. *Journal of Social Psychology, 30,* 17–37.

Green, R. (1987). *The "sissy boy syndrome" and the development of homosexuality.* New Haven, CT: Yale University Press.

Greenacre, P. (1953). Certain relationships between fetishism and faulty development of the body image. *Psychoanalytic Study of the Child, 8,* 79–98.

Haldeman, D.C. (1994). The practice and ethics of sexual orientation conversion therapy. *Journal of Consulting and Clinical Psychology, 62,* 221–227.

Harry, J. (1983). Defeminization and adult psychological well-being among male homosexuals. *Archives of Sexual Behavior, 12,* 1–19.

Harry, J., & DeVall, W.B. (1978). *The social organization of gay males.* New York: Praeger.

Hartstein, N.B. (1996). Suicide risk in lesbian, gay, and bisexual youth. In R.P. Cabaj & T.S. Stein (Eds.), *Textbook of homosexuality and mental health* (pp. 819–837). Washington, DC: American Psychiatric Press.

Herdt, G. (1989). Introduction: Gay youth, emergent identity, and cultural sense at home and abroad. In G. Herdt (Ed.), *Homosexuality and adolescence* (pp. 1–23). Binghampton, NY: Harrington Park Press.

Herdt, G. (1994). *Third sex, third gender: Beyond dimorphism in culture and history.* New York: Zone Books.

Herdt, G. (1996). Issues in the cross-cultural study of homosexuality. In R.P. Cabaj & T.S. Stein (Eds.), *Textbook of homosexuality and mental health* (pp. 65–82). Washington, DC: American Psychiatric Press.

Herek, G.M. (1996). Heterosexism and homophobia. In R.P. Cabaj & T.S. Stein (Eds.), *Textbook of homosexuality and mental health* (pp. 101–113). Washington, DC: American Psychiatric Press.

Herek, G.M., & Capitanio, J.P. (1996). "Some of my best friends": Intergroup contact, concealable stigma, and heterosexuals' attitudes toward gay men and lesbians. *Personality and Social Psychology Bulletin, 22*(4), 412–424.

Herek, G.M., & Glunt, E.K. (1993). Interpersonal contact and heterosexuals' attitudes toward gay men: Results from a national survey. *Journal of Sex Research, 30,* 239–244.

Herek, G.M., Kimmel, D.C., Amaro, H., Melton, G.B. (1991). Avoiding heterosexist bias in psychological research. *American Psychologist, 46,* 957–963.

Hirschfeld, M. (1948). *Sexual anomalies.* New York: Emerson Books.

Hooker, E. (1957). The adjustment of the male overt homosexual. *Journal of Projective Techniques, 21,* 18–31.

Humphreys, L. (1970). *Tearoom trade: Impersonal sex in public places*. Chicago: Aldine Atherton.

Jacobs, R.J., Rasmussen, L.A., & Hohman, M.M. (1999). The social support needs of older lesbians, gay men, and bisexuals. *Journal of Gay and Lesbian Social Services, 9*(1), 1–30.

Jones, B.E., & Hill, M.J. (1996). African American lesbians, gay men, and bisexuals. In R.P. Cabaj & T.S. Stein (Eds.), *Textbook of homosexuality and mental health* (pp. 549–561). Washington, DC: American Psychiatric Press.

Kennedy, H.C. (1980). The "third sex" theory of Karl Heinrich Ulrichs. *Journal of Homosexuality, 6*, 103–111.

Khan, M.M.R. (1966). Foreskin fetishism and its relation to ego pathology in a male homosexual. In H.M. Ruitenbeek (Ed.), *Psychoanalysis and male sexuality* (pp. 235–268). New Haven, CT: College and University Press.

Kimmel, D.C. (1989). *Adulthood and aging: An interdisciplinary, developmental view*. New York: Wiley.

Kinsey, A.C., Pomeroy, W.B., & Martin, C.E. (1948). *Sexual behavior in the human male*. Philadelphia: Saunders.

Kinsey, A.C., Pomeroy, W.B., Martin, C.E., & Gebhard, P.H. (1953). *Sexual behavior in the human female*. Philadelphia: Saunders.

Kirkpatrick, M. (1996). Lesbians as parents. In R.P. Cabaj & T.S. Stein (Eds.), *Textbook of homosexuality and mental health* (pp. 353–370). Washington, DC: American Psychiatric Press.

Kite, M.E. (1991). Psychometric properties of the homosexuality attitude scale. *Representative Research in Social Psychology, 19*, 79–84.

Klinger, R.L. (1996). Lesbian couples. In R.P. Cabaj & T.S. Stein (Eds.), *Textbook of homosexuality and mental health* (pp. 339–352). Washington, DC: American Psychiatric Press.

Krafft-Ebing, R. von (1978). *Psychopathia sexualis*. New York: Scarborough Book, Stein and Day. (Original work published 1886)

Kramer, M.W. (1969). Identity formation in male and female adolescent homosexuals. In J.H. Masserman (Ed.), *Dynamics of deviant sexuality* (pp. 51–59). New York: Grune & Stratton.

Kurdek, L.A. (1995). Lesbian and gay couples. In A.R. D'Augelli & C.J. Patterson (Eds.), *Lesbian, gay, and bisexual identities over the lifespan: Psychological perspectives* (pp. 243–261). New York: Oxford University Press.

Langevin, R. (1983). *Sexual strands*. Hillsdale, NJ: Erlbaum.

Langevin, R. (1985). Introduction. In R. Langevin (Ed.), *Erotic preference, gender identity, and aggression in men: New research studies* (pp. 1–13). Hillsdale, NJ: Erlbaum.

Laumann, E.O., Gagnon, J.H., Michael, R.T., & Michaels, S. (1994). *The social organization of sexuality: Sexual practices in the United States*. Chicago: University of Chicago Press.

Leitenberg, H., & Henning, C. (1995). Sexual fantasy. *Psychological Bulletin, 117*, 469–496.

LeVay, S. (1996). *Queer science*. Cambridge, MA: MIT Press.

Levenson, E. (1983). *The ambiguity of change*. New York: Basic Books.

Lewes, K. (1988). *The psychoanalytic theory of male homosexuality*. New York: Simon & Schuster.

Loney, J. (1973). Family dynamics in homosexual women. *Archives of Sexual Behavior, 2,* 343–350.

Maccoby, E.E. (1998). *The two sexes: Growing up apart, coming together.* Cambridge, MA: Harvard University Press.

Marmor, J. (1996). Nongay therapists and gay men and lesbians. In R.P. Cabaj & T.S. Stein (Eds.), *Textbook of homosexuality and mental health* (pp. 539–545). Washington, DC: American Psychiatric Press.

Marmor, J. (1998). Homosexuality: Is etiology really important? *Journal of Gay and Lesbian Psychotherapy, 2*(4), 19–28.

Marquis, J.N. (1970). Orgasmic reconditioning: Changing sexual object choice through controlling masturbation fantasies. *Journal of Behavioral Therapy and Experimental Psychiatry, 1,* 263–271.

McGuire, R.J., Carlisle, J.M., & Young, B.G. (1965). Sexual deviations as conditioned behaviour: A hypothesis. *Behavioral Research and Therapy, 2,* 185–190.

McNaught, B. (1993). *Gay issues in the workplace.* New York: St. Martin's Press.

McWhirter, D.P., & Mattison, A.M. (1984). *The male couple: How relationships develop.* New York: Prentice Hall.

McWhirter, D.P., & Mattison, A.M. (1996). Male couples. In R.P. Cabaj & T.S. Stein (Eds.), *Textbook of homosexuality and mental health* (pp. 319–337). Washington, DC: American Psychiatric Press.

Meyer-Bahlburg, H.F.L. (1977). Sex hormones and male homosexuality in comparative perspective. *Archives of Sexual Behavior, 6,* 297–325.

Meyer-Bahlburg, H.F.L. (1979). Sex hormones and female homosexuality: A critical examination. *Archives of Sexual Behavior, 8,* 101–119.

Michaels, S. (1996). The prevalence of homosexuality in the United States. In R.P. Cabaj & T.S. Stein (Eds.), *Textbook of homosexuality and mental health* (pp. 43–63). Washington, DC: American Psychiatric Press.

Mitchell, W., Falconer, M.A., & Hill, D. (1954). Epilepsy with fetishism relieved by temporal lobectomy. *Lancet, 2,* 626.

Money, J. (1977). Paraphilias. In J. Money & H. Musaph (Eds.), *Handbook of sexology* (pp. 917–928). Amsterdam, The Netherlands: Elsevier/North-Holland Biomedical Press.

Money, J. (1986/1993). Transcultural sexology: Formicophilia. In *The Adam principle* (pp. 334–340). Buffalo: Prometheus Books.

Money, J. (1987/1993). Masochism: On the childhood origins. In *The Adam principle* (pp. 302–304). Buffalo: Prometheus Books.

Money, J. (1988). Lovemaps and paraphilia. In *Gay, straight, and in-between* (pp. 126–185). Oxford, England: Oxford University Press.

Murphy, T.F. (1997). *Gay science: The ethics of sexual orientation research.* New York: Columbia University Press.

Nakajima, G.A., Chan, Y.H., & Lee, K. (1996). Mental health issues for gay and lesbian Asian Americans. In R.P. Cabaj & T.S. Stein (Eds.), *Textbook of homosexuality and mental health* (pp. 563–581). Washington, DC: American Psychiatric Press.

Nicolosi, J. (1993). *Healing homosexuality.* Northvale, NJ: Aronson.

Patterson, C.J., & Chan, R.W. (1996). Gay fathers and their children. In R.P. Cabaj & T.S. Stein (Eds.), *Textbook of homosexuality and mental health* (pp. 371–393). Washington, DC: American Psychiatric Press.

Peplau, L.A., & Cochran, S. (1990). A relationship perspective on homosexuality. In D.P. McWhirter, S.A. Sanders, & J.M. Reinisch (Eds.), *Homosexuality/heterosexuality: Concepts of sexual orientation* (pp. 321–349). New York: Oxford University Press.

Pillard, R.C. (1997). The search for a genetic influence on sexual orientation. In V.A. Rosario (Ed.), *Science and homosexualities* (pp. 226–241). New York: Routledge & Kegan Paul.

Plummer, K. (1989). Lesbian and gay youth in England. *Journal of Homosexuality, 17,* 195–223.

Porter, R., & Teich, M. (1994). *Sexual knowledge, sexual science: The history of attitudes to sexuality.* Cambridge, England: Cambridge University Press.

Powers, B., & Ellis, A. (1995). *A manager's guide to sexual orientation in the workplace.* New York: Routledge & Kegan Paul.

Powers, B., & Ellis, A. (1996). *A family and friend's guide to sexual orientation.* New York: Routledge & Kegan Paul.

Powers, W.K. (1986). *Sacred language: The nature of supernatural discourse in Lakota.* Norman: University of Oklahoma Press.

Rachman, S. (1966). Sexual fetishism: An experimental analogue. *Psychological Record, 16,* 293–296.

Rachman, S., & Hodgson, R.J. (1968). Experimentally induced "sexual fetishism": Replication and development. *Psychological Record, 18,* 25–27.

Raymond, D. (1992). In the best interests of the child: Thoughts on homophobia and parenting. In W.J. Blumenfeld (Ed.), *Homophobia: How we all pay the price.* Boston: Beacon Press.

Rosabal, G.S. (1996). Multicultural existence in the workplace: Including how I thrive as a Latina lesbian feminist. In A.L. Ellis, & E.D.B. Riggle (Eds.), *Sexual identity on the job: Issues and services* (pp. 17–28). Binghampton, NY: Harrington Park Press.

Rosario, V.A. (1997a). *The erotic imagination: French histories of perversity.* New York: Oxford University Press.

Rosario, V.A. (Ed.). (1997b). *Science and homosexualities.* New York: Routledge & Kegan Paul.

Rousseau, J.-J. (1928). *The confessions of Jean-Jacques Rousseau.* New York: Brentano's. (Original work published 1782)

Rust, P.C. (1993). "Coming out" in the age of social constructionism: Sexual identity formation among lesbian and bisexual women. *Gender and Society, 7,* 50–77.

Saghir, M.T., & Robins, E. (1973). *Male and female homosexuality.* Baltimore: Williams & Wilkins.

Savin-Williams, R.C. (1990). *Gay and lesbian youth: Expressions of identity.* New York: Hemisphere.

Scasta, D. (1998). Issues in helping people come out. *Journal of Gay and Lesbian Psychotherapy, 2*(4), 87–97.

Sell, R.L., Wells, J.A., & Wypij, D. (1995). The prevalence of homosexual behavior and attraction in the United States, the United Kingdom, and France: Results of national population-based samples. *Archives of Sexual Behavior, 24,* 235–248.

Shavelson, E., Biaggio, M.K., Cross, H.H., & Lehman, R.E. (1980). Lesbian women's perceptions of their parent-child relationships. *Journal of Homosexuality, 5,* 205–215.

Shields, S.A., & Harriman, R.E. (1984). Fear of male homosexuality: Cardiac responses of low and high homonegative males. *Journal of Homosexuality, 10,* p. 53–67.

Silverstein, C. (1981). *Man to man: Gay couples in America.* New York: Morrow.

Spence, D. (1982). *Narrative truth and historical truth: Meaning and interpretation in psychoanalysis.* New York: Norton.

Stein, E., & Pillard, R. (1993). Evidence for queer genes: An interview with Richard Pillard. *GLQ, 1,* 98.

Stein, T.S. (1996). A critique of approaches to changing sexual orientation. In R.P. Cabaj & T.S. Stein (Eds.), *Textbook of homosexuality and mental health* (pp. 525–537). Washington, DC: American Psychiatric Press.

Stein, T.S. (1998). Social constructionism and essentialism: Theoretical and clinical considerations relevant to psychotherapy. *Journal of Gay and Lesbian Psychotherapy, 2*(4), 29–49.

Stekel, W. (1952). *Sexual aberrations* (Vol. 1). New York: Liveright. (Original work published 1923)

Stoller, R. (1985). *Presentations of gender.* New Haven, CT: Yale University Press.

Stolorow, R.D. (1975). Addendum to a partial analysis of a perversion involving bugs: An illustration of the narcissistic function of perverse activity. *International Journal of Psycho-Analysis, 56,* 361–364.

Storms, M.D. (1979). Sexual orientation and self-perception. In P. Pliner, K.R. Blankstein, & I.M. Spigel (Eds.), *Perceptions of emotions in self and others: Advances in the study of communication and affect* (Vol. 5, pp. 165–180). New York: Plenum Press.

Storms, M.D. (1980). Theories of sexual orientation. *Journal of Personality and Social Psychology, 38,* 783–792.

Storms, M.D. (1981). A theory of erotic orientation development. *Psychological Review, 88,* 340–353.

Storr, A. (1964). *Sexual deviation.* Baltimore: Penguin.

Tafoya, T.N. (1996). Native two-spirit people. In R.P. Cabaj & T.S. Stein (Eds.), *Textbook of homosexuality and mental health* (pp. 603–617). Washington, DC: American Psychiatric Press.

Thompson, N.L., Schwartz, D.M., McCandless, B.R., & Edwards, D.A. (1973). Parent-child relationships and sexual identity in male and female homosexuals and heterosexuals. *Journal of Clinical and Consulting Psychology, 41,* 120–127.

Tripp, C.A. (1987). *The homosexual matrix* (2nd ed.). New York: New American Library. (Original work published 1975)

Troiden, R.R. (1988). *Gay and lesbian identity: A sociological analysis.* Dix Hills, NY: General Hall.

Vreeland, C.N., Gallagher, B.J., III, & McFalls, J.A., Jr. (1995). The beliefs of members of the American Psychiatric Association on the etiology of male homosexuality: A national survey. *Journal of Psychology, 129,* 507–517.

Wagman, M. (1967). Sex differences in types of daydreams. *Journal of Personality and Social Psychology, 7,* 329–332.

Weinberg, M.S., & Bell, A.P. (1972). *Homosexuality: An annotated bibliography.* New York: Harper & Row.

Weinrich, J.D., Grant, I., Jacobson, D.L., Robinson, S.R., McCutchan, J.A., & HNRC Group. (1992). Effects of recalled childhood gender nonconformity on adult genito-erotic role and AIDS exposure. *Archives of Sexual Behavior, 21,* 559–585.

Weinrich, J.D., Snyder, P.J., Pillard, R.C., Grant, I., Jacobson, D.L., Robinson, S.R., & McCutchan, J.A. (1993). A factor analysis of the Klein sexual orientation grid in two disparate samples. *Archives of Sexual Behavior, 22,* 157–168.

Werner, D. (1979). A cross-cultural perspective on theory and research on male homosexuality. *Journal of Homosexuality, 4,* 345–362.

Whitam, F.L. (1980). The prehomosexual male child in three societies: The United States, Guatemala, Brazil. *Archives of Sexual Behavior, 9,* 87–99.

CHAPTER 6

Love Relationships

PAMELA C. REGAN

THE LOVE RELATIONSHIPS that we form over our lifetimes have important individual, interpersonal, and societal consequences. For example, such relationships may provide us with the opportunity to engage in socially sanctioned sexual activities, to reproduce and pairbond, to establish social support networks, and to experience a host of positive affective experiences, including warmth, trust, and intimacy. Indeed, surveys reveal that most individuals regard satisfying love relationships as essential for their personal happiness (for a review, see Berscheid & Reis, 1998).

Love clearly is linked with a variety of consequential events, including the formal establishment of a sexual/romantic pairbond through cohabitation and marriage. Research indicates that people typically express their feelings of love for each other prior to marriage discussions (King & Christensen, 1983). In addition, the assumption that marriage must be predicated on love has become increasingly accepted in Western societies. Over 30 years ago, Kephart (1967) asked a sample of young men and women whether they would marry someone with whom they were not in love if that person possessed all the other qualities they desired in a spouse. Approximately one-third (35%) of the men and three-fourths (76%) of the women said yes. However, by the mid-1980s, these numbers had changed, and love was seen as an essential prerequisite for marriage by *both* sexes: Simpson, Campbell, and Berscheid (1986) asked the same question of their participants, and 86% of the men and 80% of the women considered love the primary basis for marriage (i.e., they would *not* marry someone they did not love even if that person was "perfect" in every other respect). Moreover, longitudinal studies indicate that the amount of love the members of a couple actually feel for each other predicts such important future relational events as marriage and relationship endurance. C. Hill and Peplau (1998) followed a sample of couples over a 15-year period and reported that those who experienced greater love at the beginning of their study were more likely to actually get married and to stay married than those who were less in love.

Thus, love—and the relationships it produces and fosters—plays a significant role in human lives, and a solid understanding of love becomes important to social and behavioral scientists, particularly those who wish to treat couples embroiled in distressed love relationships. The first goal of this chapter is to present some of the more commonly utilized typologies of love and their associated measurement instruments. Second, I consider the type of love most closely associated with sexuality: passionate love. Third, I explore the nature of love relationships, including the attributes that people seek in potential love partners, and the theoretical frameworks that can be used to predict and explain these preferences. Finally, I examine the darker side of love relationships, including unrequited love, obsession, mismatched love styles, and loss of desire and passion, as well as various ways to alleviate or minimize these potentially problematic occurrences.

CONTEMPORARY TYPOLOGIES OF LOVE

The study of love is not new. Throughout history, thinkers from a number of disciplines have speculated on the nature of love. For example, religious theoretician C.S. Lewis (1960/1988) outlined four types or varieties of love, based on earlier distinctions made by Greek philosophers. Affection, called *storge* (pronounced "stor-gay") by the Greeks, is described by Lewis as "the humblest and most widely diffused of loves" (p. 31). Affectionate love resembles the strong attachment seen between parents and offspring, is often experienced for and by a diversity of love objects (e.g., family members, pets, acquaintances, lovers), and consists of feelings of warmth, interpersonal comfort, and satisfaction in being together. This love type is based on familiarity and repeated contact. The second variety of love depicted by Lewis is friendship, or *philias*. Common interests, insights, or tastes, coupled with cooperation, mutual respect, and understanding, form the core of this love type. More than mere companionship, Lewis argues that "Friendship must be about something, even if it were only an enthusiasm for dominoes or white mice" (p. 66). *Eros*, or "that state which we call 'being in love'" (p. 91), is the third variety of love. Unlike the other love types, eros contains a carnal sexual element that Lewis refers to as *Venus*. In addition to this sexual desire component, erotic love is characterized by idealization of the beloved, preoccupation with thoughts of him or her, and a short life span. The final love type is charity, also referred to as Christian love. This selfless love has no expectation of reward, desires only what is "simply best for the beloved" (p. 128), and allows us to love those who are not lovable (a state Lewis reminds us is experienced by everyone at some time).

Numerous other taxonomies that specify types or varieties of love have been proposed (for reviews, see S. Hendrick & Hendrick, 1992; Sternberg & Barnes,

1988). Two of the more common contemporary typologies are those developed by Sternberg (e.g., 1986, 1988a, 1988b) and Lee (e.g., 1973, 1988).

The Triangular Theory of Love

Sternberg (e.g., 1986, 1988a, 1988b) conceptualizes love in terms of three basic components that form the vertices of a triangle: intimacy, passion, and decision/commitment. The intimacy component is primarily emotional or affective in nature and involves feelings of warmth, closeness, connection, and bondedness in the love relationship. The passion component is motivational and consists of the drives that are involved in romantic and physical attraction, sexual consummation, and related phenomena. The decision/commitment component is largely cognitive and represents both the short-term decision that one individual loves another and the longer-term commitment to maintain that love.

According to Sternberg (1986, 1988b), these components combine to produce eight different love experiences or types:

1. Nonlove (no intimacy, passion, or decision/commitment): Casual interactions characterized by the absence of intimacy, passion, and decision/commitment. Nonlove describes the majority of our transient, casual relationships.
2. Liking (intimacy alone): Friendship that contains intimacy and emotional closeness but no passion or decision/commitment. That is, one cares for the friend but does not feel passion for that individual or the desire to love that individual for the rest of one's life.
3. Infatuation (passion alone): An infatuated, "love at first sight" experience that is characterized by high degrees of attraction and psychophysiological arousal in the absence of any real emotional intimacy and decision/commitment.
4. Empty love (decision/commitment alone): Often seen at the end of long-term relationships (or at the beginning of arranged marriages) in which the couple is committed to each other but lacks emotional involvement and passionate attraction.
5. Romantic love (intimacy + passion): Liking (emotional intimacy) coupled with physical attraction and its concomitants.
6. Companionate love (intimacy + decision/commitment): Essentially a long-term, stable, and committed friendship that is characterized by high amounts of emotional intimacy, the decision to love the partner, and the commitment to remain in the relationship. This type of love is often seen in long-term marriages in which sexual attraction has faded.
7. Fatuous love (passion + decision/commitment): Couples who love fatuously base their commitment to each other on passion in the absence of deep emotional intimacy. These "whirlwind" relationships are typically unstable and at risk for termination.

8. Consummate love (intimacy + passion + decision/commitment): Consummate or "complete" love results from the combination of all three components. According to Sternberg, this is the type of love many individuals strive to attain, particularly those in romantic relationships.

Sternberg (1986, 1988b) also argues that people's relationships—their love triangles—differ with respect to total amount (area) and balance (shape). For example, some individuals feel a high amount of love for the partner and roughly equal amounts of the different components. The love triangle characterizing their relationship thus has a large physical area and a balanced (equilateral) shape. A smaller, isosceles triangle can be used to represent a relationship in which the individual feels less total love and significantly more intimacy than passion and decision/commitment.

Although conceptually interesting, this theory has not received strong empirical support. For example, Sternberg (1988a) created a 45-item scale based on his previous theoretical work. Sample items include "I communicate well with _____" (from the Intimacy subscale); "Just seeing _____ excites me" (from the Passion subscale); and "I view my relationship with _____ as permanent" (from the Commitment subscale). C. Hendrick and Hendrick (1989) administered this scale to a group of 391 unmarried men and women. Their results indicated not only that all three subscales were highly intercorrelated (with an average correlation of .75), but that the instrument formed a unifactorial scale. In other words, the Triangular Theory of Love Scale appears to measure one global construct or relationship dimension rather than three distinct elements or components of love. Nonetheless, the theory remains conceptually interesting and appears to capture the love experiences of many individuals.

THE COLORS OF LOVE (LOVE STYLES)

Another contemporary theory of love, and one that has produced a widely used measurement instrument and spawned myriad research efforts, is the typology developed by Lee (e.g., 1973, 1977, 1988). In this novel approach, each variety of love (or love style) is likened to a primary or secondary color (hence the title of Lee's 1973 book, *Colours of Love*). According to Lee, there are three primary colors or styles of loving. The first, *eros*, is an intensely emotional experience that is similar to passionate love. In fact, the most typical symptom of eros is an immediate and powerful attraction to the beloved individual. The erotic lover is "turned on" by a particular physical type, is prone to fall instantly and completely in love with a stranger (i.e., experiences "love at first sight"), rapidly becomes preoccupied with pleasant thoughts about that individual, feels an intense need for daily contact with the beloved, and wishes the relationship to remain exclusive. Erotic love also has a strong sexual component; for example, not only does the erotic style of loving always begin with a strong physical attraction, but the erotic lover usually seeks some form of sexual involvement early in the relationship.

The second primary color of love is *ludus,* or game-playing love. The ludic lover views love as a game, to be played with skill and often with several partners simultaneously. Commitment is antithetical to ludus. Ludic lovers prefer a variety of physical types, avoid seeing the partner too often, believe that lies and deception are justified, expect the partner to remain in control of his or her emotions, and view sexual activity as an opportunity for pleasure rather than for intense emotional bonding.

Storge is the third primary love color. Described by Lee as "love without fever or folly" (1973, p. 77), storge resembles Lewis's concept of affection in that it is stable and based on a solid foundation of trust, respect, and friendship. Indeed, the typical storgic lover views and treats the partner as an "old friend," does not experience the intense emotions or physical attraction to the partner associated with erotic love, prefers to talk about and engage in shared interests with the partner rather than to express direct feelings, is shy about sex, and tends to demonstrate his or her affection in nonsexual ways. Essentially, storge is highly similar to deep friendship.

Like the primary colors, the primary love styles can be combined to form secondary colors or styles of love. The three secondary styles identified by Lee (1973) contain features of the primaries, but also possess their own unique characteristics. *Pragma,* a combination of storge and ludus, is "the love that goes shopping for a suitable mate" (p. 124). The pragmatic lover has a practical outlook to love and seeks a compatible lover. He or she creates a shopping list of features or attributes desired in the partner, and will select a mate based on how well that individual fulfills the requirements. Pragmatic love is essentially a faster-acting version of storge that has been quickened by the addition of ludus.

Mania, the combination of eros and ludus, is another secondary love style. Manic lovers lack the self-confidence associated with eros and the emotional self-control associated with ludus; rather, this obsessive, jealous love style is characterized by self-defeating emotions, desperate attempts to force affection from the beloved, and the inability to trust in and to enjoy any mutuality of feeling the beloved does display. The manic lover is eager to fall in love. He or she begins immediately to imagine a future with the partner, wants to see the partner daily, tries to force the partner to show love and commitment, distrusts the partner's sincerity, and is extremely possessive. Noting that the manic lover "will abase and abuse himself [or herself] in the hope of winning the partner's love" (1973, p. 27), Lee concluded that mania produces distress in both partners (the manic lover and the beloved) and rarely ends happily.

The last secondary color of love is *agape,* a combination of eros and storge. Agape is similar to Lewis's concept of charity, and represents an all-giving, selfless love style that implies an obligation to love and care for others without any expectation of reciprocity or reward. This love style is universalistic in the sense that the typical agapic lover feels that everyone is worthy of love and that loving others is a duty of the mature person. With respect to personal love relationships, agapic lovers will unselfishly devote themselves to the partner, even stepping aside in favor of a rival who seems more likely to meet the partner's needs. Interestingly, although Lee felt that many lovers respected the agapic ideal, he also believed that it did not exist in practice. That is, the give-and-take that characterizes most adult romantic relationships, along with the tendency of lovers to consistently place the beloved before other individuals, precludes the occurrence of purely altruistic love. Near agapic experiences do, however, characterize some relationships, and were labeled by Lee as storgic eros.

This classification scheme inspired the development of a 50-item true-false instrument designed to measure each of the six love styles (Hatkoff & Lasswell, 1977; Lasswell & Lasswell, 1976). This original scale subsequently was revised substantially by Hendrick, Hendrick, and colleagues (C. Hendrick & Hendrick, 1986; C. Hendrick, Hendrick, Foote, & Slapion-Foote, 1984), who created new items and incorporated a Likert-type response format. The resulting 42-item Love Attitudes Scale (LAS) appears to reliably measure the six love styles (i.e., six distinct, nonoverlapping dimensions emerge from factor analysis, the items in each subscale are highly correlated, and the subscales have low intercorrelations with each other). A second major revision was undertaken several years later, when C. Hendrick and Hendrick (1990) recrafted the LAS so that all of the items refer to a specific love relationship (as opposed to more general attitudes about love). In addition, they created a shorter, 28-item version of the scale (C. Hendrick, Hendrick, & Dicke, 1998). The complete scale, along with its shorter version, is reproduced in Table 6.1.

The LAS has been used in numerous empirical investigations. In general, the results of these studies reveal robust group differences in love experience. For example, women tend to be relatively more storgic and pragmatic (and, in some studies, more manic) than men, whereas men tend to be more ludic than women (e.g., C. Hendrick & Hendrick, 1986, 1988; C. Hendrick et al., 1984, 1998; S. Hendrick & Hendrick, 1987, 1995). Sex role also appears to be associated with love style. Specifically, individuals with an androgynous sex role seem to adopt an erotic and pragmatic approach to love, those with a masculine sex role endorse a ludic love style, and those with a feminine sex role score highest on mania (e.g., W. Bailey, Hendrick, & Hendrick, 1987).

Demographic and personality variables also are related to love style. For example, highly religious men and women tend to endorse a storgic, pragmatic, and agapic approach to love (e.g., S. Hendrick & Hendrick, 1987). They adopt a sensible, practical, altruistic style of loving others that may be particularly suited to their religious or moral beliefs. In addition, self-esteem appears to be positively correlated with an erotic love style and negatively correlated with a manic love style (e.g., C. Hendrick & Hendrick, 1986). These results make sense insofar as eros, which involves intense emotional experiences and some degree of risk taking, clearly requires a high amount of self-esteem and ego

Table 6.1
The Love Attitudes Scale

Instructions

Please answer the following items as honestly and accurately as possible. Whenever possible, answer the questions with your current partner in mind. If you are not currently dating anyone, answer the questions with your most recent partner in mind. Otherwise, answer in terms of what you think your responses would most likely be.

Response scale

1 = strongly agree
2 = moderately agree
3 = neutral
4 = moderately disagree
5 = strongly disagree

Items

Eros

  1. My partner and I were attracted to each other immediately after we first met.
*2. My partner and I have the right physical "chemistry" between us.
  3. Our lovemaking is very intense and satisfying.
*4. I feel that my partner and I were meant for each other.
  5. My partner and I became emotionally involved rather quickly.
*6. My partner and I really understand each other.
  7. My partner fits my ideal standards of physical beauty/handsomeness.

Ludus

  8. I try to keep my partner a little uncertain about my commitment to him/her.
*9. I believe that what my partner doesn't know about me won't hurt him/her.
*10. I have sometimes had to keep my partner from finding out about other lovers.
 11. I could get over my love affair with my partner pretty easily and quickly.
*12. My partner would get upset if he/she knew of some of the things I've done with other people.
 13. When my partner gets too dependent on me, I want to back off a little.
*14. I enjoy playing the "game of love" with my partner and a number of other partners.

Storge

 15. It is hard for me to say exactly when our friendship turned into love.
 16. To be genuine, our love first required *caring* for a while.
 17. I expect to always be friends with my partner.
*18. Our love is the best kind because it grew out of a long friendship.
*19. Our friendship merged gradually into love over time.
*20. Our love is really a deep friendship, not a mysterious, mystical emotion.
*21. Our love relationship is the most satisfying because it developed from a good friendship.

Pragma

 22. I considered what my partner was going to become in life before I committed myself to him/her.
 23. I tried to plan my life carefully before choosing a partner.

Table 6.1 *(Continued)*

24. In choosing my partner, I believed it was best to love someone with a similar background.
*25. A main consideration in choosing my partner was how he/she would reflect on my family.
*26. An important factor in choosing my partner was whether or not he/she would be a good parent.
*27. One consideration in choosing my partner was how he/she would reflect on my career.
*28. Before getting very involved with my partner, I tried to figure out how compatible his/her hereditary background would be with mine in case we ever had children.

Mania

29. When things aren't right with my partner and me, my stomach gets upset.
30. If my partner and I break up, I would get so depressed that I would even think of suicide.
31. Sometimes I get so excited about being in love with my partner that I can't sleep.
*32. When my partner doesn't pay attention to me, I feel sick all over.
*33. Since I've been in love with my partner I've had trouble concentrating on anything else.
*34. I cannot relax if I suspect that my partner is with someone else.
*35. If my partner ignores me for a while, I sometimes do stupid things to try to get his/her attention back.

Agape

36. I try to always help my partner through difficult times.
*37. I would rather suffer myself than let my partner suffer.
*38. I cannot be happy unless I place my partner's happiness before my own.
*39. I am usually willing to sacrifice my own wishes to let my partner achieve his/hers.
40. Whatever I own is my partner's to use as he/she chooses.
41. When my partner gets angry with me, I still love him/her fully and unconditionally.
*42. I would endure all things for the sake of my partner.

Adapted from Hendrick, C. and Hendrick, S. (1990). A relationship-specific version of the Love Attitudes Scale. *Journal of Social Behavior and Personality, 5,* 239–254. Starred items are included in the short form of the scale. From Hendrick, C., Hendrick, S. S., & Dicke, A. (1998). The love attitudes scale: Short form. *Journal of Social and Personal Relationships, 15,* 147–159.

strength. Similarly, mania is almost by definition an esteem-draining experience, insofar as it is characterized by uncertainty, self-doubt, and mistrust of the relationship and the partner.

Finally, there are robust multicultural and cross-cultural differences in love experiences. Within the United States, Asian American adults score lower on eros and higher on pragma than Caucasian, Latino, and African American adults (e.g., C. Hendrick & Hendrick, 1986). Latino groups, by contrast, often score higher on ludus than Caucasian groups (e.g., Contreras, Hendrick, & Hendrick, 1996). Cross-cultural comparisons reveal, for example, that Americans tend to endorse a more storgic and manic approach to love than do the French, who, in turn, tend to demonstrate higher levels of agape (e.g., Murstein, Merighi, & Vyse, 1991).

These group differences notwithstanding, it is important to keep in mind that not all individuals exhibit one approach or style of loving. Some men and women may adopt numerous love styles. Similarly, a person's love style may change over his or her lifetime or during the course of a given relationship. For example, manic feelings and responses may be more common at the beginning stages of a romantic relationship, when one or both partners are uncertain as to their feelings and the future of the relationship. Over time, however, these feelings may be replaced by more erotic, storgic, or agapic feelings.

THE PROTOTYPE APPROACH TO LOVE

Some researchers, rather than following the "top-down" or theoretical approach to love taken by Lewis, Sternberg, Lee, and others, instead have adopted "bottom-up" or empirically driven techniques to delineate the nature of love. One such technique, the prototype approach, involves collecting data directly from men and women about their knowledge and beliefs—their mental representations—of the concept of love. Researchers who utilize the prototype approach are interested in exploring what people think of when they are asked about love, how they differentiate love from related concepts (e.g., liking), how they form their conceptualizations of love, and how these conceptualizations or mental representations influence their behavior with relational partners.

According to Rosch (e.g., 1973, 1975, 1978), an early pioneer in the use of prototype analysis, natural language concepts can be viewed as having both a vertical and a horizontal dimension. The former concerns the hierarchical organization of concepts, or relations among different levels of concepts. Concepts at one level may be included within or subsumed by those at another, higher level. For example, the set of concepts *mammal, dog,* and *collie* illustrate an abstract-to-concrete hierarchy with superordinate, basic, and subordinate levels. Using the methods originally developed by Rosch, some researchers have investigated the hierarchical structure of the concept of love. Shaver, Schwartz, Kirson, and O'Connor (1987) provide evidence that *love* is a basic-level concept contained within the superordinate category of *emotion* and subsuming a variety of subordinate concepts that reflect types or varieties of love (e.g., *passion, infatuation, liking*).

Concepts also may be examined along a horizontal dimension. This dimension concerns the differentiation of concepts at the same level of inclusiveness (e.g., the dimension on which such subordinate-level concepts as *collie, German shepherd,* and *golden retriever* vary). According to Rosch, many natural language concepts or categories have an internal structure whereby individual members of that category are ordered in terms of the degree to which they resemble the prototypic member of the category. A prototype is the best, clearest example of the concept (e.g., the golden retriever is the "doggiest" dog). When utilizing prototypes, individuals decide whether a new item belongs within a particular concept by comparing the item with the concept's prototype.

The prototype approach has been used to explore the horizontal structure of a variety of interpersonal concepts, including love. Fehr and Russell (1991), for example, asked men and women to generate as many types of love as they could in a specified time, and then asked another sample of individuals to rate these love varieties in terms of prototypicality or "goodness-of-example." Of the 93 subtypes generated, *maternal love* was rated as the best or most prototypical example of love, followed by *parental love, friendship, sisterly love, romantic love, brotherly love*, and *familial love. Infatuation*, along with *sexual love* and *puppy love*, was considered one of the least prototypical examples of love.

Other researchers have focused on identifying the prototypic features (as opposed to types) of love. For example, in an early demonstration, Fehr (1988) asked one group of participants to list the characteristics of the concept "love" (Study 1, p. 560), and a second group to rate how central each feature was to the concept of love (Study 2). Her results revealed that love is believed to contain such central features as *trust, caring, honesty, friendship, respect*, and *loyalty*. Features considered peripheral or unimportant to the concept of love include *see only the other's good qualities, butterflies in stomach, uncertainty, dependency*, and *scary*. Similar results have been reported by Luby and Aron (1990) and Shaver et al. (1987). More recently, Aron and Westbay (1996) extended Fehr's work by exploring the underlying structure of the prototype of love. These researchers found evidence that the 68 prototypic love features identified by participants in Fehr's (1988) study could be reduced reliably to three latent dimensions (i.e., passion, intimacy, and commitment) that resemble those included in Sternberg's Triangular Theory of Love typology.

PASSIONATE LOVE: THE "SEXIEST" KIND OF LOVE

Of all the varieties of love that have been identified by theorists and researchers, passionate love (also called erotic or romantic love) has received the lion's share of attention. This particular type of love has assumed special importance in interpersonal relationships research and in theoretical discourse on love for a number of reasons: passionate love is generally sought after by individuals and exalted in Western culture; passionate love has become the sine qua non of the marriage contract; and the absence of passionate love may be a factor in relationship dissolution (e.g., Berscheid, 1985; Burgess & Wallin, 1953; Goode, 1959; Kazak & Reppucci, 1980; Kephart, 1967; Simpson et al., 1986; Spaulding, 1971). In addition, not only is passionate love intricately associated with these and other significant individual and interpersonal events, but current social psychological discourse suggests that passionate love is the type of love most closely associated with sexuality. This section explores how passionate love is defined, the ways in which it is measured or assessed, and recent empirical evidence examining the relation between passionate love and different aspects of human sexual response.

DEFINING PASSIONATE LOVE: WHAT DOES IT MEAN TO "BE IN LOVE"?

Passionate love, or the state of "being in love," consists of a number of basic features. First and foremost, this type of love is an intensely emotional experience. Berscheid and Walster (1974), two of the first social scientists to speculate on the nature of "being in love," suggest that people experience passionate love when a minimum of two conditions are met: (1) They are extremely aroused physiologically (an essential ingredient for any strong emotion), and (2) they believe that this arousal is caused by the partner and therefore appropriately labeled "passionate love." In addition, passionate love is assumed to be fueled by and associated with both positive and negative emotions, and the passionate lover is presumed to alternate among states of joy, fulfillment, and ecstasy when the relationship is going well and bouts of emptiness, anxiety, and despair when it is not. For example, Berscheid and Walster discuss the "hodgepodge of conflicting emotions" (p. 359) associated with passionate love, and, more recently, Hatfield and Rapson (1990) describe the "continuous interplay between elation and despair, thrills and terror" (p. 128) they believe to be integral to the experience of being in love. Interestingly, however, research on beliefs about passionate love (e.g., Regan, Kocan, & Whitlock, 1998) and on correlates of passionate love in dating couples (e.g., Sprecher & Regan, 1998) suggests that passionate love is more strongly associated with positive emotions than with negative emotions, with one important exception: Jealousy is clearly related to feelings of passionate love (i.e., not only do men and women associate jealousy with the state of being in love, but those who love passionately also tend to report feeling jealous).

Second, in contrast to more durable types of love (e.g, companionate, conjugal, storgic, or friendship-based love), passionate love is viewed by most theorists as an inherently unstable, short-lived phenomenon. For example, Berscheid (1983) concludes that passionate love and other intense emotional experiences have a "swift onset" but are "distressingly fragile." Sternberg (1988b) states that the rapid development of intense passion inevitably leads to habituation; over time, the partner is no longer as "stimulating" as he or she once was and can no longer produce the intense arousal previously felt by the lover. Some research supports these theoretical contentions. With a sample of 197 couples, Sprecher and Regan (1998) examined whether the number of months that each couple had been dating was related to the amount of passionate love they reportedly felt for each other. These researchers found evidence that passionate love indeed is related to relationship duration; specifically, the longer a couple had been together, the lower their passionate love scores (although scores were high in all couples).

Third, passionate love contains a strong sexual component. In fact, current social psychological discourse suggests that sexuality is one of the dimensions that differentiates passionate love from other varieties or types of love experience (Aron & Aron, 1991; S. Hendrick & Hendrick, 1992; Regan & Berscheid, 2000). As discussed earlier, Lee (e.g., 1973, 1977, 1988) concluded that passionate (or what he terms erotic) love always begins with a strong physical attraction, and he noted that the erotic lover seeks early sexual involvement with the partner and is "eager to get to know the beloved quickly, intensely—and undressed" (1988, p. 50). Tennov (1979) and, more recently, Berscheid (e.g., 1985, 1988) and Regan (1998a, 1998c) argue that sexual desire or attraction is a necessary feature of the passionate love experience. Other theorists include such additional sexual phenomena as arousal, excitement, gratification, and activity in their conceptualizations of passionate love (e.g., Berscheid & Walster, 1974; Hatfield & Rapson, 1987, 1993; Hatfield & Sprecher, 1986). This is not to say that other types of love are sexless; certainly, it is possible to feel desire for someone we love companionately and to engage in sexual activities with that person. However, sexuality appears to play the strongest role in the passionate love experience.

Assessing Passionate Love: How Do We Measure "Being in Love"?

There are two commonly used ways to assess passionate love: single-item self-report measures and multi-item scales. Single-item measures typically focus on the quantity or the intensity of passionate love experienced by an individual. Figure 6.1 provides some examples.

Although these global, single-item measures are easy to use and appear to be relatively reliable (see, e.g., Sprecher & Regan, 1998), many researchers choose to use larger, multi-item scales that have been developed specifically to measure the various theoretically important elements of passionate love. Several different passionate love scales have been constructed over the years, including measures by Swensen and colleagues (Swensen, 1961; Swensen & Gilner, 1963); Pam, Plutchik, and Conte (1975); Critelli, Myers, and Loos (1986); C. Hendrick and Hendrick (1986); and Hatfield and Sprecher (1986). Of these, two are particularly worthy of note: Erotic Subscale of the Love Attitudes Scale developed by C. Hendrick and Hendrick (1986), discussed above, and the Passionate Love Scale developed by Hatfield and Sprecher (1986).

The Passionate Love Scale represents perhaps the best measure of passionate love currently available. Drawing on past theoretical conceptualizations, previously developed measures, and in-depth personal interviews, Hatfield and Sprecher (1986) crafted a series of items designed to assess the cognitive, emotional, and behavioral components of the passionate love experience.

1. How much passionate love do you feel for _____?

    1   2   3   4   5   6   7   8   9

    None   A great deal

2. Rate the intensity of your feelings of passionate love for your current partner.

    1   2   3   4   5   6   7   8   9

    Very little   Extremely intense
    feeling   feeling

3. How strongly are you in love with _____?

    1   2   3   4   5   6   7   8   9

    Not at all   Extremely
    strongly   strongly

4. How strong are your feelings of passionate love for your partner?

    1   2   3   4   5   6   7   8   9

    Very weak   Very strong

  or

    1   2   3   4   5   6   7   8   9

    Not at all   Extremely
    strong   strong

5. How often do you experience feelings of passionate love for your partner?

    1   2   3   4   5   6   7   8   9

    Never   Extremely often

  or

    _____ times a day
    _____ times a week
    _____ times a month

6. How often did you experience passionate love in your relationship during the last month?

    1   2   3   4   5   6   7   8   9

    Never   Sometimes   Extremely often

Figure 6.1   Examples of Single-Item Self-Report Questions to Assess Passionate Love.

Subsequent administration and revision of this original set of items resulted in a 30-item scale that reliably discriminates between feelings of passionate love and other types of love (e.g., companionate love). Of particular interest is the fact that the scale contains a number of items that directly or indirectly refer to sexuality, including the following:

Sometimes my body trembles with excitement at the sight of _____.

I take delight in studying the movements and angles of _____'s body.

I want _____ physically, emotionally, mentally.

I melt when looking deeply into _____'s eyes.

I sense my body responding when _____ touches me.

The complete scale is represented in Table 6.2.

RESEARCH ON THE SEXUAL COMPONENT OF PASSIONATE LOVE

Well, I can't speak for anyone else, but for me, the only way I'd have sex with someone was if we were deeply in love. If two people are in love, then sex seems like a natural way to express those feelings. (19-year-old woman interviewed by the author)

I've had sexual intercourse with a number of different partners—some I didn't know at all and who I never saw again after the sex, and some I had lasting relationships with. I have to say that the best, most comfortable, most satisfying sex I've ever had is with my current girlfriend (who I hope will be my wife). I'm not saying I didn't enjoy the other sexual relationships I've had, but sex with someone you love is definitely better. We (my girlfriend and I) feel totally comfortable with each other. I know that I can trust her, and I feel free to communicate openly with her about sex and all other aspects of our relationship. There's much more freedom and openness and satisfaction to the sex if you're in a committed relationship with someone you love. (31-year-old man interviewed by the author)

I love everything about him—I want him all the time and I think about him all the time. I am so in love with him that I get weak even writing down these words. I can't concentrate, I can't sleep, I don't want to eat. I get so excited when I know that I'm going to see him, and then when I do see him, I can't breathe I'm so full of want. When we're together I can't wait for him to touch me, to kiss me, to hold me. And then I want more! This is how I know that I'm really in love— these feelings just keep growing stronger and stronger. This is *it!* (24-year-old woman interviewed by the author)

As these quotations illustrate, love and sexuality appear to be intricately connected in the eyes of many individuals. Indeed, as noted above, contemporary theorists and researchers who have speculated on the nature of passionate love have linked it with a variety of sexual phenomena. Many of the existing conceptualizations and measures of passionate love contain an interesting mixture of sexual elements, including *physical or sexual attraction/desire* (e.g., Berscheid, 1988; Critelli et al., 1986; Hatfield, 1988; Hatfield & Walster, 1978; C. Hendrick & Hendrick, 1986; Lee, 1973; Pam et al., 1975; Regan, 1998a, 1998c; Shaver & Hazan, 1988; Sternberg, 1988a, 1988b; Tennov, 1979), *sexual excitement* (e.g., Critelli et al., 1986; Hatfield & Walster, 1978), *physiological and/or sexual arousal* (e.g., Critelli et al., 1986; Hatfield & Sprecher, 1986; Hatfield & Walster, 1978; Shaver, Hazan, & Bradshaw, 1988), *sexual deprivation* (e.g., Hatfield & Walster, 1978), *sexual satisfaction and/or sexual gratification* (e.g., Berscheid & Walster, 1974; C. Hendrick & Hendrick, 1986; Shaver et al., 1988; Walster & Berscheid, 1971), *sexual involvement* (e.g., C. Hendrick & Hendrick, 1986; Lee, 1973, 1988), and *sexual activity* (e.g., Buss, 1988b; Shaver & Hazan, 1988;

Table 6.2
The Passionate Love Scale

Instructions

We would like to know how you feel when you are *passionately in love*. Some common terms for passionate love are *romantic love, infatuation, love sickness,* or *obsessive love*. Please think of the person whom you love most passionately *right now*. If you are not in love right now, please think of the last person you loved. If you have never been in love, think of the person you came closest to caring for in that way. Try to tell us how you felt at the time when your feelings were the most intense.

Response scale

1	2	3	4	5	6	7	8	9
Not at all true			Moderately true					Definitely true

Items

1. Since I've been involved with _____, my emotions have been on a roller coaster.
2. I would feel deep despair if _____ left me.
3. Sometimes my body trembles with excitement at the sight of _____.
4. I take delight in studying the movements and angles of _____'s body.
5. Sometimes I can't control my thoughts; they are obsessively on _____.
6. I feel happy when I am doing something to make _____ happy.
7. I would rather be with _____ than with anyone else.
8. I'd get jealous if I thought _____ were falling in love with someone else.
9. No one else could love _____ like I do.
10. I yearn to know all about _____.
11. I want _____—physically, emotionally, mentally.
12. I will love _____ forever.
13. I melt when looking deeply into _____'s eyes.
14. I have an endless appetite for affection from _____.
15. For me, _____ is the perfect romantic partner.
16. _____ is the person who can make me feel the happiest.
17. I sense my body responding when _____ touches me.
18. I feel tender toward _____.
19. _____ always seems to be on my mind.
20. If I were separated from _____ for a long time, I would feel intensely lonely.
21. I sometimes find it difficult to concentrate on work because thoughts of _____ occupy my mind.
22. I want _____ to know me—my thoughts, my fears, and my hopes.
23. Knowing that _____ cares about me makes me feel complete.
24. I eagerly look for signs indicating _____'s desire for me.
25. If _____ were going through a difficult time, I would put away my own concerns to help him/her out.
26. _____ can make me feel effervescent and bubbly.
27. In the presence of _____, I yearn to touch and be touched.
28. An existence without _____ would be dark and dismal.
29. I possess a powerful attraction for _____.
30. I get extremely depressed when things don't go right in my relationship with _____.

Adapted from Hatfield, E. and Sprecher, S. (1986). Measuring passionate love in intimate relationships. *Journal of Adolescence, 9,* 383–410.

Swensen, 1961; Swensen & Gilner, 1963). Although these phenomena do not represent the same, or in some instances even similar, concepts, it is clear that passionate love is considered by many researchers to be a sexualized experience. Indeed, a growing body of empirical evidence now links this type of love with three particular elements of sexuality: sexual activity, sexual excitement, and, most important, sexual desire.

Passionate Love and Sexual Activity

Sexual activity plays a very definite role in passionate love and the kinds of emotionally committed relationships with which it is associated. Not only may sexual or physical contact be an important component of this type of love (Knox, 1975), but sexual activity between two individuals may serve to express, promote, or enhance feelings of passionate love (see, e.g., Neubeck, 1972). In an early work, noted theorist and sex researcher Havelock Ellis (1922) explained: "Apart from any sexual craving, the complete spiritual contact of two persons who love each other can only be attained through some act of rare intimacy. No act can be quite so intimate as the sexual embrace" (p. 68).

Some empirical evidence reveals that sexual activity is, in fact, one way that a couple expresses and communicates feelings of passionate love. For example, Buss (1988b) asked a sample of 100 men and women to think of people who "have been or are currently in love" and to list acts or behaviors these individuals have performed that reflect their feelings. Several behaviors involving sexual intimacy were viewed as integral to the passionate love experience, including such acts as "he gave her a prolonged hug," "she nuzzled him," "he made love to her," and "she spent the night with him." Similar results were reported by Marston, Hecht, Manke, McDaniel, and Reeder (1998). These researchers interviewed a sample of in-love couples about the ways they communicated their feelings of passion to each other. The most common method of expressing passion was through sexual activities, including "making love."

In addition, not only may sexual activity allow individuals to demonstrate their feelings of passionate love, but feelings of passionate love, in turn, may serve to justify sexual activity. Numerous studies indicate that most men and women view sexual intercourse as more appropriate, and as more likely to occur, in committed, love-based relationships than in casual or less "serious" relationships (e.g., Carroll, Volk, & Hyde, 1985; Michael, Gagnon, Laumann, & Kolata, 1994; Roche, 1986; Sherwin & Corbett, 1985; Sprecher & Hatfield, 1996). In an early study, for example, Reiss (1964) reported that men and women from a national probability sample of the U.S. population as well as students from five high schools and colleges were increasingly more accepting of premarital sexual intercourse between two people as their relationship became characterized by correspondingly greater amounts of affection and commitment (i.e., as the relationship progressed from relatively little affection to strong affection, and then to love and engagement). Similar results were found two decades later by Sprecher, McKinney, Walsh, and Anderson

(1988). Increasing numbers of participants in that study viewed sexual intercourse between two people as acceptable as their relationship stage progressed from casually dating (41%), to seriously dating (72%), to pre-engaged (77%), and, finally, to engaged (82%). More recently, Sprecher and Hatfield (1996) asked a sample of 1,043 men and women to indicate how acceptable sexual intercourse was at different relationship stages. Their results indicated that with each increase in relationship commitment (i.e., as a couple moved from first date to casually dating to seriously dating to pre-engaged to engaged), there was a corresponding increase in the number of men and women who expressed acceptance of sexual intercourse.

In much the same way that sexual activity is considered appropriate between partners who are involved in a committed, love-based relationship, the *absence* of love or emotional intimacy seems to be sufficient reason to abstain from sexual activity. Sprecher and Regan (1996) surveyed a sample of 97 virgin men and 192 virgin women about the reasons for their sexual status. The single most important reason endorsed by both sexes for their virginity was "I have not been in a relationship long enough or been in love enough." The least important reason for both sexes was "I lack desire for sex." In other words, these young adults felt sexual desire and wanted to engage in sexual intercourse, but had not yet experienced sufficient amounts of passionate love to justify that activity.

Not surprisingly, perhaps, the perceived association between sexual activity and love is usually stronger among women than men (although this is changing as women are becoming more accepting of premarital and casual sexual activity; Oliver & Hyde, 1993). For example, Robinson, Balkwell, and Ward (1980) asked male and female college students to write down their first five responses to various sexual concepts and terms. When exposed to the stimulus words "sex" and "intercourse," women responded with words indicative of love (e.g., love, loving, being in love, loved, loving each other) and marriage or commitment (e.g., being engaged, husband, wife, serious relationship) more often than did men. Additional support for the notion that women associate sex with love to a greater extent than do men is indirectly provided by a study conducted by Hatfield, Sprecher, Pillemer, Greenberger, and Wexler (1988). These researchers found that, although both the dating and married men and women in their sample expressed roughly equal satisfaction with their current sexual relationship, women wanted to receive love and intimacy from the sexual encounter above all else and wished that their dating or marriage partner would talk more "lovingly" and be more "warm and involved" during a sexual encounter. Men, by contrast, were less concerned with the emotional aspects of the sexual encounter and more concerned that their partner be initiative of and experimental in sexual encounters.

Research on the reasons men and women choose to engage in and abstain from sexual intercourse reveals a similar sex difference. For example, Carroll and colleagues (1985) discovered that men and women cite different motives for participating in sexual activity. Although the majority of both men and women in this study felt that the most important reason for engaging in intercourse was feeling loved or needed, more women (45%) than men (8%) felt that emotional involvement was "always" a prerequisite for sex. Similar results were reported by Christopher and Cate (1985). These researchers asked college-age, virgin men and women to indicate how important several factors would be in their decision to have sexual intercourse with an ideal partner for the first time. They found that women were more likely than men to rate relationship factors (e.g., love for partner) as a salient issue (but recall that Sprecher & Regan, 1996, found no sex difference with respect to relationship reasons for abstinence among adult virgins).

In sum, there is strong evidence that sexual activity is associated with the experience of passionate love; many men and women consider sexual activity an appropriate way of communicating their feelings of love and passion to the partner, and many view passionate love as sufficient justification for engaging in sexual activity (and, similarly, feel that the absence of love is reason enough to abstain from intercourse).

Passionate Love and Sexual Excitement

Research also suggests that physiological (i.e., sexual excitement, sexual arousal) aspects of sexuality are associated with feelings of passionate love. For example, in the process of validating the Passionate Love Scale, Hatfield and Sprecher (1986) found that people who are more passionately in love experience higher levels of sexual excitement when thinking about the partner than those who are less passionately in love. Similar results have been reported by Sprecher and Regan (1998). These researchers were interested in exploring whether two types of love—passionate love and companionate love (a stable, affectionate love based on trust and friendship)—are associated differentially with a variety of interpersonal events and phenomena. They asked a sample of 197 heterosexual couples to complete the Companionate Love Scale (adapted from Rubin's 1970 love scale) and a shortened version of Hatfield and Sprecher's (1986) Passionate Love Scale, as well as global, single-item measures of each love type. Couples also indicated how often they had experienced "sexual excitement" for the partner in the past month, and completed a 6-item sexual intimacy scale that assessed, for example, sexual satisfaction, ability to express sexual interest to the partner, and the partner's perceived interest in sex. The results revealed that both passionate and companionate love were positively correlated with these two sexuality variables. However, for both men and women, the experience of sexual excitement was more strongly correlated with passionate love scores than with companionate love scores, whereas feelings of sexual intimacy were more strongly related to companionate love scores than to passionate love scores. These results indicate that different aspects of sexuality are more (or less) associated with particular types or varieties of love. Specifically, intense, physiological components of sexuality (e.g., sexual excitement) appear to be important features of the passionate love experience, whereas low-key, subjective sexual feelings related to closeness, warmth, satisfaction, and compatibility (i.e., sexual intimacy) are an important part of the companionate love experience.

PASSIONATE LOVE AND SEXUAL DESIRE

Many passionate lovers do not engage in sexual activity with their beloved, and many people who are not passionately in love with their partners nonetheless engage in satisfying sexual relations with those individuals. In addition, it is possible to become sexually aroused or excited by individuals with whom one is not in love. Consequently, although sexual activity and sexual excitement may be associated with passionate love, these sexual phenomena are not essential features of the passionate love experience. Another aspect of sexuality, sexual desire (also called sexual attraction), does, however, appear to be a necessary condition for passionate love. Indeed, the notion that sexual desire is a distinguishing feature of passionate love is a common theme running through love discourse in such diverse disciplines as sexual pathology and medicine (e.g., H. Ellis, 1897–1928/1901–1928, 1933/1963; Krafft-Ebing, 1886/1945), psychiatry and psychoanalysis (e.g., A. Ellis, 1954; Freud, 1908/1963, 1912/1963; Reik, 1945), existential philosophy (e.g., Fromm, 1956), and theology (e.g., Lewis, 1960/1988). In addition, contemporary social psychological discourse on love suggests that the experience of passionate love is strongly associated with sexual desire (see, e.g., Regan & Berscheid, 2000).

A growing body of empirical evidence now supports these theoretical statements. Berscheid and colleagues, for example, argue that the experience of "love" is fundamentally different from the experience of "being in love," and they present evidence that passionate love (the state of "being in love") is characterized by a greater amount of sexual attraction than is "love." For example, Ridge and Berscheid (1989) asked a sample of undergraduate men and women whether they believed there was a difference between the experience of being in love with and that of loving another person; fully 87% emphatically claimed that there was a difference between the two experiences. In addition, when asked to specify the nature of that difference in an open-ended response format, participants were more likely to cite sexual attraction (i.e., sexual desire) as descriptive of the "in love" experience.

More recently, using what they term a "social categorical method," Berscheid and Meyers (1996) asked a large sample of undergraduate men and women to list the initials of all the people they currently loved, the initials of all those with whom they were currently in love, and the initials of all those toward whom they currently felt sexual attraction/desire. For each individual respondent, the authors calculated the probability that persons named in the "sexually desire" category were also named in the "in love" and "love" categories. These sets of probabilities then were averaged across respondents. The results indicated that

85% of the persons listed in the "in love" category were also listed in the "sexually desire" category, whereas only 2% of those listed in the "love" category (and not cross-listed in the "in love" category) were listed in the "sexually desire" category. Thus, the objects of respondents' feelings of passionate love (but not their feelings of love) also tended to be the objects of their desire.

Research conducted by Regan and her colleagues also provides evidence that passionate love is a qualitatively different experience from such other varieties of interpersonal attraction as loving and liking, and that sexual desire in particular is one of its essential components. For example, Regan, Kocan, et al. (1998) conducted a prototype study to investigate how people conceptualize the state of being in love. As discussed earlier, the prototype approach (e.g., Rosch, 1975, 1978) is a standard social cognition paradigm used to investigate how people organize or represent a concept, such as passionate love, in their cognitive systems, and it allows researchers to determine the central (highly distinguishing or essential) and peripheral (less distinguishing or essential) features of a concept. These researchers asked 120 undergraduate men and women to list in a free-response format all of the features they considered to be characteristic or prototypical of the state of passionate love ("being in love"). Out of 119 features spontaneously generated by the participants, sexual desire received the second-highest frequency rating (65.8%). In other words, when thinking of passionate love, two-thirds of the participants automatically thought of sexual desire. In addition, this feature was viewed as more important to the passionate love concept than kissing (cited by only 10% of participants), touching/holding (cited by 17.5%), and sexual activity (cited by 25%). These results certainly support the notion that sexual desire is more essential to the passionate love experience than behavioral sexual events, at least in the minds of young adults.

Two recent person-perception experiments provide additional support for these prototype results. Person-perception experiments are commonly used in social psychological research and essentially involve manipulating people's perceptions of a relationship and then measuring the impact of that manipulation on their subsequent evaluations and beliefs. In the first experiment, Regan (1998a) provided a sample of 60 undergraduate men and women with two self-report questionnaires ostensibly completed by "Rob" and "Nancy," a student couple enrolled at the same university. The members of this couple reported experiencing no sexual desire for each other or a high amount of sexual desire for each other, and were currently engaging in sexual activity with each other or were not sexually active. Participants then estimated the likelihood that the partners experienced passionate love as well as a variety of other relationship events. The results indicated that both men and women believed that dating partners who experience sexual desire for each other are more likely to be passionately in love with each other (as well as more likely to experience a variety of other relationship events) than dating partners who do not desire each other sexually, regardless of their current level of sexual activity.

A second experiment, a conceptual replication of the first, confirmed these results (Regan, 1998a). Here, 48 men and women received information about the members of a heterosexual dating "student couple" who ostensibly reported that they were currently passionately in love with each other, that they loved each other, or that they liked each other. Participants then estimated the likelihood that the members of the couple experienced sexual desire for each other and the amount of desire that they felt for each other. Analyses revealed that participants perceived couples who are passionately in love as more *likely* to experience sexual desire than couples who love each other or who like each other. Similarly, couples who are passionately in love were believed to experience a greater *amount* of sexual desire for each other than couples who love each other or who like each other. Interestingly, sexual desire was believed to be no more likely in a "loving" relationship than in a "liking" relationship, and greater amounts of sexual desire were not believed to occur in loving relationships than in liking relationships. Again, it seems that sexual desire is viewed, at least by young men and women, as an important feature or component of passionate love relationships—and not of relationships characterized by feelings of loving (i.e., companionate love) and/or liking (i.e., friendship).

Research with actual dating couples, although sparse, also suggests that sexual desire and passionate love share a unique connection. For example, Regan (in press) found that the self-reported amount of sexual desire experienced by men and women for their dating partners was significantly positively correlated with the level of passionate love they felt for those individuals. Their feelings of desire were unrelated, however, to the amount of companionate love and liking they experienced for their partners.

In sum, passionate love is a sexualized experience that is strongly associated with feelings of sexual desire or attraction for the partner, that tends to result in the occurrence of sexual activity, and that appears to be linked with sexual arousal and excitement.

LOVE RELATIONSHIPS

The emotional responses that we have toward another individual, whether passionate or companionate, can propel us into initiating, entering, and maintaining a relationship with that person. This section examines general theoretical approaches to love relationships, as well as current empirical research on partner selection (i.e., what characteristics do men and women seek in their potential partners?), partner attraction and retention (i.e., how do people gain and keep the attention of a partner?), and partner choice (i.e., what types of partner do men and women actually obtain?).

THEORETICAL APPROACHES TO LOVE RELATIONSHIPS

There are a number of theoretical frameworks that have been developed to explain the dynamics of love relationships. The first broad class of approaches, subsumed under the rubric of *social context* frameworks, focuses on proximal mechanisms—that is, forces located in the contemporary social, cultural, and historical milieu—that may influence partner preferences, attraction strategies, choices, and relationship outcomes. Social exchange or equity models of relationship development and maintenance represent one such framework (e.g., Blau, 1964; Hatfield, Traupmann, Sprecher, Utne, & Hay, 1985; Murstein, 1970, 1976; Walster, Walster, & Berscheid, 1978; for a recent review of social exchange models relevant to sexuality and relationships, see Sprecher, 1998). According to these models, the process of partner selection and relationship formation resembles a "stock market" (Cameron, Oskamp, & Sparks, 1977) in which men and women players attempt to maximize their rewards and make social interaction as profitable as possible by exchanging their own assets—beauty, health, intelligence, a sense of humor, kindness, wealth, status, and so on—for desirable attributes in a partner. Essentially, an individual's own value as a potential partner represents his or her bargaining power and thus is presumed to influence the extent to which he or she is able to purchase a high-value partner. Assuming that we all seek the best possible value in a potential mate, high-value individuals (those with high amounts of desired characteristics and thus a great deal of purchasing power) will pair with others of equally high value, and lower-value or "poorer" persons inevitably will form liaisons with lower-value, or less expensive, others. In other words, this process is presumed to result in the pairing of individuals of roughly equal value (Murstein, 1970). Mistakes are costly. For example, in his 1970 discussion of the early stages of marital choice, Murstein notes that although an individual may run less risk of rejection if he or she seeks a less desirable partner (low cost), the rewards of such a conquest are correspondingly low (low profit); at the same time, the increased likelihood of rejection (high cost) associated with seeking a partner who is substantially more desirable than oneself (high profit) renders this enterprise equally risky. Consequently, an accurate perception of one's own qualities and what one has to contribute or offer to a relationship is extremely important.

Other social context theories focus on sex differences in (heterosexual) love relationships. For example, social role theorists (e.g., Eagly, 1987; Eagly & Karau, 1991) posit that people develop expectations for their own and others' behavior based on their beliefs about sex-appropriate behavior and attributes. Such beliefs and expectations are assumed to arise from the distribution of men and women into different social roles in natural settings; specifically, the sexes are believed to possess attributes suited for the roles each typically occupies (for men, these roles continue to be primarily occupational and economic; for women, these roles are traditionally domestic). Consequently, sex differences in interpersonal, romantic, and/or sexual behavior are caused in part by the tendency of people to behave in a manner consistent with their sex roles. To the extent that people prefer others to behave in accordance with existing sex-role stereotypes, traditionally "male" characteristics and attributes (e.g., have a high-paying job, display assertiveness and aggression) may be valued more by women than by men when considering and selecting a potential partner, and traditionally "female" characteristics and attributes (e.g., be nurturant and emotionally expressive) may be valued more by men than by women.

Other social forces undoubtedly also act to shape men's and women's interpersonal behavior. Recall that women tend to associate sexual activity with love more than do men (i.e., women are less permissive with respect to uncommitted sexual activity, generally require love as a prerequisite for sexual activity, and often abstain from sexual activity in the absence of a committed, loving relationship). This robust sex difference may originate from sex-specific social and cultural scripts and differential learning histories and patterns of reinforcement and punishment. Oliver and Hyde (1993), for example, discuss Mischel's (1966) application of social learning theory to sex differences in sexual and romantic behavior. According to this perspective, men generally receive more positive reinforcement than do women for seeking out and engaging in sexual activity, whereas women generally receive more reinforcement for confining their sexual activity to committed, love-based relationships (also see Hogben & Byrne, 1998). Similarly, script theorists point to sociocultural norms and expectations that teach that sexual experience is an important aspect of masculinity but not femininity, and that men should seek short-term sexual liaisons, whereas women should limit their sexual activities to socially sanctioned, long-term relationships (e.g., Gagnon & Simon, 1973; Reiss, 1967, 1981, 1986a, 1986b; Simon, 1974; Simon & Gagnon, 1986). The different patterns of reinforcement and punishment that men and women receive for their sexual and romantic behavior, coupled with the existence of normative beliefs about male and female sexuality, may encourage men to have relatively more permissive standards with respect to sexual activity in romantic relationships. Those same social forces encourage women to adopt less permissive standards and to seek partners who will demonstrate commitment and a desire for a long-term union.

A second broad class of theoretical approaches to love relationships focuses on distal rather than on contemporary mechanisms. *Evolutionary models* are based on the principles of natural selection originally articulated by Darwin (1859, 1871). These models consider the ways sexual and romantic behavior might be affected by evolved psychological heuristics that were selected because they overcame obstacles to reproduction located in the human ancestral past and therefore maximized gene replication and reproductive success. Several factors are posited to affect partner preferences, choices, and relationship outcomes, including the potential partner's physical or genetic fitness; his or her emotional fitness or willingness to invest in the reproductive partner, the reproductive relationship, and resulting offspring; and paternity certainty, or the estimated likelihood that offspring produced with a particular partner are indeed one's own (e.g., Buss & Kenrick, 1998; Cunningham, Druen, & Barbee, 1997; Gangestad & Simpson, 1990; Kenrick, 1994; Trivers, 1972).

Parental investment-based evolutionary models, like the majority of social context frameworks, posit sex differences in romantic and sexual behavior. For example, Kenrick and colleagues' (Kenrick, Groth, Trost, & Sadalla, 1993; Kenrick, Sadalla, Groth, & Trost, 1990) qualified parental investment theory suggests that women, who invest more direct physiological resources in their offspring than do men (e.g., contributing body nutrients during pregnancy and lactation), will be more sensitive to resource limitations and thus particularly attentive to a potential partner's social status, which is presumably related to his ability to provide resources in the form of food, material possessions, and physical protection. Men, on the other hand, are assumed to be constrained by access to women who can produce viable offspring and thus should be relatively more sensitive than women to characteristics that reflect reproductive capacity (e.g., health and its presumed observable index, physical attractiveness, and youth).

Other evolutionary perspectives, most notably attachment-based models, recognize that our biological design, which is rooted in our hunter-gatherer roots, favors the formation of enduring relationships and few sex differences in interpersonal behavior. For example, the life span strategies theory proposed by Cunningham and colleagues (e.g., Cunningham et al., 1997; Rowatt et al., 1997) relies on principles of attachment (Bowlby, 1973) to explain partner preferences and behavior in love relationships. Noting that human offspring are characterized by a period of dependency that extends well beyond infancy, this perspective argues that successful pairbonding and childrearing depend for *both* sexes on the ability to select an ideal attachment figure: a mate who can and will provide sustained social and emotional support. Consequently, both men and women are presumed to be particularly desirous of partners who possess prosocial personality characteristics and interpersonal attributes. (For additional discussion of the pair bond maintenance function of the attachment system, see Kirkpatrick, 1998; Miller and Fishkin, 1997; and Zeifman and Hazan, 1997.)

The preferences, choices, and behaviors that men and women demonstrate as they enter, maintain, and terminate love relationships undoubtedly are influenced by both contemporary and distal mechanisms. As will become evident from the following discussion, each of the aforementioned theories and perspectives sheds some light on human love relationships.

Partner Preferences: What Do Men and Women Seek in Their Potential Partners?

Scholars from a variety of disciplines have become interested in examining the traits men and women desire in romantic partners, in part because such preferences have implications for people's behavior and their interpersonal relationships. For example, men and women may actively attempt to initiate relationships with those individuals who possess certain desirable attributes or characteristics, and avoid or terminate relationships with individuals who do not meet or who no longer meet these selection criteria.

Researchers in this area generally explore the perceived desirability of various personality traits or other individual attributes in a potential partner. Some researchers use a ranking procedure in which participants order features in terms of their importance or desirability (e.g., Buss & Barnes, 1986; Regan & Berscheid, 1997; Sprecher, Regan, McKinney, Maxwell, & Wazienski, 1997). Others utilize a rating procedure in which participants evaluate the importance or desirability of features with Likert-type scales (e.g., Wiederman & Allgeier, 1992), or a percentile ranking procedure in which participants indicate how much of a particular characteristic they would like a potential partner to possess relative to other same-sex peers (e.g., "I would like my potential dating partner to score above 75% of all other same-age men/women on intelligence"; Kenrick et al., 1990, 1993; Regan, 1998b, 1998d). Still other researchers employ content analyses of personal ads in an attempt to delineate the dynamics of partner preference and mate selection (e.g., Cameron et al., 1977; S. Davis, 1990; Deaux & Hanna, 1984; Kenrick, Keefe, Bryan, Barr, & Brown, 1995; Smith, Waldorf, & Trembath, 1990).

Numerous studies reveal a robust preference pattern such that men and women overwhelmingly prefer intelligent, honest, and emotionally stable partners who are attractive and who possess a "good" or "exciting" personality (e.g., Buss & Barnes, 1986; Howard, Blumstein, & Schwartz, 1987; Regan & Berscheid, 1997; Sprecher, Sullivan, & Hatfield, 1994; Sprecher et al., 1997). For example, in one early study, R. Hill (1945) asked a sample of college students to rank order a list of 18 characteristics in terms of their importance in a dating partner. The most important attributes, according to his participants, were "dependable character," "emotional stability," "pleasing disposition," and "mutual attraction." Other researchers have since replicated these results using the same list of features (e.g., Hudson & Henze, 1969; McGinnis, 1959). More recently, Regan, Levin, Sprecher, Cate, and Christopher (1998) asked 561 undergraduates to rate the importance of a series of characteristics in choosing a potential long-term, romantic partner. Their results revealed that, for both sexes, the most important constellation of features centered around the potential partner's personality. Specifically, men and women preferred that a potential partner possess high amounts of expressiveness, openness, humor, friendliness, and sociability. In addition, participants sought a partner who was sexually desirable (i.e., who was physically attractive, sexy, and athletic) and who demonstrated socially appealing traits (e.g., warmth, kindness, intelligence, ambition).

In addition to exploring what people seek in potential partners, some researchers have begun to examine the attributes that people seek to *avoid* when selecting a date or mate. For example, Cunningham, Barbee, and Druen (1996; also see Rowatt et al., 1997) argue that the extended time commitment involved in human reproduction requires that individuals evaluate their partners not only in terms of the positive qualities they offer but also in terms of whether their negative qualities can be endured. Research on these undesirable partner attributes, deemed "social allergens" by Cunningham and his colleagues, indicates that men and women are repulsed by individuals who consistently violate social norms (e.g., overconsume alcohol, gamble often, smoke, lie to and gossip about others, arrive late, are often angry). In addition, they seek to avoid partners who display bad habits (e.g., have poor table manners, a gullible or cynical personality, a loud speaking voice, and a shrill laugh, and who violate personal space rules) or who appear to be highly oversexed (e.g., look longingly at members of the opposite sex, brag about sexual prowess, talk often about past relational partners, have had many previous romantic partners).

In general, men and women have highly similar preferences with respect to their long-term, romantic partners. As noted above, these preferences tend to center around such internal, prosocial characteristics as honesty, intelligence, a dependable character, and an emotionally stable personality. In addition, these preferences are remarkably stable over time, with some exceptions that can be explained by the changing social roles of the sexes. For example, chastity or sexual inexperience has declined in importance, perhaps due to increased sexual freedom for both sexes (e.g., Sprecher et al., 1997). There are only two attribute categories on which men and women demonstrate consistent differences; namely, physical appearance attributes and social status characteristics. Specifically, when considering a potential date or marriage partner, men tend to emphasize physical attractiveness more than women, and women tend to emphasize social or economic position more than men (e.g., Buss & Barnes, 1986; Goodwin, 1990; Greenlees & McGrew, 1994; Harrison & Saeed, 1977; Howard et al., 1987; Regan & Berscheid, 1997; Sprecher et al., 1994; Wiederman & Allgeier, 1992; for reviews, see Feingold, 1990, 1992). For example, Sprecher and her colleagues (1994) asked a large national sample of men and women to indicate how willing they would be to marry someone who possessed a variety of characteristics. They found that men were significantly less willing than women to marry someone who was "not good looking," whereas women were significantly less willing than men to marry a partner who was "not likely to hold a steady job" and who "would earn less than you." It also should be noted, however, that neither sex was highly willing to marry individuals with these attributes. Thus, these results should not be interpreted as indicating that attractiveness is *un*important to women or that social status does *not* matter to men when considering a potential partner. To the contrary, women as well as men prefer physically attractive partners, and men as well as women tend to prefer mates who are at least equal to their own current or estimated social status (Regan, 1998b, 1998d). In sum, appearance and status are important, albeit differentially so, to both sexes.

Other variables appear to be more strongly associated than is sex or gender with partner preferences. A team of researchers led by Buss (1989) surveyed over 10,000 men and women representing 32 countries about their preferences in a marital partner. Their results revealed robust cross-cultural differences. For example, the characteristic "chastity" was highly valued in Asian cultures, including Taiwan, China, Indonesia, and India, and more so than in any other cultures. In Western European cultures (e.g., France, Sweden, Norway, West Germany), chastity was considered irrelevant (indeed, a few respondents even jotted down in the margins of their questionnaires that it was *un*desirable in a romantic partner). The second largest cultural difference was found on items related to domestic skills and domesticity, that is, "good housekeeper" and "desire for home and children." These particular attributes were most highly desired in African and South American samples. Samples of individuals who placed low value on these characteristics included North America (i.e., United States and Canada), and the majority of Western European countries. In addition to these cross-cultural differences, some researchers using multicultural samples (i.e., ethnically diverse samples drawn from within one country) found that preferences differ as a function of ethnicity. Sprecher et al.'s (1994) study revealed that Caucasian women report significantly less willingness than African American women to marry a man who lacks a steady job, whereas African American women are less willing to marry a man who is not good-looking (also see Sparrow, 1991).

Other individual difference variables also are related to partner preferences. For example, Hester and Rudolph (1994) report that individuals with an extroverted personality type (i.e., E types) place more importance on a potential partner's "exciting personality" than do introverted (I) types. In addition, although the preference patterns of homosexual men and women generally resemble those of their heterosexual counterparts (e.g., J. Bailey, Gaulin, Agyei, & Gladue, 1994; Kenrick et al., 1995; Laner, 1977; Lee, 1976), Howard et al. (1987) found that male homosexuals and lesbians preferred more than heterosexuals a romantic partner who was expressive (i.e., affectionate, compassionate, expresses feelings, romantic).

Current Research Directions

This examination of partner preferences would be incomplete without mentioning several new research directions. First, many researchers now recognize that mating relationships may range from the extremely short term and explicitly sexual (e.g., one-night stands, flings) to the long term and romantically committed (e.g., steady dating, cohabiting, marriage), and that preferences for each type of relationship may be fundamentally different (e.g., Buss & Schmitt, 1993; Kenrick et al., 1990, 1993; Regan & Berscheid, 1997). For example, a growing body of research suggests that casual sex partners are primarily selected on the basis of external, physical attributes (e.g., Regan & Berscheid, 1995, 1997; Regan & Dreyer, 1999), whereas long-term romantic partners are evaluated mostly in terms of their ability to provide emotional warmth and to create and sustain positive social interaction (e.g., Regan, 1998d; Regan, Levin, et al., 1998).

Second, there is increasing recognition that people do not rigidly adhere to their ideal preferences, but instead commonly take into account the constraints placed on their desired choices by such variables as their own characteristics and attributes, their relative freedom to pursue a partner, and the quality and quantity of available partners in the surrounding field, and consequently alter or compromise their ideal preferences. A creative field study conducted by Pennebaker and colleagues (1979) provides evidence that partner preferences are, in fact, somewhat malleable. At three preselected times—9:00 P.M., 10:30 P.M., and midnight (half an hour before closing)—these researchers entered various drinking establishments near a college campus and asked randomly selected men and women to evaluate the attractiveness of the opposite- and same-sex individuals present at that time. Their results indicated that, as closing time neared and the period remaining to select, approach, and secure a partner decreased, the perceived attractiveness of opposite-sex (but not same-sex) bar patrons increased significantly. Assuming that those individuals actually did not alter their appearance over the course of the evening, this study certainly suggests that the criteria that men and women employ when choosing a partner are not set in stone and that people can and do modify their standards as a function of various selection pressures (e.g., decision time).

Indeed, a growing body of empirical work indicates that individuals may distinguish between the quality and/or quantity of characteristics that they ideally desire and those with which they would be satisfied in a potential partner. Some researchers have explored *minimum* selection standards, or the lowest amount of various attributes that people find acceptable in potential partners. For example, Kenrick et al. (1993) and, more recently, Regan (1998b) asked young adults to report their lowest levels of acceptability (in the form of percentile scores) for a variety of partner characteristics at different levels of relationship involvement. The results of both studies revealed that men and women generally expressed higher minimum standards as the relationship context shifted from short term (casual sex) to long term (romantic). In addition, women were more selective than men, particularly when considering a partner for casual sexual relations.

Other researchers have examined compromise in the form of the *relative importance* that individuals place on particular partner attributes. Cunningham and colleagues (e.g., Cunningham, Barbee, & Pike, 1990; Cunningham et al., 1997) have conducted several studies exploring the "trade-offs" that men and women make when faced with a choice between partners who possess different constellations of positive characteristics. They reported, for example, that both men and women selected individuals who combined physical attractiveness with a pleasing personality over those who possessed the mix of physical attractiveness and wealth or the combination of a pleasing personality and wealth. Similarly, a recent series of studies by Jensen-Campbell, Graziano, and West (1995) revealed that the impact of dominant (proactive, agentic) behavior on a man's perceived dating desirability was moderated by

his level of agreeableness. Specifically, women participants preferred dominant men, but only if they also demonstrated high levels of agreeable, prosocial
behavior.

In sum, men and women distinguish among different types of partner, and
they also appear willing to modify their ideal preferences by establishing minimum standards for various attributes and by selectively choosing one characteristic or combination of characteristics over others.

PARTNER ATTRACTION AND RETENTION: HOW DO MEN AND WOMEN ATTRACT AND KEEP THEIR PARTNERS?

In addition to exploring the characteristics that individuals prefer in their potential partners, a number of researchers have investigated the behaviors and
events that people enact to attract and retain a long-term partner (e.g., Buss,
1988a; Buss & Dedden, 1990; Cashdan, 1993; Hirsch & Paul, 1996; Schmitt &
Buss, 1996; Walters & Crawford, 1994). One of the first studies to investigate
this topic was published by Buss in 1988 (1988a). He provided 107 newlywed
couples with a list of 101 acts or behaviors, and asked them to indicate how
often they had engaged in each one when they first met their spouse and while
they were dating their spouse. Both sexes tended to flirt, "act nice," demonstrate a sense of humor, touch the other person, and maintain good grooming
when trying to attract a partner. In addition, men more than women displayed
and boasted about their resources (e.g., "drove an expensive car," "flashed a
lot of money," "bragged about his accomplishments," "bought an expensive
stereo") and athleticism (e.g., "lifted weights," "talked about how good he was
at sports," "flexed his muscles," "acted like he was interested in sports").
Women more than men emphasized their appearance, engaging in such tactics
as wearing makeup, jewelry, perfume, and fashionable clothing, dieting, tan-
ning, and styling their hair. Buss then gave a list of these same behaviors to a
sample of undergraduates and asked them to rate how *effective* they would be
at attracting long-term partners for men and for women. In accord with the
earlier sex differences, he found that acts involving resource display were
viewed as more effective for men than for women in attracting a mate. Similarly, acts involving enhancing physical appearance were viewed as more effective for women than for men. However, Buss concluded that, despite these clear
sex differences, there were even greater sex similarities in the mate attraction
acts performed by men and women. For example, the acts performed most frequently and considered most effective for both sexes involved displaying sympathy, kindness, good manners, helpfulness, and humor.

More recently, and using a procedure similar to that employed by Buss
(1988a), Walters and Crawford (1994) asked a sample of men and women to
nominate acts or behaviors that they had used to compete with other members of the same sex when attempting to attract a partner. A second set of participants then indicated how frequently they themselves had engaged in the

nominated actions. The results revealed that men demonstrated athletic ability (e.g., "I arm wrestled other guys"), used risk in athletics (e.g., "I played sports that are fairly dangerous, such as hockey, football, or lacrosse"), demonstrated status (e.g., "I physically fought with another guy"), and displayed resources (e.g, "I spent money entertaining women") more frequently than did women. Conversely, women altered their appearance (e.g., "I dressed to make my breasts appear larger") and attracted attention to their appearance (e.g., "I wore makeup to something at which it is not usually worn, e.g., the beach, in order to look better than other women") more often than did men. As in the earlier Buss study, however, the sex similarities far outweighed the sex differences. Not only were there no sex differences on 18 out of 26 tactics, but the most frequently reported male *and* female tactics involved demonstrating domestic ability (e.g., cleaning house), acquiring athletic ability (working out), and emphasizing and displaying an attractive appearance.

Interestingly, the activities used by men and women to attract a partner and to compete with potential rivals for a partner's affections are highly similar to the behaviors performed by men and women when attempting to retain a current mate. In another study, Buss (1988c) asked undergraduate students to list and evaluate "the things that people do when they want to prevent their partner from getting involved with someone else" (p. 296). The most frequently performed acts by men involved complimenting the partner on her appearance; sitting next to her and touching or embracing her when other men are around; going out of the way to be kind, nice, and caring; being helpful and extremely affectionate; looking "nice" and dressing nicely to maintain her interest; acceding to her sexual requests; and purchasing gifts for her. Similarly, women reported most often complimenting the partner on his appearance; being nice, kind, affectionate, helpful, and caring; dressing nicely and using makeup to appear attractive; sitting next to the partner and holding his hand or touching him when other women are around; and buying him small gifts. Violent acts and derogation behaviors (e.g., harming the potential rival, spreading rumors about the potential rival's reputation, hitting or slapping the partner) were rarely performed. As before, men more than women displayed resources (e.g., bought gifts, flowers, expensive dinners), and women more than men enhanced their appearance (e.g., used makeup, wore the latest fashions). In addition, men were more likely than women to report using tactics of partner concealment (e.g., refusing to introduce the partner to same-sex friends, removing the partner from gatherings where other men were present), submission (e.g, giving in to the partner's "every wish," changing to please the partner), violence against the rival (e.g., hitting, fighting with, slapping, or vandalizing the property of a man who made a pass at the partner), and threats against the rival (yelling at, staring coldly at, confronting, and threatening to hit a man who looked at the partner). Despite these differences, Buss notes that men and women generally utilize highly similar tactics and acts to retain their partners.

PARTNER CHOICE: WITH WHOM DO PEOPLE TYPICALLY PAIR?

In addition to studying people's preferences in long-term partners and the behaviors they use to attract and retain their mates, researchers also have examined actual mating choices. Much of this research focuses on identifying and comparing the mating systems (i.e., the norms that govern partner selection) that exist across cultures. A number of mating systems have been identified, including endogamy (i.e., inbreeding or the pairing of genetically related individuals); exogamy (i.e., outbreeding or the pairing of genetically unrelated relatives); polygyny (i.e., a mating system in which men pair with multiple women); polyandry (i.e., a system in which women pair with multiple men); and monogamy (i.e., a system in which two individuals pairbond). Despite the panoply of systems that may govern individuals' partner choices, some universals in human pairbonding appear to exist. For example, all known human societies practice marriage or some other form of socially sanctioned, long-term pairing between men and women (Daly & Wilson, 1983). Similarly, there is strong cross-cultural evidence for the universality of the experience of romantic or passionate love (Jankowiak & Fischer, 1992). In addition, some mating systems are more prevalent than others. Daly and Wilson (1983) examined pairbonding phenomena in 849 human societies. Their results indicated, for example, that polygyny is far more common than polyandry. Specifically, 708 cultures practiced the former, only 4 followed the latter, and the remaining 137 were monogamous.

The majority of Western cultures, like our own, practice monogamy, or the bonding of two individuals in a committed relationship. The most typical form of monogamous pairing that occurs is homogamy. Also called assortative mating or assortment, homogamy is defined as the pairing of similar individuals, that is, persons who resemble one another on one or more characteristics. With the exception of biological sex, such that men tend to prefer to mate with women and vice versa, individuals seem to assort along a large variety of dimensions. For example, reviews of the literature on assortment generally reveal positive correlations between marital partners on such characteristics as age, race, ethnicity, education level, socioeconomic status, religion, and physical attractiveness, as well as on a host of personality traits and cognitive abilities (e.g., Berscheid & Reis, 1998; Buss, 1985; Murstein, 1980). In other words, regardless of our preferences, we seem to ultimately pair with similar others.

LOVE GONE BAD: PROBLEMATIC ASPECTS
OF LOVE RELATIONSHIPS

Human interaction and personal relationships have the potential to provide us with extremely positive outcomes, including attachment and pairbonding, social support, love, happiness, satisfaction, and well-being. However, there is another side to close relationships, a destructive and dysfunctional side that only recently has come to receive systematic attention from relationship theorists and researchers (for discussion, see Spitzberg & Cupach, 1998). This section examines the "darker" aspects of love relationships.

UNREQUITED LOVE

For many individuals, passionate love is an overwhelmingly positive experience, characterized by trust, commitment, sharing, honesty, joy, and acceptance. However, passionate love—particularly when it is unrequited—has the potential to be just as strongly associated with negative affective states, including jealousy, depression, and anxiety. In one of the first studies to attempt to explore the dynamics of unrequited love, Baumeister, Wotman, and Stillwell (1993; also see Baumeister & Wotman, 1992) asked 71 unrequited lovers to write autobiographical accounts of their experiences as would-be suitors and rejectors. Their results indicate that unrequited love is a negative experience for both the rejector and the rejected lover. Specifically, although roughly one-fourth of the rejectors reported feeling flattered by the attentions of their potential lovers, the majority also viewed these unwanted advances as annoying, felt uncomfortable and guilty about delivering a rejection message, and experienced a range of negative emotions, including anger and resentment. Would-be lovers, on the other hand, reported feelings of longing for and preoccupation with the love object, fears of rejection, and lowered self-esteem.

Unrequited love thus can be, and frequently is, a highly negative experience for both the rejector and the would-be suitor, and, unfortunately, there is no easy panacea for recovering from romantic rejection. Individuals who find their passionate overtures rebuffed by the ones they love may need to restore and bolster their self-esteem by focusing on their good qualities and/or other positive relationships they currently have or have had in the past. Those who reject the romantic advances of another may need to engage in self-justification as a way of coming to terms with their feelings of guilt about causing pain to another individual.

OBSESSION

> At first I thought it was sort of cute and romantic that he wanted to be with me all the time. He would ask me to give him a detailed account of my day, all the places I went, the people I talked with, the things I did. When I would go to a friend's house or to visit my mom, he would call several times just to see if I was there. I felt flattered that I had a boyfriend who loved me so much. But then it got out of hand. I mean, he wouldn't even let me drive to the store by myself! Sometimes he would even stand really close to me and listen when I was on the phone. After we broke up, he began calling me at home, usually several times a night. He also started calling me at work, which made things difficult for me with my boss. So I stopped taking his calls at work and I changed to an unlisted number at home. I think what really made me realize that I needed to take some action and tell

people what was going on was when he started spying on me. One morning, I was standing by the window looking outside and I noticed his car. He was just sitting there, watching me. I have no idea how long he had been there, but it really scared me. I felt trapped and violated. (32-year-old woman interviewed by the author)

I met a woman I thought I liked. She was attractive, bright, seemed to have a good sense of humor and to be stable and well-grounded. We went out on a couple of dates and it turned out that we didn't have that much in common, so I didn't pursue the relationship. No big breakup or anything, we just weren't suited to each other. That should have been the end of it, but it wasn't. She lived about 10 miles from me, and she would drive over to my neighborhood, park in front of my house, and then go jogging around the block for what seemed like hours. I would see her as she passed my house again and again, every single day. She began to eat in the local restaurants I frequented. She called my house and left messages about getting together to "work things out." She was everywhere I went and she did her best to invade every single moment of my day. My friends laughed about it and made jokes about what a lucky guy I was to have this woman chasing after me, but believe me it wasn't funny. Fortunately, I relocated due to my job and I haven't seen her since. (46-year-old man interviewed by the author)

Many individuals experience unreciprocated passionate or romantic attachment. Although these unrequited love occurrences are for the most part unpleasant (see discussion above), the majority of people manage to negotiate them successfully. In some cases, however, these experiences produce or are associated with obsessive thinking, psychopathology, and even violent behavior (Meloy, 1989; Mintz, 1980). We turn now to the phenomenon of obsessive relational intrusion (ORI).

ORI is defined as "repeated and unwanted pursuit and invasion of one's sense of physical or symbolic privacy by another person, either stranger or acquaintance, who desires and/or presumes an intimate relationship" (Cupach & Spitzberg, 1998, pp. 234–235). Stalking may be viewed as an extreme form of ORI in which prior acquaintance between the victim and the pursuer is not necessary. Specifically, ORI is motivated by a desire on the part of the pursuer to form a relationship with the love object, whereas stalking may be motivated by a desire for intimacy (in which case, it is appropriately viewed as a manifestation of ORI), a desire to punish the target for a presumed transgression, or the fact that the target meets some previously established criteria for assault. Whatever the motivation behind these behavior patterns, survey data reveal that stalking and ORI are far more common than traditionally has been supposed. For example, a large national survey of 16,000 adults indicated that 8% of women and 2% of men have been stalked at some time in their lives (Tjaden & Thoennes, 1997). In addition, surveys using college student samples find that sizable numbers have experienced some form of ORI (e.g., F. Coleman, 1997; Fremouw, Westrup, & Pennypacker, 1997; Spitzberg & Cupach, 1996). Although most stalking victims are female and most stalkers are male (Tjaden &

Thoennes, 1997), men and women appear to be equally at risk for ORI victimization (Spitzberg & Cupach, 1996).

In sum, relatively high percentages of men and women receive unwanted attention from other individuals. This unwanted attention takes a variety of forms. For example, approximately 22% of the individuals who rejected the advances of others in Baumeister et al.'s (1993) unrequited love study reported that their would-be suitors engaged in such unscrupulous behaviors as lying about the nature of the relationship to other people and promising to go out as platonic friends but subsequently using the occasion for romantic overtures. Other individuals report receiving unwanted letters, notes, phone calls, visits, or gifts, or being followed or watched by a pursuer (e.g., Herold, Mantle, & Zemitis, 1979; Jason, Reichler, Easton, Neal, & Wilson, 1984; Roscoe, Strouse, & Goodwin, 1994). To date, the most exhaustive list of ORI behaviors was developed by Cupach and Spitzberg (1997; Spitzberg & Cupach, 1996). These researchers argue that ORI behaviors run the gamut from mildly intrusive, invasive, and threatening (e.g., receiving unwanted gifts, notes, or messages, being repeatedly asked for a date) to moderately intrusive, invasive, and threatening (e.g., reputational sabotage, watching or spying) to extremely intrusive, invasive, and threatening (e.g., home invasion, verbal threats, physical and/or sexual assault, property damage). Not surprisingly, the milder forms of ORI behavior are the most frequently experienced. For example, the majority of participants in their studies reported that their pursuer repeatedly called and argued with them (73%), asked them if they were seeing someone romantically (72%), called and hung up without speaking (70%), begged them for another chance (64%), watched or stared at them from a distance (62%), refused to take hints that he or she was not welcome (61%), made exaggerated claims about his or her affection (61%), gossiped or bragged about the relationship with others (61%), checked up on them via mutual acquaintances (58%), and constantly apologized for past transgressions or wrongs (57%). Less common but significantly more invasive and threatening behaviors included threatening physical harm (30%), following the target from place to place (27%), damaging the target's property or possessions (26%), exposing himself or herself to the target (26%), forcing the target to engage in sexual behavior (16%), taking photos without the target's knowledge or consent (11%), sending a multitude of e-mail messages (11%), recording conversations without the target's consent (8%), breaking into the target's home or apartment (8%), and sending offensive photographs (5%).

ORI can have a variety of consequences for the targeted individual. As illustrated by the work of Spitzberg, Cupach, and others (e.g., Meloy, 1996; Mullen & Pathé, 1994), violent behavior can occur and have a range of deleterious physical effects. In addition, victims of ORI often experience a panoply of psychological and emotional reactions, including fear, anxiety, hopelessness, paranoia, depression, self-blame, and aggression or hostility (e.g., Cupach &

Spitzberg, 1997; Hall, 1996; Herold et al., 1979; Mullen & Pathé, 1994; Spitzberg, Nicastro, & Cousins, 1998; Wallace & Silverman, 1996). Interpersonally, ORI targets may lose the ability to trust other people, and they may avoid and/or otherwise curtail their social and work-related activities.

One fundamental question for researchers in the areas of ORI and stalking concerns coping responses to victimization. What responses, for example, are most effective at minimizing or eliminating stalking or intrusive behavior? What strategies can victims use to reduce their risk of negative outcomes in these situations? Unfortunately, there is little systematic empirical work in this area. Some researchers have attempted to identify the constellation of responses typically made by individuals who have been harassed, stalked, or pursued by obsessive relational intruders. The results of these pioneering studies suggest that many targets simply ignore the situation or make no response at all. For example, based on their data, Baumeister et al. (1993) concluded that most people lack a clear script for responding to unwanted romantic attention. This "scriptlessness" produces feelings of confusion and self-blame on the part of the target and contributes to a passive avoidance of the would-be lover or the situation. In addition, they reported that those targets who actively rejected the lover often did so in ways that failed to effectively convey the rejection message (also see Burgoon et al., 1989; Jason et al., 1984). More recently, Spitzberg and Cupach (1996, 1998; also see Spitzberg et al., 1998) surveyed a group of young adults and identified five general coping categories: (1) direct interaction (e.g., have a serious talk with the person, yell at the person); (2) protection or formal coping (e.g., obtain a restraining order, call the police); (3) avoidance (e.g., ignore the pursuer, avoid eye contact with the person); (4) retaliation (e.g., hit the pursuer, ridicule the person); and (5) informal coping (e.g., obtain caller ID on the telephone, ask others for advice). Although the effectiveness of these types of responses is unknown to date, some professionals believe that statements and actions that directly and unequivocally convey rejection and/or disinterest (e.g., "I am not interested in dating you, my feelings about you will not change, and I know that you will respect my decision and direct your attention elsewhere") are most effective at managing unwanted attention (e.g., De Becker, 1998). Additional research clearly is needed to inform victims, clinicians, and law enforcement workers about the efficacy of various forms of intervention in cases of stalking and ORI.

MISMATCHED LOVE STYLES

What happens if you consider that your attraction to another person is typical of the love I call eros, but the partner's approach to love is not eros but some other kind such as ludus or storge? (Lee, 1973, p. 41)

When a lover whose preferred type of loving is storge becomes involved with a partner whose understanding of true love is some other type, difficulties naturally occur. (p. 80)

Unrequited passion and obsession are not the only potentially problematic outcomes or occurrences associated with loving another individual. There are several other ways in which love relationships can go awry. In particular, it is possible that an individual's style of loving may influence the quality and even the quantity (i.e., duration or length) of his or her romantic relationships. Certainly, each type of love style is associated with a degree of personal and interpersonal risk. For example, after interviewing a large sample of men and women, Lee (1973) concluded that some erotic lovers are prone to jealousy and possessiveness; that some ludic lovers may experience guilt at violating social and relational norms about love (e.g., romantic relationships should be monogamous, committed, and long-term); and that some storgic lovers may be perceived as unexciting and passionless by partners who do not share their friendship-based approach to love. Perhaps the most potentially destructive love style, however, is mania, the combination of eros and ludus. Called "demonic love" by Lee, mania is characterized by extreme jealousy, helpless obsession, and unhappiness. Although manic attachments may develop into a more mature and lasting love, this is unusual. It is no wonder, then, that men and women who adopt this approach to love often demonstrate lowered levels of self-esteem (C. Hendrick & Hendrick, 1986). The aftermath of manic love may enable people to realize the amount of emotion they are capable of experiencing for another individual, and thus may contribute to their personal growth. In general, however, manic love is unhealthy love.

In addition, as illustrated by the quotations cited above, the pattern of a couple's love style (i.e., whether they endorse the same style of loving or not) may influence relationship outcomes. Interestingly, only a few researchers have examined the role of love styles in ongoing romantic relationships. In general, and in accord with the research on assortative mating reviewed earlier, there is a tendency for individuals to pair with others who share the same love style (e.g., K. Davis & Latty-Mann, 1987; S. Hendrick, Hendrick, & Adler, 1988). In addition, some love styles are related to relationship satisfaction and longevity. For example, S. Hendrick and colleagues (1988) surveyed 57 dating couples on a variety of interpersonal measures. Their results indicated that an erotic love style predicted overall dyadic adjustment; that is, the more passionately men and women loved, the greater the level of satisfaction they felt in their relationships. Additional analyses revealed that women's scores on eros, agape, and ludus were related to their partners' self-reported satisfaction. Specifically, women who loved passionately or selflessly tended to have highly satisfied partners, whereas women who adopted a game-playing approach to love had less satisfied partners. Finally, the researchers recontacted a subsample of couples two months after the time of their initial participation and asked them about the status of their relationship. They found that couples who had terminated their relationship originally scored higher on ludus and lower on eros than couples who were still together. Game playing and lack of passionate involvement are not conducive to relationship longevity.

In sum, manic and ludic approaches to love may increase the likelihood of negative interpersonal outcomes. Future research on the impact of mismatched love styles (e.g., a manic lover paired with an erotic lover, a storgic lover paired with a ludic lover) on relationship adjustment is recommended.

PASSIONLESS PASSIONATE LOVE

> It's not that I don't desire him anymore, it's simply that I don't desire him *as much*. In a way, our relationship is stronger now, built more solidly on other, less sexual feelings. But there are times when I have to admit I become a bit nostalgic for the passion that we've lost. It used to be that I would glimpse him making a certain gesture, or hear his voice on the phone, or catch the scent of his cologne, and I would literally be infused with this feeling of desire, of need, of sheer *want*. And it was almost indescribable, a mingling of the physical and the emotional. But we've been together for a long time, and somehow, somewhere that feeling just faded. I love him deeply, maybe more than I ever did before, and I know that we'll grow old together, but it's not the same. (35-year-old homosexual man interviewed by the author)

As illustrated in the above quotation, passion frequently fades over time in love relationships. Research suggests that the longer a couple has been involved in their relationship, the less passionate love they will feel for each other (e.g., Sprecher & Regan, 1998). To some extent, we owe this occurrence to our biological design; our bodies simply are not equipped to sustain the intense emotional and physiological arousal associated with passion and desire.

Although many couples do experience a decline in the intensity of their feelings, they also may find that passion gradually merges with or is replaced by other, less intense but equally positive feelings (e.g., companionate love). Why, then, do so many couples interpret a decrease in passion as a serious relationship issue? This section examines whether loss of passion—more specifically, of sexual passion—represents a significant problem for love relationships.

Consider the following scenarios:

Scenario 1. Sonja and John engage in sexual intercourse seven or eight times a week. Each feels a high amount of sexual desire in general and for the partner, has sexual thoughts and daydreams several times during each day, and enjoys acting out sexual fantasies and trying new sexual techniques. Their sexual encounters typically result in mutual orgasm, and they both report feeling quite satisfied with the sexual aspects of their relationship.

Scenario 2. Chris and Cynthia have sex approximately once a month. Although they indicate feeling attracted to each other, they do not consider sex to be an essential or important aspect of their relationship. They are relatively uncomfortable with sexual displays of affection and prefer to express their feelings through shared activities and nonsexual forms of intimacy.

Scenario 3. Judy and Greg engage in sexual intercourse once a week. Judy experiences high amounts of sexual desire for Greg, openly expresses her feelings, and is typically the initiator of sexual contact. Greg is less interested in sexual intercourse, but generally accepts Judy's sexual invitations and enjoys the subsequent sexual interactions.

These couples differ in their levels of sexual desire, the frequency with which they engage in sexual activity, the openness of their communications about sex, and the amount of enjoyment they draw from their sexual encounters. Are any of these couples, by definition, in a "troubled" relationship? Prior to answering this question, there are a number of factors that must be considered.

Consideration #1: Sexual Variables Are Strongly Associated with Relationship Adjustment and Quality

Of all the aspects of sexuality that have received attention from theorists and researchers, sexual desire appears to be the most strongly associated with relational variables. For example, people often interpret a loss or absence of sexual desire as a sign that a couple has "fallen out of love" with each other and that their relationship is dysfunctional, abnormal, or in need of some form of professional intervention (e.g., Regan, 1998a). Indeed, as a growing number of couples enter therapy with the aim of increasing one partner's (or both partners') diminished sexual desire, it has become clear that the experience of sexual desire is intricately connected to the quality of the relationship. For example, "emotional conflict with partner" was cited as the most common cause of inhibited sexual desire among married men and women in a survey of 400 physicians (Pietropinto, 1986), and many clinicians now focus on the dynamics of the couple's relationship in seeking to understand and treat sexual desire disorders (e.g., Fish, Fish, & Sprenkle, 1984; Kaplan, 1979; Regas & Sprenkle, 1984; Talmadge & Talmadge, 1986; Trudel, 1991).

In addition, at least two studies provide empirical support for the hypothesis that sexual desire disorders signal the existence of other problems in a couple's relationship. Stuart, Hammond, and Pett (1987) administered a dyadic adjustment scale to 59 married women who were diagnosed with inhibited sexual desire (ISD) and to 31 married women who reported normal sexual desire. The women in the ISD group scored significantly lower in marital adjustment than did women in the non-ISD group, and the spouses of women in the ISD group also reported significantly lower overall satisfactory adjustment in their marriage and lower levels of affection than the spouses of non-ISD women. Stuart and colleagues also asked respondents to rate their subjective feelings about the quality of their relationship with their spouse. ISD women were significantly less satisfied with the way interpersonal conflict was resolved and with their own and their spouse's listening ability, and they reported experiencing significantly lower levels of emotional closeness, romantic feelings, and love toward their spouse.

A longitudinal study conducted by Hallstrom and Samuelsson (1990) also suggests that relationship properties may affect the experience of sexual desire. On two occasions six years apart, the authors interviewed 497 women who were married or cohabiting with a male partner. Women were asked about the present degree of their sexual desire (i.e., whether they perceived it as strong, moderate, weak, or absent), and to report whether they received insufficient emotional support from their spouse (yes/no) and lacked a confiding relationship with him (yes/no). Although causality cannot be determined from this correlational design, a *decrease* in self-reported sexual desire over time was predicted by a perceived lack of a confiding relationship with and insufficient support from the spouse at the first interview.

Other sexual variables also appear to be linked with the quality of a couple's relationship. Several researchers have documented the association between relationship satisfaction and sexual satisfaction in a wide variety of couple types, including married and cohabiting heterosexual partners, and cohabiting homosexual male (gay) and female (lesbian) couples (e.g., Greeley, 1991; Hatfield, Greenberger, Traupman, & Lambert, 1982; Hunt, 1974; Kurdek, 1991; Schenk, Pfrang, & Rausche, 1983). A similar correlation has been found between relationship satisfaction and the frequency with which a couple has sexual intercourse (e.g., Donnelly, 1993). For example, people who feel that their marriage is fair and equitable are more satisfied with their sex life and report having sex more often than those who feel that their relationship is inequitable (Hatfield et al., 1982). Couples who enjoy spending time together and who share social activities and hobbies also have sex with greater frequency than couples who share few outside activities (e.g., Blumstein & Schwartz, 1983). Conversely, relationships filled with conflict and those in which one or both partners have threatened to leave are characterized by low frequency of sexual intercourse (e.g., Donnelly, 1993; Edwards & Booth, 1976).

Insofar as sexual desire, sexual satisfaction, and frequency of intercourse are associated with satisfaction, closeness, and other significant relational events, it is important to recognize that a sudden or prolonged absence or change in the experience of these sexual variables may signal the existence of some degree of interpersonal difficulty. In sum, a couple's relationship in the bedroom often is related to their relationship outside of the bedroom.

Consideration #2: Sexual Desire, Activity, and Satisfaction Are
Associated with Numerous Nonrelational Variables

It is equally important to recognize, however, that a variety of factors may influence the experience of sexual desire, the occurrence of sexual intercourse, and the level of sexual satisfaction, many of them having little to do with the partner or the relationship. For example, some women experience regular fluctuations in sexual desire that correspond to the hormonal phases of the menstrual cycle (for review, see Regan, 1996). Other factors that reliably are associated with decreased or absent sexual desire include poor physical health, older age, drug use, depressed mood, and negative emotional states (e.g., anger, hostility, anxiety, stress; for a review of this literature, see Regan & Berscheid, 2000). Similarly, the intensity and frequency of sexual desire will fluctuate over an individual's life span and during the course of a given relationship (e.g., Kaplan, 1979; Levine, 1984, 1987; Regan & Berscheid, 1999). For example, the level of sexual desire experienced by adults may fluctuate along a spectrum of values ranging from "driven" to "avoidant" (Levine, 1984), and people also differ in the chronic amount of sexual desire they experience (Kaplan, 1979).

Like sexual desire, the frequency with which couples engage in sex is affected by a variety of nonrelational factors, including age, physical disability, and illness (e.g., Blumstein & Schwartz, 1983). There are also certain times over the life span when sexual frequency may decline due to lack of time and opportunity (for additional discussion, see Regan & Sprecher, 1995). For instance, involvement in other roles (e.g., demanding jobs and parenthood) is associated with decreased sexual activity (Greenblat, 1983). In addition, different types of partners have sex more or less frequently than others. In general, gay male couples and heterosexual cohabiting couples tend to have intercourse more frequently than married couples (e.g., Blumstein & Schwartz, 1983; Call, Sprecher, & Schwartz, 1992; Michael et al., 1994). Lesbian couples, on the other hand, have sex less frequently than all other couple types, although they engage in more nongenital physical contact (e.g., cuddling, hugging).

Thus, changes in sexual desire, frequency, and satisfaction commonly occur over the course of any given relationship, are associated with many nonrelational events, and do not necessarily reflect a change in overall relationship function or quality.

Consideration #3: The Decline of Passion May Signal the Rise of Other, Equally Positive Feelings

Third, a general loss of passion (or of desire) may not indicate a problem in the relationship or an irrevocable loss of love for the partner, but rather may signal the development of a second, more durable type of love; namely, companionate love (e.g., S. Coleman, 1977; Safilios-Rothschild, 1977; Sternberg, 1988b). This love, similar to Lee's concept of storge, is built on a solid foundation of warmth, friendship, respect, and interpersonal trust, and frequently is seen in long-term married or cohabiting couples (e.g., Hatfield & Rapson, 1993).

Conclusions

Declines in the more passionate aspects of a love relationship do not necessarily spell tragedy for a couple or foreshadow the end of their union. There is no "right" amount of desire and activity that characterizes love relationships; rather, couples must judge for themselves what is "normal" with respect to sexuality and passion. Thus, each of the three couples in the scenarios depicted above would be considered functional—if the members are satisfied with the role sexuality plays in their relationship. It is only when one or both partners disagree about or are troubled by some aspect of their sexual life (e.g., mismatched levels of sexual desire, poor sexual communication, lack of sexual enjoyment) that professional intervention may be helpful.

CONCLUSION

The love relationships that men and women form over the course of their lifetime with romantic partners have significant individual, interpersonal, and societal consequences. Understanding the types of love that exist, the ways to assess these various love types, the association between love and sexuality, and the dynamics of mate selection and partner choice can enable clinicians, researchers, and laypersons to alleviate the problems and difficulties that often arise in these important relationships.

REFERENCES

Aron, A., & Aron, E.N. (1991). Love and sexuality. In K. McKinney & S. Sprecher (Eds.), *Sexuality in close relationships* (pp. 25–48). Hillsdale, NJ: Erlbaum.

Aron, A., & Westbay, L. (1996). Dimensions of the prototype of love. *Journal of Personality and Social Psychology, 70,* 535–551.

Bailey, J.M., Gaulin, S., Agyei, Y., & Gladue, B.A. (1994). Effects of gender and sexual orientation on evolutionarily relevant aspects of human mating psychology. *Journal of Personality and Social Psychology, 66,* 1081–1093.

Bailey, W., Hendrick, C., & Hendrick, S.S. (1987). Relation of sex and gender role to love, sexual attitudes, and self-esteem. *Sex Roles, 16,* 637–648.

Baumeister, R.F., & Wotman, S.R. (1992). *Breaking hearts: The two sides of unrequited love.* New York: Guilford Press.

Baumeister, R.F., Wotman, S.R., & Stillwell, A.M. (1993). Unrequited love: On heartbreak, anger, guilt, scriptlessness, and humiliation. *Journal of Personality and Social Psychology, 64,* 377–394.

Berscheid, E. (1983). Emotion. In H.H. Kelley, E. Berscheid, A. Christensen, J.H. Harvey, G. Levinger, E. McClintock, L.A. Peplau, & D.R. Peterson (Eds.), *Close relationships* (pp. 110–168). New York: Freeman.

Berscheid, E. (1985). Interpersonal attraction. In G. Lindzey & E. Aronson (Eds.), *The handbook of social psychology* (3rd ed., Vol. 2, pp. 413–484). New York: Random House.

Berscheid, E. (1988). Some comments on love's anatomy: Or, whatever happened to old-fashioned lust? In R.J. Sternberg & M.L. Barnes (Eds.), *The psychology of love* (pp. 359–374). New Haven, CT: Yale University Press.

Berscheid, E., & Meyers, S.A. (1996). A social categorical approach to a question about love. *Personal Relationships, 3,* 19–43.

Berscheid, E., & Reis, H.T. (1998). Attraction and close relationships. In D.T. Gilbert, S.T. Fiske, & G. Lindzey (Eds.), *The handbook of social psychology* (4th ed., pp. 193–281). Boston: McGraw-Hill.

Berscheid, E., & Walster, E. (1974). A little bit about love. In T.L. Huston (Ed.), *Foundations of interpersonal attraction* (pp. 355–381). New York: Academic Press.

Blau, P.M. (1964). *Exchange and power in social life.* New York: Wiley.

Blumstein, P., & Schwartz, P. (1983). *American couples.* New York: Morrow.

Bowlby, J.C. (1973). *Attachment and loss: Vol. 2. Separation: Anxiety & anger.* London: Hogarth Press.

Burgess, E.W., & Wallin, P. (1953). *Engagement and marriage.* Philadelphia: Lippincott.

Burgoon, J.K., Parrott, R., LePoire, B.A., Kelley, D.L., Walther, J.B., & Parry, D. (1989). Maintaining and restoring privacy through communication in different types of relationships. *Journal of Social and Personal Relationships, 6,* 131–158.

Buss, D.M. (1985). Human mate selection. *American Scientist, 73,* 47–51.

Buss, D.M. (1988a). The evolution of human intrasexual competition: Tactics of mate attraction. *Journal of Personality and Social Psychology, 54,* 616–628.

Buss, D.M. (1988b). Love acts: The evolutionary biology of love. In R.J. Sternberg & M.L. Barnes (Eds.), *The psychology of love* (pp. 100–118). New Haven, CT: Yale University Press.

Buss, D.M. (1988c). From vigilance to violence: Tactics of mate retention in American undergraduates. *Ethology and Sociobiology, 9,* 291–317.

Buss, D.M. (1989). Sex differences in human mate preferences: Evolutionary hypotheses tested in 37 cultures. *Behavioral and Brain Sciences, 12,* 1–49.

Buss, D.M., & Barnes, M. (1986). Preferences in human mate selection. *Journal of Personality and Social Psychology, 50,* 559–570.

Buss, D.M., & Dedden, L.A. (1990). Derogation of competitors. *Journal of Social and Personal Relationships, 7,* 395–422.

Buss, D.M., & Kenrick, D.T. (1998). Evolutionary social psychology. In D.T. Gilbert, S.T. Fiske, & G. Lindzey (Eds.), *The handbook of social psychology* (4th ed., Vol. 2, pp. 982–1026). New York: McGraw Hill.

Buss, D.M., & Schmitt, D.P. (1993). Sexual strategies theory: An evolutionary perspective on human mating. *Psychological Review, 100,* 204–232.

Call, V.R.A., Sprecher, S., & Schwartz, P. (1992). *The frequency of sexual intercourse in American couples: A national sample.* Paper presented at the Annual Meeting of the National Council on Family Relations, Orlando, FL.

Cameron, C., Oskamp, S., & Sparks, W. (1977). Courtship American style: Newspaper ads. *Family Coordinator, 26,* 27–30.

Carroll, J.L., Volk, K.D., & Hyde, J.S. (1985). Differences between males and females in motives for engaging in sexual intercourse. *Archives of Sexual Behavior, 14,* 131–139.

Cashdan, E. (1993). Attracting mates: Effects of paternal investment on mate attraction strategies. *Ethology and Sociobiology, 14,* 1–24.

Christopher, F.S., & Cate, R.M. (1985). Anticipated influences on sexual decision-making. *Family Relations, 34,* 265–270.

Coleman, F.L. (1997). Stalking behavior and the cycle of domestic violence. *Journal of Interpersonal Violence, 12,* 420–432.

Coleman, S. (1977). A developmental stage hypothesis for nonmarital dyadic relationships. *Journal of Marriage and Family Counseling, 3,* 71–76.

Contreras, R., Hendrick, S.S., & Hendrick, C. (1996). Perspectives on marital love and satisfaction in Mexican American and Anglo couples. *Journal of Counseling and Development, 74,* 408–415.

Critelli, J.W., Myers, E.J., & Loos, V.E. (1986). The components of love: Romantic attraction and sex role orientation. *Journal of Personality, 54,* 354–370.

Cunningham, M.R., Barbee, A.P., & Druen, P.B. (1996). Social allergens and the reactions that they produce: Escalation of annoyance and disgust in love and work. In R.M. Kowalski (Ed.), *Aversive interpersonal behaviors* (pp. 189–214). New York: Plenum Press.

Cunningham, M.R., Barbee, A.P., & Pike, C.L. (1990). What do women want? Facialmetric assessment of multiple motives in the perception of male facial physical attractiveness. *Journal of Personality and Social Psychology, 59*, 61–72.

Cunningham, M.R., Druen, P.B., & Barbee, A.P. (1997). Angels, mentors, and friends: Trade-offs among evolutionary, social, and individual variables in physical appearance. In J.A. Simpson & D.T. Kenrick (Eds.), *Evolutionary social psychology* (pp. 109–140). Mahwah, NJ: Erlbaum.

Cupach, W.R., & Spitzberg, B.H. (1997, February). *The incidence and perceived severity of obsessive relational intrusion behaviors.* Paper presented at the Western States Communication Association convention, Monterey, CA.

Cupach, W.R., & Spitzberg, B.H. (1998). Obsessive relational intrusion and stalking. In B.H. Spitzberg & W.R. Cupach (Eds.), *The dark side of close relationships* (pp. 233–263). Mahwah, NJ: Erlbaum.

Daly, M., & Wilson, M. (1983). *Sex, evolution, and behavior* (2nd ed.). Belmont, CA: Wadsworth.

Darwin, C. (1859). *On the origin of the species by means of natural selection, or, preservation of favoured races in the struggle for life.* London: Murray.

Darwin, C. (1871). *The descent of man, and selection in relation to sex.* London: Murray.

Davis, K.E., & Latty-Mann, H. (1987). Love styles and relationship quality: A contribution to validation. *Journal of Social and Personal Relationships, 4*, 409–428.

Davis, S. (1990). Men as success objects and women as sex objects: A study of personal advertisements. *Sex Roles, 23*, 43–50.

Deaux, K., & Hanna, R. (1984). Courtship in the personals column: The influence of gender and sexual orientation. *Sex Roles, 11*, 363–375.

De Becker, G. (1998). *The gift of fear: Survival signals that protect us from violence.* New York: Dell.

Donnelly, D.A. (1993). Sexually inactive marriages. *Journal of Sex Research, 30*, 171–179.

Eagly, A.H. (1987). *Sex differences in social behavior: A social-role interpretation.* Hillsdale, NJ: Erlbaum.

Eagly, A.H., & Karau, S.J. (1991). Gender and the emergence of leaders: A meta-analysis. *Journal of Personality and Social Psychology, 60*, 685–710.

Edwards, J., & Booth, A. (1976). Sexual behavior in and out of marriage: An assessment of correlates. *Journal of Marriage and the Family, 38*, 73–81.

Ellis, A. (1954). *The American sexual tragedy.* New York: Twayne.

Ellis, H. (1901–1928). *Studies in the psychology of sex* (Vols. 1–7). Philadelphia: Davis. (Original work published 1897–1928)

Ellis, H. (1922). *Little essays of love and virtue.* New York: Doran.

Ellis, H. (1963). *Psychology of sex.* New York: The New American Library of World Literature. (Original work published 1933)

Fehr, B. (1988). Prototype analysis of the concepts of love and commitment. *Journal of Personality and Social Psychology, 55*, 557–579.

Fehr, B., & Russell, J.A. (1991). The concept of love viewed from a prototype perspective. *Journal of Personality and Social Psychology, 60*, 425–438.

Feingold, A. (1990). Gender differences in effects of physical attractiveness on romantic attraction: A comparison across five research paradigms. *Journal of Personality and Social Psychology, 59,* 981–993.

Feingold, A. (1992). Gender differences in mate selection preferences: A test of the parental investment model. *Psychological Bulletin, 112,* 125–139.

Fish, L.S., Fish, R.C., & Sprenkle, D.H. (1984). Treating inhibited sexual desire: A marital therapy approach. *American Journal of Family Therapy, 12,* 3–12.

Fremouw, W.J., Westrup, D., & Pennypacker, J. (1997). Stalking on campus: The prevalence and strategies for coping with stalking. *Journal of Forensic Sciences, 42,* 664–667.

Freud, S. (1963a). "Civilized" sexual morality and modern nervousness. In P. Rieff (Ed.), *Sexuality and the psychology of love* (pp. 20–40). New York: Collier Books. (Original work published 1908)

Freud, S. (1963b). The most prevalent form of degradation in erotic life. In P. Rieff (Ed.), *Sexuality and the psychology of love* (pp. 58–70). New York: Collier Books. (Original work published 1912)

Fromm, E. (1956). *The art of loving.* New York: Harper & Row.

Gagnon, J.H., & Simon, W. (1973). *Sexual conduct: The social sources of human sexuality.* Chicago: Aldine.

Gangestad, S.W., & Simpson, J.A. (1990). Toward an evolutionary history of female sociosexual variation. *Journal of Personality, 58,* 69–96.

Goode, W.J. (1959). The theoretical importance of love. *American Sociological Review, 24,* 38–47.

Goodwin, R. (1990). Sex differences among partner preferences: Are the sexes really very similar? *Sex Roles, 23,* 501–513.

Greeley, A.M. (1991). *Faithful attraction: Discovering intimacy, love, and fidelity in American marriage.* New York: Doherty.

Greenblat, C.S. (1983). The salience of sexuality in the early years of marriage. *Journal of Marriage and the Family, 45,* 289–299.

Greenlees, I.A., & McGrew, W.C. (1994). Sex and age differences in preferences and tactics of mate attraction: Analysis of published advertisements. *Ethology and Sociobiology, 15,* 59–72.

Hall, D. (1996, March). *Outside looking in: Stalkers and their victims.* Paper presented to the Academy of Criminal Justice Sciences Conference, San Francisco.

Hallstrom, T., & Samuelsson, S. (1990). Changes in women's sexual desire in middle life: The longitudinal study of women in Gothenburg. *Archives of Sexual Behavior, 19,* 259–268.

Harrison, A.A., & Saeed, L. (1977). Let's make a deal: An analysis of revelations and stipulations in lonely hearts' advertisements. *Journal of Personality and Social Psychology, 35,* 257–264.

Hatfield, E. (1988). Passionate and companionate love. In R.J. Sternberg & M.L. Barnes (Eds.), *The psychology of love* (pp. 191–217). New Haven, CT: Yale University Press.

Hatfield, E., Greenberger, R., Traupman, P., & Lambert, M. (1982). Equity and sexual satisfaction in recently married couples. *Journal of Sex Research, 18,* 18–32.

Hatfield, E., & Rapson, R.L. (1987). Passionate love/sexual desire: Can the same paradigm explain both? *Archives of Sexual Behavior, 16,* 259–278.

Hatfield, E., & Rapson, R.L. (1990). Passionate love in intimate relationships. In B.S. Moore & A. Isen (Eds.), *Affect and social behavior* (pp. 126–152). Cambridge, England: Cambridge University Press.

Hatfield, E., & Rapson, R.L. (1993). *Love, sex, and intimacy: Their psychology, biology, and history.* New York: HarperCollins.

Hatfield, E., & Sprecher, S. (1986). Measuring passionate love in intimate relationships. *Journal of Adolescence, 9,* 383–410.

Hatfield, E., Sprecher, S., Pillemer, J.T., Greenberger, D., & Wexler, P. (1988). Gender differences in what is desired in the sexual relationship. *Journal of Psychology & Human Sexuality, 1,* 39–52.

Hatfield, E., Traupmann, J., Sprecher, S., Utne, M., & Hay, J. (1985). Equity and intimate relationships: Recent research. In W. Ickes (Ed.), *Compatible and incompatible relationships* (pp. 91–117). New York: Springer-Verlag.

Hatfield, E., & Walster, G.W. (1978). *A new look at love.* Reading, MA: Addison-Wesley.

Hatkoff, T.S., & Lasswell, T.E. (1977). Male-female similarities and differences in conceptualizing love. In M. Cook & G. Wilson (Eds.), *Love and attraction: An international conference* (pp. 221–227). Oxford, England: Pergamon Press.

Hendrick, C., & Hendrick, S.S. (1986). A theory and method of love. *Journal of Personality and Social Psychology, 50,* 392–402.

Hendrick, C., & Hendrick, S.S. (1988). Lovers wear rose colored glasses. *Journal of Social and Personal Relationships, 5,* 161–183.

Hendrick, C., & Hendrick, S.S. (1989). Research on love: Does it measure up? *Journal of Personality and Social Psychology, 56,* 784–794.

Hendrick, C., & Hendrick, S.S. (1990). A relationship-specific version of the love attitudes scale. *Journal of Social Behavior and Personality, 5,* 239–254.

Hendrick, C., Hendrick, S.S., & Dicke, A. (1998). The love attitudes scale: Short form. *Journal of Social and Personal Relationships, 15,* 147–159.

Hendrick, C., Hendrick, S.S., Foote, F.H., & Slapion-Foote, M.J. (1984). Do men and women love differently? *Journal of Social and Personal Relationships, 1,* 177–195.

Hendrick, S.S., & Hendrick, C. (1987). Love and sex attitudes and religious beliefs. *Journal of Social and Clinical Psychology, 5,* 391–398.

Hendrick, S.S., & Hendrick, C. (1992). *Liking, loving, & relating* (2nd ed.). Pacific Grove, CA: Brooks/Cole.

Hendrick, S.S., & Hendrick, C. (1995). Gender differences and similarities in sex and love. *Personal Relationships, 2,* 55–65.

Hendrick, S.S., Hendrick, C., & Adler, N.L. (1988). Romantic relationships: Love, satisfaction, and staying together. *Journal of Personality and Social Psychology, 54,* 980–988.

Herold, E.S., Mantle, D., & Zemitis, O. (1979). A study of sexual offenses against females. *Adolescence, 14,* 65–72.

Hester, C., & Rudolph, K. (1994). The effects of personality, gender, and age on ranked characteristics of the ideal romantic partner. *Journal of Psychological Type, 29,* 14–23.

Hill, C.T., & Peplau, L.A. (1998). Premarital predictors of relationship outcomes: A 15-year follow-up of the Boston Couples Study. In T.N. Bradbury (Ed.), *The developmental course of marital dysfunction* (pp. 237–278). New York: Cambridge University Press.

Hill, R. (1945). Campus values in mate-selection. *Journal of Home Economics, 37,* 554–558.

Hirsch, L.R., & Paul, L. (1996). Human mate mating strategies: I. Courtship tactics of the "quality" and "quantity" alternatives. *Ethology and Sociobiology, 17,* 55–70.

Hogben, M., & Byrne, D. (1998). Using social learning theory to explain individual differences in human sexuality. *Journal of Sex Research, 35,* 58–71.

Howard, J.A., Blumstein, P., & Schwartz, P. (1987). Social or evolutionary theories? Some observations on preferences in human mate selection. *Journal of Personality and Social Psychology, 53,* 194–200.

Hudson, J.W., & Henze, L.F. (1969). Campus values in mate selection: A replication. *Journal of Marriage and the Family, 31,* 772–775.

Hunt, M. (1974). *Sexual behavior in the 1970s.* Chicago: Playboy Press.

Jankowiak, W.R., & Fischer, E.F. (1992). A cross-cultural perspective on romantic love. *Ethnology, 31,* 149–155.

Jason, L.A., Reichler, A., Easton, J., Neal, A., & Wilson, M. (1984). Female harassment after ending a relationship: A preliminary study. *Alternative Lifestyles, 6,* 259–269.

Jensen-Campbell, L.A., Graziano, W.G., & West, S. (1995). Dominance, prosocial orientation, and female preferences: Do nice guys really finish last? *Journal of Personality and Social Psychology, 68,* 427–440.

Kaplan, H.S. (1979). *Disorders of sexual desire and other new concepts and techniques in sex therapy.* New York: Simon & Schuster.

Kazak, A.E., & Reppucci, N.D. (1980). Romantic love as a social institution. In K.S. Pope (Ed.), *On love and loving* (pp. 209–227). San Francisco: Jossey-Bass.

Kenrick, D.T. (1994). Evolutionary social psychology: From sexual selection to social cognition. *Advances in Experimental Social Psychology, 26,* 75–121.

Kenrick, D.T., Groth, G.E., Trost, M.R., & Sadalla, E.K. (1993). Integrating evolutionary and social exchange perspectives on relationships: Effects of gender, self-appraisal, and involvement level on mate selection criteria. *Journal of Personality and Social Psychology, 64,* 951–969.

Kenrick, D.T., Keefe, R.C., Bryan, A., Barr, A., & Brown, S. (1995). Age preferences and mate choice among homosexuals and heterosexuals: A case for modular psychological mechanisms. *Journal of Personality and Social Psychology, 69,* 1166–1172.

Kenrick, D.T., Sadalla, E.K., Groth, G., & Trost, M.R. (1990). Evolution, traits, and the stages of human courtship: Qualifying the parental investment model. *Journal of Personality, 58,* 97–116.

Kephart, W.M. (1967). Some correlates of romantic love. *Journal of Marriage and the Family, 29,* 470–474.

King, C.E., & Christensen, A. (1983). The relationship events scale: A Guttman scaling of progress in courtship. *Journal of Marriage and the Family, 45,* 671–678.

Kirkpatrick, L.A. (1998). Evolution, pair-bonding, and reproductive strategies: A reconceptualization of adult attachment. In J.A. Simpson & W.S. Rholes (Eds.), *Attachment theory and close relationships* (pp. 353–393). New York: Guilford Press.

Knox, D. (1975). *Marriage: Who? When? Why?* Englewood Cliffs, NJ: Prentice-Hall.

Krafft-Ebing, R. von. (1945). *Psychopathia sexualis* (12th ed.). New York: Pioneer. (Original work published 1886)

Kurdek, L.A. (1991). Sexuality in homosexual and heterosexual couples. In K. McKinney & S. Sprecher (Eds.), *Sexuality in close relationships* (pp. 177–191). Hillsdale, NJ: Erlbaum.

Laner, M.R. (1977). Permanent partner priorities: Gay and straight. *Journal of Homosexuality, 3,* 21–39.

Lasswell, T.E., & Lasswell, M.E. (1976). I love you but I'm not in love with you. *Journal of Marriage and Family Counseling, 38,* 211–224.

Lee, J.A. (1973). *Colours of love: An exploration of the ways of loving.* Toronto, Canada: New Press.

Lee, J.A. (1976). Forbidden colors of love: Patterns of gay love and gay liberation. *Journal of Homosexuality, 1,* 401–418.

Lee, J.A. (1977). A typology of styles of loving. *Personality and Social Psychology Bulletin, 3,* 173–182.

Lee, J.A. (1988). Love-styles. In R.J. Sternberg & M.L. Barnes (Eds.), *The psychology of love* (pp. 38–67). New Haven, CT: Yale University Press.

Levine, S.B. (1984). An essay on the nature of sexual desire. *Journal of Sex & Marital Therapy, 10,* 83–96.

Levine, S.B. (1987). More on the nature of sexual desire. *Journal of Sex & Marital Therapy, 13,* 35–44.

Lewis, C.S. (1988). *The four loves.* New York: Harcourt Brace. (Original work published 1960)

Luby, V., & Aron, A. (1990, July). *A prototype structuring of love, like, and being in-love.* Paper presented at the International Conference on Personal Relationships, Oxford, England.

Marston, P.J., Hecht, M.L., Manke, M.L., McDaniel, S., & Reeder, H. (1998). The subjective experience of intimacy, passion, and commitment in heterosexual love relationships. *Personal Relationships, 5,* 15–30.

McGinnis, R. (1959). Campus values in mate selection: A repeat study. *Social Forces, 36,* 368–373.

Meloy, J.R. (1989). Unrequited love and the wish to kill: Diagnosis and treatment of borderline erotomania. *Bulletin of the Menninger Clinic, 53,* 477–492.

Meloy, J.R. (1996). Stalking (obsessional following): A review of some preliminary studies. *Aggression and Violent Behavior, 1,* 147–162.

Michael, R.T., Gagnon, J.H., Laumann, E.O., & Kolata, G. (1994). *Sex in America: A definitive survey.* Boston: Little, Brown.

Miller, L.C., & Fishkin, S.A. (1997). On the dynamics of human bonding and reproductive success: Seeking windows on the adapted-for-human-environmental interface. In J.A. Simpson & D.T. Kenrick (Eds.), *Evolutionary social psychology* (pp. 197–235). Mahwah, NJ: Erlbaum.

Mintz, E.E. (1980). Obsession with the rejecting beloved. *Psychoanalytic Review, 67,* 479–492.

Mischel, W. (1966). A social-learning view of sex differences in behavior. In E.E. Maccoby (Ed.), *The development of sex differences* (pp. 56–81). Stanford, CA: Stanford University Press.

Mullen, P.E., & Pathé, M. (1994). Stalking and the pathologies of love. *Australian and New Zealand Journal of Psychiatry, 28,* 469–477.

Murstein, B.I. (1970). Stimulus-value-role: A theory of marital choice. *Journal of Marriage and the Family, 32,* 465–481.

Murstein, B.I. (1976). *Who will marry whom? Theories and research in marital choice.* New York: Springer.

Murstein, B.I. (1980). Mate selection in the 1970s. *Journal of Marriage and the Family, 42,* 777–792.

Murstein, B.I., Merighi, J.R., & Vyse, S.A. (1991). Love styles in the United States and France: A cross-cultural comparison. *Journal of Social and Clinical Psychology, 10,* 37–46.

Neubeck, G. (1972). The myriad motives for sex. *Sexual Behavior, 2,* 51–56.

Oliver, M.B., & Hyde, J.S. (1993). Gender differences in sexuality: A meta-analysis. *Psychological Bulletin, 114,* 29–51.

Pam, A., Plutchik, R., & Conte, H.R. (1975). Love: A psychometric approach. *Psychological Reports, 37,* 83–88.

Pennebaker, J.W., Dyer, M.A., Caulkins, R.S., Litowitz, D.L., Ackreman, P.L., Anderson, D.B., & McGraw, K.M. (1979). Don't the girls get prettier at closing time: A country and western application to psychology. *Personality and Social Psychology Bulletin, 5,* 122–125.

Pietropinto, A. (1986). Inhibited sexual desire. *Medical Aspects of Human Sexuality, 20,* 46–49.

Regan, P.C. (1996). Rhythms of desire: The association between menstrual cycle phases and female sexual desire. *Canadian Journal of Human Sexuality, 5,* 145–156.

Regan, P.C. (1998a). Of lust and love: Beliefs about the role of sexual desire in romantic relationships. *Personal Relationships, 5,* 139–157.

Regan, P.C. (1998b). Minimum mate selection standards as a function of perceived mate value, relationship context, and gender. *Journal of Psychology and Human Sexuality, 10,* 53–73.

Regan, P.C. (1998c). Romantic love and sexual desire. In V.C. de Munck (Ed.), *Romantic love and sexual behavior: Perspectives from the social sciences* (pp. 91–112). Westport, CT: Praeger.

Regan, P.C. (1998d). What if you can't get what you want? Willingness to compromise ideal mate selection standards as a function of sex, mate value, and relationship context. *Personality and Social Psychology Bulletin, 24,* 1294–1303.

Regan, P.C. (in press). The role of sexual desire and sexual activity in dating relationships. *Social Behavior and Personality.*

Regan, P.C., & Berscheid, E. (1995). Gender differences in beliefs about the causes of male and female sexual desire. *Personal Relationships, 2,* 345–358.

Regan, P.C., & Berscheid, E. (1997). Gender differences in characteristics desired in a potential sexual and marriage partner. *Journal of Psychology and Human Sexuality, 9,* 25–37.

Regan, P.C., & Berscheid, E. (2000). *Lust: What we know about human sexual desire.* Thousand Oaks, CA: Sage.

Regan, P.C., & Dreyer, C.S. (1999). Lust? Love? Status? Young adults' motives for engaging in casual sex. *Journal of Psychology & Human Sexuality, 11.*

Regan, P.C., Kocan, E.R., & Whitlock, T. (1998). Ain't love grand! A prototype analysis of romantic love. *Journal of Social and Personal Relationships, 15,* 411–420.

Regan, P.C., Levin, L., Sprecher, S., Cate, R., & Christopher, S. (1998). *Partner preferences: What characteristics do men and women desire in their short-term sexual and long-term romantic partners?* Manuscript submitted for publication.

Regan, P.C., & Sprecher, S. (1995). Marital sex. In D. Levinson (Ed.), *Encyclopedia of marriage and the family* (pp. 456–461). New York: Macmillan.

Regas, S.J., & Sprenkle, D.H. (1984). Functional family therapy and the treatment of inhibited sexual desire. *Journal of Marital and Family Therapy, 10,* 63–72.

Reik, T. (1945). *Psychology of sex relations.* New York: Grove Press.

Reiss, I.L. (1964). The scaling of premarital sexual permissiveness. *Journal of Marriage and the Family, 26,* 188–198.

Reiss, I.L. (1967). *The social context of premarital sexual permissiveness.* New York: Holt, Rinehart, and Winston.

Reiss, I.L. (1981). Some observations on ideology and sexuality in America. *Journal of Marriage and the Family, 43,* 271–283.

Reiss, I.L. (1986a). *Journey into sexuality: An exploratory voyage.* New York: Prentice-Hall.

Reiss, I.L. (1986b). A sociological journey into sexuality. *Journal of Marriage and the Family, 48,* 233–242.

Ridge, R.D., & Berscheid, E. (1989, May). *On loving and being in love: A necessary distinction.* Paper presented at the annual convention of the Midwestern Psychological Association, Chicago.

Robinson, I.E., Balkwell, J.W., & Ward, D.M. (1980). Meaning and behavior: An empirical study in sociolinguistics. *Social Psychology Quarterly, 43,* 253–258.

Roche, J.P. (1986). Premarital sex: Attitudes and behavior by dating state. *Adolescence, 21,* 107–121.

Rosch, E.H. (1973). On the internal structure of perceptual and semantic categories. In T.E. Moore (Ed.), *Cognitive development and the acquisition of language* (pp. 111–144). New York: Academic Press.

Rosch, E.H. (1975). Cognitive representations of semantic categories. *Journal of Experimental Psychology, 104,* 192–233.

Rosch, E.H. (1978). Principles of categorization. In E.H. Rosch & B.B. Lloyd (Eds.), *Cognition and categorization* (pp. 27–48). Hillsdale, NJ: Erlbaum.

Roscoe, B., Strouse, J.S., & Goodwin, M.P. (1994). Sexual harassment: Early adolescent self-reports of experiences and acceptance. *Adolescence, 29,* 515–523.

Rowatt, T.J., Cunningham, M.R., Rowatt, W.C., Miles, S.S., Ault-Gauthier, L.K., Georgianna, J., & Shamblin, S. (1997, July). *Men and women are from Earth: Life-span strategy dynamics in mate choices.* Paper presented at the meeting of the International Network on Personal Relationships, Oxford, OH.

Rubin, Z. (1970). Measurement of romantic love. *Journal of Personality and Social Psychology, 16,* 265–273.

Safilios-Rothschild, C. (1977). *Love, sex, and sex roles.* Englewood Cliffs, NJ: Prentice-Hall.

Schenk, J., Pfrang, H., & Rausche, A. (1983). Personality traits versus the quality of the marital relationship as the determinant of marital sexuality. *Archives of Sexual Behavior, 12,* 31–42.

Schmitt, D.P., & Buss, D.M. (1996). Strategic self-promotion and competitor derogation: Sex and context effects on the perceived effectiveness of mate attraction tactics. *Journal of Personality and Social Psychology, 70,* 1185–1204.

Shaver, P.R., & Hazan, C. (1988). A biased overview of the study of love. *Journal of Social and Personal Relationships, 5,* 473–501.

Shaver, P.R., Hazan, C., & Bradshaw, D. (1988). Love as attachment: The integration of three behavioral systems. In R.J. Sternberg & M.L. Barnes (Eds.), *The psychology of love* (pp. 68–99). New Haven, CT: Yale University Press.

Shaver, P.R., Schwartz, J., Kirson, D., & O'Connor, C. (1987). Emotion knowledge: Further exploration of a prototype approach. *Journal of Personality and Social Psychology, 52,* 1061–1086.

Sherwin, R., & Corbett, S. (1985). Campus sexual norms and dating relationships: A trend analysis. *Journal of Sex Research, 21,* 258–274.

Simon, W. (1974). The social, the erotic, and the sensual: The complexities of sexual scripts. In J.K. Cole & R. Deinstbier (Eds.), *The Nebraska Symposium on Motivation, 1973* (pp. 61–82). Lincoln: University of Nebraska Press.

Simon, W., & Gagnon, J.H. (1986). Sexual scripts: Permanence and change. *Archives of Sexual Behavior, 15,* 97–120.

Simpson, J.A., Campbell, B., & Berscheid, E. (1986). The association between romantic love and marriage: Kephart (1967) twice revisited. *Personality and Social Psychology Bulletin, 12,* 363–372.

Smith, J.E., Waldorf, V.A., & Trembath, D.L. (1990). "Single white male looking for thin, very attractive . . ." *Sex Roles, 23,* 675–685.

Sparrow, K.H. (1991). Factors in mate selection for single Black professional women. *Free Inquiry in Creative Sociology, 19,* 103–109.

Spaulding, C.B. (1971). The romantic love complex in American culture. *Sociology and Social Research, 55,* 82–100.

Spitzberg, B.H., & Cupach, W.R. (1996, July). *Obsessive relational intrusion: Victimization and coping.* Paper presented at the International Society for the Study of Personal Relationships conference, Banff, Alberta, Canada.

Spitzberg, B.H., & Cupach, W.R. (Eds.). (1998). *The dark side of close relationships.* Mahwah, NJ: Erlbaum.

Spitzberg, B.H., Nicastro, A.M., & Cousins, A.V. (1998). Exploring the interactional phenomenon of stalking and obsessive relational intrusion. *Communication Reports, 11,* 33–47.

Sprecher, S. (1998). Social exchange theories and sexuality. *Journal of Sex Research, 35,* 32–43.

Sprecher, S., & Hatfield, E. (1996). Premarital sexual standards among U.S. college students: Comparison with Russian and Japanese students. *Archives of Sexual Behavior, 25,* 261–288.

Sprecher, S., McKinney, K., Walsh, R., & Anderson, C. (1988). A revision of the Reiss premarital sexual permissiveness scale. *Journal of Marriage and the Family, 50,* 821–828.

Sprecher, S., & Regan, P.C. (1996). College virgins: How men and women perceive their sexual status. *Journal of Sex Research, 33,* 3–15.

Sprecher, S., & Regan, P.C. (1998). Passionate and companionate love in courting and young married couples. *Sociological Inquiry, 68,* 163–185.

Sprecher, S., Regan, P.C., McKinney, K., Maxwell, K., & Wazienski, R. (1997). Preferred level of sexual experience in a date or mate: The merger of two methodologies. *Journal of Sex Research, 34,* 327–337.

Sprecher, S., Sullivan, Q., & Hatfield, E. (1994). Mate selection preferences: Gender differences examined in a national sample. *Journal of Personality and Social Psychology, 66,* 1074–1080.

Sternberg, R.J. (1986). A triangular theory of love. *Psychological Review, 93,* 119–135.

Sternberg, R.J. (1988a). *The triangle of love: Intimacy, passion, commitment.* New York: Basic Books.

Sternberg, R.J. (1988b). Triangulating love. In R.J. Sternberg & M.L. Barnes (Eds.), *The psychology of love* (pp. 119–138). New Haven, CT: Yale University Press.

Sternberg, R.J., & Barnes, M.L. (Eds.). (1988). *The psychology of love.* New Haven, CT: Yale University Press.

Stuart, F.M., Hammond, D.C., & Pett, M.A. (1987). Inhibited sexual desire in women. *Archives of Sexual Behavior, 16,* 91–106.

Swensen, C.H. (1961). Love: A self-report analysis with college students. *Journal of Individual Psychology, 17,* 167–171.

Swensen, C.H., & Gilner, F. (1963). Factor analysis of self-report statements of love relationships. *Journal of Individual Psychology, 19,* 186–188.

Talmadge, L.D., & Talmadge, W.C. (1986). Relational sexuality: An understanding of low sexual desire. *Journal of Sex & Marital Therapy, 12,* 3–21.

Tennov, D. (1979). *Love and limerence.* New York: Stein and Day.

Tjaden, P., & Thoennes, N. (1997). *Stalking in America: Findings from the national violence against women survey* [Report to the National Institute of Justice and Centers for Disease Control and Prevention]. Denver, CO: Center for Policy Research.

Trivers, R.L. (1972). Parental investment and sexual selection. In B. Campbell (Ed.), *Sexual selection and the descent of man* (pp. 136–179). Chicago: Aldine.

Trudel, G. (1991). Review of psychological factors in low sexual desire. *Sexual and Marital Therapy, 6,* 261–272.

Wallace, H., & Silverman, J. (1996). Stalking and post traumatic stress syndrome. *Police Journal, 69,* 203–206.

Walster, E., & Berscheid, E. (1971). Adrenaline makes the heart grow fonder. *Psychology Today, 5,* 47–62.

Walster, E., Walster, G.W., & Berscheid, E. (1978). *Equity: Theory and research.* Boston: Allyn & Bacon.

Walters, S., & Crawford, C.B. (1994). The importance of mate attraction for intrasexual competition in men and women. *Ethology and Sociobiology, 15,* 5–30.

Wiederman, M.W., & Allgeier, E.R. (1992). Gender differences in mate selection criteria: Sociobiological or socioeconomic explanation? *Ethology and Sociobiology, 13,* 115–124.

Zeifman, D., & Hazan, C. (1997). A process model of adult attachment formation. In S. Duck & W. Ickes (Eds.), *Handbook of personal relationships* (2nd ed., pp. 179–195). Chichester, England: Wiley.

CHAPTER 7

Sexual Fantasy and Erotica/Pornography: Internal and External Imagery

DONN BYRNE and JULIE A. OSLAND

IMAGINARY DEPICTIONS ARE ubiquitous in our everyday lives. We think about what we have done, might do, and plan to do. For entertainment or educational purposes, we seek external depictions of what others have done or could have done. Such depictions may be as fleeting as a stray thought or as elaborate as a three-hour movie or a 700-page novel. The content of these internal and external images runs the gamut from daily chores to hostility and violence, and from meal planning to sexual pleasure. We deliberately conjure up images of that which we fear, as well as of that which we desire. As far as we can discern from the cave drawings and pottery creations of our prehistoric ancestors, human beings have been attempting to record and communicate such images for a considerable period of time.

In contemporary society, when such imagery involves financial planning, the story of a sinking luxury liner, an account of a serial killer, or dessert recipes, it is considered a normal part of human existence. When the context is sexual, however, we tend to be much more judgmental and thus circumspect in communicating our personal fantasies to others and in seeking out the fantasies created by others. We lie, pass laws, try to shield children and adolescents from the possible dangers of such images, and quite often respond with embarrassment and anxiety, as well as with curiosity and titillation (Byrne, 1997b). We don't have PG-13 cookbooks or R-rated mutual fund reports. Restrictions and warnings on television are more likely to involve sexual themes (such as Presidential Grand Jury testimony) than any other aspect of human behavior.

Somehow, sex is in a category by itself. We know that internal and external imagery on a wide variety of topics can be emotionally arousing and cognitively informative, and we know that one possible result is motivation to engage in the depicted activity. That is, after all, what advertising and propaganda are all about. Though some of us worry most about aggressive motivation, a greater proportion of the population seems to worry most about the consequences of sexual motivation. With these evaluative problems continually hovering in the background, the following material is an attempt to summarize some of what we know about the content and the effects of sexual fantasy and erotica/pornography.

SEXUAL FANTASY

Conceptualizing sexuality as a combination of physical and mental components has become a truism. It appears to be generally accepted that the mind is the body's most reliable "erogenous zone." Our mental processes can, in fact, either facilitate or inhibit our responsiveness to tactile stimulation. The power of imagination is such that, even in the absence of physical stimulation, erotic thoughts can create subjective arousal, as well as the various physiological reactions associated with sexual excitement.

In the following discussion, the definition of sexual fantasy follows that of Leitenberg and Henning (1995), in which the term "refers to almost any mental imagery that is sexually arousing or erotic to the individual. The essential element of a deliberate sexual fantasy is the ability to control in imagination exactly what takes place" (p. 470). Such activity ranges from fleeting images in daydreams to deliberate efforts to achieve and maintain sexual excitement. This definition omits dreams that occur during sleep because they are not under the deliberate control of the dreamer. Note that night dreams can also bring about physiological arousal and even orgasm, but dream content is even more difficult to study than the content of deliberate fantasies and will not be included in our discussion.

In any event, what do we know about the internal events that are labeled "sexual fantasies"?

METHODOLOGICAL ISSUES IN THE STUDY OF SEXUAL FANTASY

Unlike the study of overt behavior such as aggression or altruism, investigations of fantasy cannot deal directly with the phenomenon in question. That is, fantasies are directly accessible only to the individual, and the correspondence between what occurs in one's head and what is communicated to investigators (or to anyone else) is undoubtedly less than perfectly veridical. As a result, the actual research question is: What do we know about the verbal self-reports of these internal events?

As in most preparadigmatic fields of science (Byrne, 1997a), there is little consistency in the way self-reported sexual fantasies are assessed. Three somewhat different methodologies have been utilized, each characterized by multiple operational variations: (1) participants are sometimes provided with a list of fantasy themes and asked to indicate the specific scenarios that they have imagined personally; (2) participants are sometimes asked to recall and describe the fantasies they have had during a specified time period (e.g., the past week, past month, past year, etc.); (3) participants are sometimes requested to keep a daily record of their sexual fantasies as they occur, either by using a checklist or by writing descriptive summaries, throughout a delimited time period. Each approach has limitations, and the extent to which they produce parallel, partially overlapping, or completely divergent results is a matter of conjecture.

In addition to inconsistencies, consider just a few of the specific problems associated with each approach. Preformulated lists of fantasies may reflect the experiences and biases of the investigator(s) and may omit specific content that is important to a given individual. In filling out an open-ended fantasy questionnaire, people differ in their ability to remember past thought processes accurately, in their idiosyncratic decisions as to what is socially acceptable and unacceptable to report about one's thoughts, and in their verbal ability; all such differences contribute to error variance in unknown ways. Keeping a daily diary permits the reporting of fantasies beyond those suggested by a checklist and reduces the problem of recall. Nevertheless, individual differences in social desirability concerns and verbal skills remain. Also, it takes a truly dedicated participant to whip out a journal and begin writing a composition each time he or she engages in a sexual fantasy. In addition, for each of the three methods, assessment issues arise, including the frequency of occurrence of each fantasy theme (as opposed to presence-absence) and the relative importance of rare and creative fantasies versus commonly shared ones (Smith & Over, 1991). Of overriding importance is the need to determine the most meaningful way to categorize content material. Will it prove most useful to code fantasies in terms of such categories as dominance-submission, sex with strangers or with familiar partners, two-person versus group sex, forced versus consensual sex, normative versus uncommon sexual practices, and various additional specifics?

Though it may sound overly pedantic to stress these dull problems of inconsistent methodology and potentially unreliable or inaccurate responses, it is difficult (and, in fact, probably impossible) to build a meaningful empirical and theoretical superstructure on such a flimsy, jerry-built base. Thus, one might do well to consider the following discussion of fantasy differences associated with gender, sexual orientation, race, or whatever as suggestive rather than definitive. To coin a phrase, it takes a heap of consistency to make data meaningful. Note that consistent methodology does not guarantee a meaningful empirical and conceptual framework, but that inconsistent methodology does guarantee an empirical and conceptual mishmash. To discuss what is known and seek the glimmer of common findings and meaningful generalizations, it is necessary to pretend for a moment that the previous statement is irrelevant.

GENDER DIFFERENCES IN SEXUAL FANTASY

Males and females are consistently found to differ in many aspects of sexuality, so differences in their sexual fantasizing and in their sexual fantasies would not be unexpected.

Frequency

Investigators most often report that men engage in sexual fantasies more frequently than is true for women. For example, Ellis and Symons (1990) found that men were twice as likely as women to report having fantasized about sex at least once a day. Hsu et al. (1994) and Wilson and Lang (1981) also reported that men have sexual fantasies more often than women. Others, however, report no gender differences in the frequency of sexual fantasies (e.g., Jones & Barlow, 1990; Knafo & Jaffe, 1984). One suspects that the apparent inconsistency is simply a matter of methodological variation across investigations. There is somewhat greater agreement about gender differences in fantasy content.

One difficulty may involve specifying exactly what is meant by fantasy. Jones and Barlow (1990) made what appears to be an important distinction between sexual urges and sexual fantasies. They defined a sexual urge as a sexual thought initiated by an external event and a sexual fantasy as an internally generated sexual thought. Based on these definitions, men and women did not differ in how often they reported having sexual fantasies. Similarly, there were no gender differences in the engaging in fantasy during masturbation. With respect to sexual urges, however, men reported having such thoughts twice as frequently as did women. Specifically, men reported having slightly more than 4.5 sexual urges per day, whereas the frequency for women was approximately 2 per day.

Additional distinctions are suggested by Byers, Purdon, and Clark (1998). Some sexual thoughts are perceived as unwanted and unacceptable, whereas others are evoked purposely and with accompanying pleasure. Among college undergraduates, men reported a greater number of sex-related intrusive thoughts than did women. Specific intrusive thoughts common to both men and women (reported by more than 50% of the respondents) included having sex in a public place and having sex with an authority figure. Uncommon thoughts among both genders (reported by fewer than 20% of the respondents) included sexual acts with a child, masturbating in a public place, and sex with an animal or inanimate object. Intrusive sexual thoughts occurred most often among those erotophilic individuals who characteristically respond to sexual cues with positive rather than negative affect (Fisher, Byrne, White, & Kelley,

1988), those who engage frequently in vivid sexual daydreaming (Giambra & Singer, 1998), and those who also engage in nonsexual obsessive thinking (Bouvard, Mollard, Cottraux, & Guerin, 1989).

Content

The images identified across investigations vary, but some common threads emerge. For men, Smith and Over (1991) identified five themes as sexually arousing. These content areas were identified as sensual, genital, public sex, sexual dominance-submission, and sexual aggression. Male participants reported genital themes to be the most sexually arousing and sexual aggression to be the least arousing. The frequency of fantasizing about each theme was strongly associated ($r = .70$) with reported arousal. If arousal is the goal of fantasy generation, it is logical for individuals to initiate the most arousing themes in their imagination more frequently than the least arousing themes.

Among women, Meuwissen and Over (1991) identified five content areas that are slightly different from those for men: sensual, genital, sexual power, forbidden sex, and sexual suffering. Again, frequency and arousal were positively but slightly less strongly associated ($r = .57$) than was true for men.

Other investigators using other operations also report gender differences in fantasy content. For example, Ellis and Symons (1990) found that men were much more likely than women to report fantasies about multiple partners, to indicate that the fantasy target is purely an object of sexual desire rather than a romantic partner, and to substitute one partner for another during the course of a given fantasy. Also, male fantasies were found to focus on visual images (e.g., partner attractiveness, genital details) to a greater degree than contextual images (e.g., emotional reactions of self or partner, tactile stimulation). These tendencies were reversed in female fantasies, with the greatest emphasis placed on personal characteristics and the emotional context.

Hsu et al. (1994) found gender differences in 17 (out of 55) specific fantasies. For example, 25.9% of males versus 11.3% of females said they fantasized about forcing a partner to submit at least once during the prior three months. In related research, Knafo and Jaffe (1984) reported that women were more likely than men to engage in imagery involving submission and being forced to surrender. Men were more likely than women to imagine scenes dealing with their sexual prowess or dominance (such as engaging in sex involving the interaction of multiple partners). Leitenberg and Henning (1995) report analogous gender differences in content. These different themes seem to reflect gender stereotypes, with men taking an active role and women a passive role.

Focusing on a different aspect of content, McCauley and Swann (1978) found that men were more likely than women to fantasize about previous or current sexual experiences, and women were more likely than men to engage in "fictional" fantasies, that is, imagining activities that they had not actually experienced. Further, subjective sexual arousal corresponded with these differences. That is, women more than men indicated that fictional fantasies were sexually arousing, whereas men more than women indicated that reality-based fantasies were arousing (McCauley & Swann, 1980). These authors also investigated the function of such fantasies during intercourse. Women said that engaging in fictional fantasies during intercourse decreased their concerns about their ongoing behavior and made the sexual activity more enjoyable. Men, in contrast, engaged in reality-based fantasies to help them control and direct their sexual excitement.

In their study of intrusive sexual thoughts among college students, Byers et al. (1998) also found that, compared to women, men reported more thoughts involving active, aggressive themes and fewer thoughts of being sexually victimized. Men also indicated greater sexual arousal in response to their most upsetting intrusive thoughts than did women.

Attempting to generalize across quite different investigations using different methodologies, we can suggest the emergence of some commonality with respect to gender differences in fantasy content. The fantasies of men tend to feature an attractive, desirable sex object whose appearance is all-important but whose personal identity is irrelevant and with whom genital contact is the primary goal. Men tend to imagine themselves in a dominant, active, and sometimes aggressive role, engaging in explicit sexual acts such as oral-genital stimulation. In contrast, the fantasies of women focus on their own personal and physical responses, in a passive and sometimes submissive role with a single partner. Women tend to stress romance and a positive emotional tone, even if the partner is coercing them. Women also are likely to stress how the partner responds to them, with caressing and touching as essential elements. Men report a preference for scenarios that plunge straight ahead toward climax, whereas women prefer a gradual buildup to sexual interaction with a partner who caters to their emotional as well as their sexual needs.

SEXUAL ORIENTATION AND SEXUAL FANTASY

As would be expected, the sexual fantasies of heterosexuals and homosexuals differ for both men and women. The major difference involves the gender of the other person or persons in the fantasy. Specifically, gays and lesbians are more likely than their heterosexual counterparts to fantasize about sex with someone of their own gender and also about having sex with a stranger (Masters & Johnson, 1979; Price, Allensworth, & Hillman, 1985).

Hurlbert and Apt (1993) reported that homosexual and heterosexual women are equally likely to engage in fantasy while interacting with a partner, though the straight research participants indicated a more positive attitude toward such fantasies than did lesbian participants.

Among male homosexuals, fantasy content is found to fall into two general categories (Lehne, 1978) that suggest a combination of the typical feminine and masculine themes found in research on heterosexuals. Most gay fantasies (58%) emphasized themes of affection, love, and relationships. The remaining fantasies (42%) involved sexually explicit elements such as specific sexual acts. Further, much like straight males, gay males tend to have fantasies based on reality rather than fiction.

It appears that gay males differ from straight males primarily with respect to the gender of the imagined sex partner, and gays are also more likely than straights to emphasize the relationship with that partner.

SEXUAL FANTASIES: FUNCTION, ORIGIN, AND BEHAVIORAL EFFECTS

It is well established that sexual fantasies commonly are frequently initiated by both males and females, but questions remain as to why individuals engage in fantasies about sex, where the fantasies originate, and what effects they may have on overt behavior.

The Function of Sexual Fantasies

At one level, sexual fantasies would seem to be employed simply for the enjoyment they engender, and this self-initiated positive experience is equally characteristic of many other types of fantasy. That is, people also weave fantasy scenarios about romance, revenge, achievement, and many other aspects of human behavior. For these other topics, however, we seldom conduct research asking about gender differences in frequency and content or the role of sexual orientation. Maybe we should.

Beyond enjoyment of the fantasies qua fantasies, people also initiate internal erotic scenes and stories because they serve an important adjunct function in the *sexual response cycle* as individuals progress from initial arousal to orgasm (Ellis, 1942; Kaplan, 1979; Masters & Johnson, 1966). Erotic fantasies aid individuals in attaining, enhancing, and maintaining sexual arousal during masturbation as well as during interpersonal sexual activity. This seems to be a practice that is both innocuous and utilitarian.

Potential problems begin to arise, however, when one asks where the fantasies originate. Even more problematic is the concern that fantasy content is not only a reflection of behavior in which the individual has previously engaged (as it often is) but also a motivator of and instructional guide to behavior in which the individual has never before engaged. If the fantasies sometimes (perhaps usually) have an external origin and if the content sometimes motivates dangerous, criminal, or otherwise unacceptable actions, then societal self-protection becomes an issue. What do we know about the origin and the behavioral effects of fantasies?

Origin of Fantasy Content

There would seem to be only two ways in which specific fantasies originate. Least likely (except for a small and highly creative subset of our species) is the imaginative development and elaboration of totally original themes. We see such creativity in the work of novelists, painters, sculptors, and other artists, both currently and historically. Most of us, however, are consumers or imitators rather than creators of original artistic productions. As a consequence, the vast majority of individual fantasies probably originate in the creative fantasies of others. When we imagine sexual themes, we are usually indebted to what other individuals have done, said, written, drawn, photographed, or otherwise communicated to us in a variety of forms. In the simplest terms, the creative private thoughts of some are communicated publicly to others who incorporate them in their own private thought processes. In effect, our minds are repositories of the countless images to which we have been exposed.

If this analysis is correct, we find common themes in the sexual fantasies of research participants because they obtained those basic fantasies from the same cultural milieu. Untold numbers of people around the world share many other images as well: the Wicked Witch of the West threatening Dorothy and Toto, too, the *Titanic* slipping beneath the waves, the shooting of President Kennedy in Dallas, the climax of the *1812 Overture,* and so on. When the subject is sexual, presumably there would be only limited interest in the words and pictures to which you have instant access, and no one would know what they were unless you told them. Such fantasies become a matter of general interest and concern, however, if they are reflected in your behavioral actions.

External Images as Behavior Motivators?

This is the crucial juncture, because if your fantasies lead you to act, then there is reason to be inquisitive about what the fantasies are, because your behavior could become a public safety issue. And if the fantasies originate in the culture, then society has reason to raise an alarm about what kinds of fantasies are communicated to the general public. Assume, for example, that stories and movies of child sexual abuse were widely disseminated, then incorporated in the fantasy life of most citizens. If these fantasies then provided the script for subsequent behavior, strong arguments could be made for the importance of regulating the flow of such thematic material.

Before we jump to such conclusions, however, it is crucial to examine what the most common external sexual images are, whether they in fact influence private fantasies, and the extent to which private fantasies actually lead to corresponding overt behavior. For this reason, we examine several aspects of erotica and pornography before we return to behavioral effects.

EROTICA/PORNOGRAPHY

External sources of sexual imagery are omnipresent. Humans have depicted erotic material at least from the time they first began to create cave drawings and pottery. By 600 B.C., Etruscan sexual art had become amazingly diverse with depictions of oral sex, intercourse in myriad positions, and bestiality. Over the centuries, each advance in communication and art has brought with it new ways to create and communicate erotic portrayals in words and pictures. In 1874, when photography was still new, police raided a studio near London and confiscated over 130,000 "obscene" photographs.

Definitional problems abound, but we follow the suggestions of Fisher and Barak (1991, p. 66), primarily because we share their views. Thus, *erotica* involves the verbal or pictorial presentation of "nonviolent, non-degrading, and consensual sexual activity." The term *pornography* is reserved for similar material that contains violent, degrading, and/or nonconsensual sexual activity. Note that the content of pornography most often involves male aggression and dominance directed against females.

Obviously, this distinction between erotica and pornography is value-laden, and the terminology varies somewhat from investigator to investigator. In a more general sense, the term pornography is applied to whatever material is considered objectionable, and people differ greatly with respect to what they perceive as objectionable. For example, many individuals readily label a nude painting or a TV script containing sexual innuendoes as pornographic (e.g., Eliasberg & Stuart, 1961), and others respond positively to and are most aroused by depictions of sexual violence, degradation, and force (Prentky et al., 1989). Such material can be viewed as not offensive but as a valid expression of free speech. U.S. Supreme Court Justice Potter Stewart made a famous confession about the label pornography when he stated, "I can't define it, but I know it when I see it." Except for admittedly arbitrary definitions based on content (such as the one adopted here), the distinction between erotica and pornography is in the eye of the beholder.

We will discuss the study of the behavioral correlates of sexual fantasy, erotica, and pornography shortly, but it is worth noting at the outset that there is a prevailing assumption that some or all forms of sexual presentation are harmful to the individual or to society, especially to children. The accuracy of this assumption remains an open question, but the laws prohibiting or regulating sexual content in movies, on television, and on the Internet are an accurate and confusing reflection of our fears and uncertainty about potential negative effects.

Erotica/Pornography: Content and Prevalence

The immediate effects of sexual depictions on sexual arousal is perhaps the best documented and least controversial aspect of what is known in this area of research. Whether assessed by devices designed to measure objectively the physiological changes in male and female genitals or paper-and-pencil scales that evoke subjective self-reports, sexual arousal is found to occur for both genders in response to verbal or pictorial sexual material. Further, Davis and Bauserman (1993) report that films are more arousing than still pictures, audiotapes, or written vignettes of the same sexual activity. Similarly, photographs are more arousing than drawings.

It has been estimated that the erotica/pornography industry currently earns about $8 billion a year. Attempts to categorize the content of this material encounter some of the same problems involved in studying the content of individual fantasies. Different investigators select different categories. For example, content analysis of X-rated videos by Cowan, Lee, Levy, and Snyder (1988) indicated that only 37% of the sexual scenes fit the definition of erotica; the remainder could be classified as pornography

Despite the vocal assumptions of antipornography crusaders, research suggests that violent pornography is not really very pervasive (Donnerstein, Linz, & Penrod, 1987). In sex-oriented magazines such as *Playboy,* the level of violent sexuality has consistently been found to be 5% or less, and even that level is found to be decreasing over time (Malamuth & Spinner, 1980; Scott & Cuvelier, 1987).

The content of the vast majority of explicit movies, videotapes, and magazines designed for heterosexual audiences consists of heterosexual couples or groups engaging in the same sexual behavior that is commonly described in surveys of self-reported sexual behavior: foreplay and intercourse (genital-genital, oral-genital, or anal-genital). The men and women in these depictions are primarily White, but cultural diversity is served by the periodic inclusion of Blacks (mostly men) and Asians (mostly women). Only an *extremely* small segment of the market involves depictions of relatively unusual acts (e.g., sado-masochism, bestiality, urophilia) or nonnormative participants (e.g., dwarfs, amputees, hermaphrodites).

The incorporation of these external images into internal ones has been shown to depend in part on cognitive factors. For example, arousal and incorporation can be inhibited by fears of responding inappropriately. When viewers are told beforehand that others like themselves find such material very arousing, arousal levels increase (Norris, 1989). Research participants do not even become aroused in the presence of sexually explicit auditory material if the cognitive interference is created by instructions to engage in nonsexual cognition (Geer & Fuhr, 1976). The external images are perceived, but the individual is too busy with other cognitive tasks to process the stimuli and thus incorporate them among his or her personal fantasies. When the external images are visual as opposed to auditory, extraneous cognitive activity is less disruptive, especially for males (Przybyla & Byrne, 1984). As in research on sexual fantasies, men seem more attuned to visual cues than is true for women (Money, 1985).

The next step—the inclusion of these arousing images in the individual's subsequent fantasies—has not been a focus of research interest. It seems obvious, however, that we learn and can subsequently recognize and recall a significant proportion of the verbal and pictorial material that we encounter. Effortlessly, we remember movie scenes, novel plots, and the appearance of actors and actresses. It seems highly unlikely that when some scenes, plots, and performers involve sexual interactions, we fail to remember and subsequently think about what we have witnessed.

Are any of these public depictions and their replay in the private fantasies of members of the audience associated with their reenactment in the overt behavior of individuals? That is not a question for which a definitive answer is readily available. We now describe what is known on this topic, but the best (and undoubtedly disappointing) answer is: Yes, sometimes, depending on the behavior depicted, various dispositional characteristics of the individual, and situational constraints.

BEHAVIORAL CORRELATES OF SEXUAL FANTASIES

We begin with what is known about the behavioral correlates of sexual fantasies and go on to describe the role of erotica and pornography when they are responsible for the fantasies.

Are Thoughts Associated with Actions?

Several investigations report a positive relationship between the frequency of engaging in sexual fantasy in general and the frequency of sexual behaviors such as intercourse and masturbation (e.g., Coles & Shamp, 1984), as well as the number of sexual partners one has had (e.g., Jones & Barlow, 1990; Wilson & Lang, 1981). Though it is tempting to conceptualize the fantasy-behavior association as an antecedent-consequent relationship, correlational research obviously does not permit that conclusion. It is possible that fantasy leads to behavior, or that behavior leads to fantasy, or that some other variable (e.g., attitudes about sexuality) leads to both fantasy and behavior. We will very shortly address the issue of whether or not fantasy has a causal effect on overt behavior.

A less controversial question is whether the content of specific sexual fantasies is associated with corresponding sexual acts. For example, are individuals who think about and are aroused by thoughts of sexual contact with other species also more likely to engage in acts of bestiality? Though we are not aware of this content-specific association between fantasy and behavior, that sort of finding would not be surprising.

A much more common and more important content question deals with the relationship between coercive (or rape) fantasies and the overt behavior of those who report such fantasies. We have noted that submission fantasies ("I imagine that I am being overpowered") are more common among women than among men, whereas dominance fantasies ("I imagine that I am forcing a woman to submit") are more common among men than among women. Does this fact imply that all men are potential rapists and/or that all women unconsciously want to be raped? Neither assertion is in any way justified by the differential association of gender with submission versus dominance fantasies, but we will discuss what research has to tell us about the two possibilities.

Women as the (Willing?) Targets of Sexual Coercion

Though women report being aroused by submission fantasies, the resulting fantasy sex is ordinarily quite different from the brutal reality of an actual rape (Mosher & Anderson, 1986). As Leitenberg and Henning (1995) point out, in fantasy, a woman can orchestrate the details of the interaction, but the opposite is true in the criminal act of rape. These investigators point out that, in addition, one meaning of the submission fantasy is that the woman is so sexually attractive that a man (in fantasy, an attractive man) cannot control his desire for her. The mutual attraction is such that he uses the minimal amount of coercion necessary to overcome her token resistance. A woman seldom creates imagery in which there is genuine fear, pain, revulsion, and humiliation.

Why is this sanitized rape scenario arousing? In addition to the woman's being in control and being the cause of the male's arousal, the female actively enjoys the "rapist's" inability to resist her charms (Leitenberg & Henning, 1995). Also, playing the submissive role allows the woman to experience guilt-free pleasure while engaging in otherwise unacceptable sexual acts with an inappropriate partner. The fact that she is "forced" to do such things absolves her of blame because the fantasized activity is ostensibly not her responsibility (Knafo & Jaffe, 1984).

A more straightforward suggestion is that women think about (and often are aroused by) images of being coerced because they are more likely than men to have had such experiences. For example, women are statistically more likely than men to have been the victims of childhood sexual abuse (Leitenberg & Henning, 1995). As a result, it is possible that the submissive role has been paired with sexual arousal for women and that submissive fantasies would therefore be more prevalent among them than among men.

Some feminist observers have placed gender differences in this type of fantasy in a broader and more general context than child abuse. For example, Brownmiller (1975) indicates that women have had to accept a subservient role in a male-dominated society in which sexual aggression is commonplace. As a result, female fantasies of subservience are simply a reflection of the fact that they have accepted the position of inferiority and submission in a patriarchal culture.

Despite the interest in the general question and the controversy surrounding the competing explanations for gender differences in submissive sexual imagery, many potentially important empirical questions have not yet been addressed. For example, are women who report having the most frequent and most arousing submissive sexual fantasies more likely to become the target of sexual coercion than are women who do not report a high frequency of these fantasies? If so, is the fantasy behavior a precursor of the coercive experiences? If so, do the fantasies serve as scripts in their precoercive interactions with men? What is the source of submissive fantasies? Do women who do and do not have such fantasies differ in their childhood sexual experiences?

Do they differ in their attitudes about the relative place of men and women in society?

These questions remain unanswered as yet, but a few of the issues related to "guilt-free pleasure" seem to have been explored extensively in research. For example, are actual coercive experiences characterized by guilt-free pleasure? No. For example, children who have been sexually exploited by an adult often do report that the experience involved pleasure (Gil, 1985), as well as negative emotions (Scott & Flowers, 1988), but the long-range effects have uniformly been found to be negative. For example, guilt and sexual maladjustment are commonly experienced (LaBarbera, 1984; Meiselman, 1980; Silbert, 1989; Tsai & Wagner, 1978). Similarly, among teenage and adult female targets of harassment, date rape, and stranger rape, the reports almost always involve negative rather than positive immediate and long-term reactions (Beazlie, 1981; Benson & Thomson, 1982; Burgess & Holmstrom, 1985; Murnen, Perot, & Byrne, 1989). At the very least, it does not appear that positive experiences as the target of sexual aggression serve as the origin of pleasurable rape fantasies. And, to date, there are no findings indicating that such fantasies increase the likelihood of being the target of coercive acts.

Men as Initiators of Sexual Coercion

Though no connection between common female sexual fantasies and their overt behavior has been established, the story for men is quite different. As we indicated in discussing fantasy content, men are more likely than women to fantasize about dominating and forcing a sexual partner (Sue, 1979). Further, in male-female interactions, men are much more likely to dominate and forcibly to obtain sexual gratification than are women (Byrne, 1991; Greendlinger, 1985; Hogben, Byrne, & Hamburger, 1996; Kanin, 1957; Kanin & Purcell, 1977).

More directly relevant to the general question, there is a consistent relationship between having coercive fantasies and engaging in coercive behavior (Greendlinger & Byrne, 1987). That is, those undergraduate men who most frequently report having coercive fantasies (such as having a woman tied to a bed, struggling with a woman to obtain sex, and forcing a woman to have sex) also are most likely to report having used coercive sexual techniques (including lies, threats, and the use of force) to obtain a sexual goal.

The question of why males engage in fantasies of sexual domination and find them arousing seems much more commonsensical than the comparable question about why women engage in fantasies of sexual submission and find them arousing. Perhaps violence and aggression are as American and masculine as apple pie. Perhaps not. In any event, it is relatively easy to make the case that dominant sexuality more often leads to reward rather than punishment (Hogben & Byrne, 1998). Further, dominance fantasies reflect the values and norms of a patriarchal culture. They are repeatedly portrayed throughout the media as entertainment. Strong men dominate weak men, men dominate women, and men dominate this planet and outer space as well. Further, a sociobiological underpinning is provided by the proposal that reproductive success is enhanced by the male's ability to compete with and banish rival males and to overcome any reluctance of fit females to copulate (Leitenberg & Henning, 1995).

In addition to self-reported fantasies about coercive sex, males who are sexually aggressive also are found to have a consistent amalgam of beliefs and attitudes that at least support and perhaps foster their treatment of women. For example, males who behave in sexually coercive ways also are found to accept a variety of rape myths as factual (Burt, 1980), hold adversarial beliefs about male-female relationships (Burt & Albin, 1981), have a proclivity for many forms of aggression (Hogben, Byrne, & Hamburger, 1999), accept interpersonal violence as normative (Burt & Albin, 1981), hold traditional stereotypes about sex roles (Burt, 1980), and endorse hypermasculine values (Mosher, 1991).

Though there is a great deal of evidence linking various male dispositional components to coercive sexuality, additional data are needed to answer the same kind of questions that we raised about female behavior. That is, are coercive fantasies actually a precursor of coercive actions? Do the fantasies serve as scripts in interactions with women? What is the source of coercive fantasies? Do men who do and do not have such fantasies differ in their childhood sexual experiences?

Sexual Fantasies and Other Sexual Offenses

The most serious and frightening possibility is that the violent sexual fantasies of some individuals play a role in the commission of sex crimes. And, if so, it would seem possible that the presence of such fantasies might be used to predict future criminal sexual behavior. If those two hypotheses could be confirmed, the prospect is raised of altering current violent sexual fantasies as a way to prevent future sexual crimes. To date, these propositions go far beyond what has been empirically established.

The only clear and consistent finding is that sex offenders fantasize about the sexually deviant acts in which they have previously engaged. For example, in a group of convicted sexual criminals, about 80% reported masturbatory fantasies that were directly related to their offenses (MacCulloch, Snowden, Wood, & Mills, 1983). In another investigation of convicted killers, 86% of serial sexual murderers reported violent sexual fantasies such as rape, murder, or both. Among those who had committed only one sexual murder, 23% reported such fantasies (Prentky et al., 1989).

This rather dramatic association between *prior* offenses and fantasy once again cannot be interpreted as evidence that the fantasies led to the behavior. Summing up their review of the literature on this topic, Leitenberg and Henning (1995, p. 488) conclude, "there is no evidence that sexual fantasies, by themselves, are either a sufficient or a necessary condition for committing a sexual offense." For example, data demonstrating that adult sexual offenders had sexually aggressive fantasies as children have been sufficiently inconsistent to permit any firm conclusions (MacCulloch et al., 1983; Marshall, Barbaree, & Eccles, 1991; Ressler, Burgess, & Douglas, 1988; Schlesinger & Kutash, 1981).

The need for additional research in this area was pinpointed by Leitenberg and Henning, (1995). Specifically needed are (1) studies of the sexual fantasies of children between the ages of 5 and 12, (2) cross-cultural and historical studies of fantasies to distinguish sociobiological and sociocultural sources of fantasy content, and (3) longitudinal studies of fantasy across the life span to understand the development of fantasy preferences, how content changes over time, and the interactive effects of fantasy and behavior.

THE BEHAVIORAL EFFECTS OF EXPOSURE TO EROTICA AND/OR PORNOGRAPHY

Just as fantasies evoke sexual arousal and are associated with overt behavior, there is also evidence that erotica is arousing and that it affects behavior (Fisher & Barak, 1991).

Benign and Beneficial Behavioral Effects

Beginning with the report of the U.S. President's Commission on Obscenity and Pornography in 1970 and 1971, research has consistently indicated that short-term exposure to erotica produces small, transient increases in whatever sexual acts are already practiced by individuals or couples (e.g., Fisher & Byrne, 1978a). Fisher (1986) points out that this effect has been found cross-culturally, and that it has been documented among both student and nonstudent samples.

How one responds to such findings depends, of course, on how one evaluates acts such as masturbation, oral sex, nonmissionary position intercourse, or whatever. If one perceives such behavior as immoral or undesirable, one might conclude that the general public should be protected from exposure to erotica. For others, the fact that erotica facilitates normative, consensual, nonaggressive sexuality as opposed to aggressive and predatory sexuality would be viewed as a positive feature of such material. It is possible to go further and suggest that the message of erotica promoting safer sex in the form of condom use (Wright & Kyes, 1996) or of erotica promoting sex in the context of a loving relationship (Fisher & Byrne, 1978b) is clearly in the public good.

Negative Behavioral and Attitudinal Effects

The focus of a great deal of research has been directed toward the potentially negative effects of erotica and pornography. One familiar question involves the effect of pornography on male attitudes about and male behavior toward females. It has frequently been proposed that pornography engenders hostility toward women, and a number of investigations have provided support for this hypothesis. For example, Malamuth (1981) found that after being exposed to violent rape material or to a depiction of mutually consenting sex, men in the former group were more likely than those in the latter group to write a story with sexually violent content. Exposure to sexual violence also increases male acceptance of violence against women and acceptance of rape myths such as the assertion that women secretly desire to be raped (Malamuth, 1981).

Other studies have consistently reported that men who are exposed to violent pornography subsequently behave more aggressively toward a female experimenter or research confederate than men not so exposed (Fisher, 1986). In one experiment, Donnerstein and Berkowitz (1981) directed a female confederate to anger some of the male participants but not others. These males were then shown either a brief neutral film, an erotic film, or a pornographic film depicting violence. After watching the film, the participants were given an experimental task in which they could deliver an electric shock to the confederate. Compared to participants who viewed either the neutral or the erotic film, those who had been provoked and then exposed to sexual violence administered higher levels of shock. The investigator reported that the shock levels were especially high when the violent pornography portrayed the woman as deriving pleasure from her sexual violation.

An additional hypothesis predicts that degrading pornography should engender calloused attitudes toward women and erroneous conceptions of sexual behavior. The rationale for this hypothesis is that women in such material are usually portrayed as easily aroused sexually, indiscriminate in their choice of sexual partners, and ready and eager to gratify any sexual wish expressed by a man. In an experimental test of the proposed negative attitudinal effects, exposure to sexually degrading material led the participants to overestimate the base rate of nonnormative sexual behavior, to express less support for the women's liberation movement, and to respond to a rapist less punitively (Zillmann & Bryant, 1984). Later research (Zillmann & Bryant, 1986) also found that repeated exposure to degrading pornography results in an increased desire to view sexually violent pornography as well as depictions of several relatively uncommon sexual activities. These investigators concluded that such findings provide evidence that long-term exposure to pornography decreases satisfaction with the physical attractiveness of one's partner and the quality of her sexual performance and increases the desire for emotionally uncommitted sexual involvement.

Problems with Drawing Conclusions about the
Adverse Effects of Pornography

As consistent and convincing as these various findings may be, Fisher and Barak (1989, 1991) observe that since the 1980s, there has been an accumulation of new evidence that is inconsistent with concluding a causal link between pornography and negative attitudes and behavior toward women; they have summarized four criticisms of the previous conclusions.

Overly Simplistic Theory.   Fisher and Barak (1991) suggest that much of the research is based on the "monkey see, monkey do" theory of media effects.

Though research on modeling behavior does suggest that people are influenced by what they see and hear, it is far from an instant and universal tendency to imitate whatever is observed in any sort of presentation. Humans are not warm-blooded copier machines. Fisher and Barak point out that this is a reductionist view that fails to take into account humans as social perceivers who rely on cognition to define and interpret events. That is, consumers of pornography are cognizant of the many social reinforcement contingencies and the norms that dictate appropriate and inappropriate behavior.

In addition, modeling has been described as a gradual three-step process that results in shifts in the probability of new behavior only for some portion of those who are exposed to the models (Byrne, 1977). At step 1, repeated exposure (Zajonc, 1968) to portrayals of a given sexual behavior is likely to increase one's positive evaluation of that behavior over time. This effect occurs, however, only among those individuals who are not extremely negative in the first place and only among those who choose to be exposed to such material. No one is forced to buy tickets to a given movie, to rent a given videotape, to tune in a given TV channel, or to visit a given Web site. At step 2, for those whose evaluative responses have become more positive as a function of repeated exposure, there is increased likelihood of incorporating images of the behavior in question into masturbatory and coital fantasies (Schmidt & Sigusch, 1973). The third step involves acting out the fantasy in overt behavior, and this is the step most inhibited by considerations of right versus wrong, appropriate versus inappropriate, legal versus illegal, and fulfilling versus self-destructive. Though a very small percentage of the population may lack such regulatory controls, it is unrealistic to attempt to shield them from all potential sources of unacceptable models, of which pornography is only a small fragment (Fisher & Barak, 1991).

Inconsistent Effects of Pornography in the Laboratory.   Investigators have found it difficult to replicate the negative effects of either degrading or violent pornography. For example, Linz (1989) compared and reviewed the results of experiments dealing with the trivialization of rape as a function of exposure to degrading pornography and found no consistent pattern of results. He concluded that the existing data *do not* provide evidence that exposure to nonviolent pornography has negative effects on attitudes toward rape or rape victims. Similarly, with violent pornography, Fisher and Grenier (1994) have had difficulty in replicating the negative effects reported by Malamuth (1981) and others. In their attempts to replicate the earlier finding, research participants who viewed pornographic films did *not* differ afterward from viewers of neutral or erotic films in the sexual fantasies they wrote, attitudes toward women, acceptance of interpersonal violence, or belief in rape myths.

Laboratory versus the Real World.   The problem is not that there is something wrong with laboratory research. Experiments in controlled settings are essential to most fields of science. Yet, this truth does not mean that every experiment is instantly generalizable to the real world. For example, research participants in a laboratory experiment often have a restricted array of both stimulus and response choices. In the outside world, people don't *have* to watch violent pornography. In fact, given a choice, research participants are three times more likely to watch G-, R-, and X-rated films than depictions of bondage, sadomasochism, and bestiality (Zillmann & Bryant, 1986). People also have a greater freedom to choose how they respond. Consider the Donnerstein and Berkowitz (1981) experiment in which male participants were provoked by a female confederate, then exposed to different types of films, and subsequently given the opportunity to respond to her with electric shock. Rather than restricting the response possibilities to levels of shock, Fisher and Grenier (1994) gave the participants the choice of shocking the confederate, talking to her on an intercom, or terminating their participation in the experiment. Only 12.5% of the participants chose shock. In natural settings, we typically have many possible behavioral choices as alternatives to an aggressive one.

An additional consideration in the study of unacceptable behavior in the laboratory is that research participants tend to be free of various restraints on what they do. They need not experience guilt about hurting another person because the experimenter has told them to push the shock button, for example. They need not fear retaliation from the person who received shock because they are in a controlled setting under the protection of an institution such as a university.

Absence of Data Supporting Pornography's Impact on Real-World Behavior.   Perhaps because of the differences between the laboratory and the outside world just outlined, attempts to find parallels between the effects of pornography in the lab and pornography elsewhere have not met with notable success. Despite the assumptions about the power of pornography and the laws enacted on the basis of those assumptions, Fisher and Barak (1989, 1991) point to repeated failures to demonstrate that exposure to aggressive pornography increases sexually aggressive behavior. For example, they noted that at least five studies examined the use of pornography by sex offenders and did not find a link between such material and sexually violent behavior. In addition, studies seeking to demonstrate that an increase in the availability of pornography in a given society and the frequency of reported sex crimes have produced, at most, inconsistent findings.

WHAT CAN WE CONCLUDE?

First and foremost, we must emphasize the need for methodological consistency in research in this field and the need for a great deal of additional research on the questions raised in this chapter. These exhortations may appear banal and obvious, but they are not trivial. Investigators have discovered a great deal about the role of sexual fantasies and about the emotional, attitudinal, and behavioral effects of erotica and pornography, but many important issues remain unresolved. We have noted some of them in this chapter.

Second, it seems fair to state that people are at least as responsive to sexual images as to other types of images that bombard us each day. Further, we incorporate a great many of these external images into our cognitive processes in the form of both information and fantasy scenarios. Though much remains to be learned, it is clear that we use sexual fantasies as a source of entertainment, as a facilitator of sexual excitement and release, and (at times) as guides to our attitudes and behavior. It is the last of these uses that is the source of the greatest amount of societal concern. Unfortunately, this topic is also the one on which research findings have shed as much confusion as enlightenment. Sexuality arouses extreme emotional reactions and extreme attempts to rationalize and justify our positive and negative emotions. It is, therefore, not surprising that some of the research, some of the findings, and some of the conclusions about the findings consist of a mixture of what is rational and what is not so rational. We all need to work on that.

The influence of subjective factors based on beliefs, emotions, and values is not, however, limited to the study of human sexuality or to behavioral science in general. As Francis Bacon pointed out in 1620 in the *Novum Organum:*

> The human understanding is no dry light, but receives infusion from the will and affections; whence proceed sciences which may be called "science as one would." For what a man had rather were true he more readily believes. Therefore he rejects difficult things from impatience of research; sober things, because they narrow hope; the deeper things of nature, from superstition; the light of experience, from arrogance and pride; things not commonly believed, out of deference to the opinion of the vulgar. Numberless in short are the ways, and sometimes imperceptible, in which the affections color and infect the understanding.

REFERENCES

Beazlie, F.S. (1981). Coital injuries of genitalia. *Medical Aspects of Human Sexuality, 15,* 112, 116–117, 120–121.

Benson, D.J., & Thomson, G.E. (1982). Sexual harassment on a university campus: The influence of authority relations, sexual interest, and gender stratification. *Social Problems, 29,* 236–251.

Bouvard, M., Mollard, E., Cottraux, J., & Guerin, J. (1989). Étude préliminaire d'une liste de pensées obsédantes [A preliminary study of a list of obsessive thought]. *L'Encephale, 15,* 351–354.

Brownmiller, S. (1975). *Against our will: Men, women, and rape.* New York: Simon & Schuster.

Burgess, A., & Holmstrom, L. (1985). Rape trauma syndrome and post traumatic stress response. In A.W. Burgess (Ed.), *Rape and sexual assault: A research handbook* (pp. 46–60). New York: Garland.

Burt, M.R. (1980). Cultural myths and supports for rape. *Journal of Personality and Social Psychology, 38,* 217–230.

Burt, M.R., & Albin, R.S. (1981). Rape myths, rape definitions, and probability of conviction. *Journal of Applied Social Psychology, 11,* 212–230.

Byers, E.S., Purdon, C., & Clark, D.A. (1998). Sexual intrusive thoughts of college students. *Journal of Sex Research, 35,* 359–369.

Byrne, D. (1977). The imagery of sex. In J. Money & H. Musaph (Eds.), *Handbook of sexology* (pp. 327–350). Amsterdam, The Netherlands: Elsevier.

Byrne, D. (1991). Double standard or *macho* myopia? *Playboy, 38*(2), 42.

Byrne, D. (1997a). An overview (and underview) of research and theory within the attraction paradigm. *Journal of Social and Personal Relationships, 14,* 417–431.

Byrne, D. (1997b). Why would anyone conduct research on sexual behavior? In G.G. Brannigan, E.R. Allgeier, & A.R. Allgeier (Eds.), *The sex scientists* (pp. 15–30). New York: Addison Wesley Longmans.

Coles, C.D., & Shamp, M.J. (1984). Some sexual, personality, and demographic characteristics of women readers of erotic romances. *Archives of Sexual Behavior, 13,* 187–209.

Cowan, G., Lee, C., Levy, D., & Snyder, D. (1988). Dominance and inequality in X-rated videocassettes. *Psychology of Women Quarterly, 12,* 299–311.

Davis, C.M., & Bauserman, R. (1993). Exposure to sexually explicit materials: An attitude change perspective. *Annual Review of Sex Research, 4,* 121–209.

Donnerstein, E., & Berkowitz, L. (1981). Victim reactions in aggressive erotic films as a factor in violence against women. *Journal of Personality and Social Psychology, 41,* 710–724.

Donnerstein, E., Linz, D., & Penrod, S. (1987). *The question of pornography: Research findings and policy implications.* New York: Free Press.

Eliasberg, W.G., & Stuart, I.R. (1961). Authoritarian personality and the obscenity threshold. *Journal of Social Psychology, 55,* 143–151.

Ellis, B.J., & Symons, D. (1990). Sex differences in sexual fantasy: An evolutionary psychological approach. *Journal of Sex Research, 27,* 527–555.

Ellis, H. (1942). *Studies in the psychology of sex* (Vols. 1 & 2). New York: Random House. (Original work published in seven volumes, 1896–1928)

Fisher, W.A. (1986). The emperor has no clothes: On the Fraser and Badgley committee's rejection of social science research on pornography. In J. Lowman, M.A. Jackson, T.S. Palys, & S. Gavigan (Eds.), *Regulating sex: An anthology of commentaries on the findings and recommendations of the Badgley and Fraser reports* (pp. 159–176). Burnbay, BC: Simon Fraser University.

Fisher, W.A., & Barak, A. (1989). Sex education as a corrective: Immunizing against possible effects of pornography. In D. Zillmann & J. Bryant (Eds.), *Pornography: Recent research, interpretations, and policy considerations* (pp. 289–320). Hillsdale, NJ: LEA.

Fisher, W.A., & Barak, A. (1991). Pornography, erotica, and behavior: More questions than answers. *International Journal of Law and Psychiatry, 14,* 65–83.

Fisher, W.A., & Byrne, D. (1978a). Individual differences in affective, evaluative, and behavioral responses to an erotic film. *Journal of Applied Social Psychology, 8,* 355–365.

Fisher, W.A., & Byrne, D. (1978b). Sex differences in response to erotica? Love versus lust. *Journal of Personality and Social Psychology, 36,* 119–125.

Fisher, W.A., Byrne, D., White, L.A., & Kelley, K. (1988). Erotophobia-erotophilia as a dimension of personality. *Journal of Sex Research, 25,* 123–151.

Fisher, W.A., & Grenier, G. (1994). Violent pornography, antiwoman thoughts, and antiwoman acts: In search of reliable effects. *Journal of Sex Research, 31,* 23–38.

Geer, J.H., & Fuhr, R. (1976). Cognitive factors in sexual arousal: The role of distraction. *Journal of Consulting and Clinical Psychology, 44,* 238–243.

Giambra, L.M., & Singer, J.L. (1998). The sexual daydreaming scale of the imaginal processes inventory. In C.M. Davis, W.L. Yarber, R. Bauserman, G. Schreer, & S.L. Davis (Eds.), *Handbook of sexuality-related measures* (pp. 234–235). Thousand Oaks, CA: Sage.

Gil, V.E. (1985, September). *In thy father's house: Incest in conservative Christian homes.* Paper presented at the meeting of the Society for the Scientific Study of Sexuality, San Diego.

Greendlinger, V. (1985). *Dispositional and situational variables as predictors of rape proclivity in college men.* Unpublished doctoral dissertation, University at Albany, State University of New York.

Greendlinger, V., & Byrne, D. (1987). Coercive sexual fantasies of college men as predictors of self-reported likelihood to rape and overt sexual aggression. *Journal of Sex Research, 23,* 1–11.

Hogben, M., & Byrne, D. (1998). Using social learning theory to explain individual differences in human sexuality. *Journal of Sex Research, 35,* 58–71.

Hogben, M., Byrne, D., & Hamburger, M.E. (1996). Coercive heterosexual sexuality: Similar or dissimilar male-female experiences in dating relationships. *Journal of Psychology and Human Sexuality, 8,* 69–78.

Hogben, M., Byrne, D., & Hamburger, M.E. (1999). *Legitimized aggression and sexual coercion: Individual differences in cultural spillover.* Paper submitted for publication. University at Albany, State University of New York.

Hsu, B., Kling, A., Kessler, C., Knapke, K., Diefenbach, P., & Elias, J.E. (1994). Gender differences in sexual fantasy and behavior in a college population: A ten-year replication. *Journal of Sex & Marital Therapy, 20,* 103–118.

Hurlbert, D.F., & Apt, C. (1993). Female sexuality: A comparative study between women in homosexual and heterosexual relationships. *Journal of Sex & Marital Therapy, 19,* 315–327.

Jones, J.C., & Barlow, D.H. (1990). Self-reported frequency of sexual urges, fantasies, and masturbatory fantasies in heterosexual males and females. *Archives of Sexual Behavior, 19,* 269–279.

Kanin, E.J. (1957). Male aggression in dating-courtship relations. *American Journal of Sociology, 63,* 197–204.

Kanin, E.J., & Purcell, S.R. (1977). Sexual aggression: A second look at the offended female. *Archives of Sexual Behavior, 6,* 67–76.

Kaplan, H.S. (1979). *The new sex therapy.* New York: Brunner/Mazel.

Knafo, D., & Jaffe, Y.(1984). Sexual fantasizing in males and females. *Journal of Research in Personality, 18,* 451–462.

LaBarbera, J.D. (1984). Seductive father-daughter relationships and sex-roles in women. *Sex Roles, 11,* 941–951.

Lehne, G.K. (1978). Gay male fantasies and realities. *Journal of Social Issues, 34*(3), 28–37.

Leitenberg, H., & Henning, K. (1995). Sexual fantasy. *Psychological Bulletin, 117,* 469–496.

Linz, D. (1989). Exposure to sexually explicit materials and attitudes toward rape: A comparison of study results. *Journal of Sex Research, 26,* 50–84.

MacCulloch, M.J., Snowden, P.R., Wood, P.J.W., & Mills, H.E. (1983). Sadistic fantasy, sadistic behaviour and offending. *British Journal of Psychiatry, 143,* 20–29.

Malamuth, N.M. (1981). Rape fantasies as a function of exposure to violent-sexual stimuli. *Archives of Sexual Behavior, 10,* 33–47.

Malamuth, N.M., & Spinner, B. (1980). A longitudinal content analysis of sexual vio-lence in the best-selling erotic magazines. *Journal of Sex Research, 16,* 226–237.

Marshall, W.L., Barbaree, H.E., & Eccles, A. (1991). Early onset and deviant sexuality in child molesters. *Journal of Interpersonal Violence, 6,* 323–336.

Masters, W.H., & Johnson, V.E. (1966). *Human sexual response.* Boston: Little, Brown.

Masters, W.H., & Johnson, V.E. (1979). *Homosexuality in perspective.* Boston: Little, Brown.

McCauley, C., & Swann, C.P. (1978). Male-female differences in sexual fantasy. *Journal of Research in Personality, 12,* 76–86.

McCauley, C., & Swann, C.P. (1980). Sex differences in the frequency and functions of fantasies during sexual activity. *Journal of Research in Personality, 14,* 400–411.

Meiselman, K.C. (1980). Personality characteristics of incest history among psycho-therapy patients: A research note. *Archives of Sexual Behavior, 9,* 195–197.

Meuwissen, I., & Over, R. (1991). Multidimensionality of the content of female sexual fantasy. *Behaviour Research and Therapy, 29,* 179–189.

Money, J. (1985, September). *Pornography as related to criminal sex offending and the his-tory of medical degeneracy theory.* Paper presented at the U.S. Justice Department Hearings, Houston.

Mosher, D.L. (1991). Macho men, machismo, and sexuality. *Annual Review of Sex Re-search, 2,* 199–247.

Mosher, D.L., & Anderson, R.D. (1986). Macho personality, sexual aggression, and re-actions to guided imagery of realistic rape. *Journal of Research in Personality, 20,* 77–94.

Murnen, S.K., Perot, A., & Byrne, D. (1989). Coping with unwanted sexual activity: Normative responses, situational determinants, and individual differences. *Journal of Sex Research, 26,* 85–106.

Norris, J. (1989). Normative influence effects on sexual arousal to nonviolent sexually explicit material. *Journal of Applied Social Psychology, 19,* 341–352.

Prentky, R.A., Burgess, A.W., Rokous, F., Lee, A., Hartman, C., Ressler, R., & Douglass, J. (1989). The presumptive role of fantasy in serial sexual homicide. *American Journal of Psychiatry, 146,* 887–891.

Price, J.H., Allensworth, D.D., & Hillman, K.S. (1985). Comparison of sexual fantasies of homosexuals and of heterosexuals. *Psychological Reports, 57,* 871–877.

Przybyla, D.P.J., & Byrne, D. (1984). The mediating role of cognitive processes in self-reported sexual arousal. *Journal of Research in Personality, 18,* 54–63.

Ressler, R.K., Burgess, A.W., & Douglas, J.E. (1988). *Sexual homicide: Patterns and mo-tives.* Lexington, MA: Lexington Books.

Schlesinger, L.B., & Kutash, I.L. (1981). The criminal fantasy technique: A comparison of sex offenders and substance abusers. *Journal of Clinical Psychology, 37,* 210–218.

Schmidt, V., & Sigusch, F. (1973). Women's sexual arousal. In J. Zubin & J. Money (Eds.), *Contemporary sexual behavior: Critical issues in the 1970s* (pp. 117–143). Balti-more: Johns Hopkins University Press.

Scott, J.E., & Cuvelier, S.J. (1987). Violence in *Playboy* magazine: A longitudinal analy-sis. *Archives of Sexual Behavior, 16,* 279–288.

Scott, R.L., & Flowers, J.V. (1988). Betrayal by the mother as a factor contributing to psychological disturbance in victims of father-daughter incest: An MMPI analysis. *Journal of Social and Clinical Psychology, 6,* 147–154.

Silbert, M.H. (1989). The effects on juveniles of being used for pornography and prostitution. In D. Zillmann & J. Bryant (Eds.), *Pornography: Research advances and policy considerations* (pp. 215–234). Hillsdale, NJ: LEA.

Smith, D., & Over, R. (1991). Male sexual fantasy: Multidimensionality in content. *Behaviour Research and Therapy, 29,* 267–275.

Sue, D. (1979). Erotic fantasies of college students during coitus. *Journal of Sex Research, 15,* 299–305.

Tsai, M., & Wagner, N.N. (1978). Therapy groups for women sexually molested as children. *Archives of Sexual Behavior, 19,* 417–427.

Wilson, G.D., & Lang, R.J. (1981). Sex differences in sexual fantasy patterns. *Personality and Individual Differences, 2,* 343–346.

Wright, S.S., & Kyes, K.B. (1996). The effects of safer-sex stories on college students' attitudes toward condoms. *Journal of Psychology & Human Sexuality, 8,* 1–17.

Zajonc, R.B. (1968). Attitudinal effects of mere exposure. *Journal of Personality and Social Psychology Monographs Supplement, 9,* 1–27.

Zillmann, D., & Bryant, J. (1984). Effects of massive exposure to pornography. In N.M. Malamuth & E. Donnerstein (Eds.), *Pornography and sexual aggression* (pp. 115–138). Orlando, FL: Academic Press.

Zillmann, D., & Bryant, J. (1986). Shifting preferences in pornography consumption. *Communication Research, 13,* 560–578.

PART III

DESEXUALIZED GROUPS

CHAPTER 8

Disabled Sexual Partners

LINDA R. MONA and P. SÁNDOR GARDOS

T HE SEXUALITY OF persons with disabilities has been an area of research that has been slow to progress. There has also been debate about where disability-related issues fit within the context of human sexuality. Some textbooks have a separate chapter; others have included it within the information on aging. Disability scholars have argued that the unique experience of disability should be explored as a separate entity. Disability is, in fact, a distinct social experience and can be experienced at all ages and affect people at various stages throughout life. Fortunately, with the growing consciousness of disability, following the advent of the Americans with Disabilities Act (ADA) in 1990, the social experience of this community has been more readily recognized. Under this heightened general awareness, psychologists and other academicians have questioned how to include this community within the scope of behavioral sciences. Indeed, sexuality has been one of the last areas studied from a psychological perspective.

This chapter explores the social, functional, and behavioral influences and products of disability and sexuality. Past research has focused on the sexual *functioning* of persons with disabilities. This approach has viewed psychological issues as a *consequence* of the disability rather than a product of society's constrained notions of beauty, attractiveness, and suitability as a partner.

Given that much of the material in this chapter frames disability from a social or minority model experience, we have made a conscious choice to use the terms such as "disabled person" and "disability community." Many individuals from the rehabilitation disciplines advocate for "person-first language" (i.e., "person with a disability") and claim that this usage of words is most respectful to this population because it emphasizes the person first and the disability second. However, many disability studies scholars and disability rights activists argue that disability is the primary lens with which they view life and

309

feel comfort and pride in referring to themselves as disabled persons. Our choice of phrasing was made in an attempt to be respectful of all sectors of the community and to acknowledge the social experience of disability. This is not to say that functional ability and medically related issues do not affect the sexual expression of persons with disabilities. They do play an important role, but it is not the only role. Both of these perspectives will be explored and explained in subsequent sections.

Additionally, this chapter attempts to explore sexuality issues across multiple disabilities. Specifically, this chapter has been shaped to be inclusive of persons with physical, developmental, sensory, and cognitive disabilities, as well as chronic health conditions. Some authors have taken this approach in the past, but they focused primarily on functional and medically related effects of disability on sexual activity (Sipski & Alexander, 1997). This chapter combines that approach with a psychosocial perspective.

We begin by looking at the various ways in which disability has been approached through history and continue on to discussions about sexuality and society, education, relationships, specific conditions, pregnancy, parenting, and clinical treatment, all as viewed through the lens of a psychological and research-based approach to the understanding of sexuality and disability.

HISTORICAL MODELS OF DISABILITY

Persons with disabilities and the psychological variables that influence their lives have historically been largely ignored by psychology and the social-behavioral sciences. However, this population has begun to be investigated more extensively in recent years by disability studies scholars and other academicians. Three main models of viewing disability have been apparent throughout history (Longmore, 1993). The *moral model* views disability as a punishment for a sin or as the result of engaging in negative behavior. Thus, the moral model maintains that disabilities are self-inflicted. This mind-set dates back to the early 1900s. For example, in 1911, the Chicago court system upheld "ugly wards," which prohibited interaction in the social arena by those individuals who were deemed aesthetically disgusting. The Chicago statute prohibited any

> person with disease, maimed, mutilated, or in any other way deformed so as to be an unsightly or disgusting object, or improper person to be allowed in or on the public ways or in other public places in this city or to expose himself to public view. (cited in Longmore, 1993, p. 2)

The second model of disability, the *medical model*, views disability in terms of how to fix or cure the condition so that the person can assimilate into the able-bodied majority. According to this model, there is only one way to move from the disability state of being to a normal state of being: by overcoming the disability (Longmore, 1993). This is accomplished by displaying an unconquerable spirit to become as able-bodied as possible. The basic message of the medical model has sometimes been seen as "It is not okay to be disabled and you must do as much as possible to return to an able-bodied state." This type of rhetoric reinforces society's beliefs that the primary solution to the problems of disabled people is the pursuit of a cure.

The third model is the *minority model*, which suggests that physical appearance and health status play no role when talking about disability. This perspective maintains that because disabled people are different from the majority culture, they must define themselves as a minority group (Gill, 1995; Longmore, 1993). According to this model, it is the social and architectural environments that prevent disabled people from flourishing in today's world. This is the only model that removes the socially defined "problem" of disability from the disabled person and places it in the outside world. It is this view that has been employed most recently by disabled historians and theorists.

According to Gill (1995), more recent work in the area of disability points to two contrasting models of disability. First, the medical model of disability, already defined, views disability as a deficiency, as being negative, and as residing within the individual. Accordingly, the remedy for disability-related problems is a cure or normalization of the individual, and the agent of remedy is a professional. In contrast, Gill defines the *interactional model* of disability as viewing disability as a difference; being disabled in itself is neutral, and disability derives from the interaction between the individual and society. Within the context of this model, the remedy for disability-related problems is to change the interactions between individuals and society. The agent of remedy in this case can be the individual, an advocate, or anyone who affects the arrangements between individual and society.

Although these models have served as potentially useful heuristic devices, it is unclear to what degree disabled persons view themselves through such lenses. We present them primarily as a conceptual framework to help approach and understand this topic. Despite the fact that there is not yet a strong body of research supporting any one of these models, we believe that a minority-based model that also acknowledges the importance of both medical and psychosocial considerations provides the most comprehensive means to approach the topic of sexuality and disability.

SOCIETAL INFLUENCES ON THE SEXUAL EXPRESSION OF PEOPLE WITH DISABILITIES

Throughout history, persons with disabilities have been viewed as less than completely human. This mind-set dates back to the eugenics movement, which made its way to the United States in 1905 (Hubbard, 1997). Much of the rhetoric argued for the prohibition of marriage between individuals who were deemed racially, religiously, physically, and/or mentally inferior. The stated intent was to ensure that a higher quality stock of individuals was propagated.

The first sterilization law was enacted in 1907; by 1931, 30 states had compulsory sterilization laws on their books (Hubbard, 1997). Although these laws were aimed primarily at the "feeble-minded," they also included persons with epilepsy and "other diseased and degenerate parsons" (Ludmerer, 1972). Thus, there is a long history of declaring that people with disabilities should not only not have the same access as others—but not even exist! Interestingly, many of these antidisability efforts have centered on sexuality and/or the right to procreate.

Even though many of these laws have changed, and there is now more understanding of persons with disabilities, the media continue to promote false accounts and depictions of the sexual lives of the disability community. Media images of sexual attractiveness that focus on perfectly shaped, able-bodied persons have created normative standards of beauty and attractiveness in American culture. Persons with disabilities are not typically included within these standards and thus may receive the message that they are not included in this group or perceived as sexual beings. For example, Heatherington (1993) suggests that "persons with disabilities are not portrayed as sexy in advertisements or in television and film, a person with a disability is never seen as the love-heroine or the person who 'wins over' their desired love interest." Heatherington further notes that media influences have been one of the largest "culprits" in the expression of incorrect information about disabled persons' sexuality.

The effects of the media, and societal attitudes in general, are broad and affect the way able-bodied people view individuals with disabilities, in addition to the manner in which people within the disability community view themselves. Some research has looked at able-bodied persons' attitudes toward the sexuality of disabled individuals. Many women have reported that they see a woman with a disability as unsuitable for romantic partnership because of such characteristics as fragility, immaturity, and emotional and physical dependency (Hanna & Rogovsky, 1986). Furthermore, Unger, Hilderbrand, and Mardox (1982) found that college students and clinicians rate disabled women as unattractive compared to matched able-bodied peers. From a behavioral perspective, Scotti, Slack, Browman, and Morris (1996) found that college students view various sexual behaviors (i.e., public and private displays of affection, safer sex behaviors alone or between male-female partners) of persons with mental retardation as being somewhat less acceptable than those same behaviors engaged in by able-bodied college students. Attitudes of caregivers of people with developmental disabilities accept sexual expression among members of this community, but acceptance seems to be limited by type of activity (Chapman & Pitceathly, 1985; Mulhern, 1975). Specifically, masturbation and kissing were viewed as acceptable whereas intercourse was not. As in modern racial relations, though there may be an *intellectual* acceptance, it has yet to translate on a deeper emotional level.

The way that people with disabilities view themselves sexually is also clearly shaped by societal messages. For men with disabilities, issues of masculinity, sexual assertiveness, and/or sexual competence often arise. Specifically, gender-related concepts of being strong and virile (e.g., the ability to communicate easily, move one's body freely, as well as achieve and sustain an erection) are often incongruent with many disabilities. Similarly, on a psychological level, some women with disabilities may feel that they do not meet societal norms of attractiveness and gender-related expectations (e.g., lack of sex appeal or confidence in the ways that their bodies move). Thus, in view of the importance of the psychological experience of sexuality, the literature assessing the sexual self-views of disabled people is of particular interest.

DISABILITY AND THE DEVELOPMENT OF SEXUAL SELF-CONCEPT AND SEXUAL SELF-ESTEEM

Research examining the relationship between self-constructs and sexuality in persons with disabilities has expanded in recent years (Brown, 1988; DeHaan & Wallander, 1988; Fitting, Salisbury, Davis, & Maydin, 1988; Mona, Gardos, & Brown, 1994). In the past, it had been thought that an individual's sense of his or her sexuality was subsumed under his or her general feelings of self-esteem, attractiveness, and adequacy to perform sexual acts (T. Cole, 1975; Romano, 1975). Similarly, Helminiak (1989) suggested that sexual self-acceptance (e.g., comfort with one's body as a sexually responsive organism) is critical for the development of positive self-esteem.

Within the realm of sexual self-constructs, several disability-specific factors have been examined. Two main theoretical notions have been most often used. T. Cole (1975) and S. Cole (1988) made a distinction between congenital and acquired disabilities. According to this perspective, individuals with a congenital disability (a genetically transferred condition occurring from birth or early childhood) will integrate their disability into all aspects of their sexual development. By contrast, when a disability is acquired, both gender role and sexual development of the individual are interrupted; thus, problems are accentuated because expectations of masculinity and femininity are already firmly in place. S. Cole's theory also makes a distinction between disabilities that are stable and those that have ongoing health changes (including progressive illnesses). It is proposed that a stable disability can be understood and planned for; thus, a lifestyle can be pursued with realistic goals and reliable expectations. This differs markedly from a progressive disability, which is characterized by a continual state of change where the notion of spontaneity and the ability to plan ahead are severely compromised.

An alternative theory postulates that individuals with lifelong disabilities are socialized from childhood into a disabled role—which is often an asexual one (Rousso, 1982). More specifically, Rousso notes that individuals with earlier age-of-onset disabilities often have problems putting their disability into its proper perspective, demystifying sexuality, developing a positive body image, mastering social skills, and understanding their own sexual functioning. However, Rousso (1984) adds that children with congenital disabilities, having never been nondisabled, "may experience themselves disabled yet intact," with the disability being an instrumental part of their identity (p. 262). As has been noted earlier, however, society often maintains negative attitudes toward people with disabilities, and therefore, disabled children may find it difficult to reconcile these two opposing views, feeling intact yet finding no societal confirmation for this belief. Rousso (1984) indicates that positive, nurturing parental figures greatly influence the ways these children develop self-knowledge and positive self-values.

Although such notions may seem to make logical sense, few empirical studies have examined the effect of age of onset of disability on the sexual self. Some work has pointed to low self-concept for individuals with earlier age-of-onset disabilities (Hayden, Davenport, & Kendel, 1979; Wabrek, Wabrek, & Burchell, 1978). These findings have been explained by the group's extended infantalization (childlike treatment from society), overprotection by parents and others, and social isolation. The self-concept of women with later age-of-onset disabilities does, however, appear to strengthen as a function of time since the onset of the condition (i.e., duration of disability) (Fitting et al., 1988).

DeHaan and Wallander (1988) found no significant differences in the effect of age of onset on general self-esteem among women with disabilities. Also, no significant relationships were found between duration of disability and overall self-concept. These results may be attributed to the fact that only women from a college population were studied; thus, their opportunity for education and exposure to the social world may have provided them with the resources necessary to build a higher self-concept. Overall, for both earlier and later age-of-onset groups, self-concept seems to correlate with the ability to engage in social situations; that is, those who participate in more social arenas seem to see themselves in a more positive light (Fitting et al., 1988).

An additional study (Mona et al., 1994) explored age of onset of disability on a continuum among a sample of 43 women with noticeable mobility impairments. This study found that as age of onset of disability increased, sexual self-esteem ratings decreased. This finding was congruent with S. Cole's (1988) assertion that when a disability is acquired later in life, notions of the sexual self may be interrupted; problems may occur as a result of this sudden alteration in the way in which one has known oneself.

Bullard and Knight's (1981) research indicated that severity of handicap, age of onset of disability, and age of first sexual experience did not relate significantly to sexual difficulties for persons with disabilities. Furthermore, it was the person's attitude that the disability limited possibilities for sexual expression that was most influential. However, because attitudes and other socialization processes are acquired during childhood and adolescence, it seems possible that people with earlier age-of-onset disabilities may differ from those with later age-of-onset disabilities in the ways they define their social roles.

Although there is still much we do not understand about the development of the sexual self in persons with a disability, it is clear that sex education not only has an impact, but is an area that must be carefully examined in its own right. We turn to this topic in the next section.

SEX EDUCATION AND DISABILITY

Sex education for people with disabilities has been a topic widely discussed within the literature. Educational programs have been developed for certain disability groups, but few outcome studies on their effectiveness have been conducted. The following section reviews the research on sex education among individuals from specific disability groups. Unfortunately, as will be apparent, there is no specific research on sex education for people with mobility impairments; most existing programs focus instead on sensory or developmental disabilities.

DEVELOPMENTAL DISABILITIES

Mildly mentally retarded teenagers and adults are rarely provided with sexuality education (Garret, 1971; Hall & Morris, 1976; Hall & Sawyer, 1978; Kempton, 1978). This is unfortunate, given that research on developmentally disabled populations has indicated that sex education greatly increases contraceptive, reproductive, and hygienic knowledge; improves social skills; and reduces inappropriate sexual behavior (Demetral, 1981; Green, 1983; Zylla & Demetral, 1981).

An important factor with developmentally disabled individuals is the views of their parents or guardians about sexuality. The attitudes of personal assistants and/or guardians are important because they often make decisions for persons with developmental disabilities. In one study, 62% of parents were uncomfortable with or unsure about their ability to provide sex education for their developmentally disabled children, even thought 80% of them believed that the family should assume major responsibility (Alcorn, 1974). Turner (1970) sampled the attitudes of parents of developmentally disabled children and noted that the majority of children were not receiving sex education. Furthermore, although mothers were in favor of children's receiving information on hygiene and menstruation, they were not as open about their children's getting information about masturbation and other sexual behaviors. According to Ruble and Dalrymple (1993), parents of children with autism reported that the more verbal skills the child had, the more likely that the child had some knowledge and understanding about sexuality. Similarly, the more verbal the child, the more likely he or she was to have received sex education. However, verbal level had no influence on the sexual behaviors of this sample; a wide range of activities were reported: 65% touched their genitals in public, 28% removed clothing in public, 23% masturbated in public, and 18% touched the opposite sex inappropriately.

Many sex education programs address only some of the issues associated with the sexuality of people with developmental disabilities. According to

Hinsburger (1987), all of the following should be considered when devising a sex education program for people with developmental disabilities: developing a strong sense of self-concept, establishing skills to form relationships with peers, developing social skills, acquiring knowledge about sexuality, developing a positive attitude toward sexuality, addressing negative experiences with sexuality in the past, accepting the sexual behavior of others, and increasing personal power.

McDermott, Kelly, and Spearman (1994) studied the effectiveness of a program specifically designed to increase the use of birth control among women with developmental disabilities. There was a significant shift to permanent birth control for the treatment group, from 42.5% at baseline to 68% after one year. Women also tended to move from no birth control to permanent birth control and from temporary to permanent. This program took place through a family planning clinic's at-home visitation program. The curriculum comprised 30 lesson plans, including bodily functions and hygiene, self-esteem and assertiveness, refusal skills, sexuality and socialization, understanding birth control, proper use of contraception, prevention of sexually transmitted diseases, responsibilities of parenthood, nutrition during pregnancy, child nurturing, child discipline, and coping with prenatal stress. Even though this program seems to have been effective, the fact that so many participants switched to permanent methods of birth control is of some concern. Although this is a valid choice for many women, historically, the medical community has overemphasized these methods for women with cognitive and developmental disabilities, thinking that they could not be taught to use other methods reliably. We must regard these issues as important and advocate for comprehensive education for those with disabilities, including the full range of contraceptive choices.

DEAF/HARD-OF-HEARING

Efforts associated with exploring sex education for the deaf began as early as 1940. Blish (1940) advocated having sex education added to the curriculum, as well as building parental cooperation, developing strict guidelines for teacher preparation, and promoting a school team approach. Over the succeeding years, many researchers have examined the sources of sex education for deaf youth and advocated the need for sex education (Craig & Anderson, 1966; Hill, 1971).

An important milestone occurred in the late 1970s, when sexual signage was developed, allowing individuals who use sign language to communicate more effectively about sexual topics. Since that time, information about sex education for the hard-of-hearing has blossomed. Love (1983) discovered in an attitudinal study that 50% of teachers agreed that teaching about hygiene, sexually transmitted diseases, dating, pregnancy, marriage, birth control, sexual intercourse, and deviant sexual behaviors was vital, and 30% to 40% thought that homosexuality, incest, divorce, masturbation, abortion, and sterilization were topics worth addressing.

Despite these advances and the greater acceptance of sex education for the deaf, Swartz (1995) discovered significant differences with regard to sex knowledge between samples of hearing and deaf college freshmen. Specifically, the data suggested that deaf college freshmen lagged behind hearing college freshmen in nearly every aspect of sex knowledge.

This lack of knowledge may well be caused by a lack of educational materials specifically targeted to this population. Getch and Denny (1998) sent a survey to all deaf schools in the United States (including state schools). Out of 92 questionnaires, 76 were returned, with results indicating that teachers were spending more than two hours per week modifying material for their sexuality curriculum to make it accessible for their students. The need for culturally specific sex education for the deaf is quite apparent (Gannon, 1998).

Much of education regarding HIV/AIDS has tried to tackle the lack of basic health information and the higher risk of HIV transmission that has been seen in the deaf community. Barres (1992) observed youth who were deaf and noted that they were eight years behind in terms of their knowledge and awareness about HIV/AIDS. Doyle's (1995) study indicated that most of his White deaf college student sample had moderate to general knowledge about AIDS. However, even though 67% reported that they had discussed safer sex with a partner, fewer than 50% indicated that they would actually use safer sex.

BLIND, VISUALLY IMPAIRED, AND DEAF-BLIND

According to Schuster (1986), sex education for visually impaired children contains distortions that may promote negative stereotyping of blind children. However, some of Schuster's assumptions of determinants of gender in early adulthood and imagery used to describe blind children have been brought into question. Vaughan and Vaughan (1987) suggested that because visually impaired children are deprived of the major mode of learning about gender differences and appropriate sexual conduct, parents must reevaluate current social taboos against physical contact and generate naturalistic experiences to aid the child in the identification of gender differences, anatomical functioning, and interpersonal skills associated with expressing sexuality, for example through the use of anatomically correct dolls. Specific, age-appropriate intervention strategies from infancy to adulthood within the family context may be important. The relationship of psychosexual concepts to ego identity has been stressed, and it is noted that the blind child experiences frustration at each level of formation of a self-concept because the lack of vision limits contact with reality (Schuster, 1986).

Love (1983) investigated parent and staff attitudes toward sexuality instruction for sensory-impaired students at the Alabama Institute for the Deaf and Blind. A questionnaire was developed and disseminated to 603 parents/

guardians and to 265 staff members. Participants provided data in areas including instruction, grouping of students by gender, and persons responsible for instruction. Individuals' attitudes toward these areas were examined in terms of race, gender, and income. The responses showed strong agreement between parents and staff about the need for instruction about human sexuality. Contrary to the notion that parents of children with sensory impairments are resistant to human sexuality instruction for their children, findings confirmed that parents and staff are not only supportive of but eager for instruction in this area.

Love (1983) discussed the increasing need for accessible educational materials for persons with visual impairments. Parents and professionals have actively sought materials to be converted to Braille or audiotape so that sexual information can be more readily available. The Sex Information and Education Council of the United States surveyed the extent and nature of sex education programs for persons with visual impairments and the use of special materials and facilities. Two hundred and seventy-three institutions and organizations, including public schools, residential programs for the blind, and multiservice agencies, were sent questionnaires. A number of patterns were observed, including the following: public school programs seemed best planned and most fully developed in content, but because mostly visually oriented material was used, many visually disabled people experienced difficulty in understanding the concepts presented. Although residential schools appeared best equipped in materials and facilities, many programs were considered to be in need of further planning and development because of their newness. Multiservice agencies usually treated sex education as part of their counseling services on an individual/as-needed basis (Bidgood, 1971).

EFFECTS OF TYPES OF DISABILITY ON SEXUAL ACTIVITY/BEHAVIOR

The following section provides a summary of relevant psychological and physiological information on a variety of disabilities.

SEXUALITY AND SPINAL CORD INJURY

For a number of historical reasons, the sexuality of men with spinal cord injuries (SCIs) is one of the most understood areas of sexuality and disability. These reasons include the fact that substantial research funds have been allocated toward studying veterans' postwar injuries, many persons with SCIs stay as inpatients in hospital settings and thus become a captive audience for researchers, and penile functioning is considered to be more important and easier to study than vaginal responsiveness. However, in recent years, there has been a marked increase in research on the sexual functioning and psychosexual experience of *women* with SCIs (Charlifue, Gerhart, Menter, Whitnsck,

& Manley, 1992; Komisaruk & Whipple, 1995; Sipski & Alexander, 1997). Although individuals with SCI represent a minority of the disability community, it is the area in which the most research has been conducted. That this section is longer then others reflects that fact, and should not be taken to imply a greater prevalence or importance of this group versus other disabled communities.

Various psychosocial factors affect the sexual self and sexual expression of persons with SCI. Persons who acquire SCI often experience a sense of loss about their able-bodied sexual self and a transition into a state of feeling asexual (S. Cole, 1988). Physical changes that affect body appearance and function may influence the manner in which persons with SCI view themselves sexually and the way that others perceive them as well.

An additional factor affecting the sexual self-definition of persons with SCI is the loss of physical sensation in the genitals and erogenous zones. Depending on the level of injury, individuals with SCI often lose the ability to feel their body becoming sexually aroused and sometimes may not be capable of experiencing a physiological orgasm. This loss is experienced at both the physical and psychological levels. Specifically, persons with SCI have reported feelings of loss over physical sensation, but a more striking sense of loss has been reported over the inability to experience a physiological orgasm with oneself and/or a partner (Gulley, 1993). Some individuals with SCI do report "moving orgasm into the head and having a mental orgasm," but most only feel this way after a period of grieving over the loss of the physiological orgasm experience (Gulley, 1993). Money (1960) noted that orgasm was reported by women and men with SCI, but labeled these experiences as phantom orgasms. In addition, Perduta-Fulginiti (1992) reported that some women with SCI report nongenital orgasms that produce intense physiological pleasure and similar subjective physical sensations during the orgasm phase of the sexual response pattern.

The adjustment process associated with the loss of genital and erogenous zone sensation appears to be complex and comprised of several levels of adaptation. Persons living with SCI are confronted with becoming familiar with a new sense of body image, self-concept, and social identity. This interplay between psychological and physical adjustment processes may be mediated by social and cultural definitions of sexual attractiveness, in addition to able-bodied sexual standards promulgated by society. In general, following injury, persons with SCI need to reevaluate images of sexual attraction, seek to redefine sexuality as a whole, and become familiar with new body functions and sensations.

The degree to which men with SCI experience neurological erectile dysfunction depends on the area of the spinal cord that has been injured (i.e., level within the cervical, thoracic, lumbar, or sacral potions of the spinal cord) and how completely the spinal cord has been damaged. Injuries to the front segments of the cord are most likely to affect sexual function, especially if both left and right sides of the cord are involved (Torrens, 1983). Two spinal areas

that are important to erectile function have been identified as the sacral segments S2 to S4 (exit points for parasympathetic nerves) and T12 and L3 (which
contain the roots of the parasympathetic ganglia) (Schover & Jensen, 1988). Injuries to the sacral area of the cord result in a much higher rate of erectile dysfunction (Yalla, 1982). Men with injuries below the T10 level but above the S2
level often have the fullest and most sustained erections, given that both spinal
erection centers remain intact (Torrens, 1983). However, fewer than one-third
of all men with SCI can achieve and maintain erections sufficient for penile-
vaginal intercourse (Yalla, 1982).

The small amount of existing research that does address physiological sexual response in women with SCI is contradictory and difficult to interpret,
primarily because the degree or completeness of injury is often unspecified
(Komisaruk & Whipple, 1995). Overall, the major physical changes in the
sexual functioning of women with SCI are a decrease or lack of vaginal lubrication, lack of the ability to perceive tactile stimulation (particularly genital),
lack of motor function, and an inability to achieve physiological orgasm
(Perduta-Fulginiti, 1992). Research has suggested that some women with SCI
complain of inadequate lubrication, and approximately 50% report an inability to achieve orgasm (Charlifue et al., 1992). Only one questionnaire study to
date has attempted to determine the impact of different degrees of SCI on
vaginal lubrication; it found self-report means of obtaining this information
to be inadequate because many subjects were unaware of their ability to lubricate (Sipski, 1991). That is, most of the 25 female participants were unable
to positively identify whether or not they were actually experiencing vaginal
lubrication (Sipski, 1991).

In a more recent study examining vaginal lubrication in women with SCI,
Sipski, Alexander, and Rosen (1995) explored the sexual responses of 13
women with complete SCI. Women with complete SCI responded sexually to
erotic audiovisual stimulation similarly to able-bodied women in those functions that were controlled neurologically above the level of their injuries
(Sipski et al., 1995). Genital vasocongestion did not occur in women with complete SCI because the neurological pathway was blocked; however, reflex genital vasocongestion did occur in women with complete SCI despite a lack of
subjective arousal (Sipski et al., 1995).

Although it has been suggested that women with complete SCI cannot experience orgasms other than phantom ones (Money, 1960), subjective reports by
women do not support these claims (Komisaruk & Whipple, 1995; Sipski et al.,
1995; Whipple & Komisaruk, 1992). More recent research has focused on the
nature of sexual response to vaginal and cervical stimulation in women with
complete SCI at selected levels of the spinal cord that should block or allow
passage of genital sensory input to the brain (Komisaruk & Whipple, 1995).
These studies have revealed vaginal sensation and the experience of physiological orgasm in some women diagnosed with complete SCI (Komisaruk & Whipple, 1995; Sipski et al., 1995; Whipple & Komisaruk, 1992). These results

suggest the existence of a sensory pathway, the vagus nerve, that bypasses the spinal cord, carrying sensory input from the vagina and cervix directly to the brain (Komisaruk & Whipple, 1995). It is by the vagus nerve that researchers explain the experience of physiological orgasm by women with SCI (Komisaruk & Whipple, 1995; Whipple & Komisaruk, 1992).

MULTIPLE SCLEROSIS

Multiple sclerosis (MS) is a neurological condition, characterized by breakdown of myelin and the development of plaques throughout the brain and the spinal cord (McFerlin & McFarland, 1982). Age of onset is typically between 20 and 40 years of age, with women more commonly affected than men. Typical symptoms are visual defects, cognitive deficits, numbness, weakness or lack of control over limbs, and lack of coordination. Sexual dysfunction associated with MS has been investigated for many years (Lundberg, 1978). Erectile dysfunction for men is common and is associated with urinary and bladder difficulties, and ejaculatory problems are associated with spinal cord damage (Betts, 1996). Similarly, changes in sexual function are very common for women with MS and typically occur early in the condition but tend to be milder, especially at first. Lowered sexual desire as well as decreased or absent lubrication are almost as common as diminished orgasmic capacity, changes in orgasmic quality, and inability to reach orgasm. Lundberg and Hulter (1996) acknowledged the importance of treatment and issued therapeutic recommendations, but no outcome research on this type of approach exists.

In one study (Dupont, 1996), 72 women and 44 men aged 23 to 60 years with MS and their partners were questioned about their sexual and marital satisfaction, specific sexual difficulties caused by MS, and their ways of coping with sexual problems. Demographic data, impact and acceptance of MS, cognitive functioning, and mood state were also measured. Results indicated that both male and female participants had sex lives that were greatly affected by their disability. Problems included indirect physical changes, direct sexual dysfunctions, and concerns about future changes, as well as changed priorities, expectations, and communications with partner. Men had higher levels of sexual dysfunction and talked to their doctors more frequently. Three percent of women and 25% of men had been to a sex therapist. Spouses also indicated high levels of sexual dysfunction, including "nonsensuality." Relationship difficulties were present in a third of the sample, with female partners being the most dissatisfied. Interestingly, sexual dysfunction in patients was not associated with age, duration of illness, or mood state.

It has been estimated that more than 50% of women and 75% of men with MS experience some form of sexual dysfunction during the course of their condition (Mattson, Petrie, Srvastava, & McDermott, 1995; Valleroy & Kraft, 1984). Sexual areas affected include temporary or long-term disinterest in sex, inability to achieve orgasm, difficulty engaging in intercourse because of physical changes, and complete lack of erection. Fatigue may also discourage people from engaging in sexual activity, and depression, cognitive changes, and relationship side effects also play a major role. The drugs used to treat MS can also have a negative influence (e.g., antidepressants, antispasmodics, anti-anxiety agents). Several coping methods have been suggested: plan sex early in the morning to avoid fatigue problems; use side or rear entry to avoid hip abductors spasming in women with MS; use vibrators when sensitivity is affected (Smeltzer & Kelley, 1997).

DIABETES

Approximately 16 million Americans have diabetes, a disorder that affects the ability of the body to produce or properly respond to insulin (Tilton, 1997). There are two different classifications of diabetes: insulin-dependent diabetes (IDD), occurring most commonly in young people, and non-insulin-dependent diabetes (NIDD), typically occurring in adults with a genetic predisposition.

With regard to sexual functioning, men with diabetes tend to experience problems with libido, erectile dysfunction, and orgasm, as well as a decrease in sexual activity (Tilton, 1997). Although it is commonly reported by clients, there is some degree of controversy about the extent to which libido is affected by diabetes. In a study of 314 men with diabetes (with all participants developing the condition before the age of 60), 160 individuals reported some type of sexual dysfunction (Schoffling, Federlin, Ditschuneit, & Pfeiffer, 1963). Half of this group reported a decrease in libido. Jensen (1981) studied 80 diabetic men and found that 44% reported some sexual dysfunction and 31% indicated a decrease in sexual desire. One study investigated 40 diabetic men along with 40 matched controls who did not have diabetes. Compared to controls, diabetic men had significantly lower levels of erotic drive, sexual arousal, enjoyment and satisfaction. What must be remembered is that problems in these areas co-existed with sexual attitudes and body image (Schiavi, Stimmel, Mandeli, Schreiner-Engel, & Ghizzani, 1995). Given that a higher number of men with diabetes experience erectile dysfunction as a consequence of their condition, it is believed that decreases in libido may be attributed to their feelings of loss resulting from not being able to achieve an erection (Tilton, 1997).

Erectile dysfunction is the most common sexual dysfunction reported by men with diabetes, occurring in up to 50% of individuals (Tilton, 1997). The strongest predictor in diabetic men is the presence of autonomic neuropathy (e.g., Baum, Neiman, & Lewis, 1988). However, hormonal abnormalities (e.g., increased incidence of abnormal levels of testosterone) and vascular difficulties (e.g., inadequate vascular blood flow to the penis) have also been implicated in erectile problems in men with diabetes (Buvat et al., 1985; Jensen, 1981). Not surprisingly, as erectile dysfunction increases in men with diabetes, frequency of sexual activity appears to decrease (Jensen, 1981; Tilton, 1997). On a positive note, effects on ejaculation or orgasm are much less frequent than problems with erection and libido (Jensen, 1981; Tilton, 1997).

Psychological factors common in sexual dysfunction in diabetic men include depression, anxiety about future health, and a negative body image (Jensen, 1985). Jensen found that both clinicians' ratings of couple's acceptance of diabetes and the number of psychological symptoms reported by the individual with diabetes were good predictors of sexual functioning. In a study of 77 men aged 30 to 85 years, 64% experienced some degree of erectile dysfunction and 71% reported "severe erectile difficulties." Of the 45 men in marital relationships who reported erectile dysfunction, 58% reported negative effect on their relationship. Decline in sexual and nonsexual affection, withdrawal of the husband from sexual activity, refusal of the wife to participate in sexual activity with her husband, and initiation of extramarital sexual relationships by the husband or the wife were all reported (Schmitt & Neubeck, 1985). Of course, it is highly probable that performance anxiety plays a large factor in many men with diabetes, due to societal gender-role messages about male virility.

Whereas a lot of research has been conducted on the sexual issues of diabetic men, little is known about how this condition affects the sexual expression of women, though many clearly have problems with libido, lubrication, and orgasm. Specifically, Jensen (1981) found that 27% of women with diabetes reported sexual dysfunction, compared with 25% of age-matched controls. The most frequently reported dysfunction was a decrease in libido. Though hypoactive sexual desire is reported to be characteristic of diabetic women in some studies, the prevalence is not much different from that in the general population (Spector, Leiblum, Carey, & Rosen, 1993).

Similar to men with diabetes, women may experience difficulties with their vascular system, thereby influencing the blood flow to the genital region. For women, this can influence the ability to lubricate in the vaginal region. Jensen (1981) found that 25% of diabetic women reported inadequate vaginal lubrication, but this did not necessarily result in sexual dysfunction. Of course, women can sometimes compensate for this condition by using external lubrication.

Two recent studies have examined sexual arousal in women with diabetes. Albert and Wincze (1990) compared five women with IDD with five age-matched controls who watched erotic videos. Using vaginal plethysmography, results indicted that diabetic women displayed significantly lower levels of vaginal blood flow than did able-bodied participants. However, the authors did not factor in neuropathy as a possible causative agent. Another study used labia minora temperature to compare women with IDD to able-bodied matched controls (Slob, Koster, Radder, & Van der Werff ten Bosch, 1990). Vaginal responsiveness while watching erotic films was measured using this technique. Women in this study were free from neuropathy and did not show a marked difference in arousal compared to nondiabetic women. It should be noted that this study has been criticized because temperature-based methods to evaluate vaginal blood flow are not as well established as vaginal plethysmography. On the whole, research on orgasm in women with diabetes has been inconclusive, with reported ranges of dysfunction from 10% to 33% (Tilton, 1997). For a more thorough review of sexual functioning in women with diabetes, see Enzlin, Mathieu, Vanderschueren, and Demyttenaere (1998).

Little research has been conducted on sexual satisfaction and psychosexual feelings of women with diabetes. Results have been mixed in regard to the effect on relationships, with results showing both no differences in marital satisfaction to low levels of marital satisfaction compared to nondiabetic controls (Newman & Bettelson, 1986; Young, Koch, & Bailey, 1989).

CARDIAC AND PULMONARY CONDITIONS

Of all chronic cardiac conditions, coronary artery disease (CAD) is the most known for its effect on sexual function (Stitik & Benvento, 1997). Men with CAD often have problems with erectile dysfunction, premature ejaculation, orgasm, and libido. However, controversy exists over the frequency with which each occurs (Scalzi, 1982; Sjogren & Fugl-Meyer, 1983). Some literature has reported orgasmic difficulties, sexual aversion, and sexual pain disorders among women with coronary conditions, but insufficient data are available at this time to estimate whether there is an increased prevalence in these women compared to women without cardiac conditions (Stitik & Benvento, 1997).

Etiologies of sexual dysfunction among persons with cardiac conditions include both psychological and physiological causative factors. Psychological variables found to be associated with sexuality difficulties in cardiac patients include loss of sexual desire, decrease in sexual activity, depression, anxiety about the recurrence of cardiovascular symptoms, and denial about their condition (Blocker, 1985; Hellerstein & Friedman, 1970). Physiological causative factors include diminished cardiac reserve, angina during sexual activity, and cardiac medications that often effect sexual dysfunction (Blocker, 1985; Hellerstein & Friedman, 1970).

Many people with CAD fear dying during sexual activity, which obviously can lead to psychological problems and inhibition in sexual acivities. Papadopoulos (1978) found that fear of death during intercourse among post-MI individuals was reported by 51% of women and 34% of men. Fear is also apparent in individual's sexual partners (Connie & Evans, 1982). However, individuals are usually tested before being told it is safe for them to resume normal activities. People must be educated that the relative risk of a heart attack during sexual activity is low and, in fact, is similar in people with and those without a history of cardiac disease (Stitik & Benvento, 1997). Furthermore, regular exercise can decrease and perhaps eliminate the slight possibility of a heart attack during sexual activity (Muller, Mittleman, Maclure, Sherwood, & Tofler, 1996). Treatment in these situations focuses primarily on counseling, with therapists often recommending being aware of timing and environment for sexual activity (often best in the morning with rest periods before and after), as well as sexual positioning (avoiding pressure to the chest).

Similar to patients with cardiac disorders, individuals with chronic pulmonary disease may experience difficulties with sexual function. Unfortunately, there has been little research conducted in this area. Chronic obstructive pulmonary disease (COPD) has been the most commonly studied pulmonary condition in terms of its effects on sexuality (Stitik & Benvento, 1997). Individuals with COPD may experience shortness of breath, which often leads to diminished activity tolerance. Sexual activity, in particular, can be difficult because the sexual act often requires an increase in respiratory rates to 40 to 60 breaths a minute (Hahn, 1989). Similar to other cardiac conditions, difficulty may occur with certain sexual positions. For example, if a man with COPD is lying on his back with his partner on top of him, pressure to the chest may cause discomfort (Rabinowitz & Florian, 1992). Medications for COPD may also affect the ability to achieve and maintain an erection (Stitik & Benvento, 1997). Education and counseling that address these sorts of issues can be of enormous benefit to these clients.

CEREBROVASCULAR DISEASE

Sexuality after cerebrovascular accidents (CVAs), or stroke, is influenced by both physical and psychological changes. Erectile dysfunction in men and a decrease in vaginal lubrication in women are the most common sexual manifestations poststroke. Other difficulties include diminished libido, poor arousal, orgasmic difficulties, reduced frequency of intercourse, and premature ejaculation (Aloni, Ring, Rozenthul, & Schwartz, 1993; Monga, 1986; Monga & Kerrigan, 1997).

The sexual problems in individuals poststroke are rarely a consequence of the stroke itself; rather, they are often the result of a variety of associated medical conditions such as the presence of diabetes hypertension or CAD. These physiological circumstances are sometimes intermixed with psychosocial factors including anxiety, loss of self-esteem, social role changes, fear of rejection from a partner, and poor coping skills (Monga & Kerrigan (1997).

Monga and Kerrigan (1997) suggested that many problems associated with sexual difficulties following CVAs can be prevented by integrating information on sexual function into a comprehensive stroke rehabilitation program with appropriate education of professional staff.

NEUROMUSCULAR, ARTHRITIS, AND CONNECTIVE TISSUE CONDITIONS

The sexual ramifications of some disorders (e.g., neuromuscular conditions such as muscular dystrophy and arthritic conditions such as osteoarthritis and lupus) are not caused directly by the disability, but rather by consequences associated with the condition. For example, muscle weakness, joint limitation, and fatigue can affect sexual expression in a variety of ways. Some research has pointed toward low sexual desire among people with these conditions;

however, this information is confounded with the higher incidence of associated depression (Bach & Bardach, 1997; Nadler, 1997). In addition, a decrease in libido may result from the use of steroids and other drugs prescribed to treat these conditions (Blake, Maisiak, Alarcon, & Brown, 1987).

Learning about appropriate sexual positioning can be of great benefit in treating these conditions. The Arthritis Foundation (1997) provides detailed literature on sexual positions that place less pressure on joints and thus provide for a more enjoyable sexual experience.

CANCER

Sexual function is affected in individuals following a diagnosis of cancer from both physical and psychological bases. The primary sex organs and their neurovascular supply may be injured by the disease process itself. In addition, treatment options such as chemotherapy, radiation, surgery, and hormone manipulations may all affect sexual expression (Waldman & Eliasof, 1997).

Prostate cancer is the most frequently diagnosed form of cancer for men. Depending on the specific nature of the cancer, the removal of the prostate may be necessary. This typically results in 100% of men experiencing erectile dysfunction, with only 10% to 15% regaining any type of erection over time (Perez, Fair, & Ihde, 1989). Newer forms of nerve-sparing radical prostatectomies, however, can preserve erectile function in close to 70% of men (Brender & Walsh, 1992). Testicular and penile cancer are much less common but can inevitably affect sexual functioning and sexual self-perception (Waldman & Eliasof, 1997).

In contrast, women can experience breast, ovarian, endometrial, cervical, vulvar, and vaginal cancers. Breast cancer is the most frequently occurring cancer in women, with more than 182,000 new cases diagnosed yearly (American Cancer Society, 1995).

In both genders, colorectal and bladder cancer are also prevalent. Cancer of the colon or rectum is the most common form that affects both genders (American Cancer Society, 1995). Bladder, colon, and rectum cancer can also affect sexual functioning at all levels, including sexual desire, arousal, and orgasm phases (Waldman & Eliasof, 1997).

Feelings of disbelief, sadness, anxiety, and depression are common following a diagnosis of cancer. Obviously, these feelings can have a direct effect on sexual functioning. According to Waldman and Eliasof (1997), even though men and women may experience different types of cancer and forms of treatments, the psychological effects seem to be universal. Specifically, individuals with cancer may have difficulty coping with their body image following treatment that has dramatically changed their physical appearance. Redefining perceptions of oneself and the family and other social roles can be a slow process. For these reasons, persons with cancer may not be interested in their sex lives early in their diagnosis. Nevertheless, it is helpful to initiate a conversation with these individuals to provide a forum to speak about such issues when they are ready.

TRAUMATIC BRAIN INJURY

Sexual expression following traumatic brain injury (TBI) has been relatively unexplored. Clinical and anecdotal information tells us that sexual function declines after TBI, but little empirical evidence exists to explain this phenomenon (Sandel, 1997). Animal literature suggests varying consequences of brain lesions on sexual behavior, but extrapolation to humans has been speculative (Sandel, 1997). The percentage of people who have reported sexual dysfunction after TBI has ranged widely, probably due to the heterogeneity of populations studied (Davis & Schneider, 1990; Garden, Bontke, & Hoffman, 1990; Kreutzer & Zasler, 1989).

Proposed etiologies of sexual functioning post-TBI are based solely on animal models that account for the brain's role in sexual functioning (Sandel, 1997). For example, the brain stem, thalamus, hypothalamus, and limbic structures are all involved in the sexual response cycle (Sandel, 1997). Psychologically, individuals with TBI are often aware that they "feel different" postinjury and often struggle with understanding their sexual feelings and the fact that their arousal seems to be different.

Similarly, studies that have focused on patients with mild brain injuries have provided inconsistent findings. In one study of 19 people with TBI, 53% reported decrease in libido and 42% indicated some type of erectile dysfunction (Sandel, 1997). On the other hand, researchers investigated 50 individuals with brain injuries at six or more months following injury and found that 50% reported an increase in frequency of sexual intercourse, and the other half noted a decrease (Oddy, Humphrey, & Uttley, 1978). Severity of injury, time since injury, and locus of lesion may all affect sexual function in individuals with TBI. See Sandel (1997) for more specific information.

Although no data exist on the effectiveness of hormonal agents on the improvement of sexual desire among persons with TBI, Sandel (1997) proposes that use of these agents may be worth studying within this population. In therapy, use of verbal and nonverbal strategies can both be important, depending on the severity of the injury (Medlar, 1993).

ESTABLISHING AND MAINTAINING INTIMATE RELATIONSHIPS

Success in establishing and maintaining romantic and sexual relationships is a frequently discussed topic in the disability community and often brings forth feelings of frustration. Nevertheless, many persons with disabilities do in fact establish healthy, fulfilling relationships. What are the social factors that influence dating and the development of intimate relationships among persons with disabilities? There are several plausible explanations for the range of experiences reported by this community. For example, people growing up with disabilities may not have had the normative experiences with early flirtations and the development of age-appropriate social skills that typically help with early dating experiences. Architectural and monetary barriers often exclude disabled persons from interacting in the social arena. This lack of exposure to relevant life experiences can influence a person with a disability to feel unskilled in romance. In addition, the negative societal views of persons with disabilities as desirable partners also contribute to frustrations with dating among persons with disabilities.

How do people with disabilities feel about marriage? Are disabled people successful at maintaining romantic relationships? Are they satisfied with this part of their lives? How do gay and lesbian individuals with disabilities fare with dating and relationships? These questions are addressed below.

THEORETICAL VIEWS ON DISABILITY, DATING, AND RELATIONSHIPS

When compared with the rest of the population, persons with disabilities wait longer to begin dating and to experience first voluntary sexual contact (Gill, 1996). Gill offers two explanations that may explain the romantic disadvantages experienced by women with disabilities. The first explanation is based on aesthetics and argues that much of a woman's value in our society rests on her conformity with narrow prescriptions of physical attractiveness. Women with disabilities may be judged as flawed or defective as sexual partners if they do not fit traditional aesthetic gender roles. This is supported by the fact that women with cognitive and learning disabilities have higher rates of marriage than other disability groups (Wagner, D'Amico, Marder, Newman, & Blackorby, 1992). Gill's second explanation focuses on function. Women who depart from the traditional role and duties delineated for them by society are viewed as incapable partners. Seen as unable to care for their partners and children and/or unable to coordinate social and domestic events, such women may not be seen as desirable partners.

REPORTED VIEWS ON DATING AND RELATIONSHIPS

Bleszynska (1995) examined how 47 young able-bodied, 36 blind, and 44 persons using wheelchairs, all aged 20 to 30, evaluated marriage. Specifically, the importance of values related to marriage and family and the types of needs satisfied through these institutions of social life were explored. Participants were asked to evaluate such phenomena as love, sexual life, and parenthood as well as to express their attitudes and opinions on conjugal infidelity. The results did not indicate any significant differences in attitudes and views presented among the groups.

In personal accounts and narratives, a prevailing theme is the difficulty disabled men and women experience finding a partner (Bowe, 1981; Brightman,

1984; Duffy, 1981; Roth, 1981). Despite this commonality, in the end, many more disabled men than women find and develop relationships that they define as satisfying.

DATING, MARRIAGE, AND DISABILITY

In a recent study, dating issues among 250 single women with physical disabilities and 180 single women without disabilities were examined to determine differences between the groups (Rintala et al., 1997). Dating outcomes included satisfaction with dating frequency, perceived constraints on attracting partners, perceived personal barriers to dating, societal barriers to dating, and communication problems. Women with disabilities were disadvantaged on all but perceived communication problems compared to women without disabilities. Women whose disabilities occurred before their first date were older at the time of their first date than women who were either not disabled or disabled after their first date.

An early study on the dating behavior of institutionalized people with mental retardation revealed that sexual behavior was limited to necking and kissing (Edgerton & Dingman, 1964). There was little evidence of lack of impulse control, and most modeled their dating behavior on nondisabled peers. Research also suggests that some people with developmental disabilities are capable of maintaining happy and stable marriages with individuals with or without developmental disabilities (Craft & Craft, 1979; Edgerton, 1973; Hall, 1975).

Franklin (1977) reported that disabled women were less likely than able-bodied women to be married, more likely to marry later in life, and more likely to get divorced. Bowe (1980) and Hanna and Rogovsky (1986) reported similar findings from the Current Population Survey's data of the early 1980s. Whereas 60% of both men with disabilities and women without disabilities are married, only 49% of disabled women are married. However, the data do not reveal how much the presence of a woman's disability affects her choices or chances of being in a long-term relationship with a man or a woman.

Hanna and Rogovsky (1986) analyzed the 1985 population survey dividing a subsample of ever-married-but-not-widowed men and woman into three categories: nondisabled, mildly disabled, and severely disabled. They found that more women than men in all categories were divorced, whereas no significant differences emerged between "severely disabled women" and other groups. Only 14% of men termed severely disabled were divorced, but 26% of severely disabled women were. Whereas men's rates of separation were 3%, 5%, and 7% for each category of disability status, women's rates of separation were 4%, 6%, and 11%, respectively. Thirty-seven percent of the severely disabled women, as contrasted with 22% of severely disabled men, were once married but are no longer married for reasons other than death of a spouse. For both men and women whose disabilities occurred before marriage, the literature reveals considerable apprehension about finding a mate. Asch and Sacks (1983) reviewed a large number of published autobiographies of persons with disabilities and noted the dearth of information about intimate relationships; however, of those who did live with adult partners, nearly all were men.

Mathews (1983) found that only 5 out of the 45 women interviewed in her study were married, and more than half reported no sexual relationship since becoming disabled. Only half the women in Duffy's (1981) study of 75 women had ever been married. The only group of disabled adults in which women are more likely to marry than men are those defined as "retarded." One fascinating difference reported by Sandowski (1989) is that more men than women abandon marriages when their spouse becomes ill or disabled.

Women who acquire disabilities after marriage experience high rates of separation and divorce (Hannaford, 1985). In general, research on persons with SCI has focused on marital issues before and after onset of injury (Crewe, Athelstan, & Krumberger, 1976; El Ghatit & Hanson, 1976). However, little has been written about the difficulties of meeting others and developing intimate/marital relationships as a disabled person (Yoshida, 1994). Yoshida looked at 35 paraplegics living in the general community, including 28 men and 7 women. Forty-three percent of individuals within the sample were single before SCI. Relationships were viewed along five major variables that determined whether or not someone was a potential desirable partner: acceptance of the individual, awareness of and assistance with accessibility, altered divisions of labor, comfort with sexuality, and long-term goals and plans. A third of the participants were married postinjury, with only a small portion separated or divorced postinjury.

Milligan and Neufeldt (1998) examined courtship experiences through interviews of eight able-bodied women, 23 to 43 years of age, who made post-SCI marital commitments to men with SCI. The findings suggest a substantial overlap with existing models of courtship, but there were significant individual factors and external social forces influencing relationship development in the context of disability. Specifically, participants described their mates as positively adjusted to their disability and as demonstrating autonomous attitudes that, along with personality variables, were considered important elements of attraction. Participants revealed an openness to a relationship with a partner with SCI, prior personal experience with disability, flexibility regarding role performance, acceptance of disability and need for assistance, an attitude aimed at fostering their partner's independence, and resiliency when faced with social disapproval (Milligan & Neufeldt, 1998).

An additional study explored the effects of acquiring a disability after being married among 21 couples where one partner had become disabled since marriage (Parker, 1993). This investigation examined couples' sexual relationships and the ways that disability and caring affected it; both partners' views about the nature and meaning of marriage and how this related to their continuing relationship; and a comparison of different marriages and the same marriages at different points in time. Five factors were found to affect the likelihood of a couple's staying together: quality of marriage before the onset of disability, sense of duty, severity of spouse's impairment coupled with lack of other forms of support, time, and practical considerations (Parker, 1993).

GAY AND LESBIAN INDIVIDUALS WITH DISABILITIES

Gay and lesbian persons with disabilities have struggled to be acknowledged by both the disability and gay and lesbian communities. In fact, people with disabilities often feel excluded from the gay community (McDaniel, 1995; Thompson, 1994). Specifically, some women with disabilities have indicated that they feel unwelcome at lesbian events because the events are often planned in inaccessible locations and do not include interpreters for deaf persons (McDaniel, 1995). It has been argued that similar disability stereotypes exist within gay and lesbian communities and that it is difficult for persons with disabilities within this community to partner (McDaniel, 1995; Thompson, 1994). Furthermore, gay men and lesbians who cannot pass as able-bodied may therefore decide to pass as heterosexual because they are already stigmatized as a result of their disability (Appleby, 1994). Some may pass temporarily or make their illnesses known only after a dating partner knows them and is less likely to stereotype them (Hillyer, 1993).

Within the social context of disability, one author has drawn parallels between disability politics and the gay pride movement to illustrate how different minority groups share experiences while retaining distinct qualities (Corbett, 1994). Through exploring this relationship, issues such as normalism, passing, and challenging prejudice are explored within the context of gay and lesbian disabled persons' experiences of dual oppression.

Experiencing broad social pressures that stem from one's identity can have psychological effects on one's comfort with oneself. For example, one study of deaf and hard-of-hearing gay men found that 30% to 40% reported wishing that they were heterosexual. However, 81% of the hard-of-hearing gay men noted that they were happy with their romantic lives and almost 100% stated that they were pleased with their sex lives (Swartz, 1995). Interestingly, this sample's discomfort with being gay in society did not seem to affect their satisfaction with their sexual expression. An additional study involving the deaf gay community commented on the patterns of support among deaf homosexuals and lesbians. Data were obtained from personal interviews and questionnaires sent to professionals and agencies serving both homosexual and deaf communities. Deaf homosexual men face further problems from the deaf community; deafness is an isolating disability, and homosexuality is taboo within this isolation. Interestingly, there does not seem to be any viable network of support among any of the traditional channels of professions such as psychiatry, medicine, and social work, nor among the families of deaf homosexuals. The primary support system appears to be the deaf homosexual community itself, exemplified by nationwide organizations (Zakarewsky, 1979).

A study examining a younger sample of 144 individuals, 19 to 26 years of age, and 398 letters to a sexologist's advice column suggested that the main problems of gay and lesbian disabled persons are difficulties in finding a partner, conflicts with family not accepting their homosexuality, and lack of acceptance of their own homosexual orientation because of religious and environmental motivations (Lew-Starowicz, 1994).

PREGNANCY, CHILDBIRTH, AND PARENTING WITH A DISABILITY

Given that the subject of sexuality and disability has received little attention, it is no surprise that pregnancy, childbirth, and parenting within the disability community have also been understudied areas. As with more general sexuality issues, pregnancy, childbirth, and parenting among people with disabilities have been topics filled with much controversy. Common questions include: Can a woman with a disability get pregnant? How can men and women with disabilities actually take care of children and parent properly? Do people with disabilities produce disabled children? If so, why would they want to procreate? Obviously, some of these questions can be easily answered by appropriate education regarding the specific nature of a given disability. However, many of these questions contain value-laden judgments about whether or not people with disabilities actually have the capability and the right to parent. A historical exploration of these issues will provide some foundation for exploring these questions.

HISTORICAL CONTEXT

Various laws throughout history have supported sterilization of people with disabilities. For example, in the 1920s, political efforts were made to force sterilization of people with epilepsy, developmental disabilities, and psychiatric disabilities. By 1937, 28 states had adopted eugenics sterilization laws aimed primarily at women for whom "procreation was deemed inadvisable" (Saxton, 1998, p. 379).

Society has accepted assumptions that prenatal screening and selective abortion can reduce the incidence of disease and disability, thus improving quality of life (Saxton, 1998). However, according to Hubbard (1997), prenatal testing and selective abortion are direct byproducts of the eugenics movement. In addition, Hubbard points out that if a test were developed to diagnose skin color prenatally and individuals advocated for selective abortion based on these results, most people would be horrified. But it is still permissible and even commonplace to make decisions about avoiding or terminating pregnancy based on fetal abnormalities.

Even though many negative societal attitudes have prevailed, a sizable number of women and men with disabilities have chosen to be parents in a variety of ways. Some people with disabilities have written narratives about becoming parents and being parents (Jacobson, 1993; Pischke, 1993; Zola, 1993). This material focuses on both the parents' and the children's reaction to disability within the family unit. This section explores the limited amount of both phenomenological and empirically based data that we have on this topic.

PREGNANCY AND DELIVERY

In recent years, data have begun to accumulate on pregnancy and delivery issues for women with disabilities. For example, Jackson (1997) examined pregnancy and delivery pre- and postinjury among 472 women with SCIs. Specifically, certain pregnancy complications were found to be more common among these women, including urinary tract infections, disability-related difficulties (e.g., development of pressure sores), labor symptoms (e.g., abnormal pains and increased spasticity), and issues surrounding the method of delivery (e.g., increased incidence of cesarean sections in postinjury pregnancies, higher frequency of vacuum or forceps delivery, and fewer spontaneous vaginal deliveries) (Jackson, 1997). Rogers (1997) examined pregnancy in women with disabilities from a more qualitative, experiential context. This author interviewed 14 women with various types of physical disabilities and identified three problem areas with regard to the pregnancy experience: (1) difficulties with the attitude of physicians, (2) quality of communication between physicians/health care providers and patients, and (3) lack of information about the effect of the disability on pregnancy.

FERTILITY

Women with disabilities and chronic conditions may experience difficulties with fertility based on physiological alterations that may affect regulation of ovulation or secretion of certain hormones (Welner, 1997). Specifically, women with SCIs often experience changes in their menstrual patterns and/or the absence of a menstrual period (Yarkony, 1992). Similarly, women with TBIs, MS, epilepsy, and diabetes also may experience alterations in hypothalamic function leading to difficulties with hormonal regulation and menstruation (Welner, 1997). However, an assortment of reproductive techniques exists that can assist people with disabilities with fertility. For more details on reproductive technologies, see Colon (1997).

Ejaculatory dysfunction appears in men with a variety of disabilities and chronic conditions (e.g., SCI, MS) and can be traced to four different etiologies: functional, pharmacological, anatomical, and neurological (Linsenmeyer, 1997). Clearly, these four etiologies cover many men with disabilities (e.g., if men do not have functional, anatomical, or neurologic difficulties, they may be on medication that may inhibit ejaculation). Treatment for such conditions includes pharmacological agents, vibratory stimulation, electro-ejaculation, and aspiration from the vas deferens. Research suggests that pharmacologic treatments range in effectiveness (producing an ejaculation) from 55.5% (Chapelle, Roby, Yakovleff, & Bussel, 1988) to 59.7% (Gutmann & Walsh, 1971). A less intrusive means of treating infertility in men with SCI is through vibratory stimulation using a vibrator that produces impulses that travel from the penis to the sacral cord by way of the pudendal nerve to trigger a sacral ejaculation reflex. Effectiveness ranges from 5.9 % (Beckerman, Becher, & Lankhorst, 1993) to 30% (Slaten & Linsenmeyer, 1993).

ADOPTION

Although accurate statistics are not available on what percentage of disabled women and men choose adoption as the means to become parents, the topic has been widely discussed by academicians and social service agencies. Within the context of private adoption agencies, many prospective parents experience not being chosen by birth mothers based on their perceived inability to care for a child (L. Poole, personal communication, November 15, 1996). Given this dilemma, many people with disabilities have successfully sought out international adoption as an alternative and have had success in finding a child in this manner. In another approach, some people with disabilities have specifically sought out disabled children to adopt. Reasons given for this desire include wanting the child to grow up with a parent similar to himself or herself, wanting to have a child of the same culture, and knowing that it is unlikely that the child will be adopted, given that most couples are seeking a "perfect infant" (C. O'Toole, personal communication, May 10, 1997).

PARENTING

Most parents with disabilities confront many of the same issues that other parents confront with their children. However, societal constraints influence one's ability to parent in a variety of ways. For example, there are frequently negative attitudes about disabled parents' ability to care for their able-bodied children, as well as difficulties with access (wheelchair, interpreters) to their children's school and school-related events. Of course, there are physical, sensory, and cognitive limitations that some parents may face (e.g., not being able to play with the child on the floor, not being able to see the child's homework, not being capable of communicating verbally on a child's level).

SEXUAL ABUSE AND DISABILITY

As awareness has increased concerning the topic of sexuality in persons with disabilities, concerns about sexual abuse have also surfaced. As a dimension of the general study of disability, abuse has only recently been addressed by scholars and has yet to be the subject of much empirical, scientific investigation (Nosek, 1996). The increased vulnerability of the disability community to sexual abuse can be seen in various contexts. Persons with physical disabilities often use personal assistants to facilitate their daily living needs; these assistants are typically family members, paid employees, and/or volunteers. Due to the personal and quite important role that these individuals play within this community, trust is imperative. However, screening for personal assistance providers can be difficult, and people with physical disabilities may be at higher risk in these situations. Furthermore, people with physical disabilities are at risk for violence on an everyday basis as they interact within their world; it is often difficult to fight off an attacker when one has diminished physical strength.

Persons with developmental and cognitive disabilities often use personal assistants to advise them on appropriate decision making or interpretation of interpersonal interactions and events. Therefore, people with these types of disabilities become very vulnerable when they need assistance in interpreting sexually related situations. Whether making personal decisions about appropriate sexual partners or interpreting sexual advances that they have experienced, many persons with cognitive impairments rely on others. Therefore, not only may it be difficult for the person with a developmental disability to understand a sexual abuse situation, he or she may not even know how to label it as such. This may also have some effect on accurate reporting of sexual abuse among this population. Furthermore, it is important to acknowledge that children with serious disabilities have a much higher risk of residing in institutions where significantly higher rates of abuse are well documented (Crossmaker, 1991).

Not surprisingly, Sobsey and Varnhagen (1989) propose that society's expectations and treatment of people with disabilities may contribute more to the increased risk of abuse than the disability itself. In addition, attitudes toward disability may shape the way society views imposed sexual behavior in this population. For example, given that people with disabilities are often seen as nondesirable partners, it could be viewed that any type of sexual contact would be welcomed by this group. Although this notion may seem preposterous to many, attitudes about the sexual lives of people with disabilities have changed very little over the years. In fact, some studies attribute causation of the abuse to stress imposed on the family by a child's disability (Bristol & Schloper, 1984). However, the actual literature has in fact documented an *inverse* relationship between severity of disability and incidence of abuse (e.g., Benedict, White, Wulff, & Hall, 1990). Other explanations and related factors (e.g., psychological, social, and cultural aspects of the family and characteristics of the parents such as their own history of maltreatment and their coping skills) have been proposed as important considerations when exploring abuse among children with disabilities (Garbarino, 1987).

SEXUAL ABUSE OF CHILDREN

Much of the literature on sexuality and disability has focused on the prevalence of abuse among children with disabilities. Doucette (1986) reported on a study of women with a variety of disabilities and found that the individuals within this sample were about 1.5 times more likely to have been sexually abused as children than women without disabilities. Furthermore, a survey of 62 women found that 50% of women with disabilities reported being sexually assaulted as a child compared to 34% of women without disabilities (Ontario Ministry of Community and Social Services, 1987). Alarmingly, individuals with developmental disabilities may be three times more vulnerable to sexual victimization than those without disabilities (Burke & Bedard, 1995). Other data on children with developmental disabilities suggest similar findings. Muccigrosso (1991) claims that 90% to 99% of persons with developmental disabilities have been sexually exploited by the age of 18. Most of these studies, however, focus on children with severe cognitive impairments (Nosek, 1996). Sullivan and Knutson (1998) instead looked at children who are deaf and hard-of-hearing and identified several risk factors for maltreatment as well as the most common types of abuse. The most prevalent types of maltreatment in descending order of magnitude were neglect, physical abuse, sexual abuse, and emotional abuse. Fortunately, there are a number of treatment programs specifically for deaf children who have been abused (LaBarre, 1998), but outcome information is not available.

Forty percent of women with disabilities in Doucette's (1986) study had experienced some kind of sexual abuse; 12% had been raped. In a qualitative study, 11 out of 31 women with physical disabilities reported experiencing some kind of sexual abuse (Nosek, 1996). Unique vulnerabilities to abuse experienced by women with disabilities include social stereotypes of asexuality and passivity, lack of adaptive equipment, inaccessible home and community environments, increased exposure to medical and institutional settings, dependence on perpetrators for personal assistance, and lack of employment options (Nosek, Howland, & Young, 1997).

Although few data are available on sexual abuse of males, it is expected that rates would be similarly higher than among nondisabled peers.

SEX EDUCATION AND ABUSE

Sex education may play an important role in both preventing and reporting sexual abuse. McCabe, Cummins, and Reid (1994) described a comparison between the level of sexual knowledge and experience of sexual abuse among 30 people with mild developmental disabilities living in group homes. Results of this study indicated a lower level of sexual knowledge among people with disabilities but no differences between the groups in the level of incest and other unwanted sexual activities. A high percentage of people with developmental disabilities believed that "someone else decides about their level of sexual experience," were less likely to know the meanings of the terms "incest" and "rape," and were less likely to know what to do if they encountered a situation of unwanted touching and to be able to say no to unwanted touching (McCabe et al., 1994).

Recent efforts have been made to provide education about sexual abuse prevention to children with developmental disabilities (Rappaport, Burkhardt, & Rotatori, 1997). To that end, it has been recommended that social reasoning abilities be measured initially and that children first learn about their bodies. Resources useful for primary educators are special education teachers, social workers, nurses, and psychologists who provide services to children with developmental disabilities (Rappaport et al., 1997).

Treatment of Sexual Abuse

People with disabilities who experience sexual abuse often experience difficulty obtaining treatment services that are accessible and appropriate to their needs (Mansell, Sobsey, Wilgosh, & Zawallich, 1997; Sobsey & Doe, 1991). For example, Nosek (1996) found that 64% of shelters investigated in Texas were not wheelchair-accessible. In addition to wheelchair access, several other societal and environmental restrictions on people with disabilities may prevent access to treatment programs (e.g., lack of transportation for wheelchair users and persons who are blind, appropriate Braille signage on facilities, interpreter services for people who are deaf or hearing impaired, and personal assistant services for those who need help with activities of daily living). Schaller and Fieberg (1998) discussed recovery from sexual abuse among women with disabilities within a social framework and suggested that several areas (i.e., health care, transportation services and attendant care, and vocational counseling) of the lives of those in the disability community need to be understood before providing treatment. Furthermore, Nosek et al. (1997) note that policy changes are needed to increase training for all types of service providers in abuse interventions to improve architectural and attitudinal accessibility of programs for battered women, increase the responsiveness of adult protective services, increase options for personal assistance, expand the availability of affordable and accessible legal services, and improve communication among community services.

Nosek and Howland (1997) have also proposed sexual abuse assessment and treatment intervention guidelines for health care providers working with people with disabilities. Even though no outcome data on this specific approach are yet available, this treatment plan is quite comprehensive. According to these guidelines, the first step for assessment providers is to abandon the belief that no one would ever abuse a woman with a disability. Other components of the guidelines include preparing counselors to feel more comfortable initiating a question about sexual abuse with members of the disability community and to be aware of the constellation of symptoms presented by victims of abuse. For more details on this assessment and treatment plan, see Nosek and Howland.

CLINICAL CONSIDERATIONS
AND APPLICATIONS

Many therapists are daunted when faced with a disabled client who has a sexual concern. Although there are a number of specific disability-related issues to consider, it is really not much different from dealing with any client who may be from a different ethnic or racial background or sexual orientation. All of the typical therapeutic skills and approaches still apply. Basically, therapists need to be encouraged and trained to ask questions relevant to a particular disability and the social experience of that condition (S. Cole, 1988). Even though many persons with disabilities are quite adept at educating others about the nature of their disability, it is professionally ethical and responsible to make oneself knowledgeable about clients' cultural experiences. We therefore present some general thoughts about issues to consider when dealing with a disabled client before moving on to a few case examples.

The Sexuality Information and Education Council of the United States (SIECUS) suggests that sex therapy with disabled clients should be based on a number of assumptions and goals: that people with disabilities, like other persons, are sexual human beings; that normative sexual expression and sexual adjustment need to be encouraged though not be imposed on persons who have disabilities; and that sexuality and understanding and sensitivity to its interrelationship with disability ought to be an integral part of any health care and rehabilitation program (Worthington, 1988).

SPECIFIC DISABILITY FACTORS

As stated earlier, awareness of different classifications of disabilities (i.e., congenital versus acquired, stable versus progressive) helps the therapist to understand the impact of the disability on sexual development, function, and sexual self-perception and facilitates discussion of these issues (S. Cole, 1988).

Among individuals who have an acquired disability, postdisability sexual adaptation usually is more dependent on predisability adjustment (including sexual knowledge, attitudes, experience, and general psychological adjustment) than on the actual disability. Even though it is important to understand the effect that a disability has on the person's life, it should not be assumed that any sexual difficulties are a direct result of the disability. Not only could such problems fall into more common categories such as relationship/interpersonal distress, but even if the disability is a factor, it may have far more to do with the client's underlying frustrations at having to deal with negative societal beliefs about disability than actual physical, developmental, or cognitive limitations.

Among clients who have lifelong disabilities, the impact of being seen as asexual and the infantalization and patronization by family, caretakers, and society should never be underestimated (DeLoach, 1994). Often, disabled persons have not been given the opportunity for age-appropriate developmental sex play and flirting. For example, it is rare that parents of children with disabilities actually encourage them to flirt with peers at early ages. In addition, disabled individuals may be lacking in basic knowledge about sexuality. Because to this day many parents and guardians find it difficult to think of their children as sexual beings (which may be greatly exaggerated when the child is disabled), most youths still get their initial sex information in a furtive manner—often from peers. Due to the potential isolating effects of having a disability, this source of early sexual information is often not available to children with disabilities.

Sensory impairments may also hamper the acquisition of accurate sexual knowledge. Even if teenagers are given appropriate sex education in a mainstreamed educational program, it may be very difficult for them to translate the topography and logistics to their frame of reference. For example, we know of one visually-impaired college freshman who, though he could recite the technical aspects of anatomy and reproduction, was unclear as to where in a woman's body the vagina was located. Thus, clients may lack basic understanding of their own sexual functioning as well as that of others.

Although disabled persons may be used to dealing with medical professionals ad nauseam about issues related to other aspects of their body and its function, physicians and patients are often unsure of how to approach the topic of sexual functioning. For example, very few rehabilitation centers require, or even offer, sex counseling. One study showed that only a little over 40% of participants had received some type of sexuality counseling, and all subjects indicated a need for more information than they had received (Zwerner, 1982). Topics notably lacking were sexual complications related to disability, sexual positions, birth control methods and their side effects, and orgasm. Thus, some clients may require specific training in basic social/sexual engagement skills.

Conversely, therapists must not assume that others in society are as understanding or accepting of disability as they might be. There are several actual barriers to socialization that are not simply caused by poor social skills on the part of the client. There is legitimate social stigma associated with having a disability that clients experience and cope with on a daily basis. The task becomes learning how to differentiate those situations where the client can improve the situation from those settings in which the client may lack power in facilitating a positive change.

It is also vital that various types of activities other than penile-vaginal intercourse be approached as valid sexual behaviors. For persons with certain physical disabilities, "traditional" sex may be painful, difficult, or even impossible. This situation is exacerbated when both members of a couple have significant disabilities. Although personal assistance services are designed so that disabled persons can "receive assistance from another individual with activities that one would typically accomplish on one's own if one did not have a disability," most social service agencies do not include sexual positioning or expression as part of typical personal assistance services (World Institute on Disability, 1993, p. 3). It may thus be necessary to work directly with personal assistance providers or help the disabled individual develop ways to discuss these issues with providers.

With regard to working with disabled clients who are gay or lesbian, some guidelines have been introduced to assist health care professionals (McAllan & Ditillo, 1994). These practical suggestions include: (1) understanding and countering myths, (2) understanding the reality of what it means to be gay or lesbian, (3) learning about your own biases, (4) learning skills and using available resources, and (5) returning to the roots of comprehensive rehabilitation.

Because of the frequently isolating effects of having a disability, group therapy as well as peer support and mentoring can be particularly useful. This can serve to demystify and provide encouragement and support when dealing with issues related to sexuality. In a very real sense, it can serve as an alternative to the peer education that many disabled persons were not given as children. Encouraging people with disabilities to meet with others in their own community can not only provide support, but also create a forum for receiving practical suggestions from those with similar disabilities. For individuals with more recent disabilities, it can instill a sense of hope and optimism that disability need not be the end of sex. For those settings in which there are simply not enough individuals to form a regular group, there are a number of excellent books and videos that contain first-person accounts of the sexuality of disabled persons (Sexuality Information and Education Council of the United States [SIECUS], 1992).

One recent innovation that can have great therapeutic benefit for many individuals with disabilities is the Internet (see Cooper, Boies, Maheu, & Greenfield, this volume). As the saying goes, "In cyberspace, no one knows that you are a dog." So it is with individuals with disabilities who have spent their lives experiencing discrimination and social stigma. The Internet serves as a level playing field where those with disabilities of various kinds can access support, community, and information, as well as practice flirting and sexual engagement skills in an anonymous manner. It is especially advantageous to those individuals who normally use personal assistance providers, interpreters, or the like to communicate with others, allowing them a level of privacy they may otherwise lack. Virtually no disability, whether mobility, sensory, or other, prevents an individual with appropriate adaptive technology from communicating via the Internet, and on his or her own time frame. Indeed, for the most severely disabled, this may be their primary, or even only, way of communicating with the outside world (Gardos & Mona, 1994). It is especially pertinent to sexual communication because research has shown that communicating through a computer often allows individuals to speak more easily, openly, and honestly about sensitive topics (Erdman, Klein, & Greist, 1985). Finally, issues of transportation and accessibility are moot when communicating via the use of the computer.

It can be helpful for therapists to have a basic understanding of various disabilities and the types of issues they might raise. Although there is a paucity of data and real-life examples of therapeutic situations involving sexuality and people with disabilities, based on the research cited to this point and our own experience as psychotherapists, we present the following recommendations and case studies.

Persons with visual and hearing impairments may experience problems with communication with others, a factor that influences the initial meeting of two persons, in addition to the relay of information about sexual wants and desires. It is often taken for granted that eye contact is usually the first step in establishing contact with a potential dating/sexual partner. Blind and some visually impaired individuals do not have this option. How, then, does a first encounter play out for these people? Other means of communication are employed, such as verbal gesturing, speech, and touching of the hands and arms of the other person. Subsequent initiation of sexual activity may be difficult unless a comfortable level of verbal communication has already been established. Similarly, persons who are deaf or hearing impaired may have difficulties with initial communication. A large majority of these individuals use sign language as the primary or sole means of communication. Some persons with hearing impairments are proficient in reading lips. However, this means that the person with whom they are speaking must be facing them the entire duration of the conversation. How do these ways of communication influence the sexual lives of these individuals? First of all, sign language is not a language known by much of the hearing world. Usually, if a hearing person has a friend, relative, or lover with a hearing impairment, he or she may know sign language. But, what are the chances of meeting one of these people in a social situation? Due to this communication barrier, initial meetings with hearing persons can be difficult or impossible. Dating or participating in sexual activity with others who may have hearing impairments or deafness may at times seem more inviting based on the ability to have a private conversation. However, if a deaf person chooses to date a hearing person who does not use sign language, then a sign language interpreter would most likely need to be present. Thus, privacy is sacrificed in the process and, as a result, sexual communication may be hampered. None of this, of course, is to say that potential sexual and dating partners cannot learn how to utilize sign language, and this does occur often.

Persons with mobility impairments also comprise a varied group of individuals. Some persons use crutches or walkers to ambulate; others use prosthetics. Persons who use wheelchairs do so because of paralysis caused by stoke or spinal cord injury, muscular or bone conditions, or limb amputations. In general, individuals who are wheelchair users can vary over a wide range of physical agility. Those persons who do not experience loss in physical sensation often experience some difficulty in finding comfortable body positions in which to engage in sexual activity. Depending on the disability status of a disabled person's partner, physical limitations may or may not be a serious problem. That is, when an able-bodied person is involved in sexual activity with a mobility impaired person, he or she may be able to move around or move the partner's body around so that a mutually comfortable position can be obtained for kissing, touching, oral sex, penile-vaginal intercourse, or anal intercourse. However, if both members of a couple have disabilities, a personal assistant or third party may need to be involved for the facilitation of sexual activity.

For individuals with complete or total paralysis, a slightly different process may occur during sexual activity. This condition usually arises after a stroke or spinal cord injury. In these situations, a large adjustment is made in the ways that these individuals express themselves sexually. Often, people must relearn how to be sexual by becoming reacquainted with their bodies. This is best accomplished through self-touch to discover what feels good. For some individuals with spinal cord injuries, depending on the level of injury, the ability to experience a physiological orgasm is no longer possible, but society has historically promoted sex as genital- and orgasm-focused. Persons with spinal cord injuries often speak about how difficult it is to lose the ability to have the sexual release of physiological orgasm. However, as they become more familiar with their bodies, many people begin to notice an increase in level of arousal when different areas are stimulated. Whether it be the neck, ears, arms, nipples, or any other area responsive to tactile stimulation, persons with various forms of paralysis often report feeling sexually aroused even if a physiological orgasm does not occur.

Although problems of communication may seem more prevalent among those with hearing and visual impairments, persons with mobility impairments deal with these concerns as well. Negotiating sexual desires and comfortable positions can be quite difficult. Although it may be better to discuss disability and sexually related matters prior to engaging in activity, life circumstances do not always allow this. Therefore, disabled persons often practice what they plan to say in a given situation before it actually happens. This reduces anxiety when the actual time comes to engage in sexual activity. Partners of persons with disabilities sometimes fear that asking questions about potential sexual activity may be offensive. However, if a level of trust and communication has already been established, questions of this nature are usually welcomed by disabled individuals because they create an open forum in which to discuss these topics.

Persons with developmental disabilities experience social constraints similar to those with physical disabilities. However, many people mistakenly think that any type of cognitive impairment precludes the ability to think for oneself and make decisions. Personal assistants often help those with developmental disabilities to interpret social circumstances; then, the individuals are capable of understanding and making their own decisions. This process can play out in dating and sexual arenas as well as in general life situations. For example, persons with developmental disabilities may ask for assistance in deciding who may be a suitable dating partner or which sexual activities they may want to engage in with their partner. Given the delicate nature of the role that this type of assistant plays in this person's life, careful selection of the assistant is essential.

Physically disabled people confront architectural obstacles daily that prevent access to social situations. In order for individuals with disabilities to leave the house and enter the "real world," a great deal of planning and scheduling usually takes place. In fact, one major obstacle faced by persons with disabilities is having the opportunity to enter the social world to meet potential dating and sexual partners. Becauase of transportation, communication, and financial barriers, persons with disabilities may have limited experience in the dating and sexual domains of life; thus, anxiety is increased in these particular situations.

Case Examples

Case 1

Consider the potential difficulties confronted by Bob, a diabetic person with a severe visual impairment who would like to go on a dinner date to a restaurant. First, Bob would have to arrange for transportation, especially if the dating partner were also blind or visually impaired and could not drive. This would include finding the money for a taxi or a bus. The bus route would have to be navigated and the estimated duration of the ride learned. Furthermore, the route to gain entrance into the restaurant must be known. Before he arrives at the restaurant, he would need to know if the menu were available in Braille. If not, he would have to have another person read the entire menu. Obviously, this would not be a completely spontaneous evening. However, this does not mean that it could not turn out to be a spectacular romantic and sexually provocative date; it is simply different from the norm.

As far as sexual activity is concerned, Bob may or may not choose to discuss sexually related matters with his partner prior to sexual involvement. That is, his partner may be wondering if sexual activity is different for Bob compared to sighted men. This communication process typically helps with facilitating a deeper level of intimacy. The other issue that would have to be addressed is the fact that Bob requires a vacuum erection device to obtain an erection. Although this method works well for him, it would require the understanding and cooperation of his partner. He or she may not know what to do or how to assist in his preparations. Thus, persons with disabilities are frequently placed in the dual role of trying to reassure and make their partners comfortable, while, at the same time, coping with their own frustrations and possible embarrassments. Luckily, therapists can be very helpful in this area.

Case 2

Cindy is 80% deaf and uses sign language to communicate. She would like to go out to lunch and the movies with a hearing dating partner who knows some sign language. Cindy realizes that at a restaurant, she will have to either point to the desired item on the menu or have her partner order for her. After having difficulty communicating with her partner throughout lunch, she knows that she will not be able to walk into just any movie theater and receive closed captioning of the script or assisted listening devices, an issue she has already discussed with her partner. One of two options is available: find a theater that offers appropriate accommodations for Cindy's disability or go to her home and watch a rented movie that she knows is closed captioned.

Cindy's ease in being sexual with her partner on this date may or may not be problematic. That is, if difficulties with communication have ensued throughout the date, there may be some problems with communicating about sexual activity. If relatively few communication problems have occurred, Cindy and her partner may feel comfortable engaging in sexual expression. Cindy may want to talk with her partner about how to communicate with each other during sexual activity. For example, an agreement to maintain a fair amount of eye contact and use basic signing skills may be warranted. In addition, leaving the lights on may help with facilitating this type of communication.

Case 3

Gloria, a person using a manual wheelchair, wishes to go to the symphony and to dinner following the show with her partner. First, wheelchair seating must be obtained in the appropriate theater section. Questions about wheelchair-accessible restrooms would then be asked so that Gloria would know whether or not she would be able to access this part of the building. Then, transportation arrangements must be made; because she does not have the money to purchase a modified wheelchair lift van, she often must use public transportation. Fortunately, her partner owns a car. But it is a small sports car, and it is difficult, though not impossible, to get Gloria and her chair into the vehicle. Once she is lifted into the vehicle, a potentially uncomfortable transfer, her partner disassembles her chair, placing it in the back seat of the car. Luckily, Gloria does not use an electric wheelchair, which would not be able to be taken apart as easily and placed into a regular-sized car. Once they arrive at the theater, an appropriate disabled parking place must be located because alternative parking would involve the need to access stairs. Before choosing a restaurant, similar issues would need to be considered, including parking, building access, and restroom accommodations.

With regard to sexual activity, Gloria may want to discuss sexuality issues with her partner before any sexual interactions take place. Specifically, she may tell him or her about her physical limitations, or lack thereof, how she has enjoyed sex most in the past, and so on. Again, communication is important in facilitating the sexual experience. Some people may choose to discuss these topics as they arise in the context of sexual activity. This approach can also work and may be a more spontaneous way of being with one's partner.

It may seem overwhelming for able-bodied persons to consider the amount of planning involved in the lives of persons with disabilities. In view of these case examples, it may seem that spontaneity is completely lacking in the romantic lives of disabled people. However, this is not true. What is true is that spontaneity is different; that is, a lot of disabled people *plan* their spontaneity. For example, Bob could have arranged to have a friend dress as a chauffeur and drive him and his partner to a given restaurant; Cindy could have previously chosen a sexy foreign film and learned the theater location prior to her date; and Gloria could have planned to wear no underwear beneath her dress so that when her partner picked her up, not only would he or she be surprised but a break in the routine would have occurred. These are just a few ideas of the ways members of the disabled community can live their romantic lives and use nonnormative means of spicing things up.

Once therapists understand the numerous real-world issues that their clients face, as well as the practical implications of their disability, it should be possible to support the development of these individuals' sexual selves. Most important, even if therapists understand and appreciate the issues detailed in this chapter, their helping potential will be useless if their practices are not accessible. On a purely practical basis, therapists must be aware of the accessibility of the facilities in which they work. This includes the availability of wheelchair-accessible parking, close proximity to public transportation, wheelchair ramps, and architectural layout of the external building. For example, for those with mobility and visual impairments, the therapist must be prepared to give the client specific directions on how to navigate the office. In addition, therapists must challenge themselves with the possibility of working with sign language, voice interpreters, or personal assistants within the context of the therapy session. Overall, it is important for the therapist to take note of the ways the office itself is designed in addition to personal awareness of disability-related issues to best accommodate and help people with disabilities.

CONCLUSION

Sexuality and disability is a vital yet often overlooked and misunderstood topic. In particular, the psychosocial influences on the sexual lives of the disability community have previously been overlooked in favor of purely medically focused models. It is imperative to remember the roles of societal influences and definitions on the sexual lives of people with disabilities. As members of this community fight for equal rights, including architectural access, medical insurance, and the need for personal assistance, an equally important effort is taking place around being acknowledged as sexual human beings and having rights to be sexual partners and parents. In other words, let us not forget the political ramifications of excluding people from social domains and not giving them the opportunity to interact with others and develop intimate relationships. It is only by recognizing the importance of all of these factors and the disability experience in a holistic manner, and by understanding the existing research and theoretical literature, that we can begin to form a true appreciation of a research-based approach to this area of human sexuality, and thus truly serve our clients and community as well-informed psychologists.

REFERENCES

Albert, A., & Wincze, J.P. (1990). *Sexual arousal in diabetic females: A psychophysiological investigation.* Unpublished manuscript. Providence, RI: Brown University.

Alcorn, D.A. (1974). Parental views of sexual development and education of the trainable mentally retarded. *Journal of Special Education, 8,* 119–130.

Aloni, R., Ring, H., Rozenthul, N., & Schwartz, J. (1993). Sexual function in male patients after stroke: A follow-up study. *Sexuality and Disability, 11*(2), 121–128.

American Cancer Society. (1995). *Cancer facts and figures 1995.* New York: Author.

Americans with Disabilities. (1990). Washington, DC: U.S. Department of Justice.

Appleby, Y. (1994). Out in the margins. *Disability and Society, 9*(1), 19–32.

Arthritis Foundation. (1997). *Living and loving: Information about sexuality and intimacy. Arthritis information* [Brochure]. Atlanta, GA: Author.

Asch, A., & Sacks, L. (1983). Lives without, lives within: The autobiographies of blind women and men. *Journal of Visual Impairments and Blindness, 77*(6), 242–247.

Bach, J.R., & Bardach, J.L. (1997). Neuromuscular diseases. In M.A. Sipski & C.J. Alexander (Eds.), *Sexual function in people with disability and chronic illness: A health professional's guide.* Gaithersburg, MD: Aspen.

Barres, B. (1992). Facing AIDS, Part I and II. *Hearing Health, 8*(2/3).

Baum, N., Neiman, M., & Lewis, R. (1988). Evaluation and treatment of organic impotence in the male with diabetes mellitus. *Diabetes Educator, 14*(2), 123–129.

Beckerman, H., Becher, M.D., & Lankhorst, G.J. (1993). The effectiveness of vibratory stimulation in anejaculatory men with spinal cord injury. *Paraplegia, 31,* 689–699.

Benedict, M.I., White, R.B., Wulff, L.M., & Hall, B.J. (1990). Reported maltreatment in children with multiple disabilities. *Child Abuse and Neglect, 14,* 207–217.

Betts, C.D. (1996). Pathophysiology of male sexual dysfunction in multiple sclerosis. *Sexuality and Disability, 14*(1), 41–55.

Bidgood, F.E. (1971). A study of sex education programs for visually handicapped persons. *New Outlook for the Blind, 65*(10), 318–323.

Blake, D.J., Maisiak, R., Alarcon, G.S., & Brown, S. (1987). Sexual quality of life of patients with arthritis compared to arthritis free controls. *Journal of Rheumatology, 14,* 570–576.

Bleszynska, K. (1995). Values attributed to marriage by persons with physical disabilities. *International Journal of Disability, Development & Education, 42*(3), 203–210.

Blish, S. (1940). Problems involved in sex education in residential school for the deaf. *Volta Review, 42.*

Blocker, W.P. (1985). Cardiac rehabilitation. In L. Halstead & M. Grabois (Eds.), *Medical rehabilitation.* New York: Raven Press.

Bowe, F. (1980). *Rehabilitating America.* New York: Harper & Row.

Bowe, F. (1981). *Comeback: Six remarkable people who triumphed over disability.* New York: Harper & Row.

Brender, C., & Walsh, P. (1992). Prostate cancer: Evaluation and radio therapeutic management. *Cancer Journal for Clinicians, 42,* 223–240.

Brightman, A.J. (Ed.). (1984). *Ordinary moments: The disabled experience.* Baltimore: University Park Press.

Bristol, M.M., & Schloper, E. (1984). A developmental perspective on stress and coping in families of autistic children. In J. Blacker (Ed.), *Severely handicapped young children and their families* (pp. 91–142). Orlando, FL: Academic Press.

Brown, D.E. (1988). Factors affecting psychosexual development of adults with congenital physical disabilities. *Physical & Occupational Therapy in Pediatrics, 8*(2), 43–58.

Bullard, D., & Knight, S. (Eds.). (1981). *Sexuality and physical disability: Personal perspectives.* St. Louis, MO: Mosby.

Burke, L., & Bedard, C. (1995). A preliminary study of the association between self-injury and sexual abuse in persons with developmental handicaps. *Sexuality and Disability, 13*(4), 327–330.

Buvat, J., Lemaire, A., Buvat-Herbaut, M., Guieu, J.D., Bailleul, J.P., & Fossati, P. (1985). Comparative investigations in 26 impotent and 26 nonimpotent diabetic patients. *Journal of Urology, 133,* 34–38.

Chapelle, P.A., Roby, B.A., Yakovleff, A., & Bussel, B. (1988). Neurologic correlations of ejaculation and testicular size in men with complete spinal cord section. *Journal of Neurology, Neurosurgery, and Psychiatry, 51,* 197–202.

Chapman, J.W., & Pitceathly, A.S. (1985). Sexuality and mentally handicapped people: Issues of sex education, marriage, parenthood, and care staff attitudes. *Australian and New Zealand Journal of Developmental Disabilities, 10,* 227–235.

Charlifue, S.W., Gerhart, K.A., Menter, R.R., Whitnsck, G.G., & Manley, M.S. (1992). Sexual issues of women with spinal cord injuries. *Paraplegia, 30,* 192–199.

Cole, S.S. (1988). Women, sexuality, and disabilities. *Women and Therapy, 7*(203), 277–294.

Cole, T.M. (1975). Sexuality and physical disabilities. *Archives of Sexual Behavior, 4*(4), 389–403.

Colon, J.M. (1997). Assisted reproductive technologies. In M.L. Sipski & C.J. Alexander (Eds.), *Sexual function in people with disability and chronic illness: A health professional's guide* (pp. 557–575). Gaithersburg, MD: Aspen.

Connie, T.A., & Evans, J.H. (1982). Sexual reactivation of chronically ill and disabled adults. *Journal of Allied Health, 11*(4), 261–270.

Corbett, J. (1994). A proud label: Exploring the relationship between disability politics and gay pride: Representation and disabled people [Special issue]. *Disability & Society, 9*(3), 343–357.

Craft, A., & Craft, M. (1979). *Handicapped married couples.* London: Routledge & Kegan Paul.

Craig, W., & Anderson, P.E. (1966). The role of residential schools in preparing deaf teenagers for marriage. *American Annals of the Deaf, 111,* 488–498.

Crewe, N.M., Athelstan, G.T., & Krumberger, J. (1976). Spinal cord injury: A comparison of pre-injury and post-injury marriages. *Archives of Physical Medicine and Rehabilitation, 60,* 252–256.

Crossmaker, M. (1991). Behind locked doors: Institutional sexual abuse. *Sexuality and Disability, 9,* 201–220.

Davis, D.L., & Schneider, L.K. (1990). Ramifications of traumatic brain injury for sexuality. *Journal of Head Trauma Rehabilitation, 5,* 31–37.

DeHaan, C.B., & Wallander, J.L. (1988). Self-concept, sexual knowledge and attitudes, and parental support in the sexual adjustment of women with early- and late-onset disability. *Archives of Sexual Behavior, 17*(2), 145–161.

DeLoach, C.P. (1994). Attitudes toward disability: Impact on sexual development and forging of intimate relationships. *Journal of Applied Rehabilitation Counseling, 25*(1), 18–25.

Demetral, G.D. (1981). Does ignorance really produce irresponsible behavior? *Sexuality and Disability, 4,* 151–160.

Doucette, J. (1986). *Violent acts against disabled women.* Toronto: DisAbled Women's Network.

Doyle, A. (1995). AIDS knowledge, attitudes, and behaviors among deaf college students: A preliminary study. *Sexuality and Disability, 13*(2), 107–134.

Duffy, Y. (1981). *All things are possible.* Ann Arbor, MI: Garvin.

Dupont, S. (1996). Sexual function and ways of coping in patients with multiple sclerosis and their partners. *Sexual & Marital Therapy, 11*(4), 359–372.

Edgerton, R.B. (1973). Some socio-cultural research considerations. In F.F. De La Cruz & G.D. LaVeck (Eds.), *Human sexuality and the mentally retarded.* New York: Brunner/Mazel.

Edgerton, R.B., & Dingman, H. (1964). Good reasons for bad supervision: Dating in a hospital for mentally retarded. *Psychiatric Quarterly Supplement, 2,* 221–223.

El Ghatit, A.Z., & Hanson, R.W. (1976). Marriage and divorce after spinal cord injury. *Archives of Physical Medicine and Rehabilitation, 57,* 470–477.

Enzlin, P., Mathieu, C., Vanderschueren, D., & Demyttenaere, K. (1998). Diabetes mellitus and female sexuality: A review of 25 years' research. *Diabetic Medicine, 15*(10), 807–808.

Erdman, H.P., Klein, M.H., & Greist, J.H. (1985). Direct patient computer interviewing. *Journal of Consulting and Clinical Psychology, 53,* 760–773.

Fitting, M.D., Salisbury, S., Davis, M.H., & Maydin, D.K. (1988). Self-concept of spinal cord injured women. *Archives of Sexual Behavior, 7,* 143–156.

Franklin, P. (1977). Impact of disability on the family structure. *Social Security Bulletin, 40,* 3–18.

Gannon, C.L. (1998). The deaf community and sexuality education. *Sexuality and Disability, 16*(4), 283–293.

Garbarino, J. (1987). The abuse and neglect of special children: An introduction to the issues. In J. Garbarino, P.E. Brookhouser, & K.J. Authier (Eds.), *Special children–special risks: The maltreatment of children with disabilities* (pp. 3–14). New York: Aldine.

Garden, F.H., Bontke, C.F., & Hoffman, M. (1990). Sexual functioning and marital adjustment after traumatic brain injury. *Journal of Head Trauma Rehabilitation, 5,* 52–59.

Gardos, P.S., & Mona, L.R. (1994). The use of computers and on-line services in conducting sexuality research with people who have physical disabilities. *Sexuality and Disability, 12*(4), 251–259.

Garret, J. (1971). Sex education: A second opinion. *Special Education, 60,* 16–17.

Getch, Y.Q., & Denny, G. (1998). Sexuality education for students who are deaf: Current practices and concerns. *Sexuality and Disability, 16*(4), 269–281.

Gill, C.J. (1995, July). *Disability and the responsive campus.* Paper presented at the National Meeting of the Association on Higher Education and Disability, San Jose, CA.

Gill, C.J. (1996). Dating and relationship issues. *Sexuality and Disability, 14*(3), 183–190.

Green, D.R. (1983). A human sexuality program for developmentally disabled women in a sheltered workshop setting. *Sexuality and Disability, 6,* 20–24.

Gulley, S. (1993). *Sexuality reborn* [Film]. C. Alexander & M. Sipski (Producers). West Orange, NJ: Kessler Institute for Rehabilitation.

Gutmann, L., & Walsh, J.J. (1971). Prostigmine assessment test of fertility in spinal men. *Paraplegia, 9,* 39–51.

Hahn, K. (1989). Sexuality and COPD. *Rehabilitation Nursing, 14,* 191–195.

Hall, J.E. (1975). Sexuality and the mentally retarded. In R. Green (Ed.), *Human sexuality: A health practitioner's text* (pp. 181–195). Baltimore: Williams & Wilkins.

Hall, J.E., & Morris, H.L. (1976). Sex knowledge and attitudes of institutionalized retarded adolescents. *American Journal of Mental Deficiency, 1,* 382–387.

Hall, J.E., & Sawyer, H.W. (1978). Sexual policies for the mentally retarded. *Sexuality and Disability, 1,* 34–43.

Hanna, W.J., & Rogovsky, B. (1986). *Women and disability: Stigma and "the third factor."* College Park: University of Maryland, Department of Family and Community Development, College of Human Ecology.

Hannaford, S. (1985). *Living outside inside.* Berkeley, CA: Canterbury Press.

Hayden, P., Davenport, S., & Kendel, M. (1979). Adolescents with myelodyspasia: Impact of physical disability on emotional maturation. *Pediatrics, 64,* 53–59.

Heatherington, C. (1993). *Sexuality reborn* [Film]. C. Alexander & M. Sipski (Producers). West Orange, NJ: Kessler Institute for Rehabilitation.

Hellerstein, H.K., & Friedman, E.H. (1970). Sexual activity and the post coronary patient. *Archives of Internal Medicine, 125,* 987–999.

Helminiak, D.A. (1989). Self-esteem, sexual self-acceptance, and spirituality. *Journal of Sex Education & Therapy, 15*(3), 200–210.

Hill, A. (1971). Some guidelines for sex education of the deaf child. *Volta Review, 43*(2), 120–125.

Hillyer. (1993). *Feminism and disability.* Norman: University of Oklahoma Press.

Hinsburger, D. (1987). Sex counseling and the developmentally handicapped: The assessment and management of seven critical problems. *Psychiatric Aspects of Mental Retardation Review, 6,* 41–46.

Hubbard, R. (1997). Abortion and disability. In L.J. Davis (Ed.), *The disability studies reader* (pp. 187–200). New York: Routledge.

Jackson, A.B. (1997). Pregnancy and delivery. In D.M. Krotoski, M.A. Nosek, & M.A. Turk (Eds.), *Women with physical disabilities: Achieving and maintaining health and well-being.* Baltimore: Brookes.

Jacobson, N. (1993). Learning about disability from children. In F.P. Haseltine, S.S. Cole, & D.G. Gray (Eds.), *Reproductive issues for people with physical disabilities* (pp. 63–66). Baltimore: Brookes.

Jensen, S.B. (1981). Diabetic sexual dysfunction: A comparative study of 160 insulin treated diabetic men and women and an age-matched control. *Archives of Sexual Behavior, 10*(6), 493–504.

Jensen, S.B. (1985). Emotional aspects in diabetes mellitus: A study of somatopsychologic relations in 51 couples in which one partner has insulin-treated diabetes. *Journal of Psychosomatic Research, 29,* 353–359.

Kempton, W. (1978). Sex education for the mentally handicapped. *Sexuality and Disability, 1,* 137–146.

Komisaruk, B.R., & Whipple, B. (1995). The suppression of pain by genital stimulation in females. *Annual Review of Sex Research, 6*, 151–186.

Kreutzer, J.S., & Zasler, N.D. (1989). Psychosexual consequences of traumatic brain injury: Methodology and preliminary findings. *Brain Injury, 3*, 177–186.

LaBarre, A. (1998). Treatment of sexually abused children who are deaf. *Sexuality and Disability, 16*(4), 321–324.

Lew-Starowicz, Z. (1994). Problems of disabled persons with a homosexual orientation. *International Journal of Adolescent Medicine and Health, 7*(3), 233–239.

Linsenmeyer, T.A. (1997). Management of male fertility. In M.L. Sipski & C.J. Alexander (Eds.), *Sexual function in people with disability and chronic illness: A health professional's guide.* Gaithersburg, MD: Aspen.

Longmore, P. (1993, August). *What is disability? Revolutions in ideology and consciousness.* Paper presented at the Disabled and Proud: The 1993 Gathering of College Student Leaders with Disabilities, Minneapolis, MN.

Love, E. (1983). Parental and staff attitudes toward instruction in human sexuality for sensorially impaired students at the Alabama Institute for Deaf and Blind. *American Annals of the Deaf, 128*(1), 45–47.

Ludmerer, K.M. (1972). *Genetics and American society.* Baltimore: Johns Hopkins University Press.

Lundberg, P.O. (1978). Sexual dysfunction in patients with multiple sclerosis. *Sexuality and Disability, 1*, 218–222.

Lundberg, P.O., & Hulter, B. (1996). Female sexual dysfunction in multiple sclerosis. *Sexuality and Disability, 14*(1), 65–72.

Mansell, S., Sobsey, D., Wilgosh, L., & Zawallich, A. (1997). The sexual abuse of young people with disabilities: Treatment considerations. *International Journal for the Advancement of Counseling, 19*(3), 293–302.

Mathews, G.F. (1983). *Voices from the shadows: Women with disabilities speak out.* Toronto: Women's Educational Press.

Mattson, D.H., Petrie, M., Srvastava, D.K., & McDermott, M. (1995). Multiple sclerosis: Sexual dysfunction and its response to medications. *Archives of Neurology, 52*, 862–868.

McAllan, L.C., & Ditillo, D. (1994). Addressing the needs of lesbian and gay clients with disabilities. Sexuality and disability: Dimensions of human intimacy and rehabilitation counseling practice [Special issue]. *Journal of Applied Rehabilitation Counseling, 25*(1), 26–35.

McCabe, M.P., Cummins, R.A., & Reid, S.B. (1994). An empirical study of the sexual abuse of people with intellectual disability. *Sexuality and Disability, 12*(4), 297–306.

McDaniel, J. (1995). *The lesbians' couples guide: Finding the right woman and creating a life together.* New York: HarperCollins.

McDermott, S., Kelly, M., & Spearman, J. (1994). Evaluation of a family planning program for individuals with mental retardation. *Sexuality and Disability, 12*(4), 307–317.

McFerlin, D.E., & McFarland, H.F. (1982). Multiple sclerosis. *New England Journal of Medicine, 307*, 1183.

Medlar, T.M. (1993). Sexual counseling and traumatic brain injury. *Sexuality and Disability, 11*, 57–71.

Milligan, M.S., & Neufeldt, A.H. (1998). Postinjury marriage to men with spinal cord injuries: Women's perspectives on making a commitment. *Sexuality and Disability, 16*(2), 117–132.

Mona, L.R., Gardos, P.S., & Brown, R.C. (1994). Sexual self-views of women with disabilities: The relationship among age-of-onset, nature of disability, and sexual self-esteem. *Sexuality and Disability, 12*(4), 261–277.

Money, J. (1960). Phantom orgasm in the dreams of paraplegic men and women. *Archives of General Psychiatry, 3,* 373–382.

Monga, T.N. (1986). Sexual dysfunction in stroke patients. *Archives of Physical Medicine and Rehabilitation, 67,* 19–22.

Monga, T.N., & Kerrigan, A.J. (1997). Cerebrovascular accidents. In M.A. Sipski & C.J. Alexander (Eds.), *Sexual function in people with disability and chronic illness: A health professional's guide.* Gaithersburg, MD: Aspen.

Muccigrosso, L. (1991). Sexual abuse prevention strategies and programs for persons with developmental disabilities. *Sexuality and Disability, 9,* 261–272.

Mulhern, T.J. (1975). Survey of reported sexual behavior and policies characterizing residential facilities for retarded citizens. *American Journal of Mental Deficiency, 79,* 670–673.

Muller, J.E., Mittleman, M.A., Maclure, M., Sherwood, J.B., & Tofler, G.H. (1996). Triggering myocardial infarction by sexual activity: Low absolute risk and prevention by regular physical exertion. *Journal of the American Medical Association, 275,* 1405–1409.

Nadler, S. (1997). Arthritis and other connective tissue diseases. In M.L. Sipski & C.J. Alexander (Eds.), *Sexual function in people with disability and chronic illness.* Gaithersburg, MD: Aspen.

Newman, A.S., & Bettelson, A.D. (1986). Sexual dysfunction in diabetic women. *Journal of Behavioral Medicine, 9*(3), 261–270.

Nosek, M.A. (1996). Sexual abuse of women with physical disabilities. In D.M. Krotoski, M.A. Nosek, & M.A. Turk (Eds.), *Women with physical disabilities: Achieving and maintaining health and well-being.* Baltimore: Brookes.

Nosek, M.A., & Howland, C. (1997). Sexual abuse and people with disabilities. In M.L. Sipski & C.J. Alexander (Eds.), *Sexual function in people with disability and chronic illness.* Gaithersburg, MD: Aspen.

Nosek, M.A., Howland, C.A., & Young, M. (1997). Abuse of women with disabilities. *Journal of Disability Policy Studies, 8*(1/2), 157–175.

Oddy, M., Humphrey, M., & Uttley, D. (1978). Subjective impairment and social recovery after closed head injury. *Journal of Neurology, Neurosurgery, and Psychiatry, 41,* 611–616.

Ontario Ministry of Community and Social Services. (1987, April 1). Disabled women are more likely to be battered, survey suggests. *The Toronto Star,* p. F9.

Papadopoulos, C. (1978). A survey of sexual activity after myocardial infarction. *Cardiovascular Medicine, 3,* 821–826.

Parker, G. (1993). Disability, caring and marriage: The experience of young couples when a partner is disabled after marriage. *British Journal of Social Work, 23*(6), 565–580.

Perduta-Fulginiti, P.S. (1992). Sexual functioning of women with complete SCI: Nursing implications. *Sexuality and Disability, 10*(2), 103–118.

Perez, C.A., Fair, W.R., & Ihde, D.C. (1989). Carcinoma of the prostate. In V.T. DeVita, S. Hellman, & S. Rosenburg (Eds.), *Cancer principles and practices in oncology* (3rd ed., pp. 1023–1058). Boston: Jones & Bartlett.

Pischke, M.E. (1993). Parenting with a disability. In F.P. Haseltine, S.S. Cole, & D.B. Gray (Eds.), *Reproductive issues for people with physical disabilities* (pp. 57–60). Baltimore: Brookes.

Rabinowitz, B., & Florian, V. (1992). Chronic obstructive pulmonary disease: Psychosocial issue and treatment goals. *Social Work in Health Care, 16*(4), 60–86.

Rappaport, S.R., Burkhardt, S.A., & Rotatori, A.F. (1997). *Child sexual abuse curriculum for the developmentally disabled.* Springfield, IL: Thomas.

Rintala, D.H., Howland, A.A., Nosek, M.A., Bennett, J.L., Young, M., Foley, C.C., Rossi, C.D., & Chanpong, G. (1997). Dating issues for women with physical disabilities. *Sexuality and Disability, 15*(4), 219–242.

Rogers, J.G. (1997). Pregnancy and physical disabilities. In D.M. Krotoski, M.A. Nosek, & M.A. Turk (Eds.), *Women with physical disabilities: Achieving and maintaining health and well-being.* Baltimore: Brookes.

Romano, M.D. (1975). *Sexuality and the disabled female.* Bloomington, IL: Accent on Living.

Roth, W. (1981). *The handicapped speak.* Jefferson, NC: McFarland.

Rousso, H. (1982). Special considerations in counseling clients with cerebral palsy. *Sexuality and Disability, 5*(2), 78–88.

Rousso, H. (1984). Disabled yet intact: Guidelines for work with congenitally disabled youngsters and their parents. *Child and Adolescent Social Work, 1*(4), 254–269.

Ruble, L.A., & Dalrymple, N.J. (1993). Social/sexual awareness of persons with autism: A parental perspective. *Archives of Sexual Behavior, 22*(3), 229–241.

Sandel, M.E. (1997). Traumatic brain injury. In M.L. Sipski & C.J. Alexander (Eds.), *Sexual function in people with disability and chronic illness: A health professional's guide.* Gaithersburg, MD: Aspen.

Sandowski, C.L. (1989). *Sexual concerns when illness or disability strikes.* Springfield, IL: Thomas.

Saxton, M. (1998). Disability rights and selective abortion. In R. Solinger (Ed.), *Abortion wars: A half century of struggle, 1950–2000* (pp. 374–393). Berkeley: University of California Press.

Scalzi, C.C. (1982). Sexual counseling and sexual therapy for patients with myocardial infraction. *Cardiovascular Nursing, 18,* 13–17.

Schaller, J., & Fieberg, J.L. (1998). Issues of abuse for women with disabilities and implications for rehabilitation counseling. *Journal of Applied Rehabilitation Counseling, 29*(2), 9–17.

Schiavi, R.C., Stimmel, B.B., Mandeli, J., Schreiner-Engel, P., & Ghizzani, A. (1995). Diabetes, psychological function, and male sexuality. *Journal of Psychosomatic Research, 39*(3), 305–314.

Schmitt, G.S., & Neubeck, G. (1985). Diabetes, sexuality, and family functioning. *Family Relations, 34,* 109–113.

Schoffling, K., Federlin, K., Ditschuneit, H., & Pfeiffer, E.F. (1963). Disorders of sexual function in male diabetics. *Diabetes, 12*(6), 519–527.

Schover, L.R., & Jensen, S.B. (1988). *Sexuality and chronic illness: A comprehensive approach.* New York: Guilford Press.

Schuster, C.S. (1986). Sex education of the visually impaired child: The role of parents. *Journal of Visual Impairment & Blindness, 80*(4), 675–680.

Scotti, J.R., Slack, B.S., Browman, R.A., & Morris, T.L. (1996). College student attitudes concerning the sexuality of persons with mental retardation: Development of the perceptions of sexuality scale. *Sexuality and Disability, 14*(4), 249–263.

Sexual Information and Education Council of the United States. (1992). Sexuality and disability: A SIECUS annotated bibliography of available print materials. *SIECUS Report, 20*(6), 15–21.

Sipski, M.L. (1991). Spinal cord injury: What is the effect on sexual response? *Journal of the American Paraplegia Society, 14*(2), 40–43.

Sipski, M.L., & Alexander, C.J. (Eds.). (1997). *Sexual function in people with disability and chronic illness: A health professional's guide.* Gaithersburg, MD: Aspen.

Sipski, M.L., Alexander, C.J., & Rosen, R.C. (1995). Physiological parameters associated with psychogenic sexual arousal in women with complete spinal cord injuries. *Archives of Physical and Medical Rehabilitation, 76,* 811–818.

Sjogren, K., & Fugl-Meyer, A. (1983). Some factors influencing quality of sexual life after myocardial infarction. *International Rehabilitative Medicine, 5,* 197–201.

Slaten, W., & Linsenmeyer, T.A. (1993). A survey of fertility programs for spinal cord injured men. *Journal of the American Paraplegia Society, 16*(2), 109.

Slob, A.K., Koster, J., Radder, J.K., & Van der Werff ten Bosch, J.J. (1990). Sexuality and psychophysiological functioning in women with diabetes mellitus. *Journal of Sex and Marital Therapy, 16*(2), 59–69.

Smeltzer, S.C., & Kelley, C.L. (1997). Multiple sclerosis. In M.L. Sipski & C.J. Alexander (Eds.), *Sexual function in people with disability and chronic illness.* Gaithersburg, MD: Aspen.

Sobsey, D., & Doe, T. (1991). Patterns of sexual abuse and assault: Sexual exploitation of people with disabilities [Special issue]. *Sexuality and Disability, 9*(3), 243–259.

Sobsey, D., & Varnhagen, C. (1989). Sexual abuse and exploitation of people with disabilities: Toward prevention and treatment. In M. Csapo & L. Gougen (Eds.), *Special education across Canada: Challenges for the 90's.* Vancouver: Center for Human Development and Research.

Spector, I.P., Leiblum, S.R., Carey, M.P., & Rosen, R.C. (1993). Diabetes and female sexual function: A critical review. *Annals of Behavioral Medicine, 15*(4), 257–264.

Stitik, T.P., & Benvento, B.T. (1997). Cardiac and pulmonary disease. In M.L. Sipski & C.J. Alexander (Eds.), *Sexual function in people with disability and chronic illness: A health professional's guide.* Gaithersburg, MD: Aspen.

Sullivan, P.M., & Knutson, J.F. (1998). Maltreatment and behavioral characteristics of youth who are deaf and heard-of-hearing. *Sexuality and Disability, 16*(4), 295–319.

Swartz, D.B. (1995). Cultural implications of audiological deficits on the homosexual male. *Sexuality and Disability, 13*(2), 159–181.

Thompson, D. (1994). The sexual experiences of men with learning disabilities having sex with men: Issues for HIV prevention. *Sexuality and Disability, 12*(3), 221–242.

Tilton, M.C. (1997). Diabetes and amputation. In M.L. Sipski & C.J. Alexander (Eds.), *Sexual functioning in people with disability or chronic illness: A health professional's guide.* Gaithersburg, MD: Aspen.

Torrens, M.J. (1983). Neurologic and neurosurgical disorders associated with impotence. In R.J. Krane, M.B. Siroky, & I. Goldstein (Eds.), *Male sexual dysfunction* (pp. 55–62). Boston: Little, Brown.

Turner, E.T. (1970). Attitudes of parents of deficient children toward their child's sexual behavior. *Journal of Social Health, 40,* 548–549.

Unger, R.M., Hilderbrand, & Mardor, T. (1982). Physical attractiveness and assumptions about social deviance: Some sex-by-sex comparison. *Personality and Social Psychology Bulletin, 8,* 293–301.

Valleroy, M.L., & Kraft, G. (1984). Sexual dysfunction in multiple sclerosis. *Archives of Physical Medicine and Rehabilitation, 65,* 125–128.

Vaughan, J., & Vaughan, C.E. (1987). Sex education of blind children re-examined. *Journal of Visual Impairment and Blindness, 81*(3), 95–98.

Wabrek, A., Wabrek, C., & Burchell, R. (1978). The human tragedy of spinabifida, spinal myelomenigeocela. *Sexuality and Disability, 1,* 210–217.

Wagner, M., D'Amico, R., Marder, C., Newman, L., & Blackorby, J. (1992). *What happens next? Trends in postschool outcomes of youth with disabilities* (The second comprehensive report from the national longitudinal transistion study of special education students). Office of Special Education Programs, U.S. Department of Education.

Waldman, T.L., & Eliasof, B. (1997). Cancer. In M.L. Sipski & C.J. Alexander (Eds.), *Sexual function in people with disability and chronic illness: A health professional's guide.* Gaithersburg, MD: Aspen.

Welner, S.L. (1997). Management of female infertility. In M.L. Sipski & C.J. Alexander (Eds.), *Sexual function in people with disability and chronic illness: A health professional's guide* (pp. 537–556). Gaithersburg, MD: Aspen.

Whipple, B., & Komisaruk, B.R. (1992). Current research trends: Spinal cord injuries. In F.B. Haseltine, S.S. Cole, & D.B. Gray (Eds.), *Reproductive issues for persons with physical disabilities* (NIH Conference Proceedings) (pp. 197–207). Baltimore: Brookes.

World Institute on Disability. (1993). *Attending to America.* Oakland, CA: Author.

Worthington, G.M. (1988). Coping strategies for burn survivors and their families. In N.R. Bernstein, A.J. Breslau, & J.A. Graham (Eds.), *"For beauty passed away": Perspectives on sexuality and cosmetic disabilities.* New York: Praeger.

Yalla, S.V. (1982). Sexual dysfunction in the paraplegic and quadriplegic. In A.H. Bennett (Ed.), *Management of male impotence* (pp. 182–191). Baltimore: Williams & Wilkins.

Yarkony, G.M. (1992). Spinal cord injured women: Sexuality, fertility, and pregnancy. In P.J. Goldstein & B.J. Stern (Eds.), *Neurologic disorders of pregnancy* (2nd rev. ed., pp. 203–222). Mt. Kisco, NY: Futura.

Yoshida, K.K. (1994). Intimate and marital relationships: An insider's perspective. *Sexuality and Disability, 12*(3), 179–189.

Young, E.W., Koch, P.B., & Bailey, D. (1989). Research comparing the dyadic adjustment and sexual functioning concerns of diabetic and nondiabetic women. *Health Care for Women International, 10,* 377–394.

Zakarewsky, G.T. (1979). Patterns of support among gay and lesbian deaf persons. *Sexuality and Disability, 2*(3), 178–191.

Zola, I. (1993). And the children shall lead us. In F.P. Haseltine, S.S. Cole, & D.B. Gray (Eds.), *Reproductive issues for persons with physical disabilities* (pp. 67–69). Baltimore: Brookes.

Zwerner, J. (1982). A study of issues in sexuality counseling for women with spinal cord injuries. *Women & Therapy, 1*(3), 91–100.

Zylla, T., & Demetral, G.D. (1981). A behavioral approach to sex education. *Sexuality and Disability, 4,* 40–48.

CHAPTER 9

Older Adult Sexuality

JOHN M. KELLETT

Tho' I am past ninety, and too old
T' expect preferment in the Court of Cupid,
and many winters made me ev'n so cold
I am become almost all over stupid.

Yet I can love and have a mistress too,
As fair as can be and as wise as fair,
and yet not proud, nor anything will do
To make me of her favour to despair.

To tell you who she is were very bold;
But if I' th' character your self you find
Think not the man a fool tho' he be old
Who loves in body fair, a fairer mind.

—THOMAS HOBBES, 1679,
the year of his death

THE FIRST DEBATE I won was when, at 11, I persuaded a group of school friends that there was no truth in the exciting idea that penises could be put into girls to create babies. Their use as water pistols was accepted, but this new use had a strange attraction. The argument was decided when we realized that if it were true, our parents must have done this—which we all realized was inconceivable. After all, our parents were "old people." Paradoxically, adults in Western society think and worry about the potential sexual activity of their children but try not to think about it at all with regard to their parents.

The elderly may certainly *fall* in love, as described by Hobbes, but this is not the same as being able to *make* love. Like most popular beliefs, this contains a kernel of truth. Sexual activity does decline during the later part of adult life. However, our natural diversity of sexual preferences is limited by the predominantly youthful images portrayed in the media and in pornography. Women are particularly vulnerable to one aspect of ageist stereotypes, the loss of physical beauty. The sexual appeal of women is in part dependent on retaining the smooth skin of a child, a feature that is destroyed by age. The double standard of aging results in the fact that elderly men are more often pictured with their young conquests than are elderly women with theirs.

Although men's physical attractiveness is not as much of a liability with age, the age-related decline in erectile functioning is often perceived as such. Because of the male tendency to equate sexual behavior with penetration and intercourse, many men lose sight of the potential importance and satisfaction associated with the noncoital sexual behaviors. After all, human sexuality serves two biological functions: the first is reproduction and the second is bonding. Touch and related "grooming" behavior, which contributes to bonding, is an important part of ape behavior. Humans direct this behavior primarily toward their children, their pets, and their lovers. Although the reproductive purpose of sex becomes less important in old age in the male, and absent in the female, the bonding function remains. Unfortunately, some men give up on noncoital sexual behavior, which is so important to emotional bonding, when penetrative sex becomes impossible. This often leads to emotional isolation and mutual recrimination. Other men go to various lengths to continue penetration. For example, they may inject their penises with vasodilators or pay surgeons to implant prostheses in the belief that their marriages will fall apart if they fail to maintain erections.

PATTERNS OF SEXUAL BEHAVIOR

The first and most extensive survey of sexual behavior was by Kinsey and his colleagues. They published their work on the male in 1948 and on the female in 1953. There remain several unanswered questions about this survey (Maslow & Sakoda, 1952; Reisman, 1990). Unfortunately, weaknesses in their sampling techniques limit some of the interpretations that can be made about older adults. They were well aware of these limitations and made no claims for reliability. Although they surveyed over 2,800 men and 1,800 women aged 16–20, they sampled only 26 men and 10 women over the age of 70. Furthermore, their finding that 75% of men were impotent at 80 was based on a sample of 4.

Nevertheless, the graph of the age of onset of permanent impotence is an exponential curve typical of aging phenomena. Kinsey's table of sexual outlets in older adulthood is instructive, with the only exception to a general decline in activity being male intercourse with prostitutes. Like most surveys, Kinsey's concentrates almost exclusively on orgasmic and usually coital sex, and perhaps for that reason alone there was a similar and earlier decline in female activity. This seems to reflect women's need for a potent partner in order to be themselves sexually active. (Whereas over half the men in the UK over 80 live with a partner, this only applies to one in five women in that age range.)

Kinsey's survey provided certain other information about aging. For example, although the researchers did not question respondents about foreplay per se, they did establish that petting to orgasm was a relatively rare activity that reached its maximum for people in their thirties. One surprising finding was the absence of any homosexual activity in postmenopausal women, which may be a cohort effect or a reluctance to admit such activities to the male interviewer.

The only comparable survey of sexual behavior was that of Wellings, Johnson, and Wadsworth (1994) in the UK. This survey included interviews with 8,384 men and 10,942 women and, unlike Kinsey's, used a proper sampling frame. However, the object was to examine behavior likely to cause infection with the HIV virus, and therefore they concentrated on the young and excluded people over the age of 59. Nevertheless, within that age range, the survey confirmed the decline in sexual activity with aging, noting a median frequency of coitus per four weeks in married couples of 7 aged 16 to 25, 5 aged 35 to 44, and 2 for women aged 45 to 59 and 3 for men in that age group. These frequencies are all much lower than those obtained earlier by Kinsey in the United States.

Janus and Janus (1993) studied sexual behavior in the United States, obtaining 2,765 completed questionnaires (61% response rate) supplemented by 125 interviews. The statistics regarding frequency of sexual activity with age showed that age had much less effect than suggested by earlier surveys. Table 9.1 presents a summary of their frequency data.

Older women (16%) were less likely to masturbate than younger women (35%) and older men (23%). Although only 3% of women aged 51 to 64 had never experienced orgasm during coitus, 9% of those over the age of 65 had never done so. Unlike earlier researchers, the Janus team did discuss foreplay and concluded that older men obtained greater pleasure than younger men from foreplay and also from warmth and intimacy after the act.

Table 9.1
Frequency of Sexual Activity with Age

	M	F	M	F	M	F	M	F	M	F
Age	18–26		27–38		39–50		51–54		65+	
N	254	268	353	380	282	295	227	230	212	221
>1/wk	53%	46%	60%	49%	54%	39%	63%	32%	53%	41%
"rarely"	13%	17%	9%	12%	8%	21%	8%	21%	11%	22%

Source: Adapted from Janus and Janus (1993), p. 25.

There was no evidence that the older adults were more conservative in their attitudes, with 39% supporting the statement "Traditional sex roles have no place in modern society." This compared with 27% of men and 31% of women in the youngest group (18–26).

Osborn, Hawton, and Gath (1988) took advantage of a survey of two gyne-cological practices to assess the level of sexual dysfunction in women 59 and under. The older women themselves did not complain more of dysfunction than the younger women. However, researchers found that operationally de-fined sexual difficulties were more prominent in the older group, as shown in Table 9.2.

The type of surveys presented above give little information on the quality of sexual life. For this we have to rely on self-report studies such as the Consumer Union report by Brecher (1984) and the Hite report (1976). Hite analyzed 3,019 questionnaires largely completed by readers of women's magazines in the United States. However, more than half the questionnaires did not include the respondent's age. The older women Hite did identify by age often expressed a greater enjoyment of sex, though several reported difficulty finding a partner.

To assess the effects of the menopause, Hallstrom (1977) sampled 800 women from Gothenburg, Sweden, in four age strata: 38, 46, 50, and 54. He noted a lower interest in sex with age but found that these associations were lost when controlling for the menopause. Controlling for age, there were still significant reductions of libido with the climacteric. This suggested that the menopause caused a reduction in activity. Hallstrom found that the decline was much greater in the lower socioeconomic status (SES) groups and those with mental illness. Thus, he agrees with Masters and Johnson (cited in Hallstrom, 1977) "that the psyche plays a part at least equal to, if not greater than that of an un-balanced endocrine system in determining the sex drive of women during the postmenopausal period of their lives" (pp. 237–238). Cutler, Garcia, and McCoy (1987) also found a decline in libido, which they associated with the lower levels of estrogen.

Hawton, Gath, and Day (1994), using the same sample reported above, se-lected 34 women who had ceased menstruation and compared them to 34 of the same age who were still menstruating. They found that the frequency of

Table 9.2
Prevalence of Sexual Dysfunctions in Females by Age

Dysfunction	Age				
	35–39	40–44	45–49	50–54	55–59
Reduced libido	4%	8%	16%	29%	28%
Vaginal dryness	8	12	16	26	22
Infrequency of orgasm	5	8	14	22	35

Source: Adapted from Osborn, Hawton, and Garth (1988).

sexual activity was little influenced by the menopause. Rather, it was influenced by age, especially that of their partner. To control for cohort effects, McCoy and Davidson (1985) followed up 43 women from the premenopause to one or more years thereafter. They confirmed a slight decrease in sexual interest, coital frequency, and sexual responsiveness. The effect of estrogens is discussed in greater detail below. However, in a comprehensive review of the subject, Riley (1991) states that reduced levels of vaginal lubrication and hence dyspareunia are the only features that have been confirmed to be associated with lower levels of estrogen.

Cross-sectional surveys of older adults tend to concentrate on finding the factors that correlate with sexual activity. For example, Persson (1990), using a sample of 70-year-olds from Gothenburg, Sweden, compared the 76 men (46% of sample) and 36 women (16% of sample) who had had intercourse in the previous month with those who had not. Limiting the comparison to those still married, the sexually active men reported having experienced a stronger sex drive in their twenties than had the less active men. Although other authors (e.g., Marsiglio & Donnelly, 1991; Pfeiffer & Davis, 1972) implicate physical health as a strong correlate of frequency of coitus for older adults, clearly sex drive in youth remains an important consideration. As for women, it is not surprising that a much smaller percentage reported recent intercourse. The frequency of coitus is usually governed by men: women who had younger partners were more active than women with older partners. Clearly, the impression that women reduce their activity at a younger age than men is a direct result of women having partners who are older than themselves.

Using data from the Baltimore Longitudinal Study (Shock et al., 1984), Martin (1981) reported on a cross-sectional sample of 188 upper SES volunteers who were male, married, and aged 60–79. Current level of sexual activity was correlated with activity at ages 20 to 34, and less strongly with measures of health. Most striking were data on the 85 (out of the total sample of 750) who lacked potency. The authors concluded that the lack of potency was not due to performance anxiety but to lack of motivation. Only a third of the total sample wanted an increase in sexual vigor. In other words, the loss of activity in the elderly men was not so much precipitated by erectile failure that then induced performance anxiety, but rather, it was associated with loss of drive. Further, those affected were content to allow this state of affairs to continue.

The lack of desire for coitus does not necessarily indicate a complete loss of sexual desire. Weizman and Hart (1987) found that 59% of those men they sampled at age 60 to 65 preserved their frequency of coitus, and 15% of them continued to masturbate. At ages 66 to 71, only 49% preserved their frequency of coitus, but 32% continued to masturbate. In case the aging reader should become too despondent, it is worth noting the unusual study by Bretschneider and McCoy (1988) of the sexual behavior of 102 men and 100 women aged 80 to 102 years (see Table 9.3). Nearly 66% of the men and 30% of the women had coitus at least yearly. There are some important caveats. First, the sample was

Table 9.3

Percentage of 80- to 102-Year-Olds Engaging in Sexual Behaviors

Behavior	Men				Women			
	Never	>1/yr	>1/mo	>1/day	Never	>1/yr	>1/mo	>1/day
Petting	18	17	38	28	36	25	22	17
Masturbation	28	31	41	0	60	27	11	2
Coitus	38	34	26	3	70	20	10	0

selected for their unusual health and wealth. Second, the data were gathered by questionnaire completed in the presence of the researcher. This method suffers from validity problems. For example, Solstad and Hertoff (1993) found that a rate of erectile failure (in 51-year-old Danish men) of 4% from a questionnaire turned out to be 40% on interview.

Cross-sectional studies are unable to distinguish cohort effects from age effects. For example, those who experienced their adolescence during the Depression may have had a very different experience and expectation of sexuality from those who did so during the Second World War. A comparison of the sexual histories of Martin's (1981) sample showed marked cohort effects. With increasing age at interview, men reported later onset of petting, coitus, and marriage; more abstinence before marriage; less interest in erotic stimuli; and less marital breakdown. By contrast, longitudinal studies allow the researcher to identify age changes unconfounded by cohort. Researchers at Duke University have undertaken several such longitudinal studies.

In the first, published in 1968, Pfeiffer, Verwoerdt, and Wang followed 284 community volunteers over a two-year period. The most common reason for stopping intercourse was death of the spouse (mean age for stopping was 68 for men and 60 for women). Six percent of the sample actually increased their activity over the two years. The figures are likely to be reliable because when both partners were interviewed separately, the congruence of responses was very high. George and Weiler (1981) published findings from the second Duke study in which they followed a randomly selected group of older adults. They found that the decline in activity over the six-year follow-up was much less than would be predicted from prior cross-sectional studies. This suggests that the majority of the "decline" noted by cross-sectional studies is likely to be a cohort effect, those born between 1905 and 1914 remaining less active than those born between 1915 and 1924. Furthermore, the current availability of effective birth control has reduced the fears of an unwanted pregnancy and allowed couples to express their sexuality more freely. Under these circumstances, the next generation of older adults is likely to be much more sexually active than their predecessors.

In a 6-year study of menopausal women, Hallstrom and Samuelsson (1990) found that two-thirds reported no change in desire over that time. Loss of desire was related to relationship problems and an increase in desire was related to the resolution of a problem. However, unlike the loss of sexual interest found in the cross-sectional survey mentioned above, SES played no part in the loss of desire. This suggests that social class only exerts its effect on the older cohort going through the menopause.

PHYSICAL CHANGES OF AGING

The physical changes of aging have been detailed by Masters and Johnson (1966), who studied the sexual response of 34 female volunteers aged 51 to 80 and 39 males aged 51 to 90. Their findings are in Tables 9.4 and 9.5.

Gerontologists have long emphasized that the most characteristic feature of aging is its variability. Psychological, anatomical, and chronological age become increasingly divergent. Consequently, there are exceptions to the generalization of broad decline for all older adults, and the more sexually active are more similar to younger groups than to older groups. The cause of the reduction in physiological arousal with age is unknown. Without hormone replacement therapy (HRT), menopausal women experience a sudden drop in levels of estrogens and progesterone with a rise in the levels of luteinizing hormone (LH) and luteinizing hormone-releasing hormone (LHRH). This leads to

Table 9.4
Aging Changes in the Male

Sexual Response Phase	Response	Status		
		Retained	Retained but Reduced	Lost
Excitement	Penile erection	yes	(often only complete at orgasm)	
Plateau	Nipple erection		yes	
	Testicular elevation		yes	
	Sexual flush			yes
	Re-erection			yes
	Scrotal vasocongestion			yes
Orgasm	Ejaculatory power		yes	
	Rectal and ejaculatory contractions		yes	
	Ejaculatory inevitability			yes
	Prostatic contractions			yes
Resolution	Duration		yes (briefer)	

Note: Refractory period may extend to 24 hours.
Source: Adapted from Masters and Johnson (1966).

Table 9.5

Aging Changes in the Female

Sexual Response Phase	Response	Status		
		Retained	Retained but Reduced	Lost
Excitement	Nipple erection	yes		
	Clitoral tumescence	yes (delayed w/o direct stimulation)		
	Vasocongestion labia minor		yes	
	Vaginal lubrication		yes	
	Expansion inner ⅔ vagina		yes	
	Uterine elevation		yes	
	Breast engorgement			yes
	Sexual flush			yes
	Swelling labia majora		yes	
Plateau	Clitoral retraction	yes		
	Areola engorgement		yes	
	Secretion from Bartholin's glands		yes	
	Orgasmic plateau		yes	
Orgasm	Rectal and orgasmic contractions		yes	
Resolution	Duration		yes (briefer except nipple erection)	

Source: Adapted from Masters and Johnson (1966).

thinning of the vaginal epithelium, loss of fat deposits, and ultimately dyspareunia. However, regular coitus appears to preserve vaginal function. Many steroids, including testosterone, have been suggested as the source of female libido. Certainly, testosterone supplements after oophorectomy appear to increase libido (Sherwin, Gelfand, & Brender, 1985) but not after the natural menopause (Dow, Hart, & Forrest, 1983). Riley (1991), reviewing the effects of HRT on sexuality, points out that there is no consistent effect of estrogen replacement on sexual desire in women. It certainly reduces dyspareunia due to atrophy and has antidepressant action of its own (Gregoire, 1990), possibly antagonized by progesterone (Holst, Backstrom, Hammarback, & van Schoultz, 1989).

The role of hormones in the decreasing libido and erectile failure of the aging male is even more obscure. Orchidectomy in young males removes the proceptive drive but not the ability of the male to respond with an erection to sexual stimuli. Davidson et al. (1983) and Schiavi, Schreiner-Engle, White, and Mandell (1991) related sexual activity in old age to levels of free testosterone and came to similar conclusions. Davidson et al. found that sexual activity with orgasm only correlated ($r = .2$) with levels of free testosterone but correlated negatively ($r = -.34$) with age, whereas Schiavi et al. found no significant correlation with free testosterone but a strong negative correlation with age ($r = -.42$). However, frequency of sexual desire correlated strongly with both ($r = .52$). These results are consistent with other evidence suggesting that testosterone is more important in causing desire than in causing erectile function (O'Carroll & Bancroft, 1984). Rowland, Greenleaf, Dorfman, and Davidson (1993) studied penile sensitivity in a sample of 39 sexually functional, healthy men aged 29 to 81. They found a significant reduction with age in penile sensitivity to vibratory and electrical stimulation, to somatosensory evoked potentials, and to autonomic response to ischemia.

To investigate this further, we have compared two age-matched groups of older men: 28 with erectile failure and 25 without. The following measures were used: height, weight, age of first coitus, current desire and interest, pilocarpine-induced sweating, pulse ratio (with deep breathing) valsalva, blood pressure, penile blood pressure and index, collagen (skin fold thickness), testosterone and testosterone/sex hormone binding globulin (SHBG) ratio, prolactin, T4, LH, blood glucose, and alcohol and tobacco intake. Two measures separated the groups: a vascular index combining the presence of peripheral pulses with a history of ischemic heart disease ($p < .008$) and pilocarpine-induced sweating ($p < .0001$). Both of these age-related changes suggest that the cause of erectile failure in older men is the result of both vascular factors and autonomic failure, though the absence of any effect of vagal function was surprising. Once again, it confirms the limited effect of endocrine factors.

However, this does not mean that reduction in levels of testosterone in old age can be ignored. Morley et al. (1993) treated two groups of mildly hypogonadal men with either testosterone enanthate I.M. or a placebo and found an increase in muscle strength and osteocalcin levels in the experimental group. In an open study (Morley & Kaiser, 1992), the treated group appeared to experience an increase in libido. These results cannot be taken to support the notion of a male climacteric nor the need for hormone replacement in most older men. However, they do suggest that the loss of erectile function with aging is largely due to peripheral degeneration of autonomic and somatic nerves.

DISEASES THAT AFFECT SEXUAL FUNCTION

The physiological process associated with sexual arousal involves several nervous and organ systems beginning with perception of the stimuli and ending with resolution. Ultimately, relaxation of smooth muscle leads to vasodilation and the filling of cartilaginous sacs with blood. In men, this leads to erection. In women, the increased blood supply causes the labia majora to swell and the clitoris to become erect. The lining of the vagina produces a lubricant transudate. Orgasm is produced by sympathetic outflow via L2 roots. Clearly, many diseases can cause dysfunction. Though Somerset Maughan may have portrayed the sufferers of tuberculosis as having increased drive, all disease except mania leads to a loss of drive. Certain diseases are likely to present with a sexual dysfunction and should be considered during evaluation. These include diabetes, hypertension, and the side effects of medication. Table 9.6 displays a partial list of problems and causes.

The most common disease to present with sexual dysfunction is diabetes. Usually, this is due to autonomic neuropathy, a largely irreversible effect of the disease. Further, hyperglycemia itself, catecholamine secretion from hypoglycemia, dyspareunia from vaginal thrush, and atheroma affect sexual function. In some cases, sexual counseling may restore some sexual function and conceal a medical problem. Therefore, a medical exam is an essential component of any assessment of sexual dysfunction.

An ever increasing number of older adults suffer dementia, which may cause sexual difficulties in two ways. The first concerns the retention of drives and physical ability with the loss of the social skills necessary for access to an appropriate partner. This pattern is seen in frontal or subcortical dementia such as Huntington's chorea and Pick's disease. Alzheimer's disease, representing a second pattern, is characterized by an early loss of libido in men and probably reflects a fall in levels of LHRH (Oram, Edwardson, & Millard, 1981). There is little research in this area on women. Libido is often difficult to measure in demented women, who retain receptive drive but lose whatever proceptive drive they may have had. The loss of proceptive drive in male Alzheimer's patients

Table 9.6
Physiological Difficulties Associated with Sexual Dysfunction

Problem	Possible Causes
Diminished or distorted perception	Macular degeneration, depression, anxiety, schizophrenia
Autonomic failure	Steele-Richardson syndrome, autonomic neuropathy, motor neuron disease (e.g., multiple sclerosis)
Low LH	Hemochromatosis, chromophobe adenoma, prolactinoma
Testicular failure	Postorchitis, myotonia dystrophica
Spinal cord and nerve root pressure	Trauma, degenerative diseases
Damage to peripheral nerves	Diabetes, neurofibromatosis, rectal cancer, post-pelvic surgery
Peripheral vascular disease	Pelvic steal syndrome
End organ disease	Pyronie's disease of the penis, sickle cell disease, venous leak syndrome, vaginitis, uterine cancer, trauma

is striking, whereas women with the disease may continue to accept male advances (Zeiss, Davies, Wood, & Tinklenberg, 1990). Nevertheless, Morris, Morris, and Britton (1988) reported a better quality of relationship if the caregiver and patient continue to share sexual contact.

Loss of libido is a cardinal symptom of depression, and this loss may be exacerbated by treatment (see below). Low libido and erectile failure are also found in Parkinson's disease, probably due to low levels of dopamine. Here, however, increasing levels of dopamine can induce an unwelcome increase in sexual drive, as, of course, occurs in mania. A significant loss of weight from various causes such as anorexia suppresses the hypothalamic secretion of sex hormone releasers, which can also decrease libido.

Many diseases of the rectum and prostate that require surgery are likely to affect sexual function directly by damage to the nervi erigentes which run near the rectum and prostate gland. Even where surgery has been successful in removing cancer of the rectum or prostate, there is often difficulty with erections, although some of this may be psychogenic. Dunsmuir and Emberton (1996) followed up 3,965 men after a transurethral resection for prostatic hypertrophy. Although erectile failure has often been attributed to this operation, only 26% of respondents reported a deterioration of erectile response, whereas 20% reported an improvement. Much more significant was the effect of the surgical procedure on ejaculation: 77% of respondents reported retrograde ejaculation, and 52% reported an absent or altered ejaculatory sensation. Because only 1,190 respondents were, or attempted to be, sexually active after surgery, the main changes appear to have concerned ejaculation rather than erectile functioning. The follow-up was done at three months and does not take into account the changes after that time. Interestingly, more people reported being sexually active after surgery than before. Furthermore, urologists are curiously prone to leave in catheters as a way of treating urethral obstruction and incontinence in older patients without considering the effects on coitus.

Feelings about the disfigurement associated with mastectomy have often been implicated in sexual dysfunction. However, a study comparing lumpectomy and mastectomy found little difference: 28% of the mastectomy group reported loss of sexual interest compared to 32% of the lumpectomy group (Fallowfield, Baum, & Maguire, 1986). The authors concluded that fear of cancer predominates over feelings about disfigurement, a fear that may be greater after lumpectomy than mastectomy.

Hospitalization may separate a couple for the first time. The return home, often with stitches in place, a scar, or new medication, leaves the couple in doubt as to the safety of further coitus. These doubts will be reinforced if the issues are not addressed or if dressings or catheter directly interfere with coitus. Silence from the surgical team may leave the impression that sexual intercourse is out of the question, resulting in an abstinence that will continue. I have even seen patients who have been told by their general practitioner to sleep apart to allow the ex-patient to sleep in peace!

The effect of the menopausal drop in estrogens has been addressed above. This can be exacerbated by a vaginal infection or by a urinary infection inflaming the outflow from the bladder.

Prolapse of the bladder and urethra cause discomfort during coitus and stress incontinence. Detrusor instability can also cause micturition after intercourse. Surgery to correct prolapse usually improves sexual function after the surgery is allowed to heal. However, repair of rectal prolapse may narrow the vagina and cause dyspareunia.

Major surgery for cancer may damage the vagina and necessitates sexual counseling. Furthermore, disfiguring operations are likely to affect body image and attitudes toward intimacy. Recovery will depend on the attitude of the partner and the couple's ability to share physical affection. Clearly, the first priority with cancer surgery is to save life, but some treatments have adverse effects on sexual function. For example, I have a patient who had radiotherapy for a pituitary tumor such that the hypothalamus was damaged and could not respond to testosterone. The treatment was correct, but he needed to be advised about its effects on his sexual life. A more common example is the use of antiandrogens in the treatment of prostate cancer.

The effect of diabetes in men (Fairbairn, McCulloch, & Wu, 1982) and admission to the hospital have already been addressed. Diabetes also affects female function, not only by increasing susceptibility to vaginal thrush, but also through reducing parasympathetic function (Wincze, Albert, & Bansal, 1993).

There is evidence that sexual dysfunction precedes myocardial infarction (Kellett, 1987), whether by a shared mechanism of loss of vagal tone, atheroma, or depression. Marital conflict itself can also predict myocardial infarction. However, because loss of potency might cause marital conflict, it is difficult to be certain of the exact direction of effects in this complex chain (see Kellett, 1987, for a detailed discussion).

The public tend to interpret the breathlessness of orgasm as straining the heart or lungs and fear resuming coitus after an admission for myocardial infarction or respiratory failure. Orgasm causes overbreathing, the purpose of which is unknown. It causes alkalosis, and this has been shown to increase suggestibility. Thus, one explanation for the overbreathing is to increase sexual imprinting on one's partner, an effect facilitated by face-to-face coitus. Indeed, resumption of intimacy is likely to reduce the risk of recurrence and should be gently encouraged by medical professionals.

Arthritis, especially of the spine, may render intercourse painful and can be helped by analgesics and use of pillows. Hypertension (by promoting atheroma) commonly causes erectile failure and may be made worse by medication, as discussed earlier. However, alpha blockers like prazosyn improve potency. Obviously, nonpharmacological methods of reducing blood pressure such as a vegetarian or low-salt diet, meditation, and loss of weight may improve sexual function as well.

EFFECTS OF DRUGS ON SEXUAL FUNCTION

This subject has been extensively reviewed by Riley, Peet, and Wilson (1993). It is likely that the pleasure of orgasm is caused by endorphins. The effect of opiate addiction is to so swamp the brain with exogenous endorphins that the natural release at orgasm has no noticeable effect. One should not therefore be surprised to find that opiates reduce libido, an effect antagonized by naloxone, and opiate withdrawal can cause spontaneous orgasm. Most drugs of addiction appear to reduce libido, including alcohol and benzodiazepines (Riley & Riley, 1986), but not tobacco, which may, however, hasten menopause (Abel, 1985).

It may seem a paradox that the most commonly used aphrodisiac in Western society, alcohol, should suppress libido. Moreover, it was shown to have a dose-related inhibitory effect on penile engorgement in men watching erotic films (Farkas & Rosen, 1976; Rubin & Henson, 1976). Chronic alcoholism has an inhibitory effect on both sexes (Covington, 1983; Forrest, 1983; Mandell & Miller, 1983). Women also show the same reduction in genital blood flow when they drink alcohol and then watch an erotic film. However, unlike men, they report more psychological arousal with alcohol (G. Wilson & Lawson, 1976).

Testosterone appears to act through dopamine 2 receptors (Hyppa, Rinne, & Sonninen, 1970). Drugs that reduce testosterone, such as estrogens, progesterone, cyproterone acetate, flutamide, and LH analogues (e.g., goserelin, leuprorelin, and buserelin), all reduce libido in men. The dopamine blockers, the standard antipsychotic drugs, have a similar action without affecting levels of testosterone. However, the newer antipsychotics, such as clozapine and olanzapine, have less effect on dopamine 2 sites. Rather, they have greater effects on dopamine 4 sites and block $5\text{-}HT_2$ sites; thus, they have less effect on libido.

The serotonin-specific reuptake inhibitors stimulate $5\text{-}HT_2$ sites and reduce libido, although some, such as fluvoxamine and, more specifically, nefazodone, spare this area and do not inhibit ejaculation or libido. The traditional tricyclics are generally less specific and may have some inhibitory effect. A new antidepressant, mirtazepine, is an alpha 2 blocker, which by comparison with yohimbine, might be expected to improve sexual arousal. Other antidepressants said to improve erections and libido are trazodone and viloxazine. Mention should be made of a rare and paradoxical syndrome of excessive proceptive sexuality independent of mania occurring on clomipramine and other selective serotonin reuptake inhibitors (SSRI) (McLean, Forsythe, & Kapkin, 1983).

Epileptics often suffer from low libido, which has been attributed to their anticonvulsants. However, if the dose is increased to stop the seizures, the libido increases (Spark, Wills, & Royal, 1984; see below).

Drugs used to control hypertension are commonly implicated in the inhibition of physiological arousal, particularly the thiazide diuretics, beta blockers, and clonidine. However, the effect of beta blockers is more complicated. Metaprolol, a pure blocker, has no effect, unlike propranolol. Salbutamol, a beta agonist, actually inhibits the sexual response (C. Wilson, 1993). The calcium antagonists and angiotensin converting enzyme (ACE) inhibitors appear to be free of such side effects.

Levels of free testosterone are reduced by most of the anticonvulsants (except valproate) and cimetidine. Other drugs reported to inhibit sexual function include bromocriptine, verapamil, flecainide, ketokonazole, metoclopamide, sulfasalazine, baclofen, clofibrate, some of the nonsteroidal anti-inflammatory drugs (NSAIDs) (Davies, & D'Mello, 1991) and digoxin (Neri, Aygen, Zuckerman, & Bahary, 1980).

Sexual dysfunction is reported as a side effect of most new drugs. However, people who find that they must take a new drug may have a variety of reasons to experience stress, itself a cause of sexual dysfunction (possibly mediated by a rise in prolactin). Thus, it may be difficult to establish whether the dysfunction is caused by the drug or the stress associated with taking it. For some short-acting drugs whose continuity is not essential, a 24-hour drug holiday may help to establish the role of the drug in causing the dysfunction. Benzodiazepine hypnotics probably have the greatest effect on the general population. Morgan, Dalloso, Ebrahim, Arie, and Fentem (1988) found that 16% of a sample aged over 65 were regularly taking hypnotics.

SOCIAL FACTORS

The tendency of women to marry men older than themselves and the lower life expectancy of men ensures the demographic isolation of older women. Men and women in their early fifties tend equally to live with partners. In their late sixties, 83% of men and only 55% of women are living with their spouse. By the age of 80, these figures have fallen to 58% and 16%, respectively, and there are more than twice as many women as men (Miret, 1995).

Freed from the anxiety of adolescent experiments in sexual expression, those older adults not overly inhibited by the strictures placed on their cohort may be expected to be in a sexual nirvana. However, the young can be surprisingly censorious of the sexuality of their parents. Often with a misplaced loyalty to the deceased parent, the surviving parent is ruthlessly subjected by the children to the demand that his or her love life be platonic. For example, when a 95-year-old man married his mistress of 15 years, his son accused him of being of unsound mind and pursued him across the globe to try to prevent the ceremony. Pension arrangements may discourage the surviving widow from living with her lover (because her late husband's pension will be stopped if it appears that she has other support), and yet extramarital sex is still beyond the pale.

Advertising and the media generally play on the sexual attraction of the young adult. Magazines for women place emphasis on preserving youth, with hair dyes and skin creams designed to disguise the effects of aging. Clothing is displayed on models with childlike, androgynous physiques, the antithesis of the maternal body of the middle-aged woman. The self-conscious woman who can disguise her aging body with a girdle, makeup, and lustrous clothing finds it difficult to shed these defenses with her lover.

In one case, a 60-year-old, rather dominating woman sent her husband to a sexual dysfunction clinic when he could not respond to her demands to penetrate her when she was clothed. She did not appreciate that visual stimuli were essential to excite her husband, nor that tenderness should enable physical intimacy to occur. For the current older adult cohort, stimulation may be seen as the province of the brothel rather than the bedroom. The husband is banished to the prostitute while his wife is increasingly unable to respond to the morally permitted sex: quick penetration in the dark! Mutual masturbation, considered the coitus of the impotent, is despised, leaving the elderly to create a space in their double bed that cannot be crossed.

In 1984, Brecher, sponsored by the Consumer Union, surveyed the experience of sexuality in people over 50 in the United States. The report was based on 4,246 questionnaires completed in 1978 and 1979. Not surprisingly, loneliness affected 16% of currently single respondents compared to 6% of the currently married. Eighty-six percent of male respondents were sexually active compared to 68% of females. However, this was a self-selected sample. Of particular interest are the written comments of those without partners:

> I am so old and lonely that sometimes I think I just don't give a damn what happens to me any more. Nobody else cares, and it's a very lonely road you can't see until you get there." (61-year-old widow, p. 142)

> I have been widowed, alone, for eight years, so my sex life is zero—nothing. My wife was sick nine years, so there have been 17 years of inactivity. I'm sure I am useless for there hasn't been an erection for years. I would go to a prostitute but I live in a small town where there are none (that I know of). . . . Being old . . . and ugly is a terrible combination—so I keep myself busy in my yard, reading. . . . But I do miss a woman very much. . . . Being lonely and old is just as bad as being lonely and young. I know both. . . . No love, not even anyone to touch, or hold their hand." (67-year-old widower, p. 144)

The relative lack of attention devoted to sex in old age in our society is not typical of the world as a whole. Winn and Newton (1982) looked at the attitudes of 106 traditional societies and concluded: "Although some decline in the sexual activity of aged males is recorded in a significant proportion of the societies studied, many cultural groups have expectations for continued sexual activity for older men that imply little, if any, loss of their sexual powers until very late in life" (p. 289). Regarding females, they write, "Older women frequently express strong sexual desires and interests, . . . engage in sexual activity in many instances until extreme old age, . . . and may form liaisons with much younger men" (p. 294). In other words, rather than hiding their sexuality, the elderly may exaggerate their sexual prowess in such societies.

Increasing mental and physical frailty drives many into institutions, where cultural norms may be more rigorously expressed. In 1996, 25% of those aged over 84 in England lived in institutional care, compared to only 1% aged 65 to 74 (Age Concern, 1996). Such homes are not designed to cope with residents' sexual behavior, which can arouse anxiety in both the staff and the relatives. Does a mildly demented lady who chooses to spend afternoons in bed with a more competent male resident represent a case of sexual exploitation, or an opportunity to partake of life's few remaining pleasures?

Most surveys, however, show that staff are fairly liberal in their attitudes. For example, Damrosch (1982) gave qualified nurses enrolled in a graduate nursing course case vignettes in which a 68-year-old female target was presented in two conditions: sexual activity mentioned or not mentioned. Although the sexually active client was rated as less popular with staff, she was rated higher on the nine remaining scales (e.g., mentally alert, cheerful, more enjoyable as a patient). Earlier, Kaas (1978) compared the attitudes of staff and other residents in a nursing home and found the staff more liberal than the residents.

Szasz (1983) invited all 90 nursing staff working on a long-stay unit for elderly males to choose two sorts of sexual behavior that would cause a problem and one that should be encouraged. Staff had little difficulty accepting sexual behavior in private but, not surprisingly, found it difficult to cope with overt sexual approaches to them. Privacy is generally considered important for sexual activity, but institutions do not often provide this. Staff have to walk a fine line between stopping the exploitation of the demented and allowing a couple to express themselves sexually. Relatives may object because of considerations of the feelings of the other, noninstitutionalized parent, or even because newfound love may mean they will have to share their inheritance. For example, one 80-year-old widow was assiduously courted by a 40-year-old tour guide. She was delighted but perhaps underestimated the effect the size of her fortune had on his devotion. The well-meaning attempts by her son to stop the marriage were thwarted by her evident mental health.

Residential homes must provide double bedrooms to allow couples to live together. But professionals should also be aware that entry into a home may provide the opportunity for a painful marriage to dissolve without the humiliation of divorce. A room for visiting spouses or lovers is another potential solution for institutions. But this can expose the resident to ridicule, so a policy of home leave may work better. Sloane (1993) has suggested a number of ways in which nursing staff can handle the sexuality of their residents.

The departure of the children from the household may remove one reason for staying together, thus freeing a hostile couple to separate. However, there may be a lessening of hostility because people with combative and neurotic personalities that prevent them from being successful and flexible may tend to be outlived by those who are better at accepting conflict. In addition, the changes of aging often lead to a loss of drive; indeed, one might say that apathy is the predominant emotion. Thus, older adults may experience lessened marital conflict and a willingness to accept conditions that would drive a younger couple to separation. This tendency to accept conflicts, in fact, is a potential difficulty, resulting in a marked resistance to seek help.

Another characteristic of aging is variability. Previous "unusual" interests may become "eccentricities" and even "deviance." The characteristic aforementioned loss of drive, however, seems to prevent such deviant desires from being put into practice. For example, a sadomasochist may use stronger pornography but be less likely to hire a prostitute.

The ability of older adults to express their sexuality depends on their notion of the role of sex in old age. As mentioned above, they are likely to pick up negative messages from the media where terms like "dirty old man" are used to diminish the acceptability of their sexual interest. Unencumbered sexual expression demands the ability to be comfortable with one's own body. But an older woman who relies on a youthful body image for her self-esteem is likely to find nudity unpleasant and sex, therefore, stressful. Society generally allows community-dwelling older adults the freedom to engage in any private sexual behavior they choose. The relative lack of available male partners would seem to make intimate relations between women more likely, though few eroticize their relationships.

The single gay man is sometimes vulnerable to various types of exploitation by younger partners, just as the heterosexual man may be exploited by the younger woman. Certainly, the preference of older heterosexual men for young women is replicated by the older gay man for younger same-sex partners (Harry & DeVall, 1978). Dorfman, Walters, and Burke (1995) measured levels of depression and social support in 56 gay men and lesbians (33 men and 23 women) and 52 heterosexuals (20 men and 32 women). The levels of depression showed no significant differences, but social support differed. Gay men had less family support but more support from friends than did heterosexuals. This difference was found to a lesser extent for women. The gay men and lesbians in these studies were selected from gay support groups, however, and are unlikely to be typical of the larger gay population.

Whereas the cohort effect is considerable in heterosexuals, it is likely to be even greater for older homosexuals who have lived most of their lives in a manifestly homophobic society. Friend (1991) suggests that the importance of affirming one's homosexuality to adjust successfully to being gay is similar to the approach to successful aging of being proud of one's age. On the other hand, Lee (1987) studied 47 older homosexual men and concluded that successful aging was similar to that for heterosexual males, including enjoying health and wealth and avoiding conflict, even if this involved hiding one's homosexuality. This could be seen as a sensible approach to society before homosexual rights become established.

SEXUAL DYSFUNCTION AND TREATMENT

Older adults are at risk for the same range of dysfunctions encountered by young and middle-aged adults. There is, however, an increased likelihood of erectile failure in older men. It is important to remember that, as with young men, this may have various causes, such as fear of women or penetration, fear of failure, venous leak, autonomic neuropathy, vascular insufficiency, and so on. Heterophobia, or a more general social phobia, and premature ejaculation tend to be disorders of youth, whereas older adults more commonly present with disorders of physiological arousal.

As sexual dysfunction has many causes, so its treatment can come from many different disciplines, including urology, gynecology, genitourinary medicine, geriatrics, psychiatry, psychology, and general practice. Furthermore, within psychiatry, there are different disciplines of psychotherapy—many given by those without medical qualifications. This emphasizes the role of the primary care physician in choosing the correct specialist and the need to create a specialty within medicine that can encompass the variety of skills (Gregoire, 1990; Kellett, 1990).

Among the current psychological treatments, the cognitive behavioral approach is often considered first. Before behavioral treatments were popularized by the pioneering work of Masters and Johnson in the 1970s, the psychosomatic movement in the United Kingdom advocated a system of treatment based on the principles of psychoanalysis. Balint (1964) taught family planning doctors the means by which physical examination reveals psychological conflicts, which can be treated by counseling, eschewing the more esoteric interpretations of classical dynamic psychotherapy. Family planning doctors rarely treat the couple together and rely on change through insight. Other schools of psychotherapy have also established systems of treatment such as transactional analysis and cognitive therapy.

However, most interventions begin with the taking of a sexual history, which includes not only an accurate account of the presenting problem, but also of the life experiences of the individual, to identify possible etiological factors. For example, a man brought up by a demanding and androphobic mother may feel threatened by other adult women; perhaps a similar problem has arisen in previous relationships. Medical considerations also exist; medical conditions and drugs currently taken (including tobacco and alcohol) must be documented. At this stage, a physical examination is helpful and should include pulse variation on deep breathing or a Valsalva maneuver, blood pressure sitting and standing, peripheral pulses, examination of external genitalia, internal examination if relevant and requested, neurological examination to exclude a peripheral neuropathy and nerve root lesion of L2 and S2 (ankle reflex), and a general assessment to detect gross physical disease such as anemia and liver disease. A blood screen to detect diabetes is useful, and if the presenting symptom is loss of libido, a hormone assay of free testosterone, prolactin, and T4 should be conducted.

After an independent assessment of the partner, joint counseling may begin. Just as with young people, older adults may benefit from sensate-focus exercises, stop-start and squeeze techniques to help premature ejaculation, and vaginal trainers for vaginismus. Not only do these exercises desensitize the couple to aspects of petting, but they learn a repertoire of acts they can use if for any reason intercourse is impossible. A woman is more likely to respond if she feels attractive, which can be increased by a new hairstyle, pretty underclothes, or the use of makeup. Her partner can be reminded of the value of tokens of affection including flowers and dates. These obvious interventions must not be overlooked for older adults.

By the time a couple present, they are usually set within their conflict and will resist change, such that the exercises have to be described in detail, including times and places for carrying them out. Transferring sexual activity from the bedroom (with its reminders of failure) to another room may help.

The privacy of intimate behavior makes its modification peculiarly susceptible to education through the use of sex manuals. Although manuals written for younger people can be useful, Wendy Greengross and Sally Greengross (1989) of Age Concern have written a brief sex manual specifically for the elderly. This sensitively deals with the sexual problems of this age group, as does a well-known book by Butler and Lewis (1976).

Sometimes, education alone can be an effective treatment. It is often assumed that older adults are sufficiently experienced and have no need of education. Nothing can be further from the truth. They learned their sexual techniques from the myths and old wives' tales of the past. Education not only provides current knowledge, but it also removes faulty learning (e.g., male continence is damaging and ejaculation is weakening, especially by masturbation). Such a program should include instruction on the anatomy and physiology of genital function, using the couple as each other's model. An older woman and her partner may benefit from viewing her vaginal structure using a mirror. There are various models that simplify sexual function, including the arousal circuit and the ladder concept (Stanley, 1981). The former accounts for performance anxiety by indicating how anxiety can inhibit parasympathetic stimulation through its effect on the hypothalamus, thus leading to a vicious circle of increasing failure of arousal (e.g., erection), producing further performance anxiety. The latter demonstrates the importance of sharing sexual acts with the partner even with different needs, as, for example, being prepared to cuddle while the other masturbates to orgasm. Thus, the need for one to experience closeness typified by a cuddle, while the other wants full intercourse, can be satisfied if the first holds the second while he or she masturbates. While synchronous orgasm may be a desirable dream, most sex is a compromise.

Differences between the sexes must be explained to a couple as being more than anatomical. For example, men are more aroused by visual stimuli, women by tactile; men by more overt eroticism than that which excites women. As a result, the woman can easily mislabel her partner's arousal as impersonal and degrading, and the man may see her as being sickly sentimental. The woman may even judge her feelings of arousal as sickness, the vasocongestion of the pelvis being a source of pain rather than pleasure. The couple may be challenged to consider such arousal a genuine compliment rather than sexual exploitation.

Medication can usefully be combined with psychotherapy, but the use of either will depend on the wishes of the patient. For example, an older man who wishes to impress his new partner by his potency will not want conjoint counseling but will appreciate the possibility of inducing an erection with an intracavernosal injection. Once a relationship has been established, the vacuum system may be preferred. Either way, the partner will need reassurance that the patient's erectile failure is not the result of the partner's unattractiveness. Before Viagra (sildenofil), oral drugs for erectile failure were yohimbine plus oxpentifylline for vascular insufficiency. Drugs injected intracavernosally are papaverine, alprostadit, phentolamine, and moxisylyte hydrochloride, and experiments are underway to alter the method of administration per urethra and transdermally. It is yet to be determined how Viagra will transform this field. Low libido may respond to hormonal treatments. Dopamine agonists may be indicated if the problem is associated with Parkinson's disease and hyperprolactinemia, but low libido is one of the most difficult problems to treat. Premature ejaculation responds to SSRIs such as sertraline and paroxetine. Anorgasmia is possibly helped by an alpha agonist midrodrine.

A problem of female arousal, lack of vaginal lubrication, can be relieved by commercial lubricants. But the woman thus spared of dyspareunia may still be deprived of the sensation of engorgement. Commercial lubricants are also indicated for the vaginal dryness that comes with menopause. However, it may be difficult for an older woman to initiate the purchase of such a product as well as to evaluate competing brands.

As far as hormone replacement therapy (HRT) is concerned, estrogen (accompanied by progesterone in those who retain their uterus) prevents vaginal atrophy. The slightly greater risk of breast cancer is more than outweighed by the reduction in ischemic heart disease, osteoporosis, and Alzheimer's disease. The newer, selective estrogens are likely to make HRT more acceptable. The role of HRT in males is more controversial. Though testosterone levels do fall with age, they are rarely below the young adult normal range. However, an increase in binding globulin may cause a reduction in the effective levels of testosterone. The St. Louis group has shown that testosterone improves muscle strength in hypogonadal elderly men in a double-blind study (Rahmawati et al., 1997). As yet, their reports on improvement in libido are limited to open studies. They did not find that testosterone increased occurrence of prostatic cancer. De Lignieres (1993) used dihydrotestosterone, which, theoretically, should be equally effective in correcting the effects of testosterone deficiency while reducing the size of the prostate. More specific androgens may be the answer.

CONCLUSION

A truism of geriatric medicine is that most disorders are multifactorial, which has the corollary that effective treatment can take many forms, ideally in combination. For example, a man who worries that his declining potency is upsetting his wife may find that she is more concerned by his frequent attempts at coitus, which intensifies her arthritis, and she would prefer a more platonic relationship. Her arthritis may respond to paracetamol before coitus, and his erections improved by changing from a thiazide to a loop diuretic. Furthermore, their daily hassles may be reduced by a move to a retirement community, which might improve their sex life.

The role of the geriatrician is to treat the whole person. Sexuality remains an important part. Learning to be at ease in this area of medicine is crucial if one is to help patients fully enjoy their old age. Often, this can be achieved only if inquiry into the sex life is as routine as a question about the bowels. Many patients will laugh and claim that they "gave up" years ago (to which the rejoinder should be "Why?"), but they are rarely offended by the question. The newly widowed can be asked more gently whether they still have or miss a sex life. This is likely to produce far less offense than ignoring the successful new relationship that preoccupies the same widow.

Some patients are reluctant to enter into a conversation about an area in which they regard themselves as far from successful. Would this stop us from asking a bronchitic his or her exercise tolerance, or a drinker his or her intake of alcohol? The very secrecy of our intimate lives inhibits our patients from bringing up the subject themselves. The doctor must have the courage to raise the subject in the first place. Once raised, the patient will be grateful for the opportunity to discuss the topic with a sympathetic professional who offers the possibility of treatment.

In this way, patients are freed to make their own choices. We should be as wary of being sexual evangelists as of causing ridicule to the sexually active. Finally, we should also emphasize the importance of intimacy without penetration as one form of sexual expression in life.

REFERENCES

Abel, E. (1985). *Psychoactive drugs and sex*. New York: Plenum Press.
Age concern. (1996). Fact sheet. London.
Balint, M. (1964). *The doctor, his patient, and the illness*. London: Pitman Medical.
Brecher, E.M. (1984). *Love, sex and aging: A consumer union report*. Boston: Little, Brown.

Bretschneider, J., & McCoy, N. (1988). Sexual interest and behavior in healthy 80- to 102-year-olds. *Archives of Sexual Behavior, 17,* 109–129.

Butler, R., & Lewis, M. (1976). *Sex after sixty.* New York: Harper and Row.

Covington, S. (1983). *Sex and alcohol: What do women tell us?* Sixth World Congress of Sexology, Washington, DC.

Cutler, W., Garcia, R., & McCoy, N. (1987). Perimenopausal sexuality. *Archives of Sexual Behavior, 16,* 225–234.

Damrosch, S. (1984). Graduate nursing students' attitudes toward sexually active older persons. *Gerontologist, 24,* 299–302.

Davidson, J., Chen J., Crapo, L., Gray, G., Greenleaf, W., & Catania, J. (1983). Hormonal function and sexual function in aging men. *Journal of Clinical Endocrinology and Metabolism, 57,* 71–77.

Davies, M., & D'Mello, A. (1991). *Drugs and sexual function.* Harpenden: Ridge.

de Lignieres. (1993). Transdermal dihydrotestosterone treatment of "andopause." *Annals of Medicine, 25,* 235–241.

Dorfman, R., Walters, K., & Burke, P. (1995). Old, sad, and alone. *Journal of Gerontological Social Work, 24,* 29–44.

Dow, M., Hart, D., & Forrest, C. (1983). Hormonal treatment of sexual unresponsiveness in post menopausal women: A comparative study. *British Journal of Obstetrics and Gynecology, 90,* 361–366.

Dunsmuir, W., & Emberton, M. (1996). There is significant sexual dysfunction following TURP. *British Journal of Urology, 77,* 161A.

Fallowfield, L., Baum, M., & Maguire, G. (1986). Effects of breast conservation on psychological morbidity associated with diagnosis and treatment of early breast cancer. *British Medical Journal, 293,* 1331–1334.

Farkas, G., & Rosen, R. (1976). The effects of ethanol on male sexual arousal. *Journal of Studies on Alcohol, 37,* 265–272.

Fairbairn, C., McCulloch, D., & Wu, F. (1982). The effects of diabetes on male sexual functions. *Clinics in Endocrinology and Metabolism, 11,* 749–767.

Forrest, G. (1983). *Alcoholism and human sexuality.* Springfield.

Friend, R.A. (1991). Older lesbian and gay people: A theory of successful aging. *Journal of Homosexuality, 13,* 99–118.

George, L., & Weiler, S. (1981). Sexuality in middle and late life. *Archives of General Psychiatry, 38,* 919–923.

Gregoire, A. (1990). Physical vs. psychological: A need for an integrated approach. *Sexual and Marital Therapy, 5,* 103–104.

Gregoire, A., Kumar, R., Everitt, B., Henderson, A., & Studd, J. (1996). Transdermal estrogen for treatment of severe postnatal depression. *Lancet, 347,* 931–933.

Greengross, W., & Greengross, S. (1989). Living, loving and aging. *Age Concern.* London.

Hallstrom, T. (1977). Sexuality in the climacteric. *Clinics in Obstetrics and Gynecology, 4,* 227–239.

Hallstrom, T., & Samuelsson, S. (1990). Changes in women's sexual desire in middle age: The longitudinal study of women in Gothenberg. *Archives of Sexual Behavior, 19,* 259–268.

Harry, J., & DeVall, W. (1978). Age and sexual culture among homosexually oriented males. *Archives of Sexual Behavior, 7,* 199–209.

Hawton, K., Gath, D., & Day, A. (1994). Sexual function in a community sample of middle-aged women with partners: Effects of age, marital, socioeconomic, psychiatric, gynecological, and menopausal factors. *Archives of Sexual Behavior, 23,* 375–395.

Hite, S. (1976). *The Hite report: A nationwide study on female sexuality.* New York: Macmillan.

Holst, J., Backstrom, T., Hammarback, S., & van Schoultz, B. (1989). Progestogen addition during oestrogen replacement therapy: Effects of vasomotor symptoms and mood. *Maturitas, 11,* 13–20.

Hyppa, M., Rinne, V., & Sonninen, V. (1970). The activating effect of L-dopa treatment on sexual function and its experimental background. *Acta Neurologica Scandinavica, 43,* 232–234.

Janus, S.S., & Janus, C.L. (1993). *The Janus report on sexual behavior.* New York: Wiley.

Kass, M. (1978). Sexual expression of the elderly in nursing homes. *Gerontologist, 18,* 372–378.

Kellett, J. (1987). Treatment of sexual disorder: A prophylaxis for major pathology? *Journal of the Royal College of Physicians, 21,* 58–60.

Kellett, J. (1990). Physical vs. psychological: A need for an integrated approach. *Sexual and Marital Therapy, 5,* 101–104.

Kinsey, A.C., Pomeroy, W.B., & Martin, C.E., (1948). *Sexual behavior in the human male.* Philadelphia: Saunders.

Kinsey, A.C., Pomeroy, W.B., Martin, C.E., & Gebhard, P.H. (1953). *Sexual behavior in the human female.* Philadelphia: Saunders.

Lee, J.A. (1987). What can homosexual aging studies contribute to theories of aging? *Journal of Homosexuality, 13,* 43–71.

Mandell, W., & Miller, C. (1983). Male sexual dysfunctions related to alcohol consumption: A pilot study. *Alcoholism, 7,* 65–69.

Marsiglio, W., & Donnelly, D. (1991). Sexual relations in later life: A national study of married persons. *Journal of Gerontology, 46,* S338–S344.

Martin, C.E. (1981). Factors affecting sexual functioning in 60–79 year old married males. *Archives of Sexual Behavior, 10,* 399–420.

Maslow, A., & Sakoda, J. (1952). Volunteer error in the Kinsey sample. *Journal of Abnormal and Social Psychology, 47,* 259–262.

Masters, W., & Johnson, V. (1966). *Human sexual response.* London: Churchill.

McCoy, N., & Davidson, J. (1985). A longitudinal study of the effects of menopause on sexuality. *Maturitas, 7,* 203–210.

McLean, J.D., Forsythe, R., & Kapkin, I.A. (1983). Unusual side effects of clomipramine associated with yawning. *Canadian Journal of Psychiatry, 28,* 569–570.

Miret, P. (1995, Autumn). Living together in Great Britain. *Population Trends,* 37–39.

Morgan, K., Dallosso, H., Ebrahim, S., Arie, T., & Fentem, P. (1988). Prevalence, frequency and duration of hypnotic drug use among elderly living at home. *British Medical Journal, 296,* 601–602.

Morley, J.E., & Kaiser, F.E. (1992). Impotence in elderly men. *Drugs and Aging, 2,* 330–334.

Morley, J.E., Perry, H., Kaiser, F., Kraenzle, D., Jensen, J., Houston, K., Mattammal, M., & Perry, H. (1993). The effects of testosterone in old hypogonadal males: A preliminary study. *Journal of American Geriatric Society, 41,* 149–152.

Morris, L., Morris, R., & Britton, P. (1988). The relationship between martial intimacy, personal strain, and depression in spouse caregiver of dementia sufferer. *British Journal of Medical Psychology, 61,* 231–236.

Neri, A., Aygen, M., Zukerman, Z., & Bahary, C. (1980). Subjective assessment of sexual dysfunction of patients on long-term administration of digoxin. *Archives of Sexual Behavior, 9,* 343–347.

O'Carroll, R., & Bancroft, J. (1984). Testosterone therapy for low sexual interest and erectile dysfunction in men: A controlled study. *British Journal of Psychiatry, 145,* 146–151.

Oram, J., Edwardson, J., & Millard, P. (1981). Investigation of cerebrospinal fluid neuropeptides in idiopathic senile dementia. *Gerontology, 27,* 216–223.

Osborn, M., Hawton, K., & Gath, D. (1988). Sexual dysfunction among middle-aged women in the community. *British Medical Journal, 296,* 959–962.

Persson, G. (1990). Sexuality in a 70 year old urban population. *Journal of Psychosomatic Research, 24,* 335–342.

Pfeiffer, E., & Davis, G. (1972). Determinants of sexual behavior in middle and old age. *Journal of the American Geriatric Society, 20,* 151–158.

Pfeiffer, E., Verwoerdt, A., & Wang, H. (1968). Sexual behavior in aged men and women. *Archives of General Psychiatry, 19,* 753–923.

Rahmawati, S., Morley, J., Kaiser, F., Perry, H., Patrick, P., & Ross, C. (1997). Testosterone replacement in older hypogonadal men: A 12-month randomized controlled trial. *Journal of Clinical Endocrinology and Metabolism, 82,* 1661–1667.

Reisman, J. (1990). *Kinsey, sex and fraud: The indoctrination of people.* USA: Vital Issues Press.

Riley, A. (1991). Sexuality and the menopause. *Sexual and Marital Therapy, 6,* 135–146.

Riley, A., Peet, M., & Wilson, C. (1993). *Sexual pharmacology.* Oxford, England: Clarendon Press.

Riley, A., & Riley, E. (1986). The effect of single dose diazepam on female sexual response induced by masturbation. *Sexual and Marital Therapy, 1,* 49–53.

Rowland, D., Greenleaf, W., Dorfman, L., & Davidson, J. (1993). Aging and sexual function in men. *Archives of Sexual Behavior, 22,* 545–556.

Rubin, R., & Henson, D. (1976). Effects of alcohol on male sexual responding. *Psychopharmacology, 47,* 123–124.

Schiavi, R., Schreiner-Engel, P., White, D., & Mandell, J. (1991). The relationship between pituitary-gonadal function and sexual behavior in healthy aging men. *Psychosomatic Medicine, 53,* 363–374.

Sherwin, B., Gelfand, M., & Brender, W. (1985). Androgen enhances sexual motivation in females: A prospective cross-over study of sex steroid administration in the surgical menopause. *Psychosomatic Medicine, 47,* 339–351.

Shock, N., Greulich, R., Costa, P., Andres, R., Lakatta, E., Arenberg, D., & Tobin, J. (1984). *Normal human aging: The Baltimore longitudinal study of aging.* Washington, DC: U.S. Department of Health and Human Services.

Sloane, P. (1993). Sexual behavior in residents with dementia. *Contemporary Long Term Care, 16,* 16, 69, 108.

Solstad, K., & Hertoff, P. (1993). Frequency of sexual problems and sexual dysfunction in middle-aged Danish men. *Archives of Sexual Behavior, 22,* 51–58.

Spark, R., Wills, C., & Royal, H. (1984). Hypogonadism, hyperprolactinaemia, and temporal lobe epilepsy in hyposexual men. *Lancet, 1,* 413–417.

Stanley, E. (1981). Sex problems in practice. *British Medical Journal, 282*, 1281–1283.

Szasz, G. (1983). Sexual incidents in an extended care unit for aged men. *Journal of the American Geriatric Society, 31*, 407–412.

Weizman, R., & Hart, J. (1987). Sexual behavior in healthy married elderly men. *Archives of Sexual Behavior, 16*, 39–44.

Wellings, K., Johnson, A.M., & Wadsworth, J. (1994). *Sexual behavior in Britain.* London: Penguin Books.

Wilson, C. (1993). Pharmacological targets for the control of sexual behavior. In A. Riley, M. Peet, & C. Wilson (Eds.), *Sexual pharmacology.* Oxford, England: Clarendon Press.

Wilson, G.T., & Lawson, D.M. (1976). Effects of alcohol on sexual arousal in women. *Journal of Abnormal Psychology, 85*, 489–497.

Wincze, J., Albert, A., & Bansal, B. (1993). Sexual arousal in diabetic females: Physiological and self-report measures. *Archives of Sexual Behavior, 22*, 587–595.

Winn, R., & Newton, N. (1982). Sexuality in aging: A study of 106 cultures. *Archives of Sexual Behavior, 11*, 283–298.

Zeiss, A.M., Davies, H.D., Wood, M., & Tinklenberg, J.R. (1990). The incidence and correlates of erectile problems in patients with Alzheimer disease. *Archives of Sexual Behavior, 19*, 325–332.

PART IV

ISSUES OF CULTURAL CONCERN

CHAPTER 10

HIV/AIDS and Sexuality

MICHAEL W. ROSS and LENA NILSSON SCHÖNNESSON

T HE ACQUIRED IMMUNE Deficiency Syndrome (AIDS) and infection with the causative organism, human immunodeficiency virus (HIV), have revolutionized the field of human sexuality in the past two decades. AIDS was first identified in 1981 as a group of rare opportunistic infections and malignancies in homosexually active men in the United States and HIV was identified in France in 1983. As a result, issues of sexuality, sexual minorities, and sexually transmissible infections and risk behaviors associated with such infections have become common in psychology and medicine as well as in the media. Such a focus on sexual behaviors, their risks, and their physical and psychological consequences, as well as on interventions to modify risks, has provided extensive research funding to the area of human sexuality research. Medically, HIV and AIDS have become known for their protean manifestations. Psychologically, the same could also be said, given the multiple areas of sexual behavior and sexual psychology on which HIV/AIDS have an impact. Further, HIV infection has become established in every country of the globe, thus making an understanding of cross-cultural issues in sexuality central to interventions to reduce HIV transmission. This chapter is divided into two major sections: understanding the sexual and related risk behaviors associated with HIV transmission, largely derived from social psychology, and understanding the psychological responses to HIV transmission, largely derived from clinical psychology.

SEXUAL AND RISK BEHAVIORS
AND HIV TRANSMISSION

There are substantial psychological data dealing with attitudes, beliefs, and behaviors associated with risk of HIV transmission, and we review representative studies in the central areas that relate to transmission. Perhaps most important for prevention of HIV transmission, research can also indicate which factors are involved in transmission by noting which interventions can reduce transmission risk. The majority of the work has been carried out with men who have sex with men, but we discuss other areas of significance for sexual transmission where they add to the psychological understanding of HIV and AIDS. It is important to note that there is a lot in common in HIV prevention, and in response to HIV infection, regardless of the mode of sexual transmission of the virus. Thus, focusing on the sexual orientation of the individual may obscure the fact that similar psychological processes are at work in everyone. However, issues such as power in relationships may disproportionately impact women, whereas issues of stigma may disproportionately impact gay men, and issues of the effect of intoxication on sex may disproportionately impact drug users. Nevertheless, the core issues will have relevance to each of these groups.

Sexual Transmission

HIV is transmitted by sexual behavior that transfers infected body fluids (including semen) from one individual to another during penetrative sex (most commonly, vaginal and anal intercourse, although the virus may also be transmitted, but with lower efficiency, during oral sex). Its transmission rate will be significantly increased by the presence of other sexually transmissible diseases, whether ulcerative (e.g., syphilis, herpes, or chancroid) or mucosal (e.g., gonorrhea or chlamydia). The sexual orientation of the parties is irrelevant: it must be noted that heterosexual anal or vaginal intercourse, homosexual anal intercourse, and oral sex, regardless of the gender of the participants, will transmit the disease. One of the myths about sexual behavior that was exploded early in the course of the epidemic was that anal intercourse was associated only with male homosexual activity. Data suggest that the most common sexual activities for homosexually active men are mutual masturbation (an activity that carries no risk) followed by oral sex, with anal intercourse ranking only third. Ross (1986), in a pre-AIDS study of gay men in Australia, Sweden, Finland, and Ireland, found that in the countries where there was a better developed gay subculture, sexual practices tended to be more specialized and the range of preferences was not only greater but that people had more specific preferences for particular acts. Similarly, studies in heterosexual women attending British gynecologic facilities showed that at least 1 in 12 reported engaging in anal intercourse (Bolling, 1977). In countries where reliable contraception is either unavailable or is discouraged for religious or other reasons, anal intercourse may be the most common form of contraception. Some traditional sexual practices, such as drying the vagina with particular herbal or other preparations, or frequent douching, which may have the same effect, may also increase the probability of HIV transmission through microtrauma of the dry vaginal walls.

Men Who Have Sex with Men

Definitions of terms are important because many men who have sex with men (MSMs) may not identify themselves as homosexual. Their sexual activity with other men may be situational (e.g., in prison) or episodic (e.g., in adolescence or when away from home). Indeed, in many societies, the "homosexual" is defined only as the receptive partner. Carrier (1985) notes that in many Latin and Mediterranean societies, a man who has sex with other men is not stigmatized unless he is the receptive partner. The classic study of Humphreys (1970) of men who have sex with men in public toilets found that over half were heterosexually married and were engaging in sex because it was less lonely than masturbation or afforded a quick and easy form of sexual release without any attachment or obligation. He classified men using public conveniences as places for sexual gratification into four groups: "trade," ambisexuals, gays, and closet queens. Humphreys's trade group comprised working-class married men. Two-thirds took an insertor role in fellatio in sexual encounters. Ambisexuals were married men with high income; two-thirds of this group were insertees in fellatio and saw themselves as bisexual. The gay group were individuals who were unmarried, had no preference for sexual roles, and had independent occupations. The "closet queens" were also unmarried but in lower-middle-class occupations in which they were dependent on others for employment, and they avoided the homosexual subculture. They preferred to play the insertor role, at least until they lost their attractiveness.

Ross (1983), in his study of heterosexually married homosexual men, noted that a significant proportion of gay men have had sex with women, and in Kinsey's classic work on male sexuality (Kinsey, Pomeroy, & Martin, 1948), it was reported that over one-third of men had had a sexual experience to orgasm with another man. However, Kinsey's work was not based on a random sample, and subsequent work by Laumann, Gagnon, Michael, and Michaels (1994) based on random sampling has suggested that this proportion is considerably lower: less than 5%. Based on a random sample in Australia, Ross (1988b) found that 11% of men reported ever having had sex with another man, and 6% reported doing so in the past 12 months.

These considerations are important because the term "homosexual" refers to behavior. In this chapter, those who identify themselves as predominantly homosexual are referred to as "gay." However, it is important to note that the gay subculture in the United States and in other Western countries is a recent development historically. In most parts of the world, men who have sex with other men do not have a gay identity available to them culturally, and most are married, because marriage is regarded as a family obligation and unrelated to sexual preference. Even in Western countries, men who are in smaller towns or rural areas do not have access to gay satellite cultures and may be unacculturated into the gay subculture (Ross, Fernández-Esquer, & Seibt, 1996). More recently, the term "men who have sex with men" emphasizes that it is the behavior, rather than the identity, that confers risk for HIV infection. It is also important to note that not all sexual behaviors between men can transmit HIV (such activities as mutual masturbation and frottage are without risk).

Contexts of Risk

Risk should not be conceptualized as only an individual-level variable. The context may confer a degree of risk. This can best be characterized by noting that people may be completely safe in their sexual behavior for HIV (or any other STD) transmission at one time or place but not at another. Thus, the context may also contribute to the variance of risk behavior. Such contexts include bars, clubs, bathhouses, circuit parties, business trips, pay days, and bedrooms. Attitudes and beliefs may be context-specific, as may substance use or abuse. The immediate context may also determine outcome: availability of condoms, time constraints, risk of police harassment, discovery, darkness, and similar considerations. Coxon (1996) calls several of these the "3D theory": "It was dark, I was drunk, and I didn't have a condom" (p. 172). The issue of state- and context-dependent learning may also be a contributor; skills and knowledge learned in one context may not be recalled in another, because the situation may act as a learning cue (Jenkins, 1974). Indeed, the situation may interact with cognitions, affects, and partners to account for a substantial proportion of the variance of risk. Kelaher, Ross, Rohrsheim, Drury, and Clarkson (1994) randomly presented situational vignettes, varying on seven dimensions, to gay men in bars and bathhouses. They found that they could explain over one-third of the variance of unprotected anal intercourse using the variables of attraction to partner, condom availability, and perceptions of attractiveness to partner.

Further, the interpersonal context for safety in a sexual situation in which there is a risk of HIV transmission also plays a significant part in what sexual activity is engaged in and whether it is safe or not. In any interaction between two people, only about half the variance may be accounted for by each partner. Whereas much attention has been paid to risk cognitions, risk affects may prove to be more important, such as being "in love" or in a state of high arousal. In such circumstances, affects may override cognitions.

Situations may also have implications for perceptions. Perceptions may be based on folk beliefs about sex and risks of sex or particular partners. Lowy and Ross (1994) looked at the "folk construction" of sexual risk in gay men and found that epidemiological constructs were transformed into personal risk concepts. Men used several categories of signifiers of risk: age, appearance, diction, and HIV knowledge, along with epidemiological factors. This epidemiological fallacy takes variables that in a large population may be associated with lower risk of HIV infection—such as few partners, being the insertive partner in anal intercourse, being in a stable relationship, and past history of infrequent anal intercourse—and translates them into individual risk data. Along with emotional needs and sexual arousal, these are transformed into pseudo-epidemiological models of risk to determine the actual risk of each potential partner. Lowy and Ross found that rather than the absolutes of "safe," "safer," and "unsafe" sex, men created their own cognitive schema of safety gradients by extrapolating epidemiological data and principles and applying them to individual cases. The attribution of risk for HIV or other STD infection is remarkably consistent. Chapman and Hodgson (1988) found that for heterosexual men and women, a person who was thought to be likely to carry an STD or HIV was dirty and perceptably unattractive.

Cognitions that are associated with risk behavior are thus central to understanding the continued transmission of HIV. Gold and colleagues (Gold & Skinner, 1992; Gold, Skinner, Grant, & Plummer, 1991; Gold, Skinner, & Ross, 1994) looked at the rationalizations and thought processes associated with unprotected anal intercourse in Australian gay men. Respondents were asked to recall a sexual encounter in which they had engaged in this risk behavior and a safe encounter. Of the sample of 250, 30% had known that they were HIV-infected. Over 90% of the sample reported at least one of these groups of self-justifications: reactions to being in a negative mood state; being already infected and having nothing to lose; getting "what you can while you can"; dislike of condoms; the resolution to withdraw before ejaculation, used with a partner whom the respondent did not know well; and confidence in oneself and a desire to demonstrate confidence in the partner. The mood state variables showed that in the unsafe encounter, the older respondents had been in a better mood at the start of the evening and the younger respondents in a more negative mood, emphasizing the importance of *risk affects.* For the uninfected men, the major self-justification involved inferring from perceptible characteristics (e.g., healthy looking) that the partner was uninfected or inferring that because he was not using a condom, he must be uninfected. Unfortunately, this same act (not using a condom) was used by those already infected to infer that the partner was also infected!

Attitudes and beliefs associated with risk and with safety have been the focus of extensive research in gay and bisexual men. In a test of the Theory of Reasoned Action, Fishbein et al. (1992) found that attitude was the best variable explaining intention to adopt 15 sexual practices, whereas Ross and McLaws (1992) found that subjective norms were the significant factor explaining intention to use condoms. Cochran, Mays, Ciarletta, Caruson, and Mallon (1992) found both attitudes and subjective norms significantly explained intention to adopt safe sex recommendations. Ross and McLaws suggest that the stage of development of the epidemic may influence whether norms or attitudes played the more dominant role in intention to engage in safe behavior. However, Godin, Savard, Kok, Fortin, and Boyer (1996) found in a Canadian study that perceived behavioral control, as hypothesized in the Theory of Planned Behavior, along with personal normative belief and perceived subjective norm, was the best predictor of intention to use condoms. Further, perceived behavioral control was the best predictor of having sex without anal intercourse. Godin et al. concluded that interventions in gay and bisexual men should attempt to increase perception of behavioral control. Cognitive change interventions have been the most common, largely because of the measurability and modifiability of attitudes and beliefs.

Attitudes toward Condom Use

Attitudes toward condoms and condom use have been reviewed by Ross (1992), who found (1988a) that the major dimensions of attitudes toward condoms in this population were seeing condoms as unerotic and unreliable; level of protection from infection; availability; interruption of sex; and having a responsibility to use, and comfort in using, condoms. In a longitudinal study of factors that predicted condom use in gay men, Ross (1992) found that a more assertive and forceful personality style was associated with increased condom use, probably through making it easier to raise the issue of condom use with sexual partners. Further, he found that beliefs in the ability of condoms to protect from infection and their greater availability were also associated with increases in use over six months. Variables associated with lack of change to safer sex included dysphoric mood state and level of psychological distress. However, in a comparison of attitudes and assertiveness in heterosexual and homosexual men, Treffke, Tiggeman, and Ross (1992) found that general social assertiveness was negatively associated with condom use in heterosexual men, but positively associated in homosexual men (condom-specific assertiveness was related to condom use in both groups). In a Canadian study, Godin et al. (1996) also found that in men with HIV disease, the best predictor of safe sex practices was degree of perceived behavioral control over condom use, along with a perceived responsibility to use condoms. The importance of attitudes toward changes in sexual practices (including condom use) was further confirmed by Fishbein et al. (1992), who found in a multisite study in the United States that attitude was the best factor explaining intention to adopt these behaviors.

In a criticism of both the "relapse" and "negotiated safety" accounts of unsafe sex, Coxon (1996) reports on sexual diary studies of homosexual men in the United Kingdom. He argues that the role of cognitive processes, decision, negotiation, consideration, and reasoning is overstressed, and that the avoidance of condoms is often as much a matter of waiting for the partner to object as it is a prenegotiated condition. He suggests that those who come closest to the ideal of choice, responsibility, and negotiation are those already HIV seropositive. Cognitions and rational calculations such as subjective expected utility theory, then, should not be the only target of interventions. Offir, Fisher, Williams, and Fisher (1993) looked at inconsistent HIV prevention among gay men and found that participants engaged in a process of cognitive distortion to maintain consistency between perceptions of their inconsistent preventive behavior and themselves as low-risk individuals. In such cases, they suggest strategies to make individuals aware of their cognitive dissonance and rationalizations may be the most effective form of intervention.

Alcohol and Drugs

There has been a great deal of speculation about the role of alcohol and drugs in unsafe behavior. Paul, Stall, and Davis (1993) reported a 32% increase in frequency of unprotected anal intercourse in their San Francisco sample of gay and bisexual substance abusers, and they reported that two-thirds of their sample were "always" intoxicated during unprotected anal intercourse. Stall, McKusick, Wiley, Coates, and Ostrow (1986) found that men who used three or more drugs during sexual activity were more than four times more likely to engage in risky sexual behavior in a bathhouse or bar setting than those who did not combine drugs. However, in a sexual diary study in the U.K., Weatherburn et al. (1993) found that although 30% of their sample used alcohol in sexual encounters, there was no statistically significant difference between alcohol users and nonusers in the prevalence of risky sex. Supporting this, in those who used alcohol, there was no dose-response effect with quantity of alcohol and sexual safety. Thus, although multiple substance users may be at higher risk than nonusers, other factors may account for the risk or interact with substance use. Lewis and Ross (1995), in a major qualitative study of gay circuit (dance) parties in Australia, found that substance use and unsafe sex were often associated with a desire to escape from a stigmatized everyday reality that included homonegative environments, fear of HIV/AIDS, and the pervasiveness of HIV infection and risk in their subculture, and a desire to celebrate their sexuality in a "safe" context. Paradoxically, this "safe" context could also provide a context in which unsafe behavior could occur, often aided by cognition- and affect-altering substances and "magical" thinking. However, when one looks at samples of injecting drug users, and within them compares gay, bisexual, and heterosexual men, the gay men exhibit the safest sexual behaviors, followed by bisexual men, with heterosexual men being the least safe. There was little overlap between safety in sexual behavior and safety in drug using behavior, suggesting the importance of considering other risks besides the sexual for HIV transmission in gay men (Ross, Wodak, Gold, & Miller, 1992). Although the data on alcohol and drug use as risks factors for unsafe sex suggest that they may function as contextual markers rather than risks as such, drugs as disinhibitors may be a useful focus of interventions. However, drug use and unsafe sex are more likely both behaviors resulting from an underlying trait: sensation seeking.

Sensation Seeking

A possible personality dimension of risk behavior is sensation seeking. Early studies of STDs have consistently found that extroversion was one of the better predictors of STD risk and STD infection. Kalichman et al. (1994) found that sensation seeking predicted HIV risk behavior in homosexual men, and even with substance use controlled, sexual adventurism and sensation seeking were major predictors of unsafe sexual behavior. This has also been confirmed in heterosexual men: Bogaert and Fisher (1995) were able to predict a significant proportion of the variance of partner numbers using sensation-seeking measures. It appears that there is a constellation of disinhibition, including Eysenck's (1978) psychoticism and extroversion, and sensation seeking significantly related both to safety and partner numbers. Eysenck found that extroverts have intercourse earlier, more frequently, with more different partners, and in more different positions than introverts; they also engage in more varied sexual behavior outside intercourse and engage in longer foreplay.

INTERVENTIONS

Despite knowing something about the variables underlying risk behavior—personal, situational, attitudinal, attributional, affective—we need to recognize that many of these are not readily modifiable. Attempting to change personality is close to impossible, and as we have already noted, attitudinal changes may be overridden by affects. Nor can we assume that behavioral interventions will be effective with only one administration. Like some vaccines, they may require "booster" administrations to maintain their effectiveness. A further drawback is that many interventions have been based on North American samples, where the focus is on the individual. It is not clear how these may translate into contexts where the individual has limited degrees of freedom and the community and social expectations frame behavior, risk, and prevention. It may be most helpful to characterize interventions by the target group and cover the range of theories and approaches within this framework.

Men Who Have Sex with Men

The literature on risk and interventions with MSMs has been reviewed extensively by Ross and Kelly (1999), and we report some of this evidence in this chapter. Many of the interventions to reduce HIV risk were pioneered in MSM populations, given that it was in this target group that HIV/AIDS first manifested itself in the United States and in western Europe. As a consequence, the greatest amount of literature and the greatest amount of sophistication in theory and design exists in this area of intervention.

Face-to-face and individual-level interventions have been based largely on three theories: the Theory of Reasoned Action/Theory of Planned Behavior; social cognitive theory; and the Health Belief Model. A combination of these has been described in the AIDS Risk Reduction Model. Ross and Kelly (1999) note that most have a number of common characteristics. They combine risk reduction with exercises to promote positive attitudes toward safer sex, encourage change from current high-risk sexual behavior, teach behavioral risk reduction skills (such as condom use and sexual negotiation), and reinforce behavior change attempts. Valdiserri, Pultman, and Curran (1995) followed 450 gay men who were randomly assigned to one of two groups. The first group consisted of a safer sex education program that provided information about

AIDS, risk behavior, and safer sex practices, and common misconceptions about HIV and AIDS. The second provided the same information, but in addition provided role plays and psychodrama to enable participants to practice safer sex negotiation skills, and group activities to reinforce safer sex norms. Follow-up was at 6 and 12 months. Condom use in the men who had attended the information-only program was 11% higher than at baseline, whereas for the skills-building program attendees, the increase was 44%. These data illustrate the advantage of including skills as well as information in intervention programs. It is widely accepted that information is a necessary but not sufficient condition to change risk behaviors (Ross & Rosser, 1989).

Kelly, St. Lawrence, Hood, and Brasfield (1989) examined the impact of a longer and more intensive intervention in gay men in the southern United States. Their intervention consisted of 12 75-minute, small group (8–15 people) sessions. Their sample of 104 men were recruited from (predominantly White) gay community venues and were randomly assigned to intervention or a waiting-list control group. The group facilitators addressed risk knowledge and risk reduction education; skills training and skills practice in areas including sexual negotiation, assertiveness, and condom use; and risk-reduction self-management and problem-solving skills involving identifying and modifying ways to handle situations that seem to act as triggers to high-risk behavior. Group discussions centered on self-esteem, relationship issues, and personal and community responsibilities to prevent HIV transmission. Follow-up occurred at 8 and 16 months. Compared to the delayed-intervention control group, the intervention group increased their condom use from 23% at baseline to 77% at 8-month follow-up; at 16 months, the figure was 60%. The average number of unprotected anal intercourse occasions in the previous four months was 7.8 at baseline, which was reduced to 0.7 at follow-up (Kelly, St. Lawrence, & Brasfield, 1990). In a later study, Kelly et al. (1990) found that a shorter, seven-session intervention also produced an effect of comparable size.

Peterson et al. (1996) carried out a similar intervention in San Francisco with an African American population also recruited from community venues. Random assignment was to one three-hour risk reduction workshop, three such workshops, or a waiting-list control group. These workshops included risk reduction education and assertiveness and sexual negotiation skills training, as well as discussion to encourage self-esteem and positive identity. Follow-ups were carried out at 12 and 18 months. Control group members showed little change in sexual risk behavior, and the single-workshop participants showed a small change, but those in the three-workshop program reported significantly reduced risk (from 45% at baseline to 20% at the 18-month follow-up).

Community-level HIV prevention in gay men has been pioneered by Kelly et al. (1991, 1992). Their interventions were based on men in gay bars in small cities in the southern United States. Men entering these bars were surveyed to establish a community baseline, and then one city served as intervention with the other two serving as controls. The intervention, which was based on Rogers's (1983) diffusion of innovation theory, identified from the baseline survey people who were regarded as "opinion leaders" who, because they were popular and well-liked, would serve as role models for behavior change. People nominated by bartenders and patrons as opinion leaders were approached and asked to participate in the study. They were given four sessions of training in which they were taught about the characteristics and delivery of prevention messages, and they were taught how to commence conversations with strangers in bars. The intervention utilized a "traffic light" symbol in the bars; when people asked about its meaning, this was an opportunity to explain that the red symbolized unsafe behaviors, the amber safer sex, and the green safe sex practices—and to initiate a conversation to encourage safer practices.

Surveys of men entering the intervention city's gay bars at three and six months following the intervention showed a decline in unprotected anal intercourse from 37% to 28% over the previous two months. Receptive unprotected anal intercourse followed the same pattern, with a 30% decline. No such change was found in the two control cities, indicating that this campaign was successful. Subsequent work by Kelly et al. (1997) has replicated this in a larger study in eight additional small cities in the United States. This replication reported that the average number of unprotected anal intercourse occasions declined from 1.7 in the past two months to 0.6, and the numbers of occasions of anal intercourse protected by condoms in the same period increased from 45% to 67%.

Youth and HIV Prevention

Adolescents with hemophilia constitute nearly half of reported AIDS cases in teenagers in Britain. Forsberg, King, Delaronde, and Geary (1996) identified barriers to safer sex in this group. They noted that whereas only 20% indicated that peers influenced their sexual behavior, 86% indicated that partners significantly impacted their sexual decisions. Only 31% of the sexually active adolescents said that they told every partner of their HIV infection. In these adolescents, fear of rejection or a negative reaction from the partner and lack of communication skills were the major barriers to disclosure of HIV status and to practice of safer sex. Obviously, interventions in this group should involve development of communication skills and self-efficacy (Forsberg et al., 1996).

Koopman, Rotheram-Borus, Henderson, Bradley, and Hunter (1990) have identified five domains that are relevant in preventing HIV infection in adolescents: self-efficacy, perception of HIV as a threat, perception of oneself as being in control in high-risk sexual situations, peer support for safe sex acts, and expectation to act to avoid pregnancy. In a sample of low-income African American adolescents, Reitman et al. (1996) found that lower self-efficacy, higher perceived risk, and being male were significantly associated with high-risk behavior. Regardless of their behavior, though, most adolescents, did not perceive themselves as being at risk of HIV infection, suggesting that in this group, as in other adolescents, perceptions of invulnerability are the greatest barrier to protective behaviors. Reitman et al. also suggest that there may be different correlates for protective behaviors (such as condom use) and for high-risk behavior (unprotected sex with multiple partners). For condom use, predictors were increased age and positive attitudes toward condoms.

Interventions to reduce risk in substance-dependent adolescents may be targeting one of the most difficult groups to reach. St. Lawrence et al. (1994) undertook an intervention that consisted of five sessions including risk education, social competency skills (sexual assertion, partner negotiation, and communication skills) technical skills (condom use), and problem-solving training. Following training, the percentage of adolescents who reported sexual activity in high-risk contexts two months later decreased from 19% to 5% for coercion into unwanted sexual activity, from 11% to 5% for exchange of sex for drugs, and from 44% to 31% for combining substance abuse with sexual activity. However, the authors note that the durability of these changes is not known.

Innovative approaches to youth to prevent sexual acquisition of HIV and other STDs may be appropriate. Traeen (1992) describes mobilization of the youth culture using the medium of rock music (although lack of a specific message limited the success of the intervention). Luna and Rotheram-Borus (1992) note that there have been several successful interventions with street youth and that the most successful have been both culture- and gender-specific. Attention to youth is particularly important as this is a period of emerging sexual behavior and experimentation. In areas where the HIV seroprevalence is high, a large number of infections may occur while people are still in adolescence, and thus attention to adolescent sexuality is probably the most important single area of HIV prevention.

Drug Users

While injecting drug use (IDU) is in itself a separate area of HIV prevention, it is important to note that a significant amount of HIV transmission in IDUs may also be sexual. Further, IDUs may also act as a bridge for infection to other areas of the community through sexual transmission. Ross, Wodak, Miller, and Gold (1993) found that a greater proportion (75%) of the partners of female IDUs were other IDUs, compared with the partners of males who were IDUs (59%). Fewer than 5% had had no sexual partners in the prior year. In the same study, 12% of the last contact for females and 13% for males were members of the same sex. Ross et al. (1992) also found that there were significant differences across sexual orientation in IDUs, with homosexual men having the lowest risk behaviors, bisexual intermediate, and heterosexual the highest. This suggests that preventive education in one sexual area will have some impact on sexual behavior in another. However, Wodak, Stowe, Ross, Gold, and Miller (1995) found that there was no significant relationship between being safe in sexual behavior and being safe in injecting behavior, with 17% of the injectors being safe on both sexual and injecting behaviors, 51% being unsafe on either injecting or sexual behavior but not both, and 33% being unsafe on both. Clearly, one cannot assume that prevention messages will cross domains as discrepant as drug use and sexual practices.

Heterosexual Contact

In general, prevention of HIV infection in heterosexual populations follows the same theories and approaches as in other populations. What makes it different from prevention in populations of MSMs and similar to adolescents is that in many Western countries, heterosexual men and women assume that they are not at risk. Part of this problem can be attributed to risk reduction campaigns that associated their targets as gay men rather than particular sexual acts that did not distinguish among classes of persons. As a result, people may not identify themselves as being at risk.

Interventions that reduce risk of sexual transmission of HIV in high-prevalence areas have been successful in targeting heterosexual men and women. Deren, Davis, Beardsley, Tortu, and Clatts (1995) looked at a large population in Harlem, New York, including drug users and their sexual partners. Six-month follow-up indicated that significant reductions in risk behaviors occurred regardless of intervention group or even if no intervention had occurred! Nevertheless, many respondents still reported significant levels of risk behavior at follow-up. The authors concluded that, methodological considerations aside, it may be that just interviewing respondents at baseline and follow-up has an impact on risk behavior, or that diffusion of the program through the community as well as exposure to people in the community becoming ill and dying may have overwhelmed the impact of their interventions. When there is a high visibility of the impact of HIV in a community, denial and perception of it as someone else's problem are difficult. Unfortunately, given the years between infection and the appearance of symptoms and death, infection is likely to have spread through a community before it becomes obvious.

One of the difficulties in interventions with heterosexual people is that of power differentials, particularly for women. Where the woman is in a relatively powerless situation or where condom use may be interpreted by a male partner as evidence that she has been unfaithful, the woman is not able to insist on use of a condom, or if she does raise the topic, she may be at risk of violence and rejection. Nevertheless, the impact of a supportive other may also be overestimated. In an intervention to examine the impact of including a supportive person compared with a traditional solo intervention, Nyamathi, Flaskerud, Keenan, and Leake (1998) studied homeless and drug-dependent women in Los Angeles. The intervention consisted of eight 45-minute, small-group sessions providing culturally sensitive AIDS education. Coping enhancement strategies were added to the basic program as well. Outcomes indicated that, compared with baseline, where 49% of women reported having sex with multiple partners, by 6 months only 11% did; this figure remained stable at 12 months. At baseline, 90% reported unprotected sex; this had dropped to 62% at 6 months and did not decline further. Whereas support may not be a relevant issue in this population, clearly even in difficult situations, significant risk reduction is possible and sustainable over the short term and up to a year.

The issue of power and sexual behavior has been addressed by Wingood and DiClemente (1998). The main elements that characterize relations between men and women are division of labor, structure of power, and the structure of cathexis (emotional investment). Power imbalances within relationships include such issues as control, authority, and coercion within heterosexual relationships. This imbalance allows men to dominate or abuse (psychologically or physically) their female partners. The authors suggest that the structure of cathexis means that women fail to negotiate safer sex with their partners because of the perception that it undermines the trust and intimacy in relationships. Even if they know that the partner is unfaithful, they may feel that the trust and intimacy in their relationship are too important to risk. This approach offers a perspective of how being a woman may lead to risk of HIV or STD infection, and that unplanned pregnancy may have more to do with power imbalance than with carelessness. Further, Wingood and DiClemente note, women in physically abusive relationships are less likely to use condoms. Clearly, interventions that address the structure of gender inequality are needed, including not just education, but also self-efficacy training and negotiation skills. For women for whom being sexually assertive is not associated with their culture or gender role, interventions that affect the power dynamics of relationships may offer a better chance to protect against STDs, including HIV infection.

PSYCHOLOGICAL RESPONSE TO HIV INFECTION

As we write this, the HIV epidemic has raged for over 20 years and has been recognized for 17. The natural disease process is relatively well understood, and enormous progress in medical treatment has been accomplished over the years. It is possible to manage and postpone HIV-related symptoms and diseases, but the infection is still not curable. Life expectancy for people with HIV in Western countries is much longer today than it was a decade ago. In 1994, a new category was introduced at the International AIDS Conference: "long-term nonprogressor." This refers to people whose HIV-seropositive serostatus has been established unequivocally, yet who have remained immunologically healthy and physically asymptomatic for 12 years or longer (Rabkin, Remien, & Wilson, 1994). The time span has also changed with respect to survival after being diagnosed with AIDS, yielding long-term survivors.

In 1996, the treatment of HIV disease changed dramatically when triple "combination therapy" including protease inhibitors became the new standard of treatment. Although protease inhibitors appear to provide much benefit, we still do not know about their long-term benefits, side effects, the development of resistance to them, or the psychological impact of taking a new medication that may work only for a short time or not at all. The triple combination therapy arouses both hope and caution as well as skepticism among some people with HIV. A psychological consequence of this new treatment is that those women and men who are long-term nonprogressors or long-term survivors face another survival issue that is related to the future. This new situation—to be "offered" a life perspective—means that their "death-oriented" life attitude is challenged. Paradoxically, a potential life perspective can also induce life anxiety.

Whereas the response of the body to HIV infection has a more finite range of possibilities, the psychological response of the person with HIV to the condition may encompass a wide range of reactions and adaptations across the life span and across the phases of the disease. Our understanding of the psychological, social, and sexual aspects of the drama of HIV infection and its psychological processes has, however, been slow in coming, partly because there has been less clinical outcome research than prevention research. Most of the HIV-related psychosocial research is cross-sectional and mainly focused on gay men. Although HIV infection rates among women continue to accelerate, there is an embarrassing void of studies regarding the gender-specific psychological, social, and sexual situation of women who have HIV. Whereas the vast majority of empirical research has focused on the impact of HIV disease as such, little research has specifically investigated the impact of physical, social, and/or sexual HIV-related stressors on psychological well-being, and even less on quality of life among people living with HIV.

The drama of HIV infection starts with the decision to seek testing for HIV, which is the final step of an emotional-cognitive decision-making process. Most people struggle with rational versus emotional forces in the process, and the final decision may be difficult to make. The waiting period for the test result is usually perceived as stressful. Some describe it as almost unbearable, filled with worries and horrifying fantasies; others report emotional numbness. The immediate reactions to HIV-seropositive diagnosis can indeed be expressed in a diversity of ways: shock, chaos, aggressiveness, grief, hopelessness, sadness, anxiety, confirmation, and "relief." To protect oneself psychologically from the strong, painful, and overwhelming emotions related to HIV status disclosure, one may make use of various defense mechanisms, such as emotional numbness, denial, and repression. The influence of HIV seropositivity is similar to the impact of some cancer-related diagnoses. However, the research also suggests that, given related issues of stigmatization, discrimination, possible lack of social support, and the uncertainty of disease progression, the impact of the HIV seropositive test will have ramifications far beyond the time surrounding the test and the delivery of the result (Nilsson Schönnesson & Ross, 1999).

Despite the new combination therapies of protease inhibitors, we argue that HIV is still a trauma in that it is unusual and also threatens survival (Janoff-Bulman, 1995). The core of the trauma is its basic survival threat or, in Lifton's (1980) wording, "death imprint." However, the person living with HIV is also confronted with social and sexual threats. We discuss the response to HIV largely in terms of the clinical and psychotherapeutic literature as this provides our best understanding of the person, rather than the "research subject," in this situation.

THE HIV SCENARIO

Physical Threats

The individual's physical survival is abruptly challenged by the diagnosis of HIV, as the infection illuminates our fragility as human beings and life's finitude through death. People with HIV must live with various physical threats. These include stressors such as uncertainty and worries about the disease progression and its potential patterns of HIV-related symptoms and diseases as well as treatment concerns.

HIV threatens not only one's physical but also one's psychological survival. From a psychodynamic perspective, the conception of one's own body plays a crucial role in the development of the self and construction of reality. Consequently, the body is also important to self-image and self-esteem. By extension, when HIV attacks the body, it evokes not only fear of physical death but also fears about losing one's sense of body boundaries, losing one's self, and ultimately dying psychologically. Dementia or brain lesions constitute a terrifying threat to psychological survival. Sometimes, becoming dependent on others is a blow to psychological survival.

The body also plays an important role in one's strivings for affirmation and acknowledgment as a sexual person. People with HIV may experience their sexual self-esteem as heavily affected because their bodies do not match the image of the "perfect body." Others talk about their perception of losing their sexual attraction when symptoms start to develop. For example, the necessity to carry a port-a-cath for medical reasons may likely be a problem for an individual's sense of being a sexual person.

Social Threats

Discrimination and aloneness are both manifestations of the stigmatization of HIV infection (Goffman, 1963). This results in a potential threat to the individual's social existence, a "social death" (Ross & Ryan, 1995). The individual may suffer far more from the HIV stigma than from the diagnosis itself. Gay men, drug users, and prostitutes with HIV are thus faced with multiple stigmatization: the stigma associated with the sickness itself as well as the stigma of their marginal social status. Disclosure of one's HIV status adds to the negative consequences of the disease itself.

Because HIV infection is a heavily stigmatized disease, self-disclosure is a charged issue and a potent stressor for people living with HIV, regardless of whether or not they choose to reveal their status (Holt et al., 1998). But disclosure also acts as "a mechanism by which the individuals contend with their infection" (p. 54), and it may facilitate more effective coping and psychological adaptation to the disease. Disclosure is not a fixed state but rather a dynamic process. In this section, we discuss self-disclosure as it relates to the social network domain.

People with HIV wrestle with whom to tell in their social network and when to tell them about their HIV status. The aim of the self-disclosure process is to come out about one's HIV seropositivity to significant others. Indirectly, one also strives for interpersonal security, self-esteem, self-acceptance, and control over one's life. Some select carefully whom to tell; others feel they must "tell the world." The HIV disclosure process may echo gay men's gay identity-formation process (Ross, Tebble, & Viliunas, 1989), in that the individual in both cases has to manage a stigmatized status. In the self-disclosure process, the individual is confronted with the dilemma created between the psychological need for authenticity, affirmation, and respect, and the fear of being rejected and abandoned, of being "punished" for being authentic. In general, self-disclosure is the result of a long and well-thought-out process that takes into account contextual issues and potential consequences, both immediate and long term. Motives for disclosure may differ depending on the potential "target" of disclosure. Most often, the motive is to break the psychological isolation and/or the sense of denying and failing oneself. Other motives may be to live in accordance with the dictates of one's conscience or to halt rumors. In some cases, disclosing might not be carefully considered but rather impulsive, a reflection of internal psychological conflicts. There are also individuals who decide not to disclose their HIV status to anyone. Fears of rejection, abandonment, disruption of social ties, and the reactions of others are common sources of reluctance to tell others. Another source may be regret about bringing sadness to others, in particular to parents and close friends. Others stress the private character of the matter. Some may socially withdraw for fear of unintentionally "revealing" their HIV status or as a consequence of a sense of HIV-related shame or lack of self-esteem. Among some gay men, a contributing factor may be their childhood and adolescent experiences of being rejected and deprived of affirmation.

However, *not* sharing one's HIV status may result in feelings of having denied and failed oneself, eventually leading to self-blame and reduced self-esteem. Thus, the individual is in a no-win situation: on the one hand, he or she needs support; on the other hand, he or she fears that seeking support will lead to rejection.

One solution may be to seek out others in the same situation or, in self-psychological terminology, to seek twinship bonds (i.e., the experience of feeling an essential alikeness with others) (Kohut, 1971). Some become active in body-positive groups or organizations that supply them with a subculture and a feeling of belonging. Positive reinforcement and the social and psychological support of others provide confidence and may facilitate disclosure.

There is no doubt that self-disclosure can have negative consequences, such as discrimination in the workplace, in health care systems, and in insurance matters. Discrimination may also take place in more indirect ways. Negative remarks about people with HIV or AIDS, jokes, and patronizing, demeaning attitudes are other examples of "informal" discrimination. People with HIV may be transferred at work from one post to another out of "consideration" or a "best for you" attitude.

The fear of aloneness or interpersonal isolation lurks not only in the self-disclosure decision process but also after disclosure. But it is important to remember that the fear and experiences of interpersonal isolation may be reinforced, colored, and compounded by earlier psychological conflicts and problems. Sometimes, the individual "blames" HIV for his or her intimacy problems, although on closer examination, these problems may have existed long before the HIV diagnosis. In a Swedish qualitative study (Nilsson Schön-nesson & Ross, 1999), men talked about aloneness in terms of feelings of being abandoned and a feeling of being invisible. The latter emotion has an existential quality in that it represents a sense of being no one, of experiencing psychological death. Those men who were in the terminal disease phase were also occupied with thoughts of being an outsider. From a physical perspective, the advanced disease process may severely limit social interaction and the sick person may express fear of becoming completely socially isolated. An additional threat to social existence within the gay communities is the multiple losses and accompanying grief that many gay men experience. Thus, chosen social isolation can function as a protective shelter from anticipated separation and emotional suffering.

Sexual Threats

In the course of the infection, the individual's sexual existence in terms of sexual activity and intimacy is exposed to HIV-related psychological, social, and medical threats. For gay men, the gay identity and lifestyle are also similarly exposed.

Persons with HIV are faced with two major sexual dilemmas that bear on their sexual existence. One is related to protected sex and the other to self-disclosure of one's HIV status. These dilemmas may be compounded by a sense of being plague-stricken, unattractive, and "not good enough" as a sexual individual. In addition, HIV disease progression and physical deterioration may have an impact on sexual desire, physical functioning, and sexual ability.

The Protected Sex Dilemma.   The core of the HIV sexual behavioral scenario is to find a psychological equilibrium between protected sex and sexual well-being. This is a continuing process, and, to many, the equilibrium has to be re-captured over and over again. There are demands on and expectations of people with HIV to change their sexually risky behaviors and to maintain these changes during the rest of their lives. These expectations are a potential source of stress and frustration.

The sexual behavioral dilemma of people with HIV is very often looked at from a solely cognitive and rational perspective. To do justice to the complexity of sexual behavior change, we also have to address the psychological aspects of the individual's sexuality (Nilsson Schönnesson & Ross, 1999). First, we must be aware that people create sexual behavioral scripts that may differ from situation to situation and from partner to partner. Some of the behaviors are perceived as more pleasurable than others and some are more important than others to sexual satisfaction. Consequently, to change one's sexual life pattern may decrease joy, pleasure, and satisfaction. Little research has been done in this area, and the few studies that do exist show that when unprotected sex is related to sexual pleasure and/or sexual importance, it is more difficult to refrain (Ekstrand & Coates, 1990; Nilsson Schönnesson & Dolezal, 1998; Stall, Ekstrand, Pollack, McKusick, & Coates, 1990).

Another important psychological aspect is the boundless or regressive dimension of sexuality: One gives in physically and psychologically to another person without constraints. A person living with HIV is deprived of this sexual boundlessness and has to replace it with sexual boundary. But there is a paradox: The sexual act has an existential value in that it symbolizes life and its continuity, but when the individual practices protected sex, the sexual act symbolizes death.

A third psychological aspect is the psychological representation of sexual behaviors. For example, unprotected sex (regardless of HIV status) represents intimacy, a merger with one's partner, and trust. Therefore, condoms are perceived as a barrier to intimacy.

Thus, given the fact that protected sex implies the need to relinquish the hedonistic, boundless, and symbolic meaning of one's sexuality, it is understandable that sexual behavioral changes are often linked with feelings of loss, suffering, rage, grief, and accompanying mourning. To those gay men whose identification is strongly vested in sexual performance, sexual behavioral changes may be construed as an "identity death." It is notable that our empirical knowledge is almost nonexistent with respect to what extent people with HIV may experience psychological and/or sexual distress as a consequence of their sexual behavior changes.

The Self-Disclosure Dilemma.   The core of the self-disclosure dilemma is (like disclosure to social networks) fear of rejection and social isolation. The individual is faced with the difficult decision of timing of disclosure in the sexual context in order to run the lowest risk of rejection.

The dilemma can be solved in different ways. The solutions are not necessarily fixed but may change over time contingent upon intrapersonal factors and social/sexual contexts. With respect to disclosure, some individuals decide not to tell anyone, and some to always inform the sexual partners. Others decide not to inform casual partners, but as long as protected sex is practiced, potential steady partners are always told. Others solve the dilemma by continuing to engage in unprotected sex. Another solution is to make the behavioral changes necessary to practice sexual behaviors that are negatively loaded. Still another way is to change the sexual risky practices and find new, nonrisky, positively loaded ways of expressing one's sexual desire. Sexual abstinence or self-quarantine is another solution. Some individuals withdraw sexually because the sexual behavioral changes and/or self-disclosure carry a psychological price that is too high. Self-quarantine may also be generated by fears of rejection, abandonment, perception of blame and guilt, and discredited identity. To others, the next-to-optimal solution is to restrict one's cruising areas to the body-positive groups.

Intimacy. HIV infection constitutes a threat to intimacy. To some people, the infection is such an insurmountable barrier that love relationships are perceived as unattainable. The barrier is not necessarily the infection itself (i.e., the fear of transmission), but rather is associated with a negative self-image due to the negative psychological and social consequences of HIV. To others, the barrier is the individual's sense of not being worthy to be loved or to love. Still others are so afraid to disclose their HIV status that they do not dare to expose themselves to potential partners.

Although clinicians are aware that HIV infection has introduced a tragic element into the lives of many heterosexual and gay couples, distressingly little attention has been paid to psychosocial and psychosexual consequences of and strains on the relationship. The sparse empirical research has mainly focused on gay couples and in particular, on couples with serodiscordant HIV status. It is likely that the serodiscordant population is of greater concern to public health interest because of the potential risk of HIV transmission. We think this attitude is unfortunate in that couples with HIV-seropositive concordance status run the risk of being excluded from psychological and health care services. These couples struggle with the same external and relational issues and stressors that their discordant counterparts do. In addition to relational issues that typically confront any couple, the couple with HIV is also faced with specific HIV-related stressors linked to the disease, the sexual and the social domains of the relationship.

Some potential stressors within the *disease domain* are the uncertainty as to disease progression and future planning and caretaking concerns. When the couple has not disclosed their HIV status to their social network or disagrees about whether or when to tell others, it is a stressor on the *social domain* of the relationship. The danger of secrecy of HIV is that the couple becomes socially isolated. Potential stressors within the *sexual domain* are the sexual dilemma of protected/unprotected sex and also medical threats that may have an impact on sexual desire, functioning, and ability. Another sexual domain issue is pregnancy. The conflict emerging from the desire to have children is a central issue to many women with HIV. The unfulfilled wish for a child often manifests itself in emotional distress and/or psychosomatic complaints. It is also not uncommon for gay men to express grief related to their lost fatherhood. The parenthood issues have, however, been neglected in research, perhaps partly for moral and ethical reasons.

The members of the couple may perceive disease and social and sexual stressors diversely in terms of their seriousness, complexity, and salience, and also in timing, which may lead to further conflicts within the relationship. It is quite common that talking about HIV and related topics are avoided in both serodiscordant and HIV-seropositive concordant couples. Reoccurring reasons for not discussing these topics include not wanting to worry or upset the other, hurt or make the other feel bad, or burden the other. Paradoxically, this avoidance may aggravate conflicts and difficulties within the relationship. But we have to acknowledge that the basis of the avoidant attitude is the fear of rejection and ultimately separation.

Gay couples, in contrast to straight couples, are exposed to specific stressors related to their same-gender preference. They may experience the negative attitudes of others and be looked upon as "deviant." They may lack support, validation, and acknowledgment of their needs within the relationship. In those male couples where one or both members have HIV, the intensity of this experience is magnified.

Gay Identity and Lifestyle.   The gay identity and lifestyle are also exposed to HIV-related stressors. As sexual and social circles are interwoven in the gay scene, this may have a negative impact on gay men with HIV and their participation in gay subcultures. When a man perceives himself as less attractive and/or is less psychologically healthy, he is less inclined to be part of the social scene and thus also withdraws from the sexual scene. He may also withdraw from gay friends because of depression, low self-esteem, fear of abandonment, guilt, or shame. This may lead to loss of subcultural support. Alternatively, the gay man may be rejected by his friends due to his HIV status.

Psychological Functioning

Given the threats to the individual's physical, social, and sexual existence and the related psychological issues (e.g., loss, mourning, control, despair), it is not surprising that people living with HIV can suffer virtually any form of psychological distress. It should be remembered, though, that stress vulnerability might oscillate over time and also be selective; for example, an individual may be affected by sexual threats but not by social threats.

Some people appear to be minimally affected psychologically by HIV. It may be viewed as a turning point or a challenge, and the individual may be resilient and have a positive outlook. Others have great difficulties in adapting and may experience more or less intense psychological distress in the course of the disease. This is reflected on a continuum from psychiatric disorders to transient mood symptoms. Depression, in particular, has received a good deal of attention. Women score higher on psychological distress than do their male counterparts (Havens, Mellins, & Pilowsky, 1996). As with other life-threatening illnesses, such as cancer (Allebeck & Bolund, 1991), HIV has the potential to induced suicidal ideation. Although there is some evidence that people with HIV are at an increased risk of suicide compared to those without the infection (Catalan & Pugh, 1995), Sherr (1995), because of methodological problems, under-scores the difficulties in gauging the prevalence of suicide. Further, she points out that many researchers have focused only on death by suicide "rather than exploring the extreme mental health burden brought about by suicidal thoughts, attempts, completion, and bereavement" (p. 109).

There seems to be consensus among researchers that an earlier psychiatric history, depression, and a history of attempted suicide are better predictors of current suicidal activity than an HIV diagnosis or diagnosis of HIV-related symptoms or diseases. We suggest that it is necessary to make a distinction between suicide in the context of clinical depression and "acute" or impulse-driven suicide on the one hand, and, on the other hand, philosophical suicide or "self-determined" or "accelerated" death (Rabkin et al., 1994). The latter refers to a kind of contingency plan: killing oneself if medical conditions become unbearable. The possibility of choosing time of death may give the person a sense of personal control—to be in charge of death—and of sustaining human dignity.

People with HIV may also experience less severe but still psychologically painful HIV-related reactions. These can be summarized under the heading of mood distress, including global assessment of degree of distress, as well as emotions such as anger, aloneness, resignation/hopelessness, helplessness, and despair. Clement, Gramatikov, Laszig, et al. (1997) note, however, that it is impossible to draw any conclusions with respect to associations among mood distress, HIV status group, and disease phases, in that the methodologies of the studies are too heterogeneous. Psychological distress also represents a risk factor for developing sexual symptoms, which, in turn, may reinforce perceived distress. Psychological distress may also be superimposed on sexual symptoms that are of a medical character.

People living with HIV are confronted with separation, grief, and mourning processes because HIV-related threats are ultimately related to potential losses. Gay men in particular are also faced with the sickness and death of many of those around them. American authors (e.g., Hays, Chauncey, & Tobey, 1990; Wright, 1998) talk about "disenfranchised grief" among gay men: "That is, given society's homophobia, men who lose friends and loved ones to AIDS do not have adequate opportunity to mourn their deaths" (Wright, 1998, p. 2). Common symptoms of pervasive loss are depression, survival guilt, and shame of being gay. As the trauma of loss is ongoing, it gets integrated into the personality, becomes chronic, and complicates the mourning process.

Thus, women and men who have HIV may respond to their disease and related threats and stressors with a range of distress symptoms; people have unequal success when dealing with the same hardships. How can we account for these individual differences? The hitherto most studied stress mediators in HIV-related psychosocial research are coping and social support. Similar to non-HIV studies, research on the impact of coping on psychological distress within the HIV realm indicates that the use of "negative" coping styles such as wishful thinking, avoidance, isolation, and fatalism is associated with increased distress and diminished well-being. Conversely, problem solving, positive reappraisal, and seeking information are related to decreased psychological distress.

There seems to be consensus among researchers that access to social support and perceptions of feeling supported are important buffers against the negative psychological consequences of stressful experiences. When it comes to life-threatening diseases, it is highly likely that social support needs and type of support may vary over the course of the disease. Empirical findings also imply that gay men perceive partners and close friends as more supportive and helpful than family members in dealing with HIV infection. Just as social interactions can be of support, they can also be a source of stress if they are unhelpful or negative (e.g., insensitivity, disconnecting, forced optimism, and blaming). Negative interactions may have important adverse consequences on psychological functioning and may be particularly salient for people with HIV, given the stigma attached to the disease.

THE PSYCHOLOGICAL LANDSCAPES OF THE HIV SCENARIO

In an effort to understand and appreciate the meaning of living with HIV, we employ as a frame of reference the concept of the psychological landscape. The individual psychological landscape corresponds to the existential, the adaptation, and the self contexts. As these contexts may vary across individuals and over the disease phases, there is not one psychological landscape, but potentially as many as there are people with HIV.

Existential Context

When we are confronted with a boundary situation (Jaspers, as cited in Yalom, 1980) that threatens our physical and psychological survival, such as HIV disease, we often become aware of the givens of existence and their importance to us. The ultimate concerns or givens of existence are meaning, death, freedom, and existential isolation (Yalom, 1980).

HIV-related threats and psychological issues may not only affect psychological functioning but also engender crisis in *meaning* of life. Our search for meaning in life, which is an ongoing process, is based on our needs for overall perceptual frameworks and for a system of values or beliefs to interpret and make sense and order out of our lives and our place in the world. So we formulate our own assumptive worlds or view of life. HIV disease attacks the individual's assumptive world or view of life, which may become shattered as the person's sense of purpose or control and self-worth are more or less violated. As a consequence, he or she may experience chaos. Depth, duration, and the character of the crisis may vary within the individual depending on the kind of HIV-related threat or psychological issue he or she encounters. The HIV-related crisis of meaning may raise existential questions such as Why did it happen? Why me? The person tries to answer these questions to reconstrue or restore the basic, implicit assumptions (i.e., the view of life) he or she held about the self and the world prior to the traumatic event. One aspect of this readjustment process is the search for meaning in the adverse experience (Taylor, 1983), that is, the individual's psychological need to find an explanation for why the traumatic event, such as HIV infection, occurred.

Another way that may help the person to restore his or her sense of meaning in life is the kind of attribution (or representation) he or she assigns to HIV infection as such. These representations are ways to make sense of, or to construe, a psychological interpretation frame to, or mentally depict, HIV. It may represent, for example, personal growth, spiritual growth, limitation, finitude, punishment, persecutor, and prison. One could argue that limitation, finitude, and prison all symbolize a cul de sac, which could be interpreted as the symbol of the final boundary of life, death. A qualitative study among gay men (Nilsson Schönnesson & Ross, 1999) showed that the HIV representations changed over the disease phases from a concrete perception of death to psychological representations of prison and persecutor.

In the psychotherapeutic/counseling setting, the theme of *death* is not only related to or brought up in the terminal phase of life. Death thoughts can be evoked at the death of a friend or lover, which in turn stirs up emotions and reflections related to one's own death. Another context within which thoughts of death may occur is when the individual prepares (in fantasy or in reality) for his or her own funeral and will.

Fear and anxiety surround death. Death anxiety may emerge from either fear of pain and suffering associated with dying or from fear about what happens after life. From an existential point of view, however, "ceasing to be" is the central anxiety of death (Kastenbaum & Aisenberg, 1972). There are various models for understanding contributing factors to death fear and anxiety. One argues that the individual's past experience with death and the general state of a person's psychological well-being determine the level of death anxiety (Templer, 1976). Others suggest that there are three determinants of death anxiety: past-related regret (the individual feels guilty for not having accomplished what he or she expected to accomplish), future-related regret (realization that the future necessary for completion of goals and tasks may no longer be available), and meaningfulness of death (Tomer & Eliason, 1996). According to the model, a person will experience high death anxiety when he or she feels much past and future regret and/or perceives death as meaningless.

The fear of death is of such a magnitude that it has to be repressed. In an attempt to cope with these fears and anxieties, one may construct adaptive defenses such as denial, repression, displacement, and rationalization. Another strategy to circumvent the reality of death and its related anxiety is to immerse oneself in symbolic immortality. One may also develop defense strategies such as the belief in the existence of an ultimate rescuer and a delusional belief in one's specialness and inviolability. Thinking of affectionate care from family and friends, holding the conviction that one will meet dead friends and family members, marveling at one's rich life, and anticipating a union with nature are examples of strategies that people in the terminal phase may use to protect themselves from being overwhelmed by death fear and anxiety.

However, death salience may also cause an increased sense of life vulnerability and lead to personal positive change in self-concept, self-esteem, and view of life. Like patients with terminal cancer, many people with HIV describe a reassessment of life priorities, increased sensibility to one's needs and wishes, and a stronger self.

Freedom is another given of existence. One aspect of freedom is responsibility and awareness of one's responsibility: Each individual is the creator of his or her world, life design, choices, and actions. It also implies that people have to make decisions and to act on them. However, human beings find it difficult to decide when they cannot predict the potential consequences, and to make a decision always means to relinquish something else. We would argue that within the HIV realm, it is important to acknowledge existential responsibility to understand why individuals may have difficulties making decisions (e.g., regarding medical treatment). The individual may hesitate because he or she cannot anticipate or know for sure about the consequences of the medical treatment. However, if the individual decides not to take medication, that also implies consequences.

Many people talk about the fear of being rejected or abandoned by others. We suggest that underlying this fear is an even deeper fear, that of *existential isolation.* The strong focus on intimate relationships often functions as a means to keep existential isolation within manageable bounds. But love, says Yalom (1980), "does not take away our separateness—that is a given of existence and can be faced but never erased" (p. 370).

After insight into the inescapable limitations of existence, aloneness, and vulnerability, the individual may experience *existential anxiety.* This kind of anxiety reaction has to be separated from neurotic anxiety, which is generated from unconscious, internal, repressed conflicts. However, the nucleus of all anxiety is the fear of being alone, separated, and helpless. Although existential and neurotic anxiety stem from different sources, there is a link between the two: existential anxiety can be reinforced, colored, and exceeded by non-worked-through internal conflicts from the first years of life. Early losses and unhealed grief can affect worries of annihilation disproportionately strongly.

HIV Adaptation Processes

Symbolically, the life situation of a person with HIV can be pictured in the following way: His or her familiar ground is changed into a more or less new and unknown one. The person with HIV is confronted with the overall question, How can I achieve, at least temporarily, psychological and sexual well-being and carry on a satisfying and meaningful life? The answers to these questions are found in the individual's subjective HIV-adaptation process. In other words, we suggest that quality of life is the ultimate goal of the adaptation process. However, it appears to be more accurate to talk about adaptation processes, as the person with HIV is faced with various HIV-related threats and psychological issues in the course of the disease. Thus, he or she needs to adapt to different crises, events, and situations that may be more or less taxing. Depending on the adaptation process of a given crisis, event, or situation, it exerts an influence on psychological functioning and quality of life, which may be affected in a positive or a negative way. Moreover, we suggest that the way the adaptation unfolds in the face of certain threats and issues is most important for achieving a sense of high overall quality of life. This varies across individuals. In other words, neither psychological functioning nor quality of life is a fixed phenomenon, and they are highly personal.

The most common theoretical model used to describe the individual's adaptation process is Kübler-Ross's (1970) five-stage model of grief. Her model describes the emotional reactions (denial, isolation, anger, bargaining, depression) and the coming to terms with (acceptance of) dying and death. According to the model, the emotional reactions disrupt the individual's psychic equilibrium. To restore it, the person has to pass through stages such as the shock stage, the reaction stage, and the working-through stage and, finally, to reach the new orientation stage. However, no empirical studies support stage models among people with HIV (Hoffman, 1991). The stage-crisis model runs the risk of being perceived in a normative and/or hierarchical way. It tends to give the impression that there is a "right" or "normal" way to react or respond to a threat or that one approach is "better" or more "mature" than others. For those people with HIV who believe that they are not reacting in the "right" way, this may evoke feelings of guilt or of being abnormal.

We would also argue that the stage model approach does not do justice to the complexity of psychological and social mechanisms involved in the adaptation processes. We therefore suggest a theoretical framework in which the HIV adaptation processes are viewed as a spiral model considering the reoccurring character of HIV-related threats and psychological issues (Nilsson Schönnesson & Ross, 1999). Further, we argue that HIV adaptation processes can be understood as a function of psychological metabolism; in other words, metabolizing is necessary to achieve adaptation (Nilsson Schönnesson, 1992). The concept of metabolizing is used here as a metaphor to describe an individual's active (more or less consciously) internal process of coming to grips with a given HIV threat or psychological issue. Every time the person is confronted with such an issue, it may evoke psychological and cognitive chaos accompanied by a range and often a combination of emotions. The extent to which the individual's psychological equilibrium and sense of self are threatened and manifested in psychological distress is dependent on the person's life history, personality, and current life context. Based on life history and personality, the individual develops a repertoire of HIV-related psychological, social, and cognitive tools. By means of these tools and one's personality, the actual threat and/or psychological issue and its concomitant emotions are metabolized cognitively and mentally (incorporated, contained, and digested). The aim of psychological metabolism is to bring an ordering out of the chaos, and in that way to restore the disrupted equilibrium and consequently minimize feelings of psychological suffering. However, the person's metabolizing is not always constructive in terms of reducing the chaotic scenario. Regardless of the "success" of the psychological metabolism, it has to be kept in mind that a given metabolizing makes sense and can be understood within the context of the individual's life conditions.

Yet, the individual HIV adaptation process is complicated by the fact that the self, which plays an important role in the adaptation process, may be more or less destabilized by, among others, the HIV-related threats and issues. Therefore, the individual may have to struggle more or less simultaneously not only with adapting to HIV threats and psychological issues but also with restoring his or her shattered self. We therefore suggest that the HIV-disease adaptation processes interact with the self-adaptation processes.

The Self Context

Self psychology offers a useful psychodynamic bridge between the physical, social, and sexual consequences and the intrapsychic effects of HIV. The self, which is the third part of the individual's psychological landscape, can be viewed as a filter through which HIV-related threats and psychological issues are mediated and understood. It is important to remember that many gay men become more susceptible to the attack of HIV because of a vulnerable cohesive self (more or less poor self-image, a sense of inadequacy, a low self-esteem) that antedates their HIV diagnosis. This is a result of, among other things, psychological interpersonal difficulties during childhood and adolescence and social antigay attitudes and values (homophobia) and their internalization.

Various psychological stressors compromise the self, and the consequence is a more or less shattered self. The *wasting disease* is one psychological stressor. As stated before, the body is an integral part of the self. Thus, when HIV attacks the body's immune system, it also assails the individual's psychological immune system, the self, which has a psychological life-giving function.

Bearing in mind the drama of the HIV disease scenario and all of its adaptational tasks and challenges, it is not surprising that people with HIV may, at least sometimes, experience an imbalance between the burdens and their available resources and subsequently various degrees of *mood distress.* Such an unbalanced mode of living may contribute to destabilizing the self.

A third psychological stressor on the self is the potential *external and internal HIV persecutors.* The former refers to the potential stigmatizing and rejecting environment. But the individual may also become his or her own, internal, persecutor. He or she may internalize the negative societal attitudes toward HIV (just as the gay man internalizes the societal antigay attitudes), and thus they become more or less integral parts of the individual's self. The negative HIV image haunts the individual in terms of psychological persecutors such as guilt, shame, self-blame, degradation, and devaluation. The individual may also perceive as persecutors feelings of, among others, anxiety, helplessness, powerlessness, and hopelessness. Both the external and internal HIV-related persecutors thus threaten the self with destabilization.

The self can also be destabilized in that the HIV disease may function as a "radar" of *psychological conflicts,* for example, in relation to intimacy and self issues in terms of mirroring needs.

Vulnerability to the psychological stressors differs across people and may change over time, and so does their impact on the self. Thus, the self may oscillate between a shattered and a restored self over time. The ways in which individuals perceive, approach, and adapt to the psychological stressors depend on a variety of psychological, cognitive, and social factors.

THE HIV SCENARIO OVER THE DISEASE PHASES

The HIV drama changes its gestalt in the course of the disease progress over four phases (asymptomatic, mild symptomatic, severe symptomatic, and terminal) as a result of physical and HIV-related psychological processes and processes within the psychological landscapes. Our qualitative study of gay men with HIV (Nilsson Schönnesson & Ross, 1999) in psychotherapy/counseling showed that regardless of level of disease process, the HIV infection was experienced by the men as an insidious persecutor, but its character changed over time. In the asymptomatic disease phase, the persecutor was related to time, whereas in the mild symptomatic phase, the persecutor caused bewilderment, and in the severe symptomatic phase, it caused fear. The insidious persecutory character of the HIV disease was confirmed in the terminal phase. Regardless of disease phase, medication issues were discussed and reflected upon by the vast majority of the men.

The data also indicated that physical, psychological, and existential death-related themes and issues were of vital concern to the men during the whole course of the disease process. However, at the beginning of the disease process, death was talked about in an indirect way in terms of boundaries and finitude, whereas in the severe symptomatic and terminal phases, death was related to both indirectly (e.g., death symbols) and directly (e.g., longing for death). Fear of psychological death was salient in particular during the mild symptomatic phase. The gay men in the terminal phase oscillated between the realization of being mortal and the sense of being immortal, and they also experienced an ambivalent attitude toward death.

With respect to psychological issues, HIV represented limitations to the men regardless of where in the disease process they were. Control issues were more salient in the asymptomatic and the severe symptomatic disease phases, and experiences of aloneness in the terminal phase. In the first two disease phases, the men experienced a decline in their sexual interest and/or desire.

Although feelings of helplessness, hopelessness, and despair were encountered over the whole disease process, they were particularly salient in the severe symptomatic and terminal phases, as was hope.

The defense mechanism of denial was typical of the early phases of the disease, whereas the "death rescuer"-defense was in service in the severe symptomatic and terminal phases. In addition, avoidance, projection, and magical thinking were recognized in all four disease phases.

The shattered self was manifested in all phases except the terminal disease phase. The HIV infection appeared to trigger internal intimacy conflicts as well as mirroring needs in the asymptomatic and mild symptomatic phases. As stated earlier, the shattered self can be restored, which, among the gay men, was manifested as an increased sense of control, choice, vitality, and self-respect.

THE NEW MEDICATION AND ITS CONCERNS

Given the protease inhibitor and other drug combination therapies, to what extent does the "makeup" of the HIV scenario and its psychological landscapes change? Although empirical studies have yet to be conducted, based on our current clinical experiences, we suggest that much of what has been said above appears to be applicable today. We believe, however, that it is important to pay attention to which combination treatment group is under consideration. We propose that those who are newly diagnosed and asymptomatic may need to talk about their worries and uncertainties related to the medication (HIV threats). Also important to this group are the existential questions—the indirect manifestations of death such as limitations, restrictions, and boundaries. Although the new medication postpones HIV-related symptoms, it does not limit the infectiousness and consequent sexual boundaries. Thus, regardless of new HIV treatment, the individual faces sexual dilemmas (threats to sexual existence). Another potential existential concern is the fear of psychological death and aloneness by means of stigmatization and discrimination (threats to social existence). Further, we believe that the new combination treatments can never remove the traumatic element of the HIV diagnosis and its attack on the self. Therefore, we also must be alert to the extent to which the individual experiences a shattered self.

Those who are long-term nonprogressors or long-term survivors present a somewhat different clinical challenge. Many of them have repeatedly struggled with the psychological processes. Protease inhibitors are but one more area of uncertainty to them, another condition that fosters a reevaluation of their view of life. Those individuals who have cycled through episodes of health and illness for years and now have regained their health may feel psychologically depleted. They may feel depleted of the ability to reintegrate into health, despite feeling physically sound and even able to return to work and the psycho-social activities that they had abandoned.

SUMMARY

The issue of boundaries is central to the process of dealing with HIV disease. These boundaries are not only the nebulous ones between chronic and terminal disease, between illness and health, and between hope and despair, but the ultimate boundary that death presents and the existential concerns that all of these raise. Boundary issues may emerge in many guises: the ultimate boundary of life and death, sexual boundaries symbolized by the condom or limits on sexual practices, social boundaries marked by discrimination, boundaries of disclosure marked by the shadow of the closet door, and boundaries of physical functioning imposed by the response of the body to disease. Such boundaries are perceived as obstacles in the individual's life imposed by HIV, that is, external boundaries manifesting external control. On an existential level, external boundaries/control can be perceived as representing psychological death. Other boundaries such as those associated with disclosure, in relationships with lovers, families, friends, or health personnel and boundaries of the self are perceived as positive in that they impose order and structure, that is, internal control. As the disease progresses, the individual perceives increasingly that he or she is losing internal control, which is reflected in feelings of helplessness, hopelessness, and powerlessness. Overall, this is the wish to control the ultimate boundary, death. One of the stressors of living with HIV is the lack of precision of these boundaries and the uncertainty as to which side one may be on—as well as the need to set boundaries in many aspects of life and relationships. For this reason, living with HIV involves living on the boundaries.

CONCLUSION

HIV/AIDS raises major issues regarding sexuality and, indeed, has had the beneficial effect of making discussion of sexuality a more accepted phenomenon of the last decade of the twentieth century. However, most applied research has focused on prevention. In this chapter, we have attempted to deal equally with issues of sexuality in the infected, a literature that relies heavily on clinical psychology and psychotherapy because issues of sexuality and sexually related disease impact the entire lifestyle. It is clear that HIV has had a significant impact on sexual attitudes, beliefs, and behaviors, but it is also clear that for the uninfected, the changes are not sufficient to eliminate HIV transmission. HIV has been to the last two decades of the twentieth century what the "sexual revolution" of the late 1960s was to the decades before that: a major change of direction. Nevertheless, we must also remember that sexuality is associated with pleasure and power, among other factors, and that it is remarkably difficult to isolate it or attempt to change its direction independent of other aspects of the individual. The impact of HIV infection on the infected person illustrates this starkly.

REFERENCES

Allebeck, P., & Bolund, C. (1991). Suicides and suicide attempts in cancer patients. *Psychological Medicine, 21,* 976–984.

Bogaert, A.F., & Fisher, W.A. (1995). Predictors of university men's number of sexual partners. *Journal of Sex Research, 32,* 119–130.

Bolling, D.R. (1977). Prevalence, goals and complications of anal intercourse in a gynecologic population. *Journal of Reproductive Medicine, 19,* 120–124.

Carrier, J.M. (1985). Mexican male bisexuality. In F. Klein & J. Wolf (Eds.), *Bisexualities: Theory and research* (pp. 75–85). New York: Haworth Press.

Catalan, J., & Pugh, K. (1995). Suicidal behavior and HIV infection: Is there a link? *AIDS Care, 7,* S117–S121.

Chapman, S., & Hodgson, J. (1988). Showers in raincoats: Attitudinal barriers to condom use in high-risk heterosexuals. *Community Health Studies, 12,* 97–105.

Clement, U., Gramatikov, L., Laszig, P., et al., (1997). *Förderschewerpunkt AIDS, Bereich Sozialwissenschaften des BMFT/BMBT.* Methodische integration von empirischen Studien zur Lebensqualität, psychischen Verarbeitung und sexuellen Verhalten HIV-Infizierter. Absclussbericht. Psychosomatische Klinik, Universität Heidelberg.

Cochran, S.D., Mays, V.M., Ciarletta, J., Caruson, C., & Mallon, D. (1992). Efficacy of the theory of reasoned action in predicting AIDS-related risk reduction among gay men. *Journal of Applied Social Psychology, 22,* 1481–1501.

Coxon, A.P.M. (1996). *Between the sheets: Sexual diaries and gay men's sex in the age of AIDS.* London: Cassell.

Deren, S., Davis, W.R., Beardsley, M., Tortu, S., & Clatts, M. (1995). Outcomes of risk-reduction interventions with high-risk populations: The Harlem AIDS project. *AIDS Education and Prevention, 7,* 379–390.

Ekstrand, M.I., & Coates, T.J. (1990). Maintenance of safer sexual behaviors and predictors of risky-sex: The San Francisco men's health study. *American Journal of Public Health, 80,* 973–977.

Eysenck, H.J. (1978). *Sex and personality.* London: Abacus.

Fishbein, M., Chan, D.K.S., O'Reilly, K., Schnell, D., Wood, R., Beeker, C., & Cohn, D. (1992). Attitudinal and normative factors as determinants of gay men's intentions to perform AIDS-related sexual behaviors: A multi-site analysis. *Journal of Applied Social Psychology, 22,* 999–1011.

Forsberg, A.D., King, G., Delaronde, S.R., & Geary, M.K. (1996). Maintaining safer sex behaviors in HIV-infected adolescents with hemophilia: The Hemophilia behavioral evaluative intervention project committee. *AIDS Care, 8,* 629–640.

Godin, G., Savard, J.M., Kok, G., Fortin, C., & Boyer, R. (1996). HIV seropositive gay men: Understanding adoption of safe sex practices. *AIDS Education and Prevention, 8,* 529–545.

Goffman, E. (1963). *Stigma: Notes on the management of spoiled identity.* Englewood Cliffs, NJ: Prentice-Hall.

Gold, R.S., & Skinner, M.J. (1992). Situational factors and thought processes associated with unprotected intercourse in young gay men. *AIDS, 6,* 1021–1030.

Gold, R.S., Skinner, M.J., Grant, P.J., & Plummer, D.C. (1991). Situational factors and thought processes associated with unprotected intercourse in gay men. *Psychology and Health, 5,* 259–278.

Gold, R.S., Skinner, M.J., & Ross, M.W. (1994). Unprotected anal intercourse in HIV-infected and non-HIV-infected gay men. *Journal of Sex Research, 31,* 59–77.

Havens, J.F., Mellins, C.A., & Pilowsky, D. (1996). Mental health issues in HIV-affected women and children. *International Review of Psychiatry, 8,* 217–225.

Hays, R.B., Chauncey, S., & Tobey, L.A. (1990). The social support networks of gay men with AIDS. *Journal of Community Psychology, 18,* 374–385.

Hoffman, M.A. (1991). Counseling the HIV-infected client: A psychosocial model for assessment and intervention. *Counseling Psychologist, 19,* 467–542.

Holt, R., Court, P., Vedhara, K., Nott, K.H., Holmes, J., & Snow, M.H. (1998). The role of disclosure in coping with HIV infection. *AIDS Care, 10,* 49–60.

Humphreys, R.A.L. (1970). *Tearoom trade: A study of impersonal sex in public places.* London: Duckworth.

Janoff-Bulman, R. (1995). *Shattered assumptions. Towards a new psychology of trauma.* New York: Free Press.

Jenkins, J.J. (1974). Remember that old theory of memory? Well forget it! *American Psychologist, 29,* 785–795.

Kalichman, S.C., Johnson, J.R., Adair, V., Rompa, D., Multhauf, K., & Kelly, J.A. (1994). Sexual sensation seeking: Scale development and predicting AIDS-related behavior among homosexually active men. *Journal of Personality Assessment, 62,* 385–397.

Kastenbaum, R., & Aisenberg, R. (1972). *Psychology of death.* New York: Springer.

Kelaher, M.A., Ross, M.W., Rohrsheim, R., Drury, M., & Clarkson, A. (1994). Dominant situational determinants of sexual risk behaviour in gay men. *AIDS, 8,* 101–105.

Kelly, J.A., Murphy, D.A., Sikkemma, K.J., McAuliffe, T.L., Roffman, R.A., Solomon, L.J., Winett, R.A., Kalichman, S.C., & Community HIV Prevention Research Collaborative. (1997). Randomized, controlled community-level HIV prevention intervention for sexual-risk behavior among homosexual men in U.S. cities. *Lancet, 350,* 1500–1505.

Kelly, J.A., St. Lawrence, J.S., & Brasfield, T.L. (1990). Predictors of vulnerability to AIDS risk behavioral relapse. *Journal of Consulting and Clinical Psychology, 59,* 163–166.

Kelly, J.A., St. Lawrence, J.S., Diaz, Y.E., Stevenson, L.Y., Hauth, A.C., Brasfield, T.L., Kalichman, S.C., Smitt, J.E., & Andrew, M.E. (1991). HIV risk behavior reduction following intervention with key opinion leaders of a population: An experimental community-level analysis. *American Journal of Public Health, 81,* 168–171.

Kelly, J.A., St. Lawrence, J.S., Hood, H.V., & Brasfield, T.L. (1989). Behavioral intervention to reduce AIDS risk activities. *Journal of Consulting and Clinical Psychology, 57,* 60–67.

Kelly, J.A., St. Lawrence, J.S., Stevenson, L.Y., Hauth, A.C., Kalichman, S.C., Diaz, Y.E., Brasfield, T.L., Koob, J.J., & Morgan, M.G. (1992). Community AIDS/HIV risk reduction: The effects of endorsement by popular people in three cities. *American Journal of Public Health, 82,* 1483–1489.

Kinsey, A.C., Pomeroy, W.B., & Martin, C.E. (1948). *Sexual behavior in the human male.* Philadelphia: Saunders.

Kohut, H. (1971). *The analysis of the self.* New York: International Universities Press.

Koopman, C., Rotheram-Borus, M.J., Henderson, R., Bradley, J.S., & Hunter, J. (1990). Assessment of knowledge of AIDS and beliefs about AIDS prevention among adolescents. *AIDS Education and Prevention, 2,* 58–70.

Kübler-Ross, E. (1970). *On death and dying.* London: Tavistock.

Laumann, E.O., Gagnon, J.H., Michael, R.T., & Michaels, S. (1994). *The organization of sexuality: Sexual practices in the U.S.* Chicago: University of Chicago Press.

Lewis, L.A., & Ross, M.W. (1995). *A select body: The gay dance party subculture and the HIV/AIDS pandemic.* London: Cassell.

Lifton, R.J. (1980). The concept of the survivor. In J.F. Dimsdale (Ed.), *Survivors, victims, and perpetrators: Essays on the Nazi holocaust.* Washington, DC: Hemisphere.

Lowy, E., & Ross, M.W. (1994). "It'll never happen to me": Gay men's beliefs, perceptions and folk constructions of sexual risk. *AIDS Education and Prevention, 6,* 467–482.

Luna, G.C., & Rotheram-Borus, M.J. (1992, Fall). Street youth and the AIDS pandemic. *AIDS Education and Prevention,* (Suppl.), 1–13.

Nilsson Schönnesson, L. (1992). Traumatic and adaptation dimensions of HIV infection. In L. Nilsson Schönnesson (Ed.), *Sexual transmission of HIV infection: Risk reduction, trauma, and adaptation* (pp. 1–12) New York: Haworth Press.

Nilsson Schönnesson, L. (1995). Living with HIV: Dead end and/or turning point. In D. Friedrich & W. Heckman (Eds.). *AIDS in Europe: The behavioral aspect: General aspects* (Vol. 1, pp. 89–101). Berlin: Edn Sigma, Rainer Bahn Verlag.

Nilsson Schönnesson, L., & Dolezal, C. (1998). HIV-related risk factors among Swedish gay men. *Scandinavian Journal of Sexology, 1,* 51–62.

Nilsson Schönnesson, L., & Ross, M.W. (1999). *Coping with HIV infection: Psychological and existential responses in gay men.* New York: Plenum Press.

Nyamathi, A., Flaskerud, J., Keenan, C., & Leake, B. (1998). Effectiveness of a specialized vs. traditional AIDS education program attended by homeless and drug-addicted women alone or with supportive persons. *AIDS Education and Prevention, 10,* 433–446.

Offir, J.T., Fisher, J.D., Williams, S.S., & Fisher, W.A. (1993). Reasons for inconsistent AIDS-preventive behaviors among gay men. *Journal of Sex Research, 30,* 62–69.

Paul, J.P., Stall, R., & Davis, F. (1993). Sexual risk for HIV transmission among gay/bisexual men in substance abuse treatment. *AIDS Education and Prevention, 5,* 11–24.

Peterson, J.L., Coates, T.J., Catania, J.A., Hauck, W.W., Acree, M., Daigle, D., Middleton, B.L., & Hearst, N. (1996). Evaluation of an HIV risk reduction intervention among African American homosexual and bisexual men. *AIDS, 10,* 319–325.

Rabkin, J., Remien, R., & Wilson, C. (1994). *Good doctors, good patients: Partners in HIV treatment.* New York: NCM.

Reitman, D., St. Lawrence, J.S., Jefferson, K.W., Alleyne, E., Brasfield, T., & Shirley, A. (1996). Predictors of African American adolescents' condom use and HIV risk behavior. *AIDS Education and Prevention, 8,* 499–515.

Rogers, E. (1983). *Diffusion of innovations.* New York: Free Press.

Ross, M.W. (1983). *The married homosexual man: A psychological study.* London: Routledge & Kegan Paul.

Ross, M.W. (1986). *Psychovenereology: Personality and lifestyle factors in sexually transmitted diseases in homosexual men.* New York: Praeger.

Ross, M.W. (1988a). Attitudes toward condoms as AIDS prophylaxis in homosexual men: Dimensions and measurement. *Psychology and Health, 2,* 291–299.

Ross, M.W. (1988b). Prevalence of classes of risk behaviors for HIV infection in a randomly selected population. *Journal of Sex Research, 25,* 441–450.

Ross, M.W. (1990). Psychological determinants of increased condom use and safer sex in homosexual men: A longitudinal study. *International Journal of STD and AIDS, 1,* 98–101.

Ross, M.W. (1992). Attitudes toward condoms and condom use: A review. *International Journal of STD and AIDS, 3,* 10–16.

Ross, M.W., Fernández-Esquer, M.E., & Seibt, A. (1996). Understanding across the sexual orientation gap: Sexuality as culture. In D. Landis & R. Bhagat (Eds.), *Handbook of intercultural training* (2nd ed., pp. 414–430). Thousand Oaks, CA: Sage.

Ross, M.W., & Kelly, J.A. (1999). Interventions to reduce HIV transmission in homosexual men. In J.L. Peterson & R.J. Diclemente (Eds.), *Handbook of HIV prevention.* New York: Plenum Press.

Ross, M.W., & McLaws, M.-L. (1992). Subjective norms about condoms are better predictors of use and intention to use than attitudes. *Health Education Research, 7,* 335–339.

Ross, M.W., & Rosser, B.R.S. (1989). AIDS risks and education: A review. *Health Education Research, 4,* 273–284.

Ross, M.W., & Ryan, L. (1995). The little deaths: Perceptions of HIV, sexuality, and quality of life in gay men. In M.W. Ross (Ed.), *HIV/AIDS and sexuality* (pp. 1–21). New York: Harrington Park Press.

Ross, M.W., Tebble, W.E.M., & Viliunas D. (1989). Staging of psychological reactions to HIV infection in asymptomatic gay men. *Journal of Psychology and Human Sexuality, 2,* 93–104.

Ross, M.W., Wodak, A., Gold, J., & Miller, M.E. (1992). Differences across sexual orientation on HIV risk behaviours in injecting drug users. *AIDS Care, 4,* 139–148.

Ross, M.W., Wodak, A., Miller, M.E., & Gold, J. (1993). Sexual partner choice in injecting drug users from a "critical incident" measure: Its implications for estimating HIV spread. *Sexological Review, 1,* 77–92.

Sherr, L. (1995). Suicide and AIDS: Lessons from a case note audit in London. *AIDS Care, 7,* S109–S116.

Stall, R.D., Ekstrand, M.I., Pollack, I., McKusick, L., & Coates, T.J. (1990). Relapse from safer sex: The next challenge for AIDS prevention efforts. *Journal of Acquired Immune Deficiency Syndromes, 3,* 1181–1187.

Stall, R.D., McKusick, L., Wiley, J., Coates, T.J., & Ostrow, D.G. (1986). Alcohol and drug use during sexual activity and compliance with safe sex guidelines for AIDS: The AIDS behavioral research project. *Health Education Quarterly, 13,* 359–371.

St. Lawrence, J.S., Jefferson, K.W., Banks, P.G., Cline, T.R., Alleyne, E., & Brasfield, T. (1994). Cognitive-behavioral group intervention to assist substance-dependent adolescents in lowering HIV infection risk. *AIDS Education and Prevention, 6,* 425–435.

Taylor, S.E. (1983). Adjustment to threatening events: A theory of cognitive adaptation. *American Psychologist, 41,* 1161–1173.

Templer, D.I. (1976). Two-factor theory of death anxiety: A note. *Essence, 1,* 91–93.

Tomer, A., & Eliason, G. (1996). Toward a comprehensive model of death anxiety. *Death Studies, 20,* 343–365.

Traeen, B. (1992). Learning from the Norwegian experience: Attempts to mobilize the youth culture to fight the AIDS epidemic. *AIDS Education and Prevention,* (Suppl.), 43–56.

Treffke, H., Tiggeman, M., & Ross, M.W. (1992). The relationship between attitude, assertiveness and condom use. *Psychology and Health, 6,* 45–52.

Valdiserri, R.O., Pultman, T.V., & Curran, J.W. (1995). Community planning: A national strategy to improve HIV prevention programs. *Journal of Community Health, 20,* 87–100.

Weatherburn, P., Davies, P.M., Hickson, F.C.I., Hunt, A.J., Coxon, A.P.M., & McManus, T.J. (1993). No connection between alcohol use and unsafe sex among gay and bisexual men. *AIDS, 7,* 115–119.

Wingood, G.M., & DiClemente, R.J. (1998). Partner influences and gender-related factors associated with noncondom use among young adult African American women. *American Journal of Community Psychology, 26,* 29–51.

Wodak, A., Stowe, A., Ross, M.W., Gold, J., & Miller, M.E. (1995). HIV risk exposure of injecting drug users in Sydney. *Drug and Alcohol Review, 14,* 213–222.

Wright, M. (1998, January 12–15). *AIDS survivor syndrome and being HIV positive.* Paper presented at the second European Conference on the Methods and Results of Social and Behavioral Research on AIDS, Paris, France.

Yalom, I. (1980). *Existential psychotherapy.* New York: Basic Books.

CHAPTER 11

Adolescent Sexuality

ROBERTA L. PAIKOFF, ANTHONY McCORMICK,
and LYNDA M. SAGRESTANO

T he developmental period of adolescence has only recently been of interest to scholars who are focused on normative processes of behavior and development.[*] Prior to the early 1980s, the majority of work on adolescent development was undertaken from the perspective of clinical study and problem behavior, in part due to the influence of psychodynamic approaches to the study of this age period (A. Freud, 1948) as well as very early writings on adolescent turmoil and stress (Hall, 1904). These scholarly approaches have been substantiated to the lay public by a variety of media portrayals of adolescents as difficult and rebellious (with the "pathological" being "normal" for this age period) (A. Freud, 1948); indeed parents and others who interact with children do expect difficulty when asked about interactions with adolescents (Goodnow & Collins, 1990; Holmbeck & Hill, 1988).

Much of the work in modern adolescent psychology has been aimed at affirming or debunking stereotypic notions of adolescent storm and stress (Hill, 1980; Offer & Schonert-Reichl, 1993; Steinberg, 1987). This has been particularly true of much of the work in adolescent-family relationships (Holmbeck, Paikoff, & Brooks-Gunn, 1995; Laursen, Coy, & Collins, 1998; Paikoff & Brooks-Gunn, 1991; Steinberg, 1988, 1990) and in mood lability or depressive affect (Brooks-Gunn, Warren, Rosso, & Gargiulo, 1987; Buchanan, Eccles, & Becker, 1992). Work in adolescent sexuality, however, has lagged behind, and it is only recently that scholars have attempted to take a normative approach to issues of adolescent sexuality (Brooks-Gunn & Paikoff, 1993, 1997; Fine, 1988; D. Moore

[*]This work was completed with assistance from the National Institute of Mental Health, Office on AIDS, and the William T. Grant Foundation. We thank Marisela Ramirez and Michelle Whitaker for their assistance with manuscript preparation.

& Rosenthal, 1993; Paikoff, 1995a, 1997; Turner & Feldman, 1999). On some level, this is quite ironic, given that pubertal change, often considered the cornerstone of adolescence, is also a central factor in changing issues of sexuality from childhood to adolescence.

Pubertal changes mark the development of a reproductively mature individual, which is a central change from childhood to adulthood. These changes also create the major social and cultural reasons that adolescent sexuality has been considered primarily from the perspective of "problem behavior" in U.S. society, rather than as an aspect of normative development. In this chapter, we examine the major factors we believe contribute to normative development of sexuality in adolescence, as well as some of the social/cultural concerns or "problems" that have been considered, all from the perspective of understanding major developmental tasks that contribute to healthy sexual development during this age period. We also discuss efforts to promote health and to prevent risk with regard to consequences of adolescent sexuality (e.g., unintended pregnancies and sexually transmitted diseases). Finally, we briefly discuss possible clinical applications of this information.

HEALTHY SEXUAL DEVELOPMENT DURING ADOLESCENCE

Elsewhere, we have discussed four major tasks of healthy sexual development in adolescence (Brooks-Gunn & Paikoff, 1993): (1) experiences with pubertal changes, (2) coping with sexual arousal, (3) expression of sexual arousal (e.g., decisions with regard to sexual behaviors), and (4) for those youth who engage in intercourse behaviors, fertility management to maintain health and prevent early pregnancy. The majority of work conducted on healthy sexual development has fallen into areas 1, 3, and 4, and this review will concentrate on them.

EXPERIENCES WITH PUBERTAL CHANGES

The pubertal changes of adolescence are the most all-encompassing biological changes since the first year of life, leaving few if any cells in the body unaffected. Elsewhere (Connolly, Paikoff, & Buchanan, 1996), we have defined puberty as a multifaceted process including multiple overlapping events, ranging from biological processes (e.g., hormonal and physiological changes) to the physical and social changes that are visible to others.

The hormonal changes of puberty complete a maturational process begun prior to birth (e.g., during gestation). By midgestation, the area of the brain that directs pubertal development (within the hypothalamus) is already fully developed. In girls, gonadotropins (follicle-stimulating hormone [FSH] and luteinizing hormone [LH]) surge and the ovary functions at a pubertal level for the first few months after birth; these functions are then suppressed to a very low level until the endocrinological changes begin, toward the end of childhood. In boys, gonads (sex organs) are secreting androgens during the fetal period. The androgens are responsible for development of male internal and external organs (Brooks-Gunn & Reiter, 1990). Levels of all sex hormones are found in both boys and girls; amounts of different hormones contribute to the development of male versus female genitalia.

Initial hormonal changes of puberty begin between 6 and 8 years of age in normal boys, and involve increased secretion of dehydroepiandrosterone (DHEA), dehydroepiandrosterone sulfate (DHEAS), and other androgens. The process is called adrenarche, as these secretions originate in the adrenal gland. The precise reason these hormonal secretions begin when they do is not clear, although adrenocorticotropic hormone (ACTH) and the other hormones discussed above do enhance androgen production. After adrenarche, more visible secondary sex changes begin to occur, such as development of axillary and pubic hair. In addition, other physical changes associated with maturity, such as increased body odor, facial skin oiliness/acne, and a brief acceleration of bone growth (e.g., adolescent height spurt) and maturation (Kletter & Kelch, 1993; Parker, 1991), begin shortly thereafter. A couple of years after adrenarche occurs, gonadarche (increases in the secretion of gonadotropin and a reactivation of the hypothalamic-pituitary-gonadotropin-gonadal axis, which has been dormant since early infancy) occurs. Although adrenarche precedes gonadarche, no causal relationship between the two has been found.

The majority of sexual reproductivity changes of puberty for both genders begin due to maturation of the central nervous system (CNS), which allows for pulsatile secretion in sleep of gonadotropin-releasing hormone (GRH) by the hypothalamus. Pubertal bone age is a far better predictor of CNS maturity than chronological age; body mass and nutrition also contribute to CNS maturity. Indeed, most cross-cultural differences in pubertal development can be linked on some level to these physical differences (given that the age at which puberty begins has been getting progressively younger over time, and tends to be younger in Western, more developed, and wealthier cultures) (Brooks-Gunn & Reiter, 1990). One consistent cross-ethnic difference that is likely linked to these changes as well is the earlier pubertal age of African American children relative to White children. This change is consistent with the earlier developmental timetables of African American youth relative to White youth more generally (C. C. Bell, personal communication, September 20, 1995). Maturity of the CNS impels GRH's secretion of LH and FSH (Rosenfield, 1991), both of which are also secreted in nighttime pulsatile surgings. Ultimately, these secretions result in increased production of the gonadal hormones (primarily, testosterone in the testes and estrogen in the ovaries).

The visible signs of puberty have been well documented in the literature (Marshall & Tanner, 1970; Tanner, 1971; Tanner, Whitehausen, & Takaishi, 1966). For both boys and girls, physical changes include a time of rapid growth in height (the "adolescent growth spurt"), as well as changes in the proportion and distribution of fat and muscle (for boys, this is generally an increase in muscle; for girls, an increase in fat) and skin changes (oiliness, acne). During the adolescent growth spurt, the velocity of height growth is about doubled for approximately one year, with the peak height velocity at about 10.5 centimeters a year for boys, and 9 centimeters a year for girls. Timing of pubertal events can vary widely across individuals and cultures, but on average, girls' peak height velocity occurs about two years before that of boys.

Other physical changes at puberty (and those most directly relevant to adolescent sexuality) are those that signal reproductive maturity, both in terms of development of primary sexual characteristics (development of the genitalia and ovaries) and secondary sexual characteristics (such as facial or axillary hair and breast growth). Although onset of puberty and rate of pubertal change vary substantially for youth, the sequence of pubertal events is generally quite similar within genders. For boys, growth of the testes and scrotum are among the first signs of puberty, with slight growth of the pubic hair occurring shortly thereafter. Approximately one year later, the growth spurt and penile growth occur. Initial spermarche (first ejaculation of seminal fluid) occurs approximately two years after the initial physical signs of puberty. The appearance of axillary hair is a relatively late event in puberty, and it occurs along with the beginning of facial hair growth (Brooks-Gunn & Reiter, 1990; Connolly et al., 1996; Tanner, 1971).

For girls, thelarche (breast budding or beginning of breast growth) is usually the initial physical sign of pubertal growth. Pubarche (growth of pubic hair) follows shortly thereafter for most girls, although in one-fifth to one-third of girls, breast budding follows pubic hair growth (Brooks-Gunn & Reiter, 1990; Tanner, 1971). The uterus, vagina, labia, and clitoris develop at approximately the same time as the breast, and axillary hair generally appears approximately one year after pubic hair. Menarche (the onset of menstrual periods) is a relatively late event of puberty, and almost always occurs during the deceleration of the growth spurt. Initial menstrual cycles are irregular, with approximately half anovulatory (in which no egg is produced) during the first two years of menstruation. The majority of girls will establish regular menstrual periods by about two years after menarche first occurs (Rosenfield, 1991; Tanner, 1971).

As mentioned earlier, there is substantial variability in the rate of pubertal change, as well as the timing of the onset of puberty and association among various pubertal events (Brooks-Gunn & Reiter, 1990; Petersen & Taylor, 1980; Tanner, 1971). For boys, it may take anywhere from 2 to 5 years for genitalia to develop fully and still be within the normal range. For girls, it may take anywhere from 1.5 to 6 years to progress through the changes of puberty and still be within the normal range. Why some adolescents take a very short time to pass through puberty and others a very long time is not known; however, it is hypothesized that this may be related to the integration of hormones that control the events of puberty within the individual (Rosenfield, 1991; Tanner, 1971).

Psychological responses to pubertal change have been extensively studied, especially with regard to girls (Brooks-Gunn & Ruble, 1982; Brooks-Gunn & Warren, 1985, 1988; Brooks-Gunn et al., 1987; Brooks-Gunn & Zahaykevich, 1989; Petersen & Taylor, 1980; Petersen, Tobin-Richards, & Boxer, 1983; Richards, Boxer, Petersen, & Albrecht, 1990). In general, responses to pubertal change have been more positive than would be expected from a "storm and stress" or "pathology" perspective. Although responses range from the negative to the positive, most young people report neutral to more positive reactions to particular pubertal changes, although girls do report more dissatisfaction with their bodies overall than do boys (Attie, Brooks-Gunn, & Petersen, 1990). Negative experiences postmenarche have been linked to feeling unprepared for menarche, experiencing early maturation relative to peers, and receiving negative information from others (Brooks-Gunn & Reiter, 1990; Brooks-Gunn & Ruble, 1982; Ruble & Brooks-Gunn, 1982). Pubertal changes are seldom discussed with others (this is particularly true for changes in secondary sex characteristics) (Brooks-Gunn & Zahaykevich, 1989). Few studies have focused specifically on how adolescents do communicate with others regarding these physical changes. However, in one study, young women reported that out of all their social interactions, parents were most likely to tease them about their developing bodies; their primary response was anger (Brooks-Gunn & Zahaykevich, 1989).

Pubertal status (e.g., the physical changes of puberty) has been distinguished from pubertal timing (one's maturational status relative to one's peers), with more overall links between psychological functioning and timing rather than status. In general, early maturation has been linked to increased risk of behavioral problems for both boys and girls (Duncan, Ritter, Dornbusch, Cross, & Carlsmith, 1985; Magnusson, 1988; Magnusson, Stattin, & Allen, 1985) and to eating problems in girls (Graber, Brooks-Gunn, Paikoff, & Warren, 1994). In addition, early physical maturation has been linked to earlier onset of sexual activity for girls (Udry & Billy, 1987), whereas hormonal factors have been linked to early onset of sexual activity for boys (Udry, Talbert, & Morris, 1986).

Extensive research has been conducted with regard to the impact of pubertal change on parent-child relationships, with mixed findings (Holmbeck et al., 1995; Laursen, Coy, & Collins, 1998; Paikoff & Brooks-Gunn, 1991). Although numerous studies have reported relatively slight increases in conflict and emotional distance between parents and children at puberty, larger scale meta-analyses have failed to detect these effects (Holmbeck & Hill, 1991; Laursen et al., 1998; Paikoff & Brooks-Gunn, 1991; Steinberg, 1987, 1989, 1990). Findings suggest that conflict, where it does exist, may be most pronounced for mothers and daughters in White, two parent, middle-class families (Holmbeck & Hill, 1991; Paikoff & Brooks-Gunn, 1991). In a recent study of urban, African American families (primarily female-headed and one-parent), we found these differences to be more pronounced for mothers and sons, suggesting that contextual and family structural factors are likely to influence gender-based findings in this area (Sagrestano, McCormick, Paikoff, & Holmbeck, 1999). In general, parent-child conflicts in this area have been thought of as implying autonomy bids or issues of separation; gender-based differences may imply particular cultural beliefs about restriction of activities based on gender, due to concerns over sexuality or other health risks (e.g., gender intensification hypotheses) (see Lynch, 1983; Sagrestano et al., 1999).

In summary, the literature to date suggests that adaptation to pubertal changes (particularly in terms of the timing of these changes) may be important during the adolescent years, especially with regard to short-term psychological and behavioral issues. Problem behaviors have more often been considered in this arena than more normative behaviors, and this is the lens through which adolescent sexuality has most often been examined. Few longitudinal studies have been conducted, but those that have underscore the importance of pubertal timing in certain areas of psychological functioning at least through early adulthood (Graber et al., 1994) and perhaps for the longer term as well (Peskin, 1967).

COPING WITH SEXUAL AROUSAL

Although it is clear that sexual arousal increases and becomes more conscious after pubertal changes occur, very little research has been conducted on normative processes of sexual arousal among adolescents. As in many areas of pubertal development, the experiences of girls and boys likely diverge, with girls reluctant to acknowledge feelings of arousal, and boys likely to discuss these issues only in joke form and not with regard to their own feelings (Brooks-Gunn & Paikoff, 1993). A factor seldom mentioned in consideration of coping with feelings of sexual arousal is the object of sexual desire. By the time they reach middle childhood or the late elementary school years, the majority of youth are aware of sexual or romantic feelings toward same-sex individuals, other-sex individuals, individuals of both sexes, or no individuals (Paikoff & Brooks-Gunn, 1994). Many children and young adolescents engage in playful sexual behavior with persons of the same sex, but do not later report feelings of sexual attraction to same-sex individuals. Sexual play with both same- and other-sex partners during childhood is considered part of the normative process of sexual development, and probably reflects a healthy expression of children's curiosity about their genitals. We are not aware of any prospective data on the development of sexual identity (Boxer & Cohler, 1989; Paikoff & Brooks-Gunn, 1994; Savin-Williams, 1990).

EXPRESSION OF AROUSAL: SEXUAL BEHAVIORS DURING ADOLESCENCE

Normative sexual behaviors for adolescents include the range of sexual behaviors in which adults engage, from kissing to petting to various forms of vaginal, oral, and anal intercourse. However, the majority of information available on the sexual behavior of adolescents focuses on the behaviors that have been considered of concern to the larger social culture: in particular, heterosexual intercourse behavior, pregnancy, and sexually transmitted disease rates. Elsewhere (Sagrestano & Paikoff, 1997), we have written extensively about these behaviors in conjunction with the goals of *Healthy People 2000* (U.S. Department of Health and Human Services [DHHS], 1991). The majority of year 2000 goals set out for American youth (delaying onset of sexual behavior, reducing adolescent pregnancy, increasing contraceptive use) have not yet been achieved in the late 1990s.

The number of youth initiating sexual behavior has increased over the past decade, and studies indicate that although African American youth (particularly males) are likely to be earliest in onset of these behaviors (followed by Hispanics, Whites, and Asians) (D. Moore & Erickson, 1985), the gap between ethnicities is narrowing as White youth and females of all ethnicities begin sexual activity at younger ages (Brooks-Gunn & Furstenberg, 1989; Hayes 1987; Sagrestano & Paikoff, 1997). Urban minority youth have been most intensively studied in this area, in part due to the focus on "problems" of early sexual behavior and the tendency of investigators to focus on minority youth when problematic development or pathology is of interest (Gibbs, 1998; Spencer & Dornbusch, 1990). Studies suggest that the median age of onset of sexual activity for urban youth is 12 to 14 (Jemmott & Jemmott, 1992; Keller et al, 1991; S. R. Levy et al., 1995; S. R. Levy, Lampman, Handler, Flay, & Weeks, 1993; Stanton et al., 1994), suggesting that programs promoting abstinence must begin in the late elementary school years (Paikoff, 1997). Earlier onset of intercourse is linked to more frequent intercourse, more sexual partners, and earlier pregnancy (Center for Disease Control [CDC], 1991; Roosa, Tein, Reinholtz, & Angelini, 1997).

As mentioned earlier, very little information is available about ages at which young people undertake sexual behaviors prior to intercourse. Work that has been conducted does suggest ethnic differences in progression from earlier sexual experiences to intercourse, with African American youth likely to progress from kissing and petting directly to intercourse, whereas White youth may progress to intercourse after extensive sexual behaviors such as kissing and petting over time (Brooks-Gunn & Paikoff, 1993). In our work, we have examined links between other heterosocial behaviors and intercourse for urban African American pre- and young adolescents, finding that playing running and chasing games (where boys chase girls or vice versa) is associated with early exposure to sexual intercourse more than kissing or petting, most likely due to the higher frequency of occurrence of playing these games, with few preadolescent youth reporting more sexually oriented play in these situations (Paikoff, 1995a).

In addition, we have been interested in mapping out the progression from heterosocial to heterosexual behavioral development in urban, African American youth. We have developed a contextual model examining youth's progression from complete supervision and/or public play, to participation in situations of sexual possibility (e.g., heterosocial, private, unsupervised situations) (Paikoff, 1995a, 1997). In our study of urban, African American youth during the transition to adolescence, we found that although very few (2%) had engaged in sexual intercourse during the preadolescent period (ages 10–12), a significant minority (24%) had been in situations of sexual possibility. By early adolescence (12–14 years of age), the majority of youth had been in situations of sexual possibility, with a significant minority (21%: 30% of boys and 14% of girls) experiencing sexual intercourse (McCormick, Paikoff, Parfenoff, & Foster, 1998; Paikoff et al., 1997).

We also have been interested in adolescents' reasons for considering but not engaging in sexual behavior. In two samples of urban, African American youth, we have consistently found that youth report that they do not engage in sexual intercourse behaviors for a variety of individually based reasons (e.g., did not feel ready, were afraid, felt it wasn't right). Youth of both genders seldom report contextually based reasons (e.g., had no willing partner, were afraid of being "busted") as factors in choosing not to become involved in sexual intercourse behaviors (Paikoff, McCormick, McCormick, McKay, & McKinney, 1998). These results suggest that interventions may need to aim at changing *contexts* so that they are more facilitative of delaying sexual intercourse behavior and bolster individually based beliefs that are already present for many youth.

Although adolescents are having sex at earlier and earlier ages, rates of adolescent pregnancy have decreased (though not to the levels suggested by DHHS), and contraceptive use has increased among youth (Sagrestano & Paikoff, 1997). When sexually experienced youth are considered, 9% of 14-year-olds, 18% of 15- to 17-year-olds, and 22% of 18- to 19-year-olds become pregnant each year. These rates stand in sharp contrast to many other Western cultures, where views regarding adolescent sexuality diverge substantially from our own (Alan Guttmacher Institute, 1994; Brooks-Gunn & Paikoff, 1997). Much has been written about the more open Western societies and their lower teenage pregnancy rates and higher contraceptive usage (Alan Guttmacher Institute, 1994). Clearly, cultural factors heavily influence youth's sexual and decision-making behaviors and are among the most all-encompassing (and therefore most difficult) such influences to change, as they involve shifts in both public policy and overall cultural mores. Rates increase with age due to both increased fecundity (reproductive maturity) and more frequent intercourse among older teens. As with early onset of sexual experience, African American adolescents are most likely to become pregnant, followed by Hispanic and White adolescents, mirroring differential rates of sexual experience across ethnic groups.

Whereas teenage pregnancy has often been the focus of study with regard to teenage sexuality (particularly among minority youth) (Paikoff, 1995a, 1995b, 1997; Spencer & Dornbusch, 1990), limited data have considered the male role (e.g., adolescent fathers, and men who impregnate teenagers). Studies have consistently suggested that teenage girls are impregnated by men, on average, five years their senior (Males & Chew, 1996), and a majority of these fathers are over 18 regardless of the age of the woman (Alan Guttmacher Institute, 1994; Henshaw, 1992). This statistic raises a couple of concerns. First and foremost, it is likely that many teenaged girls are engaging in acts of intercourse that society would designate as statutory rape. It remains unclear whether this legal designation is relevant, particularly at older ages, because so little is known about teenagers' understanding of their sexual experiences and their decision-making abilities vis-à-vis adults in this arena (Beyth-Morom & Fischhoff, 1997; Brooks-Gunn & Paikoff, 1993; Paikoff, 1995a). Second, when considered in tandem with rates of sexual activity discussed earlier, the statistic is difficult to reconcile; that is, if more teenage males than females are sexually experienced, why are fewer males impregnating young women? It is possible that teenage boys are sexually involved either with younger girls who have not reached reproductive maturity or with older girls who sexually initiate them. In either case, these acts may be considered statutory rape as well (with boys either as victims or victimizers). Little is known about the potential psychological effects of early sexual experience that is societally defined as rape or coercion but perceived by the child or young adolescent as consensual.

The majority of teenage pregnancies, including those among married teens, are unintended (Alan Guttmacher Institute, 1994; Henshaw, 1992). Approximately 50% of these pregnancies are resolved by childbirth, with 14% miscarrying and 35% being terminated. When teenagers give birth, they are likely to experience disruption or cessation of education (Upchurch & McCarthy, 1990) and fewer employment opportunities (Hayes, 1987); their offspring are likely to face increased health and developmental risks (Ketterlinus, Henderson, & Lamb, 1990; Rosenthal, 1993) and more adjustment problems over time (Furstenberg, Brooks-Gunn, & Morgan, 1987). These problematic outcomes, however, are highly associated with factors such as poverty and related issues, such as access to health care (Coley & Chase-Lansdale, 1999; Hayes, 1987), and over the long term (e.g., 10 to 15 years post-childbirth), substantial diversity exists in outcomes for teenage mothers (Coley & Chase-Lansdale, 1999; Furstenberg et al., 1987).

FERTILITY MANAGEMENT

From both a societal perspective and from the perspective of most adolescents themselves, teenage pregnancies and sexually transmitted diseases are unwanted sequelae to early sexual involvement. The majority of youth do make some effort to protect themselves from unintended pregnancy, but few do so in a way that ensures such protection, and still fewer in a way that ensures protection from sexually transmitted disease as well as pregnancy (Sagrestano & Paikoff, 1997). Although the majority (80%) report using some form of contraceptive at last intercourse (DHHS, 1991), only approximately 50% report using condoms. A minority of youth, approximately one-third, report that they use contraceptives all the time (DHHS, 1991); such inconsistency in use is particularly problematic when sexually transmitted diseases are considered. Adolescents who do not use contraceptives at first intercourse are more likely than those who do to become pregnant, suggesting that use at first intercourse may serve as a marker for more consistent use (Roosa, Tein, Reinholtz, & Angelini, 1997). Links between contraceptive use and age (within the adolescent age range) are not consistently documented, although several studies report that youth who begin sexual activity at an earlier age are less likely to use contraception (CDC, 1991).

In summary, much of the demographic work undertaken to date helps us to portray normative adolescent sexual behaviors with regard to intercourse, pregnancy, and contraceptive use. Nevertheless, very little is known about the behavioral precursors to intercourse, the meaning of these behaviors to youth, and about healthy sexual development in homosexual youth (Brooks-Gunn & Paikoff, 1997; Paikoff, 1995b, 1997; Savin-Williams, 1990).

PROGRAMS TO ASSIST WITH HEALTHY SEXUAL DEVELOPMENT DURING THE ADOLESCENT YEARS

Given the cultural concerns over various health-compromising consequences that have been linked with adolescent sexual behavior (and determined "problems" by society), it is not surprising that many programs have been developed aimed at assisting young people during this time of development. Programs range from extremely broad and comprehensive ones that focus on multiple goals (of which delaying initial sexual onset and/or reducing adolescent pregnancy may be one or two of a long list) to targeted programs that emphasize only sexual behavior and perhaps focus specifically on one or two targeted aspects of sexual behavior (e.g., delaying onset of sexual behavior, decreasing rates of sexually transmitted disease or pregnancy). The emergence of HIV/AIDS has dramatically effected the focus of many programs, which now emphasize delaying onset of sexual behavior, with very specific recommendations for contraceptive use to reduce risk of HIV/AIDS (Kirby, Barth, Leland, & Fetro, 1991; Kirby & DiClemente, 1994). In general, a distinction can be made between broad-based versus more targeted programs.

Broad-based approaches embed consequences of adolescent sexual behavior within larger contexts and provide a more comprehensive approach, viewing the underlying context as the true "problem" inherent in youth's development. Such programs attempt to change contexts under the assumption that if the context affords more nonrisky and attractive opportunities for youth, risky behaviors will decrease, due to an increasing set of reasons and motivations to delay early sexual experience (Sagrestano & Paikoff, 1997). Such programs may provide skills training in a variety of arenas, ranging from academic skills to career planning and job placement (Allen, Philliber, Herrling, & Kuperminc,

1997; Hunter-Geboy, Peterson, Casey, Hardy, & Renner, 1985; Jollah & Alston, 1988; Philliber & Allen, 1992; Sipe, Grossman, & Milliner, 1988). Some such programs also include even more personalized services, such as counseling (Philliber & Allen, 1992; Sipe et al., 1988), family work (Nicholson & Postrado, 1992), and direct discussion of fertility-related issues (Jollah & Alston, 1988; Sipe et al., 1988).

Do such broad-based programs assist with the targeted outcomes of delaying initial sexual activity and promoting responsible sexual behavior? Evaluations of these programs tend to be less rigorously and meticulously conducted than basic evaluation research standards would dictate (Card, Peterson & Greeno, 1992; Dryfoos, 1990; Kelly, Murphy, Sikkemma, & Kalichman, 1993; K. Moore, Miller, Glei, & Morrison, 1995; Oakley, Fullerton, & Holland, 1995; Zabin & Hirsch, 1987), partly due to the nature of the programs and the outcomes themselves. In general, broad-based programs utilize a model that specifies long-term outcomes but are less likely to include funds for long-term evaluation. Evaluation that has been conducted, however, has found a number of such programs do reduce teenage pregnancy (Berrueta-Clement, Schweinhart, Barnett, Weikart, & Epstein, 1984; Jollah & Alston, 1988; Nicholson & Postrado, 1992; Philliber & Allen, 1992) and increase effective contraceptive use (Jollah & Alston, 1988; Nicholson & Postrado, 1992; Sipe et al., 1988). Recent partnerships between agencies delivering programs and research institutions and companies have resulted in more comprehensive evaluations of some of these programs as well, with positive results (Allen et al., 1997).

More targeted programs, in contrast, focus essentially on sexual behavior and rely on models that suggest that the best way to change behavior is to change the individual, so that the context becomes less and less relevant, as the individual finds himself or herself equipped with skills to respond positively to challenges regardless of context. Targeted programs include the traditional school-based sex education programs (as well as other programs that are school- or agency-based and focus on sexuality) and school-based health clinics. These programs generally operate from a social psychology or social-cognitive model, and work to improve knowledge regarding sexual reproduction, contraception, pregnancy, and sexually transmitted disease, as well as to improve problem-solving and behavioral refusal skills with regard to risky sexual situations (Howard & McCabe, 1992; Jemmott, Jemmott, & Fong, 1992; Kirby et al., 1991; S. L. Levy et al., 1994; S. R. Levy et al., 1995; Pittman & Govan, 1986; St. Lawrence et al., 1995; Schinke & Gilchrist, 1984; Walter & Vaughan, 1993). Few of these programs are delivered in the format of the traditional, classroom lecture, with most relying on more innovative formats such as small group discussion (Stern, 1988), personal counseling (Stern, 1988; Zabin, Hirsch, Smith, Streett, & Hardy, 1986), role playing (Schinke & Gilchrist, 1984), and clinic-based intervention and provision of family planning services (Edwards, Steinman, Arnold, & Hakanson, 1980; Galavotti & Lovick, 1989; Kirby, 1991; Zabin & Hirsch, 1987).

Importantly, virtually no evidence exists to suggest that such school-based programs increase adolescent sexual activity or result in more risk-taking behaviors (Grunseit, Kippax, Aggleton, Baldo, & Slutkin, 1997; Kirby, 1991). A number of programs have reported increases in knowledge and more positive attitudes (Jemmott, Jemmott, & Fong, 1992; McKay, Paikoff, & McKinney, 1998; Stern, 1988; Walter & Vaughan, 1993), delay of the onset of sexual intercourse behavior (Howard & McCabe, 1992; Pittman & Govan, 1986; Zabin & Hirsch, 1987), increased intentions to use condoms (Jemmott, Jemmott, Spears, Hewitt, & Cruz-Collins, 1992; S. R. Levy et al., 1995), increased contraceptive use (Galavotti & Lovick, 1989; Stern, 1988; St. Lawrence et al., 1995; Zabin & Hirsch, 1987), contact with fewer partners (Jemmott, Jemmott, & Fong, 1992), and decreased pregnancies (Zabin & Hirsch, 1987).

In addition to programs specifically aimed at reaching adolescents, some intervention and research programs have focused on examining familial factors, either in their role of influencing adolescent sexual development or for their possible ameliorative effect when included in an intervention program (Furstenberg, 1976; Jemmott, Jemmott, & Outlaw, 1998; Krauss & Goldsamt, 1998; Leland & Barth, 1993; Madison et al., 1998; Nathanson & Becker, 1986). Early work found that parents and older siblings have an important role to play in educating youth about sexual development; parent-child communication with specific value messages (even so vague as "If you're doing it with him, you better be using something") was associated with increased contraceptive use among teenagers (Fox & Inazu, 1980; Furstenberg, 1976). More recently, a series of intervention programs have been undertaken to promote health, delay initial onset of sexual behavior, and promote healthy use of contraceptives as appropriate, with the particular goal of involving families as educators of their children (DiLorio et al., 1998; Jemmott et al., 1998; Krauss, 1998; Madison et al., 1998) and of influencing more global family processes (such as communication, supervision, and monitoring) as well. Although much has been written about the growing importance to youth of peers and their beliefs systems, parents (or other trusted adults) remain primary in their role in socialization of value and belief systems throughout the adolescent and early adulthood period, highlighting the importance of parents' possessing accurate knowledge and the willingness to communicate with their children regarding sexuality and its potential consequences (Parfenoff & McCormick, 1997). Far less is known, however, about the potentially vital role parents or other trusted adults may play in setting an example of healthy adult sexual relationships and communicating to their offspring the joys, beauty, and healthy values of loving sexual relationships.

IMPLICATIONS FOR NORMATIVE DEVELOPMENT

Although programs have not been undertaken for their relevance to the study of normative development, findings from intervention research do have the potential to inform basic research and vice-versa (Sroufe & Rutter, 1984). In general, findings of evaluative interventions suggest that adolescent sexual behavior is somewhat malleable, both by programs that aim to change context and by programs that aim to ameliorate individual skills and problem-solving abilities. Probably both approaches are needed to provide the best opportunities for healthy development in terms of adolescent sexual well-being. More detailed information regarding healthy adolescent sexual development has not been forthcoming from evaluations to date; however, this is likely to change as more basic developmental researchers become involved in intervention evaluation (e.g., Allen et al., 1997; Paikoff & McKay, 1995). Indeed, in our own intervention work, instruments used for basic research purposes have been used in intervention adaptations as well; thus, we will have access to comparative, detailed data about youth's heterosocial and heterosexual experiences over time, which will provide much-needed baseline data as well as data on possible behavioral changes as a result of intervention (Paikoff & McKay, 1995; Paikoff et al., 1997).

It should be clear from the text so far, that although much is known about adolescent sexual behavior in certain areas, a review of knowledge to date still tells us very little about normative patterns of development in adolescence as they are relevant to understanding the development of healthy sexuality (Brooks-Gunn & Paikoff, 1993; Parfenoff, Paikoff, Brooks-Gunn, Holmbeck, & Jarrett, 1995). Indeed, reviews of the literature in this area tend to raise more questions than they can provide answers for. We still know very little about the ways in which adolescents construct their understanding and approach to sexuality, particularly at earlier ages (see Brooks-Gunn & Paikoff, 1997; D. Moore & Rosenthal, 1993; Turner & Feldman, 1999, for analyses of this issue in older adolescents and college students).

It is still the case that very few studies have examined adolescent sexual development in conjunction with more normative developmental issues, and thus very limited data exist on the interplay between sexual development and other processes, such as family and peer relationships. We are forced to rely on a discrete series of studies that address aspects of these issues but fail to present a complete picture. Based on intervention, basic science, and cross-cultural data, we are left with a strong role for both the individual and the context in determining healthy or less healthy adaptations to adolescent and young adult sexuality. Much more is known, however, about individually based factors that *result* from early sexual exploration and early pregnancy than those that lead to it (though this is changing as the need for more prospective study is recognized) (Paikoff, 1997; Parfenoff et al., 1995). The effect of context has been recognized and "blamed" for many of the problems we face with regard to adolescent sexuality, but few studies have mapped out the specific details of contexts that encourage healthy adolescent sexuality and those that are less positive (e.g., are there factors specific to sexuality in determining healthy contexts?). There remains much work to be done in creating a "whole person" view of healthy adolescent sexuality.

IMPLICATIONS FOR CLINICAL PRACTICE

Although not much substantial information is available in certain areas of adolescent sexuality, what is known leads to several areas of potential importance for clinicians working with pre- and young adolescents. On the most basic level, a full understanding of the age-related changes in sexual behavior is key to conducting a thorough intake interview and to assisting in determining initial health in social and sexual arenas. Although few clinical training programs undertake such comprehensive screenings, it seems important to minimally ascertain of new patients whether or not they have been sexually involved, particularly given the very young ages at which many youth initiate sexual intercourse behaviors (Jemmott, Jemmott, & Fong, 1992; S. L. Levy et al., 1994; Paikoff et al., 1997; Stanton et al., 1994). Such interviewing techniques might best be accomplished by beginning with an understanding of pubertal changes in the youth (e.g., asking about pubertal milestones that are accessible to the early adolescent, such as height, growth of secondary sexual characteristics, appearance), then moving to feelings about these changes, and more specifically to feelings about changes with regard to his or her own ideas regarding sexuality. One of the areas in which developmental studies could inform clinical efforts is a thorough examination of the research instruments used to discuss puberty and sexuality with pre- and young adolescents to phrase questions appropriately by age, race, and gender.

In general, age-related changes in pubertal development and sexual behavior must lead the thoughtful clinician to two somewhat conflicted approaches. The first is to ensure that these topics are raised at a relatively early age for youth (in almost every case, research dictates that these issues are of potential concern to youth at a significantly younger age than adults would perceive to be likely, or that clinicians will find comfortable). The second, however, is to ensure that youth who are not concerned with these issues or involved sexually (or who may be late physical maturers) do not feel pressured or belittled for their lack of experience or interest. It is certainly clear, based on existing empirical studies, that raising these issues into the consciousness of youth is unlikely to provoke sexual behavior that was not considered previously. However, the sensitive clinician will want to approach asking such questions from a nonjudgmental perspective with respect to both ends of the behavioral and developmental spectrum.

Although it is tempting to assume that certain youth may be at less risk than others (in particular, more affluent White suburban youth), recent data suggest that the sexual behavior of adolescents is becoming more rather than less similar across racial and socioeconomic lines (Brooks-Gunn & Furstenberg, 1989; Sagrestano & Paikoff, 1997). As mentioned earlier, few studies have been conducted regarding pre- and early adolescent sexual behavior; those that have almost always have drawn from inner-city minority populations as part of an intervention program (Jemmott & Jemmott, 1992; Keller et al., 1991; S. L. Levy et al., 1994; Paikoff et al., 1997; Stanton et al., 1994). Although this allows us to comment on minority samples, it does not allow us to assume that more affluent, majority samples would differ substantially from this group. In the absence of data to the contrary, it seems appropriate to proceed as discussed above for all adolescents, with particular wording perhaps more sensitive to specific age, gender, or racial/ethnic groups.

Issues of homosexuality and homoerotic feelings present further complications to clinical approaches to adolescent sexuality (Boxer, & Cohler, 1989; Savin-Williams, 1994, 1998; Savin-Williams & Diamond, 1999). Again, clinicians will need to be sensitive to the feelings of youth in considering how and when such topics are broached. Research reports have suggested that homosexual youth are more likely to experience symptoms of depression and suicidality (most likely due to their adaptation in a culture that perceives homosexuality quite negatively); however, specific methodological issues make interpretation of these studies problematic (Savin-Williams, 1994).

Homosexual and bisexual youth may be at risk for clinically significant problems such as running away, school-related troubles, substance abuse, prostitution, and suicide; it is likely that these problems are related to the significant life stressors of being homosexual or bisexual in a majority heterosexual youth culture (Savin-Williams, 1994, 1998). Thus, clinicians should be sensitive to potential life stressors in high-risk youth who are homosexual or bisexual, but should exercise caution in framing the problem as individually based without considering the substantial social and cultural factors operating for these youth.

Sexual identity is a personal and individual definition, and can be considered almost completely separately from sexual behavior. It is important for clinicians to distinguish between physical health concerns (which are enhanced by knowledge that an adolescent has participated in particular high-risk sexual behaviors) and psychological health concerns (which are more likely to stem from an individual's feelings about his or her sexual identity or sexual behaviors). These are especially important distinctions with regard to sexuality; for example, although many male youth may report engaging in anal intercourse with persons of the same sex, it may be that only a small subset of those youth will identify themselves as homosexual or bisexual (Savin-Williams & Diamond, 1999). Yet all of those youth will be at similar physical health risk, whereas the psychological concerns or risks may vary. For concerns with regard to physical health, it will be important to assess risk level quickly, as ongoing exposure to risk enhances the likelihood of early pregnancy or a potentially severe, or even fatal, sexually transmitted disease. More psychological concerns may be allowed to unfold more gradually (dependent on their relation to and the severity of psychological symptoms) and probably will be much thornier issues to tackle therapeutically. Unfortunately, the basic research literature provides very little guidance with regard to these issues.

What is the role of the clinician in treating an adolescent engaging in high-risk sexual behavior? In practice, the role surely varies dramatically, from no discussion of the issue (unless raised by the patient) to specific guidance and concerns regarding promotion of health and prevention of sexual health risk. Given the potentially fatal consequences of high-risk sexual behavior, those of us engaged in the study of basic sexual development would like to see clinicians take a more proactive role than is often the case, and to make recommendations regarding health and safety based solely and specifically on behavior rather than on morality or judgmental factors.

In certain cases, clinicians will be in conflict, given that their own religious, spiritual, or personal beliefs may preclude certain types of intervention (such as contraceptive use, or termination of an unintended pregnancy). It is fully understandable for clinicians to refrain from such advice giving, but perhaps most defensible to provide the patient with potential alternative referrals, so that all aspects of decision making consonant with the patient's belief system can be considered. In the opposite case (e.g., where patients' beliefs conflict with potential health goals), it may also be worth making referrals to clergy, or considering how behavior may be brought "in line" with religious or spiritual beliefs (e.g., because most religious beliefs that do not condone contraceptive use or pregnancy termination also do not condone premarital intercourse, it may be helpful to consider behavioral strategies that involve abstinence). For clinicians without personal concerns regarding such advice, recommendations of protective behaviors that ensure physical health as well as prevention of pregnancy (e.g., latex condoms), as well as assistance in negotiating personal safety (e.g., understanding that levels of physical risk vary with partners' past and current behaviors; communicating effectively with potential sexual partners) will be of particular assistance.

It is also of critical importance for clinicians to consider contextual factors in understanding particular behaviors of adolescence. Numerous social contextual factors influence whether or not adolescents become involved sexually and whether or not they are willing and able to take on the task of promoting their own health by preventing pregnancy and sexually transmitted disease (Alan Guttmacher Institute, 1994; CDC, 1991; Jemmott & Jemmott, 1992; Paikoff, 1997; Paikoff et al., 1997). It is clear that although individually based skills programs do work, they are most successful when potential contextual barriers to individual behavior are systematically addressed (Jemmott & Jemmott, 1992; Kirby, 1991). Thus, a full knowledge of when sexual behaviors occur and how the adolescent feels about them (e.g., does the adolescent perceive himself or herself to have choices regarding these behaviors, and how may such choices are seen as constrained?) will assist in choosing specific ways that behavioral health goals may be met.

A final clinical issue involves dealing with those youth who have already given birth or fathered children. Two things are clear from the literature on teenage childbearing: that childbirth and parenting are major stressors for many youth (and many adults, for that matter); and that substantial diversity exists in the long-term outcome of both teenage parents and their offspring.

For clinicians working with such youth, acknowledging potential stressors and helping youth problem-solve around these stressors to meet their own goals, as well as linking them to a variety of social services and programs they are eligible for, will be most helpful. To meet these goals, however, it is important for the clinician to get a thorough understanding of the factors that may influence outcomes in this particular situation (e.g., is the young person living with his or her own parents? Such arrangements have been found useful for relatively young teenage parents, but merely cause additional stress for older teenagers). A thorough and detailed knowledge both of the patient and of the scientific literature regarding factors that may influence outcomes for the patient will allow for more detailed treatment plans to be made and specific goals to be set and followed.

In conclusion, although much is known about adolescent sexuality, there is still substantial progress to be made, particularly in our understanding of the basic processes of normative development as they are interrelated with adolescent sexuality. It is only through understanding healthy and normative sexual development that we will be able to take the most sensible steps toward assisting youth where healthy sexual development has gone awry.

REFERENCES

The Alan Guttmacher Institute. (1994). *Sex and America's teenagers.* New York: Author.

Allen, J.P., Philliber, S., Herrling, S., & Kuperminc, G.P. (1997). Preventing teen pregnancy and academic failure: Experimental evaluation of a developmentally based approach. *Child Development, 64,* 729–742.

Attie, I., Brooks-Gunn, J., & Petersen, A.C. (1990). The emergence of eating problems: A developmental perspective. In M. Lewis & S. Miller (Eds.), *Handbook of developmental psychopathology* (pp. 409–420). New York: Plenum Press.

Berrueta-Clement, J., Schweinhart, L., Barnett, W., Weikart, D., & Epstein, A. (1984). *Changed lives: The effects of the Perry preschool programs on youths through age 19.* Ypsilanti, MI: High-Scope Educational Research Foundation.

Beyth-Morom, R., & Fischhoff, B. (1997). Adolescents' decisions about risks: A cognitive perspective. In J. Schulenberg, J.L. Maggs, & K. Hurrelmann (Eds.), *Health risks and developmental transitions during adolescence* (pp. 110–135). New York: Cambridge University Press.

Boxer, A.M., & Cohler, B.J. (1989). The life course of gay and lesbian youth: An immodest proposal for the study of lives. *Journal of Homosexuality, 17,* 315–355.

Brooks-Gunn, J., & Furstenberg, F.F., Jr. (1989). Adolescent sexual behavior. *American Psychologist, 44,* 249–257.

Brooks-Gunn, J., & Paikoff, R.L. (1993). "Sex is a gamble, kissing is a game": Adolescent sexuality and health. In S. Millstein, A.C. Peterson, & E. Nightingale (Eds.), *Promoting healthy behavior during adolescence* (pp. 180–208). New York: Oxford University Press.

Brooks-Gunn, J., & Paikoff, R.L. (1997). Sexuality and developmental transitions during adolescence. In J. Schulenberg, J. Maggs, & K. Hurrelmann (Eds.), *Health risks and developmental transitions during adolescence* (pp. 190–219). New York: Cambridge University Press.

Brooks-Gunn, J., & Reiter, E.O. (1990). The role of pubertal processes in the early adolescent transition. In S.S. Feldman & G.R. Elliott (Eds.), *At the threshold: The developing adolescent* (pp. 16–53). Cambridge, MA: Harvard University Press.

Brooks-Gunn, J., & Ruble, D.N. (1982). Menarche: Fact and fiction. In G.C. Hongtadarum, R. McCorkle, & N.F. Woods (Eds.), *The complete book of women's health* (pp. 52–58). Englewood Cliffs, NJ: Prentice-Hall.

Brooks-Gunn, J., & Warren, M.P. (1985). Measuring physical status and timing in early adolescence: A developmental perspective. *Journal of Youth and Adolescence,*14(3), 163–189.

Brooks-Gunn, J., & Warren, M.P. (1988). The psychological significance of secondary sexual characteristics in 9- to 11-year-old girls. *Child Development, 59,* 161–169.

Brooks-Gunn, J., Warren, M.P., Rosso, J., & Gargiulo, J. (1987). Validity of self-report measures of girls' pubertal status. *Child Development, 58,* 829–841.

Brooks-Gunn, J., & Zahaykevich, M. (1989). Parent-child relationships in early adolescence: A developmental perspective. In K. Kreppner & R.M. Lerner (Eds.), *Family systems and lifespan development* (pp. 223–246). Hillsdale, NJ: Erlbaum.

Buchanan, C.M., Eccles, J.S., & Becker, J.B. (1992). Are adolescents the victims of raging hormones? Evidence for activational effects of hormones on moods and behavior at adolescence. *Psychological Bulletin, 111,* 62–107.

Card, J.J., Peterson, J.L., & Greeno, C.G. (1992). Adolescent pregnancy prevention programs: Design, monitoring, and evaluation. In B.C. Miller, J.J. Card, R.L. Paikoff, & J.L. Peterson (Eds.), *Preventing adolescent pregnancy* (pp. 1–27). Newbury Park, CA: Sage.

Centers for Disease Control. (1991). *HIV/AIDS surveillance report.* Atlanta: Author.

Coley, R., & Chase-Lansdale, P.L. (in press). Teenage pregnancy. *American Psychologist.*

Connolly, S.D., Paikoff, R.L., & Buchanan, C.M. (1996). Puberty: The interplay of biological and psychosocial processes in adolescence. In G. Adams, R. Montemayor, & T. Gullota (Eds.), *Psychosocial development in adolescence: Advances in adolescent development* (Vol. 8). Newbury Park, CA: Sage.

DiLorio, C., Dudley, W., Childers, K., Resnicow, K., Manteuffel, B., Wang, T., Denzmore-Nwagbara, P., & Rodgers-Tillman, G. (1998, July). *Social cognitive predictors of maternal sex based communication with adolescents.* Paper presented at the NIMH Family & AIDS Conference, Washington, DC.

Dryfoos, J.G. (1990). *Adolescents at risk: Prevalence and prevention.* New York: Oxford University Press.

Duncan, P.D., Ritter, P.L., Dornbusch, S.M., Cross, R.T., & Carlsmith, J.M. (1985). The effects of pubertal timing on body image, school behavior, and deviance. *Journal of Youth and Adolescence, 14,* 227–235.

Edwards, L., Steinman, M., Arnold, K., & Hakanson, E. (1980). Adolescent pregnancy prevention services in high school clinics. *Family Planning Perspectives, 12,* 6–14.

Fine, M. (1988). Sexuality, schooling, and adolescent females: The missing discourse of desire. *Harvard Educational Review, 58*(1), 29–53.

Fox, G.L., & Inazu, J.K. (1980). Mother–daughter communication about sex. *Family Relations, 29,* 347–351.

Freud, A. (1948). *The ego and the mechanism of defence* (C. Baines, Trans.). New York: International Universities Press.

Furstenberg, F.F., Jr. (1976). Premarital pregnancy and marital instability. *Journal of Social Issues, 32,* 67–86.

Furstenberg, F.F., Jr., Brooks-Gunn, J., & Morgan, S.P. (1987). *Adolescent mothers in later life.* New York: Cambridge University Press.

Galavotti, C., & Lovick, C. (1989). School-based clinic use and other factors affecting adolescent contraceptive behavior. *Journal of Adolescent Health Care, 10,* 506–512.

Gibbs, J.T. (1998). High-risk behaviors in African American youth: Conceptual and methodological issues in research. In V.C. McLoyd & L. Steinberg (Eds.), *Studying minority adolescents* (pp. 55–86). Mahwah, NJ: Erlbaum.

Goodnow, J.J., & Collins, W.A. (1990). *Development according to parents: The nature, sources and consequences of parents' ideas.* Hillsdale, NJ: Erlbaum.

Graber, J.A., Brooks-Gunn, J., Paikoff, R.L., & Warren, M.P. (1994). Prediction of eating problems: An 8-year study of adolescent girls. *Developmental Psychology, 30,* 823–834.

Grunseit, A., Kippax, S., Aggleton, P., Baldo, M., & Slutkin, G. (1997). Sexuality education and young people's sexual behavior: A review of studies. *Journal of Adolescent Research, 12*(4), 421–453.

Hall, G.S. (1904). *Adolescence: Its psychology and its relations to physiology, anthropology, sociology, sex, crime, religion, and education* (Vol. 1). Englewood Cliffs, NJ: Prentice-Hall.

Hayes, C.D. (Ed.). (1987). *Risking the future: Adolescent sexuality, pregnancy, and childbearing* (Vol. 1). Washington, DC: National Academy of Sciences Press.

Henshaw, S.K. (1992). Abortion trends in 1987 and 1988: Age and race. *Family Planning Perspectives, 24,* 85–86.

Hill, J.P. (1980). *Understanding early adolescence: A framework.* Chapel Hill: University of North Carolina, Center for Early Adolescence.

Holmbeck, G.N., & Hill, J.P. (1988). Storm and stress beliefs about adolescence: Prevalence, self-reported antecedents, and effects of an undergraduate course. *Journal of Youth and Adolescence, 17,* 285–306.

Holmbeck, G.N., & Hill, J.P. (1991). Conflictive engagement, positive affect and menarche in families with seventh-grade girls. *Child Development, 60,* 130–148.

Holmbeck, G.N., Paikoff, R.L., & Brooks-Gunn, J. (1995). Parenting adolescents. In M. Bornstein (Ed.), *Handbook of parenting* (Vol. 1, pp. 91–118). Hillsdale, NJ: Erlbaum.

Howard, M., & McCabe, J.A. (1992). An information and skills approach for younger teens. In B.C. Miller, J.J. Card, R.L. Paikoff, & J.L. Peterson (Eds.), *Preventing adolescent pregnancy* (pp. 83–109). Newbury Park, CA: Sage.

Hunter-Geboy, C., Peterson, L., Casey, S., Hardy, L., & Renner, S. (1985). *Life planning education: A youth development program.* Washington, DC: Center for Population Options.

Jemmott, J.B., & Jemmott, L.S. (1992). Increasing condom-use intentions among sexually active Black adolescent women. *Nursing Research, 41,* 273–279.

Jemmott, J.B., Jemmott, L.S., & Fong, G.T. (1992). Reductions in HIV risk-associated sexual behaviors among black male adolescents: Effects of an AIDS prevention intervention. *American Journal of Public Health, 82,* 372–377.

Jemmott, J.B., Jemmott, L.S., Spears, H., Hewitt, N., & Cruz-Collins, M. (1992). Self-efficacy, hedonistic expectancies, and condom-use intentions among inner-city black adolescent women: A social cognitive approach to AIDS risk behavior. *Journal of Adolescent Health, 13,* 512–519.

Jemmott, L.S., Jemmott, J.B., & Outlaw, F. (1998, July). *Empowering mothers to save their children: Translation of research to benefit families.* Paper presented at the NIMH Family and AIDS Conference, Washington, DC.

Jollah, M., & Alston, S. (1988, November). *Mantalk: A pregnancy prevention program for teen males.* Paper presented at the annual meeting of the American Public Health Association, Boston.

Keller, S.E., Bartlett, J.A., Schleifer, S.J., Johnson, R.L., Pinner, E., & Delaney, B. (1991). HIV-relevant sexual behavior among a healthy inner-city heterosexual adolescent population in an endemic area of HIV. *Journal of Adolescent Health, 12,* 44–48.

Kelly, J.A., Murphy, D.A., Sikkemma, K.J., & Kalichman, S.C. (1993). Psychological interventions to prevent HIV infection are urgently needed: New priorities for behavioral research in the second decade of AIDS. *American Psychologist, 48,* 1023–1034.

Ketterlinus, R.D., Henderson, S.H., & Lamb, M.E. (1990). Maternal age, sociodemographics, prenatal health and behavior: Influences on neonatal risk status. *Journal of Adolescent Health Care, 11,* 423–443.

Kirby, D. (1991). School-based clinics: Research results and their implications for future research methods. *Evaluation & Program Planning, 14,* 35–47.

Kirby, D., Barth, R.P., Leland, N., & Fetro, J.V. (1991). Reducing the risk: Input on a new curriculum on sexual risk-taking. *Family Planning Perspectives, 23*(6), 253–263.

Kirby, D., & DiClemente, R.J. (1994). School-based interventions to prevent unprotected sex and HIV among adolescents. In R.J. DiClemente & J.L. Peterson (Eds.), *Preventing AIDS: Theories and methods of behavioral interventions* (pp. 117–139). New York: Plenum Press.

Kletter, G.B., & Kelch, R.P. (1993). Disorders of puberty in boys. *Adolescent Endocrinology, 22,* 455–477.

Krauss, B.J. (1998, July). *Destigmatizing HIV.* Paper presented at the NIMH Family and AIDS Conference, Washington, DC.

Krauss, B.J., & Goldsamt, L.A. (1998, July). *Helping mothers and fathers to communicate with their children about HIV-related risk.* Paper presented at the NIMH Family and AIDS Conference, Washington, DC.

Laursen, B., Coy, K.C., & Collins, W.A. (1998). Reconsidering changes in parent-child conflict across adolescence: A meta-analysis. *Child Development, 69*(3), 817–832.

Leland, N.L., & Barth, R.P. (1993). Characteristics of adolescents who have attempted to avoid HIV and who have communicated with parents about sex. *Journal of Adolescent Research, 8,* 58–76.

Levy, S.L., Handler, A.S., Weeks, K.A., Lampman, C., Flay, B.R., & Rashid, J. (1994). Adolescent risk of HIV as viewed by youth and their parents. *Family Community Health, 17,* 30–41.

Levy, S.R., Lampman, C., Handler, A., Flay, B.R., & Weeks, K. (1993). Young adolescent attitudes towards sex and substance use: Implications for AIDS prevention. *AIDS Education and Prevention, 5,* 340–351.

Levy, S.R., Perhats, C., Weeks, K., Handler, A.S., Zhu, C., & Flay, B.R. (1995). Impact of a school-based AIDS prevention program on risk and protective behavior for newly sexually active students. *Journal of School Health, 65,* 145–151.

Lynch, M. (1983). The intensification of gender-related role expectations during early adolescence. In J. Brooks-Gunn & A. Petersen (Eds.), *Girls at puberty* (pp. 201–228). New York: Plenum Press.

Madison, S.M., Bell, C.C., Scott, R., McKinney, L., Paikoff, R.L., McKay, M.M., & CHAMP Collaborative Board. (1998, July). *Let's take it a step further: Transferring a university-community collaborative HIV prevention program to the community.* Oral presentation at the NIMH Family and AIDS Conference, Washington, DC.

Magnusson, D. (1988). *Individual development from an interactional perspective: A longitudinal study.* Hillsdale, NJ: Erlbaum.

Magnusson, D., Stattin, H., & Allen, V.L. (1985). Biological maturation and social development: A longitudinal study of some adjustment processes from mid-adolescence to adulthood. *Journal of Youth and Adolescence, 14*(4), 267–283.

Males, M.A., & Chew, K.S.Y. (1996). The ages of fathers in California adolescent births, 1993. *American Journal of Public Health, 86,* 565–568.

Marshall, W.A., & Tanner, J.M. (1970). Variations in the pattern of pubertal changes in boys. *Archives of the Diseases of Childhood, 45,* 13.

McCormick, A., Paikoff, R., Parfenoff, S.H., & Foster, T. (1998, March). *Normative sexual behavior in urban African American youth.* Symposium presented at the seventh biennial meeting of the Society for Research on Adolescence, San Diego, CA.

McKay, M.M., Paikoff, R.L., & McKinney, L. (1998, July). *Preliminary effects of an urban HIV prevention program: The CHAMP family program.* Paper presented at the NIMH Family and AIDS Conference, Washington, DC.

Moore, D.S., & Erickson, P.I. (1985). Age, gender, and ethnic differences in sexual and contraceptive knowledge, attitudes, and behavior. *Family and Community Health, 8,* 38–51.

Moore, D.S., & Rosenthal, D. (1993). *Sexuality in adolescence.* New York: Routledge & Kegan Paul.

Moore, K., Miller, B., Glei, D., & Morrison, D. (1995). *Adolescent sex, contraception, and childbearing: A review of recent research.* Washington, DC: Child Trends.

Nathanson, C.A., & Becker, M.H. (1986). Family and peer influence on obtaining a method of contraception. *Journal of Marriage and the Family, 48,* 513–525.

Nicholson, H.J., & Postrado, L.T. (1992). A comprehensive age-phased approach: Girls incorporated. In B.C. Miller, J.J. Card, R.L. Paikoff, & J.L. Peterson (Eds.), *Preventing adolescent pregnancy* (pp. 110–138). Newbury Park: Sage.

Oakley, A., Fullerton, D., & Holland, J. (1995). Behavioral interventions for HIV/AIDS prevention. *AIDS, 9,* 479–486.

Offer, D., & Schonert-Reichl, K. (1993). "Myths or truths of adolescence?": Reply. *Journal of the American Academy of Child and Adolescent Psychiatry, 32,* 1077–1078.

Paikoff, R.L. (1995a). Early heterosexual debut: Situations of sexual possibility during the transition to adolescence. *American Journal of Orthopsychiatry, 65,* 389–401.

Paikoff, R.L. (1995b). *Family based intervention to prevent HIV risk exposure for urban adolescents.* NIMH Grant Proposal.

Paikoff, R.L. (1997). Applying developmental psychology to an AIDS prevention model for urban African-American youth. *Journal of Negro Education, 65,* 44–59.

Paikoff, R.L., & Brooks-Gunn, J. (1991). Do parent-child relationships change during puberty? *Psychological Bulletin, 110,* 47–66.

Paikoff, R.L., & Brooks-Gunn, J. (1994). Psychosexual development across the life span. In M. Rutter, D.F. Hay, & S. Baron-Cohen (Eds.), *Development through life: A handbook for clinicians* (pp. 558–582). Oxford, England: Blackwell Scientific.

Paikoff, R.L., McCormick, A., McCormick, S.H., McKay, M.M., & McKinney, L. (1998). *Interviewing pre and young adolescents about heterosocial and heterosexual experiences: Longitudinal and cross-sample comparisons.* Manuscript in preparation.

Paikoff, R.L., & McKay, M.M. (1995). *Family-based intervention to prevent adolescent HIV risk*. NIMH Grant.

Paikoff, R.L., Parfenoff, S.H., Williams, S.A., McCormick, A., Greenwood, G.L., & Holmbeck, G.N. (1997). Parenting, parent-child relationships, and sexual possibility situations among urban African American preadolescents: Preliminary findings and implications for HIV prevention. *Journal of Family Psychology, 11*(1), 11–22.

Parfenoff, S.H., & McCormick, A. (1997). *Parenting preadolescents at risk: Knowledge, attitudes, and communication about HIV/AIDS*. Paper presented at the Biennial meeting of the Society for Research in Child Development, Washington, DC.

Parfenoff, S.H., Paikoff, R.L., Brooks-Gunn, J., Holmbeck, G.N., & Jarrett, R.L. (1995). *Early sexual behavior and the risk for HIV/AIDS in early adolescence: The contribution of family and contextual factors*. Unpublished manuscript, Institute for Juvenile Research, University of Illinois, Chicago.

Parker, L.N. (1991). Adrenarche. *Endocrinology and Metabolism Clinics of North America, 20*(1), 71–83.

Peskin, H. (1967). Pubertal onset and ego functioning. *Journal of Abnormal Psychology, 72*, 1–15.

Petersen, A.C., & Taylor, B. (1980). The biological approach to adolescence: Biological change and psychological adaptation. In J. Adelson (Ed.), *Handbook of adolescent psychology* (pp. 117–155). New York: Wiley.

Petersen, A.C., Tobin-Richards, M., & Boxer, A. (1983). Puberty: Its measurement and its meaning. *Journal of Early Adolescence, 3*, 47–62.

Philliber, S., & Allen, J.P. (1992). Life options and community service: Teen outreach program. In B.C. Miller, J.J. Card, R.L. Paikoff, & J.L. Peterson (Eds.), *Preventing adolescent pregnancy* (pp. 139–155). Newbury Park, CA: Sage.

Pittman, K., & Govan, C. (1986). *Model programs: Preventing adolescent pregnancy and building youth self-sufficiency*. Washington, DC: Children's Defense Fund.

Richards, M.H., Boxer, A.M., Petersen, A.C., & Albrecht, R. (1990). The relationship of weight to body image in pubertal girls and boys from two communities. *Developmental Psychology, 26*, 313–321.

Roosa, M.W., Tein, J., Reinholtz, C., & Angelini, P.J. (1997). The relationship of childhood sexual abuse to teenage pregnancy. *Journal of Marriage and the Family, 59*, 119–130.

Rosenfield, R.L. (1991). Puberty and its disorders in girls. *Endocrinology and Metabolism Clinics of North America, 20*(1), 15–42.

Rosenthal, M.B. (1993). Adolescent pregnancy. In D.E. Stewart & N.L. Stotland (Eds.), *Psychological aspects of women's health care: The interface between psychiatry and obstetrics and gynecology*. Washington, DC: American Psychiatric Press.

Ruble, D.N., & Brooks-Gunn, J. (1982). The experience of menarche. *Child Development, 53*, 1557–1566.

Sagrestano, L., McCormick, S.H., Paikoff, R.L., & Holmbeck, G. (1999). Pubertal development and parent-child conflict in low-income, urban, African-American adolescents. *Journal of Research on Adolescence, 9*, 85–107.

Sagrestano, L., & Paikoff, R.L. (1997). Preventing high risk sexual behavior, sexually transmitted diseases, and pregnancy among adolescents. In R. Weissberg, T.P. Gullotta, R.L. Hampton, B.A. Ryan, & G.R. Adams (Eds.), *Healthy children 2010* (pp. 76–104). Newbury Park, CA: Sage.

Savin-Williams, R.C. (1990). *Gay and lesbian youth: Expressions of identity.* Washington, DC: Hemisphere.

Savin-Williams, R.C. (1994). Verbal and physical abuse as stressors in the lives of lesbian, gay male, and bisexual youths: Associations with school problems, running away, substance abuse, prostitution, and suicide. *Journal of Consulting and Clinical Psychology, 62,* 261–269.

Savin-Williams, R.C. (1998). Lesbian, gay, and bisexual youths' relationships with their parents. In C.J. Patterson & A.R. D'Augelli (Eds.), *Lesbian, gay, and bisexual identities in families* (pp. 75–98). New York: Oxford University Press.

Savin-Williams, R.C., & Diamond, L.M. (1999). Sexual orientation. In W.K. Silverman & T.H. Ollendick (Eds.), *Developmental issues in the clinical treatment of children* (pp. 241–258). Boston: Allyn & Bacon.

Schinke, S.P., & Gilchrist, L.D. (1984). *Life skills counseling with adolescents.* Baltimore: University Park Press.

Sipe, C., Grossman, J.C., & Milliner, J. (1988). *Summer training and education program (STEP): A report of the 1987 experience.* Philadelphia: Public/Private Ventures.

Spencer, M.A., & Dornbusch, S.M. (1990). Challenges in studying minority youth. In S.S. Feldman & G.R. Elliot (Eds.), *At the threshold: The developing adolescent* (pp. 123–146). Cambridge, MA: Harvard University Press.

Sroufe, L.A., & Rutter, M. (1984). The domain of developmental psychopathology. *Child Development, 55,* 17–29.

Stanton, B., Li, X., Black, M., Ricardo, I., Galbraith, J., Kaljee, L., & Feigelman, S. (1994). Sexual practices and intentions among preadolescent and early adolescent low-income urban African-Americans. *Pediatrics, 93*(6), 966–973.

Steinberg, L.D. (1987). Recent research on the family at adolescence: The extent and nature of sex differences. *Journal of Youth and Adolescence, 16,* 191–197.

Steinberg, L.D. (1988). Reciprocal relation between parent-child distance and pubertal maturation. *Developmental Psychology, 24*(1), 122–128.

Steinberg, L.D. (1989). Pubertal maturation and parent-adolescent distance: An evolutionary perspective. In G.R. Adams, R. Montemayor, & T.P. Gullotta (Eds.), *Biology of adolescent behavior and development* (pp. 71–97). Newbury Park, CA: Sage.

Steinberg, L.D. (1990). Patterns of family interaction as a function of age. In S.S. Feldman & G.R. Elliott (Eds.), *At the threshold: The developing adolescent* (pp. 255–276). Cambridge, MA: Harvard University Press.

Stern, M. (1988). Evaluation of a school-based pregnancy prevention program. *TEC Newsletter, 19,* 5–8.

St. Lawrence, J.S., Brasfield, T.L., Jefferson, K.W., Alleyne, E., O'Bannon, R.E., & Shirley, A. (1995). Cognitive-behavioral intervention to reduce African-American adolescents' risk for HIV infection. *Journal of Consulting and Clinical Psychology, 63,* 221–237.

Tanner, J.M. (1971). Sequence, tempo, and individual variation in growth and development of boys and girls aged twelve to sixteen. In J. Kagan & R. Coles (Eds.), *Twelve to sixteen: Early adolescence* (pp. 1–24). New York: Norton.

Tanner, J.M., Whitehausen, R.H., & Takaishi, M. (1966). Standards from birth to maturity for height, weight-height velosity and weight velosity, British children, 1965. *Archives of the Diseases of Childhood, 41,* 455–471.

Turner, R., & Feldman, S.S. (1999). *The functions of sex in everyday life.* Manuscript in preparation.

U.S. Department of Health and Human Services, Public Health Service. (1991). *Healthy people 2000: National health promotion and disease prevention objectives* (DHHS Publication N. PHS 91-50212). Washington, DC: U.S. Government Printing Office.

Udry, J.R., & Billy, J.O.G. (1987). Initiation of coitus in early adolescence. *American Sociological Review, 52,* 841–855.

Udry, J.R., Talbert, L., & Morris, N.M. (1986). Biosocial foundations for adolescent female sexuality. *Demography, 23,* 217–228.

Upchurch, D.M., & McCarthy, J. (1990). The timing of a first birth and high school completion. *American Sociological Review, 55,* 224–234.

Walter, H.J., & Vaughan, R.D. (1993). AIDS risk reduction among a multiethnic sample of urban high school students. *Journal of the American Medical Association, 270,* 725–730.

Zabin, L., & Hirsch, M. (1987). *Evaluation of pregnancy prevention programs in the school context.* Lexington, MA: Lexington.

Zabin, L., Hirsch, M., Smith, E., Streett, R., & Hardy, J. (1986). Evaluation of a pregnancy prevention program for urban teenagers. *Family Planning Perspectives, 18,* 119–126.

CHAPTER 12

Genital Surgery on Children below the Age of Consent

HANNY LIGHTFOOT-KLEIN, CHERYL CHASE,
TIM HAMMOND, and RONALD GOLDMAN*

FEMALE GENITAL MUTILATION

A WATIF IS readying herself for admission to University Hospital, where she is about to give birth to her third child. Her two older children were born in a remote town in Somalia. Within recent years, the family has fled to the United States, where her husband is presently pursuing graduate studies.

Several of Awatif's compatriots, in similar situations, help her pack the small satchel that she will take with her. Selva, who has already given birth in a U.S. hospital, elicits an outburst of uproarious laughter from the others when she impishly advises Awatif, "Don't forget to tell them all about your car accident!"

To the uninitiated outsider, such an outburst of merriment is meaningless. To these women, however, Selva's admonition plays upon a familiar, well-worn inside joke and touches a shared anxiety, one that all of them have experienced. The laughter in response to Selva's mocking advice is fueled by the absurdity of the remark and by the fear it elicits in them.

Awatif's pudendum is perfectly smooth. It is devoid of all features save for a five-inch medial scar that runs from the mons veneris down to a severely reduced vaginal aperture. Her condition is the result of ritual genital mutilation.

---

*"Female Genital Mutilation" was written by Hanny Lightfoot-Klein, "Intersex Genital Mutilation" was written by Cheryl Chase, and "Male Genital Mutilation" was written by Tim Hammond and Ronald Goldman.

She was subjected to this in early childhood, much as all of the other women in her culture were.

Awatif has not been in a car accident or any other such accident. However, if the examining doctor, nurse, or midwife has had no previous exposure to or understanding of her special condition, as is all too often the case, it is practically a certainty that she will be asked "What happened to you? Were you in a car accident?" Such a question may be cause for mirth when the patient is among her peers. However, in a medical setting, it elicits a justifiable anxiety that the health practitioner will not know how to deal with the unique problems that are part and parcel of her physical condition, or understand and respect the demands of propriety that her culture imposes on its women (Lightfoot-Klein, 1991b).

Scope of the Problem

There have been an estimated 200,000 immigrants into the United States in the past decade from countries where female genital mutilation (FGM) is customary. The women among these immigrants constitute a practically invisible, silent entity as far as U.S. medical services are concerned (Garb, 1990). The primary reason for the lack of recognition is the profoundly subordinate status of women in the cultures that institutionalize FGM. To obtain medical treatment, women from such cultures must first obtain the permission of their husbands or other custodial male relatives. Furthermore, the women can then be examined or treated only in their presence. In many of the cultures from which these women originate, a woman is considered to have been dishonored if a man other than her husband touches her body. A husband may divorce his wife on the spot under a religious legality that makes divorce ludicrously easy for men, while stringently curtailing the rights of women (Saadawi, 1982).

FGM is ubiquitous at all levels of society in at least 28 countries in Africa (U.S. Department of State, 1997). It is also practiced sporadically on the Arab Peninsula and occasionally in some regions of Asia. In Africa alone, along an uninterrupted belt across the center of the continent and along the length of the Nile, an estimated 115 million to 130 million women have been genitally mutilated (U.S. Department of State, 1997).

Origins of the Practice

Female sexual mutilation is an ancient blood ritual that is known through the writings of Herodotus to have been culturally embedded in Africa at least 2,500 years ago. The practice may have multiple origins, but they are obscure. Available historical resources and anthropological findings can furnish only educated guesses on how the practice actually arose (Lightfoot-Klein, 1989a).

In the original adoption of any practice, whatever its nature, there is always some culturally relevant reason. With the progression of time and evolution of culture, different reasons may be substituted and the original reasons completely forgotten and lost (Montague, 1946). Thus, genital ablation practices may have their origins in a group's effort to control the forces of nature or to placate ancestral spirits to ensure or limit fertility. Quite possibly, they may have taken the place of human sacrifices: a valued part is offered up to ensure the well-being of the whole (Lightfoot-Klein, 1989a). A similar notion clearly appears to have been operative in the beginnings of male foreskin ablation among Jews, as chronicled in the Old Testament. Over time, these religiously based, deity-appeasing reasons may have been replaced by the group's more sociologically based desire to control women's sexuality, thus ensuring the virginity of a girl being prepared for womanhood and marriage (Davis, 1975).

THE PROCEDURES

In communities that perform genital ablations as an integral element of the rites of passage, one is not simply born a woman. One becomes a respected person and an integrated female only after implementing the socially designated course to dignity and status, which culminates in a partial removal of the genitals (Lionnet, 1992). Regional practices differ. Among some peoples, partial or total ablation of the clitoris is customary. Among others, the procedure includes excision of the inner labia. The most drastic excisions occur in the Horn of Africa as well as in western areas of sub-Saharan Africa, Northern and Central Sudan, Egypt, Djibouti, Somalia, Sierra Leone, Mali, parts of Kenya, and Ethiopia (U.S. State Department, 1997).

In these regions, FGM includes total ablation of the clitoris and excision of the inner labia. Additionally, the outer labia are "shelled out." The remaining skin is sewn together over the wound, down to the perineum, so as to form a chastity belt made of the girl's own flesh. Only a tiny opening, the circumference of a straw or match stick, is left. This may or may not be minimally adequate for passing urine and menstrual fluid (Lightfoot-Klein, 1989a). This widely practiced extensive procedure is called infibulation or Pharaonic circumcision, and it is a source of pride in the Sudan, where the bulk of my research was carried out. The Sudanese take great pride in "scraping the girls clean" (Lightfoot-Klein, 1989a). This sense of pride allows people in Sudan to speak freely even to a Western woman about the practices; however, in other parts of Africa, for example, Kenya, Ethiopia, and Sierra Leone, it is taboo to speak of them to any outsider, and a vow of silence is an integral part of the ritual (M. Barrie, 1997, personal communication; M. Ramsey, 1994, personal communication).

In Somalia and parts of Ethiopia, introcision, an even more drastic and damaging procedure, is added. In this procedure, most of the vaginal musculature is deeply incised or scraped away. Ostensibly, this is done to make childbirth easier. However, not only does childbirth become more difficult, but this additional mutilation makes sexual intercourse as painful and undesirable for a woman as possible. In these cultures, an excised and perfectly smooth pudendum is valued as beautiful and sexually desirable, whereas an intact organ is variously regarded as repulsive, filthy, foul smelling, dangerous to the life of an emerging newborn, and hazardous to the health and potency of the husband (Assaad, 1980; Dareer, 1982). In Sudan, for example, it is believed that if the clitoris is not cut, it will grow to the size of a goose's neck and dangle between the legs, in competition with the husband's penis. This notion elicits great anxiety and revulsion among men.

Whereas clitoridectomy and excision are practiced by Africans of various religious and cultural orientations, infibulation is performed almost exclusively by Islamic peoples. It appears to be a regional rather than a religious practice, however, as it predates Islam by at least 1,200 years and is not customary among an estimated 80% of the world's Moslems (Lightfoot-Klein, 1989a). It is altogether possible, however, that this estimate is not accurate. Because so many Islamic women's lives are shrouded in secrecy, few if any facts concerning the condition of their genitals have escaped from behind the veil. Thus, the amount of information available to the West remains sparse and of uncertain reliability.

Most sexual mutilation rituals are still carried out among the village populace without the benefits of anesthesia or antibiotics and with rudimentary, unsterile instruments such as razors, scissors, and kitchen knives (Lightfoot-Klein, 1989b). Practitioners are more often than not medically untrained older women, often with failing eyesight, and the ceremony is generally performed on the earthen floors of huts, under inadequate lighting conditions, on struggling children forcibly held down. The mutilations may be carried out in the cities by midwives with some medical training, or by nurses or local doctors, using local anesthetic. However, by Western standards, the circumstances would not pass as sterile conditions, and the operation is still life-threatening (Lightfoot-Klein, 1989a).

As might be expected, immediate complications include hemorrhage, shock due to excruciating and prolonged pain, infection, septicemia, tetanus, gangrene, and retention of urine due to occlusion. Fistulas may be created in the struggling child by accidental damage to the urethra and anus, causing lifelong incontinence (Koso-Thomas, 1987; Lightfoot-Klein, 1993a; Verzin, 1975). Although no exact statistics exist on how many fatalities result from the rituals, medical estimates run high. In Sudan, where the bulk of my research was carried out and where the procedures are generally extreme and highly damaging, medical estimates of fatalities ran variously from 10% to 30%. This information was obtained through personal interviews with more than 30 gynecologists, pediatricians, residents, and interns between 1979 and 1984.

When a girl has been infibulated so that only a tiny opening remains proximal to her perineum, it is prevented from closing up totally by the insertion of a straw. Thereafter, she is able to urinate only by laboriously squeezing out her urine drop by painful drop (Beck-Karrer, 1996; Lightfoot-Klein, 1991b).

THE LIFELONG CONSEQUENCES OF FGM

The physical consequences of these drastic mutilations are far-reaching and lifelong. Because the rituals permeate entire regions and are carried out, for the most part, on small girls, no basis for comparison with intact women exists. Therefore, the cause-and-effect relationship between the procedures and their consequences later on in life is not understood by the populace (Lightfoot-Klein, 1989c). Disabling infections are common. As progressively more and more urinary debris accumulates behind the blockage, infections occur and may ultimately spread through the entire reproductive and renal systems. Further, gynecological and genitourinary complications may develop, for example, keloid and calculus formation, abscesses and cysts, dyspareunia and hemocolpus (Dareer, 1982; Koso-Thomas, 1987; Lightfoot-Klein, 1989a; Verzin, 1975).

The problem created by a tight infibulation is compounded yet further when the girl matures sexually and begins to menstruate (Beck-Karrer, 1996; Lightfoot-Klein, 1989a, 1991b, 1994b). It is virtually impossible for a tightly infibulated virgin to express her menstrual blood. Much of it may eventually clot behind the infibulation and simply remain there. A normal 4- to 5-day menstrual period stretches into as many as 10 to 15 days. A girl is often so disabled by pain and toxicity that she is unable to attend school or hold a job (Lightfoot-Klein, 1989a, 1991b, 1994b).

When a girl marries, her infibulation has to be torn open by her bridegroom. Generally, he accomplishes this by creating a rip which he then gradually enlarges with repeated attempts to penetrate her vagina, over an excruciatingly painful period of days, weeks, or even months, until the tear is large enough to allow intercourse. Whereas it is considered shameful for a man not to be able to penetrate his wife with his penis, in the opinion of Sudanese doctors, most men are actually not able to do this, no matter what they would have one believe. According to the doctors, the "wall of flesh" created by the fibrous and hardened mat of scar tissue that constitutes an infibulation cannot be broken down by mere human flesh. The truth of the matter is that most men resort to "the little knife" themselves, or, if this does not work, they secretly pay a midwife not only for her services but for her silence. Several of the doctors I spoke to related incidents in which they broke several scalpels in an effort to deinfibulate an anesthetized patient.

When the woman gives birth, the fibrous, inelastic scar tissue of her infibulation prevents her from dilating more than 4 cm of the 10 cm required to pass a fetal head. It must therefore be cut in an anterior direction and tightly resutured once more after she has given birth. The agonizing process of her husband's reopening her vagina is repeated after each birth. I personally witnessed more than 100 births in hospital delivery rooms and on the earthen floor of village huts. Not a single birth was possible without three-inch incisions lateral to one or both sides of the infibulation scar.

Persistently recurring infections are an integral part of this process due to the overwhelmingly septic conditions under which it takes place. Hemorrhage is common (Lightfoot-Klein, 1989a). Predictably, the lives of excised and infibulated women are characterized by recurring episodes of extreme anxiety, phobia, and depression in the face of anticipated and inescapable pain (Lightfoot-Klein, 1989b). These may be expected to occur at the time of the anticipated mutilation, at the onset of menstruation, at marriage, and with the birth of each child (personal interviews with Sudanese psychiatrists; see Lightfoot-Klein, 1989a).

RATIONALE AND MISCONCEPTIONS

It is difficult to understand why these profoundly damaging practices continue to exist. However, the women who are sexually mutilated have grown up in cultures where female circumcision is a matter of course. They regard it as altogether normal and are persuaded that it is absolutely necessary for their health, well-being, and social acceptability. Within the cultural framework of these societies, a girl who has not been circumcised is regarded as foul, unmarriageable, and deserving only of pity (Lightfoot-Klein, 1989b). With the exception of the Western-educated, the men and women I interviewed expressed shock and genuine concern when I revealed that my own sex organs were altogether intact. They feared for my welfare in my thereby unmarriageable, unprotected state, and they manifested genuine anxiety on my behalf for all the evil that would most assuredly befall me.

Adherents to FGM firmly believe that this practice carries with it an impressive array of what are in actuality totally nonexistent health benefits (Koso-Thomas, 1987). Genital mutilation is believed to promote cleanliness, provide immunity against all manner of disease, enhance fertility, make conception and childbearing easier, prevent acutely dreaded malodorous vaginal discharge, and prevent vaginal parasites and the contamination of mother's milk. Infibulation is further believed to prevent uterine prolapse. When genitally mutilated women do fall ill, it is assumed that this is brought on by supernatural causes. It is often argued that genital ablation and infibulation maintain good health in a woman. Moreover, circumcision is credited with having healing powers. It is claimed to have cured women suffering from melancholia, nymphomania, hysteria, insanity, and epilepsy, as well as kleptomania and proneness to truancy (Koso-Thomas, 1987). This phenomenon has its parallel in the United States. The greater part of the U.S. population has been similarly persuaded of the salubrious advantages of ablation of the foreskin of its male progeny. The myth that it provides health benefits and protection against a spate of dreadful diseases continues to be believed and acted on, in spite of mounting scientific evidence to the contrary (see Hammond & Goldman, "Male Genital Mutilation," in this chapter).

Beginning in the early nineteenth century, clitoridectomies and hysterectomies were performed on thousands of adolescent girls in the United States and England for similarly bogus health reasons and as a presumed cure for masturbation. The last case recorded in the United States occurred in 1955 (Feibleman, 1997).

"Surgical corrections of nature's mistakes" in the form of clitoral surgery to infants born with enlarged clitorises or ambiguous genitalia, performed largely to alleviate the anxiety of parents and to make the genitals "look more normal," is a cultural practice still holding sway in the United States (see Chase, "Intersex Genital Mutilation," in this chapter).

An intact vulva is regarded in sub-Saharan Arab Islamic Africa as the mark of a slave or prostitute. In a culture where a family's honor is measured largely by the sexual deportment of its women, a tightly infibulated introitus is testimony to a girl's unviolated chastity and thereby, all importantly, the unsullied honor of her family (Saadawi, 1980): "To keep the young girl pure and the married woman faithful, genital operations are maintained among Africa's most valued traditions" (Ogunmodede, 1979 p. 30).

In an extensive study of 3,210 women and 1,545 men in Sudan, Dareer (1982) found that 82.6% of women and 87.7% of men interviewed were in favor of continuing Pharaonic circumcision. Lightfoot-Klein's (1989b) in-depth interviews with more than 400 respondents resulted in similar findings (1989a). The most common reason given for supporting the mutilations was "It is custom." Furthermore, the likelihood exists that the number of people actually favoring continuation of the practice is much higher than that. Under Sudanese law, Pharaonic circumcision has been a punishable offense since 1956, although clitoridectomy remains legal. In spite of the law, Pharaonic circumcision continues more or less unabated. Youseff (1973) observed, "The laws against infibulation have not been obeyed because the custom is still an integral, positive-functioning component of the familial complex, and so, indirectly of the entire socio-cultural system" (p. 335). Within the cultures practicing these rites, they are regarded as an indispensable purification.

The presumed purifying functions of cutting off a girl's genitals are multiple. Women's intact sex organs are believed to be the source of irresistible temptation to unbridled promiscuous sexuality. Their removal is considered necessary to attenuate the girl's sexual sensitivity and reduce her sex drive (Giorgis, 1981; Lightfoot-Klein, 1989b). Whereas genital sensitivity appears, in fact, to be considerably reduced in some, although by no means all, genitally mutilated women, there is evidence that the sex drive is not so affected. According to the observations of Burton (1954), the nineteenth-century explorer who studied this phenomenon firsthand, the sex drive tended to become intensified rather than reduced in genitally mutilated women. He conjectured that this was so because sexual satisfaction was made more difficult by the mutilation. Both of these attributes are considered dangerous in a "decent" woman who is worthy of carrying on a family's lineage. The problem is believed to be solved by removing the offending parts, in other words, her genitals. Infibulation in particular is believed (quite falsely) to serve as a deterrent to rape, while effectively guarding the girl against her own errant sexual impulses. An intact infibulation assures the bridegroom that the purity, chastity, and honor of his bride and, consequently, the honor of both his family and hers are unsoiled. It is common knowledge among people in the cities, however, that if a girl is not a virgin, she need only have herself reinfibulated before marriage to appear to be one. In Sudan and other infibulating cultures, the rather curious notion of "renewable virginity" exists. Thus, if a girl is raped, has had a premarital or adulterous affair, or remarries after having been widowed or divorced, she is reinfibulated and becomes a "virgin" once more.

Uncircumcised girls are often subjected to great peer pressure, so that many eventually press their families for their own circumcisions. They are ridiculed by those who have already undergone the rite for "still having that disgusting thing dangling between [their] legs," and they are taunted for "smelling bad" (Lightfoot-Klein, 1989a, p. 72).

PSYCHOLOGICAL EFFECTS

The rites of FGM themselves are couched in mystery, so that the girl does not have a clear idea beforehand of what is about to happen to her. Although she has a vague notion that her flesh will be cut and that there will be pain and bleeding, these matters are glossed over, and her attention is more or less successfully diverted from these anxiety-producing aspects of the event. The social benefits she is about to reap are impressed upon her and joyfully celebrated. The day of circumcision is represented as the most important day in her life, the culmination of her preparation for respected womanhood. A festive atmosphere prevails; she is the center of all attention and receives many coveted gifts.

A change of heart or an escape is not possible. She is generally not yet of an age when she can run away. Increasingly, most genital mutilations are performed on small children because they are easier to manage (Lightfoot-Klein, 1989a). It is not until the circumciser actually cuts into her flesh that the little girl realizes the enormity of what is happening to her.

In view of the extensive trauma involved, one would expect to see some profound personality changes commonly occurring in young girls who have undergone genital mutilation. For example, a lively and outgoing child might become timid and withdrawn. Verzin (1975) reports that he discussed this on many occasions with various local doctors and that they tended to report that they had not observed such a change. Not a single doctor among the many that I spoke with was able to recall even one girl being brought to him for becoming timid and withdrawn. Such behavioral manifestations are accepted not only as perfectly normal in a girl, but even desirable. One doctor, whose family I lived with for some months, told me that the only difference he noticed after his own daughters had been Pharaonically mutilated was that they were "less hyperactive" than before, and that this was, in any event, as it should be.

Other observers, however, categorically state that there is considerable evidence that a child becomes withdrawn in the first year or two following her mutilation. This tends to give place to an observable pride when girls are a few years older and before the complications associated with menstruation set in.

Obviously, their self-esteem has been enhanced by having proven themselves worthy to become responsible, marriageable women and by having earned their family's approval and gratitude for upholding family honor.

By way of further explanation, Sudanese psychiatrists cite the cohesive and warmly supportive influence of the extended family as a powerful force for creating emotional stability and adaptability in girls and which also helps them to come to terms with their trauma. My personal observations tend to verify that the emotional life of children in Sudan, as well as in some other parts of Africa, is characteristically rich and joyful. They tend to develop in an atmosphere of enviable love and emotional security relative to the experience of the average child in the Western world. This emotional security helps them overcome the seemingly insurmountable trauma of the genital mutilation. It also tends to further the likelihood of a strong marital bonding for both sexes in later life, which, in turn, enables women to overcome the equally horrendous traumas of deinfibulation and childbirth (Lightfoot-Klein, 1989a). Although I did witness some evidence of depression, acute phobia, anxiety, despair, and other emotional disturbance among girls and women on a day-to-day basis in the areas I studied, it was generally not highly visible. Many towns and villages have their madman or madwoman, but major psychiatric breakdown as a consequence of FGM is not often seen. This observation was validated by all the health professionals consulted for this study. However, it must be understood that depression resulting in impotence in men is considered in these cultures to be a health problem of major concern. On the other hand, women's anxiety, depression, despair, or phobic manifestations, no matter how acute, are simply not within the definition of serious emotional disturbance in these cultures. In fact, some anxiety, fear, and distress may be encouraged to keep women in their subordinate role.

On one occasion, I stayed with some teachers at a girls' secondary school in a small town. When night fell, I announced my intention to sleep in the garden of the school courtyard. My announcement was greeted with exclamations of horror from the young teachers. They fluttered about me nervously, like hens whose adopted duckling charges are hastening toward the water.

"Oh, you must not do that!" they implored. "It is terribly dangerous."

"But how can it possibly be dangerous, here in the garden?" I asked.

"Robbers will rob you!" they exclaimed.

"How can there be robbers when there is a high wall around us, the gates are locked tightly, and there is a watchman outside the gate? Do not be afraid. No one will rob me."

"Oh you must not do it!" they pleaded. "The wild dogs will eat you!"

"The dogs are all outside the gate, and cannot come in. Do not worry. The dogs will not eat me."

"But there are evil spirits that come in the night, and they will harm you."

"There are no evil spirits, and even if there were, closed doors would not stop them. No, all the spirits are good, and Allah will watch over me."

"But, the watchman will see you!"

"Well then, the watchman is a kindly old man, and if he sees me, he will watch over me. You will see. Nothing bad will happen."

They stood there, wringing their hands, helpless and frightened. "But we are afraid," they finally said.

"Why are you so afraid?" I asked.

"Because they teach us to be afraid. From the beginning, when we are little, little girls, they teach us to be afraid."

"Afraid of what?"

"Afraid of everything. We sleep wrapped up in our blankets, with the covers over our heads, with all the windows bolted and shuttered, and the doors locked. We huddle together, and still we are afraid. We are always afraid."

And they did indeed all sleep wrapped round and round tightly like mummies, in their hot airless chamber. I came into their room in the morning, after one of them had unlocked, unhooked, unlatched, and unbolted the door. The little room was airless and sweltering with the heat of many bodies, and I could hardly bear to enter it. One by one, they crawled out of their cocoons, and each embraced me, as though I was freshly risen from the dead. They were so happy and relieved that indeed I had come to no harm.

"Allah is merciful. Praised be Allah!" they exclaimed over and over again. "But were you not afraid?" they marveled. "Were you really not afraid?"

Later, we spoke together of their greatest fear, the one that is always with them, the one that has been with them from early childhood on, the one that never leaves them. It is the most terrible, potent fear of all. It governs their waking hours and pervades their dreams. It is their fear of being raped (Lightfoot-Klein 1989a, pp. 215–216).

THE POLEMICS OF AFRICANISM

It generally comes as a shock to Westerners to find that even educated women, as well as men, may be among the ancient blood ritual's staunchest advocates. They justify the mutilations as an integral part of their tradition and unity as a people. They defend it against what they perceive to be yet another imperialist attempt to destroy their identity as Africans. Sad to chronicle, there have been a plethora of such attempts throughout colonial history, beginning with the well-meaning, albeit misguided, efforts of Christian missionaries and culminating in laws imposed by oppressive colonial rulers (Obiora, 1997):

> If it is deemed necessary to introduce laws to combat a custom as sensitive as female circumcision, a genuine attempt must be made to grasp the full socio-psychological implications of these laws in order to avoid their undesirable results or unintended consequences. (Babiker Badri, cited in Obiora, 1997, p. 289)

The embittered defense of the practices by many African intellectuals is virtually impossible for Westerners to understand. Westerners, perceiving the practices from outside the culture, can only regard them as barbaric anachronisms. In the view of Lerner (1986), the mutilations become somewhat more comprehensible once it is understood that uncircumcised women, particularly in sub-Saharan Arab Islamic societies, have historically been slaves, prostitutes, and other non-male-protected women of low caste, whose sad lot in life has always rendered them and, even more tragically, their children easy prey to rapists, marauders, and slavers.

Genital mutilation, by contrast, has for centuries been a way to ensure for wives and daughters the protection of a male-dominated compound. It is for these powerfully persuasive reasons that the honest efforts of Western governments to simply do away with "the barbaric practice" fail. This occurs with both African immigrants to Western countries and in the attempts of Western feminists to educate Africans to leave their daughters genitally intact. Ironically, the outraged opposition to such Western interference with millennia-old blood rituals comes most often not from men, but from women. Moreover, with very few exceptions, the efforts of Western feminists to bring about change in Africa have all too often been clumsy, crassly insensitive, ignorant of African culture, and self-serving:

> I have visited villages where, at a time when the village women are asking for better health facilities, lower infant mortality rates, pipe-borne water and access to agricultural credit, they are presented with questionnaires . . . on female circumcision. There is no denying that certain statistical relationships can be established between such variables, however that is not a priority from the point of view of those who make the research subjects. (Achola Pala, cited in Obiora, 1997, p. 297)

On the brighter side, a growing number of Western women and men, working alongside activist, educated Africans, have sought out long-term, firsthand experience with different African cultures at the grassroots level. When such individuals have been willing to listen rather than insist on dictating their own belief systems, they have gleaned an understanding of how to begin to unravel the conundrum of FGM. They are acutely aware that statistical analyses based on highly questionable data, as well as academic writings with no hands-on experience (that do little more than rehash what has been written by others about the issues involved), have little if anything to contribute to a solution.

AND WHAT ABOUT THE AFRICAN WOMAN ON OUR OWN SHORES?

"If we care about the genitals of these women, we need also to care about their feelings" (Lane & Rubenstein, cited in Obiora, 1997, p. 327). And what of the African woman in today's ever increasing migration into the countries of Europe and the Americas? When a genitally mutilated woman is living in her own country, where every woman has been enculturated as she has, she is prone to accept her suffering as being simply "a woman's lot." In Western countries, what has been done to her in her native country in the name of social acceptability is abhorred as the ultimate form of abuse. All too often, it becomes quite clear to her that neither her presence nor her problems are welcome, and she is likely to be overwhelmed by feelings of confusion and alienation (Lightfoot-Klein, 1994). If her awareness grows, she may understand for the first time that there is a connection between the mutilation she has been subjected to in childhood and the recurrent episodes of pain and disability that she yet suffers as a consequence. Added to her physical pain, she is now likely to experience the emotional suffering that comes with the realization that she has been robbed of an irreplaceable part of her body, the possession of which is taken completely for granted by women native to her new environment (Lightfoot-Klein, 1994).

Quite possibly, the result may be a profound shift in the way she perceives herself and the society that has created her affliction. Because she has so little power, this new awareness will only serve to heighten her confusion and emotional suffering. But will it prevent her from creating yet another generation of mutilated daughters, either by finding a practicing circumciser somewhere in the African community of her adoptive country, or by sending her daughters home "to the grannies" to be mutilated when their time comes? How can we help such women? How can we, first of all, ease their suffering and thereby open a door that may persuade them not to deal with their daughters as they themselves have been dealt with?

There are no comfortable solutions. No matter in which direction the genitally mutilated woman turns, she finds herself trapped. If she opposes genital mutilation on a personal level and refuses to subject her own daughters to the rituals, her family will almost certainly cast her out. If she finds the courage to break her vow of silence and speak out against it publicly, not only she but her entire family will become pariahs and will be subjected to insults, ostracism, threats, and even violence.

Even if she is no longer convinced that the ritual is either necessary, beneficial, or even "perfectly normal," she may find herself unable to defy the social compulsions or, for that matter, her own driving and ill-understood repetition compulsion, the acknowledged by-product of violence perpetrated on small children. It is not surprising that not many such women, even those who live in the relative anonymity of the Western world, have the courage to speak out and actively work against the practices. Those who do are certainly to be admired and are deserving of our most compassionate support. If lifestyle options other than marriage become open to the woman, and consequently to her daughters through education, such options may well form the beginnings of some meaningful change. Consistent, appropriate medical care, backed by an understanding of the woman's complicated culture and its stringent demands, would seem to be a logical first step in helping her to break free from the past and its oppression.

Furthermore, it is essential that we educate our own medical and psychological caretakers to enable them to deal knowledgeably and sensitively with such patients. We need to caution doctors not to put them on display as medical curiosities, but rather to help them reach an understanding of how their childhood mutilation is afflicting their bodies currently, and how their medical problems may be managed most effectively. Because they have generally been raised in a loving environment by a caring extended family, circumcised women are likely to cling to the notion that the mutilation was performed as an act of love and for their own benefit. They will declare with pride and conviction that the circumcision was done for them, not to them. It is important that prospective psychotherapists remember this, in order to not represent or refer to these loving caretakers, the carriers-on of a tradition of which they themselves have been victims, as sadists or bloodthirsty monsters.

At a broader level, sensitively planned and respectful reeducation is needed to begin the arduous process of dissolution of this deeply ingrained, age-old custom. It must be based on careful assessments, nurtured rapport, and insight into the mentality of each individual African woman and her family. Care must be taken as well to encourage the women, and when possible their families, to continue the more positive customs that are also a part of their heritage. It is to be hoped that through these efforts, genital mutilation will begin to lose its stranglehold on the populace. However, we cannot expect this to be an easy task.

INTERSEX GENITAL MUTILATION

> Genital ambiguity is "corrected" not because it is threatening to the
> infant's life but because it is threatening to the infant's culture.
>
> —Suzanne Kessler (1990, p. 25)

CULTURAL PRACTICE OR RECONSTRUCTIVE SURGERY?

"New Law Bans Genital Cutting in United States," reads the headline on the front page of the *New York Times* (Dugger, 1996). The law seems clear enough: "Whoever knowingly circumcises, excises, or infibulates the whole or any part of the labia majora or labia minora or clitoris of another person who has not attained the age of 18 years shall be fined under this title or imprisoned not more than 5 years, or both." Yet this law was not intended and has not been interpreted to protect the approximately five children per day in the United States who are subjected to excision of part or all of their clitoris and inner labia simply because doctors believe their clitoris is too big (Coventry, 1998; Dreger, 1998a). There is even a medical standard for how big is too big: over 0.9 cm, about 3/8 of an inch (Kessler, 1998).

Sexual anatomies, and genitals in particular, come in many sizes and shapes. Doctors label children whose sexual anatomies differ significantly from the cultural ideal as "intersexuals" or "hermaphrodites." Medical practice today holds that possession of a large clitoris, or a small penis, or a penis that has the urethra located anywhere other than at the tip is a "psychosocial emergency" (Meyers-Seifer & Charest, 1992). The child would not be accepted by the mother, would be teased by peers, and would not be able to develop into an emotionally healthy adult (American Academy of Pediatrics, 1996). The medical solution to this "psychosocial problem" is surgery—before the child reaches 3 months of age, or even before the newborn is discharged from the hospital (Parker, 1998). Although parental emotional distress and rejection of the child and peer harassment are cited as the primary justifications for cosmetic genital surgery, there has never been an investigation of nonsurgical means, such as professional counseling or peer support, to address these issues.

The federal Law to Ban Female Genital Mutilation (1996) notwithstanding, girls with large clitorises are "normalized" by excising parts of the clitoris and burying the remainder deep within the genital region (Oesterling, Gearhart, & Jeffs, 1987). And boys with small penises? Current medical practice holds that intersex children "can be raised successfully as members of either sex if the process begins before 2½ years" (American Academy of Pediatrics, 1996, p. 590). Because surgeons cannot create a large penis from a small one, the policy is to remove the testes and raise these children as girls. But first they "carve a large phallus down into a clitoris, creat[ing] a vagina using a piece of [the child's] colon," marveled one science writer, who spoke only to physicians and parents, not to any of the identified patients who were the nominal beneficiaries of this miracle technology (Hendricks, 1993, p. 10). "You can make a hole, but you can't build a pole," quipped one surgeon to Hendricks (p. 15). Efforts to create or extend a penile urethra in boys whose urethra exits other than at the tip of the penis, a condition called hypospadias, frequently lead to multiple surgeries, each compounding the harm (Stecker, Horton, Devine, & McCraw, 1981). Heart-rending stories of the physical and emotional carnage are related by victims of these surgeries in "Growing Up in the Surgical Maelstrom" (Devore, 1999) and, with black humor, in "Take Charge: A Guide to Home Catheterization" (Nicholson, 1999).

"Reconstructive" surgeries for intersex infant genitals first came into widespread practice in the 1950s. Indeed, one enthusiastic surgeon even cited the tradition of clitorectomy in Africa as evidence that the practice is not harmful (Gross, Randolph, & Crigler, 1966). Intersexuality is treated as shameful, and physicians discourage open discussion by their patients. Indeed, they recommend lying to parents and to adult intersex patients (Natarajan, 1996). Thus, until recently, most victims of these interventions suffered alone in shame and silence (Dreger, 1998b; Kemp, Groveman, Anonymous, Tako, & Irwin, 1996).

By 1993, the accomplishments of a progression of social justice movements— civil rights, feminist, gay and lesbian, bisexual and transgender—helped make it possible for intersexuals to speak out. Initially, according to newspaper reports (e.g., Angier, 1996; Mulgrew, 1997), physicians scoffed at assertions that intersexuality was not shameful and that medically unnecessary genital surgeries were mutilating and should be halted. One surgeon from Johns Hopkins, the institution primarily responsible for developing the current medical model, dismissed intersex patient-advocates as "zealots." Others cited the technological imperative: doctors "don't really have a choice" whether or not to perform surgery (Szasz, cited in Mulgrew, 1997).

By 1997, the intersex movement had gathered enough strength for advocates to visit Congress and ask that the Law to Ban Female Genital Mutilation be enforced to protect children not only against practices imported from other cultures but also against this uniquely American medicalized form of mutilation. Their work won coverage in the *New York Times* (Angier, 1997) and on NBC's *Dateline* (Shapiro, 1997). In 1998, *Urology Times* reported a small but growing "new tidal wave of opinion" from physicians and sex researchers supporting the activists (Scheck, 1998). Unfortunately, the struggle of intersex activists against American medicalized genital mutilation has yet to attract significant support or even notice from feminists and journalists who express outrage over traditional African surgeries (Chase, 1998).

What Are the Long-Term Outcomes of These Surgeries?

All parties agree that there has been a shocking lack of follow-up after surgery, and few objective data are available: "Long term results of operations that eliminate erectile tissue [i.e., surgery routinely performed on intersex children] are yet to be systematically evaluated" (Newman, Randolph, & Parson, 1992, p. 192). "Past decisions about gender identity and sex reassignment when genitalia are greatly abnormal have by necessity occurred in a relative vacuum because of inadequate scientific data" (Reiner 1997a, p. 224). "There is a dearth of systematic knowledge about the psychosocial functioning of hypospadias patients at various ages. . . . Besides, to what extent patients' perception of their penile appearance is related to their psychosocial functioning has never been investigated" (Mureau, Slijper, Slob, & Verhulst, 1997).

In 1996, demonstrators picketed the annual meeting of the American Academy of Pediatrics (AAP), protesting the group's continuing support of cosmetic genital surgery on infants and refusal to open a dialogue with patient-advocate groups. The AAP reacted by dispatching a spokesperson with a press release reasserting confidence in its policy of addressing the "emotional, cognitive, and body image" concerns of intersexuals with genital surgery between 6 weeks and 15 months of age. Meanwhile, inside the meeting, surgeon David Thomas spoke to assembled pediatric specialists, acknowledging that "the people who are picketing the AAP at the moment do have a point," and that psychological issues surrounding intersexuality and cosmetic genital surgery "are poorly researched and understood" ("Is Early Vaginal," 1997). Johns Hopkins pediatric urological surgeon Robert Jeffs, reacting to the demonstration, conceded to a journalist that he had no way of knowing what happens to patients after he performs surgery on them: "Whether they are silent and happy or silent and unhappy, I don't know" (Barry, 1996, p. 7).

What is clear is that genital surgery can cause such physical harm as scarring, chronic pain, chronic irritation, and reduction of sexual sensation, as well as psychological harm. Indeed, apart from the harm specific to genital surgery, surgery is never without risk. Even surgeons from Johns Hopkins, an institution that continues to perform and to promote the surgery, told journalist McCroy (1998) that "there is no medical necessity to reduce the size of a clitoris" (p. 18) and, in a published reply to a critical letter, acknowledged that the surgery "does not guarantee normal adult sexual function" (Chase, 1996, p. 1140).

Perhaps more important than physical harm is the psychological harm that has been reported by former patients. Schober (1998) reported that a sex therapist, H. Martin Malin, discussing patients who had been subjected to early genital surgeries, noted they had been told that vaginoplasties or clitorectomies had been performed because of the serious psychological consequences they would have suffered otherwise. In spite of the surgeries, or perhaps because of them, the patients still reported long-standing psychological distress.

FOR WHOSE BENEFIT ARE THESE SURGERIES PERFORMED?

There is a growing realization that surgeries are performed on intersex infants to alleviate the emotional distress of the parents and other adults (e.g., Oesterling et al., 1987). Surgery must be performed during the first few weeks of life, says surgeon John Gearhart; "Otherwise, every time the mom, dad, or auntie changes the diaper, everybody gets upset. You cannot have a child who causes the auntie, when she pulls down the diaper, to say, 'My God!'" (Hendricks, 1993, p. 12).

Suzanne Kessler (1990), in her ethnography of the physicians who perform these surgeries, concluded, "Genital ambiguity is 'corrected' not because it is threatening to the infant's life but because it is threatening to the infant's culture" (p. 25). However, as Schober (1998) argues, although surgeons believe they can maximize a child's acceptance by the family, they do so without knowing the psychological cost to the infant patients in their adulthood.

BUT DON'T YOU WANT TO BE NORMAL?

Genital surgery is irreversible: once removed, a clitoris, penis, or testicle can never be restored. Scarring produced by surgery can never be undone. There are many documented cases of people who have lived apparently emotionally healthy and productive lives with their atypical anatomy intact. Some of these actually refused surgery when it was offered (Fausto-Sterling, 1993; Young, 1937). Like large clitorises, small penises are capable of providing sexual arousal, genital pleasure, and orgasm. The men investigated by Reilly and Woodhouse (1989) were able to live satisfying lives as men with no impairment of sexual function; they had small penises that would be judged "inadequate" according to current medical protocols. Surgeons argue that genital surgeries must be performed on intersex children to save them from feeling different from other children or being marginalized by society. But many children grow up with physical differences that may cause them to be marginalized, yet we do not advocate using plastic surgery to eliminate all physical differences. For instance, children of racial minorities are often marginalized, teased, and even subject to violence. Yet few would condone using nonconsensual plastic surgery during infancy to eliminate racial characteristics.

Prejudice against people with unusual genitals is culturally determined. Some cultures have high regard for people with intersex genitals (Herdt, 1994; Roscoe, 1987). Even awareness of this cultural relativity does not seem to dampen the enthusiasm of some clinicians for surgery. For instance, pediatric endocrinologist Marie New recognizes that during the European Middle Ages and Renaissance, "hermaphrodites were integrated quite forthrightly into the social fabric" (New & Kitzinger, 1993, p. 10), but she does not question today's medical policy of early cosmetic surgery.

Kessler (1997) provides evidence that adults, asked to imagine having been born with atypical genitals, would not have wanted their parents to permit cosmetic genital surgery on them. Shouldn't this raise doubts about the ethical nature of the surgeries? Perhaps adults allow surgery on infants because they find it difficult to imagine a child as a future sexual being; in contrast, when asked to consider genital surgery on themselves, they are aware of and value their sexual functioning over cosmetics. The growing body of first-person narratives by intersex people and accounts uncovered by historians provide a wealth of examples of people who bitterly regretted having been subjected to "normalizing" genital surgery (including some whose surgery did not occur until adolescence) and of people who were happy to have escaped surgery (Chase, 1997a, 1997b; Dreger, 1998b, 1999).

Finally, cosmetic genital surgery does not provide "normal"-looking genitals. Reporting on the cases of a dozen girls aged 11 to 15 who had undergone clitoroplasty and vaginoplasty, Scheck (1997) cited pediatric urologist David Thomas, who concluded that the results were "indifferent and, frankly, disappointing." Over time, reconstructions showed visibly different appearance from the original cosmetic result, with the clitorises withered and obviously nonfunctional. All required some additional vaginal surgery (Scheck, 1997). Even surgeries performed by leading experts had poor outcomes: "Even after surgery, [boys and men] perceive differences in penile appearance . . . because hypospadias surgery never produces a perfectly normal penile appearance" (Mureau et al., 1997, p. 373).

Surgeons insist that cosmetic genital surgeries performed on intersex infants are not "mutilations" because their intent is to help, not to harm, the infant. But "mutilation" is a value judgment. Surely, in determining whether or not a particular form of genital cutting is a mutilation, professionals should give the greatest weight to the experience of the person whose genitals are cut, rather than to the person doing the cutting. Parents in sub-Saharan Africa who have traditional cutting performed on their daughters believe that they are doing what is best for their child.

WE CONTROL YOUR SEX AND GENDER

The current medical model insists that doctors can make any child into any sex that they wish. But there is clear evidence that this is little more than wishful thinking. For instance, surgeons insist that genetic females with a condition called congenital adrenal hyperplasia (CAH) who are born with enlarged clitorises or even with male genitals are clearly, universally, and inevitably female. In these cases, asserts John Hopkins surgeon John Gearhart, "There is not controversy there . . . the child is going to be a female" (cited in McCroy, 1998, p. 18). But before medical interventions began in the late 1950s, many such individuals lived their entire lives as men (Young, 1937). Today, a significant number of CAH individuals also choose, in their teens or as adults, to live as men even after having undergone drastic "modern" interventions such as removal of the penis (Meyer-Bahlburg et al., 1996; Money, Devore, & Norman, 1986; Zucker et al., 1996).

The most dramatic refutation of the "We control your sex and gender" thesis is the case of "John/Joan" (Diamond & Sigmundson, 1997b). "John" was born in the 1960s, one of a pair of identical male twins with typical sex anatomy and genitals. John's penis was accidentally destroyed during circumcision when he was 8 months old. A team of physicians and sexologists at Johns Hopkins determined that the best course was to raise him as a female. His testes were removed, cosmetic surgery was performed on his genitals, and his parents were instructed to raise him as a girl and to conceal his true history from him. For decades, medical literature cited this case as a glowing success story and as proof that physicians were justified in assigning intersex children a sex according to surgical convenience above any other consideration.

However, it turns out that "John/Joan" was not a success story, but an unmitigated disaster. The follow-up in Diamond and Sigmundson (1997b), reported in more detail in Colapinto (1997), reveals that John never felt female, that he resisted physicians' attempts to further feminize his body through hormones and additional cosmetic genital surgery, and that today he lives as a man, is married to a woman, and is the adoptive father of her children. The medical model tolerates no ambiguity about a child's sex. Thus, the medical team actively resisted "Joan's" attempts to avoid additional feminizing procedures, such as estrogen and vaginoplasty.

WHERE DO WE GO FROM HERE?

What the intersex activist movement and its professional allies are recommending is not terribly radical. Before the late 1950s, intersex children were raised either as girls or as boys and made their way in the world as best they could, usually without any professional help. Sometimes, they changed sex, without any professional help. Today, knowledge of genetics, embryology, and endocrinology could allow medical experts to make a better guess about which sex would be most comfortable as a label for an intersexed child (Diamond & Sigmundson, 1997a; Reiner, 1997b). But just because professionals give a child a label, it does not follow that doctors must perform surgery to make the child's genital appearance more closely approximate what is implied by the label.

Furthermore, with some specialized training, mental health professions would be well equipped to address the emotional distress of the parents and of the child as he or she grows up. The nascent intersex patient advocacy movement is struggling to create the infrastructure to provide peer support for both parents and intersexuals. In fact, some intersex adults themselves are now beginning to choose psychotherapy as a profession, with the intention of offering the type of help they wish they and their families could have had. Support groups have sprung into existence all over the world; many are listed at the Web site of the Intersex Society of North America (http://www.isna.org).

The controversy has drawn the attention of scholars from outside the medical profession, including medical historians, bioethicists, social psychologists, sociologists, sex researchers, and anthropologists. Their investigations have revealed the extent to which the traditional medical practice lacks scientific basis and suffers from a virtual absence of long-term follow-up. At the end of 1998, a special issue of the *Journal of Clinical Ethics* brought together much of this work for the first time in one volume. Every contributor (including a pediatric endocrinologist, a pediatric psychiatrist, and a pediatric urologist) calls for drastic changes in medical practice (Dreger, 1998c). An indication of how polarized the issue has become is that Alice Dreger, the editor of the special issue, reports that none of the physicians advocating infant surgery whom she invited to contribute to the issue were willing to do so. Thus, the surgical literature continues to present surgery as uncontroversial, the ethics literature unanimously condemns the practice, and the two communities do not speak to each other.

Medical practices that were once professionally respectable but have now been eliminated because of social condemnation include forced sterilization for eugenic purposes; hysterectomy and oophorectomy for psychological disorders in women (practiced at least until the end of World War II); lobotomy, electroshock, and aversion therapy for treatment of homosexuality (practiced at least through the 1960s); clitoral excision or cauterization for elimination of masturbation (practiced at least through the 1950s); radiation experiments on institutionalized handicapped children; and syphilis experiments on impoverished African American men. "Genital reconstruction" of intersex infants should finally be added to this list.

The federal Law to Ban Female Genital Mutilation (1996) permits excisions when "necessary to the health of the person on whom it is performed." But the law also says that in determining whether surgery is necessary, "no account shall be taken . . . of any belief . . . that the operation is required as a matter of custom or ritual." At what point is standard medical practice simply "a matter of custom"?

MALE GENITAL MUTILATION

Although no documents record the number of girls and boys who fall victim to genital cutting customs, one can reasonably estimate that approximately 100 million females (Toubia, 1994) and more than 650 million males (Vital Abstracts of the U.S., 1994) are alive in the world today who were subjected as children to various forms of involuntary genital mutilation. Each year around the world, an estimated 2 million girls and 13 million boys (Denniston & Milos, 1997) are subjected to "circumcision" customs, occurring in a wide variety of either developing or developed nations. The severity and rationalizations for altering children's healthy genitals differ between genders, as well as from circumciser to circumciser and from culture to culture. The customs may be carried out on the dirt floor of a village hut or in an urban hospital. The highly respected circumcisers may be local barbers, influential tribal or religious leaders, or medical professionals. Parents who offer their children to the circumciser may be sheep-herding Nomads, middle-class laborers, or college-educated professionals. In all cases, social, religious, or historical imperatives demand the removal of a misunderstood, often feared or despised, portion of the genitals, a removal that the adults sincerely believe to be in the child's "best interests."

Although the vast majority of male circumcisions in the world occur under the same rudimentary and unsanitary conditions as female circumcision, the U.S. custom of male genital alteration is a medical routine. In a world where 80% of males are genitally intact (Wallerstein, 1985), the United States is the last developed nation to continue subjecting the majority of its male newborns to circumcision for nontherapeutic and nonreligious reasons. Consequently, the United States has long been a battleground for progressive and reactionary forces in the campaign to protect male children from genital cutting. Annually, over 1.25 million infants are subjected to unanesthetized genital surgery in the United States. The American national average rate of circumcision fluctuates at around 60% (U.S. National Center for Health Statistics, personal communication, 1996), down from a high of about 85% around 1970. Rates vary by region, from 80% in the Midwest, where social conformity is highly valued, to 34% in the West, where the constraints of tradition and family pressure are weaker. The persistence of male circumcision (like female circumcision) may be due to an undervaluing of the benefits of intact genitals and a minimization of the adverse consequences of genital alteration.

MALE GENITAL ANATOMY AND FUNCTION

During sexual arousal, the flaccid penis becomes erect and increases in length about 50%. As it elongates, the sleeve of preputial tissue unfolds, providing the skin necessary for full expansion of the penile shaft (Figure 12.1). This double fold consists of an outer layer of epidermal tissue and an equal layer of inner mucosal tissue (Figure 12.2). The two layers of preputial tissue account for 50%

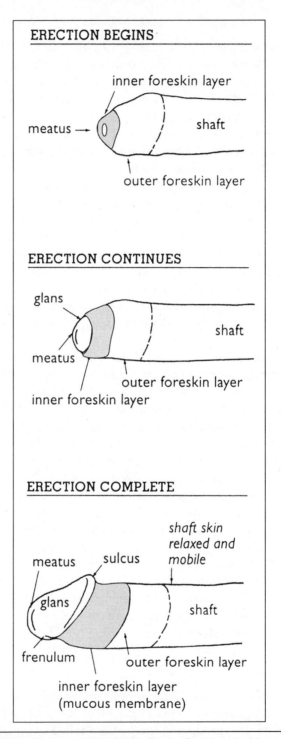

Figure 12.1   Erection Process of the Intact Penis. Reprinted with permission from *Circumcision Exposed: Rethinking a Medical and Cultural Tradition* by Billy Ray Boyd. © 1998. Published by The Crossing Press, P.O. Box 1048, Freedom, CA 95019.

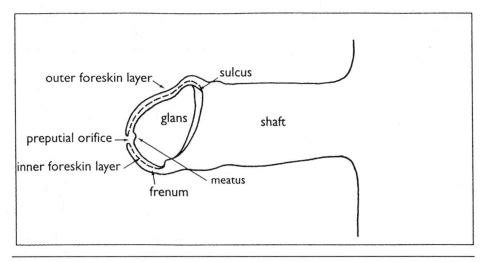

Figure 12.2   Inner and Outer Foreskin Layers. Reprinted with permission from
Circumcision Exposed: Rethinking a Medical and Cultural Tradition by Billy Ray Boyd.
© 1998. Published by The Crossing Press, P.O. Box 1048, Freedom, CA 95019.

or more of the penile shaft skin (Taylor, Lockwood, & Taylor, 1996). Recent case
reports demonstrate that the inner and outer linings of the average adult prepuce
form a total tissue surface area of 64 to 90 cm^2 (10–14 sq. in.) (Werker, Terng, &
Kon, 1998). The prepuce provides a platform for several nerves and is "an important component of the overall sensory mechanism of the human penis" (Taylor
et al., 1996, p. 291). The prepuce is specialized tissue, richly supplied with blood
vessels, highly innervated, and uniquely endowed with stretch receptors. The
inner surface of the prepuce displays a transversely arranged zone of mucosal
ridged bands that merge with the densely nerve-laden frenulum on the under-
side of the glans penis. This ridged band zone is richly endowed with Meissner's
corpuscles, similar to nerve endings in the fingertips and lips. When the prepuce
is retracted, the ridged band zone is everted on the penile shaft and available for
external stimulation (Taylor et al., 1996).

Because the prepuce is a moveable sheath, two of its other functions are
readily identifiable. In its static position (usually covering the glans), it maintains the glans as an internal organ, protecting it in much the same way that
the female prepuce (clitoral hood) protects the clitoris. In both male and female, the prepuce keeps these internal organs moist, sensitive, and out of contact with a harsh external environment (dirt, drying effects of air, and
abrasiveness of clothing). Without the protective foreskin, the normally mucosal surface of the glans penis dries out and forms several layers of dead protective tissue (keratinization) (Bigelow, 1995).

The gliding function of the foreskin both causes and responds to sexual
stimulation. Stretching the foreskin forward over the glans or backward toward the body activates preputial nerve endings, enhancing sexual excitability
and contributing to the male ejaculatory reflex (Milos & Macris, 1994). Both

the glans and the foreskin itself benefit from the stimulation of the foreskin as it glides back and forth over the corona of the glans. In the intact male, masturbation involves the manipulation of this gliding foreskin. Circumcised men must use compensatory techniques.

Lubrication is another significant function of the foreskin. When an intact male engages in heterosexual intercourse, the moist, nonkeratinized mucosal surfaces of the glans penis and inner foreskin layer move back and forth across the mucosal surfaces of the labia and vagina, providing nontraumatic sexual stimulation to both partners (Milos & Macris, 1994). A recent scientific review also indicates that the inner mucosal lining of the male prepuce, like other human mucosa, demonstrates immunological functions, thereby reducing an intact male's risk of contracting sexually transmitted diseases (Cold & Taylor, 1999; Fleiss, Hodges, & Van Howe, 1998). Thus, the foreskin is an important, purposeful aspect of male sexuality, without which "the fundamental biological sex act becomes, for the circumcised male, simply satisfaction of an urge and not the refined sensory experience that it was meant to be" (Falliers, 1970, p. 2194).

Medicalization of a Ritual

A recent biocultural analysis describes childhood circumcision as "low-grade neurological castration" (Immerman & Mackey, 1998, p. 372), resulting in traumatic neurological reorganization and/or atrophy of brain circuitry and sexual desensitization from glans keratinization. Perhaps this is a primitive effort to limit male sexual excitability and to produce a male who is more amenable to group authority figures. The authors propose positron emission tomography (PET) and/or magnetic resonance imaging (MRI) to detect differences in the somatosensory cortex when it receives stimuli from the genitalia of circumcised men compared with similar cortical areas of genitally intact men. Experience suggests, however, that circumcision "does not reduce sexual drive, but leads to compensatory behaviors including sexual compulsivity, altered sexual practices, and other personal/societal consequences" (Hammond, 1999, p. 5). The control of children's sexuality through circumcision is consistent with the motivations of religious authorities in the past (Aldeeb Abu-Sahlieh, 1994; Boyd, 1998) and with those of nineteenth-century physicians (Comfort, 1967; Wallerstein, 1980).

No action has entrenched the practice of male genital mutilation more than its legitimization through the medical profession. Circumcision evolved from a religious ritual or puberty rite into routine surgery for "health" reasons in the English-speaking countries during the nineteenth-century, when the etiology of most diseases was unknown (Milos & Macris, 1992). Victorian antisexual attitudes were largely responsible for a theory that masturbation caused a wide array of mental and physical ills. In a naïve attempt to prevent or cure masturbation, various forms of control were imposed on children of both sexes (Paige, 1978). These included religious lectures, diets of bland foods, physical apparatuses (chastity belts, straitjackets, genital cages, and spiked penile rings), carbolic acid on the clitoris, and surgical interventions. For boys, sewing the foreskin almost completely shut (infibulation) or circumcision was effective at reducing or eliminating the mobility of this erogenous tissue (Comfort, 1967). None of these was effective, however, at eliminating masturbation.

In the United States, despite the various reasons put forth to perpetuate this genital alteration (which most of the world has never considered), the American medical community has consistently failed to prove conclusively that circumcision carries any significant advantage over the intact state for the vast majority of men. This failing was recognized in 1971, when the American Academy of Pediatrics (AAP) convened a task force on circumcision to study the issue. It concluded that there are no valid medical indications for circumcision in the neonatal period. The task force thoroughly refuted claims that circumcision reduced or eliminated risks of penile cancer, cervical cancer, and sexually transmitted diseases. It clarified that the alleged problem of phimosis (nonretractile foreskin) was, in fact, a normal manifestation of infant and early childhood anatomy that resolves as the penis develops. It asserted the benefits of good hygiene over surgical intervention. Finally, it recognized that the parental decision-making process was rarely based on medical factors but rather was strongly influenced by emotion and custom. This, perhaps more than any other reason, is why newborn circumcision continued unabated in the United States even after the AAP's decisive statement, which was reiterated in 1975 (AAP Committee on Fetus and Newborn).

By the mid-1980s, articles had appeared in law journals questioning the legality of imposing medically unnecessary circumcision on healthy infants. In California at that time, a lawsuit was brought to the state Appellate Court questioning parents' assumed rights to consent to medically unnecessary surgery on their children (Bonner & Kinane, 1989). Although unsuccessful, the case may have threatened the medical community. Shortly thereafter, new medical "evidence" emerged to justify circumcision: reduced risk of urinary tract infections (UTIs) as well as speculation that the foreskin increases a man's risk of contracting HIV/AIDS.

In 1989, this "evidence" prompted the AAP to convene a new circumcision task force to revisit the issue. Although recognizing that the UTI studies were "retrospective in design and may have methodological flaws" and "the study population may have been influenced by selection bias" (AAP Report of the Task Force on Circumcision, 1989, p. 389), the task force concluded that infant circumcision "has potential medical benefits and advantages, as well as [inherent] disadvantages and risks"(p. 390). The fact that "potential" does not equal "proven" was lost on the U.S. media, which reported that this otherwise neutral statement constituted a "reversal" of the AAP's opposition to infant circumcision.

Since 1989, new research demonstrates that an increased risk of UTI is not associated with the presence or absence of a foreskin but with congenital anomalies of the male urinary tract (Mueller, Steinhardt, & Haseer, 1997) and that there is no proof that lack of circumcision is a risk factor for increased UTI

(Thompson, 1990). Studies of HIV infectivity reveal that the alleged importance of circumcision is inconclusive, often due to selection bias (DeVincenzi & Mertens, 1994; Van Howe, 1999). The preponderance of evidence indicates that the risks of penile cancer, cervical cancer, and sexually transmitted diseases (STDs), including HIV/AIDS, are not the result of being intact or circumcised, but of sexual behaviors (Poland, 1990). Circumcision does not confer protection from AIDS or any other STD. Good hygiene, limiting one's sexual partners, and use of condoms are a more reliable means of STD riskreduction than is sexual surgery.

For every problem that circumcision was once alleged to prevent or treat, there are now effective alternative methods of nonsurgical prophylaxis and treatment that respect the patient's genital integrity (Doctors Opposing Circumcision, 1997). In other medically advanced English-speaking nations with a prior history of male circumcision, medical associations have adopted positions less ambiguous than that of the American Academy of Pediatrics:

Australia (infant circumcision rate less than 10%):

> The Australian Medical Association will continue to discourage circumcision of baby boys in line with the Australian College of Paediatrics. ("Circumcision Deterred," 1997, p. 5)

> The possibility that routine circumcision may contravene human rights has been raised because circumcision is performed on a minor and is without proven medical benefit. (Australian College of Paediatrics, 1996, p. 1)

> Neonatal male circumcision has no medical indication. It is a traumatic procedure performed without anesthesia to remove a normal functional and protective prepuce. We are opposed to male children being subjected to a procedure, which had they been old enough to consider the advantages and disadvantages, may well have opted to reject the operation and retain their prepuce. (Australian Association of Paediatric Surgeons, 1996, p. 1)

Britain (infant circumcision rate less than 1%):

> Where conditions can effectively be treated conservatively, it is accepted good practice to do so. . . . Therefore, to circumcise . . . where medical research has shown other techniques to be at least as effective and less invasive would be unethical and inappropriate. (British Medical Association, 1996, p. 1)

Canada (infant circumcision rate less than 25%):

> Circumcision of newborns should not be routinely performed. (Canadian Paediatric Society, 1996, p. 769)

In 1999, the AAP released a new circumcision policy, stating that any potential medical benefits were not significant enough to recommend that circumcision be routinely performed and that it is not essential to a child's well-being.

By making an unequivocal call for pain medication, it recognized that the extreme pain and trauma of circumcision cannot be ignored. The AAP Task Force on Circumcision acknowledged reports that "penile sensation and sexual satisfaction are decreased for circumcised males" (AAP Task Force on Circumcision, Policy Statement, 1999, p. 687).

It left open the possibility, however, for physicians to cut the genitals of any boy without medical need if a parent requests it for cultural reasons. This policy conflicts with two related AAP policies. Its Committee on Bioethics stated that pediatric health care providers "have legal and ethical duties to their child patients to render competent medical care based on what the patient needs, not what someone else expresses" (AAP Committee on Bioethics, 1995, p. 315). The AAP also advised its members against participation in any form of genital cutting for girls for cultural reasons (AAP Committee on Bioethics, 1998), including removal of the clitoral hood, which many physicians admit is less severe than amputating a boy's foreskin.

Psychosocial Motivations to Circumcise

Our science is affected by our cultural values, and circumcision reflects a cultural value rooted in neither science nor medicine. Despite the possible immediate harmful effects of male circumcision and potential adverse long-term effects, it is difficult for us to change because the practice is deeply embedded in American culture. Circumcision of infants may be a reenactment of the trauma of one's own circumcision. A survey of randomly selected primary care physicians showed that circumcision was more often supported by doctors who were older, male, and circumcised (Stein, Marx, Taggart, & Bass, 1982). Defending circumcision requires minimizing or denying the harm and perhaps overstating medical claims about its alleged protective effects. Religious beliefs may also be used to defend circumcision.

Parents are solicited by hospital personnel to make a decision about circumcision. This may imply to them that it is a beneficial practice. Those parents who agree to circumcision of their newborn son are typically not aware of counter-information and may not understand what circumcision does (Terris & Oalmann, 1960). Doctors say they circumcise because parents request it, but parents choose it because doctors do it (Briggs, 1985). Communication between physician and parents about circumcision is often insufficient for informed consent, largely because of emotional discomfort with the subject. The discussion may instead include incorrect tacit assumptions by doctor and parent about what the other really wants or means (Briggs, 1985). These assumptions lean toward the decision to circumcise. The parents' lack of expertise leads them to defer to the doctor's knowledge. Although doctors do not require that parents choose circumcision, and parents believe they are freely making their own choice, doctors do exercise control over the parents' decision by controlling information and sometimes making a recommendation (Briggs, 1985; Patel, 1966).

A national study of 400 pediatricians and obstetricians indicated that two-thirds of doctors took a neutral position on circumcision when advising parents (Herrera, Cochran, Herrera, & Wallace, 1983), but this may not provide accurate and complete information to those who are asked to make the decision (Goldman, 1997). Even when doctors advise against circumcision, their continued willingness to perform it at parental request suggests to parents that circumcision may not be harmful.

The importance of conformity in the circumcision decision is illustrated by a survey of parents of 124 newborn males born at a Denver hospital. The results showed that for parents making the circumcision decision, social concerns outweighed medical concerns. Parents' reasons for circumcising were based mainly on an interest that the baby look like his father, brothers, and friends. Only 23% of the uncircumcised fathers had circumcised sons. In contrast, 90% of the circumcised fathers had circumcised sons. The authors concluded that the circumcision decision has a strong base in social and cultural beliefs (Brown & Brown, 1987).

In a study at a Baltimore hospital, social conformity was a major consideration among parents making the circumcision decision. A group of parents was given special information on circumcision, which concluded that circumcision is not medically necessary. A control group in the study was not given any special information on circumcision. The circumcision rates of the two groups were not statistically different. The researchers concluded that parents found social reasons alone sufficient to choose circumcision (Herrera et al., 1983). However, there is no empirical evidence to support the assumption that a boy would want to be circumcised if his father or peers are circumcised (Goldman, 1999).

The following factors call into question the validity of the decision to circumcise for social or "matching" reasons:

- The circumcision status of the father is not necessarily known or important to a male child.
- A circumcised boy who "matches" others may nevertheless have negative feelings about being circumcised (Goldman, 1997).
- It is not possible to predict prior to circumcision how a boy will feel about it later.
- As a growing minority in the United States, most uncircumcised men are happy to be intact.
- An intact man who is unhappy about it can choose to be circumcised, but this is rarely done. The estimated rate of adult circumcision in the United States is 3 in 1,000 (Wallerstein, 1980).
- An intact man who is unhappy about his status may feel differently after learning more about circumcision and the important functions of the foreskin (Goldman, 1997).
- The social factor is much less of an issue for boys born today because of the overall trend away from circumcision.

Consequences of Circumcision

Parents' Responses

The typical hospital circumcision is done out of view of the parents in a separate room. However, a few are observed by parents, and many Jewish ritual circumcisions are done in the homes of the parents. There are no studies of how these parents respond to observing their son's circumcision. Personal accounts vary and may include strong emotions such as grief, horror, and shock. Some parents regret their son's circumcision and report that they wish they had known more about circumcision before they consented to it (Goldman, 1997; Goodman, 1999; O'Mara, 1993; Pollack, 1995).

Effects on the Infant

In neonatal circumcision, most surgical complications are immediately apparent, such as hemorrhage, infection, skin loss in excess of that intended, urinary retention, iatrogenic hypospadias or epispadias, penile amputation, and death. From these and other consequences, one investigator concluded, "[Male circumcision] is not harmless and cannot be recommended without unequivocal proof of benefit" (Thompson, 1990, p. 195).

The question of pain is often raised in debates about circumcision. Some doctors believe that the newborn nervous system is not sufficiently developed to register or transmit pain impulses (Katz, 1977; Tilney & Rosett, 1931). However, this belief has been called "the major myth" of physicians regarding infant pain (Schechter, 1989). Anatomical, neurochemical, physiological, and behavioral studies confirm that newborn responses to pain are "similar to but greater than those in adult subjects" (Anand & Hickey, 1987, p. 1326). In one study, infants circumcised without anesthesia (reflecting common practice) experienced not only severe pain but also increased risk of choking and difficulty breathing (Lander, Brady-Freyer, Metcalfe, Nazerali, & Muttit, 1997). Increases in heart rate of 55 beats per minute have been recorded during circumcision, about a 50% increase over the baseline (Benini, Johnson, Faucher, & Aranda, 1993). After circumcision, the level of blood cortisol (stress hormone) increased by a factor of three to four times the level prior to circumcisions (Gunnar, Malone, Vancer, & Fisch, 1985). As a surgical procedure, circumcision has been described as "among the most painful performed in neonatal medicine" (Ryan & Finer, 1994, p. 232). Investigators reported, "This level of pain would not be tolerated by older patients" (Williamson & Williamson, 1983, p. 40). Using a pacifier during circumcision reduced crying but did not affect hormonal pain response (Gunnar, Fisch, & Malone, 1984). An infant also may go into a state of shock to escape the overwhelming pain (Goldman, 1998). Therefore, although crying may be absent, other body signals demonstrate that severe pain is always present during circumcision.

There is disagreement among physicians about using anesthesia during circumcisions. Prior to the mid-1980s, anesthesia was not used because infant pain was denied by the medical community. That belief has changed among many physicians, but an anesthetic (local injection, the best option tested) still is not typically administered due to a lack of familiarity with its use as well as the belief that it introduces additional risk (Ryan & Finer, 1994). Although there is indication that the risk is minimal, most physicians who perform circumcisions do not use anesthetics even after they are taught how. When an anesthetic is used, it relieves only some but not all of the pain, and its effect wanes before the postoperative pain does (Stang, Gunnar, Snellman, Condon, & Kesterbaum, 1988).

Circumcision results in behavioral changes in infants that have been shown to interfere with parent-infant bonding and feeding (Anand & Hickey, 1987). Researchers conclude that circumcision has "behavioral and psychological consequences" (Richards, Bernal, & Brackbill, 1976, p. 310). The AAP Task Force on Circumcision (1989) notes increased irritability, varying sleep patterns, and changes in infant-maternal interaction after circumcisions. Canadian investigators report that during vaccinations at age 4 to 6 months, circumcised boys had increased behavioral pain response and cried for significantly longer periods than did uncircumcised boys. The authors believe that "circumcision may induce long-lasting changes in infant pain behavior" (Taddio, Katz, Ilersich, & Koren, 1997, p. 602). One study suggests that circumcision may permanently alter the structure and function of developing neural pathways (Walco, Cassidy, & Schechter, 1994).

Studies investigating circumcision pain have referred to circumcision as traumatic (Lander et al., 1997; Taddio et al., 1997). From the perspective of the infant, all the elements in the *DSM-IV* description of traumatic events can be applied to the experience of circumcision: the procedure involves being forcibly restrained, having part of the penis cut off, and experiencing extreme pain. Based on the nature of the experience and considering the extreme physiological and behavioral responses of the infant, circumcision traumatizes the infant.

Later Effects on the Child

The negative impact of circumcision on the mother-child relationship is perhaps as evident from some mothers' distressed responses as it is from the infants' behavioral changes. The disrupted mother-infant bond has far-reaching developmental implications (Arend, Gove, & Sroufe, 1979; Donovan & Leavitt, 1985; Kestenbaum, Farber, & Sroufe, 1989; Reite & Capitanio, 1985; Vandell, 1980) and may be one of the most important adverse impacts of circumcision.

Surgical complications can become more evident as the child develops. These include prominent scarring, meatal stenosis (when the meatus—urinary opening—shrinks or closes due to ulceration of an unprotected glans, sometimes necessitating a surgical reopening of the meatus), and painful skin bridges (a tethering of the mucosal tissues of the corona and shaft, formed during the healing process when tissue of the glans fuses with the remaining inner foreskin tissue on the shaft behind the sulcus) (Sathaye, Goswami, & Sharma, 1991).

Effects on the Man

Surgical complications from infant circumcision may become more prominent and troublesome in adulthood (Snyder, 1989). Unlike adult circumcision (Money & Davidson, 1983), the adverse outcomes on men's well-being from infant circumcision have never been monitored or investigated by the medical community. The only systematic approach to documenting these consequences is an ongoing survey of more than 500 circumcised men conducted by the National Organization to Halt the Abuse and Routine Mutilation of Males (NOHARMM). Titled *Awakenings: A Preliminary Poll of Circumcised Males,* the published findings of the survey (Hammond, 1999) revealed that circumcised respondents suffered a wide range of consequences from this surgery they did not choose.

Various religious backgrounds were represented by respondents. The majority were from Christian families (77%), for whom circumcision is not a religious mandate. Respondents from religious minorities with a tradition of circumcision reported less physical harm than did Christian respondents, but higher degrees of emotional and psychological distress over their circumcision. (Jewish males accounted for more than 4% of the respondents, although they account for only 2% of the U.S. male population).

There was significant variability in how the effects of circumcision manifest themselves due to the following factors: (1) type of circumcision method; (2) expertise of the circumciser (often, hospital circumcisions are delegated to less experienced medical students and residents); (3) zealousness of the circumciser (which can determine how much or how little skin is removed); (4) nonuse of anesthesia; (5) how the injury heals (scars can be erogenous, painfully hypersensitive, or numb to sensation); (6) age at circumcision (the younger the age at which children experience pain, either by abuse or surgery, the deeper and more serious is its traumatic impression) (Green, 1983; Levy, 1945); and (7) presence or absence of cultural indoctrination (convincing a child that his circumcision is a mark of normalcy, superiority, or holiness may ameliorate trauma and resentment by offering social enfranchisement, but may also be shattered later by contradictory knowledge and awareness).

The physical and sexual harm reported by respondents included (1) progressive sensory deficit in the glans (61%); (2) excess stimulation required to reach orgasm, leading to sexual dysfunctions and orgasmic difficulties (40%); (3) prominent scarring (33%); (4) insufficient shaft skin to cover the erect penis (27%); (5) erectile bowing/curvature from uneven skin loss (16%); (6) pain and bleeding upon erection (17%); (7) painful skin bridges (12%); and (8) physical anomalies that included beveling deformities of the glans and meatal stenosis (20%).

Many respondents reported that they had to resort to prolonged and excessive thrusting to stimulate the residual nerve endings in the penis to trigger orgasm. This, and the unnatural dryness of the circumcised penis, often made coitus painful for them and their partners (O'Hara, 1999).

Reported psychological damage included feelings of (1) sexual mutilation (60%); (2) unnaturalness, abnormality, or lack of wholeness (57%); (3) resentment/depression (59%); (4) rage (52%); (5) physical violation (46%); (6) low self-esteem and inferiority to intact men (50%); and (7) betrayal over what was done to them (30%). In circumcising cultures such as the United States, these forms of psychological disturbances are not yet recognized. Therefore, few mental health professions are trained to treat them as such.

We must acknowledge that this survey group is a self-selected population of men who are well-educated about male anatomy and the effects of circumcision. However, three separate men's body image surveys demonstrate that dissatisfaction with this involuntary genital alteration is not uncommon among circumcised men. In 1989, an Australian *Forum* survey discovered that "Quite a lot of circumcised men (20%) were dissatisfied with the way they had been cut" (Badger, 1989, p. 14), and "18% of the circumcised men would rather not have been" (p. 15). In 1992, a survey of almost 200 American men by the magazine *Journeymen* (Boynton, 1993) found that 20% of circumcised respondents expressed dissatisfaction with their circumcised condition, and only 3% of uncircumcised respondents registered dissatisfaction with being intact. Conversely, the survey found that 78% of intact male respondents were happy with their genital status compared to a 38% satisfaction rate among the circumcised. Another U.S. survey in 1996 (*Men's Forum*) revealed that 50% of respondents circumcised as infants were unhappy about it, versus 3% of intact respondents who were unhappy that they had not been circumcised at birth.

In general, however, men have no acceptable means of expressing negative feelings about circumcision. Illustrative of this, the *Awakenings* survey found that 54% of respondents had not sought help for their perceived harm for the following reasons: (1) felt no recourse was available (43%); (2) embarrassment (19%); (3) feared ridicule (17%); and (4) mistrusted doctors (11%).

Many of the survey respondents (53%) were undergoing uncircumcision procedures (foreskin restoration). These nonsurgical methods involve a gradual process of skin expansion that applies gentle tension on the penile shaft skin. The resulting new growth of skin approximates the look, feel, and function of a prepuce, with a corresponding increase in self-esteem and sexual enhancement (Bigelow, 1995).

Respondents credited a fair amount of their knowledge and awareness about the foreskin and circumcision to two sources. One was the National Organization of Restoring Men (NORM). This (now international) self-help group was begun in 1990 to offer circumcised men moral and technical support in regaining their physical integrity through nonsurgical foreskin restoration. The other source, *The Joy of Uncircumcising!* by Jim Bigelow (1995), details the histories of circumcision and uncircumcision as well as the various methods of restoration.

Infant circumcision appears to be the only surgery that later prompts the patient to deliberately invest time, money, and effort to "undo" the effects of the physician's scalpel. Like the long-term effects on men of infant circumcision, the outcomes of restoration have yet to be studied by the medical community.

Awakenings respondents demonstrated that two important factors affect circumcision satisfaction levels: knowledge of foreskin functions and awareness of how circumcision impacts penile functioning. A higher degree of this knowledge and awareness corresponds to a lower level of circumcision satisfaction. The less accurate information a man has about the foreskin and circumcision, the more positively he views the circumcised condition. Respondents reported that, prior to obtaining this knowledge and developing their awareness, they denied that circumcision had damaged their bodies or their sexuality. Any challenge to their previous concept of the correctness of circumcision had been met with defensiveness or anger.

SUMMARY

The foreskin, together with the glans, is an integral part of the pleasure dynamics of movement, sensation, and lubrication that occur during masturbation, foreplay, and sexual intercourse. Pro-circumcision empiricists pursue a search for scientific evidence that supports prophylactic benefits of surgery. Their findings remain narrow and ambiguous. A disturbing silence exists in the medical community, however, regarding the normalcy of the intact foreskin, loss and grief associated with circumcision, and circumcision's impact on a man's overall psychosexual development.

Increasing numbers of circumcised men are restoring themselves and, like their African female counterparts, are breaking historical silence to challenge these childhood assaults (Boyd, 1998; Dillon & Hammond, 1995). Although important distinctions remain between the practices of male and female circumcision, they share more similarities than differences. The functional anatomy of the female genitals is identical to that of males (Toubia, 1994). The social motivations of both customs parallel each other (Lightfoot-Klein, 1989a). The paucity of scientific evidence on the sexual and psychological effects of these practices is due in part to the historical silence of the majority of victims, for whom the psychological effects are likely to be subtle and buried beneath layers of denial, mixed with resignation and acceptance of social norms (Goldman, 1997; Toubia, 1994). In many respects, the shared core issue is not severity, but sovereignty (Van Howe, Svoboda, Dwyer, & Price, 1999).

The health hazards and psychological risks to children from male genital cutting are a sociocultural, health, and human rights problem. Eradication efforts must be empathic, not alienating. They must recognize all forms of cultural manipulation and mutilation of males, whether physical or psychological, as a form of genital and sexual abuse that subjects the child to the whims of an adult. It must not be equated too closely, however, with child abuse. Genital mutilation is undertaken with "good intentions" based on "normalizing" a child, whereas child abuse isolates a child. Discussion must begin on where to draw the line between the parental desire to cute male genitals and society's obligation to protect children from harm. Such discussions are already underway in many cultures where circumcision is endemic.

REFERENCES

Aldeeb Abu-Sahlieh, S. (1994). *To mutilate in the name of Jehovah or Allah: Legitimization of male and female circumcision.* Amsterdam, The Netherlands: Middle East Research Associates or http://www.moslem.org/circumcision.htm

American Academy of Pediatrics, Committee on Bioethics. (1995). Informed consent, parental permission, and assent in pediatric practice. *Pediatrics, 95,* 314–317.

American Academy of Pediatrics, Committee on Bioethics. (1998). Female genital mutilation. *Pediatrics, 102,* 153–156.

American Academy of Pediatrics, Committee on Circumcision. (1989). Report of the task force on circumcision. *Pediatrics, 84,* 388–391.

American Academy of Pediatrics, Committee on Fetus and Newborn. (1971). *Standards and recommendations for hospital care of newborn infants* (5th ed.). Evanston, IL: Author.

American Academy of Pediatrics, Committee on Fetus and Newborn. (1975). Report of the ad hoc task force on circumcision. *Pediatrics, 56,* 610–611.

American Academy of Pediatrics, Section on Urology. (1996). Timing of elective surgery on the genitalia of male children with particular reference to the risks, benefits, and psychological effects of surgery and anesthesia. *Pediatrics, 97,* 590–594.

American Academy of Pediatrics, Task Force on Circumcision. (1999). Circumcision policy statement. *Pediatrics, 103,* 686–693.

Anand, K., & Hickey, P. (1987). Pain and is effects in the human neonate and fetus. *New England Journal of Medicine, 317,* 1321–1329.

Angier, N. (1996, February 4). Intersexual healing: An anomaly finds a group. *New York Times,* p. E14.

Angier, N. (1997, May 13). New debate over surgery on genitals. *New York Times,* p. B7.

Arend, R., Gove, F., & Sroufe, L. (1979). Continuity of individual adaptation from infancy to kindergarten: A predictive study of ego-resiliency and curiosity in preschoolers. *Child Development, 50,* 950–959.

Assaad, M.B. (1980). Female circumcision in Egypt: Current research and social implications. *Studies in Family Planning, 11,* 3–16.

Australasian Association of Paediatric Surgeons. (1996). *Guidelines for circumcision* [Brochure]. Kerstan, Queensland: Author.

Australian College of Paediatrics. (1996). *Position statement on routine circumcision of normal male infants and boys* [Brochure]. Parkville, Victoria: Author.

Badger, J. (1989). Circumcision: What you think. *Australian Forum, 20,* 10–29.

Barry, E. (1996, November 22). United States of ambiguity. *The Boston Phoenix,* pp. 6, 8.

Beck-Karrer, C. (1996). *Lowinnen sind sie: Gesprache mit somalischen Frauen und Männer uber Frauenbeschneidung in Afrika* [They are lionesses: Conversations with Somali women and men about female circumcision]. eFeF Verlag Bern, Switzerland.

Benini, F., Johnson, C., Faucher, D., & Aranda, J. (1993). Topical anesthesia during circumcision in newborn infants. *Journal of the American Medical Association, 270,* 850–853.

Bigelow, J. (1995). *The joy of uncircumcising!* Aptos, CA: Hourglass Book.

Bonner, C., & Kinane, M. (1989, July/August). Circumcision: The legal and constitutional issues. *The Truth Seeker, 1*(Suppl.), S1–S4.

Boyd, B.R. (1998). *Circumcision exposed: Rethinking a medical and cultural tradition.* Freedom, CA: Crossing Press.

Boynton, P. (1993, May 20). Letter detailing survey results to T. Hammond. *Journeymen.*

Briggs, A. (1985). *Circumcision: What every parent should know.* Earlysville, VA: Birth and Parenting.

British Medical Association. (1996). *Circumcision of male infants: Guidelines for doctors* [Brochure]. London: Author.

Brown, M.S., & Brown, C.A. (1987). Circumcision decision: Prominence of social concerns. *Pediatrics, 80,* 215–219.

Burton, R. (1954). *Love, war and fancy: Notes to the Arabian nights.* London: Kimber.

Canadian Paediatric Society, Fetus and Newborn Committee. (1996). Neonatal circumcision revisited. *Canadian Medical Association Journal, 154,* 769–779.

Chase, C. (1996). Re: Measurement of evoked potentials during feminizing genitoplasty: Techniques and applications [Letter to the editor]. *Journal of Urology, 156,* 1139–1140.

Chase, C. (1997a). *Hermaphrodites speak!* [Video] San Francisco: Intersex Society of North America.

Chase, C. (Ed.). (1997b, Fall/Winter). Special issue on intersexuality. *Chrysalis: The Journal of Transgressive Gender Identities.*

Chase, C. (1998). Hermaphrodites with attitude: Mapping the emergence of intersex political activism. *GLQ: A Journal of Gay and Lesbian Studies, 4,* 189–211.

Circumcision deterred. (1997, January 6–20) *Australian Medicine,* 5.

Colapinto, J. (1997, December 11). The true story of John/Joan. *Rolling Stone,* 54–73, 92–97. Available: http://www.infocirc.org/infocirc/rollston.htm.

Cold, C., & Taylor, J. (1999). The prepuce. *BJU International, 83*(Suppl. 1), 34–44.

Comfort, A. (1967). *The anxiety makers: Some curious preoccupations of the medical profession.* Camden, NJ: Nelson.

Coventry, M. (1998, Summer). The tyranny of the esthetic: Surgery's most intimate violation. *On the Issues: The Progressive Women's Quarterly,* pp. 16–23, 60–61. Available: http://www.momensnet.apc.org/onissues/su98coventry.html.

Dareer, A. (1982). *Woman why do you weep?* London: Zed Press.

Davis, E.G. (1975). *The first sex.* New York: Penquin Books.

Denniston, G.C., & Milos, M.F. (1997). *Sexual mutilations: A human tragedy.* New York: Plenum Press.

DeVincenzi, I., & Mertens, T. (1994). Male circumcision: A role in HIV prevention? *AIDS, 8,* 153–160.

Devore, H. (1999). Growing up in the surgical maelstrom. In A.D. Dreger (Ed.), *Intersexuality in the age of ethics.* Frederick, MD: University Publishing Group.

Diamond, M., & Sigmundson, H.K. (1997a). Management of intersexuality: Guidelines for dealing with persons with ambiguous genitalia. *Archives of Pediatrics and Adolescent Medicine, 151,* 1046–1050. Available: http://www.afn.org/nsfcommed.

Diamond, M., & Sigmundson, H.K. (1997b). Sex reassignment at birth: A long term review and clinical implications. *Archives of Pediatric and Adolescent Medicine, 150,* 298–304. Available: http://www.afn.org/nsfcommed.

Dillon, L., & Hammond, T. (1995). *Whose body, whose rights?* [Video]. (Available from University of California Center for Media and Independent Learning, Berkeley or http://www.noharmm.org/wbwr.htm)

Doctors Opposing Circumcision. (1997). *Male health and genital care: Modern alternatives to circumcision.* (Chart available from 2442 NW Market St., Suite 42, Seattle, WA, 98107 or http://weber.u.washington.edu/~gcd/DOC/altern.html.)

Donovan, W., & Leavitt, L. (1985). Physiologic assessment of mother-infant attachment. *Journal of the American Academy of Child Psychiatry, 24,* 65–70.

Dreger, A.D. (1998a). "Ambiguous sex"—or ambivalent medicine? Ethical issues in the medical treatment of intersexuality and "ambiguous sex." *Hasting Center Report, 28*(3), 24–35.

Dreger, A.D. (1998b). *Hermaphrodites and the medical intervention of sex.* Cambridge, MA: Harvard University Press.

Dreger, A.D. (1999). *Intersexuality in the age of ethics.* Frederick, MD: University Publishing Group.

Dreger, A.E. (Ed.) (1998c). Special issue on intersexuality. *Journal of Clinical Ethics, 9*(4).

Dugger, C. (1996, October 12). New law bans genital cutting in the United States. *New York Times,* p. 1.

Falliers, C.J. (1970). Circumcision. *Journal of the American Medical Association, 214,* 2194.

Fausto-Sterling, A. (1993). The five sexes: Why male and female are not enough. *The Sciences, 33,* 20–25.

Feibleman, P. (1997, Winter). Natural causes. *Doubletake,* 41–47.

Fleiss, P.M., Hodges, F., & Van Howe, R. (1998). Immunological functions of the human prepuce. *Sexually Transmitted Infections, 74,* 364–367.

Garb, M. (1990, April). Tribal identity or child abuse? *American Medical News.*

Giorgis, B.W. (1981). *Female circumcision in Africa.* United Nations Economic Commission for Africa, African Training and Research Centre for Women and Association of African Women for Research and Development, Addis Ababa.

Goldman, R. (1997). *Circumcision: The hidden trauma.* Boston: Vanguard.

Goldman, R. (1998). *Questioning circumcision: A Jewish perspective.* Boston: Vanguard.

Goldman, R. (1999). The psychological impact of circumcision. *BJU International, 83*(Suppl. 1), 93–102.

Goodman, J. (1999). Jewish circumcision: An alternative perspective. *BJU International, 83*(Suppl. 1), 22–27.

Green, A. (1983). Dimensions of psychological trauma in abused children. *Journal of the American Association of Child Psychiatry, 22,* 231–237.

Gross, R.E., Randolph, J., & Crigler, J.F. (1966). Clitorectomy for sexual abnormalities: Indications and technique. *Surgery, 59,* 300–308.

Gunnar, M., Fisch, R., & Malone, S. (1984). The effects of a pacifying stimulus on behavioral and adrenocortical responses to circumcision in the newborn. *Journal of the American Academy of Child Psychiatry, 23,* 34–38.

Gunnar, M., Malone, S., Vance, G., & Fisch, R. (1985). Coping with aversive stimulation in the neonatal period: Quiet sleep and plasma cortisol levels during recovery from circumcision. *Child Development, 56,* 824–834.

Hammond, T. (1999). A preliminary poll of men circumcised in infancy or childhood. *British Journal of Urology International, 83*(Suppl. 1), 85–92.

Hendricks, M. (1993, November). Is it a boy or a girl? *Johns Hopkins Magazine,* 10–16.

Herdt, G. (Ed.). (1994). *Third sex, third gender: Beyond sexual dimorphism in culture and history.* New York: Zone Books.

Herrera, A. (1983). [Letter to the editor]. *Pediatrics, 71,* 670.

Herrera, A., Cochran, B., Herrera, A., & Wallace, B. (1983). Parental information and circumcision in highly motivated couples with higher education. *Pediatrics, 71,* 234.

Hurwitz, R., Applebaum, H., & Muenchow, S. (Producers). (1990). *Surgical reconstruction of ambiguous genitalia in female children* [Video]. (Available from Cine-Med, Inc. 127 Main Street North, PO Box 745, Woodbury, CT, 06798)

Immerman, R.S., & Mackey, W.C. (1998). A proposed relationship between circumcision and neural reorganization. *Journal of Genetic Psychology, 159,* 367–368.

Is early vaginal reconstruction wrong for some intersex girls? (1997, February). *Urology Times,* 10–12.

Katz, J. (1977). The question of circumcision. *International Surgery, 62,* 490–492.

Kemp, B.D., Groveman, S.A., Anonymous, Tako, H.D., & Irwin, K.M. (1996). Sex, lies and androgen insensitivity syndrome. *Canadian Medical Association Journal, 154,* 1829–1833.

Kessler, S. (1990). The medical construction of gender: Case management of intersexual infants. *Signs: Journal of Women in Culture and Society, 16,* 3–26.

Kessler, S. (1997). Meanings of genital variability. *Chrysalis: The Journal of Transgressive Gender Identities, 2,* 33–38.

Kessler, S. (1998). *Lessons from the intersexed.* New Brunswick, NJ: Rutgers University Press.

Kestenbaum, R., Farber, E., & Sroufe, L. (1989). Individual differences in empathy among preschoolers: Relation to attachment history. *New Directions for Child Development, 44,* 51–64.

Koso-Thomas, O. (1987). *The circumcision of women: A strategy for eradication.* London: Zed Books.

Lander, J., Brady-Freyer, B., Metcalfe, J.B., Nazerali, S., & Muttit, S. (1997). Comparison of ring block, dorsal penile nerve block, and topical anesthesia for neonatal circumcision. *Journal of American Medical Association, 278,* 2157–2162.

Lerner, G. (1986). *The creation of patriarchy.* New York: Oxford University Press.

Levy, D. (1945). Psychic trauma of operations in children. *American Journal of Diseases of Children, 69,* 7–25.

Lightfoot-Klein, H. (1989a). *Prisoners of ritual: An odyssey into female genital circumcision in Africa.* New York: Haworth Press.

Lightfoot-Klein, H. (1989b). Rites of purification and their effects: Some psychological aspects of female genital circumcision and infibulation (Pharaonic circumcision) in an Afro-Arab Islamic society (Sudan). *Journal of Psychology and Human Sexuality, 2,* 79–91.

Lightfoot-Klein, H. (1989c). The sexual experience and marital adjustment of genitally circumcised and infibulated females in an Afro-Arab Islamic society (Sudan). *Journal of Sex Research, 26,* 375–393.

Lightfoot-Klein, H. (1991). Orgasm in ritually circumcised African women. In P. Kothari & R. Patel (Eds.), *Proceedings of the first international conference on orgasm* (pp. 121–130). Bombay, India: VRP.

Lightfoot-Klein, H. (1993a). Disability in female immigrants with ritually inflicted genital mutilation. In *Women in Therapy* (pp. 187–194). Binghamton, NY: Haworth Press.

Lightfoot-Klein, H. (1993b). Genital mutilation, female. In B.K. Rothman (Ed.), *Encyclopedia of childbirth* (pp. 160–162). Phoenix, AZ: Baruch Oryx Press.

Lightfoot-Klein, H. (1994a, May–June). The bitter lot of women: In conversation with Nawal el Saadawi. *Freedom Review, 25,* 3.

Lightfoot-Klein, H. (1994b). Female genital mutilation. In V. Bullough (Ed.), *Encyclopedia of human sexuality* (pp. 205–208). New York: Garland.

Lightfoot-Klein, H. (1997). Similarities in attitudes and misconceptions about male and female sexual mutilation. In G.C. Denniston & M.F. Milos (Eds.), *Sexual mutilations: A human tragedy.* New York: Plenum Press.

Lightfoot-Klein, H., & Shaw, E. (1991). Special needs of ritually circumcised women patients. *Journal of Obstetrics, Gynecology, and Neo-Natal Nursing, 20,* 102–107.

Lionnet, F. (1992). Women's rights, bodies and identities: The limits of universalism and the legal debate around excision in France. In M. Mutman & M. Yegenogin (Eds.), *Inscriptions, Vol. 6: Orientalism and Cultural Differences, 98,* 107–109.

McCroy, W. (1998, February 13). Does intersex "corrective" surgery do more harm than good? *Baltimore's Gay Paper,* 16–18.

Men's Forum. (1996, March 10). Circumcision uncut. *Men's Confidential,* 10.

Meyer-Bahlburg, H., Gruen, R.S., New, M.I., Bell, J.J., Morishima, A., Shimshi, M., Bueno, Y., Varga, I., & Baker, S.W. (1996). Gender change from female to male in classical congenital adrenal hyperplasia. *Hormones and Behavior, 30,* 319–322.

Meyers-Seifer, C.H., & Charest, N.J. (1992). Diagnosis and management of patients with ambiguous genitalia. *Seminars in Perinatology, 16,* 332–339.

Milos, M., & Macris, D. (1992). Circumcision: A medical or a human rights issue? *Journal of Nurse-Midwifery, 37,* 87S–95S.

Milos, M., & Macris, D. (1994). Circumcision: Male-effects upon human sexuality. In V. Bullough & B. Bullough (Eds.), *Human sexuality: An encyclopedia* (pp. 119–121). New York: Garland.

Money, J., & Davidson, J. (1983). Adult penile circumcision: Erotosexual and cosmetic sequelae. *Journal of Sex Research, 19,* 289–292.

Money, J., Devore, H., & Norman, B.F. (1986). Gender identity and gender transposition: Longitudinal outcome study of 32 male hermaphrodites assigned as girls. *Journal of Sex and Marital Therapy, 12,* 165–181.

Montague, M.F.A. (1946). Ritual mutilation among primitive peoples. *Ciba Symposia, 8,* 421–436.

Mueller, E.R., Steinhardt, G., & Naseer, S. (1997, September). Incidence of genitorinary anomalies in circumcised and uncircumcised boys presenting with initial urinary tract infection by six months of age. *Pediatrics, 100*(Suppl.), 58.

Mulgrew, I. (1997, April 7). Controversy over intersex treatment. *Vancouver Sun,* p. 1.

Mureau, M., Slijper, F.M.E., Slob, K., & Verhulst, F.C. (1997). Psychosocial functioning of children, adolescents, and adults following hypospadias surgery: A comparative study. *Journal of Pediatric Psychology, 22,* 371–387.

Natarajan, A. (1996). Medical ethics and truth-telling in the case of androgen insensitivity syndrome. *Canadian Medical Association Journal, 154,* 568–570.

National Organization to Halt the Abuse and Routine Mutilation of Males. (1994). *Awakenings: A preliminary poll of circumcised men.* (Available from P.O. Box 460795, San Francisco, CA 94146)

New, M.I., & Kitzinger, E. (1993). Pope Joan: A recognizable syndrome. *Journal of Clinical Endocrinology and Metabolism, 76,* 3–13.

Newman, K., Randolph, J., & Parson, S. (1992). Functional results in young women having clitoral reconstruction as infants. *Journal of Pediatric Surgery, 27,* 180–184.

Nicholson, S. (1999). Take charge: A guide to home catheterization. In A.D. Dreger (Ed.), *Intersexuality in the age of ethics.* Frederick, MD: University Publishing Group.

Obiora, A.L. (1997, Winter). Bridges and barricades: Rethinking polemics and intransigence in the campaign against female circumcision. *Case Western Reserve Law Review, 47,* 275–378.

Oesterling, J.E., Gearhart, J.P., & Jeffs, R.D. (1987). A unified approach to early reconstructive surgery of the child with ambiguous genitalia. *Journal of Urology, 138,* 1079–1084.

Ogunmodede, E. (1979). End this mutilation. *People, 6*(1), 30–31.

O'Hara, K., & O'Hara, J. (1999). The effect of male circumcision on the sexual enjoyment of the female partner. *BJU International, 83*(Suppl. 1), 79–84.

O'Mara, P. (Ed). (1993). *Circumcision: The rest of the story.* Santa Fe, NM: Mothering.

Paige, K.E. (1978). The ritual of circumcision. *Human Nature,* 40–48.

Parker, L.A. (1998). Ambiguous genitalia: Etiology, treatment, and nursing implications. *Journal of Obstetric, Gynecologic, and Neonatal Nursing, 27,* 15–22.

Patel, H. (1966). The problem of routine circumcision. *Canadian Medical Association Journal, 95,* 578–581.

Poland, R. (1990). The question of routine neonatal circumcision. *New England Journal of Medicine, 322,* 1312–1314.

Pollack, M. (1995). Circumcision: A Jewish feminist perspective. In K. Weiner & A. Moon (Eds.), *Jewish women speak out* (pp. 171–185). Seattle: Canopy Press.

Reilly, J.M., & Woodhouse, C.R.J. (1989). Small penis and the male sexual role. *Journal of Urology, 142,* 569–571.

Reiner, W.G. (1997a). To be male or female—that is the question. *Archives of Pediatric and Adolescent Medicine, 151,* 224–225.

Reiner, W.G. (1997b). Sex assignment in the neonate with intersex or inadequate genitalia. *Archives of Pediatric and Adolescent Medicine, 151,* 1044–1045.

Reite, M., & Capitanio, J. (1985). On the nature of social separation and social attachment. In T. Field & M. Reite (Eds.), *The psychobiology of separation and attachment* (pp. 223–258). New York: Academic Press.

Richards, M., Bernal, J., & Brackbill, Y. (1976). Early behavioral differences: Gender or circumcision? *Developmental Psychology, 21,* 310.

Roscoe, W. (1987). Bibliography of berdache and alternative gender roles among North American Indians. *Journal of Homosexuality, 14,* 81–171.

Ryan, C., & Finer, N. (1994). Changing attitudes and practices regarding local analgesia for newborn circumcision. *Pediatrics, 94,* 230–233.

Saadawi, N. (1980). *The hidden face of Eve: Women in the Arab world.* London: Zed Press.

Saadawi, N. (1982). Circumcision of girls. In *Seminar on traditional practices affecting the health of women and children in Africa* (pp. 217–228). Alexandria, Egypt: WHO/EMRO Technical.

Sathaye, U.V., Goswami, A.K., & Sharma, S.K. (1991). Skin bridge: A complication of paediatric circumcision. *British Journal of Urology, 66,* 331.

Scheck, A. (1997, August). Attitudes changing toward intersex surgery, but for the better? *Urology Times,* 44–45.

Scheck, A. (1998, February). Intersexuality takes a conservative turn. *Urology Times, 1,* 32–33.

Schechter, N. (1989). The undertreatment of pain in children: An overview. *Pediatric Clinics of North America, 36,* 781–794.

Schober, J.M. (1998). Long-term outcomes of feminizing genitoplasty for intersex. In P. Mouriquant (Ed.), *Pediatric surgery and urology: Long term outcomes.* London: Saunders.

Shapiro, N. (Executive Producer). (1997, June 17). *Dateline: Gender limbo.* New York: NBC. (Available: 800-420-2626)

Snyder, J.L. (1989, July/August). The problem of circumcision in America. *The Truth Seeker,* 39–42.

Stang, H., Gunnar, M., Snellman, L., Condon, L., & Kestenbaum, R. (1988). Local anesthesia for neonatal circumcision. *Journal of the American Medical Association, 259,* 1507–1511.

Stecker, J.F., Horton, C.E., Devine, C.J., & McCraw, J.B. (1981). Hypospadias cripples. *Urologic Clinics of North America: Symposium on Hypospadias, 8,* 539–544.

Stein, M., Marx, M., Taggart, S.L., & Bass, R.A. (1982). Routine neonatal circumcision: The gap between contemporary policy and practice. *Journal of Family Practice, 15,* 47–53.

Taddio, A., Katz, J., Ilersich, A.L., & Koren, G. (1997). Effect of neonatal circumcision on pain response during subsequent routine vaccination. *The Lancet, 349,* 599–603.

Taylor, J., Lockwood, A., & Taylor, A. (1996). The prepuce: Specialized mucosa of the penis and its loss to circumcision. *British Journal of Urology, 77,* 291–295.

Terris, M., & Oalmann, A. (1960). Carcinoma of the cervix. *Journal of the American Medical Association, 174,* 1847–51.

Thompson, R. (1990). Routine circumcision in the newborn: An opposing view. *Journal of Family Practice, 31,* 189–196.

Tilney, F., & Rosett, J. (1931). The value of brain lipoids as an index of brain development. *Bulletin of the Neurological Institute of New York, 1,* 28–71.

Toubia, N. (1994). FGM and the responsibility of reproductive health professionals. *International Journal of Gynecology and Obstetrics, 46,* 127–135.

U.S. Department of State. (1997). *Female genital mutilation.* Washington, DC: Author.

Vandell, D. (1980). Sociability with peers and mothers in the first year. *Developmental Psychology, 16,* 355–361.

Van Howe, R. (1999). Does circumcision influence sexually transmitted diseases? A literature review. *British Journal of Urology International, 83*(Suppl. 1), 52–62.

Van Howe, R., Svobada, J., Dwyer, J., & Price, C. (1999). Involuntary circumcision: The legal issues. *BJU International, 83*(Suppl. 1), 63–73.

Verzin, J.A. (1975). Sequelae of female circumcision. *Tropical Doctor, 5,* 163–169.

Vital Abstracts of the United States. (1994). *Religious populations of the world* [On-line]. Available: http://www.medaccess.com/census95/95s/1350.htm.

Walco, G., Cassidy, R., & Schechter, N. (1994). Pain, hurt, and harm. *New England Journal of Medicine, 331,* 542.

Wallerstein, E. (1980). *Circumcision: An American health fallacy* (p. 48). New York: Springer.

Wallerstein, E. (1985). Circumcision: The uniquely American medical enigma. *Symposium on Advances in Pediatric Urology, Urologic Clinics of North America, 12,* 123–132.

Werker, P.M.N., Terng, A.S.C., & Kon, M. (1998). The prepuce free flap: Dissection feasibility study and clinical application of a super-thin new flap. *Plastic and Reconstructive Surgery, 102,* 1075–1082.

Williamson, P., & Williamson, M. (1983). Physiological stress reduction by a local anesthetic during newborn circumcision. *Pediatrics, 71,* 40.

Young, H.H. (1937). *Genital abnormalities, hermaphroditism, and related adrenal diseases.* Baltimore: Williams & Wilkins.

Youseff, N. (1973). Cultural ideals, feminine behavior and kinship control. *Comparative Studies in Society and History, 15,* 326–347.

Zucker, K.J., Bradley, S.J., Oliver, G., Blake, J., Fleming, S., & Hood, J. (1996). Psychosocial development of women with congenital adrenal hyperplasia. *Hormones and Behavior, 30,* 300–318.

CHAPTER 13

Paraphilias

JAY R. FEIERMAN and LISA A. FEIERMAN

T
O MANY LAY persons and to some professionals as well, there is often nothing more peculiar about human behavior than those behaviors that are called *paraphilias*. For readers not familiar with the term, paraphilias are a group of definably stereotyped, repetitive, sexually motivated behaviors that occur predominantly or exclusively in afflicted males.

According to John Money (1986), the most widely published contemporary author on the paraphilias, in legal terminology, a paraphilia is a perversion or deviancy; in the vernacular, it is kinky or bizarre sex. Money contrasts paraphilia to *normaphilia*, which is a condition of being erotosexually in conformity with the standard, as dictated by custom, religion, or legal authority. We will leave the "what ought to be" to philosophy and moral theology and concern ourselves here with what is most common or average. There are ranges of human behavior to which, when not too extreme, non-mentally ill persons appear to conform. These behaviors include the various components of human reproductive behavior and even some of the behaviors associated with paraphilias.

Indirect measures suggest that many paraphilic behaviors are common enough in human populations to be considered species-atypical traits, such as left-handedness or exclusive homosexual behavior. The indirect measures rely on self-report, which have questionable reliability but are nevertheless the best source of data on the prevalence of these behaviors. Crepault and Couture (1980) studied the self-reported sexual fantasies of 94 men during masturbation or intercourse. Of those reporting sexual fantasies, 61.7% fantasized sexually initiating a young girl, 33% raping a woman, 11.7% being humiliated, 5.3% engaging in sexual activity with an animal, and 3.2% sexually initiating a young boy.

Briere and Runtz (1989) studied the self-reports of 193 male undergraduates regarding possible sexual interest in children. Twenty-one percent reported being sexually attracted to children, 9% fantasizing sex with a child, 5% masturbating to fantasies of sex with children, and 7% indicated a likelihood of actual sexual involvement with a child if they could be assured that no one would know and that they would not be punished.

Templeman and Stinnett (1991) surveyed 60 undergraduate males about child molestation and other types of paraphilias. Three percent reported a history of sexual contact with girls under 12, 42% voyeurism, 8% obscene phone calls, 35% frottage, 2% exhibitionism, 5% coercive sex, and a total of 65% reported some category of sexual misconduct. When asked about their desire for specific sexual contact, 5% reported a desire to have sex with girls under 12, 54% a desire for voyeuristic experiences, and 7% a desire for exhibitionistic experiences.

Some men report paraphilic fantasies and behavior; most men report that pictures depicting a distressed model in bondage, that is, showing the facial expression of "fear," are more sexually stimulating to them than are pictures in which the female model displayed positive, that is, "neutral" or "happy," affect (Heilbrun & Self, 1988). It should be appreciated, however, that many adult men exhibit both paraphilic and nonparaphilic sexual behavior (Weinberg et al., 1994).

Much of the description of paraphilias in this chapter is written with heterosexual male bias in language. The paraphilias are infrequent in homosexual and heterosexual women. Homosexual males, however, do engage in paraphilic behavior, the frequency of which, compared to heterosexual males, is incompletely studied. There are some paraphilias, such as sadomasochism, that appear to be more common among homosexual than heterosexual males (Gosselin & Wilson, 1980). There are other paraphilias, such as fetishism, that appear to be infrequent or absent in transsexual males, most of whom are sexually attracted to other individuals who have penises.

In contrast to many other behaviors that are readily observable, such as aggressive acts, the paraphilic behaviors of human males occur infrequently and covertly. As a result, even educated health care and behavior professionals know very little about these behaviors from direct observation. The first real description of at least some paraphilias was published in 1886 in German by Krafft-Ebing in his epic work, *Psychopathia Sexualis*. Some of the words for the particular paraphilias (e.g., fetish, sadism, masochism) had already crept into the English language by the early twentieth century (e.g., McDougal, 1926), and partial translations into English of Krafft-Ebing's work had been published by the same time. However, the complete English-language version of Krafft-Ebing's classic work was published only relatively recently (Krafft-Ebing, 1965). By the 1950s, several other publications on paraphilias, which were translations of earlier German works, were also available in English (e.g., Stekel, 1952). The following example illustrates how little was known in the professional literature about the paraphilias even in the mid-twentieth century. In one of the first empirical monographs describing the characteristics of two of the most common paraphilias, pedophilia and exhibitionism, Mohr, Turner, and Jerry (1964) commented that in reviewing the literature on pedophilia and exhibitionism, there was no systematic account of pedophilia and only one book specifically devoted to exhibitionism (i.e., Rickles, 1950).

The *Diagnostic and Statistical Manual of Mental Disorders (DSM-IV)* (American Psychiatric Association [APA], 1994) states that the essential features of a paraphilia are recurrent, intense, sexually arousing fantasies, sexual urges, or behaviors generally involving (1) nonhuman objects, (2) the suffering or humiliation of oneself or one's partner, or (3) children or other nonconsenting persons, that occur over a period of at least six months (Criterion A). For some individuals, paraphilic fantasies or stimuli are obligatory for erotic arousal and are always included in sexual activity. In other cases, the paraphilic preferences occur only episodically (e.g., perhaps during periods of stress), whereas at other times, the person is able to function sexually without paraphilic fantasies or stimuli. The behavior, sexual urges, or fantasies cause clinically significant distress or impairment in social, occupational, or other important areas of functioning (Criterion B).

The common paraphilias listed in *DSM-IV* (APA, 1994, pp. 522–532) include the following:

Exhibitionism: exposure of one's genitals to an unsuspecting stranger

Fetishism: the use of nonliving objects, such as female undergarments

Frotteurism: touching and rubbing against a nonconsenting person

Pedophilia: sexual activity with a prepubescent child

Sexual masochism: the act (real or simulated) of being humiliated, beaten, bound, or otherwise made to suffer

Sexual sadism: when the psychological or physical suffering of the victim is sexually exciting

Transvestic fetishism: cross-dressing

Voyeurism: the act of observing an unsuspecting person who is naked, in the process of disrobing, or engaging in sexual activity

Paraphilia Not Otherwise Specified: This category is included for paraphilias that do not meet the criteria for any of the specific categories. Examples include, but are not limited to, telephone scatologia (obscene phone calls), necrophilia (corpses), partialism (exclusive focus on a part of the body), zoophilia (animals), coprophilia (feces), klismaphilia (enemas), and urophilia (urine).

THEORIES OF PARAPHILIAS

Psychological tests cannot reliably identify paraphiliacs; neither can life history data (Garland & Dougher, 1990). Nevertheless, there are a variety of psychological theories of the causes of paraphilias that are presented for their historical importance.

HAVELOCK ELLIS'S THEORY OF EROTIC SYMBOLISM

Although Ellis attributes the term "erotic symbolism" to Eulenburg from 1895, Ellis first used the term in the 1906 edition of his *Studies in the Psychology of Sex* (see Ellis, 1936). Under erotic symbolism, Ellis included practically all of what he called the aberrations of the sexual instinct. Erotic symbolism is for all practical purposes synonymous with what we now call the paraphilias. Ellis argued that the term "symbolism" gives the key to the process that makes these "perversions" intelligible. Ellis (1936) wrote:

> In all of them—very clearly in some, as in shoe fetishism; more obscurely in others, as in exhibitionism—it has come about by causes congenital, acquired, or both, that some object or class of objects, some act or group of acts, has acquired a dynamic power over the psycho-physical mechanism of the sexual process, deflecting it from its normal adjustment to the shoe of a beloved person of the opposite sex. There has been a transmutation of values, and certain objects, certain acts, have acquired an emotional value which for the normal person they do not possess. Such objects and acts are properly, it seems to me, termed symbols, and that term embodies the only justification that in most cases these manifestations can legitimately claim. (preface, p. v)

Ellis elaborated:

> By "erotic symbolism" I mean that tendency whereby the lover's attention is diverted from the central focus of sexual attraction to some object or process which is on the periphery of that focus, or is even outside of it altogether, though recalling it by association of contiguity or of similarity. It thus happens that tumescence . . . may be provoked by the contemplation of acts or objects which are away from the end of sexual conjugation. (p. 1)

In addition to recognizing the isolation of parts of the whole, Ellis (1936) saw that some cases of what he called erotic symbolism involve symbols that are not parts of humans or even of animals; rather, such a symbol has "parasitically rooted itself on energy which normally goes into the channels of healthy human love having for its final end the procreation of the species" (p. 2). Ellis made the point that the disorders of erotic symbolism are only quantitative variations from normalcy. For example, Ellis regarded exhibitionism as

> a symbolic act based on a perversion of courtship. The exhibitionist displays the organ of sex to a feminine witness, and in the shock of modest sexual shame by which she reacts to that spectacle, he finds a gratifying similitude of the normal emotions of coitus. (pp. 93–94)

Ellis (1936) grouped the phenomena of erotic symbolism into four great classes, on the basis of the objects or acts that cause arousal (p. 11): normal parts of the body (e.g., hand, foot, breasts, secretions), abnormal aspects of the body (e.g., lameness, squinting, the pitting of smallpox), inanimate objects (e.g., shoes, aprons, handkerchiefs, statues [pygmalionism]), and various acts (e.g., whipping, experiencing personal odors, watching climbing and swinging).

Psychoanalytic Theories

There is no psychoanalytic theory that encompasses all of the paraphilias. However, there is a fairly large psychoanalytic literature on sadism and masochism. For Freud (1924), the erotogenic type of masochism was primary among five types. Freud postulated that both masochism and sadism were the products of the encounter between eros and thanatos (a death instinct), in which the libido renders a portion of the death instinct harmless by directing it toward objects in the real world; there, it manifests itself as the desire for mastery, destruction, or the will to power. A portion of the instinct is placed directly in the service of the sexual function as true sadism, and another portion remains within the person as the origin of masochism.

Berliner (1958) developed a psychoanalytic theory of sadism and masochism without the need of postulating a death instinct. He postulated that maternal hate, mistreatment, nonlove, and the wish for infanticide, which the infant experiences as if they were maternal love, can cause sadomasochism. Berliner postulated that the aggressive element in sadomasochism derives from (1) repressed hostility toward the bad love object, (2) the attempt to extort love from the object through suffering, and (3) the indictment of the love object to induce guilt that might then motivate the object to give love after all.

Menaker (1979) developed an adaptationist rather than a conflict type of psychoanalytic theory of sadomasochism. Menaker postulated that masochism is an adaptive response to a nonnurturing mother. A variety of other psychoanalytic theories of sadomasochism have included its relationship to narcissism (Bernstein, 1957), parental inconsistency (Bromberg, 1959), seductive and sadomasochistic games played by the parents during formative periods (Lowenstein, 1957), and parental persecution (Eisenbud, 1967).

Learning Theories

Under natural conditions, learning almost always results in behavior modification that is adaptive to the current environment (Lorenz, 1987). Exceptions exist, such as phobias, in which the adaptation is to an ancestral environment rather than to the current one. In addition, in comparison to other adaptations in biology, most behavioral adaptations are reversible. The exception is those modifications caused by imprinting during a critical stage in development. Paraphilias resemble imprinted learning because of their relative immutability. They are amenable to behavior modification, however. Just as one can teach a duck not to go into the water, one can teach a paraphiliac, at least on a short-term basis if the treatment is continuous, not to act out the behavior of the paraphilia. It is because of the short-term success of behavior modification in the treatment of paraphilias that learning theories of paraphilias have developed.

Because the patterns of paraphilias appear relatively consistent over time and across different societies (Ellis, 1936), there must be innate predisposition to the development of particular paraphilias. However, behavior does not form within a vacuum, and there is also evidence, albeit anecdotal, that life events, especially between 4 and 6 years of age, can influence the specific characteristics of the paraphilia. In addition, as will be expanded on later in this chapter, general characteristics of familial conspecifics (members of the same species) in early infancy also influence the general characteristics of later objects of sexual attraction.

KURT FREUND'S EMPIRICAL-BEHAVIORAL THEORY

Kurt Freund (1988; Freund, Scher, & Hucker, 1983) conceptualized paraphilias as specific examples of a generic condition that he called the "courtship disorders." Freund argued that the sequence of activities in the course of typical human sexual interaction can be seen as a succession of four phases. The first phase is initial partner choice, which involves scrutinizing the potential partner visually. The second is pretactile interaction, which involves posturing, smiling, and verbal communication. The third phase involves tactile interaction, and the fourth phase involves genital union.

Freund then asserted that the courtship disorders can be seen as an exaggeration, a distortion, or part of one of the four normal phases, and that if the remaining phases are at all represented in these behaviors, their representation is only vestigial. He argued that these courtship disorders lead to ejaculation either on the spot or later, through masturbation, as the patient replays these situations in his imagination. Based on empirical penile plethysmography, Freund was able to show that there is cross-arousal among the paraphilias associated with the courtship disorders (see Table 13.1).

Table 13.1

Percentage of Patients with One of the Indexed Anomalies Who
Show Evidence of an Additional Such Anomaly

Indexed Anomaly	Additional Anomalies			
	Voyeurism	Exhibitionism	Toucherism	Rape
Voyeurism		73.5	33.7	18.4
Exhibitionism	27.9		26.4	10.5
Toucherism	26.6	54.8		16.1
Rape	11.5	17.3	12.8	

Source: Adapted from "Courtship Disorder: Is This Hypothesis Valid?" by K. Freund, 1988, *Annals of the New York Academy of Sciences*, p. 528. Copyright 1988 by the New York Academy of Sciences. Adapted with permission of the publisher.

JOHN MONEY'S INTERPRETATIVE/PSYCHODYNAMIC THEORY

To understand Money's classification of the paraphilias, one first has to understand his concept of the "lovemap," which is defined as follows:

> A lovemap is not present at birth. Like a native language, it differentiates within a few years thereafter. It is a developmental representation or template in your mind/brain, and is dependent on input through the special senses. It depicts your idealized, romantic, erotic, and sexualized relationship. A lovemap exists in mental imagery first, in dreams and fantasies, and then may be translated into action with a partner or partners. (1986, p. xvi)

Money goes on to classify "lovemap pathology" as being (1) hypophilia (sexual hypoactivity), (2) hyperphilia (sexual hyperactivity), or (3) paraphilia (sexual activity that is off target). According to Money, in all three of the lovemap pathologies, there is a cleavage between love and lust in the design of the lovemap (see also Fisher, 1998).

Money believes that in hypophilia, the cleavage is such that lust is dysfunctional and infrequently used, whereas love and love bonding are intact. In hyperphilia, lust displaces love and love bonding, and the genitalia function in the service of lust alone, typically with a plurality of partners and with compulsive frequency. In paraphilia, love and love bonding are compromised because the genitalia continue to function in the service of lust, but according to the specifications of a "vandalized" and redesigned lovemap and often with compulsive frequency.

The term paraphilia has been defined by Money (1986) as

> a condition occurring in men and women of being compulsively responsive to and obligatively dependent upon an unusual and personally or socially unacceptable stimulus, perceived or in the imagery of fantasy, for optimal initiation and maintenance of erotosexual arousal and the facilitation or attainment of orgasm [from Greek, para- + -philia]. Paraphilic imagery may be replayed in fantasy during solo masturbation or intercourse with a partner. (pp. 266–267)

Although descriptively colorful and intuitively insightful, this definition of a paraphilia is taxonomically limited by its inclusion in a heterogeneous category of a "condition." Conceptualizing the paraphilias in the category of a condition limits one's ability to systematically understand paraphilias by what is not known about other, taxonomically equal conditions. Furthermore, Money's (1986) current classification of the individual paraphilias, which is the most complex classification of which we are aware, is not systematic, where systematic is defined as classification based on definable variation of a common theme.

Money (1986) also sees a paraphilia as a strategy for turning tragedy into triumph according to the principles of opponent-process theory. This strategy preserves sinful lust in the lovemap by dissociating it from saintly love, which Money sees as one of the doctrines of Christendom. Money goes on to say that the idea that religious parables, strategies, or formulas undergo transformation so as to be scarcely recognizable in their new guise, as in paraphilia, has not hitherto been recognized (i.e., the evolution, or phylogeny, of paraphilias).

According to Money (1986), paraphilias are not generated at random. Rather, they are characterized by triumph wrested developmentally from sexuoerotic tragedy by means of a strategy that incorporates sinful lust into the lovemap with certain requirements. The six categories are outlined in Table 13.2.

Money (1986) believes that the 40 or so paraphilias, distributed among these six categories, have not only an individual, or ontogenetic, history but also a species, or phylogenetic, history. He argues that there are specific phylogenetic components, or *phylisms*, which, should they become ontogenetically entrained, or recruited, into the lovemap, change its childhood development from normaphilic to paraphilic. Money sees the gender transpositions, such as bisexual, homosexual, and transsexual, and transvestite phenomena to be independent of the mechanisms underlying the formation of the lovemap and paraphilias.

THE PSYCHOBIOLOGICAL PERSPECTIVE ON PARAPHILIAS

In contrast to Money's (1986) perspective, it may be easier to understand the paraphilias by defining as well as describing them on the basis of overt behaviors. A *behavior*, including behaviors associated with the paraphilias, can be defined as the movement of voluntary muscles in space and over time. Unlike Money's concept of conditions, behaviors are measurable (Martin & Bateson, 1986) as well as systematically classifiable.

THE PSYCHOBIOLOGICAL PERSPECTIVE ON BEHAVIOR

THE STRUCTURE, ORIENTATION, AND TIMING OF BEHAVIOR

Overt behavior, like anatomy, has structure, defined by the description of muscle contractions in space and time (see Ekman & Friesen, 1975; Scherer & Ekman, 1982). *Movement* is the first component of behavior. *Orientation*, the second component, refers to the direction of the behavior, for example, the direction of the gaze. Orientation is a very important component of courtship behavior, because the behavior of one individual acts as the releaser of behavior in that individual toward whom the behavior is oriented.

The third component of behavior, *time or timing*, has two aspects: the moment during which the behavior occurs and the velocity with which it is executed. When behaviors are executed at velocities slower or faster than usual, this can be a signal. In fact, courtship behaviors may be signaled not by type but by slow velocity. Examples are touching or picking up an object or walking at a slower than usual velocity, which causes the individual with whom one is interacting to pay more attention than usual.

Table 13.2
John Money's Categories of Paraphilia

1. *Sacrificial/Expiatory:* requires reparation or atonement by way of penance and sacrifice, for it irrevocably defiles saintly love
   a. *Asphyxiophilia:* sexual excitement by self-strangulation and asphyxiation up to, but not including, loss of consciousness
   b. *Autassassinophilia:* sexual excitement by stage-managing the possibility of one's own masochistic death by murder
   c. *Bondage:* sexual excitement by either constraining (sadism/dominance) or being constrained (masochism/submission) with rope, chains, tape, or other equipment
   d. *Erotophonophilia:* sexual excitement by stage-managing and carrying out the murder of an unsuspecting sexual partner
   e. *Masochism/Submission:* sexual excitement by having someone impose abuse, torture, punishment, discipline, humiliation, obedience, and servitude
   f. *Sadism/Dominance:* sexual excitement by being the authority who imposes abuse, torture, punishment, discipline, humiliation, obedience, and servitude
   g. *Symphorophilia:* sexual excitement by stage-managing the possibility of a disaster, such as a conflagration or traffic accident, and watching for it to happen

2. *Marauding/Predation:* sex must be stolen, abducted, or imposed by force, for it irrevocably defiles saintly love
   a. *Biastophilia (raptophila, rape):* sexual excitement by the surprise attack and continued violent assault of a nonconsenting, terrified, and struggling stranger
   b. *Hybristophilia:* sexual excitement by being with a partner known to have committed an outrage or crime, such as rape, murder, or armed robbery
   c. *Kleptophilia:* sexual excitement by illicitly entering and stealing from the dwelling of a stranger or potential partner
   d. *Somnophilia:* sexual excitement by intruding upon and awakening a sleeping stranger with erotic caresses, including oral sex, not involving force or violence

3. *Mercantile/Venal:* sex must be traded, bartered, or purchased and paid for, not freely exchanged, for it irrevocably defiles saintly love
   a. *Chrematistophilia:* sexual excitement by being charged or forced to pay, or being robbed by the sexual partner for sexual services
   b. *Troilism:* sexual excitement by observing one's partner on hire or loan to a third person while engaging in sexual activities, including intercourse, with that person

4. *Fetishistic/Talismanic:* a token, fetish, or talisman is substituted for the lover, for lust irrevocably defiles saintly love
   a. *Coprophilia:* sexual excitement by being smeared with and/or ingesting feces
   b. *Fetishism:* sexual excitement by contact with an object, substance, or part of the body belonging to the partner
   c. *Hyphephilia:* sexual excitement by touching, rubbing, or feeling of skin, hair, leather, fur, and fabric, especially if worn in proximity to erotically significant parts of the body
   d. *Klismaphilia:* sexual excitement by being given an enema by the partner
   e. *Mysophilia:* sexual excitement by self-degradation by smelling, chewing, or otherwise utilizing sweaty or soiled clothing or articles of menstrual hygiene

Table 13.2 *(Continued)*

f. *Olfactophilia:* sexual excitement associated with smells and odors emanating from parts of the body, especially the sexual and adjacent parts

g. *Transvestophilia (transvestism):* sexual excitement associated with wearing clothes, especially underwear, of the other sex

h. *Urophilia (urolagnia):* sexual excitement by being urinated upon and/or swallowing urine

5. *Stigmatic/Eligibilic:* the partner must be, like a pagan infidel, unqualified or ineligible to be a saint defiled

   a. *Acrotomophilia:* sexual excitement by being with partners who are amputees

   b. *Apotemnophilia:* sexual excitement by becoming an amputee oneself

   c. *Autonepiophilia:* sexual excitement by impersonating a baby in diapers and being treated as one by the partner

   d. *Ephebophilia:* sexual excitement by being with a partner who is an adolescent

   e. *Formicophilia:* sexual excitement by the sensation produced by small creatures such as snails, frogs, ants, or other insects creeping, crawling, or nibbling the genitalia and perianal area

   f. *Gerontophilia:* sexual excitement by being with someone who is parental or grandparental in age

   g. *Gynemimetophila:* sexual excitement by being with partners who are sex-reassigned, male-to-female transsexuals

   h. *Morphobilia:* sexual excitement by particularizing and making prominent one or more of the bodily characteristics of the partner

   i. *Necrophilia:* sexual excitement by sexual interaction with a corpse

   j. *Nepiophilia:* sexual excitement by being with a partner who is a baby in diapers

   k. *Pedophilia:* sexual excitement by being with a partner who is a prepubertal child

   l. *Stigmatophilia:* sexual excitement by being with a partner who has been tattooed, scarified, or pierced for the wearing of gold jewelry (bars or rings), especially in the genital region

   m. *Zoophilia:* sexual excitement by engaging in sexual activity with a nonhuman animal

6. *Solicitational/Alluritive:* an invitiatory act belonging to the preliminary or proceptive phase is substituted for the copulatory act of the central or acceptive phase, thus ensuring that saintly love is not defiled by sinful lust

   a. *Autagonistophilia:* sexual excitement by being observed or being on stage or on camera

   b. *Exhibitionism (peodeiktophilia):* sexual excitement by evoking surprise, dismay, shock, or panic from a stranger by illicitly exhibiting an erotic part of the body, including the genitals

   c. *Frotteurism:* sexual excitement by rubbing, especially the genital area against the body of a stranger in a densely packed crowd

   d. *Mixoscopia (scoptolagnia, scoptophilia):* sexual excitement by watching others engaging in sexual intercourse

(continued)

Table 13.2   *(Continued)*

---

   e. *Narratophilia:* sexual excitement by using words and telling stories commonly classified as dirty, pornographic, or obscene in the presence of the sexual partner

   f. *Pictophilia:* sexual excitement by viewing pictures, movies, videos of activities commonly classified as dirty, pornographic, or obscene, alone or in the presence of the sexual partner

   g. *Telephone scatophilia (telephonicophilia):* sexual excitement from deception and ruse in luring or threatening a telephone respondent, known or unknown, into listening to, and making personal explicit conversation in the sexuoerotic vernacular

   h. *Toucheurism:* sexual excitement by being touched by a stranger

   i. *Voyeurism:* sexual excitement from the risk of being discovered while covertly or illicitly watching a stranger disrobing or engaging in sexual activity

---

Source: Compiled from Money, 1986.

REPRODUCTIVE BEHAVIORS

There are conceptual differences between reproductive behavior and sexual behavior. Reproductive behavior means all of the behaviors necessary to pass one's genes on to the next generation. Not all reproductive behavior is overtly sexual (e.g., caring for a dependent offspring), and not all overtly sexual behavior is reproductive (e.g., masturbation). As will be shown, sexual behavior is a type of reproductive behavior. However, as merely a type of reproductive behavior, it is too narrow a concept by which to understand the paraphilias.

To fully understand the basic differences in reproductive behavior between males and females, one must appreciate the phylogenetic history of these differences in species that are precursors to humans (Medicus & Hopf, 1990). There are four basic principles of vertebrate psychobiology that are useful in understanding male-female differences in human reproductive behavior:

1. A male makes more germ cells (sperm) in an hour than a female makes (eggs) in a lifetime. As a result, males behave carelessly in regard to these germ cells and are more careless in disposing of them. Said another way, males have more ammunition.

2. Males and females invest differently in what it takes to produce an offspring. A male's investment can be as little as the effort to produce one ejaculate of sperm. The female, however, has to nourish the offspring internally through gestation and then rear the offspring to the point where it can be independent. According to evolutionary theory, the sex that invests more in the offspring is the sex that does most of the choosing of the individual with whom it will merge genetic material. In humans, the scenario is that males make offers and females choose whether or not to

accept the offers, a phenomenon that is often called "female choice" (Trivers, 1985).

3. Females do not increase the number of offspring produced by mating with more than one male at a time. Males, on the other hand, increase the number of offspring they produce in direct proportion to the number of different females with whom they mate. Number of offspring produced is not the same, however, as reproductive success. Hrdy (1997) makes a compelling argument that, similar to humans' closest primate relatives, human females sneak opportunistic copulations with high-status males to improve their reproductive success. Nevertheless, in relative terms, males are still more promiscuous than females.

4. In most vertebrate males, the moods associated with fear and sex are "functionally distant," and the moods associated with aggression and sex are "functionally proximate." In females, the opposite is true: the moods associated with fear and sex are "functionally proximate," and the moods associated with aggression and sex are "functionally distant." This observation was first made by Oehlert (1958) in her observation of the male/female differences in behavior of a particular bony fish (*cichlid*). These ideas were later extended to humans to some degree (Beck & Bozman, 1995). When moods are functionally proximate (e.g., as sex and aggression are in males), it means that the two moods can occur easily together or can easily alternate. Being in one mood facilitates being in the other mood. In contrast, when two moods are functionally distant (e.g., as sex and aggression are in females), it means that the two moods can occur together only with difficulty or can alternate with difficulty. This relationship may be helpful in understanding some paraphilias such as sadism, masochism, and biastophilia (rape). This relationship is seen in Table 13.3, taken from Medicus and Hopf (1990).

Table 13.3

The Relationship between Sex and the Moods of Fear and Aggression in Prototype Vertebrate Males and Females

Sex	Fear (of mate)	Aggression (toward mate)
Male	No effect, or inhibits sexual mood	No effect, or facilitates sexual mood
Female	No effect, or facilitates sexual mood	No effect, or inhibits sexual mood

Source: Adapted from "The Phylogeny of Male/Female Differences in Sexual Behavior," by G. Medicus and S. Hopf, 1990, *Pedophilia: Biosocial Dimensions*, p. 134. Copyright 1990 by Springer-Verlag New York, Inc. Adapted with permission of the authors.

Reproductive behaviors can be divided into four main components, based on the function of the behaviors:

1. *Proceptive behavior:* Behavior that functions to facilitate the meeting and interaction of the adult male and female in a mating context, so that an eventual merger of gametes (sperm and egg) and/or bonding can occur.
2. *Receptive behavior:* Behavior that functions to maintain and reinforce the pairbond between an attached male and the female adult, so that neither one will desert the offspring.
3. *Conceptive behavior:* Behavior that functions to cause orgasm and, in males, ejaculation. Actual union of the gametes, the sperm and egg, can potentially occur.
4. *Parental behavior:* Behavior whose function is caring for offspring to ensure that offspring that are born survive to reproductive age.

Proceptive Behavior

In the field of male-female differences in behavior, no type of behavior is more striking than proceptive behavior, also called courtship behavior. Human females indicate that they are in a sexual mood through behavioral signals that can be sent specifically to particular males. These signals, which have been widely studied (e.g., Eibl-Eibesfeldt, 1989; Grammer, 1995; Moore, 1985; Perper, 1985; Perper & Weiss, 1997), are highly directional. Many of the female courtship signals are what we generally consider *feminine behavior,* which is defined as any behavior that is present in both males and females but is more common in females. Many of the behaviors that are considered feminine are, in actuality, submissive behaviors (Morris, 1977), reflecting the phylogenetic origins of the functional proximity of the sexual and fearful moods in females (Medicus & Hopf, 1990). Examples of feminine behavior include taking smaller steps, movements and positions that tend to make the overall body size smaller, smiling, and a head toss that exposes the neck.

Important in the consideration of proceptive behaviors of males is *resource accrual ability,* the male's ability to accrue resources that could be used to provision his offspring. A male's desirability to females in many vertebrate species, including humans, is heavily influenced by the male's resource accrual ability. Human males display symbols of high resource accrual ability (e.g., expensive watches and cars) and can also brag about their resources. However, in terms of the proceptive behaviors of females, they use their appearance and body movements to visually interest males. Males use their words to auditorially interest females. Among human proceptive behavior, females are as vulnerable with their ears as males are vulnerable with their eyes.

Receptive Behavior

Once a female signals to a male that she accepts his proceptive offer, the behaviors that follow are bond-promoting interactions. Among humans, these behaviors include looking into each other's eyes, hugging, kissing, holding

hands, and grooming. Such behaviors strengthen the interpersonal bonds between individuals, bonds that, it is expected, will last at least long enough for
the offspring to be capable of self-ambulation (Fisher, 1992).

In contrast to proceptive behaviors, receptive behaviors show few sex differences; that is, the receptive behavior of males is similar to the receptive behavior of females. Many receptive behaviors appear to have their origins in the
types of interactions that parents have with their offspring. It is, therefore, not
surprising that the "terms of endearment" are often diminutive (e.g., as in referring to a lover as "baby").

Conceptive Behavior

Conceptive behaviors are the behaviors that, under the right conditions, lead to
conception. However, not all of the instances in which conceptive behaviors are
expressed allow individuals to be open to conception. Examples include heterosexual intercourse when a woman is not fertile, same-gender orgasmic interactions, and masturbation. Nevertheless, the behaviors are very similar in males
and females. Much of conceptive behavior consists of direct genital stimulation;
rhythmic, forward-and-backward pelvic movements; increased frequency and
depth of respiration; increased heart rate; and sometimes vocalizations.

Parenting and Provisioning Behaviors

These include feeding, protecting, grooming, and soothing offspring usually
until they are able to care for themselves. There is a significant sex difference
in these behaviors in mammals. Females have a greater biological investment
in offspring, which includes nourishing them from their own bodies (Trivers,
1985). In humans, although parenting and provisioning behavior can be exhibited by both mothers and fathers, the pattern of behavior is consistent with the
basic mammalian pattern, and females exhibit more of the behavior.

Because of the relevance to understanding pedophilia, it should be mentioned that some of the behavioral motor patterns associated with parenting
have certain similarities to the behavioral motor patterns associated with receptive sexual behaviors between adults, although there are some easily distinguishable differences between the two. During the early phase of adult-adult
receptive behaviors, and also in parenting behavior, there is close, friendly
physical contact between the individuals that is not sexual. In contrast to parenting behaviors, the nonsexual receptive behaviors between two adults, as
well as between a pedophile and a child, can escalate over time in terms of both
intensity and involvement of the genitals to become sexual and potentially
conceptive behavior. Parenting behaviors do not escalate in this manner.

APPETITIVE AND CONSUMMATORY BEHAVIOR

In the context of behavioral biology (ethology), behavior can be further divided
into appetitive and consummatory components, a distinction first made by
Craig (1918). Eibl-Eibesfeldt (1975) refined the definitions:

Observations on intact animals have shown that fluctuations in their responsiveness to external stimuli are in part caused by built-in physiological mechanisms that act as "drives." These mechanisms motivate or cause an animal to actively seek, in what we call *appetitive* behavior, for stimuli situations that allow certain behavior patterns (according to the "mood" of the animal) to discharge. (Mood is defined as a specific readiness to act [p. 48].) Behavioral analyses of motivation reveal that motor patterns occur in sets, sharing identical fluctuations of the releasing thresholds and thus pointing to underlying common physiological mechanisms. At the same time other behavior patterns are excluded. (p. 64)

The concepts of appetitive and consummatory behavior are easily understood in terms of eating behavior (which will help the reader understand their application to sexual behavior). Hunger motivates the search for food. This search is appetitive behavior, motivated by the "appetite" to eat. Once the food is found, the individual carries out other types of appetitive behaviors, such as digging up or pulling down vegetable matter or hunting prey. Last, the acquired food is consumed by biting, chewing, and swallowing, which is the consummatory behavior. In industrialized societies, the process may be driving to a restaurant (appetitive behavior) and then eating the food (consummatory behavior).

Appetitive and consumatory patterns are seen in sexual behavior as well. Sexual desire motivates the search for a partner. Appetitive behavior might involve going to a location to exhibit the behaviors that signal interest or readiness (proceptive behavior). A person with a partner may increase behaviors such as gazing or touching (receptive behavior), which signal interest or readiness for actual sexual behavior (consumatory behavior).

With regard to paraphilic behavior, the appetite for sexual behavior is probably no different from the appetite for nonparaphilic sexual behavior. However, what one does to release the consummatory sexual behavior, which is more likely to be a penis ejaculating outside of a vagina, will depend on the particular paraphilia. A pedophile will go to where children are present. A voyeur will go to where he can see disrobing or unclothed persons. A frotteur will go to a crowded place where he can rub against unsuspecting persons.

The actual interaction with the child, the looking at a disrobing person, the rubbing against an unsuspecting victim, all are part of the conceptive behavior, inasmuch as the ideal situation for the paraphiliac may be to ejaculate during this process. If ejaculation is not possible during the actual process, for example, in a crowded subway, it occurs as soon as possible afterwards.

THREE EMOTION CATEGORIES IN MAMMALIAN REPRODUCTION: LUST, ATTRACTION, AND ATTACHMENT

Fisher (1998) proposed that mammals, including humans, exhibit three primary emotion categories for mating and reproduction: (1) the sex drive, or lust, characterized by the craving for sexual gratification; (2) attraction, character- ized by increased energy and focused attention on one or more potential mates, accompanied in humans by a feeling of exhilaration, "intrusive think- ing" about a mate, and the craving for emotional union with this mate or po- tential mate; and (3) attachment, characterized by the maintenance of close social contact in mammals, accompanied in humans by feelings of calm, com- fort, and emotional union with a mate.

In terms of ethology, what Fisher (1998) called emotion would better be called *mood*, which is a specific readiness to act. Relative to the component of mating and reproduction that has to do with paraphilias, one would be in a mood to have genital sexual release, or orgasm, by whatever stimuli or behav- ior would facilitate this process. Fisher argued that, whereas the attraction sys- tem is primarily associated with the catecholamine neurotransmitters (see also Kafka, 1997), and the attachment system is primarily associated with the pep- tides, vasopressin, and oxytocin, the lust system is primarily associated with estrogen and testosterone, the sex hormones. There are other variables, how- ever, because the selective serotonin reuptake inhibitor antidepressants (SSRIs), which act on the indoleamine serotonin by increasing its concentra- tion in the synaptic cleft, tend to decrease both the appetitive and consumma- tory components of sexual behavior, including paraphilic sexual behavior.

Fisher (1998) argued that the data suggest that, during the course of ho- minid evolution, the constellations of neural correlates associated with lust, at- traction, and attachment became increasingly independent of one another, enabling hominids to exercise mating flexibility and engage (sometimes simul- taneously) in a range of primary and secondary opportunistic reproductive strategies. One result of this independence is the capacity to develop flexibil- ity. Within this conceptualization, males would be more prone to the develop- ment of paraphilias because they have the need to be, and are, more flexible, because opportunistic matings, in which lust is separated from attraction and attachment to a specific individual, is more reproductively beneficial to males than to females. However, there is evidence that human females engage in more promiscuous extrapair matings with higher-status males than originally believed (Hrdy, 1997).

THE PSYCHOBIOLOGY OF PARAPHILIC BEHAVIORS

PROXIMATE CAUSES OF PARAPHILIC BEHAVIOR

To conceptualize a behavior from the psychobiological framework, one should analyze the behavior from four perspectives: (1) proximate cause, (2) ultimate cause (evolutionary), (3) development, and (4) function (Tinbergen, 1951).

It is our contention that current understanding of the behaviors associated with the paraphilias is incomplete because investigators have not explicated the behaviors from the four required perspectives. Nevertheless, we believe that these perspectives are the appropriate place from which to start. In this section, we develop this perspective in greater detail.

It is important to understand *cause* in psychobiology as having *proximate* and *ultimate* components. Questions about cause are often posed as Why questions: for example, Why are some adult men sexually attracted to children? Ultimate Why questions are often broad, for example, questions about the sexual behavior of men in general. Proximate Why questions are specific, for example, Why did this particular man engage in this particular behavior? We cover the ultimate, or evolutionary, answer to the Why question under the heading Ultimate (Evolutionary) Causes of Paraphilic Behaviors, which follows. This section is concerned with the proximate Why questions about the causes of a particular individual's particular behavior.

In science, when one sets out to "prove" proximate causality, one usually designs a series of controlled scientific experiments, holding certain variables constant and changing others. One then looks at the effects of the changed variables on some measurable outcome. One assumes that the change in the measurable outcome is caused by the changed variable. In interpreting these types of experiments, one must keep in mind the nature of the measurable outcome. There is a significant difference between behavior, which is the most meaningful measurable outcome, and speech about behavior (e.g., answered questions about behavior). It is also possible to measure physiological outcomes (e.g., sexual arousal), because such outcomes are an indirect measure of the behaviors that they motivate.

It is useful to separate proximate causes of behavior into those factors that are external to the organism and those factors that are internal to the organism. In doing this, one should remember that this is a heuristic process only, and that because an organism is always in some environment, internal and external factors never act in isolation from each other.

Mainly External Factors

In the original work on the biology of the behavior of whole organisms, Konrad Lorenz (1981) and Niko Tinbergen (1951), in the process of trying to understand the proximate mechanisms by which behavior could evolve by natural selection, discovered the behavioral units of inheritance, which they termed *fixed action patterns.* These fixed action patterns lie between reflexes and complex, intentional behaviors. Examples of fixed action patterns include the behavioral patterns associated with aggression, fear, and courtship. For example, when an adult human male is in a fighting mood, his face configures into an aggressive display, bearing the teeth; his hand configures into a fist; his posture becomes erect, his chest expands, his volume of speech increases, and the pitch deepens. All of this occurs "automatically," without the need to execute these separate behaviors volitionally.

Lorenz (1981) and Tinbergen (1951) realized that some of these fixed action patterns can occur spontaneously, such as when one is alone, in addition to being released by specific *releasing stimuli*. For example, a man in a room by himself thinking about a maddening situation can execute aggressive behaviors, albeit probably not with the same intensity as he would in the real situation. Many of the releasing stimuli of fixed action patterns are "social" and are released by certain behaviors of conspecifics.

In regard to the external (to the individual) proximate causes of human paraphilic behavior, the most obvious proximate cause is the releasing stimulus itself. For example, if one is sexually attracted to any particular paraphilic stimulus, seeing the appurtenances of the paraphilia or an example of the class of object or individual that defines the paraphilia will increase the likelihood of the paraphilic occurrence. As an example, if a voyeur (Peeping Tom) sees through a window someone of the preferred age, gender, and so forth disrobing, it is more likely that voyeuristic behavior would occur than if a nonvoyeur were in the same situation.

One could argue that the object of the paraphilia is not a proper cause because the object is the paraphilia. However, appreciate that if one is not a voyeur, the sight of a disrobing individual would not necessarily cause one to stop and would not cause continued looking, often over hours. Appreciate also that at least in the *DSM-IV* (APA, 1994) definition of voyeurism, the paraphilia is defined on the basis of a fantasy, urge, or behavior. However, only behavior is directly observable and measurable.

In addition to the releasing stimulus/object of the paraphilia, context is an important proximate cause of paraphilic behavior. Sexual behavior is very conditionable, and otherwise neutral contexts can be conditioned so that they evoke sexually motivated behaviors. The most obvious context is physical location. If one is used to exhibiting paraphilic behavior in a certain location, the likelihood of the paraphilic behavior increases in that location because the location itself is capable of evoking sexual motivation in the individual.

Evoking a sexual mood, especially in men, is both easy and common and is the mainstay of the advertising industry. Such evoked sexual moods in men are not necessarily coexistent with the moods of romantic love toward a specific individual. Sexual moods can be rapidly induced in men outside the context of the moods of romantic love. Because paraphilic behavior is also an example of sex without love (some forms of pedophilia being perhaps the lone exception), the mood to execute the paraphilia is also easily conditioned by various contexts.

As an example of how easy sexual moods are to condition, in dairy bulls, who are ejaculated by an electronic vibrating machine for sperm collection to be used in artificial insemination of dairy cows, signs of restlessness are evident as soon as the bulls hear the noises associated with the machine. In fact, they start their snorting chorus as soon as they hear the opening of the door to the closet in which the machine is kept (J. R. Feierman, personal observation).

Sexual conditioning is not limited to bulls (Lalumiere & Quinsey, 1998). Rachman and Hodgson (1968) showed that adult men with no prior sexual interest in boots were able to be classically conditioned to become aroused by boots when pictures of boots were paired with pictures of nude women. Conditioning took place only when the conditioned stimulus (boots) preceded the unconditioned stimulus (pictures of nude women). Because such a demonstration is a laboratory curiosity, it is unlikely that the boots would retain the ability to evoke sexual arousal if the association were not periodically reinforced. What distinguishes naturally occurring paraphilias from laboratory-conditioned curiosities is the ability of the association to continue without the need for periodic reinforcement in the paraphilias, similar to imprinted associations.

It is difficult for a mental health professional or academic behavioral researcher to study the effects of specific stimuli on the execution of paraphilic behavior. As previously noted, paraphilic behavior is executed both covertly and infrequently. Often, the information available (e.g., an arrest record) is merely that the paraphilic behavior occurred. One can then look at various factors (e.g., the context in which the paraphilia occurred) as a way of retrospectively trying to understand external proximate causes.

One very obvious external cause is the social and organizational contexts and situations in which a paraphiliac is more likely to encounter paraphilia-related situations. For example, it is not surprising that pedophiles are attracted to situations that give access to children, such as youth group leadership.

Another factor that starts out initially as a proximate external (to the individual) cause of paraphilic behavior (or almost any sexual behavior) is substances such as alcohol or drugs. Alcohol is probably the most commonly used disinhibitor of behavior, and sexual behavior, for a variety of reasons, is very prone to disinhibition. There are other drugs that may influence the execution of paraphilic behavior, both disinhibitory drugs (e.g., cocaine, amphetamine) and inhibitory drugs (e.g., SSRI antidepressants such as fluoxetine, paroxetine, and sertraline), as well as progesterone (e.g., Depo-Provera).

Mainly Internal Factors

Kinsey, Pomeroy, and Martin (1948) coined the term *total sexual outlet* to stand for the total of the six chief sources of orgasm for the human male: masturbation, nocturnal emission, heterosexual petting, heterosexual intercourse, homosexual relations, and intercourse with animals of other species. Kinsey et al. found that the means for total sexual outlet (i.e., orgasms per week) for 14,084 males of different ages in his sample population were as follows: adolescence–15 = 2.86; 16–20 = 2.87; 21–25 = 2.85; 26–30 = 3.01; 31–35 = 2.64; 36–40 = 2.36; 41–45 = 1.98; 46–50 = 1.78; 51–55 = 1.50; 56–60 = 1.20; 61–65 = 0.84; 66–70 = 0.65; 71–75 = 0.13; 76–80 = 0.01; 81–85 = 0.00 (p. 220, Table 44).

As can be seen, the total sexual outlet is relatively high from adolescence to middle adulthood and falls off significantly in old age. The total sexual outlet for a 26- to 30-year-old man is twice that of a 51- to 55-year-old man. The sexual outlet for a 51- to 55-year-old man is twice that of a 66- to 70-year-old man. The total sexual outlet of a 66- to 70-year-old man is five times higher than that of a 71- to 75-year-old man.

Assuming that paraphilic sexual outlet is proportional to total sexual outlet throughout the life span in men, Kinsey et al.'s (1948) data of total sexual outlet in men would predict that paraphilic behaviors should be the most frequent between adolescence and middle adulthood and should be less frequent in elderly men. The frequency of paraphilic behavior throughout the life span, both in terms of arrest records and self-report, shows that the expression of paraphilic behavior over the life span correlates well with male total sexual outlet frequency over the same time period.

Relationship between Internal and External Factors

Gestalt perceptual psychology offers some insight into the proximate causes of paraphilic behavior. Gestalt perception is the process by which the parts are integrated, by a central nervous system integrating mechanism, into a whole. One way of looking at paraphilias is as a breakdown of the Gestalt mechanisms usually associated with sexual attraction to the entirety of the stimulus. At least in some paraphilias, the sexual attraction is greater for a particular part than for the whole. Before this topic is discussed further, however, it should be appreciated that the mechanism of "normal" sexual attraction is poorly understood, making it especially difficult to specify where the normal mechanism goes awry.

In an earlier publication concerning pedophilia, Feierman (1990) discussed the relationship among various factors associated with the stimuli of sexual attraction. Three characteristics of the stimuli were identified:

Stimulus discriminability: the amount of detail (information) in the stimulus

Stimulus fitness: the degree to which sexual attraction to the stimulus increases reproductive success (i.e., facilitates getting one's genes into the next generation)

Stimulus potency: the amount of stimulus necessary for achieving a standard response, such as a certain amount of attention or sexual arousal

Also identified was one characteristic of the perceiving individual's nervous system, *stimulus discriminative ability*, which was defined as the degree to which the numerous animate, inanimate, and contextual attributes of, or that are associated with, another individual (or object) can be matched to the numerous attributes in the prototype on one's lovemap. Last, the term *stimulus resemblance* (previously called stimulus discrimination), which is a property of both the lovemap and the stimulus, is defined as the degree to which the stimulus resembles the lovemap. Variations on stimulus discriminative ability may account for the predisposition to develop paraphilias.

When a sexually attractive stimulus first becomes present in the environment, there is a series of steps that the perceiver follows: awareness, attention, orientation (in space), approach, and finally, contact with the stimulus. To understand the perceiving individual's initial attraction to the stimulus, one should understand the relationship between two properties of the stimulus: (1) the capacity of the stimulus to evoke initial stimulus appetence (as in appetite) in the perceiver and (2) the stimulus's discriminability, which has been defined as the amount of detail (information) in the stimulus.

Sexually evocative stimuli can be familiar to an individual in two ways. First, the stimulus (often very basic shapes, movement, color, odor) can be "phylogenetically familiar," in that the perceiving individual's nervous system has been selected (by ancestors who were attracted to the stimulus outreproducing ancestors who were not attracted to the stimulus) over eons of evolutionary time to find the stimulus "innately" sexually attractive. A nonsexual but familiar example of attraction to a phylogenetically familiar stimulus is any kitten's innate attraction to crinkling and rustling sounds or to a mouse-sized object on a string being pulled away from the kitten. Second, the stimulus can also be "ontogenetically familiar," in that the perceiving individual's nervous system has been conditioned by exposure to the stimulus during sexual arousal in the lifetime (early-formative or critical-period years) of the individual. A familiar nonsexual example of attraction to an ontogenetically familiar stimulus is any kitten's conditioned response, for example, coming to be fed when it hears a can opener. These relationships can be seen in Table 13.4.

Looking at Table 13.4, one can think about where the various paraphilias described earlier in this chapter should fall in terms of their phylogenetic-versus-ontogenetic familiarity. For example, Table 13.4 would predict that the proceptive paraphilia voyeurism is based mainly on phylogenetic familiarity (innate sexual attraction to the female body), and that another proceptive paraphilia, fetishism (e.g. sexual attraction to black bras), is based mainly on ontogenetic familiarity (conditioned during the individual's lifetime).

Table 13.4
Relationship betwen Four Properties of a Potentially Sexually Attractive Stimulus to One Another and to the Perceiving Individual

Type of Familiarity of the Stimulus to the Perceiver	The Stimulus's Capacity to Evoke Initial Stimulus Appetence in the Perceiver	The Stimulus's Discriminability
Phylogenetic (evolutionary)	high	low
Ontogenetic(conditioned)	low	potentially high

Source: Adapted from "A Biosocial Overview of Adult Human Sexual Behavior with Children and Adolescents," by J. Feierman, *Pedophilia: Biosocial Dimensions*, p. 16. Copyright 1990 by Springer-Verlag New York, Inc. Adapted with permission of the author.

ULTIMATE (EVOLUTIONARY) CAUSES OF PARAPHILIC BEHAVIORS

This is the big Why question. Why are some men sexually attracted to children? Why are some men sexually aroused by giving pain to or receiving pain from another individual? Why are some men sexually attracted to rubber, leather, shoes? To answer these questions at the evolutionary level, one needs to ask, How does it increase an adult male's inclusive fitness by being sexually attracted to children, pain, rubber, leather, or shoes? If these questions cannot be answered, is there an ultimate (evolutionary) cause of paraphilic behavior?

The frequency of certain peculiar male sexual behaviors, such as sexual attraction to certain categories of objects or certain hierarchal relationships (i.e., dominance and submission), is too systematized to be due to chance alone. "Systematized" means that the objects and relationships to which one develops paraphilic attractions seem to be finite and definable. For example, there are no known paraphilias defined by sexual attraction to wrist watches, belt buckles, or keys.

The *objects* of sexual attraction seem to fall into two categories: (1) phylogenetically familiar, such as objects that smell (rubber, leather), or objects that are associated with immobilization, dominance, and control; and (2) ontogenetically familiar, such as highly discriminable objects of sexual attraction that are placed near the female breasts, genitals, and face (e.g., lace).

Gosselin and Wilson (1980) surveyed identical and fraternal twins regarding key fantasy items, self-rated sex drive, and overall sexual satisfaction. Higher intraclass correlation in identical than in fraternal twins would suggest that the item is phylogenetically (genetic predisposition) rather than ontogenetically (conditioned) familiar. Table 13.5 gives support to the notion that some paraphilias, such as dominance and submission, have largely phylogenetic origins, whereas other paraphilias, such as specific clothes fetishes (e.g., garter belts) have ontogenetic origins.

Another line of evidence that paraphilias have genetic predispositions is the case study of identical twins by Gorman (1964), in which both identical twins

Table 13.5

Intraclass Correlation of Identical and Fraternal Twins on Various Sexual Items

Item	Identical Twins	Fraternal Twins
Being whipped or spanked	0.36	0.13
Being excited by material or clothing	0.37	0.50
Wearing clothes of the opposite sex	0.80	0.43
Sex drive	0.42	0.02
Sexual satisfaction	0.52	0.17

Source: Adapted from "Family Background and Upbringing," by C. Gosselin and G. Wilson, 1980, *Sexual Variations: Fetishism, Sadomasochism and Transvestism*, p. 115. Copyright 1980 by G. Wilson and C. Gosselin. Reprinted with permission of the authors.

developed rubber fetishes at ages 5 and 6, although they both reported that neither knew of the other's attraction to rubber until both were age 10. Age 4–6 is an important period in terms of neuropsychological development, as will be discussed later in this chapter.

The *parts* of sexual attraction seem to fall into two categories: (1) exaggeration of normal, fitness-related features, such as extra large (fecund) or extra small (youthful) breasts; and (2) similarity to objects with which one is already familiar. Examples of the latter are such characteristics as skin tone, clear complexion, hair texture and color, and facial features. These may be related to the more general mechanism of sexual attraction where individual males appear to be attracted to persons who are both healthy and similar, but not identical, to women they have seen in their early formative period (roughly ages 4–6). The preference for such objects may involve a more general mechanism underlying aesthetics, as in art and the perception of beauty (Eibl-Eibesfeldt, 1989).

In trying to understand paraphilias at the distant level of evolution, or phylogeny, one is forced to ask, Are any of the paraphilias adaptive? Further, there are two ways to consider this question: Adaptive now? or Adaptive at some time in the evolutionary past of our species? There are some rare conditions, such as hemophilia, whose prevalence in the population approximates the mutation rate of the genes responsible for the conditions. There are other conditions, such as sickle cell trait and disease, whose population prevalence is too common to be present solely on the basis of the mutation rate. In such conditions, one may find a mechanism that could account for the higher than expected prevalence, such as increased survival from malaria in individuals who carry the sickle cell trait.

There are several mechanisms by which genetically influenced traits can exist in a population at a prevalence higher than one would expect based on the mutation rate of genes that simply influence such traits, including behaviors: (1) the trait could have been previously adaptive, (2) the trait is a by-product of selection, or (3) the trait survives because of frequency-dependent selection or (4) a change or increase in the nongenetic determinant. Following are examples of how each of these mechanisms could be operative in the relatively frequent expression of paraphilic behavior.

Previously Adaptive Trait

Pedophilia, although socially and legally abhorrent now, was normative only several millennia ago in ancient Greece (Dover, 1978) and has been referred to as pedagogical pedophilia, or "Greek love." Parents selected the best adult male tutor for their young male children. The relationship between the adult male tutor and the young child was loving and sexual as well as pedagogical. Such sexuoerotic, intergenerational, male-male behavior may have facilitated adult male to adult male bonding across generations, especially in all-male bands, within social groups. Similarly, the most common pattern in group-living primates is where the young males disperse and form relationships with adult males, when they change social groups at puberty (Pusey & Packer, 1986). Similar intergenerational male-male sexual relationships have been found among medieval clerics and their young male acolytes (Quinn, 1989) as well as among samurai warriors (Saikaku, 1990).

By-Product of Selection

If it is assumed that traits influenced by multiple genes exist in populations in normal distributions, selection will have made persons with the optimal amount of the trait most common in the population. However, on either side of the optimal amount of the trait, there will be some individuals with slightly less or slightly more than the optimal amount of the trait, as well as even fewer individuals with much less or much more than the optimal amount of the trait. To use by-product of selection as a mechanism, one first must decide what paraphilia-related trait could exist in a population so that an average amount would be adaptive but less or more than average would be less than optimally adaptive. As an example, getting pleasure out of looking at partially clad, nubile females in moderation is pleasurable to the average heterosexual male. Too little of this trait could lead to no sexual interest in nubile females, and too much of this trait could lead to looking behavior at the expense of the other behaviors that should naturally follow the looking, that is, to voyeurism.

Frequency-Dependent Selection

It has been proposed that some psychiatric disorders, such as antisocial personality disorder, could be examples of adaptive traits that exist in low numbers in the population as a function of frequency-dependent selection (Harpending & Sobus, 1987). Sociopaths could be cheaters or unfair reciprocators, a strategy that works only at low population frequency. Another example may be biastophilia, the paraphilia exemplified by a male violently forcing himself sexually on an unwilling female (rape).

As explained by Trivers (1985), the sex that invests the greater amount of effort in the rearing of offspring is the sex that has the greater decision-making power over with whom to merge its germ cells. Females are therefore a limiting resource for which males compete. From an evolutionary biology perspective, low-status males who cannot successfully compete would be more likely to rape (Shields & Shields, 1983; Thornhill & Thornhill, 1983). However, this frequency-dependent-selection scenario does not explain the exceptions: those high-status males with the same predilection.

Increase or Change in the Nongenetic Determinant

In some Native American tribes of the Southwest, as many as a quarter of adults have Type II diabetes, presumably because their digestive system and pancreas evolved to digest a very different and sparser diet than is available today. The resulting inability to handle the available volume of sugar, carbohydrates, and fats results in diabetes and obesity. The relevant analogy to paraphilias considers the significant increase in sexual opportunities simply by the increased numbers of interactions we all have on a daily basis, with the vast increase in possible attractions. Our ancestors did not evolve in crowded subways or with access to large groups of nonrelated children or adults.

Degeneration

In 1886, the first German edition of Krafft-Ebing's epic *Psychopathia Sexualis* (1965) gave credence to the now archaic concept of degeneracy, written about previously in French in the nineteenth century by Morel and by Magnan. According to Magnan, healthy humanity is set on a course of progressive evolution, but individuals can be affected in such a way that their ascending evolution is stopped, and they then embark on a degenerative course, eventually leading to their extinction. The degeneration is passed on by heredity, becoming more severe with each generation, leading to sterility until the line becomes extinct (Hoenig, 1977).

Krafft-Ebing (1965) was heavily influenced by Darwin. He classified all psychiatric disorders into one of two types: psychoneurosis, which develops in a fit brain, and psychic degenerations, which develop in an invalid brain, damaged by hereditary and unfavorable environmental influences. The perversions, which was the earliest way in which the paraphilias were conceptualized, were considered an example of the latter type. Krafft-Ebing accepted Binet's (1887) conceptualization that fetishes were caused by associative learning, but with the stipulation that perversity can take place only if degeneration has prepared the ground.

DEVELOPMENT OF PARAPHILIC BEHAVIORS

In studying the effects of rearing conditions on later sexual-object choice, D'Udine (1990) found that in rodents, altricial (born relatively immature) species were more behaviorally plastic (modifiable) than were nonaltricial species. This observation across species is important because humans, especially when compared to other primates, are a very altricial species.

There are numerous developmental theories of paraphilias. The most common one, in reference to pedophilia in particular, is based on a rich, anecdotal literature and is called the "abused/abuser hypothesis of pedophilia." The hypothesis states that having been sexually abused oneself in childhood will cause one to be sexually attracted to (and therefore sexually abuse) children when one reaches adulthood. The problem with this widely held notion is that there is little evidence supporting it (Garland & Dougher, 1990). Until recently, the predominant view of the cause of homosexuality was also developmental via recruitment (Bell, Weinberg, & Hammersmith, 1981). This developmental view of homosexuality was heavily influenced by Freud's libido theory (Halberstadt-Freud, 1977), which gave the theoretical rationale for the misguided attempts at changing sexual orientation through psychotherapy (Aardweg, 1985).

Ideally, to understand the development of paraphilias, one should follow the psychosexual development of an unselected population of children. Because of the rarity of some of the paraphilias, as well as the ethical dilemmas such research with children would pose, such studies have not been done. In instances where childhood behavior is easily noticeable, as in effeminate male children, follow-up studies are possible, as represented by the now-classic prospective study of effeminate boys by Green (1987). In instances where childhood behavior is not easily noticeable, as in the childhood of persons who develop paraphilias in adulthood, health care providers' and behavior researchers' knowledge of variant psychosexual development comes from retrospective self-report.

As indicated earlier, self-report is always a dubious route to truth. Given that warning, the following is known from retrospective self-report. Freund and Kuban (1993) found, for example, that pedophiles report that the development of erotic sex preference (i.e., attraction for males versus females) precedes that of erotic age preference (i.e., prepubertal, peripubertal, or postpubertal). In a retrospective study of five adolescent males with asphyxiophilia, Friedrich and Gerber (1994) found that these boys self-reported that choking, in combination with physical or sexual abuse, had occurred. Each boy appeared to have paired choking with sexual arousal.

There is another literature on the developmental origins of sadomasochistic paraphilias. For reasons that are not entirely clear, sadomasochism and its variation, bondage and dominance, are also closely related to two fetishes, leather and rubber. Using self-report methods with persons with various sexual variations as well as normal controls, Gosselin and Wilson (1980) found that "leatherites" and "rubberites" self-reported approximately six times the rate of sadomasochistic fantasies as normal controls.

One would assume, even based on self-report data, that persons with sadomasochistic paraphilias would report more corporal punishment in childhood than would persons with other paraphilias and normal controls. Interestingly, this is not what Gosselin and Wilson (1980) found. At least in retrospective self-reports, there were no differences in this childhood antecedent among sadomasochists, rubberites, leatherites, transvestites, and controls.

Analogy of Paraphilias to the Development of Language Capability in Humans

The development of the capability to use symbolic language to communicate information between conspecifics offers an analogous developmental circumstance to the development of the capacity to express sexual behavior. Humans are born with the innate ability to easily acquire language through cultural transmission (Chomsky, 1965, 1969). Chomsky's work contradicted the work of Skinner (1957), who thought that the development of the capacity to use symbolic language could be explained solely on the basis of simple conditioning: Children learn grammatical rules easily; they learn the exceptions later.

Because paraphilias (e.g., sadomasochism and pedophilia) fall into predictable categories across societies with markedly different traditions and because there is a higher concordance rate for certain paraphilias (e.g., sadomasochism) in identical versus fraternal twins (Gosselin & Wilson, 1980), there is evidence of an innate component involved in the development of paraphilias. At this time, the mechanisms by which this innate component interacts with environmental components are not understood. Nevertheless, the innate component of paraphilias as a variation of sexual behavior can be roughly analogous to the innate component of language, the so-called innate grammar, though it is only expressed in some individuals.

Children learn a new language with the greatest ease between ages 4 and 6. This is also the time when life event trauma, such as abuse, is the most likely to lead to significant psychopathology (e.g., dissociative disorder) in children so predisposed to develop these disorders. Money (1986) asserted:

> Conjecturally, the most vulnerable years for lovemap vandalism are likely to be between ages five and eight. The systematic observations and studies of childhood erotosexual development needed to confirm this conjecture remain to be done . . . but after puberty, the lovemap, if it changes, does so chiefly by decoding what has already been encoded into it. Once a lovemap has been formed, it is, like native language, extremely resistant to change. (p. 19)

The late Konrad Lorenz claimed in 1985 that he believed his lifelong fascination with geese was related to his discovery of them (and the fact that they became imprinted on him) at age 6 (J. R. Feierman, personal communication, 1985). Lorenz stated:

> I became imprinted on them [geese] the same way that they became imprinted on me. I was only six years old at the time. My young playmate at the time [who later became his wife] was seven years old when we discovered imprinting together. She never developed the attraction to geese that I did. I was six and she was already seven years old. That I believe is important.

Interestingly, in reference to Lorenz's geese, when the geese matured, they courted humans rather than other geese, showing that at least some of the characteristics of the parent (imprinted object) are carried over to the lovemap as characteristics of a desired sexual partner. The relationship between parental imprinting and later attributes to which one is sexually attracted may be important in regard to the etiology of paraphilias. Lorenz wrote of the relationship between the "parental and sexual companion" in his very influential "Companion" paper (1935/1970), the terminology for which is found in Lorenz (1981):

> Imprinting which determines the object of instinctive behavior patterns related to conspecifics in the young bird frequently results through the influence of

parents and siblings, yet it must nevertheless determine the behavior of the young bird to *all* conspecifics. Thus, in the *imprinted* schema of the conspecific, as with the innate equivalent, only *supra-individual-species-characteristic* characters may be derived from the image of parents and siblings, to be permanently imprinted. It is amazing enough that this should succeed in normal, species-typical imprinting, but it is astounding that a bird reared by, and imprinted to a human being should direct its behavior patterns not toward *one* human but towards the species *Homo sapiens*. A jackdaw for which the human has replaced the parental companion, and which has consequently become completely "humanized," will thus direct its awakening sexual instincts not specifically towards its former parental companion, but (with the complete unpredictability of falling in love) towards any one relatively unfamiliar human being. The sex is unimportant, *but the object will quite definitely be human.* It would seem that the former parental companion is simply not considered as a possible "mate."

But how does such a bird recognize our conspecifics as "human beings"? (Lorenz, 1970, pp. 131–132)

Lorenz (1970) goes on to expand upon what he calls the "innate schema" of the sexual companion:

> Innate releasing mechanisms associated with sexual behavior patterns usually have nothing to do with imprinting. The responses concerned first awaken some time after the completion of all imprinting processes. Frequently, releasers of infantile instinctive behavior patterns determine imprinting of the later sexual object. Generally, the conspecific inducing such imprinting (parent or sibling) does *not* possess any of the releasers relevant to sexual instinctive behavior patterns, and if these are in fact present, they are never presented to the young bird. Thus, there is no question of imprinting of the sexual companion of a young female through factors emanating from the father and brothers, or of the converse process of imprinting of young males induced by female members of the family. The releasing mechanisms determining imprinting have no immediate relationship to sexual responses—the imprinted characters are always characteristic for an entire species (i.e., for both males and females). Having said on p. 132 that a bird only acquires *supra-individual* characters of the companion through imprinting, we must add at this juncture that imprinting of the sexual companion only involves non-sexual species-specific characters. (p. 186)

The ideas quoted from Lorenz may be useful in the understanding of paraphilias in two ways. First, there must be biological variation in the perceptual apparatus of the infant in regard to what degree of generality it imprints upon in the parent figure. Second, if some individuals imprint on more specific characteristics of the parent, rather than on more general characteristics, could some of these specific characteristics be the characteristics that later give rise to paraphilias? In addition, if the characteristics that the infant becomes imprinted on are the nonsexual characteristics, so, too, the reader should remember, are the objects of paraphilias. For example, paraphilias rarely involve the genitals per se. What about characteristics that occur in both sexes, such as complexion, hair color, and general body build? Where does idiosyncratic preference stop and paraphilia start?

Progressing beyond infancy, the onset of puberty coincides with the last major step in brain development, with the elimination of some 40% of neuronal synapses (Huttenlocher, 1979). There is more behavioral flexibility prior to puberty than there is after puberty. For example, any language that is learned prior to puberty can be articulated like a native, without an accent. However, once puberty occurs, any language learned will be spoken with the accent of the language the individual spoke prior to puberty.

In reference to paraphilias, the best evidence is that they are present at the time of, or shortly after, puberty, when the behaving individual seeks out the stimuli represented in his lovemap for sexual gratification. This is no different from nonparaphilic lovemap seeking. The characteristics that a nonparaphilic male finds sexually gratifying also appear to have been incorporated in the lovemap prior to puberty. Upon reaching puberty, the behaving individual simply searches to find the outward manifestations of his or her inner map (see Figure 13.1).

FUNCTION OF PARAPHILIC BEHAVIORS

Under natural circumstances, most behaviors can be said to have a *function*, where function is defined as the adaptiveness of the particular behavior. How do the consequences of the behavior contribute to the survival and reproduction of the individual? Tinbergen (1951) classified some of the main behavioral functions into (1) feeding behavior, (2) escape behavior, (3) mating behavior, (4) fighting behavior, and (5) care-of-offspring behavior.

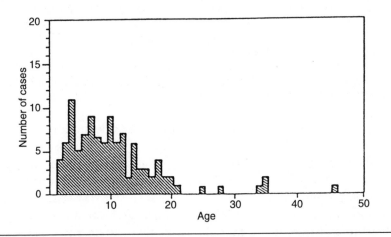

Figure 13.1 Lovemap Seeking for Both Paraphilic and Nonparaphilic Males. The ages at which 100 rubber fetishists first recognized their attraction to rubber. Reprinted from "Family Background and Upbringing," by C. Gosselin and G. Wilson, 1980, *Sexual Variations: Fetishism, Sadomasochism and Transvestism*, p. 128. Copyright 1980 by G. Wilson and C. Gosselin. Reprinted with permission of the authors.

Within Tinbergen's classification, it would be tempting, but wrong, to assume that paraphilic behaviors fall solely within the functional group of mating behaviors. Even if one were to assume this, one could just as easily argue that paraphilias are the antithesis of adaptive mating behavior, because in most paraphilias, ejaculation occurs without a chance of conception. In addition, sadomasochism has an aggressive component that would fall within the realm of fighting behavior, and there are aspects of pedophilia that would fall within the realm of care-of-the-offspring behavior (Feierman, 1990).

Because paraphilias are at least as prevalent as other species-atypical traits, such as left-handedness or exclusive homosexual behavior, it is legitimate to ask whether paraphilias are adaptive. If they were adaptive, their function would be to promote the genetic propagation of genes of paraphilic persons into subsequent generations. One should not assume that just because a behavior is labeled as being indicative of a mental illness it is not adaptive. Premature ejaculation, under some mating situations, could very well be adaptive ("survival of the quickest").

In terms of mating functions, we know of no data that would suggest that paraphilic males mate (i.e., ejaculate in potentially conceptive females) more successfully than do nonparaphilic males. Kafka and Prentky (1992) studied what they called nonparaphilic sexual addictions (NPSAs), which they described as sexually arousing fantasies, urges, or activities that are culturally sanctioned aspects of normative sexual arousal and behavior. These activities, however, increase in frequency or intensity (for greater than six months duration) so as to preclude or significantly interfere with the capacity for reciprocal affectionate sexual activity. As an example, they cited ego-dystonic promiscuity. In both paraphilic and NPSA males, NPSAs exhibited the most common form of ejaculatory sexual behavior. In addition, both the paraphilic and the NPSA males had higher than average total sexual outlets, and the predominant sexual outlet was masturbation.

In terms of parenting functions, some aspects of pedophilia involve behavioral motor patterns for certain aspects of pedophilic sexual behavior that are similar to the behavioral motor patterns used to parent children. Adult male–juvenile male pedophilia has been normative historically in the West and the East, and it is possible that although the behavior is abhorrent today, it most likely served some adaptive function in the past (see Feierman, 1994, and earlier discussion of "Previously Adaptive Trait" in this chapter).

In terms of fighting behavior, male aggression most certainly evolved to deal with aggression in other, conspecific males. It is likely that the functional proximity (ease of simultaneity and rapid alternation) between aggressive and sexual moods and behavior in males, discussed previously (Medicus & Hopf, 1990), is not fortuitous. Natural selection would favor functional proximity whenever it would be adaptive. In terms of intergroup warfare, which can be viewed as Darwinian survival of the fittest, fertile females have historically been a spoil of war for men.

As previously mentioned, a controversial argument has been made that biastophilia (rape) is an evolved, facultative, alternative reproductive strategy that can be adaptive when the benefit outweighs the cost for males who cannot effectively compete for the resources and status necessary to attract and reproduce successfully with desirable females (Shields & Shields, 1983; Thornhill & Thornhill, 1983). Given this scenario, the function of biastophilia (which is both aggressive and sexual) can be conceptualized as aggression-facilitated mating. However, some biastophiles even show sexual excitement on a plethysmograph to images of nonsexual violence toward women (Fedora et al., 1992).

Given these exceptions (pedophilia, sadomasochism, and biastophilia), current research cannot easily identify adaptive functional components with any other paraphilic behaviors. Although Kafka and Prentky (1992) argued that paraphilias differ from NPSAs on the basis of qualitative versus quantitative deviations from normalcy, respectively (with the added caveat that paraphilias are not socially sanctioned and NPSAs are), most paraphilias can also be conceptualized as a hypertrophy of what in moderation would be adaptive. Given that most biological traits have normal distributions in their degree of expression within populations, most paraphilias can be conceptualized as too much of a characteristic, the function of which in moderation would be adaptive.

THE TREATMENT OF
PARAPHILIC BEHAVIORS

There are six main modalities of treatment for paraphilias. They are not mutually exclusive, and most treatment programs utilize a combination of several modalities. These methods are behavioral modification, cognitive therapy, psychodynamic psychotherapy, group therapy, 12-step programs, and pharmacological therapy (see Kilmann, Sabalis, Gearing, Bukstel, & Scovern, 1982). The International Conference on the Treatment of Sex Offenders and the Association for the Behavioral Treatment of Sexual Abusers have proposed standards of care for the treatment of paraphilic sex offenders (Coleman & Dwyer, 1990).

One of the most difficult problems in evaluating the efficacy of any modality of treatment is the problem of defining relapse. Many paraphilias are victimless. However, others are clearly criminal and are, therefore, likely to be under-self-reported. Rearrest rates produce harder data, but it cannot be assumed that those who get rearrested are a random representation of paraphiliacs. Penile plethysmography can measure the effects of treatment on arousal. However, sexual arousal is context-dependent, and the issue is not arousal but the subsequent behavior that the arousal may or may not motivate.

Behavioral modification is the main component of most treatment programs for paraphilias (Abel, 1988; Barnard, Fuller, Robbins, & Shaw, 1989). This treatment rests on the assumption that paraphilias are primarily learned behaviors. Irrespective of the degree to which they are learned behaviors, they are reinforced by the environment, and there is good evidence that they are amenable, at least in the short term, to behavioral modification techniques. The principle is to decrease the strength of deviant sexual arousal and to increase nondeviant sexual arousal. The procedures used include aversive techniques, covert sensitization, masturbatory-satiation technique, shame therapy, biofeedback, and others. The procedures used to increase nondeviant sexual arousal include masturbatory conditioning and fading, systematic desensitization, aversion relief, and social skills retraining.

Cognitive therapy rests on the assumption that paraphiliacs justify their behaviors through self-deceptive and distorted thinking, which is based on false assumptions, misperceptions, and self-serving interpretations. Because the emphasis is on trying to correct distorted thought patterns, a diary is often kept and then used as the focus of therapy. This therapy may also include educational material, including books and movies from the victim's standpoint, or even meeting with victims and their advocates. Group therapy and role playing may also be used (Marshall & Barbaree, 1990; Murphy, 1990; Nelson & Jackson, 1989).

Group psychotherapy is a cost-effective way of treating paraphiliacs, although the outcomes are mixed. The usual form of treatment is confrontation and consensus building, based on the social needs of the individual to be accepted by the group.

Psychodynamic therapy is based on the ideological construct that the paraphiliac underwent significant childhood traumas that caused considerable psychological conflict with subsequent repression of the feelings associated with the traumatic experience; the feelings are then acted out in adult life in terms of paraphilic behaviors in an attempt to relieve the psychic discomfort. The outcome data on the use of psychodynamic psychotherapy to treat paraphilias are mixed and, in general, weak, probably because the underlying assumptions are false (e.g., see Garland & Dougher, 1990). It is very likely that the real therapeutic benefit from one-on-one psychotherapy has nothing to do with the ideological assumptions underlying it. Rather, the benefit more likely stems from the paraphiliac's wanting to please the caring therapist, with whom an intense, interpersonal relationship forms as the therapist tries to ideologically indoctrinate the paraphiliac.

Twelve-step programs, based on the model of Alcoholics Anonymous (AA), are also commonly used. Patrick Carnes is the strongest proponent of this form of therapy (Carnes, 1989). Such programs are based on the assumption that paraphilias are sexual addictions, similar to substance-use disorders such as alcoholism. Twelve-step programs can be helpful in preventing the acting-out of any problematic behavior. Such programs require the belief in a "higher power," which for many nonreligious persons is a hindrance. Apart from the higher power aspect, these programs also help the paraphiliac make at least psychological restitution to other persons who may have been adversely affected by the paraphiliac's behavior.

Pharmacological treatment rests on the assumption that the frequency and intensity of male sexual behavior is dependent on the level of the circulating male sex hormone, testosterone. There have been five main treatments: castration, cyproterone, progesterone, SSRIs, and, most recently, the gonadotropin hormone-release analogue, triptorelin. Basing his paper on preliminary work conducted in the early 1960s by Neumann and colleagues from Germany, Money (1970) was the first to write in English about the use of progesterone in the treatment of paraphilias. Freund (1980) has reviewed the efficacy of various pharmacological treatments. When taken, frequently by long-acting injection, these agents cause a significant decrease in both paraphilic and nonparaphilic sexual behavior. Triptorelin looks very promising in preliminary studies (Rösler & Witztum, 1998; Thibaut, Cordier, & Kuhn, 1996). As mentioned previously, SSRI antidepressants tend to decrease both appetitive and consummatory components of sexual behavior, which have implications for treatment (see, Balon, 1998; Kafka, 1994).

Irrespective of the method of treatment, most sex offender programs for paraphiliacs include a relapse-prevention program (Laws, 1989), and many have instituted case management programs as well (Lehne, 1994). Regardless of the type of treatment, paraphilias are not "curable." They are, however, treatable in terms of decreasing the probability of the occurrence of the behavior.

The efficacy of the treatment for the paraphilias has been difficult to evaluate, as pointed out by many authors of review articles (Furby, Weinrott, & Blackshaw, 1989; Greenberg, 1998; Hanson & Bussiere, 1998; Richer & Crismon, 1993). Problems in evaluating efficacy include lack of random assignment to treatment and control groups, diagnostic and treatment heterogeneity, and outcome measure as well as length of follow-up heterogeneity. Nevertheless, there are certain generalities that hold across most studies. Good prognosis is associated with nondeviant sexual arousal patterns, familial acts, first offenders, lack of concomitant personality disorders, and completion of treatment. Nontreatment results in relapse/recidivism rates anywhere from 10% to 90+%, if patients are followed for several years.

Treatment of almost any type, but especially when psychosocial and pharmacological treatments are combined, can reduce the relapse/recidivism rates at least by half, versus psychosocial treatment alone, which is less successful (Rice, Quinsey, & Harris, 1991). Recidivism rates for treated incest offenders average 4%–10%, nonincest pedophiles 10%–40%, rapists (biastophiles) 5%–35%, and exhibitionists 25%–71% (Abel, Mittelman, Becker, Rathner, & Rouleau, 1988; Berlin et. al., 1991; Marshall & Barbaree, 1990; Meyer, Cole, & Emory, 1992). Although rarely used in the United States and fraught with ethical issues, surgical castration produces recidivism rates in the 3%–5% range for a variety of sexual offenses, even with long follow-up times (Ortmann, 1980; Willie & Beier, 1989).

Nevertheless, on a short-term basis, the outcome rates of any of the described treatments are significantly better than no treatment at all and are at least as good as the outcome rates for many other *DSM-IV* psychiatric disorders. As with all treatment, therapeutic decisions should be based on evidence of efficacy in the literature rather than on the latest theoretical fad or on personal or anecdotal reports. In addition, because treatment merely reduces the probability of the behavior's expressing itself, rather than eliminating the cause of the behavior, treatment should be lifelong and not time-limited.

Finally, clinicians who treat people with paraphilias must be both nonjudgmental and comfortable with their own sexuality.

REFERENCES

Aardweg, G.V.D. (1985). *Homosexuality and hope: A psychologist talks about treatment and change.* Ann Arbor, MI: Servant.

Abel, G.G. (1988). Behavioral treatment of child molesters. In A.J. Stunkard & A. Baum (Eds.), *Perspectives on behavioral medicine* (pp. 223–242). New York: Erlbaum.

Abel, G.G., Mittelman, M., Becker, J.V., Rathner, J., & Rouleau, J.L. (1988). Predicting child molesters' response to treatment. *Annals of the New York Academy of Sciences, 528,* 223–234.

American Psychiatric Association. (1994). *Diagnostic and statistical manual of mental disorders* (4th ed.). Washington, DC: Author.

Balon, R. (1998, October–December). Pharmacological treatment of paraphilias with a focus on antidepressants. *Journal of Sexual and Marital Therapy, 24*(4), 241–254.

Barnard, G.W., Fuller, A.K., Robbins, L., & Shaw, T. (1989). *The child molester: An integrated approach to evaluation and treatment.* New York: Brunner/Mazel.

Beck, J.G., & Bozman, S. (1995, December). Gender differences in sexual desire: The effects of anger and anxiety. *Archives of Sexual Behavior, 24*(6), 595–612.

Bell, A.P., Weinberg, M.S., & Hammersmith, S.K. (1981). *Sexual preference: Its development in men and women.* Bloomington: Indiana University Press.

Berlin, F.S., Hunt, W.P., Malin, H.M., Dyer, A., Lehne, G., & Dean, S. (1991). A five-year plus follow-up survey of criminal recidivism within a treated cohort of 406 pedophiles, 111 exhibitionists and 109 sexual aggressives: Issues and outcome. *American Journal of Forensic Psychiatry, 12,* 5–28.

Berliner, B. (1958). The role of object relations in moral masochism. *Psychoanalytic Quarterly, 27,* 38–56.

Bernstein, I. (1957). The role of narcissism in moral masochism. *Psychoanalytic Quarterly, 26,* 358–377.

Binet, A. (1887). *Du fetischisme dans l'amour.* Paris: Revue Philosophique.

Boyd, R., & Richerson, P.J. (1985). *Culture and the evolutionary process.* Chicago: University of Chicago Press.

Briere, J., & Runtz, M. (1989). University males' sexual interest in children: Predicting potential indices of "pedophilia" in a nonforensic sample. *Child Abuse & Neglect, 13,* 65–75.

Bromberg, N. (1959). Stimulus-response cycles and ego development: With specific reference to the masochistic ego. *Journal of the American Psychoanalytic Association, 7,* 227–247.

Bullough, V.L. (1976). *Sexual variance in society and history.* Chicago: University of Chicago Press.

Bullough, V.L. (1990). History in adult human sexual behavior with children and adolescents in Western societies. In J.R. Feierman (Ed.), *Pedophilia: Biosocial dimensions* (pp. 69–90). New York: Springer-Verlag.

Carnes, P. (1989). *Contrary to love: Helping the sexual addict.* Minneapolis: Compcare.

Chomsky, N. (1965). *Aspects of the theory of syntax.* Cambridge, MA: MIT Press.

Chomsky, N. (1969). Language and the mind. *Psychology Today, 13,* 424–432.

Clutton-Brock, T.H., & Harvey, P.H. (Eds.). (1978). *Readings in sociobiology* (pp. 52–97). San Francisco: Freeman.

Coleman, E., & Dwyer, M. (1990). Proposed standards of care for the treatment of sex offenders. *Journal of Offender Rehabilitation, 15,* 4–15.

Craig, W. (1918). Appetites and aversions as constituents of instincts. *Biological Bulletin of Woods Hole, 34,* 91–107.

Crepault, C., & Couture, M. (1980). Men's erotic fantasies. *Archives of Sexual Behavior, 9,* 565–581.

Darwin, C. (1859). *The origin of species.* London: Murray.

Darwin, C. (1871). *The descent of man, and selection in relation to sex.* New York: Appleton.

Darwin, C. (1872). *The expression of the emotions in man and in animals.* New York: Appleton.

Dawkins, R. (1976). *The selfish gene.* New York: Oxford University Press.

Dover, K.J. (1978). *Greek homosexuality.* Cambridge, MA: Harvard University Press.

D'Udine, B. (1990). The modification of sexual behavior through imprinting: A rodent model. In J.R. Feierman (Ed.), *Pedophilia: Biosocial dimensions* (pp. 221–241). New York: Springer-Verlag.

Eibl-Eibesfeldt, I. (1975). *Ethology: The biology of behavior* (2nd ed.). New York: Holt, Rinehart and Winston.

Eibl-Eibesfeldt, I. (1989). *Human ethology.* Hawthorne, NY: Aldine de Gruyter.

Eisenbud, R.J. (1967). Masochism revisited. *Psychoanalytic Review, 54,* 5–27.

Ekman, P., & Friesen, W.V. (1975). *Unmasking the face: A guide to recognizing emotions from facial cues.* Englewood Cliffs, NJ: Prentice-Hall.

Ellis, H. (1936). *Studies in the psychology of sex* (Vol. 2). New York: Random House.

Fedora, O., et al. (1992, February). Sadism and other paraphilias in normal controls and aggressive and nonaggressive sex offenders. *Archives of Sexual Behavior, 21*(1), 1–15.

Feierman, J.R. (1990). A biosocial overview of adult human sexual behavior with children and adolescents. In J.R. Feierman (Ed.), *Pedophilia: Biosocial dimensions* (pp. 8–68). New York: Springer-Verlag.

Feierman, J.R. (1994). Pedophilia: Paraphilic attraction to children. In J.J. Krivacska & J. Money (Eds.), *The handbook of forensic sexology: Biomedical and criminological perspectives* (pp. 49–79). Amherst, NY: Prometheus.

Fisher, H.E. (1992). *Anatomy of love: The natural history of monogamy, adultery and divorce.* New York: Norton.

Fisher, H.E. (1998). Lust, attraction, and attachment in mammalian reproduction. *Human Nature, 9,* 23–52.

Freud, S. (1924). *The economic problem in masochism: Collected papers* (Vol. 2). London: Hogarth.

Freund, K. (1980). Therapeutic sex drive reduction. *Acta Psychiatrica Scandinavica, 62*(Suppl. 287), 5–38.

Freund, K. (1988). Courtship disorder: Is this hypothesis valid? Human sexual aggression: Current perspectives. *Annals of the New York Academy of Sciences, 528,* 172–182.

Freund, K., & Kuban, M. (1993). Toward a testable developmental model of pedophilia: The development of erotic age preference. *Child Abuse & Neglect, 17,* 315–324.

Freund, K., Scher, H., & Hucker, S. (1983). The courtship disorders. *Archives of Sexual Behavior, 12,* 369–379.

Friedrich, W.N., & Gerber, P.N. (1994). Autoerotic asphyxia: The development of a paraphilia. *Journal of the American Academy of Child and Adolescent Psychiatry, 33,* 970–974.

Furby, L., Weinrott, M.R., & Blackshaw, L. (1989). Sex offender recidivism: A review. *Psychological Bulletin, 105,* 3–30.

Garland, R.J., & Dougher, M.J. (1990). The abused/abuser hypothesis of child sexual abuse: A critical review of theory and research. In J.R. Feierman (Ed.), *Pedophilia: Biosocial dimensions* (pp. 488–509). New York: Springer-Verlag.

Gorman, G.F. (1964). Fetishism occurring in identical twins. *British Journal of Psychiatry, 110,* 255–256.

Gosselin, C., & Wilson, G. (1980). *Sexual variations: Fetishism, sadomasochism and transvestism.* New York: Simon & Schuster.

Grammer, K. (1995). *Signale der liebe* [Signal of love]. Munchen: Deutscher Taschenbuch Verlag GmbH & Co. K.G.

Green, R. (1987). *The "sissy boy syndrome" and the development of homosexuality.* New Haven, CT: Yale University Press.

Green, R. (1994). Sodomy laws. In J.J. Krivacska & J. Money (Eds.), *The handbook of forensic sexology: Biomedical and criminological perspectives* (pp. 34–48). Amherst, NY: Prometheus.

Greenberg, D.M. (1998). Sexual recidivism in sex offenders. *Canadian Journal of Psychiatry, 43,* 459–465.

Halberstadt-Freud, H.C. (1977). Freud's libido theory. In J. Money & H. Musaph (Eds.), *Handbook of sexology: History and ideology* (Vol. 1, pp. 45–56). New York: Elsevier.

Hanson, R.K., & Bussiere, M.T. (1998). Predicting relapse: A meta-analysis of sexual offender recidivism studies. *Journal of Consulting and Clinical Psychology, 66,* 348–362.

Harpending, H., & Sobus, J. (1987). Sociopathy as an adaptation. In J.R. Feierman (Ed.), The ethology of psychiatric populations. *Ethology and Sociobiology, 8*(Suppl. 3), 63S–72S.

Heilbrun, A.B., Jr., & Self, D.T. (1988). Erotic value of female distress in sexually explicit photographs. *Journal of Sex Research, 24,* 47–57.

Hoenig, J. (1977). The development of sexology during the second half of the 19th century. In J. Money & H. Musaph (Eds.), *Handbook of sexology: History and ideology* (Vol. 1, pp. 5–20). New York: Elsevier.

Hrdy, S.B. (1997). Raising Darwin's consciousness: Female sexuality and the prehominid origins of patriarchy. *Human Nature, 8,* 1–50.

Huttenlocher, P.R. (1979). Synaptic density in human frontal cortex: Developmental changes and the effects of aging. *Brain Research, 163,* 195–205.

Kafka, M.P. (1994, September). Sertraline pharmacotherapy for paraphilias and paraphilia-related disorders: An open trial. *Annals of Clinical Psychiatry, 6*(3), 189–195.

Kafka, M.P. (1997, August). A monoamine hypothesis for the pathophysiology of paraphilic disorders. *Archives of Sexual Behavior, 26*(4), 343–358.

Kafka, M.P., & Prentky, R. (1992). A comparative study of non-paraphilic sexual addictions and paraphilias in men. *Journal of Clinical Psychiatry, 53,* 345–350.

Kilmann, P.R., Sabalis, R.F., Gearing, M.L., II, Bukstel, L.H., & Scovern, A.W. (1982). The treatment of sexual paraphilias: A review of the outcome research. *Journal of Sex Research, 18,* 193–252.

Kinsey, A.C., Pomeroy, W.B., & Martin, C.E. (1948). *Sexual behavior in the human male.* Philadelphia: Saunders.

Krafft-Ebing, R., von. (1965). *Psychopathia sexualis: With especial reference to the antipathic sexual instinct* (Trans. from the 12th German ed. and Intro. by Franklin S. Klaf). New York: Stein and Day. (First German edition published in 1886)

Krivacska, J.J. (1994). Paraphilic prevention: Social and legal implications. In J.J. Krivacska & J. Money (Eds.), *The handbook of forensic sexology: Biomedical and criminological perspectives* (pp. 397–421). Amherst, NY: Prometheus.

Lalumiere, M.L., & Quinsey, V.L. (1998). Pavlovian conditioning of sexual interests in human males. *Archives of Sexual Behavior 27*(3), 241–252.

Laws, D.R. (Ed.). (1989). *Relapse prevention with sex offenders.* New York: Guilford Press.

Lehne, G.K. (1994). Case management and prognosis of the sex offender. In J.J. Krivacska & J. Money (Eds.), *The handbook of forensic sexology: Biomedical and criminological perspectives* (pp. 265–283). Amherst, NY: Prometheus.

LeVay, S. (1994). *The sexual brain.* Cambridge, MA: MIT Press.

Lorenz, K.Z. (1970). A consideration of methods of identification of species-specific instinctive behavior patterns in birds. In K. Lorenz (Ed.) & R. Martin (Trans.), *Studies in animal and human behavior* (Vol. 1). Cambridge, MA: Harvard University Press. (Original paper published in 1935)

Lorenz, K.Z. (1981). *The foundations of ethology.* New York: Springer-Verlag.

Lorenz, K.Z. (1987). Foreword. In J.R. Feierman (Ed.), The ethology of psychiatric populations. *Ethology and Sociobiology, 8*(Suppl. 3), iiiS–ivS.

Lowenstein, R. (1957). A contribution to the psychoanalytic theory in masochism. *Journal of the American Psychoanalytic Association, 5,* 197–234.

Marshall, W.L., & Barbaree, H.E. (1990). Outcome of comprehensive cognitive behavioral treatment programs. In W.L. Marshall, D.R. Laws, & H.E. Barbaree (Eds.), *Handbook of sexual assault: Issues, theories, and treatment of the offender* (pp. 363–385). New York: Plenum Press.

Martin, P., & Bateson, P. (1986). *Measuring behavior: An introductory guide.* Cambridge, England: Cambridge University Press.

McDougal, W. (1926). *Outline of abnormal psychology.* New York: Scribner's.

Medicus, G., & Hopf, S. (1990). The phylogeny of male/female differences in sexual behavior. In J.R. Feierman (Ed.), *Pedophilia: Biosocial dimensions* (pp. 122–149). New York: Springer-Verlag.

Menaker, E. (1979). *Masochism and the emergent ego.* New York: Human Sciences.

Meyer, W.J., III, Cole, C., & Emory, E. (1992). Depo-provera treatment for sex offending behavior: An evaluation of outcome. *Bulletin of the American Academy of Psychiatry and the Law, 20,* 249–259.

Mohr, J.W., Turner, R.E., & Jerry, M.B. (1964). *Pedophilia and exhibitionism.* Toronto: University of Toronto Press.

Money, J. (1970). Use of androgen-depleting hormone in the treatment of male sex offenders. *Journal of Sex Research, 6,* 165–172.

Money, J. (1986). *Lovemaps: Clinical concepts of sexual/erotic health and pathology, paraphilia, and gender transposition in childhood, adolescence, and maturity.* New York: Irvington.

Money, J. (1988). *Gay, straight, and in-between: The sexology of erotic orientation.* New York: Oxford University Press.

Moore, M.M. (1985). Nonverbal courtship patterns in women: Context and consequence. *Ethology and Sociobiology, 6,* 237–248.

Morris, D. (1977). *Manwatching: A field guide to human behavior.* New York: Abrams.

Mosher, D.L. (1994). Public policy and sex offenses: Social tolerance versus criminalization. In J.J. Krivacska & J. Money (Eds.), *The handbook of forensic sexology: Biomedical and criminological perspectives* (pp. 369–396). Amherst, NY: Prometheus.

Murphy, W.D. (1990). Assessment and modification of cognitive distortions in sex offenders. In W.L. Marshall, D.R. Laws, & H.E. Barbaree (Eds.), *Handbook of sexual assault: Issues, theories, and treatment of the offender* (pp. 331–342). New York: Plenum Press.

Nelson, C., & Jackson, P. (1989). High risk recognition: The cognitive behavioral chain. In D.R. Laws (Ed.), *Relapse prevention with sex offenders* (pp. 167–177). New York: Guilford Press.

Oehlert, B. (1958). Kampf und Paarbildung einiger Cichliden. *Zeitschrift fur Tierpsychologie, 15*(2), 141–174.

Ortmann, J. (1980). The treatment of sexual offenders, castration and antihormonal therapy. *International Journal of Law and Psychiatry, 3,* 443–451.

Perper, T. (1985). *Sex signals: The biology of love.* Philadelphia: Institute for Scientific Information Press.

Perper, T., & Weiss, D.L. (1997). Proceptive and rejective strategies of U.S. and Canadian college women. *Journal of Sex Research, 23,* 455–480.

Pusey, A.E., & Packer, C. (1986). Dispersal and philopatry. In B.B. Smuts, D.L. Cheney, R.M. Seyfarth, R.W. Wrangham, & T.T. Struhsaker (Eds.), *Primate societies* (pp. 250–266). Chicago: University of Chicago Press.

Quinn, P.A. (1989). *Better than the sons of kings: Boys and monks in the Early Middle Ages.* New York: Peter Lang.

Rachman, S.J., & Hodgson, R.J. (1968). Experimentally induced "sexual fetishism." *Psychological Record, 18,* 25–27.

Rice, M.E., Quinsey, V.L., & Harris, G.T. (1991). Sexual recidivism among child molesters released from a maximum security psychiatric institution. *Journal of Consulting and Clinical Psychology, 59,* 381–386.

Richer, M., & Crismon, M.L. (1993). Pharmacotherapy of sexual offenders. *Annals of Pharmacotherapy, 27,* 316–320.

Rickles, N.K. (1950). *Exhibitionism.* Philadelphia: Lippincott.

Rösler, A., & Witztum, E. (1998). Treatment of men with paraphilia with a long-acting analogue of gonadotropin-releasing hormone. *New England Journal of Medicine, 338,* 416–422.

Saikaku, I. (1990). *The great mirror of male love* (P.G. Schalow, Trans.). Stanford: Stanford University Press. (Original work published in 1687)

Scherer, K.R., & Ekman, P. (1982). *Handbook of methods in nonverbal behavior research.* Cambridge, England: Cambridge University Press.

Shields, W.M., & Shields, L.M. (1983). Forcible rape: An evolutionary perspective. *Ethology and Sociobiology, 4,* 115–136.

Skinner, B.F. (1957). *Verbal behavior.* London: Methuen.

Stekel, W. (1952). *Sexual aberrations: The phenomena of fetishism in relation to sex.* New York: Liveright. (English translation of 1923 German version)

Symons, D. (1979). *The evolution of human sexuality.* New York: Oxford University Press.

Templeman, T.L., & Stinnett, R.D. (1991). Patterns of sexual arousal and history in a "normal" sample of young men. *Archives of Sexual Behavior, 20,* 137–150.

Thibaut, F., Cordier, B., & Kuhn, J.M. (1996). Gonadotropin hormone releasing hormone agonist in cases of severe paraphilia: A lifetime of treatment? *Psychoneuroendocrinology, 21,* 411–419.

Thornhill, R., & Thornhill, N.W. (1983). Human rape: An evolutionary analysis. *Ethology and Sociobiology, 4,* 137–173.

Tinbergen, N. (1951). *The study of instinct.* New York: Oxford University Press.

Trivers, R.L. (1976). Foreword. In R. Dawkins (Ed.), *The selfish gene.* New York: Oxford University Press.

Trivers, R.L. (1985). *Social evolution.* Menlo Park, CA: Benjamin/Cummings.

Weinberg, M.S., et al. (1994, December). Homosexual foot fetishism. *Archives of Sexual Behavior, 23(6),* 611–626.

Willie, R., & Beier, K.M. (1989). Castration in Germany. *Annals of Sex Research, 2,* 103–133.

Wilson, E.O. (1975). *Sociobiology: The new synthesis.* Cambridge, MA: Belknap Press of Harvard University Press.

CHAPTER 14

Sexuality and the Internet:
The Next Sexual Revolution

AL COOPER, SYLVAIN BOIES, MARLENE MAHEU,
and DAVID GREENFIELD

This chapter addresses the impact of technology on human sexual behavior by examining how the Internet may affect interpersonal communication and allow freer access to all manner of sexual pursuits. The psychology of Internet sexuality is explored based on the clinical and theoretical positions of experts, along with empirical evidence gathered to date in this rapidly developing area of human sexuality. Implications for mental health professionals are discussed; these include preventive, ameliorative, and facilitative interventions as well as ethical and research considerations. Finally, thoughts about how the Internet may impact sexuality in the not too distant future are also offered.

The information age will likely change people's lives more dramatically in the next 20 years than in any previous period in history. An estimated 15 million people go on-line each day and spend an average of 9.8 hours a week visiting some of the 200 million web pages available (Computerworld, 1998). Work, school, and even social activities will be increasingly dependent on and centered around computers (Cooper, 1997). Each week, more than 300,000 new pages are added to the World Wide Web, and the number of its users is expected to reach 94.2 million by 2001 (Computerworld, 1998). Since its inception, the Internet has been associated with sexuality in a kind of synergistic dance, each fueling the transformation of the other. The influence of the Internet on sexuality is likely to be so significant that it will ultimately be recognized as the cause of the next "sexual revolution."

THE POWER OF THE INTERNET

The Internet has become a powerful communication medium with the potential to influence and redefine aspects of interpersonal relations, including sexual interactions. People are turning to the Internet for a wide range of sexual pursuits, including access to sexual information and sexually explicit material. An estimated 9 million individuals recently visited the five most popular adult web sites in one month (Goldberg, 1998). Yet, even as the web continues to expand exponentially, little is known about how this new reality is affecting sexuality in America and around the world.

The three key factors that appear to give the Internet its power with regard to sexual expression have been described as the "Triple A Engine" (Cooper, 1998): access, affordability, and anonymity. These three elements make the Internet a unique forum in which to pursue sexual interests and to distinguish it from the more conventional media (e.g., magazines, videotapes, television) featuring erotic and sexual material.

Internet access is characterized by ease, convenience, and availability to increasing numbers of people in all aspects of their lives. This easy accessibility has contributed to sex as the most searched topic on the Internet (Cooper, 1998; Freeman-Longo & Blanchard, 1998) and to its widespread use for sexual pursuits (Goldberg, 1998). On-line, people can find a web site to satisfy any sexual need or desire they may have without having to delay gratification. Consumerism is further facilitated by the seemingly unlimited availability of products, services, and people. The Internet is a virtual store open 24 hours a day for social and business transactions. With millions of users on-line, someone who knows how to navigate the World Wide Web can, at any moment, find a kindred spirit with a similar sexual interest or desire.

Affordability is based on the universal economic construct of supply and demand. The seemingly infinite number of sites and products of every conceivable kind means the supply is plentiful and thus prices are kept down. In many cases, consumers who know their way around the Net can even find free sexually related services (Hapgood, 1996). Additionally, the decreasing costs of server space, combined with increases in banner and link advertising, help keep user fees low.

The last factor, anonymity, is perhaps the most relevant to sexual behavior. The belief, whether true or not, that one's identity is concealed, seems to have a powerful effect on sexuality. Branwyn (1993) observed that using the Internet increases the sense of freedom, willingness to experiment, pace of self-disclosure, and ability to talk openly about one's sex life, sharing, questions, concerns, and fantasies. People who might be hesitant publicly to view or purchase sexually explicit material or engage in certain sexual activities may find that they have less inhibition when protected by the anonymity they feel on-line.

THE BREADTH OF THE
INTERNET-SEXUALITY CONNECTION

The relationship between the Internet and psychosexual well-being reflects a complex and multidimensional phenomenon. It might be best understood by examining the various aspects of Internet usage. As a communication tool, the Internet offers a means to promote mental health through innovative methods. However, it can also be abused, and this may be associated with difficulties in psychosocial functioning. The effects of the Internet on sexuality have previously been grouped in three broad categories: commercial aspects, negative patterns, and positive connections (Cooper, 1998).

COMMERCIAL ASPECTS

Sexuality has been one of the financial engines of the initial growth of the Internet (Hapgood, 1996), as some of the money made from sexual sites was used to develop new computer products servicing on-line communication. Adult entertainment commodities (videos, web sites, "altsex" sites, personals) have been some of the largest revenue producers and have underwritten much of the initial technological development. They also contribute to the immense popularity of the World Wide Web. In addition, the Triple A of the Internet is facilitating the commerce of sexual products. Condoms, lingerie, vibrators, videos, books, and other aids as well as sexual educational materials are easily obtained with little embarrassment and great ease. It is predicted that on-line sex stores will outpace adult mail-order catalogues and three-dimensional outlets within a few years (Semans & Winks, 1999).

POSITIVE CONNECTIONS

In a world of sexual problems, pitfalls, and prejudices, the Internet offers myriad positive ways to impact sexuality and sexual connections between people. The proliferation of virtual communities around common interests (e.g., pro-choice or pro-life interests, leather aficionados) or shared experiences (e.g., rape survivors, herpes sufferers, paraplegics) is one positive trend that can be noticed on-line. The sense of community and belonging derived from such contacts can have salubrious psychological effects on individuals, thereby contributing to the changing political and societal perceptions of these groups. Through the Internet, isolated and disenfranchised individuals (e.g., gay and lesbian youth, persons with disabilities) can come together and find social support.

Another important development is the rapid increase in the number of specific web sites that offer opportunities to educate people on sexual matters (e.g., sexual dysfunction, safe sex practices, information on reproduction, abstinence, sexually transmitted diseases). This type of information has the potential to help people overcome the anxiety many feel about sexuality (e.g., Williams,

1994). Professionals also need to be kept informed of developments, and there are analogous educational resources available to them through most of the major sexuality organizations. These organizations have their own sites as well as on-line methods of informing and educating their memberships. These methods include listserves that encourage the exchange of views on controversial issues, and bulletin boards where recent research findings can be posted.

On-line communication allows experts to share information more easily with those who are interested but who otherwise might be constrained by logistical factors (e.g., geographical location, time, money). Similarly, the large number of people on-line allows sex educators to deliver services on very narrow and specialized topics (e.g., oral sex techniques for those over 50 who are in a new relationship) to populations that might otherwise be neglected. A number of directions have been suggested in Cooper's (1998) review of these issues. For instance, classes instructing parents how to talk with teens about safe sex could be offered via the Internet to a rural village in Mexico. The developer of a new medication for sexual problems could hold a virtual class from her laboratory in England and reach physician-enrollees scattered around the globe. Last, an on-line class on sexual enrichment for same-sex partners in a long-term relationship could reach people who might otherwise be too far away or too embarrassed to attend.

The Internet also provides a relatively safe forum in which people can engage in sexual experimentation. Despite the ethical and moral issues related to on-line sexual encounters, some of these liaisons might nevertheless have a therapeutic purpose or effect. On-line users may hear of sexual practices that challenge their beliefs and expand their present conceptualizations. Visitors to an on-line chat room may learn about certain sexual practices from others or experiment themselves in that on-line environment. Thus, for example, individuals curious about group sex could first try it on-line and then decide whether or not they wanted to participate in a three-dimensional situation.

On-line sexual experimentation may also facilitate identity exploration and development. Leiblum (1997) indicated that one can create a new persona online, and this may be a fairly common occurrence. For example, one can have the experience of being treated as a member of the opposite sex by presenting oneself as such. Cooper, Scherer, Boies, and Gordon (1999) found that users who had gone on-line for sexual pursuits at least once indicated that they occasionally pretended to be a different gender (5.1%), a different age (47.8%), or a different race (38.2%). Greenfield (1999) also found that 50% of those in their survey admitted to misrepresenting some aspect of themselves.

The Internet may ultimately help one to find a romantic partner, influence the type of person chosen, or affect the nature of the relationship a couple develops. Sophisticated users can utilize the Internet as "the mother of all computer dating services." Reports abound of those who have become romantically involved with another person while on-line (Leiblum, 1997). This can occur either as a result of a carefully thought out plan and investigation of on-line resources (e.g., free personal ads, paid dating services, sex or romance chat rooms) or through the serendipity of casual interactions around common interests. The Internet can considerably broaden the pool of individuals people have the opportunity to meet relative to their usual social circles.

NEGATIVE PATTERNS

The Internet can negatively impact people's lives in a variety of ways. Individuals can go on-line for their social and sexual needs and spend increasing amounts of time there rather than investing energy in real-world relationships. The results can be avoidance or neglect of personal relationships (Greenfield, in press). Individuals with otherwise empty and unsatisfying lives may be more at risk (Freeman-Longo & Blanchard, 1998) and likely to repeat the mood-altering experience the computer can provide. Mood states evoked by on-line sexual and social interactions include a reduction in loneliness, improved self-esteem, and even euphoria, and these feelings may act as positive reinforcements for continued excessive Internet usage (Young, 1997).

Conversely, on-line communication may increase isolation or create a sense of pseudo-intimacy. Whether or not it is actually possible to develop true intimacy through the Internet has been questioned. Schnarch (1997) noted that a large part of the attraction of cyberdating is the "whole notion of emotional contact without risk, exposure, or being known" (p. 17). He noted that people may present themselves only in the ways they are most comfortable. Thus, they prevent the possibility of being fully known by their partners and limit their own self-awareness. The use of fantasy may support creativity, but it is unclear how it ultimately impacts the development of intimacy.

The Internet may become an outlet for a number of sexual issues, including unresolved sexual difficulties, unfocused sexual energy, and the repetition of traumatic experiences. The Triple A may contribute to on-line sexual activity for those with ongoing problems with sexual compulsivity as well as for those who may have particular psychological predispositions or vulnerabilities (Leiblum, 1997). A number of studies have found that some individuals may overuse or develop problems with excessive Internet usage, both in general (Young, 1997) and specifically with regard to sexual activities (Cooper, Scherer, et al., 1999).

Young (1996, 1997; Young & Rogers, 1998) warned about the dangers of excessive Internet use and found that there appears to be a correlation between time on-line and negative consequences. She reported that the "Internet addicts" in her sample used the Internet an average of 38 hours per week for nonacademic and nonprofessional purposes (Young, 1996). These users performed poorly in academic and professional spheres. In contrast, "nonaddicts" were found to be on-line an average of 8 hours a week without significant adverse consequences. Greenfield (1999) identified a similar trend. They found that those with excessive usage patterns spend nearly double the amount of time on the computer as nonaddicts, and they were far more likely to report negative repercussions.

Cooper, Scherer, et al. (1999) found a strong correlation between time spent on-line for sexual pursuits and measures of sexual compulsivity and distress. They also noted that users who did not appear to have a problem with on-line sexual activities (46.6%) reported spending less than one hour a week doing so. By contrast, the 8.5% of respondents who acknowledged spending at least 11 hours a week in on-line sexual pursuits reported the most distress and highest scores on a measure of sexual compulsivity.

Increased acceptance and prevalence of on-line activities make it difficult for one to determine at what level usage becomes excessive and easier for one to rationalize current usage patterns. The ease of access to the Internet can make it harder to decrease or discontinue going on-line, particularly for sexual pursuits.

INTERNET SEXUALITY AND PSYCHOLOGICAL FUNCTIONING

ON-LINE SEXUAL BEHAVIOR

The specific use of the Internet for sexual expression has recently received the attention of practitioners and emerged as a distinct area of research inquiry. Young (1997) suggested that sexual fulfillment, along with social support and the creation of a persona, is one of the central motivations underlying computer-mediated communication. Internet users have created a new dimension in which they can engage in their sexual pursuits, all in the comfort of home or office. Individuals can engage in "sexual talk," become involved in cyberaffairs, view sexually explicit material, and experience and explore a variety of other fantasy-supported expressions easily, safely, and with the feeling that their anonymity is assured. Sexually related behaviors that have been adapted to the Internet are also of interest. Examples include on-line sexual advice columns and web sites that disseminate sexual information, participation in sexual exchanges in chat rooms, the increased production and consumption of sexually explicit material in all forms and delivery modes, and the advent of cybersex.

Profiles of Internet Users Who Go On-Line for Sexual Pursuits

Internet sexuality has been conceptualized along a continuum reflecting normal sexual exploration to more pathological expressions (Cooper, Scherer, et al., 1999; Leiblum, 1997). How on-line sexual behavior affects or relates to people's overall psychological functioning and the expression of their three-dimensional behavior remains unclear. Social scientists may better understand Internet sexuality by examining participants' sexual behavior and experience of themselves while on-line. Cooper, Putnam, Planchon, and Boies (1999) identified three profiles of individuals who go on-line for sexual pursuits using data from the first large-scale study of Internet sexuality (Cooper, Scherer, et al., 1999). They labeled these profiles recreational, compulsive, and at-risk users.

Recreational or nonpathological users are those individuals who simply aim to satisfy their curiosity about available on-line sexual material, to experiment occasionally or gratify a sexual urge, or to search for specific sexual information. This description is consistent with Leiblum's (1997) prediction that, "For individuals who are not true sexual obsessives, the repetitiveness of the images and the unreality of the activity are doomed to eventually disappoint" (p. 25). Cooper, Scherer, et al. (1999) found that a substantial number of people (46.6%) who visit Internet sexuality sites do so in a recreational way, less than one hour per week, and with few negative consequences.

Compulsive users are individuals who exhibit sexually compulsive traits and experience negative consequences as a result. Compulsive users may have a previously established pattern of unconventional sexual practices: preoccupation with pornography, multiple affairs, sex with several or anonymous partners, phone sex, frequenting prostitutes, or any one of the more conventional paraphilias listed in the *DSM-IV* (Cooper, Putnam, et al., 1999). Cooper, Scherer, et al. (1999) found that 8.5% of respondents fall into this category based on both subjective and objective assessments. Thus, it is not surprising that the general public, as well as many social scientists, are concerned that on-line sexual behavior can be problematic and even pathological for some individuals. The danger of Internet usage for deviant and criminal sexual behavior has also been argued (Durkin & Bryant, 1995; Van Gelder, 1985), but to date, no data exist on the frequency of such activity beyond isolated reported incidents.

At-risk users include on-line users without a prior history of sexual compulsivity who have experienced some problems in their lives from their on-line sexual pursuits. At-risk users may be the most interesting group in the study of on-line sexual behavior, as they may never have had difficulty with excessive sexual behavior if it were not for the advent of the Internet (Cooper, Putnam, et al., 1999). The power of the Triple A Engine may challenge the internal defenses and coping skills of individuals with a vulnerability to, or proclivity for, sexual compulsivity. At-risk users might be further divided into two subtypes: depressive and stress-reactive. The depressive type of at-risk user tends to be either acutely or chronically depressed. For these individuals, an on-line sexual encounter may be one of few experiences powerful enough to penetrate their dysphoria. The stress-reactive type is characterized by a tendency to avail oneself of on-line sex primarily during periods of high stress. This activity may be used as a temporary escape, distraction, or means of coping with the feelings that arise from stressful situations.

ROMANTIC RELATIONSHIPS

Romantic relationships are influenced by on-line activities in a number of ways. People can use the Internet to find relationships, to improve their relationships, or to undermine their relationships.

A few authors have argued that the Internet does not just facilitate the formation of romantic relationships, but may actually improve the chances of finding the optimal partner. Rheingold (1993) observed that cyberspace provides a forum for a different type of affiliation: "In traditional kinds of communities, we are accustomed to meeting people, then getting to know them; in virtual communities we get to know someone and then choose to meet them" (pp. 26–27). Cooper (1998) agrees and suggests that the emphasis on physical appearance that characterizes most relationships in Western culture is diminished on-line, because concerns about looks are delayed until later in the development of these relationships. The relationship may already have established a foundation on similar interests or mutual respect before questions of physical attractiveness and romantic involvement arise. Thus, relationships can develop on the basis of factors other than physical appearance, and users may consider romantic involvement with a different subset of partners than they might have otherwise.

Research on attractiveness (Hendrick & Hendrick, 1983) has shown that people perceive individuals they know better to be more attractive. This suggests that individuals who develop a relationship over the Internet may have a greater chance of forming attachments that are more than just skin-deep, and those relations may even be more likely to survive over time.

Cooper and Sportolari (1997) suggested that aspects of computer-mediated relating (CMR) can actually promote and support intimacy. The on-line culture and values seem to encourage informality, mutual self-disclosure, and the sharing of personal vulnerabilities and emotions faster than traditionally happens in face-to-face interactions. This type of CMR can lead to the development of rapport, connections, and powerful feelings of intimacy. Again, particularly in the earliest stages of a relationship when it is more than a casual acquaintance but not yet consciously a romantic interest, CMR may tip the balance. Cooper and Sportolari postulated that CMR involves a sense of being both vividly real and yet not real. It involves a quality of being contained outside of time and space in what may be a model of intimate yet separate relating. CMR also allows for greater idealization and projection of sought-after attributes common in the early infatuation stage of relationships. Conversely, these loosened connections with the other person can more easily allow the expression of aggressive or demeaning tendencies. The anonymity and distance, which are other dimensions of CMR, may also facilitate the depersonalization of the other person and result in "flaming" or other harsh or aggressive outbursts.

Internet usage can also enrich ongoing relationships in a number of ways. People can use e-mail to send each other tender and affirming thoughts or keep each other abreast of activities in their daily lives. Erotic e-mail messages might also be a means of stoking sexual interest in a partner early in the day. Those in long-term relationships who are interested in keeping some spice in their love lives can search the web to find suggestions for sexual enrichment, as well as an endless supply of sexual variations from which to sample, experiment, or have as the basis for fantasy.

On-line relationships can also have a very negative effect on users' off-line relationships. Maheu (1999b) used the term *cyber-infidelity* to describe the repeated taking of sexual energy outside of a committed, monogamous relationship through action intentionally leading to sexual arousal with an identified person, place, or thing (e.g., excessive use of on-line pornography). Cyber-infidelity is seen as damaging to the core issues of trust and integrity in a relationship, because it typically involves elements of fantasy, secrecy, and a high sexual charge, paired with denial and rationalization (Leiblum, 1997; Shaw, 1997; Turkle, 1995). Partners of users having on-line sexual experiences usually experience these encounters as a form of betrayal and deception.

Despite people's recognition that cyberaffairs have a high potential for trouble, they perceive them more benignly than the typical three-dimensional affair. In an ongoing on-line survey, Maheu (1999a) found that close to 70% of respondents reported knowing someone who had a cyberaffair and believing that cyberaffairs pose a threat to traditional relationships. Yet, a majority of these sample people thought cyberaffairs were more acceptable (52%) and safer (83%) than traditional affairs. Maheu (1999b) distinguished four types of cyberaffairs (covert, overt, menage-à-trois, and group), which she linked to specific dynamics relating to a couple's capacity for intimacy. She argued that cyberaffairs are ultimately a betrayal of the self that takes away from the person's ability to build intimacy. This is consistent with Shaw's (1997) position that "Internet infidelity indicates that an individual is developed enough emotionally to find a partner, but not developed enough to be openly and compassionately oneself in relationship with that partner" (pp. 30–31).

Cyber-infidelity also challenges the concept of monogamy on personal, social, spiritual, and legal levels. Greenfield's (1999) on-line survey looked at the prevalence of these behaviors and found that approximately 15% of all Internet users engaged in on-line sexual activities and cyberaffairs. Their data point to the possibility that three-dimensional affairs may be more likely to follow these on-line experiences, particularly for those who meet their criteria for "Internet addiction."

IMPLICATIONS FOR MENTAL HEALTH PROFESSIONALS

TREATMENT OF PROBLEMS ARISING FROM ON-LINE SEXUAL ACTIVITY

Clinical considerations for the treatment of on-line sexual compulsivity have recently been presented (Cooper, Putnam, et al., 1999; Cooper, Scherer, et al., 1999; Young & Rogers, 1998). This section presents an overview of some of the major clinical issues related to on-line sexual pursuits and summarizes associated treatment strategies.

Clinicians are hearing of an increasing number of individuals who use their computers to retreat from the tensions of their marriages or relationships, creating a new class of computer widows and widowers. Clearly, this can be a source of marital discord, and there is a growing body of evidence that many Internet users develop problems in their relationships as a result of their Internet use (Cooper, Scherer, et al., 1999; Leiblum, 1997). The Triple A attraction of the Internet has the potential to turn common relational difficulties into serious troubles. Problems such as on-line sexual compulsivity and cyberaffairs bring into question the issues of commitment, intimacy, and trust for couples.

The Internet appears to pose an increased risk for the development of on-line sexually compulsive behavior in some people (Cooper, Putnam, et al., 1999; Young & Rogers, 1998). Greenfield (1999) estimated that there may be, at a minimum, 15% overlap between sexual compulsive/addictive behavior and Internet addiction. The Internet may be a haven for the sexual compulsive. The immediate access, anonymity, intensity, and time distortion all contribute to produce a powerful and reinforcing sexual experience.

Therapists need to be cognizant that persons with sexually compulsive tendencies rarely present for therapy with this behavior as their chief complaint. For example, marital problems, loss of job, legal problems, depression, loneliness, substance abuse, and/or other compulsive forms of behavior may be either consequences of or clues to a hidden problem of on-line sexual compulsivity. As with any type of therapeutic intervention, the first step should be a thorough psychological history and evaluation, including a detailed sexual history, as well as a history of computer and Internet patterns. It is important to establish whether symptoms of sexual compulsion predated an individual's use of the Internet for sexual gratification or whether the easy availability of the Internet allowed a vulnerable individual to engage in these behaviors. In addition, comorbid conditions such as depression, anxiety, obsessive-compulsive behavior, substance abuse, and other process disorders, including overuse of the Internet in general, should be considered. In most cases, initial treatment strategies will focus on helping the individual to interrupt the cycle of on-line sexual behavior and to understand the motivations and feelings that precipitate sexual urges. The identification of "triggers" helps the client to see that the behavior is something that can be controlled and that situations and emotions thought to be completely unrelated might instead be critical stimuli.

However, the nature of on-line sexual activity also suggests a need for therapeutic strategies tailored to the particular behavior patterns of the individual and the unique characteristics of Internet usage. For many people with on-line sexual issues, simply turning on the computer may become problematic. There are a number of concrete steps that therapists can take to help their clients counter the power of the Triple A Engine.

In terms of accessibility, Internet service providers (e.g., Integrity) as well as software programs (Net Nanny, Surfwatch) can filter sexual sites and materials, making them unavailable. Despite their limitations, these programs can serve as a front line of protection (Delmonico, 1997). As an extra precaution, it has been suggested that those attempting to limit their access to these materials have a trusted friend, or sponsor, hold the password to the filtering program.

The issue of affordability is countered by taking a broader view of the costs. In many cases, the actual dollar outlay of the on-line sexual behavior may be minimal because there is no shortage of sites where one can engage in sexual activity for free. However, the free sites are often set up to be "teasers" and may lead to the spending of large sums of money for access to special/premier sexual services. In either case, it is useful to explore how much the on-line sexual behavior is "costing" the patient, in terms of money, time, relationships, and self-esteem.

In dealing with the power of the Triple A Engine, it is essential to address the perception of the anonymity of the sexual activities. This is dealt with by educating people that all on-line activities can be traced, both at work and at home. In addition, individual psychotherapy can be a way to allow clients to share their secrets in a safe environment, to challenge their denial, and to understand the reasons that their sexual behaviors are so compelling. Couple therapy can also help an individual see his or her partner as a source of support instead of as an obstacle or vehicle for projected shame and self-hatred. Twelve-step programs and group therapy may be essential elements of an effective treatment package and are particularly helpful in slowly reducing the individual's desire for complete anonymity. Internet-based solutions may also be used to address anonymity. On-line individuals may get support from participating in listserves, and e-mail support groups and by going to bulletin boards, web sites, and chat rooms that focus specifically on sexual addiction (Delmonico, 1997). Individuals report that seeing others struggling with the same problem gives them strength to abstain. The best sites provide a place for individuals to develop an identity and become known and thus provide another forum in which they have both support and accountability (Cooper, Putnam, et al., 1999).

TREATMENT CONSIDERATIONS FOR DIFFERENT TYPES OF ON-LINE USERS

Cooper, Putnam, et al. (1999) developed guidelines for the treatment of the different types of consumers of on-line sexuality outlined earlier. They suggested that recreational users are not likely to talk about or be concerned with their on-line sexual behavior because, for most, it may not create difficulties in their lives. However, as was previously mentioned, anyone with a computer may be secretly engaging in on-line sexual activities or may be at risk for developing these types of problems. Therefore, therapists need to be aware of warning signs in clients who have talked about frequent computer usage either at work or at home. This is particularly important when those clients are experiencing relational problems, isolation, lack of social skills, sexual dysfunction, and long-standing patterns reflecting difficulty in establishing intimacy.

The early stages of the treatment of the at-risk user depressive type should focus on ameliorating the depression, especially when it is severe. For these clients, on-line sexual behavior may be the equivalent of self-medicating as well as a transient distraction or escape from a more pervasive chronic, negative affect. The on-line universe may be the only place where these individuals can feel totally in control. They can reinvent their lives, conjure up their own fantasies, and feel confident and competent (Delmonico, 1997). Subsequent phases of treatment will center on exploring and treating the underlying depression, clarifying the ways that the on-line sexual behavior helps the user cope, and providing more adaptive alternatives.

The goal of treatment for the stress-reactive type is to help the client understand when and how the sexual acting out is used to deal with stress. Once these patterns are clarified, alternative stress management strategies can be developed and incorporated (Cooper, Putnam, et al., 1999). These strategies may include general relaxation and cognitive coping approaches as well as specific strategies that relate to problems with anger, relationships, or work.

The approach to treatment of the sexually compulsive individual who uses the Internet parallels the traditional approaches used with similar off-line problems. As noted earlier, the initial stages of therapy focus on breaking the cycle of compulsive sexual behavior with some combination of individual therapy, 12-step program participation, and on-line support when appropriate.

On-line sexual compulsivity will often vary with relationship difficulties. The therapist should try to determine whether the relationship problems led to on-line sexual behavior or vice versa. Partners of persons with compulsive on-line sexual behavior may enable the sexual activities by maintaining emotional and physical distance and by colluding in the denial of relationship difficulties. In these relationships, it is common for each partner to shift the responsibility onto the other. The therapist's task is to help each individual acknowledge his or her respective contribution to the problems and to focus on changing what he or she can control (i.e., the individual's own behavior). In ongoing relationships, this is best accomplished in couple therapy.

THE INTERNET AS A TREATMENT MEDIUM

No discussion of sexuality and the Internet would be complete without addressing the use of the Internet as a treatment medium. In contrast to the preceding section, where the ways in which the Internet exacerbated tendencies toward excessive on-line sexual activities and sexual compulsivity were elucidated, this segment outlines how the Triple A Engine might actually have a salubrious effect for people struggling with these issues, particularly in the earliest stages of recovery.

During the critical stage when an initial breakthrough of the denial occurs, on-line venues including recovery/12-step web sites, bulletin boards, discussion groups, and so on could provide an easy, anonymous first step whereby people can examine some of their behaviors and consider whether or not a problem exists. Those afraid to be seen may be reassured by not needing to self-identify, yet still be able to "lurk," observe other participants, and "test the waters" in this low-risk way. Therapists can inform clients questioning their behaviors, as well as their family and friends, of this option. This may also provide exposure to others in recovery and offer a path when the person is ready for that next step. There are an increasing number of on-line recovery sites easily available. For a list of sites providing referrals, resources, and general information, see Cooper, Putnam, et al. (1999).

The Internet is one tool in the burgeoning field of telehealth and telemedicine. Nickelson (1998) defines telehealth as "The use of telecommunication and information technology to provide access to health assessment, diagnosis, intervention, consultation, supervision, education, and information across distance" (p. 527). The Internet makes telehealth practical and readily available to anyone with a computer. The Internet does not require any special video equipment or dedicated links. It is designed to be user-friendly and therefore affords great opportunity for accessing health care information and treatment.

There is a growing number of potential applications in the field of behavioral health care. The field of sexuality may benefit from this new modality. We may see virtual evaluations and psychological testing, for example, in forensic cases where clients are incarcerated. The potential also exists for provision of on-line education and training. There is also great opportunity for consultations regarding sexual problems where health care resources are scarce.

The Internet is particularly well suited to deal with the very sensitive and private nature of sexual concerns. Greenfield (1999) found that 43% of Internet users experience a sense of disinhibition when on-line, which allows for greater ease in communicating personal and sensitive information. Roffman, Shannon, and Dwyer (1997) suggest that the Internet may provide sexual education to millions of people across the globe either at home, work, or school. They also highlight the prospect that underserved populations may be the recipients of targeted life-enhancing and health-preserving information.

Similarly, on-line treatment adjuncts can be used to support more traditional therapies by providing clients with interactive programs and web sites that would allow them to address specific functional problems and to arrive at self-generated solutions. These programs might also be used as tools for practicing sex therapy exercises. Through the Internet, clients can practice communication and social skills and join on-line support groups. These new methods offer both a therapeutic and an economic benefit in the form of fewer office visits and reduced professional fees. The therapeutic benefits are numerous, such as the immediate accessibility and availability of on-line access; no health care practitioner can match the accessibility and geographic expansiveness of the Internet. Whether it involves adjuncts to three-dimensional treatments, information, or references, the Net can provide these easily, economically, and efficiently.

Although the ideas presented here regarding technology-mediated therapy remain to be empirically substantiated, there are clearly appropriate uses for these new technologies. General information and self-help groups are increasingly available through the Internet, but its use for psychological assessment and psychotherapy remains very controversial (Stamm, 1998). Studies that focus on understanding how the process of electronically relating may influence the nature of interpersonal relationships are needed. Care should be taken in the practice of telehealth and telemedicine; relevant legal, ethical, and professional issues are reviewed later in this chapter.

As people become more comfortable using computers, they may become more open to other forms of technology, such as CD-ROMs, DVDs, and interactive computer programs. These modalities may be very effective in providing the information and practical skills training that are particularly well suited to the treatment of some of the more common sexual concerns and dysfunctions. For example, a computer program focused on sexual concerns that was recently developed allows clients to seek psychological advice and to engage in interactions that are problem-focused and psychotherapeutic (Ochs & Binik, 1998).

Newman (1997) suggests that the creation of the "information superhighway" offers new ways to discuss sexuality candidly. His example is a situation in which one person in a couple wanted to take part in an uncommon sexual activity, and this was met with reluctance by the partner. He proposed that a couple in this situation could obtain a wealth of information or more obscure sexual practices on the Internet, thereby educating themselves and perhaps relieving some of the discord. They could then bring the new data back to an ongoing therapy situation and better understand both their interests and fears. On-line discussions with others who have participated in the activity in question would provide data about how those others felt about the experience. This would allow the couple to assess more accurately the potential impact on their relationship before engaging in the activity. In addition, Newman posits that for certain people, "the reluctance is due to nervousness caused by concerns over the 'normalcy' of the behavior" (p. 45). The ability to have a wider comparison group than might otherwise be available could allow a person permission to experiment and feel comfortable with a broader range of sexual activities.

There is a need to consider philosophical and ethical positions associated with Internet sexuality and to discuss the best ways to disseminate the information so that it has a positive impact on the sexual health of young people. Children and adolescents are learning about computers at a young age. The multimedia flavor of the Internet when combined with the natural curiosity of youth can provide a new opportunity for society to influence sexual attitudes and behaviors positively.

In response to popular concerns, there has been a proliferation of software programs that allow parents to limit and monitor what children access. However, a savvy young computer user can defeat filtering software programs. Moreover, defining certain categories as "out of bounds" might actually pique an adolescent's curiosity, magnify the allure of the forbidden, and paradoxically increase temptation rather than limit it (Tannen, 1999). As an alternative, Semans and Winks (1999) suggest that parents move from feeling threatened to defending their "child's right to good sex education by exploring the resources of the web together, rather than relying on the false security of filtering software that will block access to valuable sex information" (p. 110).

Parents can also help inoculate the young person against any potential adverse effects of encountering on-line sexual situations by explaining the differences in the sexual information and web sites that young people are likely to encounter. Prior to these discussions, parents may want to spend some time reviewing sites that they think would be both helpful and age-appropriate to their children so that they have affirmative options to suggest. This type of discussion of on-line sexuality is only possible in the context of an overall decision by the family to be actively involved in the sexual education and development of their child.

ON-LINE SEXUALITY RESEARCH

The use of the Internet for sexuality survey research is a new practice (Cooper, Scherer, et al., 1999; Maheu, 1999a). The power of the Triple A Engine may serve to enhance researchers' efforts while, at the same time, creating new concerns.

The Internet might significantly enhance researchers' ability to increase and broaden a sample by making access easier to large numbers of potential study participants. It allows respondents in different parts of the country or the world to participate in the same study and, if necessary, at the same time. Researchers may also use the Internet to find sufficient numbers of respondents when the population is small and the usual recruitment techniques are not successful. As the Internet allows various "invisible" and dispersed populations a way to meet and connect, recruitment can be facilitated by the use of on-line lists of individuals who acknowledge belonging to a specific group or are linked by a common variable. This technology will give us access to populations heretofore unexamined and that remain in relative psychological obscurity.

Another advantage of Internet research is the sense of anonymity, whether justified or not, that allows researchers access to information heretofore unobtainable. Recent studies using computer-mediated technology to assess psychopathology or to measure risky sexual behavior have found that adolescents and adults respond as or more truthfully using a computer than they do either face-to-face (Hasley, 1995; Kobak et al., 1997a; Locke et al., 1992; Millstein & Irwin, 1983), over the telephone (Kobak et al., 1997b), or on paper-and-pencil questionnaires (Locke et al., 1992; Millstein & Irwin, 1983; Turner, Ku, Lindberg, Pleck, & Sonenstein, 1998). People can participate in such research with less fear of being identified in their social groups or communities.

Freed of negative social cues that discourage sexually explicit communications, and of the discomfort of face-to-face questioning, men and women are revealing more on-line than they might when interviewed in person (Cooper, Scherer, et al., 1999; Greenfield, 1999).

An additional way the Internet may facilitate sexual research is in its capacity for ongoing participation through a repeated measurement. It can also allow for the participant to provide information at specific, preidentified times. This could be particularly relevant to the study of sexual behavior. Participants could be asked to sign on soon after having sexual activity. Such an approach would allow the measurement of moods and reactions while the experience is still clear in the participant's memory.

To date, much of on-line research appears to be descriptive or quasi-experimental field research and, therefore, does not involve control groups. Several problems exist with such research, and these are detailed by some of the leading researchers in traditional quasi-experimental research design (Cook & Campbell, 1979; Maheu & Gordon, 1999). Other selection and population biases and generalizability limitations have to do with the representativeness of on-line participants as compared to the population in general. For example, are rape survivors who are willing to answer on-line questions about their rapes and their current sexuality a unique subset of the general population of rape survivors? Related issues of self-selection in testing and research participation are compounded by additional factors such as web site navigational design, form layout, color selection, and graphic display. Moreover, despite the widening range of people with access to the Internet, investigators still need to consider whether there is a socioeconomic skew. As with any other research, when and how the sample was obtained should be described in detail. For example, information should be listed regarding the referring web site or other ways the subject learned about the study.

The authenticity and appropriateness of questionnaires can be verified using available technology, and programming precautions can prevent multiple submissions by the same individual. However, if respondents are technologically sophisticated, they may defeat most common precautions. Visual inspection of every e-mail address is a time-consuming option, and even this method is not foolproof, for a determined saboteur could send each entry from a different e-mail address.

Although there may be a need for identifying duplicate entries by examining the identity of respondents, related issues of privacy ought also to be of concern to psychological researchers. All necessary efforts should be made to ensure that volunteers remain anonymous. To that effect, a description of informed consent procedures should be available to all those choosing to electronically access an interactive web page. Owners of large sponsoring web sites might promise to safeguard the privacy of respondents, but most researchers are not technologically sophisticated enough to completely assure confidentiality. Many related questions remain to be explored, such as the level to which data must be protected during the collection and after the completion of a study. For a discussion of ethical issues regarding sex research on the Internet and guidelines for such research, see Binik, Mah, and Kiesler (1999).

Because Internet studies can be distributed worldwide, researchers need to consider multicultural issues, the sociocultural context will be paramount in determining the validity of the results. For example, in societies with differing norms and definitions of sexual appropriateness, it may be difficult for an Internet researcher to ascertain whether the respondent understands Western concepts such as paraphilias, sexual assault, and so on. Similarly, the depth of the respondents' understanding of the questions will be influenced by their reading and comprehension levels and their mastery of English. How to separate respondents who fully understand the test items from those who do not remains a problem to be solved.

The social contexts and conditions under which surveys related to sexuality are conducted must also be considered. For example, although Internet users in Bulgaria might not be able to access the Internet in their homes as readily as Americans, they might have access through a coffeehouse. The usefulness of questionnaires filled out in social settings is questionable. A group of people may encourage a respondent to complete an on-line sexuality questionnaire in a humorous rather than straightforward manner. The entertainment value of such surveys might be stronger in coffeehouses, college dormitories, or settings where the novelty of access to sexual research may be the salient factor. More dramatic psychological conditions of the respondents might also be difficult to control, such as intoxication, depression, or pregnancy.

An Internet protocol research effect might need to be identical for Internet research participants based on attitudes and behaviors that are specific to the medium being used, for example, e-mail versus web site surveys. Generally, Internet research is in its infancy, and we are just starting to have a sense of its advantages and limitations. When adding another wild card, such as sexuality, to the pile, the level of complexity increases dramatically. Clearly, more attention needs to be devoted to this powerful new research tool and how it fits with what we know about more traditional sexuality research.

ETHICAL CONSIDERATIONS IN PSYCHOTHERAPY AND EDUCATION

A number of ethical concerns arise for psychologists working through electronic media to treat sexual disorders and to provide education. Such media include not only the Internet but also videoconferencing and more advanced interactive technologies. For the most part, ethical concerns at this point are just that—concerns. Concrete ethical guidelines must be developed. We present some questions and cautions in this section.

Given the context of therapeutic interaction via electronic media, what constitutes a professional relationship between a sex therapy client and therapist may need to be defined. For example, with the advent of interactive videoconferencing equipment (videophones), widely available at low cost, where will the lines be drawn among areas previously identified as education, adjuncts to an ongoing treatment, and psychotherapy? In determining these definitions, we should consider the frequency of therapeutic contact. A single web-based video session may legitimately constitute education, but seven sessions with demonstrations may be deemed surrogate treatment, and seven sessions without demonstration may constitute psychotherapy. What if the client contracts for education, but calls the therapist regularly? How many calls will be involved before the relationship moves from educational to psychotherapeutic? Does this definition of psychotherapy via technology vary according to topic? Web site interactions that include educational films and live training present an interesting dilemma for determining how these sites differ from adult entertainment sites, which state laws come into play, and what services will be reimbursable by a third party.

A level of competency in video techniques for sex education and therapy over the Internet should be established. Also, the requirement for office visits needs to be examined. For instance, do prior or concurrent face-to-face meetings legitimize e-mail provision of services such as checking homework and completing sexual assignments?

Also, providers need to develop greater cross-cultural competency. This is a medium where geographic distance is rendered irrelevant by ease of access through telephone wires that literally span the globe. As mentioned in the prior section, a professional could easily be uninformed of critical socioeconomic status, educational, cultural, or geographic issues that could influence the response set of the client.

The possibility of sexual boundary blurring and crossing by both client and practitioner may be fueled by the Triple A Engine. Transference and countertransference will undoubtedly find new forms of expression. Will on-line sex therapy become on-line sex? With videoconferenced group interaction available through technology, just how detailed an educational presentation will a practitioner offer, given that certain clients may be stimulated rather than treated by explicit discussions of symptoms or treatments?

Will videoconferencing be an accepted treatment vehicle? If yes, under what circumstances will it be acceptable or unacceptable? How proficient at various technologies does a practitioner need to be before offering professional services to consumers claiming to have problems with cybersex in e-mail chat rooms: Internet Relay Chat (IRC), Multiuser Object Oriented (MOO), and Multiuser Dungeon (MUD)?

Given the lack of scientific knowledge in the area of advanced technology, what are the implications of using the Internet to deliver assessment and treatment? Is it wise to use disclaimers to limit misunderstanding related to services being offered? Although some practitioners have already begun using disclaimers to qualify their services, empirical tests of the effectiveness of these disclaimers are lacking.

Research on the effectiveness of various forms of electronic media, including e-mail, audiostream, and video-mediated communication, has only recently been initiated (O'Conaill & Whitaker, 1997). Nonetheless, the potential benefits of these types of services in dealing with the treatment of sexual issues and disorders have been argued (Cooper & Sportolari, 1997; Odzer, 1997; Shaw, 1997).

When dealing with informed consent, just how informed of risks and benefits will our clients be when it comes to treatment through technology? Many of us barely know how our services might be compromised electronically.

Whether or not a client understands a web-based consent form, e-mail interpretation, or assignments given, and how best to correct a miscommunication is central to offering psychological services. Gathering demographic data, such as telephone number and street address, will be necessary, but how best to inform consumers of reporting laws is still undefined, although this can be both an ethical and legal obligation for therapists and researchers.

In videoconferencing, the clinician needs to be alert for the unexpected. For instance, a family member could be in the same room, off-camera, witnessing and perhaps impacting the entire therapeutic exchange, without the therapist' being aware.

A central concern throughout this section is that for much on-line communication, the environment lacks the visual and auditory cues that the majority of professionals have been trained to use in diagnosing and treating clients. For example, the ease of impersonation (e.g., pretending to be of a different gender or age or providing an inaccurate description of physical appearance) facilitated by e-mail exchange may create specific dilemmas for a well-intentioned therapist in the on-line sexual arena. The question of liability may emerge when a practitioner is providing explicit sexual education to a minor presenting as an adult.

Several other concerns need to be considered when treating mental health issues in a technology-based environment. For instance, time differences in the formulation and delivery of e-mail may also cause discrepancies in understanding on the part of the professional as well as the client. The frequency of equipment failure in various electronic media can further complicate the relationship between practitioner and client. Nonetheless, electronic media may prove to be more helpful than face-to-face contact for some people, and professionals in the health community are already successfully using regular e-mail contact with clients (Borowitz & Wyatt, 1998; Eysenbach & Diepgen, 1998; Ferguson, 1998; Spielberg, 1998).

Emergent high-risk situations may be the most difficult to assess. Imagine a scenario where a person with a sexual attraction to a child in the neighborhood sends an e-mail to the web site of a sexuality professional asking for assistance. Refusing e-mail contact from an otherwise isolated and desperate client may be unethical, but how can a therapist handle threats of danger to self or others when the client is desperate and the practitioner is located thousands of miles away?

Some state laws prohibit practicing out of state to professionals operating in specific environments. For example, in California, practitioners are prohibited from offering video-mediated service to out-of-state clients, but they can communicate by e-mail without sanctions (Telemedicine Development Act, 1996). Details of telehealth laws in various states are available (Center for Telemedicine Law, 1997; U.S. Department of Commerce, 1997). Some professions have developed their own view regarding interstate licensure and confidentiality (National Council of State Boards of Nursing, 1998). More precise definitions of psychotherapy will be needed if such exchanges start occurring with regularity in psychology.

Definitive answers to the above issues are as yet unclear, and even their importance for a successful psychotherapeutic exchange with any given population has yet to be researched. However, with the lack of information regarding the effectiveness of such practice, professionals are cautioned against delivering services to the public at large without empirical validation of their procedures. If professionals nonetheless choose to do so, it is recommended that all potential clients be given full disclosure and consent to receiving treatments that are not validated and fall outside the standard of care. Extreme caution is in order when offering either a new type of psychotherapeutic service or a new type of psychotherapeutic service delivery system.

Computer-mediated communication technologies are not new, and the literature in this area is already extensive (Stern & Faber, 1996; Waskul & Douglass, 1996; Webster & Compeau, 1996). But although the American Psychological Association (APA) outlines ethical standards providing guidelines for computer-based tests and interpretations (1986) and standards for educational and psychological testing (1985), more guidance is needed for applying these principles to behavioral telehealth and, more specifically, for applying these guidelines to the treatment of sexuality via the Internet. Another aspect to consider is which type of technology will be most effective for assessing which client. For example, research is just beginning to elucidate how technology not only transmits but also modifies communication (O'Conaill & Whittaker, 1997; Whittaker & O'Conaill, 1997).

An often unspoken but real problem is that a practitioner may have frequented cybersex web sites, chatrooms, IRCs, MOOs, MUDs, or videoconferencing sites. A technology-savvy client could trace such transactions. This would allow a client access to intimate details of the therapist's life.

Another issue involves the sexual nature of the topics to be discussed and treated by practitioners. As was pointed out earlier, electronic communication will make it more difficult for both practitioner and client to know if the other person is misusing the interactions for sexual gratification rather than using them toward a therapeutic end. Will the practitioner's options be further limited if and when it is discovered that the current or previous treatment has been inappropriately used in this way?

At the time of this publication, the Internet is not a secure medium for offering treatment (i.e., it is not protected against human, technical, or willful creation of error compromising confidentiality). Determined users can gain access to sensitive mental health information provided to and from practitioners. The type and level of security required by our professional organizations to determine appropriate security for medical records is yet to be determined (Schwatzwalder, 1994). Guidelines are being set by various organizations such as the Institute of Medicine (IOM, 1994, 1996), but a determination of their appropriateness for mental health records has not yet been made. Medical records with information related to sexual function, dysfunction, and health are especially sensitive, and professional associations specializing in these areas must be active in developing as well as monitoring laws related to these records.

THE FUTURE OF INTERNET SEXUALITY

The future of Internet sexuality rests in part on how the continuous development of technology is melded with human interactions and sexual expression and in the ability of society to integrate these changes. If on-line sexuality continues to serve people's needs, whether educational or recreational, helpful or harmful, there will be a demand for it. Leiblum (1997) agrees and points out that despite the fact that Internet sexuality is being increasingly transformed into a "medium of commercial exchange and even exploitation, its democratic and cooperative origins still contribute to its essential character and appeal and popularity" (p. 27).

Technology and Sexuality

When speculating about the various forms on-line sexuality might take in the future, there is an inherent assumption that technology will continue to play a growing role in people's interactions, sexual and otherwise. In support of this view, Turkle (1995) explains:

> As human beings become increasingly intertwined with the technology and with each other via the technology, old distinctions between what is specifically human and specifically technological become more complex. Are we living life on the screen or life in the screen? Our new technologically enmeshed relationships oblige us to ask to what extent we ourselves have become cyborgs, transgressive mixtures of biology, technology, and code. (p. 21)

A forerunner of this trend is a situation where a person engages in a sexual act in which the computer plays an integral role. For those who are interested, the option will be there to do more than just meet on-line and exchange sexual fantasies. Sensory devices, microprocessors, and minicomputers will be linked to the Internet and available for a variety of purposes, among which will be transmitting a sense of touch. This will allow for sexual opportunities and experiences that would otherwise be impossible. For example, the future may bring the use of partial- or even full-immersion sex suits, transmitting sensory information back and forth between partners. Because the exchange will simply be comprised of digitized information, it too will be modifiable, in essence "tailored" to the user's discretion to reflect preferences and other specially desired effects (Dertouzos, 1997). Participants might, for example, make themselves or their partners a different weight, height, attractiveness, gender, or even possibly add extra limbs or appendages to their bodies. The possibilities are endless.

One application of this new technology will be the ability to allow couples physically separated from each other for reasons such as military duty, college, work, or incarceration to engage in "virtual sex." Another possible use of these devices will be to enable those otherwise unable to have a sexual relationship, due to physical or psychological limitations, to have a broader range of sexual options. Finally, there may be a host of ways that these devices could be used as teaching aids and in the provision of sex therapy (Dertouzos, 1997).

SOCIAL RAMIFICATIONS

As use of the Internet for work, education, and recreation becomes increasingly interwoven into our lives, on-line gender differences will need to be addressed in both research and practice. For example, those who identify themselves as men seem to be freer to move around the sexual world of the Internet, but women seem to draw more attention and response. Therefore, factors that create barriers to female involvement on the Internet need to be examined, such as the design of software and web sites primarily for men, as well as issues related to sexual harassment and equality (Spender, 1995).

Individuals who choose to explore their sexuality on-line must be able to do so in a safe environment free of sexual harassment. Education is key in this regard. Social scientists, government policymakers, and corporate executives need to lead the way in the development of grievance procedures for complaints of sexual harassment on the Internet. All institutions sponsoring or allowing Internet communication should participate in the development and enforcement of clear policies regarding sexual harassment. Such policies must include a definitive statement that sexual harassment will not be tolerated, with definitions of the prohibited behavior and details of specific punishment, as well as procedures for how, when, and where to file complaints (Kramrae & Taylor, 1993).

As people increasingly interact with technology, human values and connections will gain an unprecedented importance worldwide. The need for intimacy and its expression through three-dimensional connections will grow. As a counterbalance to the increasing rate of change, time pressures, and involvement of electronic devices in our lives, one constant will remain. Freud called it Eros, and it is much more than a sexual act, it is a coming together in a way that is uniquely human (Cooper, 1997). This type of sharing can be started, and even nurtured, on-line, but to be fully achieved, there needs to be a place for actual physical touch and eye contact (Schnarch, 1997). Maltz (1995) agrees that in the highest form of sexual intimacy, "there is a shared sense of deep connection, a reverence toward the body and toward each other" (p. 15). This type of sexual experience is widely searched for and prized by those who are able to find it. Whether technology-assisted sexual interactions ultimately facilitate the attainment of this depth of relatedness, intimacy, and sharing remains to be seen.

MENTAL HEALTH SERVICES

The Triple A Engine allows for people to engage in all types of sexual pursuits with a freedom never before possible. This will lead to both unimagined benefits and potential costs. It is therefore vital that research go forward in this area. Social scientists and others working in the mental health field cannot simply be passengers on this vehicle, but must be conductors: leading the way, telling others of the various destinations they can visit, and anticipating and taking all possible steps to ameliorate the inevitable dangers.

Currently, the Internet is becoming even more accessible and affordable, and people are increasingly reveling in the unprecedented freedom that goes with the perception of anonymity. However, for a significant percentage of the online community, this freedom may also include a hidden chain binding those who cannot control their sexual desires. Accompanying this newfound freedom is also an unprecedented need for skills and values related to self-mastery, and there are potentially dire consequences for those who fail to develop them (Dyson, 1997). As the allure and options for on-line sexual activity increase, therapists will inevitably see growing numbers of people who excessively engage in these pursuits to the detriment of themselves and society. Therefore, it will be incumbent upon mental health professionals to be increasingly prepared to deal with clients appropriately, including taking steps to educate, to intervene early, and to have effective treatments available specifically tailored to this phenomenon, including some of the suggestions earlier in this chapter.

Despite the previously mentioned limitations that make therapy via the Internet unwise at the present time, technological advancements and clarification of ethical and legal issues may soon lead to the commonplace delivery of this mode of therapy. In fact, Internet and other remote treatments will probably be reimbursed, possibly even preferentially, by health care organizations as more cost-effective and easier to monitor for effectiveness.

CONCLUSION

The Internet will have a revolutionary impact on how we think and feel about sexuality, how we pursue our sexual interests, and even how we engage in sexual behaviors. As the Internet extends human capabilities regarding sexual issues, the challenge will be to ensure that these are channeled in ways that enhance rather than limit sexual potential and fulfillment. In and of itself, technology is neither constructive nor destructive. Rather, how it is used will determine whether this newest sexual revolution is to be welcomed or feared.

REFERENCES

American Psychiatric Association. (1994). *Diagnostic and statistical manual of mental disorders* (4th ed.). Washington, DC: Author.

American Psychological Association. (1985). *Standards for education and psychological testing.* Washington, DC: Author.

American Psychological Association. (1986). *Guidelines for computer based tests and interpretations.* Washington, DC: Author.

American Psychological Association. (1997). *Services by telephone, teleconferencing, and Internet* [A statement by the ethics committee of the American Psychological Association]. Available: http://www.apa.org/ethics/stmnt01.html

Binik, Y.M., Mah, K., & Kiesler, S. (1999). Ethical issues in conducting sex research on the Internet. *Journal of Sex Research, 36,* 82–90.

Borowitz, S.M., & Wyatt, J.C. (1998). The origin, content, and workload of e-mail consultations. *Journal of the American Medical Association, 280,* 1321–1324.

Branwyn, G. (1993). Compu-sex: Erotica for cybernauts. *South Atlantic Quarterly, 92,* 779–791.

Center for Telemedicine Law. (1997). Telemedicine and interstate licensure: Findings and recommendations of the CTL licensure task force. *North Dakota Law Review, 73,* 109–130.

Computerworld. (1998). *Commerce by numbers: Internet population* [On-line]. Available: http://www.computerworld.com/home/Emmerce.nsf/All/pop

Cook, T., & Campbell, D. (1979). *Quasi-experimentation: Design and analysis issues for field studies.* Boston: Houghton Mifflin.

Cooper, A. (1997). The Internet and sexuality: Into the next millennium. *Journal of Sex Education and Therapy, 22,* 5–7.

Cooper, A. (1998). Sexuality and the Internet: Surfing into the new millennium. *Cyberpsychology and Behavior, 1,* 181–187.

Cooper, A., Putnam, D., Planchon, L.A., & Boies, S.C. (1999). On-line sexual compulsivity: Getting tangled in the Net. *Sexual Addiction and Compulsivity: The Journal of Treatment and Prevention, 6*(2), 23–35.

Cooper, A., Scherer, C., Boies, S.C., & Gordon, B. (1999). Sexuality on the Internet: From sexual exploration to pathological expression. *Professional Psychology: Research and Practice, 30*(2), 154–164.

Cooper, A., & Sportolari, L. (1997). Romance in cyberspace: Understanding on-line attraction. *Journal of Sex Education and Therapy, 22,* 7–14.

Delmonico, D.L. (1997). Cybersex: High tech sex addiction. *Sexual Addiction and Compulsivity: The Journal of Treatment and Prevention, 4,* 159–167.

Dertouzos, M. (1997). *What will be: How the new world of information will change our lives* (pp. 142–148). New York: HarperCollins.

Durkin, K.F., & Bryant, C.D. (1995). "Log on to sex": Some notes on the carnal computer and erotic cyberspace as an emerging research frontier. *Deviant Behavior: An Interdisciplinary Journal, 16,* 179–200.

Dyson, E. (1997). *Release 2.0: A design for living in the digital age.* New York: Broadway.

Eysenbach, G., & Diepgen, T.L. (1998). Responses to unsolicited patient e-mail requests for medical advice on the World Wide Web. *Journal of the American Medical Association, 280,* 1333–1335.

Ferguson, T. (1998). Digital doctoring opportunities and challenges in electronic patient-physician communication. *Journal of the American Medical Association, 280,* 1361–1362.

Freeman-Longo, R.E., & Blanchard, G.T. (1998). *Sexual abuse in America: Epidemic of the 21st century.* Brandon, VT: Safer Society Press.

Goldberg, A. (1998, April). *Monthly users report on MSNBC.* Washington, DC: Relevant Knowledge.

Greenfield, D.N. (1999). *Virtual addiction: Help for netheads, cyberfreaks, and those who love them.* Oakland, CA: New Harbinger.

Hapgood, F. (1996). Sex Sells, Inc. *Technology, 4,* 45–51.

Hasley, S. (1995). A comparison of computer-based and personal interviews for the gynecologic history update. *Obstetrics and Gynecology, 85,* 494–498.

Hendrick, C., & Hendrick, S. (1983). *Liking, loving, and relating.* Monterey, CA: Brooks/Cole.

Institute of Medicine. (1994). In M. Donaldson & K. Lohr (Eds.), *Health data in the information age: Use, disclosure, and privacy.* Washington, DC: National Academy Press.

Institute of Medicine. (1996). In M.J. Field (Ed.), *Telemedicine: A guide to assessing telecommunications in health care.* Washington, DC: National Academy Press.

Kobak, K.A., Taylor, L.H., Dottl, S.L., Greist, J.H., Jefferson, J.W., Burroughs, D., Katzelnick, D.J., & Mandell, M. (1997). Computerized screening for psychiatric disorders in an outpatient community mental health clinic. *Psychiatric Services, 48,* 1048–1057.

Kobak, K.A., Taylor, L.H., Dottl, S.L., Greist, J.H., Jefferson, J.W., Burroughs, D., Mantle, J.M., Katzelnick, D.H., Norton, R., Henk, H.J., & Serlin, R.C. (1997). A computer-administered telephone interview to identify mental disorders. *Journal of the American Medical Association, 278,* 905–910.

Kramrae, C., & Taylor, J. (1993). Women and men on electronic networks: A conversation or a monologue? In J. Taylor, C. Kramae, & P. Ebben (Eds.), *Women, information-technology, and scholarship.* Urbana-Champaign: Center for Advanced Studies, University of Illinois.

Leiblum, S.R. (1997). Sex and the net: Clinical implications. *Journal of Sex Education and Therapy, 22,* 21–28.

Locke, S.E., Kowaloff, H.B., Hoff, R.G., Safran, C., Popovsky, M.A., Cotton, D.J., Finkelstein, D.M., Page, P.L., & Slack, W.V. (1992). Computer-based interview for screening blood donors for risk of HIV transmission. *Journal of the American Medical Association, 268,* 1301–1305.

Maheu, M. (1999a). Cyber-affairs, a reader survey. *Self-Help & Psychology Magazine, 6,* 5. Available: http://shpm.com/cgibin/cyber_survey.cgi?results=go&start=go

Maheu, M. (1999b). *Cyber-infidelity: Untangling the web.* Manuscript in preparation.

Maheu, M., & Gordon, B. (1999). *Survey of mental health practitioners on the Internet.* Manuscript in preparation.

Maltz, W. (1995). The Maltz hierarchy of sexual interaction. *Sexual Addiction and Compulsivity, 2,* 5–18.

Millstein, S.F., & Irwin, E.E., Jr. (1983). Acceptability of computer-acquired sexual histories in adolescent girls. *Journal of Pediatrics, 103*, 815–819.

National Board for Certified Counselors. (1998). *Standards for the ethical practice of web-counseling.* Available: http://www.nbcc.org/ethics/wcstandards.htm

National Council of State Boards of Nursing. (1998, April). Boards of nursing approve proposed language for an interstate compact for a mutual recognition model for nursing regulation. *Communique*, 1–4.

Newman, B. (1997). The use of on-line services to encourage exploration of ego-dystonic sexual interests. *Journal of Sex Education and Therapy, 22*, 45–49.

Nickelson, D. (1998). Telehealth and the evolving health care system: Strategic opportunities for professional psychology. *Professional Psychology: Research and Practice, 29*, 527–535.

Ochs, E.P.P., & Binik, Y.M. (1998). A sex-expert computer system helps couples learn more about their sexual relationship. *Journal of Sex Education and Therapy, 23*, 145–152.

O'Conaill, B., & Whitaker, S. (1997). Characterizing, predicting, and measuring video-mediated communication: A conversational approach. In K.E. Finn, A.J. Sellen, & S.B. Wilbur (Eds.), *Video-mediated communication* (pp. 107–131). Mahwah, NJ: Erlbaum.

Odzer, C. (1997). *Virtual spaces: Sex and the cybercitizen.* New York: Berkley.

Rheingold, H. (1993). *The virtual community: Homesteading on the electronic frontier.* Reading, PA: Addison-Wesley.

Roffman, D.M., Shannon, D., & Dwyer, C. (1997). Adolescents, sexual health, and the Internet: Possibilities, prospects, and challenges for educators. *Journal of Sex Education and Therapy, 23*, 49–55.

Schnarch, D. (1997). Sex, intimacy, and the Internet. *Journal of Sex Education and Therapy, 22*, 15–20.

Schwatzwalder, R. (1994). The brave new world of biotechnology on-line. *Database, 17*, 103–105.

Semans, A., & Winks, C. (1999). *The women's guide to sex on the web.* San Francisco: HarperCollins.

Shaw, J. (1997). Treatment rationale for Internet infidelity. *Journal of Sex Education and Therapy, 22*, 30–31.

Spender, D. (1995). *Nattering on the net: Women, power and cyberspace.* North Melbourne, Australia: Spinifex Press.

Spielberg, A.R. (1998). On call and on-line: Sociohistorical, legal, and ethical implications of e-mail for the patient-physician relationship. *Journal of the American Medical Association, 280*, 1353–1359.

Stamm, B. (1998). Clinical applications of telehealth in mental health care. *Professional Psychology: Research and Practice, 29*, 536–542.

Stern, S.E., & Faber, J.E. (1996). *The lost e-mail method: Milgram's lost letter technique in the age of the Internet.* Paper presented at the 1996 Society for Computers in Psychology Conference, Chicago.

Tannen, D. (1999, February 22). Freedom to talk dirty. *Time*, p. 24.

Telemedicine Development Act. (1996). Cal. Stat. Chapter 864.

Turkle, S. (1995). *Life on the screen: Identity in the age of the Internet.* New York: Simon & Schuster.

Turner, C.F., Ku, L., Lindberg, L.D., Pleck, J.H., & Sonenstein, F.L. (1998). Adolescent sexual behavior, drug use, and violence: Increased reporting with computer survey technology. *Science, 280,* 867–873.

U.S. Department of Commerce. (1997). *Telemedicine report to Congress.* Available: http://www.ntia.doc.gov

Van Gelder, L. (1985, October). The strange case of the electronic lover. *Ms, 94,* 99, 101–104, 117, 123–124.

Waskul, D., & Douglass, M. (1996). Considering the electronic participant: Some polemical observations on the ethics of on-line research. *The Information Society, 12,* 129–139.

Webster, J., & Compeau, D. (1996). Computer-assisted versus paper-and-pencil administration of questionnaires. *Behavior Research Methods, Instruments, and Computers, 28,* 567–576.

Whitaker, S., & O'Conaill, B. (1997). The role of vision in face-to-face and mediated communication. In K.E. Finn, A.J. Sellen, & S.B.Wilbur (Eds.), *Video-mediated communication* (pp. 23–49). Mahwah, NJ: Erlbaum.

Williams, M.A. (1994). The Chicago study at a glance. *Contemporary Sexuality, 28,* 2.

Young, K.S. (1996, August). *Internet addiction: The emergence of a new clinical disorder.* Paper presented at the 104th annual convention of the American Psychological Association, Toronto.

Young, K.S. (1997, August). *Internet addiction: What makes computer-mediated communication habit forming?* Paper presented at the 105th annual convention of the American Psychological Association, Chicago.

Young, K.S., & Rogers, R.C. (1998). The relationship between depression and Internet addiction. *CyberPsychology & Behavior, 1,* 25–28.

PART V

SEXUAL
VICTIMIZATION

CHAPTER 15

The Aftermath of Child Sexual Abuse: The Treatment of Complex Posttraumatic Stress Reactions

CHRISTINE A. COURTOIS

Over the past twenty years, all forms of child sexual abuse have been recognized as traumatic stressors with high potential for serious intrapsychic and interpersonal consequences. These consequences may emerge at the time of the abuse and continue across the life span, especially with a lack of intervention and treatment; alternatively, the victim may be rather asymptomatic immediately postabuse only to have symptoms emerge in delayed fashion later in life. The latter may occur as a result of triggers that are internal or external to the individual and also as a result of issues and crises associated with normal development that serve as reminders of the abuse and awaken dormant effects. It is estimated that approximately half of all victims of child sexual abuse suffer significant psychological damage, that a quarter suffer some effects, and another quarter are relatively unscathed, although these figures may be conservative due to victim denial and minimization. These findings are also limited by the research methodology used and the samples studied (Briere & Runtz, 1993; Carlson, Furby, Armstrong, & Shlaes, 1997; Finkelhor, 1990, 1994; Green, 1993; Polusny & Follette, 1995; Russell, 1986). It should be assumed by clinicians that both the occurrence of child sexual abuse and its effects are highly variable; assessment and treatment must take this variability into account. It should also be assumed that more research on child sexual abuse is needed to understand the full range of its effects as well as the effects of the individual's total family environment and upbringing and other impactful life events including revictimization.

The focus in this chapter is on those individuals whose sexual abuse was objectively severe enough and/or subjectively experienced as severe enough to warrant one or more psychiatric diagnoses and the need for mental health treatment in adulthood. This chapter has as its purpose the articulation of the most common long-term symptoms and aftereffects of sexual abuse into three main diagnostic categories: posttraumatic reactions and disorders, dissociative disorders, and characterological disorders. An encompassing diagnostic formulation of complex posttraumatic stress disorder is presented to assist the clinician in understanding the often daunting and complicated symptom picture presented by many adults who report severe and chronic sexual abuse in their histories. Such an overarching diagnostic formulation assists in the conceptualization of intervention targets and in the application of a planful model of posttraumatic treatment that is sequenced and titrated.

CHILD SEXUAL ABUSE AS TRAUMATIC

Child sexual abuse is a form of interpersonal victimization that has many traumatizing elements and characteristics that put the child victim at risk for serious initial and long-term aftereffects. Child sexual abuse can be defined as

> a sexual act imposed on a child who lacks emotional, maturational, and cognitive development. The ability to lure a child into a sexual relationship is based upon the all-powerful and dominant position of the adult or older adolescent perpetrator, which is in sharp contrast to the child's age, dependency, and subordinate position. Authority and power enable the perpetrator, implicitly or directly, to coerce the child into sexual compliance. (Sgroi, Blick, & Porter, 1982, p. 9)

Incestuous sexual abuse encompasses any form of sexual activity or contact between a child and a parent, sibling, extended family member, stepfamily member, and even encompasses quasi-family members (e.g., mother's boyfriend). The presence or absence of a blood relationship between incest participants is not as important as the kinship ties and roles between them (note that the exact legal definition of incest and the required age and age difference varies by state).

Prevalence studies show that sexual abuse is not rare and occurs at all socioeconomic levels, in different ethnic and cultural groups, and in urban, suburban, and rural locales. These studies document an occurrence rate of all forms of sexual abuse at 15% to 33% in the general population of American women and between 35% and 75% of women in clinical populations. Although fewer men report experiencing sexual abuse, researchers estimate that approximately 13% to 16% of American men were so abused during childhood, with a prevalence rate of sexual abuse estimated at between 13% and 23% within male clinical samples (Polusny & Follette, 1995). Of these, abuse by family members constitute approximately 33% to 50% of the perpetrations against girls and 10% to 20% of the perpetrations against boys (Finkelhor, 1994).

Female children are therefore more likely to be sexually and incestuously abused; however, the sexual and incestuous abuse of boys must be recognized and not minimized, as has been the case until fairly recently.

Patterns of occurrence of sexual abuse are highly variable. Specific characteristics of occurrence have been found to correlate with the severity of its impact. The most significant include the following: age of the child at onset and termination (on average, abuse that begins when a child is either preverbal or in latency usually has more serious consequences: the younger child is more damaged by not understanding the behavior, the older child by understanding and being shamed by it); duration of the abuse (abuse of longer duration is, on average, more damaging); relationship between perpetrator and victim and the age difference between them (abuse by males usually occurs at more severe levels than abuse by females, abuse by parents has more severe consequences than abuse by any other relative, and abuse of a child by an adult has more adverse consequences than abuse by a peer, on average); use of force and coercion (the more forceful and coerced, the more damaging); type of sexual behavior (oral, anal, or vaginal penetration is more damaging than nonpenetrative sexual activity such as fondling and kissing); and number of occurrences and number of perpetrators (multiple experiences of sexual abuse by the same or different perpetrators are not uncommon and, quite understandably, hold additional potential for damage).

The most common sexual abuse scenario is one involving escalating sexual contact over a period of time with someone known to the child (i.e., an acquaintance or family member). Although sexual abuse can be short-lived or even a one-time occurrence (this is more the case when perpetrated by a complete stranger), it often occurs repeatedly in the context of the relationship. The most common progression is for a young child to be gradually enticed and "groomed" into sexual activity (usually beginning with special attention, kissing, hugging, fondling, exhibitionism, and oral contact) and presented as part of a special relationship as appropriate. At this early stage, the child's sexual response is encouraged and is later used as blackmail to keep the child involved (e.g., "You're so sexy, I couldn't help myself"; "It made you feel good and you responded so you must have liked it"; "You wanted the attention"; "If you tell anyone, I'll tell them how much you liked it" or, alternatively, "If you tell anyone, I'll hurt you, your pets, members of your family"). Children are easily manipulated by such ploys and stay silent due to shame and fear of being blamed or hurt, and to protect others. Silence and secrecy then give the abuser license to escalate the sexual contact, ultimately to involve full intercourse in many cases. Although this progression is the norm, some cases of sexual abuse involve oral, vaginal, or anal penetration right from the start and some are forceful and even violent from early on. Some perpetrators are sadistic in orientation and take pleasure in their victim's pain. Still other forms of sexual abuse are milder and are kept at levels of touching and observation. Yet, even with such "mild" exposure, the psychological toll can be high.

Child sexual abuse has been found to have a range of potential consequences for victims (Albach & Everaerd, 1992; Briere, & Runtz, 1993; Carlson,
Furby, Armstrong, & Shlaes, 1997; Courtois, 1979, 1988, 1997; Finkelhor, 1990,
1994; Finkelhor & Browne, 1985; Herman, 1981, 1992b; Meiselman, 1978;
Polusny & Follette, 1995; Roth & Batson, 1997; Russell, 1986). The dynamics of
incest compound the dynamics found in extrafamilial sexual abuse. Its occurrence within a family, perpetrated by someone in close proximity or relationship on whom the child depends for nurturance, protection, and nonsexual
contact, profoundly disrupts and complicates family relationships. Instead of
allowing conditions of safety and security conducive to healthy development,
intrafamilial sexual abuse creates conditions of betrayal, conflict, ambivalence,
dual relationships, rivalry, and secrecy. Most often, the occurrence of incest is
aided and abetted by particular family dynamics, many of which are dysfunctional. These include other incestuous relationships (within the nuclear and/or
extended family network, sometimes spanning generations), mental illness,
substance abuse problems, and other forms of family violence (spouse abuse,
verbal and emotional abuse, substance abuse (often across generations) with
accompanying patterns of denial, secrecy, and shame. Most often, when incest
occurs within the nuclear family (i.e., between parent/stepparent and child or
between siblings), parents are immature and unable to provide functional parenting. Incest occurs most often for several primary reasons: when a parent
turns to a child to meet unmet emotional needs that become sexualized, when
other types of abuse occur within the family, or when children are left vulnerable to abuse by others due to the vacuum of unmet needs created by emotional and/or physical neglect in the family. The duration of the average case of
incest is four years, during which the sexual contact usually intensifies from
less to more physically intrusive.

Children caught in any sexually abusive situation are often relatively powerless to stop it without outside assistance. They are trapped and dependent,
especially when the abuse occurs within the nuclear family. Consequently,
they must cope as well as they can, often with a variety of behavioral strategies
such as hiding, running away, fighting back, and withdrawing. When behavioral strategies are not successful or available, the child may have to accommodate emotionally to the abuse or escape via alterations in consciousness and
splitting (discussed further below). Whatever the behavioral, psychological, or
dissociative coping strategy, the chronically abused child at some point blames
himself or herself and feels responsible for the abuse and its continuance. The
abused child frequently arrives at the conclusion that he or she is bad, deserving of abuse and undeserving of good attention. This internalization of badness paradoxically allows the child to maintain an image of the perpetrator as
good (an essential survival strategy when the perpetrator is a parent or other
family member) and, in so doing, to maintain essential emotional attachments.

The sense of blame and badness is further consolidated when and if the
child discloses the abuse and is blamed for it rather than assisted or if it is observed and not stopped. Denial and disavowal of overt sexual abuse and incest

(with or without attempts at disclosure) are, unfortunately, quite common. Another pattern is for the abuse to be confronted and for it to stop for a time, only to resume at a later date if the abuser has not lost access to the child or has not had effective treatment. Abused children are also at risk of being revictimized by the original abuser or by others. They may be especially vulnerable due to the unresolved effects of prior abuse. For example, in families where incest has occurred, it is not unusual for the family to reconsolidate in the same relational pattern after a disclosure or intervention. An abuser might be emboldened (and even enraged at having the original abuse acknowledged) if intervention attempts were overly lenient or ineffective.

In recent years, some studies have begun to systematically examine the impact of child sexual abuse on boys. The responses of boys are surprisingly similar to those of girls; they too show marked early and long-term impact. This is despite the fact that their abuse is more often perpetrated by males and is therefore homosexual and perpetrated at levels that are more objectively serious than the abuse of girls. Where differences between boys and girls are found, they seem to be in the areas of additional shame and greater reluctance to disclose experiences of sexual abuse and in a tendency to externalize rather than internalize anger (Finkelhor, 1990). Boys may also have more sexual identity and orientation difficulties than girls by virtue of having been abused by a member of the same sex.

Of particular importance to all victims is the fact that child sexual abuse occurs over the course of the child's formative years. When it follows this course, it can be chronic trauma that impacts, becomes entwined with, and distorts (by either regressing or accelerating) the child's maturation. And, if this were not enough, many of today's adult survivors were additionally handicapped by having been abused during the "Age of Denial" (Armstrong, 1982), when child sexual abuse was neither acknowledged nor discussed publicly and when incestuous abuse was all but dismissed under the influence of Freud's repudiation of his seduction theory in favor of the oedipal or fantasy theory. In contrast, incest and other forms of child sexual abuse (along with child abuse in general) was "rediscovered" in recent years (Summit, 1982) and has received unprecedented public exposure via the mass media. Adult survivors have therefore gone from one extreme to another, from disavowal on the one hand to saturation coverage on the other. For many previously abused adults, this dramatic change has had the effect of disturbing long-dormant reactions and effects and has led many of them to seek assistance and symptom relief.

SEXUAL ABUSE AFTEREFFECTS

Research on child sexual abuse has documented a host of nonspecific psychological correlates such as depression, anxiety, and low self-esteem, as well as numerous interpersonal difficulties. A more specific pattern has emerged when samples of abused versus nonabused (by self-report) individuals are compared. In their recent review of the immediate and long-term impacts of child sexual abuse, Briere and Elliott (1994) noted the following: "Although a definitive causal relationship between such difficulties and sexual abuse cannot be established using current retrospective research methodologies, the aggregate of consistent findings in this literature has led many to conclude that childhood sexual abuse is a major risk factor for a variety of problems" (p. 54). These potential impacts are reviewed here in several broad categories: posttraumatic reactions, emotional effects, self-perceptions and cognitions, physical effects, and interpersonal effects (inclusive of sexual and social effects).

POSTTRAUMATIC REACTIONS

Studies of child sexual abuse victims and their adult survivor counterparts have documented a range of posttraumatic reactions, including intrusive and reexperiencing symptoms; numbing, detachment, and avoidance symptoms (including but not limited to dissociation, substance abuse, addictions and compulsions, eating disorders, suicidality, self-mutilation, and other self-harmful activities); and arousal symptoms such as startle response, hyperarousal, hypervigilance, and sleep disturbance due to night terrors and nightmares. These will be discussed in more detail below along with dissociative reactions.

EMOTIONAL EFFECTS

Depression, anxiety, and associated conditions such as suicidality, anxiety attacks, and phobias and emotions such as grief, guilt, anger, rage, fear, hopelessness, despair, emptiness, emotional detachment, and confusion have been routinely documented in this population. The emotional pain associated with sexual abuse is often very intense. Additionally, many survivors, whose security within a family has been disrupted by childhood abuse, have not learned to recognize, tolerate, or manage their emotions very well. As a result, many have impaired impulse control and act out their emotions in impulsive and destructive behavior to self and others, including the reenacting of their own abuse through the abuse of others. Some survivors modulate strong emotion via avoidance strategies, including emotional numbing and detachment, dissociative reactions, self-medication via addictions (drugs, food, self-harm), and compulsive behaviors and relationships.

SELF-PERCEPTIONS AND COGNITIONS

The self-perceptions of sexually abused individuals are predominantly negative and include feelings of low self-esteem and self-worth, stigma, guilt, shame, self-blame, and oftentimes a globally impaired sense of self. Psychosexual development has often been either stunted or accelerated in these individuals, resulting in further difficulties in relating to others. Many abused children display cognitive and intellectual impairment associated with delayed and arrested development possibly due to biochemical and neurophysiological alterations that may also render them more susceptible to repeat abuse (Perry, 1993a, 1993b) although it should also be noted that many victims and survivors have superior intellectual capacities and high levels of functioning. These cognitive deficits may extend into adulthood and compromise adult functioning. In addition, may adult survivors have developed distorted cognitions about self, others, and the world as a result of shattered assumptions (Janoff-Bulman, 1992), a common aftermath of any severe traumatization but especially likely when the trauma is interpersonal and involves significant betrayal, premeditation, and conflicted attachment dynamics. Distorted cognitions in terms of self and relations with others involving issues of hope, safety, trust/dependency, power, esteem, independence, and intimacy are most evident in trauma survivors (McCann & Pearlman, 1990a).

PHYSICAL EFFECTS

A range of physical effects can stem from direct and indirect damage sustained during the abuse. Recent research is documenting physiological and neurological effects of traumatization, effects that can compromise the child victim's later physical maturation and that might compound over time. Disorders involving the immune, central nervous, endocrine, digestive, reproductive, respiratory, cardiac, and other body systems have been noted or speculated about and are increasingly the subject of research investigation (Perry, 1993a, 1993b; Golding, Cooper, & Geroge, 1997). Quite a large number of adult survivors have long histories of health problems and complaints, many of which defy formal medical diagnosis. Additionally, a number of somatization effects have long been associated with a history of childhood sexual abuse (Courtois, 1988, 1993).

INTERPERSONAL EFFECTS

Interpersonal effects include an impaired ability to trust others, a tendency to feel isolated and alienated from others, a desire for anonymity, interpersonal constriction, difficulty forming healthy adult relationships, and a tendency to be revictimized, especially sexually and physically. Other interpersonal problems include a failure to resolve adolescent developmental tasks, such as separation from family due to trauma bonding and incomplete or conflicted psychosexual development, and difficulty with attachment and sustained intimate attachments, including parenting. A range of sexual difficulties including sexual dysfunctions and abuse-based questions of sexual identity and orientation have been identified in both men and women survivors. Additionally, reproduction and childbirth may pose greater than average challenges for a subset of women survivors (Courtois, 1988; Maltz, 1991; Maltz & Holman, 1987; Westerlund, 1992).

Many of these interpersonal effects extend to the social and occupational domains as well. A variety of social effects have been identified, ranging from exemplary functioning (and compulsive overfunctioning/workaholism in some cases) at one extreme to a total inability to function at the other. Whereas some adult survivors are able to make significant social and occupational contributions, others are so debilitated that they are found among the homeless and the chronically mentally ill (Harris, 1998). Another pattern that has been observed is that of survivors who function relatively well until hit by some sort of midlife crisis that functions as a trigger to dormant posttraumatic and other associated psychiatric conditions, notably major depression and anxiety, at which point they become debilitated and symptomatic.

It is important to note that, despite the listing of negative effects reviewed above, symptoms are highly variable. No one symptom is pathognomic of a history of incest/sexual abuse, nor is there a single universal or uniform impact or certainty that any given individual will develop a posttraumatic disorder (Briere & Elliott, 1994; Carlson et al., 1997; Finkelhor, 1990, 1994; Neumann, Houskamp, Pollock, & Briere, 1996; Yehuda, 1998; Yehuda & McFarlane, 1995). A number of modulating or mediating factors that can exacerbate or lessen the impact are under investigation. These include, predictably, the circumstances of abuse most conducive to more severity of response (reviewed above) and such moderating variables as the child's generic makeup, personal hardiness and other characterological and resiliency factors, his or her preabuse functioning and experiences (including bonding and early infant-caregiver attachment), the objective severity of the abuse, its subjective interpretation, available explanation and intervention, and significant restorative relationships at the time of the abuse or later (Browne & Finkelhor, 1986; Wyatt, Newcomb, & Riederle, 1993).

All of these issues notwithstanding, the available research data on the effects of sexual abuse accumulated over the past two decades, when interpreted in aggregate form, give strong support for a host of initial and sustained deleterious consequences (see literature reviews and meta-analyses by Beitchman et al., 1991, 1992; Briere & Elliott, 1994; Briere & Runtz, 1993; Browne & Finkelhor, 1986; Carlson et al., 1997; Finkelhor, 1990, 1994; Green, 1993; Kendall-Tackett, Williams, & Finkelhor, 1993; Neumann et al., 1996; Polusny & Follette, 1995). Incest, above and beyond other types of sexual abuse, is correlated with more serious consequences due to having more risk factors and due to its entrapping and ongoing nature, its impact on psychosexual development, and its betrayal of family ties and responsibilities (Cole & Putnam, 1992; Courtois, 1988; Herman, 1981; 1992a, 1992b; Meiselman, 1978; Russell, 1986; Strick & Wilcoxon, 1991) . The research of Browne and Finkelhor (1986) and Russell (1986) documented that approximately 40% of all victim/survivors of child sexual abuse suffer aftereffects serious enough to require therapy at some point in their lives. It is to this subgroup of the most severely impacted sexual abuse victims that I now turn.

COMPLEX POSTTRAUMATIC STRESS REACTIONS

As research and clinical data have accumulated, it is evident that victims of child sexual abuse (especially of the type that is repetitive and long-lasting and escalates over time) resemble victims of other forms of chronic trauma (i.e., hostage situations, concentration camps, political torture, other forms of ongoing domestic violence); furthermore, the posttraumatic stress reactions they suffer differ from the aftereffects of more circumscribed and time-limited traumatic events (i.e., rape, accidents, and natural disasters). A condition of captivity and entrapment is characteristic of the type of interpersonal trauma that involves ongoing contact with and subordination to a perpetrator-captor. Furthermore, ambivalent attachment between victim and perpetrator often results (even more so when a close family member or acquaintance is involved), a relationship dimension that complicates the victimization experience. This often necessitates the use of strong defenses and psychological accommodation and adaptation to the abuse. Defensive strategies, such as deliberate suppression of memory and attempts to avoid reminders, and alterations of consciousness, especially dissociation, allow an individual to compartmentalize the trauma in the interest of self-integrity and survival. The repeated use of these defensive patterns can have serious characterological repercussions, especially, but not exclusively, for children (Putnam, 1997); however, they may also be quite adaptive, at least for a time.

These three components of the complex posttraumatic stress response—posttraumatic reactions, dissociation, and characterological deformations—are discussed next as they characterize many of the most seriously damaged sexual abuse survivors.

COMPLEX POSTTRAUMATIC STRESS DISORDER

Victims of chronic sexual abuse trauma have a wide array of initial and long-term psychological symptoms that Herman (1992a, 1992b) and other clinician-researchers have organized into a diagnosis they termed complex posttraumatic stress disorder (complex PTSD) or alternately disorders of extreme stress, not otherwise specified (DESNOS), to differentiate it from generic posttraumatic stress disorder (PTSD) as currently defined in the *Diagnostic and Statistical Manual IV (DSM-IV)* (American Psychiatric Association, 1994). This new diagnostic formulation has been field-tested for inclusion in the *DSM*; preliminary results are that complex PTSD includes additional criteria and aftereffects not currently accounted for in the criteria for standard PTSD (Ford & Kidd, 1998; Herman, 1993; Pelcovitz, van der Kolk, Roth, Mandel, Kaplan, & Resick, 1997; van der Kolk, Roth, Pelcovitz, & Mandel, 1993; Zlotnick, Zakriski, Shea, Costello, Begin, Pearlstein, & Simpson, 1996). Despite these findings, the new diagnosis has not yet achieved official sanction and is not included in the 1994 edition of the *DSM-IV*; therefore, it cannot be given as an official diagnosis.

Nevertheless, the diagnostic model is useful conceptually both for the understanding and cataloguing of the range of reactions presented by victims of prolonged trauma (including sexual abuse) and to the planning and sequencing of treatment.

Three broad areas of psychological disturbance have been identified in this diagnostic formulation (Chu, 1992, 1998; Herman, 1992a, 1992b). The first involves the various psychiatric and posttraumatic symptoms (discussed above) and their complexity, diffuseness, and tenacity over the life span (although, as noted above, they can be dormant for years or may emerge and submerge periodically). The second involves the characterological changes such as identity disturbances, problems with emotions and their regulation, and interpersonal distress. The third includes vulnerability to repeated harm or revictimization experienced by many survivors, either self-inflicted (interpreted as reenactments of the original abuse and often in the service of affect discharge and modulation) or caused by others. All of these may occur in conjunction with dissociative coping mechanisms common in this population.

DISSOCIATIVE DISORDERS

Research has provided substantiation that individuals with dissociative disorders frequently report histories of traumatization, particularly severe childhood physical, sexual, and emotional abuse (Chu & Dill, 1990; Putnam, 1989, 1997; Spiegel, Hunt, & Donershine, 1988; Swett & Halpert, 1993), and incestuous abuse that began at an early age and that was severe and continuous (Pribor & Dinwiddie, 1992; Strick & Wilcoxon, 1991). Dissociation is generally defined as involving a separation of mental processes that are normally integrated (such as ongoing consciousness, emotions, identity, and memory). It is a normal human capacity that is quite adaptive but, when used to excess, creates problems for the individual and thus becomes maladaptive. Pathological dissociation involves alterations that interfere with an individual's ability to have a stable unitary identity and a personal consciousness that are intact rather than fragmented. In *DSM-IV,* five different dissociative disorders are identified: dissociative amnesia, dissociative fugue, derealization, dissociative identity disorder (formerly multiple personality disorder), and dissociative disorder, not otherwise specified. At present, PTSD is categorized in the *DSM* as an anxiety disorder. Many researchers and clinicians believe it could just as easily be categorized as a dissociative disorder, given the alternation between numbing and reexperiencing found in posttraumatic responses. This vacillation is seen by many as inherently dissociative. If dissociation is placed on a continuum from normal and nonpathological at one pole and abnormal and pathological at the other, PTSD would be around the midpoint. Complex dissociative PTSD responses would be toward the abnormal pole. The treatment of patients with this diagnostic picture requires attention to the posttraumatic as well as the dissociative dimensions.

CHARACTEROLOGICAL DISTURBANCES

According to Herman (1992a), "Survivors of childhood abuse develop . . . complex deformations of identity. A malignant sense of the self as contaminated, guilty and evil is widely noted. Fragmentation in the sense of self is also common, reaching its most dramatic extreme in multiple personality disorder" (p. 386). Characterological disturbances are now well documented as correlated with a history of severe sexual abuse and incest (Briere, 1989, 1996b, 1996c; Cole & Putnam, 1992; Courtois, 1988, 1997; Davies & Frawley, 1994) as well as with other forms of chronic trauma (Herman, 1992a, 1992b; Wang, Wilson, & Mason, 1996). An impoverished sense of self characterized by internal fragmentation, difficulty with the regulation of affect and the maintenance of self-integrity, and impaired object relations including the inability to trust and to have intimate relationships with others characterize many adult survivors. Additionally, a characterological depression with complications and with atypical impulsive and dissociative features has been noted as a hallmark of some incest survivors (Gelinas, 1983).

Many of these features have historically been encompassed in the Axis II diagnosis of borderline personality disorder (BPD), leading some clinicians to speculate about the impressive overlap between a history of abuse and symptoms of borderline personality. This diagnosis (along with its companion diagnosis, hysteria) has been applied almost exclusively to women, usually in a pejorative and disparaging manner. Patients diagnosed with BPD have been viewed as unreliable, unstable, manipulative, deceptive, and difficult to treat due to their use of primitive defenses (especially splitting and projective identification), their fragile and discontinuous sense of self and others, their difficulty forming ongoing attachments, and their difficult and often tumultuous relationships (including therapy). As more is learned about the traumatic antecedents of these diagnoses, they can be understood as, at least in part, posttraumatic adaptations. The overlap between BPD and PTSD is increasingly acknowledged (Briere, 1984, 1989, 1996b; Kroll, 1993; Waites, 1993), as is a relation to the dissociative disorders, particularly dissociative identity disorder (Horevitz & Braun, 1984; Ross, 1989, 1997).

It is worth noting again that not all adults with a history of significant childhood sexual abuse develop this overlapping triad of posttraumatic, dissociative, and personality disorders; however, their association and manifestation are observed in a substantial subpopulation of survivors of severe repetitive sexual abuse. Complex dissociative posttraumatic stress reactions should be given consideration as applicable to the most chronic and disabled patients who present for treatment with complicated symptomatology, and should be anticipated and considered a diagnostic rule-out among those patients who report serious and multiple forms of abuse in childhood. This diagnostic formulation assists the clinician to provide a transtheoretical therapy directed by principles of trauma-based treatment but involving other psychotherapeutic orientations and modalities as well (e.g., psychodynamic, object relations, cognitive behavioral, or solution-focused, depending on the theoretical orientation of the treating clinician) (Courtois, 1997).

The remainder of this chapter provides an overview of a treatment model for patients for whom this triad of symptoms is diagnosed and for whom the diagnostic conceptualization of complex posttraumatic stress disorder is applicable. The treatment model is sequenced and titrated to the needs and capacities of the individual patient and is directed toward personal development, skill building, and self-management in addition to trauma resolution and mastery. Because abuse occurs in an interpersonal context and results in developmental disruptions, the interpersonal and personal "lessons of abuse" are projected onto the therapeutic relationship. The treatment model incorporates a strong emphasis on this relational dimension as providing both information about the personal and interpersonal damage of the abuse and an opportunity to rework and transform it in the therapeutic relationship.

Although this model addresses dissociative behaviors and issues, it is not specialized enough for the patient diagnosed with dissociative identity disorder (DID). Therapists treating DID can use this model as the foundation for their treatment but, of necessity, need additional information and training. Texts by Kluft (1985), Kluft and Fine (1993), Loewenstein (1991), Putnam (1989, 1997), Ross (1989, 1997), and Spira (1996) are highly recommended as essential reading when treating this disorder.

A TREATMENT MODEL FOR COMPLEX PTSD

The professional training programs of most psychotherapists do not incorporate attention to the treatment of interpersonal victimization and associated posttraumatic conditions. This circumstance is particularly unfortunate and can have very serious implications because the large majority of practicing psychotherapists have traumatized patients in their caseloads at some point (in fact, they may be hard-pressed not to treat trauma because of the association between trauma and later mental health consequences). This deficiency in training means that clinicians must meet their training needs for working with traumatized individuals through continuing education, consultation and supervision, focused reading, and on-the-job training. It is to be hoped that this omission of victimization and traumatization from the curriculum will change before too long in response to a variety of pressures and influences, among them the legal challenges and controversy surrounding the treatment of delayed/false memories in adult abuse survivors and the recommendations of a number of professional organizations and task forces (e.g., the recommendations of the American Psychological Association Working Group on the Investigation of Memories of Childhood Abuse and the American Psychological Association Presidential Task Force on Family Violence) (American Psychological Association, 1996a, 1996b).

The need for formal curricular inclusion is urgent because interpersonally traumatized patients present therapists with a host of challenges (transference-based in many cases, but also related to other aspects of the therapy relationship) not found in other treatment populations. A therapist's lack of awareness and knowledge of these issues can lead to misalliances and therapeutic efforts that exacerbate and retraumatize rather than heal. These can be dangerous to both patient and therapist (Pearlman & Saakvitne, 1995; Perlman, 1999; Wilson & Lindy, 1994). Additionally, a therapist is more prone to be personally affected by working with trauma and hearing about atrocities especially of the type described in this chapter, that is, trauma that is human-induced, premeditated, directed at a child, escalating in intrusion, possibly sadistic in nature and intent, and violating perhaps the strongest of human taboos, sex between family members, especially between a parent and a child. Work with trauma has been recognized as having great potential to vicariously traumatize the helper, causing personal changes in perceptions of self and others and in life assumptions similar to those experienced directly by the victim/patient (McCann & Pearlman, 1990b; Pearlman & Saakvitne, 1995). A therapist's experience of vicarious traumatization, if not recognized and managed, can be a factor in derailing treatment. Finally, and most pertinent to the trauma population of adult sexual abuse survivors under discussion in this chapter, the stress associated with this work has recently intensified due to allegations put forth by "false memory" proponents that therapists who are misinformed, naïve, or entangled in problematic countertransference or vicarious traumatization are suggesting or implanting false memories of abuse. Lawsuits and licensing board challenges against therapists are being encouraged as a routine recourse to family members who feel they have been falsely accused based on memories suggested or inappropriately managed by therapists.

The implications of these training issues and the complexities and demands of this treatment are that therapists must supplement their degree training with additional specialized information, must stay current with the literature (on trauma, trauma treatment and the evolving standard of care, transference and countertransference issues, and particularly memory issues) because treatment methodologies are under development and changing rapidly. Therapists must institute strategies for self-care including personal and professional support and opportunities for ventilation or discharge of affect. It is also recommended that therapists monitor the composition of their caseloads and not treat abuse/trauma cases exclusively. Solo practitioners should be especially vigilant regarding their own needs and should create opportunities for collaboration and consultation to counter their professional (and perhaps personal) isolation.

In working with abuse survivors, as with other chronically traumatized patients, the therapist must take care to provide a treatment frame establishing conditions of interpersonal safety, security, and consistency. The therapist is responsible for the establishment, communication, and maintenance of clear limits and boundaries, taking care to be neither too rigid nor too loose. Therapists doing trauma work must maintain a stance of openness and empathy to the patient and must guard against an overly abstinent nonresponsive style; nevertheless, the therapist must set clear limits in personal and professional availability and not overdisclose his or her personal life to the patient. It is advisable to establish a respectful atmosphere and to maintain a collaborative stance toward the therapy process and treatment goals. These are in marked contrast to conditions of past abuse and are often simultaneously comforting to and anxiety-producing for the patient. Another important stance on the part of the therapist is to convey that recovery is the responsibility of the patient and that the patient has the strength, resiliency, and ability to heal. Such a stance establishes from the start that the therapist is not a rescuer who is available without limitation. Finally, the therapist must also communicate respect for the patient's defenses and survival strategies and for the traumatic content itself.

The treatment must be carefully paced with attention to the patient's defenses and ability to tolerate and work safely with the traumatic material and the emotions it generates (i.e., without being overwhelmed and retraumatized and without resorting to numbing strategies or to harm to self or others). Some writers have referred to this titration approach as working within a therapeutic window (Briere, 1996b, 1996c) or maintaining an affective edge with the patient (Cornell & Olio, 1991), where the survivor patient is neither overstimulated nor underchallenged regarding the resolution of traumatic aftereffects. In recent years, increased attention has been directed toward establishing safety, teaching self-management and coping strategies, increasing social connection and support, and deliberately controlling the intensity and pace of the work to help the patient maintain "present-day" functioning versus an exclusive focus on the historical trauma (referred to as healing tasks versus abreaction by Kepner, 1995). The critical importance of both sequencing and titrating the process and therapeutic tasks in the treatment of the complex symptom picture of this population cannot be overemphasized.

The Length, Titration, and Sequencing of the Therapy Process

A general consensus is evident among clinicians who specialize in the treatment of complex posttraumatic reactions associated with child sexual abuse (Briere, 1989, 1996b, 1996c; Brown & Fromm, 1986; Chu, 1992, 1998; Courtois, 1988, 1991, 1994, 1997, 1999; Davies & Frawley, 1994; Dolan, 1991; Gil, 1988; Herman, 1992b; Jehu, 1988; Kepner, 1995; Kirschner, Kirschner, & Rappaport, 1993; Meiselman, 1990; Sgroi, 1989; van der Kolk, McFarlane, &Weisaeth, 1996; Walker, 1994). Optimally, the therapy has an overarching structure and sequence but is also individually tailored to the needs, capacities, and goals of each patient and thus can vary considerably. It is, on average, therapy that is of longer rather than shorter duration, although some short-term treatments and interventions have been developed (Dolan, 1991; O'Hanlon & Bertolino, 1998) and are to be recommended according to each patient's resources and motivation.

An ethical and treatment complication of major proportions has been created by managed care limitations because adult survivors often need longer and more intensive treatment than is allowed by many plans. Both patient and therapist have the responsibility to monitor coverage and resources. It goes without saying that the patient who loses the ability to afford treatment in the middle of the process is placed in a precarious position. Of necessity, when finances are limited, psychotherapy must be attenuated. In such a circumstance, treatment is generally best focused on educational and cognitive-behavioral strategies that include the direct teaching of a variety of skills for general self-management, symptom reduction, and personal stabilization. The trauma, when it is addressed, is handled from a cognitive and educational perspective. The patient is educated about abuse and posttraumatic reactions with the aim of normalizing and validating reactions and aftereffects. As Jehu (1988) found in his research, the provision of information can sometimes have the effect of disrupting cognitive distortions and misperceptions that underlie depressive symptomatology to such an extent that depressive symptoms begin to clear up.

Longer-term treatment is nevertheless generally acknowledged as necessary for many abuse survivors with complex PTSD due to the pervasive and developmental/characterological effects of the abuse, the compounding of effects over time, and the complexity and tenacity of both symptoms and defenses. Uncovering of the intense affect associated with the long-term trauma response must proceed at a pace that is tolerable to the patient and that does not precipitate decompensation. Therapy has been found to optimally proceed in three general stages, each with specific tasks and goals. These stages should be considered dynamic and fluid rather than static or lockstep and are helpfully conceptualized as a healing spiral (Kepner, 1995). The patient might work on issues and make progress only to regress and then relearn the same issues, but in more depth and with more insight over the course of the treatment. Explaining and anticipating the back-and-forth nature of treatment and treating relapses as predictable and as opportunities for relearning can be quite helpful to the patient and can counter feelings of disempowerment and failure that are so characteristic in this population. Additionally, it has become a given among therapists experienced with this population that patient needs and goals evolve over the course of treatment and that the resolution of one issue often precedes the emergence of others; this circumstance should also be anticipated and explained to the patient as expectable and, again, not as an indication of failure.

The Preliminary Phase

This phase involves intake, initial assessment and diagnosis, and development of a treatment plan. It includes education about the therapy process and the therapeutic relationship and informed consent for the treatment. Individuals who seek treatment might present in many different ways and with a wide array of symptoms. Of necessity, assessment should precede treatment planning and implementation. A broad psychosocial assessment should be undertaken. It is recommended that all assessments include questions about childhood trauma and family violence along with the more standard areas of inquiry (i.e., mental status, family history, developmental milestones, etc.). Where warranted, specialized assessment of posttraumatic and dissociative symptoms can supplement the more generic areas of assessment. A number of questionnaires and psychometric instruments specific to trauma and dissociative symptoms are now available (Bernstein & Putnam, 1986, 1993; Briere, 1995; Loewenstein, 1991; Stamm, 1996; Steinberg, 1993), as are books and articles devoted to the topic of trauma assessment (Briere, 1996a; Carlson, 1997; Courtois, 1995; Steinberg, 1995; Wilson & Keane, 1996).

The assessment of the patient's personality and functioning determines the goals and pace of treatment. The maxim of "self-work before trauma work" (Briere, 1996b, 1996c; Linehan, 1993; McCann & Pearlman, 1990a) is now widely accepted as a given in this therapy. It refers to strengthening and bolstering the patient *before* any direct work on the trauma is undertaken. Many therapists have erred by approaching traumatic material too soon and without adequate stabilization of the patient, including attention to whether the patient has the capacity to cope with the intense emotions that might result from directed attention and reexposure to traumatic experiences. When traumatic material is discussed prematurely or without adequate preparation, destabilization and relapse to "tried and true" (albeit dysfunctional) coping mechanisms are likely to occur. When other defenses and methods for containing strong emotion are in place, patients have other personal resources to draw upon.

Early on, therefore, therapeutic attention needs to be directed to a variety of stabilization tasks: development of self-capacities, coping skills, and defenses; shoring up the patient's ability to identify, tolerate, and regulate emotion; development and maintenance of a support network; development and maintenance of personal safety (both in relationships and in terms of self-harm); stabilization of associated conditions such as acute depression, anxiety, and hyperarousal; teaching of stress management; assessment of the need for psychotropic medication; stabilization of dissociative reactions through the teaching of grounding, self-awareness, and "safe place" techniques; lessening the use of dissociation over time; lessening of self-mutilation, acute suicidality, or any life-threatening behavior including addictions and compulsions; and resolution of any current life crisis. Many other practicalities are also addressed in this treatment phase, including the patient's general level of function in terms of relationships, family and parenting, employment and occupational stability, and financial and other resources.

The first phase of treatment is often the most lengthy phase, especially for highly compromised and symptomatic patients. For some survivors, in fact, it might constitute their entire treatment, without much time or attention devoted to the trauma per se. Others who are functioning moderately well and have adequate psychological defenses and emotional resources at the outset usually move through this stage more expeditiously.

The Trauma Resolution Phase

This phase is also shaped to conform to the needs and defenses of the individual. As a general rule, uncovering and working with traumatic material proceeds slowly and carefully, with ongoing attention to titration and not overwhelming the patient. An approach-avoid strategy to the traumatic material has been proposed by Horowitz (1976/1986) to parallel the phasic alteration of the trauma response. The intent of such a strategy is to increase the patient's ability to approach and tolerate the traumatic content and emotion while simultaneously lessening avoidance and numbing and to process the material enough to achieve resolution and a decrease of posttraumatic symptomatology. This strategy involves a deliberate focus on the details of the trauma, in this case, on the sexual abuse. The patient is encouraged to remember and talk about the specifics of the abuse and to reconnect whatever was previously dissociated or disowned. At times, triggers are deliberately introduced to stimulate memory and to facilitate emotional discharge, but the triggers are carefully titrated. At whatever point the patient feels overwhelmed by the material, triggers or prompts are decreased or removed, and the patient is encouraged to utilize the previously learned coping and self-soothing strategies.

Many traumatized individuals have memory discontinuities but "know more than they know they know" (Courtois, 1991, 1992) or know and don't know simultaneously. They may de-repress and re-repress their knowledge repeatedly during this phase as they gradually accommodate acknowledgment of the abuse and the strong emotions associated with it (Briere, 1996a, 1996b; Courtois, 1991, 1992, 1997; Meiselman, 1990). Strong emotions typically emerge during this phase, including intense grief as the interpersonal betrayals and losses associated with sexual abuse are tallied and faced directly. Eventually, emotional ventilation gives way to assimilation, resolution, and the development of new meaning later in this phase of the work. At its most basic level, the patient resolves issues of self-blame secondary to a deeper understanding of the abuse scenario, including the perpetrator's motivations and any contributory personal or family dynamics. Obviously, this phase is taxing—for both patient and therapist. The therapist may have to provide more than usual amounts of availability and support during the period of greatest destabilization. The patient's support system should also be mobilized to provide additional assistance on an "as needed" basis.

The Postresolution or Reconnection Phase

The third phase builds on the work of the first two but involves a much more centered patient, one more ready to deal with present-day and future concerns. This phase is seen as analogous to more generic therapy in that patients deal with residual personality issues, relationship and sexuality issues, occupational and other life-planning issues, and any unresolved or pressing abuse-related concerns and courses of action, such as family disclosure (if not done previously), family mediation, forgiveness, and survivor missions. The work of this phase is generally easier than the two preceding phases because the patient is freed from much of the posttraumatic symptomatology and is likely to be more engaged in personal development and anticipation for the future. Options that were previously foreclosed are now open.

Termination is the final task for which considerable time may be needed. The patient is encouraged to review the course and progress of the treatment, to grieve its end, and, more specifically, to grieve the loss of the ongoing relationship with the therapist. The patient is also encouraged to view termination as transformation and as a very positive event in the healing process (Quintana, 1993). Although termination ought to be a clearly demarcated event, return in the future for "tune-ups" or "check-ins" should not be precluded. These patients may have a resurgence of symptoms due to normal developmental age/stage issues or to an unanticipated trigger or crisis. Of necessity, the therapist must be scrupulous about not allowing any dual relationships and blurred boundaries to develop, even after the therapy has ended. Abuse survivors, more than any other therapeutic population, need the assurance of a "clean" therapeutic relationship, that is, one unencumbered by dual or conflicted roles, so that a return to the "safe place" of therapy is assured if needed (Herman, 1992b).

TRANSFERENCE AND COUNTERTRANSFERENCE ISSUES

The treatment of patients with complex posttraumatic reactions is arduous work and poses a number of challenges for the clinician, many of which are evident in the transference and countertransference and others that are due more to the personality and functioning of the therapist. In general, the patient can be expected to project upon and reenact salient issues from past relationships, including the relational and abusive messages that accompany sexual abuse and the coping mechanisms learned during the abuse and later. Many of these are similar to those identified in borderline personality (Herman, 1992b), including superficial compliance, mistrust, overdependence, and overidealization offset by disillusionment and rejection, rage, entitlement, shame, a high degree of defensiveness, fear, and anxiety, all in innumerable combinations and permutations. Additionally, these reactions occur within a relational field that is posttraumatic and dissociative (Loewenstein, 1993) and hence highly changeable, confusing, and challenging for the therapist.

Rather than dismiss these reactions as bothersome or insignificant, the therapist must assess them for their thematic content and for how the trauma might be communicated or reenacted in coded form in the therapeutic interaction. A detailed discussion of these issues is beyond the scope of this chapter, but the therapist is well advised to anticipate the most common transference and countertransference issues and to become familiar with strategies for their management so that these critical issues are not overlooked or mismanaged. The reader is referred to articles by Chu (1988) and Lowenstein (1993) that detail some of the dissociative and posttraumatic issues at play in this treatment and to seven recently published books for more thorough discussion of transference and countertransference issues in treating traumatized patients (Chu, 1998; Courtois, 1988, 1999; Davies & Frawley, 1994; Pearlman & Saakvitne, 1995; Perlman, 1999; Wilson & Lindy, 1994).

SUMMARY

This chapter has reviewed common aftereffects found to be correlated with a history of child sexual abuse. It then discussed elements of complex posttraumatic stress disorder, a diagnostic conceptualization and proposed encompassing diagnosis for the various long-term aftereffects of severe child sexual abuse, including incest. This diagnosis encompasses posttraumatic, dissociative, and other psychiatric symptoms along with the characterological features and deformations found in many adult survivors. A treatment model attending to the various elements of the diagnostic formulation was presented along with the rationale for a sequenced and titrated treatment. The treatment is specifically oriented toward self-management and the safe processing of emotionally overwhelming material in the context of a relationship that offers validation, safety, and consistency. It is also focused on the development of a sense of safety in relationship and an increased capacity to trust others.

REFERENCES

Albach, F., & Everaerd, W. (1992). Postraumatic stress symptoms in victims of childhood incest. *Journal of Psychotherapy and Psychosomatics, 57,* 143–151.

American Psychiatric Association. (1994). *Diagnostic and statistical manual of mental disorders* (4th ed.). Washington, DC: Author.

American Psychological Association. (1996a). *Final report of the working group on investigation of memories of childhood abuse.* Washington, DC: Author.

American Psychological Association. (1996b). *Violence and the family: Report of the American Psychological Association presidential task force on violence and the family.* Washington, DC: Author.

Armstrong, L. (1982). The cradle of sexual politics. In M. Kirkpatrick (Ed.), *Women's sexual experience: Explorations of a dark continent* (pp. 109–125). New York: Plenum Press.

Beitchman, J., Zucker, K., Hood, J., daCosta, G., & Ackman, D. (1991). A review of the short-term effects of childhood sexual abuse. *Child Abuse and Neglect, 15,* 537–556.

Beitchman, J., Zucker, K., Hood, J., daCosta, G., Ackman, D., & Cassavia, E. (1992). A review of the long-term effects of child sexual abuse. *Child Abuse and Neglect, 16,* 101–118.

Bernstein, E., & Putnam, F. (1986). Development, reliability, and validity of a dissociation scale. *Journal of Nervous and Mental Disease, 174,* 727–735.

Bernstein, E., & Putnam, F. (1993). An update on the dissociative experiences scale. *Dissociation, 6*(1), 16–28.

Briere, J. (1984, April). *The effects of childhood sexual abuse on later psychological functioning: Defining a post-sexual abuse syndrome.* Paper presented at the annual meeting of the American Psychological Association, Los Angeles.

Briere, J. (1989). *Therapy for adults molested as children.* New York: Springer.

Briere, J. (1995). *Trauma symptom inventory professional manual.* Odessa, FL: Psychological Assessment Resources.

Briere, J. (1996a). *Psychological assessment of posttraumatic states in adults.* Washington, DC: American Psychological Association.

Briere, J. (1996b). A self-trauma model for treating adult survivors of severe child abuse. In J. Briere, L. Berliner, J.A.Bulkley, C. Jenny, & T. Reid (Eds.), *The APSAC handbook on child maltreatment.* Thousand Oaks, CA: Sage.

Briere, J. (1996c). *Therapy for adults molested as children: Beyond survival* (2nd ed.). New York: Springer.

Briere, J., & Elliott, D.M. (1994). Immediate and long-term impacts of child sexual abuse: Special issue on the sexual abuse of children. *The Future of Children, 4*(2), 54–69.

Briere, J., & Runtz, M. (1993). Childhood sexual abuse: Long-term sequelae and implications for psychological assessment. *Journal of Interpersonal Violence, 8,* 312–330.

Brown, D., & Fromm, E. (1986). *Hypnotherapy and hypnoanalysis.* Hillsdale, NJ: Erlbaum.

Browne, A., & Finkelhor, D. (1986). Impact of child sexual abuse: A review of the research. *Psychological Bulletin, 99,* 66–77.

Carlson, E.B. (1997). *Trauma assessments: A clinician's guide.* New York: Guilford Press.

Carlson, E.B., Furby, L., Armstrong, J., & Shales, J. (1997). A conceptual framework for the long-term psychological effects of traumatic childhood abuse. *Child Maltreatment, 2,* 272–295.

Chu, J.A. (1988). Ten traps for therapists in the treatment of trauma survivors. *Dissociation, 1,* 24–32

Chu, J.A. (1992). The therapeutic roller coaster: Dilemmas in the treatment of childhood abuse survivors. *Journal of Psychotherapy Practice and Research, 4,* 351–370.

Chu, J.A. (1998). *Rebuilding shattered lives: The responsible treatment of complex posttraumatic and dissociative disorders.* New York: Wiley.

Chu, J.A., & Dill, D.L., (1990). Dissociative symptoms in relation to childhood physical and sexual abuse. *American Journal of Psychiatry, 147*(7), 887–892.

Cole, P., & Putnam, F. (1992). Effect of incest on self and social functioning: A developmental psychopathology perspective. *Journal of Consulting and Clinical Psychology, 60,* 174–184.

Cornell, W., & Olio, K. (1991). Integrating affect in treatment with adult survivors of physical and sexual abuse. *American Journal of Orthopsychiatry, 61,* 59–69.

Courtois, C.A. (1979). Characteristics of a volunteer sample of adult women who experienced incest in childhood and adolescence. *Dissertation Abstracts International, 40A,* 3194A.

Courtois, C.A. (1988). *Healing the incest wound: Adult survivors in therapy.* New York: Norton.

Courtois, C.A. (1991). Theory, sequencing, and strategy in treating adult survivors. In J. Briere (Ed.), *Treating victims of child sexual abuse* (pp. 47–60). Newbury Park, CA: Sage.

Courtois, C.A. (1992). The memory retrieval process in incest survivor therapy. *Journal of Child Sexual Abuse, 1*(1), 15–31.

Courtois, C.A. (1993). Adult survivors of sexual abuse. In B.A. Elliott, K.C. Halverson, & M. Hendricks-Matthews (Eds.), *Primary care clinics in office practice: Special issue on family violence and abusive relationships* (pp. 433–446). Philadelphia: Saunders.

Courtois, C.A. (1994). Treatment of incest and complex dissociative traumatic stress reactions. In L. Vandecreek, S. Knapp, & T.L. Jackson (Eds.), *Innovations in clinical practice: A source book* (Vol. 13, pp. 37–54). Sarasota, FL: Professional Resource Press.

Courtois, C.A. (1995). Assessment and diagnosis. In C. Classen (Vol. Ed.) & I.D. Yalom (Series Ed.), *Treating women molested in childhood: A volume in the Jossey-Bass library of current clinical technique* (pp. 1–34). San Francisco: Jossey-Bass.

Courtois, C.A. (1997). Healing the incest wound: A treatment update with attention to delayed memory issues. *American Journal of Psychotherapy, 51,* 464–496.

Courtois, C.A. (1999). *Recollections of sexual abuse: Treatment principles and guidelines.* New York: Norton.

Davies, J., & Frawley, M. (1994). *Treating the adult survivor of childhood sexual abuse: A psychoanalytic perspective.* New York: Basic Books.

Dolan, Y.M. (1991). *Resolving sexual abuse: Solution-focused therapy and Ericksonian hypnosis for adult survivors.* New York: Norton.

Finkelhor, D. (1990). Early and long-term effects of child sexual abuse: An update. *Professional Psychology: Research and Practice, 21*(5), 325–330.

Finkelhor, D. (1994). Current information on the scope and nature of child sexual abuse: Special issue on the sexual abuse of children. *The Future of Children, 4*(2), 31–53.

Finkelhor, D., & Browne, A. (1985). The traumatic impact of child sexual abuse: A conceptualization. *Journal of Orthopsychiatry, 55,* 530–541.

Ford, J.D., & Kidd, P. (1998). Early childhood trauma and disorders of extreme stress as predictors of treatment outcome with chronic posttraumatic stress disorder. *Journal of Traumatic Stress, 11*(4), 743–761.

Gelinas, D. (1983). The persisting negative effects of incest. *American Journal of Psychiatry, 46,* 313–332.

Gil, E. (1988). *Treatment of adult survivors of childhood abuse.* Walnut Creek, CA: Launch Press.

Golding, J.M., Cooper, M.L., & George, L.K. (1997). Sexual assault history and health perceptions: Seven general population studies. *Health Psychology, 16*(5), 417–425.

Green, A.H. (1993). Child sexual abuse: Immediate and long-term effects and intervention. *Journal of the American Academy of Child and Adolescent Psychiatry, 32,* 890–902.

Harris, M. (1998). *Trauma recovery and empowerment: A clinician's guide for working with women in groups.* New York: Free Press.

Herman, J.L. (1981). *Father-daughter incest.* Cambridge, MA: Harvard University Press.

Herman, J.L. (1992a). Complex PTSD: A syndrome in survivors of prolonged and repeated trauma. *Journal of Traumatic Stress Studies, 5,* 377–391.

Herman, J.L. (1992b). *Trauma and recovery.* New York: Basic Books.

Herman, J.L. (1993). Sequelae of prolonged and repeated trauma: Evidence for a complex posttraumatic syndrome (DESNOS). In J.R. Davidson & E.B. Foa (Eds.), *Posttraumatic stress disorder: DSM-IV and beyond* (pp. 213–228). Washington, DC: American Psychiatric Press.

Horevitz, P.P., & Braun, B.G. (1984). Are multiple personalities borderline? In B.G. Braun (Ed.), *Psychiatric Clinics of North America, 7,* 69–87.

Horowitz, M. (1986). *Stress response syndromes.* New York: Jason Aronson. (Original work published 1976)

Janoff-Bulman, R. (1992). *Shattered assumptions: Towards a new psychology of trauma.* New York: Free Press.

Jehu, D. (1988). *Beyond sexual abuse: Therapy with women who were childhood victims.* New York: Wiley.

Kendall-Tackett, K.A., Williams, L.M., & Finkelhor, D. (1993). Impact of sexual abuse on children: A review and synthesis of recent empirical studies. *Psychological Bulletin, 113,* 164–180.

Kepner, J.I. (1995). *Healing tasks: Psychotherapy with adult survivors of childhood abuse.* San Francisco: Jossey-Bass.

Kirschner, S., Kirschner, D.A., & Rappaport, R.L. (1993). *Working with adult incest survivors: The healing journey.* New York: Brunner/Mazel.

Kluft, R.P. (1985). *Childhood antecedents of multiple personality.* Washington, DC: American Psychiatric Press.

Kluft, R.P., & Fine, C. (Eds.). (1993). *Clinical perspectives on multiple personality disorder.* Washington, DC: American Psychiatric Press.

Kroll, J. (1993). *PSTD/borderlines in therapy: Finding the balance.* New York: Norton.

Linehan, M. (1993). *Cognitive-behavioral treatment of borderline personality disorder.* New York: Guilford Press.

Loewenstein, R.J. (Ed.). (1991). Special issue on multiple personality disorder. *Psychiatric Clinics of North America, 14.*

Loewenstein, R.J. (1993). Posttraumatic and dissociative aspects of transference and countertransference in the treatment of multiple personality disorder. In R. Kluft & C. Fine (Eds.), *Clinical perspectives on multiple personality disorder.* Washington, DC: American Psychiatric Press.

Maltz, W. (1991). *The sexual healing journey: A guide for survivors of sexual abuse.* New York: HarperCollins.

Maltz, W., & Holman, B. (1987). *Incest and sexuality: A guide to understanding and healing.* Lexington, MA: Lexington Books.

McCann, I.L., & Pearlman, L.A. (1990a). *Psychological trauma and the adult survivor.* New York: Brunner/Mazel.

McCann, I.L., & Pearlman, L.A. (1990b). Vicarious traumatization: A contextual model for understanding the effects of trauma on helpers. *Journal of Traumatic Stress, 3*(1), 131–149.

Meiselman, K.C. (1978). *Incest: A psychological study of causes and effects with treatment recommendations.* San Francisco: Jossey-Bass.

Meiselman, K.C. (1990). *Resolving the trauma of incest: Reintegration therapy with survivors.* San Francisco: Jossey-Bass.

Neumann, D.S., Houskamp, B.M., Pollock, V.E., & Briere, J. (1996). The long-term sequelae of childhood sexual abuse in women: A meta-analytic review. *Child Maltreatment, 1,* 6–17.

O'Hanlon, B., & Bertolino, B. (1998). *Even from a broken web: Brief, respectful solution-oriented therapy for sexual abuse and trauma.* New York: Wiley.

Pearlman, L.A., & Saakvitne, K.W. (1995). *Trauma and the therapist.* New York: Norton.

Pelcovitz, D., van der Kolk, B., Roth, S., Mandel, F.S., Kaplan, S., & Resick, P.A. (1997). Development of a criteria set and a structured interview for disorders of extreme stress (SIDES). *Journal of Traumatic Stress, 10,* 3–17.

Perlman, S.D. (1999). *The therapist's emotional survival: Dealing with the pain of exploring trauma.* Northvale, NJ: Jason Aronson.

Perry, B. (1993a). Neurodevelopment and the neurophysiology of trauma: I. Conceptual considerations for clinical work with maltreated children. *The Advisor, 6*(1), 14–18.

Perry, B. (1993b). Neurodevelopment and the neurophysiology of trauma: II. Clinical work along the alarm-fear-terror continuum. *The Advisor, 6*(2), 14–20.

Polusny, M.M., & Follette, V.M. (1995). Long-term effects of child sexual abuse: Theory and review of the empirical literature. *Applied and Preventive Psychology: Current Scientific Perspectives, 4*(3), 143–166.

Pribor, E.F., & Dinwiddie, S.H. (1992). Psychiatric correlates of incest in childhood. *American Journal of Psychiatry, 149,* 52–56.

Putnam, F.W. (1989). Diagnosis and treatment of multiple personality disorder. New York: Guilford Press.

Putnam, F.W. (1997). *Dissociation in children and adolescents: A developmental perspective.* New York: Guilford Press.

Quintana, S.M. (1993). Toward an expanded and updated conceptualization of termination: Implications for short-term, individual psychotherapy. *Professional Psychology: Research and Practice, 24,* 426–432.

Ross, C.A. (1989). *Multiple personality disorder: Diagnosis, clinical features, and treatment.* New York: Wiley.

Ross, C.A. (1997). *Dissociative identity disorder: Diagnosis, clinical features, and treatment of multiple personality.* New York: Wiley.

Roth, S., & Batson, R. (1997). *Naming the shadows: A new approach to individual and group psychotherapy for adult survivors of childhood incest.* New York: Free Press.

Russell, D.E.H. (1986). *The secret trauma: Incest in the lives of girls and women.* New York: Basic Books.

Sgroi, S.M. (1989). *Vulnerable populations* (Vol. 1). Lexington, MA: Lexington Books.

Sgroi, S.M., Blick, L.C., & Porter, F.S. (1982). A conceptual framework for child sexual abuse. In S.M. Sgroi (Ed.), *Handbook of clinical intervention in child sexual abuse* (pp. 9–39). Lexington, MA: Lexington Books.

Spiegel, D., Hunt, T., & Donershine, H.E. (1988). Dissociation and hypnotizability in post-traumatic stress disorder. *American Journal of Psychiatry, 145,* 301–305.

Spira, J.L. (Ed.). (1996). *Treating dissociative identity disorder.* San Francisco: Jossey-Bass.

Stamm, B.H. (1996). *Measurement of stress, trauma, and adaptation.* Lutherville, MD: Sidran Press.

Steinberg, M. (1993). *Structural clinical interviews for DSM-IV dissociative disorders (SCID-D).* Washington, DC: American Psychiatric Press.

Steinberg, M. (1995). *Handbook for the assessment of dissociation: A clinical guide.* Washington, DC: American Psychiatric Press.

Strick, F.L., & Wilcoxon, A. (1991). A comparison of dissociative experiences in adult female outpatients with and without histories of early incestuous abuse. *Dissociation, 4,* 193–199.

Summit, R. (1982). Beyond belief: The reluctant discovery of incest. In M. Kirkpatrick (Ed.), *Women's sexual experience: Explorations of the dark continent.* New York: Plenum Press.

Swett, C., & Halpert, M. (1993). Reported history of physical and sexual abuse in relation to dissociation and other symptomatology in women psychiatric inpatients. *Journal of Interpersonal Violence, 8,* 545–555.

van der Kolk, B.A., McFarlane, A.C., & Weisaeth, L. (Eds.). (1996). *Traumatic stress: The effects of overwhelming experience on mind, body, and society.* New York: Guilford Press.

van der Kolk, B.A., Roth, S., Pelcovitz, D., & Mandel, S. (1993). *Complex post-traumatic stress disorder: Results from the DSM-IV field trial for PTSD.* Washington, DC: American Psychiatric Press.

Waites, E.A. (1993). *Trauma and survival: Post-traumatic and dissociative disorders in women.* New York: Norton.

Walker, L.E.A. (1994). *Abused women and survivor therapy: A practical guide for the psychotherapist.* Washington, DC: American Psychological Association Press.

Wang, S., Wilson, J.P., & Mason, J.W. (1996). Stages of decompensation in combat-related posttraumatic stress disorder: A new conceptual model. *Integrative Physiological and Behavioral Science, 31,* 237–253.

Westerlund, E. (1992), *Women's sexuality after childhood incest.* New York: Norton.

Wilson, J.P., & Keane, T.M. (1996). *Assessing psychological trauma and PTSD.* New York: Guilford Press.

Wilson, J.P., & Lindy, J.D. (Eds.). (1994). *Countertransference in the treatment of PSTD.* New York: Guilford Press.

Wyatt, G.E., Newcomb, M.D., & Riederle, M.H. (1993). *Sexual abuse and consensual sex: Women's developmental patterns and outcomes.* Newbury Park, CA: Sage.

Yehuda, R. (Ed.). (1998). *Psychological trauma: Section of American Psychiatric Press review of psychiatry* (Vol. 17). Washington, DC: American Psychiatric Press.

Yehuda, R., & McFarlane, A.C. (1995). Conflict between current knowledge about posttraumatic stress disorder and its original conceptual basis. *American Journal of Psychiatry, 152,* 1705–1713.

Zlotnick, C., Zakriski, A.L., Shea, M.T., Costello, E., Begin, A., Pearlstein, T., & Simpson, E. (1996). The long-term sequelae of sexual abuse: Support for a complex posttraumatic stress disorder. *Journal of Traumatic Stress, 9,* 195–205.

CHAPTER 16

Rape and Sexual Aggression

KAREN S. CALHOUN and AMY E. WILSON

T HE PAST TWO decades have seen an increasing awareness of rape as a major social problem. Research has documented its effects on victims and delineated many of the societal, individual, and situational factors involved. Services have greatly improved for victims, the legal system has become more sensitive, and prevention programs are growing. In spite of all this, there is no evidence that rates of rape are decreasing as rapidly as rates for other violent crimes. We live in a society with a high tolerance for violence of many kinds. Rape is the most underreported violent crime, and controversy has surrounded how prevalence rates are determined and what constitutes sexual assault. In this chapter, we give a brief overview of the literature as it relates to both the victims and the perpetrators of adult sexual assault.

Although there is some variation from state to state in the legal definition of rape, generally rape may be defined as nonconsensual vaginal, anal, or oral penetration, obtained by force, by threat of injury or bodily harm, or when the victim is incapable of giving consent (e.g., due to impairment by drugs or other intoxicants) (Koss, 1992, 1993a; Searles & Berger; 1987). This definition encompasses stranger rape, acquaintance rape, marital rape, rape of males, and homosexual rape. However, it does not include forms of sexual assault not involving penetration such as attempted rape, forced sex play, or nonconsensual fondling. Furthermore, this definition does not address the problem of sexual coercion, which occurs at an alarming rate across college campuses (Finley & Corty, 1993; Koss, Gidycz, & Wisniewski, 1987). Thus, it is important to consider forms of sexual aggression that may not meet legal definitions of rape, as these too have serious negative social and psychological consequences for victims, as well as for the community at large. The term "sexual aggression" is used in a general way here to encompass rape as well as forms of sexual trespass that involve less force or do not involve actual penetration. "Sexual coercion" is used to describe methods of aggressing that are not necessarily as violent or forceful. In the literature, these terms are not clearly differentiated and often are used interchangeably.

Although legal definitions may appear straightforward, difficulties arise when interpreting criteria such as force and consent. This is especially true in cases of acquaintance rape, in which the victim has had some previous relationship with the offender and therefore may be perceived as having consented to some degree. Similarly, force is often questioned in cases not involving a weapon, such as when the perpetrator uses the weight of his body to restrain the victim, or twists her arm or holds her down during the assault (Harney & Muehlenhard, 1991). Again, these less overt forms of aggression are more likely to occur in acquaintance assaults (Koss, Dinero, Seibel, & Cox, 1988).

Much recent research has focused on the phenomenon of date rape, as prevalence studies have suggested that 78% to 89% of all rapes are perpetrated by an acquaintance (Koss et al., 1987; Russell, 1984). Contrary to popular belief, victims of date rape are as traumatized, or more traumatized, than victims of stranger rape (Koss et al., 1988). Like victims of stranger assault, date rape victims often suffer severe long-term consequences affecting their physical and psychological health. They often feel less safe, less confidant, less trustful, more powerless, and more wary of intimacy than before the assault. Additionally, they are less likely than stranger assault victims to label their experience as rape, and very rarely report the incident to the police or seek treatment, with some estimates as low as 5% (e.g., Koss, 1988). Yet, what most clearly distinguishes victims of acquaintance rape from other sexual assault victims is their increased tendency toward self-blame, as well as specific difficulties with feelings of trust and interpersonal safety as a result of their prior relationship with the perpetrator. Furthermore, it is not only the individual circumstances of acquaintance rape that make this assault so difficult for victims, but also the social context in which it occurs. Whereas other types of victims may experience an increase in social support following an assault, victims of acquaintance rape are often blamed for the assault due to their prior involvement with the perpetrator (Gidycz & Koss, 1991).

Sexual assault that takes place within marriage is perhaps the most widely ignored problem of all, with most states not even acknowledging it as a legal possibility until the mid-1980s (Monson & Langhinrichsen-Rohling, 1998). Women were presumed to give consent when they signed a marriage license and lost their right to say no in the eyes of the law. Marital rape has largely been ignored by researchers until recently, so empirical data are sketchy. Yet, it is clear that the problem is not an uncommon one. Surveys indicate that 10% to 14% of married women have been raped by their husbands (Kilpatrick, Best, Saunders, & Veronen, 1988; Russell, 1990). Although research is limited, marital rape appears to be most commonly perpetrated by men who also physically batter. The incidence of rape reported by battered women in shelters ranges from 33% to 59% (Monson & Langhinrichsen-Rohling, 1998), whereas community samples of women in nonbattering relationships show an incidence of 10% or less (e.g., Finkelhor & Yllo, 1985). Research on women in shelters indicates that the more frequent and severe the nonsexual violence, the greater the occurrence of marital rape (Bowker, 1983; Frieze, 1983). A limitation of research in this area is that the vast majority of studies rely on wives' reports of their husbands' behavior, and few have studied the husbands themselves. In addition, the correlates of sexual aggression in marriage are largely relatively unexplored at this point, so caution should be used in generalizing from other sexual aggression situations and populations.

PREVALENCE

Much research has addressed the topic of rape prevalence, noting the limitations of federal incidence data, the great disparity in findings across studies, and the plethora of methodological problems (Harney & Muehlenhard, 1991; Koss, 1992, 1993a, 1993b). Such problems previously resulted in vast underreporting and underdetection of rape; more recent studies have employed more sensitive measures of sexual assault, resulting in more accurate prevalence rates across many populations of women. For example, the landmark study conducted by Koss et al. (1987) emerged from the premise that, given the hesitancy of sexual assault victims to report their experiences, as well as the inadequacies of measurement methods, national crime statistics fail to accurately reflect the scope of rape. Therefore, Koss et al. administered the Sexual Experience Survey (SES) to a national sample of college women and men. Unlike other instruments, the SES asks about a range of coercive sexual experiences in behavioral terms, never requiring victims and perpetrators to label their experiences/behaviors as rape. Results of this study revealed the high prevalence of sexually coercive interactions among college students. The convergent validity of the SES with individual clinical interview data was also established in this study.

Koss et al. (1987) surveyed 6,159 students on 32 college campuses nationwide and found that 54% of women reported experiencing some form of sexual victimization. Whereas 12.1% had experienced attempted rape, 15.4% reported experiences that met the legal definition of rape. Among college men, 25% acknowledged involvement in some form of sexual aggression, 3.3% admitted to attempted rape, and 4.5% admitted to rape. Similarly, Finley and Corty (1993) found that approximately 30% of college women have experienced nonconsensual sex obtained through force, threat of force, or verbal coercion, whereas approximately 15% to 25% of college males admit to obtaining sexual intercourse through the use of force, threat of force, or verbal coercion. The authors conclude that by the time female students are beyond their first year, approximately 1 in 3 will experience nonconsensual sexual penetration or psychologically pressured intercourse.

In a national telephone survey of adult women conducted by the National Victim Center (Kilpatrick, Edmunds, & Seymour, 1992), 14% of respondents reported experiences that met the legal definition of completed rape. However, given that this study did not include women under 18, women with no phone service (e.g., living in homeless shelters), women in the military, or women living in college residences, this figure may be conservative (Koss, 1993b). Future prevalence studies should address these limitations; as Koss (1993a) suggests, "the burden of sexual violence in people's lives has yet to be adequately captured" (p. 218).

RISK FACTORS

In an attempt to further our understanding of rape and sexual assault, recent research has attempted to identify risk factors for sexual assault. Situational factors, victim characteristics, perpetrator characteristics, and numerous other variables have been examined in terms of their association with greater risk of victimization. Although several factors have been clearly and consistently identified, research in this area has failed to yield a well-specified model by which future victimization can be predicted.

One of the most consistent factors associated with the risk of sexual assault is the consumption of alcohol (Abbey, 1991; Abbey, Ross, McDuffie, & McAuslan, 1996; Koss & Dinero, 1989; Muehlenhard & Linton, 1987). For example, Kanin (1984) interviewed 71 self-disclosed date rapists and found that two-thirds reported drinking excessively prior to the assault. Similarly, in a national college sample, Koss (1988) found that 74% of perpetrators and 55% of victims reported that they had been drinking prior to the assault. It has been hypothesized that alcohol may disinhibit perpetrators and increase aggression, alter men's perceptions of nonconsent/resistance cues, impair the victim's ability to perceive cues of danger, and impair the victim's ability to fight off an attack from her assaulter (Abbey et al., 1996; Koss & Dinero, 1989; Richardson & Hammock, 1991). Yet, there is still much debate regarding the specific role that alcohol plays in sexually coercive interactions. Although both victims and perpetrators report greater general consumption of alcohol than their peers (Kanin, 1984; Koss & Dinero, 1989), and much research has focused on alcohol as a risk factor for sexual assault (Abbey, 1991; Abbey et al., 1996; Muehlenhard & Linton, 1987), alcohol as a means of coercion has received little attention. Most recently, Kosson, Kelly, and White (1997) found that among their large sample of college men, 21% reported using alcohol and/or drugs as a means of coercion to impair their victims. This is consistent with research suggesting that men often hold high expectancies for alcohol to increase sexual arousal and heighten interest in violent/deviant stimuli (Roehrich & Kinder, 1991). Given this conjoint propensity to consume greater amounts of alcohol and hold higher expectancies for sexual risk taking and disinhibition, it follows that sexual situations involving these individuals may have a higher probability of resulting in coercive interactions.

Studies examining victim characteristics (i.e., personal history, behavior, attitudes) have been inconclusive in determining risk factors for sexual assault. Although it was previously thought that attitudinal variables such as rape myth acceptance and gender-role conformity were associated with victimization, Koss and Dinero (1989) found that these factors failed to discriminate rape victims from nonvictims in a national sample of female college students. In fact, the authors found that, among a selection of numerous psychological, situational, and "vulnerability-creating" variables, only previous sexual trauma was a significant predictor of adolescent/adult victimization. That is, the study failed to yield a model that would accurately differentiate the majority of sexual assault victims from nonvictims. Similarly, in a longitudinal study, Himelein (1995) investigated variables including previous abuse and victimization, prior consensual sexual experience, alcohol use, assertiveness, sexual beliefs and attitudes, and rape myth acceptance. Himelein found that previous victimization, alcohol use, and sexual conservatism correlated significantly with college victimization. However, among these variables, the best predictor of sexual victimization in college dating was precollege sexual victimization in dating. But, although history of victimization appears to be a consistent predictor of sexual victimization, the mechanism by which this potentiates future risk is unknown.

CONSEQUENCES OF RAPE FOR THE VICTIM

The effects of rape on the victim are numerous and diverse. Immediate reactions may include numbness and disorientation, denial, disbelief, loneliness, and feelings of vulnerability and helplessness. Somatic symptoms such as headaches, dizziness, fatigue, and sleep disturbance may also ensue. These initial symptoms may be followed by emotional lability, emotional numbing, anger, intense fear, and persistent feelings of shame and guilt. Longer-term consequences of sexual assault may include depression, fear and anxiety, low self-esteem, and sexual dysfunction (see Resick, 1993). Symptoms of posttraumatic stress disorder (PTSD) such as nightmares, intrusive thoughts of the event, hyperarousal, irritability, emotional distancing from others, and avoidance may also emerge. Victims have also reported social adjustment difficulties, relationship dysfunction, and a sense that the world is no longer a safe and trustworthy place for them. Deleterious effects on physical health have been documented as well (Kimerling & Calhoun, 1994; Koss, Woodruff, & Koss, 1991), even after controlling for rape-related injuries and diseases. These include a wide range of health problems, some of which appear to be tension-related and some that may be related to immune suppression. Self-ratings of health as well as medical utilization rates and cost of medical care all indicate poorer outcomes for victims than for matched controls. Other health risks to the victim include pregnancy and infection with sexually transmitted diseases. HIV infection is a largely ignored but very real risk for victims. Those women least able to protect themselves are the most vulnerable. Kimerling, Armistead, and Forehand (1999) compared a group of low-income inner-city African American women who were HIV-infected with a demographically matched comparison group who were not infected. Prevalence rates for all types of criminal victimization were significantly higher in the HIV-infected group. Rates of crime in the noninfected group were close to general averages for urban-dwelling women. Rape victims (31% of the infected sample) were over three times as likely to be infected with HIV.

Difficulties in sexual functioning are also common among sexual assault survivors (Becker, Skinner, Abel, & Cichon, 1986). The type of sexual problems experienced vary a great deal, and clear data regarding rape victims are difficult to extract given that some studies include child sexual abuse survivors in their samples. Issues related to trust, intimacy, and emotional numbing may play a role in the development of sexual dysfunctions following assault. When assessing sexual dysfunction among sexual assault survivors, the woman's ability to achieve orgasm should not be used as the sole criterion for sexual adjustment, as many victims report long-term loss of sexual satisfaction despite being orgasmic (Feldman-Summers, Gordon, & Megher, 1979). Victims with PTSD may be especially at risk for sexual dysfunction (Letourneau, Resnick, Kilpatrick, Saunders, & Best, 1996). Because engaging in sex can trigger flashbacks in some victims and cause them to reexperience the loss of control of their bodies that they experienced during the attack, partners must be very patient and allow the woman to control the pace of sexual activity in the aftermath of an assault. The full range of sexual dysfunctions has been reported by rape victims, with many reporting more than one type of dysfunction. The fact that some victims avoid sex altogether for long periods increases the difficulty of getting accurate data in this area. Those reporting good sexual adjustment prior to the assault and/or a supportive partner following the assault seem to recover most quickly in this area of functioning. Becker (1989) has outlined a treatment approach especially designed for sexual assault and abuse survivors that aims to help them regain a sense of control over their sexuality; it includes education about assault/abuse effects, a special focus on body image issues, and many more traditional elements of sex therapy.

Several preassault and contextual variables have been found to be associated with victims' reactions to rape. For example, Resick's (1993) review of the literature suggests that prior psychological functioning and previous life stressors (such as prior victimization) may be related to recovery from sexual trauma. Research examining contextual variables specific to the assault such as relationship to the perpetrator, degree of force, and use of a weapon has been inconsistent, suggesting that these factors may not be related to severity of reaction. However, Kilpatrick et al. (1987) found that a victim's cognitive appraisal of life threat at the time of the assault predicted the later development of PTSD. Similarly, recent findings strongly suggest that individuals who perceive overwhelming threat during a traumatic event and "dissociate" are more likely to develop PTSD than those who do not (e.g., van der Kolk, van der Hart, & Marmar, 1996).

Postassault variables such as immediate postassault functioning and social support have also been found to play an important role in the impact of rape (Resick, 1993). For example, Rothbaum, Foa, Riggs, Murdock, and Walsh (1992) found that psychological functioning at two weeks postassault was predictive of later functioning. Resick has suggested that social support following sexual assault may play an important role in victim recovery, possibly serving to mediate the severity of postassault reactions. However, more research is needed to fully understand the complex process of surviving and adjusting to rape-related trauma.

Rape-Related PTSD

Among the most prevalent reactions to sexual assault is the development of PTSD. In fact, rape trauma produces higher rates of PTSD than other life-threatening events, including aggravated assault and natural disasters (Resick, 1993). PTSD is an anxiety disorder involving symptoms such as hyperarousal, intrusive memories, emotional numbing, nightmares, increased startle response, hypervigilance, and avoidance of situations that remind the individual of the traumatic event. Approximately 31% of all rape victims develop PTSD during their lifetime, resulting in an estimated 3.8 million adult women in the United States with rape-related PTSD (1992). In addition, several studies have suggested that fear and anxiety-related arousal persist long after other PTSD symptoms have remitted (e.g., Calhoun, Atkeson, & Resick, 1982), even in the absence of PTSD (Rothbaum et al., 1992).

Rothbaum et al. (1992) investigated the course of PTSD and related symptoms experienced by rape victims following assault. Female rape victims were assessed approximately 12 days after their assault and were then assessed weekly for 12 weeks. Results showed that PTSD symptoms were present in the majority of victims immediately following the assault, then decreased sharply throughout the first month. At the time of the initial assessment, approximately 94% of victims met symptom criteria. Five weeks after the assault, only 65% met criteria for PTSD. Following this period was a more gradual decline in symptomology for the next two months, such that by 13 weeks postassault, only 47% continued to meet criteria. However, for those women who developed persistent PTSD, symptoms decreased only slightly during the first month, after which they stabilized and remained severe. Rothbaum et al. concluded that persistent PTSD can be identified in victims within the first two weeks following assault.

Many theories have been proposed in an attempt to explain the development of PTSD following an assault. For example, behavioral theories have suggested that classical conditioning and operant avoidance account for the persistence of PTSD symptoms. Although this may account for fear and avoidance following trauma, many have argued that behavioral theories alone fail to account for the broad range of PTSD symptoms and ignore important cognitive factors. In an attempt to develop a more comprehensive model that incorporates cognitive factors into a theory of PTSD development, Foa and Kozak (1986) proposed a cognitive-behavioral (information processing) model of PTSD that takes into consideration the importance of "meaning" assigned to the experience by victims. In this theoretical framework, victims of assault develop a "fear structure," or network in memory that includes information about (1) the feared stimulus situation, (2) the verbal, behavioral, and physiological responses to the situation, and (3) "interpretive information about the meaning of the stimulus and response elements of the structure" (Foa, Steketee, & Rothbaum, 1989, p. 166). Foa et al. argue that when events violate "formerly held basic concepts of safety," this fear structure is likely to develop, resulting in PTSD. Foa et al.'s theory is also consistent with findings that perceived threat at the time of the assault may be more predictive of PTSD than actual threat (Kilpatrick et al., 1987).

REVICTIMIZATION

Another consequence of sexual assault that has only recently begun to be recognized and empirically examined is the phenomenon of revictimization. Recent research strongly suggests that once a woman has been victimized in childhood or adolescence, she enters a "vicious cycle" whereby her risk of future victimization greatly increases (Fromuth, 1986; Gidycz, Coble, Latham, & Layman, 1993; Gidycz, Hanson, & Layman, 1995; Himelein, 1995; Koss & Dinero, 1989; Mandoki & Burkhart, 1989). For example, in a prospective study of prior assault and adult revictimization, Gidycz et al. (1993) obtained subjects' histories of child and adolescent sexual assault, then assessed subjects nine weeks later for sexual assault experiences occurring during that time period. Gidycz et al. found that women with a history of adolescent rape or attempted rape were almost twice as likely to experience a sexual assault during the nine-week period. Extending these findings, Gidycz et al. (1995) followed subjects over a nine-month period and found that a woman's chances of being victimized during a given quarter were related to victimization in the preceding quarter. That is,

> women who were victimized during their initial quarter of participation were approximately three times as likely as those not victimized during that time to be revictimized during their second quarter of participation. Furthermore, among the small subset of women [N=59] for whom 9-month follow-up data were available, those victimized during their second quarter of participation were approximately 20 times as likely as those not victimized during that time to be revictimized during their third quarter of participation. (p. 24)

Given these striking results, Gidycz et al. (1995) concluded that a strong yet perplexing link exists among sexual victimization experiences. This is consistent with other studies (e.g., Himelein, 1995; Koss & Dinero, 1989) suggesting that previous sexual trauma is a significant predictor of adolescent/adult victimization.

However, the mechanism by which sexual victimization may potentiate future risk is unclear. It has been hypothesized that poor recognition of risk for potential danger may mediate the relationship between subsequent victimization experiences, given that a woman's responses in a potentially threatening situation are contingent on her ability to perceive and respond to threat cues (Meadows, Jaycox, Orsillo, & Foa, 1997; Meadows, Jaycox, Webb, & Foa, 1996; Wilson, Calhoun, & Bernat, in press). This factor may be especially relevant to victims of acquaintance sexual assault, given that the social context of the assault and relationship with the perpetrator play key roles in the woman's ability to respond to potential threat (Norris, Nurius, & Dimeff, 1996). Wilson, Calhoun, and Bernat (in press) employed experimental analogue methodology to investigate the impact of victimization on judgments of when a man's sexual advances are placing a woman at risk for sexual assault. They found that women with a history of multiple victimization experiences exhibited poorer risk recognition than either single-incident victims or nonvictims. Furthermore, women who scored low on PTSD arousal symptoms took significantly longer to recognize that the woman in the scenario was in danger of sexual assault than nonvictims or victims with higher levels of PTSD arousal symptoms. Although further research in this area is needed, these initial findings suggest that PTSD-related symptoms may serve a buffering effect, increasing sensitivity to threat cues that portend a sexually coercive interaction.

Studies of psychological functioning as a potential mediator of the relationship between prior victimization and future risk have resulted in inconsistent findings. Several studies have found higher levels of adjustment problems among revictimized women. For example, Atkeson, Ellis, and Calhoun (1982) found that multiple-incident victims exhibited poorer interpersonal and psychological adjustment than single-incident victims. Zeitlin, McNally, and Cassiday (1993) found that retraumatized women had greater difficulty identifying and describing their feelings, exhibited a paucity of fantasy life, and demonstrated a tendency toward speech and thought closely tied to external events. Gidycz et al. (1993) found that women with a history of child or adolescent sexual victimization exhibited poorer adjustment prior to their most recent adult sexual assault than did adult victims with no such history.

Other studies have failed to support these findings. Gidycz et al. (1995) failed to find adjustment a significant predictor of subsequent victimization. Marhoefer-Dvorak, Resick, Hutter, and Girelle (1988) found no differences between single- and multiple-incident victims on any of several standardized measures of psychological functioning. Sorenson, Siegel, Golding, and Stein (1991) found that multiple-rape victims from a community sample were not more likely to be more psychologically maladjusted than single-incident victims. Such studies support a conclusion that personal characteristics of women initially victimized are not risk factors for subsequent assault.

Several studies in related areas have also proposed factors that may be related to risk of future victimization. For example, Roth, Wayland, and Woolsey (1990) found that women reporting multiple victimization experiences exhibited a greater use of denial. By denying the traumatic event and its impact, victims may fail to adequately process the experience and thus demonstrate maladaptive behaviors that place them at greater risk for future assault. This is consistent with results of a study by Layman, Gidycz, and Lynn (1996) that suggest that sexual assault victims who "acknowledge" their experience as rape exhibit more PTSD symptoms than those who do not so label their experiences. Additional findings that "unacknowledged" rape victims were more likely to have another sexual encounter with the perpetrator following the assault led the authors to conclude that failure to label the assault experience as rape may perpetuate the cycle of victimization.

The relationship between sexual assault and feelings of powerlessness has been addressed repeatedly in the literature. For example, in their conceptualization of the impact of child sexual abuse, Finkelhor and Browne (1985) addressed the way victims of repeated abuse come to feel "powerless to thwart others who are trying to manipulate them or do them harm" (p. 536). That is, following repeated victimization, a person's sense of self-efficacy and coping responses may become impaired, thereby perpetuating the risk of revictimization. Consistent with this framework, Norris et al. (1996) found that previously victimized women reported believing in a greater likelihood of experiencing a future assault, as well as a lower probability of successfully resisting an assault. At the same time, these same women reported engaging in a greater number of risk-related behaviors than nonvictims. Further research is necessary to more clearly identify factors that may predict future risk.

CLINICAL IMPLICATIONS:
TREATMENT OF RAPE VICTIMS

Given the prevalence of rape, its psychological impact on the victim, and the high percentage of women who develop PTSD following an assault, the identification of effective treatments for victims of sexual assault is of utmost importance. Much of the recent treatment outcome research involving rape-related trauma has targeted treatment of rape-related PTSD (Foa, Hearst-Ikeda, & Perry, 1995; Foa & Rothbaum, 1998). However, clinicians working with this population must also be prepared to address additional issues such as depression, sexual dysfunction, low self-esteem, somatic symptoms, and the intense feelings of shame and guilt that often follow an assault experience. Yet, given that PTSD symptoms are the most common among this population, most treatments are aimed at reducing posttraumatic symptoms such as anxiety, hyperarousal, and avoidance.

Available treatments for rape victims include crisis intervention, hypnotherapy, psychodynamic treatments, and cognitive-behavioral treatments (Foa & Meadows, 1997). However, the majority of empirical studies have examined the efficacy of cognitive-behavioral interventions, and thus they have received the most empirical support. Among these interventions are exposure-based treatments, cognitive restructuring, anxiety management, and multicomponent interventions that combine various aspects of these treatments (Foa & Meadows, 1997).

Foa et al. (1995) have proposed that a brief cognitive-behavioral intervention shortly following sexual assault can accelerate the rate of improvement of PTSD-related symptoms among victims. The treatment consists of four two-hour sessions involving psychoeducational training, relaxation training, imaginal exposure, in vivo exposure, and cognitive restructuring. Although results indicated significant differences in the treatment and control groups at two months postassault, rates of PTSD at five months postassault were too low in both groups to evaluate accurately. However, this study is the first of its kind to report success in the prevention of persistent PTSD following assault and thus represents an important contribution to the literature.

Much research has examined the efficacy of exposure-based treatments such as systematic desensitization, imaginal exposure, in vivo exposure, and flooding. Among the most successful of these in the treatment of rape victims has been imaginal exposure. Exposure treatments are based on the premise that a victim's "fear structure" must be dismantled through activation of the fear memory combined with the inclusion of new information that is incompatible with the current fear structure. The result is the formation of a new memory, which facilitates reduction in PTSD symptoms (Foa, Rothbaum, & Steketee, 1993; Foa et al., 1989). Foa, Rothbaum, Riggs, and Murdoch (1991) developed an exposure treatment protocol consisting of nine biweekly 90-minute sessions. The first two sessions involved information gathering and treatment rationale, followed by seven sessions of imaginal exposure. Clients were encouraged to describe the rape experience in detail. The narrative was repeated several times during each session to facilitate habituation. Additionally, sessions were tape-recorded and clients were instructed to listen to the tape once each day. At the end of the treatment, clients were educated about ways that their avoidance of feared situations may maintain and increase their PTSD symptoms.

Stress inoculation training (SIT) is another cognitive-behavioral treatment that has received much attention in the literature. SIT is a multicomponent treatment that was developed to teach victims coping skills for managing their fear and anxiety following an assault (Kilpatrick, Veronen, & Resick, 1982). It includes elements such as psychoeducational training, deep muscle relaxation, breathing control exercises, covert modeling, communication skills via role play, thought-stopping techniques, and guided self-dialogue, with homework supplementing in-session exercises (Foa et al., 1993).

Cognitive processing therapy (CPT) is a multicomponent treatment based on cognitive models of information processing (Foa & Rothbaum, 1998). CPT was developed by Resick and Schnicke (1992) for use with rape victims, and combines elements of exposure with cognitive restructuring. The goal of CPT is to change emotional reactions to feared situations through exposure to the situation while actively confronting cognitive distortions and maladaptive beliefs. Exposure in CPT involves having clients write about the event in detail (including sensory memories, feelings, and thoughts), then read it aloud. Cognitive re-structuring focuses specifically on the rape-relevant themes of safety, power, trust, esteem, and intimacy. Studies comparing CPT to no-treatment controls have suggested that CPT may be an effective treatment for PTSD in rape vic-tims (Foa & Rothbaum, 1998; Resick & Schnicke, 1992). However, further re-search must be conducted before the efficacy of CPT can be established (Foa & Rothbaum, 1998).

Comparisons of the various cognitive-behavioral treatments for rape victims suggest that, although several of the interventions appear to be effective at post-treatment, they may differ in terms of the longevity of their effects, their ease of implementation, and their generalizability to various groups. For example, Foa et al. (1993) reviewed the treatment literature on rape-related PTSD, focusing primarily on the comparative efficacy of cognitive-behavioral treatments includ-ing exposure, cognitive therapy, and SIT. Although research has indicated the ef-fectiveness of both SIT and exposure, the authors argue that exposure appears to have the most potent long-term effects. For example, in a study comparing expo-sure, SIT, supportive counseling, and a no-treatment control, exposure was found to be the most effective treatment at 3.5-month follow-up (Foa et al., 1991). However, the authors note that further research is necessary to identify factors that may impact treatment outcome, such as demographic variables, circumstan-tial variables related to the assault, and postassault functioning. In a more recent review, Foa and Rothbaum (1998) argue that there is no evidence to date that combined treatments are more effective than individual protocols. Therefore, the authors recommend exposure treatment over other cognitive-behavioral treatments because of its strong and consistent empirical support, its ease of im-plementation, and its relative simplicity (as compared to more intellectually de-manding multicomponent treatments).

MALE PERPETRATORS

Male sexual aggression against women has not been well understood until re-cently, when research began to address a broader range of populations than in-carcerated sex offenders, and to examine multiple, interactive factors. Studies have documented the widespread nature of the problem as well as the level of tolerance it receives in our society. Samples of college men have been studied extensively and a few community samples have been studied. The areas re-searched include motivations, sexual arousal, cognitions, affect, personality, and developmental trajectories. Results have documented the complex, multi-determined nature of sexual aggression and led to the proposal of several the-oretical models that attempt to integrate this knowledge.

The prevalence of sexually aggressive men on college campuses was well documented by Koss et al. (1987) in a multicampus study of over 6,000 stu-dents. In that study, 8.9% of the college men sampled admitted to acts that met legal definitions of rape and attempted rape, although they did not acknowl-edge their behavior as rape. Only 1 of 131 completed rape perpetrators labeled the act as rape. By contrast, 84% indicated that their behavior definitely was not rape. They typically attributed more responsibility to the woman than to themselves. Most of these men (85%) knew their victims, and 61% said their victims were dates, consistent with other research indicating that most sexual aggressors (approximately two-thirds) are acquainted with their victims. Although the mean age of the sample was only 21, these men had committed an average of 2.29 rape incidents since the age of 14, thus confirming results from studies of incarcerated offenders that rape is indeed a recidivist crime. The rape perpetrators differed from nonrapists in the sample in a number of ways. For example, they scored higher on the MMPI Psychopathic Deviancy Scale, held more rape-supportive beliefs, drank more, read more pornography, were more sexually experienced, became sexually active at an earlier age, were more hostile toward women, and reported having friends who seemed to view women as sex objects. A startling finding was that the primary emotion these men reported having following the incident was pride. This is in stark contrast to the primary emotions reported by female victims in the same study, which were fear, anger and depression.

Each of the characteristics Koss et al. (1987) described has been well documented in other studies of college men and in incarcerated rapists. Perhaps the most studied set of variables is these groups' attitudes about sex and about relationships with women. Rape myth acceptance (Burt, 1980), the endorsement of false beliefs such as that "women enjoy rape" and that women are often to blame for their own rape, has been demonstrated in study after study comparing sexually aggressive men with their nonaggressive peers. Aggressives also endorse adversarial beliefs about relationships between the sexes, seeing them as inherently exploitative, and view the use of force and coercion as acceptable in intimate relationships (Burt, 1980). Hostility toward women has also been well documented among college and community samples as well as prison samples (e.g., Malamuth & Check, 1983). Muehlenhard and Falcon (1990) found a sexual dominance factor to contribute significantly to the prediction of sexual aggression. Other researchers have focused on beliefs and values regarding masculinity. The attitude being masculine means being aggressive, competitive, and tough has been labeled "hypermasculinity" by Mosher and Sirkin (1984), who developed a scale to measure these beliefs. The scale has three subscales: calloused sexual beliefs, violence as manly, and danger as exciting. The calloused sexual beliefs subscale has most consistently been associated with use of force in sexual encounters (e.g., Mosher & Anderson, 1986). Bernat, Wilson, and Calhoun (1999) found that sexually coercive college men high in calloused sexual beliefs showed significantly more willingness than those low on this scale to allow an audiotaped date rape depiction to continue when instructed to indicate when the man in the tape should stop. Bernat, Calhoun, and Adams (in press) supported this finding and also found that the physiological sexual arousal of self-identified sexually aggressive men who were high on calloused sexual beliefs was not inhibited by cues of force and resistance, as it was in men who were noncoercive and in men with a history of sexual coercion but who were low in calloused sexual beliefs. Although Mosher and Anderson (1986) did not find that the hypermasculinity subscales predicted sexual arousal, they did predict self-reported use of force as well as lower levels of disgust and other negative reactions to an audiotaped rape scenario. Studies such as these provide strong evidence that attitudes and beliefs are correlated with sexual aggression and need to be targets of intervention.

A lack of empathy for victims is commonly observed in sexually aggressive men (e.g., Scully & Marolla, 1984). Malamuth (1984) cited lack of empathy as one of the factors mediating sexual aggression. Marshall, Hudson, and Jones (1995) suggested that calloused sexual beliefs represent a set of cognitive and affectively mediated responses that reflect a lack of empathy for victims. Most intervention programs for sex offenders include a heavy emphasis on empathy training because offenders commonly fail to recognize the harm done by their behavior. Empathy is known to have a negative relationship to general aggression as measured by questionnaires, and some studies support the assumption that empathy has an inhibitory effect on aggression (Miller & Eisenberg, 1988). However, this relationship is impacted by situational factors and affective states in complex ways. In addition, the concept of empathy is multidimensional, encompassing the ability to take another's viewpoint as well as to experience vicariously another person's emotions (Davis, 1983). The ability to take another's perspective in the absence of other aspects of empathy may allow some sexually aggressive men to use their ability to anticipate feelings and reactions in attempts to more effectively manipulate people and situations. More research into the role of empathy is warranted.

Social skills and social interaction styles of rapists and sexually aggressive men have received limited study. One of the early hypotheses concerning incarcerated rapists was that social skills deficits limited their ability to attract consenting partners and social skills training (Becker, Abel, Blanchard, Murphy, & Coleman, 1978). However, support for this hypothesis has been mixed at best with incarcerated rapists, and few social skills deficits have been identified among college samples. In fact, in certain ways, college men may have a skills advantage, as in the example of perspective taking. Kelley (1989) had college men interact with trained female confederates in situations requiring them to attempt to persuade an unwilling woman to do them a favor. The sexually coercive men were significantly more persistent in their efforts at persuasion and used a wider variety of persuasion tactics, trying different approaches rather than taking no for an answer. In short, they were more manipulative than men with no history of sexually coercive behavior. The sexually coercive men were rated by confederates as more appropriate in their use of nonverbal cues such as eye contact and facial expression, but less appropriate in their tendency to appear overly dramatic.

Interest in a finer-grained analysis of rapists' social skills has been stimulated by observations that date rape often seems to involve a failure to understand and/or act on cues that a woman is not interested in sex. In fact, studies have shown that sexually aggressive men tend to ignore negative cues and interpret neutral or even negative signs as encouragement or interest in sex. Murphy, Coleman, and Haynes (1986), for example, found that sexual aggressors in a community sample misinterpreted women's assertive behavior as hostile. Abbey (1982, 1987) has found that men have a more sexualized view of interpersonal interactions than do women, and often misperceive friendliness by women as sexual interest. Although this perception is not limited to sexually aggressive men, it can lead to sexual coercion in some instances. Misperceptions of women's sexual arousal has also been associated with date rape. Kanin (1984) reported that over 90% of date rapists he studied gave as reasons for forcing sex on their dates their own perceptions of the women as highly aroused and their subsequent ignoring of the women's attempts to signal a desire to stop. The pervasiveness of alcohol use in acquaintance rape situations further serves to facilitate cognitive distortions while also serving as a disinhibitor of aggressive behavior. McFall (1990) hypothesized specific social skills deficits in sexually coercive men, based on his Social Information Processing Model (1982). This model describes three major components of communication: decoding (the ability to correctly receive, perceive, and interpret incoming communications), decision skills (correctly generating appropriate ways of reacting to a communication and evaluating potential outcomes of a response), and enactment skills (skills required to execute a response and adjust responses as needed). Lipton, McDonel, and McFall (1987) found that incarcerated rapists were more likely than nonrapists to make mistakes in interpreting women's behavior, but not men's, when viewing videotaped interactions. They more often interpreted women's negative cues as positive. McDonel and McFall (1991) found similar results with college students, supporting the hypothesis that the major problem sexually aggressive men have in interactions with women is one of misperceiving negative cues as positive, encouraging ones. This misperception is more likely to occur when the situation is ambiguous or when the man is motivated by his own arousal to attend selectively to indicators of encouragement.

Antisocial personality characteristics have been the focus of considerable study due to observations that sexually aggressive men often appear impulsive, adventurous, nonconforming, lacking in empathy, and unconcerned about social norms. They fail to consider the long-term consequences of their behavior and instead focus on their short-term needs, such as desire for pleasure (Ward, Hudson, Johnston, & Marshall, 1997). Studies of incarcerated sex offenders provide support for the antisocial hypothesis. For example, some have a history of nonsexual criminal activity (Knight & Prentky, 1990), and they often score high on measures of psychopathic or antisocial characteristics (e.g., Armentrout & Hauer, 1978; Serin, Malcolm, Khanna, & Barbaree, 1994). Lisak and Roth (1988) found that sexually aggressive men were more impulsive and had less respect for the rules of society than did nonaggressive men. Whereas convicted rapists are often diagnosed with antisocial personality disorder (Groth, 1979), sexually aggressive men in the general population are much more variable in regard to antisocial tendencies. The college populations most often studied are unlikely to have criminal histories. However, there is considerable evidence of sub-threshold levels of psychopathic traits. Rapaport and Burkhart (1984) found that the Socialization Scale (Gough, 1960) differentiated self-reported sexually aggressive men from those who had not engaged in coercive sexual behavior. This indicates that the sexually aggressive men were less well socialized and more likely to engage in an antisocial lifestyle. Socialization scores have been found to predict criminal history and substance abuse among college students (Kosson, Steuerwald, Newman, & Widom, 1994). These men are, in fact, more prone to alcohol and drug abuse (White & Humphrey, 1994; White, Humphrey, & Farmer, 1989). They are also more sexually promiscuous, starting sex at an earlier age and having more sex partners than other men (Malamuth, Sockloskie, Koss, & Tanaka, 1991). Kosson, Kelly, and White (1997) examined psychopathy-related personality traits in sexually aggressive college men and found that those most closely resembling psychopaths on two dimensions of psychopathy had the highest frequency of sexual aggression. The two dimensions, impulsive antisocial lifestyle and callous exploitation of others, interacted so that those with both types of traits were more likely to use force and engage in a variety of forms of aggression, especially the use of alcohol and controlled substances to obtain sex from an unwilling or unwitting partner.

Sexual arousal has been the target of considerable research with sexually aggressive men, especially convicted sex offenders. Sexual arousal to depictions of forced sex has been found to differentiate sexual aggressors from their nonaggressive peers in both college populations (e.g., Bernat, Calhoun, & Adams, in press; Malamuth, 1986) and incarcerated rapists (e.g., Barbaree, Marshall, & Lanthier, 1979; Lalumiere & Quinsey, 1994). In the majority of cases, this arousal does not so much indicate a preference for forced sex, as was once thought, as a lack of concern about whether sex is consensual or not. Except for sadistic rapists, who are rare, sexual arousal is usually greater in response to depictions of consenting sex. But most rapists' arousal is not impaired by the use of force or manipulation in the face of resistance, as is that of nonrapists (Abel, Barlow, Blanchard, & Guild, 1977; Barbaree & Marshall, 1991). This has led to a theoretical model of sexual aggression, called the inhibition model (Barbaree et al., 1979; Malamuth, Heim, & Feshbach, 1980). According to this model, sexual aggression is likely to occur when cues of nonconsent and force fail to inhibit sexual arousal. Barbaree et al. (1979) proposed that rapists lack the same strength of inhibition as nonrapists, and a number of studies have provided empirical support for this model. In several studies, the disinhibition has been furthered by situational factors, such as alcohol (Barbaree, Marshall, Yates, & Lightfoot, 1983), being angered by a woman (Yates, Barbaree, & Marshall, 1984), and victim-blaming conditions (Sunberg, Barbaree, & Marshall, 1991).

Sexual arousal is only one element in sexual aggression, operating in conjunction with other disinhibiting factors in men who are susceptible due to antisocial tendencies, peer pressure, lack of empathy, or a combination of individual characteristics. Burkhart and Stanton (1988) have posited that, for sexually aggressive men, sex becomes "motivationally overdetermined," that it serves many other motives than sexual excitement and pleasure, including power and dominance. Sexual arousal may play a stronger role in acquaintance rapes that are preceded by some level of consensual sexual activity (Blader & Marshall, 1989).

DEVELOPMENT OF SEXUAL AGGRESSION

Research with adult sexual aggressives points clearly to the early development of a number of contributing factors, including general aggressive and anti-social tendencies, and attitudes condoning aggression and hostility toward women. A history of delinquency is commonly found in studies that examine predictors of both sexual and physical aggression (e.g., Malamuth et al., 1991; Malamuth, Heavey, Linz, & Barnes, 1995). However, relevant data are limited and largely retrospective in nature. Longitudinal studies are especially limited. In the past, studies on the development of delinquency and violent behavior have failed to focus on sexual aggression and studies of sexual aggression have rarely included adolescents. Most of the information we have about adolescent sexual aggression and its developmental antecedents comes from studies of juvenile offenders. Because only the most violent and habitual perpetrators are likely to be incarcerated, such studies may have limited generalizability, but they are somewhat instructive, as researchers have begun to trace the developmental trajectory for delinquent children. Patterson, DeBaryshe, and Ramsey (1989) proposed a model of the development of antisocial behavior and aggression in youngsters. Poor parenting in the preschool years results in a child who is inadvertently reinforced for engaging in coercive behavior. As the coercive cycle escalates in the family, more severe forms of deviant behavior, such as hitting and physical attacks, emerge on the part of the child and the parents. When the child goes to school, his coercive behavior results in rejection by normal peers and in academic failure. Rejected children who achieve poorly in school tend to spurn conventional norms and self-select into deviant peer groups that promote antisocial behavior. It is unclear how well this pattern holds for sexual aggression. Some studies of adolescent sex offenders offer support. For example, Kavoussi, Kaplan, and Becker (1988) found that the most common psychiatric diagnosis of adolescent sex offenders was conduct disorder. Becker, Cunningham-Rathner, and Kaplan (1986) found that 28% of a sample of adolescent sex offenders had been arrested previously for nonsexual crimes and 16% to 18% had experienced physical or sexual abuse as children, consistent with the Patterson et al. model. However, this was a small sample (67), and most of their offenses were child molestation, not rape. Other studies have not been supportive of the model's generalizability to sexually aggressive groups. Fagan and Wexler (1983), for example, found that adolescent sex offenders were less likely than nonsexual offenders to come from broken homes and committed fewer delinquent acts, although they were more likely to have been victims of abuse.

The most frequently studied age group in the area of sexual aggression is college-age men and women. Yet, the roots of the behavior and very often the behavior itself are manifest before that age. White and Koss (1993) emphasized the importance of research with adolescent samples, citing the high prevalence of actual sexual aggression in this group as well as the importance of developing heterosocial skills that will lead to later positive relationships with women. In one of the few large-scale studies of adolescent sexual aggression, Ageton (1983) found delinquent peer group association to be the best predictor of the behavior. Peer endorsement of intercourse in general and of forced sexual acts specifically predicted sexual aggression. Consistent with Ageton's findings are the results of a smaller prospective study of a community sample of male adolescents followed into young adulthood (Calhoun & Bernat, 1997; Calhoun, Bernat, Clum, & Frame, 1997). The best predictor of sexual aggression in young adulthood was self-reported delinquency. Examined longitudinally, sexual as well as physical aggression was best predicted by socialized aggression and conduct disorder, as rated by teachers during the senior year of high school. Self-rated anger during the senior year also contributed significantly to the equation. However, socialized aggression was by far the strongest predictor, accounting for 38% of the variance, indicating that peer-related delinquent and antisocial behavior is a potent factor in the development of later aggression, especially when combined with anger. The overlap between sexual and physical aggression was somewhat lower in this community sample than in Hannan and Burkhart's (1993) college sample; 9% versus 17% reported past incidents of both. The developmental trajectory that leads to each of these types of violence against women, separately and in combination, would provide valuable insights and should be the focus of future study.

THEORIES OF SEXUAL AGGRESSION

Many theoretical notions have been proposed to explain sexual aggression. However, most are limited in their focus on one or two primary factors that may form only part of the complex picture. Empirical research in recent years has revealed the complexity and multifaceted nature of this behavior, and modern theories must take into account a wide range of interacting determinants. Currently, viable theories are integrative in nature, incorporating multiple and overlapping influences. Some include attempts to develop typologies, usually along dimensions of motivation, level of violence, emotional disturbance, or associated criminal behavior. Typologies have also been proposed for subpopulations such as marital rapists (e.g., Monson & Langhinrichsen-Rohling, 1998). However, typologies are somewhat arbitrary and may have limited usefulness for purposes of treatment and prevention. Theoretical models that integrate the many dimensions on which sexually aggressive men are known to vary may lead to more useful subtypes that can guide treatment and prevention development (Swartz & Cellini, 1995).

Marshall and Barbaree (1990a) have proposed an integrated theory based on an inhibition model of sexual offending that focuses on the failure of rapists and other sexually aggressive men to appropriately inhibit the readiness to aggress sexually that is conferred to them by biological inheritance. They state, "As we see it, the task of human males is to acquire inhibitory controls over a biologically endowed propensity for self-interest associated with a tendency to fuse sex and aggression" (p. 257). Social inhibitions must be learned through good parenting and social influences. Socialization processes act on these biological predispositions through learned patterns of behavior to overcome the influence of hormones and brain centers. Because sex and aggression appear to have similar neural substrates and the same endocrines can activate both, inhibitions must be acquired that separate these two tendencies. These inhibitions are acquired through a combination of three environmental influences: childhood experiences, especially parenting; the sociocultural context; and transitory situational factors. In childhood, attitudes and behaviors are learned that point the child in a prosocial or an antisocial direction. Violent parenting, or the use of harsh and inconsistent discipline without love, may leave the child with strong feelings of hostility and an emotional detachment from others. Many of these children learn that aggression is a good way to get what they want. Stereotypical masculine behavior and attitudes may be adopted to gain confidence and esteem. A sociocultural environment that fosters male dominance, negative attitudes toward women, and a high tolerance for violence reinforces the early learning, and easy access to pornography that often fuses sex and aggression further defeats the development of inhibitions. The result is a man who is vulnerable to transitory situational factors that can disinhibit weak behavior controls, such as alcohol, anger, and even sexual arousal.

A quadripartite model of sexual aggression has been developed by Hall (1996; Hall & Hirschman, 1991) to account for the behavior of rapists and other types of sex offenders. It includes four etiological factors, or "motivational precursors," that also define characteristics of relatively discrete subtypes: deviant physiological arousal, cognitive disinhibitors, affective dyscontrol, and developmentally related personality problems. All four factors may be present in a given case, but some will be relatively more important than others in the development of an individual pattern of sexual aggression, thus defining the subtype to which the man belongs. Hall and Hirschman suggested that distorted cognitions that justify sexual aggression are the most common precursors of date rape. When desires to have consensual sex are thwarted, distorted cognitions such as those represented in rape myths (e.g., "no means yes") may facilitate sexually aggressive behavior and allow a man to ignore cues of nonconsent. Even strong protests and physical resistance are sometimes believed by rapists to represent signs of arousal or encouragement. Sexual aggression of this type is often planned and less impulsive than others and the level of violence is usually low. Affective dyscontrol denotes an inability to modulate affect and a tendency to act impulsively and often violently. It is likely to be present in nonsexual forms of aggression as well. Sexual aggressors with developmentally related personality problems or disorders may have a history of aggression, delinquency, family conflicts, substance abuse, and so on. They are most likely to be violent and have the poorest treatment prognosis. Physiological arousal as a precursor has been examined in a number of laboratory studies, which are generally supportive. These four variables are not independent, but interact with each other and with situational factors.

Craig (1990) delineated a "situational" model of coercive sexuality whereby sexually coercive men selectively choose situations in which they are able to express their dispositions, actively manipulating their social environments and their evaluations of events to participate in preferred activities. In this way, coercive men choose victims, dating situations, and relationships that are compatible with their intentions and ignore stimuli that are incompatible (e.g., cues of nonconsent) to maintain a cognitively congruent self-concept. An even more integrative model has been proposed by Malamuth (1986; Malamuth, Heavey, & Linz, 1993), whose "confluence model" incorporates both sexual and nonsexual aggression against women. This multivariate model posits two primary interacting paths that lead to sexual aggression: sexual promiscuity and hostile masculinity. Sexual promiscuity, which includes both multiple partners and age at first intercourse, may result from developmental factors, such as early abuse, which lead to delinquent behavior. Sexual promiscuity provides opportunities to act out hostile masculinity in sexual aggression. Hostile masculinity, which includes hostility toward women and macho attitudes, mediates the effect of rape-supportive cognitions. The two paths must interact to lead to sexual aggression. Men who are characterized by hostile masculinity but not promiscuity are thought to act out their hostility toward women in nonsexual ways.

Although recent progress has been made in the development of more comprehensive explanatory and predictive models of sexual aggression, there is still no generally accepted theory or set of theories. As Hall (1996) pointed out, this leaves researchers and clinicians without a common language to translate research findings into treatment and prevention, which may interfere with integration and hamper progress.

TREATMENT OF PERPETRATORS

Treatment programs for sexually aggressive men have been limited almost exclusively to convicted rapists: those in prison or on parole or probation. Whereas these groups are often motivated to change their behavior to stay out of trouble and reclaim their lives, sexually aggressive men in the community are not a treatment-seeking population. The usual motives for seeking help in changing behavior, such as emotional distress, guilt, or desire to improve relationships with others, do not apply to them. Therefore, most programs have been aimed at adjudicated sex offenders. Usually, rapists are treated together with other types of sex offenders. Treatment outcome data are often reported without breaking down these groups. Other methodological problems common to this area increase the difficulty of evaluating treatment effectiveness. As pointed out by Marshall and Barbaree (1990b), these programs carefully select prisoners who are motivated for treatment and most likely to benefit from it, excluding the most dangerous offenders. Control groups are rare and often inadequate, and follow-up data, especially longer-term outcomes, other than rearrest rates, are not often collected. Marshall and Barbaree concluded that the outcome data for prison programs indicates that they are much less effective in the treatment of rapists than of child molesters, exhibitionists, and other types of sex offenders. If the methodological confounds are overlooked, the recidivism rates reported for combined groups of sex offenders after treatment are around 10%. Results from treatment programs that have reported data separately indicate that rapists are the least responsive to treatment. For example, Maletsky (1987) reported that 26.5% of rapists reoffended based on police records. This was over twice as high as any other group of treated offenders.

Treatment programs tend to be similar in that they cover the same topics, though with different emphases. The major treatment targets, as described by Marshall and Barbaree (1990b), include sexual behaviors and interests, social difficulties, and cognitive distortions that contribute to the deviant behavior. Deviant sexual preferences are targeted in rapists because of the assumption that they prefer forced sex to sex with a consenting partner, which may be true in individual cases but not for the group (Barbaree, 1990). Techniques for reducing deviant arousal include aversive therapy, covert sensitization, and masturbatory retraining. These techniques aim to reduce the strength of the deviant stimulus and substitute arousal to more appropriate stimuli. They are combined with sex education and treatment of any sexual dysfunctions that make consenting sex unsatisfying.

Treatment of social difficulties may include a number of different elements. The exact combination used depends on the specific deficits in each case. Heterosocial skills training is usually offered to increase the possibility of success with consenting adult partners. This has been controversial due to fear that it may give rapists better skills they might use to entrap victims, so selection and monitoring of participants is important. Some programs (e.g., Marshall & Barbaree, 1990b) target a broad range of social functioning, including social problem solving, assertiveness, and conflict resolution. Empathy training is a common element in these programs as well, because of the consistent finding that rapists are markedly lacking in empathy for their victims as well as others.

Cognitive distortions are targeted because distorted thinking patterns so often are found to maintain the behavior of sex offenders. Specific targets of treatment usually include negative attitudes about women and denial of the harmful effects of their attacks on women, including impact on the family and friends of the perpetrator as well as the victim. Acceptance of responsibility for their behavior is an important target as well. Cognitive therapy is often used to change these maladaptive thought patterns. Treatment may include individual or group formats, or both. Usually, some combination is used.

PREVENTION

Effective prevention of sexual assault requires a comprehensive approach that attacks the problem at all levels. Primary prevention should target the developmental precursors, including child abuse and delinquency. On a societal level, the attitudes and images that foster disrespect for women, rape myths, viewing women as sex objects, and promoting hypermasculinity need to be changed. Inequality, in a general sense, adds to the perception held by many rapists that women deserve less consideration, as they can be viewed as second-class citizens. Rape-supportive cognitions may be fostered by societal tolerance of other forms of abuse of women, such as sexual harassment in colleges and in the workplace. Research on the cognitive association of power and sex concepts supports the conclusion that sexual harassment and sexual assault may be points along a continuum (Bargh, Raymond, Pryor, & Strack, 1995). Power and dominance have long been acknowledged as primary motives for sexual aggression, especially in feminist models (Darke, 1990; Herman, 1990). The association between sex and power has also been shown to be closer in men who engage in sexual harassment than in men who do not (Pryor & Stoller, 1994).

Society needs to reevaluate the common belief that pornography is harmless, especially as it impacts young men whose attitudes about women are still developing. Although pornography does not lead directly to sexual aggression, even so-called soft porn often portrays women as enjoying dominance and even becoming sexually aroused by rape. Attempts should be made to inoculate young men against the influence of these images in the same way that is recommended for countering effects of media violence. In addition, the dangers of underage drinking should be taken more seriously, especially when combined with other risk factors. The legal system must take "date-rape" drugs more seriously, and women must be warned about their rapid spread.

Rape prevention programs have become common on college and university campuses. However, empirical evidence regarding their effectiveness is limited (McCall, 1993). In response, Hanson and Gidycz (1993) evaluated a sexual assault prevention program focusing on psychoeducational information, the identification of situational variables associated with sexual assault, and the discussion of preventive strategies. They followed participants for nine weeks and found that although the intervention was effective in reducing the incidence of sexual assault for women with no prior history of sexual assault, it failed to decrease the incidence of sexual assault among women with moderate or severe sexual assault histories. Although these results are promising for prevention of assault among nonvictims, given the high rates of revictimization among college women, prevention programs targeting this vulnerable population are needed.

A report of a pilot program for women who have been victimized previously was presented by Marx, Calhoun, Wilson, Meyerson, and Britt (1998). In addition to the elements described by Hanson and Gidycz (1993), the program included several other aspects aimed at factors thought to contribute to the vulnerability of this group. These included personal risk identification, problem solving in social situations, and assertiveness. Evaluation of the program after a nine-week follow-up period showed that it was effective in preventing the most serious form of revictimization, rape, and that participants in the prevention group reported greater improvements in psychological adjustment than did the control group.

Campus rape prevention programs specifically aimed at men have a shorter history than those for women, and data on their effectiveness are even more scarce. Methodological problems abound, including lack of control groups, lack of outcome measures other than self-report, lack of follow-up, and a focus on measuring attitude change alone. These programs tend to include psychoeducational elements, rape awareness, victim impact information, and group discussion. All-male groups led by male facilitators, often peers, seem to work better than coed groups (Berkowitz, 1994). Attitude change is usually measured immediately following the program, and thus it is not surprising that programs often report attitude change. Schewe and O'Donohue (1996) attempted to go beyond the usual evaluations by including a no-treatment control group and measures of rape proclivity to compare two model-based prevention programs for high-risk college men. One program targeted rape-supportive cognitions and the other targeted victim empathy and awareness of negative consequences for the men as well as the victims. Both groups were more effective in changing some attitudes, compared to the control group. Only the group that targeted rape-supportive cognitions changed attraction to sexual aggression, which is a measure of rape proclivity. However, sexual assault behavior itself was not assessed and outcome measures were completed immediately after the completion of the programs, with no follow-up to determine how lasting the changes might be. Nevertheless, this is a promising development in the prevention area.

It is clear that much more emphasis on prevention is needed and more efforts should be aimed at men. The problem is complex and multifaceted and will take concerted efforts at all levels to impact.

REFERENCES

Abbey, A. (1982). Sex differences in attributions for friendly behavior: Do males misperceive females' friendliness? *Journal of Personality and Social Psychology, 42,* 830–838.

Abbey, A. (1987). Perceptions of personal avoidability versus responsibility: How do they differ? *Basic and Applied Social Psychology, 8,* 3–19.

Abbey, A. (1991). Acquaintance rape and alcohol consumption on college campuses: How are they linked? *Journal of American College Health, 39,* 165–169.

Abbey, A., Ross, L.T., McDuffie, D., & McAuslan, P. (1996). Alcohol and dating risk factors for sexual assault among college women. *Psychology of Women Quarterly, 20,* 147–169.

Abel, G., Barlow, D.H., Blanchard, E., & Guild, D. (1977). The components of rapists' sexual arousal. *Archives of General Psychiatry, 34,* 895–903.

Ageton, S.S. (1983). *Sexual assault among adolescents.* Lexington, MA: D.C. Heath.

Armentrout, J.A., & Hauer, A.L. (1978). MMPIs of rapists of adults, rapists of children, and non-rapist sex offenders. *Journal of Clinical Psychology, 34,* 330–332.

Atkeson, B.M., Ellis, E.M., & Calhoun, K.S. (1982). An examination of differences between multiple-incident and single-incident victims of sexual assault. *Journal of Abnormal Psychology, 91,* 221–224.

Barbaree, H.E. (1990). Stimulus control of sexual arousal: Its role in sexual assault. In W.L. Marshall, D.R. Laws, & H.E. Barbaree (Eds.), *Handbook of sexual assault.* New York: Plenum Press.

Barbaree, H.E., & Marshall, W.L. (1991). The role of male sexual arousal in rape: Six models. *Journal of Consulting and Clinical Psychology, 59,* 621–630.

Barbaree, H.E., Marshall, W.L., & Lanthier, R.D. (1979). Deviant sexual arousal in rapists. *Behaviour Research and Therapy, 17,* 215–222.

Barbaree, H.E., Marshall, W.L., Yates, E., & Lightfoot, L.O. (1983). Alcohol intoxication and deviant sexual arousal in male social drinkers. *Behaviour Research and Therapy, 21,* 365–373.

Bargh, J.A., Raymond, P., Pryor, J.B., & Strack, F. (1995). Attractiveness of the underling: An automatic power—sex association and its consequences for sexual harassment and aggression. *Journal of Personality and Social Psychology, 68,* 768–781.

Becker, J. (1989). Impact of sexual abuse on sexual functioning. In S. Leiblum & R. Rosen (Eds.), *Principles and practice of sex therapy: Update for the 1990s* (pp. 298–318). New York: Guilford Press.

Becker, J., Abel, G.C., Blanchard, E.B., Murphy, W.D., & Coleman, E. (1978). Evaluating social skills of sexual aggressives. *Criminal Justice and Behavior, 5,* 357–367.

Becker, J., Cunningham-Rathner, J., & Kaplan, M.S. (1986). Adolescent sex offenders: Demographics, criminal and sexual histories, and recommendations for reducing future offenses. *Journal of Interpersonal Violence, 1,* 431–445.

Becker, J., Skinner, L., Abel, G., & Cichon, J. (1986). Level of postassault sexual functioning in rape and incest victims. *Archives of Sexual Behavior, 15,* 37–49.

Berkowitz, A.D. (1994). *Men and rape: Theory, research, and prevention programs in higher education.* San Francisco: Jossey-Bass.

Bernat, J.A., Calhoun, K.S., & Adams, H.E. (in press). Sexually aggressive and nonaggressive men: Sexual arousal and judgments in response to date rape and consensual analogues. *Journal of Abnormal Psychology.*

Bernat, J.A., Wilson, A.E., & Calhoun, K.S. (1999). Sexual coercion history, calloused sexual beliefs and judgments of sexual coercion in a date rape analogue. *Violence and Victims, 14,* 1–14.

Blader, J.C., & Marshall, W.L. (1989). Is assessment of sexual arousal in rapists worthwhile? A critique of current methods and the development of a response compatibility approach. *Clinical Psychology Review, 9,* 569–587.

Bowker, L.H. (1983). Marital rape: A distinct syndrome? *Social Casework: The Journal of Contemporary Social Work, 64,* 347–352.

Burkhart, B.R., & Stanton, A.L. (1988). Sexual aggression in acquaintance relationships. In G. Russell (Ed.), *Violence in intimate relationships* (pp. 43–65). Great Neck, NY: PMA.

Burt, M.R. (1980). Cultural myths and support for rape. *Journal of Personality and Social Psychology, 38,* 217–230.

Calhoun, K.S., Atkeson, B., & Resick, P. (1982). A longitudinal examination of fear reactions in victims of rape. *Journal of Counseling Psychology, 29,* 655–661.

Calhoun, K.S., & Bernat, J.A. (1997, March). *Longitudinal prediction of sexual and physical aggression among a sample of young men.* Paper presented at the Southeastern Psychological Association meeting, Atlanta.

Calhoun, K.S., Bernat, J.A., Clum, G.A., & Frame, C.L. (1997). Sexual coercion and attraction to sexual aggression in a community sample of young men. *Journal of Interpersonal Violence, 12,* 392–406.

Craig, M. (1990). Coercive sexuality in dating relationships: A situational model. *Clinical Psychology Review, 10,* 395–423.

Darke, J.L. (1990). Sexual aggression: Achieving power through humiliation. In W.L. Marshall, D.R. Laws, & H.E. Barbaree (Eds.), *Handbook of sexual assault.* New York: Plenum Press.

Davis, M.H. (1983). Measuring individual differences in empathy: Evidence for a multidimensional approach. *Journal of Personality and Social Psychology, 44,* 113–126.

Fagan, J., & Wexler, A. (1983). Explanations of sexual assault among violent delinquents. *Journal of Early Adolescence, 3,* 363–385.

Feldman-Summers, S., Gordon, P.E., & Megher, J.R. (1979). The impact of rape on sexual satisfaction. *Journal of Abnormal Psychology, 88,* 101–105.

Finkelhor, D., & Browne, A. (1985). The traumatic impact of child sexual abuse: A conceptualization. *American Journal of Orthopsychiatry, 55,* 530–541.

Finkelhor, D., & Yllo, K. (1985). *License to rape: Sexual abuse of wives.* New York: Holt, Rinehart and Winston.

Finley, C., & Corty, E. (1993). Rape on campus: The prevalence of sexual assault while enrolled in college. *Journal of College Student Development, 34,* 113–117.

Foa, E., Hearst-Ikeda, D., & Perry, K. (1995). Evaluation of a brief cognitive-behavioral program for the prevention of chronic PTSD in recent assault victims. *Journal of Consulting and Clinical Psychology, 63,* 948–955.

Foa, E., & Kozak, M.J. (1986). Emotional processing of fear: Exposure to corrective information. *Psychological Bulletin, 99,* 20–35.

Foa, E., & Meadows, E. (1997). Psychosocial treatments for posttraumatic stress disorder: A critical review. *Annual Review of Psychology, 48,* 449–480.

Foa, E., & Rothbaum, B. (1998). *Treating the trauma of rape: Cognitive behavioral therapy for PTSD.* New York: Guilford Press.

Foa, E., Rothbaum, B., Riggs, D., & Murdock, T. (1991). Treatment of PTSD in rape victims: A comparison of cognitive-behavioral procedures and counseling. *Journal of Consulting and Clinical Psychology, 59,* 715–723.

Foa, E., Rothbaum, B., & Steketee, G. (1993). Treatment of rape victims. *Journal of Interpersonal Violence, 8,* 256–276.

Foa, E., Steketee, G., & Rothbaum, B. (1989). Behavioral/cognitive conceptualizations of post-traumatic stress disorder. *Behavior Therapy, 20,* 155–176.

Frieze, I.H. (1983). Investigating the causes and consequences of marital rape. *Signs, 8,* 532–553.

Fromuth, M. (1986). The relationship of childhood sexual abuse with later psychological and sexual adjustment in a sample of college women. *Child Abuse & Neglect, 10*, 5–15.

Gidycz, C., Coble, C., Latham, L., & Layman, M. (1993). Sexual assault experience in adulthood and prior victimization experiences. *Psychology of Women Quarterly, 17*, 151–168.

Gidycz, C., Hanson, K., & Layman, M. (1995). A prospective analysis of the relationships among sexual assault experiences: An extension of previous findings. *Psychology of Women Quarterly, 19*, 5–29.

Gidycz, C., & Koss, M.P. (1991). The effects of acquaintance rape on the female victim. In A. Parrot & L. Bechhofer (Eds.), *Acquaintance rape: The hidden crime* (pp. 270–283). New York: Wiley.

Gough, H.G. (1960). Theory and measurement of socialization. *Journal of Consulting and Clinical Psychology, 24*, 32–30.

Groth, A.N. (1979). *Men who rape.* New York: Plenum Press.

Hall, G.C.N. (1996). *Theory-based assessment, treatment, and prevention of sexual aggression.* Oxford, England: Oxford University Press.

Hall, G.C.N., & Hirschman, R. (1991). Toward a theory of sexual aggression: A quadripartite model. *Journal of Consulting and Clinical Psychology, 59*, 662–669.

Hannan, K., & Burkhart, B. (1993). The topography of violence in college men: Frequency and comorbidity of sexual aggression. *Journal of College Student Psychotherapy, 8*, 219–237.

Hanson, K., & Gidycz, C. (1993). Evaluation of a sexual assault prevention program. *Journal of Consulting and Clinical Psychology, 61*, 1046–1052.

Harney, P., & Muehlenhard, C. (1991). Rape. In E. Grauerholz & M. Koralewski (Eds.), *Sexual coercion: A sourcebook on its nature, causes, and prevention* (pp. 3–15). Lexington, MA: Lexington Books/D.C. Heath.

Herman, J.L. (1990). Sex offenders: A feminist perspective. In W.L. Marshall, D.R. Laws, & H.E. Barbaree (Eds.), *Handbook of sexual assault.* New York: Plenum Press.

Himelein, M. (1995). Risk factors for sexual victimization in dating: A longitudinal study of college women. *Psychology of Women Quarterly, 19*, 31–48.

Kanin, E. (1984). Date rape: Unofficial criminals and victims. *Victimology: An International Journal, 9*, 95–108.

Kavoussi, R., Kaplan, M., & Becker, J. (1988). Psychiatric diagnoses in adolescent sex offenders. *Journal of the American Academy of Child and Adolescent Psychiatry, 27*, 241–243.

Kelley, S.P. (1989). *Heterosocial behavior of sexually coercive and non-coercive college males.* Unpublished doctoral dissertation, University of Georgia.

Kilpatrick, D.G., Best, C.L., Saunders, B.E., & Veronen, L.J. (1988). Rape in marriage and in dating relationships: How bad is it for mental health? *Annals of the New York Academy of Sciences, 528*, 335–344.

Kilpatrick, D.G., Edmunds, C.N., & Seymour, A.K. (1992). *Rape in America: A report to the Nation.* Arlington, VA: National Victim Center.

Kilpatrick, D.G., Veronen, L., & Resick, P. (1982). Psychological sequelae to rape: Assessment and treatment strategies. In D. Dolays & R. Meredith (Eds.), *Behavioral medicine: Assessment and treatment strategies* (pp. 473–479). New York: Plenum Press.

Kilpatrick, D.G., Veronen, L., Saunders, B., Best, C., Amick-McMullen, A., & Paduhovich, J. (1987). *The psychological impact of crime: A study of randomly surveyed crime victims.* Washington, DC: National Institute of Justice.

Kimerling, R., Armistead, L.P., & Forehand, R. (1999). Victimization experience and HIV infection in women: Associations with serostatus, psychological symptoms and health status. *Journal of Traumatic Stress, 12,* 41–58.

Kimerling, R., & Calhoun, K.S. (1994). Somatic symptoms, social support, and treatment seeking among sexual assault victims. *Journal of Consulting and Clinical Psychology, 62,* 333–340.

Knight, R.A., & Prentky, R.A. (1990). Classifying sexual offenders: The development and corrobation of taxonomic models. In W.L. Marshall, D.R. Laws, & H.E. Barbaree (Eds.), *Handbook of sexual assault* (pp. 23–52). New York: Plenum Press.

Koss, M.P. (1985). *Hidden rape: Survey of psychopathological consequences.* Final report NIMH Grant #MH 29602.

Koss, M.P. (1988). Hidden rape: Incidence, prevalence, and descriptive characteristics of sexual aggression and victimization in a national sample of college students. *Aggressive Behavior, 14,* 136–146.

Koss, M.P. (1992). The underdetection of rape; Methodological choices influence incidence estimates. *Journal of Social Issues, 48,* 61–75.

Koss, M.P. (1993a). Detecting the scope of rape: A review of prevalence research methods. *Journal of Interpersonal Violence, 8,* 198–222.

Koss, M.P. (1993b). Rape: Scope, impact, interventions, and public policy responses. *American Psychologist, 48,* 1062–1069.

Koss, M.P., & Dinero, T. (1989). Discriminant analysis of risk factors for sexual victimization among a national sample of college women. *Journal of Consulting and Clinical Psychology, 57,* 242–250.

Koss, M.P., Dinero, T., Seibel, C., & Cox, S. (1988). Stranger and acquaintance rape: Are there differences in the victim's experience? *Psychology of Women Quarterly, 12,* 1–24.

Koss, M.P., Gidycz, C., & Wisniewski, N. (1987). The scope of rape: Incidence and prevalence of sexual victimization in a national sample of higher education students. *Journal of Consulting and Clinical Psychology, 55,* 162–170.

Koss, M.P., Woodruff, W.J., & Koss, P.G. (1991). Criminal victimization among primary care medical patients: Prevalence, incidence, and physician usage. *Behavioral Sciences and the Law, 9,* 85–96.

Kosson, D.S., Kelly, J., & White, J. (1997). Psychopathy-related traits predict self-reported sexual aggression among college men. *Journal of Interpersonal Violence, 12,* 241–254.

Kosson, D.S., Steuerwald, B.L., Newman, J.P., & Widom, C.S. (1994). The relation between socialization and antisocial behavior, substance use, and family conflict in college students. *Journal of Personality Assessment, 63,* 473–488.

Lalumiere, M.L., & Quinsey, V.L. (1994). The discriminability of rapists from nonrapists using phallometric measures: A meta-analysis. *Criminal Justice and Behavior, 21,* 150–175.

Layman, M., Gidycz, C., & Lynn, S. (1996). Unacknowledged versus acknowledged rape victims: Situational factors and posttraumatic stress. *Journal of Abnormal Psychology, 105,* 124–131.

Letourneau, E., Resnick, H., Kilpatrick, D., Saunders, B., & Best, C. (1996). Comorbidity of sexual problems and posttraumatic stress disorder in female crime victims. *Behavior Therapy, 27,* 321–336.

Lipton, D.N., McDonel, E.C., & McFall, R.M. (1987). Heterosocial perception in rapists. *Journal of Consulting and Clinical Psychology, 55,* 17–21.

Lisak, D., & Roth, S. (1988). Motivational factors in nonincarcerated sexually aggressive men. *Journal of Personality and Social Psychology, 55,* 795–802.

Malamuth, N.M. (1984). Aggressive pornography: Individual differences and aggression. In N.M. Malamuth & E. Donnerstein (Eds.), *Pornography and sexual aggression* (pp. 19–52). New York: Academic Press.

Malamuth, N.M., (1986). Predictors of naturalistic sexual aggression. *Journal of Personality and Social Psychology, 50,* 953–962.

Malamuth, N.M., & Check, J.V.P. (1983). Sexual arousal to rape depictions: Individual differences. *Journal of Abnormal Psychology, 92,* 55–67.

Malamuth, N.M., Heavey, C.L., & Linz, D. (1993). Predicting men's antisocial behavior against women: The interaction model of sexual aggression. In G.C.N. Hall & R. Hirschman (Eds.), *Sexual aggression: Issues of etiology, assessment, and treatment* (pp. 63–97). Washington, DC: Taylor & Francis.

Malamuth, N.M., Heavey, C.L., Linz, K., & Barnes, G. (1995). Using the confluence model of sexual aggression to predict men's conflict with women: A 10-year follow-up study. *Journal of Personality and Social Psychology, 69,* 353–369.

Malamuth, N.M., Heim, M., & Feshbach, S. (1980). Sexual responsiveness of college students to rape depictions: Inhibitory and disinhibitory effects. *Journal of Personality and Social Psychology, 38,* 399–408.

Malamuth, N.M., Sockloskie, R.J., Koss, M.P., & Tanaka, J.S. (1991). Characteristics of aggressors against women: Testing a model using a national sample of college students. *Journal of Consulting and Clinical Psychology, 59,* 670–681.

Maletsky, B. (1987, May). *Data generated by an outpatient sexual abuse clinic.* Paper presented at the 1st annual conference on the Assessment and Treatment of Sexual Abusers, Newport, OR.

Mandoki, C., & Burkhart, B. (1989). Sexual victimization: Is there a vicious cycle? *Violence and Victims, 4,* 179–190.

Marhoefer-Dvorak, S., Resick, P.A., Hutter, C., & Girelle, S. (1988). Single- versus multiple-incident rape victims: A comparison of psychological reactions to rape. *Journal of Interpersonal Violence, 3,* 145–160.

Marshall, W.L., & Barbaree, H.E. (1990a). An integrated theory of etiology of sexual offending. In W.L. Marshall, D.R. Laws, & H.E. Barbaree (Eds.), *Handbook of sexual assault* (pp. 257–275). New York: Plenum Press.

Marshall, W.L., & Barbaree, H.E. (1990b). Outcome of comprehensive cognitive-behavioral treatment programs. In W.L. Marshall, D.R. Laws, & H.E. Barbaree (Eds.), *Handbook of sexual assault* (pp. 363–385). New York: Plenum Press.

Marshall, W.L., Hudson, S.M., & Jones, R. (1995). Empathy in sex offenders. *Clinical Psychology Review, 15,* 99–113.

Marx, B., Calhoun, K.S., Wilson, A.E., Meyerson, L., & Britt, D. (1998, November). *The prevention of sexual revictimization: A preliminary investigation.* Paper presented at the annual meeting of the Association for Advancement of Behavior Therapy, Washington, DC.

McCall, G. (1993). Risk factors and sexual assault prevention. *Journal of Interpersonal Violence, 8,* 277–295.

McDonel, E.C., & McFall, R.M. (1991). Construct validity of two heterosocial perception skill measures for assessing rape proclivity. *Violence and Victims, 6,* 17–30.

McFall, R.M. (1990). The enhancement of social skills: An information-processing analysis. In W.L. Marshall, D.R. Laws, & H.E. Barbaree (Eds.), *Handbook of sexual assault: Issues, theories and treatment of the offender* (pp. 311–330). New York: Plenum Press.

Meadows, E., Jaycox, L., Orsillo, S., & Foa, E. (1997). *The impact of assault on risk recognition in ambiguous situations.* Poster presented at the 31st annual meeting of the Association for the Advancement of Behavior Therapy, Miami Beach, FL.

Meadows, E., Jaycox, L., Webb, S., & Foa, E. (1996). Risk recognition in narratives of rape experiences. In S. Orsillo & L. Roemer (Chairs.), *The use of narrative methodologies to explore cognitive and emotional dimensions among women with posttraumatic stress disorder.* Symposium conducted at the 30th annual meeting of the Association for the Advancement of Behavior Therapy, New York.

Miller, P.A., & Eisenberg, N. (1988). The relation of empathy to aggressive and externalizing/antisocial behavior. *Psychological Bulletin, 103,* 324–344.

Monson, C.M., & Langhinrichsen-Rohling, J. (1998). Sexual and nonsexual marital aggression: Legal considerations, epidemiology, and an integrated typology of perpetrators. *Aggression and Violent Behavior, 3,* 369–389.

Mosher, D.L., & Anderson, R.D. (1986). Macho personality, sexual aggression, and reactions to guided imagery of realistic rape. *Journal of Research in Personality, 20,* 77–94.

Mosher, D.L., & Sirkin, M. (1984). Measuring a macho personality constellation. *Journal of Research in Personality, 18,* 150–163.

Muehlenhard, C.L., & Falcon, P.L. (1990). Men's heterosocial skill and attitudes toward women as predictors of verbal sexual coercion and forceful rape. *Sex Roles, 23,* 241–259.

Muehlenhard, C.L., & Linton, M.A. (1987). Date rape and sexual aggression in dating situations: Incidence and risk factors. *Journal of Counseling Psychology, 34,* 186–196.

Murphy, W.D., Coleman, E., & Haynes, M. (1986). Factors related to coercive sexual behavior in a nonclinical sample of males. *Violence and Victims, 4,* 255–278.

Norris, J., Nurius, P., & Dimeff, L. (1996). Through her eyes: Factors affecting women's perception of resistance to acquaintance sexual aggression threat. *Psychology of Women Quarterly, 20,* 123–145.

Patterson, G.R., DeBaryshe, B.D., & Ramsey, E. (1989). A developmental perspective on antisocial behavior. *American Psychologist, 44,* 329–335.

Pryor, J.B., & Stoller, L.M. (1994). Sexual cognition processes in men high in the likelihood to sexually harass. *Personality and Social Psychology Bulletin, 20,* 163–169.

Rapaport, K., & Burkhart, B.R. (1984). Personality and attitudinal characteristics of sexually coercive males. *Journal of Abnormal Psychology, 93,* 216–221.

Resick, P. (1993). The psychological impact of rape. *Journal of Interpersonal Violence, 8,* 223–255.

Resick, P., & Schnicke, M. (1992). Cognitive processing therapy for sexual assault victims. *Journal of Consulting and Clinical Psychology, 60,* 748–756.

Richardson, D., & Hammock, G. (1991). Alcohol and acquaintance rape. In A. Parrot & L. Bechhofer (Eds.), *Acquaintance rape: The hidden crime* (pp. 83–95). New York: Wiley.

Roehrich, L., & Kinder, B. (1991). Alcohol expectancies and male sexuality: Review and implications for sex therapy. *Journal of Sex & Marital Therapy, 17,* 45–54.

Roth, S., Wayland, K., & Woolsey, M. (1990). Victimization history and victim-assailant relationship as factors in recovery from sexual assault. *Journal of Traumatic Stress, 3,* 169–180.

Rothbaum, B., Foa, E., Riggs, D., Murdock, T., & Walsh, W. (1992). A prospective examination of post-traumatic stress disorder in rape victims. *Journal of Traumatic Stress, 5,* 455–475.

Russell, D. (1984). *Sexual exploitation: Rape, child sexual abuse, and workplace harassment.* Beverly Hills: Sage.

Russell, D. (1990). *Rape in marriage.* Indianapolis: Indiana University Press.

Schewe, P.A., & O'Donohue, W. (1996). Rape prevention with high-risk males: Short-term outcome of two interventions. *Archives of Sexual Behavior, 25,* 455–469.

Scully, D., & Marolla, J. (1984). Convicted rapists' vocabulary of motive: Excuses and justifications. *Social Problems, 31,* 530–544.

Searles, P., & Berger, R. (1987). The current status of rape reform legislation: An examination of state statutes. *Women's Rights Law Reporter,* pp. 25–43.

Serin, R.C., Malcolm, P.B., Khanna, A., & Barbaree, H.E. (1994). Psychopathy and deviant sexual arousal in incarcerated sexual offenders. *Journal of Interpersonal Violence, 9,* 3–11.

Sorenson, S., Siegel, J., Golding, J., & Stein, J. (1991). Repeated sexual victimization. *Violence and Victims, 6,* 299–308.

Sunberg, S.L., Barbaree, H.E., & Marshall, W.L. (1991). Victim blame and the disinhibition of sexual arousal to rape vignettes. *Violence and Victims, 6,* 103–120.

Swartz, B.K., & Cellini, H.R. (1995). *The sex offender.* Kingston, NJ: Civic Research Institute.

van der Kolk, B., van der Hart, O., & Marmar, C. (1996). Dissociation and information processing in posttraumatic stress disorder. In B. van der Kolk, A. McFarlane, & L. Weisaeth (Eds.), *Traumatic stress: The effects of overwhelming experience on mind, body, and society* (pp. 303–330). New York: Guilford Press.

Ward, T., Hudson, S.M., Johnston, L., & Marshall, W.L. (1997). Cognitive distortions in sex offenders: An integrative review. *Clinical Psychology Review, 17,* 479–508.

White, J.W., & Humphrey, J.A. (1994, July). *Alcohol/drug use and sexual aggression: Distal and proximal influences.* Paper presented at the meeting of the International Society for Research in Aggression, Delray Beach, FL.

White, J.W., Humphrey, J.A., & Farmer, R. (1989, March). *Antisocial behavioral correlates of self-reported sexual aggression.* Paper presented at the Southeastern Psychological Association, Washington, DC.

White, J.W., & Koss, M.P. (1993). Adolescent sexual aggression within heterosexual relationships: Prevalence, characteristics, and causes. In H.W. Barbaree, W.L. Marshall, & S.M. Hindson (Eds.), *The juvenile sex offender* (pp. 182–202). New York: Guilford Press.

Wilson, A., Calhoun, S., & Bernat, J. (in press). Risk recognition and trauma-related symptoms among sexually revictimized women. *Journal of Consulting and Clinical Psychology.*

Yates, E., Barbaree, H.E., & Marshall, W.L. (1984). Anger and deviant sexual arousal. *Behavior Therapy, 15,* 287–294.

Zeitlin, S., McNally, R., & Cassiday, K. (1993). Alexithymia in victims of sexual assault: An effect of repeated victimization? *American Journal of Psychiatry, 150,* 661–663.

CHAPTER 17

Therapists' Sexual Feelings and Behaviors: Research, Trends, and Quandaries

KENNETH S. POPE

R ESEARCH SUGGESTS THAT it is common for therapists to experience sexual feelings for at least one patient over the course of a career. National studies found that slightly more than 8 out of 10 psychologists (87%) and social workers (81%) reported feeling sexually attracted to one or more patients (Bernsen, Tabachnick, & Pope, 1994; Pope, Keith-Spiegel, & Tabachnick, 1986). A sizable minority of therapists seem to carry with them—in the physical absence of the client—sexualized images of the client. About 27% of male psychologists and 30% of male social workers—compared with 14% of female psychologists and 13% of female social workers—reported engaging in sexual fantasies about a patient while engaging in sexual activity with another person (i.e., not the patient). About 46% of psychologists reported engaging in sexual fantasizing (regardless of the occasion) about a patient on a rare basis; an additional 26% reported more frequent fantasies of this kind (Pope, Tabachnick, & Keith-Spiegel, 1987).

Participants in these studies were asked to describe the characteristics or qualities of patients to whom they were attracted. Psychologists in the 1986 study named 997 descriptive characteristics that were sorted into 19 content categories. Interestingly, and perhaps not surprisingly, the most frequently named characteristic was "physical attractiveness." With two exceptions, there were no statistically significant differences in the frequency with which male and female therapists mentioned each characteristic. But there were two significant gender differences: male therapists far more often than female therapists mentioned "physical attractiveness" (209 times for male therapists vs. 87

times for female therapists); female therapists significantly more often than male therapists mentioned "successful" (27 times for female therapists vs. 6 times for male therapists). Table 17.1 presents the list of client characteristics for the 1986 and 1994 studies.

Simply feeling this sexual attraction, without necessarily feeling tempted to act on it, troubles many therapists. A *majority* of therapists (63% of the psychologists, 51% of the social workers) reported that experiencing sexual attraction to a patient made them feel guilty, anxious, or confused.

But if sexual attraction by itself tends to be guilt-inducing, anxiety-provoking, and confusing to most therapists, it occurs within an emotionally complex process (i.e., therapy) or context that often involves intense feelings. Table 17.2 presents findings from three national studies suggesting the extent to which therapists may encounter intense feelings or occasions for intense feelings.

It is not just that when therapists go to work, they go to a setting in which a wide variety of intense, complex feelings may occur; it is also that therapists bring to the setting their own emotional patterns, vulnerabilities, and histories,

Table 17.1

Characteristics of Clients to Whom Psychotherapists Are Attracted

	Social Workers[1]	Psychologists[2]
Physical attractiveness	175	296
Positive mental/cognitive traits or abilities	84	124
Sexual	40	88
Vulnerabilities	52	85
Positive overall character/personality	58	84
Kind	6	66
Fills therapist's needs	8	46
Successful	6	33
"Good patient"	21	31
Client's attraction	3	30
Independence	5	23
Other specific personality characteristics	27	14
Resemblance to someone in therapist's life	14	12
Availability (client unattached)	0	9
Pathological characteristics	13	8
Long-term client	7	7
Sociability (sociable, extroverted, etc.)	0	6
Miscellaneous	23	15
Same interests/philosophy/background to therapist	10	0

[1] Social work data are from Bernsen et al. (1994).

[2] Psychology data are from Pope et al. (1986).

Table 17.2
Sexual and Other Occasions for Intense Emotion in Therapy

Behavior	Study 1	Study 2	Study 3
Feeling sexually aroused while in the presence of a client			57.8%
A client seems to become sexually aroused in your presence			18.2
A client seems to have an orgasm in your presence			3.2
Noticing that a client is physically attractive			95.8
Telling a client that you find him or her physically attractive			38.9
Telling a sexual fantasy to a client			6.0
Engaging in sexual fantasy about a client	71.8%		
Feeling sexually attracted to a client	89.5		87.3
A client tells you that he or she is sexually attracted to you			73.3
Disclosing details of current personal stresses to a client		38.9%	
Lying on top of or underneath a client			0.4
Crying in the presence of a client	56.5		
Telling a client that you are angry at him or her	89.7		77.9
Raising your voice at a client because you are angry at him or her			57.2
Having fantasies that reflect your anger at a client			50.9
Feeling hatred toward a client			31.2
Telling clients of your disappointment in them	51.9		
Feeling afraid that a client may commit suicide			97.2
Feeling afraid that a client may need clinical resources that are unavailable			86.0
Feeling afraid because a client's condition gets suddenly or seriously worse			90.9
Feeling afraid that your colleagues may be critical of your work with a client			88.1
Feeling afraid that a client may file a formal complaint against you			66.0
Flirting with a client			19.6
Kissing a client			5.6
Using self-disclosure as a therapy technique	93.3		

Source: Study 1: A national survey of 1,000 psychologists with a 46% return rate (Pope, Tabachnick, & Keith-Spiegel, 1987).
Study 2: A national survey of 4,800 psychologists, psychiatrists, and social workers with a 49% return rate (Borys & Pope, 1989).
Study 3: A national survey of 600 psychologists with a 48% return rate (Pope & Tabachnick, 1993).

including their experiences as patients. Table 17.3 presents some aspects of therapists' own experiences as patients. This national study found that about 90% of the female therapists and about 80% of the male therapists had been in therapy. Among the 35 major issues on which the therapy had focused, the following dozen (beginning with the most frequently mentioned) were among the most common: depression or general unhappiness, marriage or divorce, general relationship problems, self-esteem and self-confidence, anxiety, career, family of origin, loss or abandonment, stress, dependence, sexual conflicts, and sexual assault or abuse. A majority (61%) reported that, regardless of the major focus of therapy, they had experienced at least one episode of what they described as clinical depression. Over a fourth (29%) reported having felt suicidal, and 4% reported making at least one suicidal attempt. Twenty percent of those who had been in therapy reported keeping a significant secret from the therapist. A majority of these secrets were, according to the participants, sexual in nature. Interestingly, therapy evaluated as successful by the participants was positively correlated with an absence of secrets withheld from the therapist.

Findings from a national study summarized in Table 17.4 suggest that about one third (33%) of the participants reported having experienced some form of sexual or physical abuse as a child or adolescent, and slightly over a third (37%) reported having experienced some form of abuse during adulthood. Overall, about one third (33%) of the male therapists and slightly over two-thirds (70%) of the female therapists reported some form of abuse during childhood, adolescence, or adulthood.

EDUCATION ABOUT SEXUAL FEELINGS

That therapy, a process that can involve such intense and often uncomfortable feelings such as fear, anger, and hatred, is carried out by therapists who have their own emotional histories, vulnerabilities, and patterns underscores the importance of the therapist's competence in the area of sexual feelings. Training programs must enable therapists to avoid responding to such feelings in a way that harms patients or interferes with therapeutic tasks. Unfortunately, the research suggests that adequate training in this area is rare. Only 9% of the psychologists and 10% of the social workers reported that their graduate school and internship training on this topic was adequate (Bernsen et al., 1994; Pope et al., 1986). Most psychologists and social workers reported no training in the area of sexual attraction to patients.

This widespread neglect of the issue in training programs may make it difficult for therapists to acknowledge, understand, and respond to their own feelings of attraction in a safe and appropriate way. "How can the extant population of psychotherapists be expected to adequately address [these issues] if we pay so little attention to training in these matters?" (Koocher, 1994, p. viii). The lack of attention to this topic may also create the misleading impression that few therapists experience sexual attraction to their patients.

Table 17.3

Therapists' Reports of Their Experiences as Patients

Codes: 0 = never, 1 = once, 2 = rarely (2–4 times), 3 = sometimes (5–10 times), 4 = often (over 10 times).

Item	0	1	2	3	4
In your own personal therapy, how often (if at all) did your therapist ($N = 400$):					
cradle or hold you in a nonsexual way	73.2	2.7	8.0	8.8	6.0
touch you in a sexual way	93.7	2.5	1.8	0.3	1.0
talk about sexual issues in a way that you believe to be inappropriate	91.2	2.7	3.2	0.5	1.3
seem to be sexually attracted to you	84.5	6.2	3.5	3.0	1.5
disclose that he or she was sexually attracted to you	92.2	3.7	1.0	1.3	0.8
seem to be sexually aroused in your presence	91.2	3.7	2.2	0.8	1.3
express anger at you	60.7	14.3	16.8	5.7	1.8
express disappointment in you	67.0	11.3	14.8	4.7	1.3
give you encouragement and support	2.5	0.8	6.2	21.8	67.5
tell you that he or she cared about you	33.7	6.7	19.5	21.8	16.3
make what you consider to be a clinical or therapeutic error	19.8	18.0	36.2	19.0	5.5
pressure you to talk about something you didn't want to talk about	57.5	7.5	21.3	8.8	4.0
use humor in an appropriate way	76.7	8.8	10.0	2.2	1.5
use humor in an inappropriate way	5.2	2.5	12.5	35.0	43.5
act in a rude or insensitive manner toward you	68.7	13.0	12.0	4.0	1.5
violate your rights to confidentiality	89.7	4.5	2.7	1.3	1.8
violate your rights to informed consent	93.2	3.2	1.3	0.3	0.3
use hospitalization as part of your treatment	96.2	1.8	0.5	0.5	1.0
In your own personal therapy, how often (if at all) did you ($N = 400$):					
feel sexually attracted to your therapist	63.0	8.0	14.0	7.5	6.5
tell your therapist that you were sexually attracted to him or her	81.5	6.2	5.5	3.0	2.7
have sexual fantasies about your therapist	65.5	8.0	12.8	7.0	5.2
feel angry at your therapist	13.3	9.5	32.7	28.5	15.0
feel that your therapist did not care about you	49.5	13.0	19.0	12.3	5.5
feel suicidal	70.0	8.5	9.5	8.3	3.0
make a suicide attempt	95.5	2.5	1.0	0.0	0.0
feel what you would characterize as clinical depression	38.5	15.8	16.0	16.5	12.5

Source: Pope & Tabachnick (1994).

Table 17.4
Percent of Male and Female Therapists Reporting Having Been Abused

Type of Abuse	Men	Women
Abuse during Childhood or Adolescence		
Sexual abuse by relative	5.84	21.05
Sexual abuse by teacher	0.73	1.96
Sexual abuse by physician	0.0	1.96
Sexual abuse by therapist	0.0	0.0
Sexual abuse by nonrelative (other than those previously listed)	9.49	16.34
Nonsexual physical abuse	13.14	9.15
At least one of the above	26.28	39.22
Abuse during Adulthood		
Sexual harassment	1.46	37.91
Attempted rape	0.73	13.07
Acquaintance rape	0.0	6.54
Stranger rape	0.73	1.31
Nonsexual physical abuse by a spouse or partner	6.57	12.42
Nonsexual physical abuse by an acquaintance	0.0	2.61
Nonsexual physical abuse by a stranger	4.38	7.19
Sexual involvement with a therapist	2.19	4.58
Sexual involvement with a physician	0.0	1.96
At least one of the above	13.87	56.86
Abuse during Childhood, Adolescence, or Adulthood	32.85%	69.93%

Source: The table summarizes a national study by Pope & Feldman-Summers (1992).

> In light of the multitude of books in the areas of human sexuality, sexual dynamics, sex therapies, unethical therapist-patient sexual contact, management of the therapist's or patient's sexual behaviors, and so on, it is curious that sexual attraction to patients per se has not served as the primary focus of a wide range of texts. The professor, supervisor, or librarian seeking books that turn their *primary* attention to exploring the therapist's *feelings* in this regard would be hard pressed to assemble a selection from which to choose an appropriate course text. If someone unfamiliar with psychotherapy were to judge the prevalence and significance of therapists' sexual feelings on the basis of the books that focus exclusively on that topic, he or she might conclude that the phenomenon is neither wide-spread nor important. (Pope, Sonne, & Holroyd, 1993, p. 23)

To the extent that formal training programs fail to discuss sexual attraction to patients (which is, of course, not the same as the topic of therapist-patient sexual involvement), they may be unintentionally modeling for trainees the view that sexual attraction to patients is taboo, is abnormal, and is not to be acknowledged, let alone studied and discussed.

A TOPIC NOT JUST FOR THE INTELLECT

One factor that may make sexual issues in therapy difficult to address and easy to neglect in training programs is that they often evoke emotional reactions that are sometimes surprising, uncomfortable, and difficult to acknowledge. The following seven scenarios and questions, which are adapted from Pope, Sonne, and Holroyd (1993), illustrate aspects of therapy that may evoke such reactions. These exercises invite readers to reflect on their own emotional responses. They address the reader directly in the second person to allow identification with the fictional therapist in each scenario. Each set of questions begins by inviting readers to identify the feelings evoked by the scenario.

Scenario 1: The Movie

It has been an extremely demanding week, and you're looking forward to going to the new movie with your life partner. The theater is packed but you find two seats on the aisle not too close to the screen. You feel great to have left work behind you at the office and to be with your lover for an evening on the town. As the lights go down, you lean over to give your partner a passionate kiss. For some reason, while kissing, you open your eyes and notice that, sitting in the seat on the other side of your partner and watching you is a therapy patient who has, just that afternoon, revealed an intense sexual attraction to you.

- What do you feel?
- If you were the therapist, what, if anything, would you say to the patient at the time of this event? What would you say during the next therapy session?
- How would the patient's presence affect your subsequent behavior at the theater?
- How might this event affect the therapy and your relationship with the patient?
- What, if anything, would you say to your partner, either at the theater or later, about what had happened? Are there any circumstances under which you would phone the patient before the next scheduled appointment to discuss the matter?
- Imagine that during a subsequent therapy session, the patient begins asking about whom you were with at the theater. How would you feel? What would you say?
- What if the patient is a business client of your partner (or knows your partner in another context) and they begin talking before the movie begins. What feelings would this discovery evoke in you? What would you consider in deciding how to handle this matter?
- To what extent do you believe that therapists should be free to "be themselves"? To what extent should they behave in public as if a patient might be observing them?

Scenario 2: Marriage Counseling

You have just completed your third marriage counseling session with a couple who have been together for four years. As you walk back to your desk, you find that one of them has left a note for you. Opening the note, you find the client's declaration of overwhelming feelings of love for you, the desire for an affair, and a promise to commit suicide if you tell the other member of the couple about this note.

- What do you feel?
- Would you initially address this matter privately with the client who left the note or with the two clients as a couple? What do you consider as you make this decision?
- How would your understanding of and response to this client's "love" for you differ, if at all, if you were conducting individual rather than couple counseling?
- What feelings does the client's threat of suicide evoke in you? How do you address this issue?
- As you imagine this scenario, do you tend to believe that the other client is aware of his or her partner's loving feelings toward you?
- When you see a couple in therapy, what ground rules, agreements, or formal contracts do you create regarding confidentiality, "secrets," and the scheduling of sessions with only one member of the couple? Do you provide any of this information in written form?
- When providing couple counseling, do you keep one chart for the couple or individual charts for the two clients? How do you decide what information should be included in (or excluded from) the charts? Would you include the note described in the scenario in the chart?

Scenario 3: Sounds

You are working in a busy mental health center in which the doors to the consulting rooms, while offering some privacy, are not completely soundproofed. As long as therapist and client are talking at a normal level, nothing can be heard from outside the door. But words spoken loudly can be heard and understood in the reception area.

A patient, Sal, sits in silence during the first five minutes of the session, finally saying, "It's been hard to concentrate today. I keep hearing these sounds, like they're ringing in my ear, and they're frightening to me. I want to tell you what they're like, but I'm afraid to."

After offering considerable reassurance that describing the sounds will be OK and that you and Sal can work together to try to understand what is causing the sounds, what they mean, and what you might do about them, you notice that Sal seems to be gathering the courage to reveal them to you.

Finally, Sal leans back in the chair and imitates the sounds. They build quickly to a very high pitch and loud volume. They sound exactly like someone becoming more and more sexually aroused and then experiencing an intense orgasm.

You are reasonably certain that these sounds have been heard by the receptionist, some of your colleagues, the patients sitting in the waiting room, and a site visitor from the Joint Commission on Accreditation of Healthcare Organizations who is deciding whether the hospital in which your clinic is based should have its accreditation renewed.

- What do you feel?
- As you imagined the scene, was the client male (e.g., Salvador) or female (e.g., Sally)? Does the client's gender make any difference in the way you feel?
- If Sal began to make the sounds again, would you make any effort to interrupt or to ask the client to be a little quieter? Why?
- If none of the people who might have heard the sounds mentioned this event to you, would you make any effort to explain what had happened?
- Imagine that just as Sal finishes making these sounds, someone knocks loudly on the door and asks, "What's going on in there?" What do you say or do?
- Would your feelings or behavior be any different if the sounds were of a person being beaten rather than having an orgasm?
- How would you describe this session in your chart notes?
- If you were being supervised, would you feel at all apprehensive about discussing this session with your supervisor?
- What approach do you usually take toward your clients making loud noises that might be heard outside the consulting room?

SCENARIO 4: INITIAL APPOINTMENT

In independent practice, you've been working in your new office for about a year. In the past few months, several of your patients have completed therapy and new referrals haven't been coming in. It has become difficult to cover your expenses. Finally, a prospective patient schedules an initial appointment. During the first session, the patient says that the problem is sexual in nature and asks if you are comfortable and experienced in working with that sort of problem. You answer truthfully that you are. You are told that the patient will only be able to work with a therapist of a particular sexual orientation, without specifying what that orientation is. Then the patient asks, "What is your sexual orientation?"

- What do you feel?
- Imagine that the question takes you by surprise. What might you say to the patient if the question took you off guard?

- Reflect on the various ways you might respond to this question. If you had adequate time to consider the question, how do you think you would respond? Is this response different from the one you might tend to make if the question caught you off guard?
- Imagine that the patient has been in therapy with you for six months and then asks this question. Would you give a different answer than if he or she were a new patient?
- If you were choosing a therapist, would the therapist's sexual orientation make any difference in your decision?
- Do you believe that there are any false stereotypes about therapists based on their sexual orientation? If so, what are they? How, if at all, do they affect therapy research, theory, and training? How, if at all, do they affect hiring practices, promotions, and formal or informal policies within mental health facilities? How, if at all, have they affected your training and practice? What feelings do these false stereotypes that you believe exist evoke in you?
- Do you believe that there are any actual group differences among therapists based on their sexual orientation? If so, what are they? How, if at all, do they affect therapy research, theory, and training? How, if at all, do they affect hiring practices, promotions, and formal or informal policies within mental health facilities? How, if at all, have they affected your training and practice? What feelings do these group differences that you believe exist evoke in you?
- How do you decide what kinds of personal information to reveal to a patient?

SCENARIO 5: SIZE

During your first session with a new patient, he tells you that he has always been concerned that his penis is too small. Suddenly, he pulls down his pants and asks you if you think it is too small. (Consider the same scenario with a new patient who is concerned about the size of her breasts.)

- What do you feel?
- What would you, as therapist, *want* to do first? Why? What do you think you *would* do first? Why?
- What difference would it make if this were a patient whom you had been treating for a year rather than a new patient?
- How, if at all, would your feelings and actions be different according to whether treatment were conducted on an inpatient or an outpatient basis?
- How, if at all, would your feelings and actions differ according to the gender of the patient?
- Imagine that the male and female patients in the scenario are 15 years old. What feelings does the scenario evoke in you? What do you do? What

fantasies occur to you about what might happen after the event described in the scenario?

Scenario 6: Reaction

A client begins describing sexual fantasies in great detail. You find that you become sexually aroused and are blushing. The patient notices that you seem different somehow and asks you, "What's wrong?"

- What do you feel?
- Is it likely that you will respond to the client's question directly? Why or why not?
- What do you consider as you decide what to do next?
- As you imagine yourself becoming sexually aroused in front of a patient, what feelings do you experience? Would you mention these feelings to the client? To a supervisor? To a colleague? To a supervisee?
- As you imagine yourself blushing in front of a client, what feelings do you experience? Would you reveal these feelings to the client? To a supervisor? To a colleague? To a supervisee?
- What effects do you imagine your arousal and blushing might have had on the client?
- As you first imagined this scenario, was the client sexually aroused while describing the fantasies?
- Are you aware of any desire for the client to continue describing the fantasies? Any desire to move closer to the client? Any desire to extend the length of the session? Any desire that the session were already over? Any desire that the client had not described the fantasies in such detail? Any wish that you had met this client outside of the therapeutic relationship so that you could enjoy a sexually intimate relationship? Any desire to terminate or transfer this client?
- The session is now over and you are preparing to meet with your supervisor. Are you any more eager or reluctant to meet with your supervisor than you customarily would be? Do you believe that you would describe the client's fantasies in great detail to your supervisor? Would you mention your own sexual arousal to your supervisor?
- You describe this session to a colleague. The colleague says, "I think you must have been acting seductively. In some subtle ways, you must have been giving signals encouraging the client to talk in a way that would stimulate you sexually." What do you feel when your colleague says this? What do you think?
- You describe this session to a colleague. The colleague says, "I think this client was trying to seduce you." What do you feel when your colleague says this? What do you think?

- You describe this session to a colleague. The colleague says, "Aren't you concerned that this client might file a complaint against you for sexual misconduct?" What do you feel when your colleague says this? What do you think?
- You describe this session to a colleague. The colleague says, "Some people have all the luck. I wish one of my clients would do that!" What do you feel when your colleague says this? What do you think?
- When a client describes sexual fantasies in great detail, under what circumstances might you fail to include any mention of the topic in the client's chart? Under what circumstances might you include detailed descriptions of the fantasies in the chart? What are your feelings and thoughts as you anticipate the possible consequences of including or omitting sexual material while charting?
- You are now sitting in your office five minutes before the next session with this client. Do you find yourself either more or less eager to meet with this client than you usually are? In future sessions, would you make any effort to encourage or discourage the client from describing sexual fantasies in great detail?

SCENARIO 7: THE GOAL

Your patient describes to you her troubled marriage. Her husband used to get mad and hit her ("Not too hard," she says) but he's pretty much gotten over that. Their sex life is not good. Her husband enjoys anal intercourse, but she finds it frightening and painful. She tells you that she'd like to explore her resistance to this form of sexual behavior in her therapy. Her goal is to become comfortable engaging in the behavior so that she can please her husband, enjoy sex with him, and have a happy marriage.

- What are you feeling when the patient says that her husband used to get mad and hit her? What are you thinking?
- What are you feeling when she says that she finds anal intercourse frightening and painful? What are you thinking?
- What do you feel when she describes her goals in therapy? What are you thinking? In what ways do you believe that your feelings may influence how you proceed with this patient?

WHAT PERCENTAGE OF THERAPISTS ENGAGE IN SEX WITH THEIR PATIENTS?

Although the research suggests that a great majority of therapists experience, at least occasionally, sexual attraction to a patient, a relatively small minority, according to the research, engage in sex with a patient. Table 17.5 presents findings from the eight national self-report studies that have been

Table 17.5

Self-Report Studies of Sex with Clients Using National Samples of Therapists[a]

Study	Publication Date	Discipline	Sample Size	Return Rate (%)	% Reporting Sex with Clients	
					Male	Female
Holroyd & Brodsky[b]	1977	psychologists	1,000	70	12.1	2.6
Pope, Levenson, & Schover	1979	psychologists	1,000	48	12.0	3.0
Pope, Keith-Spiegel, & Tabachnick	1986	psychologists	1,000	58.5	9.4	2.5
Gartrell, Herman, Olarte, Feldstein & Localio[c]	1986	psychiatrists	5,574	26	7.1	3.1
Pope, Tabachnick, & Keith-Spiegel[d]	1987	psychologists	1,000	46	3.6	0.4
Akamatsu[e]	1988	psychologists	1,000	39.5	3.5	2.3
Borys & Pope[f]	1989	psychiatrists, psychologists, & social workers	4,800	56.5	0.9	0.2
Bernsen, Tabachnick, & Pope	1994	social workers	1,000	45.3	3.6	0.5

[a] This table presents only national surveys that have been published in peer-reviewed scientific and professional journals. Exceptional caution is warranted in comparing the data from these various surveys. For example, the frequently cited percentages of 12.1 and 2.6, reported by Holroyd and Brodsky (1977), exclude same-sex involvements. Moreover, when surveys included separate items to assess posttermination sexual involvement, these data are reported in footnotes to this table. Finally, some published articles did not provide sufficiently detailed data for this table (e.g., aggregate percentages); the investigators supplied the data needed for the table.

[b] Although the gender percentages presented in the table for the other studies represent responses to one basic survey item in each survey, the percentages presented for Holroyd & Brodsky's (1977) study span several items. The study's senior author confirmed through personal communication that the study's findings were that 12.1% of the male and 2.6% of the female participants reported having engaged in erotic contact (whether or not it included intercourse) with at least one opposite-sex patient; that about 4% of the male and 1% of the female participants reported engaging in erotic contact with at least one same-sex patient; and that, in response to a separate survey item, 7.2% of the male and 0.6% of the female psychologists reported that they had "had intercourse with a patient within three months after terminating therapy" (p. 846; see also Pope, Sonne, & Holroyd, 1993).

[c] "Respondents were asked to specify the number of male and female patients with whom they had been sexually involved" (p. 1127); they were also asked "to restrict their answers to adult patients" (p. 1127).

[d] The survey also included a question about "becoming sexually involved with a former client" (p. 996). Gender percentages about sex with current or former clients did not appear in the article but were provided by an author. Fourteen percent of the male and 8% of the female respondents reported sex with a former client.

[e] The original article also noted that 14.2% of male and 4.7% of female psychologists reported that they had "been involved in an intimate relationship with a former client" (p. 454).

[f] This survey was sent to 1,600 psychiatrists, 1,600 psychologists, and 1,600 social workers. In addition to the data reported in the table, the original article also asked if respondents had "engaged in sexual activity with a client after termination" (p. 288). Six percent of the male and 2% of the female therapists reported engaging in this activity.

Source: Adapted from Pope (1994), and used with written permission.

published in peer-review journals (for additional data sets, see http://idealist .com/memories). These studies, beginning in 1977, draw on self-reports from 5,148 therapists. Psychology, psychiatry, and social work are each represented by at least two studies conducted in different years. Pooling the data from all eight studies reveals that about 4.4% of the therapists report engaging in sex with at least one patient.

When all the data are statistically analyzed, there is a significant effect due to gender, which will be discussed later. There is also a significant effect due to year of the study: each year, there are about 10% fewer self-reports of therapist-patient sex than the previous year. When data are based on self-report relying on retrospective memory, there are always concerns that such findings may be due to participants changing their self-reports rather than actual changes in the population (see, e.g., Pope, 1990). However, it is possible that each year the population of therapists includes about 10% fewer therapists who have engaged in sex with their patients than the year before.[1]

Statistical analysis of the data from all eight studies reveals no significant effect due to profession. That is to say, psychologists, psychiatrists, and social workers report engaging in sex with their patients at about the same rates. Although, in looking at the percentages in Table 17.5, it may seem that the professions differ in their rate, statistical analysis of the data suggests that such differences are due to differences in years that the studies were conducted and to the fact that there is a confounding correlation between the professions and the years they were studied. A statistical model incorporating the data from all studies allowed assessment of the predictive power of each variable (i.e., profession and year) once the variance accounted for by the other variable had been subtracted. Year of study reveals significantly more predictive power once effects due to profession have been accounted for than the predictive power of profession once effects due to year have been taken into account. Once year of study is taken into account, significant differences among professions are gone.

COMMON SCENARIOS OF THERAPIST-PATIENT SEXUAL INVOLVEMENT

The research literature, public records from civil suits and licensing hearings, clinical case accounts, and other available databases allowed an analysis of patterns among situations in which therapist-patient sex occurs, from which the 10 most common scenarios emerged (Pope & Bouhoutsos, 1986).

---

[1] This does not, of course, mean that the field would be free, at the end of 10 years, of therapists who sexually exploit their patients, a conclusion that was suggested by a workshop participant. According to this reasoning, because the figure would be 10% lower each year, at the end of 10 years it would be 100% (i.e., 10 years times 10%) lower. The research suggests that on average, the figure will be only 90% of the figure *for the previous year*.

ROLE TRADING

In the role trading scenario, therapist and patient seem to exchange roles. The therapist in essence becomes the "patient." The actual needs of the patient are ignored; it is the therapist whose needs and wants become the focus of the therapy and the therapeutic relationship. It becomes the task of the patient to meet the needs and fulfill the wants of the therapist. The process is similar in some respects to what happens in some incestuous families in which the abused child becomes the "parent" to the actual parents, learning to anticipate and meet their sexual, emotional, and other needs.

SEX THERAPY

In this scenario, the therapist undertakes the fraudulent exercise of trying to convince the patient that sex with the therapist is a legitimate, appropriate, safe, and effective treatment for the patient's problems. Sometimes, offenders present this option as the only way to help the patient. In some cases, the patient may have initially described a sexual problem or concern, but this is not essential. Regardless of the patient's presenting complaints or other difficulties that may arise during subsequent sessions, the therapist can present sexual activity as the patient's only way "to grow," "to learn how to trust," "to learn how to be spontaneous," "to find the authentic self," "to overcome debilitating inhibitions," "to explore," "to learn how to achieve true intimacy," "to try out different parts of her or his self," "to experiment with new ways of being," "to integrate mind and body and spirit," and so on. The bizarre way in which therapists may attempt to rationalize sex abuse of patients as part of an innovative treatment plan is illustrated by a 71-year-old therapist who "admitted sexually assaulting a 17-year-old boy . . . by whipping him on the buttocks, hands and feet while the boy was naked." The therapist had maintained that such whippings were part of an innovative treatment "to help [the patient] overcome a drinking problem" ("Therapist Sentenced for Whipping Patient," 1987, p. 3B).

As If. . .

Here, the therapist pretends that the patient's cognitive dynamics that are elicited by the therapeutic situation would have occurred, in light of the therapist's supposed charm, outside the therapeutic situation. During moments of great stress, a fragile patient may experience feelings of being tiny and virtually powerless, and may feel that the therapist is an all-powerful, intensely attractive, godlike figure. An offender therapist in this scenario assumes that the patient has just experienced a wonderfully accurate insight into the therapist's true nature.

SVENGALI

In this scenario, the therapist uses the power of the therapeutic situation to create and nurture an extreme dependence on the part of the patient. The therapist makes decisions for the patient, and attempts to recreate the patient into a new personality of the therapist's choosing.

DRUGS

This scenario is enacted when the therapist uses cocaine, alcohol, or other drugs to bring about a sexual relationship with the patient. In some instances, only the patient takes the drugs, often presented as if they were prescribed medicine. In other instances, the therapist may share the drugs with the patient.

RAPE

When the therapist resorts to physical force, threats of violence, or other forms of intimidation to sexually exploit the patient, the rape scenario has been enacted. In many instances, the therapist may warn the patient that no one will believe the patient's account, that it will come down to the word of a respected therapist against an obviously "disturbed" or even "crazy" mental patient, that the patient is psychotic and any claims of a sexual relationship with the therapist are obviously the result of a delusion, a hallucination, a false memory, or a vivid dream. One patient used this threat as the title of her book describing rape at the hands of a prominent therapist: *You Must Be Dreaming* (Noel & Watterson, 1992).

TRUE LOVE

In this scenario, the therapist uses rationalizations that misrepresent or deny altogether the professional and fiduciary relationship with the patient and the inherent clinical, legal, and ethical duties that the therapist owes to the patient. These rationalizations are similar to those used by some incest perpetrators and other child sex abusers, that is that intercourse with a young child was not only legitimate but morally right because it was a case of true love. "True love" is one of several claims made by a prominent media psychologist who had his license revoked on the basis of accusations that he had had sex twice a week with a female patient 15 years younger for a one-year period. The psychologist maintained that

> he was in love with the woman, to the point of considering divorcing his wife and marrying the patient. But he maintained he didn't have sexual relations with her . . . until . . . after she had stopped going to him for treatment. Also, he said he was having impotency problems at the time, and was far too busy to have had an affair with her. (Bloom, 1989, p. B-1)

It Just Got Out of Hand

Here, the therapist tries to justify the sexual exploitation of the patient as if it were unintentional, an accident. Some therapists may make claims about the unintentional nature of the sexual exploitation that are so extreme that the therapist claims to have been unaware that sexual contact was taking place. For example, a psychologist who was 44 years older than his female patient was found to have sexually assaulted her. The psychologist testified that

> he remembered clearly that all he did was sit next to her and drape his arm around her shoulder. "It was a reassurance and kind of reinforcement of what she had been accomplishing." He emphasized, "I meant if my hand inadvertently got in the area of her breast, I was unaware of it." ("Therapist Guilty in Sexual Assault," 1988, p. 28)

As another example, here are a psychiatrist's responses during cross-examination as he testifies about his relationship with a patient:

Q. Did there ever come a time that she . . . performed fellatio on you?
A. . . . Whether there was oral-genital contact in the course of therapy, I am not certain.
Q. In what respect are you uncertain?
A. I am not certain that it did occur.
Q. Were there ever any instances in which you took your clothes off in front of this patient?
A. I don't recall.
Q. Did you ever lie on top of her?
A. I don't recall.
Q. Did you ever penetrate her?
A. I don't recall.
Q. Did she ever manually stimulate you sexually?
A. I don't recall. (Plaisil, 1985, p. 190)

Time Out

Here, the therapist refuses to acknowledge and take account of the fact that the therapeutic relationship and therapist's responsibilities do not cease to exist between scheduled appointments or outside the therapist's office. The therapist may, for example, invite the patient over for a relaxed lunch or game of tennis. Once a social relationship has been established, and the therapist and patient can share meals, play games, and hang out with each other as friends, there is no perceived barrier, according to this rationalization, for them to allow the closeness of friendship and play turn sexual, as long as it occurs during the "time outs" of socialization, play, and friendship between sessions or outside the office.

HOLD ME

In this scenario, the therapist takes advantage of the patient's desire for nonerotic physical contact and possible confusion between erotic and nonerotic contact. Although offender therapists may exploit the patient's desire for and confusion about nonerotic contact, that by no means indicates that nonerotic contact with patients is wrong per se or a high-risk behavior. Some forms of physical contact between therapist and patient are quite common. National studies suggest that at least 97% of therapists offer or accept a handshake from a client, about 81%–82% hug a client, about 89% accept a hug from a client, and 60% hold a client's hand (Pope et al., 1987; Pope & Tabachnick, 1993). To date, there are no research data published in peer-reviewed scientific or professional journals supporting the notion that therapists who engage in nonsexual physical contact with patients are at higher risk to become sexually involved with patients (Pope, Sonne, & Holroyd, 1993, p. 281). Holroyd and Brodsky (1980), who conducted the first national study of therapist-patient sexual contact, found that the research did suggest that sexual intercourse with patients was associated with *differential* touching:

> Erotic contact not leading to intercourse is associated with older, more experienced therapists who do not otherwise typically touch their patients at a rate different from other therapists (except when mutually initiated). Sexual intercourse with patients is associated with the touching of opposite-sex patients but not same-sex patients. It is the differential application of touching—rather than touching per se—that is related to intercourse. (p. 810)

Unfortunately, even if therapists do not believe that nonsexual touching (i.e., touching that is not differential according to gender) increases the risk for engaging in sex with patients, they may fear that colleagues who are aware of the touching will be critical of them, perhaps suspecting that they are engaging in or are at increased risk for sexually abusing a patient. Many therapists may be suffering from a *touch anxiety* that is similar to that experienced by many adults who avoid physical contact with (or sometimes even proximity to) children: "In regard to increasing public acknowledgment of child sexual abuse: Adults may be reluctant to hold children and to engage in nonsexual touch that is a normal part of life" (Pope & Vasquez, 1991, p. 105). Therapists "may go to great lengths to ensure that [they] maintain physical distance from . . . [clients] and under no circumstances touch them for fear that this might be misconstrued" or that it may subject therapists "to an ethics complaint or malpractice suit" (p. 105). Both patients and therapists are badly served when decisions about treatment are based solely on avoidance of being sued. The ways in which normal, nonsexual human touch have been made to seem inherently dangerous, wrong, and harmful unfortunately represent one of the many ways in which the small, atypical group of therapists who have violated the prohibition against therapist-client sexual intimacies have not only exploited their clients but also helped to create an atmosphere in which [even the most normal human experiences and acts] seem dangerous and daunting for the vast majority of therapists who, whatever their sexual feelings toward patients, would never seriously consider violating the prohibition and placing their patients at risk for great and lasting harm. (Pope, Sonne, & Holroyd, 1993, p. 45)

A HISTORY OF THE PROHIBITION

It is not uncommon for therapists defending themselves in civil suits against charges of sexually abusing a patient—when there is such clear evidence that the abuse occurred as to preclude a defense of "I didn't do it"—to make some version of the following claim (especially when there is a delay of years before the case comes to trial):

When I became sexually involved with this patient (or more often: when I was seduced by this patient), there wasn't a prohibition against sexual relations, which is a quite recent notion. The time in question was a time of great experimentation in the field. For many, you might even say it was a time of "anything goes." We were eager to try out almost any approach that might help the patient get better, even if the method was unorthodox. There is a relatively new theory that it is not the best practice and I probably agree, in light of this new theory, that it may be safer to refrain from such involvements. But it really isn't fair to judge my actions then on the basis of such a new idea.

Such claims may seem quite persuasive to jurors, especially if they are supported by the testimony of expert witnesses. Despite such claims, however, the prohibitions against therapist-patient sex, like those against rape and incest, have a long history. Although therapist-patient sex can appear in many forms, as the previous section illustrates, it was recognized as an abhorrent departure from safe, responsible, and appropriate practice by the health care profession in its ancient Hippocratic beginnings. The Hippocratic Oath states clearly: "In every house where I come, I will enter only for the good of my patients, keeping myself far from all intentional ill-doing and all seduction, and especially from the pleasures of love with women and men" (*Dorland's Medical Dictionary*, 1974, p. 175). The prohibition actually has earlier origins, appearing in the code of the Nigerian healing arts, which predated the Hippocratic Oath (see Pope, 1994). The prohibition was reaffirmed specifically at the origins of "talking" therapy. Freud articulated the prohibition against sex with a patient.

Therapist-patient sexual involvement was not named *explicitly* in the professional ethics codes until the mid-1970s. The reason was that it was assumed to occur so rarely, if at all, and to be so clearly unethical that explicit mention of it was unnecessary. Physical assault of patients is still not mentioned *explicitly* in the professional ethics codes for the same reasons: it is assumed to occur only on the most rare basis and it is clearly understood to be unethical. Were it to be discovered that a substantial minority of therapists were actually engaging in physical assaults on their patients and attempting to justify it as acceptable practice, the professional ethics codes would need to address the matter explicitly. It is difficult to overstate the degree to which therapists refused to believe that incidents of therapists engaging in sex with their patients occurred with any greater frequency than, for example, incidents of therapists engaging in violent physical assaults on their patients. The first peer-reviewed study that used actuarial data from existing archival information to address the notion that therapist-patient sex might actually occur was published in *American Psychologist* in 1971. The study reviewed all malpractice suits that had occurred during a 10-year period under the professional liability insurance plan provided specifically for members of the American Psychological Association. Although this report noted the large number of suits alleging therapist-patient sex, it contained no mention of *any* valid allegation of such offenses. The report blamed the false reports of women as accounting for the majority of *all* malpractice suits. It also set forth as unqualified fact the supposed reason for this epidemic of false allegations:

> The greatest number of [all malpractice] actions are brought by women who lead lives of very quiet desperation, who form close attachments to their therapists, who feel rejected or spurned when they discover that relations are maintained on a formal and professional level, and who then react with allegations of sexual improprieties. (Brownfain, 1971, p. 651)

Prior to this study, psychologists such as Harold Greenwald and Bertram Forer either had formally proposed to their psychological societies that research be conducted to determine whether therapist-patient sex actually occurred or they had actually collected data. In regard to the former, a petition was circulated in the local society that Greenwald be expelled; in regard to the latter, the board of directors of the local psychological society, who had sponsored the collection of data, resolved to prohibit presentation of the findings in any public forum (e.g., journal publication, psychology convention presentation) because it was "not in the best interests of psychology to present it publicly" (for more detailed discussion and documentation of these events, see Pope, Sonne, & Holroyd, 1993).

As a result of this lack of any systematically collected data suggesting that therapist-patient sex was anything but an extremely rare, virtually nonexistent phenomenon, comparable to therapists' violent physical assaults on patients, there was no perceived need to name it explicitly in the professional ethics codes. However, even though therapist-patient sex was not explicitly named, it clearly fell under categories of behaviors prohibited by various sections of the ethics codes, and offenders could be held in violation of the code. For example, Hare-Mustin (1974), a former chair of the American Psychological

Association's (APA) Ethics Committee, published an article three years before her association's ethics code made explicit mention of therapist-patient sex. The article demonstrated that APA's 1963 *Ethical Standards of Psychologists* contained standards that prohibited therapist-patient sexual involvement. Hare-Mustin emphasized that in light of "a review of principles relating to competency, community standards and the client relationship that genital contact with patients is ethically unacceptable" (p. 310). Holroyd, who was senior author of the first national study of therapist-patient sex, testified that the 1977 code did not represent any change in the standards regarding sexual activities with patients:

ADMINISTRATIVE LAW JUDGE: Was it [the 1977 ethics code] a codification of what was already the standard of practice?
HOLROYD: Yes, it was making it very explicit in the ethics code. . . .
ADMINISTRATIVE LAW JUDGE: What I am asking is whether or not the standard of practice prior to the inclusion of that specific section in the [1977] ethics code, whether or not that changed the standard of practice.
HOLROYD: No, it did not change the standard of practice. The standard of practice always precluded a sexual relationship between therapist and patient.
ADMINISTRATIVE LAW JUDGE: Even though it was not expressed in the ethics codes?
HOLROYD: From the beginning of the term psychotherapy with Sigmund Freud, he was very clear to prohibit it in his early publications. (*In re Howland*, 1980, pp. 49–50)

This ancient prohibition has gained judicial recognition. For example, over two decades ago, Presiding Justice Markowitz of the New York Supreme Court noted evidence that from the time of Freud to the present, therapist-patient sex had been viewed as harmful: "Thus from [Freud] to the modern practitioner we have common agreement of the harmful effects of sensual intimacies between patient and therapist" (*Roy v. Hartogs*, 1976, p. 590).

That the prohibition against therapist-patient sex has remained constant over so long a time and throughout so many diverse cultures reflects to some extent the shared recognition in the professional community that such involvement places the patient at risk for exceptional harm. Until relatively recently, this recognition was based mainly on individual observations and case studies, common sense, and theory. Only in the past few decades has a diverse array of systematic investigations informed our understanding with empirical data.

INITIAL RESEARCH

That current claims about the frequency and consequences of therapist-patient sex can be based on and tested against systematically collected data is due in part to the pioneering work of Masters and Johnson. Their data, based on relatively large samples, were published in *Human Sexual Response* (Masters & Johnson, 1966) and *Human Sexual Inadequacy* (Masters, & Johnson, 1970). Their studies formed the basis of five fundamental observations.

First, in their various samples, they found a number of cases in which people reported sexual involvements with their therapists. This finding suggested that, contrary to the notions previously discussed, therapist-patient sex was *not* a phenomenon of such rarity that it virtually did not occur.

Second, the researchers concluded, based on the available evidence, that most of these reports of sexual involvement with therapists had actually occurred, although a minority appeared to be invalid. The possibility that many of the researchers' judgments might represent false positives was explored. The researchers emphasized that the occurrence of therapist-patient sex would still be significant even if only one-fourth of the reports were valid (Masters & Johnson, 1970).

Third, the reports included all possible pairings of therapist and patient (i.e., male therapist and female patient, male therapist and male patient, female therapist and female patient, and female therapist and male patient) as well as instances of group sex.

Fourth, instances involving male therapists and female patients were the most common.

Fifth, the researchers were able to consider therapist-patient sex against the background of other events in the participants' lives because extensive data were collected about each person's background, development, and sexual history and functioning. The effects of sexual involvement with a therapist could be compared to consensual sexual involvement with a spouse or nontherapist partner, long- and short-term extramarital sexual relationships, and forms of sex abuse such as incest and rape. In light of the negative effects that tended to appear associated with therapist-patient sex, Masters and Johnson (1975) concluded that such involvements tended to constitute a "tragedy" for the patient. The results of their research led them to state that therapist-patient sex was functionally equivalent to criminal rape:

> We feel that when sexual seduction of patients can be firmly established by due legal process, regardless of whether the seduction was initiated by the patient or the therapist, the therapist should be sued for rape rather than malpractice, i.e., the legal process should be criminal rather than civil. (p. 1)

This initial large-scale research made it difficult for therapists to continue denying that therapist-patient sex was a virtually nonexistent phenomenon and prompted the national self-report studies summarized in Table 17.5. It also led to systematic studies gathering information about patients who were sexually involved with a therapist. Table 17.6, for example, presents data from 958 patients who were sexually involved with a therapist. One out of 20 of these patients were minors at the time that the sexual involvement with the therapist reportedly

Table 17.6
Characteristics of 958 Patients Who Had Been
Sexually Involved with a Therapist

	N	%
Patient was a minor at the time of the involvement	47	5
Patient married the therapist	37	3
Patient had experienced incest or other child sex abuse	309	32
Patient had experienced rape prior to sexual involvement with therapist	92	10
Patient required hospitalization considered to be at least partially a result of the sexual involvement	105	11
Patient attempted suicide	134	14
Patient committed suicide	7	1
Patient achieved complete recovery from any harmful effects of sexual involvement	143	17*
Patient seen pro bono or for reduced fee	187	20
Patient filed formal (e.g., licensing, malpractice) complaint	112	12

*17% of the 866 patients who experienced harm
Source: Adapted from Pope & Vetter (1991, p. 431).

occurred. Although much of the literature on therapist-patient sex seems to imply that the patients are virtually always adults, in many cases they are minors, sometimes quite young. A national study focusing exclusively on patients who were minors at the time they were sexually involved with a therapist found that most (56%) were female patients, ranging in age from 17 down to 3 (Bajt & Pope, 1989; for additional studies, see http://idealist.com/memories/). The average age of these girls who had been sexually involved with a therapist was 7. The boys ranged from 16 down to 7 at the time they were sexually involved with a therapist; the average age of these boys was 12.

Findings from the initial research conducted by Masters and Johnson and others led to the discovery of demographics such as gender (discussed in the next section) that seem to be significantly associated with therapist-patient sex. They also led to the question, are there specific factors aside from a fundamental demographic such as gender that might help identify patients who are at increased risk for sexual exploitation by a therapist? It is easy to assume the role of armchair psychologist and speculate on any number of clinical or personal history factors that might make a patient more vulnerable to sexual exploitation. The vast array of possible characteristics, however, have tended to find no empirical support in research studies. Bates and Brodsky (1989) considered the diverse risk factors that have been hypothesized, at one time or another, to put certain patients at higher risk for therapist-patient sex. Their analysis led them away from the personal history or characteristics of the client and to the prior behavior of the therapist: the most effective predictor of whether a client will become sexually involved with a therapist is whether that therapist has previously engaged in sex with a client (Bates & Brodsky, 1989). Their analysis is reminiscent of what happened when rape reached epidemic proportions in Tel Aviv. The prime minister's cabinet (mostly males) spent considerable time trying to discern which women seemed to be putting themselves at risk for rape (e.g., those women who had a tendency to venture out after it got dark, or those who tended to walk alone). The cabinet decided that because women who engaged in these activities seemed to be placing themselves at risk for rape, it would make sense to enact a law setting a curfew for women. Prime Minister Golda Meier revealed the assumptions underlying this analysis by suggesting, "Why not a curfew for the men? They are the ones doing the raping" (Unger, 1979, p. 427).

GENDER PATTERNS

Masters and Johnson's discovery of a gender pattern in therapist-patient sex was supported by subsequent studies. Peer-reviewed published findings from three kinds of surveys—those based on reports by subsequent therapists working with patients who have been sexually involved with a previous therapist, those based on therapists' self-reports about their own sexual involvements with patients, and those based on patients' own self-reports—strongly suggest that therapists who engage in therapist-patient sex are overwhelmingly, although not exclusively, male, and that patients who become sexually involved with a therapist are overwhelmingly, although not exclusively, female.

Surveys of therapists, published in peer-review journals, asking how many, if any, patients have reported sexual involvement with a prior therapist have revealed stark gender contrasts. Of the patients reported to have been sexually involved with a previous therapist in these studies, 94% were female and 6% were male (Bouhoutsos, Holroyd, Lerman, Forer, & Greenberg, 1983), 91% were female and 9% were male (Gartrell, Herman, Olarte, Feldstein, & Localio, 1986), and 87% were female and 13% were male (Pope & Vetter, 1991).

The national studies based on therapists' anonymous self-reports of their own sexual involvement with patients summarized in Table 17.5 indicate the percentages of male and female therapists reporting sex with a patient. The gender differences are not always statistically significant for the sample size in these studies when the base rate of the reported behavior was extremely low. However, in *none* of these studies does the percentage of female therapists who report engaging in sex with a patient equal or exceed the percentage of male therapists who report a sexual relationship. The proportion of male to female percentages ranges from 1.5 to 9 (i.e., in the latter case, the percentage of male therapists reporting sexual involvement is nine times as large as the percentage of female therapists reporting such involvement). Pooling the data from all eight studies in Table 17.5 reveals that 6.8% of the male therapists and 1.6% of the female therapists reported engaging in sex with at least one patient.

Data based on patients' anonymous self-reports supplement the data based on reports by subsequent therapists and on therapists' anonymous self-reports. In one study, about 2.19% of the men and about 4.58% of the women reported engaging in sex with their own therapists (Pope & Feldman-Summers, 1992).

A fourth source of data (in addition to those provided through reports by subsequent therapists, therapists' anonymous self-reports, and patients' anonymous self-reports) supports the hypothesis that sexually involved therapists are overwhelmingly (although not exclusively) male and that sexually involved patients are overwhelmingly (although not exclusively) female. Data from licensing disciplinary actions suggest that about 86% of the therapist-patient cases are those in which the therapist is male and the patient is female (Pope, 1993).

It is worth noting that in some studies, the proportion of cases involving a dyad of male therapist and female patient is quite high. Bouhoutsos et al. (1983), for example, reported a landmark study in which it was found that sexual involvement between a male therapist and a female patient constituted 92% of the instances in which a subsequent therapist reported that a patient had been sexually involved with a previous therapist. Gartrell et al. (1986) found that 88% of the "contacts for which both the psychiatrist's and the patient's gender were specified occurred between male psychiatrists and female patients" (p. 1128).

This gender pattern, which persists even when the overall percentages of male and female therapists and of male and female patients are taken into account, provides a context for attempts to understand and address the phenomenon of therapist-patient sex, but it is a pattern and context not clearly understood. Holroyd and Brodsky (1977), who conducted the first national study of therapist-patient sex, concluded their discussion of the data by outlining major unresolved issues: "Three professional issues remain to be addressed: (1) that male therapists are most often involved, (2) that female patients are most often the objects, and (3) that therapists who disregard the sexual boundary once are likely to repeat" (p. 849). In subsequent work, Holroyd (1983) suggested that this gender pattern tended to reflect sex-role stereotyping and bias. Noting the vast majority of cases in which a male therapist engaged in sex with a female patient, she stated that "sexual contact between therapist and patient is perhaps the quintessence of sex-biased therapeutic practice" (p. 285). Holroyd and Brodsky's (1977) landmark research prompted a second national study focusing on not only therapist-patient but also professor-student sexual relationships.[2] Findings from these and related studies suggested that the gender pattern might be linked to role power and role vulnerability:

---

[2] For subsequent studies of student-teacher sexual relationships in mental health training programs, see Carr, Robinson, Stewart, and Kussin (1991), Glaser and Thorpe (1986), Pope (1989), Pope and Vetter (1992), and Robinson and Reid (1985).

When sexual contact occurs in the context of psychology training or psychotherapy, the predominant pattern is quite clear and simple: An older, higher status man becomes sexually active with a younger, subordinate woman. In each of the higher status professional roles (teacher, supervisor, administrator, therapist), a much higher percentage of men than women engage in sex with those students or clients for whom they have assumed professional responsibility. In the lower status role of student, a far greater proportion of women than men are sexually active with their teachers, administrators, and clinical supervisors. (Pope, Levenson, & Schover, 1979, p. 687; see also Pope, 1994)

A clear, comprehensive, and useful understanding of how therapists could place those who have come to them for help at risk for severe and lasting harm and of how the profession has responded to this phenomenon is unlikely to emerge from denial of this obvious, marked gender imbalance and the context that it creates.

WHEN THE MAJORITY MASKS THE MINORITY

One example of how a predominant pattern has tended to mask less frequent occurrences has already been noted: Therapist-patient sex is often discussed as if it were solely an activity between adults, ignoring the instances in which the patient is a minor. The predominant gender pattern has seemed to contribute to a failure to attend adequately to the *relatively* small minority that involve other dyads (such as female-female or male-male), triads, or larger groups. Benowitz (1991), for example, noted that many early research reports tended to use exclusively the pronoun *he* for sexually involved therapists, as if a female therapist would never sexually exploit a patient (p. 2). She also observed that until relatively recently, "sexual abuse of women clients by women psychotherapists was largely invisible publicly" (p. 3). Attempts to acknowledge, attend to, and understand how the predominant male gender pattern influences professional responses to therapist-patient sex must lead to an increased awareness of instances for which this predominant pattern does not hold and must not lead to a denial, discounting, or trivialization of these less frequent types.

To acknowledge and attempt to address the significant gender differences that have consistently emerged from the diverse national studies of dual relationships does not, of course, imply that men are the only perpetrators, that women are the only victims/survivors, or that victimization of male clients is somehow less damaging or important. As with the phenomenon of incest to which certain dual relationships have often been compared in terms of nature, dynamics, and consequences (Chesler, 1972; Gabbard, 1989; Marmor, 1961; Pope, 1989; Pope & Bouhoutsos, 1986; Siassi & Thomas, 1973), women may take advantage of a more powerful role, engage in rationalization, and cross boundaries serving to protect those who are vulnerable, and men may be harmed. But to affirm one obvious point—that unethical behavior needs to be recognized and prevented, regardless of gender—need not mask another obvious point: that a higher proportion of male than female psychologists engage in sexual and nonsexual dual relationships of the sort that are expressly prohibited by the Ethical Principles (APA, 1981) and that a significantly disproportionate number of female clients and students are harmed and exploited. (Borys & Pope, 1989, pp. 290–291)

HOW THERAPIST-PATIENT SEX AFFECTS PATIENTS

The work of Masters and Johnson described in a previous section was followed not only by studies revealing gender patterns but also by diverse systematic investigations into the effects of therapist-patient sex on patients (see, e.g., Bouhoutsos et al., 1983; Butler & Zelen, 1977; Feldman-Summers & Jones, 1984; Herman, Gartrell, Olarte, Feldstein, & Localio, 1987; Pope & Vetter, 1991; Sonne, Meyer, Borys, & Marshall, 1985; Vinson, 1987; see also http://idealist .com/memories/). Approaches to learning about effects have included studies of patients who returned to therapy with a new therapist as well as patients who sought no additional course of therapy after their sexual involvement with a therapist. The consequences for clients who have been sexually involved with a psychotherapist have been compared to those for matched groups of therapy patients who have not been sexually involved with a therapist and of patients who have been sexually involved with a (nontherapist) physician. Subsequent treating therapists (of those patients who undertook a subsequent therapy), independent clinicians, and the patients themselves have assessed the effects of therapist-patient sex on patients. Standardized psychological tests and other assessment instruments have supplemented behavioral observation, clinical interview, and other methods of obtaining data. These diverse approaches to systematic study have yielded findings consistent with the firsthand reports of individual patients (e.g., Bates & Brodsky, 1989; Freeman & Roy, 1976; Noel & Watterson, 1992; Plaisil, 1985; Walker & Young, 1986).

The following reactions have emerged from the research as frequently associated with therapist-patient sex (see, e.g., Hare-Mustin, 1992; Mann & Winer, 1991; Pope, 1994; Pope & Bouhoutsos, 1986; Pope, Sonne, & Holroyd, 1993; Sonne, 1989). Several qualifications are crucial. First, although research studies suggest that these reactions are common, they are by no means inevitable. Clinicians should never assume that these reactions necessarily occurred for an individual patient who was sexually involved with a therapist. An adequate assessment must never fail to evaluate whether each of the common responses is present but also must never reflexively assume that any particular response is inevitably present. Each patient is unique and experiences "this destructive event in his or her own way in the context of his or her unique life" (Pope & Bouhoutsos, 1986, p. 21). Second, this pattern of common reactions is a useful, research-based descriptive construct, but it should never be used in forensic contexts as proof that a patient was or was not sexually involved with a therapist. Third, it can help guide consideration of possible treatment plans and in matching patients to modalities that are most likely to be helpful. For example, in evaluating the outcome of the UCLA Post Therapy Support Program for patients who had been sexually involved with a therapist, Sonne (1989; see also Sonne et al., 1985), reported:

> The group experience appeared specifically helpful for all clients in alleviating 5 of the 10 major aspects of . . . therapist-patient sex syndrome . . . : emptiness and isolation, guilt, emotional lability or dyscontrol, increased suicidal risk, and cognitive dysfunction (i.e., flashbacks, intrusive thoughts, nightmares). Improvement in the 5 other aspects (impaired ability to trust, ambivalence, suppressed rage, sexual confusion, and identity and role reversal) tended to be more dependent on the specific dynamics of the individual client.
>
> Clients who struggled with continuing and intense issues of mistrust and ambivalence were least likely to benefit from the group and tended to be most disruptive of effective group process. (p. 113)

COGNITIVE DYSFUNCTION

Sexual involvement with a therapist often impairs cognitive functions, particularly in the areas of attention and concentration. Intrusive thoughts, unbidden images, memory fragments, nightmares, and flashbacks—sometimes experienced as if they were happening in the present—may plague the patient. This pattern of cognitive reactions sometimes represents an aspect of a posttraumatic stress disorder.

GUILT

Many patients who are sexually exploited by a therapist experience intense irrational guilt about the event. The guilt is irrational because it is always and without exception the therapist's responsibility to refrain from engaging in sexual involvement with a patient. It is the therapist who is licensed by the state and charged with the responsibility to refrain from any behavior that would place the patient at undue risk for severe harm and specifically to avoid engaging in sex with a patient. It is the therapist whose ethics code prohibits using a patient for sexual pleasure.

This irrational guilt is similar to the experience of many who have experienced rape or incest. Although the responsibility for refraining from rape always falls on the rapist and never on the one who is being raped, women, men, and children who have been raped may feel intense and lasting guilt. They may criticize, accuse, blame, and interrogate themselves: Why didn't I have a weapon so I could protect myself? Why didn't I struggle more? Why didn't I make a lot of noise or cry for help? Why didn't I dress so that I covered all my skin, hid my shape, and protected my body? Why didn't I try to reason the rapist out of it? Why did I ever go anywhere that I could be raped? Adults who, as children, experienced incest may misleadingly see in their own personality and behavior apparent confirmation that they feel guilty for good reason:

They secretly sought or enjoyed the parent's attention, approval, and love. They must have been too sexual and provocative. They did too much hugging of the parent and longed for affection. They had "bad" thoughts or fantasies or impulses. Their bodies sometimes responded while their parent bathed them or toweled them dry in ways that must have been "asking for" the parent's incestuous behavior.

Patients may feel irrational guilt not only about sex with the therapist but also about breaking the silence, speaking about "secret" events that the therapist wanted to conceal from others, and loosening the bond with which the previous therapist had drawn the patient into the abuse:

> Many patients who are sexually exploited by their therapists refuse to reveal the unethical behavior, often explaining that it would be a betrayal of their intimacy with the therapist. One wonders if access to a patient in an exploitive way is often gained by therapists through appeal to the patient's longing for intimacy. (Lebe & Namir, 1993, p. 18)

It is possible that gender, a topic discussed in an earlier section, may play a role in how the guilt is experienced and expressed. Carr and Robinson (1990) wrote, "Women are often programmed to take responsibility for and feel guilty about relationships and their problems. The almost universal expression of guilt and shame expressed by women who have been sexually involved with their therapists is a testament to the power of this conditioning" (p. 126). Comparing therapist-patient sex to rape, Davidson (1977) wrote:

> Women victims in both instances experience considerable guilt, risk loss of love and self-esteem, and often feel that they may have done something to "cause" the seduction. As with rape victims, women patients can expect to be blamed for the event and will have difficulty finding a sympathetic audience for their complaint. Added to these difficulties is the reality that each woman has consulted a therapist, thereby giving some evidence of psychological disequilibrium prior to the seduction. How the therapist may use this information after the woman decides to discuss the situation with someone else can surely dissuade many women from revealing these experiences. (p. 48)

IMPAIRED ABILITY TO TRUST

Therapy often seems based on a remarkable degree of trust. Patients often walk into the office of a complete stranger and begin disclosing personal information about themselves that no one else will be permitted to hear. Therapists often ask questions that would be unwarranted, intrusive, and offensive if asked by someone else. Recognizing the powerful nature of the "secrets" that patients tell their therapists, all states recognize some form of confidentiality for the therapeutic process and some form of therapist-patient privilege. With a relatively few explicitly listed exceptions, therapists are prevented from disclosing, in the absence of the patient's informed consent to waive confidentiality, to third parties what patients say during the course of therapy.

The therapeutic process is similar in some ways to surgery. Surgical patients allow themselves to be physically opened up in the hope that their condition will improve. They must trust that surgeons will not take advantage of their vulnerable state to cause harm or abuse them in any way. Similarly, therapy patients undergo a process of psychological opening up in the hope that their condition will improve. They must trust that therapists will not take advantage, harm, or exploit.

Freud (1924/1952) originally observed this similarity. He noted that the newly developed "talking therapy" was "comparable to a surgical operation" (p. 467) and emphasized that "the transference especially . . . is a dangerous instrument . . . . [I]f a knife will not cut, neither will it serve a surgeon" (p. 471). To acknowledge the potential harm that could result from psychotherapy was fundamental:

> It is grossly to undervalue both the origins and the practical significance of the psychoneuroses to suppose that these disorders are to be removed by pottering about with a few harmless remedies. . . . [P]sychoanalysis ... is not afraid to handle the most dangerous forces in the mind and set them to work for the benefit of the patient. (Freud, 1915/1963, p. 179)

Smith (1984) applied this surgical analogy to a therapist's decision to engage in sex with his or her patients:

> The specifics of these sexual engagements . . . clearly indicate the therapist's sadistic impulses. The rationalizations . . . are in truth based on efforts to disguise this hidden sadistic meaning. These rationalizations are not unlike some surgeons who discover exactly the same indications for surgery over and over again. . . . As Karl Menninger (1938) has indicated, some doctors are obsessed with cutting out thyroid glands, others with excising ovaries, others go after pieces of intestine, but it is the compulsion of cutting that drives them, not the objective realities of the patient's condition. The same repetition-compulsion can be found in the sexually abusing therapist, and it is the element of sadism that seems to stand at the forefront of the therapist's behavior. (pp. 93–94)

These analyses clarify the trust that vulnerable patients accord to professionals—therapists or surgeons. Patients must be able to trust that a therapist will do nothing that knowingly and needlessly places them at risk for deep, pervasive, and lasting harm.

AMBIVALENCE

Patients who have been sexually exploited by a therapist may find themselves caught between two opposing sets of impulses: (1) to escape from the abuse and the lasting effects of the abuse, to seek justice and restitution for the offense, and to move on with life, recovered and empowered, and (2) to deny the abuse or to redefine it or fantasize it as not abusive, to cling to and protect the offender, and to avoid or minimize any discomfort to the offender. This form of ambivalence is similar to that which many survivors of incest experience. For example, a young daughter experiencing incest may sometimes want to keep the secret, to affirm that it is her responsibility (or fault), to make sure that her father is not forced to leave the home, and to see that nothing happens that might make her father mad or unhappy; at other times, she may seek escape, safety, and healing. Similarly, a battered partner may try to cling to, pacify, shield, and please the batterer, even though these impulses compete with efforts to seek help, relief, restitution, and justice.

Ambivalence is one of the most paralyzing, painful effects that therapist-patient sex causes. The patient finds no stability in the world: if things ever seem to begin settling into a stable pattern, the opposite pole of the ambivalence asserts itself, and the world turns inside out again. The patient finds no way to make sense of the world. No description of the evolution of events seems to fit. The abusive therapist may appear, for example, to offer the tenderness, concern, and validation that the patient has always sought while also—as the patient reflects upon the emerging events—robbing the patient not only of tenderness, concern, and validation but also of the chance that these positive elements will ever enter the patient's life.

ISOLATION AND EMPTINESS

Many sexually abused patients report feeling both isolated and empty. Here is how one patient described the emptiness: "It is as if I don't really exist without him. I'm not there, not myself. He's the only one who can fill me up, not sexually but in terms of who I am." The emptiness seems associated with isolation. It is as if what has happened to patients who have been sexually exploited by a therapist has changed them so severely that they do not feel they can rejoin the world of humans, that their identity has been dehumanized and altered to such an extent that they cannot communicate with others.

These feelings of isolation and emptiness may be at odds with what the patients know on an intellectual level. Even though they may intellectually know that others have been through similar experiences, it feels as if they alone have been selected. These descriptions resemble those of some incest and rape survivors: however much they may know intellectually that they are not the only people to have been molested or raped, it *feels* as if they were singled out.

Some may feel as if the sexual involvement with the therapist has made them "dead" or permanently numb and hollow, and that there is no fullness, fulfillment, or "life" to their experience. They may be waiting to die, believing that there is no way for them to reenter the world of other people. For some, separation from the therapist with whom they were sexually involved is terrifying. In 1912, Elma Pálos wrote to Sándor Ferenczi, who had been her therapist and sexual partner (as well as the therapist and sexual partner of her mother), "This being alone that now awaits me will be stronger than I; I feel almost as if everything will freeze inside me. . . . If I am alone, I will cease to exist" (cited in Brabent, Falzeder, & Giampieri-Deutsch, 1993, pp. 383–384). Walker (Walker & Young, 1986) provided a detailed report of an extreme sense of emptiness and isolation:

> By this time, of course, I had given up on the rest of my life. I lived the twenty-four hours of every day for the five- or ten-minute phone conversations with my Zane [the therapist with whom she was sexually involved]. If it hadn't been for my appointments with him twice a week, I would never have gotten out of bed. . . .
>   I had withdrawn to the point where I spent all of my time, except for when I went to see Zane, in the bedroom with the shades drawn. I never knew when it was day or night, whether [my husband] was at work, or downstairs, or somewhere on a trip. I kept the television on because I couldn't stand the quiet. (pp. 71–72)

Feeling empty and isolated may be related to the abuse of trust, discussed previously. Patients may understandably believe (or be led to believe) that therapy is a safe environment in which they can open themselves to a deeply trusting relationship. When that relationship is abused, they may feel that they have lost the self that they placed within the supposedly safe environment (emptiness) and lack the ability to be recognized, respected, and taken seriously by another person (isolation). The abusive therapist may have encouraged—through commands, threats, "prescriptions," or subtle manipulation—the patient's social isolation to help reinforce the patient's dependency, the therapist's power, and the likelihood that the secret of the abuse would not be disclosed to others (Pope & Bouhoutsos, 1986).

EMOTIONAL LABILITY

Emotional lability can be one of the most disconcerting effects of therapist-patient sex. Emotions seem to lose their reliability and customary patterns. Emotional changes occur suddenly, swiftly, and without apparent reason. Talking about a seemingly neutral event gives way to unexpected fear. Talking about a joyful event becomes the occasion for wrenching sobs. Emotional intensity may alternate with emotional numbness. The person may rarely experience what he or she would call a normal emotion.

Before the therapist-patient sex, the patient may have experienced emotions as familiar aspects of his or her interior life and they may have served as guides to understanding events and experiences. After sex with the therapist, emotions may become so frighteningly alien and seemingly unconnected with environmental events or internal processes that the patient feels that both inner and outer life are out of control. In extreme instances, the person may feel helpless vis-à-vis his or her own emotions, as if under attack from a powerful but unpredictable enemy.

SUPPRESSED ANGER

Sexually exploited patients are often—with good reason—angry. The anger is often suppressed and may begin to emerge only months or years after all contact with the abusive therapist has ended. There are diverse reasons why the anger is suppressed or sometimes turned inward on the patient. Sometimes, the offender has been exceptionally careful to intimidate, manipulate, or coerce the patient into avoiding any expression or even recognition of anger. Therapists are trained to understand emotions and may attempt to shape a vulnerable patient's reactions to his or her own emotions. Sometimes, the suppression may come about not so much through the therapist's sophisticated skills as through simple force. One sexually abused patient described her therapist's tendency to angrily yell at her whenever she, (the patient) was angry or even irritated. Eventually, the patient had trouble knowing when she was angry. She grew fearful that those around her might become angry at her. She often went to sessions with her subsequent therapist and sat silently for long periods of time, occasionally saying, "You're mad at me, aren't you?" During the early phase of the subsequent therapy, no words or behavior by the subsequent therapist would reassure her that the therapist was not angry at her. She lived in terror of her own anger and of the consequences should it ever emerge.

Some patients fear that any feelings of anger, should they emerge, will obliterate their sense of self or destroy those around them. Sonne (1987) wrote, "Although the patient may occasionally acknowledge her intense rage, she will more often suppress her anger for fear of being overwhelmed by it, or of harming its object (the therapist) or others" (p. 119). As one patient reported, "More often than not, I was on the edge of boiling over with rage, and I walked around barely contained" (Noel & Watterson, 1992, p. 211).

SEXUAL CONFUSION

Sex with a therapist may prompt a period of extreme confusion about the patient's sexuality. The therapist-patient sex leads some to believe that they are "only good for sex." They are convinced that they have no value except in their ability to respond to another person's sexual wants and needs. The experience with the offender therapist generalizes to other relationships. For other patients, therapist-patient sex is followed by sex with other people as reenactments of the relationship with the therapist. For those who feel empty and isolated, reenacting with others the sexual behaviors previously experienced with the exploitive therapist seems to represent an attempt to fill up the self and break through the isolation.

For still others, sex—and particularly casual sex or sex from which the patient derives little pleasure—becomes a way to express the feelings of irrational guilt. Some patients have remarked that it is as if their participation in uncomfortable, demeaning, or dangerous sexual activities seemed to express the conviction "I am worthless and this is all I deserve." One patient was told by her male therapist that if she ever wanted to get well, she must repeatedly pull up her dress, take down her underpants, and masturbate while the therapist watched. She was told that she secretly wanted to do this and that it was necessary in order for her to overcome the sexual inhibitions that were making her miserable. Long after the recurrent sexual relationship with the therapist stopped, she reported a pattern that she seemed to follow almost against her will: As if in a trance, she would think of her therapist, go find a man she had never met before, and follow the commands of her therapist as if she were actually hearing them. Because she did not know these men, she was subjecting herself to danger and abuse. She was, in fact, physically forced to perform sexual acts against her will and was threatened, beaten, and almost killed during some encounters. None of the men wore a condom; consequently, she suffered a sexually transmitted viral infection. As she later talked during a subsequent therapy about her confused behavior, she described how she had frequently hoped that she would die during one of the encounters.

Another patient who had been sexually involved with a male therapist described her subsequent sexual behavior in these terms:

> Once in a while, maybe every six months, she would feel the urge to have a glass of wine at dinner, then go out and pick up a strange man and spend the night with him at a hotel or motel. She wanted to be with men who didn't ask a lot of questions, who, like herself, were interested in being with someone just for the night, then separating. . . .
>
> Fortunately, in her few sexual forays, she did not meet a Jack the Ripper; neither the poet nor the drummer treated her with anything but respect. She had a dim awareness that her escapades, seldom though they occurred, showed how little she cared what she did with her life. (Freeman & Roy, 1976, pp. 115, 117)

Some patients express sexual confusion not through engaging in specific patterns of sexual activities but rather through careful avoidance of any sexual activity. Female patients who participated in the earliest therapy groups in 1982 and 1983 at the UCLA Post Therapy Support Program for patients who had been sexually involved with a therapist

> expressed a cautiousness or even disgust with their sexual impulses and behavior as a result of sexual involvement with their previous therapists. For some female clients who identified themselves as heterosexual before they were involved sexually with female therapists, there tended to be significant confusion over their "true" sexual orientation. (Sonne, 1989, pp. 106–107)

In some cases, the confusion about sexuality can spill over into other aspects of the patient's cognitions and affects:

> In some cases the trauma has been so profound that the patient has difficulty accurately distinguishing sexual impulses, sensations, or feelings from affects or other experiences. Thus a patient who becomes extremely angry or anxious

may label the experience as "sexual arousal." Situational cues that seem to the patient to have nothing to do with sex may elicit sexual fantasies, impulses, arousal, or behavior. Such reactions may be part of the patient's more general feelings of being "out of control." (Pope & Bouhoutsos, 1986, p. 103)

The loss of a safe and fulfilling sense of sexuality and eroticism from the patient's life can be at once devastating, paralyzing, disempowering, and demoralizing. Cut off from this source of potential information, connection, and fulfillment, a patient may become less able to be open to and to integrate feelings, as suggested in this passage from Audre Lorde (1978):

> We have often turned away from the exploration and consideration of the erotic as a source of power and information, confusing it with its opposite, the pornographic. But pornography is a direct denial of the power of the erotic, for it represents the suppression of true feeling. Pornography emphasizes sensation without feeling.
>
> The erotic is a measure between the beginnings of our sense of self, and the chaos of our strongest feelings. It is an internal sense of satisfaction to which, once we have experienced it, we know we can aspire. For once having experienced the fullness of this depth of feeling and recognizing its power, in honor and self-respect we can require no less of ourselves. (p. 3)

INCREASED SUICIDAL RISK

Research suggests that about 1 in every 100 patients who have been sexually involved with a therapist will take his or her own life, and that about 14% will make at least one suicide attempt (Bouhoutsos et al., 1983; Pope & Vetter, 1991):

> Depression, suicidal concerns, and pressures toward self-mutilation and subtle mechanisms of self-harm are frequent issues. The exploited patient may have minimal self-esteem and be grieving not only the previous therapist but numerous other losses occasioned by the misadventure that took place. Guilt may intensify these issues, as may ongoing pressures from the previous therapist in some egregious instances. It is not uncommon for the majority of the early course of subsequent therapies to be dominated by such concerns. Many patients will need to rely on a supportive network of concerned others if hospitalization is to be averted; some will need hospital stays. The success of organic therapies for depressions in this group is mixed; responses to them are often incomplete. (Kluft, 1989, p. 496)

One woman who had become sexually involved with her therapist described her attempt to end her life:

> I do not remember clearly planning anything. I just went straight for the medicine cabinet as soon as I got home, and I lined up all of the bottles of pills I had accumulated. For no reason that makes sense to me now, I removed all the labels first and flushed them down the toilet. I got a big glass of juice from the kitchen, because I knew I would need it to swallow pills, and then I emptied them into my hand and swallowed them a handful at a time.

After I had done it, I had the most marvelous feeling. Maybe it was the peace of mind I had originally sought through therapy. Whatever the source, I lay on my bed and felt light, peaceful, calm. I remember thinking that nobody would ever hurt me again. (Walker & Young, 1986, pp. 51–52)

ROLE REVERSAL AND BOUNDARY DISTURBANCE

It is common for patients who have become sexually involved with a therapist to appear to exchange roles: The therapist gradually shifts the focus of the sessions from the patient to the therapist; the patient's legitimate clinical needs fade in importance, and the therapist's personal needs emerge as the sole matter of importance. This transition often starts with the therapist's gradually increasing self-disclosure. Whatever the supposed rationale for the personal disclosures in this context, they serve to introduce the personal desires of the therapist into the therapy and to ease the clinical needs of the patient aside. Eventually, the therapist's sexual desires not only blot out the need for legitimate treatment but also overcome any reluctance to place the patient at risk for deep, pervasive, and lasting harm. Rather than the therapist's fulfilling the clinical, legal, and ethical responsibilities to address the patient's clinical needs, the patient becomes a means to fulfilling the therapist's personal desires. Therapist and patient appear to change roles.

The therapeutic process tends to generalize to other aspects of the patient's life. When therapy is positive, appropriate, and effective, the help that the patient receives tends to reach beyond the limited time that the patient spends with the therapist during a session and beyond the course of therapy itself. The benefits tend to last beyond termination; otherwise, termination would mark the loss of all therapeutic gains. When therapists use the therapeutic process to express their sexual impulses at the expense of the patient, the negative effects likewise often generalize to the patient's experiences outside sessions and beyond termination of the meetings with the abusive therapist. Often, the patient, through the violation and exploitation of the therapeutic process, learns to ignore or suppress personal needs and to strive to gratify the needs of others.

The iatrogenically induced refusal to acknowledge, respect, or care for the self can disturb the patient's sense of boundaries. The customary boundaries that define, mediate, and protect the self may be broken, blurred, or dissolved to meet the needs of other people more immediately and completely.

SPECIAL TREATMENT FOR OFFENDERS

By allowing some therapists who have engaged in sex with a patient to resume practice, the profession has created an interesting exception to the standards of accountability, integrity, and trust recognized for other professions. Historically, when professionals explicitly authorized by the state (through licensure or similar means) to hold special positions of trust significantly violate that trust, it has been understood that they have waived their right to resume those positions under any conditions. Part of the context for understanding therapist-patient sex and attempting to address the phenomenon is formed by the what Keith-Spiegel (1977) described over two decades ago as the "sanctuary provided by the profession for those who engage in sexual intimacies with clients" (p. 2).

If a judge were convicted of abusing the power and trust inherent in the position of judgeship by allowing bribes to determine the outcome of cases, numerous sanctions, both criminal and civil, might follow. However, even after the judge "paid the debt" due society by the abuse of power and trust, the judge would not be allowed to resume the bench, regardless of any "rehabilitation."

> Similarly, if a preschool director were discovered to have sexually abused the students, he or she would likely face both civil and criminal penalties. The director might undergo extensive rehabilitation efforts to help reduce the risk that he or she would engage in further abuse of children. However, regardless of the effectiveness of the rehabilitation efforts, the state would not issue the individual a new license to found and direct a new preschool.
>
> Neither of these two offenders would necessarily be precluded from practicing their professions. The former judge and preschool director, once rehabilitated, might conduct research, consult, publish, lecture, or pursue other careers within the legal and educational fields. However, serving as judge or as preschool director are positions that involve such trust—by both society and the individuals subject to their immediate power—that the violation of such an important and clearly understood prohibition against abuse of trust (and power) precludes the opportunity to hold such positions within the fields of law and education. (Pope & Vasquez, 1991, pp. 110–111)

It is worth noting that returning sex offenders to licensed status may be deterring patients from filing licensing complaints. Sexually abused patients who file licensing complaints provide an unpaid service (i.e., licensing tribunals do not grant financial awards to the prevailing party) to the profession and to future potential victims of the therapist. It is a service that is likely to cost them in terms of time, effort, and discomfort (e.g., through cross-examination by the offender's attorney). To file a licensing complaint, they must waive the privilege and privacy in regard to their therapy and mental status. The most private aspects of their lives may become a matter of public record and receive extensive publicity during an administrative hearing. The defense attorney may raise questions and allegations about the patient and press various lines of attack to discredit his or her character. One attorney skilled in trying therapist-patient sex cases (and who had previously defended people accused of rape) emphasized that in therapist-patient sex cases, like rape cases, one of the most frequent aspects of the "defense includes trying to prove that the victims are promiscuous, trying to prove the clients were asking for it" (Terwilliger, 1989, p. D1). The following passage illustrates the kind of cross-examination that patients may encounter when they make formal allegations that they were involved sexually with a therapist and that the involvement harmed them in sexual and other private aspects of their lives.

"During the period of a year and a half that you were married, did you have satisfactory sexual relations with your husband?"

"It was satisfactory in the beginning. It was not satisfactory at the end," she said. . . .

"When did you start having the lesbian relationships?" he asked.

"About 1963," she said. . . .

He questioned her about sex with Dr. Hartogs, asking if she had engaged in cunnilingus, and she said, "That's correct." . . .

"Were there days when you had sexual intercourse with him three times a day?"

"There was an occasion, yes," she replied. . . .

"You weren't forced into that, were you?"

"I was not physically tied down, no."

"But you enjoyed sex with him, didn't you?" (Freeman & Roy, 1976, pp. 146–150)

Another patient encountered the following questions from the defense attorney:

Could I mentally control vaginal lubrication? At what angle were my legs spread? Did I have orgasms? . . . Have you ever had occasion to swap sexual partners with anybody? . . . And when you engaged in sex, did you just have intercourse with these people or would you have oral sex with them, too? (Bates & Brodsky, 1989, p. 66)

The defense attorney also decided to take "a photograph of [the plaintiff] to circulate at local bars . . . in order to gather information about [the patient's] social life" (Bates & Brodsky, 1989, pp. 105–106).

As a final example, five former patients found themselves confronted with the following information, which became a matter of public record, in a licensing disciplinary hearing:

Five of the [psychiatrist's] former patients testified that the [psychiatrist] had used his role as their psychiatrist to influence them to engage in sexual relations with him. Over the department's objections, the hearing officer allowed the [psychiatrist] to present evidence of each of these women's sexual histories, even to the extent of allowing testimony as to the names and numbers of their sexual partners, their pregnancies outside marriage, their aborted pregnancies, and their experiences as victims of incest and sexual abuse as children. (*Department of Professional Regulation v. Wise*, 1991, p. 714)

Patients who have been sexually abused by a therapist may view their efforts to help the profession rid itself of sexually abusive therapists and to protect future patients from harm as ineffective in light of the profession's allowing these offenders to return to practice. Especially in light of the steep costs (e.g., placing the most private aspects of their lives, such as may be reflected in the offender therapist's chart notes, into the public record and facing vigorous and detailed cross-examination, as illustrated above), abused patients may believe that the profession is more concerned with protecting and enabling offenders than ensuring patient safety and welfare and that filing a licensing complaint is pointless. Continuing this practice may suppress the apparent rather than the actual scope of the problem, as reflected in the number of licensing complaints and disciplinary actions.

The ease with which perpetrators are able to achieve "rehabilitated" status and return to practice reflects a stance that therapists have a special exemption from the standards of integrity applicable to others, such as judges and preschool operators, in whom society in general and patients in particular invest special trust. This exemption may be related to a variety of factors:

1. The profession may have nurtured a deep and pervasive sense of entitlement (see, e.g., Gilbert & Scher's 1989 discussion of this theme in regard to therapist-patient sex): There may be a closely held belief that therapists who sexually exploit patients are inherently entitled to resume practice. This entitlement places the professional beyond the mechanisms of accountability and responsibility applicable to others who hold regulated (e.g., through governmental licensure) positions of great trust.

2. The profession may tend to accept decisions to expose, in the absence of informed consent, unsuspecting patients to the risks of entering therapy with a known (but not to the patients) offender. Putting unsuspecting patients at risk for abuse by therapists who are known offenders is often defended by denying that there is a legitimate right to informed consent and by stating that everyone lives in a world of risks. Reliance on this logic implies that no one need be informed of any risks in research because life itself involves risk, and that the right to informed consent is meaningless. A member of the pesticide regulatory board charged with protecting citizens against undue risks from pesticides provided a vivid example of this reasoning. Discussing the use of Chlordane, which kills termites, the regulatory board member stated, "Sure, it's going to kill a lot of people, but they may be dying of something else anyway" ("Perspectives," 1990, p. 17).

   The executive officer of the California Board of Psychology brought this particular informed consent issue into focus:

   > In much more trivial matters that do not threaten the safety of citizens, we would not think of proceeding with such an experiment until there is reliable evidence that a product or procedure is both safe and effective. To take the example of therapists who sexually abuse their patients, who can name even one independently conducted study published in a scientific or professional journal showing that any rehabilitation intervention has ever worked? When someone claims to have an effective treatment, drug, or intervention, we test *first* for safety and effectiveness and *then* approve it for general use. But pressures to protect abusive and dangerous licensees from accountability may have resulted in ignorance of this fundamental principle.

If in fact there is no evidence based on independently conducted studies published in scientific or professional journals which establishes the effectiveness of rehabilitation programs for therapists who have sexually abused their patients, then are not all interventions currently used—both by definition and in actuality—trial interventions? Who is exposed to the harm caused by bogus or ineffective trial interventions that enable abusive therapists to return to practice? Is it not the consumers? A review [by Bates and Brodsky, 1989, p. 141] of the research on consumers who are likely to be sexually victimized in therapy reveals: "The best single predictor of exploitation in therapy is a therapist who has exploited another patient in the past." Even the Insurance Trust of the American Psychological Association acknowledged that "the recidivism rate for sexual misconduct is substantial." Do those who place consumers at risk of harm on the basis of experimental or trial diversion methods not have a responsibility to obtain informed consent of these consumers as they study and research their methods? According to the Nuremberg Code, the first principle of trying out procedures is to obtain the "voluntary consent" of those who are placed at risk. Consumers simply should not be used as guinea pigs, without their knowledge or consent, while diversion programs test as-yet-unvalidated procedures. (O'Connor, 1992, p. 4)

O'Connor not only set forth evidence and argument but also appealed to the profession's conscience: Until there is "evidence based on independently conducted studies published in scientific or professional journals which establishes the effectiveness of rehabilitation programs for therapists who have sexually abused their patients," trial rehabilitation interventions must be tested "*first* for safety and effectiveness and *then* [approved] for general use." According to O'Connor, any use of unvalidated rehabilitation interventions should, in accordance with the Nuremberg Code, inform subsequent patients of a perpetrator that they are being placed at risk for substantial harm as part of an investigation to test the "safety and effectiveness" of a rehabilitation intervention, should document clearly that they are aware of the risks and are voluntarily consenting to assume the risks, and that they are aware of the means by which they are (or are not) being compensated for serving as research subjects and assuming the associated risks.

3. The profession may view its members, including those who sexually abuse patients, as possessing such important skills that patients cannot or must not do without them. As one licensing board member stated about an offender: "He contributes significantly to our society . . . and we thought that resource should not be denied to patients" (cited in English, 1992, p. 41). Unless all therapists are viewed as so important and skilled that permanent license revocation is unthinkable, this approach suggests that there may be at least two different standards or mechanisms of accountability: one for those renowned for their skills, and the other for everyone else.

4. The profession may view itself as possessing such effective skills that to ask for evidence that a particular intervention (i.e., rehabilitation) actually works is viewed as an affront to be answered on the basis of authority and self-esteem rather than evidence (e.g., "I am just sure that rehabilitation works. I wouldn't do therapy and value myself as a therapist if I didn't believe that people can change and that I am effective at bringing about that change. I've returned many therapists to practice and testified on their behalf in countless suits, and I would never have done that had I doubted that I was able to help these people or that it was well within my clinical skills to determine whether any of them would offend again."). One of the major difficulties—or strengths, depending on one's point of view—of this form of self-assurance is that the forms of assessment and intervention that it supports (e.g., astrology, phrenology, past-life regression) appear to be limitless.

5. The profession may have become adept, especially in regard to cases of abuse in which the perpetrators are predominantly male and the survivors are predominantly female, at denying or discounting the perpetrator's responsibility and accountability by shifting the focus toward the behaviors or characteristics of the victim/survivor. What the individual said, wore, thought, fantasized about, or otherwise did becomes the basis for concluding that the individual caused the abuse or must at least assume a significant share of the responsibility or accountability for being abused. Both the professional and popular literature provide examples of the tendency to focus on ways in which people not only consent to but also elicit, cause, or share accountability for being sexually exploited (see Pope, 1994, for examples), but some of the least subtle examples come from the courts:

- A judge declined to convict two adult men of raping an 8-year-old girl because she was, in the judge's opinion, "a willing participant" ("Judge Urged to Resign," 1985, p. A6).
- A judge refused to confine an individual who pled no contest to sexual assault of a 16-year-old girl because rape, according to the judge, is a "normal" reaction to the girl's "provocative clothing" (i.e., blue jeans, a blouse over a turtleneck sweater, and tennis shoes) ("A Woman's a Sex Object," 1977, p. 2).
- A judge took a 5-year-old girl's "character" into account in discounting the responsibility of the 24-year-old man who sexually assaulted her. According to the judge, she was "an unusually sexually promiscuous young lady. No way do I believe that [the adult] initiated the sexual contact" ("Unbelievable," 1983, p. F2).
- The defense of a man charged with sexually assaulting a girl is that he was her victim. The man, who was 6'8" tall and weighed 240 pounds, claimed that the "5-year-old girl raped him." According to testimony, he

"told a probation officer that the girl would climb into bed and molest him" ("Son of Retired Police Officer Sentenced for Sexually Assaulting a Child," 1998)

6. Therapists who sexually abuse patients and those who enable them to resume practice may characterize what offenders have done as a "mistake in judgment" due to unhappiness, personal stress or distress, the absence of adequate support and nurturing by important others, burnout, financial pressures, trying to do too much, unrequited love, difficult work conditions, role strain, not enough positive feedback, preoccupation with family issues, poor work habits, wanting to please too many people, unfulfilled longings, unresolved life questions, the fast pace of modern society, a bad diet combined with not enough sleep and exercise, existential uncertainty or angst, inadequate planning, not living up to potential, well-intentioned gaffes, or inattentiveness.

   There is considerable difficulty and distortion in trying to equate (1) decisions about whether to engage in a prohibited activity that puts a vulnerable patient at risk for deep and lasting harm to (2) difficult professional judgments such as whether a specific patient is likely to commit suicide if not hospitalized, the partners in a committed relationship will be better served by individual or conjoint therapy, or a 16-year-old single mother would benefit more from an adult or an adolescent day-treatment program. The prohibition against therapist-patient sex is clear, long-standing, and without exception (i.e., there are no conditions under which it is acceptable for a therapist to engage in sex with a therapy patient). Therapists do not clinically assess patients to arrive at a judgment about whether to engage in sex with them and if so how often and under what circumstances. Although the therapists in some of the documented cases noted earlier in the scenarios of therapist-patient sexual involvements make this claim, therapists do *not* engage in sex with their patients by mistake (in judgment or otherwise), unintentionally, or without realizing it. It is difficult to find documentation of *any* case in which the therapists were either so out of touch with fundamental reality that they lacked understanding that they were engaging in sex with a patient or so lacking in voluntary motor control that they were unable to prevent themselves from engaging in the sexual act. Engaging in sex with a patient is a prohibited activity that places a patient at risk for pervasive and lasting harm, that may lead to a patient's suicide. Engaging in sex with a patient is not an unintentional mistake that the therapist didn't even notice.

7. Professionals sometimes try to enable those who offend to continue practice by attributing the commission of sexual abuse by therapists to some form of mental illness, psychiatric or psychological impairment, the result of debilitating emotional wounds, and so on. According to this approach, a disorder was the necessary condition that caused the offense;

once the disorder is alleviated through rehabilitative treatment, there could be no reasonable alternative to allowing the perpetrator to continue practicing. Rapp (1987) remarked on a licensing board's directing some sexually exploitive therapists to "seek psychotherapy. Such an event tempts one to raise Szasz's specter of the danger of medicalizing all abhorrent acts and of the 'therapeutic state.' . . . Whether [such therapy to rehabilitate offenders] should ever occur is an open question" (p. 194).

RESEARCH AND REHABILITATION

Whether therapists, unlike others such as judges or preschool teachers who are licensed or otherwise authorized by the state to hold special positions of public trust, are entitled to resume practice after violating that trust, is a separate issue from what O'Connor (1992) noted was the lack of any "independently conducted study published in a scientific or professional journal showing that any rehabilitation intervention has ever worked" (p. 4).

One difficulty may be that many of the rationales set forth by defense attorneys to licensing boards to demonstrate rehabilitation are based on some combination of therapy and education. The premise that therapy will eliminate any real risk of reoffending and thus justify returning to practice is based on reasoning outlined in items 6 and 7 in the prior section. The premise that education will be helpful is based on the stereotype that less well-educated therapists are those who are at risk for sexually abusing patients, and that supplying the education eliminates (or at least lessens) the risk. This stereotype is similar to the view that it is the lower-class, uneducated misfit (e.g., the lonely man in the tattered raincoat by the school playground) who tends to be the child molester.

Research has not supported (and tends to contradict) these two rationales. No study published in a peer-review scientific or professional journal has provided validation for the hypothesis that therapists who undertake personal therapy are less likely to become sexually involved with patients. For example, Gartrell et al. (1986) conducted a national study in which they found that psychiatrists who had completed a personal course of therapy or psychoanalysis were in fact *more* likely to have engaged in sexual relations with a patient. (For discussion of the absence of research studies demonstrating that personal therapy eliminates or even reduces a therapist's risk for sexually abusing a patient, see Gechtman, 1989.)

Similarly, no research published in a peer-review journal has provided validation for the hypothesis that therapists who are well educated or received more professional recognition from their peers are less likely to become sexually involved with patients. For example, Gartrell et al. (1986; see also Gartrell, Herman, Olarte, Feldstein, & Localio, 1989) found that psychiatrists who had engaged in sex with a patient were *more* likely than nonoffenders to have completed an accredited residency. Similarly, a national study of psychologists found that those who had attained high levels of competence and achievement (as measured through such factors as APA Fellow status and American Board of Professional Psychology (ABPP) diplomat status) reported higher rates of sexual involvement with their patients than was reported by more general samples of psychologists (Pope & Bajt, 1988). A review of various types of offending therapists provided examples of perpetrators who had held such positions as director of an educational program, licensing board chair, chair of the ethics committee of a large state professional association, president of a state professional association, hospital chief of staff, and tenured professor (Pope, Sonne, & Holroyd, 1993). One study suggested a possible relationship between therapist-patient sex and an aspect of training: people who, as students during graduate training, engaged in sex with their professors and clinical supervisors were later, as therapists, statistically more likely to engage in sex with their patients (Pope et al., 1979). This may seem like a contradiction in view of the fact that the majority of therapist perpetrators are men and the majority of student victims are women. However, having had sex with a professor or supervisor is obviously not the only variable associated with whether an individual later, as a therapist, has sex with patients. As a result, the numbers of men who have sex with patients can still, logically, be greater than those of women. (For a more extended discussion of the statistical and methodological aspects of this apparent contradiction, see Pope, 1994, and Pope, Butcher, & Seelen, 1999).

O'Connor's (1992) noting the absence of any independent research published in peer-review journals demonstrating any rehabilitation effort to be successful is interesting in light of how easy it would be to exploit the low base rate of reporting therapist-patient sex to provide a pseudodemonstration of rehabilitation effectiveness. Perpetrators, of course, may continue to engage in sex with patients during or after rehabilitation (i.e., as long as they have access to patients). Bates and Brodsky (1989), for example, document a vivid example.

That a "rehabilitated" therapist is engaging in sex with a patient may come to light only if the patient reports it. However, the research suggests that the base rates of patients formally reporting sexual involvement with a therapist is low. Although some studies find that perhaps only about 5% make a formal report to a licensing board (see, e.g., Pope & Vetter, 1991), the percentage appears to be significantly lower when the number of cases estimated from anonymous surveys of clinicians (who report instances in which they have engaged in abuse) are compared with complaints filed with licensing boards, ethics committees, and the civil and criminal courts. And if the clinicians in these national studies are underreporting the degree to which they are engaging in sex with patients, the base rate percentage of patients reporting to licensing boards would be still smaller.

Using the higher, 5% reporting estimate as the percentage base rate of sexually abused patients who report the offense to the licensing board, imagine a hypothetical rehabilitation program for therapists who have engaged in sex with a patient. In a formal research study, this fictional program will rehabilitate 10 offending therapists referred by the state's licensing board. Each offender undergoes several years of an extremely comprehensive rehabilitation process. At the end of the process and after a careful evaluation, the hypothetical program administrator assures the licensing board that all 10 offenders have been completely rehabilitated. But as part of this hypothetical situation, also assume that the rehabilitation program was unfortunately completely ineffective. *Every one* of these therapists will engage in sex with a future patient.

This fictional research study will avoid any temptation to look at an unrealistically short time span (because the program administrator is assuring the licensing board that all 10 offenders are safe for the full remaining length of their career, and not just for the next year or two). It will report whether any of these offenders reoffend during each five-year period for the duration that they practice.

What is the probability that even after 10, 20, or 30 years, the program appears to be *completely* effective even though it is completely ineffective (i.e., each offender reoffends with another patient)? If each of the 10 patients who are subsequently exploited by these supposedly rehabilitated therapists has a 5% probability of reporting the abuse, there is a 59.9% probability that *none* of the 10 will file a complaint. This completely ineffective program, after decades of independent evaluation, has almost a 60% chance of *appearing* to be 100% effective.

The following questions may be useful when considering claims that evidence shows any rehabilitation process to be effective:

- How many systematic investigations were completed?
- For those systematic investigations that produced evidence that the rehabilitation approach was effective, what was the size of the sample?
- How was success measured?
- Was the time period covered by the research appropriate to the hypothesis?
- What level of success did the rehabilitation program demonstrate?
- If the rehabilitation program depended on an accurate classification of offenders (i.e., offenders are divided into different types, with each type associated with a specific rehabilitation plan and "prognosis"), what are the reliability and validity of the classification system, as formally and impartially assessed?
- Was the investigation conducted by a disinterested party?
- Was the research conducted in a way that meets the highest ethical, legal, clinical, and similar applicable standards?
- Was an adequately detailed report of the research published in a peer-reviewed academic, scientific, or professional journal?
- How has the apparently low rate of reporting been taken into account in the validation study? (Pope, Butcher, & Seelen, 1999, pp. 171–186)

The lack of research data validating any rehabilitation program and the likelihood of recidivism (i.e., reoffending by those who have already been through a rehabilitation program) emphasizes the need for the profession to rethink what Holroyd and Brodsky (1977) identified over two decades ago as one of the three major issues to be addressed in this area: "that therapists who disregard the sexual boundary once are likely to repeat" (p. 849). The American Psychological Association Insurance Trust (1990), with access to a substantial set of actuarial and historical data, concluded that the "recidivism rate for sexual misconduct is substantial" (p. 3). The executive directors of the California licensing boards for psychology, social work, and marriage and family counseling emphasized that for therapists who become sexually involved with a patient, the "prospects for rehabilitation are minimal and it is doubtful that they should be given the opportunity to ever practice psychotherapy again" (Callanan & O'Connor, 1988, p. 11). The California Department of Consumer Affairs (1990) published its findings in a document that was sent to all licensed therapists and counselors in California. This document stated that "80 percent of the sexually exploiting therapists have exploited more than one client. In other words, if a therapist is sexually exploiting a client, chances are he or she has done so before" (p. 14).

WHAT TO DO WHEN YOU DON'T KNOW WHAT TO DO

The research reviewed in this chapter suggests that although it is common for many therapists to experience sexual attraction, fantasies, arousal, and excitement in regard to a patient, only a relative few choose to knowingly violate a fundamental clinical, ethical, and legal responsibility, engage in sex with a patient, and thereby place that patient at substantial risk for deep and lasting harm. It is likely that most readers of this chapter have experienced a diverse array of sexual thoughts or feelings about at least one patient, but also likely that only a very few have or would sexually exploit a patient.

Even if the overwhelming majority of therapists are not at risk for choosing to engage in any sexual relations with a patient, the research suggests, as discussed earlier, that sexual feelings per se may make most therapists feel guilty, anxious, or confused. Sexual daydreams, impulses, and reactions may make it difficult for therapists to decide whether a particular intervention makes sense as a legitimate component of the treatment plan. The following section, which is taken from the book *Sexual Feelings in Psychotherapy* (Pope, Sonne, & Holroyd, 1993) and is used with permission, suggests a set of 10 considerations that might be useful to therapists facing these dilemmas. An important assumption and theme is that there are no clear, one-size-fits-all answers to what sexual feelings about patients mean or what their implications for the therapy are. Various theoretical orientations provide different, sometimes opposing ways of approaching such questions. Each person and situation is unique. Each therapist must explore and achieve a working understanding of his or her own unfolding, evolving feelings and the ways they may provide a source of guidance about what to say or do next. A cookbook approach may hinder rather than help this process.

A companion theme places fundamental trust in the individual therapist, adequately trained and consulting with others, to draw his or her own conclusions. Virtually all therapists have learned primary resources for helping themselves explore problematic situations. They may, for example, (1) introspect, (2) study the available research and clinical literature, (3) consult, (4) seek supervision, and (5) begin or resume personal therapy. But there are times when, even after the most sustained exploration, the course is not clear. The therapist's best understanding of the situation suggests a course of action that seems productive yet questionable and perhaps potentially harmful. To refrain from a contemplated action may shut the door to the therapist's spontaneity, creativity, intuition, and ability to help; to refrain may stunt the patient's progress or impede recovery. However, to engage in the contemplated action may lead to disaster. It may be helpful for therapists, having reached an impasse, to examine the potential intervention in light of the following considerations.

CONSISTENCY OF COMMUNICATION

This consideration invites the therapist to review the course of therapy from the start to the present: Has the therapist clearly and consistently communicated to the patient that sexual intimacies cannot and will not occur, and is the contemplated action consistent with that communication? The question of sexual intimacy may not arise with all patients. If the question does arise, it may not surface until therapy is well underway. Although approaches to therapy seem to have an almost infinite variety, there is probably no therapist who begins with the words, "Hello, I'm Dr. _____. I want you to know that under no circumstances will we ever engage in sex." Nevertheless, therapists must and do communicate the ground rules of therapy to their patients. The communications differ in each therapy relationship, according to theoretical orientation, personal style, the unique situation, and so on. Under no circumstances should a therapist ever communicate, either explicitly or implicitly, that sexual intimacy with the patient is a possibility. No communication should be inconsistent with the fundamental prohibition against sexual intimacies between therapist and patient. *Even when the therapist would never engage in sex with a patient*, it is important to consider whether any communications have been, however unintentionally, ambiguous or misleading.

It is important to be alert to subtle or unintentional communications contrary to the prohibition against therapist-patient sex. Some therapists may enjoy and tacitly seek to encourage a patient's sexual feelings, attraction, or desire. They may be reluctant to clarify the prohibition because to do so might result in the patient's examining the feelings therapeutically (rather than expressing them in a way that the therapist finds personally arousing or gratifying) or turning his or her attention to other issues. Through words or deeds, these therapists may act in a creatively seductive manner, inviting, reinforcing, and trying to maintain the patient's sexual interest.

CLARIFICATION

This consideration requires the therapist to assess whether taking the contemplated action should be deferred until sexual and related issues have been clarified. Imagine, for example, that the patient has told the therapist that he or she would like each session to end with a reassuring hug. Assume that the therapist's theoretical approach does not preclude this form of physical contact. Assume also that the hugging might be construed as addressing one or more of the patient's important clinical needs. Finally, assume that the therapist is not sexually attracted to the patient, does not anticipate becoming sexually aroused if such brief hugs were to end each session, and that hugging does not seem to stir up any conflicts or confusions on the part of the therapist.

What issues would adding this ritualized hug to the process of therapy raise? For some patients, abusive childhood experiences may have prevented their learning that hugs can be nonsexual; for them, this sort of physical contact involves deeper levels of sexual expression. For others, the hugs may represent an attempt to please the therapist, another pattern that may have been learned in childhood. Still others may be challenging or testing a boundary. In such cases, the therapist may need to discuss these issues with the patient before making a decision about whether to end each session with a hug.

THE PATIENT'S WELFARE

This consideration is one of the primary touchstones of all therapy: Is the contemplated action consistent with the welfare of the patient? The therapist's feelings—especially when they are sexual—can be so powerful, complex, and personally immediate that they can create a context of their own. In this context, the therapist can respond to vivid personal feelings, impulses, desires, fears, and fantasies while the patient's clinical needs lose their salience.

Complex legal issues may make this consideration more difficult. In some instances, a therapist may take an action that may not be construed by all concerned as clearly consistent with the welfare of the patient. For example, a therapist may be legally required to report that the patient has engaged in child abuse or has threatened to kill a third party, even though some therapists may believe that such reports are not consistent with the welfare of the patient.

Despite the legal and related complexities, it is important to consider the degree to which any contemplated action promotes, is consistent with, is irrelevant to, or is contrary to the patient's welfare. Both therapist and patient, for example, may enjoy talking at length about the patient's sexual fantasies. But the therapist must frankly address these questions: Does such discussion serve a legitimate therapeutic purpose? Is it consistent with the patient's welfare? Does it help address the needs or questions that prompted the patient to seek therapy or that emerged during the course of therapy? Regarding the previous example (i.e., discussing at length the patient's sexual fantasies), there is no predetermined or universal answer that spans all therapeutic situations. In some instances, such discussion may be vital to the patient's progress. In others, it may be extremely destructive. Nothing can spare therapists from struggling with such questions each time they arise.

CONSENT

This consideration is another primary touchstone of therapy: Is the contemplated action consistent with the basic informed consent of the patient? Consent is one of the most difficult issues with which therapists must contend (see, e.g., Pope & Vasquez, 1998). Legal requirements for informed consent to treatment and informed refusal of treatment vary according to jurisdiction. There are often instances in which patients are subjected to interventions that are contrary to their voluntary consent. For example, a person who is actively suicidal, homicidal, or gravely disabled may, again depending on applicable law for the jurisdiction, be involuntarily hospitalized. However, patients are generally accorded rights to informed consent or informed refusal. Each act or set of actions by a therapist must be carefully considered in light of its consistency with the person's autonomy and his or her right to choose what forms of treatment to try or to avoid.

ADOPTING THE PATIENT'S VIEW

This consideration is one that invites the therapist to empathize imaginatively with the patient: How is the patient likely to understand and respond to the contemplated action? Therapy is one of many endeavors in which *exclusive* attention to theory, intention, and technique may distract from other sources of information, ideas, and guidance. Therapists-in-training may cling to theory, intention, and technique as a way of coping with the anxieties and overwhelming responsibilities of the therapeutic venture. Seasoned therapists may rely almost exclusively on theory, intention, and technique out of learned reflex, habit, and the sheer weariness that approaches burnout. There is always risk that the therapist will fall back on repetitive and reflexive responses that verge on stereotype. Without much thought or feeling, the anxious or tired therapist may, if analytically minded, answer a patient's question by asking why the patient asked the question; if holding a client-centered orientation, may simply reflect or restate what the client has just said; if Gestalt-trained, may ask the client to say something to an empty chair; and so on.

One way to help avoid responses that are driven more by anxiety, fatigue, or similar factors is to consider carefully how the therapist would think, feel, and react if he or she were the patient. Regardless of the theoretical soundness, intended outcome, or technical sophistication of a contemplated intervention, how will it likely be experienced and understood by the patient? Can the therapist anticipate at all what the patient might feel and think? The therapist's attempts to try out, in his or her imagination, the contemplated action and to view it from the perspective of the patient may help prevent, correct, or at least identify possible sources of misunderstanding, miscommunication, and failures of empathy.

COMPETENCE

This consideration focuses on competence: Is the therapist competent to carry out the contemplated intervention? Ensuring that a therapist's education, training, and supervised experience is adequate and appropriate for his or her work is an important clinical and ethical responsibility. "The Ethical Principles of Psychologists and Code of Conduct" of the American Psychological Association (1992), for example, emphasizes that

> Psychologists . . . recognize the boundaries of their particular competencies and the limitations of their expertise. They provide only those services and use only those techniques for which they are qualified by education, training, or experience. . . . They maintain knowledge of relevant scientific and professional information related to the services they render, and they recognize the need for ongoing education. (p. 3)

As an extreme example, consider a hypothetical male therapist who discovers, in the second month of work with a patient, that the patient is the victim of child sex abuse. The patient says that he or she fears the therapist and finds it difficult to talk because sexual memories keep intruding. The therapist has listened to colleagues discuss "reenactment therapy" and decides that this might be an appropriate intervention to try on a trial basis with this patient. He asks the patient to describe the memory, which involved anal intercourse. The therapist then suggests that he and the patient get down on the floor, fully clothed, to pantomime the action. Although the therapist has no real knowledge of reenactment therapy, the approach seems to make sense to him in light of his knowledge of learning theory and behavior therapy. He believes that reenacting the traumatic memory through pantomime, in the safety and security of the therapy office, will enable the patient to become systematically desensitized to the traumatic associations. He anticipates that after one or two slow, careful reenactments, the patient will no longer generalize the learned fear (as well as other negative feelings) to the therapist.

Especially if they are knowledgeable about interventions for people who were sexually abused as children, readers will probably be able to envision some likely disastrous consequences of the therapist's contemplated actions in this scenario. Whenever therapists consider possible interventions or courses of action (e.g., emotional flooding, systematic desensitization, using touch to help induce a hypnotic trance, "emergent uncovering" of sexual feelings, or psychodrama), it is crucial that they candidly assess the degree to which they have adequate knowledge and training in the area, are adequately aware of whether research supports the use of such interventions, and are knowledgeable, assuming that the intervention rests on a solid research base, about the indications and contraindications.

UNCHARACTERISTIC BEHAVIORS

This consideration invites alertness to unusual actions: Does the contemplated action fall substantially outside the range of the therapist's usual behaviors? That the contemplated action is unusual does not suggest that something is wrong with it per se. The creative therapist will likely try—with adequate attention to informed consent and informed refusal—creative interventions. The typical therapist—if there is such a person—will likely engage in atypical behaviors from time to time. But possible actions that seem considerably outside the therapist's general approaches probably warrant special consideration.

For most therapists, therapy is conducted in the consulting room. Some theoretical orientations, however, may not preclude the therapist from seeing a patient outside the office if there is clear clinical need and justification. For example, Stone (1982) described a woman suffering from schizophrenia who was hospitalized during a psychotic break. The woman heaped verbal abuse on her therapist, claiming that the therapist did not really care about her. Suddenly, the patient disappeared from the unit.

> The therapist, upon hearing the news, got into her car and canvassed all the bars and social clubs in Greenwich Village which her patient was known to frequent. At about midnight, she found her patient and drove her back to the hospital. From that day forward, the patient grew calmer, less impulsive, and made great progress in treatment. Later, after making substantial recovery, she told her therapist that all the interpretations during the first few weeks in the hospital meant very little to her. But after the "midnight rescue mission" it was clear, even to her, how concerned and sincere her therapist had been from the beginning. (p. 171)

Searching for a patient outside the hospital or office is an extremely atypical event for most, if not all, therapists. When the therapist undertakes such an atypical action, is it clear that such out-of-the-office contact is warranted by the patient's clinical needs and situation? Contemplated actions that are out of the ordinary invite extremely careful evaluation.

On a much more complex level, it is useful to consider the factors that define, reflect, or influence what is "usual" behavior for the therapist. For example, does the therapist typically use nonerotic touch (e.g., handshakes, reassuring pats on the back, or briefly holding the patient's hand to express sympathy) with patients? Careful examination of the patterns of touch may reveal bias (see Holroyd & Brodsky, 1980) or other factors that may hold important meaning or implications.

Consultation

This consideration addresses secrecy: Is there a compelling reason for not discussing the contemplated action with a colleague, consultant, or supervisor? One red flag to the possibility that a course of action is inappropriate is the therapist's reluctance to disclose it to others. One question a therapist may ask about any proposed action is this: If I took this action, would I have any reluctance for all of my professional colleagues to know that I had taken it? If the answer is yes, the reasons for the reluctance are worth examining. If the answer is no, it is worth considering if one has adequately taken advantage of the opportunities to discuss the matter with a trusted colleague. If discussion with a colleague has not helped to clarify the issues, consultation with additional professionals, each of whom may provide different perspectives and suggestions, may be useful.

Reflecting on one's motivation for seeking consultation and one's methods of selecting potential consultants can be an important part of the consultation process. In times of temptation, often there is ample motive to seek superficial, phony, or pro forma consultation as a way to obtain approval or "permission" for a questionable behavior. The apparent consultation is an attempt to quash or override doubts rather than to explore them. Methods for selecting potential consultants can help undermine or ensure the integrity of the consultation process. Only the least persistent therapist would be unable to find, in a moderate or large community, a consultant who would say yes to virtually any proposed intervention.

Making use of consultation as a regular component of clinical activities rather than as a resource used only on atypical occasions is one way to extend the process of continuing education that should be a career-long process. Consultation with a variety of colleagues on a frequent basis can strengthen the sense of community in which therapists work. It can provide a safety net, helping therapists to ensure that their work does not fall into needless errors, unintentional malpractice, or harmful actions that are due to lack of knowledge, guidance, perspective, challenge, or support. It can create a sense of cooperative venture in which the process of professional development, exploration, and discovery continues.

REFERENCES

Akamatsu, T.J. (1988). Intimate relationships with former clients: National survey of attitudes and behavior among practitioners. *Professional Psychology: Research and Practice, 19,* 454–458.

American Psychological Association. (1992). Ethical principles of psychologists and code of conduct. *American Psychologist, 47,* 1597–1611.

American Psychological Association Insurance Trust. (1990). *Bulletin: Sexual misconduct and professional liability claims.* Washington, DC: Author.

A woman's a sex object. (1977, May 27). *San Francisco Examiner,* p. 2.

Bajt, T.R., & Pope, K.S. (1989). Therapist-patient sexual intimacy involving children and adolescents. *American Psychologist, 44,* 455.

Bates, C.M., & Brodsky, A.M. (1989). *Sex in the therapy hour: A case of professional incest.* New York: Guilford Press.

Benowitz, M.S. (1991). *Sexual exploitation of female clients by female psychotherapists: Interviews with clients and a comparison to women exploited by male psychotherapists.* Unpublished doctoral dissertation, University of Minnesota, Minneapolis.

Bernsen, A., Tabachnick, B.G., & Pope, K.S. (1994). National survey of social workers' sexual attraction to their clients: Results, implications, and comparison to psychologists. *Ethics & Behavior, 4,* 369–388.

Bloom, D. (1989, March 22). Psychologist's license revoked after sex with patient. *Riverside [California] Press Enterprise,* p. B-1.

Borys, D.S., & Pope, K.S. (1989). Dual relationships between therapist and client: A national study of psychologists, psychiatrists, and social workers. *Professional Psychology: Research and Practice, 20,* 283–293.

Bouhoutsos, J.C., Holroyd, J., Lerman, H., Forer, B., & Greenberg, M. (1983). Sexual intimacy between psychotherapists and patients. *Professional Psychology: Research and Practice, 14,* 185–196.

Brabent, E., Falzeder, E., & Giampieri-Deutsch, P. (under supervision of A. Haynal). (1993). *The correspondence of Sigmund Freud and Sándor Ferenczi: Vol. 1. 1908–1914* (P.T. Hoffer, Trans.). Cambridge, MA: Harvard University Press.

Brownfain, J.J. (1971). The APA professional liability insurance program. *American Psychologist, 26,* 648–652.

Butler, S.E., & Zelen, S.L. (1977). Sexual intimacies between therapists and patients. *Psychotherapy, 14,* 139–145.

California Department of Consumer Affairs. (1990). *Professional therapy never includes sex.* Sacramento: Board of Psychology.

Callanan, K., & O'Connor, T. (1988). *Staff comments and recommendations regarding the report of the Senate task force on psychotherapist and patients sexual relations.* Sacramento: Board of Behavioral Science Examiners and Psychology Examining Committee.

Carr, M.L., & Robinson, G.E. (1990). Fatal attraction: The ethical and clinical dilemma of patient-therapist sex. *Canadian Journal of Psychiatry, 35,* 122–127.

Carr, M.L., Robinson, G.E., Stewart, D.E., & Kussin, D. (1991). A survey of Canadian psychiatric residents regarding resident-educator sexual contact. *American Journal of Psychiatry, 148,* 216–220.

Davidson, V. (1977). Psychiatry's problem with no name. *American Journal of Psychoanalysis, 37,* 43–50.

Department of Professional Regulation v. Wise. 575 So.2d 713 (Fla.App. 1 Dist. 1991). Rehearing denied March 13, 1991.

Dorland's Medical Dictionary. (1974). Twenty-fifth edition. Philadelphia: Saunders.

English, B. (1992, December 16). Medical men get a message. *Boston Globe,* p. 41.

Feldman-Summers, S., & Jones, G. (1984). Psychological impacts of sexual contact between therapists or other health care professionals and their clients. *Journal of Consulting and Clinical Psychology, 52,* 1054–1061.

Freeman, L., & Roy, J. (1976). *Betrayal.* New York: Stein & Day.

Freud, S. (1952). *A general introduction to psychoanalysis* (Rev. ed.; J. Riviere, Trans.). New York: Washington Square. (Original work published 1924)

Freud, S. (1963). Further recommendations in the technique of psychoanalysis: Observations on transference-love. In P. Rieff (Ed.), *Freud: Therapy and technique* (pp. 167–179). [Authorized English translation of the Rev. ed. by J. Riviere]. New York: Collier Books. (Original work published 1915)

Gartrell, N.K., Herman, J.L., Olarte, S., Feldstein, M., & Localio, R. (1986). Psychiatrist-patient sexual contact: Results of a national survey: I. Prevalence. *American Journal of Psychiatry, 143,* 1126–1131.

Gartrell, N.K., Herman, J.L., Olarte, S., Feldstein, M., & Localio, R. (1989). Prevalence of psychiatrist-patient sexual contact. In G.O. Gabbard (Ed.), *Sexual exploitation in professional relationships* (pp. 3–14). Washington, DC: American Psychiatric Press.

Gechtman, L. (1989). Sexual contact between social workers and their clients. In G.O. Gabbard (Ed.), *Sexual exploitation in professional relationships* (pp. 27–38). Washington, DC: American Psychiatric Association.

Gilbert, L.A., & Scher, M. (1989). The power of an unconsicious belief. *Professional Practice of Psychology, 8,* 94–108.

Glaser, R., & Thorpe, J. (1986). Unethical intimacy: A survey of sexual contact and advances between psychology educators and female graduate students. *American Psychologists, 41,* 43–51.

Hare-Mustin, R.T. (1974). Ethical considerations in the use of sexual contact in psychotherapy. *Psychotherapy: Theory, Research and Practice, 11,* 308–310.

Hare-Mustin, R.T. (1992). Cries and whispers: The psychotherapy of Anne Sexton. *Psychotherapy, 29,* 406–409.

Herman, J.L., Gartrell, N., Olarte, S., Feldstein, M., & Localio, R. (1987). Psychiatrist-patient sexual contact: Results of a national survey: II. Psychiatrists' attitudes. *American Journal of Psychiatry, 144,* 164–169.

Holroyd, J.C. (1983). Erotic contact as an instance of sex-biased therapy. In J. Murray & P.R. Abramson (Eds.), *Bias in psychotherapy* (pp. 285–308). New York: Praeger.

Holroyd, J.C., & Brodsky, A.M. (1977). Psychologists' attitudes and practices regarding erotic and nonerotic physical contact with clients. *American Psychologist, 32,* 843–849.

Holroyd, J.C., & Brodsky, A.M. (1980). Does touching patients lead to sexual intercourse? *Professional Psychology, 11,* 807–811.

In the Matter of the Accusation Against: Myron E. Howland. (1980). Before the Psychology Examining Committee, Board of Medical Quality Assurance, State of California, No. D-2212. Reporters' Transcript, Vol. 3.

Judge urged to resign after child rape decision. (1985, July 18). *Los Angeles Herald Examiner,* p. A6.

Keith-Spiegel, P. (1977, August). *Sex with clients.* Paper presented at the annual meeting of the American Psychological Association, Washington, DC.

Kluft, R. (1989). Treating the patient who has been sexually exploited by a previous therapist. *Psychiatric Clinics of North America, 12,* 483–500.

Koocher, G.P. (1994). Foreword. In K.S. Pope (Ed.), *Sexual involvement with therapists: Patient assessment, subsequent therapy, forensics* (pp. vii–ix). Washington, DC: American Psychological Association.

Lebe, D., & Namir, S. (1993, December). *Boundary dilemmas posed by contemporary psychoanalytic theories.* Paper presented at the meeting of the American Academy of Psychoanalysis, New York.

Lorde, A. (1978). *Uses of the erotic: The erotic as power.* Trumansburg, NY: Crossing Press.

Mann, C.K., & Winer, J.D. (1991). Psychotherapist's sexual contact with client. *American jurisprudence proof of facts* (3rd series, Vol. 14, pp. 319–431). Rochester, NY: Lawyers Cooperative.

Masters, W.H., & Johnson, V.E. (1966). *Human sexual response.* New York: Bantam Books.

Masters, W.H., & Johnson, V.E. (1970). *Human sexual inadequacy.* New York: Bantam Books.

Masters, W.H., & Johnson, V.E. (1975, May). *Principles of the new sex therapy.* Paper presented at the annual meeting of the American Psychiatric Association, Anaheim, CA.

Noel, B., & Watterson, K. (1992). *You must be dreaming.* New York: Poseidon.

O'Connor, T. (1992). Diverting justice: Unanswered questions on diverting licensees from discipline. *California Regulatory Law Reporter, 12*(4), 4–5.

Perspectives. (1990, April 23). *Newsweek,* p. 17.

Plaisil, E. (1985). *Therapist.* New York: St. Martin's/Marek.

Pope, K.S. (1989). Student-teacher sexual intimacy. In G.O. Gabbard (Ed.), *Sexual exploitation within professional relationships.* Washington, DC: American Psychiatric Press.

Pope, K.S. (1990). Therapist-patient sexual involvement: A review of the research. *Clinical Psychology Review, 10,* 477–490.

Pope, K.S. (1993). Licensing disciplinary actions for psychologists who have been sexually involved with a client: Some information about offenders. *Professional Psychology: Research and Practice, 24,* 374–377.

Pope, K.S. (1994). *Sexual involvement with therapists: Patient assessment, subsequent therapy, forensics.* Washington, DC: American Psychological Association.

Pope, K.S., & Bajt, T.R. (1988). When laws and values conflict: A dilemma for psychologists. *American Psychologist, 43,* 455.

Pope, K.S., & Bouhoutsos, J.C. (1986). *Sexual intimacies between therapists and patients.* New York: Praeger/Greenwood Press.

Pope, K.S., Butcher, J.N., & Seelen, J. (1999). *The MMPI, MMPI-2, and MMPI-A in court: A practical guide for expert witnesses and attorneys* (2nd ed.). Washington, DC: American Psychological Association.

Pope, K.S., & Feldman-Summers, S. (1992). National survey of psychologists' sexual and physical abuse history and their evaluation of training and competence in these areas. *Professional Psychology: Research and Practice, 23,* 353–361.

Pope, K.S., Keith-Spiegel, P., & Tabachnick, B.G. (1986). Sexual attraction to patients: The human therapist and the (sometimes) inhuman training system. *American Psychologist, 41,* 147–158.

Pope, K.S., Levenson, H., & Schover, L.R. (1979). Sexual intimacy in psychology training: Results and implications of a national survey. *American Psychologist, 34,* 682–689.

Pope, K.S., Sonne, J.L., & Holroyd, J. (1993). *Sexual feelings in psychotherapy: Explorations for therapists and therapists-in-training.* Washington, DC: American Psychological Association.

Pope, K.S., & Tabachnick, B.G. (1993). Therapists' anger, hate, fear, and sexual feelings: National survey of therapists' responses, client characteristics, critical events, formal complaints, and training. *Professional Psychology: Research and Practice, 24,* 142–152.

Pope, K.S., & Tabachnick, B.G. (1994). Therapists as patients: A national survey of psychologists' experience, problems, and beliefs. *Professional Psychologist: Research and Practice, 25,* 247–258.

Pope, K.S., Tabachnick, B.G., & Keith-Spiegel, P. (1987). Ethics of practice: The beliefs and behaviors of psychologists as therapists. *American Psychologist, 42,* 993–1006.

Pope, K.S., & Vasquez, M.J.T. (1998). *Ethics in psychotherapy and counseling: A practical guide* (2nd ed.). San Francisco: Jossey-Bass.

Pope, K.S., & Vetter, V.A. (1991). Prior therapist-patient sexual involvement among patients seen by psychologists. *Psychotherapy, 28,* 429–438.

Pope, K.S., & Vetter, V.A. (1992). Ethical dilemmas encountered by members of the American Psychological Association: A national survey. *American Psychologist, 47,* 397–411.

Rapp, M.S. (1987). Sexual misconduct. *Canadian Medical Association Journal, 137,* 193–194.

Robinson, W.L., & Reid, P.T. (1985). Sexual intimacies in psychology revisited. *Professional Psychology: Research and Practice, 16,* 512–520.

Roy v. Hartogs. (1976). 381 N.Y.S. 2d 587; 85 Misc.2d 891.

Smith, S. (1984). The sexually abused patient and the abusing therapist. *Psychoanalytic Psychology, 1,* 89–98.

Sonne, J.L. (1987). Proscribed sex: Counseling the patient subjected to sexual intimacy by a therapist. *Medical Aspects of Human Sexuality, 16,* 18–23.

Sonne, J.L. (1989). An example of group therapy for victims of therapist-client sexual intimacy. In G.O. Gabbard (Ed.), *Sexual exploitation in professional relationships* (pp. 101–127). Washington, DC: American Psychiatric Press.

Sonne, J.L., Meyer, C.B., Borys, D., & Marshall, V. (1985). Clients' reaction to sexual intimacy in therapy. *American Journal of Orthopsychiatry, 55,* 183–189.

Son of retired police officer sentenced for sexually assaulting a child. (1998, April 30). *Associated Press* wire report.

Stone, M. (1982). Turning points in therapy. In S. Slipp (Ed.), *Curative factors in dynamic psychotherapy* (pp. 259–279). New York: McGraw-Hill.

Terwilliger, C. (1989, October 16). Client says she sued doctor to save herself and others. *Cedar Springs [Colorado] Gazette Telegraph,* pp. D1–D2.

Therapist guilty in sexual assault. (1988, April 8). *Rocky Mountain News,* p. 28.

Therapist sentenced for whipping patient. (1987, September 1). *Minneapolis Star and Tribune,* p. 3B.

Unbelievable. (1983, January 24). *Los Angeles Herald Examiner,* p. F2.

Unger, R.K. (1979). *Female and male: Psychological perspectives.* New York: Harper & Row.

Vinson, J.S. (1987). Use of complaint procedures in cases of therapist-patient sexual contact. *Professional Psychology: Research and Practice, 18,* 159–164.

Walker, E., & Young, T.D. (1986). *A killing cure.* New York: Holt, Rinehart and Winston.

Author Index

659

Subject Index